The Heritage of Man

A HISTORY
OF THE WORLD

THE HERITAGE OF MAN

A HISTORY OF THE WORLD

by Goldwin Smith

CHARLES SCRIBNER'S SONS, NEW YORK

MAPS BY SAMUEL H. BRYANT

TITLE-PAGE DRAWING
BY DEAN ELLIS

TO

PATRICK D'ALTON

NOBLE HARBINSON

WILLIAM SEILER

"I am certain of nothing but of the holiness of the heart's affections, and the truth of imagination."

—JOHN KEATS

Acknowledgments

IT IS a special pleasure to acknowledge my debt to Professor Geoffrey Bruun for his criticisms and suggestions. His great knowledge, his patience and understanding, have saved me from all sorts of errors.

I appreciate deeply the expert advice and thoughtful corrections of Professors Milton Covensky, Sidney Glazer, C. Norman Guice, Finley Hooper, Alfred H. Kelly, Harry Josselson, and T. F. Mayer-Oakes.

Mr. T. J. B. Walsh and Mr. Wallace Meyer, my editors at Charles Scribner's Sons, have earned my lasting gratitude for their generous aid and advice. No acknowledgment could adequately express my obligation to them and to all of the other members of the staff of Scribners who worked with me.

Professor Samuel N. Kramer of the University of Pennsylvania Museum, with his usual kindness, has permitted me to use his translation of the Sumerian poem that appears in Chapter 3.

I am grateful to the following publishers for their courtesy in granting permission to quote from works in which they hold copyright:

George Allen and Unwin Ltd., London, for the quotations from the translations of Sir Gilbert Murray of Aeschylus, *Prometheus Bound* (London, 1931) and Euripides, *Medea* (London, 1956); The Beacon Press, Boston, and J. M. Dent & Sons, Ltd., London, for the quotation from Arnold J. Toynbee's *Greek Civilization and Character* (London, 1924 and Boston, 1950); The University of Chicago Press for the passages from Ernst Cassirer, ed.: *The Renaissance Philosophy of Man* (Chicago, 1948) and from Henry Frankfort, Mrs. Henry Frankfort, John A. Wilson, Thorkhild Jacobsen, *The Intellectual Adventure of Ancient Man* (Chicago, 1946); The Columbia University Press for the quotation from Janet Henderson Robb, *The Primrose League 1883–1906* (New York, 1942); Constable & Company, Ltd., London, for the lines from Helen Waddell, *Lyrics from the Chinese* (London, 1938); The John Day Company, Inc., New York, for the quotation from Jawaharlal Nehru's *The Discovery of India* (New York, 1946); J. M. Dent & Sons, Ltd., London, and E. P. Dutton & Co., Inc., New York, for the lines from George Rawlinson's translation of Herodotus' *Persian Wars* (Everyman's Library, London, 1910 and New York, 1924); The Harvard University Press for the lines from the A. S. Way translation of *The Suppliants* of Euripides, Vol. III of the Loeb Classical Library (London, 1912–1916); Luzac & Company, Ltd., London, for the lines from Stephen Langdon's *Babylonian Wisdom* (London, 1923); Macmillan and Company, Ltd., London, and The Macmillan Company, New York, for the quotation from H. R. Trevor-Roper, *The Last Days of Hitler* (London and New York, 1947); Methuen & Company, Ltd., London, for the quotation from Eileen Power, *Medieval People* (London, 1924); Oxford University Press, Inc., New York, for the lines from Sir Gilbert Murray's translation of *The Bacchae* of Euripides (London, 1915) and for the quotation from Alfred Cobban, *National Self-Determination* (London, 1947); Random House, Inc., New York, for the lines from *The Tsai Shu* and the *Rigveda* in Lin Yutang, ed.: *The Wisdom of China and India* (New York, 1942); the lines from the Lewis Campbell translation of the *Agamemnon* of Aeschylus and the A. S. Way translation of the *Medea* of Euripides in *Four Famous Greek Plays* (New York, 1929); the quotation from the R. Crawley translation in the *Complete Writings of Thucydides* (New York, 1934); the lines from the Avraham Yarmolinsky translation of Alexander Pushkin's *Boris Godunov* in *The Works of Alexander Pushkin* (New York, 1936); *The Saturday Review* and Mr. Douglas V. Steere for the quotation from *The Saturday Review* (June 13, 1953).

GOLDWIN SMITH

Detroit, Michigan
August 1, 1960

Foreword to the College Edition

THIS BOOK was originally written for the general reader. Although it was not intended as a text it is now being used by an increasing number of college and university students. This educational edition is being published to meet their needs. A new binding and jacket have been provided to distinguish the college edition from the original trade volume. Apart from the addition of this Preface there has been no change in the contents of the book.

G. K. Chesterton once remarked that it was bad enough to have lost one's way but it was worse to have lost one's address. The task and pleasure of all teachers is to try to enable the students to understand the outer world of space, the backward world of time, to confront the present and anticipate the future with intelligence. It is my sincere hope that this college edition of *The Heritage of Man* may contribute to that end.

GOLDWIN SMITH

Detroit, Michigan
March 1, 1962

Foreword

So FAR as we know there are no living creatures like man elsewhere in the universe. Man is unique. Man stands alone. "Wonders are many," said Sophocles, "but none, none is more wondrous than man. . . . Cunning, cunning is man. Wise though his plans are, artful beyond all dreaming, they carry him both to evil and to good."

Man is indeed a being set apart. Cell by cell he developed into *Homo sapiens,* Man the Thinker. His brain weighs less than fifty ounces and yet the intelligence that lives in the networks of its multiple switchboards produces marvels of memory and creative power. Of all living creatures man alone has the capacity for conceptual thought. He knows that he is more than a colloidal particle swirled about by Brownian movements. He alone can carve ideas out of experience and he alone by speech and writing can transmit to his offspring their social heritage. His complex nervous system, his ingenious fingers and opposable thumb, his ability to think and move swiftly—these characteristics have enabled him to achieve and to survive.

At the beginning of this book we peer through the mists of time towards our remote ancestor *Pithecanthropus erectus,* that strange, half-enigmatic figure standing at the portals of the timeless deep. Our forefathers are coming out of dark caves and striking fire from flint. They are grasping clubs and hurling spears. They are fleeing from the wrath and greed of their foes. Soon men of art and imagination will shape objects of beauty to warm their spirits against the chill blasts and the great night without. Men of curiosity will ask questions for which there are no final answers this side of Jordan. And men of skill will always invent new things. Said Sir Francis Bacon: "Neither the naked hand nor the understanding left to itself can effect much. It is by instruments and tools that the work is done." Man thinks. He talks. He dreams. He creates. He is learning, always learning. The human race has been brought a long way by the twin gifts of reason and wonder.

In the twentieth century all our days are filled with the triumphs of natural science. As we pursue happiness, health, and survival the jet planes roar overhead and break the sound barrier with a double boom. Radio and television have become, we sometimes think, absolutely necessary parts of our daily lives. We respect and admire the engineer and the industrialist, the surgeon, the physicist, the chemist. These, surely, are the kinds of men who have made it unnecessary for us to leap from the leafy stalks in the jungles of Java or plait lianas by the Limpopo. The modern scientists, engineers, and men of business seem to us to be the creators of a new age, bold prophets of a tomorrow we hope will be bright. Let us add to our list the names of the poets, the mathematicians, the men of music, the artists. They, too, must have their honored place.

Each generation of men places a stone or two upon the foundations of the past. Our building is as yet unfinished. The story of mankind is an uncompleted tale of struggle and toil, of discovery and invention, of experiment and error, of high success and bruising failure. No man can know anything about the chapters that are yet unwritten. Nobody can draw aside the curtains of the future. We are all a little lower than the angels, a little less reliable than the minor prophets. And we all have in us a bit of the uneliminated ape.

> Created half to rise and half to fall;
> Great lord of all things, yet a prey to all;
> Sole judge of truth in endless error hurl'd;
> The glory, jest, and riddle of the world!

This book is a journal of certain experiences of mankind rebuilt out of the memory of the historian. It also contains more than a mere catalogue of memories because I have consistently sought to stress the varying trials and problems of the human race and the particular ways in which men have met the challenge of their hour. The conflicts and questions about man and society, man and the cosmos, man and himself go very deeply indeed. The root of the matter is the ultimate purpose of man in the universe. Said Abelard: "By doubting we come to the question; by inquiring we come to the truth."

I have no new or old theory of history to expound or defend. Perhaps, however, it is right and just that I should tell the reader that I do not admit the existence of any so-called "laws" of history. I reject them as I reject any forms of determinism. I do not even claim that history necessarily "teaches" patriotism or righteousness or the truth of any of my beliefs or prejudices. To make that claim or any similar ones seems to me to be unscientific, immoral, and naïve. I consider knowledge and the search for truth goods in themselves needing no defense or justification before any judgment bar. At the same time, I would declare my hope that perhaps the light of history may help us find the right roads from what has been to what is to be.

It is not, however, the task of history to explain the present. One of the clear and present dangers of contemporary writing and teaching in the field of history is the tendency to stress unduly acts and ideas in the past that seem important today. Many things that are not at all significant in our century caused the cutting of throats and the bashing of heads long ago. To try to understand the past in the scientific spirit of free inquiry and bridled imagination, the historian and the journalist and the general reader must try to enter and live in the past in mind and emotion. Our fathers did not know where they were going and neither do we. To read back into the past that which exists in the present alone is not wise.

History is the vital, vivid, and complex tale of deeds and ideas of a multitude of human beings. The world of all the yesterdays is as complex as the currents and eddies that swirl and push in the stream of history today. The chapters of history are not neat and they are not simple. To try to make them so is an unseemly and demeaning task for the servants of Clio.

The really important historians of any age have been sympathetic and imaginative artists as well as scientific detectives. When we read or write about the elusive past we must be critical and cautious explorers. We must weigh evidence carefully because we seek to find as much of the significant truth as we can. One part of the truths of history, of course, is the fact that our ancestors believed many things that were false; but they acted as if their beliefs were true and their actions made history. The sum of the matter is that there are many "truths" in history, some important and some not. And some, indeed, have fallen into oblivion forever. So far as the whole "truth" is concerned it is a pity that Pilate never got an answer.

The astronomer and the physicist probe into space. The historian probes into time—he is the high priest of continuity. He knows that there have been times of blood and murder and times when there was a great hush in the world. He knows that the generations of men pass swiftly. He remembers Emily Bronte's sentence: "I lingered round them under that benign sky, watched the moths fluttering among the heath and the harebells, listened to the soft wind breathing through the grass, and wondered how anyone could ever imagine unquiet slumber for the sleepers in that quiet earth."

Many kinds of human beings march across the pages of this book. The ranks of mankind have always contained the builders and the destroyers, the men who call themselves realists, and the mystics, the master makers of dreams. The tale of man is as confused and complex and as infinitely variable as man himself, that creature who came out of the gulfs of darkness, dreamed his dreams, and made some of them possible.

Contents

PART THREE

PART FOUR

PART I

PLATE I

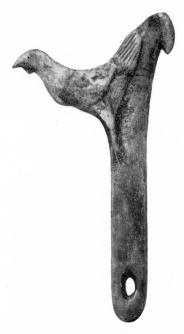

] Head of woman. Prehistoric carving in mammoth ivory

[2] Decorated spear thrower of the Old Stone Age

3] *Below:* Prehistoric sandal made of esparto grass

[4]

A razor of the early Bronze Age

[5] Bronze Age clothing

Babylonian cuneiform tablet concerning the
sale of two slaves

[6]

[9]

PLATE II

Detail of a statue of Gudea, ruler o
Sumerian city of Lagash

[7]

Hieroglyphics carved on a pillar
at Luxor

[10]

Black stone carving of Assyrian hunters

[8]

Part of the Siloam Inscription in
Jerusalem (c. 715-687 B.C.)

[11]

Right: The Siloam Tunnel cut through the rock at
Jerusalem by King Hezekiah (c. 715-687 B.C.)

Chapter 1

THE ASCENT

OF MAN

"And the earth was without form, and void; and darkness was upon the face of the deep."

—Genesis, I, 2

WE LIVE in a mysterious universe, a vast and expanding continuum that curves in upon itself. Even the power of our strongest telescope does not penetrate to the limits of the gigantic swarms of star-systems that sweep and swirl in space and time. A beam of light, traveling at a speed of slightly more than 186,000 miles a second, takes about 8 minutes to reach the earth from the sun. It would take that beam a billion years to flash across the diameter of the observable universe.

In one of the minor galaxies spins the planet Earth. Around it moves the satellite moon, its surface broken by ugly craters—unsightly ulcers that have never healed.

No man was there to witness the violent events that brought our earth into being between four and seven billion years ago. In a cosmic storm the earth was torn from the mother sun and became a ball of fire and gases rushing through the black stretches of space. Slowly the gases cooled and the earth became a molten mass. Then the basalt and the granite hardened to form an outer shell. And then the rains fell and the oceans were filled.

For more than a billion years there was no life. Slowly, in the warm saltiness of the primeval oceans, the first living cells were formed. The stream of life began. About 350,000,000 years ago a creature moved from the Silurian slime to crawl upon the land. This was the arthropod, the ancestor of crabs and lobsters and insects. Man did not appear until about a million years ago, more or less. He, too, came from the mother sea. It is a long road back to the Devonian lungfish and the coelacanth, back to the first molecules of protoplasm. That is the road man has traveled, step by step, through eons of time.

3

Over untold centuries the forces of physical geography and climate relentlessly shaped the face of the earth. Plants and animals grew and laid down the petroleum fields and the coal beds of the world. Great sheets of an ice mass spread from the bleak and barren regions of the north down to the river Thames in England and the Himalayas of northern India. Vast areas were held motionless and desolate in the hostile clutch of the savage cold. Glaciers scoured and ground the land down to the fringes of the warm belts. When the warm years came again in enormous rhythmic climatic changes the ice retreated and extended the areas of land available to human beings and animals. But again and again the harsh winds and the cold invaded the warm and comfortable lands to freeze and kill. Four times the ice drew back and returned.

Our study of early man must be closely linked to these great changes. The last cold period was about 40,000 years ago. Then the ice went back to the immense solitude of the polar caps. Only a few men, like the Eskimos, have ever lived in these frozen lands. The penguins and the polar bears move over the empty miles. The caribou contemplate the sun hanging above the red horizon.

In the whole of this vast period of time the rains and the floods sometimes came to destroy the weak and the unwary. Earthquakes and tornadoes struck and stunned. The seas and the lakes and the uplifted masses of the mountains stood as barriers to limit the comings and goings of man. The abandoned monotony of the deserts stretched in their hateful emptiness, their secrets unrevealed.

The history of man in these centuries of the long dawn was not written. There was no writing, no alphabet. Wild animals and primitive men hunted and fought and tore at one another by the riverbanks and in the steaming green of the jungles. No one ever described these battles of claws and muscles and brains because no one had any devices for recording and preserving information. For thousands of years—this early period is of enormous duration —the ancient hunting peoples moved and lived over vast tracts of land. Their progress towards civilization was pathetically slow.

Life was a battle for survival. Only the tough men and the shrewd men lived, for a while. The hostile forces of nature were all about, relentless and fearful.

Some aspects of nature were friendly and kind. There were the gentle rains, the soft winds, and the bright sun. Men lived where they could find water and food. They searched for such things as shellfish, eggs, edible plants. When they learned to hunt they sought the regions where there were animals to kill. They fished in the seas and the rivers. When they learned to grow crops they looked for spots where there was good soil and a water supply. When they began to domesticate animals they stayed close to rich pastures. Through long centuries the shepherds have kept watch by night on green hills.

It was in the warm lands that human beings first appeared. Remains of the earliest known men have been found in several places. Modern science has been able to tell us the approximate age of these human remains through the use of radioactive carbon-14. In 1891, for instance, a skullcap, some teeth, and a thighbone were discovered in Java. Those bones belonged to a man who leaped and hunted in the jungles about 500,000 years ago. Java Man, or *Pithecanthropus erectus,* is believed to be the earliest human being.

Parts of other skeletons have been found in places as widely separated as Peking and Heidelberg. Some of these bones belonged to a short and powerful creature called Neanderthal Man. He had a big head, a sloping brow, and a receding chin. He worked with flint and he used fire. The most learned scholars cannot add much more. We really know very little about the dim and distant days of man's beginnings and his first frontiers. Facts are one thing. Surmise and conjecture are another.

In 1868 the remains of the first really "modern" man were discovered. He is called the Cro-Magnon Man and he probably lived and wrestled with his environment about 50,000 years ago. We know that he was usually more than six feet tall and that he was undoubtedly an ingenious fellow. Physically, he was not unlike many modern men. Professor Carl Becker once said that if we should meet him on Pennsylvania Avenue one fine morning we would probably fail to recognize him as our remote Cro-Magnon ancestor. We would put him in a zoo and we would probably be amused, if only because his antics might parody our own on the less formal occasions of life. Professor Becker also remarked that if the tables were turned and we were dropped in the jungles of Java, the amusement, if any, would not be ours.

The Cro-Magnon Man and several similar beings lived in what we call the Paleolithic or Old Stone Age, the dawn of human history, the real beginning of the ascent of modern man. This period of slow advance lasted until about 8,000 years before Christ was born.

The men of these far-off days lived in caves or pit dwellings. They knew how to make fire. They chipped flints and they carved bones to defend themselves and to hunt the reindeer and the mammoth, the cave bear and the bison. They ate the meat of the animals they killed and covered their bodies with the hairy skins. They made primitive tools from flint, horns, and ivory. They caught fish with hooks and lines. They gathered shellfish, nuts, and fruits. Dean Inge once remarked that "the whole of nature is a conjugation of the verb to eat, active and passive."

The really important fact is that the men of the Paleolithic Age were trying, like men today, to increase their control over their physical environment. They did not want to suffer from hunger and cold. With the shaping spirits of our imagination we can peer through the smoke and the dancing shadows and see our ancestors going out to stalk their food or crouching by the fire. We can watch them making lamps by placing wicks of reindeer hair or moss in stone bowls filled with animal fat. We can look over their shoulders as they laboriously shape a club:

> . . . the prophetic soul
> Of the wide world dreaming on things to come.

The Greek poet Aeschylus once wrote about the tiny seed of flame which Prometheus hid in a fennel stalk and gave to men. He made Prometheus describe the early state of our race:

> . . . like feeble ants wind-blown
> They hid them in crannied caves, far from the day.

Aeschylus was a great poet but he was very wrong about the nature of the men of the Old Stone Age. They are not to be likened to "feeble ants" but to the muscled and uncouth pioneers of any time and place.

Men have invariably been driven by their restless spirits to seek things never desired by any other creatures on earth. From Paleolithic days they have made and admired beautiful things. Paleolithic men made bracelets of mammoth ivory, necklaces of fish vertebrae, and many kinds of magic charms. They carved small models of cave lions and mammoths. They have left several paintings in various places, especially far underground in the deep recesses of the limestone caves of France and Spain. The masterly realism of the paintings on the walls and roof of the Great Hall in the Cave of Lascaux in southern France still shine brightly in the beams of the acetylene lamps of the twentieth century, exciting our admiration and our wonder. Here the winds never penetrate and the temperature is always constant. The pictures nearly always represent animals and were probably ritualistic drawings connected with hunting. Success in the chase, it seemed, might be speeded by magic arts as well as by the hunter's skill.

The Old Stone Age slowly ended about 10,000 years ago and the first phases of the Neolithic, or New Stone Age, gradually began. As succeeding generations of men learned to polish their stone weapons or tools, they got sharper edges to cut wood or hunt animals. They made nets and baskets, rafts and boats from tree trunks. Because they learned to weave, they were able to make crude cloth and no longer relied solely on animal skins for clothing. They decorated their bodies with shells and beads and stains. They learned to use a rotary motion to drill holes in stone and wood. They invented the bow and arrow. They made bone darts and harpoons from deer antlers.

In pre-Neolithic times men had domesticated dogs. Now they began to domesticate other animals: cattle, pigs, goats, sheep. The dogs continued to help men hunt, raised the alarm when strangers approached, herded the animals that were used for meat and milk and wool. The food supply of men was increased. The population began to rise.

These men of the New Stone Age did something else of high importance: they began to plant seeds and harvest crops. Before this time, men had only gathered and hunted food. Now they began to produce it. Men improved the food and the food improved the men. When the food supply became larger and more certain the population increased still more rapidly.

This sowing and harvesting of crops occurred when a great climatic change began in Europe. As the ice sheets melted at the end of the last cold age the lands of southern Europe were slowly changed into grasslands and virgin forests of birches, pines, and ash. Most of the areas south and east of the Mediterranean Sea were gradually transformed into deserts sprinkled with a few green oases. Instead of grass and trees there appeared a bare and forbidding wasteland of sand and rock, parched riverbeds, badlands, and canyons baked by the pitiless sun. They remain unchanged today. Deserts comprise nearly 20 per cent of our planet's surface. Here live the king snakes and the kangaroo rats, the giant cactus and the sagebrush. In these vast and burning miles are the cruel illusions of the mirages of lakes and rivers and the minarets of mysterious cities dancing on the hot horizons. Deserts are deathtraps, graveyards, deadly foes of the water-cooled bodies of men.

As the sands of the new deserts swirled and spread in the convulsions that marked the end of the last ice age most of the wild animals perished or fled northward with the reindeer. Hunting became poor and meat scarce. Hence men began to seek out the green places in the mountain passes, the green belts by the rivers and lakes. All the early chapters of our history are filled with the clashes and battles of men for rich green lands, for possession and control of rivers and lakes, springs and wells.

In the green lands by the waters men planted seeds: barley, corn or maize, rice, squash, wheat. Because they sometimes had to cut down trees these men made sharper stone axes. Because they had to cultivate their crops they made stone-bladed hoes. They learned to irrigate. They reaped their grain with sickles. Having grown the grain they pounded it to make flour. Since they now had more food than they needed at once they made clay pots to store it for later use.

When the men of the New Stone Age moved towards the lakes and rivers they frequently found no caves. They made grass shelters, tents of hides, sod houses, wooden huts. They began to live together in settled villages. They worked together in communities.

The herdsmen still wandered from pasture to pasture, especially in those regions where farming was difficult. The farmers, on the other hand, usually stayed in the same place. We may be sure that then, as today, fathers and sons through many generations farmed and lived at peace in the same quiet valleys.

The men who first planted crops and domesticated animals and settled down in communities gradually made a social revolution. They were cooperating to alter the untouched world of nature. They were no longer passively accepting their environment but were trying to adapt it to human needs and purposes. This was the most significant achievement of the men of the Neolithic Age.

The Age of Stone gradually merged into the Age of Metals. Copper came first, bronze second, iron third. About 4000 B.C. an unknown Egyptian fashioned copper needles. Probably the copper he used had been found in a relatively pure state. A thousand years later copper ores, perhaps from Cyprus, were being smelted and cast into molds. Copper had advantages over stone. It was tough, light, and strong. On the other hand, it was a soft metal; it did not take a good edge; and it was expensive. Ingenious men soon discovered that harder and more useful implements could be obtained from bronze, an alloy of copper and tin or copper and zinc. Around 1300 B.C. iron began to be smelted with charcoal at the eastern end of the Mediterranean. Slowly the production and use of metals spread over Europe and Asia.

Metal industries gradually began to appear in the valleys of rivers: the Danube, Don, Elbe, Po, Rhine, and Rhone. All who could buy wanted a regular supply of metal, especially craftsmen and specialists like smiths and carpenters, boatbuilders and millers. A lively trade arose along the coasts of the Mediterranean Sea all the way to Spain and Morocco, up and down the rivers, out through the waters by the rock of Gibraltar to the west coast of Europe. Tin from Britain's Cornwall mines moved steadily on the trade routes eastward. Gold and salt, amber and copper, tin and iron, timber and lead— these became the important commodities of trade in the Age of Metals. Men and markets were coming together in a way the world had not seen before. Along the routes of trade and commerce the people prospered and real wealth increased.

The rising tides of trade made men familiar with the goods and techniques, the customs and characteristics of individuals from other regions. The result was a series of slow and subtle changes in the cultures affected by the ebb and flow of commerce. Once men began to hunt bears or plant crops together, the doors of a new world were opened and they have never closed. Since that time, men have talked and traveled and traded. They have exchanged goods and ideas. Goods and ideas make societies and cultures.

There was another significant result of the streams of the new trade. Some areas had to import essential raw materials. In order to pay for what they imported they had to increase their own productive enterprise so that they would

have a surplus of goods to exchange. Hence agriculture and industry hastened
their pace and power as a result of the pressure of necessity and demand.

Many other important things happened in the Age of Metals. From Asia
came the potter's wheel, an instrument that enabled men to make, with speed
and precision, perfectly symmetrical products, such as pots and vessels. Wheels
on carts and wagons were used in Mesopotamia by 3000 B.C., in India by
2500 B.C., in Egypt by 1600 B.C., in Sweden and China by 1000 B.C. Bricks
were manufactured in kilns in India by 2500 B.C. Wooden plows appeared in
Egypt and Mesopotamia about 3000 B.C., in China about 1400 B.C. Camels,
donkeys, oxen, and horses were used in agriculture and transport. The horse
came late; it did not appear in Egypt, for instance, until about 1600 B.C. New
ships, so essential to trade, were built with timbered keels and ribs, far superior
to the rafts used earlier.

As people moved over Europe and Asia the languages of wide areas of the
world were being shaped. To describe completely what happened several
alternative hypotheses have been suggested. It is true that none of these provides a fixed and final explanation for all of the scattered phenomena observed
by the archeologists and philologists. Nevertheless, the main outlines, so well
described by Professor J. L. Myres and Mr. Harold Peake, are clear enough to
satisfy the demands of the scholars.

About 2500 B.C. groups of warlike peoples came in a series of marauding
migrations out of a grassland area north of the Black and Caspian Seas. These
groups possessed a military superiority resulting mainly from the fact that they
had horse-drawn chariots and cut-and-thrust swords. They also brought with
them more sheep, the practice of cremation, and, to some areas, the first
wheeled vehicles. In several regions of Europe they established themselves as
an aristocracy.

In large and sweeping movements these people came. We call them Indo-
Europeans because they originally spoke various forms of an Indo-European or
Aryan language. One group rolled westward towards Greece and Italy. They
were the ancestors of such peoples as the Armenians, Greeks, Romans, and
Celts. Through long generations their language changed and many of the
changes depended upon where they stopped in the migrations. So it is that the
related Indo-European languages of Europe first arose. French, Italian, Portuguese, Spanish (the Romance languages) are all derived from Greco-Latin
languages which in turn came, with numerous changes, from the mother
Indo-European. It used to be supposed that separate languages arose out of
the parent speech by a process of fission. "Trees" were drawn to show exactly
where each group broke away from the original stem or trunk. This picture
was soon seen to be too neat, too simplified. It has now been concluded that a

large number of different dialects were probably included in the parent source from which all Indo-European languages came.

Out of the heartland of language by the Black and Caspian Seas came the Balto-Slavonic languages (Bohemian, Bulgarian, Croatian, Lettish, Lithuanian, Polish, Serbian, Russian); the Teutonic languages (Anglo-Saxon, Dutch, German, the Scandinavian languages); Greek and Latin and the Romance languages mentioned earlier together with Provençal, Catalan, Rumanian; the Celtic languages (Bretonic, Erse, Manx, Welsh, the Gaelic of Scotland, Devon, Cornwall). Today most major groups in Europe speak an Indo-European language.

There was a second wave in the dispersal of the Indo-European migrants who came out of the northland grass country. About 2000 B.C., perhaps driven by drought, a group of Indo-Europeans left their homes on the steppes and headed on horseback south and west into Persia. They became the ancient Medes and Persians. Both the old and new languages of Persia are Indo-European.

A third body of Indo-European light-skinned warriors and cattlemen surged through the mountain passes into northern India about 1500 B.C., driving their cattle before them. Today most of the numerous languages and dialects of India and Pakistan are Indo-European. The others belong to the Dravidian group of languages that have been used since time immemorial by the Indian aborigines in the Deccan and Tamil Land. Today about 13 Dravidian languages and many dialects are spoken by 60,000,000 people in southern and central India and northern Ceylon. There is also a Dravidian dialect spoken by the Brahuis of Baluchistan, an isolated island in a sea of Aryan speech.

The standard histories of language explain, usually with much technical detail, the scope and power of Grimm's law of the interchange of consonant sounds (labial, linguo-dental, guttural) in the Indo-European languages. Of all the known and established laws of the Aryan tongues Grimm's is the most important and the most fascinating. According to the shift-laws of Grimm and others, verbal equations can be made in several languages, especially in words that have to do with objects and concepts fundamental to a society.

In Latin, Greek, Sanskrit, German, Norwegian, French, and Russian the words for "brother" are: *frater, phrater, bhrata, bruder, broder, frère, brat.* The words for "mother" are: *mater, meter, mata, mutter, moder, mère, mat.* The Latin word for "father" is *pater.* In Sanskrit it is *pitar;* in Erse, *athir;* in German, *vater;* in Tocharian, *patar.* "One hundred" in Latin is *centum,* in Sanskrit *satem.* The Vedic Indians of the ninth century B.C. and the Homeric Greeks used quite similar words for "fall" and "five" and inflected them in the same way.

Another body of people, quite separate from the Indo-Europeans, were called the Semites. They lived in the southern grasslands of Arabia with their sheep and their goats, their asses and their camels. Some of them, like the Indo-Europeans, migrated from their original homeland in widely spaced waves. Centuries often divided the coming of separate migrations. The ranks of Semitic peoples include such groups as the Arameans, Assyrians, Babylonians, Hebrews, and the Phoenicians. Through the centuries languages changed and changed again. That is the reason why several different Semitic languages exist today.

Besides the differences of language among men there are the differences of race. During the long centuries of mankind's early history the human beings of the world had slowly become divided into subspecies or races. The word "race" is correctly used to describe only the physical characteristics of men, such as the size and shape of the skull, the form of the features, the color of the skin. If the word "race" is intended to describe anything else, such as nationality or language, it is incorrectly used and is without meaning. For instance, there can be no Semitic race, no Indo-European or Aryan race. These words refer to the languages men speak and to nothing else.

The main racial divisions of mankind are three: the first is the Negroid, the black-skinned, which includes the Negroes of Africa and America. The second is the Mongoloid, which includes the Japanese, the Chinese, and the American Indians. The third is the Caucasian, or white, which includes almost all Europeans, Americans, northern Africans, western Asians. These three main racial divisions are segmented into smaller groups. For instance, within the Caucasian division is the Mediterranean group (short, dark, brown-eyed) and the Nordic group (blond and blue-eyed). It is clear, of course, that there are no "pure" races today. Like many classifications, the divisions of race must be used with caution and judgment.

Thus it happened that different languages and different races emerged during the great migrations of early human history, when whole peoples surged forward to conquer, to settle, and sometimes to move to still new frontiers. Military leaders sought booty and power and scourged the lands about them. Old customs and laws were cherished and others were added. Farmers and herdsmen became fighters when it was necessary and then went back to their pastures and their plows. New discoveries and inventions added to the progress and power of mankind. Beyond the horizons always rolled the challenge of tomorrow.

The children of these remote and almost unimaginable times lived hard lives as they struggled for survival. The pace of advance was slow. In the Age of Metals, however, there was certainly a quickening of that pace—sometimes the men of those days seem almost to leap ahead; they trudged and sailed to new places; they continued to shape their languages; they smelted ores and made new tools and weapons; they traded wherever they could. It was a dynamic world and the men in it seldom paused for breath.

The outstanding feature, beyond any doubt, of the whole long period has not yet been mentioned. It is a great matter that will form a steady theme in the next few chapters. Far back in the Age of Stone men had begun to live in small communities. In the Age of Metals, as production mounted and population grew, those communities increased in size and skills. It was natural that the greatest expansion of settlement would come where effective use could be made of green fields and water. The green river valleys provided spots where men could use the improved methods of agriculture, the new devices of industry, and the advantages of trade. To these places—strategic points on all counts—came thousands of sound and sensible men to settle and work. They appeared on the banks of the Nile, the Euphrates and the Tigris, the Indus, and the Hwang Ho. There had now arrived the hour of the birth of cities and the growth of the great river civilizations of the ancient world.

Chapter 2

THE

VALLEY OF THE NILE

"But time and chance happeneth to them all."
—Ecclesiastes, IX, 11

FOR many miles the Nile river flows between steep cliffs across a waterless waste of sand and rock. There are six great rapids and cataracts. About 700 miles from the swampy Nile Delta a widening valley cut in the soft limestone brings a gash of life in the desert. This green ribbon of marvelously fertile land, flooded annually by the river, is from two to thirty miles wide. It was, and remains, one of the great crossroads of the world. For centuries Egypt has been a natural meeting place for different streams of culture brought by migrants and travelers from many lands.

Egypt today is a country of contrasts, a restless region of mingled wealth and poverty. "The tools of the peasant are those of his ancestors—the hoe, the wooden plow, the hand sickle, and the threshing board. His dwelling is a crude, fly-infested two-room hut sheltering family and chickens alike. He owns little clothing and has few comforts. Like three-quarters of his fellow-countrymen, he is afflicted with disease." Through the centuries this has been the lot of the peasant, the fellahin. Around him press his fellows in a heavily crowded land. Only 3.5 per cent of the land of Egypt is cultivated and habitable. Twice a year it produces crops of cotton, sugar cane, and wheat. An average of 1,200 people live on each square mile of land. In modern Japan the average is 1,000; in Java, 900; in Belgium, 700.

The culture of the land of the pharaohs and pyramids has always been self-centered and self-reliant. The people have been a proud people, often intolerant of the strangers within and the foreign lands without. The ancient Egyptians, for instance, liked flat and fertile lands and uniform landscapes like the familiar valley and Delta of the Nile. They did not like the mountainous foreign regions, dismal and dangerous, rainy and unpredictable. One Egyptian scribe

13

wrote that Syria was a dreadful place. "Shuddering seizes thee, thy hair stands on end, thy soul lies in thy hand. The ravine is on one side of thee while the mountain is on the other."

Although archeologists have found artifacts dating from 15,000 B.C. in Egyptian graves on the desert margins of the Nile valley, the main streams of ancient Egyptian culture do not begin until about 5000 B.C. The period of Egyptian history after 2900 B.C. is called the Dynastic period because Egypt was then ruled by the pharaohs. This Dynastic age is itself divided into five parts: the Old Kingdom (2900–2300 B.C.); the Feudal Age (2300–2100 B.C.); the Middle Kingdom (2100–1780 B.C.); the Hyksos domination (1780–1580 B.C.); and the Empire (1580–525 B.C.).

In the pre-Dynastic years of Egyptian history the country was divided into several city-states or nomes. Sometimes they were at war; sometimes they cooperated for economic reasons, especially for the building of canals and irrigation works. About 5000 B.C. all the city-states were fused into two kingdoms, Lower Egypt in the north and Upper Egypt in the south. After one earlier attempt at consolidation the two kingdoms were finally united about 2900 B.C. Tradition says that the founder and leader of this unified state was Menes, who therefore became the founder of the first of the five dynasties that ruled in Egypt during the period of the Old Kingdom. The intertwined lotus and papyrus on the carved Egyptian thrones always symbolize the kingdom of united Egypt.

The Old Kingdom ended about 2300 B.C. in complete confusion. The reasons for the collapse seem to have been the ambitions and rivalries of the pharaoh's senior servants governing the provinces, the heavy taxes, and the persistence of local loyalties. In the so-called Feudal Age between 2300 B.C. and 2100 B.C. the years were marked by the competition of petty tyrants, by anarchy and destruction, by the invasions of nomads from outside the country, and by recurrent famine. "Gold and lapis lazuli are hung about the necks of slave girls. But noble ladies walk through the land and mistresses of houses say: 'Would that we had something to eat. . . .' Behold they that possessed beds now lie on the ground. He that slept with dirt upon him now stuffeth for himself a cushion."

At last the leaders in the capital city of Thebes succeeded in bringing order. Then began the capable and famous Eleventh and Twelfth Dynasties and the period of Egyptian history called the Middle Kingdom. For about 300 years there was social progress and prosperity broken only by sporadic instability and disruption. At the end of the Twelfth Dynasty, however, there came 200 years of internal dislocation and civil disorder. The nobles revolted against the pharaohs and the whole Nile valley was broken again into warring states. Such weakness tempted invaders from outside, and around 1780 B.C. they swept in and conquered.

The invasion of Egypt was impelled by the concurrent Indo-European migrations farther north. The foreign invaders were the semibarbarous Hyksos, a Semitic people from western Asia. Among these militant and hungry tribesmen may have been some Indo-European adventurers.

The Hyksos had a strong army and swift chariots. It was from them that the Egyptians acquired the horse and the chariot—these chariots were the first wheeled vehicles seen on the banks of the Nile.

Until 1580 B.C. the alien Hyksos controlled Egypt and brought a dark age. Then the Egyptians began a successful rebellion in the south against their overlords. The Hyksos who were not killed or enslaved were forced to flee. The Empire now began with Aahmes I, a national hero and founder of the Eighteenth Dynasty.

During the period of the Empire the pharaohs of the Eighteenth, Nineteenth, and Twentieth Dynasties deliberately adopted a policy of aggressive imperialism. This idea may have been borrowed from the Hyksos' schemes of statecraft. The Egyptians were not prepared to be content with the expulsion of the Hyksos. They lusted for further victories and more conquests of land. They also liked booty. At the same time, of course, they wanted to protect themselves against further attacks from western Asia by striking first to conquer strategic areas with their armies and their fleets.

The formidable Thothmes III (1490–1436 B.C.) of the Eighteenth Dynasty led his powerful armies to victory over Syria, Palestine, and Phoenicia. The Tell el-Amarna cuneiform tablets—part of the Egyptian archives discovered in 1887—indicate that Thothmes collected much tribute in Syria, thus adding considerably to the economic surplus of Egypt. It also seems that he forced Nubia and Assyria to pay him tribute and Cyprus and Crete to ally themselves with him. For Egypt these were years of power and stability. Plunder added to the treasures brought by profitable trade, and Thebes became a rich and magnificent symbol of the might of the pharaohs. It was indeed the Golden Age of Egypt. Thothmes III made great monuments to commemorate his victories. One of them stands today in Central Park in the city of New York.

The peoples Thothmes III had vanquished were not content. They would not permit the Egyptians to manage their empire in peace. Frequent revolts, especially in Syria, weakened the power of Thebes. Luxury and corruption did their inevitable work among the upper classes at home.

It is true that there were a few outstanding leaders among the successors of Thothmes III. One of these was Amenhotep III (1398–1361 B.C.), a pharaoh of wealth, power, and reputation. The ruins of his palaces and public works remain to show us something of the imperial magnificence of his age. From Amenhotep's point of view, big things were better than small ones. He was obsessed with bigness: big temples, avenues, monuments, pillars, palaces. Professor John A. Wilson once remarked (in *The Burden of Egypt*) that Amenhotep III "started that passion for the colossal which characterized the later Empire."

There were other pharaohs who were not in the tradition of the warrior Thothmes III. Amenhotep II was an athlete and sportsman. Amenhotep IV was an eccentric religious reformer. Tutankhamen was weak. Destiny called them to be kings; but the fates had denied them the gifts to do the job.

Ramses II (1290–1224 B.C.) and Ramses III (1195–1164 B.C.) were the last of the really able pharaohs in the Nineteenth and Twentieth Dynasties. Ramses II almost restored the power of the Empire—but "almost" is seldom enough. He did conquer a part of Palestine and southern Syria again. He fought a long and exhausting war with the Hittites, then at the height of their power and the rulers of a great empire. He carved on temple walls an account of the Battle of Kadesh, which he declared to be a glorious victory over the Hittites. Historians know that Kadesh was not in fact a triumph for Ramses II. The truth is this: Ramses was ambushed by the Hittites, fought his way out, and was lucky to escape alive. It was this escape that he magnified into a stunning victory.

The arrogant inscriptions Ramses II placed on the temple walls of Karnak, Abydos, Luxor, Abu-Simbel, and elsewhere were put there to strengthen the chances of his fame among men in the centuries ahead. He also built great monuments. In the cliffs at Abu-Simbel in Nubia there were carved four statues of this proud Ramses II, each ninety-four feet high. Today they have almost come to the same end as the stone figure of Ozymandias, who was once "king of kings":

> Two vast and trunkless legs of stone
> Stand in the desert . . . Near them, on the sand,
> Half sunk, a shattered visage lies. . . .
> Nothing beside remains. Round the decay
> Of that colossal wreck, boundless and bare
> The lone and level sands stretch far away.

The reign of Ramses III was dark and difficult. Egypt was attacked by Libyans, Philistines, Sicilians, and other groups of the "Sea Peoples" who had seized Cyprus, Anatolia, part of Syria, shattered the Hittite Empire, and turned towards Egypt. Ramses III did succeed in repelling the assaults. It was no mean achievement.

After Ramses III came a series of weak and vacillating rulers. Some very able men have had very silly sons. Under the incompetent successors of Ramses III the land of Egypt declined in prestige and power. It was her sunset era. Libyan and Nubian barbarians came into the land. Libyan kings ruled from the thrones of the pharaohs. Then some Nubians seized power. Around 670 B.C. the Assyrians invaded, plundered, killed, and enslaved. After the wide

Assyrian Empire fell Egypt was left independent for a short period and enjoyed a brief economic and cultural renaissance called the Saitic Revival. Then Cambyses of Persia came and conquered in 525 B.C. In 332 B.C. the mighty Alexander the Great was to extend his hungry empire to embrace the Nile Valley.

Such is a swift summary of the salient military and political points in the tale of the rise and decline of early Egypt. So it was that strong men ruled and weak men faltered in hours of confusion and disorder. The wicked despoiled and conquerors came with sudden violence. When we consider how complex is the total story it seems impertinent to recite it so briefly. There are certainly perils in doing so, but many activities of men are in fact very fugitive when regarded in the broad canvas of the history of a whole state or a whole world. They have their day and pass. Nor can we afford to believe that the regnal years of pharaohs and the political patterns of the state are the sole pillars and grounds of the total history of ancient Egypt.

Many years ago the English historian Freeman said that "History is past politics." Fortunately, modern scholars have no patience with that blinkered vision. They feel that it is their function to try to understand as many aspects of the past as they can. The empire of the historian has broadened so steadily in recent decades that it now includes provinces the very existence of which were unsuspected not so long ago. The historian knows that neither in the present nor the past does a human being live by politics alone. He buys and sells. He plows the fields, digs ditches, and loafs in the sun. He paints with oil and whitewash. He writes poetry and he makes music. He beats, beheads, and tortures. He worships and he prays. Page upon page the list could run and the sum would not be said.

What may be written about the land of ancient Egypt that has little to do with the details of thirty dynasties or twenty wars? What of the pharaohs? the nobles and the lower classes, those hewers of wood and drawers of water? the arts and crafts? the gods? Not every man is like the war horse of the Scriptures who "saith among the trumpets Ha, ha and he smelleth the battle afar off, the thunder of the captains, and the shouting." There are other ends that matter, such as the worship of the gods and the arts and crafts of peace.

The pharaohs emerge into the light of history as the rulers of the unified Egyptian state that appeared around 2900 B.C. According to one of their titles they were the Lords of the Two Lands of Upper and Lower Egypt. By right of conquest they were indeed Lords because they were regarded as the legal owners of the whole Nile valley and the Delta. As owners of all this fertile land they were entitled to collect in tributes the whole surplus product of the soil. Their servants did collect that surplus; they transported it on the Nile to royal granaries. The revenues were fantastic.

Such a system, quite satisfactory from a palace point of view, might not have been maintained for long if the power of the pharaohs had been deemed to depend only upon the ownership rights obtained by conquest. In fact, the authority of the pharaoh rested upon something else: his supposed divinity. Here is the earliest example of the "divine right of kings" in human society. Royal claims of divine right have always been hard to challenge. The heretics are often few, the believers many. "The gods had sent the pharaohs forth to lead mankind." It was dangerous to dispute, easy to acquiesce. Said the pharaoh:

> Give heed to my utterances. Hearken to them.
> I speak to you. I make you aware
> That I am the son of Ra who issued from his body.
> I sit upon his throne in rejoicing since he established me
>   as king, as lord of this land.
> My counsels are good. My plans come to pass.
> I protect Egypt. I defend it.

So far as we know there were really not many who were prepared to dispute the divinity of the Lord of the Two Lands and the Ruler of the Nile. Who dared risk the anger of the gods? The pharaoh was considered to be possessed of supernatural attributes. He was an immortal being. He alone held the magic power to control the coming of the annual river flood with its burden of fertile silt, the daily rising of the sun, the fertility of the live-stock, the fate of the crops, the rains and the waters. He could give immortality to faithful servants. The pharaoh was "the lord of the sweet breeze" from the Mediterranean. He was the link between ordinary mortals and the great gods.

There were other boons given to the Egyptians by the pharaohs. Those monarchs made the rules of the land and many of their laws were good. They often gave effective leadership, order, and strength to the state. They built and financed the great canals and irrigation works and the storehouses for wheat and linen. They policed the frontiers, especially against the prowling and land-hungry Nubians. They sent expeditions to get the copper of Sinai, the timber of Lebanon, the perfumes of Arabia.

Below the pharaohs were the powerful and wealthy nobles, the governors and the stewards with great estates and profitable hereditary offices. Many nobles were also priests in the religious system of Egypt. The office of priesthood often became hereditary and profitable. It seems that most of the time the governors, stewards, priests, and other servants of the pharaohs were able and active assistants in the state. In some periods, of course, corruption, robbery, and jobbery were common. In any age there are a few downright scoundrels about. The petty pilferers, the big-time racketeers, and the like are old characters in the human drama.

At the base of the rather stable social pyramid were the crowded ranks of the common people, the peasants, artisans, miners, soldiers, and the workers who built the pyramids with no wheeled vehicles to aid them, no cranes or windlasses, only ropes, cradles, levers, ramps, and corded muscles lifting and pulling in the agony of the sun.

Two things were of overwhelming importance in the life of the Egyptian. In the first place, he saw that the sun blazed daily and banished the hated darkness and cold. The sun, it seemed, was the source of life. Secondly, the Egyptian saw that once a year the Nile river was swelled with the spring floods that brought the fertile mud. Here, then, were two miracles: the daily rebirth of the sun and the annual rebirth of the river.

It was natural that the sun god Ra should be considered the greatest of all the gods. Legend said that Ra was the first king of Egypt. The sun, said the Egyptians, was probably moved by a boat or pushed by a giant beetle across the sky. Perhaps it was a great falcon. In the night the sun sailed on a ship through an underworld called the Dat. The water under the earth was called Nun. This was believed to be the water that fed the Nile. These ideas are all described in the famous Egyptian *Book of the Dead*.

There were many other gods and goddesses: Osiris, king of the region of the dead after he was murdered by his brother Seth; Shu, god of the air; Nut, the sky goddess; Geb, the earth god; Horus, son of Osiris; Anubis, the jackal-headed god who waited to conduct the spirits of men to the everlasting shades.

The Egyptians believed that they would survive after death if they observed the proper rituals and formulas of their religion. Each individual had his own *ka,* the mysterious other-side of his being which came into existence at the physical birth of his body and lived on after the body died. This is the reason why the tombs of Egypt, "the castles of eternity," contain food and equipment for the use of the dead in the next world. A ferryman in a magic boat, according to one Egyptian idea, would take the dead to the Field of Reeds, filled with fertile soil and everlasting spring. There the welcoming gods would wait, "their white sandals on their feet."

The inhabitants of ancient Egypt had rather clear views about the nature of the earth and the universe. The earth, they said, was a great flat platter with a bent and roughened rim. Inside the bottom of this platter were the rich plains of the Nile valley called "The Great Green." The platter floated in the waters under the earth called Nun, mentioned earlier. Overhead was the arched vault of the sky resting upon four posts and partly supported by Shu, the goddess of the air.

Thus it was that in the days of ancient Egypt, as in the days before and after, men sought to understand and explain the universe. They were "searching in the dark for the key to the lock of the truth."

The Egyptians, like many other peoples, made a script with vivid pictorial symbols standing for ideas, words, and sounds. The Egyptian script, called hieroglyphic, lasted for 3,000 years. Some of the pictures and diagrams came to be used with the phonetic value of single consonants to spell out names. The Egyptians, however, used a variety of signs to stand for the same sounds and usually jumbled phonograms and ideograms all together. They never came near to inventing an alphabet. The Egyptian script was first deciphered by the Frenchman Jean François Champollion from the famous Rosetta Stone, which was found in the Nile valley in 1799. The same inscription was repeated on the stone in Greek and in two forms of Egyptian writing.

In addition to the messages or records carved on stone there were others written with ink on papyrus, a reed native to the Nile valley. The pith and fiber in a single strip of reed were pounded flat. When the leveled pulp was dried into a smooth mat it was ready for the written words. Papyrus was the best writing material available through all the ages of antiquity.

The Egyptians also made the first calendar, probably the best monument to Egyptian learning. Always concerned with practical affairs, the Egyptians calculated that the spring flooding of the Nile valley, the most important event of the year, occurred when the dog star Sirius rose above the horizon in the morning. Because this happened every 365 days the Egyptians made a solar calendar. They divided the year into 12 months of 30 days each and had 5 days left over. Some peoples, such as the Chinese, watched the moon and studied its phases. Naturally enough, they made and used a lunar calendar.

Arts and crafts were developed to a high level by the Egyptians. Their mural paintings, for instance, were made on a dry surface with colors that are still brilliant. Their skillful use of the artistic principle of parallel rhythm was continued through several centuries. They manufactured rich jewelry, dyes and cosmetics, glass and enamel. They tempered iron in the later phases of the Age of Metals. They knew quite a bit about astronomy, engineering, mathematics, chemistry, and physics. True, their contributions to astronomy and mathematics were decidedly inferior to those of the Babylonians and Chaldeans. At the same time, their accurate knowledge and skill in the planning and execution of engineering projects are clearly shown in the building of the proud pyramids. These structures are the most celebrated group of royal tombs and monuments on earth, especially the three on the Gizeh plateau.

Most of the massive pyramids were built between 3200 and 2300 B.C. on the west bank of the Nile near the ancient city of Memphis. The mastabas

—mud-brick structures placed over burial pits—belong to an earlier age. Of the eighty pyramids the largest is the Great Pyramid of Gizeh (Cheops), a royal tomb built on the desert plateau by the architect Khufu-onek near the beginning of the Fourth Dynasty (about 2600 B.C.). The British Houses of Parliament and St. Paul's Cathedral could easily be put inside the base of this pyramid (13.1 acres). In its outer facing are 2,300,000 separate blocks of Tura limestone, the weight of each averaging about 2½ tons. The Greek historian Herodotus tells us that the construction required the labor of 100,000 men, and it may well be so. The four sides of the pyramid are almost exactly in line with true north, south, east, and west. The structure is 481 feet high and each side measures 756 feet. (Many more fascinating statistical details are to be found in I. E. S. Edwards' *The Pyramids of Egypt*.) Some of the stones were so tightly fitted more than 4,000 years ago that a knife cannot be inserted in the joints today. "The Great Pyramid of Egypt," Professor James H. Breasted once wrote, "is . . . a document in the history of the human mind. It clearly discloses man's sense of sovereign power in his triumph over material forces. For himself and for his sovereign the pharaoh's engineer was achieving the conquest of immortality by sheer command of material forces."

On the great causeway leading to the Gizeh Pyramid rests the huge lion with the human head of the pharaoh that is called the Great Sphinx. It is 240 feet long. The royal cobra headdress lies upon its forehead 66 feet above the sand.

In 1954, several archeologists, digging in the sand near the south face of the Great Pyramid, found a row of limestone blocks sealed with pink gypsum. In an underground chamber beneath these stones was a 6-decked ship 125 feet long and 17 feet wide. Apparently this was the ship built to convey the spirit of Cheops to the happy Field of Reeds.

The mighty temple ruins of Luxor and Karnak always bring to the beholder an awareness of the engineering glory that once belonged to Thebes and Egypt. At Karnak there stand today a colossal pylon and rectangular towers before a colonnaded hall. Each column in the Great Hypostyle Hall is 70 feet high. There are 136 of these columns, and they once supported the roofs of the aisles on each side of the nave. The capitals were each capable of holding 50 standing people. The hall itself is 170 feet long and 338 feet across the nave and the flanking aisles.

Karnak and Luxor are connected by an avenue of sphinxes. In the famous Valley of the Kings rock cliffs contain the tombs of pharaohs. "All these were honored in their generations." There are several temples, including the one belonging to Queen Hatshepsut's high priest, with all its columned glories. Two statues of Amenhotep III rise to a height of more than seventy feet. All about are granite obelisks and carved figures, imperturbable, formal and conventionalized in design and execution, suggesting power and confidence.

One of the many texts carved in the chambers and corridors of the pyramids says: "I protect the chapel of thy tomb. I ward off the intruding stranger. I hurl the foes to the ground and their weapons with them. I destroy thine adversaries in their lurking-place, blocking it that they come forth no more." Fortunately the words of the shadowy defenders of the pyramids have not always proved true.

There is another Egyptian inscription: "Generations pass away and others go on since the time of the ancestors. They that build buildings their places are no more."

Chapter 3

THE LAND

BETWEEN THE RIVERS

"Who is tall enough to reach up to heaven?
Who is broad enough that he might encompass the earth?"
—*Dialogue of Pessimism* (Mesopotamia, c. 2500 B.C.)

NORTH and east of Egypt lies the land called the Fertile Crescent. It begins near Egypt, curves along the eastern rim of the Mediterranean, swings towards the Arabian Desert, sweeps east and south to the Persian Gulf and the waterless central basin of Iran.

In ancient days the soil of the Crescent land was rich and the crops were abundant. For long centuries production and commerce flourished. Men grew fat and prospered. Vineyards and groves of date palms stood beside the panorama of the bright-sailed boats of the fishermen on the lakes. The long caravans moved from the old city of Damascus by the Barada river, from Tyre, Nineveh, and Babylon. Haggling merchants from Tarsus met silversmiths and swordsmen from Ephesus by the white houses shining in the sunlight.

If you travel northeast from Egypt through the land of Goshen you will come to Palestine, to Jerusalem and the region of the Dead Sea. Then you will reach Samaria and Syria, the places where the men of Tyre and Sidon once traded in the sun. Here, too, the Hittites once raided from their northern strongholds. Here and beyond lie the home of the Phoenicians and the mountains of Lebanon, land of the great cedars. And beyond Palestine to the east is Mesopotamia.

Mesopotamia lies between the Tigris and the Euphrates, two famous rivers in the early history of mankind. In the lower parts of that land by the once desolate marshes of the Tigris-Euphrates delta there arose the civilization of Sumer. This happened about 4000 B.C.

The early Sumerians, a non-Semitic people, probably came from the mountain fastnesses of central Asia. They lived a hard life of struggle and toil, working as farmers and cattle breeders, fishermen and boatmen, merchants and artisans. They built houses of sun-dried bricks on the mud flats. Along the numerous irrigation ditches the fig trees and the wheat and barley crops swayed in the sun. A new device called the wheel appeared. Herds of cattle and flocks of sheep multiplied. Many Sumerians became excellent metalworkers and craftsmen. The merchants, busy with the tasks of trade, counted their profits in the evening and waited for another day of pleasure on the morrow. It was in Sumer that there first began among merchants the practice of using bills of credit, bills and receipts, interest taking, all steps of high importance in economic history. Temple priests often kept elaborate records of business transactions—some of them are in the world's museums today.

The men of these times also came to use the highly convenient device of money. This brief sentence does not mean that a suitable system of currency suddenly grew out of a state of barter. Such developments usually take a long time; they are the results of experiments and accidents, trials and errors, rule of thumb. What does not work is discarded; what does work is kept and improved.

Long before the appearance of money there were exchanges between groups —such as tribes and families—in the form of reciprocal gifts or rough barter. Only later were there such exchanges between individuals. In these distant days there gradually emerged several units of value. It was quite natural that one of these units would be cattle, the wealth of many early peoples. The Latin word *pecunia,* meaning money, appears in the Latin plural *pecua,* which means cattle of all kinds. In some areas other kinds of units of value were used, such as salt, shells, and skins.

When hard money was first devised it probably took the form of iron bars. Later exact amounts of gold, silver, or copper were measured out to settle payments. Still later, bars of metal with their values stamped upon them were used. About 700 B.C. coins of fixed weight and content appeared —the idea and practice first arose in Lydia. The use of metal as money obviously had many advantages. It was durable, of fairly constant value, and was easily transported and guarded.

In these years of the Age of Metals patterns of life were steadily changing. With the increase of trade and the rise of cities came a concentration of capital and a greater division of labor. The growing cities had to import essential raw materials and the exporting societies—such as Anatolia, Cyprus, and Syria—grew more familiar with the cultures of their customers. Everybody, it seemed, learned from everybody else, sometimes a little and sometimes a lot. Quick eyes and shrewd brains are always necessary if anything of importance is to happen at all in any age. The steady interchange of ideas and techniques among men of many lands was mentioned earlier. It bears repetition. Keys to the understanding of peoples and their times are found in the bazaars of Kabul and Jerusalem and in the workers' huts as well as in the palaces of Thebes and Babylon.

In the land of Sumer and the nearby kingdom of Akkad to the north several independent city-states arose, each governed by wealthy and despotic priest-kings. These rulers had great political and moral power. They had the physical force to compel obedience; they controlled the army, the granaries, and the irrigation systems. They were believed to be partly divine. The kings, it was said, were creators of property, the protectors of the poor. Sumerian inscriptions hailed the king as "The Shepherd of the People" and the "Waterer of the Field."

The lands of each city were also believed to be owned by one or more gods. The rulers in the imposing temples were looked upon as holders of the land in trust for the gods. There were four "great" gods, seven who decided the fates of men, and about fifty others, including the lesser gods of Salt and Wine. The mightiest god was Anu, or Shamash, the god of the sun, the rain, and the sky—and therefore of fertility. Second in rank was Enlil, god of the storm. The god of the plague was called Nergal. In a land where Nature showed herself to be terrifying and powerful it was fitting that the people should turn to such gods of rain and lightning, flood and storm. They were more concerned with this life than with the drab afterworld they called Sheol.

The city-kingdoms, with wonderful names like Eshnunna, Shuruppak, Legash and Ummah and Kish, battled among themselves for property and power and water rights. Cruel and bloody wars among these urban cultures brought tragic consequences, especially to poor and humble men and women struggling against their fates. These things were no less bitter because they were long ago and the people who suffered then lie in dust and darkness now.

The clash of arms is often matched by the quiet triumphs of peace. So it was with the Sumerians. Like the Chaldeans after them, the men of Sumer used sundials and waterclocks and carefully observed the movements of the sun and the stars. They divided the week into seven days, the day into twenty-four hours (really twelve double hours), the hour into sixty minutes, the minute into sixty seconds. They also invented a system of numerical notation. The numbers 1 to 9 were expressed by straight lines, 10 was expressed by a circle, 20 by two circles—a decimal system. Multiplication tables were often used, especially to calculate areas of land and volumes of such things as brick piles. The Sumerians, like the Egyptians, were also skilled in the use of fractions.

There were other signal achievements. The Sumerians developed a standardized system of weights and measures. They improved their medicine and their surgery. They used the water level and the square. They built water-control gates and reservoirs. They invented the dome, the vault, and the arch —probably because the post and lintel construction used in Egypt was impossible in Sumeria or any land that did not have large stones.

The ziggurat—the word means pinnacle or top of the mountain—was the towering part of the palace temple. It was the architectural symbol of all Mesopotamia, as the pyramid was the symbol of Egypt. The typical ziggurat consists of several massive and monotonous stories with outside staircases or ramps, each stepped back and smaller than the one below it. At the summit stands a shrine. The famous temple at Ur built in honor of the moon god Nannar and the king of the Chaldees, had four ziggurats. The great ziggurat of the temple of Marduk at Babylon was the Biblical Tower of Babel.

The Sumerian skill in arts and crafts is justly famous. They excelled in gem carving, sculpture, and metalwork. The excavations of Sir Leonard Woolley at Ur have uncovered finely fashioned gold and silver headdresses, beads, helmets, and spears. Over the trade routes of the known world moved Sumerian caravans carrying the products of their hands and tools. To the markets of the ancient trade centers these goods traveled, together with grains and dates, leather and wool.

The men of Sumer also developed a system of writing on clay tablets and cylinders, later protected by seals. They pressed out their characters with reeds. These characters were wedge-shaped or cuneiform (from *cuneus*: wedge). In their writing the Sumerians used about 350 syllabic signs. They never made an alphabet. Nevertheless, they were able to communicate quite effectively with their fellows and with scholars today. Thousands of their burnt-clay cylinders and tablets contain such varied things as statements of government tax accounts, famous episodes in Sumerian history, poems, proverbs, pictures. There were also epic tales like the long mythological story *Gilgamesh* which recounted the adventures of a Sumerian Ulysses and the coming of a great flood which lasted for seven days and almost destroyed the world. The epic *Gilgamesh* is one of the sources for the tale of Noah.

Dr. Samuel N. Kramer, the distinguished professor of Assyriology in the University of Pennsylvania, has translated and given permission to quote the song which a Sumerian poet wrote about 2000 B.C. in the proud city of Nippur:

> In those days there was no snake, there was no scorpion,
>   there was no fox,
> There was no lion, there was no dog, no wolf,
> There was no fear, no terror.
> Man had no rival.
> In those days the land of Shubur, the place of plenty,
>   of righteous decrees.

Harmony tongues Sumer, the great land of the decrees of
  the princeship.
Uri, the land possessing all that is needful
The land Martur resting in security
The whole universe, the people in unison
To Enlil in one tongue give praise.

About 2300 B.C. a Semite ruler named Sargon I attacked Sumeria from
his kingdom of Akkad in the north. Sargon had superior military power and
striking ability. Before his armies Sumeria fell. So did Syria and Assyria.
Soon, however, other conquerors came, more barbaric groups like the Guti,
one by one. In a time of breakup and insecurity a contemporary sadly asked
"who was king, who was not king?"

The rule of these less civilized tribes brought darkness. An inscription
at Ur said the invaders were "a host whose onslaught was like a hurricane,
a people who had never known a city." There was now little commerce, little
temple or household industry. The triumphant barbarians did not understand
the civilization of the Sumerians or Sargon. What they did not understand
they tried to destroy.

About 2100 B.C. the Babylonians swept over the land of Sumer, shortly
after the so-called Third Dynasty of Ur had been established with wide authority. These Babylonians were not uncivilized or barbarous—far from it.
The capital of a new empire rose swiftly in the desert at Babylon, a fine spot
on the Euphrates. Today the ruins of Babylon are deserted. The nearest
modern city is Bagdad, seventy miles north on the Tigris. But 4,000 years
ago proud Babylon was crowded and wealthy and rejoiced in its strength.

Ancient Babylonia included all the lower half of the area between the
Tigris and the Euphrates. The upper northeast half was the land of the
Assyrians, so expert at the war they loved. To the northwest of the Babylonian
Empire were the Hittites, to the east the Persians. Zoning outwards from
Babylon, as from all the fertile river-valley centers of higher civilization, were
the barbarian tribes, usually nomadic, in various stages of the local Age of
Metals. In the desert south of Babylonia were many tribes of Semitic nomads.
The tale of these tribes is one of chaos and rivalry all through history. To
the far northeast of Babylon were the barbarians of the steppes. These peoples
stretched from beyond the Caspian to western Europe. All of the barbarian
peoples hunted and pastured and—like all hungry land-pirates—they raided
and looted across the borders into Mesopotamia and into any other rich and
civilized areas. They lurked along the caravan routes. To many a troubled
merchant the cloud of dust on the horizon betokened the danger and death
coming over the dunes.

The sixth and most successful Babylonian king was Hammurabi, who ruled about 1750 B.C.—until recently the date was thought to be two centuries earlier. This king conquered all of Mesopotamia and established the first centralized government for the whole Valley of the Two Rivers. He was indeed one of the greatest rulers of the ancient world.

Hammurabi is particularly famous for the fact that his reign marked a high level in the expansion of Babylonian commerce and for the great list of laws that he made for all his people. He collected and improved old rules and made new ones. Then he carved the 282 sections of his code on a stone shaft nearly 8 feet high where everybody could see and read. The code, enforced by royal judges, is the oldest one we know about.

There are several ideas of right and wrong revealed by the code. Its opening said that justice should prevail in the land; that the wicked and the evil-doers should perish; that the strong should not defraud the weak. If a robber was not caught, the state compensated the man who was robbed. If a contractor was careless in building a house and it fell down and hurt or killed somebody the builder was executed or mutilated. Punishments varied in their severity. The higher the rank of a culprit in society, the heavier was the penalty.

Throughout the code is invoked the principle of *lex talionis,* "an eye for an eye." The law said: "If a son strike his father, they shall cut off his fingers." A slave who disputed with his master was to have his ears cut off. When a wife had been less than satisfactory the punishment was fixed: "If she has not been economical but a gadder about, has neglected her house and belittled her husband, they shall throw the woman into the street." Hammurabi's code, with its many sections about the primitive idea of rights, responsibilities, and justice, was a milestone in human history.

The Babylonians were especially active in the fields of the arts and sciences. They made such accurate records of the movements of the heavenly bodies that they were able to predict some eclipses. They named five of the planets and the twelve signs of the zodiac. They were skillful in metalwork, sculpture, carpet and tile making. They wrote prose and poetry and spent much time in astrology and the magic arts.

As a result of the work of Sir Henry Rawlinson modern scholars have been able to translate a large number of the Babylonian writings that have been rescued from the past. After Sir Henry had identified 14 of the 39 letters of the Persian alphabet he began to study the famous Behistun inscription cut in a cliff more than 300 feet above the Persian Royal Road between Susa, near the Persian Gulf, and Sardis, in Lydia. The inscription, written in Persian, Susian (a Persian dialect), and Babylonian, tells of a suppression of a revolt against Darius I of Persia (521–486 B.C.). By comparison of the three sections of the inscription Sir Henry was able to read the Babylonian passages.

After Hammurabi died his power crumbled. Babylon was divided by civil wars. Foreign tribes invaded the once mighty empire. The barbarous Kassites from the east maintained an uneasy grip for nearly 600 years after 1650 B.C.

It has been claimed that the Kassites first brought the horse into Babylon to take its place beside the donkey and the camel. If the Kassites really did bring the horse into Mesopotamia the importance of the event must not be misunderstood. The coming of the horse did not mean that there was available a major new supply of nonhuman power. Commandant Lefebvre de Noëttes and others have proved that animal strength was used most ineffectively in antiquity. The ancients had no nailed shoes to put on their animals. They were unable to harness one animal in front of another. Their high-yoke harness was satisfactory for the ox but not for the horse. It pressed upon the neck of the horse and he could not breathe freely or pull effectively. That is the reason why slaves, not horses, were still used to pull heavy weights. Not until the late ninth and early tenth century A.D. did there appear the horseshoe, the tandem harness, and the modern rigid horse collar.

In 729 B.C. the strong and ruthless Assyrians came and conquered. They diverted the waters of a canal over the city of Babylon, and the prophecy of Jeremiah in a sense came true. At the height of their power the Assyrians captured and sacked Damascus (733 B.C.), Jerusalem, and Thebes. They ruled over Syria, Egypt, Phoenicia, and Israel—Judah was never conquered, probably because the plague struck the armies of the Assyrian king Sennacherib.

The Assyrian homeland was an area of limited resources in the upper valley of the Tigris; when the population pressed against the food supply the Assyrians moved to expand by war. War was their way of life and they tried to make violence pay. Their armies, cruel, ferocious, greedy, and efficient, swept to victory. They had heavy bows, iron swords, lances, breastplates, helmets, shields, swift horses, and the first battering rams. Despite their considerable achievements in art—their development of bas-relief, for instance —their genius was essentially military.

> The Assyrian came down like the wolf on the fold
> And his cohorts were gleaming in purple and gold. . . .

Empires, like men, grow strong and pass away. The Assyrians, so able in war, were not skilled in government. They were able to hold on to their power and territory for only about 150 years. In 612 B.C. the Chaldeans from the northern grasslands destroyed Nineveh, that proud Assyrian capital founded on war and loot. These Chaldeans gathered the shattered Assyrian power and built an empire for themselves.

They rebuilt Babylon, and the whole land was soon called Chaldea. Their astronomers and mathematicians won fame in the ancient world. They were the most capable scientists in all of the history of Mesopotamia, especially in the field of astronomy. For more than 150 years they mapped the heavens, recorded eclipses, and the like. These things, of course, they did to help themselves predict the future prepared for men by the gods. Astronomy was therefore close to astrology.

Chaldea's Nebuchadrezzar II made the Hanging Gardens of the new Babylon, one of the ancient world's seven wonders. He sacked and destroyed Jerusalem, blinded King Zedekiah, and dragged away many of the children of Israel into "the Babylonian Captivity." After a strange fate befell the proud Nebuchadrezzar his unwieldy empire sickened. Its weakness tempted a mighty robber, the ruler of the Persians in the north. Chaldea's King Belshazzar saw the handwriting on the wall at his famous feast: *Mene, mene, tekel, upharsin.* (Daniel v:25–30)

The homeland of the conquering Persians was a high and dry plateau south and east of the Persian Gulf. The center of that plateau was a salt desert. Only the borderlands were fertile, and there the Persians lived. In the hills to the north were the Medes, a kindred Indo-European people. It was these Medes who once helped the Chaldeans to destroy the proud empire of the Assyrians. Through most of their history the Medes and the Persians stood together.

About 550 B.C. a king named Cyrus ruled both the Persians and the Medes. There is no doubt that he was a military genius and a wise statesman—it is not usual in human history to find both of these qualities united in one man. What ability Cyrus had Cyrus used. About 546 B.C. his horsemen conquered the Lydians, famous in history for their rich King Croesus and for the fact that they were probably the inventors of coined money. By 540 B.C. Cyrus overran the weakened Chaldean Empire. Belshazzar, weighed in the balance, was found wanting. Cyrus won his victory, as he was supposed to have said, "without a battle and without fighting." His capture of Babylon, for instance, was accomplished in large part by the successful activities of fifth columnists within the city.

Cyrus was seldom idle. There were other conquests. Soon a great Persian Empire stretched from India to the Nile valley. We have seen, for example, that in 525 B.C. Cambyses, the son of Cyrus, conquered Egypt. Despite the dangerously long frontiers and frequent internal revolts the Persian Empire lasted for two centuries.

Cambyses was murdered on the way back from Egypt and the throne was seized by his cousin Darius. Darius I ruled over the Persian Empire as

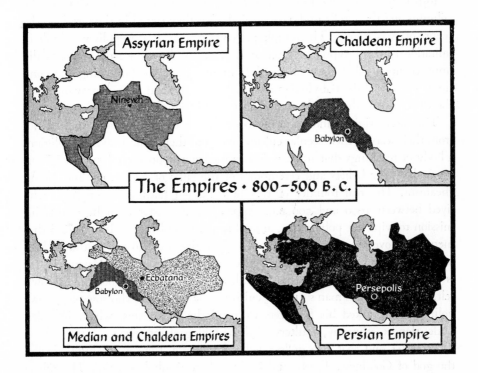

a benevolent despot from 521 to 486 B.C. He reorganized the state administration, dividing the empire into twenty provinces, each under a satrap or
governor. He hired secret police, "the eyes and ears of the king," to watch
the governors, and he sent out special inspectors every year to watch everybody and everything. In all the Persian provinces Darius was careful not to
interfere with the religions or the customs of the subject peoples. He was
also shrewd enough to allow them a large share in the rights and responsibilities of local government. He gained still more prestige and power by building magnificent military and trade roads to connect the provinces with the
four Persian capitals: Babylon, Ecbatana, Persepolis, and Susa. He constructed
several fleets—his galleys were all about the waterways of the empire and
beyond. When Darius I was upon the throne there was no rebellion. Security
was established. Peace prevailed.

Most of the Persian culture was derived from other civilizations, especially
from Mesopotamia, Egypt, and Palestine. This was to be expected, for the
Persians were a semibarbaric people when they first came into the light of
history. They copied the terraced buildings and the decorations of Babylonia
and Assyria. It was strange that they never used either the arch or the vault

—instead they took the Egyptian column. They imitated the flutings of the columns and the scrolls under the capitals that they found in the Greek settlements of Asia Minor. The temple-palace of Xerxes at Persepolis was built in imitation of the Egyptian temple at Karnak. At least once the Persians did improve upon what they obtained from one place by borrowing a second time. They used the Babylonian cuneiform writing, and then, borrowing from the Phoenicians, they made an alphabet of thirty-nine letters.

The most original and enduring contribution of the Persians resulted not from their wars or their secular culture but from their ethical revealed religion, a body of teachings that made a deep impression upon several later religions, particularly the beliefs and ceremonies of the cults of Mithraism and Manicheanism. The real founder of this new Persian faith was Zoroaster, who lived between 1000 and 500 B.C. Apparently Zoroaster thought it was his mission to wipe out polytheism, animal sacrifice, and magic. He insisted that men must love one another. "Whoever shall give meat to one of the faithful he shall go to paradise." In another place Zoroaster wrote: "That nature alone is good which shall not do unto another whatever is not good for its own self." He said it was man's duty to cultivate the soil: "He who sows corn sows holiness." He asked his followers to avoid the major sins, which included pride, slander, gluttony, adultery, and the taking of interest.

Zoroaster said that two gods ruled the universe. One was Ahura-Mazda, the god of Goodness, Truth, and Light, whose symbol was fire. The other, Ahriman, was the god of Evil, Darkness, and Deceit. The universe was a battleground for these evenly matched adversaries. Man was in the center. Since he was possessed of free will, he must help one side or the other.

The doing of good deeds, asserted Zoroaster, was more important than meditation. After 12,000 years the god of Goodness would triumph. At the end of 9,000 years the second coming of Zoroaster would be the signal for the approach of the end. A messiah would come to prepare the good for eternal paradise. Ahura-Mazda would hurl Ahriman into an abyss and the dead would rise from their graves to be judged.

The most successful kings make errors. Probably the greatest mistake of Darius I was his decision to conquer Greece. He failed and failed completely. In 481 B.C. the Persian King Xerxes tried again. He, too, was defeated. A century and a half later the power of Alexander the Great, brilliant son of Philip of Macedon, was to crush the Persian weakling Darius III. Then the Persian Empire crashed. The hoarded gold of Persian kings tumbled into Alexander's outstretched hands in 332 B.C. It is said that Alexander then sighed for more worlds to conquer.

Chapter 4

BY THE SHORES
OF THE GREAT SEA

"He heapeth up riches, and knoweth not who shall gather them."
—Psalms, XXXIX, 6

Most of the rivers of our world have long been arteries of trade and travel. In months of flood they have deposited fertile soil in their valleys to grow rich harvests for those who till and sow. They have made green pastures for the shepherd and the herdsman. The fish in their waters have fed the hungry angler. It is not to be wondered that the first settled civilizations appeared in river valleys like those along the Nile, the Tigris, and the Euphrates.

Meanwhile the nomadic tribes in the steppes and the desert wandered from stream to spring, hunting, plundering, trading, pasturing their sheep and their cattle where they could. In some regions there were many traveling tribesmen, in other areas few. At the eastern end of the Mediterranean, for instance, the groups who came into the land usually stayed and settled, at least for a while. They fished and traded, labored in the vineyards, planted where there was good earth and watched their flocks on the hills.

From many parts of the ancient world men came to the lands by the eastern edge of the Mediterranean Sea. The mingling of peoples began in the mist of prehistory and it continues still. Many groups are known to have drifted or flooded into the coastal region long before the Christian era. The whole area was always a melting pot and often a battlefield and a highway for conquerors.

Three peoples at the eastern end of the Mediterranean were of particular importance in the history of the Near East and the ancient world: the Hittites, the Phoenicians, and the Hebrews.

After 2000 b.c. there appeared in the Near East the Hittite Empire, a power that once extended over most of Asia Minor. Until 1500 b.c. the Hittite territories grew. Somewhere around 1200 b.c., after long conflicts with Egypt, the Hittite Empire dissolved and faded into history.

Only in the last hundred years have scholars discovered how strong and wide was the area controlled by the Hittites. Extensive search has unearthed many monuments, clay tablets, ruined cities. Remarkable discoveries were made by such men as Archibald Henry Sayce, that imaginative and daring English orientalist. Much has been salvaged from the wrecks of the once proud and frowning palaces of long-vanished monarchs. Despite these discoveries our sources of knowledge and comprehension of that ancient world are still too few. Evidence about the origins of the Hittites is still too vague and incomplete. Some authorities believe the Hittites were related to the Kassites. We cannot be certain. Some scholars say they were Indo-Europeans. We do not know. The realm of conjecture is usually wide; that of fact is often narrow. We are now certain that the center of Hittite power was in Anatolia, not in Syria or Palestine. We do know that the Hittites mined copper, lead, and silver; they possessed a well-developed legal system; they traded widely; their culture probably influenced the Hyksos, the Trojans, and the men of Crete. Beyond this, we are certain of little about the Hittite civilization. Some experts have even raised technical objections to the word "Hittite." At the present time the word is still used widely because we have not found a convenient or acceptable substitute. Meanwhile the indefatigable scholars search and dig and study. There must be nothing slipshod or inaccurate. Slowly the theory of today may become the fact of tomorrow. The archeologist, the epigraphist, and the historian must combine the virtues of Professor Dryasdust with those of the imaginative interpreter Sherlock Holmes. What has rightly been called "the secret of the Hittites" has yet to be solved.

Another important people lived at the eastern end of the Mediterranean in the region that is modern Syria. About them we have much more knowledge than we do about the Hittites. They were the Phoenicians, a Semitic group who probably came from the inland reaches of Mesopotamia. They kept away from the barrier hills of the north that merge into the west Asiatic steppes. They did not choose to be nomads or hunters of the badgers and bears and Syrian squirrels. They did not settle on the inland plateau. They turned instead to build their city-states on the seaboard. These Phoenicians were thus one of the early immigrant stocks who came in like the Kurds, the Yurucks, and the Armenians to find a dwelling place by the shores of the Mediterranean.

The Phoenicians developed a love for the sea that persisted for several centuries. Some of the time they were independent and free. Most of the time they were not—they were conquered and ruled by the Hittites, Egyptians, Assyrians, Chaldeans, and Persians. Yet through all the years the traffic of the Phoenician ships and caravans was flowing out of their merchant cities of Tyre, Sidon, and Aradus. The Phoenicians were indeed the great sea traders, shippers, and adventurers of the ancient peoples. Over the seas their round merchant boats and their great Tarshish ships carried their profitable

PLATE III [12]

Right: Sunk relief (limestone) from the mastaba of an Egyptian priestess (2665-2420 B.C.)

Below: Stone relief of woman spinning found in the ruins of the city of Susa, one of the four capitals of ancient Persia

[14]

reat storage jars preserved in the ruins of the ancient royal Cretan palace at Knossos

[15]

Mother and child, an example of Egyptian pottery made about 3100 B.C.

[17] Detail of mourners cut in the rock in the Buddhist Cave Temples at Ajanta, India, in the sixth century

[16] A stone relief of Buddha made by an Indian sculptor in the eighth century

[18]

Scenes from the life of Buddha were carved about 100 B.C. on the highly decorated North Gateway of the Great Stupa at Sanchi, India.

PLATE IV

cargoes of the wares of the world: gold, oil, textile fabrics, glassware, wine, purple dye-shells, copper, cedars and firs from Lebanon, perfumed spice and incense from East Africa and India, amber brought to the Phoenicians along the trade routes running from the Baltic to the Adriatic.

When the wind stood fair for distant ports the Phoenician trading vessel, large and proud, must have been as impressive a sight as another ship a poet saw in a later age:

> . . . a stately ship
> Of Tarsus, bound for the isles
> Of Javan or Gadire
> With all her bravery on, and tackle trim,
> Sails filled, and streamers waving,
> Courted by all the winds that hold them play;
> An amber scent of odorous perfume
> Her harbinger.

The Hebrew prophets Ezekiel and Isaiah drew vivid pictures of the economic power of the Phoenicians. Isaiah wrote of "Tyre, the crowning city whose merchants are princes, whose traffickers are the monarchs of the earth." Regular trade routes from the lands of the Euphrates and the Tigris led to the cities of the Phoenician merchants. By 1100 B.C. they had trading stations all through the Mediterranean. They mined gold and silver in southeast Spain, tin in the northwest. From these mines and the fisheries on the coast they drew fantastic profits.

The Phoenicians always counted for more in commerce than in politics or war. They became fearless and patient navigators and ventured into regions where nobody else dared go. It was said that in 600 B.C. a Phoenician fleet circumnavigated Africa. Their knowledge of winds and currents and their sailing skill made the Phoenicians famous everywhere. Assyrians, Egyptians, Greeks, Persians—all employed Phoenician sailors to carry goods and fight battles.

On the coast of North Africa the Phoenicians founded the famous city of Carthage in Libya in 813 B.C. They also held Cyprus as a colony and made settlements in Sicily, Malta, Corsica, and Sardinia. Thus their power grew.

It was Alexander the Great who brought final disaster to the Phoenicians. In 333 B.C. Alexander besieged Tyre for several months. When the city fell Alexander's men are said to have slain about 8,000 Tyrians and to have sold 30,000 as slaves. When Alexandria was founded in Egypt the main lines of trade began to shift and the high glory of the Phoenician cities was no more. In 64 B.C. Rome brought them all into the Roman province of Syria. Most of the Syrian harbors that once were the great shipping centers of the world have long been blocked with silt.

It has often been asserted that the Phoenicians invented and used the first phonetic alphabet around 1700 B.C. If they did invent the alphabet then they have left a more enduring monument than their achievements and glory in adventure and in trade. But there are many things in the history of mankind about which we cannot be certain. What we call the Phoenician alphabet may not have been invented by the Phoenicians. The subject is highly controversial. Amateurs in any field often claim too much too soon and too firmly, especially if they can make dramatic and exciting assertions. The experts, on the other hand, usually prefer to wait and watch for evidence that is sound and sure. In the light of present knowledge we do not know who invented the alphabet.

It may be that in some distant hour beyond our ken a nameless pioneer did shape a phonetic alphabet. Out of the gray glimmer of a dawning idea there may have come this spectacular invention. It is more probable that mankind was the hero, and not any one human being. Single, immediate, and individual discoveries were rare in the early history of mankind. Pictographs, syllabaries, and alphabets slowly grew through centuries of trial and error, mingled misfortunes and happy chance. There is often much more chance than calculation in the complex tale of man's accomplishments through the unrolling centuries.

It is certainly true that the Phoenicians helped to spread the alphabet and the new system of writing over most of the known world. The Hebrews took it, and so did the Greeks, the Romans, the Persians, the peoples of India, and scores of others. Today the so-called Phoenician system is the basis of alphabets as dissimilar as the Russian and the Arabian.

Into whatever lands the alphabet went it changed to meet the varying sounds of the languages. In some tongues a few letters were dropped and others added. For example, the Phoenicians had no vowels. About 1000 B.C. the Greeks added vowels and a few consonants. They wrote carefully on a board or tablet coated with wax, using a sharp instrument called a stylus. The Romans took their alphabet from the Greeks. We took it from the Romans, adding a *j* and a *w*.

With writing and the alphabet a permanent gift and skill were added to the human heritage. The alphabet and the pen are mighty tools. "Words," said Dr. Samuel Johnson, "are the daughters of the earth." They are indeed.

To the south of Syria and the hills of Lebanon was Palestine, the rugged land of the Hebrews lying at the gates of Mesopotamia and Egypt and playing a part in human history for more than 4,000 years.

Long ago Palestine extended about 140 miles from north to south, through cities and villages "from Dan to Beersheba." It reached eastward from the Mediterranean Sea to the pilgrim road from Damascus. In the east was a lofty steppe. In the west there were intersecting mountain peaks and ranges broken by the great fertile plain of Esdraelon. In the south there were uninviting mountains and the repellent and inhospitable deserts—the beginning of the Arabian dryness. Along the coast there stretched a rich maritime plain "flowing with milk and honey" from Lebanon to Egypt, sometimes narrow and sometimes broad, always cut and crisscrossed by the great caravan roads of the merchant traders.

Palestine was a land of contrasts. Here were the mountains and the dreary deserts and plains, the Jordan river flowing into the salt Dead Sea 1,300 feet below the level of the Mediterranean, the fish-filled waters of blue Galilee. Here were the hyena and the jackal, the gazelle and the ibex, the snakes and the lizards rustling their brittle length. And here was a great area of mingled peoples, rites, cults, and customs, a cosmopolitan region torn by jealousies and intrigues and intertribal quarrels.

The word "Hebrew" means simply "nomad" or "alien." It has no ethnic significance. In ancient days several tribes were called "Hebrews," including the Edomites, Moabites, and Israelites. Technically it is true that the Hebrews were but one tribe of Semites: the tribe of Judah whose ancient speech is used today as the religious tongue of the Jews. But the usage of generations has resulted in the fact that the word "Hebrews" has come to mean the Israelites.

The Hebrews first came out of the Arabian Desert. About 1600 B.C. some Hebrew tribesmen under the leadership of Abraham settled in northwest Mesopotamia. ("Now the Lord said unto Abraham Get thee out of the country . . . unto a land that I will show thee.") Abraham's grandson Jacob led them into Palestine. Around 1400 B.C. there was a famine in Palestine, and several tribes of the Israelites fled to the rich lands of Egypt and found themselves the slaves of the pharaoh. About 1250 B.C., in a time of Egyptian weakness and disaster, the children of Israel escaped from Egypt. Moses, their leader, took them into the wilderness and to the sacred mountain of Sinai where the Egyptians had their turquoise mines. He persuaded them to enter into a covenant to accept the great God Jehovah as lawgiver, judge, and leader in war. They agreed to obey His Ten Commandments. ("And Moses said unto God, Behold, when I come unto the children of Israel and shall say unto them, The God of your fathers hath sent me unto you; and they shall say to me: What is his name? what shall I say unto them? And God said unto Moses: I AM THAT I AM.") After about two generations the exiles moved northwards to cross over Jordan and start the slow and dreary conquest of Canaan, the Promised Land. Poets, priests, historians, and prophets began the composition of the Old Testament with the book of Genesis and the folk-memory story of the Exodus from Egypt. "He took not away the pillar of the cloud by day, nor the pillar of fire by night from before the people."

The Israelites were not the only invaders of declining Canaan. There were loosely united kindred tribes raiding and pressing from the desert. There were also attackers who surged in from the sea—the Philistines. These men probably came from Crete. It was they who gave the invaded country its name: Palestine, the country of the Philistines. In the books of Joshua and Judges the tales of the travails and triumphs of the Israelites are told with power and pathos.

About 1025 B.C. the Hebrew monarchy took the place of the rule of the "judges." There appeared the first king, a man able to bring some political organization out of the unity of religious feeling. This king was Saul, "a choice young man and a goodly," a member of the tribe of Benjamin. Saul's early days were days of promise, but his later career was leaden and unlucky. He was opposed by jealous Samuel, last of the judges, and the ambitious young David who perhaps slew Goliath and other tens of thousands. Saul and his sons were defeated and killed by the Philistines in dark years like those when Samson was wandering eyeless in Gaza.

The hero David now became king and ruled for forty years. He pressed back the Philistines. He succeeded in bringing the Twelve Tribes into a united state with a capital at Jerusalem, a city captured by David and his army. David's son Solomon built the great temple his father had planned, importing artisans from Phoenicia and gold and silver and the cedars of Lebanon to put in the national shrine. Solomon also built up a central administration, tried to keep an adequate army in being, encouraged foreign trade, and followed a shrewd diplomatic policy. Both Solomon's wisdom and his extravagance have been unduly stressed in later centuries. The evidence is not sufficient to praise him for the one or condemn him for the other.

After Solomon's death in 935 B.C. the old kingdom fell apart. The ten northern tribes broke away to form the new Kingdom of Israel and stood together in a rich, fertile, and prosperous land. The house of David in the south was left with little more than its own tribal territory in the struggling kingdom of Judah, filled with barren miles and poor shepherds. The prophets of Judah, especially Elijah and Amos, denounced the conspicuous consumption of the wicked and wealthy men of the north. One of the causes of scandal to the prophet Amos was the "Ivory House" of King Ahab at Samaria. The carved ivory inlays, once a part of the "Ivory House," are now in the British Museum. The famous "Moabite Stone" is in the Louvre.

Through the flaming words of the prophets ran always the theme of lofty spiritual and ethical concepts and the certainty of safety for those who served the Lord in faith and fear. "Ho, every one that thirsteth, come ye to the waters, and he that hath no money, come ye, buy and eat; yea, come, buy wine and milk without money and without price."

The destinies of the smaller states in the Near East have often been determined by the rivalry of great powers. Soon new dangers appeared for Israel with the emergence of the Assyrian challenge. Resistance and appeasement failed, and about 722 B.C. Israel fell. Most of the inhabitants were deported and so widely dispersed by the conquerors that they are still called the Ten Lost Tribes of Israel. The kingdom of Judah, as was earlier remarked, was not overrun by the Assyrians, perhaps because the plague struck the Assyrian army:

> And the widows of Ashur are loud in their wail,
> And the idols are broke in the temple of Baal;
> And the might of the Gentile, unsmote by the sword,
> Hath melted like snow in the glance of the Lord!

If the Assyrians did not prevail over all of Palestine, the Chaldeans did. Nebuchadrezzar II, as we have seen, seized and plundered and laid waste Jerusalem in 586 B.C. and deported and blinded Zedekiah. Thousands of the Israelites were taken prisoners to Babylon. Psalm 137 recalls the agony of exile and slavery: "By the rivers of Babylon, there we sat down, yea, we wept, when we remembered Zion. . . . How shall we sing the Lord's song in a strange land? If I forget thee, O Jerusalem, let my right hand forget her cunning."

In 538 B.C. the Chaldean Empire was overthrown in a power struggle with Cyrus of Persia. "Babylon is fallen, is fallen!" New masters ruled over the lands that had known so many. Cyrus allowed the Hebrews to return home and they rebuilt Jerusalem under Nehemiah in the fifth century B.C. Other cities faded into oblivion but not Jerusalem.

Almost always Palestine was a subordinate state in a great imperial system. Until 332 B.C. it was a vassal state of Persia. Then it was conquered by Alexander the Great. When he died Palestine was ruled by Egypt. In 65 B.C. it became a Roman protectorate, in 70 A.D. a Roman province. Thousands of people were uprooted and slowly forced to leave the land of their fathers in the "scattering abroad," or Diaspora. They wandered to new worlds to live far from the place they considered their only homeland. Not for 1,900 years were they to have a homeland again. In English, as in Hebrew, the ring of poetry is in the term used to describe the return of the Jews to the new Zion: "the ingathering of the exiles."

Scholars today are steadily working to recover from the past whatever information they can about the Palestine region and its history. In 1946 peasants at Nag Hammadi discovered 850 pages of Coptic Gnostic papyri, written about the middle of the fourth century A.D. These pages may perhaps settle the question whether or not Gnosticism is a later product of religious thought in Christianity and linked directly to such sources as Zoroaster and the Egyptian god Thot. They may also show what degree of influence the teachings of the Gnostics had upon the synthetic religion called Manicheanism.

In the Arab-Jewish war of 1948 an utterly unexpected discovery was made by Bedouin shepherds. Hidden in a cave near the Dead Sea were found eleven seriously deteriorated ancient Biblical dried-leather scrolls that were probably written in the first century B.C.–A.D. and were almost certainly taken out of the library of the Essene sect near Jericho and hidden for safekeeping in the Roman-Jewish war of 66 A.D. The Dead Sea scrolls contain, among other things, the text of a Psalm hitherto unknown, a text of Isaiah, and an unknown work, "The War of the Sons of Light Against the Sons of Darkness." There are also preserved parts of the "Book of Lamech," which is an Aramaic version of Chapters V–XV of Genesis, similar in style to the Apocryphal Books of Jubilee and Hanoch. The name of Lamech, the father of Noah, appears in several lines of the outer fragment of a scroll deciphered by scholars with the aid of infrared rays—this is the reason why the scroll has been tentatively called the "Book of Lamech." The work of Hebrew University specialists has revealed a description of Sarah's beauty, related to the Egyptian pharaoh by his princes; a narrative of Abraham's "walk through the land in the length of it and in the breadth of it"; a clear description of the War of the Five Kings; and an account of Abraham's dream that he would have a son. (See Genesis XII–XV.) Before 1948 no actual ancient copies of Biblical texts in Hebrew existed in any form earlier than the ninth century A.D. Since 1948 hundreds of fragments of Biblical and other books have been found in the cave area. These include parts of the Apocryphal Books and sections of the New Testament written in Greek. When these are studied and digested by scholars our knowledge and conclusions about Biblical texts will doubtless be extended and in some instances perhaps greatly changed.

Sometimes small communities make great contributions to the world. The people of Israel never united to form a strong state. They had no great armies and they built no wide empire. They had no strong economic power. In architecture and the arts they were usually imitators. Unlike Egypt and Mesopotamia they gave mankind nothing original in technology, nothing new in science. In these things no Hebrew genius shone.

There are other grounds for assigning a high place to Israel. The Old Testament as a body of classical literature written over several centuries is of the highest quality. There are passages of beauty and power that are not surpassed —even in translation—in any age, in any language.

When I consider the heavens, the work of thy fingers, the moon and the stars which thou hast ordained;
What is man that thou art mindful of him? and the son of man, that thou visitest him?
For thou hast made him a little lower than the angels, and hast crowned him with glory and honor.
Thou madest him to have dominion over the works of thy hands, thou hast put all things under his feet;
All sheep and oxen, yea, and the beasts of the field;

The fowl of the air, and the fish of the sea, and whatsoever passeth
through the paths of the seas.
O Lord our Lord, how excellent is thy name in all the earth!

The greatest achievement of Israel was in the spheres of religion and philosophy, in speculations and conclusions about the nature and destiny of man,
the humane ethical concepts of sin and the good life, the idea of absolute submission to the will of God, whose sublime purposes no man can know. The
deity of the Israelites was Jehovah and from Jehovah they expected mercy and
justice, safety and victory, good crops and all the blessings of this world and
the next. From His people Jehovah compelled obedience and service. In the
eyes of the children of Israel they were indeed Jehovah's people. Had He not
chosen them before all men? Had He not led them out of Egypt?

Other ages and other peoples had believed that there were many gods and
sometimes they tried to satisfy them all. The faith of the Israelites was quite
different. It was monotheistic. The children of Israel believed that there was
one God and one alone. The confused and irrational apparatus of paganism
was thrust aside. What seemed rational, clear, coherent, and ethical was
exalted. There was one God, one realm of absolute law where moral values
prevailed through time and eternity. "And God spake all these words, saying,
I am the Lord thy God, which have brought thee out of the land of Egypt,
and out of the house of bondage. Thou shalt have no other gods before me."

When later days saw the decline from high ideals and the intrusion of other
cults, especially of the gross and licentious nature worship of Baal and Ash-
toreth, the great prophets dared to stand for the divine discipline in which
they placed their faith and hope. Disaster, said the prophets, loomed for the
wicked who would forsake His ways. For a time evil men might flourish like
the green bay trees but they would finally flee and fall. The prophets set their
faces against the alien doctrines and the "strange gods." ("Yet my people have
forgotten me days without number.") They asserted the claim of Jehovah
alone to the worship of His people. They insisted upon the observance of the
moral law that He commanded. They declared that God would be just and
merciful to His covenanted people if they would return from the unrighteous
paths upon which they had wandered and strayed abroad. "Ask for the old
paths," said Jeremiah, "where is the good way, and walk therein, and ye shall
find rest for your souls."

The children of Israel were the first of mankind to conceive of history as
having purpose and direction. They saw the great drama of Man being performed on no shoddy and tinseled stage but on an earth which was the work
of the Lord. All of the characters—living, dead, and unborn—played their
parts, made their exits, and received their rewards. "For God shall bring every

work into judgment, with every secret thing, whether it be good, or whether it be evil." All mankind was moving towards some unknown end that God had willed.

Such is a part of our heritage from Israel. That heritage, including the foundations of Christianity, has touched with its power the history of nearly every Western state and civilization for 2,000 years.

In recent pages we have watched the changing face of cultures and civilizations in the Nile valley, in Mesopotamia, and along the eastern coast of the Mediterranean Sea. There generations of men sowed, starved, prospered, fought, begat children, invented tools, and worshiped at the shrines of their gods. They were unconsciously preparing mankind for the next generations and the next slow steps forward.

We turn now to Crete, an island lying in the Mediterranean southeast of Greece. On that island a brilliant primitive civilization—the first in Europe —passed through successive stages to disaster and almost to oblivion.

Sicily is the largest island in the Mediterranean; Sardinia is second; Crete is third. At its widest point, Crete stretches for 35 miles. It is 160 miles long. Its shoreline is heavily indented, and ranges of mountains, ravines, and caves are found over most of its surface. The massive White Mountains in the southwest are particularly impressive. There are only two plains, fertile and lovely, one small and one large. The big central plain of Monofasti is 37 miles long and 10 miles wide. From time immemorial Crete has been a land of the wild goats, of the cypress, of olives, oranges, and lemons. It has also been a land of violence. The ancient historian Polybius said that the history of the island was a series of civil wars. Despite the clouds of mythology and fable there is much evidence to indicate that Polybius was right. The Cretans themselves claimed that Crete was the birthplace of mighty Zeus, a god not known to have followed the paths of peace.

Lying midway between three continents, Crete was a natural stepping stone for passing peoples and cultures. These peoples and cultures came and went upon their ways, sometimes leaving important things behind and sometimes not. There is a great deal of the history of human affairs that is quite uncalculated. One of the laws of history, like one of the laws of physics, is surely the law of indeterminacy, probability, or just plain luck.

On the island of Crete there flourished between 3000 and 1500 B.C. a brilliant and strong civilization called Minoan, after Minos, a legendary king who was said to be the wise son of mighty Zeus himself. There was apparently little political unity on the island, only some cooperation in commerce and a considerable uniformity in culture. Homer once wrote that there were "a hundred cities" in Crete, and there may indeed have been. This crossroad of commerce and piracy was a busy spot. Kings and gangsters lived together there.

Profits were made and throats were cut. The island was the Singapore or Hong Kong of its day. Minoan vases and tapestries have been found in tombs and towns along the Nile, in Syria, and far inland. Several Egyptian products and a Babylonian cylinder seal have been dug up in Crete.

During the past century the picks and shovels of the archeologists have been turning up much dirt and treasure. After the Second World War, for instance, several major jobs were started and some fine discoveries made. Excavations were begun at the sites of the Greek settlements that flourished in Italy between 800 and 600 B.C., especially at Tarentum and Naxos. The American School of Classical Studies began to clear and excavate an area of about twenty-five acres in the heart of Athens where once stood the Athenian market place, the Agora. Jesuit specialists began to excavate under St. Peter's in Rome. In Cyprus a great stone mound and some tomb groups (3000–500 B.C.) were opened in 1950 at Old Paphos, the birthplace of Aphrodite. Plans were made to begin extensive work in Asia Minor and the important upper reaches of the Tigris and the Euphrates.

Most of our knowledge about the Cretan civilization has been derived from the result of the excavations of Sir Arthur Evans and Heinrich J. Schliemann and their successors during the past seventy-five years at the ruins of the Minoan palaces of Knossos, Mallia, and Phaestos. The excavations have revealed many things about the long-haired, kilted, and high-booted Cretans. Some conclusions, of course, change as new evidence appears. Until recently it was believed that no strong fortifications stood on the island because the Cretan fleet could defend it easily. Professor Chester Starr has now shown conclusively that the idea of a Minoan domination of the sea is no longer tenable. The Cretan thalassocracy is one of the many myths that will probably be repeated in books and lectures for a long time to come. "Words said too often become such ancient sounds that men forget them or are lost in them."

The most extensive archeological work has been carried out at Knossos in northern Crete. The palace site is about four miles from Candia and occupies nearly six acres on the hill of Kephala, a spot now known to be a place where human beings have lived since the days of remote antiquity. From the west a great paved road approached the palace. The building itself was a huge square structure with massive walls and bastions. In the center was a large paved court. The interior contained a maze of corridors, a council chamber with a gypsum throne, the residential east wing with its ivory-lined or stuccoed halls, private rooms, theater areas, gold-plated gaming tables—the whiffs of elegance float across the centuries. In the basements were the workshops, the broad store-rooms, and the six-foot olive-oil storage jars. The elaborate plumbing system was probably the best in all the world at that time. The whole palace of Knossos was fitted with clay tiles and copper pipes, some of them six inches in diameter. Minoan craftsmen were obviously no men of mean or petty skills.

Archeologists have rescued from oblivion several specimens of superb and specialized skill in the arts. Cretan artisans have left behind them enamel crystal plaques, animated ivory figurines, gem engravings, gold cups made with the new techniques brought by expert jewelers from Mesopotamia and beyond. All the Cretan metal products were of high quality—their swords, for instance, will rank with any made in their time. The Minoan skills, of course, were not confined to work with metals. Their pottery, often painted with egg-shell delicacy, was characteristic of the extraordinary perfection of much of their ceramic products. Their vases, for example, have never been excelled for texture, symmetry, and beauty of decoration.

In the royal halls of the palaces of Knossos, Mallia, and Phaestos are frescoes of remarkable beauty and naturalism. They depict warriors, wrestlers, pugilists, bull-hunting scenes, monkeys, flowers. Few of these paintings have in them any spirit of repose. All is action—taut muscles, flushed cheeks, excitement. True, there is one fresco that has a theme, and some passages of that theme are gentle. The craftsman painter tells the legend of Theseus, king of Athens, and the Minotaur, that Cretan monster that was half man and half bull. The reader will recall that every seven years Minos of Crete required the Greek city of Athens to send seven maidens and seven youths to be sacrificed to the Minotaur who prowled in the Labyrinth. Theseus slew the monster and was able to find his way out of the Labyrinth thanks to the ball of yarn which Ariadne, daughter of Minos, had fastened to the entrance.

In 1893 Sir Arthur Evans found about 2,000 small tablets or seal stones of clay covered with symbols representing fish, birds, human heads, and other subjects. These were characters of a distinctive pictorial form of writing used around 2500 B.C. Other tablets were found later with a well-developed linear script, apparently used about 1600 B.C. It seemed to the experts that almost all of these tablets were inventories and other business or government documents. The fact that such records were kept indicated a considerable degree of business efficiency and, probably, of legal organization. Unfortunately, it seemed that this Minoan linear script resembled none of the known languages of ancient times. By assigning to each symbol a Greek phonetic value the linguists were able to reach some ancient Greek names such as Knossos, Timenos, and Achilles. Beyond that point they could not go. They were baffled.

Early in the twentieth century more tablets in the same script were discovered in Crete. Later Professors A. J. B. Wace and C. W. Blegen found the first tablets in Minoan script at Mycenae near the Gulf of Argos and at Pylos in the extreme southwest. In 1953 Michael Ventris, using the skills he demonstrated as a code expert in the Second World War, turned to try to "break" the Cretan script by working with some of the tablets found at Pylos. As a result of his shrewd use of frequency tables and other devices of intelligence code-breaking systems Ventris convinced himself and others that the Cretan script was an early form of Greek. He finally succeeded in deciphering several hitherto baffling symbols. The work is not yet ended, but it is well begun.

Minoan religion differed from those we have observed on the mainland. It is true that the rulers did have priestly functions like many ancient kings of Egypt and elsewhere. In other ways the Cretan practices seem to have stood as a cult by themselves. There were two main divinities, female and male. The female, often a virgin Snake Goddess, was frequently represented by bare-breasted statuettes. The male god was far less important than the female. In Minoan remains there also appear frequently the emblems of the tree, the double ax, and the sacred pillar. There were no Cretan temples, only sanctuaries on mountain peaks or in caves. It seems that the violent games and sports so often depicted in the frescoes, especially bullfighting, may have had some religious significance. Certainly the Minotaur and the Labyrinth did.

Obvious signs of decadence leave no doubt that the Cretan civilization was declining by 1500 B.C. About a century or two later an earthquake cracked and tumbled and almost completely destroyed the palaces of Knossos and Phaestos. The great days of Crete were over. After the catastrophe there were slight signs of recovery, a little bit of pomp, and then slow death. Tumbled on the rocks and the grass today lie the time-scarred stones of the palaces. The clay lies brittle, hard, and dry. Little else remains to mark the center of the civilization that once spread to the isles of the Aegean and the southern lands of the Greek peninsula.

Chapter 5

INDIA:

WORKS AND WORDS

"Most Westerners still imagine that ancient history is largely concerned with the Mediterranean countries, and medieval and modern history is dominated by the quarrelsome little continent of Europe."

—Jawaharlal Nehru,

The Discovery of India, p. 184

To the north of India is the land of Afghanistan, a state about the size of Texas. There the resemblance to Texas ends, for all but a tenth of Afghanistan is barren. In the northwest tower the vast Hindu Kush mountains. In the southeast lies the blazing Desert of Death, where rest the ruins of ghost cities that were old when Alexander the Great passed by. Several readers will know about Professor W. W. Tarn's work on the Greeks in Bactria (Afghanistan) and the excavations of Professor Rodney Young of the University of Pennsylvania Museum. These studies are important—some anthropologists suspect that the origins of mankind lie north of the Hindu Kush mountains.

For more than a thousand miles on the northern frontier of India stands the towering upthrust of the ranges of the Himalayas, a wall that soars to awesome heights. There are sheer cliffs and yawning chasms, bare and windswept rocks, deep snow and bitter cold. In icy majesty looms Mount Everest, the highest peak in the world.

In the extreme northwest the Himalayas are pierced by the great Indus River which flows for 2,000 miles from its source in the Kailas glaciers southwards through the vast plains of the Punjab to the Indian Ocean. The whole broad plain of the northwest is watered by the Indus and four of its tributaries. In the northeast the mighty Ganges starts in an ice cave, drains a part of the southern slopes of the Himalayas, and sweeps for 1,500 miles through Bengal. Many rivers join the Ganges, including the long and famous Brahmaputra. A twisted network of waterways unites to drain the tableland of northern India. In India, as in Egypt and Mesopotamia, these rivers are the givers of life and the channels of commerce and communication.

In the south, behind the low sandstone Vindhya mountains and the Kistna River, lies the Deccan, a land of high plateaus, and Tamil Land. Beyond is the sea and the island of Ceylon.

It is nearly 2,000 miles from the Himalayas to the coast of Tamil Land. The kite-shaped peninsula of India contains 1,246,880 square miles—nearly half the area of the United States. It has a population of about 450,000,000. The population of all Asia is about 1,134,000,000; of Europe, 488,000,000 (excluding the U.S.S.R.); of Africa, 200,000,000; of North and Middle America, 215,000,000.

Men of the Old Stone Age did not live only in Europe and the Near East. Several primitive stone implements have been found in India, China, Africa, and elsewhere. Admittedly, the sums of our evidence and knowledge about the material cultures of prehistoric India are very imperfect. Nevertheless, what has been discovered fits quite well into the pattern of human evolution in Europe. In different parts of India a steady development can be discerned in the technique of making flint weapons, especially in the use of the flaking process. The blade industries in Sind were large and, for their times, efficient. Core-tool industries also existed in several parts of India, just as they did in Arabia, Western Europe, and in the Stellenbosch group of stone workers in South Africa. So far as other aspects of the Old Stone Age in India are concerned, conclusive evidence is lacking. Even the relative chronology of the Indian prehistoric culture is still in a provisional stage.

Most New Stone Age cultures in India appeared late. This is the conclusion of such scholars as Professor R. E. M. Wheeler, sometime director-general of archeology in India, and Stuart Piggott, professor of prehistoric archeology in Edinburgh University. There have been some enthusiastic claims made by others who insist that a very early Neolithic culture did exist in Kashmir. Their contentions have not yet been supported by sufficiently strong pillars of fact.

It seems that the Neolithic cultures thus far identified in India may have appeared as a result of folk movements from the West. Certainly the arts of metallurgy and agriculture did not arise in India. They were imported from somewhere between Asia Minor and Turkestan in the days when the local "Metal Ages" began. Nor did the men of India invent the techniques of pot painting and baking kilns. Those inventions seem to have come first in northern Persia, northern Mesopotamia, or Syria. From these places the moving and blending cultures carried the skills of making buff and black-and-red pottery into Baluchistan, in western India, and then into Sind and beyond. From very early times trade and immigration links may have somehow joined Mesopotamia, Persia, Turkestan, and Baluchistan. Such things, for instance, as pottery, stone vessels, tools, and bronze weapons may have moved back and forth by 2800 B.C. The black-and-red Quetta ware of Baluchistan does appear in Anau in Russian Turkestan and in Persia's Persepolis. The Amri, Nal, and Nandara styles of pot painting used by the men of the hills and villages of Baluchistan spread their influence into northern Persia.

The emerging webs and patterns of interrelationships are complex and fascinating. At the same time, the statements about them must not be made in the sharp tones of finality. Whatever happened was spasmodic and irregular. And sometimes, too, we are not sure about what we see and what we think we see. Professor Stuart Piggott, that learned and brilliant scholar, wrote these sentences in his *Prehistoric India:* "Did Sumerian ships put in at the mouth of the Dasht River and barter lapis-lazuli or gold for the fashionable grey-green stone pots with their sweet-smelling contents? Or did there come to the quays of Ur foreign ships of merchants speaking an uncouth tongue and worshipping strange gods? There is some evidence that this did indeed happen and that Baluchi traders settled in Sumer." The cautious scholar says: "There is some evidence" and then is silent. When there is a lot of evidence he may speak again.

It is human, of course, to wish to speculate. An ancient Indian legend tells about Indian merchants who went by sea to Babylon. They carried a peacock "trained to scream at the snapping of the fingers and dance at the clapping of the hands." Perhaps such tales contain some vague truths about trade in the misty days when merchants carried apes and ivory and peacocks to the brick cities of Sumer more than 2,000 years before Christ was born.

East of the Baluchi mountain barrier lies the land of Sind, now a part of Pakistan. Mile upon mile stretch the dreary desert salt lands and the stunted tamarisk and scrub of the Indus valley, far from the shifting mouths of the Indus River and the mangrove swamps and lagoons. Today the sun beats down upon this sandy waste. A few camels sometimes move across the horizon. There are no other signs of life.

The prospect once was otherwise. Before the southwestern monsoon shifted eastward there was no desert with its brittle salt crust, no bare clay and sand. Once, long ago, in the valley of the Indus south of the Punjab land of the Five Rivers, there was rain, grass, timber, and rich soil. There was wheat and cotton. Thousands of human beings lived and died in this fertile land. It was here in northwestern India that a great prehistoric civilization grew and prospered 4,000 years ago. Here were shaped the first phases of the civilization and culture of India.

In the midst of the desert on the right bank of the Indus are the ruins of a city, "a rose-red city half as old as time." This is the city of Mohenjodaro. If you went to Mohenjodaro now—traveling by train and bus and jeep the 200 miles from Karachi—your footsteps would echo on the paving stones as you walked along the gridiron of the carefully planned main streets. In the ruins that cover more than a square mile you would see the cracked tile drains, the crumbling houses of the wealthy, the deserted cottages of the poor.

Mohenjodaro was but one of many settlements in a great nameless civilization of Asia that flourished in its mature form in the valley of the Indus between 2500 and 1500 B.C. In that civilization cities were built and destroyed and built again. The traveler can see the ruins of some of them, the quiet ghosts of a violent past. Into the broad river plains of northern India once rolled great migrations of peoples. Some stayed and others went away. Here came mighty armies to loot and burn and butcher as they crossed and recrossed the land. Here came generations of traders with their caravans, their sneering and bad-tempered camels. Here, since the dawn of human history, has been a land of turbans, dust, bazaars, monsoon rains, squawking chickens and calm cattle, grizzled shepherds trudging after flocks of fat-tailed sheep and skittish goats. Now all is sand and silence.

The first modern discoveries in northwest India were made about a hundred years ago. They were made not by archeologists but by engineers. In 1856 two brothers, John and William Brunton, were building the East Indian Railway between Karachi and Lahore. John used the bricks of the ruined medieval city of Brahminabad to make a firm roadbed for the railway tracks. His brother William got bricks from the ruins of Harappa, the prehistoric capital of the Punjab. A few of the curious antiquities found by workmen reached expert archeologists. The source was discovered and the hunt was on. Since that day many expeditions have searched and excavated and rescued some treasures of prehistoric India from oblivion. Although much has been discovered there still remains a great deal of work to be done in studying these ancient Indian worlds. "Many things hinder sure knowledge," Pythagoras once wrote, "the obscurity of the subject and the shortness of human life."

Inside a broad area south of the Himalayan foothills there have been found the sites of nearly fifty towns and villages and two great cities, each with a complex urban organization. One city was Mohenjodaro. The other was Harappa, once a sprawling metropolis on the left bank of the Ravi in the Punjab and much later the spot where William Brunton got his bricks for the roadbed of the East Indian Railway. The two cities stood about 350 miles apart, twin capitals set in the north and south of a united empire.

In each city, in every town and village of this "Harappa Culture," there was the monotonous uniformity characteristic of a highly organized state and an efficient and ruthless central government. The pottery vessels were mass-produced by a standardized technique. The capacity and type of the utilitarian pots were all the same. The weights and measures were identical. The millions of baked bricks were the same size. Mohenjodaro and Harappa each had wide streets, protective river embankments, public baths, market places, and a towering citadel. The ground plans of the two cities were identical. Each house had the same street frontage. The granaries were run by the government. The grain production at Harappa, and probably at Mohenjodaro, was under the elaborate bureaucratic control of a highly evolved and rigid machine. Flour was made by organized groups pounding grain. Of political or social liberty there seems to have been none. It was a robot society, grim and dismal.

We cannot date the beginnings of the Harappa Culture. Its origins are quite unknown. Through about a thousand years of authoritarian rule (2500–1500 B.C.) there seems to have been no change, no modification at all, in the substance or the course of the stagnating and isolated material culture.

These comments about the soulless uniformity of the harsh and enigmatic Harappa civilization have been made upon the basis of the field work and conclusions of archeologists. All that they have said and written seems to be solidly founded upon the cumulative total of formidable evidence about the fabric and shape of the mature Harappa Culture. Our dependence upon the archeologist is particularly heavy because the unique pictographic script on the Harappa seals and stones has not been deciphered or transliterated. The language it represents is unknown. It seems to have been the only script that any part of India possessed before 1500 B.C. After the cities of northwestern India fell about 1500 B.C. there were no written documents on stone or clay until the great Asoka made his famous inscriptions around 250 B.C.

The Harappa Culture had a high level of representational art. Most of it had to do with the forms of animals and human beings. Several of the animals found in Harappa art disappeared from northwestern India a long time ago; only their bones are sometimes found. The Harappa carvings show, for instance, the famous humped bulls, the buffalo, the long-tailed sheep, the monkey, crocodile, mongoose, rat, lizard, squirrel, parrot, wolf, tiger, elephant, tortoise, deer, and jackal. There was also some fine painted pottery with the designs in black upon a deep red background. The pieces of metalwork that have been discovered were finely conceived and made by masters of their crafts. Remarkable works of sculpture have been found, including the well-known red sandstone torso of a man and the stone sculpture of a bearded man wearing a carefully embroidered garment.

About 1500 B.C. this Indus civilization, the first known to have existed in India, came to an abrupt end. Invaders sacked and killed. Archeologists have found skeletons on the staircases at Mohenjodaro, silent evidence of swift death. Until recently we did not know how or why disaster happened or who the violent intruders were. In view of the recent evidence brought forward by Mr. R. E. M. Wheeler and others it seems that we may now safely conclude that it was the invading Indo-Europeans who wrecked and plundered and brought the extinction of the Harappa civilization. It will be recalled that some of the wandering Aryans who surged eastward out of the region between the

Black and Caspian Seas went to Persia and stopped there. Others swept on their famous horses into Afghanistan. About 1500 B.C. several Aryan tribesmen pressed through the northern defiles into India. It was these fair-skinned warriors who destroyed one civilization and set about building another.

The conquering Aryans did not stop in the Indus valley. They struck to the south and there they encountered the dark-skinned Dravidians, the aborigines of India, "the most primitive of Indian types, occupying the oldest geological formation in India, a medley of forest-clad ranges, undulating plains, and terraced plateaus" in southern and central India. There is no evidence that the Dravidians came into India from outside or superseded an older population. So far as we know they were the true aborigines and their home was in and around the Deccan, from whence they spread to the north and south. Anthropologists have traced Dravidian elements in the population of northern India, even in Kashmir and the Punjab, showing that Dravidian settlers probably once lived in those regions. It is true, of course, that through many centuries in many lands the numerous blood streams of peoples have steadily mingled. Only a highly skilled anthropologist can measure and test and conclude, frequently providing for a broad margin of error.

The Aryans who came from the northern grasslands measured their wealth in terms of animals and their word for war meant "a desire for cows." They were skilled in metalwork and their society contained blacksmiths, goldsmiths, coppersmiths. They had horses and chariots. They built river boats. The father of the family was its head, its defender, its priest. Several families made up a tribe and at the head of a tribe was a king, or rajah. Year by year the Aryans spread to the east and the south in the Punjab area and beyond. The Dravidians who did not retreat were slain, enslaved, or gradually absorbed into the society of the conquerors as free men.

There is a famous collection of sophisticated Sanskrit songs and hymns called the *Rigveda*—the title means "songs of spiritual knowledge." This collection, a characteristic Indo-European gathering of sacred lore, contains 10 books and 1,028 poems or hymns probably composed by the Aryans somewhere about 1400–1500 B.C. It is as long as the *Iliad* and the *Odyssey* combined. It was transmitted orally through illiterate peoples with great precision and care. The whole *Rigveda* was preserved intact because there was a great fear of the consequences if the sacred words were varied by a syllable.

The greatest god of the *Rigveda* was Indra and more than 200 hymns were composed to him. Like the Anglo-Saxon *Beowulf*, Indra was a victorious leader and adventurer. He had great muscles. He fought bravely from his careening two-wheeled chariot. He drank and ate like a giant. He was "strong, young, immortal, and ancient." All epics must have their heroes. Men have seldom admired or loved abstractions.

The *Rigveda* tells us a great deal about the Aryans, especially the upper classes, their values, their zest for life, their deep and strong religious spirit, their sense of wonder, their desire to understand the universe. Again and again they say: "What is the purpose and meaning of man's existence upon earth?" One hymn asks: "What god shall we adore?" The dignified and moving lines about a warrior dead speak for themselves across more than 3,000 years. They need no explanation, no voice or pen of a scholar or critic:

> Betake thee to the lap of Earth the Mother, of Earth
>   farspreading, very kind and gracious . . .
> Heave thyself, Earth, nor press thee downward heavily;
>   afford him easy access, gently tending him,
> Cover him, as a mother wraps her skirt about her child,
>   O Earth.

There are many comments about values and virtue: "The riches of the liberal never waste away, while he who will not give finds none to comfort him." There are also some interesting lines about gambling:

> The gambler seeks the gambling-den and wonders, his
>   body all afire, Shall I be lucky? . . .
> Play not with dice; no, cultivate thy corn-land.
> Enjoy the gain, and deem that wealth sufficient. . . .

So appropriate to our own day are many of the passages of the *Rigveda* that it is difficult to believe that they come from one of the oldest word records of humanity.

In later days in India there were to appear many poems and prose pieces about man and the universe. One of these is called the *Upanishads,* a word that means "sitting at the feet of the teacher." The *Upanishads* probably came into existence about the sixth century B.C. Another famous work was the *Gita,* or "The Lord's Song," probably composed about 200 B.C. Every line of these famous works breathes the mental and religious atmosphere of India, asserting strongly the importance of the spirit and the denial of materialism. They have been rightly called great monuments to the intense and searching spirits of men.

The religious beliefs of Hinduism controlled many aspects of life. Throughout the whole system of faith and thought runs a pervasive sense of pessimism about the things of this world, the idea that escape is the highest good and that passivity and asceticism are to be preferred to action, violence, or indulgence. The essential problems, said Hinduism, are not worldly or humanistic; they are metaphysical. The wise and holy man tries to plumb the depths of the mystery of life. "Indian philosophers have not been humanists. Absorbed in metaphysics they have deliberately disinterested themselves in worldly affairs; and the conception of such Europeans as Bacon of a society comprehended, ordered, and transformed by the human reason has in the past left them cold."

There were priests who spent their lives teaching the faiths of Hinduism and interpreting the words of the *Rigveda,* so cumbersome and so complicated. These men were called Brahmans. To become a Brahman it was necessary to travel through four clearly described stages of life, to be subjected always to rigorous discipline and long hours of study and meditation, to follow without deviation the rules of caste and ceremony.

The Brahmans believed that the most important thing in life was learning. Said they: "All men would be made happy by intelligence, thought, and sacrifice." They established schools. They taught philosophy, religion, law, anatomy, surgery. Out of India came to the West such things as chess, the invention of zero in our number system, the use of letters as symbols in algebraic equations. The Brahmans insisted, with many other men, that the more a man understands the universe, the better he can serve and please the gods. By knowledge and detachment a person should try to lose his individual being and unite with the world soul (Brahma) that pervades all things. Becoming one with Brahma was called Nirvana. The world soul, said the Brahmans, was represented by three gods: Brahma, the Creator; Vishnu, the Preserver; and Siva, the Destroyer. They represent the great processes of life: creation, preservation, and destruction. They form today a basic part of Hindu belief.

The Brahmans also taught men to believe in the transmigration of souls or reincarnation. This, they said, was the process by which the soul achieved final perfection and obtained its deliverance by losing its identity in the world soul. Every soul, according to this teaching, has lived from the beginning in various bodies of men or animals. There was an endless wheel of birth and rebirth. The place into which a person was born depended upon his actions in his previous lives. A man's deeds in this life helped to determine his level of existence in the next. Every man must accept his lot, or Karma.

Finally, the Brahmans taught that no life should be destroyed because all life belongs to the one universal life reality or force. In India today cows are considered sacred by the Hindus and it is a crime to kill a cow. In recent years the increasingly modern-minded Hindu has looked with less favor upon his sacred cattle. In 1954, for instance, the city fathers of New Delhi rounded up about 4,000 cows and bulls wandering at large in the city. They put the captured animals in a 2,000-acre government home in the Himalayan foothills.

If all cows were sacred, not all men were. Because the Brahmans were the most influential element in society they became a caste, a superior group in the caste ladder. Soon the soldiers became a second caste and the businessmen, craftsmen, and farmers a third. The fourth and lowest caste were the unskilled workers, the servants. In addition to these four main categories there gradually arose hundreds of others, each usually connected with a particular occupation. Gradually the caste system in Indian society became more and more complex and rigid. Members in lower castes never rose in society. They were not allowed to take any part in religious activities, to become educated, to do anything other than toil and suffer. Those of the lowest class were the pariahs, the "untouchables" whose shadows would defile a person of higher caste. This aspect of Indian society has been a harsh and cruel curse to the land.

Life in the large cities was one thing. Life in the small villages was another. Thousands of villages stretch from Tamil Land to the Deccan to the valley of the Ganges and beyond. In these spots the old ways in religion, farming, and the crafts were maintained from sunset to sunset, generation after generation. Not until the twentieth century were any real attempts made to improve the living conditions of the villages, the pivots of Indian society. Uncounted men and women of the isolated village worlds have lived and died without going upon a day's journey from their huts and hovels. A boy was born into a certain caste and there he stayed. His status and occupation were determined. The laws of the Brahmans and the rules of tradition said that it must be so. The eldest male in the family usually had full authority in that group. The Panchayat, the village governing body, guarded the customs, traditions, caste rules. The individual counted for little; the group counted for much; and the rules and formulas established by men long dead seemed to count for most of all.

By 600 B.C. the Brahmans were solidly established with their teachings, their numerous and mysterious rituals and costly sacrifices. They were hostile to all change. They opposed desecrating holy words by writing them down, and essentially the transmission of Hindu religious texts—the case of the *Rigveda* was mentioned earlier—was orally from teacher to pupil until about the eighteenth century A.D. In passing it may be remarked that paper was introduced into India by the Moslems in the thirteenth century but most early manuscripts in India either decayed or were destroyed by white ants. Meanwhile, through all the years, the Brahmans asserted that only in the Right Way of life proclaimed in the past was the Truth. The present had nothing to offer, nothing to give.

It seemed, however, that the present did have something to offer. It offered revolution.

In the ninth century B.C. several reform and revolutionary movements were attempting to reduce the power of the Brahmans with their steady emphasis upon ritual and the caste system. One of these movements, called Jainism, was started by an ascetic holy man named Mahavira (the great hero). He seized upon the idea of reverence for all forms of life and made it the center of his whole gospel. The idea of nonviolence (*ahimsa:* harmlessness) became a vital element in the history and philosophy of all India. All things material, said the Jains, were evil. The most devout sometimes starved themselves to death in order to escape from the slow stains of the corrupting world. Today there are more than a million Jains in India, especially in Bombay and Rajputana. Most of them are highly literate men, noted for their success in business and the professions.

The second revolt against the dominant Brahmans and their dogmas started when Gautama Buddha, the "Indian Luther," began his crusade. This great religious leader, soon to be called "The Enlightened One," was born the son of a noble near the borders of Nepal about 563 B.C. (China's Lao Tzu was born about 570 B.C., Confucius in 551 B.C.) At the age of twenty-nine Gautama Buddha made the Great Renunciation. Like many another idealist and mystic, Buddha abandoned his wealth and deserted his family.

Seeking the answer to the planet's problems of disease, death, and pain, Buddha donned a beggar's rags and went to the forest to fast and think. There he sought the Truth by self-study and reflection. He built a religion that has literally altered the lives of millions of people. The Buddha—"The Enlightened One"—preached, like Jesus, to the rich and poor alike.

What did Buddha say? What did he teach? Relying in part upon the concepts of the *Upanishads,* Buddha said that the greatest sin is spiritual ignorance. "As rain breaks through an ill-thatched house passion will break through an unreflecting mind." A holy life is simple and moral and founded on a spirit of inquiry. A man must analyze and control his mind and desires. He must try to forget the self and its interests. The physical world will soon pass; it is all an illusion. The important life has no concern with material things. In a famous passage about the Four Noble Truths and the Eightfold Path, Buddha said that pain and sorrow would be removed by "right understanding, resolve, speech, action, living, effort, mindfulness, meditation." He also said that men must not steal, kill, lie, swear, be angry, find fault, be covetous, gossip. "Hatred does not cease by hatred at any time; hatred ceases by loving. All men tremble at punishment. All men love life. Remember that you are like unto them and do not cause slaughter." Buddha also said: "Let no man think lightly of evil, saying in his heart: 'It will not come nigh unto me.' Even by the falling of water drops a water-pot is filled; a fool becomes full of evil, even if he gathers it little by little."

Buddha thus held out hope to all men, regardless of caste, so long as they were reasonable and moderate. If you followed Buddha you had no need of Brahman rituals and sacrifices. Every man, according to Buddha, must work out his own destiny.

Although Buddha rejected the caste doctrines of Hinduism he did accept the idea of reincarnation and Karma. The soul, he said, was chained to the

Wheel of Life and Rebirth and would pass through a series of reincarnations so long as it was self-centered and self-seeking. When it was at last purged and purified of all concern for itself then it would achieve the unspeakable bliss and peace called Nirvana. There is no mention by Buddha of a Supreme Being, a personal God, or a personal immortality. Buddha said nothing about temples; but he did say a great deal about living a good life.

Soon after Buddha died he was worshipped as a god as well as a teacher and a prophet. The evils he opposed crept into the faith he founded. His simple rules were widely forgotten as rituals grew and high thin veils of incense curled before the Buddhas made of stone. Temples and monasteries were built. People prayed to Buddha, asking his help in hours of trouble.

Through the passes of the northern mountains Alexander the Great invaded India in 326 B.C. He conquered the Punjab in the northwest and a few small states in the Indus valley and prepared to weld them into one. But time did not wait for Alexander, and he had to leave his task unfinished. After his departure, however, new hands and swords did succeed in building a great state in central and northern India. Under the Mauryan dynasty this native empire had an unusual period of peace and prosperity that lasted from 322 to 185 B.C.

The third king in the Mauryan line was Asoka, who ruled from 273 B.C. to about 232 B.C. Asoka was a successful soldier who became a devout Buddhist and urged his people to follow the Eightfold Path. The able and benevolent Asoka was one of the really great men in the early history of India. He and his successors sent out missionaries to teach the ideas of Buddha, to encourage and help the weak and the unprotected, to dig wells and plant trees. These missionaries went to Syria, Macedonia, Egypt, Burma, Ceylon, Kashmir, Turkestan, and many other lands as royal messengers and agents of civilization. The dynamic message of Buddha that they preached abroad had much to do with the diffusion of cultures in the East.

For all of these activities the most credit must be given to Asoka. He was the first builder. Others continued what he began. One of the reasons why Asoka's fame endures, of course, is simply this: he did believe in good works, he kept the Buddhist faith, and he had brains enough to be tolerant.

Meanwhile only a few Buddhists really followed the doctrines of the master teacher. There were arguments about beliefs, about the multiplication of sects that corrupted the moral and practical teachings of Buddha. The revived Brahmans gradually drove Buddhism out of India. By 800 A.D. the former vital force in Buddhism was apparently extinguished in the land that saw its birth. Hinduism had triumphed again.

Abroad the tale was different. There the prophet was not without honor. The victories of the faith of Buddhism in exile were great and lasting. The mighty power of Buddha lives today in Afghanistan, Ceylon (the purest form is there), the islands of Indonesia, China, Japan, Nepal, Thailand, Tibet. More than 30 per cent of the inhabitants of the world are Buddhists. Shrines and monasteries reach from the Caspian Sea to the Pacific Ocean. Buddhism is probably India's most important gift to the world.

"Long is the night to him who is awake, long is the mile to him who is tired, long is the life to the foolish who know not the true law."

The history of early India is a complex and tortured tale. Its chapters help to show how it was that such barriers between East and West as those of custom, religion, and habits of thought became firm and formidable.

Some Western historians have been accustomed to see Europe as the focus of most of the important history, the problems and the solutions of the world. But no clear view of early and medieval history is possible unless one sees Europe within the framework of the whole stretch of the land mass from the Atlantic Ocean to the Pacific waters. We must not get bogged down by looking too carefully at Europe alone or by letting the voices of Asia recede, faint and far. To understand the superficial identity and the diverse reality called Asia one must try very hard to see the lands of that immense continent as their peoples see them. In our modern world we have sometimes failed to glance beyond the continents of Europe and America. As troubles grew slowly in the East the policies and attitudes of the West helped to sow dragons' teeth and the swords are now coming up. Unless passions are calmed and much ignorance is wiped away in the lands of the Indus, the Thames, and the Hudson then it may soon be true that

> The Stars are setting and the Caravan
> Starts for the Dawn of Nothing. . . .

Chapter 6

CHINA:

THE PACE OF CHANGE

"They clear away the grass and the bushes;
And the ground is laid open by their plows. . . .
From of old it has been thus."

—*Tsai Shu*, ancient Chinese sacrificial ode

THE two giants of the Orient are India and China. China contains about 3,850,000 square miles of land and more than 500,000,000 people. It is a country of rugged mountain ranges, wide tablelands, great plains and rivers, highlands, lowlands, deserts.

In the north is the broad valley of the Hwang Ho or Yellow River and its tributary the Wei. The fertile Yellow Plain of the Valley stretches for hundreds of miles. If the rains come slowly, all is well. If they come fast, there are floods, destruction, and death. If the rains do not come at all, then great famines starve and kill. The Chinese call the Hwang Ho River "China's Sorrow."

The people in southern China are more fortunate and more prosperous. There the land is moist and green, filled with canals and lakes, great tea and rice plantations and large cities. From the earliest times a vast river network for communication and commerce has existed in China. The Yangtze River, one of the major waterways of the world, curves for 3,000 miles towards the Yellow Sea. Its basin forms the whole of central China. Scores of tributaries join it. Among them is the great Han River, which tumbles its flood into the Yangtze at Hankow ("the mouth of the Han").

About the misty years of early Chinese history many mingled myths and legends have been told and written, such as those in the fascinating *Annals of the Bamboo Books*. It is probably not true, for instance, that the first man, Panku, created the world with a chisel and a hammer or that 13 Celestial Emperors each ruled 18,000 years. Modern scholars are interested in the discovery of facts, even though the facts are sometimes far less interesting than the shifting lights and shadows of the enchanting tales of myth and magic that are part of the heritage of China.

We know that the first civilization of the Far East developed in the Chinese river valleys, especially in the Hwang Ho region. We know that during the Stone Age men lived in villages of clay huts by the riverbank or hunted in the hills beyond the valley. They used stone tools and weapons and made black pottery. They domesticated the ox and the horse. By 2500 B.C. the peoples in the Hwang Ho valley had built strong and efficient city-states— they were later to fall upon evil days—like those in Egypt, Mesopotamia, and India. Their carefully organized government was carried on by members of a nobility of birth serving in the emperor's cabinet. They had constructed roads, canals, and irrigation systems. They knew how to use gold, silver, mercury, and lead. They worshiped a god they called Shang-ti, together with the sun, moon, stars, and the spirits of their ancestors. Their whole religious system was filled with mystery and much ritual.

As one studies and reflects upon these and other achievements in China the more obvious it becomes that detailed comparative books about early developments in Asia and Europe are sadly lacking. Professor Joseph Needham's *Science and Civilization in China* closes a part of the gap; but more bold efforts at synthesis are needed and they cannot come too soon.

The early inhabitants of eastern Asia crossed over the Bering Straits into North America. In 1955 traces of what may be the oldest civilizations in northern Canada were discovered at a caribou crossing on the banks of the Firth River in the Yukon territory. A party headed by Richard N. MacNeish, chief archeologist with the National Museum of Canada, found in the permafrost more than 8,000 artifacts of four civilizations hitherto unknown in America. The pieces of pottery and bone and stone tools and implements are identical in design and concept with those found in eastern Siberia and other parts of eastern Asia from the remains of cultures known to have flourished between 3000 and 1000 B.C.

In the years when the men of eastern Asia were probing into North America and wandering in the frontier areas of their own continent they were also building political and economic systems destined to influence their cultures and their histories for long centuries to come. Although many of the facts are hidden and the chronology is vague it seems that the Hsia ("civilized") dynasty may have reigned in China after the shadowy days of the "Model Emperors" and later rulers like Yau (who supposedly reigned from 2357 to 2258 B.C.) and Shun. The Hsia dynasty is said to have ruled in China from about 2205 to 1766 B.C. The first of the new sovereigns was also said to have been Yü, a ruler who was reputed to have had unusual and superhuman powers. It was claimed, for instance, that Yü saved his people from destruction by the floods of nine rivers by cutting canals through the hills and making nine lakes. It was also said that he divided his kingdom into nine provinces and extended his rule all the way to the Gobi Desert.

After several centuries the Hsia family may have become corrupt and weak. We are told that the eighteenth and last ruler of the dynasty, described in the ancient tales as a vicious and contemptible tyrant, was overthrown in 1766 B.C. Then he committed suicide by burning down his palace with himself inside. So runs the story.

Out of a welter of wars and plots there arose a national revolutionary hero called T'ang. He founded the Shang or Yin dynasty, which is usually said to extend from 1766 B.C. to 1122 B.C. According to Chinese historians, the first ruler of a dynasty is invariably good and the last ruler is invariably bad. For instance, Chou-sin, the last sovereign of the Shang dynasty, was described as ruthless and cruel. He had obviously lost the mandate of heaven to rule. So it was that Chou-sin was defeated in battle by his enemies in 1122 B.C., and then began the Chou dynasty, so famous in Chinese history. The period of the rule of the house of Chou lasted for nearly 900 years through the lives of 35 sovereigns (1122–249 B.C.)

The Chou family came from the duchy of Chou on the northwest frontier. At first their power reached no further than the Hwang Ho and Wei river valleys. Slowly it was extended by battle and blackmail and inheritance and marriage. The emperor allowed his brothers, uncles, cousins, and faithful servants to collect and keep taxes in certain areas and to hold and rule large fiefs or grants of territory. In return, these nobles were expected to give the emperor military aid and to help carry on the government and the central administration.

In time the result of this allocation of lands was the formation of a confederation in which several feudal states, each with its own ruler, were united under the emperor, called the "Son of Heaven" because he was the high priest of all the nation. Since the emperor was regarded as the chosen "Son of Heaven" his moral power was tremendous. He ruled with rigid ceremony in the name of Heaven like the pharaohs of ancient Egypt. In theory, he was the supreme lord. In fact, however, his actual political, military, and financial power steadily dwindled. The nobles became nearly independent rulers of nearly independent states. Meanwhile the decrease of military power in the hands of the central government meant that the vassal states warred among themselves. By battles, coups, and diplomatic ruses the smaller states were gobbled up by the larger. Bloodshed and rivalry almost inevitably occur when central authority is weak. Warlords rose and fell. This is called the period of "The Contending States" in Chinese history.

Around 1200 B.C. there seem to have been nearly 1,800 feudal principalities in China. By about 500 B.C. the number had been reduced to 52. Early in the seventh century B.C. the weakened emperor was merely the nominal head of the confederation: the actual power in the empire fell in turn to one of the five main states—this is called by the Chinese the period of the "Five Leaders." But there was no stability. Always there was rivalry, always conflict.

These years of wild civil warfare were filled with excitement and romance, heroism and cowardice. Chinese prose and poetry contain many rousing tales of the "Contending States" and the "Five Leaders." At last a warlord from the great Ch'in state conquered all his foes and the Chinese provinces were united under his authority. About 249 B.C. he claimed the title of emperor and his will prevailed. One of his successors, Shih Hwang Ti, abolished the feudal system (which had endured for about 800 years) and divided China once more into provinces. In each province he put salaried officials responsible to the emperor alone. Shih Hwang Ti built palaces and magnificent public buildings, canals and roads. Then he turned with an army of 300,000 men against the enemies from beyond his frontiers, the Tartars. Thousands of Tartars were killed and the rest were hurled back into Mongolia. To keep out the foreign invaders Shih Hwang Ti began in 214 B.C. to build a gigantic wall across the northern frontier from the sea to the farthest northwestern corner of the Chinese Empire.

About the same time Shih Hwang Ti concluded that the scholars and writers were praising the past too much and giving the heroes of the feudal days too much acclaim. He disliked the power of the "intellectuals" in the state. To Shih Hwang Ti the living heroes, such as himself, and the new ideas mattered more than those of yesterday. Everything, said he, must begin with his reign. Henceforth he, and he alone, would be called "the First Emperor." Shih Hwang therefore decreed that all books referring to the past history of the empire were to be burned and scholars refusing to obey the command were to be executed. He excepted only books relating to agriculture, divination, and medicine. It is said that about 500 scholars were killed and hundreds more banished. Not all of the books were burned. Some, including the sacred Confucian group, were hidden in bricked-up walls and caves. This was not the last time in human history that an attempt has been made to destroy books and ideas. The past is not easily wiped away.

The "burning of the books" prepared the way for the fall of the dynasty of Shih Hwang Ti. When he died in 210 B.C. rebellion broke out. His son and successor, a debauched and nerveless youth, was murdered. A second son surrendered to the rebels and he, too, was put to death. After four years of bloody dispute a new family, the Han dynasty, grasped the reins of power. This was in 206 B.C. The Han family swiftly became strong and popular. Trade increased. Learning was encouraged. A new and efficient civil service labored hard. The empire was extended beyond the Yangtze valley to the edge of Indochina. True, there were soon to be new civil wars in China.

Nevertheless, the whole country was slowly becoming a unified state, and that is what mattered to China and the world.

Until modern times almost all societies contained the princes and the nobles who were widely considered to be superior to their fellow men. So it was in early China. There were also the workers who toiled and served and lived in thatched hovels of earth. It is true that much can be said in defense of a state system in which the pivots of power are found in the palace and the great houses of men of high birth and many acres. And yet no absolute kingship and no rigid class hierarchy can ever support the idea that the dignity of every individual is sacred and inviolable. The power and comfort of the upper classes in such societies have always rested upon the sweat and sadness of the nameless men below. In ancient China, as in many other lands, the surroundings formed an atmosphere from which the individual could not escape—"they came into his belly like water and like oil into his bones." The good earth provided the farmers' food—wheat, buckwheat, and soya beans in the north and wheat, rice, and barley in the south. Men of the lower classes worked from dawn to dusk while the nobles plotted and fought and ate beef and delicate bamboo shoots.

The rules and customs of the country, always so important in China, said what was to be done and what was to be avoided. The state, for instance, decided what taxes were to be paid in grain and animals. It declared what the occupation of a young man was to be: artisan, farmer, merchant, scholar, servant, unskilled worker. The strongest social group was the family. All members of a family lived under one roof and were subject to the authority of the oldest male. Love and respect were held to be the twin foundations of all family life. Throughout the land unfaltering courtesy was the standard of good conduct.

In these early days in China the towns and cities grew rapidly and the skills of peace were multiplied. Craftsmen and merchants founded numerous guilds. Linens and silks, carved panels and couches, silken screens and brocaded gowns were heaved aboard the river boats and sold in the countless shops of China. The knowledge and the application of science steadily increased. Professor Joseph Needham and others have recently done a great deal to place the scientific contributions of China to the world in their proper perspective, a task that has long needed doing. Against the background of a formidable body of evidence Professor Needham has ventured to make an assertion startling to those of us who have been born and taught in the Western tradition: "It is my conviction that the Chinese proved themselves able to speculate about Nature as well as the Greeks in their earlier period." In applied science they certainly did not lag behind early Egypt or Mesopotamia. Very early in their history, as we have seen, they irrigated fields, deepened river beds, made canals, reservoirs, bricks, developed a system of weights and measures, invented and used a lunar calendar, grew silkworms and wove silk —they began the manufacture of silk in the Shang period (1766–1122 B.C.).

It must not be forgotten that these Chinese achievements were really re-markable for their times. The immediate heirs of the Chinese river civiliza-tions do not suffer by comparison to those of the Nile, the Euphrates, and the Indus. Mankind reached forward very gradually, through numberless generations. The reader will have been sharply aware, for instance, that the centuries before Christ was born saw very few advances in the skills of trans-portation or communication, mileposts of progress upon which so much of our contemporary world depends. We know that many chapters of the tale of man can be told in terms of his persistent enterprise in moving himself and his baggage of goods and ideas about. In the hours of his early history he shouted across the valleys to friends and foes. In the twentieth century his wireless messages circle the planet and he bounces radar off the broken sur-faces of the moon. In the time scale of the universe it is not so long ago that a proud and nervous human being first gingerly maneuvered the frail raft he had made into the waters of a river or a sea. In the light of our earth's age it is only yesterday that buffeted and bewildered explorers first saw with mindless awe the waters of the Pacific, vast and lonely under the dome of a silent sky. It is only today that jet planes flash from London to New York and from New York to Karachi. On the one hand, this kind of thing plays crushing havoc with the individual ego. On the other, it brings a surge of pride and hope for the race of men who have toiled so hard through the cen-turies and have achieved so much.

While Chinese civilization was slowly advancing on so many fronts it steadily resisted then, and it steadily resisted later, the introduction of a phonetic alphabet. In most lands the obstacles to such a procedure have been overcome without major dislocations. In China, however, it was tremendously difficult to adopt a phonetic alphabet with its simplicity and its standardizing influence on the spoken language. There are indeed very great barriers. More than 40,000 characters are found in the Chinese script. Each symbol repre-sents the word or the idea rather than the sound, and that is the reason why so many characters are necessary. Only a small educated class understands the written language. It is a difficult and complex method of communication, and to learn to read and write in China is hard indeed.

The spoken language, which is different from the written, also presents problems. There are many dialects in China and the dialect of one region is not understood by the people of another. Because there is a limited number of distinct sounds that the human throat can utter, the Chinese often have to convey their meaning by tones. There are four different tones in the Peking

Mandarin dialect and nine in the Cantonese. If this fact seems startling, it may be remembered that in the English language there are eight different sound values to the letter *a* and almost as many to the four-letter combination *ough*.

If the Chinese did not surmount their problems of written and oral communication with celerity and skill they did excel in other arts. China has no pyramids or temple ruins to bear witness to her antiquity or her genius, but for centuries her massive achievements in the fine arts have brought her wonder and applause. Consider, for instance, the growth of skill in the cutting and elaborate carving of jade. For hundreds of years the Chinese have believed in the medicinal value of jade and have regarded it highly as a symbol of virtue, "the quintessence of heaven and earth."

The greatest of the arts of China has not been the carving of jade. It has been painting, a skill whose origins are lost in the fogs of legend. We know that by 300 B.C. the delicate hair-brush, handled with such sensitive and marvelous grace by the Chinese, was already used for painting on woven silk, wooden panels, and walls whitened with lime. Again and again the Chinese artists painted the two great symbolic figures of China, the Tiger and the Dragon, the one representing the power of nature and the other the malign forces of sinister spirits. From the beginning the painting of China has been rightly famed for its restrained poise and balance, the rhythms of its delicate lines, its quiet insight into the deepest emotions of man.

In Chinese bronzes there arose a form of art that can be traced to about 2000 B.C. The daring and powerful sacrificial bronze pieces of the ancient Shang and Chou dynasties have a savage grandeur in their design. Especially impressive are the inscribed libation cups and other ceremonial temple vessels shaped in the forms of animals such as the tiger, the snake, bull, deer, and rhinoceros. There were also graceful wine vases whose delicate beauty foreshadows the lightly flowing porcelain objects of later ages. The most outstanding periods of bronze production were during the period 220 B.C.–400 A.D. and the Ming dynasty which began in the fourteenth century.

Man's first literary utterances in China—and this statement is probably true for lands elsewhere—took the form of verse. In Chinese poetry there is no blank verse; all lines are rhymed. Although most of the Chinese poetry and prose written before the sixth century B.C. has been lost, there have been rescued from the rats of time about 3,000 folk songs and lyrics. Tradition has it that Confucius (551–478 B.C.) chose and arranged the 305 ancient poems that are included in the famous *She King*, or *Book of Odes*. The *Odes* now belong to the Sacred Books of China because they form an important section of the Confucian Canon.

Many of the emotions revealed in the *Odes* are as old as mankind. Usually written in lines of four words, the poems treat of good and evil, war and death, love and dancing and happiness, the heart cries of misery, the joys of hunting and drinking. Here are four lines from the oldest drinking song known in the world:

> The dew is heavy on the grass
> At last the sun is set.
> Fill up, fill up the cups of jade
> The night's before us yet.

In these early centuries the arts of sacred dancing and music also came to be highly developed. Before 1000 B.C. eight kinds of musical instruments appeared, including wind and stringed instruments, rattles, drums, bells, musical stones, cymbals. The Chinese slowly built up a five-toned musical system, highly mathematical in all of its principles.

Quite apart from the technical and historical aspects of the growth of Chinese art and music lies the significant fact that as arts they always contain and express some aspects of the spirit of the Chinese people. All forms of art, of course, tell us something about the men and women who made them. It is often forgotten, too, that pieces of fine art are themselves symbols. They frequently carry ideas of universal validity—we usually call them "values." Symbols other than language are invariably useful in the study of the thoughts and emotions of peoples and cultures in places and times remote from our own. Especially is this true of creations that reveal something of the aesthetic appreciations of those who look and those who make. A Western poet said: "A thing of beauty is a joy forever." An Eastern sage remarked: "It is better to have a broken piece of jade than a whole tile." Both poet and philosopher were stating the same truth: all civilized and sensitive beings bow before the beautiful in nature and in art.

The philosophers of China, unlike those of India and the world of the West, have seldom been concerned with the mysteries of a divine plan in a puzzling universe. Their major interest has been turned towards the problems of man in society, the principles of morals and ethics and the pursuit of happiness. "What is right?" "What is wrong?" "What is the way to truth?"

Many men have had many answers. The name Lao Tzu, for instance, takes a high place in the ranks of those who have guided Chinese thought and contributed to the ingredients of the Chinese spirit. Despite the eminence of his name scholars know no more about his life than they do about the life of Homer. Lao Tzu—"the Venerable Philosopher"—may have been born in 570 B.C. If he actually did live—some scholars think that at least three men did the work attributed to him—it is possible that he was the curator of the Royal Library of Chou. What is important is this: a book supposedly written by Lao Tzu in his old age, called *Tao Te Ching,* or *The Book of the Way and of Virtue,* has influenced a large part of the vast Asian continent for more than 2,000 years.

Tao Te Ching is a short, mystical, poetical, and obscure treatise on metaphysics written in about 5,000 characters and usually divided into 82 chapters and 2 parts. The word *Tao* cannot be adequately translated into English or any other language. Usually translated "the Way" it contains within it many meanings made more misty by the difficulties of communication and interpretation: the way, the road, the path, the word, reason, the universal spirit, the laws of nature. To Lao Tzu the *Tao* meant that for any individual the way of virtue was in simple, spontaneous action, unfettered and untrammeled by any selfish purposes or ulterior motives. The final accomplishment of any good or natural action alone mattered. "It is the way of *Tao* not to act from any personal motive; to conduct affairs without feeling the trouble of them; to taste without being aware of the flavor; to account the great as small and the small as great; to recompense injury with kindness." A rose grows naturally, without a word or a claim or any display of pride. So a man should live and grow with humility, compassion, and serenity. The individual, "without striving or crying," should govern himself "as a little child." No man should ask or want too much because these wants, like the love of money, are the roots of many evils.

Human beings who are really wise, said Lao Tzu, never strive or fight their fates or their fellows. They compromise and submit with untroubled spirits to every push and blow of men and fortune. Serene and humble individuals must learn to accept the relativity of all values in the worldly affairs of active men. They must learn to pause and quietly contemplate the eternal rhythm of life and the many processes of nature in all their mystery. Only by taking this way, said Lao Tzu, can men reach the passionless understanding that is the good life. Part of this conclusion, of course, is a philosophical concept found throughout the East: the idea that happiness and truth are to be found within the mind and not in a mindless submergence in purposeless activity. "Controlling oneself in the Orient became a more urgent matter than knowing and controlling the outer world." The Christian faith also says that it is better for a man to be able to govern himself than to take a city.

In his short book Lao Tzu stressed frequently a basic principle of early Taoism: men must learn to scorn and renounce society and return to contemplate, as mentioned above, the beauty and serenity of nature and her laws, fixed and immutable—it will be noted that this intuitive and introspective view of nature suggests again that Lao Tzu had little trust in intellectual apprehension. All people, said the sage, should live a simple life without interference from the outside government. "The greater the number of statutes, the greater the number of thieves and brigands." This position is very close to philosophical radicalism.

PLATE V

[19]

Above: Chinese jade head of a horse. Han
dynasty (206 B.C.—220 A.D.)

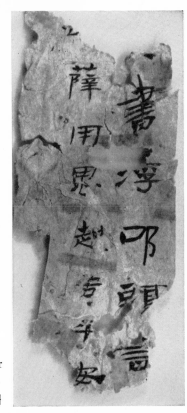

Right: A piece of the world's most ancient paper
made in China between 25 and 220 A.D.

[20]

[22]

]

Chinese ceremonial vessel in the form of an elephant (early
Chou dynasty c. 1000 B.C.)

Ancient Greek statue of a lyre player
(Cycladic marble)

[23] The Acropolis of Athens

[24] *Left:* An ancient Greek computer. The Greeks used several devices of this kind to aid them in their calculations.

[25]

Right: Silver coin (tetradrachm) of Athens. Note the owl to the side of the olive branch.

Below: Detail from a decoration on a Corinthian vase (c. 575-550 B. C.) [26]

PLATE VI

Lao Tzu was certain that if the government were in the hands of wise men like himself, then all would be well. "A government conducted by sages would free the hearts of the people from inordinate desires, fill their bellies, keep their ambitions feeble and strengthen their bones. They would constantly keep the people from knowledge and free from desires." But the government was not in the control of a philosopher-king like Lao Tzu. In the circumstances Lao Tzu did not rebel against the evils of political disorder and decadence. He submitted. He withdrew. The American philosopher John Dewey once remarked: "While saints are engaged in introspection burly sinners run the world."

There was another Chinese philosopher who was not prepared to abandon the field of battle to the government or anybody else. This man was Confucius, whose name is known wherever civilized men assemble. We know that Confucius had at least one conversation with Lao Tzu in 517 B.C. The two men whose influence was so great upon all subsequent generations of Chinese—although their professed followers departed far from the original teachings—must have had a very interesting talk indeed. Their ideas were so different, so firmly held. An old Chinese proverb says: "Parties whose principles are different cannot take counsel together." It is sometimes so.

The greatest philosopher and scholar of China was Confucius—"the philosopher K'ung." More than any other person he epitomizes Chinese thought through the centuries. He was indeed a wise human being.

Confucius was born in 551 B.C. and died in 478 B.C. His lineage was noble —he was the descendant of Shang kings. On the other hand, his purse and stomach were often empty and he spent several years of his life seeking food and money and patrons. Those years were not peaceful, because the Chou Empire was declining and the result was turmoil, misrule, battles, crimes, misery, and famine. Clan fought clan and state battled state. "In those days there was no king in China and every prince did what was right in his own eyes." All about were abuses.

At the age of twenty-two Confucius began to teach philosophy, poetry, and music. "When I have presented one corner of a subject and the pupil cannot himself make out the other three, then I do not repeat my lesson." Unlike the Taoists, Confucius and his followers—one of them was the distinguished philosopher Mencius—did not stand aside from human life. They became instead reformers and humanists. "If any ruler," said Confucius, "would submit to me as his director . . . for three years I should attain the realization of all my hopes." For many years he apparently dreamed of being the leader of a great reformation that would bring China back to the habits and moral rules that prevailed in the long-past Golden Age. Confucius knew that he could advise princes how to rule by giving them sage counsels about morality and justice and moderation. To his sad dismay, nobody in authority accepted him or his advice. The princes would not listen. Some of them dismissed him as a wind-laden busybody. The way of a reformer is always hard when he tilts against vested interests and arrogant power.

When Confucius was fifty-two years old he became the chief magistrate of the city of Chung-tu. It seemed to him that his prince was unduly interested in the dancing girls and not active enough in following the excellent advice of his chief magistrate. The result was a violent quarrel. Confucius was then forced to resign, and he spent the rest of his life wandering through the provinces of China and teaching all who would come to hear and study. To hundreds of disciples he became a revered and inspired teacher of great moral truths.

Throughout his life Confucius denounced the moral laxity and political darkness of his age. Restraint upon evil, he repeated, was always a stimulus to good. Even the weak must fight evil and the slow men run from it. "Oppressive government," Confucius declared, "is fiercer and more feared than a tiger." He insisted always that if princes practiced right behavior and sound ethics, then their subjects would do likewise. The power of right example would always triumph. "Not more surely does the grass bend before the wind than the masses yield to the will of those above them."

The sage of China seldom said anything about the place of man in the universe or his relation to any Supreme Being. He was mainly concerned with man as he is and his duties to society. The teaching of Confucius became essentially a conservative, ethical teaching, a series of secular instructions about right behavior. His faith was a sincere faith in man. All men, he said, must love the truth. They should live rational and ethical lives here on earth. All men of reason and good will must obey the golden rule and behave virtuously toward their neighbors. The greatest values are found in human relationships. "The higher man has nine things which are subjects with him of thoughtful consideration. In regard to the use of his eyes he is anxious to see clearly. . . . In regard to his demeanor he is anxious that it shall be respectful. In regard to his speech he is anxious that it shall be sincere. In regard to his doing of business he is anxious that it shall be reverently careful. In regard to what he doubts about he is anxious to question others. When he is angry he thinks of the difficulties his anger may involve him in. When he sees gain he thinks of righteousness."

The pith and point of the maxims of Confucius are known all over the civilized world. "What you do not like when done to yourself do not do unto others." "The cautious seldom err." "What the superior man seeks is in himself; what the small man seeks is in others." "Learning, undigested by thought, is labor lost; thought unassisted by learning is perilous." "When you hear words that are distasteful to your mind you must inquire whether they are not right." "The ultimate effect of shielding men from the results of their folly is to fill the world with fools."

These ideas, and many more, are to be found in the six Confucian classics, said to have been edited by Confucius himself. Of special interest to thoughtful men today are *The Book of Poetry, The Book of Philosophy,* and *The Canon of History.* The human race will be poorer if it ever loses the wit and wisdom of Confucius. "I do not expect to find a saint today. But if I find a gentleman I shall be quite satisfied." "Men are born pretty much alike, but through their habits they gradually grow further and further apart from each other." "The young people should be good sons at home, polite and respectable in society. They should be careful in their conduct and faithful, love the people and associate themselves with the kind folks. If, after learning all this, they still have energy left, let them read books."

It is said that Confucius died in 478 B.C., a melancholy and disappointed man. His hopes had been frustrated, his aims unachieved. After his death the tide began to roll the other way. For more than 2,000 years pilgrims have come to a magnificent gate at the entrance to the avenue of cypresses that leads to a severely simple tomb. On that tomb is this inscription: "The most sagely ancient teacher; the all-accomplished, all-informed king." In Peking stands a great temple. Thousands more have risen in cities and towns throughout the land. It may be that sometimes Confucius' own words are quoted still:

> The great mountain must crumble
> The strong beam must break
> The wise man must wither away like a plant.

Lao Tzu and Confucius were among those men of China who were not mainly concerned with the external world of science and industry and material things. They did not seek new sources of power or instruments of precision. They never tried to train their hands and eyes to subdue the physical forces of nature. They turned instead to other problems of duty, morality, and the principles of right living.

We do not know when men first began to ask questions about these things, or about death and disillusionment and the destiny of man. What is the meaning of existence? Why does man, who alone knows and aspires, live but a brief moment in an indifferent universe? Why is it that men live to know, struggle to attain, and die defeated in the end? We do know something about the teachings of superior sages, philosophers, and prophets in the small and harsh worlds of the early centuries: Isaiah and Job and Zoroaster, Buddha and Lao Tzu and Confucius. In varied ways these wise men told their followers how to resist the tidal pull of evil and to transcend the frustrations of the insecure and impermanent world of the flesh. They spoke of such things as the ways of fortitude, or moderation, or good works, or the renunciation of the wicked material world. Every man knows for himself whether or not they were right. In any event, they tried to be right. "It is better to light one candle than to curse the darkness."

We now turn away from China to the turquoise blue waters of the Mediterranean Sea and the land of ancient Greece, a place of imperishable glory. The keynote to that glory is the Greek answer to the problems of knowledge and beauty and the nature of man. The Greeks tried to see life steadily and whole in the clash of strife and the calm of peace. Whenever we look at their works we are assailed by the concentrated awe of generations of spectators. What work of the hand of man can take its place beside the Parthenon, bright in the noonday sun? Who in the ranks of men can hopefully challenge Plato and Aristotle? The foot-slogging armies have long since perished. The great artists and philosophers of mankind are as immortal as anything human can be.

Chapter 7

GREECE:

WARRIORS DEAD

"You are privileged to contemplate day by day the manifestations of our country's power. Be her lovers, and, when her greatness fills your understanding, realize that it is the achievement of men—men who dared for her and planned for her and faced death for her and who never felt that failure in an enterprise was a reason for depriving their country of their valor, the noblest offering that they could lay at her feet. . . . The sepulchres of heroes is the whole earth. . . . Nothing is immortal but the spirit of honor. . . . For where the rewards of valor are, there will valiant men be gathered together."

—The Funeral Oration of Pericles,
Thucydides, *The Peloponnesian War*, Book II

FROM time beyond memory ships and men have moved over the waters of the Mediterranean Sea. Today, as yesterday, the traveler observes in the sunlight the lambent crests of cobalt waves blurring in the distance under a bowl of glaring porcelain sky. By moonlight the hushed waters make a silent floor of silver, pulsing and flawless.

The centuries have seen pharaohs and kings and wealthy nobles who flourished and died; limping poverty, goaded and muzzled; gray fat rats by the slimy harbor waters and the rotting jetties; plumes of steam from the scrofulous beggars' pots; tawdry bazaar stalls spangled by bright knives. They have seen the sure and steady men who stayed in their home places, the men who knew only the streets of the city or the barns and the measured fields. They have also seen the adventurers who scudded across uncertain seas, who hazarded and battled under strange suns, who gulped what time could give.

Here the soldiers trampled on the barley fields and crushed the milk-belled amaryllis. There the columns of curdled marble lie shattered on the hill. The past and the present bring tales and truths beyond the numbering of man.

In the southeast of Europe lie the mainland and islands of Greece. Everywhere the coasts are deeply indented—the sea reaches in with a thousand arms. Almost every spot in Greece is less than fifty miles from the sea. Sheltered inlets and harbors give safe haven to the ships and the mariners. This fact has been important in the lives of the Greeks, for they have always been a maritime people. From the days of antiquity they have sailed and traded. In fact, they have had to trade to survive. Only 20 per cent of the land in Greece can be cultivated. There are few mineral resources. Greece has always depended upon the energy and skill of her traders, workmen, and bankers; upon the special products of the vine and the olive tree; upon the supply of services. Hence the Greeks shrewdly built their industry and commerce. They developed and borrowed new techniques. They became, like the Phoenicians, fishermen and smugglers and "peddlers of the sea."

Much of the story of Greece can be told in terms of the blue sea and the dividing and interlacing mountain chains. "The mountains look on Marathon —And Marathon looks on the sea." The sea provided a channel for commerce and communication. The rugged mountains, on the other hand, made barriers inside the country. It was quite natural that the inhabitants of separated slopes and narrow valleys should have organized themselves into rival city-states. All of them, mountaineers and mariners, were individualists— there was nothing monotonous about the landscape and nothing monotonous about the people. They were men of tough sinews, men of vigor and courage devoted to their own valleys and villages. Perhaps, too, the beauty of the landscape helped to stir the artistic instincts of a versatile and sensitive people. Nobody who has seen Greece can forget the compelling power stretched before his eyes: the rocky heights and precipices; the delicate shades of color; the abundant cypresses, laurels, and pomegranates; the thick hedges of aloes; the magic casements of the poet opening upon scenes not easily matched this side of paradise.

The lamps of the Cretan palaces finally guttered out soon after 1500 B.C. and the power of Crete at last collapsed. Political and economic leadership in the whole Aegean area gradually passed from Crete to Mycenae, a city on the Gulf of Argos that stood athwart the natural land route across Greece to the Adriatic. For many years the city of Mycenae, like many other regions in the Greek and Illyrian lands, had borrowed freely the numerous skills of Crete. More skills meant more power and prosperity. The merchants and craftsmen of Mycenae made her a great trading city. The commercial posts and colonies of Mycenae studded the shores and islands of the Mediterranean.

In 1876 the wealthy amateur archeologist Heinrich J. Schliemann, whose discoveries in Crete were mentioned earlier, began to dig at Mycenae. The great palace at Mycenae was surrounded by massive fortifications—the walls were so large and thick that a Greek legend says they were built by one-eyed giants called Cyclops. Among the many entrances is the impressive Lioness

Gate, where two stone lionesses lie upon a triangular stone above the gateway, watching and guarding still. In the tombs and graves of Mycenae have been found magnificent pieces of porcelain work, golden hairpins, bracelets, earrings, and finely modeled inlaid daggers. At the nearby city of Tiryns, Schliemann also discovered (1884) the ruins of a great walled palace and several treasures in the domed beehive tombs.

Among the most interesting discoveries of Schliemann were those made on the site of ancient Troy. Since Troy stood on the west coast of Asia Minor near the Hellespont it was a natural crossroads, an almost inevitable spot for human settlement. Between 1870 and 1873 Schliemann unearthed nine cities built on top of one another. He concluded that the ancient Troy of Homer and the Greek wars was the second city in the series. Later investigation convinced others that the sixth city was that of Homer's Troy. In the 1930's Professor C. W. Blegen of the University of Cincinnati, perhaps best known for his excavation of the palace of Nestor at Pylos, began further work at Troy. The results of his findings have been published in several volumes. Professor Blegen has discovered, for instance, that the Troy of the famous wars was Troy VII and not, as had earlier been believed, either II or VI.

About 1600 B.C. the fair-haired and Greek-speaking Achaeans were beginning to move down from the Danube river basin. They slowly dominated and mingled with the Aegean peoples, settled mainly in Greece, probably seized Crete, and certainly assaulted Egypt. They occupied Lesbos and attacked Asia Minor, an event that brought the siege and defeat of Troy about 1200 B.C.

The fall of Troy in the Heroic Age of Greece (1300–1000 B.C.) was vividly described about four centuries later in the rolling lines of Homer's *Iliad*, an epic rightly praised for nearly thirty centuries. It is a commonplace to say that Homer was the Bible of the Greeks. It is perhaps also stating an obvious fact to add that the works of Homer, written in the noblest of all meters, will be read as long as men stay civilized.

Many pages have been written to show that Homer was actually several men; those pages are probably matched by the ones asserting that Homer was in fact a single poet of mighty power, perhaps a Greek from Ionia, a genius blind and poor and without honor while he lived.

> Seven cities now claim Homer dead
> Through which the living Homer begged his daily bread. ·

However these things may be, we do have Homer's poetry, probably composed in the ninth century B.C. The *Iliad* describes how Helen of Sparta was carried off by Paris, a Greek from Asia Minor, and taken to Troy. In extraordinary flights of genius, "the deep-browed Homer" tells of the wrath of Achilles and the long conflict that ended with the taking of Troy. His *Odyssey* records the exciting tale of the strange wanderings of the patient and untiring Odysseus—or Ulysses—in the long voyage home from the siege and sack of Troy. Many readers of this book will recall the power of such moving scenes as the parting of Hector and Andromache, Priam's ransoming of Hector's corpse, or the meeting of Penelope and her husband. Perhaps they will reach to the bookshelf and visit again the Land of the Midnight Sun, the Island of the Winds, and the Singing Sirens. "There in the meadow they sit and all around is a great heap of bones, mouldering bodies and withering skins."

About 1100 B.C. the first waves of the light-skinned Dorians from the north surged slowly through Illyria and Macedonia into Greece. The opposition to them was apparently not strong—Greece was already weakened by such events as the earlier interruption of trade with the Syria-Palestine region caused by the long wars between the Hittites and Egypt's Ramses II. The Dorians destroyed Mycenae and set up their chief states of Argos and Sparta. They occupied Rhodes and they conquered Crete. Meanwhile they mingled and married with the Aegean peoples.

The descent of the Dorians also gave impetus to migrations from the overcrowded Greek mainland. Thousands of impoverished and desperate people fled from their accumulated debts and their oppressive landlords. The Hittite Empire had fallen; Troy was no more; the way was open for the Greeks who wanted to move over the sea into Asia Minor or to sail unchallenged to the islands of the Mediterranean. Thus they went to Lesbos and Aeolis, to Chios, Miletus, Samos, and elsewhere. A few centuries later—especially between 750 and 650 B.C.—there were other outbursts of colonization by city-states creating dependent colonies. Megara founded Byzantium and Chalcedon at strategic points at the western entrance to the Bosporus. Miletus, the main city of Ionia, founded Sinope and Abydus and several other colonies along the shores of the Sea of Marmora and the Black Sea and the coasts of Thrace. Corinth founded Syracuse on the island of Sicily and also got control of the island of Corcyra. Chalcis, the leading city of the island of Euboea, founded in Italy the cities of Cumae, Puteoli, and Naples. Sparta founded Tarentum. Greek settlers (Phocians) even moved to make a colony at Massila—now Marseilles, that proud city of France.

Every one of the cities planted abroad by Greece was soon to become a center for the spread of Greek culture. Almost at once, of course, they became points for the stimulation of trade and industry. The colonies prospered. For instance, the carpets and draperies of Miletus and the cloth of Megara were sold and shipped to the merchants of many lands. The mother city-states in Greece exported textiles, iron weapons, pottery, hides, works of art, leather goods. They imported grains, salt fish, ivory, lumber, hides, and wool. Meanwhile the shipbuilding industry, always an index to the state of the carrying trade, steadily expanded.

During these years many more city-states arose in the cup-shaped valleys rimmed by the barrier mountains. These states were usually led by an elected king who was at once a priest, a judge, and a leader in war. Despite the fact that some kings apparently claimed absolute authority and divine descent it was usually true that these kings were in fact required to consult with a council of chiefs or elders who were elected by the wealthy landowners and merchants, the members of aristocratic families. The little traders and the small farmers had few powers and rights. The slaves had almost no rights at all. The eighth-century poet Hesiod's *Works and Days* presents a vivid picture of the unsolved riddle of social justice. Overpopulated Greece has seen much misery beneath her skies. The English poet Thomas Gray said in the eighteenth century that the annals of the poor are short and simple. On the contrary, they are often long, complicated, and bitter.

Although the Greeks spoke different dialects, all literate Greeks wrote and read the same language. All Greeks worshiped the same gods who lived on Olympus, a high and snow-capped mountain in Thessaly: the sky god Zeus, "the father of gods and men" who ruled the world with lightning; Apollo, god of the sun, beauty, and the fine arts; Aphrodite, goddess of love; Dionysus, god of the grape and wine; Poseidon, ruler of the sea; Athena, warlike goddess of wisdom. To the gods the Greeks attributed human strengths and faults and follies. Sometimes, as many famous stories tell, the gods descended from Mount Olympus to share in the affairs of men. Great religious meetings

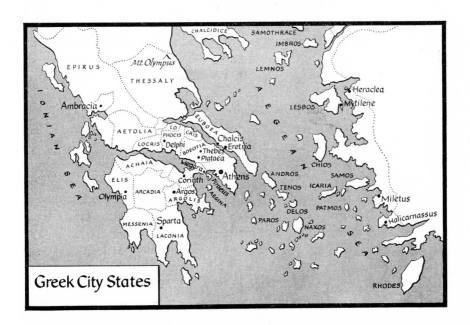

Greek City States

were held by the city-states to honor the gods. In honor of Zeus, for instance, the Olympic games were held. We hold them still, though not to honor Zeus.

By 550 B.C. the two most famous and powerful city-states were Sparta and Athens. The Spartans followed one road in government and values. The Athenians took another.

The Spartans lived in the rich river land of Laconia at the southern end of the Peloponnesian peninsula. After the so-called reforms of Lycurgus the state took control of all its citizens. When a boy was seven years old he was taken from his parents and trained by the state to fight, to endure hardships, to be hard and tough. Everywhere was the heavy hand of state control, the stern discipline of the barracks, the armed camp. It was the duty of a citizen to be an efficient soldier, to obey and serve. There was no time for fine art, philosophy, literature. No Spartan citizen might own land—it belonged to the state. No Spartan was allowed to take part in trade and commerce, to have or use money, or to travel outside Sparta.

One by one, Sparta conquered many of the neighboring Greek states, taking the richer lands and all the treasures. Some of the defeated Greeks were made slaves or serfs (helots) and others were given some poor land and left alone. The Spartans themselves became great landowners—always controlling the land and ruling thousands of subjects in the name of the all powerful police state. The rulers of such states often live in daily fear. Several decrees of the leading Spartans show how deathly afraid they were.

This Spartan state of steel contained about 25,000 Spartan citizens. They had two kings and a council of thirty men over sixty years of age. Most of the real government was done by a committee of five *ephors* elected by the citizens. Thus the Spartan citizen had a share in the government; but nobody else did. There is no need here to describe in further detail the complex system of the balanced and counterbalanced Spartan government. The most important fact is that their state was military, belligerent, totalitarian. Sparta was isolated, ringed round by an iron curtain. Inside was regimentation, stagnation, and the starvation of the spirit. It was a cold and barren existence, as ugly a business as the soul-killing paralysis existing in the states of modern dictators.

It was far otherwise in Athens. This famous city-state, born of a coalition of Attic villages, stood in central Greece about three miles from the Aegean Sea. In its early history it was ruled by a king and later by a group of harsh and unjust noble landowners. The result, of course, was almost constant conflict between the rich and poor. In 622 B.C. the discontented men in Athens were partly placated by a codification of the law prepared by the executive magistrate Draco. Whatever satisfaction they had did not last for long. Because the social and economic evils were left unchanged, popular agitation soon broke out again.

In 594 B.C. a wise and liberal aristocrat named Solon the Lawgiver carried out several justly famous reforms that helped to relieve the mounting tension. In the future, said the laws of Solon, nobody was to be sold into slavery because he owed money. Debtors who had become slaves were freed and all their debts were canceled. It was forbidden to secure any loans upon a debtor's person. A new constitution divided the people into four classes in which membership was determined by wealth. The richest men belonged to the first two classes. They were eligible for election to the magistracies, to the old council of the Areopagus and to the new Council of the Four Hundred, created by Solon. Men of the third class, the middle class, could also be elected to the Council of the Four Hundred. The fourth class, the poor farmers and city workers, had the right to participate in the popular assembly. Slaves and foreigners had no vote in the assembly or anywhere else. Under the arrangements made by Solon, new jury courts helped to bring the administration of the law under popular control by providing a machinery for appeal from the arbitrary actions of magistrates. Judges were to be chosen by lot from among all free citizens.

Solon also tried to raise the level of agricultural production by encouraging new and better methods of farming. He attempted to build up the export trade, especially in such commodities as olive oil. He did all he could to stimulate industry. He welcomed, for example, the immigration of artisans from other states and from across the seas.

The sagacious Solon probably saved Athens from a class war. He was not only a social reformer. He was also a statesman. A good case can be made for the assertion that he really began the political system that we call democracy. True, what he created was only a limited democratic system; but it was a step towards completely popular government. It is the first step that sometimes matters most. Said Solon:

> I stood with a mighty shield in front of both classes
> And suffered neither of them to prevail unjustly.

Nobody was fully satisfied with Solon's attempt to reconcile the differences between the aristocracy and the commons. The nobles thought he had gone too fast and too far. There were others who thought he had not gone far enough. The way of a reformer is always hard. Class divided against class. In these conditions it was not surprising that a clever military hero and adventurous noble named Pisistratus succeeded in his third attempt to upset the government. In 545 B.C. Pisistratus declared himself to be the true protector of the small farmer. The small farmer listened and followed Pisistratus. Many others rallied to his banners and he became the ruler, or tyrant, of Athens. In ancient Athens, it must be remarked at once, the word "tyrant" had no such dark meaning as it has today. It did not mean then that the ruler was harsh, or brutal, or wicked. It meant only that he held authority by force and without constitutional sanction. Greece had several tyrants in the city-states of the sixth century and only a few of them were really nasty men.

Pisistratus was not cruel or evil. He was a benevolent despot. He gave Athens as good rule as any state can have without liberty. With his death in 527 B.C. the prospect altered. The son who succeeded him was assassinated and the second son, an oppressive and wicked man, was driven out of Athens in 510. Thus the so-called Age of Tyrants came to a rather violent end.

At once the aristocrats tried to regain the power they had lost. In this design they were thwarted by Cleisthenes, an aristocrat who deserted the ranks of his class to become a popular leader. It was to his advantage and the advantage of Athens that Cleisthenes decided to follow the road traveled by Solon. He set up a new executive council of five hundred men chosen by lot from the different classes of the ten city and country tribes. Everybody—merchants, farmers, bankers, fishermen—was represented in the council. Below the council still stood the popular assembly. The male citizens of Athens now chose all officials. Everybody had a chance to serve his city in public office. If any man seemed to be growing too powerful or ambitious he might be banished from the city by a "want of confidence" vote of the assembly. This was the idea and practice called ostracism, a powerful weapon in the hands of the people. A man held to be "dangerous to the state" had to go into exile and stay there for a specified time. The price of liberty, it seemed, was vigilance and the popular ability to anticipate the emergence of dark designs and crooked counsels that might endanger the safety of the state.

The Athenian government in the sixth century B.C. took long strides towards the democratic operations that later made Athens famous through the centuries. Athens pointed to the road leading to individual dignity and freedom. Sparta pointed the other way.

Some historians have said that it was inevitable that Greece and Persia should fight each other. On the one hand stood Greece, composed of divided and bickering city-states on the mainland and the islands. On the other hand, the armies of Persia, in a great explosion of power, had rolled to the shores of the Aegean. After the fall of the Lydian kingdom of Croesus (546 B.C.) Persia swallowed up the Greek cities on the coasts and hills of Asia Minor. Darius I, hungry master of a mighty empire, looked across the narrow seas towards the Greek peninsula. The Greek city-states, divided among themselves, would fall easily before the Persian hosts. Darius was confident of that. He had already probed into Thrace and found soft spots. Stronger foes had stood before him and he had beaten them all.

If wars are wished for, causes can usually be found. Darius could have argued that the Spartans had been allies of the conquered Lydians; that Athens had refused too abruptly to take back the exiled son of Pisistratus as her ruler when Persia had asked her to do so; that the Greek cities were giving refuge to troublemakers fleeing from the Persian zones of control. Darius made no such charges and the Greeks made no replies. Such steps were unnecessary because a wide rebellion of the Greeks in Asia Minor provided an immediate cause for conflict. The rebels asked for aid from Greece. Athens and one other city agreed to supply ships. Persia crushed the revolt, blamed Greece for inciting and prolonging it, and turned to invade and chastise the presumptuous country.

In 492 the first Persian expedition struck at Greece by way of Macedonia. The Persian army fared well, but a storm wrecked the fleet. In 490 B.C. Darius mounted another offensive. A fleet sailed across the Aegean and landed forces that seized and burned the city of Eretria. Then a Persian army of about 20,000 men turned towards Attica and Athens. To meet the advancing foe the Athenians sent an army of 10,000 heavily armored soldiers. The two armies met at Marathon, about twenty miles northeast of Athens. The Greeks deliberately left their center weak and kept their armored and anchored flanks strong. The attacking Persians did what the Greeks expected: they caved in the Greek center. Then the powerful flanks of the Greek army charged swiftly through the arrows, closed in, encircled and throttled the Persians. When the battle ended, a Greek soldier ran from Marathon to Athens to say that the Athenians had won, that Greece was saved.

The Persian defeat at Marathon meant delay, not final victory for the Athenians. It was clear that the Persians would strike again, and that before very long. In 485 B.C. Darius I of Persia died and his son Xerxes soon began preparations for a third campaign against Greece. A pontoon bridge was built across the Hellespont. Supply depots were set up. In 480 B.C. a Persian army of about 100,000 men moved along the north coast of the Aegean to begin the drive into Greece. A Persian fleet of about 600 triremes edged slowly along the jagged and dangerous shore. In Greece, meanwhile, the Athenians, Spartans, and the men of twenty-nine other states stood together in a Hellenic League to defend their homeland.

Between the mountains and the sea there is a narrow pass called Thermopylae and here the Spartan king Leonidas decided to make a stand against the invaders. The Persian cavalry—the cavalry was usually the most efficient arm of all Oriental armies—could not be expected to do well in or about the pass of Thermopylae. When the Persian ships tried to land forces behind the Greek lines they were badly battered by a storm and mauled by the Athenian fleet. Then Xerxes tried to break through the pass by a frontal assault. For two days the Greeks held him back. When a traitor showed the Persians a secret path they were able to fall upon the Greeks from the rear. Leonidas got word in time to send away the main part of the Greek army; but he and about 300 men stayed to fight a holding action in the deathtrap. They fought until the last man fell. "In this position they defended themselves with their knives (if they still had knives to fight with) or otherwise with their hands and teeth until they were buried by the Orientals under a hail of missiles."

The deeds the heroes did that day have made their names immortal. "O passer by, tell the Spartans we lie here, obedient to their orders."

On to Athens rolled the victorious Persians. There they burned and looted. The Greeks, not yet ready to surrender, retreated to the south. Themistocles, the popular commander of the Greek fleet, had earlier had the foresight to build 200 triremes. He now concentrated the whole Greek fleet in the narrow bay between Athens and Salamis. The fleet of Xerxes was almost destroyed in the dramatic struggle that lashed the waters and broke the ships. Xerxes himself saw the battle. When it was ended, Athens ruled the sea. "And another praise have I to tell for this the city our mother, the gift of a great god, a glory of the land most high: the might of horses, the might of young horses, the might of the sea."

When the Persian communication lines were cut they were compelled to retreat. Only once again did they do battle with the Greeks. They attacked in 479 B.C. and were defeated by the Spartans and the Athenians at the battle of Plataea. They never came back. The West was saved.

In Greece there appeared a new national energy, a heightened sense of power and superiority. There also emerged an extraordinary explosion of individual genius. The Golden Age of Greece was at hand.

Yet even in the midst of that Golden Age there were years of darkness and quarrels and internecine conflict. Almost as soon as the Persians were defeated the allies who had stood together in war fell apart in peace. Athens, mainly a commercial city, wanted to keep on fighting Persia until the Eastern Mediterranean was completely open to trade. Sparta, chiefly an agricultural state, was quite content to battle no more.

Athens prevailed. She was able to bring the Aegean and Ionian cities into a great naval alliance called the Delian League because the central money chests were kept on the island of Delos. The League members finally freed the Greek cities of Asia Minor from the tenacious grasp of the Persians. Satisfied with this victory, several islands wanted to secede from the alliance. Athens would not let them get out. Instead she made them subject states, seized their fighting ships, levied tribute, and took away the treasure of the League to Athens. The Athenians used some of that treasure to rebuild their city. They also connected Athens with the Piraeus by building two long walls, thick and fortified.

Thus Athens changed the Delian alliance into an Athenian maritime empire of about 300 city-states. The bold man mainly responsible for this imperial adventure was the aristocrat Pericles, a statesman and orator who stood for thirty years (461–429 B.C.) as the unchallenged leader of the Athenians.

Athens was now the great sea power, the commercial center and financial hub of the world of Greece. City-states like Sparta—the dominant land power —and the commercial city of Corinth bitterly resented and envied the new strength of Athens, the bulging purses of the Athenian merchants, and the treasure chests of the government of Pericles. Corinth was particularly angry because Athens was directing more of her trade towards the West and thus was reducing Corinth's commerce and profit. Athens, of course, did this mainly to avoid Persian attacks and blockades in the regions of the East. Such an argument, had it been presented to Corinth, would not have fallen upon sympathetic or friendly ears.

In 457 B.C. the great conflict called the Peloponnesian War began between Athens and Sparta. Each side was supported by several city-states. The decentralization tendencies of Greece were thus given greater impetus. A conflict of power interests might provide an answer to the question: Who was to dominate the peninsula of Greece and the islands beyond?

The first part of the war lasted from 457 to 445 B.C. Led by Sparta and Corinth, the states of the Peloponnesus attacked the Athenians in central Greece. Athens, no match for Sparta on land, sued for peace in 445. The years between the making of the frail peace and 431 B.C. were years of a watchful truce, armed and tense. Then the war broke out again with violence as the Greek states began a bitter campaign of self-destruction, a long and ruinous struggle that lasted for twenty-seven years (431–404 B.C.). The whole tale was complex and bloody. We need not pause to recite the grim chapters at length. Pericles, who might have been the architect of victory for Athens, died in 429 B.C. More than a third of the inhabitants of Athens perished when a plague swept over the city. With disease and terror came the collapse of law. Athens and Sparta fought on in hope and desperation. Each truce was used to prepare for more war.

When the Athenians tried in 415 B.C. to seize the Corinthian colony of Syracuse in Sicily they lost two fleets and an army. This event was probably the turning point of the war. The famous description by Thucydides of the proud Athenians sailing away from the Piraeus to bloody disaster in Sicily was once called by John Stuart Mill "the most powerful and affecting piece of narrative perhaps in all literature." The end came ten years later. Athens was "utterly prostrate, her proud 'Long Walls' down to her port at the Piraeus being demolished to the sound of Peloponnesian flutes." She had no ships, no gold, no friends. The ruthless irony of events compelled her to surrender, helpless at last before her foes.

The Greeks, victors and vanquished, were exhausted. They saw with dismay the Persians once more swallowing Greek cities in Asia Minor. Meanwhile, Sparta and Thebes fought feebly for a barren supremacy. Men died in sordid and sad squabbles. And meanwhile, too, the eyes of a hardy king of Macedonia turned towards the south. His name was Philip. His son's name was Alexander.

At several decisive points in man's history the tide of affairs has been changed by the discovery and use of new military weapons. Sometimes, too, brilliant men of arms have broken the patterns of the orthodox and have used new concepts of tactics and strategy. If the new ways defeat the old, then the patterns of studies in the world's war colleges may be altered. The successful heretic makes the new orthodoxy and that, in turn, may yield before another triumphant rebel.

There is one major difficulty in studying and planning upon the basis of the superb strategy and tactics of such commanders as Alexander the Great or Napoleon Bonaparte. They were men of genius dealing with sets of circumstances that arose at a particular time in a particular way. The trained Sandhurst and West Point officer must not only know in precise detail the great military campaigns of the past. He must also remember Napoleon's advice to one of his generals: "If none of these orders fits the circumstances, then do what you think I would do if I were now where you are."

Philip of Macedon and his son had no new or secret weapons, such as the horses and swords of the nomads who boiled out of the northern grasslands in earlier days. Because these nomads had weapons hitherto unknown in the south they were able to doom and smash the settled men of agriculture who were used to fighting on foot with clubs and battle-axes. Then the new slowly became the usual. Soon other methods and tools of destruction came. Such instruments as longbows, gunpowder, tanks, and atom bombs mark long steps forward in the science of annihilation. Each offensive weapon demands a countercheck, a defense, a weapon more efficient than the one before. Philip and Alexander had no such novel weapons—they did improve and alter the phalanx, but it was not new. They had power made up of solid phalanxes supported by heavy cavalry and bowmen and siege weapons. And they had brains and skill and daring. "Wisdom lies in masterful administration of the unforeseen."

In 338 B.C. Philip of Macedon conquered Thebes and Athens. The weakened state of Greece made this an easy military operation. Then and later the mighty Greek orator Demosthenes delivered many speeches. He bewailed the decay of patriotism and morality. In many lands today his *Philippics* and his famous *On the Crown* (330 B.C.) are studied as models of rhetoric. Again and again Demosthenes attempted to persuade his countrymen to unite against

Philip and to fight hard. It was all to no avail. Oratory, left to itself, was not enough. In the Greek spirit there was no longer fire to fan.

When Greece was conquered Philip forged a league of all the Greek city-states except Sparta and prepared to attack Persia. It was his misfortune that he was assassinated before he had a chance to carry out his ambitious plans.

Some historians and others have described Philip as a "barbarian." One of the best definitions of "barbarian" is surely that of George Santayana: "The barbarian believes that the outflow of energy is the absolute good, irrespective of motives or consequences." In that sense, Philip was not a barbarian. He was only a barbarian in the sense that his culture was not Greek. He destroyed to build and he invaded to borrow. In any age, a real barbarian wants to crush what he cannot understand. Philip, on the contrary, wanted to learn and to use.

Philip's son Alexander the Great (356–323 B.C.) was twenty years old when he succeeded his father. He was a man of action, a fighter of skill and courage, a quick-witted man who was once a student of Aristotle, an individual with a passionate temper. He was also a dreamer of the kind T. E. Lawrence described more than 2,000 years later: "All men dream but not equally. Those who dream by night in the dusty recesses of their minds wake in the day to find that it was vanity. But the dreamers of the day are dangerous men, for they may act their dreams with open eyes, to make them possible."

Alexander invaded Asia Minor and routed the Persian armies in 334 B.C. In the following year he conquered Syria and Palestine. He took the Persian naval bases. Then he overran Mesopotamia and captured Babylon. When that was done he turned and seized Egypt, where he founded the city of Alexandria, soon to be a stronghold of Greek culture. In 331 B.C. he destroyed the main Persian forces as they shifted and dissolved near Nineveh. In 324 B.C. he ascended the Persian throne as "King of the World." Meanwhile, as the reader will recall, Alexander penetrated deeply into northern India. In all his campaigns he fought no major battle that he did not win. He brought beneath his rule all the peoples between the Nile and the Indus. He was master of an empire the like of which no man had ever ruled before. "His success looked easy only because it was so complete."

Everywhere the armies of Alexander carried the influence of Greek thought and civilization. Alexander also founded cities in his empire and hoped to make them economic and cultural centers of value to his subject peoples. To stimulate trade he put into circulation much of the precious metal he had captured. He encouraged the marriage of his soldiers with the women of the Near and Middle East—some have said that he wanted to bring about a mingling of peoples throughout his empire so that it would be united by blood as well as by arms.

It is impossible to know or say what Alexander might have done had he

lived longer. In June, 323 B.C., in the city of Babylon, Alexander died of a
fever. He was not yet thirty-three years old. So far as Alexander was concerned, the invisible shafts of Apollo had settled all questions. Euripides once
said of another event:

> . . . the end men looked for cometh not,
> And a path is there where no man thought
> So hath it fallen here.

When Alexander died his generals divided his conquests and fought and
snarled among themselves for plunder, power, and prestige. The empire of the
great Alexander was finally divided into three parts, a series of new states.
Syria, Palestine, and Persia went to Seleucus, a Macedonian nobleman. The
rule of Egypt was given to the Ptolemies, the heirs of one of Alexander's
officers. Most of Greece and Macedonia were given to the descendants of
Alexander's general Antigonus. The city-states of Greece revolted, urged on
by Demosthenes; but the revolt was smashed and all resistance to Macedonia
ended. The political and economic pre-eminence of Greece was no more. Liberty
and power once lost are not easily recovered.

There seems no reason here to describe at length the details of political
unrest and military activity in the long years following the death of Alexander.
Such a careful description would be warranted only if the emerging facts were
of significance in the total tale of mankind. They are not.

What, then, is of significance? Let us look at a few facts and ideas.

The period in Western history usually called the Hellenistic Age is said to
begin with the death of Alexander in 323 B.C. and to end about 146 B.C. It is
really impossible, of course, to impose strict chronological limits upon this or
any other epoch. History does not wait upon the deaths of kings and queens.
Only the human passion for neatness has given us many of the divisions we
find so convenient in recording the history of mankind. So far as the Hellenistic
Age is concerned, the name simply means that here was a time when Greek
culture and Greek techniques were spread over most of the known world.
Greek influence, for example, has been clearly traced to India and China. One
of the greatest triumphs of Greece came when other lands borrowed what they
could from her.

To this embracing statement another must be added. In the years of Hellenistic civilization the flow of knowledge and skills did not move solely from
Greece to the world outside. In Greece—and especially in the world beyond
her shores—there were many streams of influence. If we wish to be quite
precise about the nature of Hellenistic culture we must say that it was a
merging and mingling of the currents from Greece, from the Near East, and
from the western Mediterranean areas. At cosmopolitan Alexandria, for instance, there was often a fusing of the knowledge of East and West. The

Semites, the Egyptians, and the Greeks were all about the streets and the stalls of the great city. In her famous library there were about 500,000 papyrus rolls. It was a tragic event when a mob destroyed that storehouse of knowledge during Caesar's occupation in 47 B.C. We do not know all that was lost. We are certain that much of it was priceless.

This merging and mingling, this diffusion of ideas, habits, and techniques, is clearly traceable. Where trade goes, ideas go. Where wants exist, people prowl, probe, fight, trade, and settle. Carpets, perfumes, dyes, and tapestries came out of the Near and Middle East. Egypt began to export cotton cloth in the fourth century B.C. Tyre built more ships. Farmers learned more about crop rotation and fertilizers. Almost everyone wanted "cheap weapons to fight men and cheap tools to fight nature." And so the tale continued.

Meanwhile Greece moved into a steady political and economic dislocation and decline. This was partly the result of decentralization, the mutual hostility of the city-states on the mainland, and the falling exports. Overseas colonies were themselves producing many goods they formerly bought and imported from mother Greece. The streams of commerce slowly turned away from the Greek mainland. Alexandria rose in wealth and importance. So did such places as Antioch, Pergamum, Ephesus, and Rhodes. The center of economic gravity was no longer Athens. All the Greek cities were hurt still more in the third century B.C. when Rome isolated Syria and cut Macedon off from Greece.

The economic wounds were deep and painful. Private debt increased. Real wages fell. There came an increased concentration of land in the hands of the large landowners who grabbed the acres of the poor. Everywhere, it seemed, the strong were busy crushing the weak. Reform movements multiplied. Often there was violence and more blood stained the stones of ancient places. Countless thousands suffered and mourned. Some men stayed and endured. Others fled over the seas to happier lands and brighter fates.

Troubles seldom visit one country alone, particularly if they are economic. There were dark and heavy clouds in Syria, storms in Egypt. In the land of the Nile, where centralizing tendencies had proceeded apace under the Ptolemies, a sharp inflation occurred in the second century B.C. The Ptolemies, not without reason, were held partly responsible for it. Strikes and disorders broke out. Riots blazed in the streets. The latter part of the Hellenistic Age was a period of discontent, unrest, and uncertainty in all the lands of the eastern Mediterranean region.

Soon the prospect altered. The streets of many cities were to hear the trampling march of the Roman legions. The power of the Greek city-states was no more. Some authorities believe that their decline was speeded by malaria brought in from North Africa. It may well be so.

A new age, the age of Rome, was at hand. Rome brought peace. Rome brought order.

Chapter 8

PROFILES OF

GENIUS

"Had we never seen the stars, and the sun, and the heaven, none of the words which we have spoken about the universe would ever have been uttered. But now the sight of day and night, and the months, and the revolutions of the years, have created number, and have given us a conception of time; and the power of inquiring about the nature of the universe; and from this source we have derived philosophy, than which no greater good ever was or will be given by the gods to mortal man."

—Plato, *Timaeus*

THE land of ancient Greece covered an area of about 25,000 square miles—half the size of New York state. The city of Athens, the pride of her citizens, was unpoliced. Its streets were filthy. Only about 300,000 people lived there and more than a third of them were slaves. These Greeks were numerically insignificant. They lived in a small segment of time. Why, then, did they produce such a point of light in human history, such brain power, so many artists, inventors, mathematicians, philosophers, poets, scientists, and statesmen? And why, within a few centuries, did the flame of genius and the blazing ideas sink to ashes? There are no sure answers to these questions. We can describe, but we cannot explain, the unprecedented and golden glory of the Greek culture.

Civilized men look today with wonder and admiration upon the shining triumphs of the Greeks, those lonely leaders of the West. There are only a few individuals in our own century who can read the Greek of Plato and Sophocles and there are probably only a few who have read such books as the scholarly three volumes of Professor Werner Jaeger's *Paideia: The Ideals of Greek Culture*. And yet countless men and women understand and appreciate something of the nature of the Greek genius and the priceless legacy the Greeks left to us.

What did the Greeks believe? They believed that all culture, all progress, all achievement, were based upon lifelong education, the true mortar of society.

The pleasure and pain of the cultured man's knowledge was always to be preferred to the numbness of the ignorant and the shallow-minded. The task of the student was to learn, that of the teacher to teach. In Plato's *Laws* the Minister of Education was one of the highest officers of the state because "if man's education is inadequate or bad he becomes the most savage of all the products of the earth." It was the Greeks who first became aware of the powers of the human mind.

The Greeks also believed and taught the classical virtues of balance, clarity, courage, discipline, honor, order, patriotism, symmetry, and the wisdom of restraint. "Anger, for instance, was to them ugly. But to them it was also a vice if a man could not be moved to anger by a proper cause, and by proper people. It was a vice if he were not angry in the proper manner and for the proper length of time." The Greek civilization was life-giving and life-loving. At the same time, it praised and prized a life of poise, balance, and control. In no aspect of Greek culture do we find excess. Man should be a noble being, defiant and disdainful of the wanton forces all about him, unterrified by omnipotent death, the undismayed master of himself.

The idea that man should be the master of himself has a close connection with the nature of the Athenian state. Euripides makes Theseus reply to the Theban herald:

> No worse foe than the despot hath a state,
> Under whom, first can be no common laws,
> But one rules, keeping in his private hands
> The law: so is equality no more.
> But where the laws are written, then the weak,
> And wealthy have alike but equal right.
> Yea, even the weaker may fling back the scoff
> Against the prosperous, if he be reviled;
> And, armed with right, the less o'ercomes the great.

The probing curiosity of the Greeks reached always towards the utmost edges of what they could see and feel and sense. "The philosopher," said Plato, "is the spectator of all time and all experience." Above all, the Greeks were interested in the nature and destiny of the total human being, in all that man was and might be. That was their supreme achievement. They discovered Man.

What did the Greeks do in their particular spot in the time scale? They created the lines and forms of some of the most beautiful buildings and statues ever made. Their master works in science, poetry, drama, and philosophy bulk massively in the cultural heritage of mankind. They never lingered, like lotus eaters, within the narrow seas. Their proper business was in great waters.

One link with our world of the twentieth century is the Greek achievement in mathematics. That adventure and achievement was possible only in a society where there was unfettered freedom of mind, an essential part of what we call "the scientific spirit." Under free conditions Greek mathematicians and other men of science could not avoid or evade one question: "Are we to accept the ageless fairy tales, the legends and myths about the gods of Greece or are we to take the evidence that agrees with the evidence of our senses?" There was a second question: "To what extent is the evidence of our senses to be trusted?" More than 2,000 years later, another mathematician named Henri Poincaré remarked that "to doubt all or believe all are two equally convenient solutions, in that both dispense with thinking." One of the most powerful of man's tools of thought is mathematical reasoning, "the model and foundation of all exact sciences."

The Greeks obtained hardly any mathematical knowledge from Egypt. The Babylonians did better than the men of the Nile valley. They knew quite a bit about arithmetic and algebra. They could set up quadratic and cubic equations and their geometry was far enough along to enable them to measure some areas and volumes. But their achievements were mainly practical "rule of thumb" devices. The Greeks, as we know, used deductive reasoning. That is the chief reason why we say that all roads in mathematics lead back to the Greeks. Filled with an indefeasible desire to know, several Greeks of penetrating insight studied the problems of number, form, extension, and measurement.

It has often been said, and rightly, that a large part of the tale of man's progress can be told in terms of his skill in measurement. In the early days of the race, a cubit was the length of a man's forearm from the elbow to the end of the middle finger. Later, the yard was the distance from the fingertips to the end of one's nose. But not all men's arms were the same length. In the thirteenth century A.D., Edward I of England ordered a permanent measuring bar of iron to serve as a standard yardstick for the kingdom. The seventeenth century looked for precise standards to the swing of a pendulum. In 1793 the French government established the metric system—a meter is one ten-millionth part of the distance from the North Pole to the equator when measured in a straight line running through Paris along the surface of the earth. In modern times the most precise measurements are made with light waves. "Although a wave of green light (mercury 198) is only 1/50,000 inch in length it can be reproduced to within 1/100,000,000 of its length, and length measurements with light can be made with this accuracy." Scientists working in the field of spectroscopy today use what are called angstrom units, each of which is four-billionths of an inch. The piston is fitted to the cylinder of a Diesel engine injector with an accuracy of 25-millionths of an inch, 1/120 the thickness of a human hair. The precision-weighing balances of analytical chemists can weigh a period printed on this page.

It is to this place that man has now come with his ideas and tools of measurement. The gateway to the long road was really opened by the groping and eager Greeks with their mathematics, especially with their geometry—"the measurement of the earth."

All geometry worthy of the name depends upon deductive reasoning. The first man to merit the title of a real geometer was Thales (624–548 B.C.), a student and teacher of Miletus and later of Egypt. He is often called "the father of science." Thales, it was said long ago, "endowed geometry with rigour and founded it upon congruence and similitude." In 585 B.C. he forecast correctly an eclipse of the sun. Because Thales was indeed a scientist he was interested in many problems in the world around him. For instance, he wanted to find out more about the nature of matter, a problem that has challenged man for a long time. Thales classified all matter into four elements and said that water was the basic element. A controversy immediately arose among Greek scientists. Heraclitus of Ephesus insisted that fire was the basic element and that there was really no stability in anything, because all things were perpetually becoming and passing away. Democritus (460–370 B.C.) asked what happens when you keep dividing something like a stone or a loaf. Does it keep all its qualities intact, unimpaired and unchanged in any way? The answer of Democritus was that all matter consists of little indivisible particles he called atoms.

Let us return to mathematics. One of the great contemporaries of Thales was Pythagoras of Samos, later of Croton in Italy (582–507 B.C.). Pythagoras said that Number was the basis of all the world, and he produced an advanced system of theorems and proofs in geometry that stands unchallenged today. It is of interest to note that Pythagoras did not discover the famous theorem that bears his name: the square of the hypotenuse of a right-angled triangle is equal to the sum of the squares of the other two sides. It was known long before Pythagoras was born. In later days Pythagoras had tremendous influence upon scientific and religious thought throughout the Western world. A cult of followers when he lived attributed many ideas and discoveries to him. After he died—and it was said that he was slain by his enemies in a bean field—scores of fashionable cults arose bearing his name. Some of them flourish in the twentieth century.

There are other men and other ideas. Anaxagoras (500–428 B.C.) studied the structure of animals by dissecting them. Anaximander of Miletus (611–547 B.C.) asserted that living organisms first appeared in water—he anticipated Charles Darwin, quite vaguely, by about 2,500 years. Many scholars have regretted the fact that the written works of Anaximander upon mathematics have been lost. Hippocrates of Chios, who lived in the middle of the fifth century B.C., became a merchant and then a famous teacher of mathematics —he was no relative of the physician Hippocrates (460–370 B.C.) who attributed the cause of diseases to natural phenomena and gave the modern world the famous Hippocratic oath. The mathematician Hippocrates lived in a world far from medicine. He is known among mathematicians in many lands for presenting the problem of the Hippocratean crescents. Only the algebraic aspect of this problem has ever been solved and it was done by modern analysis and number theory. In these days—and later, of course—several difficult and celebrated problems appeared to challenge the able and nimble brains of men: squaring the circle, doubling the cube, dividing a circle into any number of equal parts, trisecting any given angle, finding an answer to the vexing quadrature problem of Hippias the Sophist, and the like.

Such were some of the ideas and some of the works of the early Greek scientists. When the Hellenistic Age began in the early fourth century B.C. another series of shining names appeared. They included Euclid, Apollonius, and Archimedes. These men would have been giants in any land, in any age.

The great bequests to mankind made by men like these came from a few small and scattered oases of the restless Hellenistic world. If we look above the clouds of definition and particulars at the major contours of the interlocking unity of the Hellenistic Age we see that the most important achievements were not made in Greece proper but in the young and virile Hellenized outposts in Africa, Asia Minor, and Italy. This is true in all the arts, in mathematics, and in science. It would not be many years before Rome would conquer Greece in a military and political sense. But the world of Greek culture would educate Rome. In time, too, Rome would educate the raw barbarians who came from the dim and distant northlands to conquer the falling empire. The Greco-Roman culture would survive and spread and Europe would stay a civilized continent.

Euclid, that leader of classical mathematics, spent most of his life in the lively, squabbling, dynamic city of Alexandria. About 300 B.C. he completed his *Elements,* a study of plane geometry that is both a signpost and a milestone. The *Elements,* the earliest mathematical work known to us, was not a highly original study in the sense that it opened many gates to new knowledge. It contains much material known to the predecessors of Euclid. Euclid's achievement was the organizing of widely scattered ideas and theorems into a system. That system and organization was so well done that it is still the basis of most elementary textbooks.

Euclid's *Conics* and his *Book of Prisms* have been lost. It is our own good fortune that they have not slipped completely into oblivion. We do have some information about them from other sources. We also know that Euclid did some brilliant studies in prime and perfect numbers and in music and perspective and that he was responsible for some plane and solid geometry conclusions that were new in his day. The fact that we have these fragments of knowledge increases our desire to possess more. Euclid seems to have been a fascinating individual. It is a pity that we cannot see his face more clearly.

Apollonius of Perga (247–205 B.C.) made a special study of the geometry of cones and conic sections. It was he who invented the terms "ellipse," "hyperbola," and "parabola." He clearly foreshadowed the analytic geometry of Descartes, who was to assert in the seventeenth century that mathematics was the most powerful instrument of the mind of man—"Give me motion and extension and I will build you the world." Appolonius must have been one of those of whom Professor Tobias Dantzig was thinking when he wrote of "the almost uncanny intuition of the Greek masters."

A third brilliant and versatile figure in the world of Hellenistic mathematicians was Archimedes (287–212 B.C.) He studied at Alexandria and then left to live at Syracuse on the island of Sicily. Before he was killed by Roman soldiers Archimedes had gained a deep knowledge of mechanics. He had explained the principle of the burning mirror, the endless screw, and the compound pulley. He had discovered specific gravity. He had calculated approximate limits for the value of *pi*. He had anticipated the integral calculus of Newton by nearly 2,000 years. He was certain that he could move the earth if he had a fulcrum strong enough to support the lever.

Perhaps a few words should be said here about the searching mind of the great Aristotle (384–322 B.C.) as he moved in one sector of the world of the science he helped to create. Aristotle made no detailed or narrow contributions in special fields of mathematics or natural science. His great achievements were in larger empires: the shaping of ideas and concepts and general laws.

Consider, for instance, the problem of motion. Aristotle said that all objects had a natural tendency to move towards the center of the universe which was at or near the center of the earth. Motion in any other direction was unnatural. An unnatural motion required a mover. In fact, said Aristotle, all things that moved required—in an Aristotelian universe—an active mover.

The Aristotelian doctrine of inertia was a doctrine of rest. The state of rest was natural and all bodies, said Aristotle, tended to return to it when left to themselves. Once a mover stopped moving an object and the impetus exhausted itself, then the object stopped, or rested, or fell vertically towards the center of the earth. The speed of a moving object was always proportional to the force exerted upon it and the resistance it met. If there were no resistance, then the speed would be infinite. Aristotle asserted that such a thing was impossible because nature abhorred a vacuum. So far as an infinite speed in an infinite universe was concerned, Aristotle simply could not conceive of an empty Euclidean space. There must be resistance and there must be gravity.

Aristotle and his followers were sometimes hard put to defend this theory of motion. For instance, it was pointed out that projectiles continued to move after they had lost contact with the mover. The Aristotelians came forward with the answer that the first disturbance caused in the air was responsible. In the case of a flying arrow, for example, the air was compressed in front of the arrow and then it had to rush around behind the arrow to stop the formation of the vacuum that nature abhorred. When it was also remarked that falling objects moved at an accelerated pace it was replied that because there was more air pressing in from above than from below there was less resistance. Aristotle himself said only that a falling object moved more rapidly because it was getting closer to the center of the earth, its natural home.

Despite many attacks and much wrangling the Aristotelian idea of motion lasted until the Middle Ages. Then the medieval mind moved with celerity and skill: "Let us suppose that there is a simplified form of motion in which there is no resistance or gravity at all. There is no doubt that objects would continue along a straight line. Now let us study all of the forces that could possibly interfere with that motion." This procedure, of course, was precisely the right one. The answers it brought, however, were to pose new questions— a disconcerting habit of nature, even in the twentieth century.

There were other men who can claim our notice and applause. In the fourth century B.C. Heracleides of Pontus said that the earth revolves on its axis every twenty-four hours. Aristarchus of Samos computed the distance of the earth to the moon and said that the sun, not the earth, was the center of the universe. In the second century B.C. the astronomer Hipparchus invented spherical and plane trigonometry. Eratosthenes measured the shadow cast by the sun in order to determine the circumference of the earth. Accidentally or otherwise, his calculation was only 200 miles in error. About the time when Christ was born Hero of Alexandria produced his famed formula for the proof of the area of a triangle. He also found algebraic formulas for a number of other areas. When James Watt worked with his steam engines in the eighteenth century he probably never knew that Hero of Alexandria had once made a tiny pinwheel engine run by steam from the spout of a pot. About 100 B.C. Poseidonius declared his belief that the tides were the work of the moon. Meanwhile, in the field of medicine, Herophilus of Chalcedon named the upper part of the intestine the duodenum. This was about 300 B.C. Around ten years later Erasistratus distinguished between the motor and sensory nerves and gave the valves of the heart the names we still use today.

Many of the erroneous ideas that came from these and later years were accepted for a long time. For example, Ptolemy (100–178 A.D.), the famous author of the *Almagest*, said that the cosmos was made up of a series of revolving concentric spheres, of which the earth was the center. The Ptolemaic theory was not decisively and finally upset and smashed until after the publication in 1543 of *On the Revolutions of the Heavenly Bodies*, by Copernicus. As a matter of fact, it took almost a hundred and fifty years for the great crescendo of conflict about the ideas of Copernicus to rise and fall. Some men, it has been said, "took nearly fifty years to see that Copernicus was bound to lead to Voltaire." Many of the ill-founded ideas that Strabo (63 B.C.–21 A.D.) brought into geography lasted until the sixteenth century. The same kind of tale is true in the field of medicine. In the second century A.D., Galen (130–200) described, not very accurately, the structure of human tissues and muscles. His description—and many other things that Galen said—were accepted almost without a murmur of dissent for more than a thousand years. As late as the sixteenth century Galen still remained to most physicians "the prince of physics" and "the lantern of surgeons." True, when Vesalius published his *On the Structure of the Human Body* in 1543 the authority of Galen was weakened; but it was weakened only upon a restricted scale and within a small circle. It took a long time to shake the power and prestige of Galen's name throughout the medical profession.

So it was that in these years of ferment the minds and hands of many men brought new ideas and new triumphs. At the end of the Hellenistic period, about 146 B.C., the curtain of history dropped abruptly in the world of science and mathematics. So far as the scientists and mathematicians were concerned the roads that led to Rome ended in a desert. Almost nothing happened, nothing at all. For a thousand years there was a long silence.

The average reader has a distaste for lists of names and dates, even those from a turbulent and exciting age. Perhaps our teachers in the schools of our youth were sensible and practical and businesslike individuals who insisted that we should remember at a flick of a pointer too many names and boundaries and years. The reckless use of such procedures stimulates no understanding, no respect for knowledge. The result may be a starving and stunting of natural curiosity. Facts and dates and names, left to themselves, are often heavy and meaningless. They should never be left to themselves.

Each name in this chapter is a label attached to a human being who was one of those who helped to lift man to his present status, such as it is. Each date tells when he was born and when he died and thus places him in the time scale. And yet this, surely, is not enough. If we study the separate achievements of the Greek mathematicians, learn their names, and place them precisely in their centuries, then we have but a part of the total tale. What matters most is not the spasmodic visitation of the names and dates of Greek scientists as we go about our twentieth-century jobs. It is the awareness of the ways in which their victories and disasters in a segment of time are a part of a wide and broad pattern of movement and growth.

In every chapter of the tale of mankind there have been some sensitive men and women who have paused to see the beauty that gleams on the heights in the sunrise. Pure mathematics, the intellectual apprehension of form and order, is one of the highest kinds of the beautiful. Consider that the Greek scientists and mathematicians—like all explorers, dreamers, and builders—saw something distant and magnetic to draw them on, something to strive towards. The passions and prejudices of the shifting and troubled present often obscure the vital fact that it has been restless men of vision who made our heritage possible. Without vision a people may perish, an earth commit planetary suicide. If men forget this potent law of evolution they will live, for a while, to bewail that day.

The soaring spirits and ideals of the Greeks are nowhere shown more clearly than in the visible splendor of their incomparable art. In the work of the Greek architects and sculptors there is an unmatched love of balance, of correct and delicate curves, of form and symmetry. In these things they are the instructors of all mankind.

After the Persian wars the Greek city-state of Athens decided that it was strong enough to get along without a fortified Acropolis. Most of the buildings on the hill had been destroyed by the Persians, and so the Greeks built new ones—without any fortifications. In 477 B.C. Ictinus, that great architect who built the Hall of Mysteries at Eleusis, began his work on the Parthenon. The master sculptor Phidias, friend of Pericles, designed the sculptures. He made the east pediment of the Parthenon. He made the great statue of Athena Parthenos, "an ivory goddess with robes of gold."

All classical Greek architecture shows the overwhelming importance that the Greeks gave to form, balance, and symmetry. Every reader knows, for instance, the balanced characteristics of the three great orders of capitals and columns: the sturdy Doric, the first to develop among the Dorian Greeks on the mainland; the simple Ionic, born in Asia Minor's Ionia; the delicate Corinthian, the last to develop and so widely used in the Hellenistic Age. In all the temples and all the other buildings of ancient Greece the essential structure may seem to be simple. It is indeed. Here is the methodical and deceptive simplicity of precise calculation, care, reason, and a keen sense of proportion. The forms used are simple: the cube, the cylinder, the oblong, the pyramid, the triangle. Everything follows the rules of balance, proportion, and symmetry. Everything is carefully adapted to the eye of the spectator. The lines are clear, like the skies and the landscape. The rows of carefully made columns are spaced at exact intervals. Every angle is precisely measured. The curvatures are corrected so that the flowing form is pleasing and unbroken and there are no awkward confusions of perspective.

All of these qualities, these rules and principles of composition, are revealed at their best in the Parthenon. For more than 2,500 years the imagination and senses of men have been staggered by its naked power. Today, despoiled and shattered by men who loved it not, the Parthenon still stands to prove that men centuries dead once reached a high moment of human endeavor. The aspiration was caught in the perfect productions of the chisel. "The mason thinks before he works, and while he works, and thinks in entire correspondence with his meaning."

It is likewise impossible to look without humility and awe at the drapery, flowing yet frozen in stone, of the Winged Victory of Samothrace. How, we ask, could any human sculptor have shaped the vigorous male beauty of Apollo of the Belvedere? Still remaining to enchant and conquer are several sculptured works of Phidias, Praxiteles, Scopas, Timotheus, and their fellows: the Farnese Bull, the Laocoön Group, the Discobolus of Myron, the Aphrodite of Melos, the Dying Gaul at Pergamum, the Hermes of Praxiteles—a marble copy of a bronze original.

The very names are poetry. "It was fairly said that wealth and power might pass to others but Athens alone had the secret of the path which raises men to the heavens."

Around 600 B.C. were the years when "burning Sappho loved and sung" on the island of Lesbos. The fragments we have of her verse show that she was a very fine technical poetess indeed. Every line is carefully finished. "Her painting of passion, which caused Longinus to quote the ode to Anactoria as an example of the sublime, has never been surpassed."

Sappho had many students but among them were none whose words echoed very far down the slopes of the years. The great literary achievements of Greece were not in the field of lyric poetry but in drama. Here were born the moving tragedies of Aeschylus, Sophocles, and Euripides and the polished intellectual satires of the incomparable Aristophanes.

If wide and exciting personal experiences help a creative artist, then Aeschylus (525–456 B.C.) was well prepared to be the founder of Greek drama. In the wars against Persia he fought with prowess in the great actions of Marathon, Salamis, and Plataea. He traveled and lived in many places. Through the years he wrote about ninety plays. Of these, seven have been saved from the rats and damp of time.

Aeschylus had powerful gifts: range and force of diction, an overwhelming and somber grandeur, lofty and vigorous language. In all the tragedies of Aeschylus the beholder sees the power of the gods upon human sinners. "Who but a god goes woundless all the way?" In the dark mysteries of life the wickedness of men bring about their fall—"the hidden reef which wrecks the bark, unable to weather the headland." In the *Prometheus* trilogy, for instance, the hero Prometheus is both victim and rebel. Slowly the audience is chilled by his violence and impiety. In the darkening suspense they feel the slow and relentless approach of fear, the imminent horror of the measured advance of calamity. At last the impending doom falls, pitiless and just. In the *Prometheus* of Aeschylus, as in the *Prometheus Unbound* of Shelley, there remains one duty and one task:

> To defy Power, which seems omnipotent;
> To love, and bear; to hope till Hope creates
> From its own wreck the thing it contemplates.

In the *Persae,* Aeschylus describes the destruction of the fleet of Xerxes. There, too, as in almost all Greek tragedy, is the theme of punishment and doom, in this case the humiliation of bulging pride. "Pride breeds sin and atonement will be made by the wrath of heaven." In the *Oresteia* trilogy is *Agamemnon,* the last and greatest work of Aeschylus. In this play of revenge and recklessness we are carried forward swiftly and steadily in the breathless progress of the action and the gradually emerging horror until we reach the height of tragic intensity and dramatic concentration. The forces of destruction gather. Man stands against fate. Then the inevitable catastrophe comes, swift and terrible.

> Ah! What is mortal life . . .
> > When prosperous
> A shadow can o'erturn it, and when fallen
> A throw of the wet sponge blurs the picture out.

At last the avenging and evil Clytemnestra, taunting and boasting, thrusts the sword into Agamemnon through the embroidered net and Agamemnon dies. Filled with horror, the audience hears the king's piteous and stifled death shriek.

"There were brave men before Agamemnon," wrote the Roman poet Horace, "but, all unwept and unknown, they are lost in the distant night, being without a divine poet."

In his later years, disgusted by what he regarded as the excesses of Athenian democracy, Aeschylus went to Sicily. There, as everywhere else, stories and traditions gathered about his name. One of the last ones, repeated still today, says that Aeschylus was killed in Sicily by an eagle dropping a tortoise to crack its shell upon his head. It is easy to smile at such tales. Men do not smile when they watch and hear the opening scenes in *Agamemnon* describing the beacons flashing to tell that Troy has fallen. The Watchman and the Chorus speak the undying lines. Aeschylus wrote them.

With the works of Sophocles (496–406 B.C.) there came a high degree of passionless detachment. "He sat like a god, holding no form of creed, yet contemplating all." Sophocles was of course concerned with the laws that govern life; but he was more deeply interested in the wonder and mystery of man himself, Alexander Pope's "glory, jest, and riddle of the world." Man was so great, so divine, and yet such a helpless plaything of the gods.

Like Aeschylus, Sophocles was a man of action. He served as a general with Pericles and was a member of several Athenian embassies abroad. From all we can learn from his contemporaries, he was an amiable and widely loved citizen. As a writer of drama he curbed his kindly and friendly emotions—except in such passages as the impassioned Ode to Love in *Antigone*—and showed his fellow citizens and those who followed after that there is nothing wrong in the universe, there is nothing right, there is only that which is. Perhaps the only real passion Sophocles ever had was a passion for the truth.

The minor poems of Sophocles have all perished and we have only seven of his hundred dramas. In them we see the strong men and the weak men who fight the battle of life with broken swords. We see the wounded honor of Ajax, the beaten innocence of Oedipus, the total devotion of Antigone, caught between the pressures of man's law and a higher commandment. We hear the dark counsels of despair:

> Oh, when the pride of Graecia's noblest race
> Wanders, as now, in darkness and disgrace,
> When Reason's day
> Sits rayless, joyless, quenched in cold decay
> Better to die, and sleep
> The never-waking sleep, than linger on,
> And dare to live, when the soul's life is gone. . . .

Again and again we see the reverence for the eternal and unwritten laws of nature and what happens in the supreme and decisive crises in individual destiny. In *Oedipus Rex*, for instance, we see at the end how Oedipus, blind, bloody, and mad, rushes away and seeks to vanish from the world. Jocasta dies by her own hand. All is over. All is done. "One touch," says a Messenger, "will send an old man to his rest." There remains but the dignity of sorrow. Sophocles folds his robes about him and walks into history.

In the stirring and tragic dramas of Aeschylus and Sophocles the characters were confronted with the gradually accumulating horrors brought upon them by the fates, the faults of their own characters, or by the iron dice tossed by careless or revengeful gods. The dramatic work of Euripides (480–406 B.C.) was of a different kind. True, Euripides was a tragic poet—about seventy-five dramas prove it—but he was not filled with the severe Attic spirit that marked the other two giants of the tragic muse. He has been called "the virtual founder of the romantic drama." Although that title is perhaps too strongly phrased it still contains much truth: with Euripides there was a romantic dawn. His *Alcestis* (438 B.C.) does seem to mark a vivid transition from a purely Hellenic drama to a drama that had a more universal appeal in taste and sentiment. Euripides, of course, knew very well that "the old faiths were losing their meaning in Athens and the old life was passing away." He has often been called a skeptical realist. This is a good description if it is not considered to be final and complete. It is wise, for instance, to remember that

he wrote many lovely and dancing lyrics as well as the critical and darkened
lines of the Chorus in *Medea:*

> Back stream the waves on the ever-running river
> Life, life is changed and the laws of it o'ertrod. . . .
> Old bards shall cease and their memory that lingers
> Of frail brides and faithless shall be shrivelled as
> with fire.

Euripides looked with distaste upon the coarser aspects of Athenian democracy. Like many scholars and thinkers, he was repelled by the noise and the
dirt and the uncouth ways of the mob. He was also troubled by political dangers, the busy tongue of his shrewish wife, and the laughter of Aristophanes.
The answer of Euripides was not to stay and fight but simply to go away.
He went to Thessaly and then to Macedonia. There he stayed and there he
died. Despite his flight from Athens, he did not die a prophet without honor.
"A poet whom Socrates called his friend, whom Aristotle lauded, whom Alexander admired, and for whom Sophocles and the city of Athens put on mourning on hearing of his death must certainly have been someone."

During these years Aristophanes (445–386 B.C.) was writing his riotous
and sensual satires, those shattering comedies penned in deadly earnest. The
line between comedy and tragedy is sometimes very narrow indeed—tragedy
often has a smiling face. Aristophanes mocked and burlesqued the customs,
institutions, morals, and manners of all his contemporaries. Several famous
Athenians felt the lash of his wit. One of the few who replied to him was
Euripides:

> My spirit loathes
> Those mockers whose unbridled mockery
> Invades great themes.

In *The Frogs* the audacious Aristophanes made sport of literary critics, a
diverting business. In *The Clouds* he tried to make ridiculous the intellectuals
of Athens, those fuzzy-minded men chasing panting abstractions through
time and space. In one of the scenes in *The Clouds,* Aristophanes has Socrates
hauled into the skies in a basket because Socrates can pursue his business of
thinking better up high in the sky. In *The Wasps,* Aristophanes described
unkindly the numerous Athenians who liked to be busy with lawsuits. In
The Birds he tilted against the government. In *Lysistrata*—which was really
a plea for peace between Sparta and Athens—he showed the military authorities in a most unfavorable light. He even portrayed women on strike and
women in the august halls of the legislature.

Despite the boisterous and often obscene qualities of his comedies Aristophanes was really a polished and sophisticated artist who knew precisely

PLATE VII

[27]

Hermes, the messenger of the gods, and the infant Dionysus by the Greek sculptor Praxiteles (c. 343 B.C.)

[28]

Left: Etruscan bronze figure of Minerva as goddess of war (6th century B.C.)

Below: Part of a bronze diploma granting Roman citizenship to some veterans and their wives

[29]

PLATE VIII

[30]

The Prima Porta statue of Caesa
Augustus discovered in 1863 in th
Villa of Livia. The cupid riding o
a dolphin indicates the descent o
Augustus from Venus (c. 13-9 B.C.

Below: The Praetorian Guard, on
of the great marble panels from th
reign of Diocletian (81-96 A.D.
discovered under the Cancelleria
Palace, Rome

[31]

what he was doing. He was able to depict with understanding and accuracy the people he pilloried in his plays. The whole human race, it seems, was his target. He could laugh at everybody, including himself. Aristophanes was never a snob; that is one reason why he was a really fine artist.

Someone once described the spirit of Aristophanes as "Monkeys and nightingales in the treetops." We see the antics of the monkeys and we hear the songs of the birds, both at the same time.

After the doers of deeds and the makers of things have finished and gone away the historian comes, like a detective, to ask questions, many questions, and to write the answers down, editing and massaging now and then. Good historians are like good journalists—all kinds of things go into their retentive brains and their notebooks. Then shrewd logic and judgment select and discard and say: "This is probably the way it happened and these are the possible consequences." The scientist and artist meet in one.

There were several historians who lived in ancient Greece. Three have been remembered to our day: Herodotus, Xenophon, and Thucydides.

Herodotus (484–425 B.C.) came from Halicarnassus in Asia Minor. He traveled over many parts of the Greek world and the lands beyond. As he went, Herodotus collected a mass of fact and fiction and, like a magpie, he held on to all of it. Much went into his enthusiastic and uncritical account of the war between the Greeks and the Persians called *The History of Herodotus of Halicarnassus*. To Herodotus the Persians were barbarians and the Greeks civilized heroes. In his writings the Greeks had the best of it because they were better fighters, more moral people, and Zeus was on their side. Herodotus is often very good reading. He is a superb storyteller—and you believe him at your peril. If his charming history is sometimes less than unprejudiced, his way of spinning his tale is fine. His epigrams, too, shine upon the page: "The truth is that the eulogy of others is only tolerable as long as the hearers feel that each could have risen to the occasion had the part fallen to them. They begrudge and refuse to believe what is beyond their range."

We need not pause to look at Xenophon (c. 430–c. 356 B.C.) for long. He is a lesser figure. He wrote upon such varied subjects as Socrates, the economy of Sparta, the Peloponnesian War (the *Hellenica*), and a Spartan king's biography. His *Anabasis,* the best known of his works, told the tale of a civil war in Persia in which Xenophon fought bravely as a Greek mercenary.

The greatest of the Greek historians was Thucydides (c. 455–c. 400 B.C.). Indeed, of all the ancient historians Tacitus (55–c.118 A.D.) alone could be considered by some to rival Thucydides. Others would say, and rightly, that Tacitus is too careless and unjust—as when he hints that Domitian poisoned Agricola or when he mocks and gibes at his foes.

Thucydides wrote *The Peloponnesian War,* a famous history recording the years of the conflict from 431 to 411 B.C. Upon the basis of this work Thucydides has a good claim to be considered the father of scientific history and historical criticism. There is no doubt of his scientific spirit and his desire to state the facts as he finds them in true relationship. He tries to be quite impersonal, to stay out of the text of his tale, to be severely objective and restrained. Any reader today who looks at his analysis of character and political history will agree that they seem shrewd and balanced and sane. In the preface to his *Peloponnesian War,* Thucydides wrote: "The absence of romance in my history will, I fear, detract somewhat from its interest. . . . I have written my work, not as an essay which is to win the applause of the moment, but as a possession for all time."

Of much value to Thucydides and to us is the fact that he did have personal knowledge of the events of much of the war. He held a command until he was exiled in 424 B.C. for his failure to save one city. He lived in exile for twenty years in Thrace; then he was assassinated. "I lived through the whole of it, being of an age to comprehend events, and giving my attention to them in order to know the exact truth about them."

Thucydides is an author more praised than read today. Customs and interests in societies rise and then falter and flag. Perhaps, even in our time, some may turn to admire Thucydides and his skillful handling of material. He has remarkable gifts as an imaginative artist, especially in constructing dialogues and speeches. He does know how to write an epigram: "The three secrets of success are to hold your own against your equals, to keep on good terms with your superiors, and to treat your inferiors with consideration." And certainly he can create emotion in the reader entirely from the events he is describing. It may be suggested that few contemporaries could match in power these graphic sentences from a description of the plague of 429 B.C.

> Some died in neglect, others in the midst of every attention. No remedy was found that could be used as a specific; for what did good in one case did harm in another. . . . The bodies of dying men lay one upon another, and half-dead creatures reeled about the streets and gathered round all the fountains in their longing for water. The sacred places also in which they had quartered themselves were full of corpses of persons who had died there, just as they were; for as the disaster passed all bounds, men, not knowing what was to become of them, became utterly careless of everything, whether sacred or profane.

With the artists and the historians always march the philosophers. The philosophers of ancient Greece, like all lovers of knowledge, were busy asking questions: "What is justice? Is virtue the same thing as knowledge? What sort of ethics ought men to follow in human relations and why? What is a *good* individual? What do we mean by *good?* Who says so? How do we know?"

The Greek philosophers would have been unhappy and maladjusted in any society mindlessly immersed in sheer activity. They would have deliberately tried to avoid the irrational and the urgent. They were deeply committed to the belief that their great business was to try to be absolutely clear about the timeless ends of mankind, to sort and organize experience, to know precisely where they stood in the light of their concepts of what were the highest goods in the universe. Aristotle, for instance, asserted that no ideal was random and meaningless—every ideal had its basis somewhere in nature. On the other hand, everything natural had an ideal fulfilment. "Perfection," as George Santayana once wrote, "is the ultimate justification of being." Plato and Aristotle both said that human ideals were the only forces that gave meaning to anything on this planet.

Plato, the greatest student of Socrates, was born in 427 B.C. and died in 347 B.C. He spent many years teaching in the Academy in Athens. It was typical of Plato's values that no candidate was admitted to the Academy unless he had mastered geometry. Plato well understood the profound fact that all scientific interpretation and adequate judgments in most other areas of thought depend upon an understanding of quantitative relationships. Logic and mathematics, political theory, science—all these go hand in hand with religion and poetry. To the winged poetic imagination of Plato was always linked devotion to exact inquiry with the tools and methods of logic. His pursuit of truth involved the hard and patient thought demanded by mathematical reasoning. The realities were to be apprehended only by the logical study of the long and difficult language of facts.

Plato wrote no systematic treatise on philosophy. Most of his works that have come down to us are written in the form of a series of dialogues such as the *Apology, Crito, Ion, Meno, Symposium, Phaedo, Phaedrus, Gorgias, Theaetetus, Laws, Timaeus, Philebus,* and the *Republic*. In the market place, in the streets, or in one of the Academy gardens the indefatigable Socrates, the leading figure in the dialogues, brings forth the problems of the matter in hand by asking questions, one by one.

> *Meno:* I suspect that what you say, Socrates, is true, and that no man wills or chooses anything evil.
> *Socrates:* Did you not say, just now, that virtue consisted in the willing or desiring things which are good, and in the having it in our power to gain them?
> *Meno:* I did say so; it is true.
> *Socrates:* Is not this will or desire according to what has been said in all men? So that, in this respect, one man is not at all better than another man?

Meno: It appears so.
Socrates: It appears, therefore, that if one man is better than another,
  he must be so in respect of this power.
Meno: Undoubtedly.
Socrates: This, therefore, as it seems, according to your account,
  is virtue, the power of gaining things which are good.
Meno: The case seems to me, Socrates, to be entirely so, as you state
  it.
Socrates: Then let us examine if this account of yours be true: for
  perhaps it may be so. You say, that to be able to gain good
  things, is a virtue.
Meno: I do.
Socrates: Then let me ask you a question. . . .

Men chained in a cave may think the shadows on the wall are real. We know, of course, that the shadows are not real. The realities are outside in the sun. So it is, said Plato, in the world of men on earth. The world of appearances is not real at all. The only true and ultimate realities are the eternal and fixed qualities behind and beyond the world of the apparently real. These realities Plato called Ideas. The world of sense perception is only a faint reflection of these final verities, these Ideas, these eternal Forms.

Everything that exists on earth, said Plato, is an inferior copy of a corresponding spiritual Idea. The whole physical world, in fact, is an imperfect copy of a perfect Idea. All spiritual Ideas have an existence apart from their earthly counterparts. The sum of all the Ideas is the Idea of the Good, the final Absolute. Virtue, asserted Plato, is knowledge—not of the world of sense but knowledge of the final truths, the Ideas.

"Of the three objects which are of universal interest to mankind, interest in wealth, in its right forms, holds the third and lowest place; midway comes the care of the body, and first the soul." In the state that rightly cares for that soul Plato sees the importance of the subordination of all to the law and not to men: "For that state in which the law is subject and has no authority, I perceive to be on the highway to ruin; but I see that the state in which the laws are above the rulers and the rulers are the inferiors of the law, has salvation, and every blessing which the gods can confer."

In Plato's ideal state, described most completely in the *Republic,* there would be a balanced society in which every man would do what he was best fitted to do by ability and training. Because not all men are fitted to take part in government, said Plato, the actual ruling should be done by highly trained and intelligent men, expert guardians, professional governors, philosopher-kings. It would be a foolish impertinence indeed to think or say that the ideas in the *Republic* or the other great dialogues could be explained or judged in a few paragraphs or pages. So far as the *Republic* was concerned, Plato knew and said that in this world the day of the philosopher-king had not yet come. He may also have known that in this imperfect planet of imperfect men "most would rather govern themselves rather badly than be governed by others, however competent those others might be."

All of Plato's writings, explained and discussed in so many volumes through so many centuries, are really concerned in one way or another with the problem of knowledge, the relations between sense and thought, the intellectual search for an understanding of the good.

> And is not the case the same with reference to the good? Whosoever cannot define it by reason, separating the idea of the good from all others, and piercing through all arguments as in a battle, eagerly contending to prove it, not according to opinion, but according to reality, and in all these cases to march forward with unerring reason, such an one knows nothing of the good itself, nor of any good whatever; but if he hath attained to any image of the good, we will say that he hath attained to it by opinion, not by science, and is dreaming and sleeping out his present life, and ere he be awakened, he will descend to the lower regions, there to sleep on to the end.

Aristotle (384–322 B.C.) was a daring adventurer in the unexplored realms of thought. He had come down to Athens from Macedonia. In Plato's Academy he became a prize student. After Plato died in 347 B.C., Aristotle went back to Macedonia and for three years tutored Alexander, Philip's royal son. About 335 B.C. he started in Athens a school of his own called the Lyceum. There he walked with his students in the garden, teaching them as Plato had taught him and Socrates had taught Plato.

It is impossible here to summarize and try to assess the vast labors of Aristotle, the versatile "master of those who know." We must be content with saying that in his day he almost literally took all knowledge for his province and that intellectually his power ranks with Plato.

Aristotle is considered the "father of formal logic," that science of the necessary laws of thought, of reasoned thinking, of the right ways of finding out how something works and how it ought to work. Perhaps Aristotle's shaping and sharpening of the tools of logic were his greatest single service to mankind.

He also wrote about astronomy. He had much to say, as we have seen, about physics and such things as laws of motion. He discoursed wisely about such varied subjects as meteorology, philosophy, psychology, metaphysics, ethics, comparative government, politics, botany, zoology, art, and poetry. The titles of some of Aristotle's works suggest to us very vividly the widely ranging competence of his mind: *The History of Animals, Ethics, Politics, Rhetoric, On Sleep, On Dreams, On Life and Death, On the Senses and the Sensible, On the Soul*. Many of Aristotle's writings have been lost; but the list of what we have saved is long and formidable. For instance, we know that Aristotle made a monumental study of the constitutions of more than a hundred city-states; we have only the *Constitution of Athens*. The *Politics* thus remains our chief source for our knowledge of Aristotle's complex political theory.

Aristotle soon abandoned the transcendental Ideas of his master Plato. He insisted that from particular material things we can form generalized concepts and that the universal is nothing more than a deduction from the particular. For instance, if we know individual tables we can shape a generalized concept of what a chair is. We cannot assert that a cow is not a horse unless we have at least some general idea of the nature of a horse. The controller of all the universe, said Aristotle, is not the sum of the Platonic Ideas but a Prime Mover that is itself unmoved but moves the world and the universe.

Happiness and the good life, asserted Aristotle, are always found in the *right* activity of the soul. The task of the legislator, then, is to make a society that enables men to live the good life. The legislator is a craftsman, an expert —the *Politics* was written for his guidance. The state should exist for the well-being of everybody. It should be a community of men in pursuit of the good. To obtain knowledge about the good, men should turn to logic and experience. "Let us remember that we should not disregard the experience of the ages; in the multitude of years, these things, if they were good, would certainly not have been unknown; for almost everything has been found out, although sometimes they are not put together; in other cases men do not use the knowledge which they have." Aristotle and Plato share a strong disapproval of men who carelessly use what minds they have. They both approve of the craftsman and the expert as leaders in an intellectual aristocracy.

Plato and Aristotle have been especially successful in convincing men that critical analyses of complex experience can only be made by those who are wary of abstractions, those cancerous verbalisms that eat into sense. "Error is never so difficult to be destroyed," said Jeremy Bentham, "as when it has its roots in language. Improper terms are the chains which bind men to unreasonable practices." The diamond-hard facts must be searched for, gazed upon, and studied. Before a problem can be mastered it must be understood. There is yet no evidence that the suprarenal glands are superior to the brains as instruments for solving problems of science, education, or anything else.

One of the wisest men who ever lived was Socrates. That strange genius had much to say about the nature and knowledge of man. He has touched many minds with fire.

Socrates was a stonemason in the city of Athens. Probably he was not entirely successful in that trade because he spent many hours doing more important things. He was an eccentric and persistent market-place talker. He left no writings, only disciples. Often barefoot and shirtless, Socrates "stalked down the street like a pelican." His physical appearance was grotesque: his eyes protruded on either side of his snub nose; his forehead bulged. Wherever he went his consuming curiosity made him stop to ask questions. "The proper study of mankind is man." All of this was very annoying and puzzling to his wife Xanthippe, that busy shrew.

The relentless questions of Socrates were not haphazard or ill conceived. He believed that by progressive methods of thinking, or dialectic, men come to more accurate understanding. He said that the first step towards real wisdom was a knowledge of one's own ignorance. Step by step, the humble inquirer and doubter convinced other men that what they thought was true was often not true at all. Everything, asserted Socrates, must be open to question. No man should turn for his faiths to his father or his fellows. He should not follow the furrows and footpaths of his ancestors because it was the comfortable thing to do. He should challenge and experiment and expose society and religion to the solvents of logical inquiry. If you are going to try to practice justice you had better find out what it is. If you are going to try to be a brave man or a good man you had better discover what bravery is and goodness is. Everything in the universe is intelligently arranged for human happiness and good. Men will follow the right way if only they know what the right way is. If you do not use right reason as a guide, said Socrates, you are wandering without chart or compass. You have lost your way. What is worse, you have lost your address.

Evil is ignorance. Virtue is knowledge, and knowledge alone. Men must think. Societies rot when men grow mentally lazy. Apathy and indolence are always great dangers to free men.

> Simple said: I see no danger.
> Sloth said: Yet a little more sleep.
> And Presumption said: Every tub must stand upon its
>   own bottom.
> And so they lay down to sleep again.

Frequently the probing questions of the tireless Socrates left a conviction of ignorance in those who talked with him, an ignorance that he sometimes pretended to share. He compared himself to a midwife bringing other men's thoughts to birth. "Unsuspected he taught them."

There have been many men in history who have stubbornly searched for truth in the rocks and the jungles, the fire of divine discontent in their marrows. Often the respectable and conservative have distrusted them—it was the respectable folk who crucified Jesus and let Barabbas go. "But the chief priests and elders persuaded the multitude that they should ask Barabbas, and destroy Jesus." They could understand Barabbas but not Christ.

So it was with Socrates, that doctor of the soul. He died a victim of politics and public distrust. In the days at the end of the Peloponnesian War it was not entirely safe to assert, as Socrates did, that everything was open to question, that only expertly trained men should run the affairs of state, or that much could be said for some new ideas and ideals in education and culture. The conservatives and the reactionaries stood together, and they put Socrates outside. They said he was corrupting the youth, "introducing strange divinities," and destroying men's faith in the old gods. Faith in the old gods dies slowly, like the embers in a protected fire. But posterity remembers and often does homage to Socrates. Those who condemned him are forgotten. Many of the values they tried to protect have been blown away, brittle leaves in the winds of the centuries.

The text of the famous trial of Socrates reminds us that the tales of human passion, persecution, and prejudice are both new and old. The causes of intolerance sometimes differ from age to age but the unfortunate end is often the same. Inch by inch the hemlock crept upwards in the benumbed limbs of Socrates and he died, condemned by those who felt that the safety of the state demanded his death. "The difficulty is not to escape death," said Socrates, "but to escape wickedness."

There were several schools teaching different philosophies in Athens. Some of them continued for hundreds of years. The Cynics were led by Diogenes of Sinope (412–323 B.C.), who perhaps looked for an honest man with a lantern and perhaps lived in a tub. He certainly led strong offensives against several social institutions, especially private property. The Cyrenaic school preached the pursuit of pleasure. The Skeptics, led by Pyrrho (360–270 B.C.), took an interesting position: they asserted that men were unhappy because they could not attain knowledge and therefore they should give up all efforts to learn.

The leader of another school, called the Stoics, was the Cyprus merchant Zeno (336–264 B.C.). He taught in the market place of Athens at the Painted Porch or colonnade (Stoa Poikile). In later days the ranks of the Stoics included famous men like Epictetus, Seneca, and Marcus Aurelius. What did the Stoics believe? What did they say? Their philosophy, briefly stated, was this: a virtuous man should always be ruled by reason; as a completely rational being he should be at harmony with himself. To act in a rational way is good. To act irrationally is evil. The contemplative life is a cold and passionless neuter—there is no virtue because there is no action at all, good or bad. The Stoics also held that the spirit of a man in doing a deed was more important than the deed itself. In later years, especially in Italy, the Stoic philosophy stressed the importance of self-discipline, the voluntary inward striving towards the qualities of a perfectly rational being who moves through the world with good will and right reason, who obeys the rules of the gods and tries to live in full and wise harmony with the moral order of the universe.

Still another important school of philosophers was led by the genial and generous Epicurus of Samos (342–270 B.C.), who taught for about thirty years in Athens. For a long time Epicurus suffered the pains and tortures of extremely bad health. There seems little doubt that the condition of his body had much to do with the constitution of his philosophy. "Vain is the discourse of that philosopher by which no human suffering is healed."

The philosophy of Epicurus has often been distorted by men of later generations. His followers began the warping, and the custom has been continued. The Epicurean philosophy is not at all what it is often popularly supposed to be. In fact, it is almost the reverse. The essentials of the original teachings of Epicurus can be rather barely and simply stated because those teachings were simple, spare, and lean. "The sum and purpose of a blessed life," said Epicurus, "is health of body and tranquillity of mind." If all fears, pains, alarms, and desires can be curbed or forced beyond the edges of awareness by deliberate acts of will, then happiness and tranquillity will come and stay as long as life. Follow a severe and simple pattern of living. So far as religion is concerned, believe and do anything that makes you more serene. Try to be tranquil. Limit your desires and avoid new wants—"Give me barley bread and water and I will vie with Zeus in happiness." Always keep your own advantage in mind—"No one loves another except for his own interest." Try to stay away from disturbing scenes or people. Never marry—it brings trouble. Do not become wealthy if you can escape it—money brings trouble, too. Do not be afraid of dying— "It does not concern the living who are alive and the dead know nothing about it."

From another part of the forest came other voices, other views. Of particular interest are the Sophists, if only because there are many of them in the world of the twentieth century. True, they may move under other banners and rejoice in other names. They may bear no labels at all. But they are Sophists just the same.

The Sophists insisted that they were concentrating upon practical things: the problems of government, law, adult education, methods of argument in debating, technical skills like carpentry and the like. They vehemently asserted that there was no place in society for "idle speculations" by a motley crew of cantankerous and befuddled philosophers talking about their fuzzy worlds and their impractical ideas in philosophy, mathematics, and science. In their opinion, sensible and level-headed men should study only those things that could be used for the practical advantage of themselves and the state. In any society, it was the utilitarian posts and props and pillars that really mattered, not the misty dreams of the sons of Socrates. A truly human philosophy, said the Sophists, must be concerned with the immediate affairs of men in a tough, hard, competitive world. (They never had a chance to read

Abraham Flexner's answer in his essay of the twentieth century: "The Usefulness of Useless Knowledge.") Some of them, like the modern relativists, insisted that there were no values or authority beyond men themselves. Knowledge is not absolute but relative to man. Good and evil, said the Sophists, depend solely upon men's views of them. The ends that we believe practical alone count in the society, the world, and the universe. Did not Protagoras say: "Man is the measure of things?"

The Sophists were skilled debaters, although it seems that they did sometimes mistake apoplexy for thought. They were too strongly inclined to answer their opponents by denunciation and not by cogent argument and to think and feel that those who were opposed to them were simply unvirtuous, perverse, deluded, or purblind. Many of their words suggest to us that they were sometimes ready to settle problems by leaping at the jugulars of those who disagreed with them. "It is human to err, but diabolical to persevere."

Like the so-called relativists of the twentieth century, the Sophists were frequently mercilessly manhandled by masters of logic. But they came back to battle. They have been coming back for twenty centuries. To them the human paradise they want upon this earth is worth fighting for.

Plato, as we would naturally expect, left no doubts about his opposition to the Sophists and their ideas. "Each of these private hirelings, which these men call Sophists, . . . teach no other things but those maxims of the vulgar which they approve when they are assembled together, and call it wisdom . . . [the Sophists] know not in reality what is handsome, or base, or good, or ill, or just, or unjust." They listen to the mob, "the great animal," and call "those things good in which it delighted and those things evil in which it was vexed." They have no other measures of good and bad. "Do they not truly appear to you as absurd teachers?"

In an age of conflicting and competing faiths many Greeks tried to take careful thought. "Thought maketh the whole dignity of man," wrote Pascal in the seventeenth century, "therefore endeavor to think well, that is the only morality." The resolute use of independent cerebral action is always necessary at times when pressures and enemies within and without a state threaten to level all society into a vast and level prairie of mass conformity. And yet it is also true that rationalistic individualism may result in a discarding of belief in many of the moral values—they are sometimes called "social myths"—that help so much to bind individuals and states together. Henry Bamford Parkes, that able and persuasive author of *Gods and Men,* has asserted that creativity ended in Athens and society became devitalized when the Athenians came to rely exclusively upon the tools of reason. Disaster was at hand when "organic life" was changed into "mechanism."

Was England's David Hume correct when he concluded in the eighteenth century that all belief is more properly an act of the affective than of the cogitative part of man's nature? He also said: "Disputes are multiplied as if everything were uncertain and these disputes are managed with the greatest warmth as if everything were certain."

However these things may be, it is still true that there was no timidity of thought in the Greeks. They were neither slogan-drugged nor sleepy. They belonged to the fellowship of those in all ages who have been concerned with their hearts and minds about the destiny of free men.

Chapter 9

ROME:

PRIDE AND POWER

"Rufus, son of Callisunus, greeting to Epillicus and all his fellows. I believe you know I am very well. If you have made the list, please send. Do thou look after everything very carefully. See that thou turnest that slave girl into cash. . . ."

—Fragment of a letter written in London about 75 A.D.

THE area of Italy is 116,226 square miles. The great peninsula is therefore about the size of the state of Arizona, two-thirds the size of California, more than twice the size of Greece. In the north the towering Alps sweep in a semicircle from the top of the Adriatic to the shores of Monaco. To the south the Italian peninsula thrusts out from the mass of central Europe into the Mediterranean for 650 miles. Upon the eastern shores beats the Adriatic, cold and stormy. On the west are the islands of Corsica and Sardinia. Beyond the tip of the projecting mainland lies Sicily, ancient island of mystery, poverty, and courage.

Back and forth across the whole length of the long land of Italy the forces of nature have placed a great chain of limestone mountains called the Apennines. In the north, these mountains traverse the country almost directly east and west in an unbroken line from the Gulf of Genoa to the Adriatic. Thus they help to divide southern Italy from the northern lands drained from the Po river basin. Further south, the Apennines hug the inhospitable east coast, leaving free from their rocky invasions the western regions with their rolling hills and fertile plains, their broad streams, their ports. South of Naples, the Apennines loop back towards the west coast and hence the hilly plains in southern Italy are on the east side of the peninsula. On the south and west coasts there are excellent harbors, always an important fact in a world of war and trade. Italy looks to the west and the south.

Of high significance in Italy's history has been her strategic location, her central position in the great inland sea. Because of her geographical situation it was inevitable that many groups would come to Italy to colonize, farm, trade, or fight. About 5000 B.C., for instance, a long-headed and dark-skinned Mediterranean people came from North Africa. Between 2000 and 1500 B.C. the sturdy Indo-European invaders pressed through the northeast passes of the Alps. Warlike tribes fought and fused. In green pastures by the Po the sheep and cattle grazed as the centuries passed. "How noiseless falls the foot of time."

To establish intelligent contact with the remote past we must always call upon the skilled archeologists. In recent years they have discovered and accumulated most impressive bodies of evidence in widely scattered regions of the earth. The remains of the fire apes in South Africa contend for our interest with the Stone Age artifacts found in Saskatchewan; and both yield before the latest reports from the excavators at the Agora in Athens. Meanwhile the archeologists have at last discovered many secrets of the Stone Age Lake Dwellers in Switzerland and in Italy's Po valley. And recently, too, much more has been revealed about the puzzling Etruscans, that mysterious and highly civilized people who swooped upon the west coast of Italy about 750 B.C. and built their walled hilltop cities.

Professor Raymond Bloch has ably presented the view that the Etruscan civilization was brought by invaders from Anatolia. Other scholars are strongly opposed to this idea. They assert that Professor Bloch and those who believe as he does—including Herodotus—are wrong, quite wrong. If all the massed evidence could be assembled and discussed in this book most readers would be so quickened to thought and feeling upon the subject that they would support the contentions of one side or the other. They would then understand why excited archeologists and historians can be so vehement about the societies of men centuries dead.

We do know that the Etruscans began mining in Elba and Tuscany and traded with southern Italy, Greece, and Carthage. They brought with them the idea and practice of the city-state organization, considerable skill in the arts and crafts of engineering, metalwork, frescoes, sculpture, and much Greek culture. The myths the Etruscans illustrated in their tomb paintings and elsewhere were almost all Greek. They had also taken over the Greek alphabet before they came to Italy and altered it to fit their language, a language we cannot read today.

There is no dispute about the distinctive and permanent value of Etruscan achievements in art. Several of their aesthetic performances were masterly. There is a sixth-century head of Hermes in painted terra cotta from Veii— that shrine of Etruscan statuary—that would rank with the most prized treasures of any modern musem. Here is nothing flat or austere. On the contrary, there is a sparked vitality and power that have no doubt changed many a casual glance into a fixed gaze of admiration. The Orator of Lake Trasimene, too, is a masterpiece in terra cotta. What has perished we cannot know.

In the north, then, were these Etruscans with their twelve cities united in a loose confederation. In the south and southeast of Italy was the urban civilization of the Greeks that had begun when the Greeks began to migrate from the motherland about 800 B.C. In the central part of the peninsula were the rural cultures of peoples like the strong Latins, the Sabines, and the Samnites of the hills.

About 600 B.C. the Etruscans conquered the west central region called Latium, the home of the Latin tribesmen. During their advance the Etruscans seized some clusters of huts on the banks of the Tiber river. These settled spots were part of a city-state that the Latins had formed in imitation of their hostile neighbors to the north. The city-state was called Rome. Legend says, of course, that Rome was founded in 753 by Romulus and Remus, descendants of Aeneas, hero of the fall of Troy whose exploits were told in Virgil's *Aeneid*. We can reject this fable shining through the mists of time. The facts of the early history of Rome are exciting enough.

The Etruscans who flooded out of Etruria knew a lot about drainage, irrigation, and building. They made fertile and healthy farmlands out of the Tuscan Maremma, the Pontine Marshes, and the Roman Campagna. They built embankments along the Po to control the waters. They constructed the drainage canal called the Cloaca Maxima near Rome's Palatine Hill. They built a big temple on the Palatine Hill dedicated to Jupiter, Juno, and Minerva, soon to be the center of Roman worship. They made an army, shortly to be skilled and strong. They built a market or forum. In time the town of Rome, located at a strategic spot on the Tiber fifteen miles from the sea, became the dominant state in central Italy. The first step had been taken on the long road to empire. Each achievement, great and small, took time. Rome was not built in a day.

There is no doubt that the Etruscan conquerors of Rome were a sophisticated, gifted, and powerful people. When we look back at what happened in Rome and Latium it is really astonishing that the virile, hayseed Romans were not absorbed and destroyed as a separate group. Instead, "they kept their farmers' tongue and their ploughmen generals. They made a place for themselves in the world of cities and then they mastered that world."

The Romans acted soon. In 509 B.C. they rebelled, tossed out the Etruscan king, Tarquin the Proud, and founded a republic. In these years the Etruscan power was waning everywhere, and it was waning fast. The Greeks of Syracuse destroyed an Etruscan fleet at Cumae (476 B.C.). The half-naked tribesmen of Gaul began slowly to press into the large, rich plains of the Po valley. The Etruscans were on their way to being absorbed into a new world and a new civilization. Their Tuscan blood would slowly mingle with that of other men from the north and the south and from over the seas. Then their distinctive qualities would be lost forever.

The makers of successful revolutions have usually described the manifold evils of the regimes they have overthrown. For centuries the Romans told of the wicked Tarquins, those alien Etruscans who had seized and held power until the patriotic Romans rose in justified revolt. It seemed, however, that the ousting of the Etruscan kings did not bring universal satisfaction. The new republic also had its troubles and its opponents.

One of the darkest of those problems was the inevitable result of class divisions within the state. There were three distinct groups: the aristocratic wealthy landowners or patricians; the plebeians, or non-noble freemen, including the artisans, tradesmen, poorer farmers, and landless workers; and the slaves. The real strength of the republic was in the self-reliant plebeians who frequently battled the raiders descending from many points of the compass on the fertile fields of Latium. At home these plebeians wanted enough land to live happily upon, a share in the government, the abolition of slavery resulting from debt, the publication of all laws. The main political power did not lie in their hands. It rested with the aristocracy, with the patricians. They stood together, congratulated one another upon their monopolistic tendencies, and tried to keep the control and influence of policy out of the hands of the lower classes.

The organization of the state was simple and efficient. There were two chief magistrates, called consuls, elected annually. In theory they were chosen from among the senators by the popular assembly composed of all men who were free and bore arms in the defense of the state. In fact they were selected by the political machines of the patricians. The consuls commanded the army, presided over certain religious ceremonies, often acted as judges. There were also 300 senators—almost all patricians—chosen for life by the consuls. The senators "advised" the consuls, summoned the assembly, decided such important questions as peace and war. The popular assembly had very few powers. Anything it did could be vetoed by the senate. The plebeians, compelled to pay heavy taxes and serve in the army, were permitted to sit in this assembly. They might take no other post in government.

Two praetors administered justice. Two censors took the census, watched over morals, and assessed property values. Two (later ten) tribunes protected, as best they could when they wanted to, the rights and interests of the plebeians. Two quaestors managed and guarded the state treasury.

In the Roman aristocratic republic there was also the office of dictator, to be filled only in times of emergency. The state might appoint a dictator with absolute power over all things and all people for a period not to exceed six months.

By slow stages the plebeians, fighting stubbornly in "the struggle of the orders," did gain some ground against the patricians. There is no need here to dwell upon the details. It is enough to state briefly a few selected facts. About 470 B.C. the plebeians compelled the aristocracy to permit the election of tribunes who were given the veto over any illegal acts of the senior magistrates. In 445 B.C.—after a committee had been sent to Greece to study the work of Solon and Cleisthenes—the plebeians obtained a codification of the laws: the Laws of the Twelve Tables. These new enactments, among other things, helped to strengthen the economic basis of the state by regularizing the transfer of property, thus aiding capital formations for economic enterprise.

In 362 B.C. a plebeian was elected to serve as one of the consuls. In 287 B.C. the noted Hortensian Law provided that decrees approved by the assembly were to become the laws of the state even if the senate did not approve and ratify. Despite these advances—far more impressive on paper than in actual operation—an oligarchy of the wealthy continued to control the state until the end of the days of the republic. To their legal powers, of course, these gentlemen added the effective instruments of influence, of robbery, jobbery, and corruption.

For more than two centuries the new republic was almost constantly at war. The population of Rome was steadily mounting. The Romans, always an aggressive people, wanted more land. They needed to expand and expand they did. Specialists in this period of history can list, one by one, the numerous wars with the Aequi, Campanians, Hernici, Volscians, the Etruscans up around Veii, and the other hostile tribesmen. The stout Romans defeated all of their enemies but one: the blond barbarian Gauls who rolled down from the north in 390 B.C. to capture and burn Rome. These Gauls had to be paid to go back to their homes in the Po valley.

Undaunted Rome recovered fast. The days of the simple farming and herding world of primitive Latium were gone forever. Swords, spears, and javelins—these were the new instruments of power. The efficiency of the Roman legion, that basic military unit, had been proved and proved again on the field of battle. The legion contained 3,000 heavily armed men, 1,200 lightly armed foot soldiers, and 300 horsemen. It was composed of small units capable of independent action. In both attack and defense the legion was a balanced tool, flexible, swift, and deadly. A Roman army was made up of three parallel divisions, each divided into maniples of 120 men. If the line of the front division broke, then a part of the rear divisions moved up to the front. Several features of the Roman arrangements are not unfamiliar to men who have served in the armies of a later age.

New wars broke out. New triumphs came to the Roman soldiers. By 290 B.C., after a desperate struggle with the Samnites in the highlands of central Italy, the Roman republic stood forth as the master of the middle sector of the peninsula. To the north were the warlike Gauls. To the south were the settlements of Magna Graecia, the highly civilized Greek cities of Sicily and the mainland.

It is difficult to stop a tide of conquest. The ambitious Romans now moved down upon the Greek colonies, those flourishing centers for the diffusion of Greek culture. The Greeks in Tarentum, alarmed and desperate, sought help. They begged Pyrrhus—able general and ambitious king of Epirus—to bring his armies from the mainland of Greece. Pyrrhus came to Tarentum, hoping to carve out a Greek empire in the West. He won several costly land battles, so costly that such triumphs are still termed "Pyrrhic" victories. Then Carthage, the temporary ally of Rome, scattered his navy. Rome defeated his army. Pyrrhus went home to Greece, there to be slain by a woman in a street brawl. The Greek colonies on the Italian mainland surrendered to Rome. By 265 B.C., a time of triumph, the Roman republic stood supreme in all the lands of Italy south of the Po and the city of Pisa.

The wars of Roman expansion had not yet ended. The conquest of southern Italy brought an immediate challenge from a powerful rival: the mighty commercial city of Carthage, the North African daughter of Phoenicia's Tyre.

The tale of Carthage, that fortified city on the gulf of Tunis, was for centuries filled with drama, gold, and glory. Within her boundaries lived about 700,000 people. Her lands in North Africa were vast and fertile. She was a trade outlet for the dates, gold, and slaves of central Africa. Her quick-eyed sailors traded with all the known world. She had colonies in Sardinia, Sicily, and Spain. No state dared challenge her sea power.

In the war against the Greeks, Carthage had fought on the side of Rome. It was an unfortunate error—the triumph of Rome meant that Carthage stood alone against a formidable foe. Had Carthage earlier held aloof, or if she had joined the Greeks, then the balance of power would not have been tilted.

Rome and Carthage soon disputed about the future of Sicily, rich in granaries and grain fields. The disjointed struggle that began in 264 B.C. between the giants of the Mediterranean was crucial. Its outcome decided whether Greco-Roman culture was to rule in the world of the West. For more than a hundred years the conflict continued and then Rome prevailed.

The truce that ended the first Punic War in 241 B.C. gave Rome Sicily and a large sum of money paid by Carthage in gold—about $5,000,000. In 218 B.C. the bitter Second Punic War broke out after Rome seized Sardinia, conquered Corcyra and Corsica, and threatened to impose another indemnity upon Carthage. By that time Rome ruled the Mediterranean. If she were to be defeated, it had to be by land campaigns. now the sole hope of Carthage. The brilliant Carthaginian general Hannibal, son of mighty Hamilcar and implacable foe of Rome, tried to do precisely that.

Hannibal's superb military gifts, his energies, his undying hatred, and his passion for revenge have all been described and stressed many times in the twenty centuries since he lived. To the amazement of his foes, Hannibal brought his army and some of his horses, mules, and elephants out of Spain and through the icy and treacherous passes of the Alps. When he reached the Po, Hannibal had only about 20,000 foot soldiers and 6,000 horsemen. He had left behind on the journey about 30,000 of his infantry and 9,000 cavalry. But he had come down into the plains of the Po. The arrival meant much. Victory would mean more. Rome was the heart of the republic and Hannibal was close to Rome.

The perilous adventures of the brilliant and daring Carthaginian are finely told by the historians Polybius and Livy. In the twenty-first book of Livy's history, for instance, the staccato sentences describing the passage through the Alps are among the most vivid and dramatic ever penned by a Roman historian. Even the reader whose knowledge of Latin has faded with the years can sense the excitement in the words describing the dizzy heights and the men and mules who sometimes fell, packs and all, to measureless depths below.

Hannibal hoped in vain for a rising in the north and a lunge against Rome by the unhappy Gauls. He hoped for an invasion by Philip V of Macedon. With the aid of a few men from Cisalpine Gaul, he finally moved into battle. No tribesmen revolted. No conqueror came from Macedonia. Hannibal was almost alone.

There were two minor victories for Carthage in the north, and then the main battle of 217 B.C. was joined at Lake Trasimene in Etruria. There Hannibal destroyed a Roman army of 40,000 men. In the next year the Romans lost two armies that were nearly annihilated at Cannae. Dark and desperate though her peril was, writhing under successive defeats, Rome still fought on. Her command of the sea around Italy meant that she could keep Hannibal's supply lines cut. Her ships could continue to prowl on the sea lanes and molest every ship that sailed from the ports of her foe. Fearful though Rome was of the skills and stratagems of Hannibal, she knew that in the end she must win. Final victory was surely a matter of time, nothing else.

To reduce the pressure at home and open other fronts, Roman legions attacked the Carthaginians in Spain, a highly sensitive spot. The two Scipios drove out Hasdrubal, famous leader of the armies of Carthage in Spain. Hasdrubal was soon to come back again to Spain, kill both Scipios, and get back the land for Carthage. Then, in 209 B.C., the Romans were to send still another Scipio to Spain. He was to force Hasdrubal to escape to Italy with his army, there to be defeated and killed.

The Romans also attacked Africa. Hannibal, so long tied down in Italy, was at last recalled to defend his homeland. In 202 B.C. he was defeated by the Roman general Scipio—soon to be hailed as "Africanus"—at Zama, near Carthage. The war was over at last. Under the terms of a harsh treaty Carthage surrendered Spain to Rome and paid the conqueror about $15,000,000. Carthage was also forbidden to wage war outside of Africa. A few years later (183 B.C.) Hannibal—"history's most glorious failure"—committed suicide. "Let us release the Romans from their long anxiety since they think it too long to wait for the death of one old man."

The Romans were not yet finished. They coveted rich North Africa. Avarice, fear, jealousy, and revenge come upon the stage. Might not Carthage recover from defeat? Carthage was a deadly enemy. "Carthage must be destroyed." Cato, who uttered these famous words, was a landowner who hoped that the competition of Carthage in oil and wines might somehow be stopped. Cato was also, of course, a patriotic Roman.

Fifty-two years after the battle of Zama, Rome treacherously attacked Carthage and began the Third Punic War. In 146 B.C. the city of Carthage fell after a desperate siege and hours of blood and butchery. It was burned, cursed, plowed up, and sown with salt. The inhabitants were sold into slavery. North Africa became a Roman province. Rome was cruel, Rome was hard. Gentleness in war has often been held to be the same thing as imbecility.

Meanwhile the Romans had conquered Spain. They enslaved Macedonia and divided it into four republics. Greece, a state that still loved liberty, was crushed beneath the heels of the trampling legions. Corinth was captured and destroyed, her people killed or sold into slavery. Within a few years, too, the Roman legions marched to conquer new provinces in Asia Minor, including Cilicia and Syria. Everywhere victory sat on the banners of the proud republic. The lands of east and west were slowly moving into the orbit of her power.

As the Roman state expanded, its difficulties multiplied. One grave problem was the land question, always a running sore in the body economic. Large landowners, many of them senators, increased their holdings and imported foreign slaves to work the estates. When the slaves were treated badly—many of them were more civilized than their masters—they became antagonistic. A lot of them were slaves because they had been captured in the Punic Wars; they had no cause to like the Romans. Numerous small yeomen farmers were evicted. It was inevitable that these men, pushed off their holdings, should resent the big landlords. The soil of Latium, overcropped and eroded, yielded smaller harvests. Then the landowners raised more animals and less grain, importing their grain from North Africa, Sardinia, and Sicily. As middle-class men like the merchants, the moneylenders, and those who held government contracts grew wealthier, they increasingly resented the position and pretensions of the patrician aristocracy. The poor grew poorer and the rich richer. A great gulf widened between those who had land and money and those who had neither. Crowded Rome swarmed with poor people, landless, jobless, homeless, hungry, bitter. The sick and the wretched despaired. Tax gatherers grew sleek and fat and slept well at night. The homely virtues of the youth of the state were widely abandoned. The crooks and the gamblers prowled and preyed.

A few reformers, like Tiberius Sempronius Gracchus, elected tribune in 133 B.C., tried to battle the creeping decadence. As leaders of the landless and workless farmers against the aristocracy, they attempted to revive agriculture, to restore the small farms by dividing the public lands and taking other acres from the die-hard senators, grown rich in trade rackets and war profiteering. Tiberius persuaded the assembly to pass a law limiting the amount of land any one person might hold to about 300 acres. Said Tiberius: ". . . the men who fight and die in defense of Italy enjoy indeed the air and light, but nothing more. . . . They fight to maintain the wealth and luxury of others, and they die with the title of lords of the earth without possessing a single clod to call their own."

The senators naturally resisted the new proposals. Before the law went into effect, Tiberius completed his term as tribune. Although the constitution said he was not eligible for re-election, Tiberius decided to run for office again. The issue was soon settled because Tiberius and about 300 of his followers were murdered and their bodies thrown into the Tiber. The respectable and the reactionary senators, the rich, the educated, the privileged—they were the ones that did it. Their interests were threatened, and with savagery they went forth, blood on their hands and bloody menace in their thoughts.

Gaius Gracchus, a tribune and a brother of Tiberius, tried to compel the government to buy grain on the open market and sell it once a month to the people at half the prevailing price. In 121 B.C. he was successful in getting the assembly to approve his proposal. The senators, for their part, insisted that the feeding of the poor out of the public purse would encourage laziness and would cost too much. The state, surely, should be saved needless expense. Gaius also proposed to extend the franchise and to reform the tax-collection system, so cumbersome and corrupt. In 120 B.C. he stood for re-election. His action was illegal and the senators made as much of it as they had in the case of his brother Tiberius. In the election Gaius was defeated and was soon declared an enemy of the state by the famous "final decree" of the senate. His followers were dispersed. Defeated and abandoned, Gaius either asked a slave to kill him or was murdered. The end was the same.

The Gracchi left no heirs but they have had several spiritual descendants in the proud rebels of later centuries. In Rome, the cries of the destitute and the outcasts and the clamors of the "forgotten men" of the masses were met by government gifts and free amusements—"bread and circuses." The state, it seemed, owed all men a living—especially when it was dangerous to deny it. The earlier senatorial comments about the folly of unnecessary expense were apparently forgotten.

Quarrels between the aristocratic senate and the popular assembly soon brought civil war, a welter of blood and butchery, the decay of constitutional government. A general named Marius became consul in the interests of himself and the senate. His successor was Sulla, a veteran and hero of the foreign wars who seized power, defended the senate, was appointed dictator, and ruled by the power of the sword and slaughter. A state that uses violence can expect to perish by the sword. The dispossessed and the discontented will wait and watch for their hour to come.

After several tangled events, Sulla retired in 79 B.C., and two men rose to power: Pompey and Julius Caesar, clever and ambitious masters of intrigue and politics. Pompey was famous as the conqueror of Palestine and Syria. Caesar, who became consul in 59 B.C., believed he could be chosen sole leader of the republic if he gained military fame. This he set out to do.

Between 58 and 50 B.C. Julius Caesar completed a series of great campaigns that added all Gaul to the lands controlled by Rome. His campaigns were marked by his calculated efficiency and his close attention to details of supply and transport. It is true that Gaul was torn by intertribal quarrels, but it still remains a tribute to Caesar's military skill that he was able to accomplish his conquests with six legions. His lucid and famous *Gallic Wars,* studied by so many generations of schoolboys, provided superb propaganda for his cause and his ambitions back in Rome.

In 55 B.C. Julius Caesar embarked from Boulogne with a force of about 10,000 men and headed towards Britain. British charioteers, infantry, and cavalry gathered on the downs above Dover to throw back the threatened attack from the sea. Caesar's legionnaires were victorious, but a gale dashed the anchored Roman transports on the shore. In the following year, Caesar left his fleet anchored "off a gentle open beach." Again a gale hammered his ships. Forty vessels were destroyed. Caesar went back to Gaul. For nearly a century no Roman soldier set foot on the shores of Britain.

Meanwhile Pompey was back in Rome. As the tide of reports about Caesar's triumphs came southwards, Pompey grew fearful and jealous. At last he was able to persuade the senate to declare Caesar a public enemy. The brave and wily Caesar moved swiftly. He knew that to lose the approaching struggle with his rival Pompey meant the loss of his power and perhaps of his life. He immediately left Gaul and crossed the Rubicon. This small stream flowing down to the east coast of Italy was important because it was the border between Cisalpine Gaul and Italy. It was thus the limit of Caesar's province and when he crossed it he was defying the laws of the republic. With his army he did cross it and he came home to defeat the armies of the senate and to rule with absolute power. He drove Pompey out of Italy and defeated him in Thessaly. Pompey, who had lost the contest, was assassinated in Alexandria.

The republic was dying. Men like Cassius and Brutus falsely accused Caesar of being a tyrant. They plotted. On March 15, 44 B.C., Caesar was murdered in the senate house at Rome.

> Liberty! Freedom! Tyranny is dead!
> Run hence, proclaim, cry it about the streets. . . .

Caesar was dead. His death was soon to be avenged.

> *Mark Antony:* O mighty Caesar! dost thou lie so low?
> Are all thy conquests, glories, triumphs, spoils,
> Shrunk to this little measure? . . .
> But yesterday the word of Caesar might
> Have stood against the world; now lies he there,
> And none so poor to do him reverence. . . .
> I am no orator, as Brutus is;
> But, as you know me all, a plain blunt man,
> That love my friend. . . .
> *Second Citizen:* Poor soul! his eyes are red as fire with weeping. . . .
> *All:* We'll mutiny!
> *First Citizen:* We'll burn the house of Brutus!
> *Third Citizen:* Away, then! Come, seek the conspirators!
> *Second Citizen:* Go fetch fire. . . .
> *Fourth Citizen:* Pluck down forms, windows, anything. . . .
> *Servant:* I heard him say, Brutus and Cassius
> Are rid like madmen through the streets of Rome. . . .

But Brutus and Cassius were not to live for long. They had an early appointment with death on the battlefield at Philippi. Dante put them both in the lowest pit in the Inferno, by the side of Judas Iscariot.

> Regions of sorrow, doleful shades, where peace
> And rest can never dwell, hope never comes.

The result of Caesar's murder at the hands of fanatics was another grim and terrible civil war. There was a sickening series of dark plots and wild assaults. Three men fought and hunted down the senators who were suspected of being in the plan to kill Caesar: Octavian, Caesar's grandnephew and adopted heir; Lepidus, Caesar's friend; Mark Antony, Caesar's lieutenant. When most of their enemies were dead the three victors in the triumvirate fell apart. Rome was once more honeycombed with intrigue. Octavian ousted Lepidus from power. Antony, who had taken control of the eastern provinces, was in Egypt with his mistress Cleopatra, an able queen of beauty and intense ambition. In 31 B.C., Octavian defeated Antony's navy at Actium, near Greece, and annexed Egypt to Rome. Antony, broken and useless, committed suicide and Cleopatra followed him.

Victorious Octavian returned to Rome in 30 B.C. and in 27 B.C. he was given the name Augustus. "In my sixth and seventh consulship, after I had put out the flames of civil war and by universal consent had become possessed of the control of affairs, I transferred the state from my own power to the will of the senate and people of Rome. For this service I received by decree of the senate the name of Augustus." As a matter of fact, Augustus held many titles in his time. He became tribune for life, first citizen, and emperor. Even when a semblance of power remained with the senate, Augustus in fact wielded full authority in an exhausted and bleeding Roman world. The army was his and he kept it loyal. He was unassailable. Rome wanted peace, an end to party passions, plots and cliques, civil discord, and external peril. Two centuries of galling trials had ended. The republic was no more. The empire was born.

Augustus, an able dictator, succeeded in a heavy task of reconstruction. With a combination of patience and relentless zeal he tightened his hold upon the provinces and his grip was sure and hard. Cruel extortions brought vast plunder. The legates of Augustus in the provinces were not greedy amateurs; they were shrewd experts. Meanwhile his legions tried to carry the eagles of Rome to new frontiers on the Rhine and the Danube. Everywhere his servants shaped and reorganized the taxation system so that efficiency increased and graft went down. Control and order were firmly established in every place but Germany; there General Varus and his legions were defeated.

The Roman peace, the *Pax Romana,* meant that more men were enabled to turn their energies to the production of wealth for themselves and the state. The shrewd Augustus encouraged superior techniques in production and trade. He also created a centralized system of courts. It is obvious that these steps, and many more, contributed to a peace and stability that the Roman lands had not seen for many decades. Even in the heart of the empire Augustus moved to bring reforms long needed. For instance, he established a fire brigade and a city police force in Rome. The really significant fact, a fact of overwhelming importance, is that there now came order, peace, stability. As between liberty and Augustan peace the Roman world chose peace. Other peoples in later distracted days did the same thing, usually to their sorrow.

In 14 A.D. the reign of the strong and diplomatic Augustus ended. It had lasted for forty-four years.

Among the rulers who followed Augustus there were some men of talent and wisdom. There were other monarchs who were base men or fools. The life of Tiberius, suspicious stepson of Augustus, whom Edward Gibbon called "dark and unrelenting," was a long misery. He could not have known that the most important event of his reign was the killing of Jesus of Nazareth. Most of the immediate successors of Tiberius were weak or vicious or both.

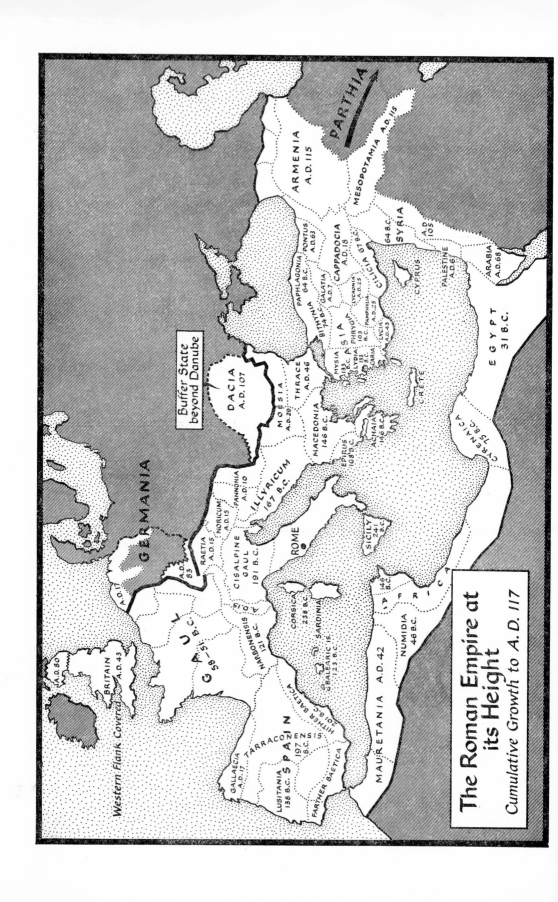

The Roman Empire at its Height

Cumulative Growth to A.D. 117

Caligula was really an untamed freak and a madman—he bestowed a consul-ship upon his horse. He was murdered by his guards. Perhaps the best that can be said of the crippled Claudius is that he performed no dark deeds of crime. He was poisoned. The profligate monster Nero murdered recklessly until the senate declared him a public enemy. Alone and despised, Nero killed himself. It is said that he exclaimed with the death rattle in his throat: "What an artist dies in me!"

After the death of Nero in 68 A.D. there were four rival emperors and a wounding year of violence and anarchy. Then came the Flavian period (69–96 A.D.) and long battles between the emperors and the senators. After Ves-pasian, Titus, and Domitian came the Antonines or "the Good Emperors" (96–180 A.D.): Nerva, Trajan, Hadrian, Antoninus Pius, and the Stoic "philosopher-king" Marcus Aurelius. The names and deeds of such monarchs stood proudly along the road to imperial wealth and glory.

With the coming of the capricious Commodus the happy age ended ab-ruptly. "Commodus attained the summit of vice and infamy." He was strangled by a young wrestler in the night. Then came Pertinax. His formidable guards murdered him. His successor was the worthless Julian, who had bought and bribed his way to the throne. A revolt pulled him down after sixty-six days. He was beheaded in the baths of the palace and the general Severus became the new emperor. Meanwhile, as usual, the lions roared and desperate gladiators fell and died before excited Romans in the forum.

It would be tedious to record at length the disasters and crimes in the gray decades after the death of Marcus Aurelius. During a period of about fifty years in the third century there were thirty emperors, more or less. The "eternal empire" was slowly crumbling and nobody was aware of it. The symptoms and causes were unknown and unperceived.

During all these years the bounds of the empire steadily expanded. Soon no power could challenge the might of Rome. In our modern museums we can see and handle the swords and shields of the tough and bronzed soldiers who set their hard-thonged feet down strongly as they marched the roads of the world.

With their weapons and skills the Roman legions conquered long miles and vast acres from the Rhine and the Danube and Hadrian's Wall in Scotland to the Sahara Desert, from the Atlantic Ocean to the Tigris and the Euphrates. Edward Gibbon rightly remarked that the Roman Empire at its height in-cluded "the fairest part of the earth and the most civilized portion of man-kind."

One of Rome's great achievements was the Roman peace, the *Pax Romana*. Roman civilization and Roman trade were everywhere protected by the watch-ful and efficient soldiers when the empire was at its height. Roman rule meant almost universal law, order, and peace. Throughout all the empire there was the Roman culture, the Roman institutions, the Latin language. Far frontiers were guarded by the legions. "The terror of the Roman arms added weight and dignity to the moderation of the Emperors. They preserved peace by a constant preparation for war." *Si vis pacem para bellum.* To the 75,000,000 people with an empire about the size of the United States the rule of Rome over all classes and masses meant peace, security, order, and stability.

> *tu regere imperio populos, Romane, memento;*
> *hae tibi erunt artes—pacisque imponere morem,*
> *parcere subjectis, et debellare superbos.*

Several achievements of the Roman civilization have stood the critical challenges of time. These were in the fields of government, law, and engineering. So far as government was concerned, the Romans wisely permitted the peoples within the empire to develop their lives in their own ways. Rome never tried to impose uniformity upon her subjects. Nevertheless, in all the Roman provinces there was established a solid system of government control and administration and an elaborate and admirable system of law. The Roman law has heavily influenced several modern legal systems, such as those of France, Spain, Italy, and the Latin American countries. The Romans are still famous, and rightly, as masters of the arts of law and administration.

The machinery of government varied in different parts of the empire. There were two classes of provinces, the one group controlled by the senate, the other by the emperor. Britain, for instance, was one of the latter class, an imperial province ruled by a governor who was the legate, or representative, of the emperor. This official, like all imperial governors, normally held his post for a term of not less than three years, and not more than five. He was responsible for civil administration and commander-in-chief of the military forces of the province.

Whenever we pause to consider a few details of Roman administration we should remember that behind the tables of organization lies one salient fact: the Mediterranean world believed that man's spiritual needs could be satisfied only by the town. "The town was at once the symptom and the symbol of all that was highest and most precious in human life, all that raises man above the beasts of the field." Because this was held to be so, the Romans tried to supply many places—such as Roman Britain—with towns as centers of Roman culture.

These urban units were sometimes large and sometimes small. Most of the settled areas had regular chessboard street plans, a forum, a market square surrounded on three sides by shops and flanked on the fourth by a town hall. There were public baths and temples. The townspeople usually came to speak Latin and to live in a Roman way.

Out in the country the inhabitants lived in villages or in country houses called villas. These villas were of various sizes. Some of the most magnificent had mosaics, frescoes, hot-air furnaces. Most had bathrooms, courtyards, and rectangular-walled farmyards in which stood barns, stables, and quarters for the workers. Beyond were the large open fields of the owners' estates. In Britain more than 500 villas have been located, mostly in the southeast low-land zone. Much of the power of Roman civilization outside of the cities was in the villas of the great landlords. The ruins of the villas, like the remains of the solid, earth-clinging temples, the coliseums, and the baths, stand as symbols of the strength and grandeur that once belonged to Imperial Rome.

Throughout the empire the Roman engineering skill built forts and roads and walls to be used and to endure. Consider, for example, what was done in Britain. First came the soldiers and then came the engineers. In 43 A.D. the Emperor Claudius gathered about 40,000 men and invaded the island. Slowly Roman authority and power advanced in the face of obstinate resistance and bloody rebellion. A network of military highways was constructed. The main arterial roads were twenty to twenty-five feet wide, usually graveled and kept open to traffic all the year round. There spread over Britain a great gridiron of communications between towns and camps and guardian fortresses. In all the empire the amazing system of radial roads, dotted by forts and legion garrisons, was a major key to the success of the Roman military conquest and government. "All roads," as the saying is, "lead to Rome."

Agricola, famous soldier and father-in-law of Tacitus, was governor of Britain from 78 to 85 A.D. He conquered Wales and thrust north of the Clyde. When the legions lost their grasp on Caledonia the Emperor Hadrian, anxious to keep the barbarians out, began to build a wall across the island from the Tyne to the Solway. It was finished about 127 A.D. This wall—one of the two great stone and mortar barriers in the north—was a continuous rampart ten Roman feet thick and twenty feet high, protected by a ditch thirty feet wide and garrisoned by troops housed in forts along its line. To dig the ditch it was necessary to move about 2,000,000 cubic yards of soil, subsoil, and rock. The wall itself contained more than 2,000,000 cubic yards of material. Often the stones had to be carried from distant quarries. It was a tremendous achievement, typical of the Romans.

In these days of wealth and pomp and pride the streams of trade grew deep and long. By land and sea the traders moved their gold and silver, their tin and their amber, their ivory, hides, Spanish fish sauce, wool, carpets, spices, perfumes, olive oil, and glazed pottery from Gaul. Great aqueducts carried water across the valleys. Bridges spanned the rivers and the gorges.

The Romans were hardheaded and practical. They were builders, not theorists. "The best men," said their own Sallust, "preferred doing to talking." They were not interested in the abstract speculations of the Greeks.

There was little advance in philosophy, none in mathematics. The Romans' borrowed some of the science of the Greeks but they added little to it. They wanted efficiency, action, and solid results. It was no accident that Julius Caesar brought an Egyptian calendar into Rome; that was the action of a practical man. Meanwhile his fellow Romans continued to trade and conquer, introduced soap, built military machines like slings and battering rams, and collected the taxes and tributes of empire.

It is true that many Romans admired and tried to imitate the genius of the Greeks. It is also true that Roman eagerness to follow in the paths of Greek culture made possible the extension into a later world of the knowledge, the ideas, and the spirit of ancient Hellas. The famous words of the Latin poet Horace are often quoted to illustrate the waves of influence that came from Athens to Rome: "Greece, taken captive, took captive her rough conqueror and brought her arts to rustic Latium."

By the side of these facts there are others. The Greek influence in the Roman Empire was less than has sometimes been asserted and assumed. Copies of Greek statues and plays were seldom successful. The architects of Rome, despite their solid achievements, built nothing that could compare with the Parthenon. When the Romans tried to borrow and to imitate they were often not quite sure what it was that they were doing. It seems that they were sometimes more successful in imitating Greek vices than Greek virtues. They could not understand the Greek spirit or the Greek view of the world and the universe. The thoughts, tastes, and tempers of the Greeks and the Romans were wholly different.

Some Romans became alarmed at the shiploads of Greek immigrants, the power of Greek teachers, the spread of Greek habits and ideas, and certain vices that were said to be peculiar to the Greeks. They feared that the alien culture might make Rome soft and weak. Rome did, of course, become soft and weak in later days; but for that the culture of Greece could not be held responsible.

Of all the arts of Rome those in the field of literature were certainly the most triumphant. Paper monuments are sometimes more enduring than bronze or brass or stone.

The growth of Latin prose and poetry was both rapid and healthy. It began and continued with the imitation of Greek models. Terence copied Menander. Lucretius acknowledged Empedocles as his master. Horace turned to Alcaeus and Sappho. Virgil wrote his *Eclogues* in admitted imitation of the pastoral poet Theocritus; in his *Georgics* he imitated Hesiod; in his *Aeneid,* Homer. The accepted standards of literary excellence required Greek models. Native vigor and inspiration were not enough.

Although the leading Latin poets imitated the Greek masters, they did much more. They wrote great poetry in their own right. The Greek models provided controls and criteria. The Roman poets supplied the material and often a genius of their own.

The later period of the republic and the early years of the empire (50 B.C.– 116 A.D.) are usually called the "Augustan Age" or the "Golden Age" of Latin literature. The poets were numerous but they were not all distinguished. Among those whose names and works were worthy of survival was Catullus (85–54 B.C.), a fresh and vigorous lyrical poet who wrote his graceful and famous songs on many subjects—from sparrows to wedding feasts. In the same century Lucretius (96–55 B.C.) merged philosophy and poetry in his brilliant and long *On the Nature of Things*. He sought to find both beauty and hope in a universe he believed was indifferent to the dreams of men. The manly Horace (65–8 B.C.) is justly famous for the themes and technical skill of his *Odes* and *Satires* and his insistence upon moderation, integrity, and the rural virtues that he believed had made Rome great. Here the master of the Latin hexameter taught his world and ours something of the beauty and melody that can be created by a sensitive weaver of words. The mind, the spirit, and the pen meet in one.

The inspired poet Virgil was born at Mantua in 70 B.C., five years before Horace and seven before Augustus. He was buried at Naples in 13 B.C. Master indeed of the "ocean-roll of rhythm," Virgil was also a patriot who loved his country "far brought from out the storied past." His pride in his homeland lives in many a majestic line. The mighty fabric of the twelve books of his *Aeneid* told the tale of Rome in noble and rhetorical poetry. Here were mingled the toils and trials of Aeneas, the wars and adventures of an ancient world, the insistence upon the virtue, the greatness, and the historic mission of the Roman people. In the sixth book of the *Aeneid*, Virgil removes all doubt, if doubt there ever was, that he is worthy to walk in glory through the avenues of history with the greatest of the epic poets. Like Homer and Dante and Milton, Virgil wrote a masterpiece.

The prose of the lawyer and consul Cicero (106–43 B.C.), the last prophet of the Roman republic, has been studied and admired for nearly twenty centuries. We have parts of about seventy of his famous orations, nearly a thousand of his letters, and several of his essays. In the *Republic* and the *Laws*, Cicero states and explains his ideas about the ideal society of man. His style is perhaps best seen in his fiery speech attacking Catiline and in his essays on friendship and old age. His sentences are carefully shaped and sometimes skillfully decorated. They are always vigorous, terse, swift, balanced, clear. Cicero had something to say and he said it. His prose was never careless, never slipshod, arrogant, foggy. He thought that language should really be a means of communication. He never forgot his hearers. Because he did make himself understood, his books and speeches are read as well as praised. The spirit of ancient humanism is at its best in Virgil and Cicero.

In the "Golden Age" and the later "Silver Age" there were many other poets and prose writers of ability and consequence. Ovid, for instance (43 B.C.–17 A.D.), wrote much about pleasure and little about morality. The *Satires* of the embittered Juvenal (60–140 A.D.) are quoted still. Sallust (86–34 B.C.) wrote his history of Catiline's conspiracy, the Jugurthine War, and other events. Livy was born in Padua in 59 B.C., and he died there in 17 A.D. His long history of Rome has not all survived. The parts we do possess show that Livy was a fine reporter of both fact and fancy. He wrote as a Roman, always conscious of the greatness of his city. The *Annals, History,* and *Germania* of Tacitus (54–116 A.D.) are often written with both brilliance and passion. Tacitus, as remarked earlier in these pages, was prejudiced and pessimistic. All his writings show it.

The *Thoughts of Marcus Aurelius,* written by the last of the "Good Emperors," is one of the world's classics. It is a wise and sad book, a superb statement of the Stoic view of the universe and the men born to live out their uncertain days in it. "The duration of human life is momentary, its substance in perpetual flux, its senses dim, its physical organism perishable, its consciousness a vortex, its destiny dark, its repute uncertain. What can see us through? One thing and one thing only—philosophy—and that means keeping the spirit within us unspoiled and undishonored . . . and taking what comes contentedly as part of the process to which we owe our own being." The philosopher-emperor Marcus Aurelius also said this to his fellows and to us: "Up and down, to and fro, round and round: this is the monotonous and meaningless rhythm of the universe. A man of average intelligence who has reached the age of forty years has seen all that has been and shall be."

A long list of names and capsule comments often make tedious reading. The most significant conclusions about the Latin writers of the classical age may be swiftly stated. In the first place, many of them could and did write well. Secondly, they formalized their style and language. Thirdly, they were mainly concerned with mankind and nature in the abstract. Finally, their prose and poetry reflected very fully the tastes and values of an era that seemed secure, prosperous, and stable. They usually avoided extremes of fervor and emotion. They deplored excesses of any kind. Again and again they insisted upon the virtues of moderation and the importance of the golden mean. Drawing upon the teachings of Epicurus and the Stoics, they exalted and stressed the importance of the laws of nature's harmony, rational balance, and a steady self-control before the blows of adverse circumstance and the careless fates.

In the last years of the empire there emerged many tremendous and cancerous changes in its strength, composition, and outlook. "A bow long bent at last waxeth weak." Immoral and impractical slips and blunders, the falling away of courage and spiritual force, marked a decline that followed slowly upon centuries of power and triumph. The hard-pressed empire split and dwindled and dissolved in smoke and blood. Her enemies growled and snapped and overwhelmed all in a common devastation. We turn now to the tale of those dark years.

Chapter 10

THE GREAT COLLAPSE

"It was at Rome, on the 15th of October, 1764, as I sat musing amidst
the ruins of the Capitol, while the barefooted friars were singing vespers
in the temple of Jupiter, that the idea of writing the decline and fall of
the city first started to my mind."

—Edward Gibbon, *Autobiography*

IN THE long tides of history individuals and civilizations have flourished
and fallen in apparent cycles of perplexing variation. The seeming patterns
of birth, growth, and breakdown in cultures, states, and religions have long
fascinated professional and amateur historians and prophets. Research, both
deep and shallow, has brought forth much speculation and theories beyond
numbering. In the past and present many men have become convinced that
they can discern certain rhythms, curves, and immutable laws controlling the
destinies of civilizations.

Christian historians have often seen history as an act of God beginning
at the creation and destined to end at the Last Judgment. At first the Israelites
said that Jehovah had selected them as instruments to carry out His purposes.
Then the Christian Church, the Moslems, and many others claimed that they
were the "chosen people." Still later, Western nation-states made similar assertions, not leaving room for India or China, Buddha or Confucius. Men
of the eighteenth-century Enlightenment believed in linear progress towards
a Heavenly City on this earth. "Every age of the world," wrote Edward
Gibbon in 1787, "has increased, and still increases, the real wealth, the happiness, the knowledge, and perhaps the virtue, of the Human Race." The
Golden Age, said the eighteenth century, was no longer in the past. It stood
over the horizons in the vast tomorrow.

The nineteenth century brought a widening belief in the inevitability of
Progress, the shining assurances of future worlds striving to be born. Surely
unimpeded achievement was the destiny of man. Somehow good would be
the final goal of all. The whole creation, it seemed, was moving towards "some
far-off, divine event." The earth declared the glories of evolution and rejoiced

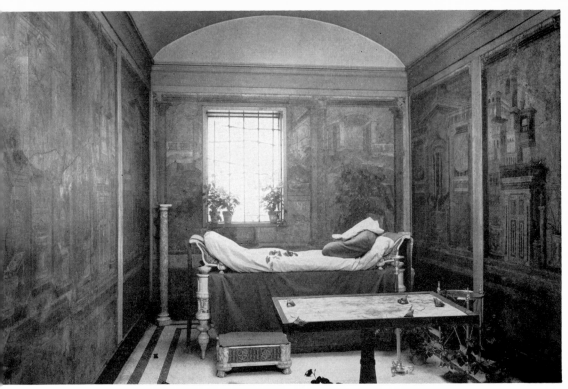

[32] Roman paintings (Pompeian) on the walls of a villa (1st century B.C.)

[33]

PLATE
IX

Battle between Romans and Germans. Detail from the Column of Marcus Aurelius, Rome

[34]

[35]

Above: An example of early Christian art from the catacomb of St. Calixtus on the Appian Way, Rome

Left: The Visitation, from a panel of the altar of Duke Ratchis in Cividale del Friuli, Italy (8th century)

[36]

PLATE X

Maison Carrée, a Gallo-Roman temple built in Nîmes about 16 B.C. and used successively as a church, consular office, and museum

in the handiwork of man while paeans of praise to Progress swirled over the seas and the everlasting hills.

In human affairs there are always those who wonder and doubt or who proclaim answers different from those their fellows find. Oswald Spengler, for instance, would have no truck with Progress. He insisted that the decline of the West was inevitable. His logic was usually excellent; his premises were not. The Marxian determinists reiterated their dogmatic assertion that the state would wither away and the relentless power of the proletariat would bring a classless society among all men. The numerous and varied conclusions about the course and curves of history contained one common idea: mankind was controlled by cycles and laws that moved inexorably upon their charted ways. No matter what human beings might do, they could not evade or avoid their determined destiny. The cosmos had no room for displaced persons or civilizations. Some would even have said that it was inevitable that there should be laws and theories of inevitability. Historians gave their pens to a cause that was both new and old. Theologians and philosophers did important work—they often do, because they ask the most important questions.

In recent years Professor Arnold J. Toynbee, famous historian and mystic, has also sought an ultimate pattern of history, a pattern holy, absolute, and unconditional. In the latter part of his *A Study of History,* in addition to maintaining his theme of "challenge and response," Professor Toynbee has stressed the religious interpretation of human life. In the future, he believes, what matters most to the world is what will emerge from the spiritual encounter of the planet's four great religions: Christianity, Islam, Hinduism, and Buddhism. Toynbee sees, in the words of Professor Frank Underhill, that "man's main purpose of existence is to discover man's relation to God; the higher religions carry us further on this path than do the secular civilizations." The "hardening of the categories" in Professor Toynbee's panoramic view of history has repelled some historians. On the other hand, all respect and admire his massive erudition. Some also praise the long ribbons of his periodic sentences and the luxuriant power of his prose. "Metaphors dead for many centuries are revived by his impartial trust, and go slowly by, their draperies billowing in the wind of Time. For as you read *A Study of History* the air of all the earth, of all the ages, is circulating around you."

Intelligent men must respect the brave attempts of learned and wondering scholars to emancipate us from local and Western points of view and to break through the traditional partitions of specialized parochial and national studies. Any carefully considered synoptic generalizations provide far-reaching challenges to all thinking men. Such challenges to the mind and spirit are desperately needed at a time when distance is being annihilated and equations of power swiftly change. For men who dwell on the boundaries of the present and the future the answers of yesterday cannot be enough. All men thinking in the new world of the twentieth century must become adjusted to the fact that the promises of tomorrow are for those who take them.

What is true in our times of troubles and hopes today was also true when the Roman Empire shook and fell. The old worlds were gone, shattered beyond recovery or repair. The strong men with their swords can always destroy; but often they cannot build; they cannot command the broken bones to knit again.

The men who survived when the rivers of civilization seemed to be running dry did not have the advantage of knowing that they were in one of the troughs or cycles of civilization. The so-called laws of history may bring but thin sips of comfort when a man is cold and a child is hungry. The warmth of a historian's study is one thing; blood on the stones of the street is another.

Between the years 180 and 193 were the reigns of Commodus, Pertinax, and Julian. As we have seen, they were short and bloody. Septimius Severus, a native African who commanded the Roman forces along the Danube, became emperor in 193 by the grace of good fortune and the support of the soldiers he led. Severus was a career army man, and to him the interests of the army came first. All the soldiers were given high pay and new privileges. The senate, the civil authority in the state, was thrust into the background. Many rights of the senators were taken away and handed over to officers of the army. Severus even confiscated some of the property of certain senators—and of businessmen, too—to keep his supporting soldiers bribed and happy. When Severus died up at England's York in 211 he had done much to build a machine of corrupt military despotism, an octopus of army bureaucracy. The old constitution was being torn up by the new army. "The army became the chattel of the soldiers."

Professor M. I. Rostovtzeff has shown that the foundations of urban civilization were destroyed by Severus and his associates. This grim African plundered towns by taxation to strengthen the army. Perhaps the underprivileged and envious peasantry assisted in the new policy. In any event, the wealth of the urban aristocracy was dissipated. As the third century passed along many people departed from the decaying cities. The ones that remained usually put up walls, a symbol of fearful hearts within. City life, upon which the process of provincial Romanization was so dependent, slowly became drained of the radiating energy it once possessed. The life blood was seeping away. More and more men refused to accept offices in the city governments. This fact, in itself apparently trivial, was a very important fact indeed because it tells a great deal about the failure of the cities to hold the allegiance of men whose support counted. The cities depended upon such men; the empire depended upon cities that were healthy and strong.

There were other tragic forces of decay that can now be seen when we look back at the changes in the economic structure of the empire. These were years of strain and anxiety, filled with ominous symptoms. During the height of her imperial power it was clear that Rome was superior to all her provinces in the techniques of production and commerce. But slowly Rome taught various parts of her skills to her subject peoples—and their natural resources were greater than hers. At the same time, Rome's labor forces, spoiled by the dole of "bread and circuses," were content to loll and loaf. The capitalist class of Imperial Rome put less and less money into productive power and more and more into luxuries of various kinds. The Romans brought luxury goods from Asia and they had few goods of their own to exchange. So more and more Roman gold flowed to Asia. This was a major reason why the Roman Empire was plagued by currency depreciation, rising prices, higher taxes.

Thus the real economic power of Rome was withering away. Without transfusions of capital and energy there could be no hope of recuperation. To a greater and greater extent the provinces were sustaining Italy. "These . . . deadly Romans . . . behold with the same passion of avarice both wealth and want. To plunder, butcher, steal, these things they misname empire; they make a solitude and they call it peace."

The Roman politicians and statesmen became more interested in booty, spoils, and plunder and more softened by the enticing baths of Capua. They wasted the material and human resources of the mines, forests, farms, and labor. They let the body economic grow weak. They failed to see that safety lay only in productive enterprise and managerial efficiency. Vitality and salvation are the same thing in the world of business, empires, and republics. Without vision and purposeful vitality a people perishes or a business goes down.

Severus was succeeded by his sons Caracalla and Geta. Caracalla, who fancied himself a brilliant army leader, murdered his brother and several others who opposed him. He gave Roman citizenship to almost every free citizen in the empire, thus really wiping out the distinction between Italy and the provinces. When Caracalla was finally assassinated—he was completely insane by that time—there followed the more than fifty years of flaming civil war and anarchy mentioned in the previous chapter. Only two of about thirty emperors died a natural death. The authority of the central government, assailed on every hand, grew steadily more feeble. Undisciplined and riotous legions plundered and killed almost at will. Production continued to fall off. Population declined and the birth rate went down. Farms were often abandoned. Thousands of yeomen farmers were steadily slipping into the ranks of the unfree or the semifree class of tenants, the *coloni*. Meanwhile, great landlords often hired alien tribesmen who had entered the empire. These men, especially from the Germanic regions, arrived at such a rapid rate that they could not be effectively absorbed. Back in the first century Juvenal had seen danger in the large number of men of alien stock and character coming into Rome. "The Orontes," he said, "has flowed into the Tiber." Juvenal was alarmed. He had cause to be.

Many taxes, steadily increased because the government had to meet its mounting expenses, could not be collected. Several people simply could not pay. Others refused because they thought that they could defy the palsied power of the state and suffer no punishment. The hand of the government was far less sure and heavy than it once had been. Trade was increasingly disrupted and the monetary system went out of control. Inflation spiraled costs and prices upward as real incomes went down. The value of some coins, especially as the central government began to debase them, fell to 2 per cent of par. Several cities and provinces began to issue their own coins. The masses of the people were being steadily impoverished. In the upper levels of society it seemed that everybody tried to grab more and more as less became available. The Roman traditions and the feeling for Rome's past were being slowly eroded and swept away. "The state offered careers, but had ceased to speak to the soul." This is one reason, incidentally, for the rise of numerous and exciting religious cults in the last days of Roman rule.

By the third century the number of small farms had decreased in almost all parts of the empire. The small farmers were running away from overtaxed land. The movement towards the concentration of large blocks of territory in the hands of big landowners, already evident in the days of the Gracchi, had continued without effective hindrance. A small monopolistic group of aristocrats held vast regions under their control. Often they raised only small crops. Large crops meant more work, more income, and more taxes. As food supplies went down the starvation levels went up. Much land went out of cultivation. What did stay in cultivation was more heavily taxed. Unwise governments have often taxed away initiative. The mainstay of any state must be the individuals who together give it being.

Such were some of the deadly trends that indicated basic weaknesses and internal softness in the empire. Civil wars, economic decline, immorality, thoughtless luxury, governmental ineptitude, widespread dismay and apathy took their inevitable toll. People who live with a sense of impending calamity are not apt to hold empires together.

Meanwhile terrorizing disturbances multiplied in these grim days in the tottering empire: in Gaul, Italy, Sicily, North Africa, Asia Minor. By 235 brigands roamed almost at will in Italy. Gusts of civil war and mindless panic leaped across North Africa in 238. In the same year the farmers in Gaul assaulted several cities and in 239 the slaves in Sicily rebelled. After 270 the armies coming back from the Near East brought a plague with them. Thousands died but the government took no steps to halt the fearful disease. Their failure to act was a symptom of their bankrupt age. Within and without the government men were making careers out of crime and deceit. The dictates of law and morality yielded before naked power and subterranean evasion. When moral dignity goes, not much is left worth measuring.

The philosopher Plotinus, the founder of Neo-Platonism, stated in dramatic language his personal view of the reasons for disaster: "The philosophers tried to show the world sound ways of government. But the barbarians, within and without, would not listen. To the barbarians, accordingly, we sadly abandoned the world."

In 284 Diocletian became emperor (he was born in 245) and took upon himself at once all the power of undisguised absolutism. Surrounded by Oriental pomp and magnificence, Diocletian was declared to be a divine ruler. His pagan subjects worshiped him as their god-king, their Sun God. Most of the rights and duties of the subordinate senate were taken away. Until his abdication and retirement in 305 Diocletian remained an autocratic monarch. He was as absolute a ruler as a man could be whose administration was crumbling and whose effective controls were daily more diminished. He believed that the only hope for the recovery of the empire lay in the concentration of power in his hands. The steps he took were often steps of skill.

In order to bolster and stabilize the cracking unity of the empire Diocletian tried to destroy the mounting power of the provincial governors, those men who were often prepared to risk revolt if they thought their own ambitions could be served. As a first step towards the stopping of the grasping and grabbing and factional strife Diocletian declared all the provinces equal to Italy. Then he created numerous political subdivisions so that the strength of the provincial governors, so potentially dangerous, was whittled away. These small units were also useful for tax-administration purposes. Meanwhile Diocletian tried to stop the governors from commanding and using the Roman legions as provincial militiamen. He created and maintained an imperial field army, a trouble-shooting body heavy in cavalry units that could move swiftly to check disturbance. He set up a large secret service. Spies and counterspies were everywhere. In a strenuous effort to ease economic pressures Diocletian tried to control and fix prices. Despite all his efforts he failed. All past and present attempts to hold price lines have been successful when, and only when, there has been efficiency at the operating levels, when officials have moved to enforce the laws and rules upon all individuals regardless of their status or the persuasions of their bribery and their blackmail. Legislation and decrees cannot do the job alone. To them must be added effective control. Diocletian could never get that control because of the nature of the corrupt and lazy bureaucracy in his empire. Nor did punishments and dismissals purge the evils away. When some men were sent out one door others of similar character came in by another.

Diocletian thought that the administration of the empire could be made more effective if there was a division of responsibility and a new precision in the chain of command. He therefore selected his general Maximian to be co-emperor, or co-Augustus, and to administer the western part of the empire —the capital of the western area was shifted from Rome to Milan. Diocletian took the eastern half. Later two subordinate "Caesars" were appointed and the unwieldy empire was divided into four parts or prefectures: Gaul and Britain; Italy, Spain, and Africa; the Danubian provinces and the Balkans; the eastern provinces. There were subdivisions called dioceses and below these were the provinces, of which there were now 101 instead of the earlier 45. Diocletian, of course, continued to be the supreme ruler.

By his new arrangements Diocletian hoped to avoid struggles about the succession. He planned to retire with Maximian in 305. He hoped that then the "Caesars" would become co-emperors. New "Caesars" would be appointed, and hence a quiet and orderly succession would be maintained and assured.

It was not to be. When Diocletian retired to Salona in 305 there came once more a period of murky plots, murder, and war. After five years Constantine emerged as another autocratic emperor. He kept many of the political reforms of Diocletian and others he abandoned. There is no need to describe the details here. It is enough to say that the work of reconstruction of Diocletian and Constantine did not and could not insure a successful government and the security of the empire. Spontaneity, energy, and imagination had been sapped away. Of initiative there was little. As the clamps of control and coercion became tighter and tighter the result was often a robot uniformity, the fatal leveling into a prairie of apathy or despair.

After Constantine died in 337 the years from the fourth to the sixth century were harsh and bleak. The vital centers of the empire continued to be threatened by the slow gangrene of decadence and stagnation, by malaria, by the trembling palsy that always exists when nerve and motor controls falter and fail. To the weakness of the body within there were added the dangers from the gnawing and biting of voracious enemies without. The overextended Roman Empire, once so robust, could not cope with the steady attacks from the Teutonic tribes in the barbaric northlands.

The Teutonic tribesmen of the Danube and the Rhine were assaulted heavily by the Asiatic Huns. These dreaded saddle nomads from the East, ugly and merciless, were not really stopped in their advance until the Romans united with the Goths to repel and defeat Attila in the fifth century at Châlons in the Marne valley. Faced by the Huns, by hungry demands resulting from their own population increase, it was inevitable that the Teutonic tribesmen were tempted by the fertile lands of the empire. The Goths, the Vandals, and the Huns—hunters and fighters all—began to press relentlessly against the bastions of the frontiers. Those defenses, strained and cracked beyond endurance, were broken and shattered at last. The waves of invaders rolled and rushed towards the final citadels.

The Burgundians moved into southern and southeastern France. The rich valley of the Rhone, for instance, was a place of wonder and delight. The Franks spread westward to set up their kingdom in northern Gaul. The Lombards swirled down from the Danube out of the Germanic lands to settle in the Po valley regions—this happened later, in the sixth century. The Jutes, Angles, and Saxons invaded Britain. The Visigoths headed towards Rome itself. In 378 their mailed cavalry defeated a Roman army and killed the Emperor Valens at Adrianople. In 410, led by the sturdy Alaric, they sacked Rome. Then they went to southern Gaul, then to Spain. The Vandals, who were really savages, stormed into Gaul and exploded into Spain. Then they burst into North Africa, where they built a formidable pirate state and a strong navy. In 455 they came back to hammer and plunder Rome. They were but faintly tinctured with the ideas and ideals of what we would call civilization. Meanwhile the Persians invaded Armenia and Mesopotamia and the Berbers killed and plundered in North Africa.

Amidst the developing calamities the murmuring legions were withdrawn from the outposts of empire, one by one. Often the soldiers and commanders of these and other legions were not to be trusted, so filled were they with aliens who knew not the traditions of Rome. By the fourth century most of the legions were mainly composed of Germans. The Italians, who packed the legions in the old days, were seldom to be seen in the ranks of the mobile forces or the garrisons any more. By Constantine's day the total strength of the Roman army was no more than 650,000. Of these about 400,000 were spread thinly in garrisons along the long frontiers. Meanwhile the fifth columnists were all about the Roman world. There was infiltration as well as flank and frontal assault.

In the wake of the withdrawal of the legions the fearful scuttled to what they hoped was safety. "The barbarians drive us to the sea. The sea drives us back to the barbarians. We are either slaughtered or drowned." The unchronicled catastrophes we can never know. The mists and mysteries of oblivion stretch far and deep.

The proud and restless Roman conquerors would forge no new provinces. Slowly and irrevocably the Roman Empire flickered in the twilight to its death. The black and red chaos that came with the collapse of Western civilization was almost an aftermath and an anticlimax. In Gaul and Britain, for instance, there is unassailable evidence that many men did not suspect that the final hour was at hand, even in a world where the alarms became each year more insistent.

The Roman Empire in the West was soon at an end. It was astounding that it had achieved so much and had lasted so long. The Eastern Roman

Empire, on the other hand, did not collapse. In Constantinople, that fine city founded around 600 B.C. by the Dorian Greeks and defended by nature and by art, the rulers of the Eastern Empire maintained their power. Constantine, who chose and renamed his great capital, was after all a Balkan man who saw the strategic and political importance of a place like Constantinople near the frontiers of Asia and Europe. These men of the Eastern Empire sheltered religion. They kept and transmitted to later centuries much of the civilization and culture that once had flourished in the vast lands ruled from the city of the seven hills. For a thousand years after Rome fell, the Eastern Empire and the civilization of Byzantium stood inviolate on the edges of the worlds of the East and West.

One fact should be stressed. The end of Rome's control of the world to the west of the approaches to Asia was but a single aspect of the retreat and decline of all ancient civilization in the West: cultural, economic, political, social, military, moral. There was not one cause, or ten, for "the fall of the Roman Empire." There were many complex and interrelated forces the total nature and impact of which we can never know.

It is well to remark that the Romans were singularly lacking in inventive skills and imagination. Their technological achievements were few. Even in war the Roman advantage was discipline, not technology or tactics—military historians will tell us how often their tactics were wrong.

Probably a good case could be made for the argument that the Romans failed in the end because they lacked imagination; they were unable to adapt themselves to forces that they could not control; they had too few "original" minds in their midst; they had gone as far as they could go, and what Professor Arnold Toynbee has called "the nemesis of the perfected technique" helped to destroy them.

When all the volumes about the decline of Rome have been written and read, when many questions have been asked and answered by the mightiest of scholars, there will still remain some problems about the strange shriveling of the spirits of men, about the alarming stillness of the once throbbing arteries in those unhappy days. Neither Marx nor Freud nor any of the most learned professors of history have a full answer. It is not to be expected that they should have complete and final replies to riddles and enigmas that often have most to do, after all, with imponderables. Description is much less difficult than explanation. Let us never confuse symptoms with causes. A recent scholar, at the end of a wise volume, summed up much in a single sentence: "Rome never fell; she turned into something else."

Conclusions like these sometimes dismay and annoy human beings who like to find neatness and order and the magic wand of finality in the answers of the experts. Be not deceived. There are few explanations of men about themselves and the cosmos that are absolutely fixed and final. Knowledge advances. Judgments change. By slow degrees the vast emptiness of error and ignorance is being reduced by the indefeasible desire of some men to rescue the truth from obscurity. Let us not—in our human pride and power —ever think that we are further along the road to knowledge than in fact we are. The signs and the mileposts can be read by humble, shrewd, and cautious men. The others, certain of too much, rush along where it is not wise to tread. They have no time to pause. In the silence they can sometimes be heard shouting in premature triumph and then clattering down to disaster and oblivion.

Chapter 11

THE CROSS
AND THE CRESCENT

"He said not: 'Thou shalt not be tempested, thou shalt not be travailed, thou shalt not be afflicted.' But He said: 'Thou shalt not be overcome.'"
—*The Book of the Lady Julian of Norwich*

"There is no piety in turning your face towards the east or west but he is pious who believeth in God, and the last day, and the angels, and the Scriptures, and the prophets; who for the love of God disburseth his wealth to his kindred, and the orphans, and the needy, and the wayfarer. . . ."
—The Koran, Sura 2:V. 172

THE creeds that have claimed the allegiance of men through the centuries have radiated their power from strange places and in numerous ways. In the dark backward of time primitive man worshiped many gods and godlings. Sometimes he turned to the Unknown God that he knew must be there. Why he insisted upon the existence of such a Being some modern psychologists, prowling and probing in the mountains and muskegs of man's inner being, have not been able to say. They have, in their opinion, sometimes explained; but they have not answered.

In every age, the spiritual assurances of revelation and reason have mingled in conflict, swirling in dark pools and fed by distant fountainheads. With prodigal energy men have raced swiftly to find the Heavenly City, so often bolted and barred against them. In one place, the shriveled ascetic has sought salvation by shuddering in penance under countless flagellations. In another, the mystic has reached out and met his Maker in the existential moment. He has stood with Mystery. A third man has used his human reason and the power of logic to bring him to the gates of understanding. "The game of getting the right answer is a hard game," says Professor Percy Williams Bridgman in *Reflections of a Physicist*. A hard game it is. A fourth man has insisted that human beings are but clots of vivified dust, akin to the brutes and the stars. A fifth is content to be like a mollusc or a polyp, to be quite apathetic, satisfied to sleep and make a mistake as long as eternity. And a sixth, in untroubled faith, simply knows that he is a child of God. Undisturbed by fears of the interstellar dark, he trusts that he will never be confounded.

In all ages, too, there have been those who have sought to pursue and demolish the men they have believed to be wicked. Many have claimed the guidance and dictation of an "inner light." They have nursed their own convictions and identified them with the will of the Almighty. Men who did not believe as they did were by them damned, drawn and quartered, or dragged flinching beneath the poised blade of the guillotine. We have not always been our brothers' keepers. Toleration has come but slowly in the history of man, and sometimes it stays not long.

Jesus Christ was born in Bethlehem in the Roman province of Judea. He said: "Thou shalt love the Lord thy God with all thy heart and with all thy soul and with all thy mind." He also said: "Thou shalt love thy neighbor as thyself." In the Holy Land He told all men that they were the children of God and that whoever believed in Him would never die. "I am the Way, the Truth, and the Life."

The New Testament contains the story of Christ and His disciples, those men who served the Lord with gladness and did not fear the power of any adversaries. Peter, of course, almost stumbled and fell. Judas did.

The chapters of the New Testament are also filled with passages that have entered into the beings of every man and woman who has shared in the Christian heritage. There is the pulsing power of the Sermon on the Mount and the tale of the Good Samaritan. There are the tiny flashes, too, like the picture of Zacchaeus, that curious little fellow who ran ahead of Jesus and climbed up into a sycamore tree to see Him. St. Luke does not say that Zacchaeus lounged, stumbled, tottered, or strolled to see Jesus. Zacchaeus ran.

Christ was crucified on Calvary. In memory of the Last Supper and the Crucifixion millions of human beings take communion today ("And in the night in which He was betrayed He took bread . . .") and repeat the simple and moving words of the Lord's Prayer and the Apostles' Creed. They are able to do this because the apostles of the Church and generations of preachers and missionaries have spread the teachings of Christ.

At the close of St. Matthew's Gospel is this familiar verse: "Go ye therefore, and teach all nations, baptizing them in the name of the Father, and of the Son, and of the Holy Ghost: teaching them to observe all things whatsoever I have commanded you: and lo, I am with you always, even unto the end of the world." So St. Paul and St. Barnabas sailed from Cyprus on their first missionary journey. For twenty centuries missionaries have followed the example of the traveling apostles. Christianity is a continuing historical process. Through valleys of shadow and persecution the dedicated Christians, clergy and laymen, have persisted in hope and faith.

In the early days of Christianity the eagles of the Roman legions cast their shadow and their power from Scotland to the lands of the eastern Mediterranean. The highest loyalty of men was asked for the Roman state. The cult of that state centered in the emperor, the mighty leader of all the Romans. Pagan Rome demanded the worship of its divine Caesar. On the other hand: "Render unto Caesar the things that are Caesar's and unto God the things that are God's." Again: "Thou shalt have no other gods before me." An inevitable result of a clash of loyalties was the persecution of Christians.

Heavy persecutions of those who followed Christ began in 64 under the Emperor Nero. St. Peter and St. Paul were martyred. St. Polycarp died at the hands of the Romans in 155. Thousands of others were tortured and burned, stoned by mobs, torn apart by the lions in the arenas, or crucified. In 249 the Emperor Decius decided that the corrupting and subversive sect of Christians must be destroyed. He made determined attempts to stamp out the whole Church organization of bishops, priests, and deacons. "The blood of the martyrs became the seed of the Church." After Decius was killed in 251 the persecutions declined. In 303 Diocletian made another attempt to crush Christianity. He failed.

In 311 the Emperor Galerius, the successor of Diocletian in the eastern part of the empire, issued his famous Edict of Toleration, a document that gave legal recognition to the Church. Two years later, Constantine, the successor of Diocletian, issued the Edict of Milan confirming and extending the decree of Galerius.

Meanwhile there had been several schisms in the Christian ranks. The Novatians, for instance, were opposed to forgiving the weak-hearted apostates who had preferred life to martyrdom. They broke away from the main body of the Church. Another rigid group, called the Donatists, also grew angry and departed. The Gnostics, too, presented a serious challenge when they insisted that the physical world was completely evil and Jesus could not have entered that physical world in a body of flesh and blood. They said that Jesus only *seemed* to have a human body. The Gnostics also claimed to have secret knowledge imparted by Jesus to a select group of disciples. That secret knowledge, they said, was the true Gospel.

In the face of the Gnostic pressure the Church turned to the known Apostolic tradition, succession, and teaching. St. Irenaeus and others worked to sift out pious legend from genuine Apostolic writing. Slowly and carefully the Church tested and formed the canon of the New Testament Scriptures in their clearest and purest form.

From the middle of the second century the Christian Fathers also wrestled with the problems of the creeds of the Church. The impact of the Gnostic assertions, of course, helped to speed the elaboration of credal statements. By the end of the third century the general form of the Apostles' Creed had taken shape. About 750 it was finally fixed as it stands today. In 325, at the Council of Nicaea, the Nicene Creed was phrased in its present form. Athanasius, Bishop of Alexandria, conducted a strong and successful defense of the principle that Christ was Incarnate God against the teachings of Arius, a presbyter at Alexandria who asserted that Christ was a kind of intermediate semidivine being, neither fully God nor completely man. The insistent language of the Nicene Creed reflects this controversy when it describes Christ as "God of God, Light of Light, Very God of very God, Begotten, not made, Being of one substance with the Father . . . Who for us men and for our salvation came down from heaven, And was incarnate by the Holy Ghost of the Virgin Mary, And was made man. . . ."

This was the great age of Church Councils: Arles (314), Nicaea (325), Constantinople (381), Ephesus (431), and Chalcedon (451). All of them developed the knowledge and organization of the expanding Church of the empire. The patriarchates of the eastern regions were established where early Christian communities had been founded by the Apostles. Antioch in Syria, Alexandria in Egypt, and Rome in the western Mediterranean became the main pivots and pillars of the organization of the Church. Greek Christianity received its own center when Constantine moved the seat of imperial administration from Italy to his city of Constantinople. In the West the primacy of Rome was unchallenged. In the East, the cities of Alexandria, Antioch, and Constantinople struggled for precedence. When Constantinople finally established its supremacy in Eastern Christendom it entered into a long battle with Rome. This struggle of giant rivals was not ended until the final rupture between the East and West in 1054. The Orthodoxy of Constantinople went one way. The Catholicism of Rome went another.

Meanwhile the political and social fabric of the Roman Empire was crumbling fast. The intellectual, evangelical, and administrative leadership of the Church continued steadily to build a bridge over which generations of men could pass to the Middle Ages. The rule of the Caesars ended. The power of the bishops survived.

Into the affairs of the world of men there was soon to explode the new religion of Islam, a creed of immense vitality. The star of Mohammed the Prophet was to blaze in Asia, Africa, and Europe. Teachings of dynamic power were to command the allegiance of millions of men. The faith of the

Moslems was a faith of passion and of strength.

Mohammed was born about 570 in the Arabian town of Mecca near the Red Sea. He was a child of the compact Koreish tribe, an aristocratic group that owned and controlled a large part of the town of Mecca. But aristocratic blood did not bring wealth to Mohammed. His early life was a long chapter of poverty. The legends about his childhood are neither credible nor interesting. We know that he was a shepherd boy, then a trader in a caravan, then a salesman. He probably had epileptic fits. Fortune may perhaps have smiled upon him when he married a middle-aged widow who owned several caravans and had much money—the riches of three continents poured along the caravan routes into Mecca. In any event, Mohammed no longer had to spend his hours in physical labor. He had leisure, time to think and dream. Once a year he went three miles away to Mount Hira to stay alone—like Buddha in the jungle, Christ in the wilderness, St. Jerome in the desert. It was there on the mountain that Mohammed first became convinced that he had a sacred mission. He said that the angel Gabriel had appeared to him and told him to become the prophet of God.

For nine years Mohammed tried to convince the busy people of Mecca that he was indeed the Prophet of Allah—the ancient Arabic name for God. It was a hard task. Some men were indifferent. Some men laughed. And some were hostile and persecuted Mohammed as a crazy crank. When he began to denounce the wealthy men of Mecca and spoke out against the prevailing practice of infanticide Mohammed found himself in real jeopardy. The re-

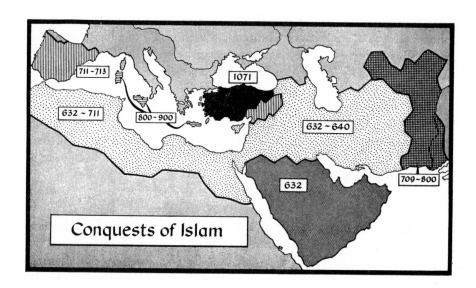

Conquests of Islam

spectable people of Mecca had had enough of him and his wild claims, his dreams and nightmares, his passions. Out he must go, and soon.

In September, 622, Mohammed wisely left Mecca and took refuge in the town of Yathreb, a strategic spot on the main caravan route to the north. This emigration of Mohammed is called the Hegira—"the Flight of the Prophet." The year 622 is the Year I of the Moslem calendar.

In Yathreb, Mohammed was successful at last. His zeal was contagious and his disciples multiplied. When he and his militant followers got control of Yathreb they changed its name to Medina, "the city of the Prophet." Mohammed built a mosque and proclaimed laws and codes of conduct for all who followed him. In 630 his efficient and enthusiastic army captured Mecca. Since that time every devout Moslem turns daily towards the holy city of Mecca. There is the sacred reddish-black meteor that is called the Black Stone. It is built into the southeast corner of the Kaaba, a cubical temple standing forty feet high on a green basalt base and covered with a black brocade embroidered in gold with texts from the Koran. The only entrance to the Kaaba is by a door that is reached by a ladder—the Door of Hope. Nearby is the sacred well of brackish water called the Zem-Zem. This is said to be the well that Joseph showed to Hagar and thus saved the life of Ishmael. Another object of devotion is the sacred stone of Abraham—tradition says that Abraham stood upon it when he built the Kaaba.

Part of the basis of the new religion of Mohammed is to be found in the teachings and ethical doctrines of the Jewish prophets, in Christianity, and in the local cults of Arabia. The 114 vivid chapters of the Koran (from the Arabic *corân:* to recite) are believed by Moslems to contain the actual will and words revealed by God directly to Mohammed. This belief is the reason for the orthodox Moslem view that the long and rhythmic Suras of the Koran are untranslatable: no synonyms can be found for the precise words God said. Every true Moslem believes in the Koran. He believes in one God, in the prophets and angels and divine laws. He accepts Mohammed's statement that God did reveal valid truth through many prophets, of which Mohammed was the last and greatest. He also accepts his master's assertion that both the Old and the New Testaments were divinely inspired. No more than their master Mohammed do the Moslems recognize the divinity of Christ. In their view, Christ was a great prophet, nothing more. Nor do the Moslems accept the Christian doctrine of the Trinity. Mohammed stated flatly that he found the concept of the Trinity opposed to monotheism.

The faithful Moslem believes in the virtue of formal prayers. Five times a day he must face Mecca—at dawn, noon, before sunset, after sunset, after dark. He must pray in Arabic according to fixed forms and rules—although he may not understand Arabic at all. He may know that Mohammed said that "an hour of justice is worth more than seventy hours of prayer." Nevertheless, it is the bounden duty of a Moslem to repeat his prayers and repeat them he does. He must also abstain from all foods in the daytime during the sacred month of Ramadan (unless he is ill or traveling—the Koran ii, 179–184). He must try to make a pilgrimage to Mecca at least once in his lifetime.

The pilgrimage (Hadj) is an important duty to every devout Moslem. If a pilgrim is fortunate he may stand before the Door of Hope—the entrance to the Kaaba high up in the wall—and see the sacred ceremony of the washing of the inside of the temple. This ceremony comes twice a year. At all times, the pilgrims who come to Mecca must wear a special two-piece garment whenever they are on the sacred ground of the holy city, and they must perform two complicated rites before they are held to have completed their pilgrimage and thus to have fulfilled their solemn obligation.

Mohammed and the Koran taught and teach that there will be the dooming and damning of a Last Judgment:

> That day mankind shall be scattered like moths
> And the mountains carded like colored wool
> Then as for him whose balances are heavy, he shall
>   enter into Bliss
> And as for him whose balances are light
> The Pit shall be his dwelling.

A Moslem also believes that there will be a resurrection of the body, a Hell and a Paradise. Those who depart into Hell, says the Koran, "shall dwell amid burning winds and in scalding water under the shade of a black smoke which is no shade, neither cool nor gracious . . . and they shall drink boiling water. . . . They shall have garments of fire fitted unto them . . . and they shall be beaten with maces of iron." On the other hand, says the Koran, he who obeys God goes to Paradise and there faces a prospect of eternal felicity: "For him who dreadeth the tribunal of the Lord are prepared two gardens, planted with shady trees. In each of them shall be two fountains flowing. In each of them shall be of every fruit two kinds. He shall repose on couches, the linings thereof shall be of thick silk, interwoven with gold."

The Moslem is required to observe the prohibition of usury. He must not eat pork, which is unclean. He may practice polygamy, which is divinely sanctioned. He must give money to the sick and the poor—practical benevolence is very important. The good things of the earth, Mohammed said, are for the faithful. He who dies in battle will inevitably go to Paradise.

> Praise be to Allah, the Lord of Creation
> The merciful, the compassionate
> Ruler of the Day of Judgment

Help us,
Lead us in the Path
The Path of those to whom Thou hast made promises
Not of those You are angry with, who walk in error.

The Moslems have never had an organized priesthood. They have no sacraments. True, the muezzin calls the faithful to prayer at the proper hours. "Allah is Allah and Mohammed is his Prophet." Every Friday there are services in the mosques where there is usually a reading of the Koran and prayers; but attendance is not one of the duties prescribed by the Moslem law.

The word "Islam" is often used to describe the Moslem faith. The word simply means "submission to the will of God." That is the highest duty, the supreme obligation. "When the sun shall be folded up . . . And when the leaves of the book shall be unrolled . . . Every soul shall know what it hath produced."

The new religion leaped like the wind over the desert and mountains. Men of many tribes rushed to the standards of Mohammed, Prophet of Allah. What he began was both a crusade and a revolution. By it the boundaries of states were defied. Before its power whole peoples surrendered.

After Mohammed died in 632 there were several "successors of the Prophet" called caliphs. These men were vested with political and religious authority. Allah was believed to rule through them. They were His representatives on earth.

The first of the four caliphs who ruled between 632 and 661 was Abu-Bekr, Mohammed's friend, adviser, and father-in-law. He and his immediate successors were militant Moslems. It was they who really began the swift expansion of Saracen power—the word "Saracen" originally meant an Arab but soon came to be applied to any Moslem no matter what his nationality might be. By 652, with the aid of the tough desert Bedouins, the caliphs had conquered large areas of the Byzantine Empire and beyond: Armenia, Cyprus, Cyrenaica, Egypt, Iraq, Mesopotamia, Palestine, Persia, and Syria. On the Tigris they built the new city of Bagdad in 750. By 700 they had swept into western Turkestan, Afghanistan, and northwest India. They surged over all of North Africa and the homes of the Berbers. They took firm hold of Morocco, "the land of the peacock's tail." They also pushed down to the edge of Middle Africa. It is no accident that in the northern part of Nigeria—that pacemaking state of modern Africa—the Fulami ruling class and the Hausa-speaking peoples are all Moslems.

In 711 the Moslems gave the name of their leader Tarik to Gibraltar—the word means "Tarik's Mountain." They crossed the straits and rolled into Spain, a land they were to live in for 800 years. After a part of Spain was subdued the conquerors pushed beyond the Pyrenees into France. There they were stopped at last. In 732—exactly a hundred years after the death of Mohammed—the Moslems were defeated at the battle of Tours by the Christian forces under Charles Martel, Charles the Hammer, leader and ruler of the turbulent western Frankish warriors. It was the strong grandson of this Charles Martel who was to be called Charlemagne and to be crowned as emperor of a new "Roman Empire" by the pope in the year 800.

In these days the Moslems turned to conquer Sicily and lunge towards the gates of Rome itself. Their vast empire—"the community of the faithful"—now reached from the Pyrenees to the Indus. Nearly half of the civilized world was under their rule.

The Moslems were remarkably tolerant. They left their subject peoples largely unmolested. Unlike the Romans, they cared little about the assimilation of all the groups in their composite empire. They did not compel them to accept the teachings of the Prophet. For instance, the Copts in Egypt and most of the Syrians remained Christian. At the same time, however, millions of men did become converts of Islam and helped in the Saracen conquests. The fact must be stressed, of course, that the actual building of the Moslem Empire was far less the result of religious factors than of other kinds of pressures that were mainly political and economic and military.

It was difficult for such a vast and heterogeneous agglomeration of peoples to be united in a strong and cohesive unit. There were grave disorders and internal conflicts, nasty incidents of sectional and factional strife. From the original teachings of Mohammed new ideas were born and nourished. Offshoots and sects multiplied. Doctrinal cleavages widened. The mystics stood against the rationalists and the strict believers denounced the liberals. Religious schisms and differences were often influenced and sometimes decided by political dislocations and economic rivalries. Meanwhile the Shiites, the Sunnites, the Sufis, and the rest fought on. The lines of open battle and quiet murder swayed back and forth.

From 661 to 750 the Ommiad dynasty ruled. Members of this family were the descendants and supporters of the interests and traditions of Fatima, the Prophet's daughter, and her murdered husband Ali. When they were triumphant in a civil war that ended in 661 the Ommiads moved the capital of the empire to Damascus, mainly because they obtained their strongest support from Syria. In 750 the Shiites and the Abbasid family—descended from an uncle of the Prophet—seized the throne. They shifted the capital to the new and dazzling city of Bagdad. From 750 to 1055 more or less benevolent despots like Harun-al-Raschid (786–809) ruled and lived lavishly. The luxury and magnificence of Harun-al-Raschid's court apparently beggared description. In comparison with the conspicuous consumption and the advanced culture of

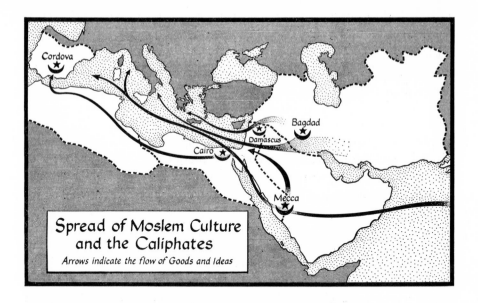

Spread of Moslem Culture and the Caliphates
Arrows indicate the flow of Goods and Ideas

his palaces the castles of his European contemporary Charlemagne were poor and barren things.

During the ascendancy of the Abbasids the prestige and power of the Moslem Empire reached their height. Commerce flourished. From all corners of the known world men came to trade and fight and live.

Time always brings in its revenges. The proud and brilliant Abbasids, like the Ommiads before them, felt their sinews of power weakening and their hands grow nerveless. The administrative system creaked and collapsed. In 756 an Ommiad escaped from the control of Bagdad and set up his own dynasty at Cordova in Spain; Cordova became a caliphate in 929. The fabulously wealthy Fatimate Caliphate was founded as an independent unit in Cairo in 969. Meanwhile the Bagdad caliphs and emirs turned more and more to the ways of the East. The efficiency of their government, never great, rapidly declined. They became the creatures of their Persian viziers. Some provincial officers rebelled against the caliphs and demanded recognition as sultans, or independent sovereigns. Then, in 1055, the Bagdad caliphs were compelled to yield to another force. They handed over all their secular powers to their Mongol mercenary troops, the Seljuk Turks who had captured effective control of Bagdad. The Abbasids were now puppets. For 200 years the real power was in the hands of the Seljuks.

During these exciting centuries the Moslems became widely famous for their energy and enterprise in the pursuits of peace. They terraced the slopes of the mountains in Spain. They irrigated the deserts in the Near East. Their fields, orchards, and vineyards produced abundant harvests of flax, olives, peaches, rice, sugar, wheat, and the like. The tentacles of their trade lines reached over all of the known world. From Africa to Russia, from Spain to the vast lands of the East went the camel caravans and ships. Out of Morocco came the red and yellow leather admired for centuries. From Mosul in Mesopotamia was exported cotton cloth (muslin). From Toledo came the famous swords. The artisans of Damascus made and shipped the embossed linen called "damask" and the fine steel that was for centuries the wonder and envy of the earth. Bagdad produced her beautiful glassware, her silks, and her pottery. Out of the East came dyes, drugs, perfumes, satins, spices, tapestries. The list might be prolonged for pages.

It was the Moslem merchants who developed and brought into wide use such familiar instruments of business as checks, letters of credit, and joint stock companies. These steps in economic enterprise had much to do with the rise of Venice in a later day, the coming of the Italian bankers, and the commercial revolutions beginning in the fifteen century. Meanwhile, the Moslem commercial empire grew. At one end were the Spanish port cities, where widehorned, creamy oxen drooled in their yokes by the high-wheeled carts and the burly and brainy boatmen and merchants bustled on the docks. Great baskets of eels and piles of red mullet lay in the stalls of the fishmarkets. Whitewinged pigeons wheeled by the wine shops. The oleander thickets were purple with bloom. Back from the turquoise Mediterranean Sea were the twisting stone veins of streets and evil entrail alleys. And far from Spain stood the Moslem cities of Cairo, Damascus, and Bagdad, dazzling in their magnificence.

Moslem culture has never had a simple or uniform pattern. It is many-sided, heterogeneous, complex. Distinctions and diversities abound—how could it be otherwise when there are 300,000,000 Moslems in the world speaking many tongues, living under many kinds of rule, dwelling in large numbers in three continents? A Chinese Moslem obviously differs from his brothers in faith in Malaya or Morocco or Saudi Arabia.

Even in the early years when the Moslem Empire first began to expand, there were innumerable cultural strands and patterns inside the world of Islam. At the same time, the Moslems steadily picked up elements from other cultures. They have always had a special genius for synthesizing the native and the foreign, the past and present. This is one reason why so many elements, apparently quite irreconcilable, have been adapted and assimilated and often transmitted to the world of the West.

The debt of the Western countries to the colorful and rich Moslem civilization is far more considerable than many people know. Even a swift reference to things embedded in our language shows how great was our borrowing long ago from such peoples as the Arabians and the Persians. These are some of their words that we use today: admiral, alchemy, alcohol, algebra, alkali, almanac, attar, azure, barge, bazaar, caravan, cipher, coffee, elixir, fez, fustian, jar, julep, lemon, lilac, lute, magazine, mattress, mecca, orange, ottoman, sherbet, sofa, sugar, syrup, tambourine, tariff, traffic, zenith, zero. On its long journey from India to Europe the game of chess picked up the term "checkmate" from the Persian *sha mat,* which means "the king is dead." Meanwhile the Moslem songs of Spain and Sicily came to delight the troubadours of Provence and the sweet singers of Padua.

In learning and science the advanced Moslem civilization gave us a great deal indeed. It was the Moslems who really founded the science of optics—most of the earlier work was not sound. They studied the velocity and refraction of light. They advanced astronomy. Through them there came to the West a Chinese product called paper, usually made of rags or pulpwood. Only the word is connected with the Egyptian papyrus; the product is not. The Moslem world also advanced many areas of algebra. By the twelfth century the clumsy Roman system of numbers began to yield to the nine numbers in the neater Arabic. The flexible and precise decimal system that we use today in arithmetic is in part the result of the Arab genius in using and extending the skills of their predecessors in India, Greece, and elsewhere. As active men of business the Moslems could swiftly appreciate the advantages of an easily handled numerical system. Perhaps, as is often claimed, the Arabs did invent the idea and use of zero. The weight of the evidence now seems to say that the claims of India are stronger and that the Moslems merely passed the practice along to us. But they certainly passed it along. They did hand over several things that they picked up half a world away.

Sometimes the Moslems turned their energy to invent and discover. For instance, they found several new substances and compounds: alum, bichloride of mercury, borax, carbonate of soda, cream of tartar, nitrate of silver, nitric and sulphuric acids, saltpeter. They also discovered several processes of sublimation and filtration. Sometimes they improved, as they did when they built their great hospitals, or when their surgical teachings became the envy of the surgeons and physicians of Europe.

Throughout the Moslem Empire moved the massive intellectual and cultural heritage of the Saracens. The brilliant achievements in arts and letters of such regions as Greece, Syria, Persia, India, and Egypt were often fused and transmitted east and west, north and south. The reader has already noted the varied kinds of things that were happening in such fields as mathematics. They were also happening in other areas. For example, the shining literature and philosophy of the Bagdad of the tenth century were widely known and quoted in the Cordova of the twelfth. Again and again the Moslems brought to Europe both new knowledge and old knowledge that had been forgotten or destroyed when Rome fell.

In the Near East and in the Western lands the Moslems saved, compiled, and translated Greek manuscripts, often aided by Jews and Christians. The sciences of the Greek world were kept and cultivated in Syria. Famous schools flourished at Alexandria, Antioch, Beirut, Junde Shapur, and Nisibis. Bagdad had a superb library. The Arab Ibn Hunain translated works of Aristotle, Galen, Hippocrates, Plato, and Ptolemy. The *Index of Sciences* of Mahmud Al-Nadim (978) has an annotated bibliography of thousands of titles of original and translated works in Arabic—most of them have now been lost.

Spain—whose Moorish and Jewish scholars did so much for Europe—had great schools at Toledo and elsewhere busy in translation work. They did their share and more in helping to give the immense fruits of Moslem learning and culture to Europe. It was through Spain that Aristotle first came to the West —in a Latin translation. If the sources of knowledge brought by the Moslems to Europe had not been available, then the later tale of the revival of learning and the Renaissance would have been different indeed. It must be added, of course, that Moslem philosophers, such as the great Averroes of Cordova (1126–1198), had a tremendous influence on European thought in the later Middle Ages and during the years of the Renaissance. The words and works of Averroes were especially influential in the development of the scholastic thought of the medieval world. He was a light from the East to the Schoolmen. Certainly few men of that day knew more about Aristotle than Averroes.

In the profession of medicine there were men like Rhazes (al-Razi), who was born in 865 and died in 925. Rhazes has been called "the greatest clinical physician of the medieval world." He wrote more than 200 works, including the first accurate description of smallpox and measles. He did much research with antidotes for poisons, styptic agents, and cauterization methods. He saw and understood the infectious nature of the plague. He wrote a huge encyclopedia of diseases that was praised and used by physicians in Europe for centuries. The renowned Avicenna (980–1037) was a philosopher, physicist, and physician. He discovered the contagious nature of tuberculosis. He described pleurisy. He asserted that diseases could be spread by the contamination of water and soil. His *Canon of Medicine* was highly regarded in Europe until the seventeenth century.

Nor were the Moslems idle in the field of literature. Probably because of the famous translation of Edward FitzGerald, the *Rubaiyat* of Omar Khayyam is the most familiar of all Persian poems. It is not by any means the best. The most widely known and quoted book of prose is, of course, the *Arabian Nights,* a collection of 1,001 stories from the eighth and ninth centuries. We

all know the personal pleasure we can derive from the *Arabian Nights* and
the *Rubaiyat*. Despite the learned praise given some other Moslem works, it
seems that enthusiastic hands will not reach for them frequently. The dust
lies on the works of many men who were once revered as gods for their
wisdom.

Because Mohammed feared the return of the worship of idols and images,
he forbade his followers to make pictorial art and sculpture in which the
human face or form appeared. This is the reason we have no statue or painting
of Mohammed and plant and animal motifs appear so often in Moslem art.

The lack of Moslem triumph in sculpture and painting is more than balanced by their mighty success in their architecture and their arts of design and
decoration. They deserve well of the world for the grandeur of the mosaics, the
twisted columns, the slender minarets of the mosques and palaces they built
from Spain to India, the bulbous domes glittering in the sun.

In most Moslem architecture the Persian and Byzantine influence is particularly strong. It can be seen in places as far apart as the Alhambra in Spain
and the Taj Mahal in India. The Byzantine thrusts of influence appear sharply
in the uses of the domes, columns, and horseshoe arches. Although the forms
vary in different parts of Islam, the main borrowings and tendencies can always be discerned. The Persian influence is distinct and certain in many of
the graceful and intricate decorations. The decorative devices of the Moslems
were later to provide inspiration and ideas for many Gothic architects in Europe. We do not easily associate Moslem influence with Gothic architecture;
but it is there, strong and clear. It is to the Moslems, for instance, that the
great Gothic craftsmen turned for their cusped arches and traceried windows.
The sculptured ornaments of the Spanish Moors found their places in many a
Gothic structure. Arabesque designs abound.

Both Persia and Byzantium share in the riot and profusion of rich color,
always characteristic of the lands to the east of the Mediterranean. The same
tastes and inclinations are obvious, of course, in the painted pottery, the
gorgeous rugs, the glazed tiles and mosaics, the brocaded tapestries, the intricate and bewildering gold and silver inlay work so rarely seen in the contemporary world of art.

Of special interest to modern man is the evidence of the painstaking precision of the Moslem and Christian artisans. Perhaps the pulse and pace of our
modern world have brought penalties as well as profits to the artisans and
artists who live and work today. Perhaps they, too, have been caught and held
by the impelling power of speed, that valuable commodity of the twentieth
century. It is sometimes forgotten that old masterpieces do not hold their
places of pride because they are old but because they were made by masters.
These men were often not concerned with becoming; they were content to
be. He who would be a mighty craftsman in any age, he who desires to make

enduring works of art, must have much skill and much patience. He must take much time. Both God and Leonardo found that one day was not enough.

In 1258 thousands of invading Mongols led by the nephew of the terrible Genghis Khan erupted out of central Asia. They captured and destroyed Bagdad. The Abbasid dynasty died. The Ottoman Turks, rough heirs of power, seized the leadership of the eastern Moslem world. Soon converted to Islam, they became fierce fanatics. After many struggles with the Byzantine Empire, especially with the Slavs of the Balkans, these Ottoman Turks finally captured Constantinople in 1453, a famous year in history. Then they swept into southeastern Europe. For the Western world the significance of these events was tremendous. All Europe was faced by the fierce challenge of the Moslem power.

Chapter 12

THE

HEIRS OF ROME

"Without adventure civilization is in full decay."
—Alfred North Whitehead
Adventures of Ideas (Cambridge edition, 1933), p. 360

WHEN the hour hand of history reached the place where the Western Roman Empire was destroyed, it must have seemed to many men that a fierce and terrible Dark Age of sterility and danger was rushing towards them out of the darkness. All about were broken beams and shattered walls, ashes and ruins to sadden and harden the eyes of the Romans. The roads that led to Rome were cut and choked. The aqueducts carried water no more. Grass grew in the chinks of the paving stones and in the vile rubble of the shattered buildings. Soon few men could read or write. Barbarian gangsters, unbookish and greedy, looted and ruled the world that once was the world of Roman law. We cannot easily conceive of the darkness of fear in the wreckage of those years, so filled with negative malignity, so poor and barren. The lives of many men, all they ever did, seemed to have become meaningless. Human thought seemed useless, hope a vain dream.

At this point a professional historian who is an expert in the history of Europe at the dawn of the Middle Ages may hasten to query and correct. It is true that the shadowy aspects of the scenes must not be stressed with dramatic sentences for which there are no sure and certain footnotes. And yet it may be submitted that the cumulative total of footnotes and references for the misty years after the fall of Rome might well lead the reader to conclude that the spirits of many a survivor wandering in the streets of Rome were leaden and desperate. He would also conclude, and rightly, that not all men were pessimists.

They were not. There are always the optimists, robust as oaks, able and pugnacious. Among all the changing scenes through which mankind has passed, there have flourished those stout men who have seen the hope beneath the harsh anatomy of magnified distress. They never see the perilous sum of the worst. They know that the maimed and weakened are still alive; that wounds will heal and bitter memories fade into soiled oblivion; that grass grows swiftly over the field of battle. Gradually the shattered spots and the frayed edges of the world of Rome were mended by steady toil in a new form. There are always the brave and deft builders, ready to start all over again. "The soul's joy lies in doing." Men of stamina climbed out of the dark night and stumbled forward. The process of advance was often interrupted, troubled, delayed, stopped, and sometimes reversed by wars and floods and famines. It is indeed possible that man might have turned towards savagery again, towards the distant darkness of the jungle and the brutality of the cave. We have no assurance that mankind may not do precisely that in the future. Our hold upon what we have and are is more precarious than many of us believe.

The tale of Western European man's recovery is long. It covers about 1,000 years. Classical civilization was gone forever. Over the horizons of time between 500 and 1500 there came a new culture and a new civilization. And yet this civilization contained a great deal that was old. Some of it was older than Rome, older than Greece. Some was recovered from the past and some had never been abandoned. "Habit," said William James, "is the great flywheel of society." The idea that the so-called Dark Ages was a period when all the past was forgotten and the present found nothing new is not a sound or acceptable idea at all. Many school children were taught a great many inaccurate things about the history of the world when we were young together. Professors and teachers sometimes lag. It is probable that the Dark Ages are now being presented in a less unfavorable light today. It is equally probable that new discoveries will show that some chapters of our history teaching need revision and correction almost as frequently as our courses in sciences and mathematics. Men seldom discover whole truths. They discover little pieces, sometimes centuries apart.

The first solid bridge from the past to the future was the Church of the Christians.

When the Goths and Vandals pillaged Rome in the fifth century the power of the Church remained unshaken. By the sixth century the bishop of Rome, soon to be called the pope, was the virtual ruler of the city. The senate was a "pithless shadow." The pope was accepted as the moral and spiritual head of the Christian community and tradition, a stable tradition that had apparently stood unmoved amidst the assaults and slaughters of violent men. Rome had been the scene of the final labors and martyrdoms of St. Peter and St. Paul. Was it not widely believed that Jesus himself had chosen St. Peter, the beloved disciple, to be the first bishop of Rome, the leader of all His followers? Was it not said to be true that the immense powers possessed by St. Peter had been inherited by the succeeding bishops of Rome? It is not to be wondered that the prestige and effective power of the pope stood unchallenged when so much around was perishing. "On this rock I will build My Church."

Before the empire collapsed the unity of its parts had aided the apostles in their hard and heavy tasks. In the second half of the fourth century Prudentius had written: "God willed peoples of discordant tongues, kingdoms of conflicting laws, to be brought together under one Empire, because concord alone knows God. Hence He taught all nations to bow their necks under the same laws and to become Romans. . . . This is the fruit of the triumph of Rome: they opened the door for Christ to enter."

When the Emperor Constantine had recognized Christianity, the organization of the Church, with its tradition of everlasting rock, had been rapidly developed. After the disintegration of the empire, the whole machinery of the Church—based on the civil administration system of the vanished empire—continued to be strong and efficient. Below the pope still stood the archbishops or metropolitans, the bishops, priests, and deacons—all established in the chain of command developed long before. The clergy declared one faith. They stood by one creed. They taught praise and prayer and they proclaimed the Word of God with its power and its glory. Of tremendous psychological importance in these days was the fact that men could see that although men's cities of stone might crumble the city of Zion endured, a refuge and a strength. Above the smoke and the wreckage the Cross of Christ still towered. When the Roman Empire broke into fragments it must have seemed to thousands of people in Europe that the Church, and the Church alone, stood among the ruins to provide a shelter from perils and storms.

It was fortunate that there were many leaders of the Church who were not only men of intense devotion but also passionate men of action, tough and determined. In an age of transition from the ancient to the medieval world these men played a decisive part in keeping the thin flame of civilization burning in the winds of barbarism.

One of these leaders was St. Augustine, bishop of Hippo, famous philosopher and theologian. It is now sixteen centuries since St. Augustine was born in 354 in northern Africa. Over the tumult of the dying agonies of Rome, over the wild years afterward, his words were heard.

St. Augustine was a student of St. Ambrose, that fearless bishop of Milan who barred the Emperor Theodosius from the Church until he accepted the discipline laid upon him for his sins. Some pagans had asserted that the grim fate of Rome had resulted from the anger of the gods whose altars had been neglected. To answer them St. Augustine, "inflamed with zeal for the Lord's house, determined to write a treatise on *The City of God* in order to refute the mistakes of some and the blasphemies of others." *The City of God,* a work of epic grandeur, stands beside St. Augustine's *Confessions* as one of the world's great books. St. Augustine stated his views with as much vigor and courage as his master, St. Ambrose. His interpretation of the meaning and destiny of man was clear and realistic. Rationalism and faith meet and merge. His logic flows smoothly, step by step.

> Whoever gives even moderate attention to human affairs and to our common nature, will recognize that there is no man who does not wish to be joyful, neither is there anyone who does not wish to have peace. For even they who make war desire nothing but victory— desire, that is to say, to attain to peace with glory. For what else is victory than the conquest of those who resist us? And when this is done there is peace. It is therefore with the desire for peace that war is waged, even by those who take pleasure in exercising their war- like nature in command or battle. And hence it is obvious that peace is the end sought for by man. For every man seeks peace by waging war, but no man seeks war by making peace.

The City of God, said St. Augustine, is an eternal spiritual community of those whose lives are centered in the things of God. "The City of God abideth forever, though the city of the world has fallen in ruins." The City of man, on the other hand, is an earthly community where men seek pros- perity and pleasure, and nothing else. If you never leave the City of Man to seek the City of God, then you will be doomed forever.

After St. Augustine came other key churchmen, valiant warriors and statesmen like Pope Gregory I, usually called Gregory the Great (540–604). Gregory was born of a famous and wealthy senatorial family, and he obtained the best education to be had in Rome. In his youth he became a lawyer and talented prefect of the city. Then he suddenly withdrew from the world and gave much of his great wealth to help the building of monasteries. In one of them he spent three years as a monk. In later days he wrote: "I remember longingly what I once was in the monastery, how I rose in contemplation above all changeable and decaying things and thought of nothing but the things of heaven; how my soul, though pent within the body, soared beyond its fleshly passions." Soon Gregory became a deacon. Then he moved to spend distasteful years as papal representative at the imperial court at Constantinople. Then he wrote his *Magna Moralia,* a commentary on the Book of Job that was popular for a thousand years. Generations of men were also influenced by Gregory's *Dialogues* and his *Pastoral Care.* Soon he became abbot of his monastery. And then, finally, he became pope. In that exalted place he was a famous reformer, administrator, and statesman.

In one frequently quoted passage Pope Gregory described the Church as "an old and violently-shattered ship, its timbers rotten, and rapidly becoming a wreck." Gregory's energetic service in the cause of Christ helped the "violently-shattered ship" of the Church to ride out the storms. The vigorous leadership of the "Servant of the Servants of God" extended the papal authority to Spain, helped to clothe and feed the poor, aided in the conversion of the Anglo-Saxon tribes in far-off England. The tireless Gregory stood forth as a mighty champion of the Church, insisting upon unity and stability among all Christians under the power of the pope. By the time of Gregory's death the Church held enormous influence over increasing thousands of individuals, including many converted Goths and Vandals, among whom Christianity had taken firm root. All roads, it seemed, were beginning to lead to Rome once more. This time, however, they were leading to the Church and the pope and not to Caesar and the senate.

To meet the needs of faith and knowledge heroic and zealous missionaries traveled into far lands. They entered into strange cities and among the savage peoples of the forests. St. Boniface went to the tribes of central Germany. St. Patrick went to Ireland. St. Columba, an Irish Scot, went to Wales and founded the famous monastery of Iona about 590. His biographer wrote: "He longed to go into strange lands and under the guidance of Christ went to the seashore with twelve companions." Aidan, a monk from Iona, founded Lindisfarne, or the Holy Isle, off the coast of Northumbria.

In 597 Augustine and forty monks were sent by Gregory the Great to begin the conversion of England. They brought the Christian message of faith and fear to Ethelbert, king of England's Kent. Ethelbert convinced himself of the honesty of Augustine at a famous interview at Thanet. He gave the Roman missionaries a dwelling place at Canterbury, provided food, and permitted them to preach their religion. As Celtic Christianity spread from the north and from Wales, Roman Christianity pressed from the south. In 664, at the famous Synod of Whitby, the representatives of rival Celtic and Roman missions debated before King Oswy of Northumbria the religious issues that divided them. What was most important was the problem of Christian unity in the British Isles. Would the Celtic Christians turn aside from the Roman Christians of all Europe? "To fight against Rome," said a debater at Whitby, "is to fight against the world." Oswy decided in favor of the usages of Rome, and the pope sent the Greek Theodore of Tarsus, the city of St. Paul, to organize a new hierarchy, a united English Church under the dominion of Canterbury.

Thus the gospel of Christ was spread. Meanwhile, too, the Church steadily continued its work in education. Through all of Europe schools were founded in the new cathedrals, in the palaces of kings and the manor houses of nobles. At the same time, the names and achievements of individual sons of the Church continued to increase. St. Jerome (d. 420), for instance, came out of Dalmatia to be a hermit in Syria. In 382 he became secretary to Pope

Damasus. He wrote numerous essays, tracts, and letters and gave Europe a new Latin version of both the Old and New Testaments. His translation became the official Vulgate of the Western Church. Boethius, born about 480, became a high official under Theodoric, the king of the Ostrogoths who was recognized as ruler of Italy in 493. Probably guilty of treason, Boethius was imprisoned and executed (524). When he was in prison he wrote the eloquent *Consolation of Philosophy*—"a golden volume not unworthy of the leisure of Plato or Tully." It was widely read and discussed and debated for more than a thousand years; and it is not yet forgotten or abandoned.

Not all devout Christians followed these roads. Some of them renounced and fled from this world to prepare for the next. There were many ascetics and hermits in the early Christian era. By the year 400 it seems that there were thousands of hermits, saints and sinners. "Some had gone out in order to make real atonement and to become saints; others to pose as such. Some fled society and its vices; others their calling and its toils. Some were simple-hearted and of indomitable will; others were sick of the whirl of life." St. Anthony went out into the desert near Alexandria—"The fish die when they are drawn to land, and the monks lose their strength in towns." Some were extremists like St. Simeon Stylites of Syria (d. 459), who lived for thirty years on the top of a pillar.

Not all men in the Church were godly and righteous. Many unworthy individuals came in, not for the first or last time in human history. Some slinked or shuffled into the congregation of the faithful because they thought they might profit from its power and status. Some came in quite boldly, brazenly asking that the Church give them opportunity to achieve their ambitions. St. Jerome once paused in the busy round of his dedicated service to God to denounce the scoundrels, the hypocrites, and the Pharisees within the walls of the Church and the ranks of the Churchmen:

> One of these men . . . I will briefly and concisely describe, in order that when you know the master you may the more readily recognize his disciples. He hastens to rise with the sun, he arranges the order of his visits, he seeks short-cuts, and the troublesome old man almost pushes his way into the bedchambers of people before they are awake. If he happens to see a cushion, a pretty napkin, or a piece of furniture, he praises it, he handles it, he admires it, he complains that he lacks such things; and he not so much begs it as he extorts it; for everyone fears to offend the city newsman. Chastity he hates, fasting he hates; what he likes is the smell of dinner, and his weakness is sucking-pig. . . . Wherever you go he is; whatever news you hear, he is either the author or the exaggerator of the report.

The faithful outnumbered the others. As the work and power of the Church increased, hundreds of monasteries, particularly in the fifth and sixth centuries, rose from Greece to Iceland. The monks went into the disciplined monastic life to devote their whole beings to God, to a united brotherhood, to self-sacrifice, and to valuable social, economic, and religious services. They built libraries, copied manuscripts, and preserved learning. They drained swamps and felled forests. "They filled the meadows with cattle and they stocked the uplands with sheep."

St. Benedict of Nursia (b. 480) gave to Western monasticism the form and organization and discipline it sadly needed. He came to his personal destiny by strange and devious roads. As a youth, "learnedly ignorant and wisely untaught," St. Benedict was gravely offended by the corrupt society of Rome. He appears, as a matter of fact, to have been in his younger days an unduly sensitive and condescending prig, proud that he was purer than other men. The lessons of the years ended that delusion. St. Benedict, like many a person before and after, learned that it is not enough to condemn sin and that one of the greatest evils of all is that of pride, of *hubris*. In his later years St. Benedict cast few stones. He was too busy helping healthy men and sinners.

The young St. Benedict left Rome and lived for three years in a cave in the Apennines. After he became the acknowledged leader of the hermits in the region he founded the renowned monastery of Monte Cassino, so badly shattered by the guns and bombs of the Second World War.

The rule of St. Benedict is famous throughout the Western world: poverty, chastity, and obedience. Each monk was required to spend about seven hours a day working with his own hands at the kind of work for which he was best fitted. He also spent about four hours in reading and study—the Benedictine monasteries soon became natural homes of learning. The monk's life was thus passed partly at work and study. It was also spent in rest and prayer and praise—"Seven times a day do I praise Thee, O Lord!" St. Benedict did not believe in extreme asceticism. Wine was permitted and good food was desirable. The laws of hospitality were never to be broken by the brothers: "All guests who come shall be received as though they were Christ." "Chiefly in the reception of the poor and of pilgrims shall care be most anxiously exhibited: for in them Christ is received the more."

In the peaceful and well-ordered monasteries, Benedictine and Cistercian and all the others, the Romans and the Goths, the nobles and the peasants prayed and worked together. Day after day, year in and year out, century after century, the bells of the cloisters rang and the monks chanted the glory of God.

The peoples who invaded the Roman Empire and overturned the structure of Europe were called the barbarians, or strangers, by the Roman world. Some of them were the Gothic Germans of the east: Alamans, Burgundians, Lombards, Ostrogoths, Vandals, and Visigoths. The others lived in the Teutonic western areas: Angles, Franks, Frisians, Jutes, Saxons, and the rest. Up in the northern Scandinavian regions were the Norsemen, destined to push out in all directions in the ninth and tenth centuries to explore and settle in Greenland and Iceland; to plant Baltic colonies; to thrust into Russia, Constantinople, Sicily, the British Isles; to establish their great state of Normandy in France. The Norsemen took no part in the upsetting of Rome. The east and west Germans had most to do with that.

One of the first descriptions of the Germans was written by the Roman historian Tacitus. He described those tribesmen as barbarians with "fierce blue eyes and reddish hair; great bodies, especially powerful for attack, but not equally patient of hard work; little able to withstand heat or thirst, although by climate and soil they have been inured to cold and hunger." The words of Tacitus are usually interesting, even if they are frequently less than accurate. The most important fact is clearly this: the Germanic peoples, courageous conquerors of Rome, had no culture worthy of the name. They were divided into independent tribes without any common political organization. The leaders of the tribes were called kings, and whatever political power they possessed was shared with the men of the aristocracy. Most of the tribal activities had to do with primitive agriculture, cattle raising, barter, hunting, and fighting. True, the German tribes had fought against the Romans, had served in the legions, had been hired hands or slaves, and had learned a little about the arts and graces of civilization. Some of them, especially among the Goths, had deserted Wotan and Thor and had embraced Christianity. From the tribes on the borderlands of Asia and Europe the Germans had learned some skills in horse riding and metalwork. They had thus accumulated a few new abilities and experiences, nothing more. Pressed by the Huns from the East, battling among themselves, hungry for land, space, and booty, envious of the wealth and warmth of the interior of the Roman world—these were the peoples who had come and conquered.

The task of shaping a new Europe fell mainly into their hands. Soon after the fall of Rome new political systems were established by the eastern Germans in the populated areas around the Mediterranean. The Visigoths carved out insecure states and set up the rudiments of ordered governments in Spain and southwest Gaul. The Burgundians did likewise in southeast Gaul. The Vandals formed spheres of influence and kingdoms in Africa, and the Ostrogoths followed suit in Italy. The western Germans occupied the lands that had formerly been the northern provinces of the Roman Empire. The Franks, for instance, moved into the lands between the Rhine and the Somme. The Bavarians settled eastward on the Danube. The Angles, Saxons, and Jutes made their way across the North Sea and the English Channel to conquer the Britons. There were many other aspects of upheaval and migration among

[37]

[38]

Above: Hero and Lion. An excellent example of Byzantine art (6-7th century)

Right: Byzantine earrings (6th century)

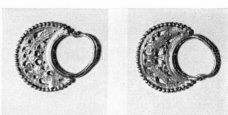

[39]

ight side of a late Roman ory diptych (c. 516 A.D.) owing Emperor Anastasius olding sceptre and mappa he cloth thrown by him into e ring as a signal for the start of games)

[40]

modern view of the great hurch of Hagia Sophia Is-nbul, the most famous exam-le of Byzantine architecture the world. It was opened by ne Emperor Justinian in 537. fter the fall of Constantino-le in 1453 the Turks made anta Sophia a Mohammedan mosque.

PLATE XI

[41]

Nativity. Ivory Carving, probably from Alexandria. (6th-7th c. A.D.)

[42]

مال هنوا فی فضال البنوی ان لا یکون هاک بل یکون والده تقدم رح ویکون شبما فضال الهواب اخی ان نب اسه حامله به تم دح والده فقال لهحمل اصند

The monk Bahira identifies Mohammed as the Prophet whose coming was foretold
in sacred texts.

[43]

This sheet from a Moslem manuscript on medicine written in 1222
or 1223 gives a recipe for cough
medicine and shows a doctor preparing it.

PLATE XII

such peoples as the Slavs and the Huns, all pointing towards the language, blood, and culture divisions of modern Europe.

Meanwhile towns and cities dwindled and decayed. The roads remained unsafe. The arteries of trade, once pulsing with the life blood of Empire, grew dry and brittle.

Probably the most significant political achievement of those years was the slow building of a great kingdom by the Frankish tribesmen. The man who was mainly responsible for the new creation was the cruel and unscrupulous Clovis, a member of the Merovingian family and hard chief of the tiny Frankish unit of Tournai. Between 481 and 511 Clovis was able to bring under his rule all the areas where Rome had once ruled in Gaul—there were still fragments of classical culture remaining there. Clovis ousted the Visigoths from southern Gaul. He defeated the Alamans—that victory gave him the upper Rhinelands—and the Burgundians. He married a Burgundian princess and through her he was converted to orthodox and Catholic Christianity in 496. The adjective "orthodox" is important because all of the other German tribes were either pagan or had accepted some heresy, usually Arianism. The leaders of the Church naturally supported Clovis against his enemies, for his enemies were also theirs. His missionaries were preaching the orthodox teachings of the Church—and Clovis sent many missionaries to spread the truth among the tribesmen of northern Europe. The conversion of Clovis was an important event in the history of the West.

Before the aggressive Clovis died in 511 he had achieved a great deal. He was an intense man in everything he did. Whether he was killing men or saving souls, his passion seems to have been much the same. His four sons and his grandsons extended the Frankish kingdom still further in the sixth century by defeating the Bavarians and the Alamans and seizing their territories. Diverse ethnic and religious elements were stitched into the patchwork of the expanding Frankish state. The various tribes and areas kept their own legal systems. Military conquest, of course, never means effective unification. Many chapters of history tell of conquerors who learned that hard fact too late. The pieces of the great Frankish kingdom were held together by the iron grip of Clovis and the two succeeding generations of strong Merovingian rulers. As soon as the grip was loosened the territories split and fell apart. Civil war came with weak government at the end of the sixth century and continued into the seventh.

It was the Carolingian Charles Martel, victor in the battle of Tours fought against the Moslems in 732, who checked the mounting dislocations in the Frankish state. Before he died he had pulled the recalcitrant Alamans and all of Aquitaine back into the kingdom of the Franks. In 751 his son Pepin the Short legally eliminated the decadent Merovingian dynasty by declaring himself "King of the Franks" and obtaining the pope's approval. Pope Stephen II crossed the Alps and anointed Pepin with consecrated oil. The whole procedure was devoid of justice; but it was quite legal. The last of the Merovingian kings was sent to die quietly in a monastery.

Pepin at once invaded Italy, drove out the Lombards who had been threatening Rome and the pope. He then handed to the pope the lands around Ravenna that the Lombards had seized earlier. When this territory was added to Rome and the adjoining papal lands there was created the belt of the famous Papal States reaching across Italy from Rome to Ravenna.

When Pepin died in 768, he was succeeded by Charles the Great, called Charlemagne. Under him the Carolingians were to reach the summit of their power. Many of the foundations were to be laid for the glories and the frustrations of the Middle Ages.

While the western half of the Roman Empire was disintegrating the fabric of the eastern half survived, part Roman, part Greek, and part Oriental. Geography, time, and circumstances united to shape events. The eastern part of the empire not only survived, but it flourished as it took over the control of the ancient imperial provinces of the Near East and transmitted some culture and much Christianity to the Slavs of Russia and the Balkans. We of the West have been so deeply impressed by the rapid advances of Europe and America since the discovery of steam, coal, electricity, oil, and atomic energy that we tend naturally to think of Britain, France, Germany, and the United States as areas of the highest importance. They are, of course, regions today of power and civilization. Long ago, in the period after the waning of Rome, the most important political and cultural unit was not in any of these lands. It was in eastern Europe in Constantinople.

Only in the last century have scholars come to understand and appreciate the debt the world owes to the Byzantine civilization of the Eastern Empire. For too long the judgment of Edward Gibbon was accepted without doubts and without research. "Byzantine history," said Gibbon, "is a tedious and uniform tale of weakness and misery." Gibbon was wrong.

Byzantine civilization was not weak and miserable, soft or effete. It was solid, rich, and splendid, and it was able to maintain and extend itself as its world ceased to look westward to Rome. In this achievement Byzantium was aided by the fact that it had a highly developed city life. There was a large population of many bloods and cultures living in Constantinople, a city with a great landlocked harbor, magnificent buildings, the impressive Hippodrome seating 80,000 spectators, and a long tradition of culture. Some visitors, it must be admitted, had grave doubts about the morals of the inhabitants of the sprawling metropolis. Professor A. A. Vasiliev, one of the greatest contemporary authorities on the Byzantine Empire, has quoted one writer who objected to the people he encountered in Constantinople: "The men are very thievish who dwell in the capital of Constantine; they belong neither to one language nor to one people; there are minglings of strange tongues, and there are very thievish men, Cretans and Turks, Alans, Rhodians, and Chians— all of them being very thievish and corrupt are considered as saints in Constantinople." These words are quoted here to remind the reader that there must be balance in our judgments about Constantinople or any other city. All was not culture and roses in Constantinople. In our own cities we know that not far from the museums of modern art there are depressed areas of which we are not proud. Lazarus always hobbles by the side of Croesus. The furtive criminal lives in the same city as the social workers and the bishops.

Law, government, and art constantly evolved in Constantinople, building upon older traditions tenaciously preserved and honored. Constantinople remained a great storehouse of classical learning until a resurgent western Europe was able and willing to take and use it again. Meanwhile artists and artisans, especially architects and painters, influenced most of the world of the West. We owe a tremendous debt to them. For centuries, too, the bustling docks of Constantinople marked it as the greatest trading port of the Christian world. Maritime enterprise in commerce has often been a bulwark of national power. Men who have grasped the trident of Neptune have usually had fair destinies. The merchants were rich, the city prosperous. "There is none like it in the world, except Bagdad, the great city of Islam." The economic and financial structure was sound; the gold besant circulated unquestioned everywhere. The strength given by wealth had to be defended in a greedy world by a strong army and navy. The Byzantine emperors built both, mainly by drawing upon enlisted men from Asia Minor. Emperors wrote books on the strategy of war.

Through the years it is true that the Byzantine Empire lost Egypt, Mesopotamia, North Africa, and Syria to Islam. On the other hand, it did continue to hold extensive territory in Asia Minor, Greece, the Aegean islands, and most of the lands that now form the Balkan states. It did hold the straits and Constantinople—the eastern buffer and gate of Europe—against successive challenges of the Moslem waves of power. Not until 1453 did the Turks seize Constantinople and turn the famous Cathedral of St. Sophia, "the fairest church in all the world," into a mosque. They obeyed the dictates of the Moslem faith and covered the beautiful mosaics with whitewash. For different reasons in a different age the Puritans of England smashed and slashed the interiors of Anglican churches.

Among the pillars of Byzantine strength and influence were the Orthodox Churches. Byzantium was a Christian monarchy. Eastern Orthodoxy accepted the theory that the emperor had both ecclesiastical and civil duties and functions and that he was the sacred representative of divine power on earth. The patriarchs of the Orthodox Church were always the ecclesiastical allies and associates of the emperor. In the Eastern Empire the Church and the state were united; they were not distinguishable one from the other.

Between the Roman Catholic Church and the Eastern Orthodox Church there soon arose a series of tensions, disputes, and schisms still unhealed. In 1054 there came the final rupture between the Eastern Orthodoxy of Constantinople and the Catholicism of Rome. Each church excommunicated the members of the other. This famous division resulted in part from ecclesiastical and theological quarrels. It resulted also from the fact that the cultures of Rome and Constantinople were and remain incompatible. The approach of Greek Orthodoxy was largely speculative, philosophical, theological. On the other hand, the nature of Roman Catholicism was much more practical and legal.

The Orthodox Churches, then and now, are bound together by a unity of faith and worship and order. At the same time, the churches in such areas as the Balkan states and Russia are really independent and self-governing national bodies, identified with different cultural scenes and characteristics. By the side of the Orthodox Churches still stand the churches that are separated from the Patriarchate of Constantinople. These "separated churches" are mainly remnants of the Monophysite and Nestorian bodies that appeared after the great theological and conciliar disputes of the fourth and fifth centuries. In the "separated" group are such bodies today as the Armenian Church, the Coptic Church of Egypt, the Ethiopian Church, and the Syrian Jacobite Church.

When the Emperor Anastasius died in 518 he was succeeded by Justin, an illiterate and able Illyrian soldier. Justin, a childless man, adopted his nephew Justinian and made him heir to the throne. He required Justinian to be taught the laws and traditions of Rome. Justinian worked hard. Because he had ability of the right kind the work proved profitable. He did find time to marry the gifted daughter of a Cypriot beekeeper. She was to be the brilliant Empress Theodora, fair of face and dark of reputation.

The Emperor Justinian (482–565) wanted to restore the fallen Empire of the West. He paid the Persians to stop being aggressive in the east, withdrew many of his troops from the Danube area, and then turned his power towards Rome. Justinian's generals Belisarius and Narses were men of shining military talents. They defeated and ousted the Vandals from North Africa in 533, seized the Balearic Islands and a short stretch of coast in Spain. They invaded and captured the Gothic kingdom of Italy amidst scenes of terrible destruction in a bitter war that lasted nearly thirty years. They were costly and exhausting victories. Justinian had a long way yet to travel before he could recover all the lost empire. He had not yet set foot upon Gaul, Germany, or Britain; and he had only a tiny bit of Spain. Soon the Lombards swept down upon the unhappy Italian peninsula and Rome was besieged and sacked again. Its greatness was gone. It was a monument surrounded by clogged malarial ditches and swamps. "No more was there a Roman Senate. The last circus had been held, the last triumph celebrated, the last consul elected." Three years after Justinian's death the Lombards had established their new kingdom firmly. Italy was again divided. As a matter of fact, the whole of Italy was not governed again by one ruler until 1870. "Justinian had no successor until Victor Emmanuel."

Meanwhile the powerful khan of the Avars led his savage nomads into the Danube valley and the Balkan regions. The restless Persians threatened to attack the empire on the flank again. The exhausting and brilliant victories of Justinian in Africa, Spain, and Italy had brought no solid or lasting results. The task of recovering the lost lands and prestige was too much for Justinian with his thinly stretched lines and his declining resources. In the circumstances the herculean task he set himself would probably have been too much for anyone. Nevertheless, Justinian still had ambitions far beyond his power. "We have good hopes that the Lord will grant us the rest of the Empire which the Romans formerly extended to the limits of the two oceans and lost through indolence." But there were no more ambitious western wars. Justinian, dying at the age of eighty-three, saw his hopes unrealized. The victories he longed for never came. The imperial heritage he thought was his stayed in other hands.

It was in the domestic affairs of the Eastern Empire that Justinian was most successful. The imperial administration was reorganized and under Justinian's orders the codification of Roman law was completed for the use of the cosmopolitan population. The famous *Code,* later supplemented by the newer decrees called the *Novellae,* was prepared by a commission of several lawyers who were instructed to collect and revise all the formal decrees since the days of Diocletian. They were also commanded to condense, digest, and codify the writings of the jurists, a large and difficult task. The result was the immortal *Digest,* a work in which about 1,500 works by 38 jurists were discussed and analyzed. The commission also published the *Institutes,* a text about first principles. The *Code, Digest,* and *Institutes* together form the *Corpus Juris Civilis,* probably the main channel through which the achievements of Roman law were passed along to posterity. It is difficult to overstress the influence of the *Corpus* in the medieval and modern worlds.

Justinian is also rightly remembered as the emperor who ordered the building of the low-domed Cathedral of St. Sophia to the glory of God. At Justinian's command numerous magnificent buildings were constructed throughout the empire. The superb churches at Ravenna would alone commend him to posterity. All the fine churches raised by Justinian form together one symbol of his militant Christianity. And yet when these things are said, it must also be remembered that Justinian was a bigot. He issued harsh edicts against pagans and sternly bullied heretics. It was he who closed the schools at Athens suspected for their "pagan" teachings and their "Hellenism." The voice of philosophy must be silenced. Philosophers, especially if they disagreed with the emperor, were obviously dangerous men.

Justinian also tried to compel his clergy, often with disastrous results, to obey his decrees about theology and doctrine. Many clergymen preferred either to follow the decisions of the councils of the Church or to go on their own ways without the interference of the emperor. Had it not been for the compromising wisdom of the Empress Theodora, the empire might have been even more sadly divided by the sterile results of stubborn and energetic persecution.

After Justinian died his successors found themselves beset with many foes and perils. These were the years, as we have seen, when the Lombards finished fixing their grasp on Italy. The Spanish lands were lost, this time for good. The Persians, who had earlier seized and plundered Antioch and Damascus, now went to war again. In 614 they captured Jerusalem, slew hundreds of Christians, and carried off the "true cross." The Emperor Heraclius finally stopped them in 622, even as he found himself pressed and plagued by the raiding barbarian Avars. In 626 those Avars joined with the menacing Persians and almost succeeded in capturing Constantinople.

It was in these years that the Prophet Mohammed stirred the vast reservoirs of Arab power. Islam was born. Before the Moslem onslaught the attacks of the Avars and Slavs seemed in retrospect less formidable. The roused and triumphant Moslems, whose amazing course of conquest has been earlier described, wrested large pieces of the Eastern Empire from the weakened hands of the emperors, so exhausted by the protracted wars. Egypt, Palestine, Syria, and the North African lands to the west fell into Moslem hands. In 673 and 717 Constantinople was besieged by the brave and bold sons of the Prophet. But Constantinople did not yield; it did not fall. The Emperor Leo III, an able man, finally pushed back the Moslems about the same time that Charles Martel was defeating them in the battle of Tours in faraway France.

Leo III was less fortunate in dealing with the internal affairs of his empire than he was on the field of battle. It was he who roused the masses to riot and slaughter when he denounced the worship of images and pictures, a step that brought the Eastern Empire once more into bitter conflict with the Church of Rome. Not until 843 was the use of pictures and images in the churches permitted by a new imperial decree.

Soon there were dangers from such restless and belligerent peoples as the

Bulgarians and the Russians. There were also brief flashes of glory. Crete, for instance, was taken back from the Saracens in the tenth century. In the early eleventh century the Bulgarians were defeated. On that occasion the strong and nasty Emperor Basil II cruelly blinded 15,000 Bulgars. Earlier, in the eighth century, the ruthless Irene had her own son blinded so that she might become empress. Such tales and facts, unpleasant to contemplate, are numerous.

Most of the time the Byzantine Empire was literally fighting for its life. Attacks from one quarter were followed by attacks from another. By the eleventh century the Venetians stretched their power over the Adriatic. The Seljuk Turks occupied Bagdad in 1055, conquered Armenia and Georgia, reached the Dardanelles in 1079, and then hurled themselves towards the inner citadels of the empire. Earlier, in 1071, they had won a great battle at Manzikert and captured the emperor. These Turks then swallowed the eastern part of Asia Minor and continued to strike and strike again. Meanwhile the Normans grabbed imperial territory in Sicily and the southern Italian mainland. In these stormy hours the empire was still further harassed by the fact that several of its leaders were incompetent and fumbling and many of its emperors were weak and vicious. Some of those emperors died by poison or the quiet knives of assassins. We are told by historians who have carefully counted the rulers of the Eastern Empire that more than sixty emperors abdicated or were murdered in the course of 800 years. The very fact that the empire survived in the long decades of manifold disaster is amazing proof of its vitality. It was certainly corrupt. It was incompetent most of the time. It was regarded as decadent for centuries. Yet for hundreds of years it maintained itself.

In the end, of course, the Byzantine Empire moved slowly and steadily towards its blood-red sunset. On the Fourth Crusade (1204) the soldiers of the Cross paused to seize and sack Constantinople in a disgraceful and familiar scene of rapacity and violence. The commercial profits of the great city passed more and more to the clutching hands of the Venetian and Genoese merchants. Internecine wars combined with religious disputes, class conflicts, economic and military palsy to weaken the sinews and nerves of the imperial administration and the people it governed. We know the result, so long delayed. In 1453, as we saw in the previous chapter, the Emperor Constantine XIII gathered his army of 9,000 men and stood against 160,000 Turks. In the rest of Europe not a sword was lifted to aid him. Constantine XIII fell, and with him fell Constantinople, the last bulwark of the Eastern Empire. The gates of Europe swung open and the Moslems entered. "Under a pile of corpses someone saw eagles embroidered in gold on a pair of shoes, and so identified the body of the last direct successor of Constantine and Augustus."

An historian of the twentieth century, looking back to the years immediately following the end of the era of Rome, notes the poisons and pressures that caused the destruction of the great empire and the events that marked one of the major turning points of history. The motives and impulses underlying the actions of men did not greatly change. Many of them are as old as the human race. Many of the tasks of human beings still remained. The rains came and went and the crops continued to grow. Conquerors may come and depart, but the land must be ploughed, the clods broken up, the seeds planted, the harvests reaped. We are often so concerned with the dramatic scenes in history that we forget the constant rhythms of the seasons and the flow of food from the fields of nameless men.

Nor were all of the arts and skills of Rome forever lost. We are still linked to Rome, just as we are linked to the invention of agriculture and the taming of fire in the primeval night. There is a continuity in all things.

There is also relentless change. In these years European man, prompt and powerful, made drastic and swift alterations in his ways and views of life after the day when the forum roared no longer and he stood blinking in the sunlight amid the ruins of the Colosseum.

This chapter has not attempted to give a comprehensive picture of the outcome of the Roman collapse. It is always useful to remember that too many serried ranks of facts, intriguing as they are, may bore and baffle all but the most learned and dedicated scholars and experts. The main broad facts of consequence are that after the Roman world fell many thousands of people endeavored, amidst great difficulties, to find new roads and destinations. True, anarchy and absurdity did have their fling—as they always do in fermenting times. Nevertheless, an unbiased observer becomes increasingly aware of the ways in which virile and determined men hastened to lift Europe out of one groove and began to set it in another. The old idea that the Dark Ages were really dark is entirely untrue and must be abandoned. This insistent comment was made at the beginning of this chapter and it bears repeating at the end.

One way or another, through the long years of contact with Christianity, a massive foundation was built for the Christendom of the Middle Ages. Christianity was a thing of the spirit, and hence often more enduring than some impermanent varnishes imposed upon aliens from without and mistakenly named "culture." A second great thing that gradually happened was the emergence in Europe of several groupings of tribes loosely called states. The greatest of these, forged with much marching and fighting, were the Frankish Merovingian and Carolingian kingdoms. Thirdly, the Roman Empire in the East did not perish. It stood, and it stood with an exciting history for a thousand years. Such have been the main themes of this chapter.

Europe was now moving into the Middle Ages towards a period of throbbing action and clashing ideas. The Middle Ages were not nearly so sleepy and static as many individuals think. The late Professor Eileen Power said they looked to her as lively as an ant heap. New skills appeared. New ideas rose and soared. New ranges of challenging thought gleamed beyond the foothills. The currents and cross-currents of the medieval centuries are many and deep. On the one hand there are the supreme achievements of men like St. Thomas Aquinas and Geoffrey Chaucer and the stirring tales of the forgers of feudalism and the makers of the Crusades. On the other, one may find the stumbling words or the broken swords of men whose names have long since perished. Between the fall of Rome and the shining centuries of the Renaissance there also stand forth, as always, the everlasting themes of love, death, honor, courage, and the familiar follies and hopes of man.

PART II

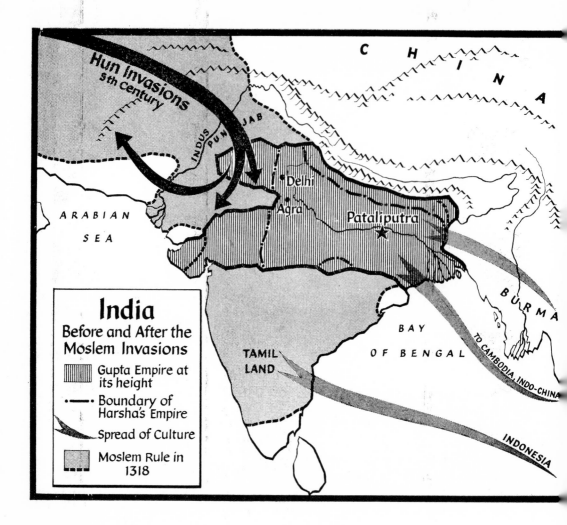

India
Before and After the Moslem Invasions

▥	Gupta Empire at its height
▬·▬·	Boundary of Harsha's Empire
◅	Spread of Culture
▦	Moslem Rule in 1318

Hun Invasions
5th Century

INDUS
PUNJAB

ARABIAN
SEA

•Delhi
•Agra

Pataliputra

C H I N A

BURMA

BAY
OF BENGAL

TAMIL
LAND

TO CAMBODIA, INDO-CHINA

INDONESIA

Chapter 13

INDIA: THE GOLDEN AGE
AND AFTER

"In the beginning rose Hiranyagarbha, born only lord of all created beings.
He fixed and holdeth up this earth and heaven. What god shall we adore
with our oblation?"

—Rigveda, X, 121

UNCOUNTED generations of men have lived and died through the gradual
changes of the centuries in India. The steps in their advance were piti-
fully slow, the reverses many, the formidable misery and poverty constant and
unrelieved. In experiences sacred and profane, in the mingling of mystery
and sweat, in the intensely moving insights and labors of a shining gallery
of saints who taught and toiled, in the crimes of cruel or careless men, in
tragic and twisted and sometimes glorious ways, the web of the cultural
heritage of India was interwoven. Turn where we will today to apply the tests
of consequences, we discover the importance of inherited patterns of belief
and action in that great land. We observe on every hand the results of passivity and assent and pathetic misdirections of human effort. Open wide the
windows over the horizons, and multitudes of human beings are seen toiling
with primitive tools and listening to the muffled voices of their ancestors.
Even in the midst of the uprooting winds of the twentieth century most
treadmill habits and traditional faiths endure, effortless and ordered, anchored
in the rocks and the ancient earth. Of such things is greatness sometimes
made.

When we peer down towards the beginning of the long avenues of India's
history we can see some of the bizarre and tantalizing events and a few personalities. Then we can see no more. The road twists back into the years of
silence behind the veil. We do know, of course, that even in the obscure
days before recorded history certain things must have been true. For instance,
the men who lived in a land like India were compelled to adapt themselves
to the relentless and rigorous demands of climate and soil. Their destinies,

habits, desires, and ideals were in part determined and set by the conditions imposed by nature.

It is also true that the subcontinent of India is a vast land with many kinds of climate and soil and with millions of human beings scattered about its miles. The country and the people must not be described as if they were the same in all times and places. Just as New York is not New Orleans, so Bombay is not Calcutta or Madras. The traveler sees that within India there are great variations between the regions, profound differences and varieties of pattern. Within all Asia there are mixed and complex swirlings so vast and bewildering that the words "East" and "Orient" are often dangerous nouns because they say so little.

In the roadless oxcart past of India, in the long interconnected chapters of empires and squabbling states, there emerged habits and attitudes that are difficult for the men of the West to comprehend. Our chapters of continuity and change in onmoving time have been different. In India, for instance, there appeared religions and philosophies highly organized and rich in their peculiar values. There came teachings that gave the peoples of India varying views of the world and the universe. These views differ vitally and radically from the ones of men who live in the western sectors of the planet. If we use the yardsticks of our own land and countrymen in any effort to understand ancient or modern India, we will fail to achieve even a semblance of understanding or informed sympathy. Then we may perhaps flee to the woods of prejudice or take refuge in platitudes without explanation. It is always easy to do that; but it is not wise.

Western eyes and minds must not judge India or any other land of Asia by Western values and Western laws. This injunction is easily given, hard to follow. It is difficult, for example, for Western man to understand the principle of nonactivity, the passionless contemplation of the world's unrolling, the idea of the negation of material things so strongly held in India. There are few citizens in the lands of Europe and America who believe that true existence is immaterial and that the material world is deceptive, transitory, and unreal. Not many Frenchmen, Englishmen, or Americans try to outleap the barriers of flesh and things. The tides of our cultures have not carried these ideas. To us they are strange and baffling. So it is that men of the West often reject, quite summarily, concepts that are external to their awareness and kept secret from their understanding. Men of Asia frequently do the same thing.

What we do not understand we sometimes denounce or evade. Such a procedure is natural and human and often comfortable. Why, it is said, should we be deeply concerned with the skinny and sour inheritance of other men? We of the West may insist that few can find intelligible the lines of the *Rigveda*. They of the East may assert that few can break through the thickets of the prose of Georg Wilhelm Hegel when the owl of Minerva takes its flight in the gathering darkness. Men of all lands sometimes forget that they "should not try a case by a code unknown to the defendant." Miss Amy Loveman, that great lady of American letters, once stated a law of human behavior in six sad words: "He who knows little rejects much."

We have seen how rulers and empires rose and perished in the bitter days of ancient India. Early invaders came along that great traffic line of the northwest, through passes and plains saturated with history. With spears and rough hands they pushed and prodded and plundered. Alexander the Great, that reckless and inspired genius, marched and trampled with his armies towards the rising sun. Other conquerors, cruel and arrogant, arrived with flurries of trumpets and flickers of unsheathed swords.

> The East bowed low before the blast,
> In patient, deep disdain;
> She let the legions thunder past,
> Then plunged in thought again.

Meanwhile, in these distant days, the whole of southeast Asia was dotted with the cultures of the peasant folks and disturbed by savage wars. Early civilizations appeared in the river deltas. Highly developed tribal organizations were shaped in Burma, Indochina, Indonesia, Malaya, the Philippines, Siam. The enduring strength of folk cultures grew in the cohesive village life. The villages were closed worlds, the centers of existence of thousands of families. Here were formed and cherished the skills in handicrafts, the beliefs in magic and ritual, the primitive worship of unseen forces, the dances and the chants, the rules and customs that still survive in the remote and green fastnesses where the voices of the outside are seldom heard or heeded. These villages stood when empires and cities were swept away. Large empires did arise on the mainland: in Cambodia, Champa, Modjopahit, and Angkor. Every one of them collapsed. They were slowly swallowed up by the conquering power of the green jungles. Even in the spots where they thrived they are now almost completely forgotten. Only dim memories drift through the mists of oblivion.

We have seen in one of the earlier chapters that a Hindu rajah named Chandragupta Maurya founded a dynasty in the Ganges valley about 320 B.C. This efficient man was mainly responsible for driving out the garrison of Alexander the Great. He was a brilliant general and an administrator who proved his excellence again and again. He was also a zealous and ambitious ruler who believed in conquering and holding whatever he could. Before his death he had built an empire of three great provinces that stretched in a broad belt over all of northern India from the Arabian Sea to the Bay of Bengal. To create this empire and to hold back his hungry enemies Chandragupta

gave first importance to the task of forging strong military forces. Because
he believed in the arguments of power Chandragupta made and maintained
a large and efficient army. He paid the price that safety and ambition demanded.

With power and stability came peace, wealth, and trade. After Alexander
the Great died Chandragupta lived upon excellent terms with Seleucus, the
general who inherited the eastern empire. In the court of Chandragupta the
linking influence of Greek and Persian culture grew strong and constant.
The court also became famous throughout the East for its pomp and luxury,
its lavish displays of gold and silver and jewels and servants. The geographer
Strabo tells us that in one of the court processions there moved "a great host of
attendants in holiday dress, with golden vessels, such as huge basins and
goblets, six feet broad, tables, chairs of state . . . buffalos, leopards, and
tame lions and rare birds in cages." It must be admitted, of course, that Strabo
should always be quoted with doubt and hesitation. He was apparently seldom
inhibited by any passion for the truth. It is he who tells us about the "wool-
bearing" trees in India and about the law in that land that said anyone discovering a deadly poison must be executed unless he also found an antidote.

In an earlier chapter we have also seen something of the work of the deeply
religious and tolerant Asoka (273–232 B.C.), a great king who in some ways
did not quite belong to his times. This grandson of Chandragupta not only
spread far abroad the teachings of Buddha but he also carried out many needed
reforms within his empire. For instance, he relaxed many harsh laws and made
many other reforms in the methods of punishing crime. His great fame then
and later rested in large part upon the fact that what he did seemed sane and
sensible. Several of his imperial edicts were carved upon numerous stone pillars and rocks. There are six main Pillar and Rock Edicts and many minor
ones. The traveler in northern India today can see some of these pillars and
rocks still standing. Their messages, carved more than 2,000 years ago, are
sometimes still legible. The finest extant example of a monolithic Asoka pillar
is the plain polished Sarnath shaft erected on the traditional site of the First
Turning of the Wheel of the Law. "Thus says he who was dear to the gods:
'Where there are stone pillars or stone slabs, there this Edict of Piety is to be
inscribed, that it may be permanent.'"

From his famous palace at Pataliputra, Asoka sent out men to build hundreds of monasteries or *viharas*. Many of his successors followed his example.
Perhaps the oldest monastery in India is at Bhaja in the western Ghats near
Poona. In most of the monasteries there are still to be seen examples of work
done by Indian artists once well described by Dr. Ananda K. Coomaraswamy
as being "men of wild, fertile, uncanny imaginations, filled with dread of the
tiger-haunted forest, the power of the storm, and the marvel of the sun that
journeys through the air."

Asoka and the men who followed him also built several *stupas* or "topes." The name and structural form of these *stupas* came from the funeral mounds in pre-Buddha days. By the time of Asoka the *stupas* were constructed to enshrine relics of the Buddha or other teachers or to mark holy spots. Each stone, rock, or brick *stupa* is built in the form of a great solid dome resting on a triple circular base set upon terraces or a paved square. Above the dome is a cubicle, or "god's house," from which projects a mast carrying one or more stone umbrellas or parasols (*chatra*), the Indian symbol of sovereignty used because Buddha was of royal birth. Like most forms of architecture, the *stupa* went through several stages of stylistic development. This statement is also true of the development of the low, massive, flat-roofed cave temples of ancient and medieval India. The famed cave temples of Ajanta and Elephanta still enchant the men and women who come to wonder or worship.

Around all *stupas* stand four stone gateways carved with decorations. There are usually several scenes from the life of the Buddha, such as the Incarnation, the Nativity, or the Enlightenment. These are never represented by human forms but only by symbols, such as the caitya tree, the umbrella, the sandals, and the Wheel. The three-pointed triratna symbol represents the "Three Jewels"—the Buddha, the Law, and the Order.

When Asoka died in 232 B.C. the Mauryan empire fell into the hands of feeble and careless men. They slowly lost what they had inherited. There is often no substitute for strength, and the later Mauryans had neither strength nor sound judgment. Weak rulers and weak states cannot expect to thrive or survive for long in a ruthless world. "It is useless for the sheep to pass resolutions in favor of vegetarianism so long as the wolves remain of a different opinion."

The Mauryan dynasty yielded to the Sunga family in 184 B.C. The Sungas then insulted and persecuted the Buddhists and squandered the wealth and power accumulated by their predecessors. In a familiar tale of terror new invaders came through the northwestern mountain passes. Greeks, Syrians, and Scythians brought Greek and Persian culture into the western Punjab when they conquered the land and settled there. These were the years when the strong Greek kingdom of Bactria reached its height of prestige and power, when there occurred the building of hundreds of pieces of Persian architecture in northwest India, and when the nomads exploding out of central Asia continued relentlessly to raid and slay. To the south, meanwhile, the Sunga dynasty yielded to the Kanva, the Kanva to the Andhra, the chiefs of a Dravidian people famous for their walled towns.

About 100 A.D. the Andhra rulers gradually gave way before the pressures of the Kushans and the other alien tribesmen from central Asia. By the time that this happened the Kushans had already overrun the Punjab and smashed the defenses of the Indo-Greek princes on the frontier. Decade after decade saw successive invasions and civil wars, a dark and bloody welter of confusion and death.

After the darkness came the light. There slowly rose to power in northern India a rajah named Chandragupta I. This man was not related to the earlier Mauryan emperor. He was an able member of the lowborn Gupta family who had married a princess and had become master of the Magadha region. In 320 he was crowned with the proud title King of Kings, and the Gupta era began. Chandragupta's son, the famous warrior Samudragupta, ruled for fifty years and conquered wide and wealthy provinces. Before he died almost all of northern India had fallen under his sway. The long miles of his empire included most of Afghanistan and Baluchistan, all of Sind, Nepal, Kashmir. He held Bengal to the mouth of the Ganges, peninsular India to the lands beyond the Narbada River. When Samudragupta died he was succeeded by Chandragupta II (375–413). This stern and strong ruler pushed the frontiers of empire still further towards the west. Under him the glory of the strong and brilliant Gupta culture reached its height. It was indeed a golden age for India, a shining chapter in the records of a long history.

Such times as these usually bring forth high cultural achievements. The Gupta period is the classical age of Indian art. A sensitive individual in the twentieth century is delighted to see the graces of perception and expression, the rhythm of the curving lines, the dignity, subtlety, and restraint of the painted or chiseled scenes and figures. In the Gupta age there is a unification of indigenous, early Asiatic, Persian and Hellenistic art forms and a steady evolution in styles. All of the art is powerful. Some of it is unhappy, painful, and terrifying. Perhaps certain works reflect the fears of cruel invaders, the racking and oppressive governments of the past, and the nameless horrors of hunger, slaughter, and other dread things in the half-alive villages and the city alleys of disease and squalor. Man has often tried to picture his nightmare fears as well as his hopes of heaven. In the East, of course, the truth to which art aspires with its formalized techniques is almost always the embodiment of imaginative symbols. In the sculpture of the Gupta artists, for instance, we see a perfected medium of explicit statement of spiritual ideas. Most Asiatic art suggests, with rich decorative resources and astounding vividness, an aloofness from the changing material world or conveys the idea of the visible and tangible universe as mere illusion, or *maya*.

Much of the work of the Gupta artists illustrates their concern with deep spiritual meaning, with the changeless values of the universe as they saw it. Consider, for instance, the numerous Buddha figures, dignified symbols of enlightenment and life everlasting.

All-Honored, Wisest, Best, most Pitiful,
The Teacher of Nirvana and the Law.

Look at the violence of Siva in the "Dance of Destruction" or the calmness of the goddess Vishnu, always the Preserver.

The words of John Fergusson, written long ago about some other aspects of Gupta art, are still true: "Some animals, such as elephants, deer, and monkeys, are better represented by the Gupta artists than in any sculpture known in any other part of the world." Anyone who has seen and admired the floral designs or the trees cut in the stone or metal would agree that they present an excellent and lasting definition of the meaning of precision and elegance. The same careful craftsmanship is to be seen in the numerous plaques and terra cottas, the bronze and copper gilt figures, the iron and steel work. Some of the finest artistry is found in the engraved steel of the tempered Dravidian swords. Skilled hands also produced magnificent brass water vessels (*lota* and *surahi*), superb decorations of metal inlay and overlay, filigree work in gold, the imbedding of jewels by soft gold bezels, silver and gold enamelings, especially in the Lahore district, sacred images and dice of cut ivory, pierced or carved plaques and inlaid doors, panel bronzes of great beauty. Their achievements in textile making were marked by many types of techniques and designs in weaving, dye-painting, and embroidery. Throughout Asia the skilled fingers of the textile makers labored, with scrupulous attention, to make the silks and velvets of Bokhara, the Kachin shirts of Burma, the striped mashrus, and the gold and cotton threads. The influence of India's arts and crafts has been clearly traced to many lands. The waves and ripples reached in the East to Bali, Burma, Cambodia, Ceylon, China, Indochina (especially the Campa art), Indonesia, Japan, Java (particularly in the seventh century), Korea, Siam, Sumatra, Tibet.

The fertile age of the Guptas also brought significant developments in poetry, art, and drama. India is not only one of the oldest nations in the world. It is also one of the most poetic. Certainly India's mystic poetry ranks among the best of its sort ever written. It was in the years when the Guptas ruled that Kalidasa, perhaps the finest of all India's poets, wrote his *Cycle of the Seasons, The Dynasty of Raghu, The Cloud Messenger, The Birth of the War-God,* and the world-famous *Shakuntala.*

> My limbs move forward, while my heart flies back
> Like a silken standard borne against the breeze.

These were the years, too, when Bhartrihari was penning his short and moving lyrics and an unknown master who called himself "King Sudraka" wrote *The Little Clay Cart,* a lovely thing. The writers of fairy tales and fables were also busy, not knowing that what they wrote would find a place in the literature of many lands. Because the Arabs borrowed the story of Sinbad from India there are few children in the civilized world who have not stayed sleepless listening to the strange and wonderful adventures of that magnificent sailor.

Nor did the scientists nod or lag. Astronomers and mathematicians calculated the diameter of the moon, predicted eclipses, found the square root of two. The chemists and their fellows made soap, glass, and cement. The medical men seem to have been wise and skillful for their times. For example, the surgeons sometimes sterilized wounds. Let us not make too much of this fact, however easy it may be to claim and assert that the physicians and surgeons of early India were far in advance of their times. It must be said, quite calmly and cautiously, that the men of India were not at all consistent in their use of sterilizing procedures and that nobody seems to be sure that they knew what they were doing. Only a careless enthusiast would venture to claim that they had any inkling of a germ theory of disease or a knowledge of the processes of infection.

Several brilliant achievements of Indian science and mathematics were exported and explained abroad. The Greeks and Arabs were strongly influenced by the men of India, and they, in turn, passed along to India many of the discoveries and inventions of the Near East and of Europe. The export and import of ideas and skills always goes on between peoples, century after century, increasing their knowledge and sharpening their curiosity. It is obvious that both direct transference and gradual osmosis are of massive importance in the growth and decay of cultures and civilizations. Some influences, of course, must remain forever unknown or obscure. At the same time, many facts about the interchange of ideas and knowledge have not been discovered because no explorers or detectives have gone looking for them. Too few careful or penetrating analyses of cultural interchange have been made or attempted by competent scholars.

Chandragupta II was a careful and persistent ruler, a master of statecraft, a solid center of gravity in the state. When he died in 413 the Gupta empire began to crack and crumble. The years of serene and unswerving progress ended. The earlier vigilance and vitality, the old confidence and strength, seem to have ebbed and drained away. The leaders of the state acted as if they were the victims of some strange and numbing malady. They slowed down, halted, and then sat still in trancelike impotence. First there came several years of ominous and sinister rumors and unsettling tensions. Then came the tests of strength as new invaders, baleful and malevolent, poured from the northwest into the Punjab and pushed towards the Indus and to Sind.

These attackers were the White Huns, a branch of the aggressive and ruthless tribesmen who were shaking both Asia and Europe. Before the power of those inspired brigands the might of Persia had fallen. They had overrun the Kushan kingdom of Kabul. Now the Gupta empire collapsed in flames and ruins. The rise of the Guptas had been almost meteoric. Their fall was calamitous.

> When sorrows come, they come not single spies
> But in battalions.

The rule of the Huns did not last long. In 528, battered by Turkish attacks on the Oxus and by powerful revolts in India, the Hun empire fell. Many of the Huns were driven out. Others retired to Kashmir, soon to be absorbed in the teeming millions.

Into the vacuum of power now came Harsha (607–647), a strong and benevolent despot of brave deeds and great decisions, a king, poet, dramatist, military genius, and patron of the arts. An inscription plate says that Harsha was one "whose fame spread beyond the four seas, and to whom submitted the other kings in power and love." According to the contemporary poet Bana, the great Harsha was frequently too cribbed, confined, and frustrated: "His energy wants scope and his fame sighs for a wider horizon; his kindly nature seeks in vain more hearts to win, his virtues exhaust the powers of number and all the fine arts are too narrow a field for his genius." Bana also tells us that Harsha became "a lion to the Huna deer, a burning fever to the king of the Indus land, a trouble to the sleep of Gujerat, a bilious plague to that scent elephant, the lord of Gandhara, a looter to the lawlessness of the Lata, an axe to the creeper of Malwa's glory."

There were many other eulogies, all of which need to be looked upon shrewdly. Fulsome flattery and adulation are clearly not the same thing as the precise facts. The really important fact is that the empire of Harsha began in the north and Harsha steadily made it larger. Before he died it seemed possible that he might be able to extend his power over all of India.

It was not to be. In 647 the childless Harsha died and with him died his empire. The disruptive forces of northern India were unleashed once more. The burdens of these chapters of Indian history seem always the same: the growth and destruction of empires. With monotonous regularity the familiar themes appear. For hundreds of years the whole land of India was plagued by warring kings and desperate peoples. In the north, victors and vanquished swayed in apparently interminable struggles. In the south, the three ancient kingdoms of Chera, Chola, and Pandya went upon their old ways, the roads of truce and war.

After the death of Harsha the rivalries of the Rajputs, the Sons of Kings, brought confusion and terror. Then, in 664, the first waves of the Moslem Arabs invaded the Punjab through the funnels of the northern passes. In 711 they conquered Sind in the name of the caliph of Damascus—this was the same year that Tarik was leading a Moorish army in the first Moslem assaults upon Spain. In 997 the Sultan Mahmud of Ghazni probed and pushed into the

plains of the north with his Turkish and Afghan armies. Mahmud was the
son of a Turkish slave. He had escaped the world of his father and had risen
to rule most of Afghanistan. It is said that he invaded India seventeen times.
His most famous attack was in 1025 when he marched to seize the temple
raised to Siva in the sacred city of Somnath. Tradition says that Mahmud
fought the Hindus for two days and then forced them to flee. Then, it is also
said, Mahmud followed the Brahman priests into the temple and there struck
the great idol of Siva "and forthwith a fountain of precious stones gushed out."
For more than 800 years the club of Mahmud and the wooden gates of
Somnath were kept at Mahmud's tomb near Ghazni. About 1840 they disappeared and probably nobody knows where they are today.

Delhi was captured by the Moslems in 1206. Rapidly the Delhi sultanate
extended its effective power and the north was soon subdued from the Indus
to the Brahmaputra. By the end of the century the Deccan had fallen before
the might of the Turks. For more than 500 years the Moslems were to rule
from their capitals at Delhi and Agra.

The Moslem march to power did not go unchallenged. There were wars
and blood-feuds. In 1219 the fighting Asiatic nomads of Genghis Khan
reached the Indus. In 1398 the mighty Tamerlane captured and pillaged Delhi
and ravaged much of the land of the north. Then he departed. Behind him
the Moslem power stood, shaken and bruised.

The fifth Moslem leader to strike into northwest India was Baber, a direct
descendant of Tamerlane. He came in 1526. After his victory at Panipat, Baber
settled his Mogul followers in the plains of Hindustan. They were probably
pleased to be such well-rewarded soldiers of "the Tiger." Baber established the
capital of the new Mogul Empire at Delhi, ancient seat of kings.

Many of the Moguls were highly successful rulers. They were also skilled
in spreading the faith of Mohammed. Nearly one-fourth of the inhabitants of
the Indian subcontinent are Moslems today. It might thus be argued that in
a sense the founder of the modern state of Pakistan was Baber, a ruthless soldier
and a missionary, "an educated and accomplished man, an elegant poet . . .
a great admirer of beautiful prospects and fine flowers." From what we read
of him it seems certain that Baber also liked fine food and lingered over his
curried shrimp and his Tandoori chicken fried with spices.

Baber died in 1530 at the age of forty-eight. The most able of his successors
was Akbar (1542–1605), "the best of the princes of the house of Tamerlane."
This contemporary of Philip II of Spain, Elizabeth I of England, and Henry
IV of France has many solid claims to fame. In the first place, Akbar was a
soldier, and a good one. Shortly after he came to the throne he began to wage
a long war to extend his power in the Punjab and the land around Delhi and
Agra. At that time he had an uneasy hold upon a belt of territory about 300

miles wide stretching from the frontier to Bengal. By 1572 Akbar ruled from his capital at Agra over more of India than any one man ever claimed before. Later he went on to seize and hold Kabul, Kandahar, Kashmir, and Sind. Only the plateau of the Deccan and the reaches of Tamil Land evaded his clutching hands. Akbar was the real founder of the Mogul Empire.

The victories of war were matched by the shining achievements of peace. Akbar's reign was marked on every hand by enlightenment, toleration, and compromise. He encouraged architects, artists, painters, and writers. He insisted upon the cooperation of Moslems and Hindus throughout the state, asserting again and again that the foundations of the empire could be made firm and lasting only if there was understanding and reasonable harmony among the people and a toleration of diverse faiths by all men.

The emperor's actions met and matched his words. He put Hindus into positions of power and trust in the government. He abolished the poll tax imposed on all non-Moslems. He forbade the slave raids formerly carried out to provide forced labor for the court. He permitted full freedom of worship. He married a Hindu princess.

In Akbar's day Persian was the official language of the Mogul court. The invaders spoke Arabic and Persian. Many of the Hindus spoke Hindi, the language of western India. Because of the mingling of Moslems and Hindus the Persian and Arabic languages were combined with Hindi to form Urdu, a language widely used in modern Pakistan. Hindi later grew into modern Hindustani. Likewise, the Sikh religion came out of a mingling of Moslem and Hindu beliefs.

There are about 6,000,000 Sikhs in Indian today. Such were a few of the long-term developments that came in part from Akbar's policies of balanced understanding and enlightened compromise.

There were other reforms. Akbar forbade child marriage, *suttee,* and trial by ordeal. He so arranged the taxation procedures that the land revenue became a steady flow into the exchequer rather than an irregular flood or trickle spasmodically and haphazardly collected. He asserted that only salaried civil-service officials could provide an adequate basis for sound and honest administration. Therefore he created such a service. He also divided his empire into fifteen provinces and put a governor in each directly responsible to the emperor. Akbar liked efficiency as well as peace and justice.

Akbar went further. He tried to establish a new universal state religion, the *Din Ilahi* or Divine Faith, a religion containing what Akbar thought was the essence of the teachings of all the faiths and the best features and practices of all the creeds. The result was a strange kind of natural philosophy. Akbar became the head of a new church in which men worshiped the sun, the divine soul or spirit that was said to give life to the universe. Despite the emperor's zeal and persuasion the unfamiliar ideas were not widely accepted. The people did not want common agreement on religion if they would find it necessary to surrender any part of their individual beliefs. They preferred to walk and worship in the old paths. About all of them stayed where they were before Akbar proclaimed his new universal church. He who ventures to touch or move the rocks of ancient faiths invites defeat. Akbar never tired or weakened in the pursuit of his hopes and the carrying out of his plans. So far as his arrangements for the introduction and adoption of his new faith were concerned, he worked hard. Nevertheless, he failed. Akbar was willing to burn and bury the old religions. His subjects were not.

Like Asoka before him, Akbar was a ruler who met and grappled with the main issues of his age. He was an example and a model for the enlightened rulers of any period—if we do not take into account his plans for a reformed religion. Akbar was able, learned, understanding, and generous. Call this statement exaggerated if you will; but it is the truth.

Akbar died in 1605. He was buried beneath a severely simple slab in the magnificent mausoleum he built near Agra. Few tombs contain nobler dust.

Most of the Mogul rulers who followed Akbar need not detain us long. We may pause to note that Shah Jehan (1627–1666), Akbar's grandson, tried to push and pull all of India into the Moslem faith. He persecuted Hindus and smashed their temples. He did succeed in conquering the Deccan. It was Shah Jehan who built the white marble Taj Mahal at Agra as a mausoleum for his favorite wife. The beauty and importance of his wife are forgotten; but the domed and minareted Taj Mahal remains one of the world's great achievements in architecture. About the same time Shah Jehan's servants and subjects constructed the splendid marble palaces at Delhi. On the walls of the one containing the Peacock Throne is the inscription: "If anywhere on earth there is a Paradise, it is here, it is here, it is here."

The last of the Moguls was Aurungzebe (1659–1707). He was a detestable and bigoted fanatic. He persecuted the Hindus with merciless zeal. The poll tax on non-Moslems that Akbar had removed Aurungzebe put back. He battered and tore down many Hindu temples. Hence he lost the support of most Hindus. The warrior Rajputs in the north deserted him. Many Moslems joined the widening ranks of the rebels.

For 500 years the Moslems had ruled in India. The Afghan and Turkish sultans had held sway from about 1200 to 1526, the year that the Mogul Empire began. Now the Mogul Empire was flickering towards its last years. The scene has been described in Lord Macaulay's *Essay on Lord Clive*. That giant of letters followed his usual custom of putting things very well: "Throughout the long reign of Aurungzebe, the state, notwithstanding all that the vigor and policy of the prince could effect, was hastening to dissolution. After his death, which took place in 1707, the ruin was fearfully rapid. Violent shocks from without cooperated with an incurable decay which was fast proceeding within; and in a few years the empire had undergone utter decomposition."

Chapter 14

CHINA AND JAPAN:

BOOKS AND SWORDS

"Under the firmament is not so great a lord, nor so mighty, nor so rich, as the great Khan; not Prester John, that is the Emperor of the high Ind, nor the Soldan of Babylon, nor the Emperor of Persia. All these are not to be compared to the great Khan, neither in might, nor in noblesse, nor in royalty, nor in riches; for in all these he passes all earthly princes."
—*The Voyages and Travels of Sir John Mandeville*

CHINA is a giant land of distances, space, and contrasts. There are the bare and treeless plains, the naked mountains, the shocking bareness of the tortured lands of the northwest, the great death-dry deserts where the winds rage and the sands cut and bodies wither in the sun. There are the boggy hollows where oil, manganese, lead, and copper lie beneath the ground. There are the low and rich river valleys. There are the high places of Sinkiang and Tibet. The old city of Mukden stands not far from the new cities of Fushun and Anshan, centers of coal and steel production, so useful in the modern world. Past and present meet and merge.

From time immemorial millions of leg-weary men have moved with a measured tread over the footpaths carrying their bamboo poles and their balanced loads. Until the edge of modern times there were few roads, few wheels in China outside the cities. The ancient codes and attitudes dictated a deep mass antagonism to some advances of technology, despite the fine achievements of several Chinese scientists and inventors. Our world of the West, so absorbed in savoring present progress and future promise, has often found it difficult to understand a land that has judged time by centuries and survived by the toil of human backs, a land where plagues and famines still strike and where more than four-fifths of the people are still illiterate.

The Chinese people have not always remained indifferent and unmoved or fixed in their traditional apathy. There have been disturbed and menacing hours, boiling and swirling like the Yangtze. Generations of families have known the fear and frenzy of combat, the pain of wounds, the agony of famine. China has seen dark muddles of intrigue and hopeless incapacity in government. Many disputes have embittered and embattled the affairs of millions of men. The weak and the exposed have fallen. The determined and the strong have survived. They have dominated and persecuted to their advantage as they increased the scars of China.

The sad and dangerous hours of the contemporary Chinese commonwealth of fear and hope cannot be understood apart from the background of the long past. Nor can the perils and problems of China be appreciated unless we remember always the pressures upon a great population steadily increasing as it moves along the road to survival. Manchuria alone is half the size of France. One-tenth of all the human race lives in the Yangtze river basin. In the immense area of China there are half a billion people who must be fed every day.

These problems of geography, population, and human nature in modern China are not nearly so strange and new as some men think. Many of the difficulties existed in a slightly different form in the Middle Ages. It is a symbol of history that the Chinese dragon should be drawn with writhing convoluted folds.

The Han dynasty began to rule in China in 206 B.C. and collapsed in 220 A.D. The result of the end of the Han rule was a period of wild and savage disorder that lasted for nearly 400 years. Then came the strong and impressive brief rule of the Sui family (589–618). They kept power and order with a large army and safeguarded their government with brutality. Many of their measures were odious and criminal. The most important part of their constructive work was the linking of the great canals of China into one vast network. This tremendous task was completed by the forced labor of thousands of men toiling in the sun day after day, year upon year.

The Sui dynasty was strong, but not strong enough. It was honeycombed with fatal ills. A sudden revolt in the army, a sudden attack in the night, and the Sui family was overthrown. "Success is never blamed."

The new rulers of China were the T'ang family, shrewd and ruthless emperors, hard-eyed and able. The governments they established were usually efficient and honest, an unusual thing in China. The whole government system was neatly organized to do the necessary tasks swiftly and well. Men discovered to be corrupt or careless or lazy lost their jobs and sometimes their heads.

The members of the T'ang family (618–906) wanted to make themselves supreme in all China and China supreme in all the East. Because they were practical men they made alliances with the northern tribes beyond the Great Wall. Many of these alien tribesmen were absorbed into China, as water is taken up by a sponge.

Slowly the might of the T'angs reached further and further until it touched and invaded Korea. The Hans had once taken much of the northern areas. The T'angs went in again and finished the job. Thus began Korea's long vassalage under the Chinese and later the Mongols. Meanwhile, Japan's watchful eye and eager arm were always ready to take advantage of an hour of weakness. Not until 1876 did Japan recognize the independence of Korea. Not until 1895 did China agree that Korea might be united and free. Half a century later Korea was divided again.

The power of the T'angs also swept far into Mongolia, Nepal, Tibet, and Turkestan. China was now in direct contact with India and Persia. From the Near East and India came traders to the water and land edges of China. The Syrians and Arabs were particularly active because they controlled most of the trade routes. Out of China went such things as spices, jades, silks, porcelain, tea, rice, and the glazed cups and the plates that we still call "china."

The T'ang period is one of the high tides of Chinese civilization. As the Gupta era was the golden age of India, so the years of T'ang rule marked the golden age of medieval China. Particularly famous are the lines and forms of T'ang painting, sculpture, and poetry. Deftly and delicately handled brushes painted some of the favorite themes of Chinese art: a bud, a branch, or a snow-capped countain. Skillful hands shaped bronze and baked clay statuettes. Silk embroidery became more and more popular and was added to the lengthening list of Chinese arts. Meanwhile more scholars studied the ancient *Bamboo Books* and the newer Buddhist *Diamond Sutra*. More tiled pagodas rose behind the Great Wall. More temple gongs were sounding. More heads were bowed to ritual. More men studied how to pursue the ancient and unchanging laws of perfection in human conduct.

There were more than 2,000 poets in China in the days when the T'ang family ruled and the greatest of them was Li Po (705–762), probably the most renowned of all the poets of the Far East. Even through the filtering lens of translation this prince of Chinese poets conveys to the Western reader a vivid idea of the power and beauty of his work. The four lines that are printed below are no doubt bruised and twisted by the difficult journey from Chinese to English; yet something of the original quality surely still remains in the English words of curve and color:

> Out in the artificial lake
> there is a pavilion of green and white porcelain;
> it is reached by a bridge of jade,
> arched like the back of a tiger.

Li Po was also a master of musical phrases and melody, a magician transforming the harshness and pain about him into a world of romance and tingling happiness. "Oh, let a man of spirit venture where he pleases and never tip his glass empty towards the moon!"

One event important for all the world happened in the days of the T'angs. Printing was invented. Block printing was first used around 750. By this method men printed from characters cut in wooden blocks; the type was non-movable, consisting of a whole set of characters cut together. Chinese block printing was usually done on large sheets of paper, and the sheets were pasted together to form a roll like a modern roll of wallpaper. With their invention the Chinese printed books, paper money, and playing cards.

About the year 1000 the Chinese invented something more important: baked-clay movable type. The new invention traveled slowly towards Europe. It took a long time to reach the fingers of Johannes Gutenberg of Germany about 1450 and William Caxton of England in 1477. In the sixteenth century William Shakespeare mingles comedy, satire, and sadness when he has Jack Cade, that fifteenth-century rabble leader, denounce the poor Lord Say because printing has been brought into England: "Thou hast most traitorously corrupted the youth of the realm in erecting a grammar school; and whereas, before, our forefathers had no other books but the score and the tally, thou hast caused printing to be used, and, contrary to the king, his crown and dignity, thou hast built a paper-mill." Shakespeare's jesting apart, the important fact is that in China, a thousand years ago, began man's journey to power presses, electrotyping, stereotyping, phototypsetting, composing machines, gravure, and all the other marvels of the printing and publishing empires of today.

The fall of the T'ang dynasty in 906 brought the chaos that so frequently comes when strong hands are removed from the helm of government. During the years between 906 and 960 there were five weak dynasties that held uncertain power and other men clutching and clamoring for it. In 960 the Sung family seemed to have established themselves rather firmly. After the first Sung ruler died in 976, however, the bright promise of the dynasty faded swiftly. Controls slipped from nerveless fingers. The central government became weak. Meanwhile the Sungs had begun to pay tribute to the threatening barbarian Tartars. The Tartars, of course, steadily raised their demands. By the middle of the eleventh century they were insisting that the Chinese pay annually a tremendous tribute: 265,000 pieces of silver and an equal number of packets of tea and pieces of silk.

The tribute payments brought no security. After the Gold Tartars had defeated the Iron Tartars in a short and bloody conflict they turned to seize all of China north of the Yangtze. This land was called Cathay, land of the north, land where the dark memories are bitter and the heritage of passive resignation is so heavy. In the face of the Tartar challenge the hapless and shaken Sungs set up a new capital at Nanking in Mansi, the south. Later they shifted the capital again, this time to Hangchow, at that time called Kinsai.

Hangchow was a rich and beautiful city in the days of the Sungs and on the eve of its conquest by the Tartars. It is said that there were twelve thousand bridges over the canals and lagoons, twelve great gates, a little blue lake, and a great park. About twenty miles away was the harbor, a wealthy trading area crowded with big ships and junks.

Meanwhile the unwashed Mongolian nomads and hunters of the northern plains were everywhere riding to conquest from their lands of Gog and Magog. The gigantic fury of the Mongol tide is difficult to exaggerate. Their hordes were widely known as the "scourge of God." The impact of their barbaric power, their terribly destructive skill with bows and arrows, shook most of Asia and a sizable portion of Europe. England's Roger Bacon called them "the soldiers of Anti-Christ."

The terrifying Genghis Khan (Temujin) was born in 1162 in the northern corner of the Gobi desert. He led the Mongols to overrun Mongolia and drove the Gold Tartars out of North China. In 1214 he seized and sacked Peking when far away in England King John was battling the barons and Magna Carta was about to be sealed. Two years later the Mongols swept over southern Manchuria and stormed at scores of city gates. Many square miles of China fell under the heavy hand of Genghis Khan. The dragon throne was toppling.

Genghis Khan did not wait to complete the conquest of all China. He lunged instead westwards with his Golden Horde and gathered much loot, loads of silk and gold and jewels. He seized Novgorod and began the conquest of Russia. His successors overran almost all of central Asia and pushed towards the Danube. They plunged into Poland and struck at Hungary. As we have seen, the Mongols also invaded India and Persia and menaced Egypt. They paused briefly to take tribute from Indochina and the island of Java. It was a long and fearful road from the Yellow River to the lands beyond the Danube.

In 1227 Genghis Khan died. For centuries his name brought echoes and folk memories of panic and death.

Despite the political darkness and the years of danger the Sung period was remarkable for its steady growth in education, thought, art, and literature. For instance, the thin porcelain of the Sung period has been rightly famous for hundreds of years because of its beauty and its form. We should also pause to note that there lived in the Sung period a highly intelligent philosopher, government servant, and publicist named Wang-An shih (1021–1086). Almost completely forgotten now, Wang-An shih was responsible for much excitement in his own day. He wanted to jettison several of the old habits and traditions of China. He was a crusader who was in a hurry. Against him, as might be expected, often stood a dull dead weight of resistance. The government did put a few of his proposals into effect when he was state councillor, and the man who looks at them from the vantage point of the twentieth century finds them startlingly modern.

In order to aid the farmers the government agreed to follow Wang-An shih's recommendation that loans be made at 2½ per cent interest a month to all farmers to buy such things as seed and equipment. As a further aid to the farmers the government accepted Wang-An shih's proposal that the state try to control prices by buying and selling commodities. As a further result of Wang-An shih's insistent pressure the standing army was reduced and local militia units were organized to provide cheaper protection. The forced-labor practices of the government were widely abolished and most men were paid for their assistance upon public-works projects.

Most of these challenging reforms and experiments were not permanent. They touched too many of the rich and powerful people in sensitive places. Solid and respectable individuals were often alienated by the wrenching and uprooting nature of Wang-An shih's proposals. One of his theories, for instance, was that the government should own and control agriculture, industry, and commerce and that the wealthy men should pay all the taxes. Such points of view do not easily become popular.

Despite its long and stout resistance the Sung dynasty was at last overthrown by the Mongols. In 1259 the remarkable Kublai Khan, grandson of Genghis, came to rule in China. He rebuilt Peking and made a summer palace at Shandu, the "Xanadu" of Coleridge's dream-poem:

> In Xanadu did Kubla Khan
> A stately pleasure dome decree. . . .

Through the years Kublai ruled with wisdom, toleration, and decency, perceiving that the Chinese culture was far superior to his own. Slowly the Mongol invaders were absorbed into China. China has conquered many who came to conquer her.

To the land of Kublai Khan came Marco Polo, that greatest of medieval travelers.

Marco, his father Nicolo, and his uncle Maffeo left their native city of Venice in 1271. They went first to Acre and from Acre they went through Persia. Then they traveled through several regions not explored by Europeans until the nineteenth century. They ascended the upper Oxus into the cold land of Pamir.

> For many a league
> The shorn and parcell'd Oxus strains along
> Through beds of sand and matted rushy isles.

Out of Pamir they moved into the dreary stretches of the Gobi desert. After thirty days in that dread world of heat and cold they reached the northwest of China and the great steppes of Mongolia. Then they moved into Cathay. The long journey had taken more than three years.

Kublai Khan welcomed the strangers from Venice. "Being introduced into the presence of the Grand Khan Kublai the travellers were received by him with the condescension and affability that belonged to his character, and as they were the first Latins who had made their appearance in that country they were entertained with feasts and honored with other marks of distinction." Marco was employed in the public service of Kublai Khan and journeyed through several provinces of China on the emperor's business. These royal missions took him to the edge of Tibet and into northern Burma.

In 1292 the Polos set sail from Zaiton on the long trip home. After delays in Sumatra, Ceylon, and southern India they traveled back by way of Tabriz, Trebizond, and Constantinople. When they reached Venice in 1295 "in worn and outlandish garb" they had difficulty in persuading their friends and relatives that they were indeed the lost Polos long since believed dead. In later days the book called *The Travels of Marco Polo* was written from Marco's dictation by a literary hack named Rusticiano of Pisa.

Marco Polo was indeed "the first traveller to trace a route across the whole longitude of Asia, describing kingdom after kingdom which he had seen with his own eyes. . . . the first traveller to reveal China in all its wealth and vastness, its huge cities, its rich manufactures, its swarming population, the inconceivably vast fleets that quickened its seas and inland waters." In his later days Marco said that in his book he "had not told one-half of what he had really seen." He probably knew that few Europeans believed his tales about the wonders he said he had seen in the dazzling court of Kublai Khan and the civilization of Cathay. Why should anyone believe, for instance, the silly story that the Chinese burned rocks? The wise men of Europe could not possibly know that the Chinese had discovered coal or that Marco was usually telling the truth about his travels, even about the dog sleds of Siberia.

In the following centuries many men were to seek the Cathay of Marco Polo. At last some sailed to the west and found it, or almost so. Still later Jesuit missionaries moved towards the frowning gates of the Forbidden Kingdom. One of these pioneers was Father Matteo Ricci (1552–1610). Against the advice of his fellow Jesuits in Portuguese Macao, Father Ricci went to the Imperial Court of China, taking his astrolabes and his quadrants with him. His knowledge of astronomy and mathematics delighted the Chinese. Not many

Woman Playing with Two Children (style of Chou Fang, c. 780-805 A.D.)

[45]

Mogul Portrait of Shah Jehan (1627-1666 A.D.) on Horseback

[47] *Above:* From "Frolic of the Animals," Japanese Scroll Painting (Heian Period, 794-1185 A.D.)

[46] *Left:* Chinese Porcelain Stoneware Vase (Sung Dynasty, 960-1279 A.D.)

PLATE XIII

[48]

Marco Polo, great[...]
of medieval travel[...]
bids farewell to V[...]
as he begins his lo[...]
journey to Cathay
in 1271.

[50]

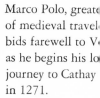

Japanese carving of Dutch trumpeter, probably 17th century

Chinese screen panel, carved talc, mounted on silk, in rosewood frame. Ch'ien Lung Period (1735-1795)

[49]

PLATE XIV

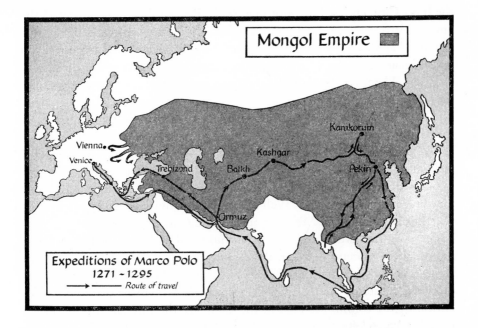

other men of Europe, apart from a few Portuguese, Dutch, and English traders, found a welcome in China. The gates to that land were not easily opened.

By the fourteenth century the proud empire of the Mongols was weakening. Many rulers before the days of the Mongols had trod the same path to disaster. Governments cannot always remain strong or hope to endure forever. When weakness appears, enemies come. When enemies come, the ambitious and the greedy gather. The reformers and the optimists assemble, too, always hoping that the world they want to build will be better than the old they are helping to destroy. They are often undeceived.

The Mongols, with the exception of Kublai Khan, were usually more successful in conquering territory than in governing it well. In 1368 a man who had once been a Buddhist monk captured Peking and overthrew the last of the Mongol emperors. This remarkable rebel, who took the name of Hung Wu when he began to rule, was the first of the Ming dynasty. He began his reign by trying to wipe away all the institutions, traditions, and memories of the Mongols. The government was returned to the hands of the Chinese. Major reforms in the educational system were completed. A large body of the laws was codified.

In the fifteenth century another Ming emperor named Yung Lo built a group of golden-tiled palaces at Peking inside a great wall. This was the Forbidden City. Around it was the Imperial City. Outside the Imperial City was

the Inner City, enclosed by great gray walls. Beyond those walls stretched the
crowded streets of the Outer City. The building of new structures by the side
of the old and all the work made necessary by the vast plan of reconstruction
was a signal achievement. It was also a symbol in stone of much of the history
of China. Here were great walls, the centers of power, the barred gates, and
the secret places.

The Mings ruled for almost 300 years (1368–1644). In the latter part of
their rule their power was weakened by internal disputes and the rivalries of
ambitious men, by famine, by rebellions, by divided authority. To these perils
and difficulties were added the attacks by the Japanese. Then there came new
invaders from Manchuria, the Manchus. Aided by Mongols and Koreans,
they broke through the Great Wall and flooded southward. In 1644 the Mings
were finally ousted. The Manchus grasped the reins of power.

For more than two centuries the Manchus stood against all challenge. With
the twentieth century, however, there came new voices and new demands in
China. As foreigners from the West pressed in to obtain concessions and territory the future of the nation was in doubt. Was it to be partitioned, like
Africa, by the British, the French, the Germans, the Russians, the Japanese?
In resistance and strength alone, it seemed, was there a chance for China to
keep her freedom. Lethargy and weakness must be replaced by vision and
deeds. Since no vision or leadership could be provided by Pu-yi, the Manchu
boy emperor, he was dethroned. The republic proclaimed by Sun Yat-sen
began in 1912.

Several of these sentences have anticipated the paragraphs of later chapters
about the running feet of modern history in the Far East. Perhaps they will
form a slight bridge to future themes and sections. Perhaps, too, they may suggest again the unbroken continuity of human history, whether it be in the
streets of Peking or in Wounded Knee, Montana. History never begins a new
chapter. Only historians do.

Three seas lie along the coast of China: the East China Sea, fed by the
Yangtze River rolling by the docks of Shanghai; the Yellow Sea, cutting
deeply into the Chinese mainland far past the Shantung peninsula and the
fortress of Port Arthur; the Sea of Japan, shallow, stormy, and filled with fish.

These three seas are separated from the Pacific Ocean by a long cluster of
islands called Japan. There are about 3,000 of these islands; nearly 600 of them
are fairly large. They stretch for about 2,500 miles along the coast of the
continent of Asia.

About 85,000,000 people live in Japan, especially on the main islands of
Honshu, Shikoku, and Kyushu. The total area of Japan is about 174,000
square miles, slightly more than the state of California. Ranges of mountains
run from north to south sending out lateral branches; throughout the whole

land mountain alternates with valley. There are three volcanic ridges. More than 100,000 people have been killed by volcanoes during the past 500 years. One of the most remarkable of the volcanic peaks is the sacred mountain of the pilgrims: snow-capped Fujiyama, famous for its curving grace and beauty. All through the islands are rivers, lakes, and fairyland waterfalls. Facts of geography like these mean that only about 12 per cent of the land is fit for farming. Fortunately the climate speeds the growth of crops. Three wet seasons in a year are a help to a farmer in any land.

Frugal and industrious, the peasants of early Japan worked on their tiny plots of land, carefully guarding their crops and their chickens from the numerous foxes, badgers, weasels, and hares. Fish, rice, and barley were their main foods. Hardship was their daily companion. Everywhere there was luxuriant growth: cherry, peach, plum, and dwarf trees, wild vines, camellias, chrysanthemums, peonies, roses, and scores of other shrubs and flowers blazing their colors in the valleys and down the mountain sides. The Japanese have always liked things of calm beauty like the tranquil lotus ponds. On the other hand, they have always had cause to fear the power of the earthquakes, the tidal waves, and the winds. The typhoons (from the Japanese *tai-fu:* great wind) often come up like thunder out of the China Sea to destroy and kill.

Tradition says that Japan was created by the god Izanagi who took his jeweled spear, dipped it in the ocean, and lifted it out. The drops that fell from the end of the spear made the islands of Japan. "The life blood of Japan," says the ancient proverb, "is the water of the sea." Izanagi also made the Sun Goddess Amaterasu O-Mikami, and she began to rule in heaven. To her grandson she gave dominion over the earth. His descendants are said to be the emperors of Japan, whose rule is thus approved by heaven.

The belief in these events is an integral part of Shinto, the native religion of the Japanese. Shinto—"the Way of the Gods"—is mainly a worship of natural forces, such as the sun, the wind, and the rain. It also teaches reverence for the sacred Emperor, the Son of Heaven descended directly from the Sun Goddess. Shinto is therefore both a religion and a patriotic expression of the national spirit. For many years Shinto shrines were partly supported by the state. Today, despite the fact that the state gives them no aid, there are still more than 80,000 brilliantly colored shrines and 15,000 Shinto priests. It is said that more than 5,000,000 visitors come annually to the Grand Shrine of Ise by the clear waters of the Isuzu River. Few visitors to the temples of Japan are disappointed. The finest of them are Kyoto, Nikko—site of the Toshogu Shrine—and Nara, where stands the 1,360-year-old Horyuji Temple, perhaps the world's oldest wooden building.

So far as the Western scholar is concerned, the history of Japan begins with the short and hairy Ainu, the aborigines of Japan. Then came the Manchu-Korean, Mongol, and Malay types from across the seas to settle and multiply in the islands. The recorded history of Japan actually starts a little before 100 A.D. when Mongol invaders from Korea brought their bronze and iron cultures and their cohesive clan societies. About these events we have a few scattered pieces of authentic information, nothing more. In 532 Buddhist missionaries came from China and Korea and by 625 there were about fifty Buddhist priests in Japan. The Buddhists thus came into conflict with Shinto. The teachings of Confucius, brought down from Korea, increased the disputes.

The Japanese also began to learn the Chinese language and some of the wisdom of China and India. Meanwhile the advance of Japan was speeded by several reforming emperors, especially Shotoku, a ruler "of gentle disposition who loved men of learning." With a mounting concern for civilized practices there slowly began to grow the elaborate social etiquette and the courtesy characteristic of many Eastern lands, the ritual patterns of the tea ceremony, the cultivation of a refined reserve, and the cloaking of inner emotions.

A part of the rigid clan system brought by the Mongols was ended by the Taikwa reforms of the seventh century. Nevertheless, the clan leaders, the local warlike feudal lords, and the petty princes remained powerful. At the upper level of Japanese society stood a group of warrior gentry, called the samurai, or knights, led by the heads of the great clans. They developed a code of right conduct and honor called *Bushido:* loyalty, courage, self-discipline, good manners, devotion to duty, physical fitness and skill reached and kept by archery, fencing, and ju-jutsu. Sometimes, it seems, the code and pattern of *Bushido* took such full command of men that they became submerged in it. They ceased to be reflecting beings and became instead unreasoning machines of the state.

In the twelfth century the leader of a feudal faction called the Minamoto established himself as a military dictator and actual ruler of Japan. He and his successors, called shoguns, held effective power in Japan until 1868. The emperor, of course, always ruled in name from the seclusion of the great imperial court at Kyoto, "the City of Peace and Tranquillity." In that once quiet place by the Kamo River a million people live today. The face of Kyoto has changed with the changing face of the rest of the land. Not all of the people who live in Kyoto today are princes or nobles or servants of the imperial court. Not all of them dress in silk or are well housed or eat steaks and sizzling sukiyaki.

The shoguns, the samurai, and the feudal lords called *daimyos* have had a deep and lasting effect upon Japanese national habits and values. These men stood near the summit of the state. They were the proud and skilled warrior class. Their boxwood bows, their three-feathered arrows, their swords, single-edged and sharp, were probably the best weapons of their kind in the medieval world. The importance of skill and spirit and *Bushido* was evident in the Japanese use of more modern weapons than bows and arrows in the Second World War. The leaders in Japan were also frequently influenced by the anti-intellectual Zen Buddhism with its emphasis upon discipline and toughness. "Zen seeks only the light man can find in himself. It tolerates no hindrance to this seeking. Clear every obstacle out of your way."

This aspect of Japanese life was stressed and fixed more firmly in the sixteenth century. An able general called Hideyoshi overcame all his enemies and brought about the political unification of Japan. He established four main divisions in the upper and middle strata of Japanese society: the warrior administrators; the peasants; the artisans; and the merchants. Hideyoshi also set up a secret police network for his protection and peace. Meanwhile he stopped brigandage, or almost so; he encouraged domestic trade; he forced out the Christian missionaries who had come after the great Jesuit missionary Francis Xavier. All the foreign merchants—except the Dutch—were also required to leave. A later edict of 1639 said: "For the future, let none, so long as the sun illuminates the world, presume to sail to Japan." The isolation of Japan had begun. The islands were to be sealed off until the middle of the nineteenth century.

During these centuries there flourished the arts of the painters, sculptors, and poets, the landscape-gardening techniques and the skills in flower arrangement marked by the familiar artistic sensitivity of the Japanese. The painters have always been interested in landscapes, birds, flowers, fish, trees, bodies in motion. In their work the Japanese artists have invariably shown their close study and minute observation of nature. They have also displayed an easy grace and facility of execution similar to the Chinese masters. Western observers are sometimes confused by the refusal of Japanese and Chinese artists to follow the laws of linear perspective. They are also often bewildered by the insistence in the Far East that it is enough for an artist to do no more than suggest an idea or an emotion. Both the poetry and the painting of China and Japan leave a great deal to the imagination of the individual who sees or reads.

From about 550 to 850 the artists of Japan studied and adopted the techniques and ends of Chinese Buddhist art. After 850 several native Japanese schools arose and the pure Chinese school retreated into the background of professional and popular interest. About 1450 the Chinese style was revived. Around 1650 it yielded to several popular styles, which in turn gave way about 1750 to the new naturalism. The last 200 years have been marked by European influences and a revived interest in Chinese painting. Throughout all of these shifting attitudes the artists of Japan have never lost the delicacy of their touch. In their paintings there is never heaviness, never discord.

Early in their history the Japanese displayed unusual gifts and skills in the decorative arts. All the civilized world knows their mastery of design and execution in carving wood and casting bronze, the beauty of their fabrics and embroidery, their gold dust in the black lacquers.

Wood carving began on a fairly large scale in the sixth century; the famous Nara school was founded 500 years later. Bronze work of a high order first appeared around 650. The idea of making lacquer was apparently first obtained by the Japanese from China, probably in the seventh century. In the eighth century they began to use the dust of gold, mother of pearl, and other designs in the black lacquer. The modern Owari lacquer, with its luster and richness, is particularly admired in Europe and the United States. The process of making superior lacquerware is long and exacting. There are fifty-five steps between a piece of cypress and the final production of a cocktail glass or a high-gloss rice bowl.

In the field of ceramics Japan became more famous for her faïence—especially the Satsuma ware—than for her pottery. In the Middle Ages and later the Japanese artists and artisans also worked to produce their water colors and woodcuts, their enameled porcelain, their tortoise shell, their embroidery, their elaborate gold and silver inlays, their carved ivory pieces, their color painting, their swords and knives. The long-taloned fingers of their weavers have made products that are famous all over the world.

Japanese literature and learning, like their art, was at first mainly transplanted from Korea and China. Soon native influences brought major changes. Among the classics in the medieval period stand the works of Hitomaro, Akahito, and Tsurayuki. At least three books are worth reading and possessing: *The Collection of a Myriad Leaves* (756), *The Collection of Odes Ancient and Modern* (905), and the *Hundred Odes by a Hundred Poets* (about 1250).

Japanese poetry has no rhyme; it has no variety of meter; it has no elasticity—its dimensions cannot be changed. One form of poem, called the *tanka*, is arranged in lines of five and seven syllables. Usually there are five lines; the first and third line contain five syllables; each of the other three lines has seven syllables. The total for the whole *tanka* must be exactly thirty-one syllables. A second type of poem is the famous *hokku*, a three-line poem that belongs to the Japanese and to nobody else. The *hokku* contains exactly seventeen syllables in the Japanese.

The following is a *hokku* written by a Shinto priest:

> I thought I saw the fallen leaves
> Returning to their branches.
> Alas, butterflies were they.

The greatest master of the *hokku* form was the Japanese poet Basho:

> Into the ancient pond
> The frog jumps
> Sound of the water!

To many Western eyes and ears such poems as these may convey little meaning or emotion. Like certain Japanese and Chinese paintings they are intended to suggest more than they state. To a receptive reader the lines of a Japanese poem may be compared to the pressing of a modern electric switch. When the poem is read the current of the reader's creative imagination does the rest. The result is light and power for the spirit. The *hokku* of Basho quoted above may bring visions of the secluded courtyard of a Buddhist temple or the mossy slopes of a monastery garden. It may evoke surging memories of a distant scene of childhood. If the *hokku* or the *tanka* creates the mood and begins the chain reactions of emotion felt in the blood and felt along the heart, then its task is done; its end as an art form is realized.

Such are a few of the outstanding features of the history and culture of ancient and medieval Japan. Increasingly isolated from all the world except China and Korea, the Japanese lived and labored and fought among themselves. Like the people of India and China, they were laying the solid foundations upon which their modern state and culture rest. "Let time be lavished," said the Greek historian Herodotus, "and everything possible happens."

Meanwhile, far away on the western side of the land mass of Europe and Asia, there came an immense increase in power and enterprise. New strands were being woven into the complex tapestry of the history of man. Europe was entering upon the great age of feudalism.

Chapter 15

THE FEUDAL WORLD

"Among the wax and wooden effigies kept at the Abbey there was a wooden head of Anne of Bohemia, the first queen of Richard II, who died of the plague in 1394 at the age of 28. The head was almost black and had a damaged nose. Cleaning and repair revealed a most interesting face. A wignail which remains was driven into the hard oak by such a violent hammer blow that its head bent over and imprisoned some brown hair. Thus we know the color of her hair, and my recovering one of her bones, stolen probably by a Westminster boy, gives us her approximate height of five feet, three inches."

—Mr. Howgrave-Graham,
Assistant Keeper of the Muniments at Westminster Abbey
(*Manchester Guardian*, February 16, 1953)

IT IS customary and comfortable to divide human history into three periods: ancient, medieval, and modern. Such an arrangement is neat and tidy. We sometimes tend to believe that when we have order, categories, and neatness, when we have placed things and people exactly as we think they should be placed, then we have reasoned rightness and truth.

The facts are quite otherwise. For instance, we cannot rightly assert that ancient history ended and medieval history commenced with the fall of Rome. We could not say that modern history really began with the Renaissance, even if we knew and agreed precisely what the Renaissance was or when it started. We use the term "Middle Ages" because our fathers and grandfathers used it and because it remains the only brief and adequate label that we can think of to describe the centuries between the last convulsions of Rome and the golden blaze of the sixteenth century. The periodization of history is a convenient device arbitrarily imposed upon a continuous flow of events, and it is nothing more. Our descendants may say that medieval history ended and the modern age began in 1960. The facts, as they see them, may warrant that conclusion.

It is also true that modern men often have numerous ideas about the Middle Ages that are demonstrably false. A little learning may be dangerous, stifling, and deceptive. Besides, the truths of history are usually wild and leaping things. They do not lie asleep and still when we peer behind the curtain of the night. They are always joined to other truths, many of which we do not understand. They often seem to change even as we think we have them fully described and finally named.

Many modern ideas and attitudes about the Middle Ages are no doubt inherited from the eighteenth and nineteenth centuries. The Age of Reason and the Age of Progress looked down upon the medieval period, believing that before the Renaissance reason was imprisoned and superstition barred the road and ruled the world. In his *Essay on Customs,* Voltaire wrote this about the medieval centuries: "It is necessary to know the history of that age only in order to scorn it." Very few men during the eighteenth and nineteenth centuries did justice to the Middle Ages. Their climate of opinion would not easily permit it. They insisted that the medieval centuries formed a barren gap of unreason in man's history. The Romantic writers of a century ago were unjust in a different way. The shaping spirits of their imagination created an idealized medieval world filled with many-colored mists and brave knights, fair ladies, fat monks, and gay troubadours, color and clangor. Similar beams and motes often are in the eyes of modern man.

It would be ridiculous and unrealistic for hopeful professors to think that thousands of their contemporaries, suddenly filled with an indefeasible desire to know, could be persuaded to study carefully the panorama of the splendor and squalor of the Middle Ages where characters with strange names appear and disappear with disconcerting abruptness in the twists and turns of a long, lamentable maze. Most human beings, these days, have other things to do. Nevertheless, all intelligent and thoughtful individuals are prepared to profit from the studies of scholars, provided that those studies are designed to provide pith and perspective and are simple, precise, and clear.

Fortunately the honorable company of professional historians in Europe and America has within its ranks several able men who have had something valuable to say and have said it without fuss or fumble. They have proved, if proof were needed, that the high wisdom historians guard and perpetuate does not have to be unfolded in polysyllabic profundities. It does not have to be a mountain of matter-of-fact statements innocent of balance or interpretation. "Nothing in education is so astonishing," wrote Henry Adams, "as the amount of ignorance it accumulates in the form of inert facts." Oscar Wilde once said of a writer: "He hunts down the obvious with the enthusiasm of a short-sighted detective." There is no need, of course, to argue by quotation. The facts are clear enough. The scholar who chokes on the dry crumbs of minutiae is not a scholar at all. One also files away the hinges of the principles of scholarship by deliberately taking refuge in jargon or obfuscating phrases. Almost anything that was thought, done, or dreamed can be stated clearly by words, music, symbolic logic, or mathematics. There

is no need to be fuzzy or confusing. Short words and short equations sometimes explode and the world shakes. "God is love," said Christ. "Working
men of all countries, unite!" said Karl Marx. "E equals mc ^{2}," said Albert
Einstein.

Ready-made formulas are often uttered about the incredible diversity of
the Middle Ages. "Clichés undefined beat in the void their ineffectual wings
in vain." Sometimes, too, the bloodless abstractions of vague "forces" and
"trends" and "influences" are discussed as if they could stand alone, apart
from the bodies and minds of men. "Avoid abstractions," said a French philosopher. "Your sentences should be full of stones, metals, chairs, tables,
animals, men and women." Let us not forget that history is the record of
things thought, known, and done by human beings and by them alone.
The substance of humanity is what matters most. England's Professor K. L.
Wood-Legh recently told a tale about an eminent historian of English law
who was busy in research on Henry II's great judge, Ranulph de Glanville.
"He once remarked to me," wrote Professor Wood-Legh, "that it would be
much easier for him to think of Glanville as a living person if only he could
know what he had for breakfast." The quotation at the beginning of this
chapter reminds us again that we are reading and writing about men and
women like ourselves, about "John Nameless, John the Miller and John the
Carter and John Trueman." Their horizons are remote from ours, but we
can bring them closer by understanding and sympathetic study.

The medieval chapters of the hot-blooded drama of human history were
made by individuals toughened on the field of battle, the cockpits of politics,
the woods and the towns and the fields. Most of them were practical men
faced by human emotions and dilemmas even as we are in the running hours
of the twentieth century. Many of their years were filled with hopes and
achievements. Far too much has been said and written about the turbulent
and chaotic politics of the Middle Ages, about the retarded economy, the
hit-and-run wars, the withered culture. It is all very interesting and pathetic;
but it is not quite true. It is the result of a gross misreading of the evidence.
The facts often lie in ambush for the unwary. When swiveling shafts of light
pick them out, then the road can be made safe again.

The darker side of medieval life, for example, is often exaggerated. In the
midst of disease, stagnant filth, and poverty there was still some laughter
and beauty. Through noisy, stinking, and narrow streets the merchants, house-
wives, vagabonds, and ruffians swarmed about their business. To our descendants the conditions of the twentieth century may seem somewhat less than
satisfactory. Arrogant in our achievements, and proud of our historical hindsight, it is easy for us to stress the evils of the Middle Ages. It is likewise
good sense to remember that human beings in any age have shown themselves

remarkably adaptable creatures; the general nature of mankind in the mass has remained fairly constant. The man of the Middle Ages, for instance, did not know what amenities of civilization lay unborn in the womb of time. Therefore he made the most of what he had and did not bewail the absence of what he knew not.

In every age of man's history there have appeared institutions and habits in society and government born of the needs and values of the human beings who lived at that time. During the Middle Ages there grew and flourished the combination of customs that is usually described by the single word "feudalism." These customs, beginning in the older parts of the Frankish kingdoms of Europe, spread over most of the Continent and lasted for hundreds of years.

The term "feudalism" clearly implies a scheme of things based upon fiefs (*feuda*): lands held from a superior individual in a society upon certain conditions, such as military service. Binding ties of vassalage and lordship were created by the ancient Frankish ceremony of homage soon to be linked to the Christian oath of fealty. In the sacred act of homage the man about to become a vassal knelt bareheaded and placed his hands between those of his lord. In becoming a vassal an individual swore that he would be the lord's "man" and would "bear faith to you of life and members and earthly honor against all other men." The lord, for his part, bound himself to give his vassal justice and protection.

Thus lord and man were presumably united in mutual and honorable loyalty. By the eleventh century the act of homage usually meant that the vassal received lands from his lord in return for which he gave special services. In most European lands in the Middle Ages there could be no man without his lord and almost every man held land of his lord on certain fixed and specified conditions.

Once, not so long ago, historians could write and talk freely about "the feudal system," quite unhampered by doubts as to the wisdom of using such a term. Today we know that the so-called "feudal system" was in fact very unsystematic indeed. Feudal contracts varied from country to country, from region to region, from age to age. Feudalism was a growing thing; it was lively and flexible; it was never fixed and frozen; it never stood still. There were many kinds of local arrangements, diverse local customs, individual agreements reached by particular negotiations.

One feudal principle, already mentioned, remained intact and constant: the principle that tenants held land from their lords under a system of primogeniture in return for certain services. These services, despite the diverse kinds of contacts, were always carefully defined. Lords and vassals in a feudal community were bound together not only by social, military, and economic ties but also by the legal bonds that often made those ties precise and effective. This was the very essence of feudalism.

For several centuries the institution of feudalism worked in Europe with considerable success. One of the main reasons for its long survival was the active idea that it contained of the mutual obligations of all men. In the intricate network of rights and duties everybody was responsible to somebody else. Nobody was entirely free. The custom was the community custom and nobody had a right to change it.

It is necessary to make all statements about feudalism very carefully. To do otherwise is dangerous. Often feudal arrangements did not develop in a fashion amenable to easy definition; rather they have had it sometimes thrust upon them. We cannot consider here the numerous details of varying feudal contracts and habits. We must be concerned only with certain broad facts. In summary, we have thus far stated that throughout the fabric of feudalism, so tightly knit in complex patterns, every man was another man's vassal; all land had its lord; each tenant received both land and personal protection; every tenant owed loyalty to his lord; both lord and vassal had rights and duties that had to be fulfilled.

Sometimes the tenants held their land by military tenure. In that case they were required to supply a stipulated number of knights for their lord's army. Sometimes they paid cash or performed nonmilitary services. All tenants were required to aid their lord by giving counsel in the lord's court or in conversation. On certain fixed occasions the vassal had to make special money payments to his lord. He was expected to help his lord in any time of trouble. There were many other feudal obligations, hallmarks of duty usually called "incidents."

All of the contracts and conventions were often less precise than the previous paragraphs might suggest. It is almost always impossible to state with exactness and brevity many of the intangible and imponderable things which help to form "a theory of society." Some of the feudal obligations were in fact not sharply defined. Feudal problems and disputes were multiplied in the Middle Ages. Oaths were not always kept. Vassals were not always given protection. Who was to control a strong king? How could a weak king control overweening or rival feudal lords?

Because European society was basically agrarian the fiefs granted to tenants were normally composed of one or more rural agricultural settlements called manors. Those manors were the normal units of land division for the purposes of feudal landholding. They were the estates controlled and supervised by a lord for his own profit. In the manor was usually a village. Dominating the village was the lord's wooden manor house. Here lived either the lord or his agent. About the manor house there usually stretched the lord's garden, meadow, stables, storehouses, implement sheds, and parts of the arable land of the great fields. The tenants of the land, usually the lower-class villeins or peasants, lived in the manorial village of huts made of wattle, plastered with mud, covered with straw-thatched roofs.

Each peasant on the manor usually had a garden, some chickens or geese, pigs, maybe cows. His hut might have a table and one or two benches. His bed was made of straw. His bread was black. He was forbidden to fish or shoot game. He seldom had meat. He held strips of land in a large open field. He held "rights of common," including the right to pasture what cattle he had on the common pasture land, to let his hogs range in the common woods. The tenants worked on the lord's land two or three days a week. They were required to pay rent to their lord in the form of a part of their crops or their livestock. They were not allowed to leave the village without the lord's permission. The gulf between the peasants and the upper classes was deep and wide. A man of low birth could rarely hold a fief from the king or any lord. The lines of birth were not easily wiped away. To be of aristocratic blood was one thing; to be of the gentry class was another; to be a yeoman or a peasant was still a third. A lord of noble birth received a particular kind of education in the age of chivalry. A lad of low birth was taught by his horny-handed father the skills he needed to plow a field or milk a cow. Every man was born under a law, into a niche in society. There, so long as the feudal customs prevailed, most men were expected to stay. It is not surprising that in England's Peasants' Revolt of 1381 this interesting question was asked:

> When Adam delved and Eve span
> Who was then the gentleman?

The structure of feudalism was based upon a set of economic conditions that made it possible. This statement, of course, is true of the institutions of any society and culture. Behind the steel pillars and the plate-glass windows of the twentieth century there are always the cash registers and men and families and the problems of meat and milk. Behind the problems of meat and milk stand the realities of a society's total energy. This fact is often overlooked.

As civilization advances, its energy needs increase. Man began with the power of his own muscles. Then he used oxen, horses, and water power. His adroit hands and nimble brain turned to devise machines to use steam, electricity, gas, and the fossil fuels of coal and oil. In the twentieth century he stood at the dawn of new revolutions and sources of power: the energy of the atom and the sun. The vast forces of nature were almost, but not quite, subordinated and manipulated by the whim and will of human beings. "Man has conquered Nature unless it should turn out that Nature has conquered man."

Energy and machines travel through time together. The horse gives way to the tractor; the hired man walks away from the stool and leaves the job to the automatic milker; the wheelbarrow yields to the bulldozer. Man finds new sources of energy or new ways to use it. Then he invents new machines or alters old ones. Man makes changes in the machines. The machines make changes in man. It is as simple or complex as that.

The environment of man is thus not constant. It has been slowly and steadily altered and enlarged by new human skills and knowledge. Much of the tale of man's advance is about the ways in which human beings made changes in the environment that they or their ancestors first found, about how they increased their sources of energy. In the fateful and formative years of the feudal world the total amount of energy available was not large by our modern standards. True, the vigor of medieval Christendom was such that by the year 1100 it had the resources to send and maintain armies in the Crusade operations more than a thousand miles away from the home bases. It is at the same time a fact that the gates to new storehouses of power had not yet been burned or blasted open. The land was still the basis of most economic activity. Most wealth came from land. Most labor was bound to the soil—the acres of ribbed loam stretched far away. Hence the major basis of the whole economic structure was still agricultural. The tools used in the fields and about the barns were still fairly primitive and most production was still for local needs.

There were a few impressive technological improvements; none of them were explosive or revolutionary. Many of the discoveries and inventions that did occur were made by humble men. For example, they had long used the water power of rivers and creeks to run mills and to grind flour. Now they found that it could be used for other jobs: in the twelfth century for grinding bark to tan leather; in the thirteenth century to saw lumber; in the fourteenth century to turn grindstones in metalwork. The reader of Professor Herbert Butterfield's *The Origins of Modern Science* will also note, for instance, that gunpowder was first used in the thirteenth century and that the mechanical clock was invented about 1271 and thus another foundation was laid for skill in precision work in industry.

In the latter part of the Middle Ages more men of ideas and intuition became interested in discovery and experiment. The pace of science slowly gathered speed. In many aspects of medieval life the shrewd observer can detect the early symptoms of the coming of unharnessed and violent winds and floods of change. Torrents of energy were soon to be let loose. They were to alter the whole tale of the West. A part of the Renaissance happened before the Renaissance began.

There were also the windmills. The building of these instruments of power was an important forward step of man in the Middle Ages. Most of the time we men of the modern world do not think about the dictating nonhuman power of the water supply in the world's history. There is, of course, an increasing awareness of some of the challenging and complex problems of the water resources of the contemporary world of the United States, problems inextricably involved with agriculture, industry, and energy production. Governmental and private studies have shown the critical problems of water supply in certain local and regional areas—more than half the area of the United States is arid or inadequately watered—and the mounting demands for fresh water in industrial and urban areas. The men of the Middle Ages, of course, faced different kinds of problems. Some of their difficulties were ended by the use of the windmill. The windmill raised water out of the ground to supply the needs of men and beasts and to irrigate the fields. The need for dams and millponds went down. More land was released for cultivation. Where there was too much water—in the Low Countries, for instance—the windmill was used to pump it away.

From the northlands of Europe there came the new northern plow with a colter, moldboard, and a horizontal share. This new tool made it possible to plow places where the soil was heavy and wet. Nor did the farmer have to cross-plow, always a sweaty and wearisome job.

In the years of the feudal age nobody knew why soil became exhausted from overcropping. Men understood nothing about nitrogen depletion or the scientific application of fertilizers—even if they had been available. They only knew that if land was allowed to lie fallow it would then grow good crops again. What was called the three-field system therefore developed in northern and central Europe and in England. One-third of the land, one field, was left to rest every year. Of the remaining two fields one was planted with a spring crop and one with a fall crop.

The productive use of land with the three-field system and the rotation of crops gave northern and central Europe an advantage over the south. It should be added, of course, that the three-field system would have been unprofitable in southern Europe because of one fact of climate: the successful operation of the three-field system really depended upon the new practice of spring plowing. In the north there was usually plenty of summer rain to fall upon the plowed land; in the south there was little. The northern summer rains thus took their place as one of the many causes for the rise of prosperity in northern Europe and the slow shift of power from the Mediterranean areas.

By the side of feudalism and agriculture moved the tides of trade and industry. Between the fifth and tenth centuries European industry and production fell off. Trade declined and population decreased. When the Moslems came to conquer several wide areas some trade lines were severed completely

and others were badly frayed. The three cities of Venice, Naples, and Bari
—and Genoa and Pisa in the eleventh century—did succeed in keeping up
their commerce with Constantinople. They were willing to trade with the
infidels for prices that meant profits. The carriers and traders of Venice, that
proud city lying upon her lagoons, were soon to pass all rivals. The "Gulf
of Venice," at the head of the Adriatic, became a great thoroughfare of
medieval commerce. Venice is mainly a Mediterranean seaport. At the same
time, it is so far north that from Venice to the great northern towns is not
far by land.

Like a magnet Venice drew into her harbor—especially by the twelfth
and thirteenth centuries—goods from many lands: ebony chessmen wrapped
in Chinese silk to cushion the jolts of caravans and ships, the metals of Germany, the wines of France, the cloth of Flanders, cloves and nutmegs from
the Indies, musk from Tibet, pearls from Ceylon, ambergris from Madagascar.
The Doge of Venice, swathed in scarlet, used "to wed the sea with rings."
In earlier years Venice fought Constantinople. She fought the pope and the
Holy Roman Empire. Her galleys defeated all rivals. She traded directly with
Syria and North Africa and captured female Slavs for Arabian harems—
hence our word "slaves." Steadily the center of maritime power shifted from
the eastern Mediterranean to the central Mediterranean. It shifted to Venice,
that city of "sea without fish, mountains without woods, men without faith,
and women without shame."

Between the ninth and twelfth centuries trade began to revive throughout
most of central Europe. More roads and bridges were built. Canals were constructed to connect rivers. Some prosperity came again to the cities of north
Italy and the towns of France and Spain along the coast of the Mediterranean.
After the Crusades began in 1096 the Italians were often happily busied in
supplying goods for the fighters in the Near East. Trade routes began to grow
lively again along the north-south land axis between the Mediterranean and
the Baltic. By the ninth century the Danes were active in trade and industry
in Britain, France, and the Netherlands. The Swedes were busy along the
trade artery southwards through Russia to Constantinople. Down that long
and dangerous road through newly proud Novgorod went amber and furs,
honey, women for the harems.

The demands of distant markets stimulated the growth of vigorous towns
in strategic areas where goods were produced or trade routes ran. Famous
and large fairs were held in the main wholesale centers, especially in the twelfth
and thirteenth centuries. At Champaign in France, at Bruges, Ypres, Lyons,
Geneva, at England's Stourbridge and Winchester these fairs attracted export
and import merchants from all over Europe and the Near East. Here they
bought and sold and made contract delivery arrangements. Here their pens
and voices made agreements that moved the goods and made the profits.

Several towns in France, Spain, and England formed the key points of political consolidation, so important in the rise of nation-states. By 1400 Milan, Paris, Venice, and Florence each had populations of more than 100,000. London had about 50,000.

Behind the strength of their wealth and their walls, most medieval townsmen controlled trade by an organization known as the merchant guild. Private capitalism and local politics were inextricably mingled. In the merchant guild were all the merchants, the buyers and sellers of goods, who wanted to hold a monopoly of the internal trade of their town. They often stood together to obtain special privileges from the king or the noble upon whose lands the town stood. The merchant guilds usually had codes of law by which all members were rigidly controlled. The regulation of community prices, for example, was very strict. The guilds also protected their members, so far as was possible, from being badly used in other towns. Several guilds resembled modern "clubs" and "brotherhoods" in their charitable activities; they often visited the sick, looked after the indigent families of deceased members, attended in a full assembly the funeral of a merchant "brother," and distributed charity to the poor. They were rather conservative bodies, not inclined to encourage initiative or invention.

There grew up alongside the merchant guilds the craft guilds, composed of all men engaged in one particular craft or "mystery." For example, the masons, weavers, carpenters, goldsmiths, ironmongers, tanners, fishmongers, and shoemakers all had their own craft guilds to regulate the affairs of their trade. Each guild included all the workers in the town who practiced its craft. No man could engage in any particular craft until he became a member of the guild. As the years passed it became increasingly difficult to obtain membership. The guilds later developed the general rule that a period of apprenticeship had to be served before a man could enter a trade. After an apprentice had worked under a contract with a master of a trade for a definite term, usually seven years, he became a journeyman. In time, if he could accumulate enough money of his own to start a shop, he might become a master craftsman.

The artisans of the craft guilds regulated the size and quality of their products. They supervised many other things. For example, a butcher was forbidden to sew the fat from good meat on lean to deceive his customers. For the welfare of the craft they fixed wages, hours of labor, quantity of production, and sometimes prices. They tried to keep a monopoly of the market for their goods. Many of the craft guilds were also benevolent, religious, and social organizations similar to the merchant guilds. They had patron saints and processions on holy days. They provided money for masses for dead members. They looked after the brethren of the trade who were ill, aged, poor, or in trouble.

The rise of towns and trade meant that there was a more widespread use of money for the purchase of goods and services. Wealth and power no longer rested solely with the land. Money changers appeared wherever trade routes ran or goods were produced. Banking families like the Bardi and Peruzzi were laying the foundations of their fortunes. The bankers of these exciting days began to devise new instruments of business, such as bills of exchange and letters of credit. Meanwhile the gains of production per capita provided the economic surplus that made a high level of civilization and culture possible. No advanced form of culture can ever prevail in a subsistence economy. The economic surplus of the twelfth century, for example, was a significant reason for the appearance of the famous "twelfth-century Renaissance" and the revival of Latin and Greek in the so-called High Middle Ages.

The shifting patterns of medieval feudalism, agriculture, trade, and industry help to explain many kaleidoscopic changes in the political history of the early Middle Ages. We turn now to look at the political achievements and failures of emperors and kings, princes and popes. As we move down this cluttered corridor of history we can see at once that there is much blood and drama, a great deal of confusion, and a considerable amount of quiet and solid building.

Charles the Great, or Charlemagne (768–814), virile king of the Franks, was a hard-grained soldier, statesman, and apostle of civilization. His tall and massive body was a symbol of his strength as a ruler. We have a great deal of information about him from the biography of his dwarf secretary Einhard, from his numerous edicts, and his capitularies, those famous instructions to the royal officials. This was the man who defeated foes from the Long Beards of Normandy to the men of the Saxon lands. This was the ruler who extended his empire from Italy to Jutland and from the Pyrenees to Bohemia. Before he died the territories of Charlemagne included all of France, parts of Germany, Italy, Spain, and the Low Countries. It was this Charlemagne, a king who never learned to read or write, who was responsible for the revival of culture usually called the Carolingian Renaissance. From all over Europe he brought scholars to his court and palace school: Alcuin from England's York; Paulinus from Aquitaine; Theodulf, a Goth and bishop of Orleans; Paul the Deacon, a Lombard; Angilbert, a Frank.

Much aid came from the British Isles, especially from Ireland, mighty in her monastic scholarship. The flood tide of Irish fame in learning had been in the fifth century. "That fierce and restless quality which had made the pagan Irish the terror of Western Europe, seems to have emptied itself into love of learning and love of God." When the scholars had fled from Europe in the years when Rome was crumbling, many of them had found refuge and safety in the shelter of Ireland's Four Seas. Some had come by the old trade routes; some had taken the three days' journey from the Loire to Cork; some had gone up the Irish Sea to Bangor. Now, after three centuries, the scholars were coming back to Europe. Some were coming to the court of Charlemagne, enthusiastic patron of the arts and sturdy defender of the cause of education.

At the king's command Alcuin introduced the beautiful reformed handwriting that excites our admiration today. Most of the writings of ancient Rome that we have in the modern world exist in their oldest form in the Carolingian copies. This rich heritage comes to us from Charlemagne. It was Charlemagne, too, who grasped and seized the valuable new ideas that we see embodied in his legal and administrative reforms. Not all the triumphs of history are marked by the fields of battle.

When Charlemagne came to the throne he immediately turned to fight the Lombards. In a series of battles he defeated them in one campaign, took their iron crown and put it on his own head. Then he gathered his army and leaped upon the Saxons east of the Rhine. In a difficult war that lasted for several years Charlemagne defeated and Christianized the Saxons and by his will they joined the Frankish Empire. Then he fought the Bavarians and the Avars. In 778 his expedition against the Spaniards failed. On the way back the Christian Basques attacked his army in the pass of Roncesvalles. Many men poured out their blood and the great Count Roland was slain. This event inspired one of the most magnificent epics of the feudal age: *The Song of Roland*.

The details of Charlemagne's conquests are unimportant. What matters is that he carved and kept an empire. What matters also is that he helped to guide men along the roads to a new age.

There had been no resident emperor in the West after the year 476. Most people seem to have believed in the tradition of the Roman Empire and some certainly looked to the Byzantine emperor at Constantinople as the chief of the Western world. By the year 799, however, the wicked Irene had seized the throne in Constantinople and had put out the eyes of her son. Such notorious deeds did not win wide approval. At the same time, Pope Leo III was in serious trouble. He had been assaulted in Rome and driven out of the city. He appealed to Charlemagne, who had much authority in the Roman states. Charlemagne went to Rome and supported Leo as lawful pope before a great council of clergy and laymen.

On Christmas Day in the year 800, as Charlemagne knelt in prayer before the altar at old St. Peter's, Pope Leo placed a diadem on his head. We are told that the assembled people shouted: "To Charles Augustus, crowned of God, great and pacific emperor of the Romans, life and victory!" The warrior Frank, fifty-eight years old and thoroughly German, was now the head of the Roman Empire.

Charlemagne usually kept his court at Aachen (Aix-la-Chapelle), famous

for its hot springs. He built there a fine little domed chapel. Because the gold
and silver and other materials he wanted were not available in his German
lands Charlemagne plundered Rome and Ravenna. This chapel, a symbol
of Charlemagne's faith and strength, was preserved inside the great cathedral
at Aachen until it was destroyed in 1945 by mightier weapons than the builders ever knew.

When Charlemagne and his successors held sway over the broad lands of
the expanded Frankish kingdom called the Empire they were not ruling a
unified realm. There was no effective administrative structure, despite the
long and detailed description of its officials to be found in many books. There
was no central administration worthy of the name. There was no adequate
public finance, no chain of command of salaried officials. The lands and the
peoples, with their deep and diverse loyalties, were held together by force.
Only a hardfisted ruler like Charlemagne could keep a semblance of political
order, peace, and unity. It is interesting to look at a map showing the extent
of Charlemagne's empire. It is better to realize what a cumbersome agglomeration of different regions and squabbling peoples the empire actually was. It
took no soothsayer to predict dislocation when the heavy hand of Charlemagne
was gone. The empire was to survive as an ideal. The imperial title was to
stay for a thousand years. In a political sense the title was a vain thing and
the empire was flimsy and frail. What counted was power. Of that valuable
commodity the empire never had much.

The river of western European history became murky and muddled after
the dominating Charlemagne died. The strong king had a weak son, Louis
the Pious, and weakness brought its inevitable results. Louis was not a warrior,
not a statesman. His three legitimate sons, all mediocre men, fought bitterly.
Two of them, Charles the Bald and Louis the German, joined to battle their
brother Lothair, who had inherited the imperial title. The nasty "war of the
three brothers" was ended by the Treaty of Verdun in 843. By its terms the
empire was split into three parts. Charles the Bald took an area that is covered
by a large part of modern France, the lands west of the Rhone and the Saône.
Lothair was given a long, heterogeneous belt of land stretching from Italy
to the North Sea—Italy, Provence, Burgundy, the western Rhinelands, and
the Low Countries; he also kept the title of emperor. Louis the German obtained lands roughly equivalent to those now included in modern Germany.
Shortly after Lothair died in 855 his brothers had divided his whole kingdom.
The great empire of Charlemagne had thus been split, and split again. A
contemporary wrote: "Where is the former grandeur of the Empire of the
Franks? If God does not intervene we shall soon be delivered defenceless to
the attacks of the pagans."

There was indeed great danger from "the attacks of the pagans." Western Europe was once more harassed by barbarian invaders. From the tumultuous

Scandinavian lands came virile men called Danes, Norsemen, Vikings, the rude men of the fiords. Forced from their lands by overpopulation, pressed by the restless spirit of adventure, these warriors and sailors must have been pleased to discover the lack of defended ramparts in the rich places to the south. They wanted to loot and burn, kill and destroy. Wherever they came they brought terror, havoc, and desolation. These were the men, as we have seen, who thrust and carried commerce down through Russia all the way to Constantinople, persistently ravaged and plundered in the Mediterranean, looted from their clinker-boats along the coasts of Aquitaine and Spain, attacked Cadiz and Seville, smashed the guard of Ireland, seized and held the Orkneys, the Shetlands, the Hebrides, the Isle of Man, Scotland, and all the northern part of England. In 841 they pillaged Rouen; in 843 they sacked Nantes and murdered the bishop in front of his altar; in 845 they captured Paris and collected a ransom. They plundered Bordeaux, Toulouse, Tours, Orléans. In 912 they obtained and kept a block of territory in France in the Seine valley. This land was soon to be called Normandy. To the Danelaw in England and to Normandy in France came settlers from the north. The people of western Europe said in the Litany, "from the fury of the Northmen, good Lord, deliver us."

When the Vikings were raiding and conquering in the north the Moslems were striking in the south. It was during these years of the ninth century that the Moslems overran Sicily, took Marseilles, and attacked the coasts of Italy and Provence and the islands of Sardinia and Corsica. They burned and plundered old St. Peter's on the edge of Rome and the great monastery of Monte Cassino to the north.

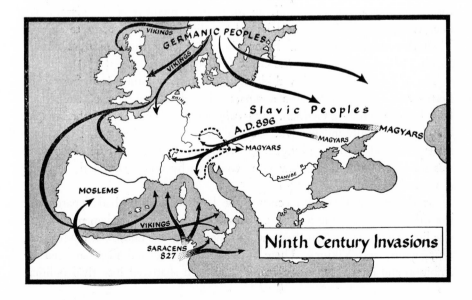

Ninth Century Invasions

To the onslaughts of Vikings and Moslems was added the violence of a third group of marauders. On the eastern rim of the empire appeared some primitive and hungry nomads from Asia, usually called Hungarians because of their relationship to the earlier Huns. These Hungarians, or Magyars, had come by the old roads over the grassland steppes and now they pressed into the lands between the Danube and the Carpathians and drove into Bavaria, Venetia, and Lombardy. Not until 955 were they finally defeated by Otto I at the battle of Lechfeld. Then they settled and mingled with the Avars in the land of modern Hungary.

Meanwhile the heirs of Charlemagne bickered and battled and broke faith. There is no need to recite here the successive phases of the struggle. Few are worth mentioning. Brother fought brother; usurpers came and claimed; disorder never stopped. Robert the Strong moved into conflict with Charles the Bald and with the Norsemen too. Louis the Stammerer, only surviving son of Charles the Bald, lived for two years after his father died and he was lucky to do that. Then came Louis III and Carloman and Charles the Simple. Only once, under the incompetent Charles III, called Charles the Fat, was the empire temporarily reunited. This third son of Louis the German was not to rule for long. In 885 the Danes attacked Paris with hundreds of Viking ships and in 886 Charles led an army to relieve Paris. Then he faltered. He "did nothing worthy of the royal majesty." Soon he bribed the Norsemen to go home. They took the bribe and went home, for a while. The dismayed and disgusted subjects of Charles III pulled him off the throne.

The empire now became completely divided. In 887 the leaders of the western kingdom proclaimed Odo, Count of Paris, the new king—his descendants were to be the Capetian kings of France. In the eastern kingdom the throne was given to Arnulf, an illegitimate member of the Carolingian line. When his son died in 911 the old Carolingian dynasty came to an end. Then there ruled Conrad of Franconia and Henry the Fowler, Duke of Saxony, whose son was Otto the Great (936–973).

The old belt of Lothair's middle kingdom now broke into fragments. Lorraine in the north became a separate kingdom, held for a while by a Frenchman, then by a German. Burgundy and Provence also became separate kingdoms, virtually independent. Beyond the Alps the kingdom of the Lombards, the land of Italy, plunged into anarchy. The empty title of emperor was held by five men in a few years and then by nobody until the coming of Otto the Great.

At the end of the ninth century the lands of Europe had departed far from the tradition of the Roman Empire and the rule of Charlemagne. There was little law or order. On the contrary, there were the raids of the Moslems, Hungarians, and Vikings. There was internal strife and massacre, fed by ambition and hate. The whole empire had been shattered into rival political units: kingdoms, dukedoms, marquisates, and the like. The papacy, too, had lost the spiritual leadership of Europe. Successive popes became involved in political strife and smirched by scandal. Christendom was divided. There was no hand to gather and weld the fragments. No voice was heard to rally and rouse the spirits of men.

During the ninth and tenth centuries in Europe there were only faint and wavering signs of the emergence of nation-states. The king of the Western Franks ruled over many tribes, ambitious and squabbling. There was no idea of a unified nation-state called "France." Nor was there as yet a dream of a single state called "Germany." The king of the Eastern Franks was the nominal leader of many tribal duchies—Bavarian, Franconian, Saxon, Swabian —and the degree of his power depended upon his sword and supporters. To the south, Italy stood divided into separate states and independent cities filled with rebellion and discord. Not for nearly a thousand years was the Italian peninsula to be united by the power and genius of Cavour, Mazzini, and Garibaldi.

Under the Saxon house of Otto the Great (936–973) the German regions saw a brief dawn of bright promise. Otto put down the rebellions of several tribal duchies. He defeated the Czechs of Bohemia and thus helped to open the gates for German migration eastward. Meanwhile he pushed his control to the Rhone. He stopped the last Magyar invasion in 955. He cooperated with the Church to win and hold its support.

For good or ill, Otto now turned away from the problems of his homeland to follow the beckoning dream of empire. In 961 he occupied Lombardy and assumed the Italian crown. In 962 he marched to Rome to help Pope John XII, that immoral profligate, and was crowned Roman emperor. What is known as the Holy Roman Empire came into existence, an empire conceived of as a continuation of both the Carolingian Empire—was not Otto a rightful successor of Charlemagne?—and the Empire of the Roman Caesars. For centuries sections of Italy and Germany formed that sprawling body in Europe.

Most of the Saxon and Salian rulers who followed Otto the Great had neither his ability nor his good fortune. The reigns were short; the rebellions were sharp and strong; the advance was always slow. In the confusion of those decades one significant fact may be noted: the Germans continued to migrate on an immense scale to the opening eastern lands. From the Elbe to the Niemen the stalwart Germans found a great plain, a rich frontier waiting for them to overrun and colonize. By the reign of Henry III (1039–1056) the German overlordship in Poland and Bohemia had been soundly established. When Hungary became a Christian kingdom the German hands and voices were seen and heard in that land more and more. If the German people had turned and moved exuberantly westwards instead of to the Eastland the later consequences for all of Europe would have been beyond calculation. The fact remains, however, that the eyes of the Germans did not gaze upon the lands to the west. They looked to Italy and the eastern advance. "The land was empty and conquest was easy." Thus the tides of these hard and fierce Germans swept eastward. The invaders appropriated, enslaved, cleared and drained land, and built houses and barns.

In France, meanwhile, a hundred years of rivalry and bloodshed followed the selection of Odo, Count of Paris, as king in 887. In 987 Hugh Capet secured the throne and the famous Capetian dynasty began its long rule. Hugh Capet had under his immediate control in the royal domain only the Île de France, a narrow strip of land with its center in Paris. Most of the other areas over which Hugh and his successors held nominal sway were really in the power of territorial princes. True, most of these princes were technically feudal vassals of the Capetians, but they obeyed their royal overlords only when they found it convenient.

Frequently the kings intervened in the affairs of the principalities. Sometimes they were successful; more often they were not. In the north and west, strong feudal states—like the duchies and counties of Burgundy, Normandy, Champagne, and Flanders—were not willing to hand over any of their powers to a Capetian king or to anybody else. In the south, the actual authority of the Capetians was likewise small. There stood the proud and strong and practically independent states of Aquitaine, Gascony, Toulouse, Barcelona, Anjou with its rich lands in the valley of the Loire. The early Capetians, handicapped by the smallness of their territories and by their meager resources, could not hope to prevail against the mighty feudal lords.

Under the first four Capetians (897–1108) the power and prestige of the crown were not shining and strong. Education, piety, and manners were not enough to win and hold power and land. No Capetian king could hope to conquer his kingdom and subdue his vassals until the royal cause and claims were backed by force and a large royal income. Such necessary power could be obtained only by forging a strong state out of the small and weak royal domain.

It was the shrewd and energetic Louis VI (1108–1137) who really began the forward march of the Capetians. He subdued all rebels inside the royal domain. He built a sound administration of loyal vassals. His courts were efficient and his taxes increased. To his skill and patience was added good fortune: his son married Eleanor, the only daughter of William X of Aquitaine. The pious Louis VII (1137–1180) thus inherited both Aquitaine and the royal Capetian domains around Paris. In 1180 Louis VII was succeeded by the crafty and determined Philip Augustus (1180–1223). This king was to add great provinces to his kingdom: Normandy, Artois, Maine, Poitou, Anjou. The kingdom of France was now more than a name.

Across the North Sea and the English Channel new chapters were being written in the long history of England. There the sea-rover Angles and Saxons and their fellows had swooped when the Romans went home forever. There the waves of Danish invaders had come in the ninth century. The *Anglo-Saxon Chronicle* recorded the "harrowing inroads of the heathen men." The Danes raided and ravaged the shores of England, splitting the skulls of monks with battle-axes, killing and stealing, burning the monasteries, loading their long ships with gold and gems, booty from ill-guarded shrines. Slowly, as we have seen, they overran the northern part of England, the Danelaw. By the Treaty of Wedmore (878) the Danish king Guthrum divided England with Alfred the Great. This arrangement lasted until the Danish king Canute was chosen to rule all England in 1016. When Canute's line died out in 1042 the English turned to the Saxon line and Edward the Confessor was crowned at Winchester.

Edward had spent much of his life in Normandy. He brought to England many Normans to hold office in his household, to be priests in his chapel, to be wine merchants. The Anglo-Danish nobles resented the Norman invasion of the court and the state. When Edward died the king's council placed upon the throne Harold, Earl of Wessex and son of Godwin, famous opponent of the Normans.

Harold's brother Tostig, the exiled Earl of Northumbria, was threatening to invade England because, as he bitterly said, Harold had betrayed him to his enemies. In any conflict the king of the Scots would probably support Tostig. There were stirrings in restless Norway, a possible prelude to attack. Most dangerous of all, Harold's cousin William, Duke of Normandy, was an ambitious candidate for the English throne.

Had Harold been wrecked in 1064 off the coast of Normandy and taken to William's court? Had Harold, to obtain his liberty, sworn an oath to be William's vassal or to support his claim to the English throne? There were many assertions about the nature of William's claim to England's crown. The Bayeux tapestry stated that "Harold took an oath to Duke William." Whatever the facts may have been, William began to prepare for the invasion of England.

Meanwhile the fleet of the king of Norway was moving against England. Tostig, Harold's brother, joined the Norwegian forces. On September 25, 1066, Harold defeated and killed both the Norwegian king and Tostig at the battle of Stamford Bridge, despite the fact that many of the English soldiers had earlier been disbanded to harvest the ripening grain.

Three days later William of Normandy landed on an undefended shore in the south. The banners that snapped in the wind had been blessed by the pope. Harold's enemy was a man familiar with all the devices of Continental warfare. To be a successful ruler in Normandy it was necessary to be a master of war. The core of William's army was an array of mailed horsemen; the infantry was a subsidiary arm. Harold's force, on the other hand, was mainly infantry, designed to fight with spear, ax, and shield. The English army probably numbered about 7,000 men, ranging from nobles to ill-armed peasants. William's force was probably smaller; but all his men were picked troops.

Harold moved swiftly southwards. On October 13 he massed his army on the brow of a steep hill, "at the grey apple tree" near Hastings. To protect his front line he dug a ditch and threw up a fence of stakes and wattled boughs; he hoped that this device would help to hold back the charge of the Norman horsemen. The center of the crowded hill was held by well-equipped nobles who locked their shields together to form a shield wall. On the flanks and in the rear were a motley crowd armed with spears, axes, swords, and clubs. Harold's only chance of victory was in the possibility that his army could fight a protracted defensive engagement until the Norman forces had exhausted themselves in attack.

In the dawn of October 14, 1066, William prepared to strike. Placed in the first rank were his archers, slingers, and crossbowmen. In the second were the heavily armed infantrymen. In the third were the feudal horsemen.

The battle lasted all day. Once the Norman lines gave way; it was William himself who rallied his forces. Afterwards the Normans were able to cut off and destroy some of their Anglo-Saxon pursuers. Later the Normans carried out several pretended flights with the same results. Norman arrows shot perpendicularly into the air killed many Englishmen within the shield wall. At last Harold fell. In the dusk the leaderless English army broke and fled along the darkening trackways; and the Frenchmen held the place of slaughter.

The battle decided the fate of a nation. The English leaders formally surrendered and accepted William as king. On Christmas Day, 1066, William was crowned in Westminster Abbey by a Saxon prelate. During the coronation ceremony the Norman knights outside the Abbey misunderstood the shouting inside and thought the crowd was attacking William. In a panic they set fire to some neighboring buildings. The flames lit up the coronation scene, symbolic of the events that had brought William to the throne.

In the sullen north William carried out a systematic devastation of the country in a campaign of sustained ferocity. As a further guard against rebellion the logical William built great castles at strategic points in England and along the Welsh border. In northern England, the massive castle of Durham arose above the charred villages and wasted dales.

To England "the stark, stern, and wrathful" William brought feudalism, efficient government, Norman culture. The Norman Conquest opened the gateways of England to new influences from Europe. The leading members of the church and state were now Normans; many held their Norman estates; and most of them were in frequent touch with the Continent from France to Rome. English and Norman soldiers fought together across the Channel. English and Norman clerics found posts on the Continent. The bursting intellectual revival of Europe was soon mirrored in England, where Norman churchmen led the way in founding English schools.

French became the language of the court, the law, the government. Educated men spoke and wrote both French and Latin. Exiled from hall, court, and cloister, English remained almost entirely a spoken tongue for about three centuries. It was in those years that it gained the suppleness and grace that are among its chief merits today. At the same time it was enriched by French words and ideas, especially those that had to do with hunting, art, cooking, religion, politics, justice, war. In the fourteenth century English again entered polite society in the works of Geoffrey Chaucer, John Wycliffe, and their fellows. Then its long and unconscious growth had left it improved and flexible, ready to develop into the language of William Shakespeare.

William the Conqueror died in 1087 and was succeeded by William II, a coarse and debased likeness of his father. In the summer of 1100, William II was hunting in the great New Forest that his father had made in Hampshire. There he was shot through the heart, perhaps by accident. Some foresters took his body up to Winchester on a cart. His younger brother Henry rode at once to seize the royal treasure. Then he seized the throne and became Henry I.

Henry I (1100–1135) was an able ruler. Stephen (1135–1154), his successor, was not. He was weak. Nothing prospered under him. Law and justice collapsed in civil war and anarchy. "Men said openly that Christ and his saints slept." The frightening confusion of his reign showed how dangerous it was to have a "soft and good" man for a king. Unchecked feudalism meant anarchy and bloodshed, tortured peasants and depopulated villages. It was fortunate that Stephen's successor was Henry II (1154–1189), one of the greatest monarchs of the Middle Ages.

Henry II held more territory in France than the king of France himself. His father Geoffrey, Count of Anjou and Maine, had conquered Normandy. In 1151, Henry inherited all of his father's lands. Then, in 1152, he married Eleanor of Aquitaine. Her dowry, added to his own French possessions, gave him control of all western France. When he succeeded Stephen as king of England in 1154 his territories reached from Scotland to the Pyrenees.

The personality of Henry counted for much in his age; it was one of the reasons why he left his mark forever upon England and her laws. Henry was twenty-one years old in 1154, scholarly, efficient, intelligent, practical, with an essentially legal turn of mind. His energy was demonic. Courtiers were amazed at this king who seemed never to grow weary. Henry was a skilled politician, preferring the tools of diplomacy to those of force and war. He was also particularly shrewd in selecting able servants. Industrious and determined, Henry tolerated no slackness in others. With him all seemed to move upon a heroic scale.

To Henry the business of kingship was an absorbing passion. He would make England a model state. There would be no anarchy among the barons when Henry II was king, for Henry intended to be master of his realm. He restored order and reorganized the central government. He suppressed the baronage. He extended the power of the central royal courts. He increased the use of writs and itinerant justices. He introduced the jury system as a normal part of royal court procedure. He added much to the common law. When he met objection or defiance he pounced swiftly and hard. The day of feudal anarchy was ended. For thirty-five years Henry II drove on towards his goals, relentless and almost unimpeded.

The fortunes of Henry II in the British Isles were not matched by his achievements across the English Channel. The strange and heterogeneous character and interests of Henry's feudal holdings in France made administration difficult. Henry's feudal lands were divided by differences in culture, language, and blood. Their economic and political desires were quite dissimilar. Before the birth of French national feeling the men of Normandy, Aquitaine, and the other provinces had no common bond to unite their interest or enthusiasm. By accident, and accident alone, they were all ruled by Henry II of England. Henry, in turn, was responsible, in varying feudal relationships, to the king of France. Beyond that political and feudal fact there was no unity in Henry's vast French domain.

To an increasing extent the kings of France coveted English territory. Amidst defiant ambitions and jealousies they were prepared to seize every chance to dislodge Englishmen from a county here, a city there, and to round off and knot up the royal lands of the kingdom of France at the expense of alien feudatories as well as French rivals. The envenomed Continental duel between England and France began when William of Normandy conquered England and the destinies of the two states athwart the Channel became intertwined. What began as essentially a French civil war became a war between states. Out of this protracted struggle two nations emerged, clearly distinguished in their religious, social, and political structure.

The problems of Henry II's French provinces occupied much of his time. He had to keep his vassals submissive and his French rivals thwarted. His Continental schemes and claims were steadily directed to retaining and extending his French possessions. Louis VII of France, on the other hand, was determined to check Henry wherever he possibly could. Louis was not an aggressive king. His temperament was placid; his resources were insignificant. "Your lord, the king of England," he once remarked, "has gold and silk and jewels and goods things in abundance. We of France have only bread and wine and gaiety." Louis was aware that his kingdom was weak and disjointed and that he could not afford to gamble his inheritance by open battle with Henry II. He preferred to rest upon his legal claims and to stir up Henry's restless and unscrupulous vassals to strike against their English master. He could also shake the throne of his powerful vassal by plotting with Eleanor, Henry's queen, and with Henry's four legitimate sons.

Between Henry and his queen a hatred burned steadily, fanned by the king's roving loves. Eleanor was powerful in Aquitaine; Henry was not. It was through Aquitaine that Eleanor struck most strongly at Henry and the weapons she used were their sons. There were four of them: Henry, Richard, Geoffrey, and John. Henry and Geoffrey died before their father; Richard and John were to succeed him upon the throne. Perhaps because of his deep affection for his sons Henry never restrained them. The harsh and ungentle methods he employed to curb other men were not used upon his children. The princes did not become either dutiful youths or gentlemen. One of the sons declared that in the Plantagenet family brother always strove against brother and son against father. "From the devil we came; to the devil we return," said Richard, the best of the four.

Henry II had no intention of surrendering any of his power to his sons so long as he lived. His sons saw their inheritance dangling before them but still beyond their grasp. They stood, discontented and impotent, waiting for the great king to die. In such circumstances the youths easily listened to the intriguing Louis VII and, above all, to their mother, Eleanor.

In 1173, Henry, Geoffrey, and Richard led revolts against their father in the eastern counties of England, in Normandy, and in Brittany. Several of the great Anglo-Norman barons seized the chance to rebel against the king who had done so much to limit their power. The Scotsmen under William the Lion came down from the north. The king of France, supported by the strong counts of Boulogne and Flanders, invaded Normandy. Thus the conspiracy of the princes grew into a dangerous coalition of all the king's enemies. But Henry was not easily overcome. In England the strength of his government showed itself; there would be no return to the days of Stephen. The royalist forces triumphed everywhere. The middle and lower classes detested the prospect of a baronial oligarchy influenced by the tempers and whims of Henry's sons. They stood by the king who had given England strong and sound government. It was the peasants of Suffolk who used pitchforks and flails to wipe out the Flemish mercenaries of the rebelling Earl of Leicester. The proud earl was taken captive and submitted to the king he had hoped to dethrone. The king of Scotland became Henry's prisoner. The revolt in Normandy collapsed.

Henry II promised the rebel princes an annual revenue, but nothing more. He still refused to share his sovereign power. To John, his favorite son, he gave land and castles in Anjou, Normandy, and England. In 1175 he sent Richard to administer the duchy of Aquitaine. Then trouble started once more. Richard's envious brothers intrigued against him. When Richard encroached upon Anjou, the fief of his brother Henry, war began between the two brothers. Henry was soon joined by Geoffrey. Then Henry II intervened and the brothers turned against the father. When Prince Henry lay ill with dysentery in 1183 it is said that in an agony of remorse he begged his father to visit his deathbed. Henry II, fearing treachery, refused to come but sent his ring in token of forgiveness and affection.

The brief interval of peace that followed Prince Henry's death was used to advantage by Philip Augustus, who had succeeded Louis VII as king of France in 1180. Wary, hard, suspicious, and able, Philip Augustus was determined to drive his English vassals out of France whatever the means he might have to use. He began by plotting with Geoffrey of Brittany, Henry II's third son. After Geoffrey died, Philip turned to Richard. In the summer of 1189 Richard defeated his father and forced him to accept a series of humiliating demands. Henry II was prematurely old, broken by labor, disease, and sorrow; he came to the formal conference with Richard and Philip Augustus a dying man.

All of Henry's sons, he believed, had betrayed him but John, and John was far away. When he left the conference Henry knew that the name of John, the son he had trusted, led the list of conspirators for whom amnesty had been demanded. At Chinon, in its summer beauty, the agony of defeat mingled with the delirium of disease. In the shadows of treachery and humiliation Henry II died on July 6, 1189, at the age of fifty-six.

Thus it was that the lands of Europe and the British Isles moved towards the end of the twelfth century. It is impossible, of course, to describe at length all of the themes and threads in the history of Europe in the early Middle Ages. To make such an attempt would invite disaster and make confusion certain. The lives of men in all times and lands take their places in far more complex landscapes than some men dream of in their philosophies. What has been written here is enough to suggest the varied aspects of the shifting economic patterns, the successive thrusts and counterthrusts in the political struggles of turbulent and dangerous centuries. Slowly, very slowly, several foundations of modern Europe were being shaped and anchored. Many of the moves of the European leaders were bold. Some were right and some were wrong. It is easier for us to express our balanced opinions on past events than it was for those who made them long ago.

Chapter 16

POPES, KINGS, AND

PEOPLE

"The human race we have divided into two parts, the one consisting of those who live according to man, the other of those who live according to God. And those we also mystically call the two cities or the two communities of men, of which the one is predestined to rule eternally with God, and the other to suffer eternal punishment with the devil."

—St. Augustine, *The City of God*

THESE are the final words of the book of *Ecclesiastes:* "Let us hear the conclusion of the whole matter. Fear God, and keep his commandments: for this is the whole duty of man. For God shall bring every work into judgment, with every secret thing, whether it be good, or whether it be evil."

In the Middle Ages thousands of men devoutly believed that "the whole duty of man" was to follow the laws of God. The basic dignity of every individual was believed to depend upon his relation to God. In the eyes of medieval man the boundary lines drawn by kings and emperors did not really fragment the planet. Despite all political and economic divisions the idea still prevailed of the universal brotherhood of man and the comprehensive fatherhood of God. Not until the sixteenth century did there arise the idea that Christian doctrines could be divided by national boundaries. In the world of the Middle Ages, in the world of St. Augustine's two cities, there lived together the evil and the vicious men, the meek and the merciful and the poor in heart. All would be judged.

All would indeed be judged. It is difficult for many modern minds to understand and appreciate medieval concern with the progress of the human soul in this world and the next. In the Middle Ages the Last Judgment was a vivid, real, and imminent event. "Men's minds were haunted by the Apocalypse and the more dismal chapters of the Prophets." The famous *Dies Irae,* written by Thomas of Celano in the thirteenth century, shows very clearly,

PLATE XV

[51]

William Longespée, illegitimate son of England's Henry II, who aided his brother King John (1199-1216) in resisting the demands of the barons, later wavered, and finally joined the enemy.

Below: An upper class English family of the fourteenth century at dinner in the great hall

PLATE XVI

Left: Christ teaching, a Byzantine mosaic of the twelfth century in the apse of the Cathedral of Cefalu, Sicily

Below: The Towers of San Gemignano, built in the eleventh century, were once proud defense points of an Italian city-republic.

[53]

[54

like several hymns in medieval missals and breviaries, the prevailing interest in the day of judgment.

> Day of wrath! O day of mourning!
> See fulfill'd the prophets' warning!
> Heaven and earth in ashes burning! . . .
> Wondrous sound the trumpet flingeth
> Through earth's sepulchres it ringeth
> All before the throne it bringeth. . . .
> Ah! that day of tears and mourning!
> From the dust of earth returning
> Man for judgment must prepare him;
> Spare, O God, in mercy spare him!

Man's relationship to God was one thing. His connection with his fellow men was another. To most medieval men a good society upon this earth seems to have meant a unified and hierarchical social and political structure in which an individual was in his "proper station" as a noble or a yeoman. God and nature had stratified all society. Men were not equal except before the Cross. Every man had his duties, his responsibilities, and his rights in that niche to which God had called him. Modern ideas of democracy would have been quite unintelligible in the Middle Ages.

The strength of the Church extended to the farthest edges of Europe. There was one Church, one revelation, one spiritual domination of the Church universal. After the Empire of Rome had crumbled, the Christian Church had become the greatest unifying force. Europe was Christendom, and the spiritual center of Christendom was at Rome. The bishops, priests, and deacons taught and guided the faithful and tried to do the same thing for the faithless. Most people in Europe could not read and could not write; but they could understand. It was not then widely believed that education meant the same thing as intelligence or that salvation waited upon literacy. The essential need was faith in the truth that brought men into the congregation and companionship of the clergy and dedicated laymen in the City of God. Those who remained outside the Church belonged to the City of Men and their fate was sure. "Man that is in honor, and understandeth not, is like the beasts that perish."

Religion was concerned with all aspects of man's life. The laws of God were mighty and would prevail and God must never be mocked by arrogant men. Such were the views of most men of the Middle Ages. Such were the beliefs of the kings and nobles as well as of other men who worked and died and lie in unremembered graves. Whenever we look at the vast canvas of the crowded medieval panorama we are sharply aware of the militant faith of Christendom. The flames and fountains of the medieval spirit can never be described or explained without reference to the commands of God, the faith and fear and hopes of man. Dr. Paul A. Zahl recently summarized a law that wise men always know: "For a believer or a philosopher hope is the essence on which life feeds, the essence before which death flees."

Secular and cynical men may assert that such faiths, past and present, are based on sterile dogmas, endlessly repeated like a beadsman's prayers. They may claim that only secret and sinister opponents of Progress can willingly deviate from the known mass laws prescribed by a liberal, secular world and the "normative values" said to be established by society and discoverable by careful measurement. Men dedicated to the purpose of proving that there is no purpose beyond themselves frequently become enmeshed and throttled by circular arguments. They often end by being what Lecomte du Noüy once called "accountants of phenomena" and nothing more. "He made a pit, and digged it, and is fallen into the ditch which he made." When the idea of causes, reaching back beyond the origins of the universe, is once discarded, then few things are comprehensible to the modern scientists or to anybody else. Not all men are satisfied to evade the issue by stopping with the statement that a hydrogen bomb can move mountains. There is a great deal in the universe that can be neither weighed nor measured. The mystical element in human experience may be the most complete reality there is. "Step by step I was led upward," said St. Augustine, "and then at last I saw Thy invisible things understood by the things that are made."

Medieval man considered that the universe was purposeful and orderly. Nature formed one rational whole. The sources of man's knowledge were two: reason and revelation. Revealed truth, said medieval man, was really quite rational. Reason and faith, asserted the philosophers and theologians, were the same thing. This claim is one of the reasons why some men of later ages insisted that the medieval period was a time when shackling superstitions ruled a trembling world. To a man of the Middle Ages there was no necessary contradiction between the answers of reason and the answers of revelation. Was not theology the queen of the sciences? Had the Church ever made a statement that had been disproved by either fact or logic? Could any structure of ideas or stone endure if the proportions were wrong?

Scholars will hasten to remark, and quite rightly, that the use of reason as an ally of faith came only by slow degrees. In the early Middle Ages it was easier to say that faith had its foundations in truth and that truth was declared by authority. Shortly after 1100, however, Abelard (1079–1142) wrote his famous *Sic et Non*. As a stimulus to debate he cited several contradictions in the teachings of the Church without comment. "We have collected diverse statements from the fathers to provoke young readers to seek out the truth with the greatest diligence, and to render them more acute by the search." Abelard was not opposed to his Church; he simply wanted to use the tools of reason to explain or defend the faith. "I know," he said, "in order that I may believe." Abelard also wrote: "Even if the sayings of the fathers do not agree, it is not to be judged that they are untrue. The seeming disagreement may come from our lack of ability to understand them, not from their mistakes."

Some strong members of the clergy thought that it was certainly impudent and perhaps dangerous to raise any questions whatever about the answers of the Church. Under the heavy pressure of such men as Bernard of Clairvaux, Abelard was compelled to stop teaching and to retire to the monastery at Cluny. Then Abelard's student Peter Lombard published his *Sentences,* a volume in which he tried to show that apparent contradictions in the teachings of the Church were not contradictions at all. In the mazes of dispute with which these years are filled one important fact emerges clearly: the power of reason was used more and more to support the doctrines of the Church. The unique intellectual triumph of the mighty system of thought called scholasticism came to be based upon faith and buttressed by reason. Despite some barren dialectics the scholastic method enhanced the position of formal logic; it trained and subtilized the minds of men to handle the materials of philosophy and theology.

Into a vast and logical scheme of the master schoolmen everything was fitted neatly. For instance, with the gradual recovery of some of the long-lost works of Aristotle, especially the *Logic,* it became necessary to reconcile his words with Church doctrines. This task was accomplished by St. Thomas Aquinas (1225–1274) in his greatest work, the twenty-two volumes of the *Summa Theologica,* a monumental synthesis of Aristotle and the orthodox teachings of the Church. St. Thomas showed that in many respects Aristotle was not in opposition to Rome. Where there was obvious conflict, Aristotle was condemned. When St. Thomas finished his impressive *Summa* it took its place as the most important theological and philosophical contribution of the Middle Ages, combining sacred and profane learning into one harmonious whole. It was an amazing intellectual feat. There were no splintered edges, no discordant notes. "An angel," said St. Thomas, "perceives the truth by simple apprehension, whereas man becomes acquainted with a simple truth by a process from manifold data." With the use of "manifold data" St. Thomas sought to embrace in one system of philosophy and theology the total sum and range of human thought, basing the whole structure on reason and faith together. His influence upon later centuries has rightly been tremendous.

Such learned works of St. Thomas as the *Summa Theologica* and the *De Regimine Principum*—a volume of advice to the king of Cyprus and princes everywhere—did not have wide circulation in their original form either in the days of manuscripts or after the coming of printing in the fifteenth century. Nevertheless, many of the ideas of St. Thomas and his fellow scholars did appear in more popular works written to instruct the laymen. This custom, of course, has continued in recent centuries. "Very few people read Newton," explained Voltaire 200 years ago, "because it is necessary to be learned to understand him. But everybody talks about him." Upon one of the pages of the wise and witty *The Heavenly City of the Eighteenth-Century Philosophers,* Professor Carl Becker listed some of the popular books written about Newtonian philosophy for the "ordinary man." "Anyone might open, instead of Newton's *Principia,* Benjamin Martin's *A Plain and Familiar Introduction to the Newtonian Philosophy, in Six Sections, Illustrated by Six Copper Plates* (1751), of which there appeared in due time five editions." Many popular and ingenious "explanations" of the theories and genius of Professor Albert Einstein have appeared on the news racks of the twentieth century. In the Middle Ages such books as the *Bible of the Poor,* the *Mirror of Salvation,* and *The Art of Dying* had great popularity. There were many illustrations of the "drifting down into the popular consciousness of the definitions of high and abstract thought."

St. Thomas, of course, was only one of the philosophers and churchmen who were thinkers of might and power in the medieval centuries. Faith is the basis of much great thought and most great writing in any age.

While the philosophers and theologians were writing and debating, the abbots and the monks in the monasteries worshiped and served God according to the rules of their orders and what they believed were the commands of God. St. Bernard of Clairvaux (1091–1153), the famous monastic reformer, watched the monks moving along the narrow road to salvation:

> Many of them, I hear, are bishops and earls, and many illustrious through their birth or knowledge; but now, by God's grace, all distinctions of persons being dead among them, the greater anyone thought himself in the world the more in this flock does he regard himself as less than the least. . . . I see them in the gardens with hoes, in the meadows with forks or rakes, in the fields with scythes, in the forest with axes. To judge from their outward appearance, their tools, their bad and disordered clothes, they appear a race of fools without speech or sense. But a true thought in my mind tells me that their life in Christ is hidden in the heavens. . . . I knew them proud and puffed up. I see them walking humbly under the merciful hand of God.

The principal strength of the Church was in her message and in the men who served her. Added to this fact was another: the universal Church of the faithful alone could provide the sacraments, those channels through which divine and invisible grace flowed to the individual and helped to assure his salvation. On the other hand, the Church alone could excommunicate, anathematize, and lay under interdicts those individuals and states that incurred its terrible wrath. "Let him be . . . accursed of heaven and earth and of all that is holy therein. Let him be accursed wherever he be, whether at home or abroad, in the road or in the path, or in the wood or in the water, or in the church. Let him be accursed living and dying, eating, drinking, lying, working, idling . . . accursed in his brain . . . in his heart . . . in his loins . . . in every joint of his body. Let him have no health . . . and may Heaven with all its virtues rise up against him to his damnation. . . ."

The spiritual hand of the Church reached over all of Europe to comfort and control the lords and serfs alike, the ladies in the castles and the peasants' wives, scrubbing in the huts and toiling in the fields. Throughout Christendom, too, was the visible evidence of the tremendous political and economic strength possessed by the clergy. Church courts handled extensive areas of law. The towers and spires of thousands of cathedrals and parish churches rose in silent majesty from Ireland to Russia, from the Baltic to the Mediterranean. Fat sheep fed on the unnumbered acres of land possessed by the Church. Into the coffers of the clergy rolled a flood of gold and silver. There were the contributions of the faithful, the constant taxes, the fines in the Church courts, the numerous bequests. Scores of sources of income fed the stream that flowed to Rome. Scholars have estimated that in the later Middle Ages the total revenues of the Church were greater than the incomes of all the secular rulers in Europe combined.

It is not surprising that the mighty institution of the Church was frequently challenged by the powers and claims of the secular states of Europe. If there had been no struggles between Church and state that would indeed have been a cause of wonder. For hundreds of years before the shattering Reformation kings and lesser laymen battled bitterly with popes and priests. Does Christianity force the citizen of a country to split his allegiance? Where stands the Church?

Every European had two loyalties, one to the spiritual Church and one to the temporal state, those twin powers of *regnum* and *sacerdotium* that governed the lives of men in the Middle Ages. To the Caesars of the states must be given some things. To the Church of God must be given others.

In the European society of the Middle Ages men lived under one principle of life, expounded in the last resort by the pope. The Church insisted that there could be no end to the validity of the natural laws of the universe. These laws, fixed and immutable, were held by the Church to be identical with the laws of Christ. "All custom and all written law which is adverse to natural law is to be accounted null and void." There was to be no gainsaying the voice of Rome. *Si Roma locuta sit, cause finita sit.*

The two loyalties to Church and state imposed upon medieval man were potentially incompatible. They could not help causing many disputes between lay rulers and the papacy. Numerous quarrels arose about the lines of demarcation between papal and royal jurisdiction. They began in the eleventh century and they lasted, sometimes in an acute form, until the explosive Reformation more than 400 years later.

In 1073 the militant and inflammatory monk Hildebrand became Pope Gregory VII (1073–1085). Hildebrand had been born in 1023 in Tuscany. After spending several years in a Cluniac monastery he became chaplain to the exiled Gregory VI in Cologne. In 1049 he returned to Rome with Leo IX. As soon as he became Pope Gregory VII he roused his Church and he roused the Western world.

Throughout Europe the zealous Gregory swiftly increased the power and claims of the papacy. Under his competent control the government of the Church became more centralized. He saw the see of Rome as an instrument for uniting Christendom more effectively than ever before. In his policy Roman imperialism and the Christian religion were combined.

The reforming Gregory and his allies had no patience with corrupt, slovenly, decadent, or somnolent churchmen. In the papal reform program that swept over Europe the government of the cathedral chapters was reorganized. A new and stricter discipline was enforced among the secular clergy. The rules of the monasteries were tightened. Schools and monasteries multiplied. These steps were all a part of the "Cluniac" reforms, named after Hildebrand's monastery of Cluny in Burgundy.

The militant Gregory VII announced that he was ready to use all the weapons of the Church, including "the lance of anathema," against those who opposed his will. He sometimes called his opponents "depraved and wicked men," sometimes "ministers of Satan and heralds of Antichrist." When Gregory moved against the Lombards he quoted the Old Testament: "Cry aloud; spare not, lift up thy voice like a trumpet and declare unto Thy people their transgressions!" When several princes were proposing to conquer Spain, Gregory said: "We suppose you know that the kingdom of Spain belonged of old to St. Peter, and that this right has never been lost, although the land has long been occupied by pagans. Therefore the ownership of this land inheres in the apostolic see alone. . . . Beware lest after you have conquered that land you wrong St. Peter in the same way the infidels do who now hold it."

It is sometimes said that among the claims of Gregory VII was the assertion that every temporal ruler must obey all the orders of the papacy. The picture is not quite so simple as that. The whole problem of the relations of Church and state in the Middle Ages is much more complicated in theory and confused in practice. It is easy and simple to say that "the spiritual and temporal powers are entrusted to two different orders, each drawing its authority from God, each supreme in its own sphere, and independent, within its own sphere, of the other. . . . the king is subject to the bishop in spiritual matters, the bishop to the king in temporal matters." On the other hand, it is easy to say that the pope "must always intervene to protect the interests of the Church and the inalienable rights of Christians." Pope Gelasius I, and many who followed after him, was conscious that no distinction between the powers of Church and state would ever be complete "and the question which is the greater of the two cannot be wholly avoided." Learned modern scholars, such as Professor C. H. McIlwain and Dr. A. J. Carlyle, are reluctant to say exactly how much temporal jurisdiction Gregory VII intended to claim. It certainly seems that Gregory was on occasion prepared to assert the ultimate supremacy of the Church over all secular powers of the world, infallible in doctrine, universal in dominion. His claims sometimes seem to have varied with the rise and decline of the actual power of the papacy. In any event, few ambitious rulers in Europe were prepared to accept the demands and controls of Gregory VII with meekness and humility.

One king who refused to obey all the commands of Gregory VII was William of Normandy, successful conqueror of the realm of England. William had invaded England under the banner of the pope and with his blessing. He was quite prepared to reform the English Church with the aid of the energetic Lanfranc, archbishop of Canterbury. At the same time, he stood adamant against the invasion of what he considered to be his sovereign rights. True, Christ had said: "Render unto Caesar the things that are Caesar's and unto God the things that are God's." Yet who could say with sureness where the laws and controls of popes and kings began and ended?

When the pope boldly demanded an oath of fealty as a formal acknowledgment that England was a fief of Rome, William refused. His sovereign rights must be left unimpaired. "Holy Father," wrote William, "your legate, coming to me on your behalf, has admonished me to do fealty to you and your successors, and to take better heed touching the money which my ancestors used to send to the Church of Rome. To the one request I consent, to the other I do not consent. I have refused to do fealty, and I do refuse, because neither did I promise it, nor, as I find, did my predecessors do fealty to your predecessors. As to the money, it was negligently collected for nearly three years when I was in France and now that I have by divine mercy returned to my kingdom what has been collected is sent by the present messenger and the rest will be sent through the messenger of our faithful archbishop Lanfranc when opportunity shall serve. Pray for me and for the estate of our realm, because we have loved your predecessors and desire sincerely to love you before all men and obediently to hear you."

William also refused to allow English churchmen to acknowledge any pope without royal consent. He commanded that no papal letters or legates should come to England unless he permitted it. In temporal matters the pope's orders must yield to the authority of the king. William insisted that he should have the power of vetoing any legislation made by an English ecclesiastical synod. He refused to permit any appeals to papal courts without his consent. He ordered that none of his tenants-in-chief should be excommunicated by the pope unless William agreed to it. There must be no papal pressure upon the secular arm of the state. William also separated the Church courts in England from the ordinary lay courts. Henceforth the ecclesiastical courts dealt with the great tracts of problems covered by canon law; the secular courts, including the vigorous courts of the shire and the hundred, administered justice in all other areas. A strong king and a strong pope had reached a stalemate.

In England the struggle for power between Church and state continued intermittently throughout the Middle Ages. William II (1087–1100) fought with Anselm, the archbishop of Canterbury. Henry I (1100–1135) also quarreled with Anselm and the pope, mainly about the problem of lay investiture, the formal presentation to an elected archbishop or bishop of the ring and staff symbolic of the transfer of office to him. The Church said that the presentation must be by a churchman. There must be no "lay investiture." On the other hand, if there was no "lay investiture," then the members of the clergy would be entirely outside royal control and wholly under the centralized power of the Church. How could the king be assured of dependence and loyalty, especially from those churchmen who held numerous offices and thousands of acres of land from the crown?

Henry II (1154–1189), busy bending the barons of feudal England to his royal will, followed his predecessors in seeking to limit the powers of the Church. He was especially concerned about the sinister dangers he saw in the strength and jurisdiction of the Church courts and the numerous appeals to Rome. With his archbishop Thomas Becket, Henry negotiated and quarreled again and again. Fearing the royal wrath, Becket fled into exile.

After six years the archbishop returned to England in 1170. He did not bring peace. After Becket challenged Henry again it is said that the king cursed his archbishop as a "turbulent priest" and apparently shouted that the royal servants would eat the king's bread but would not rid him of Becket. Four knights, fired by Henry's hasty words, crossed the Channel and killed the archbishop in Canterbury Cathedral.

This was murder. This was sacrilege. Becket became a martyr. Miracles were to be wrought in the tomb of St. Thomas of Canterbury. Over the old road of the Pilgrim's Way men and women were to trudge and ride from every shire. Prayers and pilgrimages to Canterbury became a habit, long continued. In his death, Becket had triumphed. Henry II made peace with the Church. He carried out a spectacular public act of contrition. The simple and great folk of England saw their king, warrior, and statesman on his knees before the tomb of St. Thomas of Canterbury, his back scarred with weals of penance.

In the early thirteenth century a new struggle arose between King John (1199–1216) and Pope Innocent III (1198–1216), militant and able defender of papal authority. When a dispute erupted in England about the election of the archbishop of Canterbury, Innocent III bestowed the office upon Stephen Langton, a famous theologian, scholar, poet, honest and devoted servant of the Church. John angrily refused to accept the appointment of Langton. He foolishly pitted himself against Innocent III, an agile and veteran fighter. Against such a pope, John had small chance of victory.

In 1208 Innocent placed an interdict upon England. All public church services were suspended. The bells were silent; few sacraments were given; the dead were buried without the services of a priest in unconsecrated ground. King John, of course, showed his Angevin fire and obstinacy. He seized the lands of the clergy who obeyed the pope's command. Most clergymen, having pronounced the interdict, fled from the realm.

After two years the pope warned John, his "dear son," that the papal bow was fully bent. In November, 1209, the arrow flew. Innocent III excommunicated the king. The fearful sentence cut John off from the services and sacraments of the Church and damned his soul if he died before the curse was removed. John was not cowed; he did not yield. He took from his tenants new oaths of homage and more hostages. He increased the number of his mercenary troops. He paid their wages out of the spoils of the Church, the Cistercian wool, the taxes on the towns, the coffers of the Jews. John's soldiers were faithful to his gold; and they would remain so, while the gold lasted.

Violence and terror invited opposition among John's subjects. Slowly the surging discontent became an underground movement and this, in turn, was to become an open revolt. Despite all of John's measures and gestures, the tide of hostility continued to roll against him. A mad hermit prophesied that John had less than a year to reign. From castle to village rumors raced through England that the royal cause was desperate.

At this point the shrewd Innocent III struck again. He declared John deposed, released his subjects from their allegiance, and gave his kingdom to Philip Augustus of France. The rapacious Philip answered with alacrity to the papal request that he carry out the sentence of deposition by invading England. The wily Innocent III, of course, never intended Philip to conquer England; the union of the two crowns would diminish papal power in both countries. Innocent's purpose was to frighten John.

Frighten John he did. At last the king surrendered to Innocent III and consented to accept Stephen Langton as archbishop of Canterbury; to restore all Church lands; to recall the exiled monks and bishops. He made several other promises. He handed over the kingdom of England and Ireland to the papacy and then received it back as a fief, for which he agreed to pay a token sum of 1,000 marks a year. For John this was a wise move on the chessboard. Philip Augustus would not dare to invade a fief of the papacy.

King John was now released from the excommunication. A year later the interdict was removed after John had satisfied the pope that he was carrying out the terms of his capitulation. The bells rang out and the services of the Church were performed once more. King John had lost the contest. Innocent III had won.

In Europe the extraordinary Gregory VII and his successors vigorously asserted the claims of the Church. The leaders of the states replied that their cause against Rome was sound in theory and sound in history. True, some of the secular rulers in Europe allied themselves with the papacy in conflicts with local warlords like the dukes of Germany. Often the state leaders helped the Church in bulwarking its claims to land and power. They frequently cooperated in carrying out reform programs. The administrative officers of the state were usually churchmen—they were learned and literate persons, masters of things in books and often skilled and crafty masters of men. Despite such bonds of interest and common action the state would not accept and the Church would not relinquish doctrines that came close to claims to ultimate Church supremacy. Disputes and battles flamed and fell over all of Europe, especially in France and Germany.

The tone and nature of these critical European conflicts can be illustrated by a brief chapter in the history of Germany. That chapter begins in the year 962 when Otto I was crowned emperor at Rome and the historic relationship of the Church and state was well begun. In Otto's reign and later there were several disputes about state interference with Church property. Nevertheless, until the latter part of the eleventh century there were no violent disruptions of the relations between Rome and the German states. The explosions did come in the last quarter of the eleventh century. This was the time when Gregory VII was pope and Henry IV was first king and then emperor.

When Henry IV (1056–1106) succeeded to the throne he was a six-year-old child faced by no pleasant prospect: "a Germany seething with discontent, a nobility on the point of rebellion, and in Italy a papacy under the thumb of the reforming Hildebrand and his allies." For nearly twenty years Henry struggled and survived. In the process of surviving he became toughened and crafty.

Gregory VII's relentless and passionate campaign to reform and strengthen the Church had less success in Germany than in England, France, or Italy. Many German churchmen were alienated, especially in southern Germany, when the austere and puritan Gregory commanded them to give up their wives and concubines and children. Celibacy is a hard virtue. Undaunted and obstinate, the persistent Gregory proceeded with banners unfurled and trumpets sounding. Before all things came the cause of the Church, as he understood that cause. To him the Church was "the mother and mistress of all Christianity," the only means of salvation for erring and straying men. The Church must be strong and the Church must be pure.

Upon the German clergy Gregory would and did impose his reforming decrees. Lukewarm churchmen were suspended. The pope's opponents were denounced as men who would "lay waste the Church of Christ with the flames of their vicious views." When Archbishop Siegfried of Mainz objected to the calling of a synod of the German clergy in such dangerous times of war and rebellions, Gregory's reply was swift and strong. Echoing the Scriptures, he said: "When the wolf comes the hireling fears for himself, not for the sheep. He abandons his flock and flees, leaving them to destruction." Again and again the theme of the duty of the Church shoots through his sentences: "We ought to regard it as a shameful thing that the soldiers of this world daily stand up to fight for their earthly prince and shrink not from deadly conflict, while we, who are called priests of God, will not fight for our King."

To Henry IV, king and emperor, Gregory VII sent long, frequent, and scolding letters. He was not pleased with the conduct of Henry. The language and tone of his sentences seldom varied: "It would have been more becoming to you, since you confess yourself to be a son of the Church, to owe more respectful attention to the master of the Church, that is, to Peter, prince of the apostles." The successive stages in the complex controversies between the pope and emperor grew steadily more violent and bitter.

At the end of 1075 Pope Gregory decreed that there should be no more lay investitures in Germany or anywhere else because they were against divine law. He sent his decree to Henry IV together with a hectoring letter that was really an insulting challenge. In January, 1076, an angry and headstrong Henry, proud of his recent victory over the Saxons and supported by his bishops, told Gregory of fateful decisions taken in Germany. The king asserted that Gregory had wrongfully put himself over the whole Church and was claiming an illegal authority. "Henry, king not by usurpation, but by the holy ordination of God, to Gregory, not Pope, but false monk. . . . You have never held any office in the Church without making it a source of confusion and a curse to Christian men instead of an honor and a blessing. . . . Let another ascend the throne of St. Peter, who shall not practice violence under the cloak of religion. . . . I, Henry, king by the grace of God, with all my bishops, say now unto you, 'Come down, come down, and be accursed through all the ages.' "

Gregory VII at once deposed and excommunicated Henry IV, the bishops of Lombardy, and the prelates and laymen beyond the Alps. In September, 1076, he sent letters "to the Faithful of Germany" calling upon them to oppose their emperor and save their souls. Many of the princes of Germany stood against Henry. Some wanted to depose him at once. Others said that he should be deposed unless he could get absolution within a year. Gregory VII knew the situation in Germany and he waited for Henry to surrender.

In October, 1076, faced by strong rebellion, Henry IV decided to yield to avoid complete disaster. He promised to offer obedience to the pope and to accept ecclesiastical discipline. In December he crossed the Alps. In January, 1077, Henry came as a penitent to the Tuscany castle at Canossa where Gregory VII was a guest. "He presented himself at the gate of the castle barefoot and clad only in a wretched woolen garment." There he endured the famous three-day humiliation of Canossa. "January this year was very cold and there was a great deal of snow. Seven days before the end of the month the king, his feet nipped by the cold, was admitted to the presence of the Pope. He threw himself on the cross shouting again and again: 'Spare me, blessed father! Holy father, spare me, I beseech thee!' . . . The Pope conducted Mass and they ate together in the castle of Canossa." In such words a medieval chronicler told the tale. In the telling, of course, we can be sure that the facts were slightly massaged and the events made to appear more dramatic than an unprejudiced observer might find them. Nevertheless, there was no question about the full defeat of the emperor. Canossa marked a great moral victory for the pope and the papacy.

When Henry IV was freed from the excommunication his subjects were once more bound to support him. The emperor now turned swiftly to try to rebuild his armies and his fortunes. After a long war at home with the rebels Henry was victorious. Then the struggle between Henry and Gregory VII was renewed. Gregory was finally forced out of Rome when his Norman allies seized and sacked the city. When he died at Salerno in 1085 it is said that Gregory VII's last words were: "I have loved righteousness and hated iniquity, therefore I die in exile." Nevertheless, the cause of Gregory VII and his Church had not suffered any costly or irrevocable defeat in the battle between Church and state. There were other chapters still to be written.

These later chapters were long and complex. A bare catalogue of events would list battle after battle now long forgotten except by erudite scholars. The strong popes, of course, waged their wars in the tradition of Gregory VII, often with courage and consummate skill. The strong kings, for their part, watched and guarded the ramparts of their secular states.

Innocent III, that learned and indefatigable pope of the medieval world, was not only concerned with advancing the papal power in the contest with King John of England. He was also steadily busy with a long and superb diplomatic campaign that reached out to the edges of Christendom. Under Innocent III the papacy reached the height of its medieval power. This ener-

getic leader was mainly responsible for extending the rule of the Western
Church towards Constantinople, driving the Germans out of Sicily and central
Italy, bringing a civil war in Germany, stamping down the Albigensian heresy
in France. It was Innocent III who put France and England under interdicts,
who compelled Philip Augustus, King of France, to take back his wife, who
forced the kings of England, Spain, and Portugal to hand over their countries
to Rome and receive them back as fiefs of the pope, who used the weapon
of excommunication with terrible and telling effect. So far as the Holy Roman Empire was concerned, Innocent III said bluntly: "It is the business of
the Pope to look after the interests of the Roman Empire, since the Empire
derives its origin and its final authority from the Papacy."

The successors of Innocent III also had their quarrels, their conquests, and
their defeats. Pope Gregory IX (1227–1241) and Innocent IV (1243–1254)
fought frequently, especially about clerical taxation, with the formidable
Frederick II, the last of the real medieval emperors, the Wonder of the World.
Anger, distrust, and episodes of war darkened and distracted Europe. Papal
exactions offended even the most obedient lords and princes. Louis IX of
France reminded Innocent IV that "he who squeezes too hard draws blood."
When Boniface VIII (1294–1303) tried to press the papal cause too far and
collect taxes too much he was challenged at once by Edward I (1272–1307)
of England and Philip IV (1285–1314) of France. The legislation in each
country shows how strongly resistance was mounting to the claims of Rome
stated in such papal bulls as *Clericis laicos, Ausculta filii,* and *Unam Sanctam,*
each of which asserted in a different way that the pope held both the spiritual
and the temporal swords on earth. When the agents of Philip IV, usually
called Philip the Fair, seized the doughty Boniface VIII and held him prisoner
there were strong protestations in Europe; but not a sword was lifted against
Philip. The humiliated Boniface died—it is said from shame and shock—
about a month after the disgraceful assault upon him.

In 1305, Clement V, archbishop of Bordeaux and one of the councilors
of Philip IV of France, was elected pope. He and his immediate successors
lived in Avignon on the Rhone and remained surrounded by French cardinals
and under the control of French kings. This was the period of the "Babylonian
Captivity" of the popes, a sordid and shameful story.

It was probably inevitable that the tide of nationalist feeling in the fourteenth century should have resulted in continuous clashes between the papacy
and the states of Europe. All over the Continent the sense of medieval unity
was departing. Antipapal and anticlerical sentiment swelled to new levels,
especially after the popes took up their seventy years' residence at the "sinful city" of Avignon. In those days, for instance, the opposition of Englishmen to papal authority and papal taxation mounted rapidly because many
men thought that the taxes paid to the pope were finding their way into the

money chests of France to be used by the French kings in their wars against England. In *Piers Plowman,* England's William Langland opposed the shipment of gold to Avignon:

> Till Rome-runners carry no silver over sea
> Graven or ungraven, for the robber Popes of France.

The suspicion of Rome and the lowering of papal prestige was further increased by the "Great Schism" from 1378 to 1417 when two popes, each denouncing the other, divided the Church. It was a sight at once pathetic and ridiculous.

There is no doubt that the authority of the Church was weakened in these struggles with the heads of states. The investiture controversy and other disputes led many men, even those who were not active foes of the Church, to question its claims to jurisdiction and to oppose the use of excommunication as a papal weapon. The immense and obvious wealth of the Church also caused much adverse and sometimes envious comment. The outspoken Bernard of Clairvaux wrote to the pope: "Who will permit me to see before I die the Church of God so ordered as it was in the old days, when the apostles cast their nets to fish for souls and not for gold and silver?" Many men also said that the priests were neglecting their proper duties. Still others asserted that the clergy had no business taking such a great part in temporal affairs. Slings and arrows of adverse criticism looped and thudded against the gates and walls of the Church. Numerous voices rose to demand a general reformation. The mounting chorus was joined by several members of the clergy, angry and sorrowful at the sad state of the Church they loved.

There were other persistent and jarring notes. Complacent and compliant orthodoxy was often roused and challenged by the words of the heretics. Some of these heretics were fantastic people, fanatics and madmen and excitable fellows who were only slightly demented. Others were rather steady and solid men and many who listened thought they had something to say. Several of all kinds were condemned by the Church for heresy. Tranchelm of Flanders, the insane Eon of Brittany, and Peter of Bruys were venerated by some men and burned by others.

The execution of heretics by noose and fire did not always bring the results desired by the Church. Bodies may be destroyed; but messages and memories remain. Groups of heretics began to cherish the memories of those who had died at the hands of the priests. Martyrs, whatever the cause may be, are usually dangerous foes. To bestow the gift of martyrs upon one's enemies is never politically wise. Men of the Christian Church, perhaps above all others, have cause to remember that fact. Much of the strength and glory of the Church obviously rests upon the faith and the deeds and the blood of the Christians who have died for her cause. Persecutions and burnings in the

Middle Ages did not end heresy. They killed some heretics, which is a different thing.

Several important heretics obtained quite large followings. For instance, there was Peter Waldo of Lyons. About 1170 this well-to-do merchant gave most of his money to the poor and then decided to preach. His organized followers, usually called "the good people," or the "Poor Men," steadily increased in number. All of these active Waldensians vehemently asserted that any adult might preach; that masses were valueless; that the popes and prelates deserved no obedience because they had no justified authority. In 1184 the Waldensians were excommunicated and driven from Lyons. Then they moved still further from Catholic teaching, discarding more and more dogmas and rituals. Into Germany, Italy, Spain, and France their busy missionaries went, spreading their doctrines.

There were also the men called Manicheans who kept alive the ancient belief in the eternal warfare of the twin principles of light and darkness, good and evil. The spirit of evil, they asserted, had made all things material and those things were inherently bad. An elect group of self-disciplined men were the leaders. These ascetic and perfected leaders condemned marriage, practiced vegetarianism, forbade the shedding of blood. The ordinary men in the movement were not expected to be able to imitate the leaders in all things; but they could respect and revere them.

These rebels had many names in various parts of Europe. In many areas they were called Cathari, the Pure Men. In France they were known as Albigensians, after their stronghold in the county of Toulouse. They said there was no purgatory, no hell. They asserted that they were the true Christians and that the Catholics were wrong. They denounced the worldly endowments and the immorality of the soft-living orthodox clergy.

Despite the long persecutions and crusades of the Church and the Inquisition the formidable and impassioned Albigensians and Waldensians were neither converted nor entirely crushed. The orthodox men who went on Pope Innocent III's famous Albigensian Crusade smoked the heretics out of the caves of Languedoc; they slaughtered and burned, but their will in the end did not prevail. The small remnants of the Albigensian cause that were not completely wiped out slowly and silently grew larger again, sending out offshoots from France all over Europe. Persecution has seldom been successful in the history of mankind. The men of the twentieth century, with a vivid awareness of totalitarian evils, should be particularly interested in the course and collapse of persecution in the past. Anatole France once said: "One seeks in history only for the stupidities with which he is already familiar." There will probably still be other dark chapters in the tale of man's inhumanity to man.

The European difficulties with problems of faith and heresy in the early

Middle Ages did not deeply trouble England. Most Englishmen, so far as we can tell, were rather apathetic about unorthodox speculation. In the late thirteenth century Edward I (1272–1307) was disturbed, as we have seen, about clerical invasions of what he considered the proper royal sphere of power. The tides of opinion were running against Rome mainly because the papal taxes were increasing in number and weight. This was one of the reasons why Parliament passed the Statute of Mortmain, designed to prevent future transfers of property to the Church without royal permission. This was one reason why Edward I refused to permit the collection of new taxes that Rome proposed to levy. These actions and attitudes showed opposition to the Church; they did not mark any heresy.

By the fourteenth century there were at last appearing in England several sturdy heretical doctrines born of the independent thought of the market place and the taverns. Evangelists preached in the streets and on the squares. Anticlerical feeling assumed many guises. Englishmen often discussed the ideas and actions of such men as William of Ockham and Marsiglio of Padua, two champions of the cause of the state against the claims of papal sovereignty. William of Ockham's theory of resistance to the papacy was mainly devised to support Ludwig of Bavaria, elected emperor in 1314, in his long struggle against Pope John XXII. William and Ludwig agreed that the pope was a heretic, a rather extreme conclusion. William even asserted that the Scriptures were the sole source of law. He attacked canon law, the legalism of medieval Christianity, the hierarchy in the Church. William of Ockham also claimed that the Church was really the whole body of Christian people and that the pope never did possess the authority to speak for all of the Church. He insisted that the rules of faith were the rules of the whole community of the faithful. The anticlerical pen of William of Ockham remained busy until his death, and his influence stretched down the years towards the Reformation. His ideas, and others like them, found willing ears in England. These were the kinds of things men listened to and talked about in the streets and the pubs and under the chestnut trees.

The antipapal and anticlerical spirit in England reached a new height with several enactments of Parliament. In 1343 Parliament forbade anyone to bring in letters from Avignon that might be prejudicial to the interests and rights of the English king. In 1351 the first Statute of Provisors, extended in 1390, was designed to prevent the pope from giving any English benefices to his followers. In 1353, as a result of "clamours and grievous complaints," the first Statute of Praemunire, reissued and strengthened in 1365 and 1393, forbade appeals from English courts to the papal courts "in cases of which the cognizance pertains to the court of our lord the king." In 1366 the prevailing attitude was revealed even more sharply when Englishmen refused the pope's demand for the 1,000 marks of annual tribute King John had promised to pay earlier in the century. England was then about thirty years in arrears; after 1366 she paid no more.

During these years Englishmen heard and repeated the themes of many sermons of complaint and reform, those sermons of the Middle Ages filled with brimstone and vitriol. Modern scholars, such as Professor G. R. Owst and Professor Woodburn Ross, have recovered and published with comments several rousing texts of the sermons delivered in the fourteenth century. The pulpit was surely a powerful instrument for both good and evil in those days. The excited congregations had a lot to talk about.

One of the most outstanding teachers and preachers was John Wycliffe, born in Yorkshire about 1320. Wycliffe attacked clerical wealth and immorality, defended the claim of the crown to tax ecclesiastical property, wrote several pamphlets exalting the state at the expense of the Church. In 1377 he was called before an ecclesiastical court at St. Paul's to answer for his public outcries against the clergy. Later he was summoned to a court at Lambeth. In each case Wycliffe was able to avoid having sentence pronounced upon him. He had the support of the crown and the mob.

Wycliffe soon came to write several "heretical and depraved" pamphlets and other works in English. In a series of lashing rebukes he denounced bishops, monks, parish priests, church courts; he denied the temporal authority of the clergy; he demanded the confiscation of church property. Wycliffe also denounced the doctrine of transubstantiation. He stated that a good life was more important than sacraments. "Each man that shall be damned shall be damned by his own guilt, and each man that is saved shall be saved by his own merit." Either Wycliffe or his followers translated the Bible from the Latin of the Vulgate into English. "The gospel pearl is cast abroad," lamented a churchman, "and is trodden upon by swine." Wycliffe also founded the Lollards, a word meaning mumblers or lazy folk. These "poor priests" were to go in pairs about England, barefoot and in brown gowns, to preach the Gospel. The Lollards spread everywhere their founder's hatred of the "Caesarean papacy" and the property-owning clergy.

In 1384 Wycliffe died, and his body was buried at Lutterworth. Forty-four years after his death the Council of Constance declared vengeance upon Wycliffe's remains: "In obedience hereunto Richard Fleming, bishop of Lincoln, sent his officers to ungrave him accordingly. To Lutterworth they come, take what is left out of the grave and burn them to ashes; and cast them into Swift, a neighboring brook running hard by. Thus this brook hath conveyed his ashes into Avon, Avon into Severn, Severn into the narrow seas, they into the main ocean. And thus the ashes of Wycliffe are the emblem of his doctrine, which is now dispersed all the world over."

By the late twelfth century both the secular and regular clergy had begun to enter upon a period of increasing worldliness and lethargy. The flame of the mighty monastic revival was burning less brightly. Hospitality declined. Learning and education suffered. Monasteries were no longer attracting enough able men. Many monastic orders, such as the Cluniacs and Benedictines, were sinking into spiritual degeneracy. They had become such busy and wealthy landlords that their discipline and ideals had slipped from their once high spiritual level. The material world was too much with the monks and abbots; the Heavenly City was receding over the horizon. All through the Church the zealous, crusading fires were banked. Parish priests were often ignorant; some were absentees. The bishops, with few exceptions, were not active Christian soldiers.

There was also much evidence of an increasingly secularized perspective. One churchman said that a morally good man who cared for the common weal and who did not strive for possessions too much ought not to be hindered from growing rich since he brought benefits to his community. The author of *Aucassin and Nicolette* lightly wrote: "Into Paradise . . . go those aged priests and those old cripples, and the maimed who all day long and all night cough before the altars . . . with them have I nought to do. But in Hell will I go. For to hell go the fair clerks and the fair knights. . . . There go the fair and courteous ladies who have friends, two or three, together with their wedded lords. And there pass the gold and silver, the ermine and all rich furs, harpers and minstrels, and the happy of the world."

The prospect soon altered. At the opening of the thirteenth century there began the new orders of the mendicant friars, seeking to return to the simplicity of the early days of the apostles. The first order was founded in 1216 by the Spaniard Dominic Guizman, the man whom Dante called "the athlete consecrate." This man from Castile had seen the wholesale slaughtering of the Albigensian heretics and the desolation of lovely Provence. Perhaps that experience had helped to convince him that the sword is a poor weapon on a religious crusade. Moral force is better.

The Preaching Brothers of the Dominican order at first numbered sixteen men. Soon they numbered hundreds. They went from town to town in poverty, like Christ's first disciples. Their task was to go among men to convert the sinners, fight heresy, awaken the spiritually drowsy. The crusading Dominicans were dedicated fishers of men, the prophets and missionaries of a new spiritual awakening. "Zeal must be met by zeal, lowliness by lowliness, false sanctity by real sanctity, preaching lies by preaching truth."

The second famous order of friars was the Franciscan, founded by St. Francis of Assisi. St. Francis, the son of a cloth merchant, had become weary of the vapid maunderings of his bourgeois society friends. After a serious illness he began to give so much money to charity that his father was alarmed.

The frescoes of Giotto and the poetry of Dante tell how St. Francis "took Poverty for his bride." To him the words of the Gospel were clear: "As you go, preach, saying, the kingdom of heaven is at hand. Heal the sick, cleanse the lepers, raise the dead, cast out devils; freely ye have received, freely give. Provide neither gold, nor silver, nor brass in your purses, nor scrip for your journey, neither two coats, neither shoes, nor yet staves; for the workman is worthy of his meat." With their coarse gray robes and girdles of rope the Franciscans, the "begging friars," preached the Word of God and cared for the poor, the sick, and the lonely. "They are the true doctors who, with the meekness of wisdom, show forth good works for the edification of their neighbors." St. Francis said: "I advise, warn, and exhort my brothers. . . . They shall be gentle, peaceable, and modest, merciful and humble, honestly speaking with all, as is becoming. . . . The brothers shall appropriate nothing for themselves. . . . Nor need they be ashamed, for the Lord made himself poor for us in this world. . . . This be your portion, which leads on to the land of the living."

The friars brought a great revival, like the Christians of the later Puritan, Wesleyan, and Salvation Army movements. The Dominicans were at first much more learned and intellectual than the more mystical Franciscans, for St. Francis had forbidden the Franciscans to read books. Later the Franciscans followed the Dominicans in their search for knowledge and produced some outstanding scholars.

Throughout Europe the good Samaritans of both orders did not pass by on the other side. They sought out the poor, the neglected, and the sick. They filled the stomachs of the hungry. They preached the teachings of Christ and his apostles. They offered salvation to all, in the name of the Saviour. Above all, perhaps, the friars spoke a language all understood. What they said was intelligible because it was as simple as the Gospels. They spoke with enthusiasm; to them religion was a way of life and not a form. "Woe to those who die in mortal sin," says St. Francis' beautiful Italian *Canticle of the Sun*. "Praise ye and bless my Lord, and give Him thanks, and serve Him with great humility."

In later days the fires of the apostolic spirit in the mendicant orders sank into embers. They came to enforce their discipline but laxly. They were wealthy corporations, increasingly careless about things of the spirit; and they had many enemies. Geoffrey Chaucer and others laughed at the hypocrisy of the begging brothers and the various signs of their degeneration. They perhaps forgot that once, in a crisis of religion, the friars had indeed followed in the footsteps of the Master.

Chapter 17

PATHS OF PEACE
AND WAR

"Kings are like stars—they rise and set—they have
The worship of the world, but no repose."

—Percy Bysshe Shelley, *Hellas*

THROUGH the centuries the minds and passions of human beings have been roused by many issues and causes. Great wars and lesser quarrels have divided continents, states, and villages. Disputes have leaped and flamed on the planet so long that the memory of man cannot recall anything but the old disorders and his eyes can see little but the new. The wise and honest historian always notes and stresses the complexity of human existence. He observes chapters of our past both engrossing and dull. He sees the sparks that set all kinds of things into flame. The reasons why some events happened he often cannot tell. Any attempt to impose patterns upon history are distortions that usually tell more about the historian than the world and events he is presumably seeking to describe. For instance, the good man does not always die in bed; the best general does not always win the battle; the cause that is right and sound often fails, so far as this world is concerned, before the attacks of evil men.

The final balancing of the account of many of man's endeavors is no easy task. An excellent illustration of the difficulty can easily be found in the past and present historical works upon the subject of the Crusades, that famous series of European attempts to rescue the crumbling Byzantine Empire, to oust the warlike Moslem Turks from the sands and the pink hills of Palestine, and to establish and maintain a Christian bridgehead in the Holy Land. Historians will agree upon most of the facts assembled from the primary sources. They vehemently dispute about many conclusions and about the true significance of the whole crusading movement. In the third volume of his lively *A History of the Crusades,* for instance, Steven Runciman concludes that from a military point of view "the whole movement was a fiasco," that the Crusades were "a tragic and destructive episode," and that "the Holy War itself was nothing more than a long act of intolerance in the name of God which is a sin against the Holy Ghost." Few contemporary historians will accept these assertions without major erasures and alterations. No one man, not even a Runciman, can master all the aspects of the Crusades. The superb work of some scholars has opened many doors. Beyond some of these doors, however, no man has yet peered. It is also true that upon phase after phase of man's history expert judgments differ. The magic wand of finality is not to be found or waved with wisdom in the groves of Clio.

Before the use of printing and the slow improvement of transportation and communication the interests and knowledge of most men were local and immediate. Nevertheless, the floods and eddies of spreading interest and excitement raced over wide areas of Europe to rouse men to go upon the Crusades. From Scandinavia to Sicily, from Britain to the edges of Russia, the Crusaders went to battle against the formidable Turks. These Crusades lasted from 1095 to 1291, a period of nearly 200 years. Thousands of men, listening to the violent voices of preachers like Peter the Hermit, pushed forward by the leaders of a reformed papacy, and disturbed by thorns and gadflies all about them, gathered together to "take the Cross" and go on the Crusades. Some went because they were pious and enthusiastic. Others, especially the men from the cities, were eager to lead in the expansion of commerce. Still others were curious, or odd fish, or needy and seedy adventurers, or greedy, or just plain crooks—the Emperor Alexius complained that somebody stole the lead off the roof of a church in Constantinople. Whatever their faults and follies and virtues, these men marched and bunked together on the long road to Jerusalem.

These were exciting years in the troubled history of Byzantium. Some of the events have been described in Chapter 12. The reader will recall that by the end of the eleventh century the Moslem offensives had overrun Persia and Armenia, defeated the Byzantine emperor at the battle of Manzikert (1071), seized and occupied almost all of Asia Minor. After the Turks had pressed on to complete their conquest of Syria in 1080 the emperor at Constantinople appealed to the energetic Pope Gregory VII and the armed Christians of Europe for help.

Gregory VII at once supported an expedition led by the Sicilian Norman, Robert Guiscard; but Guiscard had to return to fight the Emperor Henry IV of Germany and then he died a few months after his marauding and plundering troops had forced his ally, Gregory VII, out of Rome. Not for ten years did any further promise of aid come out of the West.

A new leadership and inspiration came in 1095 from the young, talented, and militant Pope Urban II. He planned a great Christian crusade to free the

Holy Land, organized and led by the Church. At the great Council of Clermont he appealed for the help of Europe in the task of rescuing the Holy
Land from the foul and besmirching hands of the infidel Turk. Let the
Franks and the Germans and all the rest cease from their paltry European
quarrels. Let them rise up and take the sword against the common foe. Christ
would be their leader and would go on before their armies. God would open
to the men of crowded Europe a Promised Land, "flowing with milk and
honey." He would give those who went on His Crusade pardon and absolution from all their sins. When Urban II finished his appeal, it is said that
from the throats of the assembled faithful came a single sentence: *"Dieu le
veut*—God wills it." No hand could now check or stay the power that had
been unloosed.

Raw enthusiasm is one thing. An organized military enterprise is another.
In 1095 and 1096 thousands of excited people started off for the Holy Land.
Some were turned back or were enslaved or perished on the way. Others were
killed when they got to Constantinople and crossed the Hellespont. There is
no substitute for basic training, adequate supply and communication lines,
and an effective chain of command.

Not until the fall of 1096 did the first organized Crusade get under way.
No leaders came from Henry IV's confused Germany. All of the commanders of the host were from the Frankish chivalry and some of them were men
of fame and skill: the shrewd Bohemund, son of Robert Guiscard and his
unscrupulous kinsman Tancred; Hugh, Count of Vermandois and brother
of the French king; the rash and improvident Robert, Duke of Normandy
and son of William the Conqueror; Stephen, Count of Blois; Robert, Count
of Flanders; Eustace, Godfrey, and Baldwin of Boulogne; Raymond, Count
of Toulouse, "as fanatical as a monk and as land-greedy as a Norman." And
so they set out. "This is the Lord's doing; it is marvellous in our eyes."

The Emperor Alexius of Constantinople had not expected aid like this.
Edward Gibbon said that Alexius was like "the shepherd who was ruined by
the accomplishment of his own wishes: he had prayed for water; the Ganges
was turned into his grounds, and his cottage was swept away by the inunda-
tion." The emperor was afraid of the hosts that called themselves his saviors.
He feared that they would take his capital city and anything else that they
could seize. Consequently he tried by violence, bribery, and trickery to protect himself even as he urged and pushed the Crusaders over the Hellespont
to engage the Turks. He was able to take advantage of the rivalries of the
leaders and to play them against one another. In the end the leaders all agreed
that if they conquered cities that had earlier belonged to the Eastern Empire
they would hand them over to Alexius. In return the emperor promised the
Crusaders full military support. In the subsequent events each owed much

to the other, despite charges and countercharges made, and sometimes sustained, by contemporaries then and historians later.

In the spring of 1097 the Christian forces, probably numbering about 25,000 men, crossed the strait at Constantinople and besieged Nicaea. They took Nicaea, defeated the Turks in a pitched battle, gradually pressed over the Taurus mountains into Cilicia, seized Tarsus and Edessa. In June, 1098, plagued by the wastage brought by disease, heat, and thirst, the Crusaders took and held the great city of Antioch.

Supplied by an Italian fleet, the Christian forces now advanced slowly towards Jerusalem. In July, 1099, Jerusalem fell and a general slaughter began. "And if you desire to know what was done with the enemy who were found there, know that in Solomon's Porch and in his temple our men rode in the blood of the Saracens up to the knees of our horses."

Meanwhile the conflicts among the Crusaders continued. "Each one thought of his advantage, and no one cared for the common good." Stephen of Blois, for instance, went home. Bohemund stayed in Antioch—he had it, why should he let it go? Some of the Christian leaders made alliances with the Moslems against their fellow Christians. The whole chapter of events forms a tale of confusion, fraud, and treachery. For instance, Peter the Hermit ran away; when the Emperor Alexius found out that the Crusaders were in some difficulties at Antioch he wheeled around, retreated, and waited to see what happened. When his allies won, he doubtless rejoiced.

Despite all the oaths and assurances made to the Emperor Alexius, four Latin feudal states were finally organized by the Crusaders in a bold experiment: the Kingdom of Jerusalem, the principality of Antioch, the counties of Edessa and Tripoli. The rulers of these states seldom cooperated. Rivals they were and rivals they remained. Nor could the emperor of Constantinople be expected to give any of them aid in an hour of need. To him they were intruders who had filched a part of his domain. True, they were Christians; but they were still intruders. Meanwhile the new states stood. Other military and quasi-military organizations appeared: the Knights Templar, the Teutonic Knights, the Hospitallers or the Knights of St. John.

The second Crusade came in 1147 after the Moslems had conquered Edessa (1144) and threatened again the Christian position in the Holy Land. After the vehement Bernard of Clairvaux called upon Europe to smite the infidels, Louis VII of France and Conrad III of Germany led a woefully bungled expedition that wasted away. The whole thing was a series of needless blunders. After the dark shadows of the failure of the second Crusade the Saracens moved against the Christians, slowly at first and then in a series of swift campaigns. Their famed leader, Saladin, was shrewd, cultured, merciless. In 1187, shortly after the battle of Hittim, his army swept into Jerusalem. The

Kingdom of Jerusalem shriveled away. By that time there were few Christian strongholds that had escaped the Moslem cavalry and the victorious scimitar. Saladin ruled a Turkish empire from Iraq to Cyrenaica. Once again the weight and balance of the Near East, from a Christian point of view, had been upset. The Holy Sepulchre had once more passed into the hands of the Moslems. It was to stay there for more than 700 years.

In 1189 Richard I of England, the lion-hearted knight-errant of the age of chivalry, the aged and crafty Frederick Barbarossa, Holy Roman Emperor, Philip Augustus of France, and Leopold, Duke of Austria, went forth on the third Crusade. Richard I, newly crowned king of England, swiftly collected revenues to finance his share in the holy enterprise. Somewhat less than holy were the means he used to gather money. His overseas adventures were his main interests, and he treated England as a source of supply for the financial demands of his campaigns abroad. It is said that he once remarked: "I would sell London if I could find a bidder." He was interested not in statecraft but in war. The Emperor Frederick Barbarossa, soon to be drowned in Asia Minor, and Philip Augustus were interested in both. They were quite prepared to euchre or cheat Richard if the means and the chance came along.

In July, 1190, Richard sailed from Marseilles and Philip Augustus sailed from Genoa. Richard paused to sack the Sicilian city of Messina, conquer Cyprus, and marry the beautiful Berengaria of Navarre. He then joined Philip Augustus in besieging Acre, the city with the best harbor in Palestine. When the city fell in 1191 more than 2,000 Moslems were massacred. Meanwhile the leaders and the soldiers on the Crusade filled hours of their days with fruitless bickering and rivalry. An open quarrel, born of long ill will, arose between Leopold, Duke of Austria, and Richard I. Philip Augustus was soon jealous of the exploits of the English king, who showed by his courage and leadership that his prowess was as great as his fame. Sickness, petty discords, and paralyzing spite took their inevitable toll from the forces arrayed against Saladin.

In August, 1192, Philip Augustus, pleading ill health, departed for France. Richard suspected that Philip would not be too ill to begin operations against some of the English possessions in France while his English ally carried on alone against the Saracens.

Richard intended to march down the coast and thence overland to Jerusalem. Upon that barren land the sun beat like fire; there was almost no fodder for the horses. The soldiers were fed from the baggage train and from the fleet that followed the army along the coast. Saladin's army, moving farther inland, jabbed continually at the flanks of Richard's forces. It took the army of the Crusaders three weeks to travel the sixty miles from Acre to Jaffa. Saladin was as yet unbeaten in the field. Difficulties and discords among the Crusaders increased. Should they advance at once in an attack upon Jerusalem?

Could the city be taken? If so, could it be held? A truce was finally signed with Saladin, who promised Christian pilgrims free access to the Holy Sepulchre in Jerusalem. Jaffa, Acre, Tyre, and certain other coastal ports were to stay in Christian hands. This was the conclusion of the Crusade whose prelude had been so dramatic.

In October, 1192, Richard I sailed from Palestine for England. When he disguised himself and tried to travel overland from the head of the Adriatic he was captured and imprisoned. Philip Augustus of France and Richard's brother John tried to persuade the Emperor Henry VI to keep Richard in prison. Early in 1194 the English king was released when his vassals gathered a feudal aid to provide a part of the ransom demanded by the imperial brigand: 100,000 pounds.

Preparations for the fourth Crusade began in 1201. It seems that Venice agreed, at a price, to provide ships and provisions for a year for all the Crusaders and to supply forces of her own. It was also stipulated that Venice was to receive half of all the conquests made. Later there was much dispute about the precise terms of the arrangements. After months of confusion the divided Crusaders took the Adriatic trading city of Zara for the Venetians. Then a candidate for the throne of Byzantium said that if the Crusaders would put him on the throne he would give them treasure to support their assault upon the Moslems. Thus persuaded, the Crusaders attacked and looted Constantinople, a shameless action denounced by Innocent III and many others as a crime against a Christian city. The Venetians were delighted at a chance to wound a trading rival. They joined in the plundering and brought back four gilded horses to St. Mark's. Those horses stand today not far from the remains of the Apostle which were stolen from Alexandria four centuries earlier. When the Byzantine candidate for the throne failed to keep his promises the Count of Flanders was put in his place, and so began the weak Latin Kingdom of Constantinople which lasted until 1261. In 1261 the Eastern Empire was restored. It stood as a frail shell. One of the numerous ironies of history is that the Crusaders who set out to force the Moslems from the Holy Land ended by plundering Constantinople, the main European bulwark against the Moslem tide. If Constantinople had been left alone by the crusading men of Europe, it might not have fallen in 1453 to the Turks. Nobody knows, incidentally, whether or not any of the men who went on the fourth Crusade ever reached the Holy Land. In any event, Europe was becoming fatigued by failures in the Holy War.

In 1212 hysterical and gullible peoples believed that little children, unstained by the sins of adults, could win Jerusalem without a struggle. In Germany a large number of children gathered together and marched into Italy. It was believed that the waters of the Mediterranean Sea would be pushed back by the Lord and that the children would pass safely over to the Holy

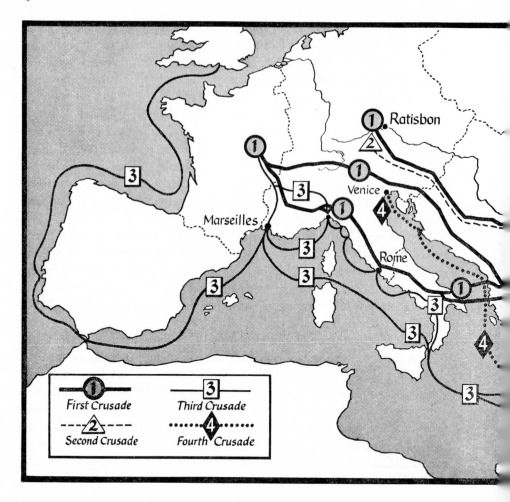

Land. The Children's Crusade was a fantastic and foolish idea, a pathetic tale of disaster and death. The little children never reached the Holy City. Those who did not die of disease or hunger or cold or heat were probably sold as slaves. To the modern mind these events seem incredible; but they did happen.

Although the Crusades did not free Palestine they did achieve several things. When the veterans came back from the Crusades they told all over Europe the tales of what they had done and seen beyond the seas. They brought strange gifts. Their horizons had been widened by travel and adventure. They brought to the West in the twelfth century such things as pepper and many other spices, watermelons, the crossbow. The kingdom of Jerusalem, lasting for two centuries, provided an open door for the flow of ideas and goods. The long exposure to the commerce and culture of the Near East thus gave a tremendous stimulus to the trade flow that was already beginning to appear

Routes of the Chief Crusades

SELJUK

KINGDOM OF ARMENIA

COUNTY OF Edessa EDESSA

TURKS

EUPHRATES R.

Antioch P. OF. ANTIOCH

Constantinople

COUNTY OF TRIPOLI

Tripoli

Sidon

Tyre

St Jean d'Acre

Caesarea

Jaffa

ARABIA

KINGDOM OF JERUSALEM

Beach head of the Crusaders

Edessa

Antioch

Tripoli

Acre

Jerusalem

Alexandria

in the eleventh century. With the mounting demand for products from the lands east of the Mediterranean came more prosperity. More people came to live in the cities along the lines of commerce. Where trade and merchants moved ideas came and stayed. In these days, as in the times before and after, there was no substitute for the conversation and contact of human beings. The whole European outlook slowly changed. It was never the same again.

Meanwhile the evolution of the European political world continued steadily. In the latter part of the Middle Ages, as so often in human history, the stage was dominated by kings and warriors, by the strong and ruthless men who forged new tools of government and beat ploughshares into swords to conquer and destroy.

At the end of the twelfth century in France, Philip Augustus (1180–1223) began to build upon the solid foundations laid by his Capetian grandfather

Louis VI. Said Philip: "I desire that at the end of my reign the monarchy shall be as powerful as in the time of Charlemagne." For more than forty years Philip fought and intrigued to achieve that desire. His main problem was to oust the English kings from the wide lands they held in France. Against England's Henry II (1154–1189) Philip had little success. He was soon to have more. During the reigns of England's Richard I (1189–1199) and John (1199–1216) Philip Augustus gathered into his eager hands many of England's French territories: Normandy, Maine, Anjou, Touraine, and Brittany. In all the expanded royal domain he reorganized the government and the machinery of justice. The competition of feudal lords was almost ended. France was becoming a truly national state with an efficient and centralized government under the immediate control of the monarch.

The process of unification and the growth of absolute monarchy proceeded slowly and relentlessly under the astute Louis IX (1226–1270) and Philip IV (1285–1314), that Philip the Fair who fought so long and successfully against Pope Boniface VIII.

In Germany the prospect was different. No German kings sought to build a united kingdom in the German regions. True, rulers like Henry the Fowler (919–936) and Otto the Great (936–973) had stopped the invasions of the Northmen, Slavs, and Hungarians and had expanded German territory to the east and north. Most of the time, however, Germany remained a loose union of the lands of great dukes like those of Bavaria, Franconia, Lorraine, Saxony, and Swabia. In many of these areas ancient tribal divisions persisted and ancient traditions stayed. Differences in such important things as language, blood, customs, and laws presented formidable obstacles to national unification and the development of an effective centralized monarchy.

It is interesting and unprofitable to speculate what might have happened in European history if the German kings had relentlessly pursued the task of shaping a unified state. The material with which the French rulers started was surely not more promising. The facts, however, cannot be changed; and the facts are that Otto the Great and his successors turned to try to build an unwieldy empire instead of a single German nation. Otto, as we have seen in earlier pages, invaded rich and tempting Italy in 951 and was crowned Roman Emperor in 967. The empire built by Charlemagne was created again, or so it seemed. Soon the flamboyant title of Holy Roman Empire was given to a congeries of sprawling lands in Germany and Italy.

The political history of the empire is a tangled web of diplomacy and war. Popes and emperors were locked in the bitter struggles between Church and state. Frederick Barbarossa (1152–1190), founder of the Hohenstaufen house, fought a coalition of Italian cities who were reluctant to pay tribute and taxes to a German ruler who fancied himself a new Caesar in a new Roman Empire. Four times the emperor led armies against them. Four times, supported by the papacy, the passionate Italian townsmen beat him back. Then the Italians saw

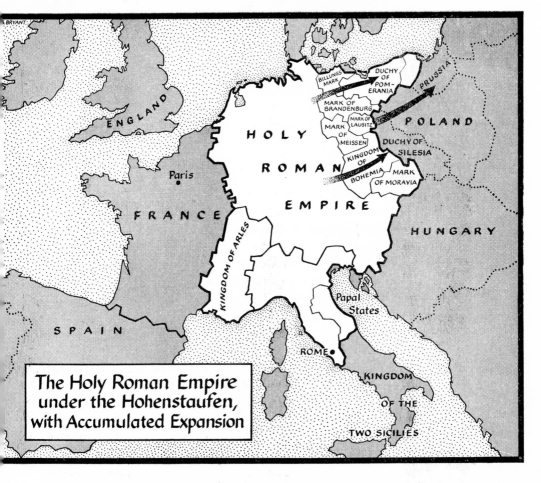

The Holy Roman Empire
under the Hohenstaufen,
with Accumulated Expansion

another danger looming. When Frederick Barbarossa's son married the heiress
to the crown of Sicily the papacy and the Italian cities feared that they would
be pressed between hostile Hohenstaufen states in Germany to the north and
in Sicily to the south.

Frederick Barbarossa never got back from the third Crusade. His grandson,
the enigmatic and mighty Frederick II, lifted Sicily to unprecedented heights
of power and culture in an intelligent despotism, supported by a German and
Saracen mercenary army. In Germany, however, the dukes and the other
nobles, left almost to themselves, became more and more independent as the
Emperor Frederick made lavish concessions to them and increased their power
by his absence. Frederick II devoted much of his energies and wealth to a long
struggle with the fiery Pope Gregory IX, the unscrupulous Pope Innocent IV,
and the Lombard League of Italy. After the controversial Frederick died in
1250 the whole empire began to crack and crumble and the Hohenstaufen
dynasty was uprooted. In 1266 the last of the Hohenstaufen was captured and
executed in Naples. The papacy and the Italian towns had won the conflict.

The Norman kingdom of Naples and Sicily soon passed into the hands of
the French Count of Anjou. So unpopular were the French rulers and their

officials that the natives of Palermo rose in the terrible Sicilian Vespers episode of 1282 and massacred all the Frenchmen they could find. The thrones of Sicily and Naples, sometimes united and sometimes not, went to the Spanish house of Aragon.

In central Italy were the Papal States and the republics of Florence and Siena. In the north were the enterprising city-states of Genoa, Milan, and Venice. Each was wealthy and powerful. Each was blessed with a great commercial empire. Each was bitterly jealous of all the others. In most of them, the rich and prominent families produced despots or oligarchies. These were the early years of the princes, doges, and podestas, often suave and cultured men and almost always unscrupulous. "A white glove," says an Italian proverb, "often conceals a dirty hand." These were the years of the condottieri, of the poisoned wines and the knives thrown silently in the night.

After a bloody and tormented period of civil war the crown of the Holy Roman Empire was given in 1273 to the upstart Rudolf of the house of Hapsburg. Except for two intervals the Hapsburgs were Holy Roman Emperors until Napoleon Bonaparte ended the empire in 1806. In the thirteenth century the Hapsburgs obtained Austria and in the sixteenth century they added Bohemia, the Netherlands, and most of Hungary. These areas—except the Netherlands—they were to hold until the end of the First World War.

Meanwhile, obviously, the last chance had passed for the appearance of a strong, effective, and coherently organized Roman Empire. In Germany the process of disintegration continued. There was no semblance of political or moral coherence. From the fourteenth century onwards the Holy Roman Emperor was chosen by seven German princes; three of these were ecclesiastical rulers—the archbishops of Cologne, Mainz, and Treves; the four secular rulers were the King of Bohemia, the Duke of Saxony, the Margrave of Brandenburg, and the Count Palatine of the Rhine. This arrangement was fixed and settled by the Golden Bull issued by the Emperor Charles IV in 1356. "Within their own territories the electors were given practically sovereign rights. . . . The Bull fixed irrevocably the supremacy of the princes and the impotence of the central power in Germany." Charles, it has been said, "legalized anarchy and called it a constitution." Because neither the emperor nor the Imperial Diet possessed much effective power many of the nobles of Germany who were not among the seven electors became almost independent rulers freed from imperial taxes, uncontrolled by any strong hand anywhere. Soon the Holy Roman Empire contained more than 300 archduchies, duchies, counties, margravates, and free cities. Rapacity, intrigue, violence, and private wars were chronic.

There were some spots of light. The Teutonic Knights were conquering and colonizing rude and primitive Prussian regions. German settlers still pushed eastwards into such areas as Bohemia and Silesia. Great city leagues were formed for the preservation of peace and the growth of trade. The power of the mighty Hanseatic League, for example, stretched far beyond the valley of the Rhine and the waters of the Baltic. In the later Middle Ages the economic strength and material wealth of the Germanies were the envy and admiration of most of Europe. By the fifteenth century there had risen a rich and variegated combination of material prosperity, political power, and genuine culture in such wealthy cities as Cologne, Nuremberg, Augsburg, Hamburg, Bremen, Lübeck, Strassburg, Magdeburg. In such places, too, a local pride and patriotism had grown and flourished so strongly that it has never been successfully challenged, even by the urgent orders of the leaders of the totalitarian Third Reich in the twentieth century.

As various states and territories moved in and out of the empire the proud and defiant people of Switzerland formed an independent nation. In 1291 three cantons in the Alps created a self-governing confederation under the overlordship of the Emperor Rudolf. In 1315 Duke Leopold of Austria attacked and tried to subdue and destroy this Swiss union. The Hapsburg soldiers were soon defeated. The Swiss had long been famous for skill in fighting in lands of mountains and ice and narrow passes. By the fifteenth century thirteen cantons, including the pivotal ones of Lucerne, Berne, and Zurich, had joined the autonomous confederation of towns and rural cantons. In 1499 the Emperor Maximilian surrendered all his claims to sovereignty in the Treaty of Basel. In the Treaty of Westphalia of 1648 Switzerland was declared to be a free and independent state. Through all the tumults and wars of later centuries Switzerland has kept her freedom in her mountain land.

Architects of national unity also appeared in the Spanish peninsula, a region that had long contained a prosperous and cultured Moslem state. Sometimes that state had been united, as in the days of the brilliant Caliphate of Cordova. Sometimes it had been fragmented, as in the years when more than twenty separate Moslem kingdoms followed the overthrow of the Cordova Caliphate in 1031. Up in the north and west there appeared and survived a few Christian communities: Aragon, León, Castile, Navarre, Portugal, and some smaller territories. Great Christian campaigns soon began to drive the Moors from Spain. Slowly the tide of reconquest pressed southwards. Patriotism and religion were fused in the whole massive movement. By the latter part of the fifteenth century the Moslems were clinging desperately to the small state of Granada, their last stronghold in western Europe. In 1492 Granada fell at last.

In 1469 Isabella of Castile and León married Ferdinand of Aragon and their lands were soon united. Early in the sixteenth century Ferdinand seized the section of Navarre that was south of the Pyrenees. Spain was now a united kingdom. By her side stood Portugal, already famous for her explorers and her expanding empire beyond the seas.

In northern Europe the three kingdoms of Denmark, Norway, and Sweden were slowly emerging. No significant political organization had yet developed in the territories along the Baltic where such peoples as the Estonians and Finns still traveled along their ancient tribal paths. In eastern Europe the Slavic Bohemians and Czechs moved into the orbit of the Hapsburgs and Austria. Poland, united with Lithuania in 1560, became a national state. The larger part of Hungary, land of the Magyars, Croats, Rumanians, and Slovaks, was divided in the sixteenth century between the Archduke of Austria and the conquering Turks. After the Turks were ousted, all of Hungary moved under the sway of the Hapsburgs. In southeastern Europe the declining Byzantine Empire approached its death and dissolution. By the end of the fifteenth century the Ottoman Turks had conquered all the Balkans and were sweeping towards Vienna.

Across the English Channel and the North Sea, William the Conqueror and his successors had long since established a unified state. Henry II (1154–1189) had succeeded in laying the firm and strong foundations of a unique and famous judicial system. The common law and the writ and jury procedures have endured. No assaults upon them have had any measure of success. Their power is felt and their language is heard in many lands of whose existence Henry II never dreamed.

The kings who followed Henry II were not strong rulers. Richard I, the romantic hero of the age of chivalry, liked and sought excitement. He rudely thrust aside all other claims, such as the moral duties and demands that the kingship of England imposed upon him. He visited his kingdom only twice. The rest of the time he lived and fought on the Continent or in the Holy Land. In 1199, when he was besieging a vassal's castle, the warrior Richard was wounded by an arrow and died in his tent outside the castle walls. When the years of Richard's life are sifted there is some gold; but there is more tinsel and lead. We have perhaps forgiven Richard too much. "After the strong man with the sword comes the weak man with the sponge."

Richard's brother John succeeded him. There is no doubt that John was arbitrary and vicious, a master of the art of the double cross. On the other hand, as Professor Sidney Painter and others have clearly shown, John was always active and often able, a hard and calculating king in a turbulent age. It was not entirely his fault that he was defeated in the struggle with Innocent III or that he lost Normandy, Maine, and Anjou to Philip Augustus of France. Nor was he entirely to blame for the disasters that fell upon him at the hands of his barons. In 1215 some of the feudal leaders of his state compelled him to accept and seal the famous document that is called Magna Carta.

Magna Carta proclaimed no abstract principles. It simply redressed wrongs and checked the trend towards strong monarchy. The significant thing is that the wrongs described in Magna Carta were substantially those of all bad government in any age and the principles of redress have altered little through the centuries. Each clause was directed to a specific problem. The words were simple and direct, the language of practical men. The Church was to have "its rights entire and its liberties inviolate." There was to be no more overriding of feudal law by tricks or chicanery. "To no one will we sell, to no one will we deny or delay right or justice," runs the famous clause 40. "No freeman shall be captured or imprisoned or disseised or outlawed or exiled or in any way destroyed, nor will we go against him or send against him except by the lawful judgment of his peers or the law of the land," stated the celebrated clause 39 about which scholars have engaged in so much controversy, discussion, and skilled speculation and scholarship.

Magna Carta was really a conservative document designed to protect the interests of the barons. It contained no new law and it stated no new liberties. It became a symbol because it did contain the idea that there were certain things a king might not do. The principle that King John was bound by the feudal contract became expanded slowly into the broader idea that in some directions any king is bound by the law. He must respect the "rights" of the subject although those "rights" are not easily defined. If the king violates these laws and rights, said the expanded principle, he may be compelled by force to observe them. Through the centuries the laws of England have been concerned with the rights of the individual man against his neighbors and the state. The moment the rules of law are destroyed or evaded both the state and the citizen are in peril.

After John came Henry III (1216–1272). He began his reign as a child. When he became a man he was weak, easily bullied, and impractical. Dante put him in that part of purgatory reserved for children and simpletons.

The feudal barons rebelled against Henry III and limited his power by the Provisions of Oxford of 1258. As a result of a series of baronial wars Simon de Montfort, the leader of the nobles, summoned in 1265 the barons of the Great Council and elected members of the middle class: the knights and burgesses of the shires and towns. This great assembly was an important step in the evolution of England's Parliament. Edward I (1272–1307), a strong king, called several Parliaments in his reign to grant money and give advice. Most famous was the Model Parliament of 1295 which contained the upper clergy, the cathedral and parish clergy representatives, nobles, elected townsmen, and knights of the shire.

The growth of Parliament was a gradual process. In the fourteenth century this new institution divided into the House of Lords and the House of Commons. Only slowly did it develop legislative procedures and powers and obtain freedom of speech. Out of the early experiences of the county courts and the experiments of men like Simon de Montfort and Edward I there emerged through the centuries the great institution that now reflects the mind and will of the British people.

By the thirteenth century England was indeed a national monarchy. The judicial system was secure. The common law was unchallenged. Parliament had become an essential part of government.

In 1307 Edward II, a hollow counterfeit of his mighty father, came to the throne of England. Twenty years later he was deposed and his son succeeded him as Edward III (1327–1377). It was in the reign of Edward III that there began the spasmodic and spectacular Anglo-French conflict usually called the Hundred Years' War. Apart from its purely military aspect the long struggle was important in the growth of English and French national feeling. On the military side, the year 1340 saw the battle of Sluys, the first great naval battle in British history. In 1346 and 1356 the battles of Crécy and Poitiers brought the first triumphs of the English longbow over the mailed French horsemen. In a famous passage the chronicler Froissart wrote that the English let fly the arrows "with such force and quickness that it seemed as if it snowed."

Not all the victories went to the English. Before Edward III died in 1377 the French had pushed their foes back into a narrow strip of land on the coast. Further disasters fell in the reign of Richard II (1377–1399). The triumphs of Edward III and the Black Prince at Crécy and Poitiers were not forgotten; the magic names told of the harvest of glory; but the lands that the armies had won had been lost again.

When men were fighting the Hundred Years' War on the Continent the stream of domestic progress in England and Europe was slowed by the virulent Black Death. Many authorities believe that this disease was some type of the deadly bubonic plague. Wherever it struck there was terror. One Englishman wrote of "the fell death" that "broke forth on every side with the course of the sun." Far away in Italy's Florence, Giovanni Boccaccio later described the plague as it swept over the land. "No physician's counsel, no virtue of medicine whatever seemed to have an effect or profit against this sickness—it spread no less rapidly than fire will spread to dry or oily things that lie close at hand." In some areas nearly all the inhabitants died. In larger towns the deadly infection raced unhindered. The records that remain tell a frightful story.

The social and economic results for England were immediate and important. Tremendous impetus was given to the decline of feudalism, to the emancipation of the serfs, and to the whole tide of social and economic discontent among the lower classes. In view of the decreased labor supply it was inevitable that the rural and urban hired workers should demand and get higher wages. The unfree peasants, villeins, and serfs who had survived the plague insisted upon their freedom. They did not want to perform any more compulsory labor; they wanted wages. The few tenants replacing those who had died wanted easier terms. The income of the landlords went down as their tenants decreased in number; their overhead costs kept going up. After the Statute of Laborers (1351) failed to limit the demands of the laboring classes there was more commutation of feudal dues and obligations into money payments. A money economy was slowly replacing goods and service payments, an event of much consequence in the Western world.

In the thirty years following the Black Death the spirit of unrest mounted as the working classes sought to make still further gains. In 1381 an abrupt explosion shook the country in the Peasants' Revolt, the first uprising of the submerged men of England on a large scale, their first fumbling attempts to act for themselves. The rebellion was crushed in a strong and cruel reaction. Nevertheless, in a new age of labor fluidity men were moving more freely as laborers about the land; as sailors over the seas; or as soldiers in foreign wars. So it was that in these long years the economic causes working towards the disappearance of villeinage and serfdom rolled ahead without effective hindrance.

Richard II was deposed in 1399, largely through the efforts of the energetic and unscrupulous Henry IV (1399–1413), first of the Lancastrian kings. Rebellion and disaffection filled his reign. "Uneasy lies the head that wears a crown." In 1413 that crown passed to the young and vigorous Henry V (1413–1422). Henry decided to reconquer the lost heritage of the Angevins and in 1415 he renewed the Hundred Years' War against France. In October, 1415, he won the great victory of Agincourt. Soon there was an uneasy peace. After Henry VI (1422–1461) came to the throne the war blazed forth again. Joan of Arc helped France's Charles VII defeat the English. She was captured, judged guilty of heresy, and burned at the stake at Rouen. The French, filled with a new pugnacity, advanced to final victory. Of all the English possessions in France only Calais was left. The Hundred Years' War was soon over.

Heroic deeds faded. The excitement of the struggle ended with death and grass. The plows run over the field of Crécy today. The hayricks rise by Agincourt.

A war in France was ended. A war in England began. Between the two royal houses of York and Lancaster there came the intermittent dynastic conflict called the Wars of the Roses. The majority of Englishmen were neutral and they did not suffer much. The weight of the war fell upon the nobles. Edward IV, first of the Yorkists, was crowned in 1461. In 1483 he was succeeded by his son, Edward V, a child twelve years of age who had the shortest and saddest reign in English history. Despite sincere attempts to prove the contrary, it seems that Richard of York was responsible for the murder of his nephew Edward V and Edward's younger brother. Less than two years later Henry Tudor defeated and slew Richard at the battle of Bosworth Field. By the fortune of battle and by act of Parliament the victor became Henry VII, first of the great Tudor line. The main political force in England was now the monarchy; and the Tudors kept it so.

In the closing lines of Shakespeare's Richard II, Henry VII spoke of the new peace:

> Abate the edge of traitors, gracious Lord
> That would reduce these bloody days again
> And make poor England weep in streams of blood.

Chapter 18

THE MEDIEVAL SPIRIT

"For history, after all, is valuable only in so far as it lives, and Maeterlinck's cry, 'There are no dead,' should always be the historian's motto."
—Eileen Power, in Preface to *Medieval People*

THE human beings on the planet Earth, spinning through the great ocean sky, have now reached the twentieth century. When modern man, baffled and breathless, pauses to look back he is at once proud and humble at where he has been and what he has done. States and societies have altered again and again. Perspectives and proportions have been swiftly changed.

The world of the twentieth century is filled with the racing nationalism of Asia and Africa, with the promises and problems of nuclear energy, with the struggles of nation-states. A few pioneer scientists, aided by the new skills in technology, have probed into time and space, into the subatomic universe and the secrets of proteins and protoplasm. New horizons replace the old. New worlds for discovery and conquest swim into our ken. Within a few decades our eyes have seen and our hands grasped wonders never dreamed of by our fathers or their fathers before them. We know, most of us quite vaguely, that we live and move in a universe of curved space and relative time. Few of us are troubled by the problems of the measurement of the energies of the beta particles of fission products. All of us are concerned with our food, our families, our health and wealth. When the scientists, those amazing high priests of our age, translate and transfer their tests and equations into something of demonstrable "usefulness" to mankind there is appreciation, wonder, and applause. Then we rapidly become accustomed to radio, television, jet airplanes, penicillin, cortisone, Salk vaccine, cobalt bombs, nuclear reactors, the wonder worlds of polymers and plastics. Each day seems to promise more news of frontiers breached and old forts fallen.

From all of these things the medieval world seems far removed, fading daily more and more into the remote and unfamiliar past. It seems a little alien world, a period of brief and hard lives, a misty age of grim stone castles and bright colors dimmed by time. We finger the manuscript that describes an

263

England studded with the king's forests and see in contrast the crowded streets of the great modern cities of Britain ablaze with the glitter of neon lights. We read that in medieval Germany a horseman usually traveled about thirty miles a day, and our reading is interrupted by the thunder of the Berlin Express. The carved sepulchers of the Middle Ages seem as remote in time as the tombs of Egypt's pharaohs.

> The garlands wither on your brow;
> Then boast no more your mighty deeds. . . .

We know a great deal about the Middle Ages—perhaps too much about the men of blood and pride and too little about the humble. Across the centuries flash the little things, the human touches, the account of a restless baby crying in the night, the tale of the strange shadow cast by the body of a man hanging from a gibbet at a crossroads in Kent in 1381. Scholars like Eileen Power—how well she knew these medieval folk!—have told us of the world of the Menagier's Wife in Paris who knew all the butchers and meat markets and how many sheep and pigs were sold there; of Madame Eglentyne, that sprightly Prioress of Chaucer's *Canterbury Tales:*

> Ful wel she sang the service divine
> Entuned in her nose ful semely.

In the world of the cottage and the hall the days of toil and pleasure folded into one another. There was bread to be baked and ale to be brewed. There were wells to be cleaned, gardens to be weeded, vines to be pruned, fleas and moths to be chased away. There was food to be cooked: black puddings, highly spiced sausages, sea fish, beef, eels, sauces, jams, pastries. There was advice to be given to the young ladies: "And before you leave your chamber and house take care that the collar of your shift, and of your *blanchet, cotte,* and *surcotte* do not hang out one over the other, as happens with certain drunken, foolish, or witless women, who have no name for their honor . . . and who walk with roving eye and head horribly reared up like a lion. . . ." Other people had their problems, too—such as the scholars and artists and poets, those "unacknowledged legislators of the world."

> The lyf so short, the craft so long to lerne,
> Th'assay so hard, so sharpe the conquering.

We know the exact number of baths King John of England took between January 29, 1209 and May 5, 1210—they cost fourpence each. The archers who carried the king's bow got fivepence a day. Sugar cost Henry II fivepence a pound. We know much about the low standards of comfort in most medieval houses—only the upper-class families had linen sheets and fur covers on their beds. We know something of the problems of firewood and candles and coal. We know that the men and women, especially those of the upper classes, usually wore full long gowns and cloaks with hoods. For hunting or working the men donned short garments girt about the waist. All shoes and boots were pointed and had no heels. Apparently insignificant facts like these, all added together, help to give us a picture of the lives of these medieval people of Europe who were the ancestors of most of us in the Western world.

Over the roads of Europe and England moved many high and humble travelers on foot or horseback. Long carts and heavy barges slowly moved the heavy goods by the roads and waterways. All about were the rogues and vagabonds. François Villon had many comrades. There were also the men who toiled in the fields, by the forge of the smith, in the shops of the craft guilds. Their sleep was heavy, less distracted than the sleep of princes. There were no printed books, no television. There were rough games, riddles, dull moral tales like the famous one of patient and bovine Griselda, rousing epics, bear baiting, hawking, wrestling, and jousting. Life was to be endured and sometimes enjoyed. Death was unavoidable. Religion promised to the hungry and poor an eternity of satisfaction. God would know and save His own. Said the Lady Julian of Norwich: "And He that shall be our bliss when we are there, He is our keeper while we are here."

In the towns of Europe there slowly appeared more action and a more lively ferment of ideas. Young men who were veterans of the Crusades did not want to go back to the quiet and lonely country fields and villages. They wanted to stay in the exciting cities, to argue and talk with their comrades and their elders. Wandering young men, hungry for adventure and knowledge, were mainly responsible for the first universities, a great event in the world's history. In the twelfth century they found scholars willing to teach them. Both teachers and students lectured, studied, and quizzed by the roadsides, in upper rooms, in any convenient place.

Several free-lance teachers settled down and attracted tramping students from distant places. At Bologna, under the influence of Gratian, arose a famous law school. At Salerno there grew up a medical school. Padua was founded in 1222, Naples in 1224. By the middle of the fifteenth century there were more than sixty universities on the Continent and in England, including Portugal's Coimbra, England's Oxford and Cambridge, Paris, Montpellier, Cracow, Prague. Soon one was to arise in Peru's Lima, far in the new world of America.

At Montpellier the medical school soon outranked all others on the Continent. At Paris, mother of all northern universities, three separate colleges attracted great teachers and thousands of students. There lectured Abelard, that genius who taught that students must be trained to think for themselves. In order to think well, a student must learn to use the tools of logic. Abelard

taught his students logic by questioning them like Socrates, by arguing with
them, by showing them where they succeeded and where they failed. Those
who help youths in a university are at least among the lesser ranks of those
who will enter the kingdom of heaven.

The universities of Europe soon formed learned guilds of masters and
scholars for the purpose of regulating their affairs. Each cooperative guild association was under a rector, and the university operated according to a set
of rules drawn up by the guild. The universities also began to obtain special
charters or privileges from the pope, emperor, or king. Under these the scholars
were usually granted the universal protection given to pilgrims and clerics.
The degrees of master and doctor given by an acceptable and chartered university gave the holder the right to teach anywhere. Every university degree
was originally a teaching license or certificate. To the bachelor, the master, and
the doctor certain specific rights and privileges were given.

Medieval universities had at first no campuses or buildings. The lecturers
usually talked in hired halls. The students lived wherever they could find a
place to sleep. They ate what they could buy cheaply, or what they could
steal. The "ancient and honourable company of scholars" often came into
dispute with the townspeople, who frequently sought to overcharge and prof-
iteer and infringe upon university rights. Then the university authorities
could, if they wished, merely stop the lectures and the whole university would
move somewhere else.

Soon the universities built halls and colleges where the students lived with
the masters. The main topics of study were logic, rhetoric, grammar, arithmetic, geometry, astronomy, and music. These subjects provided important
foundations for careers in the three great professions of theology, law, and
medicine. The young students delighted in carrying on informal and purposeful disputes with gusto, sometimes with acute and acid comments. They
were impatient with sterile routines or any rules that cramped freedom of
speculation. We may be sure that there were many kinds of youths attending
the universities: the conservatives and the liberals, the skeptics, the materialists,
the immoralists, and the mockers, the dull and the sharp. The youthful rebels,
of course, are often the best hope of mankind.

The students were not always sober and serious young people, any more
than the young men of today or only yesterday. They had their fun and their
troubles. The "town and gown" feuds, especially at Oxford and Cambridge,
sometimes assumed serious proportions. The battles between the North and
South of England at Oxford and Cambridge were often long and bloody. So,
too, were the frays among the students from the different parts of Europe.
"The Nations wrangled and disputed about the various countries and it caused
dissensions, hatreds, and virulent animosities among them and they impu-
dently uttered all kinds of affronts and insults against one another. They

[55] The Crusades of St. Louis, a French parchment painting of the early fourteenth century

Below: Baptism, from Pasquier Grenier's The Seven Sacraments, a Flemish wool and silk tapestry (c. 1475)

[56]

PLATE
XVII

PLATE XVIII

A miniature by Jean Fouquet showing a scene from "The Martyrdom of St. Appollonia," a miracle play of the fifteenth century

[58]

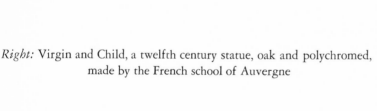

Above: An illustration from the Luttrell Psalter showing peasants carting grain in England about the year 1340

Right: Virgin and Child, a twelfth century statue, oak and polychromed, made by the French school of Auvergne

affirmed that the English were drunkards, the sons of France proud and effeminate and carefully adorned like women; the Burgundians they considered vulgar and stupid. . . . After such insults they usually came to blows."

The students also had financial troubles. In 1221 one young man wrote to his father: "Dearest father, when I was lately in Orléans I had a row with a young man, and the devil tempting me, I hit him over the head with a stick, and now I am shut up in Orléans jail. . . . The fine is ten pounds and I can't get out until it is paid." We have the father's callous answer: "I wish you full repentance of your folly. People who get into prison are as well to stay there until they realize their foolishness and I am not going to make myself poor for the likes of you." In 1220 another young man sent a letter to his father saying that he was "studying with the greatest diligence" but that he lacked money. "I respectfully beg you my father that by the promptings of divine pity you may assist me, so that I may be able to complete what I have so well begun. For you know that without clothes and food and wine your son grows cold."

Among the interesting Aularian Statutes that took their final form in 1556 at the University of Oxford were these:

> Those who engage in a game of dice, handball, fencing, or any other unseemly game disturbing to the peace and distractive to study shall be fined 4 d. Stones are not to be brought into the dining hall. If one student shall address another in a mocking tone concerning his wits, his knowledge, or his reason, whereby the peace and tranquillity of the hall is disturbed and learning suffer, he shall be fined 2 d. The men must not roll dice while the church is in session. Students are not to bring knives into the examination room. After the ringing of the bell or the sounding of the horn every student must come with haste, lest otherwise the food be divided to the prejudice of him who comes late.

Brief glimpses such as these into the days of the rise of the universities and the lives of professors and students indicate clearly enough that there are certain constants that can never be removed from the equations of history or from the hearts and brains of men. The nature and habits of youth may seem to change; but they really never do. Those who are young in heart always drink at the fountains of wonder and enthusiasm and walk the road of hope.

One of the chief errors in the writing of history is overstatement. It is often said, for instance, that during the Middle Ages the habit of most men was to rely heavily for guidance upon the static dogmatism of theology and the shackling words of authority. It is said that the men of science were expected to support the conclusions of the theologians and that the dominant emotions of the medieval period were those of acquiescence, not of questioning tumult.

Thus yoked and harnessed, the scientist was not free to experiment or investigate. He was compelled to deduce his conclusions from the cribbing and confining premises held and stated by the theologians. He could not reason from the particular facts he found to general hypotheses or firm conclusions. Thus he was not an objective scientist in the modern sense. He did not know that analysis, comparison, and synthesis must go hand in hand with description. He did not know that the proper aim of science is "to seek the simplest explanation of complex facts."

These statements are partly true. There were many fettering conditions and attitudes in that long period of history we call the Middle Ages. There were numerous difficulties and obstructive nuisances. The scientists of the earlier medieval age, for example, were handicapped by the fact that they knew little about the achievements of the Greeks. Their compilations, such as the famous *Etymologies* of Isidore of Seville, were strange and dazzling compounds of fact and theory and fancy. Only in the twelfth century, when Greek and Arabic works began to be translated, did the scientific and mathematical knowledge of the past come into Europe. The recovered facts and ideas helped to pull off several smothering blankets of misconception and ignorance.

Physics was based on the accepted theory of Aristotle's dynamics and upon the four elements—earth, water, air, and fire and their four qualities, the active ones being hot and cold and the passive dry and moist. Chemistry was also founded upon Aristotle's theories, aided by ideas of magic and alchemy. Astronomy and its twin science astrology were cast and fixed in the finite universe of Aristotle and Ptolemy. The earth was the center of that universe; the stars and planets were fixed in their places; the crystalline spheres whirled in their majestic courses. On this great stage of Ptolemy, the stage of John Milton's *Paradise Lost,* the divine drama of human salvation moved upon its relentless way.

About 1260 the Franciscan friar Bartholomew Anglicus wrote in his *Concerning the Properties of Things* that spiders were killed by the sight of a sapphire; that crocodiles weep; that the liver contains fire and is the center of kindness; that dragons like to fight elephants and fastened their wings together and sailed over the seas "to get good meat." Of the human body Bartholomew Anglicus said: "By the spleen we are moved to laugh, by the gall we are angry, by the heart we are wise, by the brain we feel, by the liver we love."

The illustrations of what can be regarded as medieval credulity and ignorance might easily be multiplied. They are sometimes quoted at length by those who desire to amuse, who delight to be condescending, or who wish to stress the fact that modern man is emancipated from the naïve delusions of his ancestors. Far too much of this kind of thing has been presented as characteristic of the Middle Ages. It is wise to remember that all men stand upon the shoulders of their predecessors. Some writers and readers of history—or what is expected to pass for history—are haunted by the unfortunate notion that most of the discoveries of man have suddenly blazed or exploded without warning or preparation. This is simply not so. Behind the insights of the giants are usually the laboratories and the workbenches of lesser men who contribute their unspectacular mites to the expanding total of human knowledge. Some of these men are living now. Some lived in the Middle Ages. It is also wise to remember that when we write or talk about the medieval period of human history we are referring to an age that stretched over a thousand years. In the habits, ideas, institutions, and attitudes of men there were tremendous variations in time and place. Only deluded enthusiasts can attribute to all the Middle Ages common qualities and quantities of belief and action. Our living heritage from medieval worlds springs from many fountains in different lands and generations.

The sum of scientific knowledge increased far more in the medieval centuries than we were taught to believe by those who asserted that the Renaissance of the sixteenth century marked the great division between ignorance and light. Neat little ways of thought often obscure accuracy. The unwarranted emphasis upon the limiting patterns of habit, thought, and action in the Middle Ages has resulted in several warping errors of perspective and understanding. Not enough has yet been written to restore the balance, despite such superb works as George Sarton's *Introduction to the History of Science* (to 1400) and Lynn Thorndike's many-volumed *History of Magic and Experimental Science*.

The Middle Ages were not years of slumber and weary decadence. Several short steps forward were taken as early as the ninth century Carolingian Renaissance in Frankish Gaul and Germany. Several more were taken in Anglo-Saxon England and Germany in the so-called Ottonian Renaissance in the tenth century. The excitement of the twelfth and thirteenth centuries brought a series of new facts and ideas to upset many cherished follies of the past. By the fifteenth century, when the Church exerted a less powerful influence than the state, the rising strength of the new philosophies and the natural sciences forced theology into a steady retreat.

The coming of doubt is often the beginning of wisdom. Probing minds began to question Aristotle's assertion that there had to be a mover to make anything move in any direction except towards the center of the earth. Some said Aristotle could not be right when he said that there could never be a complete void or vacuum in nature. In any age there are men who will ask questions and find answers that are not acceptable to their fathers. Human beings are always trying to annex and understand the realms of the mysterious. There was never any valid reason to suppose that men suddenly stopped being inquisitive in the Middle Ages.

Most men of the medieval centuries believed that Ptolemy was right: the earth was a sphere in the center of the universe. Although the geocentric theory of Ptolemy was widely accepted there were some scientists who had other ideas. Nicolas Oresme of Paris stated in the fourteenth century his theory of the daily rotation of the earth around the sun. French scholars are probably correct in saying that the essential steps preparing the way for Galileo took place in fourteenth-century Paris. It must be added, of course, that Nicolas Oresme's conclusions were not widely spread abroad or understood by the masses or by his fellow scientists. Nor is there any evidence that Copernicus or Galileo knew about the work of Oresme or about the fact that the Greek Aristarchus had said much the same thing in his heliocentric theories eighteen hundred years earlier. It often happens that scientific theories are obscured or ignored and left to lie by the wall.

In the twelfth century the mariners' compass was probably brought into Europe by the Arabs. In the thirteenth, men like the Paris Schoolman Jean Buridan were taking remarkable steps forward in what we may call physical science, especially in their discussions of uniform motion and the problems of impetus. About 1300, a new rudder, mentioned earlier, appeared upon several ships. Soon the shape, masts, and rigging were changed and improved. Miss Dorothy Burwash has described with skill and precision some later developments in the Middle Ages, especially in construction and navigation aids, that made the fifteenth- and sixteenth-century voyages and triumphs possible. In the fourteenth century Nicolas Oresme made use of coordinates in mathematics long before Descartes is supposed to have invented analytical geometry. He also used fractional exponents for powers, a discovery usually attributed to mathematicians of the sixteenth century. Albert of Saxony, also of the fourteenth century, provided Leonardo da Vinci with most of his geological information. Torricelli used in the sixteenth century the notes that Jean Buridan had prepared in the thirteenth when he was studying the possibility of a vacuum. About the fourteenth century the first blast furnaces were developed and iron-working techniques were swiftly improved. The Arabs brought westward the art of papermaking and a method of printing by carved wooden blocks. A printing press was invented either by Gutenberg of Mainz or Coster of Haarlem. This famous invention, perfected in the fifteenth century, involved the casting of metal type which could be put into a rigid frame and used over and over again.

There is no need here to print a long catalogue of names and dates. The important fact is this: the founders of modern science and technology, as suggested earlier, were not Copernicus, Galileo, Kepler, and Newton and their fellows. These giants were men of vision and genius; but they were also heirs and builders in a great tradition. This statement is a far cry from the uninhibited assurances, so often loosely given, that there is nothing—or at best but a little—worthy of concern or admiration before the days of Copernicus.

The story of Roger Bacon, for example, is magnificently compelling when read in its proper context. Here was a fiery Franciscan friar of the thirteenth century who got into a great deal of trouble. Certainly Bacon thought and talked too much about the stupidity and ignorance of his contemporaries. He made them uncomfortable; and when he made them uncomfortable they tried to beat him down. Bacon wanted to put torches to some rotten pillars of tradition. He wanted to run through the halls and rouse men to tumble out of their beds of lethargy. These were some of the reasons why state and Church authorities locked Roger Bacon up. It is not wise, surely, to permit eccentric men to shake society. Sincerely conservative and respectable men have often held the fort against the radicals and the rebels who have waved the flags of revolution. Sometimes the citadel has proved to be the fort of folly. It has fallen, and the revolution has been achieved by dreamers and patriots who have started to build anew.

Bacon did accept many current assumptions—he believed in astrology and he thought the circle could be squared. On the other hand, he insisted that a parade of formal logic could not contribute much towards finding out the secrets of nature. He thought that it was absurd to accept Aristotle blindly, particularly through translations that quite probably distorted his meaning. Bacon also remarked that the Schoolmen were far removed from their master Aristotle when they neglected nature. Why did they not study nature themselves, in the manner of their master Aristotle?

About 1267 Roger Bacon wrote his famous *Opus Majus*. His later *Opus Minus* and *Opus Tertium* were merely summaries of his *Opus Majus* with some additions on alchemy and chemistry. Bacon was a man of many interests; he not only wrote about theology, grammar, chemistry, geography, alchemy, and astrology but he also experimented in chemistry, optics, mechanics, and mathematics. He made tests and experiments with gunpowder and survived.

We come now to the fact and quality for which Roger Bacon has won a long renown. Like Albert the Great, Roger Bacon stressed the importance of the use of inductive experimental methods in seeking knowledge: "Experimental science controls the conclusions of all the other sciences; it reveals truths which reasoning from general principles would never have discovered; finally, it starts us on the way to marvellous inventions that will change the face of the world." This quotation perhaps suggests that Roger Bacon's ideas were more modern than in fact they were. Certainly he did not say that all knowledge must be tested by experiment; but he did say that experimental science provided a way to test and validate or destroy conclusions and hypotheses reached by other roads.

Many of the Greeks, in the bright days of their glory, had said the same thing. The facts of experience, they had asserted, alone may show whither man has been and where he is perhaps going. Only by a study of the facts can men hope to have any ideas—or at least any defensible ideas—about the meaning and destiny of the universe.

Such controlling conclusions are also basic to all modern scientific procedure. Roger Bacon looks back to Aristotle and forward to Enrico Fermi. The conclusions of the scientists must be rigorously checked, step by step, against the facts that are known. "A scientific law embodies a recipe for doing something, and its final validification rests in the domain of action."

The plain and unembellished tale of man's scientific achievement, as it moves forward, links and fuses together present, past, and future, not only by the successive names of men but also by their controlling beliefs. We cannot be sure that the lessons of history are the lessons we think we see. Nevertheless, it seems that scientists have grappled most successfully with their problems and challenges when they remembered the value of experiment, experience, empirical observation, and repeated testing. In the history of that practice and that idea the name of Roger Bacon shines brightly.

Of himself Roger Bacon wrote: "I recognized my own littleness, my stammering speech, and my scratching pen." At the same time he revealed his pride in the work that he had done: "It is well known that no man hath laboured in so many languages and sciences as I, nor hath laboured so hard therein."

Sometimes there is a disarming simplicity about the paragraphs describing the lives and achievements of individuals who were born and died and left their gold and their books to their sons and daughters. All is so elementary and straightforward that the unwary reader is apt to forget that the sunshine and storm recorded in the individual biographies form a part of a greater drama. There is little satisfaction—except to those who are wrongheaded and pedantic—in knowing a great deal about one page and little about all the others. The details about any segment of history can only gain and hold their full significance in the broader context of the whole, or as much of the whole as we can see. "History," said Thomas Carlyle, "is the essence of innumerable biographies."

Of importance to the race and the planet were several events that had to do with a significant sector of science and technology: the production of new weapons and the development of new warfare techniques. In our modern age we can have no grudge or grievance against men who improved the skills of slaughter, mayhem, or demolition.

In the later Middle Ages the days of the impregnable castle and the armed knights were passing away. Such a result followed the appearance of the longbow, of gunpowder and firearms. In the age of chivalry power and protection and skill in close combat were very important. They were less important after the new weapons came, because the bows and guns killed at a distance. A humble yeoman with a bow and arrow could bring down a valiant and noble knight as soon as the knight came within range—Crécy and Poitiers had demonstrated that simple fact quite conclusively. Give a yeoman a gun and he could be more dangerous still. Against gunfire a heavily armed knight was usually helpless. Broken shields, splintered lances, and crumpled bodies marked the slow death of the age of chivalry. Departing, too, were the many aristocratic principles embodied in the armored knight. Ariosto said that firearms were an invention of Beelzebub made "to ruin all the race of mankind." His comments upon guided missiles and hydrogen bombs would probably be even more emphatic.

It seemed that the offensive weapon of the new artillery demonstrated the futility of fortifications. Artillery could smash the walls of castles and forts. Thus the way was opened more completely for the centralization of power in the hands of a conquering king who had the heavy guns and the firepower to subdue his foes. And thus the way was open for the accelerated growth of nation-states under powerful rulers. Gunpowder and guns helped to doom the earlier structure of state and society. The first artillery bombardment in the world's history enabled Henry V of England to take the city of Harfleur in 1415—"Once more into the breach, dear friends. . . ." Another series of artillery attacks smashed the walls of Constantinople in 1453, and the Turks were at bay no more.

"Beauty," said St. Thomas Aquinas, "requires three things: wholeness, harmony, and radiance." Much of the art of the Middle Ages possesses these three qualities. They may be found in the symbolism of the mosaics, the wood carving, the sculpturing, the stained-glass windows, the painting, the pottery, the illustrated manuscripts so carefully made by the devout monks, the majestic Gothic cathedrals. No radiance is found in the massive medieval castles dominating the landscape; but they do possess wholeness and harmony. Despite the requirements of St. Thomas these castles have their own kind of beauty. No one, surely, who has seen them standing against the sky in the twilight will say otherwise.

Many characteristics of a civilized society are revealed in its architecture. Three kinds of style are found in the European buildings of the Middle Ages: the Byzantine, the Romanesque, and the Gothic. Each was developed slowly by master craftsmen and each possessed its individual kind of beauty and appeal. There are no limits to the search for the beautiful and the true. It is permissible to prefer Gothic to Romanesque and Byzantine; but he who denounces and despises all other kinds of architecture must be both blamed and pitied. Much important architecture, like much of the whole body of art, really exists to rouse the world of emotion, the kingdom which is within us. The human emotions do not thrive in a vacuum. The architects of the Middle

Ages knew this. Their aims were great, their achievements were great, and their fame is great.

In the early Middle Ages the eastern areas of Europe saw the continued development of Byzantine architecture, the typical form that evolved in all Moslem countries. Throughout central and southern Spain, as already re-marked, many of the buildings standing today evoke memories of the long Moslem occupation. In Venice the famous church of St. Mark was modeled upon Constantinople's St. Sophia. Throughout southern Italy the Byzantine influence was strongly felt and sometimes followed. Turn a corner in Ravenna and there may well be a dome or a minaret. In a side street of Palermo the traveler may pause before the intricate and bright design of a Moslem dec-oration.

In western Europe the prevailing form of architecture by the eleventh century was the earth-clinging Romanesque, a massive and robust style, firmly based on the Roman tradition. Horizontal lines were always predominant. The walls and pillars were thick; the arches were rounded; the solid towers suggested strength and repose. In later years the walls and pillars became higher and flat buttresses were used at points of strain and pressure. Doors and windows were deeply recessed. New forms of decoration appeared: the zigzag, the triangular dogtooth, the scallop, the beak, the signs of the zodiac. Hundreds of workmen chiseled and carved in stone the capitals, the gargoyles, and all the other decorations in the great cathedrals, the elaborate monastic buildings, and the humble parish churches by the dusty roads.

In the larger Romanesque churches heavy barrel vaults reached over the naves and thrust against the thick walls supported by huge piers. Nobody had yet figured out how to buttress the transverse arches from the outside to hold the thrust of the great weight. Because the walls had to be strong and massive there could be no large windows. This is the reason a Romanesque church with a vaulted nave is usually gloomy and grim.

From region to region in Europe there were variations in Romanesque structure. Throughout France, Italy, and Spain the aisles of the churches were usually cross-vaulted. In the early period several churches, especially in Germany, had timber roofs. In Germany, too, some churches had two tran-septs and most of them had three towers at the ends. In France and Spain there was almost always a single transept and a single apse.

Excellent examples of the Romanesque style are the Cathedral of Modena in northern Italy, Sant' Ambrosio in Milan, St. Severin in Cologne, the Abbey Church of St. George in Limburg, the Cistercian monastery at Maul-bronn, the cathedrals at Mainz, Bamberg, Verona, Toulouse, and Arles. These buildings, and many more, show how the Romanesque architecture reached a high degree of perfection in the balance of masses, spaces, and planes. The beauty of the Romanesque structure always results from its majestic proportions, its massive strength, its wholeness and harmony. Of the radiance St. Thomas Aquinas wanted, there is none.

Wholeness, harmony, and radiance are always present in the contrived innocence and lightness of the soaring Gothic cathedrals, one of the greatest architectural achievements of mankind. The purity, warmth, and vigorous life of the Gothic style lives through the centuries in the majestic and soaring vaults and spires and the great windows of the medieval cathedrals of Europe. Uncounted thousands of men and women have been swayed by the admirable excellence of what they beheld. They have lifted their eyes in silent wonder as they stood before these buildings raised by man to the glory of the living God.

The so-called Gothic style in architecture was given the name by the Renaissance scholars who thought that all things medieval were as barbarous as the Goths who overran the Roman Empire. This Gothic form of building appeared first in France and then spread. By the end of the thirteenth century it had extended over wide areas of Europe.

In contrast to the Romanesque building, the Gothic roof was supported or interlaced by pointed arches buttressed from outside and by groups of slender columns. Vaults soared to an astonishing height. Much of the thrust of the weight from above was directed downward rather than outward. The vertical thrust was directed and controlled by the judicious placing of arches, ribs, groins, and columns. Because the walls themselves carried little weight and stress there was an opportunity to use large windows filled with exquisite and multicolored stained glass. The flooding of the interior with generous light added to the effect of airy grace already achieved by the vertical lines of construction.

It is not surprising that aspects of the earlier Romanesque style, such as cylindrical columns and rounded arches, often remained in Gothic structures. It must be remembered, too, that the building of a cathedral sometimes took several generations. Cologne Cathedral, for instance, was begun in 1248 and was finished in 1880; no work was done upon the project between 1560 and 1842. The west façade of Chartres was finished about 1150; the south tower was built between 1180 and 1194; a large part of the cathedral was later completed in 1280; the northern Gothic spire was built between 1506 and 1512. Some of the smaller churches did not take so long to raise. The church of Wimphen, in the Ruhr valley, was completed in ten years (1268–1278). It happened this way: "The Dean . . . pulled down the monastery . . . as it was in a ruinous condition and then sent for a mason who was highly skilled in architecture and who had lately come from Paris. . . . the aforesaid artificer built a church of marvellous architecture, very finely decorated with the images of saints within and without, and it had windows and pillars carved like sculpture . . . so people came to it from every side, admiring the excellent workmanship and praising the artificer . . . and rejoicing that they had seen him; and his name was carried far and wide afield."

The early English Gothic, extending from about 1170 to 1280, can be recognized by the delicate tracery and geometrical patterns of the pointed lancet windows. Early English Gothic in most features of their construction are the choir of Lincoln Cathedral, rebuilt about 1200; Westminster Abbey, rebuilt in the thirteenth century; Wells Cathedral in Somerset; and Canterbury Cathedral. A magnificent example of pure early Gothic is Salisbury Cathedral, finished about 1258. From about 1280 to 1380 there appeared the fantastic traceries of the broad-windowed and decorated Gothic. An excellent example of decorated Gothic architecture is Exeter Cathedral. From about 1380 to 1500 the so-called perpendicular Gothic exhibited a blunting of the pointed arches, the tracery usually reduced to a series of vertical straight lines and squarish towers. These characteristics are perhaps best shown in the perpendicular additions made to Gloucester Cathedral in the fourteenth century.

Among the best illustrations of the flexible and evolving Gothic style in Europe, sometimes with other stylistic qualities intermingled, are the superb Notre Dame of Paris and the cathedrals of Amiens, Reims, and Cologne. There is also, of course, the incomparable Chartres. We have the words of a man who saw Chartres being built. The spirit of an age long past is in the sentences he wrote:

> The inhabitants of Chartres have combined to aid in the construction of their church by transporting the materials. . . . Since then the faithful of our diocese and of other neighboring regions have formed associations for the same object; they admit no one into the company unless he has been to confession. . . . They elect a chief under whose direction they conduct their wagons in silence and with humility. Who has ever seen—who has ever heard tell, in times past, that powerful princes of the world, that men brought up in honors and in wealth, that nobles, men and women, have bent their proud and haughty necks to the harness of carts, and that, like beasts of burden, they have dragged, to the abode of Christ, these wagons, loaded with wines, grains, oil, stone, timber and all that is necessary for the construction of the church?

Despite the widespread idea that the Gothic style means lavish and excessive decoration, the reverse is usually true. Until the later meaningless years of Gothic decline the decorative patterns were almost always unostentatious and delicate. In most of the cathedrals of Europe there are fine examples of the decorative skill of hundreds of medieval craftsmen. Particularly effective are the sculptures of the twelfth and thirteenth centuries at Chartres, Reims, and Amiens. Many of these and others elsewhere were designed to teach as well as to adorn. Several of them were symbolic and traditional, such as the carvings of the Last Judgment, the four beasts of the Apocalypse, the faces and figures of saints and Biblical characters. The minor sculptures were frequently more naturalistic and individual. Several stained-glass windows by the nave and aisle usually illustrated stories from the Scriptures or the lives of the saints. The great rose windows were made of colored glass designs and were placed to catch the rays of the setting sun and to suffuse the interior of the church with radiance and color. All of these things contributed their part to the plan and purpose of the whole church. The blended and impressive beauty of a Gothic masterpiece lies overwhelmingly above all in its total design, its logically perfected and graceful completeness. "All art," said Walter Pater, "constantly aspires towards the condition of music."

Not all of the fine buildings of the Middle Ages were built to the glory of God. Towards the end of the Middle Ages the rising tide of treasures from trade and banking resulted in the building of several fine civic structures. These were constructed for secular purposes in the midst of a rising secular spirit on the eve of the Renaissance.

Among the most impressive of these civic buildings were the Cloth Hall at Bruges, the guild houses of Brussels, the Belfry of Ghent, and the town hall of Louvain with its typically Flemish steep roof. A number of princely private residences also began to rise, especially in southern Europe. Probably the most famous of them all was the graceful and balanced Medici Palace at Florence. It was fitting that it should be so. Florence was to be one of the great cities of the approaching Renaissance. The scholarly work of Hans Baron and others has shown how great were the contributions of Florence in the growth of humanism and many other aspects of Renaissance glory. The Medici family were already possessed of a new kind of wealth and a new kind of power. The city of Florence and the Medici family were symbols and portents of an approaching era in which many values of the Middle Ages would have but narrow room.

Through the centuries of the Middle Ages the artists of Europe painted and carved to satisfy man's long hunger for beauty and imagery. In the early medieval period these artists had one main subject: the Christian faith. Religious feeling suffused the painting on the altars, the wooden panels, the miniatures on the margins of the illuminated manuscripts. The story of the Nativity, for instance, was repeated in scores of ways and forms.

Sometimes there was heavy emphasis upon one kind of art, sometimes upon another. After the rise of Gothic architecture the amount of fresco work swiftly declined because the Gothic churches had no plaster walls. The most extensive development of altar painting came in the fourteenth century. The finest achievement of the facile illuminators appeared at the same time in the *Book of Hours* made for the Duke of Berry, wealthy brother of Charles V.

In the early period of medieval art there was usually little stress upon realism. Symbolism mattered most. It is true that several artists did observe some of the disciplines of scale and proportion. Nevertheless, when they worked upon a flat surface the work stayed flat. There was no sense of depth or distance. There was seldom vitality. Only slowly were the quivering and nervous lines of the early period replaced by more stable construction. Only gradually did a swift and exciting pulse of vitality appear.

It has been remarked before that none of the history of mankind can be neatly divided into chapters or carefully sorted and separated into compartments of time and space. Some men have tried to wrench and warp the past in ways that seemed logical and reasonable. They have failed because there are so many things that simply will not fit into a pattern of neatness. "The commonest kind of trouble is that this world of ours is nearly reasonable, but not quite. . . . It looks just a little more mathematical and regular than it is; its exactitude is obvious, but its inexactitude is hidden; its wildness lies in wait."

In the later centuries of the Middle Ages there appeared numerous artists who do not easily slide into any of the categories usually associated with the period before the Renaissance. It seems that they somehow got into what we call the Middle Ages by mistake; but they are there. It has been said that they are "transition artists" or "heralds of the Renaissance." It has also been asserted that the springlike surge of the Renaissance really began quite early and that the whole concept of the nature and course and span of the Renaissance must be radically changed. About this complex subject the next chapter will have something to say. Meanwhile let us pause to look at a few of the men who seem to have leaped suddenly upon the world stage without waiting for their cues.

Up in Burgundy there lived in the fifteenth century the first and greatest of the so-called Flemish school of painters: the brothers van Eyck, Flemings serving the Duke of Burgundy. Their portraits and domestic interiors are masterpieces of realism—especially the work of Jan van Eyck (d. 1441). The famous altarpiece at Ghent, painted about 1435, is a striking example of Jan's skill. It is one of the high moments of medieval art. In most of their work the van Eycks abandoned the use of tempera—a mixture of color and gum or egg—and used oils. One result was the brilliant colors that pleased the van Eycks and drew the eyes of many Europeans. Some approved and some scorned and scolded. Others were uncertain about their judgments when confronted by the new and the unforeseen.

In a small Dominican monastery at the foot of the hill of Fiesole outside Florence lived Fra Angelico (1387–1455), called "The Angelic" by his fellow monks because of the faith and reverence that filled his life and his paintings. A hundred years after Fra Angelico's death the historian-artist Giorgio

Vasari wrote a biography of the celebrated painter in which he said: "He never took up a brush without first making a prayer. He never made a crucifix when the tears did not run down his cheeks." To the reader of the twentieth century it seems that Vasari's language is somewhat extreme and that he has massaged the truth. Nevertheless, Fra Angelico was a very godly and self-effacing monk, a devoted servant in the house of the Lord who never sought the seats or the favors of the mighty. "He that will enter Paradise must come with the right key."

Fra Angelico was also a very great artist. He once said that the goal of his life and art was the "contemplation and realization of Beauty." All his paintings show his strivings towards that goal. As he moved from the world of medieval illuminations to the portals of the Renaissance, Fra Angelico shrewdly developed a tremendous technical skill. His quick eyes made careful observations of nature. His clever fingers, touched with genius, created color effects and translucent surfaces that had never been seen before and not often since. For the Convent of Santa Maria Novella in Florence he painted in one panel the "Coming of the Magi" and "The Annunciation" with a sweep and a power his city had not seen. The backgrounds are rich and golden. The paintings are filled with glowing colors—blue, red, and pink—and soft-textured robes. The drab and putty-like figures so often seen in early medieval art are gone. Fra Angelico's Virgin, for instance, is no longer in the flat, two-dimensional tradition. All of the figures breathe vitality, just as they do in another "Annunciation" Fra Angelico painted for the Church of San Domenico in Cortona and now considered to be one of the world's great paintings.

In the fifteenth century the most prominent citizens of Florence were the Medicis, especially Cosimo de' Medici (d. 1464) and his grandson, Lorenzo the Magnificent (d. 1492). These men were bold and able capitalists, shrewd entrepreneurs, sensitive men, scholars, and patrons of the arts. It was not surprising that Cosimo de' Medici requested Fra Angelico to do the frescoes of San Marco Convent for presentation by Cosimo to the Dominicans. These frescoes are still to be seen and admired; they have withstood the damaging effects of the years more successfully than many masterpieces.

In 1445 Fra Angelico began decorating the Vatican, especially the Chapel of the Sacrament. He was still busy at this long task when he died in 1455 at the age of sixty-eight. To this humble Dominican friar had been given the power to create things of superb beauty, a gift so many men have longed for and so few through the centuries have possessed in full measure. Of Fra Angelico's paintings Vasari rightly said: "It is an incomparable pleasure to regard them, for it appears that the spirits of the blessed in heaven cannot be otherwise than these."

All the civilized world knows that the High Renaissance of the sixteenth

century brought a race of giants and a blaze of glory. It has earlier been remarked that before the years of that exploding power there were at least three
centuries of pioneers and preparation. Even if the van Eycks and Fra Angelico
had stood alone in their times our cultural heritage from that age would have
been considerable. But they did not stand alone. They lived and worked in
the midst of many other men who saw visions and dreamed dreams and were
able to come back to tell the world in creations of incomparable art.

Only a few artists can be mentioned here. Most of them had names that
ring over the centuries and make so many other periods in man's history seem
poor and barren. There was, for instance, Giotto (1276–1337), friend of
Dante and painter and builder extraordinary. It was Giotto who decorated
chapels in Padua and Florence with his frescoes, so famed for their varying
colors, their depth illusions, and their astounding realism. His frescoes at
Assisi portraying some chapters from the life of St. Francis are probably his
best, and they are in excellent condition today. A second remarkable man
was Donatello (1386–1466), rightly praised for more than five centuries for
the physical realism and beauty of his statues. Under the magic of his hands
the statues he made of the saints emerged as individual men and women; no
longer were they symbols of ideal virtues. When Donatello made angels they
were little laughing children who seemed rightly to belong to the kingdom
of heaven. His equestrian bronze statue of Gattamelata seems about to ride
away. His statue of David looks like a graceful and athletic youth from
Florence. Donatello's dramatic Mary Magdalen was finished about 1455 and
is perhaps his masterpiece. For 500 years she has stood as Donatello made
her: ragged and gaunt, haggard and lonely. Jesus, her Master, has gone. Is
there no one else to pity and befriend?

The goldsmith Lorenzo Ghiberti (1378–1455) made the famous east doors
of the baptistry in Florence that Michelangelo said were worthy to be the
gates of Paradise. Masaccio (1401–1428) was known and praised for his new
techniques and his vivid realism, especially in such words as "The Expulsion
of Adam and Eve from Eden." The two most famous works of Alessandro
Botticelli (1447–1510) were his "Birth of Venus" and his "Primavera," both
done for the Medici Palace. Uccello (1396–1475) also did his battle scenes
from the past history of Florence for the Medici Palace and was particularly
successful in finding answers to problems of perspective and composition.

There is no need to prolong the list of names and dates. Standard reference
works are filled with many facts, all pointing to the same conclusions: the
centuries that marked the close of the Middle Ages were studded with superb
achievements; the elements of realism and naturalism in Renaissance art had
their source and inspiration in the three preceding centuries and not in classical art; to an increasing extent Italian art was becoming more secular in spirit
by the fifteenth century; the achievements in painting and sculpture were not

haphazard but were parts of a movement stimulated and developed by gifted and technically skilled men.

Far back among the first dawns of history human beings began to make music. The sounds that came from their crude instruments, now found broken in ancient caves, would probably be offensive and unintelligible to modern ears. So also would be the strange rhythms of human voices echoing across the primeval valleys. The road to the days of the symphony and the concert soprano is long and difficult. In his endless search for beauty, filled with the divine urge to create, man has persistently struggled along that road.

> The man that hath no music in himself,
> Nor is not moved with concord of sweet sounds,
> Is fit for treasons, stratagems, and spoils;
> The motions of his spirit are dull as night,
> And his affections dark as Erebus.
> Let no such man be trusted.

The basis of almost all medieval music was the plain chant, a single melody sung by an individual or by a choir. This plain chant, said to have been developed by Gregory the Great, is still the foundation for much church music, especially in the Catholic and Orthodox world.

The harmonic system first appeared in the tenth century. At first the tone compositions were based most commonly upon a succession of fourths and fifths, an arrangement that sounds strange and annoying to modern men. Other intervals were soon added and the state of affairs improved considerably. It should be remarked, of course, that medieval musicians carried their new developments along contrapuntal lines rather than harmonic. They knew nothing of the modern idea of a harmony subordinate to a melody. They remained primarily interested in such things as counterpoint, an area in which England's John Dunstable obtained considerable fame in the fourteenth century.

In the Middle Ages, as in the modern world, a body of secular music arose quite apart from the Church. Harps, horns, and lyres were played with skill by both saints and rascals. Numerous rhythmical verses were recited and sung to instrumental accompaniment as the *jongleurs* assembled numerous accounts of great deeds, the *chansons de geste*. Greatest of these was the famous *Song of Roland,* mentioned in Chapter 15, that exciting tale of the mighty champion of Christendom, the chivalrous leader of the Franks who fell—so legend tells us—in a tragic hour at the hands of the Basques by the woods of Roncesvalles.

Throughout Europe in the twelfth and thirteenth centuries traveled the professional singing artists called the troubadours, singing their lyrics to the strains of the guitar, an instrument brought into Europe by the Arabs. These troubadours—and the minnesingers of Germany—sang folk songs and love songs to the ladies and to all who would listen and pay. Marie de France, Chrétien de Troyes, and many others wrote very long romances in rhymed couplets, usually complex tales of chivalry, love, and beauty. Sometimes there were epics like those about King Arthur or the Cid (Rodrigo de Bivar), shining hero of the Spanish struggle with the Moslems in the eleventh century. There were also the long allegories, in later days perhaps suitable only for drowsy maiden aunts in summer Sunday afternoons.

Not at all suitable for maiden aunts in any age were the rougher songs and darker tales called the fabliaux. These pieces of art usually had their stock characters and jests. Most of them were boisterous; some were scabrous and smutty; and most were good for a roar of male laughter and a few pennies tossed in the corner tavern or on the market square. Such popular tales, circulating through the towns and sometimes filtering out to enliven dark village evenings, are found in many times and places.

Most of the university songs of the Middle Ages are no longer sung today. Lusty lads of every college generation in our world do sing about the oysters in San Francisco Bay and the best company that ever came over from old Germany. They sing happily, which is as it should be. Perhaps, one evening, they will return for a time to the ageless swing and beat of the medieval songs. Through the doors in the evening will be heard again "Gaudeamus igitur, juvenes dum sumus" and the incomparable "Mihi est propositum, In taberna mori."

In the medieval world of prose and poetry a towering and original genius was Dante Alighieri (1265–1321). As a result of his activity in the violent arena of Florentine politics Dante was driven into exile by the supporters of Boniface VIII—"how bitter is the taste of another's bread!" For many years Dante remained one of the leading opponents of the papal claims to temporal power. His important *De Monarchia* was written to state and defend his position. In it Dante asserted that the end and purpose of all politics was nothing more and nothing less than peace among men. In his opinion, God had intended the Roman Empire to be a single sovereign state to bring and keep the peace that all men craved. Professor Franklin L. Baumer of Yale University has rightly remarked that the *De Monarchia* is "a superb statement of the medieval dream of Christian universalism."

As a politician Dante was one among many. As a poet he stood alone in his age. The lyrics in the *Vita Nuova* were finely done, but they did not promise lasting fame. Immortality came with the writing of the *Divine Comedy,* the greatest vernacular poem in Italian literature and one of the greatest in all the world. This famous poetic allegory, written in the accepted tradition, remains the most complete expression of the spiritual and intellectual climate of Dante's age. It is filled with jeweled beauty, imagination,

[60]

When Benozzo Gozzoli of Florence painted "The Journey of the Magi" in 1469 he gave faces of the Medici family to the main figures.

[61]

PLATE
XIX

The Port of Venice, detail from "The Lion of St. Mark" by Vittorio Carpaccio (c. 1465-1522)

[62] Italian Humanists, by Domenico Ghirlandaio (Florence, 1490)

[63] Sketch of a rotating bridge by Leonar Vinci (1452-1519). In the amazing noteboc this versatile genius were plans for a submar steam engine, and a flying machine.

Left: Monk writing in a scriptorium. A fifteenth ce miniature

Below: The Piccolomini Library in the Cathedral at founded by Cardinal Francesco Piccolomini (after Pope Pius II)

[64]

[65]

PLATE
XX

technical skill in language and structure, passion, sustained thought, and lofty eloquence. It is religious. It is learned. It is human.

The hero of the *Divine Comedy* is Dante, the symbol of all weary and bewildered men who have wondered about the destiny of the human soul in the universe. His spiritual guide is Beatrice, "the youngest of the angels," the personification of all beauty. She will show him, surely, how the demands of this life and the next can be reconciled.

Escorted by the poet Virgil, Dante tours the depth of Hell, where all who come abandon hope. Then he climbs the mountain of Purgatory. Then Beatrice guides him to Paradise. Dante meets and talks with many heroes and villains of the past. St. Peter agrees with Dante's theology. St. Benedict, a vivid personality, vehemently denounces the decay of the monasteries. A former pope says, quite calmly, that Boniface VIII and Clement V are coming to Hell. Meanwhile the themes and threads of patriotism and condemnation run through the verses: "Ah! servile Italy, abode of all woes, ship without pilot in wild storms, no mistress of provinces but house of ill fame. . . . Thy living sons and daughters are not free from war . . . the cities of Italy are crowded with tyrants." "See the Rome mourning in her desolate widowhood . . . by night and day she cries: 'My Caesar, why dost thou not abide with me?' " Readers who know and cherish the original text of Dante will recognize and regret the inevitable losses in translation.

Francesco Petrarch (1304–1374), the prophet of the later humanists, studied at Montpellier and Bologna and then entered the priesthood. After he had published his early verses Petrarch became increasingly opposed to some of the prevailing attitudes of his age and disdainful of his native language. More and more he turned to the past.

It was at this point that Petrarch became widely popular for several of the assertions he made and for the causes he defended. It is not wise to stress unduly his contributions to the growth of the sonnet or his reputation as a lover of Laura. These aspects of his career have their proper place, but they should be kept in it. It is more important to note that Petrarch steadily opposed the medieval philosophers and Aristotle. He did this because, he said, they "helped in no way towards a happy life." The introduction of the idea that "a happy life" in this world was one of the needed ends of philosophy was not welcomed by the defenders of medieval scholasticism. The assertions of Petrarch were an indication of the increasing secular ideals that were appearing as the influence of the Church began to be weakened. Petrarch's main inspiration was classical and pagan. He became a determined, enthusiastic, and successful student of classical learning. He tried to write like Cicero.

In the exciting last half of the fourteenth century more classical manuscripts were being discovered. More students were studying Greek and Latin.

Within a century the universities in Italy were dominated by the humanists, those men who were students and lovers of Greek and Roman letters and interested in the nature and destiny of man in this world as well as the next. They looked upon Petrarch as one of the first who pointed to the new road. He became one of the gods of the humanists. So far as their cause was concerned, they chose well.

A third man who shared and led in a shift of interest and emphasis was the learned, acute, and clever Giovanni Boccaccio (1313–1375). His most famous work was the *Decameron,* the first important piece of Italian prose. The *Decameron* is a collection of stories told in a group of men and women of the Neapolitan court who have gone out of the city to escape the great plague of 1348. Boccaccio wrote that there were those "who will say that the stories are too full of jests and merry conceits and that it ill becomes a man of weight and gravity to have written such a book." For 600 years the stories of the *Decameron,* filled with sex and excitement and sudden death, have been widely read and printed. They are tales of the faults and follies of human beings, and that is one reason they have survived.

We turn now to the greatest ballad writer of all time. François Villon was probably born in 1431 and probably died around 1489. About several chapters of his life we have no knowledge at all. We do know that he was a master of arts of the University of Paris and that he studied in preparation for admission to the Church. He lost his chance to enter when he killed a priest in a fight over a girl. We also know that Villon became a disreputable, thieving fellow who narrowly escaped hanging several times. In 1463 he was sentenced to be hanged and strangled. The sentence was changed to banishment from Paris for ten years. At this point the sources are silent. The curtain is drawn and night falls. Scholars say that Villon died about 1489 alone with his exciting memories and his poverty. We cannot be sure.

The best biography of Villon has been written by D. B. Wyndham, and the best translation of his poetry is by G. P. Cuttino. The grim and gay ballads in the *Petit Testament* and the *Grand Testament* reveal a strange spirit. Villon was a jester, a thief, and a rascal. It was this same man who would sometimes leave his roistering and dissolute companions to write about the passing vanities of the world and the ultimate sadness and mystery in all things. "A harlot was thy nurse and God thy sire."

Swinburne once said that Francois Villon was "a prince of sweet songs." True, he was that. He was also one of God's lonely men. "Myself I only know by name."

In England most of the vernacular literature in the early Middle Ages was in Norman French. The *chansons de geste* were repeated in various forms. Later there appeared the courtly and often mystical metrical romances. There were also the moralizing beast fables, the political and romantic ballads, and the coarse tales of the fabliaux, so popular on the Continent. At the same time, the Celtic legends about Arthur and Merlin appeared in both English and Norman French versions and merged in scores of folk tales. The Arthurian legend was well launched upon its amazing and prolific career. One of the outstanding English prose works of the fifteenth century was to be Sir Thomas Malory's *Morte D'Arthur,* a splendid version of the Arthur saga. Meanwhile the writing of chronicles continued apace. The most famous prose chronicles were written in the thirteenth century by Matthew Paris and Roger of Wendover. About 1205 a priest named Layamon wrote a rhymed chronicle called *Brut,* based on a legend that the Britons were descended from the Trojan Brutus and from Aeneas, founder of Rome. After Layamon several metrical chronicles appeared side by side with translations and imitations of the French.

Guilds or "companies" performed religious plays for the entertainment of the townsmen and themselves. These plays, often presented annually, were usually prepared with considerable care and enthusiasm. In the larger towns, such as Coventry, Chester, and York, the beginnings of the English drama were in part traceable to these events. From the "cycles" of mystery and morality plays and the later interludes often performed in taverns, courts, or churchyards it was not a long step to the "plays" of comedy and tragedy in the sixteenth century.

In the fourteenth century England's achievements in the making of literature were impressive. *Piers Plowman,* an earnest and sincere poem usually attributed to William Langland, was written in the vernacular. Its long and alliterative lines denounced in allegorical passages the vice and folly of the rich and preached the glory of the honest worker placing his hardened hands on the plow stilts. Also written in English were scores of tracts and anonymous poems, usually in the popular dream and allegory form. The long-submerged English language was coming swiftly into its own as Norman French declined. The English that was appearing again in polite society was supple and taut; the old inflections were gone; the vocabulary had become larger, its main flood enriched by tributary streams from many sources, especially French and Danish. The speech of the eastern midlands, of London, Oxford, Cambridge and of John Wycliffe and Geoffrey Chaucer was to be the "standard" English language.

Geoffrey Chaucer was the first of the great English poets, England's "morning star of song." He was born about 1340 and died about 1400. The bourgeois son of a wine merchant, the nimble, eager, and clear-eyed Chaucer crowded many activities into the sixty years of his life. He was a soldier in the French wars, a diplomat in Italy, a customs officer, a senior clerk. His literary achievement was thus the result of experience, shrewd observation, and travel—as well as hard work.

Chaucer's quick wit and nosing curiosity led him to experiment in new poetic forms and techniques. His work, strongly influenced by French and Italian literature, soon took second place to none in England. All this was part of the apprenticeship of the man who gave the world *The Canterbury Tales*.

Over 500 years after it was written the Prologue of *The Canterbury Tales* stirs men to wonder and admiration. In the swiftly moving camera lines of the Prologue, Chaucer precisely described the thirty pilgrims who met at the Tabard Inn in Southwark to begin their pilgrimage to the shrine of St. Thomas at Canterbury. The mixed company of the pilgrims included typical people from many classes, English to the core. There was the perfect and gentle knight, with his coat of mail; the friendly host, with his strong wine; the gross shipman and the indecent miller. There was the man of law; the lisping prioress; the five burgesses; the ploughman; the brawny, hunt-loving monk; the wanton friar; the rich doctor of physic; the hollow-cheeked "clerk of Oxenford"; the money-grabbing pardoner with his wallet on his lap full of his relics and his pardons "come from Rome all hot."

There was the buxom and amazing Wife of Bath who had been on many pilgrimages and had had five husbands: "Three of them were gode and two were badde." There was the poor parson; the merchant with his forked beard; the franklin, or small businessman: "Well loved he in the morn a sop in wine. . . . It snowed in his house of meat and drink"; the yeoman with his bow and his coat and hood of green. As the pilgrims moved at a slow pace over the rough road to Canterbury their tales revealed what they thought about the world they knew in fourteenth-century England. The tellers of the tales also told many other things about themselves. In every page of *The Canterbury Tales* there stands forth the shrewd poetic temper of Geoffrey Chaucer, his dramatic power, his gentle satire, his genial tolerance, and the universality of his sympathy.

Chapter 19

THE RENAISSANCE:
MAN IS THE MEASURE

"O supreme generosity of God the Father, O highest and most marvellous felicity of man! To him it is granted to have whatever he chooses, to be whatever he wills."

—Pico della Mirandola
Oration on the Dignity of Man

THE passion for unity," says Pieter Geyl in his *Use and Abuse of History,* "is a passion fundamentally antagonistic to history." Professor Geyl is surely right. It is true that many famous men have built neat and unified systems and philosophies of history: St. Augustine, Bossuet, Carlyle, Grotius, Hegel, Macaulay, Marx, Nietzsche, Spengler, Toynbee, and scores of others. Nevertheless, their structures have not been founded solidly and entirely upon historical facts. Their beliefs and interpretations are of continuing interest; but what they have done remains "fundamentally antagonistic to history."

The natural desire for neatness, unity, and full explanations is also evident in the works of many men who cultivated small gardens and had no desire to found widely ranging systems of thought and theory. About the period of the European Renaissance, for instance, there has been published a wealth of fact and ideas. Some scholars of earlier days attempted to shape their conclusions to show that the years of the Renaissance were fused into a unified whole with clear values and characteristics all their own. Familiar themes and theories were monotonously repeated. Tradition and hallowed repetition have often been responsible for blocking fruitful innovation and diversity.

Modern students of the Renaissance period in European history have not been content to bow before the judgments of their fathers. Many of them have asserted clearly and firmly that the enormous expansion of our knowledge makes more realistic and useful conclusions possible. They admit that there are extreme complications in their problems. Sometimes they have been baffled by what they have found. Sometimes they have been trapped by their own interpretations and challenged by those of other men. The great debates continue in the journals and in the corridors and in the seminars. Passionate disputes multiply. It is an exciting part of the academic world. Meanwhile, the general reader, that uncommitted amateur, is fascinated by the serried ranks of fact and the shining steel of logic.

Several contemporary historians have written wisely and well about the nature and meaning of the Renaissance. For instance, Hans Baron's study of the relations between humanism and the civic life of Florence will remain a milestone on the road of modern Renaissance scholarship. Readers who are interested in a full and shrewd analysis of the varying views of the historians about the Renaissance will find no better book than Wallace K. Ferguson's *The Renaissance in Historical Thought: Five Centuries of Interpretation.* Professor Ferguson belongs to no cult or school. He does believe, in the words of Lecomte du Noüy, that "simplification is always arbitrary and tends to separate us from reality."

Dangers and difficulties have multiplied as a result of the numerous attempts to define the word "Renaissance." It is hard to say, without fear of wise and wide disapproval, when the Renaissance began and when it ended. Even about its essential characteristics there is no full and firm agreement.

The "classic" conception of the Renaissance, still repeated in many books, asserted that the years of the Renaissance marked a revolt of the individual spirit and mind, stimulated by a revival of ancient culture, against the asceticism, collectivism, sterility, and iron authority of the Middle Ages. In the eyes of the literary enthusiast John Addington Symonds, for instance, the Middle Ages were centuries of inaction and apathy. The Renaissance, on the contrary, was an exciting time, "the first act in the drama of liberty." Symonds, like France's Jules Michelet, liked romance and drama. He liked to see the stage filled with things happening. He was quite sure that he could see them happening in the Renaissance. The imaginative John Addington Symonds was a creative artist, not an historian.

The most famous statement of the "classic" conclusions is still to be found in Jakob Burckhardt's *Civilization of the Renaissance in Italy* (1860). The Swiss Burckhardt attempted to describe the inner spirit of the Renaissance in Italy from the fourteenth to the sixteenth century. The first three parts of his masterpiece describe the characteristics of the state and the individual in the Renaissance and the nature and results of the revived interest in antiquity. The last three parts explain the ways in which the factors discovered and described in the earlier sections influenced the social, moral, political, and cultural life of Italy in the Renaissance period. Despite the acknowledged skill and shrewdness of Burckhardt, one of the chief objections, widely held and frequently repeated, is that his Renaissance is too frozen and static. "It has no history, no rise or development." Much controversy still gathers and flashes about the name and work of Burckhardt.

In the previous chapter it was remarked that there have recently been many conflicting interpretations of the Renaissance. There are learned scholars who deny the appearance of any sudden movement that began in Italy in the fourteenth century and spread over Western Europe in the fifteenth. They only see evolution and continuity in a long development from the Middle Ages to the twentieth century. Ernst Cassirer and others have asserted that it is futile to try to draw a dividing line between the Middle Ages and the Renaissance. One group of historians would extend the Renaissance back to include the Middle Ages. Another pushes the Middle Ages ahead to include the Renaissance.

Whatever the merits of the numerous arguments may be, it is clear in the light of modern research that the Renaissance was not a great watershed suddenly emerging in human history. It was not so decisive an event as earlier historians believed. There was no really vivid and violent contrast between tradition and innovation. The once sharp lines drawn between the Middle Ages and the Renaissance have been increasingly blurred by recent research. Vital aspects of medieval attitudes and thought continued throughout the Renaissance in the midst of new men and new ideas. The roots of the Renaissance are now known to have stretched far back into the medieval past.

It is also wise to remember that what is true about the Renaissance in one century may not be true in another. The evidence that is found about conditions in one place in Europe may have no validity a hundred miles away. Each country had its own problems and its own answers. The path and impact of the Renaissance differed in character and time from land to land. "No single set of dates is satisfactory everywhere." Some regions absorbed many elements from Renaissance Italy; some took very few. The humanism of Italy, for instance, was quite different from the humanism of northern Europe.

Among the chief characteristics of the Renaissance were the growth of interest in the achievements of the classical civilizations of Greece and Rome; an increasing concern with human activities and human motives, the "self-discovery, self-realization and self-exaltation" of man; a marked secularization of thought and culture; an accelerated growth of economic power and the monetary exchange system called capitalism; a tremendous interest in the tools and ends of education and the development of critical minds; a growing national consciousness—especially in northern Europe—and an increased centralization of nation-states; a series of magnificent achievements in art and letters, the like of which had not been seen since the golden days of Athens.

The achievements of Greece and Rome were of special interest to the men called humanists. During the Renaissance centuries these men were, or tried or pretended to be, classical scholars. They were also usually sympathetic students of human nature. For them the proper study of mankind was man. Because an enthusiasm for classical studies and a curiosity about man were supposed to have a tendency to undermine faith in the Church and its teachings, the humanists were frequently looked upon as free thinkers, skeptics, or agnostics. They were often accused, then and later, of falling into the ancient error of making relatives into absolutes, the human into the divine.

Although we usually associate the humanists with the Renaissance, the name and character of humanism has an earlier origin. The men we may call the original humanists were the individuals in the Middle Ages who studied pre-Christian literature, art, and history, particularly the human achievements of Greek and Roman poets, philosophers, orators, and historians. Hence these classical scholars were named humanists as opposed to the divines, the priests and monks whose chief study was theology. It should be remarked, of course, that the line between humanists and divines was soon blotted away. Many churchmen became humanists in an increasingly secular age. Pope Leo X, for example, made several humanists cardinals. One prelate warned another not to read the epistles of St. Paul because they might corrupt the classical purity of his prose style.

The Renaissance humanists belittled, denounced, and deplored what they called the gross ignorance, the credulous superstition, the sleep and darkness of the Middle Ages. As they scoffed, they failed to realize how great was their legacy from the medieval centuries. Like their revered master Petrarch they turned back to the classical world, to Cicero, Seneca, Livy, Sallust, Virgil, Plato, Aristotle. With enthusiasm and energy they sought to find and use the works of Greece and Rome. With excitement, and often with understanding, they studied and interpreted and frequently tried to imitate the classical writers. We have many instances of their jeweled love of "words in their best order." One man of the Renaissance asked: "Is it not a polished and eloquent, or at least a classical and chaste style, which confers an immortal reputation on an author?" An affirmative reply to the question appears again and again in clear and unequivocal terms.

The humanists were not solely concerned, of course, with classical style and literature to the exclusion of everything else. If their main endeavor had been to ape the classics there would have been but a narrow place for the rip tide of vernacular literature that was one of the glories of the Renaissance. The eager humanists, sharply conscious that they were the makers of a revolution, wanted to find new maps and anchors in the past, to grasp the treasures, use the ideas, locate the reasons for the greatness of Greece and Rome. History was therefore placed first among the necessary studies by humanists like Leonardi Bruni. To them history was a subject "which must not on any account be neglected by one who aspires to true cultivation. For it is our duty to understand the origins of our history and its development, and the achievements of peoples and kings."

The humanists also wanted to transform and broaden the Petrarchan inheritance and to create and build. They, too, would plunge to the ocean bed of the human spirit and search its caverns. They, too, would look out over magic casements and shape and paint splendid and moving things of beauty and power. Other men in other times might paddle by the shore, but they would swim far out in the flashing seas.

These men of the Renaissance looked back to the golden age of Greece and Rome and forward to a golden age of their own that posterity might respect and admire. In their work and writing they created a tradition, the tradition that they had discovered and revived the classics in the centuries following the feeble and deaf Middle Ages and had thus been responsible for a rebirth of art and letters, a true Renaissance, a decisive shift in the winds of thought and feeling and the direction of cultural history. We have seen that what they asserted about themselves was seldom challenged in the centuries that followed. Their words were strong and their claims were great. Many of our modern views about the whole course of human history first appeared in the humanist concepts of the Renaissance.

With most of the ideas and aims of the humanists the masses were not much concerned. Countless men and women were busy in the hard and narrow tasks of their daily lives. Sometimes the skies were leaden and dreary, sometimes bright. There was hay to be mowed, wine to be made, babies to be fed, disease and death to be endured. From horizon to horizon it is always the same. By the side of the eminent dwell the obscure in the unbroken links of the generations of man.

Most of the excitement and zeal in the rediscovery of the past was among the princes and popes, the aristocracy, and the rich burghers. It was they who built the libraries, spurred the search for classical manuscripts, gave currency to the new ideas, and became patrons to the scholars and artists. These were the men who encouraged such things as translations and teaching, the growth of civic humanism in the city-states, the interpretation of Greek and Roman societies with a steady emphasis upon their cultural values and concepts. They subsidized and applauded the new classicism that appeared in the arts. They delighted in encouraging and joining groups of cultivated men who gathered and worked and talked in the princely courts and fine houses. The creative artists and the intellectuals were often paid and fed and wined. The leaders in Renaissance society believed that outstanding men busy in the world of art and intellect deserved both money and honor. Sometimes, of course, there was but a precarious relationship between the belief and the performance.

Cosimo de' Medici founded the Platonic Academy at Florence. The humanist Pope Nicholas V started another at Rome. The Florentine Academy reached the height of its fame and power under Lorenzo the Magnificent—he died in 1492, the year that the Borgia Alexander VI was elected pope and Christopher Columbus first sailed westward. One of the bold projects of the Academy was to make a synthesis of all the philosophical ideas and systems ever conceived and constructed by man. Scores of scholars and detectives gathered and catalogued material from the sages of the past, from the Greeks, Egyptians, Arabs, Romans, Hebrews. It was an ambitious plan, conceived in an age of optimism. Enthusiastic men often do not understand the difficulties of what they try to do. Zeal and youth, of course, are often found together. In 1486, for instance, Pico della Mirandola, then twenty-three years old, published his *Conclusiones*. He said that he hoped to put into "a coordinated whole" all of the "annexed nine hundred theses relating to dialectics, ethics, physics, magic, mathematics." Pico della Mirandola never finished his task. The men of the Platonic Academy at Florence never made a happy synthesis of all the philosophical ideas of their predecessors. It is a comment upon them and upon their age that they thought these things possible. Their reach exceeded their grasp; but we cannot condemn them for that. Men of vigorous imagination are often undisciplined. If the men of discipline had always prevailed the world would have been the worse.

Some plans were more successful. In Venice, Aldus Manutius began in 1493 the project of printing the Greek classics. The neat and handy products of the Aldine press were soon sold over most of western Europe. In the "New Academy" of Aldus Manutius a group of scholars prepared texts for the press. The large sales had two significant results: there was a wider diffusion of classical knowledge among the upper levels of Italian society; the professional classicists found that they no longer had any monopoly of learning. The achievements of Aldus Manutius must have brought special pain to the pedants of his day. The sensitive ego of a pedant must have been bruised to know that the precious jewels of knowledge were being loosely tossed about and profaned by quite ordinary men in the markets and the forums.

The ideal man of the Renaissance climate of opinion was cultured and versatile, active on the human scene, busy for the public good with "the courtier's, scholar's, soldier's eye, tongue, sword." His character had been shaped upon the model of a superior citizen of ancient Greece or Rome. Throughout the pages of Renaissance writers we encounter themes and attitudes to life that soon become familiar: the importance of high-minded action; the necessity of knowing and using the humanistic wisdom of the ancient world; the significance of the basic dignity and worth of man; the grounds for optimism about human nature; the value of aiming at the development of all the human faculties; the rewards of a life of reason. Said Erasmus, the prince of the humanists: "I affirm that, as the instinct of a dog is to hunt, of the bird to fly, of the horse to gallop, so the natural bent of man is to philosophy and right conduct. . . . What is the proper nature of man? Surely it is to live the life of reason, for reason is the peculiar prerogative of man."

Before anyone could hope to become a refined Renaissance gentleman he must obtain what the humanists called—we have kept the words—a "liberal education." A man exposed to the "liberal arts" would be fearless and free, unhampered by the fetters of formality, ignorance, and superstition that had supposedly characterized the Middle Ages. The theme of "freedom" was often repeated. For instance, the historian Leonardo Bruni of Arezzo, probably the first true humanist of the Renaissance, wrote a literary, patriotic, and secular *History of the Florentine People* in which he said that the republic of Florence owed its glory and greatness "to the moral qualities engendered by freedom."

Good letters would lead, surely, to a good life. "We call those studies liberal which are worthy of a free man." "Men are not born, they are made." "Given time, education can work miracles in the individual and in the world at large." "Handle the wax while it is soft, mould the clay while it is moist, dye the fleece before it gathers stains." Education was the new magical element that would touch and change the powerful and the poor.

The poor would not be touched or changed so much as the upper classes. Renaissance ideas of education were essentially aristocratic. The ideal man was not only the good citizen; he was also usually the leader, the governor, the successful "complete" and "universal" man, the unusual fellow who was able to seize and hold power, dignity, and virtue all at the same time. The themes and creeds of the numerous treatises on education stress the ways in which such men could be made. Some of these books are still read and discussed today in the Western world: Baldassare Castiglione's *The Book of the Courtier,* Sir Thomas Elyot's *The Governor,* Henry Peacham's *The Complete Gentleman,* large parts of Sir Thomas More's *Utopia* and Desiderius Erasmus' *The Education of a Christian Prince.*

It was probably to be expected that much education during the Renaissance would be concerned with practical questions. Many old roads were being broken up. New ones were being blasted through the rocks and cut through the trees. Many traditions and customs were crumbling. The Church was losing power and prestige. The bustling towns had little concern with the dying world of feudalism. The humanists, as we are well aware, placed the emphasis upon man and his world, his tasks, his triumphs and tragedies. They were less concerned than some men of the Middle Ages with abstract problems or the contemplative or collectivistic life. They were interested in what most men call the practical problems of the daily world, in the active and individual doings of human beings. These were the days of the practical bankers, the practical despots in Italy, the practical capitalistic entrepreneurs

—those princes of gold now sat beside the princes of blood. The society and culture were increasingly secular, much concerned with success in the struggles of this world. When political and economic opportunity beckoned, what foolish man would falter or flee? "To be weak is miserable, Doing or suffering." There were always exceptions to the rule; but this was the rule.

In such circumstances it was not at all surprising that to the lay intelligentsia "philosophy meant ethics" and history provided "useful examples of virtue and vice." Nor is it to be wondered that art contained less allegory and more naturalism or that there was much more personal poetry, more individual painting and drama with much tears, fury, action, violent death.

In the field of education some men asserted that it was their first business to teach. Others insisted that their main task was to study and do what is now called "research." The dilemma of many professors today is suggested by a sentence written by Erasmus, one of the greatest teachers of any age, to the eminent French scholar Guillaume Budé: "You have preferred to be understood by the learned, I, if I can, by the many; your aim is to conquer, mine to teach or persuade." Several practical problems and conclusions of the classroom are of interest to the modern reader. In Roger Ascham's *The Scholemaster,* for example, we find the famous distinction between "quick wits" and "hard wits." Ascham said: "Quick wits commonly be apt to take, unapt to keep; soon hot and desirous of this and that; as cold and soon weary of the same again; more quick to enter speedily than to pierce far; even like over sharp tools whose edge be very soon turned." He concluded that it was the student of slower comprehension, "the hard wit who taketh the lesson not so speedily" who "both for learning and the whole course of study proveth always the best."

Many men of the age of the Renaissance believed that they were committed in the field of their interests and studies to a critical appraisal of all the evidence they could find. It was their duty, they said, to see that they were never charged with a blind acceptance of myths and wrongheaded conclusions. Numerous humanists attacked several inherited teachings of theology and philosophy. Some developed their own interpretations of history, and their pages, quite naturally, stressed the achievements of men through the centuries. They usually avoided the medieval insistence upon the hand of God moving in all things, punishing the wicked and helping the faithful in a world that was but the entrance to Paradise. To them the facts were clear: in this world the wicked sometimes flourished like the green bay tree; the destinies of men were mainly of their own making, fortunately or otherwise. The writing of Renaissance history was thus done by men who had a secular attitude; they had no use for flawed medieval spectacles or a predominantly theological world view.

There was some excellent critical scholarship. For instance, Rome's Lorenzo

Valla (1405–1457) discovered that the famous "Donation of Constantine," one of the main foundations of the papal claims to temporal power, was a forgery. Other humanists, like Marsilio Ficino (1433–1499) of the Medici Academy, constructed a philosophy of Christianity upon the basis of Neo-Platonism—not an easy task. Still others accepted and defended the "Aristotle-Christian universe of purpose and striving." Said Francis Bacon: "A little philosophy inclineth men's minds to atheism, but depth in philosophy brings men's minds about to religion." Some men were indifferent to religion. Some were skeptics. "The thorough skeptic is a dogmatist," said Alfred North Whitehead. "He enjoys the delusion of complete futility." Some men made the mistake of being atheists and their mistake was as long as eternity. On the other hand, a later passage in this chapter will describe some Christian humanists and mystics. They are never far away.

It is always dangerous to try to compress into a few paragraphs the numerous ideas, the altering perspectives, and the great changes in environment that appeared through several generations. For instance, the writer who leaves the impression that he is labeling the Renaissance as pagan or irreligious omits too much and says too little. Certainly there were some pagans among the educated men of the Renaissance; there were probably some in the Middle Ages. "Where God hath a temple," said Robert Burton (1577–1640), "the devil will have a chapel." The historian who stresses unduly the immoral and irreligious aspects of the Renaissance is writing perilous nonsense. "He who tries to prove too much, proves nothing." Color is fine, but perspective is better.

The conclusions of humanist critics inevitably led to demands for reform —reform of the state, reform "of the head and members of the Church." What Christian, for instance, could approve of the Borgia Pope Alexander VI (1492–1503)? Christian humanists like Desiderius Erasmus, John Colet, and Sir Thomas More castigated the clergy and put forward realistic reform programs. They were not challenging Christian teaching; they were denouncing many aspects of the life of the clergy and the institution of the Church. These are two quite different things. They should not be confused.

In the eighteenth century Voltaire wrote at length about the shining culture, the aggressive individualism, and the collapse of morality in the Renaissance. Of the court of Francis I, proud king of France, he said: "Courtesy glittered in the midst of crime; it was a robe of gold and silk covered with blood." In one sentence he described the Italy he thought he saw: "Intelligence, superstition, atheism, masquerades, poetry, treason, devotion, poison, assassination, a few great men, an infinite number of clever and yet unfortunate scoundrels: that is what Italy was!" Nineteenth-century historians stressed these themes and quoted Voltaire. His conclusions were repeated so much that men came to believe them. It is seldom difficult to accept the conclusions of a man when they meet and mesh with your own preconceived and emotionally held ideas. Most twentieth-century scholars agree that Voltaire's gleaming prose is indeed magnificent, but it is not history.

Meanwhile exuberant cults and academies flourished and faded. The vigorous and vehement humanists pushed forward their crusades and continued their disputes, sometimes with words and sometimes with fists and swords. On one occasion, we are told, there exploded a violent quarrel between two passionate Italian humanists about the relative merits of Scipio Africanus and Julius Caesar. It is difficult for an individual of the twentieth century to understand or appreciate the reasons for the excitement roused by such issues among Renaissance men. Modern quarrels, we may insist, are more sane and sensible. Our descendants, of course, will be of a somewhat different opinion. In any event, there appeared in the Renaissance days much controversy. One contemporary said: "There are the most infamous libels that have ever seen the light; there is no sort of vituperation which the antagonists do not vomit forth against each other, no obscenity or roguery of which they are not mutually accused."

The excitement was not limited to the disputes of the humanists. Demands for reform and repentance, mentioned briefly in the previous pages, were not only made by quiet and effective men like More and Erasmus but also by peculiar evangelical firebrands like Savonarola, Dominican monk of San Marco, gaunt prophet of doom. When a deadly plague struck and a French army under Charles VIII invaded Italy in 1494 Savonarola spoke like a Hebrew prophet. He persuaded the people of Florence to drive out Piero, the Medici ruler, and to welcome Charles VIII. After Charles took Naples, Savonarola expected him to turn against the immoral Pope Alexander VI. At that point Savonarola was excommunicated. Soon the Florentines turned against the violent friar. He was burned at the stake in 1498.

The events described in many a book as marking "the rise of the individual" were certainly at hand. Perhaps, of course, the "individual" of the Renaissance was as hard to locate as the "common man" of the twentieth century. Perhaps, too, he began to "rise" a little before the years of the Renaissance. Nevertheless, the humanists of the Renaissance age, as remarked earlier, did show an intense interest in the deeds and dreams and nature of man, that creature who, in Renaissance literature, was both a beast and a god.

In the tumultuous chapters of Renaissance history are written the names of many remarkable individuals who found life good, who rejoiced in it, and who felt an urgent need to express their separate personalities in as many ways as possible. They tried to be versatile and cultivated men, to serve the state and society well, and, if possible, to achieve something of consequence in the arts, the glory and delight of man.

Many of these men were uncommonly capable. Most of them seem to have possessed a real and complete spontaneity, always a useful index to the quality of a culture. "Energy is an eternal delight," said one of them. The display of energy, the search for action, and the delight in novelty were all in accord with the frequently stated aims of the Renaissance humanists.

Too much has been said, and most unwisely, about the rebellious aspects of the Renaissance and about its alleged immoral individualism. Whenever the spirits of men are really roused, whenever thousands of them realize that they are indeed individuals, then it is folly to expect that they will be wholly moral and completely Christian unless the excitement and the revival have essentially spiritual bases. "The lust of eye and pride of life" is a part of the ancient heritage of man that some may deplore but none can deny. In certain societies it has whirled and flamed for all to see. In others it has been discreetly shielded by doors and night. Several nineteenth-century writers, for instance, concluded that the men of the Renaissance were busy everywhere replacing restraint by anarchy. What they wrote was no more true than their insistence that their own society was padded with virtue and secure against the darker sins, at least in the respectable parts of their world. England's upper-class Victorians, for example, politely preferred the genteel language of their famous parlors. Nevertheless, they had not forgotten the strategy and tactics of the boudoir. To some of them discretion was the better part of virtue.

From the charming hills of Savoy to the Straits of Messina the spirit of the Renaissance in Italy spread and conquered. It was indeed an astounding age of razor-edge excitement, a lively panorama of patrons and politicians, soldiers and artists, explorers and poets, humanist popes and princes, conflicts and tensions, violence and virtue and vice. Many men who lived then and later have described the Renaissance world in words of mingled confusion and ecstasy. It is easy to forgive them for that.

Lively and exciting men and deeds sometimes obscure the deep and quiet surges of the tides of power that are actually responsible for the achievements of advanced civilizations. The really important ingredients of high cultures are usually not exciting or dramatic at all. Casual observers see the glitter and the glory. Even the sober scholar, dredging for facts and ideas, may overlook or forget certain realities.

The strength or weakness of a culture is always dictated by economic conditions. A thriving and highly developed economy invariably possesses these major characteristics: urban centers, technological advances, specialized tools, division of labor, expansion of trade, cooperative effort, freedom of choice for the individual, gains in production per capita, and "the investment of present energies for the purpose of future gains." Only vigorous economic progress can produce an economic surplus. Such an economic surplus is a necessary basis of any important cultural achievement. No advanced form of culture can prevail in a beleaguered and precarious subsistence economy.

In earlier pages it was said that the Renaissance centuries, marking the slow transition from medieval to modern modes of life and thought, were filled with men whose attitudes and actions were directly connected with practical problems, with the world of men and things. During these years, too, the number of educated laymen steadily increased. Into government, law, business, and diplomacy they brought their secular attitudes. There was an increased pace in the rise of the bourgeoisie, the artisan and mercantile classes. Money and brains came to bolster bourgeois ambition and enterprise. They counted for as much, sometimes, as birth and titles. In several lands—especially in England—the nobility and the higher bourgeoisie began to marry and merge, a practice that has since continued. Meanwhile the men of the bourgeoisie traded and bargained and worked and grew stronger. In larger sectors of society their values came to prevail. Shrewd and calculating men of the bourgeois class have always liked order, management, and the gathering and use of money for profit.

In Renaissance Italy there was much money and much profit. The fifteenth and sixteenth centuries marked a real commercial revolution. By land and sea the tides of trade increased. As the demand for money mounted, the interest rates went up. The bankers, who were both moneylenders and money-changers, grew fat and comfortable.

By the side of the glories of the Sistine Chapel and the new humanism stand the complex and turbulent changes in the world of trade and technology, the achievements in the realms of exploration, mathematics, music, and science. The tale of the Renaissance contains far more than the story of art and architecture, humanism and heresy, the coasts strewn with the wreckage of spontaneous sonnets and calculated love affairs. Podesta and prince scanned with shrewd eyes the word of Machiavelli or stayed awake thinking about the audited statements of the bankers.

Much of Italy's prosperity and many of its consequences were made possible by such veteran cities of trade as Venice, Florence, Milan, Genoa, Lucca, and Pisa. Venice, for example, still controlled a centralized empire of commerce and industry. Her galleys furrowed many waters. Her government was efficient, respected, and quite undemocratic. The city of Milan stood at the end of the trade routes that ran through the Alps into northern Europe—a strategic spot. There the Visconti family ruled until 1477. Then the Sforzas came to hold power until 1535, the year the Spaniards began a period of control that lasted for nearly 200 years.

Florence was another famous city of bankers and merchants. Here were once the medieval banking houses of the Bardi and Peruzzi families. In 1434 the strong control of Cosimo de' Medici ended the battles of factions and the long feuds. Peace—the peace imposed by power—had arrived. For sixty years the Medici family ruled Florence as despots, moving and managing quietly behind the doors and curtains of the city. The name of Lorenzo the Magnificent, who ruled from 1469 to 1492, appears again and again in any history of the Renaissance.

One of the most famous sons of Florence was Niccolò Machiavelli (1469–1527), historian, philosopher, master of Italian prose, statesman. The chief parts of Machiavelli's political theories, the cause of centuries of dispute, are to be found in his *Discourses on Livy* and the twenty-six brief chapters of *The Prince*. In *The Prince* (1513), a handbook giving advice to a ruler about the arts of political success, Machiavelli explained that although he preferred a republican form of government he was convinced that only a strong ruler could unite the Italian peninsula into one state. Machiavelli was a patriot. For "the common good" he wanted a unified Italy, free from foreign rule. A strong prince could repel foreign armies, outwit hostile and cunning kings and diplomats, and maintain peace and order at home. Power, said Machiavelli, must be maintained and extended, by the use, if necessary, of any kinds of devices, fair or foul. Machiavelli deliberately, plainly, and frankly stated his case. To him it was a case and doctrine that recognized the inescapable facts in a ruthless world, a world of force and fraud. The end justified the means. Power was its own defense, its own justification, its own excuse. Power, in fact, made its own laws, its own state morality in which there was no place for justice or mercy. If you want a naked, unashamed, and cynical body of consistent doctrine for a leader of a state, Machiavelli will provide it.

> A prudent ruler ought not to keep faith when by doing so it would be against his interest, and when the reasons which made him bind himself no longer exist. If men were all good, this precept would not be a good one; but as they are all bad and would not observe their faith with you, so you are not bound to keep faith with them. . . . it must be understood that a prince, and especially a new prince, cannot observe all those things which are considered good in men, being often obliged, in order to maintain the state, to act against faith, against charity, against humanity, and against religion.

Venice, Milan, and Florence were the strongest city-states in Italy. Each had added many square miles of territory around its walls. Each had economic strength. The triumphs of the Renaissance, a magnificent chapter in the slow ascent of man, were made possible by a coincidence of forces, one of the greatest of which was economic power.

Renaissance Italy was thus a virile land of strong and prosperous city-states, energy and enterprise, eager and passionate humanists. Despite invading armies and political turmoil there was a gleaming constellation of brilliant artists, makers of meaning and beauty. Some of their honored and familiar names suggest to us by their very sound the flight of man's spirit beyond the flux of immediate and transient things: Cellini, Giorgione, Leonardo da Vinci, Michelangelo, Raphael, Titian, Tintoretto.

Among the concentrated and dazzling achievements of the High Renaissance were those of the versatile and talented Leonardo da Vinci (1452–1519), a painter, sculptor, architect, natural philosopher, engineer, poet, musician, man of science. His fascinating notebooks show us still the variety of his interests, his numerous experiments, his consuming curiosity, and the flood of his ideas. Of many of those ideas nothing ever came. It would take many men many lives to do all the things that Leonardo hoped one day to do. His notebooks are filled with the results of his studies in light and shade, human anatomy, geometry, mechanics, and scores of other things. On one page, for example, is a sketch of a galloping horse. On another is an ingenious device to be used in a project to improve the irrigation of the Lombard plain. On a third are architectural plans for completing Milan Cathedral—Leonardo lived at Milan at the Sforza court from 1483 to 1499.

So far as his artistic work was concerned it seems that Leonardo was hard to satisfy. In Giorgio Vasari's *Lives of Seventy of the Most Eminent Painters, Sculptors, and Architects* (1550) we read that "Leonardo, with his profound intelligence of art, commenced various undertakings, many of which he never completed, because it appeared to him that the hand could never give due perfection to the object or purpose which he had in thought, or beheld in his imagination."

Fortunately for posterity Leonardo did complete several paintings. Greatest of these are the marvelously executed "The Virgin of the Rocks," the haunting "Mona Lisa," and "The Last Supper," painted on the walls of Santa Maria delle Grazie in Milan. In recent years several experts have attempted, with considerable success, to repair a part of the damage done to "The Last Supper" through the centuries by dampness and mildew.

A second giant and genius was the Florentine Michelangelo (1475–1564). Like many a genius before and after Michelangelo had no smooth road to travel. His nature, it seemed, was always to be at war with circumstances. He suffered poverty. He was plagued in later days by greedy relatives. Hostile and jealous rivals intrigued against him. He often had difficulty getting paid for his work. He was frequently tormented by the dark moods and storms of his volcanic being. He quarreled with a great many people. The confused tale of his relations with Pope Julius II, for instance, is filled with successive estrangements and reconciliations. His associates found him moody, masterful, formidable, fiery, headstrong, sensitive—accurate adjectives could be multiplied. Michelangelo was not a lovable man.

The personality of Michelangelo was one thing; his intense and eloquent art was another. Friend and foe—at least those who were capable of understanding the mighty creative power of Michelangelo's genius—admired with awe the magnificence of his technical execution. They recognized, for example, that the hands that had carved the colossal statue of David out of a huge block of marble had achieved a perfection unequaled since the Greeks.

In Michelangelo's work there is much that reminds the viewer of the attitude of the Greek dramatists: the dignity and the tragic fate of man are the only legitimate subjects for the hand and mind and heart of the artist. No man can know the thoughts and emotions of Michelangelo as he energetically shaped the twisted agony of the two "Slaves"—they are now in the Louvre. Every man who has stood before them can understand how feeble and frail are the resources of language when one seeks to describe their compelling power. Or consider the famous "Moses" in the church of San Pietro in Vincoli in Rome. Moses has come down from the mountain to find the Israelites worshiping the golden calf. The whole bearded and draped figure is alive with menace and indignation and anger.

For the tombs of the Medici in Florence, Michelangelo carved several figures representing such abstractions as Despair and Sorrow. Each conveys, with great emotional power, a sense of the tragedy of the struggles of man, his misery and his pain. For his own tomb Michelangelo made the famous Pietà, a statue of the Virgin Mary weeping over the body of Christ.

Not all of Michelangelo's work has survived. For instance, he made a bronze statue of Julius II that was placed in Bologna. When the people of that city rose against Julius II they destroyed the statue. The men of Bologna lost the cause for which they fought; some lost their lives; and all the world lost the bronze made by Michelangelo.

The chief interest of Michelangelo was in sculpture. He asserted this fact when Julius II asked him to paint a series of frescoes for the great Sistine Chapel. Finally, however, he began the tremendous task. Frequently impeded and often enraged, Michelangelo labored on. All of the work upon the vast ceiling design he did lying upon his back, hour after hour, month after month. More than 400 figures were placed upon the 6,000 square feet of ceiling. At the end of nearly five years the painting was done, a work of unsurpassed variety and grandeur, depicting epic hours in the long history of mankind: "God Dividing the Light from the Darkness," "God Creating the Earth," "The Creation of Adam," "The Fall of Man," "The Deluge," and similar events. One of the frescoes, called "The Last Judgment," was painted about 25 years later on the wall behind the altar. It is probably the most famous picture in the world. "Good painting," said Michelangelo, "is in a sense an act of devotion, for nothing enobles the soul and invites piety so much as the achievement of perfection. And perfection, of course, approaches God and unites with him."

The fame of Michelangelo rests mainly upon his work as a painter and a sculptor. He was also a poet and architect—he designed, for instance, the dome of St. Peter's. Shortly before he died in 1564—the year that William Shakespeare and Galilei Galileo were born—he wrote a description of himself that suggests the darker passages of Chapter 12 of Ecclesiastes and the irony of Voltaire or a Jonathan Swift: "I live alone, confined like the pith in a tree. My teeth are rotten like the keys of a musical instrument; my face is a scarecrow; in one ear a spider spins its web; in the other a cricket chirps all night; my catarrh rattles in my throat and will not let me sleep. This is the end to which art, which proves my glory, has brought me."

The genius of men like Leonardo and Michelangelo is not easily matched. Many lesser artists—some of them able and famous—lived and worked in the cities of Italy. In the so-called Venetian school of Italian painting three men were the leaders: Titian (1477–1576), Giorgione (1478–1510), and Tintoretto (1518–1594). Unlike the painters of Florence the men of Venice were not mainly interested in religion, philosophy, or psychology. Their secularized work was filled with the spirit of human pride in Venice, the love of lavish display, color, and rich and splendid things. It was thus not calculated to appeal to the mind but to the senses. The colors are bright and the ladies beautiful. There are many jewels and silks and satins. Even the landscapes suggest a silver and golden richness. Venetian painting contains a sensuality never seen before but often since.

Among the popular Italian artists of the Renaissance was Raphael Sanzio (1483–1520). His fluent painting, filled with color, is charming, simple, sentimental, and usually superficial. He tried and failed to capture the dynamic power of Leonardo da Vinci, an artist he greatly admired. Admiration was not enough. There had to be something more. Raphael must be numbered among the artists who almost succeeded in being great.

The versatility and skill of many other Italian artists could be described and discussed and illustrated if this book were about the Renaissance alone and not about all the world and times of man. The achievements, for example, of such men as Leo Battista Alberti (1404–1472)—one of the "universal men" of the age—and of Benvenuto Cellini (1500–1571), goldsmith, craftsman, and story-teller extraordinary, must be passed by with this brief mention and this pruned tribute. Upon writers and readers alike the demands of time and space and patience are relentless and constant.

The architects of the Renaissance departed far from the days and dreams of the Gothic masters. During the Renaissance years there was a marked attention to classical architecture, a great deal of individualistic creation, much borrowing from many sources, a strong interest in the building of secular structures, including palaces and town halls, and an almost unbroken development in the arts of decoration, such as the varied use of the arcade, the balustrade, and the cornice. Decorative skills and devices were the most important Renaissance contributions to architecture.

Emphasis upon secular and individualistic building started around the end of the fourteenth century with the work of Filippo Brunelleschi (1377–1446). His buildings in Florence mark the revival of Roman forms with the typical massiveness and horizontal lines, pediments over the windows, round arches, decorations. Men like the architect Bramante (1444–1514) carried on the Roman tradition—he died before his plans for constructing St. Peter's were carried through, and Michelangelo, as remarked earlier, made the great dome, a step that Bramante would not have approved. Andrea Palladio of Vicenza (1518–1580), a great student of classical architecture, wrote *Four Books on Architecture*, a book that has been translated into almost every European language. Palladio built many palaces, villas, and churches. His most famous work in Vicenza and Venice includes the Capuchin church of San Giorgio Maggiore and several large palaces by the Grand Canal. One of Palladio's students was England's Inigo Jones, who was mainly responsible for bringing the revived classical or Palladian style into England. The first fully classical building in England was the Banqueting Hall built in Whitehall by Inigo Jones for James I.

The sixteenth century has been called the golden age of music. One of the masters of polyphonic music was Italy's Giovanni da Palestrina (1525–1594). In Burgundy and Flanders, regions famous for their achievements in the fifteenth century, much fine work was still being produced, all of it ably discussed in Gustav Reece's *Music in the Renaissance*. All over western Europe appeared the new instruments called the violin, the harpsichord, and the spinet. The power and growth of English music was astounding. Beautiful English madrigals excited the praise and delight of all Europe. The bright genius of William Byrd, greatest of English composers, of Thomas Tallis, of Orlando Gibbons, of Thomas Morley, placed London among the exciting musical capitals of Europe. "The isle is full of noises, sounds and sweet airs, that give delight and hurt not." Meanwhile, some German authorities claimed that Orlandus Lassus, court choirmaster at Munich, was at least the equal of Palestrina.

Miracle and morality plays slowly gave way to a secular drama written in the vernacular. Some of the sources for structure and plot were classical. On the other hand, some were new, particularly in the plays that had to do with ordinary folk in the world of the Renaissance, the type of play soon to be called *commedia dell' arte*. Meanwhile the medieval interest in epic poetry continued. Ariosto's (1474–1533) *Orlando Furioso* was written in 1515 and Tasso's (1544–1595) *Jerusalem Delivered* early in the next century. Pastoral poetry in the tradition of Bion and Theocritus came from the pens of many poets and others. Men skilled in the arts of irony and satire increased their number and their power. Pietro Aretino (1492–1556) was undoubtedly the most famous—or notorious. The vitriolic pen and the lacerating phrases of this "Scourge of Princes" placed him in the front ranks of the masters of the lampoon and the satire. He belongs to the company of Voltaire and Jonathan Swift.

"From the scientific point of view," Professor George Sarton once remarked, "the Renaissance was not a renaissance." Professor J. H. Randall also said that many humanists in the field of science "seem to have displayed all the contemporary ignorance and futility of intellectual revolutionaries and to have proposed new methods distinguished chiefly by the novelty of their ignorance." Professor Randall further cautioned against accepting the "uncritical importance which pioneer thinkers of the sixteenth and seventeenth centuries made of their own turning away from the heritage of the past." He stressed the fact that "the later Middle Ages contained the roots of seventeenth-century advance with countless bonds of continuity in materials, methods, and even achievements." Professor Randall also reminded his readers that the seventeenth-century insistence on the mathematical basis of natural science was really Aristotelian—"the father of modern science turns out to be none other than the Master of them that know." Several other scholars, such as Professor Dana B. Durand and Professor Lynn Thorndike, learned professor and author of the many-volumed *History of Magic and Experimental Science* quoted earlier in these pages, have stood in basic agreement with Professor Randall.

These men are formidable scholars. Their judgments are not to be lightly challenged or ignored. It may be suggested, however, that perhaps the hour is yet too early for generalizations. Every scholar knows that there is more than one road to truth and salvation and never any simple formulas. So far as Renaissance science is concerned, it may perhaps be true, as Professor Ernst Cassirer believed, that "more studies in Renaissance science are needed, especially in the fields of botany, anatomy, physiology, shipbuilding, and navigation." There would seem to be sound and sober reasons for delaying firm and final judgments. Haste makes waste in scholarship as well as everywhere else. It may also be suggested that much may be said for the point of view stated so well by Professor Hans Baron: the view that the Renaissance *spirit* of tradition and innovation had much to do with the advance of science. The position of Professor Baron is of course not new; but it should not be opposed because it is old. Surely a critically minded modern man, whether he is a scholar or not, must be careful to see that he is being critically minded about his own adverse criticisms of Renaissance science, the conclusions of the astrologers of Chaldea, or the policies of the political party opposed to his own.

Probably the most famous scientific achievement of the Renaissance was the great work of Nicolaus Copernicus, born in Cracow and trained in Nuremberg and Italy. His *On the Revolutions of the Heavenly Bodies* was published on the eve of his death in 1543. In his book Copernicus asserted that the earth was not the center of the universe but revolved around the sun—Giordano Bruno was burned at the stake for saying the same thing in 1600. Copernicus thus stated again the heliocentric theory first advanced by Aristarchus in the third century B.C. and repeated by Leonardo da Vinci later.

Despite the numerous legends it is certain that Copernicus himself was not a careful or outstanding observer. He trusted—sometimes too much—the observations of his contemporaries and predecessors. It seemed to him that his main task was to develop a system that would reconcile all of the observations that others had recorded and all the differences in the opinions of mathematicians. In *The Origins of Modern Science,* Professor Herbert Butterfield remarks that Copernicus seems to have been stimulated in his work by the fact that "he had an obsession and was ridden by a grievance"—he resented the fact that Ptolemy had, as he thought, "cheated" his own and later generations by some questionable mathematical devices he had used to create the neat Ptolemaic system.

The sphere, said Copernicus, is the perfect shape—Copernicus was obsessed with a delight in spheres and circles. All spheres, he also said, must revolve. Therefore the dynamics of his new Copernican system depended upon that physical law. Copernicus said further that the motion of spheres through the heavens must be circular. Every heavenly body, he asserted, has gravity—thus he challenged the basis of the whole of Aristotelian theory. The idea of Copernicus, in the words of Professor Butterfield, was "a colossal synthesis." True, Copernicus was not able to clinch his arguments. He had a lot of trouble, for instance, with the question of centrifugal force. Why, too, were there not continual winds if the world was rushing through space from east to west in the way Copernicus believed? Despite these difficulties—and many more— the work of Copernicus had tremendous implications. The importance of his idea and its corollaries was soon to be seen by men like Galilei Galileo (1564–1642), Tycho Brahe (1546–1601), Johann Kepler (1571–1630), and Isaac Newton (1642–1727). The result was a revolution in theory and a new concept of the universe.

A second landmark in Renaissance science was the book *On the Structure of the Human Body* published by Andreas Vesalius in 1543, the same year as the great work of Copernicus. Vesalius, a native of Brussels, went to study at Padua. He was disturbed and displeased at the reliance of Paduan professors upon the ancient medical authorities, especially upon Galen, that Greek "lantern of all surgeons." Vesalius preferred to find what facts he could about the human body by direct examination, dissection, and study. The result—after years of labor—was the publication of *On the Structure of the Human Body,* a shining event in the history of the study of anatomy. Vesalius was a true scientist, a man who tried to lift the veil and make his judgments upon the basis of all the pertinent facts he could find. Like his contemporary Paracelsus—who was not the impostor and quack he is often made out to be—Vesalius thought that there was no substitute for direct experience, the best teacher of all.

There were several really outstanding scientists in the Renaissance period. To condemn or scoff at their errors is not wise. The growth of the scientific spirit of inquiry is what matters most. There are certain ages of mankind in which the probing curiosity of several generations is strong and steady. Such a time came in ancient Greece; it came in the Renaissance years and in the modern centuries. Without wonder, curiosity, indefatigable investigation, and mental activity the illumination of the human mind comes slowly.

In many parts of Europe discoveries and inventions in science and technology opened new gates and doors. Several locks and canals in Italy were improved by the application of the principles of hydrostatics. German mine-owners spent money and time upon the study of metallurgy. The soldiers joined the scientists in improving artillery on the one hand and fortifications on the other—another chapter in the contest between weapons of offense and defense. Musicians learned more about the mathematics of harmony. The new Gregorian calendar appeared in the form used by the Western world today—it contains an error of only one day in 3,330 years. The Flemish geographer Mercator (1512–1594) devised a system for projecting the earth's spherical form as if it were a cylinder.

Cultures do not, of course, move forward at the same pace in all places at the same time. Some attitudes and habits of men may endure long after the reason for their being has gone. Some are difficult to destroy. In 1486, for instance, the *Hammer of Witches* was published by the Inquisition, two years after the "witches bull" of Pope Innocent VIII. Despite the march of knowledge and science there was an unpleasantness about witches in Massachusetts some 200 years later. Not until the eighteenth century was the last charge against an individual for practicing witchcraft in England dismissed by Chief Justice Holt. By that time such men as Copernicus, Galileo, Kepler, and Newton had lived and lightened the world. Nevertheless, many people continued to believe in the prevalence and danger of witches. In the twentieth century the charts and charges of the astrologers have not been laid to rest by the wall. The revolutionary spirits and minds of the men of the Renaissance—and ot many another age—have not cast their power over all men or into all places. Ignorance and apathy are evil things, the constant enemies of mankind.

The Renaissance in the areas of Europe beyond Italy was based, like the Italian surge of cultural power, upon solid economic achievement. For instance, such towns as Marseilles, Barcelona, Montpellier, Hamburg, and Augsburg rose steadily to new heights of economic strength. In the fifteenth century Jacques Coeur of France became one of Europe's great bankers. Between 1450 and 1600 the Fugger family made Bavaria's Augsburg a pivot of international finance.

In northern Europe the humanistic impulses and scholarship characteristic of the Italian Renaissance were to be found in many places and persons. There was something else: a sharp and vivid interest in religion, even in the midst of much brutality and vulgarity. Northern humanists were usually less secular-minded than the humanists of Italy. It seems that they were more sober and serious and perhaps a little more moral. They were certainly more interested in ecclesiastical reform. The Christian humanism of the north was especially powerful among the laymen in Germany and the Netherlands. Men like Johannes Reuchlin, master of criticism and satire, led the numerous voices in Germany demanding the reform of the Church. The voices in the Netherlands were likewise strong and steady.

The men of northern Europe were also deeply interested in the questions and answers of the mystics. Some writers have remarked upon the fact that in the fourteenth and fifteenth centuries Germany had produced mystics like the Dominicans Eckhart and Tauler and Thomas á Kempis, said to be the mighty author of the *Imitation of Christ*. The statement is true, but it should not lead to disputable conclusions about the mysterious and mystical elements in the German *Geist* at the end of the Middle Ages. It should be remembered that Catherine of Siena had various visions and led an agitation for reform in Italy in the fourteenth century. Joan of Arc also had visions and led an army in the fifteenth century in France. All over Europe this was an age of visions and dreams and existential moments in life and literature.

Germany's Eckhart and Tauler preached the power of contemplative piety and founded the religious association of laymen called the Friends of God. Around 1400 Gerard Groot began the communistic lay brotherhood of the New Devotion, called the Brothers of the Common Life. Soon branch houses were started in various parts of Germany. The Brothers were laymen; they asked no recognition from the Church; they took no religious vows; they stressed no systematic doctrine. They simply said that men should be humble, tolerant, love their neighbors, and do reverence to God. The lay Brothers educated thousands of children and talked about the teachings of Christ to thousands of adults. There was nothing similar to this in Renaissance Italy.

Again and again there appeared in various forms the assertion that man could communicate directly with God, that he needed no mediating Church or priesthood. This idea was an explosive one, as men like Martin Luther and Sören Kierkegaard were one day to show. Here was a profound and revolutionary concept, a doctrine of tremendous implications for religion, government, and society. The rise of the new political and social claims of the individual soon brought inevitable crises in the states of Europe as kings were defied and princes tumbled down. In the sphere of religion, the challenge to the universal authority of the Church of Rome came earlier. It came not from Italy but out of Germany and Switzerland and England. The world of the West was never the same again.

Dominating the whole European stage stood the mighty figure of the influential and cosmopolitan Desiderius Erasmus of Rotterdam (1466?–1536). This balanced and moderate "Prince of Humanists," this traveling scholar, denounced the folly and stupidity of man in the world of politics, religion, and education. He scoffed at the pedants. He found "the modern race of divines" obnoxious because they "spend their lives in mere logical tricks and sophisticated cavils . . . they exhaust the mental power by a dry and biting subtlety, without infusing any vigor into the mind." He denounced the makers of war: "Perpetual peace is the source of piety and learning." Of his famous *Praise of Folly* (1511) there were twenty-seven editions in his lifetime. This book was a scourging satire directed against the smug, the stupid, the ignorant, and the slothful. Despite his ill health—the viewer can see the evidence of it in Holbein's famous paintings—Erasmus did an enormous amount of work. He wrote thousands of letters, many editions of classical works, several original books. He also published a Greek New Testament in 1516 and a Latin translation three years later. He traveled widely. He lectured often. It has been said, and rightly, that Erasmus, always a liberal rationalist and individual cosmopolitan, was "one of the greatest teachers in the history of the Western world."

The whole life of Erasmus was a long and exasperated campaign against stupidity, lack of imagination, and spiritual and intellectual darkness. "The great mass of people," he said, "are swayed by false opinions and are no different from those in Plato's cave who took the empty shadows as the real thing." At the same time, Erasmus believed, and strongly believed, that many ills of society could be removed by a rational and secular education resting mainly upon a study of the classics—his *Colloquies* was written to improve the Latin style of the students. To the moral and rational wisdom of antiquity must be added an education in the spirit and discipline of Christianity. Erasmus said: "All studies are followed by this one object, that we may know Christ and honor Him. This is the end of all learning and eloquence." He also wrote: "I do greatly dissent from those men who would not that the Scriptures should be translated into all tongues that they might be read more diligently by the private and secular men and women." These themes, so acceptable to most Christian humanists, were frequently stressed in such books of Erasmus as the *Handbook of a Christian Knight* (1503) and the *Education of a Christian Prince* (1516). With the development and extension of Christian humanism Desiderius Erasmus, "the teacher of teachers," had a very great deal to do.

The faith of Christian humanists in such a philosophy of education for a "Christian knight" was continuous and effective. They steadily stressed intellectual and ethical excellence, the virtue of human qualities, the idea of an ideal Christian order among princes and their peoples. Within the nations of Europe the ideas about humanistic education took different forms. Some centuries later there was still to be no agreement as to the nature of a liberal education.

In the Low Countries the virile painting of the van Eycks, earlier described, did not stand alone in its excellence. The same kind of brilliant color and effective realism, the same suggestions of respectable virtues and solid piety, appear in the paintings of men like Hans Memling and Roger van der Weyden. In the sixteenth century Pieter Breughel (1525?–1569) depicted, with realism and sympathy, the lot of the common man. His skillful hand used art as a weapon of political protest against the Spanish occupation of the Low Countries. Breughel's famous "Massacre of the Innocents," showing the women and children slaughtered by Spanish soldiers, roused the anger, sympathy, and patriotism of countless people.

Over in Germany, Albrecht Dürer (1471–1528) of Nuremberg was the first painter to be influenced by Italian art. His paintings, woodcuts, and engravings made his name famous then and famous now. His contemporary, Hans Holbein the Younger (1497–1543) was without doubt one of the really great painters of the world. His fame rests chiefly upon his religious art and the portraits he painted outside the Germanic world, especially in England and Switzerland. ("He is going to England," wrote Erasmus, "to pick up a few coins. . . . Here the arts are shivering with cold.") A modern critic has succinctly praised Holbein in these words: "He sought above all accuracy of form and clarity of composition, truth of expression and grace of movement." Much of Holbein's work, of course, was in opposition to German values and standards. "He developed in the direction of a classicism of an almost international character." It is certainly true that in the work of Holbein the grace of Italy was skillfully merged with the temperament of the north. For these qualities and for his imagination, the beauty of his form, and the startling objectivity of his portraits Hans Holbein won fame and honor all over the world of the West. He certainly deserved it, then and now.

Let us turn to France. There an event that had at first nothing to do with art and literature had a great deal to do with both in the end. In 1494 Charles VIII of France invaded Italy because he was greedy and ambitious. The invasion opened more widely the doors of his own land to the ideas and culture of the early Italian humanists. What had earlier been a light and spasmodic influence now became heavy and constant.

Some French humanists, like Guillaume Budé (1467–1540), were particularly influential in the world of scholarship. Other men moved beyond the universities and the libraries to the worlds outside. A renaissance among scholars is one thing; a quickening of a part of the spirits of that vague, amorphous mass we call "the people" is quite another.

France made almost no contributions to Renaissance art, a few to Renaissance science—especially in mathematics and medicine—and a great many to Renaissance literature and philosophy.

Among the giants of the French Renaissance was François Rabelais (1495?–1553). Rabelais was a brilliant and extraordinary man, a sound classical and medical scholar, who had the happy gift of being able to write in a way that the most humble person could understand. His *Inestimable Life of the Great Gargantua, Father of Pantagruel* (1532) is properly regarded as one of the world's great books. The account of the adventures of the giants Pantagruel and Gargantua gave the exuberant Rabelais a chance to scoff at and satirize the bigots, the hypocrites, the persecutors, and the puritans among men. Human nature, he insisted, was good; it should not be suppressed or thwarted. Many people, then and later, have called Rabelais obscene. "Nothing is obscene but thinking makes it so." In this large world, of course, there is room for those who prefer the polished and suave Michel de Montaigne (1533–1592), master of the essay and the epigram, the skeptic and the disenchanted man.

The achievements of Spain and Portugal were not numerous; but they were of high rank and stature. For instance, the greatest literary work ever produced in Portugal appeared in the sixteenth century: the tremendous epic called the *Lusiads* written by Luis Vaz de Camoens. Camoens (1524–1580) was the prince of Portuguese poets. The written language of Portugal today is not inaccurately called "the language of Camoens," so much did Camoens do to fix its form. In all the sixteenth century Portugal had no other artists worthy of praise or admiration. It was perhaps enough for any land to have had a man of the genius of the kind that Camoens most surely was.

Two names stand forth in Spanish Renaissance art: Luis de Morales (1517–1586) and El Greco (1541–1614)—his real name was Domenico Theotokopouli and he was born on the island of Crete. The orthodox religious paintings of Luis de Morales—especially the Madonnas and the Crucifixions—were the best in sixteenth-century Europe. El Greco, of course, was a far greater artist than Luis de Morales. His genius "fused together the solemnity of Byzantium, the pictorial glow of Venice, and the vision of the Spanish mystics." The paintings of El Greco, as the reader is well aware, are often filled with emotion, with tragedy and horror, sometimes with themes mystical and supernatural and the distortion of human figures. Characteristic of his work are the famous "Pentecost," "The Apocalyptic Vision," and the "Burial of Count Orgaz."

The most prolific dramatist of Renaissance Spain was Lope de Vega (1562–

1635), a master of plot structure and a writer who appealed to the masses. It is said that Lope de Vega wrote about 1,500 comedies and 400 religious plays. He once remarked: "More than a hundred of my comedies have taken only twenty-four hours to pass from my brain to the boards of the theater."

Outside of Spain the name of Lope de Vega is almost forgotten today except among the scholars whose business it is to know such things. On the other hand, the glory of Miguel de Cervantes (1547–1616) has spread and will remain throughout the Western world. *Don Quixote,* his masterpiece, has made countless thousands laugh. The new Spain and the world of later men could afford to see through the eyes of the sensible Sancho Panza the laughable aspects of medieval chivalry. The satirical prose of Cervantes describes how Don Quixote, slightly demented as a result of reading too many medieval romances, has a series of misadventures when he sets out at the age of fifty to be a knight-errant. Gallant, mad, lovable, futile Don Quixote tilts at windmills and thinks kitchen maids are duchesses. His faithful squire Sancho Panza, who is quite sane and quite practical, almost succeeds in protecting his master from his follies; but "almost" is not enough. Don Quixote, of course, symbolizes the outworn and bankrupt medieval ideology; Sancho Panza is the challenge of the practical and complex world of a new age. Knighthood was no longer in flower. The lance had been replaced, or almost so, by gunpowder.

The years of the later Renaissance in England may be described as disorderly, comprehensive, bubbling with a zest for life, extravagant, sensuous. In some sectors of the arts and sciences there was but small achievement; in others there was a great deal. In natural science, for example, almost nothing of consequence happened. At the end of the sixteenth century William Gilbert published his conclusions about magnetism and Francis Bacon his *Advancement of Learning.* Before the advances of the seventeenth century English medical science lay largely in the field of preventive medicine in dealing with the plague. There were not many skilled physicians and surgeons in Tudor England. Medical schools in England were still lamentably weak. The best published medical work, such as the *Treatise on Gunshot* (1548) of Thomas Gale, came from men who had been in the army. William Clowes, who produced some of the best surgical writings of his age, obtained most of his clinical experience serving with the English army in the Low Countries, where "bad surgeons slew more than the enemy."

The wide range of interests of men who lived in the reign of Elizabeth I (1558–1603) was clearly revealed in the outburst of literature that made the age one of the greatest in the world's history. The vital springs of the Renaissance spirit, Christian and worldly humanism, the impulse of exploration and discovery, the soaring nationalism, the sense of rapidly expanding horizons, the training of the judgment through logic and rhetoric, these formed a few of the stimulating sources of literature. There was a steady flow of translations; there were the clenched fists of the writers of pamphlets and controversial literature; there were scores of books written in national enthusiasm and patriotic pride. Francis Bacon's *Essays* shared pride of place with Richard Hakluyt's *Principal Navigations, Voyages, and Discoveries of the English Nation,* Richard Hooker's *Laws of Ecclesiastical Polity,* Edmund Spenser's *Faerie Queene.*

The supreme achievements of the rich Elizabethan literature were in poetry and drama. The steadily swelling stream of sonnets, epics, lyrics, and pastorals reached its full flood late in Elizabeth I's reign. It is impossible to do justice to the poets; they were so many; and they were so great. Sir Walter Raleigh's lovely "Walsingham" and "Give me my scallop-shell of quiet" stood side by side in beauty with the gems of Robert Southwell, Roman Catholic poet martyred at Tyburn in 1595. Southwell, in turn, is matched in the words of Thomas Nashe suggested by the plague year of 1593: "Beauty is but a flower . . . Dust has closed Helen's eye; I am sick, I must die. Lord have mercy on us!" In the long parade of golden names there is recalled the gnomic lines of Fulke Greville; the voices of Ben Jonson, Thomas Dekker, and Thomas Ford on the edge of the Jacobean age; the *Astrophel and Stella* sonnets of Sir Philip Sidney—"With how sad steps, O moon, thou climb'st the skies! How silently, and with how wan a face!"

Meanwhile strong impetus was given to dramatic writing by the increase in the number of theaters. A group of university men began to develop the new English drama. The variety and range of that drama was astonishing; it moved all the way from the melodramatic and turbulent duels and suicides, from the numerous corpses in Thomas Kyd's *Spanish Tragedy* to the jolly and relaxed scenes of Thomas Dekker's *Shoemaker's Holiday.* Robert Greene's *Friar Bacon and Friar Bungay* is an excellent example of the Elizabethan love of life, action, novelty: "Persia, down the Volga by canoes, Send down the secrets of her spicery."

One of the most original and vigorous of the university writers was Christopher Marlowe, author of many remarkable plays: *Tamburlaine* (1587), the *Tragical History of Doctor Faustus* (1588), the *Jew of Malta* (1593), and sections of the second and third parts of *Henry VI,* later finished by Shakespeare. Before the wilful and intellectual Marlowe died in a tavern brawl at the age of twenty-nine he had written many an unrestrained and soaring line; he stands among the world's great poets. Here, for example, is Dr. Faustus, who has sold his soul to the Devil, searching for what is forbidden to man, in the limbo between heaven and hell:

> The stars move still, time runs, the clock will strike,
> The Devil will come, and Faustus must be damned.
> Oh, I'll leap up to my God! Who pulls me down?
> See, see where Christ's blood streams in the firmament!
> One drop would save my soul—half a drop. . . . see where God
> Stretcheth out his arm and bends his ireful brows.
> Mountain and hills, come, come, and fall on me,
> And hide me from the heavy wrath of God!

The awakening muse of the drama also produced William Shakespeare, without a peer in any age, in any language. Shakespeare was born in 1564, the son of a tradesman; he did not belong to the university group; his formal education had been obtained at the grammar school of Stratford-on-Avon. When he came up to London there was nobody to know that he was to produce about forty plays, *Venus and Adonis, Lucrece,* and the sonnets.

About 1591 Shakespeare wrote *Love's Labours Lost.* After the early period of the influence of Marlowe the comedies began to appear: *The Merchant of Venice, A Midsummer Night's Dream, Twelfth Night,* and *As You Like It.* The great series of tragedies was written between 1599 and 1609: *Julius Caesar, Hamlet, Othello, King Lear.* Then, at the end, came the new notes of *Cymbeline, A Winter's Tale, The Tempest.* Shakespeare's imperishable words, the immortal characters of Hamlet, Lear, Othello, Falstaff, Shylock, the scenes where Sir Toby Belch, champion of cakes and ale, speaks to the Malvolios of all time, these are among the highest reaches of human genius.

The cross-currents of the golden age of English literature are many. On the one hand, there is the supreme achievement of William Shakespeare. On the other, one may find the stumbling epigram of an amateur whose name has long since perished. Between these two poles there stand forth in Elizabethan literature the everlasting themes of love, death, the vanity of human wishes, the last judgment, honor, courage, and the eternal follies and hopes of man.

Chapter 20

THE REFORMATION: GOD
IS THE JUDGE

"For therein is the righteousness of God revealed from faith to faith:
as it is written, The just shall live by faith."
—St. Paul, *Epistle to the Romans*, I, 17

IN THE Middle Ages most people in Europe believed that there was but one
road to God and that road was provided by the Church Universal, the
Roman Catholic Church. Through the Church alone, it was said, could an
individual obtain salvation. After the exploding religious revolutions of the
sixteenth century the prospect was altered; many new roads to God seemed
open. Instead of one Church there were many churches, sects, answers, claims,
and cults. Some said this; some said that. The unity of Christendom was
shattered and the fragments are with us still.

The Church of the sixteenth century was particularly vulnerable to attack.
Shrewd men realized that the institution that had done so much to shield and
direct Europe in the Middle Ages had ceased to meet and serve the needs of
a changing society. The power of the states had risen as the power of the
Church had diminished. No longer was the Church the chief preserver of
order or the main source of education. Meanwhile, too, the former vitality of
the Church had been slowly drained away by the vampires of time and chance.
The delays and injustices of the ecclesiastical courts were there for all to see. The
leadership was weak, inefficient, often corrupt. There were grave abuses that
could not be defended, excused, or disguised. Many devout Christians had
denounced these abuses and demanded reform, asserting that the evils could
not be long endured.

Who could approve the activities of the neo-pagan Leo X? Who could look
happily upon Alexander VI, that corrupt father of Lucrezia Borgia? Who
could sanction the evil ways of Julius II? What spiritual or moral integrity
did such men possess? Who could see with equanimity three popes excom-

municating one another? Scandals—and there were many—were sometimes exaggerated. Stories were multiplied about the body and members of the Church, about fat monks and decadent monasteries, about worldly friars who were neglecting their Father's business, about cardinals who poisoned their foes and nuns who were virgins no more. Many of the stories were true. The clergy were not all "unspotted from the world." The facts of sin and weakness had nothing to do with the faith of Christianity; they had a great deal to do with the institution that was the Church of God on earth.

Orthodox men like Erasmus, like England's John Colet, Dean of St. Paul's, Bishop Fisher of Rochester, and Thomas More, filled with the new learning and "sorrowing for the ruin of the Church"—the phrase is John Colet's— protested with skill and vigor. Some men desired to go back to what they said were the faith and practices of the early Church. Others said that any man might reach up to God without the use of priests and creeds. Men like the reformer Erasmus, writing in the spirit of John Wycliffe, wanted to see the Scriptures available to all men and women: "I would have the weakest woman read the Gospels and the Epistles. . . . I would have those works translated into all languages. . . . I long for the man in the fields to sing them to himself as he follows the plough, the weaver to hum them to the tune of his shuttle. . . ."

In the preceding centuries the Church had survived many crises and many attacks. The scene now was different: the weakened Church was not now the resilient and militant power that it once had been; its clergy was not cut from the timber of Innocent III or Gregory VII; and many of the attacks and accusations, as we have seen, came from godly men from within its own ranks.

Changing trends of life and thought had affected every aspect of European life and multiplied the frictions between Church and state. Secular forces merged with religious discontent. Such men as the bankers and the capitalist entrepreneurs often viewed with dislike a clergy that disapproved of usury, frowned upon men of business as being somehow not quite respectable or decent, and yet came with condescension to borrow money. Many laymen resented the necessity of paying what they considered to be exorbitant financial exactions to a Church already the greatest landlord in Europe, glutted with hoarded wealth, whose clergy neither toiled nor spun nor seemed to do the work of God. Princes and peoples of national states often looked upon the papacy as a foreign power with benefits, immunities, and interests prejudicial to the welfare of their homeland. Nationalism was already a mighty force in Europe.

Many eager laymen looked with jealousy, envy, and greed upon the great wealth of alien Rome. Hungry peasants—with national allegiances—scanned the broad lands of the international Church. Before the laymen of Europe the Church stood entrenched and powerful, enormously wealthy, blocking the expansion of the new economy and the new society. The attempts to explain the Reformation solely in economic terms have always been unconvincing and sometimes ludicrous; but the economic thrusts were there, strong and constant.

When Pope Leo X (1513–1521) proclaimed a plenary indulgence early in 1517 he certainly had no idea of the explosion that would follow.

For several centuries the indulgence had been a familiar part of the penitential system of the Church. The practice arose and continued in the following pattern. In the first place, the Church never claimed that it could do anything to affect the guilt of a sinner in the eyes of God. God's pardon could be obtained by sincere contrition and an appeal to Him for forgiveness. Secondly, the Church did claim the power to control and determine the punishments for sin on this earth and in Purgatory. Thus a penitent sinner was assigned in the confessional an act of penance or discipline to perform as a sign of his repentance and as a symbol of the earthly punishment sin always merits. In certain circumstances, the Church granted indulgences decreasing or remitting the penance or punishment of truly repentant people. Originally, the indulgence or privilege had been earned by specified acts of charity or devotion. Later, money was accepted for indulgences, with the understanding that the Church would use the money for charity or manifest public advantage. "In theory, the indulgence could apply only to the contrite sinner. In practice, it came to be thought of as an easier way to forgiveness than the hard road of true repentance."

The granting of indulgences for money was soon an occasion for scandal, abuse, and patent corruption. Julius II had given plenary indulgences to every person who contributed to the rebuilding of St. Peter's. Leo X promised to open the gates of Paradise to those who went on a crusade against the Turks. (*Claudo tibi portas inferni et januas aperio Paradisi.*) Leo X also proclaimed a plenary indulgence remitting all temporal punishment for those who contributed money to help rebuild St. Peter's and to reimburse Albrecht von Brandenburg for the amount he had spent to get the archbishopric of Mainz —surely a worldly undertaking. The papal agents helped to spread the idea that the indulgences freed individuals from the consequences of sin both in this world and the next: "As soon as money in the coffer rings, The soul from Purgatory's fire springs." The necessity of true repentance was often forgotten as men and women flocked to buy the indulgences. John Tetzel, for instance, was a Dominican monk active in the papal enterprise. He sold the indulgences in Germany as if they were passports to Paradise.

It was at this moment that the Saxon friar Martin Luther took a series of decisive steps. Luther was neither a profound student of theology nor a scholar learned in philosophy. He was a passionate, coarse, pious, complex, morbid, combative preacher extraordinary, a man obsessed with the problems and terrors of sin. "I am rough, boisterous, stormy, and altogether warlike; I am born to fight innumerable monsters and devils, to remove stems and stones, cut away thistles and thorns, and clear away wild forests."

To Luther corruption and hypocrisy were a challenge to civilization and an absolute barrier to salvation. As he taught and studied at Wittenberg, Luther also became more and more convinced that the Church was advertising and selling the indulgences as a mechanical scheme of salvation that was against morality, against theology, and against the laws of God. Further, he felt that too many men within and without the body of the clergy were stressing unduly the importance of good works. Man was wicked. Beads and relics, pilgrimages and indulgences, could not change that fact. Only the divine goodness and grace of God, reaching in His mercy across the gulf between Himself and miserable man, could bring salvation. "Thereupon I felt myself to be reborn and to have gone through the open doors into Paradise." Had not St. Paul declared in his Epistle to the Romans: "The just shall live by faith"? Martin Luther said that salvation came by faith and faith alone. If a man had faith, good works would follow. Every baptized Christian, every man and woman who had come to Him in simple faith, was a priest.

Martin Luther did not believe in toleration or free judgment—few men did in the sixteenth century. He did believe in religious and civil authority under God. He also believed that all truth was to be found in the Scriptures. Man is justified only by his faith in the supreme Gospel, by nothing more and nothing less. Everybody—pope, priest, and peasant, robber, merchant, banker, and beggar—is bound by the same moral laws. These laws are proclaimed in the Scriptures. Like all the laws of God, they are fixed and immutable. "All departments of life, the state and society, education and science, law, commerce, and history, were to be regulated in accordance with the law of God."

On October 31, 1517, Martin Luther nailed his Ninety-Five Theses upon the castle church door in Wittenberg. He posted these theses as topics for discussion and attacks upon several activities of the clergy. Luther was apparently not yet prepared to defy the Church or to separate from Rome. It seems probable that in 1517 he saw himself as a champion of a great reform movement rather than the leader of a blazing revolution. He certainly did not look upon himself as a rebel or as a heretic. Were not his words and views based upon the solid foundation of St. Paul and St. Augustine? Did not Erasmus, no mean authority, praise and approve the Ninety-Five Theses?

The explosive results of the posting of the famous document at Wittenberg were certainly not anticipated by anybody, including Martin Luther. Several historians have explained—it seems sometimes not difficult to explain an event after it happens—that the explosion and the fire were the inevitable results of the numerous and dangerous combustible elements in the social, economic, religious, and political situation: the widespread objections to the indulgences and the activities of men like Tetzel; the pressure of middle-class ambitions against the ramparts of the Church; the rise of secularism and capitalism; the envy and greed of some men as they looked at the wealth of the clergy; the challenges of nationalism; the lowered prestige of a Church weakened by moral and financial corruption—"God has given us the Papacy, let us enjoy it," Leo X had said; the attacks upon the sacramental system; the return of many men to the teachings of St. Augustine as they departed from the fold of St. Thomas Aquinas; the wide disapproval of other abuses in the Church— Erasmus said that European churches contained enough pieces of the true Cross to build a ship; there was on exhibit five shinbones of the ass on which Jesus rode on Palm Sunday; the archbishop of Mainz claimed—if we may believe Martin Luther—to have "a whole pound of the wind that blew for Elijah in the cave on Mount Horeb and two feathers and an egg of the Holy Ghost."

Contemporaries of Martin Luther and Leo X did not have the advantages possessed by able and shrewd modern historians. They could not collect and compare documents from hundreds of sources. They could not assess calmly the weight and value of facts and allegations. They knew only that they were suddenly shaken by a revolution, an explosion, a whirling tornado—whatever the precise word may be. Revolutions make men busy. He who hesitates may lose his cause.

To thousands of German people the impetuous Martin Luther was a hero, an incorruptible man of God. In a public debate with John Eck, a famous and skilled theologian, Luther increased the excitement and extended his influence. Many men did not see that Eck had shrewdly forced Luther into a more radical position. Luther now was saying that Church Councils might make mistakes; that John Huss—the famous rebel of earlier days in Bohemia—was not a heretic at all but an honest follower of the teachings of primitive Christianity. Meanwhile Luther wrote several pamphlets—he always had the support and cooperation of numerous printers. In these pamphlets he continued to insist that salvation came by faith; that all men of faith were bound together in a common companionship and priesthood; that they learned God's will from the Scriptures; that the priests of the Church were not necessary to salvation. Neither pope nor priest, Luther said, held the keys of the kingdom of heaven.

For three years Pope Leo X was busy with the problems involved in the election of a Holy Roman Emperor. The new emperor, the young Charles V of Spain, was occupied with the approaching coronation and the ratification of his election by the Spanish Cortes. At last, in 1520, both pope and emperor turned towards Martin Luther. A papal bull gave Luther sixty days to admit his errors. On December 10, 1520, Luther replied by burning the bull in the presence of the students and people of Wittenberg. Faced by such defiance,

Leo X acted swiftly: he declared Luther a heretic and excommunicated him.

What would the emperor do? For a time Charles V hesitated, aware of the wide support and sympathy given to Luther by the Germans, especially by the men of the important middle class. He knew, too, that Luther had a powerful protector: Frederick, Elector of Saxony. In the circumstances, Charles deemed it wise to summon Luther before the Imperial Diet—then all the leaders of the empire would share responsibility for whatever action was taken.

In 1521 Luther went to the Diet at Worms. Before the Diet he asserted that he would change his position and retract his statements only if they were disproved by the Scriptures. After several members of the Diet had gone home Charles V was able to get a sufficient number of votes to condemn Luther (May 26, 1521) and declare him an outlaw. The excommunication had marked an official break with the Church. The Edict of Worms marked an official break with the empire.

Frederick, that powerful Elector of Saxony, concealed and protected Martin Luther in the castle of Wartburg for nearly a year. Soon Charles V moved into war with France. His soldiers never enforced the Edict of Worms. Luther was left alone. Charles himself never visited Germany until 1530—he was too busy in Spain, Africa, Italy, and the Netherlands. Some men today would say that the emperor was busy in the wrong places and that imperial action in Germany might have turned the tide of Lutheranism. History is filled with such words as "if" and "might" and "but."

Meanwhile Luther developed the theory of "consubstantiation," which said that the body and blood of Christ were present in the Holy Communion *along with* the bread and wine. He kept the sacraments of the Eucharist, Baptism, and Penance; the other sacraments he abandoned. Even the sacraments of the Eucharist, Baptism, and Penance, he said, brought no grace from Heaven, only the promise of it.

Luther also asserted that he opposed monasticism, the veneration of relics, fasts, pilgrimages, the invocation of saints, many kinds of formalism. Rome, he said, was Babylon. The pope was Antichrist. So far as Luther was concerned, priests might marry—after all, according to Luther, every baptized and faithful Christian was also a priest. These doctrines, and many more, appear again and again in Luther's three most famous treatises: *On the Babylonian Captivity of the Church, To the Christian Nobility of the German Nation Respecting the Reformation of the Christian Estate,* and *Concerning Christian Liberty.* The grace of god and the faith and humility of the individual were the things that seemed to matter most to Luther. To him justification by faith continued to be the sole road to safety and salvation. To him the Scriptures were the supreme authority—he translated the New Testament into German in 1522 and the Old Testament in 1532. "I am bound by the texts of the

Bible, my conscience is captive to the Word of God. I neither can nor will recant anything, since it is neither right nor safe to act against conscience. God help me. Amen."

Many men aided the militant rebel. Philip Melanchthon of Wittenberg, a gentle scholar and theologian, helped to prepare and provide a new theology for the new church of the Lutherans. It was Melanchthon who was mainly responsible for the drafting of the *Confession of Augsburg*, the full statement of Lutheran belief published in 1530 and promptly rejected by the Imperial Diet.

There were those who now refused to travel all the way with Luther. Some had wanted moderate and reasonable reform, not revolution, not a break with Rome. Others were frankly appalled by the unwavering "justification by faith alone" doctrine. Erasmus, for example, balked at the later phases of Luther's rebellion. On the other hand, many radicals put forward an increasing variety of interpretations of the sacraments and the Scriptures, of the nature of man and God. New sects mushroomed up throughout Europe—the inevitable result of turning over to the individual the responsibility for his faith. When thousands of people concluded that they could interpret the will of God and the Scriptures all by themselves in the taverns and under the chestnut trees, then Babel was built again. Sects multiplied, all claiming the final Truths. Voices and fists were raised, as Anabaptist fought Lutheran and both fought Roman Catholics and all the other opposing groups. "By apostolic blows and knocks They proved their doctrines orthodox." Unsheathed swords dripped with the blood of Christians. "To set up Scripture as the sole authority is to separate the Bible from the life of the Church. Who, then, is to interpret the Scripture aright?" Too many men forgot that Luther said that the believer is the "servant of all" as well as the "lord of all." And too many—not for the last time—forgot in their human zeal the second commandment of Christ.

So it was that wars of religion arose in Germany, harsh and bitter. The League of Catholic States appeared in 1521 and the League of Protestant States in 1526. Not until 1555 did the exhausting struggle end, for a time. It was then agreed that the people of each state would adhere to the religion of its prince (*cujus regio, ejus religio*). This famous principle, of course, meant that there might be peace between states but not toleration within them. Regions such as the Rhineland, Austria, and Bavaria stayed within the Church of Rome. Areas like Saxony, Prussia, Brandenburg, and Hesse became Protestant and Lutheran. So, too, did many Scandinavian regions.

Luther's main support came from the princes and the busy men of the middle class. Individualistic and aggressive businessmen often found Lutheranism more congenial than the teachings of Rome. Many were to find the doctrines of Geneva's Calvin more congenial still. Several princes and peoples of Germany were delighted to break away from the confining power of Rome

—and to profit by the seizure of Church lands and treasures. Protestantism, capitalism, and nationalism often went hand in hand.

In the sixteenth century some petty German nobles were very poor, like the later "sparrow hawk" nobles of France who were said to possess only genealogical tables and rusty swords. Many of these men had an easy and simple explanation for their plight. They blamed their misery upon the fact that the Church had so much land and wealth. Led by men like Ulrich von Hutten and Franz von Sickingen they broke into the wild revolt of 1522 usually called the "Knights' War." The powerful nobles and clergy soon put the rebels down. Nevertheless, all the secular leaders had a sharp and vivid demonstration of the power of a group aroused against the wealthy Church. They were not likely to forget what happened.

Two years later the peasants revolted. Many city workers and educated men joined in the rebellion, a bloody event caused by hunger, heavy rents, spiraling prices, envy of the landed clergy, and the new points of view partly inspired by the teachings of Martin Luther. The revolt began rather quietly in southern Germany. Then its nature changed. Radicals like Thomas Münzer got control of the movement in 1524, and their simple followers were urged to burn and slay and plunder. This they did, but not for long. The revenge of the nobility was swift and savage.

Much has sometimes been made of the fact that Luther supported the nobles. His vehement pamphlet entitled "Against the Plundering and Murdering Hordes of the Peasantry" has been frequently quoted, especially the passages in which he urged every man on the side of order to pursue the peasants, to "strike, strangle, stab secretly or in public, and let him remember that nothing can be more poisonous, harmful, or devilish than a man in rebellion."

Some historians and others have strongly condemned Luther for supporting the secular princes and thus strengthening "the powerful movements towards absolute monarchies in Europe in general and the growth of the territorial states of the princes in Germany in particular." Professor Harold J. Grimm has pointed out—and quite rightly—that Luther was consistent. He supported the princes because he took literally the Biblical references to the authority of rulers in secular matters. His main task, as he saw it, was to strive for "the betterment of the souls of men." In his day most people looked upon the Peasants' Rebellion as a purely political disturbance. Men who looked at it later saw the economic and social aspects more sharply than those who lived in the sixteenth century. Luther's position must be viewed according to the attitudes of his own day and not ours.

It must also be remembered that Luther insisted that the "free Christian" must submit to "an orderly society under the protection of the government." A "Christian government which supports the Gospel" must always be upheld. "What a heinous crime it is," said Luther, "to revolt against established authority." When we consider the times in which Luther lived and the doctrines he firmly held, it is difficult to avoid agreement with Professor Grimm: "If we bear in mind Luther's life-long struggle to preserve the Gospel, we cannot justly accuse him for failing to attach his religious cause to the social and political revolution of the peasants."

Waves of political and religious revolution did not strike in Germany alone. The ramparts of the old order were weak and ill defended in the early sixteenth century. Then, as now, there were many disputes in the world of man about the word of God.

In 1519—the year that Martin Luther debated with John Eck—the first strong currents of a reform movement began to swirl through the streets of quiet Zurich, that Swiss city so rightly famed in the songs and tales of centuries. Zurich stood as one of the symbols of a bold and brave people who had ousted the Hapsburgs. Her courageous sons had served with men from other Swiss cantons in many mercenary armies of Europe and there they had kept the high reputation of the soldiers of the Swiss republic. It was in Zurich that the voice of Ulrich Zwingli (1484–1531) began to denounce the abuses of the Church and to preach an unorthodox message.

In a life of travel and adventure Zwingli had encountered many men and ideas. He was a student, too, a humanist student of Erasmus. With such a background of experience and knowledge Zwingli read the tracts of Martin Luther and what he found there persuaded him that Luther had made one major error: he had not gone far or fast enough. Zwingli was not only a patriotic, moral, and religious man; he was also a man in a hurry.

Luther had said that the body and blood of Christ in the Eucharist coexisted with the bread and wine. Zwingli said that *Hoc est corpus meum* must not be taken literally: the bread and wine, he insisted, were symbols, nothing more; the doctrine of the real presence was false. Zwingli also hastened to oppose such things as clerical celibacy, fasting in Lent, and the use of Latin in the Church services.

By 1529 the impetuous Zwingli's power had conquered six of the thirteen cantons. He tried to force the Roman Catholic eastern cantons to follow him by imposing a trade embargo. There was a darker instance of his intolerance: he "drowned Anabaptists at Zurich in a horrible parody of their insistence upon adult baptism." In Zwingli's judgment, men who disagreed with him were manifestly wrong. "Who is this that darkeneth counsel by words without knowledge?" Zwingli was not the first or last human being to be so deluded.

Soon Zwingli led the men of Zurich into battle against the recalcitrant Roman Catholic cantons. In battle Zwingli died. The time was 1531. The place was the field of Cappel, reddened with the blood of men who professed and called themselves Christians.

It was not Ulrich Zwingli who was destined to be remembered as the most famous religious reformer in Switzerland. It was John Calvin (1509–1564), one of the greatest of all the revolutionary leaders of the sixteenth century, a man of enormous knowledge, intellectual suppleness, and political acumen, a man cold, stern, and logical. John Calvin had little in common with Zwingli, except the assurance of the rightness of his ideas and his deeds.

Calvin was born in France's province of Picardy. During his youth in Paris he began to study law. Then he turned to other fields, particularly those explored and mapped by the Christian humanists. Soon he fell under Luther's influence and left the ranks of the Roman Catholics. When Francis I ousted the Protestants from Paris, Calvin went to Basel and then to Strassburg—in Strassburg he began his long friendship with the famed theologian Martin Bucer. Meanwhile, Calvin's ideas were steadily growing and hardening. He studied St. Paul, St. Augustine, and the early Greek fathers. In these years, too, his character was undoubtedly being shaped. He would soon be an austere and magnetic man of Spartan simplicity, athletic logic, piety, energy, and always lofty aims. On the surface there was calmness and ice; beneath there was fevered emotion and fire.

In 1536 John Calvin published his famous *Institutes of the Christian Religion,* a book intended to be an elementary catechism, an introduction to the major themes of Christian faith and thought. The volume was dedicated to Francis I of France and a short introduction tried to prove to Francis I that he and his fellow Roman Catholics were wrong in thinking that Protestantism was subversive. The first edition of the *Institutes* contained six chapters. A later edition had seventeen. The last expanded edition (1559) had eighty-one.

What did John Calvin say in the *Institutes* and in his sermons and essays and thousands of letters? What did he believe? What did he do? In the first place, Calvin asserted that the lordship and authority of God were absolute. "We are not our own, but we are God's." Individuals and groups must obey Him completely. They must surrender all their beings to Him. John Calvin never ceased to write and preach about the majesty of an all-righteous God and the dusty worthlessness of wicked and fallen men. Secondly, Calvin agreed with Martin Luther that men are justified by faith and that they can fulfill the divine moral laws provided that God will be merciful. The limiting words "provided that God will be merciful" are important because they lead to another significant chapter in Calvin's thought and practice, a chiseled, polished, and orderly system.

What if God does not choose to be merciful to certain human beings? Certainly, said Calvin, sinful man deserves and has a right to expect nothing but justice from the Almighty. By justice alone men are surely predestined to death, hell, and damnation. If God withholds His mercy they are lost forever. Only by the grace of God does any man have a happy fate in eternity. A doctrine of justification by faith was thus merged and mingled with a doctrine of justification by grace. The twin laws of providence and predestination, the central themes of Calvinism, were being slowly forged.

It seems that some men and women, observed Calvin, simply cannot obey God's laws. Obviously, God has not chosen to let these people into Heaven to dwell in felicity forever. In His mercy he has chosen other men to fulfill the moral laws and be saved. These elected men are chosen because Christ won for them that inestimable gift upon the Cross. The men who are not elected perish. The grace and mercy of God are not for them. They are lost and damned forever. Nobody can climb to the gates of Heaven by his own effort and determination. Piety, good will, and good works are of no avail, said John Calvin. They save nobody.

This was a harsh doctrine to men who were not chosen by God in His mercy to be of "the Elect in Jesus Christ." Many individuals who followed Calvin were assured that they would not wither and burn because they belonged to the group of the Elect. They declared sometimes that they could feel the spirit of God working within them. They were often filled with "sweet, pleasant, and unspeakable comfort" as they rejoiced in the assurance that God had chosen them to be His companions in eternity. Many Calvinists were responsible, zealous, and able men. Partly because of their beliefs and their sense of personal responsibility they were God-fearing and moral men of integrity and courage. Sometimes, too, they were stiff-necked and legalistic and cruelly intolerant. Man's ideas about the nature of God's truth have often been—quite literally—matters of life and death.

In 1541 John Calvin was invited to come to Geneva. Into that city divided by battles and sects Calvin came to establish a theocratic government under the Consistory of Elders. Within about twenty years he had united most Swiss Protestants in what came to be called the "reformed Church." To some men its Calvinistic doctrines and structures were harsh and icy. Others summoned a tepid enthusiasm. A few rejoiced in the beauty of bleakness.

The "Ecclesiastical Ordinances," those forerunners of the later "Blue Laws" in many Western lands, were strict and somber. They were enforced by the civil authorities who were expected to support and protect the church. They contained precise and detailed regulations for a simple form of worship: Bible reading, psalms, prayers, preaching, especially preaching. Most ceremonial aspects of church services were abandoned. "Sweating sermons" were to be preferred to what England's Archbishop Laud, quoting from the psalms, called "the beauty of holiness." Laud liked the organ roll of the psalms. The Calvinists found other parts of the Bible more interesting and important.

The Consistory of Geneva and the authorities of the Reformed Churches in many other lands also watched public and private morals. It was blasphemy to "defame Calvin," and wicked to play cards, to stay away from Church services, to dance. In Cromwell's day in England it was an offense to be found "walking profanely abroad on the Sabbath."

The Geneva system, in varying forms, spread its dynamic power into many lands. It reached into wide areas of Europe, into Scotland and, to a lesser extent, into England. In later days it moved into far lands beyond the seas. As the years passed, the rigid attitudes and rigorous procedures of many of the Reformed Churches slowly changed as a result of successive doses of toleration. For more than four centuries many members of the Reformed Churches have been valiant, devoted, and evangelical servants of God. They are often men of will and energy, granite morals and principles.

Throughout the European countries where Protestantism prevailed the authority of the state was greatly increased. In Germany and the Scandinavian countries, for instance, the churches became, in many respects, departments of state, important divisions of "the powers that be ordained of God."

It was also a fact that in most Protestant lands the gap between the clergy and the laymen was narrowed. This statement is particularly true of the Lutheran regions, where all true believers were deemed to form the priesthood of God. The altered relation of the clergy and laymen was obviously but one aspect of the explosive individualism released by the Reformation and the Renaissance. Both of these massive events had much to do with the later insistence upon the importance of individual human dignity in the politically democratic Western states. Not all the fountainheads of freedom first spurted in the eighteenth century.

The lifting of some barriers of authority inevitably loosed a number of undisciplined spirits who made few contributions to society. We need not pause to study or to mourn. There were also many religious sects, some of them sane and sober and some of them not. In all societies there are individuals who abuse authority when they have it. There are others who confuse freedom with the right to incite to riot. One of the central purposes of civilization is to try to find the secret of combining individual freedom with social order.

Luther and Calvin would have been shocked and angered to have seen the rampant individualism of later centuries. In the years of the Protestant Reformation most leaders were usually opposed to such things as unfettered freedom of speech and investigation. There was wide Protestant opposition, for example, to the study of natural science. Most Protestant groups insisted that there could be no salvation outside their own faith and their own church. To them, as to the Roman Catholics, dissent and heresy were often the same thing. What are called the progressive and secular aspects of most Protestant thought came after the first prophets and leaders were gone. In many respects the first phases of the Reformation were essentially conservative. This fact is often forgotten in the contemporary age where the frequent insistence upon flexibility and relativism has often caused older sanctions to crack and crumble, not always for the good of mankind.

Early followers of Luther and Calvin—and the members of several other groups—were usually stern and disciplined soldiers of the Lord. Religion was a sober business.

To many modern men and women the faith and life of their forefathers may seem frigid and uncongenial. Through the centuries there have been many interpretations and judgments about the best way to live and die.

Meanwhile the various forms of Calvinism helped to stimulate what Max Weber called "the spirit of capitalism." The Scriptures said that "a man diligent in his business" would "stand before kings and not mean men." As Professor R. H. Tawney and others have clearly shown, the course of religion and the rise of capitalism are inextricably mingled. It was, surely, a matter of duty and conscience to labor in the shops and fields, to increase capital— ethically, of course—and to use one's God-given talents so that a businesslike accounting could be given to the Lord. Those who professed the faith and accepted the disciplines of John Calvin were usually men who believed themselves to be hardheaded and practical, guided by time-tested common sense and not by theories and fancies born of the philosophers' studies. A glance at the history of Scotland and New England will illustrate—if any illustration is needed—what power in the secular world was wielded by those toughminded Calvinists.

In the first part of this chapter it was remarked that long before the Protestant Reformation there had been numerous and strong pressures for reform within the Roman Catholic Church. In all of Europe there were devout Roman Catholics who were dismayed and angered by the weakness and corruption of the clergy, high and low. To them the doctrines of men like Luther and Calvin provided no answers and the churches they founded provided no refuge. They wanted their own Church to meet the mounting emergency by setting its own house in order and marching forth to war against the foe with a new spirit and a new vigor.

The mobilization of Roman Catholic power was slow and difficult. There were also the problems of tactics and strategy. Despite the dark memories and the sad results of many earlier Church councils, especially in the Conciliar movements of the fifteenth century, it was decided to summon the leaders of the Church to meet and plan means and methods of internal reform and a vigorous campaign against the Protestants. The resulting Council of Trent met three times in long sessions: 1545–1547, 1551–1552, and 1562–1563.

At the famous Council of Trent traditional doctrines were stated once more with vigor and clarity. Major and drastic reforms, so long needed, were carried through with determination and skill—this time there was no evasion or equivocation. Sincere and zealous popes—the first was the fiery Paul III who had come to the papal throne in 1534—hastened along the paths overgrown with weeds and cut and cleaned on every hand. The upper clergy, at last roused and belligerent, labored to overcome the disasters and difficulties brought by delay and weakness. The Protestant foes were at the gates. The danger was terrible and the time perhaps short.

The Roman Catholic Church readied itself for conflict on many fronts. The hope of reconciliation—if hope there ever had been after a Roman Catholic-Protestant conference collapsed in 1540—was past. The Roman Catholics, for instance, could not alter their traditional insistence that both faith and good works were necessary for salvation. They could not surrender any of the sacraments: "If anyone saith that the sacraments of the new law were not instituted by Jesus Christ, our Lord; or that they are more or less than seven, to wit, baptism, confirmation, the Eucharist, penance, extreme unction, orders, and matrimony; or even that any one of those seven is not truly and properly a sacrament; let him be anathema." Nor could the Roman Catholic Church accept any change in the doctrine of transubstantiation. The fabric of faith of the ancient Church could not be thus rudely torn, Luther and Calvin and all the rising sects to the contrary. The dogmas of the Roman Church were the foundation stones of faith. So far as the Council of Trent was concerned, those stones would not be moved or shattered whatever the wind or weather or whatever the Protestants might assert or do.

The Roman Catholic Church did not lack weapons, men, or skill. For instance, it possessed the Inquisition, the great ecclesiastical court which in medieval and modern times has detected, tried, and punished heretics and other offenders against orthodoxy. It also used the Index, a list of books that the faithful were forbidden to read or possess.

The controls of punishment and censorship were powerful weapons in the unrelenting conflict between the Roman Catholic Church and those who belonged to its ranks no more. There also appeared many efficient missionary groups and active soldiers of reform, the spiritual descendants of the reforming orders of the thirteenth and fourteenth centuries. Greatest of these was the Society of Jesus, an intensely militant and uncompromising body of crusaders first led by the Spaniard St. Ignatius of Loyola.

St. Ignatius (1491–1556) was one of the creative geniuses of the Roman Catholic Church. The son of a poor Basque noble, Ignatius became a page in the Spanish royal court of Ferdinand and Isabella. Later he served as a soldier and was wounded. While recovering from his wounds Ignatius read books about several saints of the Church, and those books changed his life. He went into retreat and vigorously disciplined his mind and body to serve his Lord and Church. Afterwards he wrote the famous *Spiritual Exercises,* a handbook still used by his followers. Said Ignatius: "I can find God at all times, whenever I wish, and any man of good will can do the same. As the body can be exercised by going, walking, and running, so the will of man can be trained by exercise to find the will of God."

Ignatius was certain that he had indeed found the will of God. In Paris, aided by Francis Xavier and a few other men, he began the association that became the Society of Jesus, usually called the Jesuits, a military body of dedicated soldiers of God (1540). Slowly the power of the order girdled the world. It reached into the edges of Europe, into Japan, China, India, Africa, North and South America. It seemed that wherever the word of God needed preaching there went the Jesuit explorers and missionaries. In Persia, Father Gaspar Barzaeus preached to Mohammedans and Jews. In China, Father Matthew Ricci led the way for the numerous Jesuits who became advisers at the China court. Father Lorenz Nicolai went to Sweden. Marquette and Joliet explored in North America. Although temporarily suppressed (1773–1814) the Society of Jesus later grew in size and power. It is the largest order in the Roman Catholic Church today—there are more than 30,000 Jesuits and they serve in 74 nations.

Possessed of tools and men like these, it is not surprising that the Roman Catholic Church was able to throw back its foes on many fronts. Although the lands of Spain and Italy had never been seriously threatened by Protestant invaders their defenses were strengthened and supply routes and communication lines were kept open with the underground movements in Protestant areas. Protestant rebellions in Poland, Austria, and Hungary were crushed, not gently. The independent states of southern Germany were kept for Rome; the north belonged to Luther. The southern Netherlands went back to the Roman faith; the Dutch stayed with Calvin. National churches rose and flourished. Meanwhile the Roman Catholic missionaries went over the seas to teach and save. Protestant missionaries followed after.

France seemed at first securely Roman Catholic, mainly because the strong kings Francis I and Henry II ruled with hands of steel and permitted no deviations from orthodoxy. When the strong kings were dead the Protestant voices could no longer be muffled or silenced. The Huguenots—those Calvinistic Protestants—multiplied in the ranks of the French nobles and among the middle class. Unhappy France moved towards a period of bitter and bloody religious wars. Soon thousands of humble and heroic men would be locked in conflict as their pulses kept pace with the sound of the guns. For many of them, life's last grains would be running out of the glass.

Conflicting answers and opposing values in the realm of Christian faith had divided all of Europe. The agnostics and neutrals who stood on the uncharted borderlands must have been quite confused in those years of the wars of religion. Their descendants would find that their task was perhaps less difficult. In a new and more secularized age they could give their loyalties to the new nation-states. For most men there would be little difficulty about that: a man who was a Frenchman would usually fight for France. As a French Calvinist from Picardy marched towards the Rhine he might find that the man on his right was a Roman Catholic from Paris. The first enemy to fall before his fire might be a Lutheran. The wars of men continue; the ends and causes change.

The leaders of the Reformation in Europe were mainly concerned with making changes in religious dogmas and practices. They could not stop there. Side by side with the upheavals in religion came slow revolutions in other areas of the lives of men. It is sometimes possible in books to keep neatly separated the pressures and thrusts of such varied things as religion, politics, and economics. In real life such controls are not possible. There were important political and economic causes of the European Reformation and there were important political and economic consequences. What began as a series of revolts within the Church ended by becoming political, economic, and military struggles that shook the whole Continent. The souls of men are always important. So, too, are their prides, their politics, and their pockets. Some men have often preferred much money and a soft bed to poverty and virtue and the teachings of a hard Bible. Other men have been of a different opinion. The important point is simply this: it was as impossible in the sixteenth century as it is today to label and allocate precise significance to religious crusades and defeats and victories. Sometimes the use of the adjectives "political" and "economic" and "religious" merely means that you are going to try to look at the same men and events through different lenses. What the observer sees sometimes depends a great deal upon his spectacles and upon the total of his own character and personality.

When the Reformation came to England and Scotland it came swiftly. Ireland was isolated; Ireland was quite safe. Among most Irishmen no questions arose about their own steady adherence to the faith of Rome and no trouble came until successive waves of Protestant men swept into northern Ireland in a later day and the counties of Ulster became and remained a Protestant stronghold. The Irish were not yet compelled to ask or answer the difficult question facing the men of London and Edinburgh: what should be the position of a clerical organization as a part of a body politic?

The leaders of the early English and Scottish Reformation were less concerned with problems of dogma than with a revision of the relations between church and state. Their Reformation was at first primarily a political reconstruction; the reformed religion came later. Englishmen, in this rising age of nation-states, were increasingly aware of their separateness from other nations. Their emotions were becoming more and more attached to King Henry

VIII (1509–1547) and to England. They turned less and less to Rome. The emotions that linked them to Rome had never been national ones, and the fires of nationalism were now burning brightly. "I content myself with my own," said the mighty Tudor Henry VIII. "I only wish to command my subjects; but, on the other hand, I do not choose anyone to have it in his power to command me, nor will I ever suffer it."

Henry VIII was theologically orthodox. From Pope Leo X he had received the title "Defender of the Faith" for defending the seven sacraments against the attacks of Martin Luther. The king and most of his people were opposed to heresy; but they were also opposed to many practices of the Church. For centuries in England there had been waves of anticlericalism. With the coming of the critical spirit of the Renaissance the anticlerical and antipapal feeling increased. Disputes multiplied and a great body of pamphlet literature arose about the endowed wealth of the Church and Church taxation, about the corruption and muddles of the spiritual body of the Church, the degeneration of the monasteries, the decline of the mendicant orders, the evils of the ecclesiastical courts, the abuses of benefit of clergy, the increase and degradation of relics, the decline of the practice of Christian virtues. Few of the men who complained were schismatics; they simply wanted a reform of their Church.

Why should the large sums of annates and Peter's Pence collected from the people be shipped directly to the foreign city of Rome? Why should they not remain in England? Everywhere the churchmen were gathering money. "The parson sheareth, the parish priest polleth, the friar scrapeth, and the pardoner pareth; we lack but a butcher to pull off the skin."

Against this background of ferment and unrest there arose the famous series of questions connected with Henry VIII's marriage to Catherine of Aragon.

Between 1509 and 1515 Catherine had borne Henry four sons and one daughter; all had died almost at birth. A daughter named Mary, born in 1516, survived. There followed successive miscarriages and a stillborn child. To secure the succession Henry felt that a son was vitally necessary. If the strong king left only a daughter to succeed him the result might be the end of the Tudor dynasty, a civil war like that of the fifteenth century, a national weakness tempting foreign foes.

Did Henry VIII have honest doubts about the validity of his marriage? No man can say with certainty. In November, 1501, Henry's elder brother Arthur had married Catherine; five months later Arthur died. In June, 1503, Catherine was betrothed to Henry, who was then twelve years old. The canon law said that a man might not marry his deceased brother's wife. True, Pope Julius II had issued a dispensation to permit the marriage of Catherine and Henry. Was the dispensation valid? Did the curse of Leviticus (XX, 21) raise doubts in Henry's mind? In the book of Leviticus it was written that if a man marries his brother's widow "they shall be childless." Scruples of conscience may have been a terrible reality to Henry VIII; and they may not. Then, too, for Henry the attraction of Anne Boleyn, one of the queen's attendants, was strong. "The gospel light first shone in Boleyn's eyes."

Henry VIII could obtain a dissolution of his marriage with Catherine of Aragon only if the pope agreed to recognize the union as originally invalid. A contemporary records that "the king is studying the matter so diligently that I believe he knows more in this case than a great theologian and jurist." Embassy after embassy was sent to Rome. In vain Henry VIII and his aides —especially Thomas Wolsey—pressed the pope to yield.

One massive obstacle stood in Henry's way. In 1527 the Emperor Charles V was in Rome. The pope, an ally of Francis I of France, was the prisoner of Charles. Because Charles was the nephew of Catherine of Aragon it was not reasonable to expect that Henry would obtain a favorable hearing at the papal court. It was difficult for Pope Clement VII to say that the emperor's aunt had been living in sin for eighteen years, especially when the emperor's soldiers streamed about the streets of Rome. The pressure of Charles V upon the papacy was sharp and heavy. The pressure of Henry VIII steadily mounted.

In 1529 the strong-willed Henry called Parliament "to redress the enormities of the clergy." Henry knew how many Englishmen resented the authority and exactions of the pope. He also knew that the majority of those in the propertied classes would not shrink from plundering the churchmen, a wealthy and unpopular minority. So far as Henry VIII was concerned, such a procedure would increase his income; it was also to be preferred to the more orthodox methods of direct taxation.

Would Pope Clement VII be coerced? There is no doubt that the Parliament of 1529 stood behind Henry VIII. Charges of servility, terror, or packing have frequently been made and they remain unproved. Early in its sessions Parliament prohibited nonresidence of the clergy and certain other obvious abuses. The papal jurisdiction next came under scrutiny. "Though from Christian charity we abhor retaliation yet we are not so preposterously patient to endure injuries with equanimity," declared Henry VIII. Clement wrote to Henry, "admonishing him in all benevolence and threatening excommunication."

In 1531 Henry accused the whole clergy of violating the laws of England because they had recognized Thomas Wolsey as a papal legate. They voted in Convocation to pay a fine of £100,000. They were also forced to acknowledge Henry VIII to be their "especial protector, single and supreme lord, and so far as the law of Christ allows, even Supreme Head." Early in 1532 the payment of annates to Rome was suspended. The spirit of resistance was draining out of the clergy. Had not Henry VIII said that he "would not brook denial?"

In 1532 Henry appointed Thomas Cranmer to the vacant archbishopric of Canterbury. In January, 1533, Henry married Anne Boleyn. In February an act of Parliament forbade appeals to Rome. In April, Cranmer declared that Henry's marriage to Catherine of Aragon had never been valid. In June, Anne Boleyn was declared queen. In September, the princess Elizabeth was born. The English ambassador was recalled from Rome.

In 1534 the Act of Supremacy declared that "the King, our sovereign lord, his heirs and successors, kings of this realm, shall be taken, accepted, and reputed the only supreme head on earth of the Church of England . . . to the pleasure of Almighty God, the increase in virtue in Christ's religion, and for the conservation of the peace, unity, and tranquillity of this realm." The legal breach with the See Apostolic was complete.

Thus the issues between the rival powers of church and state were at last settled in England. The church was annexed to the state. Henry VIII was head of the state and head of the English national church. Parliament and convocation were now in a similar relationship to the crown. The shaping ideas of national heroes and saints, of economic nationalism, of intellectual unity, and of national solidarity had been emerging more sharply into the full light of English history. What happened in 1534 was a natural chapter in a long process.

An Act of Succession soon provided that the heirs of Henry VIII and Anne Boleyn should succeed to the throne. A few men of Roman Catholic consciences, including Sir Thomas More and John Fisher, Bishop of Rochester, were executed when they would not accept the Succession Act or acknowledge Henry VIII to be the Head of the Church. New Treasons Acts were passed. Spies and informers plied their nefarious trades. In 1536 the small monasteries, in 1539 the large monasteries, were dissolved by acts of Parliament and their property given to the king. Henry VIII gave away or sold the larger part of the monastic lands. The propertied classes who shared in the plunder from the Church were now more firmly bound to the house of Tudor and the repudiation of papal supremacy.

Henry VIII had no mind to tolerate Protestant ideas in his realm. Despite the creeping influence of Protestant voices from across the Channel, Henry VIII continued to be rigidly orthodox. All the doctrines and rituals were to be those of the Church before the separation from Rome. The Six Articles Act of 1539, for instance, provided that any individual who denied transubstantiation was to suffer the loss of life and property. Henry VIII executed both Roman Catholics who denied the royal supremacy and the heretics who denied the Catholic doctrines of the Six Articles. "It was wonderful to see adherents of the two opposing parties dying at the same time," said a contemporary, "and it gave offence to both."

Meanwhile Anne Boleyn drifted to disaster. She was convicted of adultery and executed in 1536. Henry's next queen, Jane Seymour, died in childbirth; her son survived and later became Edward VI. The further matrimonial adventures of Henry VIII need not concern us here. It is enough to say that Henry had three more wives; only one of them died on the scaffold.

Men still debate about Henry VIII's political genius and his monstrous iniquity. For good or ill, his actions were always on a grand scale. Whatever may be said about his morals and his sins, the fact remains that Henry VIII consolidated the Tudor power and strengthened England as a nation-state. His safe and prudential Reformation had made an English church a national church in name and in fact.

In January, 1547, Henry VIII died. His heir was a little boy, and two girls after him. The shocks and upheavals that followed the death of Henry are themselves evidence of his force and his power. Henry could ride the whirl-wind. Those who followed him could not.

The will of Henry VIII left the throne to his only son Edward. If Edward had no heirs the throne was to go first to Henry's daughter Mary, then to his daughter Elizabeth. In 1547 Edward was only nine years of age, a sickly and precocious child. His father's strong hand had held many forces in iron con-trol. Now men felt the grip of that hand no more. The flames of rebellion licked at the foundations of the state; through court and castle spread the slow poison of intrigue.

The council of regency was soon divided by doctrinal hatreds, by jealousies, by conflicting interests. The leader of the council was the Duke of Somerset, the uncle of Edward VI. Somerset was a soldier. He was neither a statesman nor a politician. With the approval of Edward VI, Somerset proceeded to secure the passage of laws pointing towards Protestantism. The Treasons Act of Henry VIII was largely repealed. The Six Articles Act was rescinded. Protestant preachers came in from the Continent to explain the creeds of their reformed religions.

In 1549 the first Act of Uniformity was passed. It ordered a new prayer book to be used in the churches. The book contained the beautiful English liturgy prepared by Archbishop Cranmer, who was himself strongly influenced by Protestant doctrines. The dignity and power of the new ritual, filled with "the matchless beauty of the shapèd syllable," rendered a priceless service to the national church. It also stood as a compromise between the extremes of both Protestantism and Roman Catholicism and thus angered all who did not like compromise, evasion, or obscurity.

Somerset and his pro-Protestant oligarchy proceeded to carry further the confiscation of church property. They destroyed thousands of relics, images, and shrines. Priceless treasures of medieval art were knocked down, torn, or burned. The excesses of Protestant mobs increased the divisions of opinion.

Throughout England squabbles multiplied and armed skirmishes often reddened the village greens. Meanwhile, too, economic disturbances shook the state.

Somerset was overthrown and executed as a result of the plots and power of the self-seeking and dishonest Duke of Northumberland. When Edward VI died of tuberculosis in 1553, Northumberland vainly tried to put Lady Jane Grey upon the throne. Mary Tudor, the rightful heir, defeated Northumberland and the headsman's ax ended his plots and hopes.

Queen Mary, daughter of Catherine of Aragon and Henry VIII, succeeded to the throne at the age of thirty-seven, a worn, warped, harsh, and bitter woman. Through the years of danger and persecution she had clung to her Roman Catholic religion; it was her consolation and her refuge. When Mary came to the throne in 1553 she was determined to bring Englishmen back to what she believed was the only true way, the only religion that could save their souls. Her mission, as she saw it, was to restore the Roman Catholic church to its ancient power in England.

The return of England to the Roman allegiance began swiftly. Many Protestant bishops were imprisoned. Roman Catholic bishops were placed in positions of power. An Act of Repeal referred to the legislation and practices of Edward VI's reign "whereof has ensued among us, in a very short time, numbers of diverse and strange opinions and diversities of sects, and thereby grown great unquietness and much discord, to the great disturbance of the commonwealth of this realm; and in a very short time like to grow to extreme peril and utter confusion." An Act of Uniformity and eight other acts of the reign of Edward VI were "utterly repealed, void, and annihilated" with the result that Catholic doctrine and service were restored as they had stood at the end of the reign of Henry VIII.

The third Parliament of Mary was more submissive and pro-Roman Catholic than the two before it. A second Act of Repeal repealed the Act of Supremacy and most of the antipapal laws of Henry VIII. Parliament also re-enacted the heresy acts "for the eschewing and avoiding of errors and heresies which of late have risen, grown, and much increased within this realm." About 300 Protestants were burned at the stake. Mary certainly expected that her persecution would weaken Protestantism. Here she miscalculated. The impression she created was indeed lasting, but it was the opposite of what she intended. Protestant martyrs died as the Roman Catholics Thomas More and John Fisher had perished for their faith two decades before. The Reformation was sealed with the blood of martyrs, most of them humble folk.

Queen Mary's marriage to Philip of Spain had been a mistake. When she was persuaded to help Philip in a war with France she gained nothing and she lost Calais. She had hoped for an heir and she was disappointed. Sterility was the keynote of her reign. Famine and disease sharpened discontent. Mary's ill-judged severities in the cause of Roman Catholicism sent her popularity shooting downwards at a quickened pace. The whole reign of the honest and misguided Mary was one of maladministration, discontent, defeat, bloodshed, disgrace, and persecution. The chapters of her life were dark and tragic. On November 17, 1558, Mary died of cancer. Her successor was Elizabeth I, daughter of Henry VIII and Anne Boleyn.

The hard school of experience had made Elizabeth I skeptical, subtle, watchful, wise, a queen with a peculiar political genius. Capricious as the surface of her nature might seem, the depths were usually steady and hard. Like her father before her, she craved power; and she knew that power must rest upon popular approval. It had been the habit of Henry VIII to stoop to conquer; it was also the habit of his daughter.

In dealing with the problem of religion, Elizabeth moved carefully. The Roman Catholics waited and hoped. In the first public document of the new reign an "et cetera" was placed at the end of the royal titles where Henry VIII and Edward VI had written "Supreme Head of the Church." At first Elizabeth I attended Mass; she kept her ambassador at Rome; she kept the Roman Catholic bishops and clergy in their offices. Slowly, however, the prospect altered. It was soon clear that Elizabeth and her council intended to establish a system of moderation and compromise, to place the English Church on a broad middle ground of doctrine and practice. The new state faith was to be a fiat religion to which all must publicly conform.

The famous compromise settlement was swiftly effected. The Marian legislation that had brought England back into the Roman Church was repealed. A new Act of Supremacy again abolished papal power in England. The Act of Uniformity of 1559 enjoined the use of the Second Prayer Book of Edward VI in all churches. Alterations were made to provide a form of service acceptable to as many Englishmen as possible. Doctrinally much scope was left for varying shades of belief; precise definition was carefully avoided. The Thirty-Nine Articles of 1571 purged the Forty-Two Articles of Edward VI of their extreme Protestant elements. Thus the nation in Parliament decided the nature of the established Church and the established religion. Elizabeth I hoped that this compromise settlement would meet the wishes of the majority of her people. The queen preferred to have "controversial points involved in a wise obscurity." At the same time she determined to have outward conformity and complete royal supremacy. Elizabeth I and her churchmen did not want to set the church agog with spiritual excitement. They did not demand unity of hearts or conviction. To "open windows into men's souls" was not their intention. They demanded only external conformity. On many questions of dogma and doctrine they were quite prepared to hedge; few governments were less swayed by purely religious motives.

As the years passed the Anglican compromise was loudly opposed by two groups: the Roman Catholics and the Puritans. The former rejected the Act of Supremacy. The latter demanded further Protestant reforms. For more than a hundred years these complaints were to form a central theme of English history. The Roman Catholics made several dangerous plots and spread much militant propaganda. The numerous attacks of the Puritan Protestants were usually coarse and slashing. The result of such tides of assaults was an increase of government control. In 1593, for instance, Parliament passed "an act to retain the queen's subjects in obedience," directed against "the wicked and dangerous practices of seditious sectaries and disloyal persons" and providing for imprisonment of all offenders until they should conform. In the same year an act was passed "for the better discovering and avoiding of all such traitorous and most dangerous conspiracies and attempts as are daily devised and practised . . . by sundry wicked and seditious persons calling themselves Catholics."

Meanwhile the mere passage of the years was helping to fix and establish the Church of England. In human history time and habit are often stronger forces than legislation. In the reign of Elizabeth I there also appeared several solid and sensible statements and explanations of the Anglican faith. It was clear that the body of its Catholic doctrine reached back to the wellsprings of Christianity. The apostolic succession in the clergy had continued unbroken. It was also true that the whole fabric of Anglican faith contained much of the Aristotelian and medieval conception of the universe and the state and of man's place in both. In Richard Hooker's *Law of Ecclesiastical Polity*—the prose masterpiece of the golden Elizabethan age—there appeared a clear and balanced statement of the Anglican idea of the nature of the good state and the good individual, the basic political philosophy of the Anglican Church. There were also stated and stressed the orthodox doctrines of the early church councils, the rules of the Scriptures and the creeds, the fixed laws of a changeless God "to whom all hearts are open and all desires known." The foundation of all human morality, in the judgment of Hooker, was to be found in a body of Christian beliefs and practices that binds individuals together in a companionship with one another and with God.

In the four centuries since the Renaissance and Reformation there have appeared in the Western world a bewildering array of new sects and individual interpretations of the Scriptures. In some groups, indeed, it seems that God has been replaced by man, the ruthless and devouring master of things, filled with ego-centered faiths. For them the New Jerusalem has become a secularized and earthly society of man, free from pain and want. Man, it is said, has surely conquered Nature—until some tragic headlines suggest that Nature has conquered man. All confused in brave new beliefs and myths are pragmatism and ethics, love and violence, relativism and moral absolutes. Strange things swivel and swirl around the unanchored pivots of the Unfixed and the Unsure.

Often, too, the concern and the compassion for the individual man and woman have been lost in our great modern societies so occupied with mass minds and mass action. It has sometimes been forgotten, surely, that the Gospel can never be anything but personal—"strait is the gate, and narrow is the way, which leadeth unto life, and few there be that find it." Five centuries ago Meister Eckhart said: "People should think less about what they ought to do and more about what they ought to be."

Chapter 21

BEYOND
THE UNKNOWN SEAS

" 'Sir, if any other come that hath better iron than you he will be master
of all this gold.' "
—Solon to Croesus in Francis Bacon's
Of the True Greatness of Kingdoms

M UCH of our contemporary world has obviously been shaped by successive revolutions in the making of tools and techniques of communication
and transportation. Our estimate of the culture of any society is partly marked
and measured by the answer we are given to this question: "How far and
how fast could the people move their bodies and their goods?" In the perspective of history we can see the altering scales on which men thought of distance. What was distant yesterday seems near today. Horizons shift and barriers shrink and disappear. More and more, endurance and enterprise have
become linked with new techniques and instruments and speed and power.
In the lands where there has been no change in the tools of power, civilizations have ebbed away. They are either dead or of little consequence in contemporary human affairs. Without power there is no progress. Without progress there is no power.

Our remote ancestors in the ancient river valleys made the best of the tools
and techniques that they had. They built rough rafts and boats to use on the
lakes and edges of the sea. Their descendants ventured further.

They that go down to the sea in ships, that do business in great waters;
These see the works of the Lord, and His wonders in the deep.

The reader will recall how daring and clever the Phoenician sailors were.
Their world was filled with adventure, hardship, profit, danger. "There is
danger everywhere except in heaven." The keels of the Vikings furrowed dark

338

oceans that surged and beat upon shores far from home. Chinese ships visited Africa. The Polynesians, those "Vikings of the Sunrise," thrust and searched over the waters of the Pacific.

The "Oceanic Age" of the Western world did not begin until the fifteenth century. The Europeans who sailed in that century to seek and find and trade did not know that they were beginning a new era of ocean-linked civilizations. Professor Arnold Toynbee once said that "the revolutionary Western invention was the substitution of the Ocean for the Steppe as the principal medium of world communication. This use of the Ocean, first by sailing ships and then by steamships, enabled the West to unify the whole inhabited and habitable world."

In the fifteenth century the sails that had sometimes sagged in the harbors stirred uneasily in the breeze. The new three-masted caravels were certainly more seaworthy than ships had ever been before. They were larger, too— their size was about 100 tons and they could carry a crew of about 60 men. The maps, charts, and astronomical tables had been steadily improved. In Chapter 18 it was mentioned that the mariner's compass, probably a Chinese invention, had been brought to Europe in the twelfth century. In the fourteenth century a new compass was invented: a magnetized needle rotating on a pivot independent of a ship's movements and used with a compass card. The astrolabe—that ingenious instrument used to find latitude by astronomy, the forerunner of the quadrant and the sextant—had been passed into Europe by the Arabs. About 1275 the first portolano charts appeared; these were working charts showing the contours of coasts in detail and the distances between places. The axled and hinged rudder, mentioned earlier, was first used in the Baltic and the North Sea in the thirteenth century. This rudder made it possible for the helmsman to steer large ships with big sails in the ocean. Ships thus equipped had probably taken the Scandinavian settlers to Iceland and Greenland when southern Europeans were fighting the Hundred Years' War and the Turks were closing in on Constantinople.

For a long time it was believed that a strong impetus to Western exploration and oceanic discovery came when the Turks closed the gateway to trade with the East with the seizure of Constantinople in 1453. About fifty years ago Professor A. H. Lybyer showed quite conclusively that the Turks interfered but little with Italian trade before 1516. If the trade had been large and there had been much Turkish interference, then the European price levels would have risen much more than they did. The ships of Venice and Genoa still moved in the eastern Mediterranean. The sailors still paused in the Near Eastern ports and in northern Africa to smell the sizzling shishkebab, the dust and sandalwood and myrtle. The sound conclusions of Professor Lybyer and several other scholars have not entirely prevented some men from uttering, without fear or doubt, the old tale that the Turks blocked one road to the East and the dauntless men of Europe found another. The truth is mighty, but it does not always prevail when the falsehood is dramatic and attractive. It is also often forgotten that Europe produced little that the East wanted. The Romans had suffered from a lack of goods to exchange with the East; and so did their successors.

The men of Europe who searched for new trade and trade routes were often resentful of the charges laid upon them by the Italians, those hungry middlemen. A direct water passage to the East promised to reduce prices on Eastern products. The gold and silver that was soon to flow from America provided the *quid pro quo* that Europe had previously lacked in trade with the East. The tides of trade slowly increased. The desire for participation and profit grew among several states of Europe. The Renaissance spirit of nationalism rose.

There was also the factor of religious zeal. Religion, empire, and trade are triple themes in the tales of most commercial nations.

First to adventure far upon the seas were the men of Portugal. They sailed and explored and traded. Their missionaries went out to help and save the souls of natives in distant lands. The most famous missionary of all was St. Francis Xavier, a Spaniard, a son of Navarre who worked and died in Asia.

The familiar motives of curiosity and desire for gain doubtless persuaded some Portuguese sailors to go out on strange seas towards a wider world. Some, no doubt, were knaves or fools. Some were probably fleeing from the tongues of shrewish women. Others may have been bored with the sameness of the dragging hours at the taverns and the slugging and sweating at the docks. The human dislike of monotony can often overcome the fear of the unknown and the unfamiliar, even the oft-repeated tales of the horrors beyond the horizons: the dog-headed monsters of the deep, the distant boiling seas, the bones of dead men floating amidst the weeds.

Prince Henry the Navigator (1394–1460), a younger son of King John of Portugal and grandson of England's famous John of Gaunt, became the patron of several Portuguese explorers. Prince Henry was not a seagoing man but he did understand the importance for Portugal and Europe of a search for better knowledge of the western ocean. He also wanted gold. At Cape St. Vincent he established a research center where scholars and sailors collected all the information they could find about geography and navigation. Mapmakers and mathematicians labored hard.

Of special and immediate interest were the waters along the unknown west coast of Africa. In 1312 the Genoese had rediscovered one of the Canary Islands and started a colony there. The Madeira Islands appear on a map of the fourteenth century. There had long been exciting tales of the lands where a "western Nile" was said to flow down to the Atlantic. Could men go up this mysterious river to the reputedly rich and magnificent Negro lands beyond the barren stretches of the Sahara? Could they reach the golden country of Abyssinia and the wonderful Christian kingdom of Prester John? Could they then push on to the Indies?

All of the explorations undertaken under the auspices of Prince Henry the Navigator were carefully described in the contemporary *Chronicles of Azurara,* a mine of information for later ages. From the pages of *Azurara* and elsewhere we can trace the slow Portuguese advance down the west coast of Africa and beyond. The rising public interest in geography and the wonders of the wider world soon resulted in the writing of several books, such as Antonio Galvano's *The Discoveries of the World* (1555), Roger Barlow's *A Brief Somme of Geography* (1540), Richard Hakluyt's *Principal Navigations* (1589). Meanwhile men's ideas of space and geography steadily changed. European man moved from a local view to a regional and then to a global. It was a long revolution.

In 1418 the Portuguese occupied the Madeira Islands. Soon a stream of goods flowed from Madeira to Portugal: timber, sugar, honey, the famous Madeira wine made from the malmsey grape brought in from Crete. Portuguese sailors reached the Azores in 1427. Soon the first experiments in colonization began. In 1445 the Cape Verde Islands were discovered and in 1446 a fort was built on the coast of Guinea. The mouths of the Senegal and Gambia were found. Diogo Cão reached the mouth of the Congo in 1482. Black slaves from Africa were brought into Portugal and the new colonies. More and more Portuguese ships sailed along the Gold, Slave, and Ivory Coasts.

Meanwhile the Portuguese made heavy shipments of sugar to northwest Europe. They spent large amounts of Sudanese gold in the Low Countries and in the German states, to the disadvantage of Genoa and Venice where the shortage of gold was acute. There were many ways, even in the fifteenth century, of waging economic warfare. The Atlantic ports were soon to rise in power as the glory of the Italian trading cities became faint and dim. Slowly the centers of strength and commerce were to move from the Mediterranean to the Atlantic seaboard. There they were to remain. The results were incalculable in the history of the world of the West.

Strange and horrendous tales were told of the great cape at the southern end of Africa called the Cape of Storms, soon to be named the Cape of Good Hope. For many years the Portuguese looked upon this region with doubt and superstition. Sometimes they called it the Cape of Admastor after the vengeful spirit of storms that appeared in the *Lusiads* to predict the disasters that would befall the men who sailed on to India.

Bartholomeu Dias first rounded the Cape of Good Hope in 1486. He was followed soon by Vasco da Gama, a Portuguese noble who reached the west coast of India in 1498. Vasco da Gama set out with four ships and came back to Lisbon in July, 1499, with two ships and a small spice cargo. In his long voyage he used *naus*, square-rigged and heavier vessels than the low and light lateen-rigged caravels sailed by Bartholomeu Dias and those who went before. Many sea captains were to sail their ships through the centuries around the famous cape on the road to India. Once they were past Table Mountain and Table Bay they ran before the west winds of the "roaring forties" until they hit the trade winds in the longitude of Java. They usually sailed in the old cause of spices and profits and souls and patriotism. Like the oaken men who had gone before them, they often pushed back the curtains of the unknown. Prophets and pioneers belong to all the ages of mankind.

The Portuguese now moved swiftly. Along the shores of Africa they built a chain of posts, warehouses and "factories." The great viceroy Almeida, soon to be killed by the Hottentots, fortified Mozambique and Mombasa on the east coast. The Turks and Venetians, anxious to keep some eastern commerce moving on the overland routes, blocked, for a time, the Portuguese attempts to seize Aden, near the entrance to the Red Sea. In 1506 Portugal built a naval station at Ormuz, a strategic spot at the mouth of the Persian Gulf. Meanwhile, Alfonso de Albuquerque, that quick and ruthless soldier, conquered Goa on the west coast of India. Into Portuguese hands fell Muscat and Malacca on the Malay Peninsula, a commanding spot on the road to India and China. Portuguese expeditions were sent to Banda and the Molucca Islands. Portuguese sailors reached Java and Siam. An agent was sent to Canton in 1514. Portuguese traders visited Japan in 1542. Macao was leased from China in 1557.

Portugal is said to have obtained 1,300 tons of pepper from the East in 1503, especially from Malacca, that great spice market. Large profits from eastern trade were recorded in the ledgers of Portuguese men of enterprise.

After the Portuguese came the Dutch. In the sixteenth century many men of the Low Countries read a book by their countryman van Linschoten: *A Voyage to the East Indies*. Its pages told of van Linschoten's travels, of his imprisonment by the Portuguese at Goa (1583), of the court of the Mogul Emperor Akbar, the far lands where there were "a deplorable number of heathen idols . . . some were like a cow, some were like a monkey, some like peacocks, and some like the devil." In the East, said van Linschoten, there were "great provinces, puissant cities, and immeasurable islands." Must all this be left to the Portuguese?

It would be incorrect to think that the words of van Linschoten were the main stimulus to Dutch activity overseas. His voice was but one among many. The sudden increase in the size of the known world was firing the imaginations of eager Europeans everywhere. In 1602 the Dutch East India Company was founded. In 1609 the Dutch attacked the Portuguese settlement at Amboyna and in 1610 they burned a Portuguese fleet at Malacca. To Sumatra, Borneo, and Java the Dutchmen came to build strongpoints in their expanding empire. In 1652 Jan van Riebeck put Dutch colonists ashore at the Cape of Good Hope; they were the first European settlers in Africa south of the Sahara. In Africa and the East Indies several foundation stones of the modern world were being swiftly laid.

To the waters and lands of the East soon came the sailors and merchants of England and France. The results were to be more colonies, more commerce, and war.

Across the green miles of the Atlantic lay the great triangle of the continent of North America. This vast land mass covered 9,375,000 square miles of land —Europe contained 3,762,000 square miles. Its northern limits reached to the bare white world of the arctic ice, beyond the regions of the tundra and the home of the ptarmigan, polar bears, seals, and whales. The middle area of the continent stretched for more than 3,000 miles from coast to coast. There were mountains in the east and west, great fresh-water lakes in the northwest, the Great Lakes in the east central area, the St. Lawrence River, a large central plain reaching into the arid regions of the southwest. The broad central area was drained into the Gulf of Mexico by a great river system—the Mississippi River is nearly 4,000 miles long. Far to the southwest the Colorado River leaped and roared towards the narrow Gulf of California at the bottom of canyons, one of which is more than 300 miles long and over a mile deep. Millions of trees covered much of the land. Near the western coast in the higher Sierra Madre there were the bristlecone pines that have now grown for more than 4,000 years, the oldest living things upon the planet Earth. Mexico's cypress, El Tule, has grown for 3,500 years. The giant sequoia, the General Grant, in the great forest near Mount Whitney, is about 3,200 years old.

We have seen in earlier pages (Chapter 6) how some people came from Asia to North America by way of Bering Strait and the Aleutian Islands— they were probably following game animals northward as the ice fields retreated. Evidence of man's early presence upon this continent is found in many places, and a few of them were described in Chapter 6. Several archeological remains have also been discovered in the Yukon territory of Canada, in British Columbia, Manitoba, and Ontario. On the Frank Bay site near Ontario's Lake Nipissing, for instance, Mattawan chipped stone and pottery remains related to the Arctic Dorset and Paleo-Eskimo industries were discovered in 1954. Similar discoveries of artifacts have been made at the Sheuinandah site on Manitoulin Island. A thousand miles away, on Canada's Melville Peninsula, great carved boulders stand to challenge, and sometimes to confound, the experts. In 1956, near Dallas, Texas, archeologists found camel and elephant bones. They also discovered a spearhead with a partly fluted "Clovis point" similar to those previously unearthed in New Mexico. The "Clovis point" is about 37,000 years old, the earliest trace of human beings in the New World.

Through many generations there were successive waves of migration from Asia, usually by way of the north. In later centuries, a few men were perhaps swept across the Pacific from the Polynesian islands. The modern Kon-Tiki expedition of Thor Heyerdahl proved that the Pacific could be crossed in a primitive craft. The Atlantic was certainly spanned by the Norsemen, although it is improbable that they ever pierced to Minnesota or cut runes upon a Kensington stone. Eric the Red moved beyond Iceland to found two settlements in Greenland; the first was in 985. A man named Bjarni Herjulfson discovered the mainland of America somewhere around the end of the tenth century, and Leif Ericsson soon followed to explore a part of the coast of North America.

The successors of all the early migrants were the Eskimos who lived in the long and harsh miles between the Aleutian Islands and Labrador and the numerous and diverse tribes of Mongoloid Indians who inhabited most of the temperate and tropical regions to the south. Clyde Kluckhohn, Professor of Anthropology at Harvard University, and other authorities on ethnology and linguistics agree that about a thousand languages were spoken by the ten million Indians who were scattered over America before 1492. There were many kinds of Indian groups: the nomadic and the settled, the hunting, the fishing, and the agricultural. Most cultures were primitive. A few were not.

One of the advanced cultures existed in the southwest part of North America, the home of the Pueblo Indians. Some of these Indians were cliff dwellers who settled at such places as Mesa Verde in large cave areas under the rims of canyons. Others built their settlements on the canyon floors—in Chaco canyon there stand today the ruins of more than fifty villages. Almost all of the Pueblo Indians were highly skilled in architecture, in construction, in the making of beautiful pottery. Most of them were excellent farmers. They raised beans, corn, cotton, squash—the women did all the work. For their labor in building and farming the Pueblo Indians had only wooden and stone tools. They had no iron or bronze. They had no wheels.

More than a thousand miles to the southwest a second civilization appeared. About 1,000 B.C. tribes of Mayan Indians settled in Central America. They were indeed a remarkable people. Around 600 B.C.—many dates are uncertain in Mayan history—they devised a calendar so accurate that it commands the admiration of our contemporary world. Their various scientific calculations, especially in astronomy, were models of skill and precision. They also built several fine cities. Several scholars—including Professor Clyde Kluckhohn, upon whose writings and specialized knowledge these sentences are mainly based—have noted that the evidence of cultural influence from Asiatic regions is strong: the concept of mathematical zero, for instance, was known by the men of India in one hemisphere and by the Maya Indians in the other. Professor Kluckhohn has also called attention to "the striking similarities between the Indian game of parchesi and the American game of patolli; the detailed resemblances between notions about the zodiac; certain parallels between Maya art and architecture and certain styles in southeast Asia." Here and elsewhere are interesting similarities in religious, political, and social organization. It may be remarked, of course, that the nature of the human mind and body is such that many ideas and practices could have appeared quite independently in different continents.

At first the Mayas lived in the south. There the soil was often poor and the restless people moved and moved again, always northward. In the richer lowland region of the north they finally settled, usually in spots near natural ponds and sinkholes in the limestone. In the areas that are now Yucatán, Honduras, and Guatemala they raised their cities, temples, and palaces. The ruins of some of their great buildings lie today in the silent solitude of the tangled jungles on the borders of Yucatán and Guatemala.

The Mayas were men of the land, never of the sea. They cleared small areas of the tropical forest and grew their cacao, their rubber, and their avocadoes, beans, corn, papayas, peppers, pumpkins, and squash. They had few domesticated animals. The Mayas were not usually meat eaters. In that respect they were certainly unlike most Indian tribes in America.

There were two periods of high achievement in Mayan culture. The first was between 400 and 600 A.D. The second was between 1000 and 1200 A.D. By 1200 the Mayan civilization had reached its final height. Like the ancient Greeks, the Mayans united in a confederacy of independent walled city-states. The people were protected and prosperous. In such happy circumstances it is not surprising that there was a surge of achievement in art and architecture.

The power of the golden ages of the Mayas stands out in scores of ways and places: in the limestone monuments, called stelae, raised to mark important events; in the vases, jars, turquoise mosaics, jade carvings; in the spacious courts and the finely proportioned horizontal buildings with stucco or stone veneers; in the religious representations of gods and animals: snakes, frogs, jaguars, hummingbirds—hundreds of them silently contemplate the creeping jungle in the ruins of places like Chichén Itzá.

Among the main buildings in the large courts was usually a massive, flat-topped pyramid or a great mound, and on top of it stood a temple. The Mayas, like the Aztecs and many other Indian groups, worshiped the sun with elaborate rites. The powerful priests were the respected teachers, the scientists and mathematicians, and the keepers and guardians of the records and traditions of the past.

The strength of the Mayan civilization was slowly sapped by bloody civil wars. There was also another weakness not easily defined. Somehow, it is clear, the Mayas lost the will to achieve. Their culture, once so healthy, withered and grew brittle in the sun. About 1325 the lands of their great confederacy were largely taken over by the highland Aztec Indians, who established the center of their culture on the high plateau of Mexico at the lake-city Tenochtitlán—now the site of Mexico City. The warlike Aztecs overwhelmed the Toltecs—who had come down from the north in about 1000 A.D. —and rapidly built an Aztec empire that stretched from the Gulf of Mexico to the Pacific Ocean. The main Aztec weakness was this: they never created an effective system of government to deal with their numerous subject peoples.

In their cities the Aztecs built magnificent palaces. They raised large pyramids surmounted by their temples to the god of the sun and the god of war— legend said that the war god's temple was to be built where the prickly pear was found growing in a rock upon which stood an eagle holding a serpent. As a part of their polytheistic and bloody religion the Aztecs slaughtered thousands of human beings in ritual sacrifice to placate Huitzilopochtli, the terrible sun and war god. The priests cut out the heart of a victim with an obsidian knife before the idol of the hideous war god and held up the quivering heart of the victim before the shrine. The great snakeskin drums were beaten and the fires flamed as the naked body of the victim was hurled down the steps of the temple.

No blood sacrifices were given to Quetzalcoatl, the virtuous ruler and civilizer, the god of the wind and the heavens who stood for law, order, and knowledge. Quetzalcoatl is represented in Aztec art as a feathered serpent, the composite creature that was the symbol of the earth (serpent) and the sky (eagle) and the creator of men. To honor Quetzalcoatl the Aztecs raised at Cholula the biggest pyramid and temple in all their lands. It seems that most human beings who wish to honor a man or a pagan god or commemorate an event believe that the honor is increased by the size of the temple or the monument.

Only in the lands of the Pueblo Indians, the Chichas, the Mayas, and the Aztecs had the arts and crafts reached a really high level in North and Central America. Elsewhere, as we know, were the primitive living arrangements of the Eskimos and the Indian tribesmen who were mainly buffalo hunters and fishermen and whose greatest skills were the chipping of flint arrowheads and the putting of beads on wampum. In the dense jungle lands of Central America lived other Indian tribes, those almost nameless people who advanced not at all. In the twentieth century, for instance, the forests between the Panama Canal Zone and the edges of Colombia are being explored for the first time. Here live the primitive and hostile Chicoa Indians who paint their nearly naked bodies purple, red, and yellow with tree-bark dyes. Through unnumbered centuries they have stayed in their jungle lands. Not until the middle of the twentieth century did any strangers come to see what mysterious people dwelled midway on a line between Seattle and Rio de Janeiro and athwart the route of the modern Pan-American highway.

West of the steep slopes and plateaus on the edge of the Andes in South America stretch the rhythmic alternations of fertile oases and savage deserts. Here, and high in the Andes, have been found several pieces of pottery dating back to the days—around 1200 B.C.—of the land's primitive and houseless nomadic peoples. Centuries later came the higher native cultures of such groups as the Chimus, skilled in design, pottery work, and building; the tribes and families of the lake basin area at Tiauanaco in southern Peru; the Mochicas, with their strange tale of a slow decadence and death.

About 500 miles north of Peru's city of Lima, famous for its beauty, its aristocracy, and its earthquakes, is the broad valley of Lambayeque, rich in rice and sugar cane. In this valley are now many broken towers and piles of sun-dried bricks. These are the material remnants of the Chimu Indian civilization, one of the earliest known to have existed in South America. In 1956 Peruvian archeologists found other remains of the Chavin culture of the Chimu Indians about 170 miles from Lima; these discoveries included a large granite monument, an impressive gateway, and large cylindrical obelisks. Near the modern city of Trujillo are the ruins of Chanchan, once the capital of the Chimu kingdom. The traveler today can see the broken parts of the massive brickwork walls that once enclosed the great quadrangular courts. He may find a piece of the pottery that skilled Chimu hands shaped so well. Far to the south stands the ancient fortress of Paramongas marking the southern edge of the Chimu power, long ago so proud and strong.

The Chimu civilization began rather slowly along the Peruvian coast in a few unforested valley spots where the silt from the streams coming down from the Andes had made a fertile soil. In the years before 500 A.D. the people constructed irrigation systems; built their cities of sun-dried bricks; sailed up and down the coast on their cotton-sailed balsa rafts. Then they began to move further inland, to terrace the lower slopes of the Andes, and to settle up in the mountain valleys and on the high plateaus. There they raised their potatoes, herded their llamas, goats, sheep, and alpacas; and there they prospered.

Ruin came to the Chimu civilization at the hands of the Incas, "the people of the sun" from the higher regions of the Andes; they prepared the way for invasion and full conquest by blocking the mountain streams and thus cutting off the water supplies of the Chimu lands. These interlopers did not stop with the defeat of the Chimu Indians. They extended their power steadily. More and more tribes yielded before their arms.

By 1500 the famous Inca Empire had reached its height under Huayna Capac, "the Great Inca" who died about 1523. Inca dominions stretched from what is now southern Colombia through Peru and Bolivia into Argentina and down past the Santiago region of Chile. Far up in the Andes was the famous capital city of Cuzco—it was seized by the Incas in the thirteenth century. Here was the center of the Inca realm and the Andean world. Professor Arnold Toynbee, in an apt phrase, once called Cuzco the "germ cell" of the Empire.

The Incas worshiped a sun divinity with a lightning spear and a weird halo. Strange sun-disc designs are found scattered throughout the Inca lands, especially upon the numerous stone statues. Besides the sun discs there are other symbols: ferocious jaguars, unpleasant snakes, poised condors.

One of the most sacred places in the Inca Empire was the holy Island of the Sun in Lake Titicaca—13,000 feet above sea level. Here the blue cold waters match the blue of the sky. Not far away is Mount La Raya and the Vilcañoya valley. In the distant background the sinister teeth of the higher Andes are blurred by the miles.

The Incas did more than worship their gods. They were superb silversmiths. They made and garbed themselves with fine clothes with colors rich and wild. They were remarkable builders with bricks and carefully cut and fitted stones. Their temples, palaces, aqueducts, and forts—the stout fort Sacsahuaman, for instance—show how clever they were. Their canals, gardens, and fields brought crops and comfort, especially for those lucky enough to belong to the upper levels of society. The contours of the cultivated terraces grooving the mountain sides must have been an impressive sight. All of this, and more, was excellent. At the same time, of course, there was much squalor and poverty among the lower classes. The Incas never had a written language; hence there was no literature. The picture of any civilization must not be painted too brightly. In life, as in painting, the triumphal red is not enough. There are also the somber blacks and the shrinking browns.

Like the Persians and the Romans, the Incas were master road builders. Straight out from Cuzco went four main highways; one west to the Pacific coast; one east to the Amazon jungle; one north to the city of Huaras and to Quito; and one down to Chile. The Inca Highway Expedition recently discovered the entire routes of these royal roads—they also found some side roads and the ruins of several towns long since lost and forgotten. The whole story of their work has been magnificently told by Victor W. von Hagen in *Highway of the Sun*.

There are other striking proofs of the engineering skill of the Incas. For instance, they built a great suspension bridge across the Apurimac with rope cables made from maguey plant fibers. This bridge—supposedly the one so vividly described in Thornton Wilder's absorbing novel *The Bridge of San Luis Rey*—was used by countless people through 600 years. It fell in 1890. The anchor posts have rotted away. The broken cable ends have gone.

Bartholomeu Dias and Vasco da Gama sailed the seas for Portugal. Christopher Columbus sailed for Spain.

Columbus was the son of Domenico Columbo, a bankrupt Genoese weaver and wineshop merchant. It is supposed that Columbus made many voyages in the Mediterranean Sea and along the Atlantic coasts of Europe on the ships of the merchants of great commercial houses. He was stubbornly confident in his belief that there was still another road to India, shorter and more profitable. The silks and spices and gold could be reached by sailing westward. Was not the world round? He asked the city fathers of Genoa to help him. They refused. He asked the men of Venice and Portugal and Henry VII of England. They, too, refused. Columbus turned to Spain, long a rival of Portugal. Queen Isabella, that famous lady of Castile, yielded to his arts and persuasions in the summer of 1492. Columbus was authorized to "make for India through the seas of the Ocean with three armed caravelles." Under royal sponsorship Columbus began his preparations. He was now the "Grand Admiral of the Ocean Sea." Perhaps he did not yet deserve the title; it soon would be rightfully his, in his own time and later.

After weeks of danger and difficulty, threatened by the grumblers, the mutineers, and the fearful, Columbus reached one of the islands of the Bahamas; he called it San Salvador. The date was October 12, 1492.

Columbus then visited several other islands, including Cuba and Haiti. He found that the inhabitants had no horses, no iron, no ploughs. He did find that some tribes had domesticated dogs. He did not know that other tribes had domesticated turkeys and llamas and that the Hopi Indians had been using coal as fuel for nearly 200 years. He found no wheels, although wheels were later dug up in Mexico and they were certainly used to make some of the pottery that was all about when Columbus came. After seven months Columbus returned to Spain. He left a small number of colonists at Navidad. Back to Spain he brought some American Indians, some trinkets, no gold. He had few startling tidings to report about the wonders of Cipangu and Cathay.

In September, 1493, Columbus made a second voyage. He wanted to discover more, to prove that Cuba was a part of the Asian mainland in the kingdom of the Great Khan. After three years—during which he discovered Puerto Rico and Jamaica—Columbus came back to Spain with no proof and with empty hands. In 1498 he went a third time and discovered Trinidad and the coast of Venezuela. In 1502 he sailed to the west from Cadiz. This time he explored more of the coasts of South America and the Panama isthmus. Then he came home to die in obscurity. There was still no gold. "Gold," wrote Columbus, "is the most precious of all commodities . . . he who possesses it has all he needs in this world, as also the means of securing souls from Purgatory and restoring them to the enjoyment of Paradise."

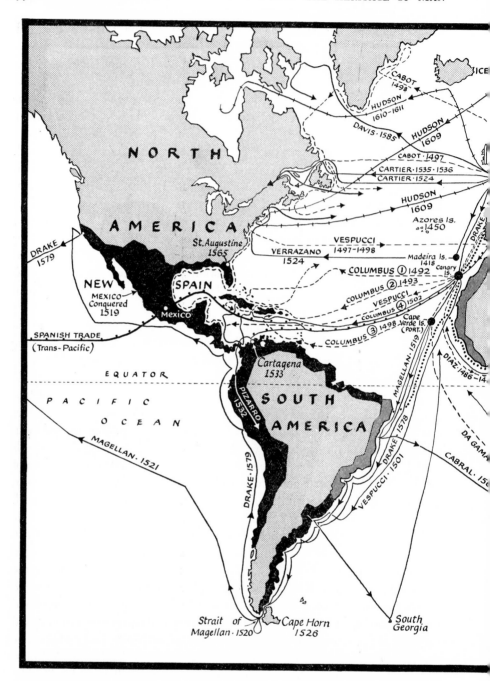

In Santa Marta square in Seville six orange trees spread their dark green leaves towards the grilled windows. Bells tell the hours in a Moorish tower a few yards away. Across the square is the fifteenth-century cathedral of Seville, second in size only to St. Peter's. Here Christopher Columbus heard his last

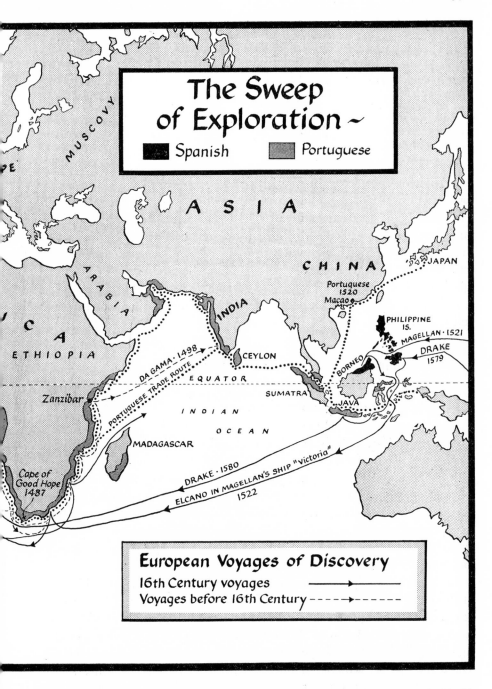

The Sweep of Exploration ~

■ Spanish ▦ Portuguese

MUSCOVY

ASIA

JAPAN

CHINA

Portuguese
1520
Macao

ARABIA

INDIA

PHILIPPINE
IS.

MAGELLAN · 1521

DA GAMA · 1498

CEYLON

DRAKE
1579

BORNEO

ETHIOPIA

PORTUGUESE TRADE ROUTE

EQUATOR

SUMATRA

JAVA

Zanzibar

INDIAN

OCEAN

MADAGASCAR

DRAKE · 1580

ELCANO IN MAGELLAN'S SHIP "Victoria"
1522

Cape of
Good Hope
1487

European Voyages of Discovery
16th Century voyages ———————→
Voyages before 16th Century ---->-------

mass. The men of Seville say that a magnificent tomb in the cathedral holds the bones of the admiral whose fame became greater after his death than it ever was when he lived.

Men still sought the road to Asia, half a world away. In 1497 the Venetian

John Cabot obtained a charter from England's frugal and cautious Henry VII "for the discovery of new and unknown lands." With his three sons Cabot sailed in the *Matthew* from Bristol. He traveled by a more northerly route than Columbus and probably landed at or near Cape Breton Island. To the northeast, Cabot's "New Found Land" stood, bleak and desolate. There were no spices, no Asiatic princes, no pearls or gold; but there were codfish. Soon Englishmen were moving out of the western ports to "adventure" to the great banks off Newfoundland. Henry VII gave £10 to John Cabot, "hym that found the New Isle."

After John Cabot great English sea captains of a later day came to search for the northwest passage to the East: Sir Martin Frobisher, John Davis, Sir Humphrey Gilbert, Henry Hudson. The bays and islands of the Canadian Arctic are the only memorials of many brave sailors. "Death was less a risk than a certainty for most of those who sailed." Meanwhile, men searched also for a northeast passage. England's Richard Chancellor and Hugh Willoughby sailed round the north of Norway. Willoughby perished, but Chancellor reached Archangel and opened the road for trade by sea between England and Russia.

> Vertue is ever sowing of her seedes;
> In the trenches for the Souldier; in the wakeful study
> For the Scholler; in the furrows of the sea
> For men of our Profession—of all which
> Arise and spring out Honor.

The enterprising French soon began to seek new dominions beyond the western seas. To the land of Canada came Jacques Cartier, whose first voyage with Verrazano was in 1524 and not, as was previously thought, ten years later. After Jacques Cartier came other men, explorers and missionaries, men like Roberval, Champlain, Nicolet, Brébeuf, Joques, La Salle, Marquette and Joliet, Groseilliers and Radisson. Then, slowly, came the later explorers who pushed far to the west: La Verendrye, Alexander Mackenzie, David Thompson, Simon Fraser, Lewis and Clark.

Far to the south, the Portuguese and Spaniards, as yet unchallenged by the English and the Dutch, claimed and carved new empires. In 1500, for example, Pedro Alvares Cabral sailed from Lisbon with thirteen ships; he reached the eastern point of South America and claimed for Portugal the land that was later to be called Brazil after the red dyewood named brazil. The following year Amerigo Vespucci, a native of Florence who had sailed on several voyages, went on a trip to explore the Brazilian coast for Portugal. He had nothing to do with planning the voyage; he held no command; but upon his return he spoke and wrote and advertised the wonders of the land mass across the seas. Vespucci was indeed a great geographer, cosmographer, and trainer of pilots and navigators. He ventured a little and discovered a little—the estuary of South America's La Plata, for instance. Had he not been a publicist his name would probably have slipped into oblivion except among the faithful scholars. Publicity has its virtues and its victories. The name of Amerigo Vespucci was soon fixed upon the new worlds. In 1541 the famous geographer Gerardus Mercator put the word "America" upon a map. There it stayed.

In 1493 Pope Alexander VI tried to prevent conflict by dividing the regions of commerce and discovery in the New World between Portugal and Spain. The papal "Bull of Demarcation" drew an imaginary line in the Atlantic 100 leagues west of the Azores and Cape Verde Islands and awarded exclusive rights to all non-Christian lands beyond that line to Ferdinand and Isabella. In June, 1494, the line was shifted 270 leagues further west by the Treaty of Tordesillas between John II of Portugal and Ferdinand and Isabella. The division awarded Africa and Asia and a part of the shoulder of the land that was to become Brazil to Portugal and the rest of America to Spain. The English, Dutch, and French refused to accept the papal decision. Their sailors, explorers, traders, and buccaneers were not disposed to respect the interests of Portugal and Spain. The keels of their ships cut many waters to reach the lands the rulers of Madrid and Lisbon so vehemently claimed. The English were particularly active in the sixteenth century. Again and again Sir Francis Drake and his fellow sea dogs of Devon seized Spanish treasure galleons, raided Spanish ports, and disrupted Spanish trade.

More strangers soon reached the world of the Aztecs and the lands far to the south:

> Rich Mexico, the seat of Montezume,
> And Cusco in Peru, the richer seat
> Of Atabalipa, and yet unspoiled
> Guiana, whose great city Geryon's sons
> Call El Dorado.

Among the Spanish explorers who came to Central America in the early sixteenth century was Vasco Nuñez de Balboa (1475–1517). Balboa was a gentleman, a hidalgo. When he was thirty-five years old he went to the West Indies to help in exploration and conquest.

During the campaigns of conquest Balboa heard of a great ocean on the other side of the mountains. He also heard misty tales about the gold to be had in a land called Peru—"more gold than there was iron in Biscay." In the fall of 1513 Balboa led about two hundred Spaniards and a thousand natives westward. One of the scouts sent ahead of the expedition was named Alonso Martin. He was the first white man to reach the Pacific, "the Great South

Sea." Late in September, 1513, Balboa claimed the land for Ferdinand and Spain. When he returned to the east coast he hastened to inform Ferdinand. Ferdinand gave him two fine titles: "Admiral of the Pacific" and "Governor of Panama." Balboa got no money from his sovereign. Perhaps he appreciated the titles; certainly he needed money.

It is said that Balboa visited the Pacific many times. Again and again he gathered facts and rumors about the mysterious and wealthy land of Peru lying somewhere far to the south. Slowly he collected men and supplies to attempt a conquest of that wonderful country, so filled with gold and silver.

The dream of Balboa never came true, not even a part of it. In 1517 he was suddenly seized by a jealous rival, the aged and greedy Pedrarias Davilla, the pitiless governor of Darien and founder of Panama City and Nicaragua. For want of a better excuse Pedrarias said that Balboa was a traitor, that he was going to throw off his allegiance to Spain and rule alone the lands he conquered. Balboa had hoped to be a wealthy conquistador. He had hoped to be a hero in Spain and to win the grace and favor of his sovereign. He was executed instead; he lies in a nameless grave because Pedrarias said that he was a traitor.

A second Spanish conqueror had slightly better luck. He was Hernando Cortes (1485–1547), a man of resolution, resourcefulness, and courage.

Hernando Cortes belonged to a noble Spanish family that had the misfortune to be poor. Young Cortes tried to study law, lost his interest, and decided to test his luck elsewhere. "The world was all before him where to choose." He chose Cuba. In 1518 he sailed from Cuba for Mexico with 10 ships, about 600 Spaniards, a few horses and cannon. In the spring of 1519 he landed in Mexico. The Aztecs greeted Cortes with amazement, admiration, and terror. Horses, armor, and firearms were outside the world of their experience. Were there not legends that white-skinned gods would come to destroy the Aztecs? Had they come at last?

The Aztec civilization had already begun to decline before Cortes arrived. It is really idle to speculate what would have happened in America if Cortes had not come, if Columbus had never sailed. The Aztecs were past their crest —and so were the Incas of Peru—and it is doubtful if even an improbable renaissance would have enabled them to lead America to any era of progress and power. What interested Cortes and his fellows most of all was not the culture of the Aztecs but their gold. When Montezuma, the Aztec sovereign, sent rich gifts to the invaders they were pleased. When he sent a helmet filled with gold dust they were overwhelmed.

The Spaniards pushed into the interior—they paused to found the settlement that was soon to be Veracruz—and captured Tenochtitlán, a rich city with palaces, twenty-five temples, numerous courts and baths, hundreds of

66] "The Fleet of the East India Company in the Roads of Batavia" (Aelbert Cuyp). The Dutch East
India Company was founded as a joint stock enterprise in 1602.

7] The Attack on the Great Temple Lienzo de Tlaxcalo,
an Indian version of the Spanish Conquest

[68]

Mask of Quetzalcoatl Aztec god of the
wind and the heavens

PLATE XXI

[69] The Fleet of England's Sir Francis Drake attacking the Spanish Colony of Santo Domingo in 158

[70]

The Indian village
of Pemeiock, Virginia,
from a water color
by John White, who
landed in Virginia
in 1587

PLATE XXII

fountains, rich wall hangings, fine furniture, elaborate pottery. Montezuma, king of the Aztecs, was seized, shackled, and declared to be a vassal of the Spanish Emperor Charles V. The Aztecs who had attacked the Spaniards at Veracruz were burned alive.

The Aztecs finally rose against the Spaniards. Cortes led the retreat to the sea; he did not leave behind his booty or his jewels; his position was not that desperate. On July 20, 1520, Cortes fought and won a battle on the plains of Otumba. If he had lost that battle the course of conquest would certainly have been different. Because he did not lose, the fate of Mexico seemed sealed and settled. Spanish expeditions invaded Guatemala and thrust into Yucatán. Meanwhile, the good and vigilant Bartholomé de Las Casas, "Father of the Indians," bishop of Chiapa in Mexico, carried on the work of God. So, too, did other priests, including the tireless Antonio de Montesinos.

Cortes went back to Spain. Soon he returned to America. In 1530 he discovered the peninsula of Lower California. After he came home again Cortes was not allowed to be governor of Mexico. But he was given several titles, large grants, and the right to make additional explorations. To the Emperor Charles V he is reputed to have said: "I am a man who has given you more provinces than your ancestors left you cities."

Soon scores of Europeans, hungry for adventure and gold, crossed the seas to America. The exploitation of the New World proceeded apace. In North America, Spanish explorers went into the swamps of Florida, into Nicaragua, up the Colorado and the Mississippi. In South America, they ascended the Paraná River to the regions that are now Paraguay and Bolivia—the famous mine of Potosí was discovered in 1545. Francisco Orellana crossed the Andes from Quito and went down the Amazon to the Atlantic. It was not long before trading ships from the Philippines unloaded their cargoes at Acapulco on Mexico's west coast; the goods were loaded on mules, carried overland and stored in warehouses or put at once on ships at Veracruz and sent on to Spain. More and more goods were funneled through Central America, goods from over the Pacific, from Chile, from Peru, from all of the great viceroyalties of Spain.

Most of the West Indies were in the Spanish Empire. More than half of the continent of South America was divided into three broad viceroyalties. The first was New Granada, with its capital at Bogotá; it included the area covered by the present states of Panama, Colombia, Venezuela, and Ecuador. The second was La Plata, which included all of the lands east of the Andes and south of Brazil, areas now a part of the states of Argentina and Paraguay and large sections of Bolivia. The third was Peru, stretching far down into southern Chile. For about 300 years the Spanish Empire in America steadily grew. In North America, for instance, it soon reached into areas now covered by the states of Texas, Florida, South Carolina, New Mexico, and California. Great was the power of Spain.

Through the years the explorers and missionaries wrote new chapters in the drama so well described by such eminent historians as William Prescott, Roger Bigelow Merriman, Herbert E. Bolton, and Edgar Prestage—several other names could be added. It may also be remarked in passing that readers will find pleasure and profit in the delightful *Knights of the Cape and Sword,* a book of legends about the colonial period translated by Muna Lee directly from Ricardo Palma's *Peruvian Traditions.* Ricardo Palma was for many years director of the Peruvian National Library at Lima; nearly a hundred years ago he put into literary form the tales he collected and rescued from oblivion.

Luis Ponce de Léon sought the fountain of youth in Florida. Pedro de Alvarado went into Guatemala; Pedro de Valdivia into Chile; Jiménez de Quesada into Colombia; Pedro de Mendoza along the River Plate; Cabeza de Vaca and Francisco Vázquez de Coronado into North America's southwest; Rodríguez Cabrillo up the Pacific coast to Oregon; Hernando de Soto into Florida and the southern Mississippi Valley.

One of the most famous of the Spanish conquistadors was Francisco Pizarro, the Spaniard who discovered and seized Peru.

Pizarro was probably born in 1475. His youth was darkened by poverty. He left Spain and came to Panama. There he served as a soldier with Balboa. Then he tried to be a cattle farmer. More and more, it seems, Pizarro was troubled by the rumors he had heard of the wealth to be found far to the south in Peru. He wanted to find that wealth.

The first plans of Pizarro were slowly shaped. A priest and a soldier—Hernando de Luque and Diego de Almagro—agreed to join him in a scheme to conquer and share Peru. In 1524 the three adventurers set out with one ship and a hundred men. They failed to reach the land they sought. Two years later they tried again. This time they found Peru. More important from their point of view, they discovered that the Incas did have jewels, silver, and gold. The tales that they had heard in Panama were true.

After months of exploration Pizarro returned to Spain in 1528. There he persuaded the Emperor Charles V to make him governor and captain-general of New Castile—the new Spanish name for Peru. In 1531 he sailed from Panama with three ships, about three hundred men, and thirty horses. There followed a darkly blotted tale of blood and treachery. Atahuallpa, king of the Incas, was kidnaped by Pizarro. A large ransom of gold was collected. Then, after a farcical and preposterous trial on a charge of treason against Charles V, Atahuallpa was sentenced to be burned. Because he was persuaded to become a Christian, Atahuallpa was not burned, but merely strangled.

Soon Pizarro conquered Cuzco. In 1535 he founded the city of Lima. The gold and silver he had desired were now in his hands. The Incas were put to work in their own mines for their new Spanish masters.

The victors soon began to quarrel. Pizarro, his brothers, and Diego de Almagro disputed about the areas of Peru that they were to control. The result was a civil war. Almagro was seized and executed. The Incas, infuriated by the crimes and the grinding oppression, rebelled and were stamped down. Pizarro was assassinated in 1541.

Meanwhile, the precious metals flowed over the seas. Between 1503 and 1660 Spain imported about a billion dollars (1960 value) of gold and silver bullion. In the history of Peru there were some shafts of sunlight: the University of San Marcos, said to be the oldest university in America, was founded in 1551 by a grant from Charles V to the Dominican monastery in Lima; the huge and elegant cathedral at Lima was begun in 1535; its cornerstone was laid by Pizarro, and his bones lie within its walls.

To the names of men like Cortes and Pizarro there must be added another: Ferdinand Magellan (1480–1521). Into a life of forty-one years Magellan crowded excitement and drama. He fought in the East and was wounded several times. In 1512 he came back to his native Portugal. In 1513 he was wounded again while on service in Morocco. Despite Magellan's combat record there seems to be little doubt that he was a poor soldier. In any event, he became disgruntled. Then he got into heavy trouble in Portugal, went to Spain, and became a naturalized Spaniard.

In 1518 the young Charles V agreed that Magellan and a few associates might sail to the west in search of the Spice Islands, the Moluccas. There were also tales about the riches of the Ryukyus, northeast of Formosa. Magellan thought that they were the Tarshish and Ophir of the Old Testament, the secret source of the wealth of King Solomon. He was quite interested in the Ryukyus.

The Emperor Charles promised that Magellan and his fellows might have one-twentieth of all the profits of the voyage, and the government of any lands that they might find was to be "vested in them and their heirs." In August, 1519, five armed ships sailed from Sanlucar under Magellan's command. The crews numbered about 280 men and included Spaniards, Portuguese, Englishmen, Germans, Frenchmen, and Italians. More than a year later—it was October, 1520—Magellan reached the southernmost point of South America. Amerigo Vespucci—who believed that there was a southern strait—had never sailed that far. Nor had Juan Díaz de Solis, the intrepid Spaniard who had been killed by the hostile Rio de la Plata Indians.

No sailor ever forgets the savage crags of Cape Horn. The bones of men lie fathoms deep along those coasts. In the wake of Magellan, hairy and tattooed men of the sea have beaten round the rocks under square sail; perished of scurvy; left their wrecked ships as their only monuments on the purple bleak beauty of the shores. Before the coming of vessels propelled by steam and sweating stokers, the hazards of the Horn tested even old tars bowlegged from the rolling decks. Ropes freeze stiff. Fulmars scream about the masthead. The "loom of the lone Falklands" gives way to islands ribbed with glaciers. Evergreens show brightly on the mass of snow. The dorsal fins of blue-gray sharks cut the waters. Past Tierra del Fuego, squalls leap out from the land, carrying the perfume of the pampas grass. Green and purple streamers of kelp float by. The water is alive with microscopic bladder and ribbon algae. On the shore by the ice the Ancient Mariner once saw "green as emerald" are schools of waddling penguins. Grave-faced seals lie heavily on the rocks. Monster narwhals wallow and spout. To the far south lies Antarctica, a continent twice as large as the United States, frozen and silent in the ever-lasting ice.

Past the Cape of the Eleven Thousand Virgins bowled the old sailing ships before the screaming winds; past Useless Bay and the Isles of the Evangelists; down to the First and Second Narrows of the great strait. Then, at last, the weary vessels reached the South Pacific. Blue in the misty distance stretched the waters.

Magellan sailed first through the strait that bears his name. He was the first European to sail upon the Pacific. The Pacific Ocean holds half of all the water that is on the face of the earth. It covers a third of the surface of the globe. At the equator it reaches halfway round the world—between the coast of Ecuador and the Malay Peninsula are 12,000 miles of water.

For more than a hundred days, the ships—three of the five were left—were beaten by storms as Magellan fought his way to the west over the wastes of the Pacific—"he would push on if they had to eat the leather of the rigging." The crews were plagued by scurvy. The food ran low.

> We ate biscuit, which was no longer biscuit, but powder of biscuits swarming with worms, for they had eaten the food. . . . We drank yellow water that had been putrid for many days. We also ate some ox hides that covered the top of the main yard to prevent the yard from chafing the shrouds, and which had become exceedingly hard because of the sun, rain, and wind. We left them in the sea for four or five days and then placed them for a few moments on the top of the embers and so ate them; and often we ate sawdust from boards. . . . The gums of both the upper and lower teeth of some of our men swelled, so that they could not eat under any circumstances and there-fore died. . . . Had not God and His blessed Mother given us so good weather, we would all have died of hunger in that exceeding vast sea.

In March, 1521, the ships reached the Marianas. In April they came to the Philippines. There Magellan was killed by the natives.

Two ships—the *Trinidad* and the *Victoria*—carried the survivors to Borneo and the Moluccas. Only the *Victoria*, a galleon of eighty-five tons under the command of Sebastián del Caño, reached Spain in September, 1522. In its hold was a cargo of spice from the Moluccas. The voyage had taken three years. Thirty-one men came home on the *Victoria*. They had sailed around the world. Magellan they had left behind in the Philippines.

Chapter 22

RUSSIA:

BLOOD AND POWER

> "Have we any assurance
> Of our poor lives? Each day disgrace awaits us;
> The dungeon of Siberia, cowl or fetters,
> And then in some lost nook at last starvation,
> Or else the halter."
>
> —Alexander Pushkin, *Boris Godunov*

THE triumphs and woes of human history are made clearer to the man who has a globe at his side or maps upon the wall. Then he may point and say: "Here is how it happened. This is the way it was." Geography and history meet in one.

The destiny of Russia has in part been shaped by the fact that the land is large, a giant sprawl upon the globe. The Soviet Union today contains about 8,436,000 square miles of territory—the United States has slightly more than 3,000,000. Says a Russian proverb: "Our greatest enemy is space."

One significant factor in Russian history has been the existence of the great widening Eurasian plain that sweeps eastward from the North European lowlands all the way to Siberia. It reaches from the Arctic south to the Carpathian Mountains on the borders of Hungary, to the Black Sea, the Caucasus, the Caspian Sea, and the mountains of central Asia.

The northern part of this broad inland plain belt is the rolling tundra region, today spotted with mining and fishing settlements and airfields. Immediately south of the tundra lands are the forest and marsh areas, the taiga. They stretch over all the long miles from Norway to the Bering Sea. South of the forests is the region of the slightly undulating steppes that cover almost all of the southern Russian lands from the Black Sea in the Ukraine—the word "Ukraine" means "borderland"—eastward to Siberia. Here the famous nomadic tribesmen of the steppes once galloped in freedom and spaces that

360

seemed to have no end. In the fertile black earth grows the yellow steppe-grass, mile upon mile towards the far horizons.

The slow rolls and heaves of the broad southern plain are often broken by ravines, sometimes by a few hills. The most important interruptions of the monotonous sweep of the steppe lands are two: the belt of the Ural Mountains and the deserts and bare semi-arid places of the south central Asiatic regions. On the outer edges of the plain area there are no ranges of mountains or other natural barriers. All is open to invasion. At different times in history the Mongols invaded from the east, the Turks from the south, the Scandinavians from the north, the Poles, Germans, and Lithuanians from the west.

Many rivers, great and small, curve and loop through the land. For hundreds of years the river roads of Russia have been her main highways, providing channels of communication, transportation, and trade. In the length of its inland waterways, about 220,000 miles, Russia today ranks first in the world. The navigable length of Russian waterways is about 62,000 miles; of United States' waterways about 29,000 miles; of Brazilian, 22,000 miles.

Early in Russian history the first trade routes began to appear in the western lowland areas. Traders from the Baltic carried their goods—furs, amber, cloth, grain—from Lake Ladoga to the Volga—the great trade artery of the Volga is about 2,200 miles long—and down to the Caspian Sea. Others went from Lake Ladoga to the Volkhov River, then to the Lovat River, and then to the Dnieper and the Black Sea. Still others used the Neva River or the Dvina River and then crossed over to the Dnieper. So started the great trade routes between the Baltic and Constantinople, a north-south economic axis of tremendous significance. Where ancient towns had stood great cities slowly grew: Kiev, Moscow, Novgorod, Kuibyshev, Astrakhan.

The traders were not the only men who went along these river roads. The reader who traces the flow of migrations in the early centuries will note how the boats of the travelers on the rivers led the way for the tribes and families who followed after, also by the rivers. In Russia, as in distant America, the explorers and settlers moved over the water networks as they became the makers of new frontiers.

Missionaries from Constantinople brought along the rivers the news that those who believed in Christ would never die. The West was taught Christianity mainly from Rome, the East mainly from Constantinople. The so-called Cyrillic alphabet, so widely used by the Slavic peoples, was based in large part upon the Greek. From their contacts with Constantinople, with the Mongols, and from their own experiences the Russians shaped a political tradition that belonged more to the East than to the West—the Turks brought a similar pattern of action and attitude into the Balkans after 1453. That political tradition was distinguished by a form of government marked—in varying degrees—with these characteristics: formality, rigidity, arbitrary authority, sometimes Oriental despotism. "The government of Russia," it was once said, "is a system of autocracy tempered by assassination." In the light of history the statement does not seem unduly harsh.

In all the land of Russia there were no ports free from ice throughout the year or even for a major part of it. Through the early centuries of her history Russia was a small landlocked state. In later days increased size meant increased frustration, especially when Russia became the world's largest continental empire. The attempts of the Russians to have and hold warm-water ports form one of the central themes of Russian history. Since the days of Peter the Great the Russian leaders have tried to get ice-free outlets. Their tactics and strategy, their devices and pressures, have frequently varied. Their ends have stayed unchanged. Meanwhile the Russian lands remained, to a large extent, isolated and insulated from Western Europe, from the newly discovered lands over the seas, from European habits of thought and areas of experience, from what we can loosely call the European "frame of reference." The modern Russian "iron curtain" was not lowered only yesterday; it will not be raised suddenly tomorrow. What Professor Geoffrey Bruun once called the "cultural watershed" between the Russian, Balkan, and Slavic peoples and Western Europe has been long in the making.

Facts of geography are always joined to other realities and forces. The long past of Russia's numerous peoples has many lights and shadows, many faces. There are the different folk-held memories of far-off battles, menacing fears, the shining years of good harvests, the grim times of famine and disease. In eastern Siberia the peoples of such cities as Yakutsk, Rhabarousk, and Birobidjan have not been closely linked through the centuries to the peoples of the Ukraine or Georgia. They have little in common with the men of Moscow, Odessa, Kiev, or Novgorod. They have been separated by space, by such things as varying methods of farming, hunting, fishing, and mining, and by differences in language, blood, religion, literature, and music. There are also such contrasts as those to be found in the different forms of art. West of the Urals, the earlier art of Russia was picturesque, intense, colorful, and romantic—consider, for instance, the beauties of the better icons. The modern art of the western regions is filled with tensions, masses, and hollows. Far to the east of the Urals the development of art was quite dissimilar. In the beginning it was touched and influenced by the East. The Oriental characteristics still remain.

Facts and factors such as these, so obvious and yet so easily forgotten, are of high importance in the variegated patterns of Russian history. The modern Russian state was not produced in the brief span of a few centuries. So vast are its spaces and so numerous its peoples that statements made about one region may not be true of another. Intelligent explanations and arguments about Russia or any other nation must always have deep foundations in the facts and ideas derived from the study of history, economics, religion, science, geography, philosophy, literature, and the like. If conclusions are based upon the soft sands of arrogant ignorance they are only important because they are dangerous. They are dangerous because they may be believed by the insensitive and the ill informed. Belief sometimes leads to action and action to disaster. It is in the tough lessons of both past and present that man must put his trust.

Early in the Christian era the Slavic tribesmen began to migrate from their homes on the slopes of the Carpathian Mountains. The western Slavs moved towards the Elbe, the Oder, and the Vistula and became the chief ancestors of the Poles, the Czechs, and the Slovaks. The southern Slavs traveled towards the Dnieper and upper Volga regions and became the main ancestors of the Russians who now live in these areas. Slowly they began to hunt, fish, farm, and settle near the southern rim of the forest lands. They founded little towns. The convenient wood of the forest meant fuel and houses and protecting forts. The black earth meant good crops. By the middle of the seventh century the Slavic tribes seemed to be firmly settled in their new lands.

They were not to remain undisturbed. In the early ninth century tall and fair-haired men came from the north to conquer and to claim tribute. These were the warlike men of Rus, often called the founders of Russia. For centuries after their coming many legends were told about them. Tradition said, for instance, that three brothers—Rurik, Sineus, and Trevor—established themselves as princes; that Rurik alone survived to rule a broad area; that he founded Novgorod and Kiev, "the mother of Russian cities." Such interesting tales are not quite true. The men of Rus were really Norsemen, a group of the enterprising people who were thrusting out of the northlands down towards the British Isles, France, and—in an "inner line" of advance through Russia —towards their careers as Varangian bodyguards of the emperor in Constantinople and their later exciting destinies in places like Sicily.

Under the rule of the Norsemen there were several dynastic struggles. The territory under their control was extended, but it was never successfully fused or welded together. Meanwhile trade increased and towns grew larger, especially places like Novgorod and Kiev. The "Kievan princes" were powerful—one ruler gathered about 200 vessels to attack Constantinople in 860. Among the most outstanding was Vladimir I, sometimes called Vladimir the Great (c.956–1015). He married Anne, the sister of the Byzantine emperor. After Vladimir's conversion from paganism the power of the Eastern Orthodox faith was slowly and steadily extended in the Russian regions beyond Kiev. Kiev itself became the center of religious faith and teaching in Russia. The famous Cathedral of St. Sophia was built at Kiev. Religious and economic bonds between Constantinople and Kiev became stronger by the decade.

About 988, Vladimir ordered all of his subjects to be baptized. Several monasteries were built. If ever the name of "Holy Russia" was deserved it would seem to have been at this time.

Not all of the realms of Vladimir I were filled with Christian peace. The times were unstable and the facts complex. Vladimir fought with Poland for many years. He imprisoned both his son and a bishop when they tried to persuade him to renounce the faith of Constantinople and embrace the truths of Rome. Vladimir I was a battling prince, tough and crafty. It is fitting that his throne should now be a treasure of the Kremlin.

When Vladimir died there followed a long period of anarchy. More than sixty principalities rose and fell. Nearly 300 princes with rival claims fought among themselves. It was a dark and bloody chapter in Russian history.

> . . . the good old rule
> Sufficeth them, the simple plan
> That they shall take who have the power
> And they should keep who can.

The proud city of Kiev was proud and strong no more. It was seized and held and lost by several combatants. Strange tribes from the steppes galloped to loot and kill.

From the north, south, and west other invaders came: the Swedes, Turks, Hungarians, Letts, and Lithuanians. Many Russians retreated to start new principalities in the upper Volga regions, the northern areas around Novgorod. For instance, the town of Moscow was founded as the clusters of fish huts grew on the banks of the Moskva River about 1147—this is the date when Moscow is first mentioned in the Russian annals.

The struggle of the princes for prestige and territory was suddenly interrupted in 1223 by the coming of the Mongols, those wild, warlike, and ferocious horsemen of the steppes whose conquests were described in Chapter 14. They defeated the Russians near the Sea of Azov and the land was at their mercy. In 1227 the fierce Genghis Khan died but the Mongols did not retreat. They continued to sweep over the plains of Russia to slaughter and steal. One Russian chronicler wrote: "For our sins unknown nations arrived. No one knew their origin or whence they came or what religion they practised. That is known only to God and perhaps to wise men learned in books."

For more than 200 years the Mongols collected taxes and tribute from the steeled and patient Russians. The history of the rule of the predatory Mongols well illustrates the constant interplay of different influences and pressures in the social, cultural, and institutional history of Russia. Some of the tales of the disorder and the agony of subjugation have been exaggerated, but only a little. The fact that the Mongols were usually tolerant in religion must be set against another fact: they were ruthless and determined marauders who burned, slaughtered, and tortured, just as many other invaders in other lands and other times. Their armies were well organized and trained. Their leaders were skilled in the crafts of tactics and strategy. In the light of their ends and purposes many of the Mongols were intelligent and practical men.

In 1237 the Mongols burned and plundered Moscow. Much violence and terror have been seen in the streets of that great city: it was burned and looted in 1293, 1382, 1547, 1571, 1739, 1748, 1753, and 1812. In 1238 the Mongols got to within sixty miles of Novgorod. In 1240 Kiev was taken and a large part of it destroyed. The curbed Russian princes became tributaries of the Great Khan. Then—the reader will remember the passages in Chapter 14— the redoubtable Mongols rode on into Poland, the west German states, Silesia, and Hungary. In 1242 they seized Trebizond; in 1258 they took Bagdad; in 1259 they overran Syria. Only Palestine and Egypt stayed in the hands of the Turks.

Intrigue and bribery at the Mongol court helped the Russian princes to obtain by devious ways some of the things they could not win by victories on the battlefield. Ivan I (1325–1341) persuaded the Mongols to accept his title as "Grand Prince of Vladimir and all Russia." He was able to have the seat of the Russian Church moved to Moscow. This step was of considerable importance in the light of later events. When the Ottoman Turks seized Constantinople in 1453 and reached out for Vienna the Byzantine Empire of the East came to an end. As the Moslems came in thousands of Christians fled or died. The minarets of mosques soon reached up towards the sky. Rome had fallen. Constantinople had fallen. Moscow now claimed to be the center of the Church of the East, the stronghold of orthodoxy, the heir of the causes and dreams of Rome and Constantinople. "Moscow is the successor of the great world capitals: ancient Rome and the second Rome—Constantinople. Moscow is the third Rome, and there will be no fourth."

When Ivan IV came to the throne in 1533 he was called "tsar," a word that comes from the Roman "Caesar." The theory behind this step was that somewhere an Orthodox Christian emperor must rule and reign. Moscow was a Holy City, the third Rome that had inherited the spiritual leadership of all Orthodoxy formerly belonging to Constantinople. In the next century the Russian Church became a separate Patriarchate of Eastern Orthodoxy. Peter the Great (1689–1725) abolished the Patriarchate and gave its powers to a central ecclesiastical committee called the Holy Synod. By this act Peter made the Church a department of the state government. It was not a wise decision.

In 1380 the Russians fought and defeated the Mongols in the great battle of Kulikovo. The Moscow princes claimed all the lands that had once been

included in the core areas of Kievan Russia. They steadily continued to drive
back the Mongols and to expand their territories and effective power. The
first steps in that direction had been taken earlier by a succession of remarkable
Muscovite leaders: Ivan I, Ivan II, Dmitri, Vasily I, and Vasily II. Then
came Ivan III, usually called the Great (1462–1505), his son Vasily III
(1505–1533), and his grandson Ivan IV (1533–1584). These ambitious
princes fought hard against the Poles and the Lithuanians—"there were only
truces to draw breath." Ivan III seized and annexed Novgorod. Muscovite
dominions soon extended to the Arctic and the Ural mountains. Scores of
independent principalities were absorbed into the growing empire. Russia in
the sixteenth century was controlled by an iron despotism. The rulers never
stopped in their ruthless careers of expansion and autocracy. In the center, of
course, was Moscow, now a strong and wealthy city in the fertile blacklands
country and lying right athwart the busy river and land trade routes.

Ivan IV began his reign at the age of three years and survived until he was
fifty-four. He was crowned "Tsar of All the Russias" in 1547. Ivan was a
strange man, a mixture of a beast and a genius. He is usually called "Ivan
the Terrible," and he merited the name. He killed his son. He had a leader
of the Church strangled. He executed thousands of the citizens of Novgorod
because he wanted to discourage republican feelings and he feared treachery.
He ruthlessly suppressed the nobles who opposed him. He organized a secret
police force—a custom the later rulers of Russia continued. He made murder
his main political weapon. His word was law. He was the state. Upon those
who disobeyed his commands a swift and terrible vengeance fell. Slaughter is
a familiar word in Russian history. Yet it was this despot who prayed for the
souls of those he killed. When he was about to die in 1584 he declared that
he wanted to be a monk. His wish was not granted.

Ivan the Terrible has other claims to the attention of posterity. He built
up his army and pushed out the frontiers of his empire. In 1552 he annexed
the Mongol khanate of Kazan and in 1556 Astrakhan. He struck towards the
Baltic and fought with the princes of Lithuania and Poland and with the
Germans, Swedes, and Danes. He moved with giant strides into the lands
beyond the Urals, far into Siberia (1581). In those days Siberia was above all
the land of furs and timber—today there are sawmills, geologists, mining
engineers, great agricultural experiments, new towns and old forced labor
camps. Great was the march of Moscow.

The Muscovite advance continued under Ivan's successors. In 1600 the
Russians reached the Pacific. In 1644 they turned south through the mountains to the Amur River, where they were stopped by Chinese soldiers. Agreements were reached later with the Manchu emperors, fixing, for a time, the
boundaries between China and Siberia. In 1741, Vitus Bering, a Dane employed by the Russians, saw Alaska and sailed ships upon the Pacific. Mean-

while the Russians bulged out the boundaries of their lands south of the Caucasus mountains and obtained control of the lowland corridor between Baku on the Caspian Sea and Batum on the Black Sea. In the nineteenth century they were to reach the edge of Afghanistan. Great Britain was then not pleased to see Russia near a gateway to India. There were spies and intrigue in the bazaars of Kabul.

In the works of many geopoliticians, always concerned with the "geographical pivots of history," we have read that the bloc of territory stretching from the Himalayas to the Arctic and from the Yangtze to the Volga is the "heartland" of the planet—nations like Great Britain and France are "rimland" powers and the United States is a "land-oceanic" one. The geopoliticians have said: "Who rules East Europe commands the Heartland. Who rules the Heartland commands the World Island. Who rules the World Island commands the World."

Facts and theories do not always meet and mesh. The roads of learned theorists and passionate prophets are always hard and long and they lead towards destinations no man can know. If the geopoliticians are right, the future of Russia is one of dazzling glory. If they are wrong, the reverse may be true.

After Ivan died there came the limping reign of the sick and saintly Feodor I (1584–1598). His energetic brother-in-law, Boris Godunov, guided Feodor and succeeded him as tsar (1598–1605). These were the days when the first "false Dmitri" entered Moscow and claimed that he was the younger son of Ivan the Terrible—he did not know that the real Dmitri had been strangled by Boris Godunov. These were also the days when the "Troublous Times" of Russia started. Finally, these were the days when serfdom darkened Russia, the autocratic days when the landlords, the princes, and the boyars got their labor when and where they wanted it on their own harsh terms. Successive generations of the serfs went on their long journey. The *Dead Souls* of the gifted Nikolai Gogol (1809–1852) still remains the best description of the tragic fate of the peasants pushed down into serfdom. His brawling and bellowing characters seem to be living beings, filled with the loves and hates, the guile and stupidity and greatness that are found in human beings everywhere, even in sad black Russia. "Let us lay aside the question of who is most to blame," says Gogol's Russian prince. "The point is that it is our task to save our country, that our country is in danger now, not from the invasion of twenty foreign races, but from ourselves."

The "Troublous Times" were marked by murders, by peasant revolts, by Polish and Swedish invasions, and by more false claimants to the throne. There were plots and butcheries all over the sprawling provinces. Only after disorder brought exhaustion did a semblance of stability come. An "Assembly of the Land" containing representatives of the clergy, the boyars, and some country and city delegates elected Michael Romanov tsar of Russia in 1613. For more than 300 years the Romanov family was to give Russia her rulers. Not until 1917 did the heirs of a new philosophy decree that matters should be otherwise.

With the coming of the Romanov dynasty there was a slackening of disorders and ferments, a decline of the inflamed upheavals of riots and repressions. True, there were still some men who told of their troubles in the streets and fields and other men who believed them. There were the workers who rose, now and then, against the men above. Not all was suddenly and completely peaceful. The voices of the insulted and the injured were almost never silent. On the other hand, for the autocratic tsars the impulse and the means to repression were strong. If they had not used them they might not have remained at the summits of power. The suppression of all democratic tendencies, the crushing of the ambitions of nobles, the full subordination of the Church—these policies have been characteristic of Russian leaders until the present day. The autocratic tradition is strong, whatever praise may be given by some lips to the "peoples' democracies" of the twentieth century.

Michael Romanov (1613–1645) was succeeded by Alexis (1645–1676); Alexis was followed by the sickly and incompetent Feodor III (1676–1682) and Feodor by the joint rule of the half-brothers Ivan V and Peter I that lasted from 1682 to 1689. During these reigns the face of Russia is not greatly changed. A little territory is added to the state, especially in the Ukraine. A few advances are evident in handicraft production, and there are improvements in agriculture and in the iron, salt, and potash works.

Ivan V died in 1689 and then Peter ruled alone. So began the reign of Peter the Great (1689–1725), "Father of the Fatherland, All-Russian Emperor." The dynamic Peter was the last tsar of Muscovy and the first emperor of Russia. In many times and places Peter has been described as a mighty builder—and a builder he certainly was. His ways were often strange and brutal. They were always autocratic. Sometimes Peter seemed to be a savage madman thrust up from the Russian ice to plague his people. Sometimes he seemed to be a genius, a ruler charged with elemental energy breaking an old world and shaping a new. The reader who wishes to have some sound conclusions of his own will find that the best biographies of the mighty tsar are the two-volume work of Eugene Schuyler and the shorter study by the British historian B. H. Sumner.

Frederick the Great of Prussia said that Peter the Great worked upon Russia "like nitric acid upon iron." Peter was certainly a prince of great virtues and colossal vices. It is difficult to look upon his activities with cold eyes and unmoved spirits even more than 200 years after his death. About the deeds of many men, living and dead, we find it hard, try as we will, to be neutral or dispassionate—our values keep getting in the way. Consider, for instance, individuals like Moses, Judas, Cleopatra, Buddha, Akbar, Henry VIII,

Louis XIV, Benedict Arnold, George Washington, Maximilien Robespierre, Napoleon Bonaparte, Adolf Hitler, Albert Schweitzer, Winston Churchill. Any man, even a little honest, must admit that the names of human beings like these bring swift reactions of pride or anger or contempt. So it is when we look at Peter the Great, that strange prince who played out his destiny on the great stage of the land of Russia.

Those who have admired Peter have praised his constructive enterprises, his dreams of the Russia that might be, his thunderstorms of genius. His opponents have denounced his breakneck reforms, so opposed to the traditions and spirit of Mother Russia. They have damned his extreme and shocking deeds. They have called him "a cruel beast of prey," a "bloodsucker," a horrible "Antichrist" who was the true child of Beelzebub, an offspring of the dark pits of Hell. In the nineteenth century, for instance, the famous Alexander Herzen wrote and apparently believed that "Peter wrought grimly and terribly against the will of his people, relying on autocratic authority and personal strength." Peter was certainly heavy-handed, reckless, and brutal in ruling his 9,000,000 subjects. How far he moved "against the will of the people" no man can be certain.

There is no doubt that with Peter all seemed to move upon a heroic scale. He ate and drank like a half-savage giant. His energy was almost demonic—witness his immense efforts in supplying the Smolensk front in 1705 or his crushing of the revolt of the Moscow garrison. When his curiosity was stirred he pressed and pursued and harassed everybody who might know some of the answers he wanted. Several of his close companions were rough and disreputable men and foreign heretics—he learned from them. He even learned from the polished and educated individuals for whom he usually showed a strong dislike. What interested him most was the learning that could be used for what he considered practical purposes. Geometry, for instance, was a useful study because it could be used to build fortifications.

Within the tumultuous being of Peter there were other forces: ambition, enterprise, courage, recklessness, obstinacy. Beyond these there were still more. Peter was a complicated character, not to be apprehended in a glance or plumbed in a paragraph. Much has been made, for instance, of his almost incredible fits of anger. When he hated, he wanted to kill—and he often did. "There are deeds of his which make humanity shudder, and frightening depths of cruelty and treachery." All these things are true. And yet—are they to be wondered at in a Peter who in the midst of the miseries and perils of youth had seen one of his uncles murdered by a mob and one of his close friends hacked to pieces? The shocks of childhood sometimes mar the man. Such queries and comments perhaps lead to a part of the explanation, never to the complex whole. Why, for instance, did Peter put his wife Eudoxia in a convent? She had done him no ill.

The power and prestige of Russia, declared Peter, must be increased. One aspect of power was obviously military strength. Therefore Peter made a new Russian army upon the model of the European armies equipped with flintlocks and artillery. It was also clear to Peter that Russia needed a navy. He ordered some of his men to cut trees from the forests along the Don and to build a fleet. The modern Soviet navy claims Peter as its founder. Peter also built a shipyard at Lake Ladoga and fortified Kronstadt.

Military and naval power must not be left untried. Peter went to war with Turkey. When he tried to take the Turkish fortress at Azov in 1695 his expedition failed. The next time Peter's fleet blocked the Turkish supply lines and Azov was forced to surrender. This was surely an excellent beginning. The results of the bright promise, however, were not happy from the Russian point of view. In 1711, for example, the Russians were defeated by the Turks in a big engagement on the Pruth.

In 1696 Peter set out to investigate the sciences and arts, especially the technical, mechanical, and manufacturing methods, of western Europe. Traveling as a sailor under the name "Peter Mikhailov" he visited Germany, the Netherlands, and England. He did not go to France, mainly because he never admired the culture of Versailles. Peter was more sharply curious about the ways in which practical men of action were making and using things. When he returned to Moscow he took with him several European mechanics and artisans and he invited more to follow after. They were willing to go to Russia, for a price; Peter was prepared to pay what they wanted, provided that they taught the Russians as much as they could of their skills. All foreigners, however, were disliked and distrusted by most Russians. Said one writer: "Acceptance of foreigners is a plague. They live by the sweat and the tears of the Russians. The foreigners are like bear-keepers who put rings in our noses and lead us around. They are Gods, we fools. They dwell with us as lords. Our Kings are their servants."

In 1698 Peter returned to Moscow to suppress a revolt of the *streltsy*, the reactionary musketeers of the royal bodyguard. The crushing of the rebellion was a savage affair. About 2,000 of the presumptuous *streltsy* were sentenced to torture and death. It is said that Peter personally cut off the heads of several of them. Disobedience must be punished.

After Peter came back to Russia there began a series of projects and decrees that stretched over a period of more than twenty years. The tireless Peter ordered the streets of Moscow to be paved. He said that only houses of stone should be built within the town. At his orders numerous canals were made. He sent many young Russians to study in Europe. Some of them never came back. He built hospitals and encouraged medical training. With his own hands Peter clipped off the mustaches and beards of his chief boyars. He started a mathematical school and a naval academy. He ordered several

European books to be translated into Russian. He simplified the Cyrillic alphabet. We have seen how he abolished the Patriarchate in the Russian Church and substituted the Holy Synod. He minted money. He established embassies at foreign courts. He changed the uniforms of his armies. The use of tobacco and the wearing of short coats were encouraged. Fiscal reforms were multiplied. Major changes were made in governmental policies of administration. Russia was divided into eight "governments" for several reasons, including the more efficient collection of taxes: Archangel, Azov, Kazan, Kiev, Moscow, St. Petersburg, Siberia, and Smolensk.

Peter also turned to develop swiftly the economic resources of Russia. He took numerous steps to stimulate industry—the cloth and arms trades, for instance—and the growth of metallurgy. It was Peter who started the iron and copper industries behind the Urals. Increased trade with Europe was declared to be a national necessity.

Peter felt strongly that only alert and able leaders could tread the new roads to national glory. His son Alexis was a weakling and so he died of terrors and tortures at Peter's orders. It was, surely, an inhuman deed; but was it not done for the sake of the new Russia? Peter was a man in a hurry, reckless of good and evil. If he had been told that he was not prudent he would probably have replied that he saw no need to be so. Was he not tsar and was there not only one tsar? What seemed to Peter to be good must be done and done swiftly. Profound changes had come before Peter's day, but they now came with hurricane force and speed. In the place of the old and the outworn must be put something better. Ivan Poroshkov, a contemporary of Peter, wrote these words: "If any land be overmuch encumbered with weeds, corn cannot be sown thereon unless the weeds first be burned with fire. In the same way, our ancient inveterate evils should also be burnt out with fire."

Only if the character of the old tsardom of Muscovy was changed, said Peter, could the proper destiny of Russia be achieved. Peter saw the future Russia as an important member of the family of European nations. To the leaders of some European states the idea that Russia, with one great leap, would join the councils of Europe seemed somewhat ominous. About their reactions it seems that Peter the Great did not deeply care. He would knock and if the door to the congresses of Europe did not open he would bash and batter it down. On occasion, Peter stated another view: Russia might become so powerful and civilized that she could afford to stand aside from the affairs of Europe. "For a few score years only," he once said, "we shall need Europe. Then we shall be able to turn our backs on her."

To some of his people the hopes and ambitions of Peter were clear. They were ready to follow him and to borrow and improve upon the accumulated experience of Europe. On the other hand, there was wide and strong opposition to Peter's plans and dreams. Against Peter stood the hard and heavy obstacles of the massed power of Russian tradition and ritual, the old ways that were sacred to so many men. The cake of time-honored custom is usually hard to break and the ancient habits hard to change. Conservative men asserted that the world of Muscovy must be a closed, isolated, and icy world of her own. The supporters of the old (*stariny*) and of the new (*novizny*) were soon joined in conflict. Meanwhile the Western world wondered about the career

Growth of Russia to 1815

Principality of Moscow ~1300	1462~1505	1670~1725	1796~1815
Principality of Moscow~1462	1505~1670	1725~1796	

of Peter the Great. Said England's Bishop Burnet: "How long he is to be the scourge of that nation or of his neighbors God only knows."

In 1700 Peter turned to try to win territory in the northwest. He sought, of course, an ice-free port. The Caspian Sea provided no outlet. Archangel, far away on the White Sea, was useless for long months every year. The Turks carefully guarded the Dardanelles and the Bosporus, the strategic gates of the Black Sea.

Charles XII of Sweden came to the throne of his land in 1697 at the age of fifteen. This youth was a military prodigy. Unaware of the peculiar genius of Charles XII, the states of Denmark, Saxony (the Elector of Saxony was also king of Poland), and Russia united to try to seize some land from the young king's realm. So began the Great Northern War.

What Charles XII achieved startled all the world of Europe. He swiftly laid siege to Copenhagen and forced peace upon Denmark. Then he turned (1700) with about 8,000 Swedes and defeated 50,000 Russians. He put up Stanislaus Leszczynski as Polish king in place of the Elector of Saxony.

Although Peter's army had been defeated in battle the Russians had been able to get a few small pieces of land in the Livonia and Narva regions. Peter, hoping to obtain still more, started to build a new Russian capital (1703) to be a gateway to the west. The new city, built partly with Swedish prisoners of war, was called St. Petersburg. It was then a symbol for those who looked ahead to an age of change as Moscow was a symbol for those boyars and merchants and others who hated Peter's scandalous innovations and steadfastly preferred the familiar ways of the long past.

The complicated military duel of the northlands lasted for more than twenty years. In 1709 Charles XII invaded Russia. In the same year he was beaten by the Russians at Poltava in the heart of the Ukraine. The defeated Charles fled to Turkey and tried without success to persuade the Sultan to help him against Russia. Charles then went back to Sweden. His head was bashed in by a cannonball when he was besieging a Norwegian town in 1718. Most of his life had been a long military campaign.

When peace terms were finally signed in 1721 Russia obtained from Sweden a parcel of territory east of the Narva, the region then called Estonia, the prize city of Riga in Livonia, all of Ingria, and a part of Karelia. These new Baltic provinces reached around the mouth of the Neva River and gave Russia a long strip of coast on the Baltic. A "window to the west" was open at last.

During the years that marked the end of his reign Peter looked and moved towards the East. In a war with Persia he obtained a few Caspian towns and there the story ended. Peter died in 1725. The achievements of his reign had opened a road for Russia that his predecessors would never have foreseen. Soon

there were to come the famous reigns of Elizabeth (1741–1761) and Catherine
the Great (1762–1796). Russia was now a part of Europe, or almost so.

> Wide stretching from these shores
> A people savage from remotest time
> A huge neglected empire, one vast mind,
> By heaven inspired, from gothic darkness called.
> Immortal Peter! first of monarchs! he
> His stubborn country tamed, her rocks, her fens
> Her floods; her seas; her ill-submitting sons.

The passage quoted here is from James Thomson's *The Seasons*, a poem
widely read and praised in the eighteenth century. To the modern reader the
language of the poet may seem to be rather exaggerated. He wrote, of course,
in another age. He also stood closer to Peter the Great than we do.

Many events and individuals in Russian history are widely recorded in the
names of persons and places, in the writings of men long dead, in songs and
legends, in the monuments and buildings of cities and towns.

Consider the cities of Moscow and Leningrad, once called St. Petersburg.

In modern Moscow stand the red battlemented walls, the yellow buildings,
and the nineteen towers of the Kremlin, a giant fortress covering more than a
hundred acres on the Korovitsky hill. This is the Kremlin of the twentieth
century, the heart of the Russian world.

Far different was the Kremlin of long ago. The earliest fortified Kremlin
was made of wooden stockades after the ancient capital of Kiev had been
seized by the Mongols in the thirteenth century. About a hundred years later
the first stone walls were built—the only Kremlin building surviving from
those days is the brick and stucco Church of the Saviour in the Forest constructed in 1330. In the fifteenth century Italian architects and engineers came
to Moscow. The Spaskiya (Saviour's) Gate was erected in 1491 by a Milanese
architect. Fieranti from Bologna built the domed Cathedral of the Assumption
in the Kremlin on the site of the old Uspenskiy Cathedral. It is famous for its
minarets surmounted by crosses, its Indian cupolas, its frescoes, its stucco, its
ornate ribs and groins, its relics of tsars and saints. In the other cathedrals of
the Kremlin are also many tombs, relics, and holy pictures. There are also
numerous bells, including the famed Tsar-Kolokol, the king of them all. There
is also an arsenal, a convent, a monastery, a library filled with rare books and
other treasures. Among the more modern structures is the severely classical
Senate building erected by Catherine the Great in the eighteenth century. In
the nineteenth century Nicholas I built the Grand Kremlin Palace, a building
made of white stone surmounted by a gilded cupola—it covers about 500,000
square feet of ground.

By the walls of the Kremlin is Red Square, stretching for a length of nearly a thousand yards. Here, through many centuries, the tsars dispensed justice. Offenders were "hanged, broken on the wheel, impaled, beaten to death, buried alive, burned in iron cages, or choked with molten lead." In Red Square today is the squat tomb of Lenin, built by Shchusev in 1930 to hold the body of the first hero of the Soviet Union. At the end of the square is St. Basil's Cathedral with its ten colorful cupolas. This cathedral, one of the wonders of Moscow, was built in 1584 by Ivan the Terrible after he had conquered the Kazan and beaten the Tartars of the Crimea.

Past and present stand side by side. Not far from the massive and depressive magnificence of the Kremlin is the tower of the University, an entrance to the great modern Moscow subway, beautiful parks and dark slum areas, crowded with the old wooden houses and the ancient ovens. Through the streets the four million inhabitants of Moscow move about their tasks and pleasures. Among the younger generations there is no memory of the rule of the Tsars. If the older men and women remember they perhaps do well to be silent.

Six hundred miles from Moscow, at a spot where the Neva River flows into the head of the Gulf of Finland in hilly northwest Russia, is the city of Leningrad, once called St. Petersburg. It has often been said that St. Petersburg was the head of the Russian state and Moscow was its heart.

Leningrad—for today, at least, Peter yields to Lenin—is the damp and cold city that Peter the Great first built on the marshy ground in 1703 so that there might be "a window through which his people might look into Europe." Peter's bones lie in a tomb on an island in the Neva. Here is the famous Fortress of St. Peter and St. Paul where nine tsars and tsarinas are buried— it is now a state prison. Below are the dungeons built in Peter's day; his pathetic son Alexis was once locked up in them. On the left bank of the Neva is the Admiralty Building, a spot from which radiate the three main street arteries of Leningrad. Nearby is a bronze statue of Peter the Great made by the French master Falconet. It shows Peter on horseback ascending a rock and pointing to the River Neva on the banks of which he founded his great city.

In Leningrad the baroque Winter Palace built by Peter's daughter Elizabeth (1762) still stands, its walls painted apple green with white trim. Within are the marble staircases, the red granite columns, the chandeliers and colored ceilings, splendors undamaged by time or war. At the edge of the macadamized "Field of Mars"—where once the Imperial Guards of Paul I and Nicholas I marched in swirling dust—there rises a statue of Suvorov, the general who defeated both the Turks and the French.

In the eighteenth century Catherine the Great built the Hermitage, a huge structure adjoining the Winter Palace on Khalturina Street. If Catherine's ghost walks the corridors it must be amazed to see what has happened to the building she raised in her time for the convenience and delight of herself and the rulers who followed after. To the original Hermitage two connected buildings were added in 1771 and 1850. Together with the vast Winter Palace the enlarged Hermitage is now the most important museum in Russia. The mazes of the Hermitage Fine Arts Gallery contain the largest and best Rembrandt collection outside of the Netherlands; two madonnas attributed to Leonardo da Vinci; Giorgione's "Judith," Titian's "Repentant Magdalene," Veronese's "Descent from the Cross"; one piece of unfinished sculpture, "The Sitting Boy" by Michelangelo; about fifty paintings by Rubens; others by Sir Joshua Reynolds, Van Dyck, Raphael, Poussin, Watteau, Manet, Monet, Renoir, Degas, Gauguin, Cézanne. There are also invaluable treasures of engravings and Greek and Scythian antiquities, Chinese porcelains, Mogul miniatures, mammoth tusks, ancient blue masks, carved chariots and reindeer.

The ugly cathedral of the Virgin of Kazan—a small-scale and bad copy of Rome's St. Peter's—is used as a museum of a different kind; it is designed to show the evil consequences of all religions and all churches. The gold-domed and gorgeous Cathedral of St. Isaac of Dalmatia is still open, we are told, for those who wish to worship in the ancient ways.

The traveler must also pause to look upon Paul's Castle. In 1801 Paul I, son of Catherine the Great, built this castle-fortress because he was afraid to live in the Winter Palace. Paul stayed in the new building for about a month, and then his nobles murdered him one winter night when the skies were dull and a satin snow covered the frozen Neva.

Such are a few of the buildings and monuments that carry the memories and echoes of the past of Leningrad. There are also the glories of the present. Leningrad has had its own university for a long time. Like Moscow, it has its modern subway. There are escalators, crystal chandeliers, eight stations with marble-faced walls, decorations of glass and silver, murals, statues, carvings, great columns. Not far away is Lenin's statue, set in front of the building where the Second Congress chose the first government of the new Russia on October 25, 1917.

In the cities, on the steppes, in the regions of the black earth, the first chapters of Russian history were made. There the sickle was first used, the hammer first lifted by a strong arm. There blood flowed, the harvests grew, and the herds increased. The last pages of this tale of blood and power have not yet been written. Perhaps they will be bloodier than the first.

Chapter 23

EUROPE:
THE NATION-STATES

"It is the chiefest point of the duty of every natural and reasonable man
to know his prince and head, to be true to his head and prince. . . . Every
man is bound to venture life, to lay out and expend goods, land, and possessions, to forsake father, mother, kindred, wife, and children, in respect of
serving his prince."

—Chief Justice Catlin, 1752. Quoted in William Cobbett, T. B. Howell, *et
al.* (eds.), *A Complete Collection of State Trials and Proceedings*, I, 1045

THE tempers and tensions of the modern era were in many ways foreshadowed by the struggles of the emerging nation-states of Europe in the
sixteenth century. To that century and scene we now turn again. The men
of the age of the Renaissance and the Reformation were not solely concerned
with the triumph of the humanists and the truths of a Christian God. In
those exciting years many practices and assumptions were altered as the overseas discoveries fired the imaginations of men and the tumbling events disturbed the worlds their fathers made.

There were sharp and enormous changes in the economic scene, the world
of industry, trade, business, and finance. The leaders and peoples of the nation-
states of the new era were steadily concerned and often troubled by what
Francis Bacon once called "the considerations of plenty and the considerations
of power." In the tale of the rise of the nation-states and their struggles for
power one word appears again and again: money.

It is sometimes said that capitalism was introduced into Europe in the sixteenth century. This statement is not quite true. Major changes from the
customary aspects of medieval economy—all pointing towards a money-
exchange system—had been taking place at least 200 years earlier. Before
the sixteenth century there existed the characteristic components of any satisfactory definition of capitalism: a system in which men own capital—land,
raw materials, instruments of production, money or other valuables—and hire

377

labor and work to produce goods and services for profit. It is true, of course, that money, that mobile instrument of power, was not to be found in large supply before the later fifteenth century. When the supply of money relative to goods and services suddenly increased dramatically—the stock of precious metals in Europe tripled between 1500 and 1650—then a great gateway to progress and power was suddenly opened.

At the same time, the new European system of credit instruments—bank notes, letters of credit, bills of exchange, promissory notes—tremendously increased the size of exchange mediums. When money supplies increased so much there came, of course, a greater exchange of goods for money and the building of an extensive price system. The tidal increase in money also resulted in a spiraling upwards of price levels—in Spain and England they rose about 300 per cent. As prices rose, wages failed to keep pace. When costs of labor were reduced profits increased. Those profits were poured back into enterprise. Soon the demands of overseas markets for European industrial goods expanded steadily. When states fought wars military supplies were in high demand and often in short supply. As prices went up, civilian demands increased. These things, and many more, pressed production upwards.

The medieval guild system could not meet the new challenge. It began slowly to decay and disintegrate on a plateau of stagnation. Guild arrangements were simply unsuitable for the changing conditions of the new world. The guilds had always clung to the idea and practice of maintaining a monopoly over a small market. Unlike the guildsmen, the new entrepreneurs stressed volume of output more than quality and monopoly price control. Soon capital, management, and manufacture tended to be no longer in the control of one man or a small group of men as had been the case in the guild system. The craftsmen steadily became more separated from the capitalist. Management and ownership often drifted apart as more and more owners ceased to manage and hired other men to perform that necessary function. The gates to the modern impersonal world of efficiency were at last opened; they were never closed again.

The guilds had other troubles. Bitter class divisions—especially in the strong and wealthy guilds of northern Italy and Flanders—disrupted the organizations that had once been so strong. Narrow guild oligarchies of rich men had long held tight controls over the lesser members of the guilds. When the lesser members objected, the result was often open war. Because the guild leaders frequently controlled the economy of the older towns they were able to hinder the development of new industries. Old theories—some of them Church-inspired—about profit, price, and payment of interest often checked or interfered with rapid economic expansion.

The rising entrepreneur of the sixteenth century wanted ready money for investment without restriction in any enterprise in any place. The flow of

American treasure and the rising production of precious metals in the mines of Europe, mentioned earlier, not only increased available capital but stimulated the ambitious men of enterprise. The accumulation of capital also improved Europe's position in trade with the East. In Chapter 9 and Chapter 21 it was remarked that in earlier days the Europeans had never been able to export enough articles to the Moslem lands and Asia to balance the flow of imports from those lands. Hence there had always been a drain of precious metals from Europe eastward. Even the sale of thousands of Slavs—especially children from the Balkans—by the Venetians to the merchants from the eastern regions had not offset the export-import imbalance.

There soon appeared upon the European stage the regulated company, joint stock company, or partnership which operated under charter but without guild restrictions. Most important, in these days, was the joint stock company. The reasons for its beginning were clear and strong. Because few individual merchants could find enough money to finance a ship's trading voyage, groups of merchants began to pool their resources and share their profits in joint ventures. Permanent companies of "merchant adventurers" were formed. England's Levant Company (1592) carried on trade for 200 years. The Muscovy Company traded with Russia. In 1600 England's famous East India Company, a joint stock enterprise, began its great career. The companies of the Netherlands grew strong and prosperous.

The ambitious European entrepreneur needed a mobile labor force that could be hired at any time and place without the interference of the guildsmen or the restrictions of the feudal lords. By the sixteenth century feudalism had almost completely disappeared in England and Holland. It was weakening in France. In the form of serfdom, however, it was being introduced into eastern and central Europe (Poland in 1496; Russia in 1597; Austria in 1627). The breakup of feudalism in western Europe, especially in the years following the Black Death of 1348–1349, was hastened by the desires of the landlords to have more money and less labor service. In England thousands of acres were turned into profitable sheeplands and thus a great mass of human labor left the rural areas for the cities or the seas.

The new capitalists almost invariably objected to local controls whether they were guild regulations, feudal customs, or cribbing and confining medieval town laws. They wanted a uniform law, suited to their requirements, that operated effectively over fairly large areas. If a law is to extend over a wide territory there must be a strong authority to enforce it. This is one outstanding reason the rising merchants, industrialists, and financiers of a new age supported the emerging national states and stood against the claims of smaller, weaker, and more cumbersome traditional medieval units such as the towns, the guilds, the dukedoms and principalities. The capitalists wanted strong kings and strong writs and arms to provide safety and security. They were willing to pay well—and to lend at high interest in emergencies—to support a strong state. The monarchs, of course, welcomed happy financial arrangements at a time when the costs of governments and standing armies were rising.

All European states were concerned about their economic strength as well as their military power. Some states, such as Portugal and Spain, hoarded bullion. Some increased domestic trade. Some stressed home industrial and agricultural production. Other states, such as the Netherlands, campaigned for free trade. Still others, such as England, pressed the production of goods and services and tried to sell abroad industrial goods in return for food and raw materials. Each state was a rival of all the others. Meanwhile, Europe's economic power grew at the expense of the outside world. And meanwhile, too, the riddles of social justice increased in number and urgency and remained unsolved.

So it was that in the sixteenth century, as a result of a series of pressures and struggles, several cardinal economic and political facts emerged in western Europe. In the first place, an industrialist capitalist class arose in the towns and cities, a class determined to destroy the customs and practices repugnant and unsuited to their tempers and contrary to their interests. Secondly, royal power was slowly consolidated within definite territorial limits. From the twelfth to the seventeenth century there had been two main obstacles to this consolidation. The first was the proud feudal vassals who had so often asserted almost complete independence in their domains. The second was the self-governing Roman Church, vehemently uttering its claims to be superior to the civil power. By the sixteenth century these twin obstacles had been virtually removed. The power of Rome had been broken and the power of kings increased. When the Church was subordinated to the state in most areas of Europe, the clergy moved slowly into the status of a privileged class. Mainly with the aid of the industrial bourgeoisie the monarchs pushed the proud nobles—this process took centuries—into the status of landed proprietors, another superior social class. "Merchants and traders," Carl Becker once wrote, "always found the turbulence of the nobility bad for business." The hour was shortly to come when the reins of power in the states of Europe would be held, more and more, by the educated, shrewd, tough men of the bourgeois class. They did not have high birth; but they did have money and brains, twin instruments of power. In a later century and in another land, John Jay said that "those who own the country ought to govern it." With that point of view not all men could agree.

A great weakness of Europe has been its inability to stop or limit conflicts among its nation-states. The kings and peoples of the continent have moved, again and again, into the agonies of war. There has been but narrow room

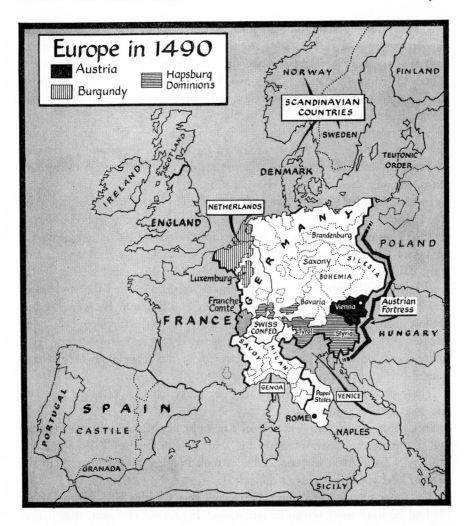

Europe in 1490
■ Austria   ▤ Hapsburg Dominions
▥ Burgundy

for the idea of a "United States of Europe." Throughout the modern age what one historian has called "the old disorder" in Europe has continued. Attempts to shape new orders of stability and security have always faltered and failed.

By the end of the fifteenth century weak feudal units dissolved in several areas of Europe when the power and gravitational attractions of emerging dynastic and national states increased. As foreign foes and quarrels multiplied, as Machiavellian power politics turned to the weapons of war, the men of Europe marched through a bloody period. The cruel and destructive conflicts that flamed and died in the sixteenth century had much to do with the shaping of the political structures and the total cultural fabric of modern Europe.

With war went diplomacy. Professor Garrett Mattingly, that shrewd and sensitive scholar, has found the origins of modern diplomacy in the fifteenth century. During the next hundred years the idea of European balance of power policies gradually grew and hardened as the rules of the complicated and dangerous game of international politics were made by kings and resident ambassadors. In theory and practice the competitive state system seemed to adhere to a maxim stated by Niccolò Machiavelli in 1512: "Let a prince, therefore, take the surest courses he can to maintain his life and state; the means shall always be thought honorable."

The three strongest nation-states in 1500 were France, Spain, and England. Each kingdom played a major part in an age of dislocations and contentions characterized by intense religious animosities, sharp dynastic and constitutional feuds, disputes about territory, rivalries in trade.

In 1494 Charles VIII of France led an army of 30,000 men across the Alps into Italy—some of the results of this dramatic event were described in Chapter 19. The ambitious Charles, who apparently thought that he shared the genius of Charlemagne and Alexander the Great, sought land and loot in Italy. His Swiss pikemen and French knights had a personal interest in the wealth of the ill-defended land. Charles, of course, presented the world with reasons for his invasion. He said that he came as a liberator. He would restore the lost liberties of Florence. He also marched to claim the kingdom of Naples. Charles asserted that the throne rightly belonged to him because genealogical tables would prove that he was a descendant of the Angevins who had conquered Naples in the thirteenth century.

These claims and deeds are a comment upon Charles VIII, his age, and the good faith of princes.

In Chapter 19 the tale was told of the flight of the Medici from Florence and the sermons of doom preached by Savonarola as Charles VIII approached the city. Charles took Florence. Charles took Naples. Such triumphs, in the divided land of Italy, were not difficult.

The other monarchs of Europe suspected that Charles VIII meant further ill. Did he have more territorial ambitions? Ferdinand of Spain, that master of the arts of intrigue, feared that Charles, drugged by success, might leap to seize Sicily. The Holy Roman Emperor felt that the whole balance of power in Italy had been upset and the prospect of French dominance filled him with jealous apprehension. The pope, too, had his doubts. Venice trembled. Would that fair city be the next to fall before the armies of Charles VIII?

The result of this tide of alarm was the formation of a short-lived alliance directed against France. United against Charles VIII were the Holy Roman Empire, the Papal States, Venice, and Spain—it did not trouble either Ferdinand or the emperor that they had earlier promised to support Charles when they accepted his bribes.

The new alliance, called the Holy League, moved to cut the French off from their home base. Charles flinched and wavered; then he chopped his way back into France along a scarlet road. The gleaming vision of empire in Italy had paled and died. Sullen and hard-eyed soldiers, disappointed and comfortless, trudged homeward. If Charles had stayed in France he would have done better.

Soon Louis XII followed Charles VIII as king. Louis, audacious and obstinate, made large plans. He put forward a genealogical claim to Milan—his grandmother was a Visconti—and also asserted that Naples belonged by right to him. To protect his venture and keep his neighbors neutral, Louis made treaties with England, Spain, Venice, and the papacy and handed over a little slice of land to the Duke of Burgundy. Then he led his armies down to Milan and drove out the Sforzas. The soldiers of the crafty Ferdinand of Aragon helped Louis to subdue Naples. All was victory. All was peace.

Then the victors quarreled. The Spaniards defeated the French. When Louis tried to invade Spain across the Pyrenees he was beaten again. In 1504 Naples was annexed to Aragon and the hope of a French province in southern Italy, earlier so marred and torn, now fell to the ground. The fates had mocked Charles VIII and now they ranged themselves against Louis XII. Through the ranks of the French armies ran the menacing symptoms of despair. About ten years later Niccolò Machiavelli wrote: "Nothing is so natural or so common as the thirst for conquest and when men can satisfy it they deserve praise rather than censure. But when they are not equal to the enterprise, disgrace is the inevitable consequence."

Some of the astute and greedy leaders of Europe now made new and resolute plans. In 1508 the cynical coalition of the League of Cambrai was formed to attack Venice and seize her rich mainland territories in the Po Valley. The new alliance contained this quartet of darkened and suspicious spirits, masters of duplicity: Ferdinand of Spain, the Emperor Maximilian, Louis XII of France, Pope Julius II. It was not surprising that Julius II was an eager member of this group; the promise of petty immediate gains often distracted Italian leaders from a contemplation of their solid and practical interests.

Within the League—it was not to be expected that the partners would trust one another—not all went well. When Ferdinand had occupied the areas he wanted, he quit. Pope Julius II would also have been ready to withdraw had he not been afraid that Louis of France and the Emperor Maximilian would euchre him out of his share of the spoils. Julius had a holy respect for property. He had an intense misgiving about the possible conduct of his allies, especially France. When the misgivings became a nightmare Pope Julius decided to form another "Holy League" to oust Louis XII and the French from Italy.

Julius II found willing allies: Ferdinand of Spain, the Emperor Maximilian, young Henry VIII of England, and the leaders of the recently defeated state

of Venice. Henry VIII attacked the north of France in 1513 and won the Battle
of the Spurs. Louis XII, defeated in Italy, discreetly chose the desolate road to
retreat. Twice he had gambled; twice he had lost.

These tangled events, described in summary fashion here, reveal the unscrupulous diplomacy, the ruthless greed, the tides of passion, treachery, and
malignant duplicity characteristic of the extraordinary rulers of the sixteenth
century. In the first Italian wars, and later, it seemed that moral and religious
factors were overbalanced by the weight of greed for land and gold. Europe
had indeed been fragmented into a warring congeries of states. The international Church no longer held universal sway over the hearts and spirits of
western man. Two hundred years earlier Dante had said that mankind required, among other things, "perpetual peace, eternal justice and the general
reign of law." The successors of Dante, it seemed, denied the validity of these
conclusions. Their secular ethics were certainly not those of Dante. The political arts of Machiavelli—the hero of *The Prince* was Cesare Borgia—did not
include justice, mercy, honor, or courage.

Was might indeed right? Was war a proper tool to test one's power in
dynastic and national controversy? Was it to be a usual tool? Would men
ever forget long hates in one consummate faith? These were some of the
questions that men in the sixteenth century might rightly ask. They were
cramping and chilling queries, first uttered hundreds of years before. They
are heard in the twentieth century, in the blood-dark midnight of the nations,
in the billion-throated terror that marks the birth agonies of a new world or
the shuddering death of the old.

The year 1520 is a key date in the tumbling events of the sixteenth century.
With the death of the Emperor Maximilian in 1519 the throne of the Holy
Roman Empire became vacant. The seven electors of the empire considered
the claims of three candidates: Charles, grandson of Maximilian and great
prince of the house of Hapsburg; Francis I of France; and Henry VIII of
England. The electors chose Charles, the logical candidate. Hence he became
the Emperor Charles V, sovereign of more territory than any European monarch had claimed and ruled since the days of Charlemagne.

Charles administered the holdings of his insane mother Joanna, the daughter of Ferdinand and Isabella of Spain. These possessions included the crowns
of Castile and Aragon, Naples, Sicily, Sardinia, Corsica, and all the Spanish
colonies overseas. Charles obtained from his father Philip all of Austria, the
Netherlands, Luxemburg, and the rest of the vast Hapsburg realms. Because
the pieces of this diverse and many-languaged empire were scattered all over
Europe they were highly vulnerable to attack. Ramshackle and arthritic, the
empire was an anachronism in an age of rising nation-states. Its very size was
a handicap when hungry enemies prowled.

The enemies of Charles V were not only hungry; they were also fearful. They dreaded a concentration of power in the hands of the Hapsburgs and the possible domination of all Europe. It was natural that they should seek to weld coalitions to smash the chances of a single man becoming master of the Continent. They could see, they were sure, the dangers of a "universal monarchy." Charles, for his part, was determined to hold together all of the Hapsburg empire. For nearly forty years a large part of his treasures and his men were drained away in this hard task. Charles was not a brilliant leader of men; he was a cautious, serious, plodding, conscientious ruler who stubbornly fought his many-sided battles "against fate, against fortune, and against time itself." Behind the glittering façade of Spain's golden and heroic century was always the grim fact of almost constant struggle and always heavy debt.

The first enemy of the new emperor was the ambitious and rather irresponsible Francis I of France, a kingdom now nearly surrounded by Hapsburg lands. Francis, already bitter about his defeat in the imperial election, decided to follow in the steps of his predecessors and strike for ground and glory in Italy. He thrust into northern Italy, pushed down to take Milan, raised the old French claim to Naples, and turned his eyes towards the Spanish kingdom of Navarre. The pope, fearful of the strength of Charles and always sensitive to the importance of the balance of power, supported the French invader. Francis even made a flimsy alliance with Henry VIII of England and another one with the Turks. So far, so good.

Then the prospects of Francis altered. It was said at the time that he "snatched defeat from the jaws of victory." The glory was lost and the money was gone. Deserted by his allies, Francis fought on, for a while. Then England's Henry VIII allied himself with Charles V. In 1521 imperial forces ousted the Frenchman from Milan. Francis invaded Italy again in 1524. He was defeated and went home. In 1525 Charles crushed the armies of Francis at the battle of Pavia. Francis was captured. "Nothing is left to me," he said, "except my honor and my life." A little later Francis got his release by promising Charles V he would abandon his Italian claims. A little later he received a message from Suleiman, the famous leader of the Moslem Turks: "There is nothing wonderful in emperors being defeated and made prisoners. Take courage, then, and be not dismayed."

There was reason for dismay. When Francis was defeated at Pavia the European balance of power was completely upset. The threat of Hapsburg hegemony had become a greater danger than ever before. How could the march of Charles V be stopped? How could the equilibrium of Europe be restored?

The princes who now opposed Charles did not give him time to take advantage of his triumphs at Pavia. The League of Cognac swiftly made war upon Charles—this League contained France, Venice, Milan, Florence, and the papacy. The emperor defeated his enemies, captured and sacked Rome (1527), made Pope Clement VII his virtual prisoner. Not until 1529 did the Treaty of Cambrai bring an armed and fitful truce. Francis I, that spendthrift Valois, withdrew once more all French claims to Italian territory. Meanwhile, Charles battled against the claims of England's Henry VIII during the years when Henry was asserting that his marriage to Catherine of Aragon, the aunt of Charles V, had never been valid. Meanwhile, too, the Protestant religious explosions had rocked the realms of Charles. The emperor, a militant Roman Catholic, was determined to destroy the strange and violent forces that he considered heretical. He swore that he would risk his "dominions, friends, body, blood, life, and soul" against the heretics. Charles struggled hard. Despite his zeal and courage, his Roman Catholic forces were pushed back by the Lutheran princes and the Schmalkaldic League. Charles failed and Luther triumphed.

There was another hampering challenge: the Turkish assault up the Danube.

While the Christian monarchs of Europe were battling one another the rugged Moslem warriors had been pressing into Europe to harry and kill. Even before Constantinople fell in the nightmare of 1453 the Bulgars and the Serbs had been subdued and submerged by the Turks. Soon the Ottoman power pushed towards Austria and Poland. The advancing soldiers ferreted out and slaughtered the men who rallied and resisted. Everywhere they brought cold-blooded atrocity and fierce massacres. The constant ally of the Turks was terror.

Selim I (1512–1520), that remarkable architect of empire, seized Syria, Mesopotamia, and Egypt, the main Moslem lands. The crack and thunder of Turkish guns was heard from the Euphrates to the Danube. Selim took the title "Caliph." He was given the keys of the Kaaba at Mecca, the symbol of the religious headship of Islam.

Suleiman the Magnificent (1520–1566) guided the Ottoman Empire to the peak of its impressive power. This ambitious and masterful ruler wanted to conquer the world for Islam. Ten times he led his armies into Europe; three times he marched into Asia. His internal reforms, wisely conceived and executed, endured for three centuries. He startled the Western world by seizing Belgrade (1521) and several other strongholds that stood athwart the road to Hungary. His galleys blockaded the island of Rhodes and took that Christian fortress from the Knights Hospitallers of St. John (1522). In an alarmed Europe there was much futile talk and many abortive negotiations about uniting to stop the spectacular Turkish drive. Nothing was done.

In 1526 Suleiman struck across the Danube and defeated the Hungarians, then friendless and alone, at the bloody battle of Mohacs. The Hungarian king—he was also king of Bohemia—was drowned while fleeing the field

PLATE XXIII

[ ] Peter the Great, disguised as a sailor, working in an Amsterdam shipyard about 1697

[72] The Black Virgin of Vladimir, a famous icon
in the St. Vladimir Church, Moscow

[73] Tsar Alexius welcoming foreign guests at a state banquet in the Kremlin, April 24, 1662

[75]

[74] The Armada Jewel. A portrait of
England's Queen Elizabeth I surrounded
by intricate gold work set with precious
stones (about 1588)

Above: Titian's famous portrait of Philip II of Sp[ain]
painted in 1553. Here Titian brilliantly suggests [the]
complex character of a monarch both strong and w[eak]

Left: This portrait of Louis XIV in his robes of s[tate]
illustrates the elegance and confidence of the sovere[ign]
and his famous age.

[76]

PLATE XXIV

of slaughter. In 1529 the Turks took Buda and laid siege to Vienna itself—
they were to attack Vienna again in 1532 and 1683.

Meanwhile Charles V made a truce with the Lutheran princes and obtained their support against the Turks. The imperial army blocked, for a
time, the advance of Suleiman. On the other hand, Turkish and French fleets,
their ships glistening in the spray, struck at Italian towns and shipping. Turkish pirates built their lairs along the coasts of North Africa. They raced out to
seize the traders' goods and gold. They killed, enslaved, and imprisoned—
"and many a one grows witless in his quiet room in hell."

In 1534 Suleiman attacked Persia and thus the Turkish fury was temporarily turned away from Vienna. The Austrian ambassador to Constantinople
wrote these words home: "only the Persian stands between us and ruin."

The respite lasted for seven years. Then the harassed land of Hungary was
invaded once more. The Turkish wave of conquest could not be stayed. When
the battles ended only a small western strip of Hungary was left in Hapsburg
hands on condition that the Turks be paid an annual tribute. All of central
Hungary stayed under Turkish rule. Transylvania was given to a prince who
was a creature of the Sultan. Turkish power was at its height. The defense
belt of the Balkans had been broken. In the midst of clamors and alarms
Europe was on the defensive. For Europe the death of Suleiman the Magnificent in 1566 was a fortunate event. The Turkish rulers that followed Suleiman
—Selim II and Murad II—were aggressive, but they were also eccentric and
incompetent.

In 1556 the Emperor Charles V, broken in health and hope, abdicated and
retired to a Spanish monastery. There he died in 1558. Titian's magnificent
portrait of Charles in his old age shows us how he looked when he moved
towards the end of his long reign.

Charles V had not completely defeated France. His brother Ferdinand had
been forced to sanction the Lutheran religion in the divided empire by the
Treaty of Augsburg of September 25, 1555. Nor had Charles removed the
threat of the Turks. He had so many problems that he left most of them unsolved. He tried to shore up his empire with cracking props. He was not by
nature agile enough to deal with all the troubles that flickered and flamed in
his sprawling lands. It is difficult to avoid speculating what might have happened in Europe if a really vital man had been the master of so great a realm
as that ruled by Charles V in the critical years of the sixteenth century.

Greatness had been thrust upon Charles. He did the best he could; but his
best was not enough. Charles was not an incompetent man; in some respects
he was brilliant; he simply could not reach a height of genius to cope with
what Sir Charles Oman once called "the extraordinary complication of hin-
drances" which fell to his lot.

Philip II of Spain (1556–1598), the son of Charles V, had fewer problems. His fate, like his father's, was to be frustration and failure in the things he tried to do. A good case can be made for the assertion that Philip's reign was a long misfortune for his state, his people, and himself.

From his father Philip II obtained Spain, Milan, Naples, the Netherlands, and all the Spanish colonies overseas. Charles V gave his brother Ferdinand I (1556–1564) the Hapsburg lands and the crown of Bohemia and Hungary. Thus the European empire of the Hapsburgs was divided. Ferdinand, elected Holy Roman Emperor in 1556, ruled from his court at Vienna. Philip stayed at Madrid. There he built the vast palace-monastery of the Escorial in a bleak and barren spot northwest of Madrid. For months at a time Philip would shut himself up in a gloomy room overlooking the high altar of the Escorial chapel. He was a strange and complex being.

Titian's portraits of Philip II—especially the famous "half-armor" painting of Philip as a young man—show with consummate art the pale and thin face, the heavy eyelids, the haughty and suspicious mien. History calls Philip "the prudent king." That he was, and more. He was a melancholy and rather dull individual, a man of frequent indecision and procrastination. He was awkward, bigoted, deceitful, hard-working, narrow, obstinate, pedantic, pettifogging, punctilious, proud, self-righteous, secretive, solemn, and filled with suspicions. He trusted few men and few men trusted him. He delighted in subterranean ways and secret plots. He was skilled in dark treachery. He has been accused of being mainly responsible for the murder of Don Carlos, his insane eldest son. But there is no proof that Don Carlos was murdered. There is proof, however, that Philip rewarded the family of the assassin of William the Silent.

Philip was also experienced in persecution. A devout Roman Catholic, he deemed it his duty to oppose and destroy the unsettling heresies of his age. Charles V had been rather liberal and generous, never a fanatic or a cruel man. All the princes of his age were guilty of some persecution, now and then. Philip II, on the other hand, wanted to root out heresy ruthlessly, with all the weapons he could find. His black and vicious crusade was disapproved and held detestable by many men, Roman Catholics and Protestants alike, even in his own times. Opposition did not change the mind of Philip. Once he wrote to the pope: "I would lose all my states, and a hundred lives if I had them rather than be lord of heretics."

The Roman Catholics of Europe usually looked upon Philip as the relentless champion of their faith and the leader of the wars against the Protestants. Such a leader the unamiable Philip tried to be. If his character had been different he might have altered the face of western Europe. Certainly he would have served far better the cause of his religion if he had wisely followed the noblest traditions of his church. The greatest symbol of the Christian Church is not a fire, a stake, or the tongues of leather lashes; it is the cross of Calvary. Men forget that unchanging fact at their peril.

Philip II seized and held the throne of Portugal. A Portuguese prince whose hereditary claims were stronger than those of Philip found himself pushed aside. Portugal was formally united to Spain in 1580. The national state of Spain was thus expanded. For the first time since the Roman Empire the Iberian peninsula was united. Also united were all the Spanish and Portuguese possessions in America, Africa, and Asia, "the wealth of Ormuz and of Ind."

The Hapsburg-Valois battles at last were stopped. Philip II of Spain and Henry II of France signed the Treaty of Cateau-Cambrésis in 1559. By the terms of this treaty France again gave up all claims to lands in Italy. The French had spent their blood and treasure in an unwise policy; again and again their armies had been rolled back beyond the Alps. Now France quit. She also abandoned her claims to the Netherlands and her active alliance with the Turks. This Treaty of Cateau-Cambrésis did not mean that there was to be a genuine and general European peace. It did mean that there would be less disturbance in some parts of the Continent. In others there would be more. France herself, for instance, was about to plunge into a series of horrible civil wars.

The new king of Spain married Mary Tudor, Roman Catholic queen of England. This event, mentioned in earlier pages, was really the work of Mary. She felt that a Spanish alliance would help her bring England back to the Roman Catholic Church. Englishmen, with pride in their nation's growing strength, saw with despair and anger the prospect of foreign intervention in English affairs. Was England to be an adjunct or satellite of Spain? Bishop Gardiner warned the queen that her course would damage the Roman Catholic cause; but Mary went ahead; she was in a hurry.

Philip came to England and tried to be diplomatic and friendly; but he could not make himself popular. Feeling against the marriage resulted in three rebellions in England. Mary was also disappointed when the results of her religious persecution seemed to be the opposite of what she intended. She was still further disappointed when her marriage to Philip brought her no heir. Her misfortunes increased when Philip persuaded her to enter a war against France and the papacy. England lost Calais, her last link with the glories of Crécy and Agincourt. It was a heavy blow to the national pride. Englishmen felt that their island kingdom had suffered by Mary's foreign marriage alliance. When Mary died in November, 1558, it was clear to Philip that England might possibly be recovered for Roman Catholicism if he married Elizabeth I. It seemed probable, however, that only by plots or by war could a Roman Catholic triumph be won.

There was also the continuing problem of the Turks. Before and after the death of Suleiman the Magnificent the Turkish corsairs roamed and dared and struck through the Mediterranean almost at will. The Turkish warriors brought agony and loss to the Italian lands, pushed the Spaniards out of the forts of Tunis, laid siege to Corfu and Malta, and attacked Cyprus. Then the pendulum swung again. The Turks met a great disaster. In 1571 a combined fleet of Spanish, papal, Venetian, and Maltese ships—there were also some from several Italian republics besides Venice—sailed under the command of Don John, half-brother of Philip II. They challenged and defeated about 200 Turkish galleys in the great battle of Lepanto off the west coast of Greece. The drama of this event is best caught and held in the lines of G. K. Chesterton's poem "Lepanto." The historian is sometimes compelled, and rightly, to yield to the poet. It may be remarked in passing that an earlier master of magic and language named Miguel de Cervantes was wounded by the Turks at Lepanto. He returned to Spain to write *Don Quixote* for the world.

Thus the Christians of Europe fought and won the battle of Lepanto. Don John of Austria and all his fellows had gone forth to war and had returned with victory. The Turks had seen "Don John pounding from the slaughter-painted poop. . . ." It seemed that the long tide of Turkish triumph would surge and shift no more in the Mediterranean Sea. Lepanto seemed decisive. Don John was Europe's hero. Said Pope Pius V: "There was a man sent from God whose name was John."

It is easy to claim too much for Lepanto. The alliance that won the battle collapsed. The Turks finally grabbed Cyprus. For a long time to come it was to be generally true that the Christian power was predominant west of Sicily, the Turkish power to the east. The victory of Lepanto did not, in the end, make all the Mediterranean safe for Christians.

The Turkish challenge by land continued. Not until the end of the seventeenth century (Peace of Karlowitz, 1699) were the Turks forced out of Hungary; then the Hapsburgs came in. Not for about two centuries was the yoke of Ottoman power to be lifted from the lands of the Serbs and the Bulgars. Only slowly did the strength of the Ottoman Empire ebb away. Then the Western powers began their long discussions about the European provinces of Turkey. Should those provinces be nursed and nourished or should the Turks be driven "bag and baggage" out of Europe? This dispute was to darken the conference rooms of Europe and redden the streets and fields of the Balkans in the nineteenth century.

Like the rulers of Spain before him Philip II believed in absolutism. All of his subjects, he insisted, must be loyal to the state and faithful children of the Church. Dissent must be crushed. "Peace and order," Philip said, "are to be maintained in my dominions only by maintaining the authority of the Holy See." There was to be but one state policy, the policy decided upon by Philip.

He was so deeply concerned with order and orthodoxy, with the careful regulation of minute details of government, that he neglected industry, trade, and commerce. The gold and silver of America were swiftly spent. Prices rose. Debts increased and taxes multiplied. The failure to encourage trade and foster industry was perhaps the greatest single sin of the Spanish government. The price the Spaniards paid, then and later, was tremendous.

In the rule of the Netherlands the autocratic Philip showed even less wisdom than at home. Charles V had been widely loved; Philip II was widely hated. The troops of Spain were stationed in the Netherlands and the nonconformists and the waverers were persecuted in that proud land. The people of the southern section, or Flanders, were similar to the French in their blood and culture and their orthodox Roman Catholic religion. These were the ancestors of the modern Belgians, skilled in the arts and industries. On the other hand, the people of the north, now modern Holland, were heavily Germanic. They were the great traders of northeast Europe, the envy of many lands. Through the centuries they had built strong local governments. The tradition of independence was a sturdy thing, as Philip discovered. There was another significant fact: many of the Hollanders held religious beliefs far from the doctrines of Rome.

The Netherlanders of the north and south were not easily cowed, even by the tyranny of Philip and his governors. They insisted upon the prerogatives of their own nobles and upon the preservation of their own traditions. They resented and protested the oppressive taxes levied by the Spaniards. The men of business were especially incensed because they knew that they were being taxed to stop them from continuing to compete with Spain. Trade was the heart of Holland: and the heart must be protected.

When the harsh Duke of Alva came to be governor of the Spanish Netherlands in 1567 the people found that he was no more intelligent and humane than his master Philip. Alva was a good soldier, but he was an intemperate and foolish man. He brought with him from Spain about 10,000 veteran Italian and Spanish mercenaries to crush resistance to his commands. Rebels must be punished. Taxes must be collected. Order must be maintained. Heretics must be rooted out. Torture and butchery, the sword, the ax, and the stake must be used as instruments of government. Such was the decision of the Duke of Alva.

The ill-disciplined soldiers also wreaked their unauthorized cruelties upon the people. Meanwhile Alva seized by treachery two nobles of the Netherlands. They were executed—on the orders of Philip II—together with hundreds of other nobles and citizens in the "Council of Blood" of May, 1568.

The Duke of Alva was recalled to Spain; but the disorders grew. Even the moderate Don John of Austria was unable to check the public fury and alarm. "The Prince of Orange," Don John wrote to Philip, "has bewitched the minds of all men. They love him, and fear him, and wish to have him as their lord." The Revolt of the Netherlands was well upon its way.

Then came another governor: the Duke of Parma. He was not like Alva, bloodthirsty and blundering. He was not like Don John, a hero and a dreamer. He was able to cajole, to conciliate, and to divide. In 1579 the Flemings formed their Catholic Union of Arras and decided that they would rebel no longer but return to their Spanish allegiance. The Dutch, on the other hand, founded their Protestant Union of Utrecht and fought on, led by William of Orange.

In 1581 the Dutch supported an Act of Abjuration, a declaration of independence. The turmoil of the War of Liberation went on, year after year. William was assassinated in 1584; but his successors continued to lead the embattled Dutchmen in obstinate campaigns. After 1584 many soldiers of Elizabeth I of England came over, often in the guise of volunteers, to grapple with the hated Spaniards. The long rebellion in the Netherlands was the "running sore" that drained the dwindling resources of Spain, nearly ruined her reputation, and weakened her national morale.

Not until 1609 was the desperate struggle finished and a truce signed. There was not yet a formal peace—it was hard for the Spaniards to recognize that the Dutch rebels had forged an independent republic; it was hard to admit that they should have the right to be Calvinists or whatever else they chose to be; it was hard to say that they might trade with all the world, even in the Spanish waters of America, India, and Africa. Finally, in 1648, Holland was formally recognized as an independent nation. Meanwhile strong Dutch fleets and vigorous Dutch traders had won the admiration and respect—and often the jealousy—of the Western world.

In the latter part of the sixteenth century the state of France, whose unity had been so hardly won, was hurt and divided by innumerable broils, brawls, and civil wars. Almost all of the French conflicts were mainly caused by religious ferments and frictions. Wars of religion have often brought installments of human misery in the history of nations. Extremists of all kinds, filled with emotions of passion and vengeance, can place the bodies and souls of men in jeopardy; few fanaticisms are more hideous or senseless than those of religion. So it was in France. Families, villages, cities and provinces were divided. The dynastic hopes of nobles became joined to the Roman Catholic or the Protestant cause. The webs of plots and counterplots stretched over the land. Assassins thrust their daggers, pressed their poisoned rings, lifted their glasses to drink the health of unsuspecting victims. Soldiers marched and killed.

Henry II of France died in 1559. Behind him he left three sons who succeeded him, one by one: Francis II, sick in body and mind; Charles IX, a light-headed psychopath; Henry III, a vicious and weak fop, sometimes made desperate by his incapacities and no longer comforted by the beauty of his earrings and his pearl necklace. Henry III was once described as "the worst ruler of the worst dynasty that ever governed." It may be so.

Catherine de' Medici, the Italian mother of these three kings, usually held the reins of power. She was a cultured, fat, immoral, vengeful, and usually competent woman whose personal inclination was towards balance, compromise, and indulgence in religious matters. It is always difficult, of course, to walk the paths of compromise, especially for individuals whose emotions are stronger than their intellects. For them it is easier to take extreme positions and defend them to the end. Toleration is usually the child of wisdom as well as of time.

For several decades three artistocratic groups wrestled for power in France. First were the Roman Catholics, led by the great and brilliant Guise family, famous for its soldiers and churchmen. Against them were ranged a second element, the Protestant Huguenots. The Huguenot faith, born in Calvin's Geneva, had made thousands of converts, militant crusaders for the Protestant cause, especially in western and southwestern France. Their ranks included two Bourbon princes and the distinguished Gaspard de Coligny, Admiral of France. A third group, usually called the Politiques, arose later in the century. They were Roman Catholics who, despite their opposition to the Protestants, strongly disliked the persons and policies of both the Guises and Catherine de' Medici. Many of them, too, simply thought that too much was being made of religious differences in France. Their Roman Catholicism was usually rather perfunctory and lukewarm.

The battle lines of the contending forces swayed and bent back and forth in fantastic fashion in the royal court and in the scattered provinces. There were really about seven tangled religious wars that erupted and died away in France in the last half of the sixteenth century. Both Roman Catholics and Protestants made foreign alliances and brought mercenary troops to add to their power and the national confusion. Many volumes have been written to describe and follow the numerous strands of plots and violence. The complete tale will probably never be told. The final judgment will certainly never be made by human beings.

At one critical hour the Guise leaders seized the Huguenot Louis, Duke of Condé, and condemned him to death. Catherine de' Medici, at that time persuaded that she should follow a path of conciliation and compromise, released Condé. She even permitted the Huguenots to worship publicly. Then she changed her mind. The result was another phase of coercion and crime, an outburst of savage persecution of Protestants, a welter of battles and plots. When prices rose and work did not bring good pay, many men became detached from their moorings and left whatever jobs and homes they had to look for money and adventure. Meanwhile rough bands roamed the country to steal and kill. Murder became an occupation, treachery a custom. Even as we write and read of these troubled years, however, it is wise to remember that not all was a chronicle of sin and shame. Among human beings there is always some goodness and glory.

One of the grim times of the religious wars came on August 24, 1572, St. Bartholomew's Day. As a result of a Guise plot, supported by excited Roman Catholic mobs, more than 4,000 Huguenots were massacred in Paris and the furious butchery spread to the provinces. The head of Gaspard de Coligny was sent to the pope. When news of the bloody event reached Spain, Philip II ordered a *Te Deum* to be sung.

The Huguenots resisted still. In such strongholds as Rouen and La Rochelle they bitterly made their plans and warmed their hopes. In 1576 the Guises formed the Catholic League—their patrons were the pope and Philip II. The Huguenots sought the aid of the English.

Soon the leaders of the Catholic League controlled the French government. Their will was supreme until Henry III, in one of his rare moments of decision, hired assassins to murder the Duke of Guise and his brother the Cardinal of Lorraine. "Now I am King of France," Henry III is supposed to have said to Catherine de' Medici. "I have killed the King of Paris." The queen mother, so the tale is told, shrewdly replied: "God grant that it may be so, but have you made sure of the other towns?"

Henry III had not. The Catholic League soon thwarted his hopes and declared him deposed. The rule of the League, once it had the state in its hands again, was violent and unpopular. Men sometimes ruin their cause by using force too long and too unwisely. Their adversaries increase their ranks and lie in wait. The hour of their chance will come.

The legitimate successor to the throne of France was now Henry of Navarre, that famous hook-nosed Bourbon prince and Protestant warrior extraordinary. Henry of Navarre was every inch a man. He really did care for the common man and the public good. The peasants and artisans knew it. So, too, did the aristocrats. Most men agreed that France might be united and peaceful if Henry were king.

In August, 1589, Henry III, that last deplorable and pathetic specimen of the Valois line, was assassinated. Henry of Navarre was now hailed as the new king, Henry IV. He was the first of the Bourbon monarchs to reign in France (1589–1610). In 1593 he became a Roman Catholic. Perhaps he did utter the words attributed to him: "Paris is well worth a mass." Perhaps he did not. He certainly did believe that a king should have the same religion as the majority of his subjects.

The really important fact is that Henry IV slowly brought a high measure of peace to a distracted nation. He pushed the Spaniards out of Amiens. In the Edict of Nantes he granted the Huguenots wide freedom of worship, judicial protection, equality of civil rights, the same chance as Roman Catholics for public office and education, the right to garrison about a hundred fortified towns. This gesture of appeasement became deservedly famous.

At the same time, with the aid of Sully, his famous minister, Henry IV guided his land back to the paths and arts of peace. Agriculture and commerce were encouraged. Such things as the administration of justice and the collection of taxes were made more efficient. Roads and bridges were repaired. The central government was strengthened and reorganized. The amiable despotism of Henry partly prepared France for the royal absolutism that was soon to come.

Philip II had hoped to bind England to the cause of Rome and the welfare of Spain by marrying England's Mary Tudor. All his plans had miscarried. Later Philip was a disappointed suitor of Elizabeth I. Still later he joined in several plots to remove Elizabeth, by murder if necessary, and to place the Roman Catholic Mary, Queen of Scots, upon the English throne. Elizabeth I and her island kingdom were the constant enemies of Spain, always hostile to the plans of the leaders of the Counter Reformation. Elizabeth helped to end the French influence in Scotland. She sent aid to the men of the Netherlands who rebelled against Spanish rule. She and her Council were mainly responsible for the execution of Mary, Queen of Scots, in 1587. She sent money to the harassed Protestant Huguenots in France. She encouraged her great sailors —men like Sir Francis Drake and Sir John Hawkins—to go on unofficial piratical expeditions against the ships and ports of the Spanish empire and of Spain.

Slowly Philip II concluded that England could not be brought back to the Roman Catholic Church or removed as a menace to Spain except by war. Philip, who had long dreamed of a Roman Catholic crusade, turned resolutely to try to crush the insolent islanders. The ports of Spain stirred with preparations for a great Armada that would sail against the obstinate and heretical English.

Against the Spanish threat Elizabeth was able to mobilize the sea dogs of England, those adventuring sailors who had broken through the Roman Catholic monopoly of power, sold Negroes, sacked Spanish treasure ships, and plundered Spanish settlements. In the name of Elizabeth and England, motivated by patriotic, personal, and religious interests, these mariners of England were anxious to enter into open war with Spain. They knew the importance of sea power; and they were eager to seize the trident of Neptune from the hands of Philip II.

Late in July, 1588, the Armada of Spain swept into the English Channel. The Spaniards planned to effect a junction with the Duke of Parma in the Netherlands; the Armada would then cover his crossing and support his troops by landing infantry forces carried from Spain.

The wind that drove the Spanish fleet towards the coast of England kept the English ships in Plymouth harbor. At last the English got their fleet out and in running fights began to hammer the Spanish galleons in swift, sharp attacks. The English avoided the traditional close-ranging and grappling action that the Spaniards had expected. There was no attempt to board the Spanish ships. The tactics of the English sailors were terribly effective. Their numerous guns pounded the Spaniards from a distance; then the light but heavily armed English ships dashed in under the Spanish guns to rake the crowded decks of the galleons with terrific broadsides. This running fight lasted for six days; the Spanish spirits ebbed away. Six Spanish ships were sunk and 4,000 Spaniards killed by English gunnery.

Then the Armada, closely pursued by the English, moved into Calais. The English at once let loose fire ships among the Spanish vessels, most of which cut their anchor cables and struggled out to run before the heavy wind. They nearly ran ashore on the Flemish sandbanks but escaped into the North Sea. The storm finished the defeat of the Armada. Crippled and leaky Spanish ships rolled around the north of Scotland, down the coast of Ireland; many of them were wrecked on the inhospitable shores. Only about fifty battered ships got back to Spain; only ten thousand men came home. Philip II was devoutly resigned to the disaster. "In God's actions reputations are neither lost nor gained. It is best not to talk of it." In England Lord Howard of Effingham wrote of the men he had led out to meet the Armada: "God send me to see such company again, when need is."

The defeat of Philip II hastened the withering of Spain, and her power declined throughout the world. When Philip II died in 1598 he left a bankrupt and crumbling empire. For Englishmen the path lay open to world commerce and trade. For Frenchmen and Hollanders the path lay open too. The Roman Catholic champion had been humbled. All over Europe, Protestants lifted up their heads and took courage. The world of the seventeenth century would be different, surely, from the sixteenth.

The seventeenth century was indeed to be different but not in the ways that many men hoped. Like many another century, it was to be, for all the Western world, a time of perils, blunders, clashes, and ugly international immoralities. Armies were to march with bloody swords in triumph and then to slump back in defeat. There were to be the armed deadlocks that cannot be called peace, then or now. The ranging vision of the historian sees other aspects of European life, which counted as much in the long run. He sees a century of achievement and adventure, a century of busy ships, of bankers, poets, and philosophers, an age studded with the names of scientists who pushed forward the frontiers of human knowledge and understanding. He knows, too, that it is sound and salutary to remember that the dramatic and exciting chapters written by princes and prelates and generals tell only a part of the tale of mankind. He thinks of the straitened lives and the forgotten worries of the peasants and the lesser townsmen, the problems and the answers discussed in the shops and taverns by the village pumps and water troughs. All men, great and small, move through their generations to shape their segments of the human story.

> Sceptre and crown
> Must tumble down
> And in the dust be equal made
> With the poor crooked scythe and spade.

Chapter 24

THE YEARS

OF CHALLENGE

"Will is power."
—German proverb

We NOW turn away from the checkered spectacle of shame and glory in the sixteenth century to the wars, the wrangles, the national rivalries, the private grudges, and the solid achievements of men and states in the era that followed the death of Spain's Philip II and England's Elizabeth I.

The first part of the seventeenth century in Europe was a continuation of the age of frustrating civil and international conflict that marked and marred the previous era. Still present were the themes of intractable religious beliefs, jealous commercial rivalry, and dynastic ambitions. At the same time, strong forces continued to change the face of the Continent. Out of the disrupted old world was slowly emerging a new. The new order, gradually shaped by decades of slow repair and reorganization, promised to bring peace and stability to the wounded lands of Europe.

After 1600 the centers of population density in Europe began to shift northward. There came a marked acceleration of population growth in France, England, the Netherlands, and the German states and a relative decline in the Mediterranean regions. In the nineteenth and twentieth centuries the population centers have steadily moved eastward because of the rapid rate of population growth in eastern Europe and the comparative birthrate decline in northwestern Europe. Such demographic trends have obviously been of great significance in the history of Europe and the world of the West.

When the population centers began to shift northward after 1600 the political pivots of power moved with them. Both of these developments were stimulated, of course, by the swift accumulation of economic strength in the lands and ports of the Atlantic regions and the decline of the Mediterranean lands, once so wealthy and so proud. Spain, Austria, and the Italian states saw their exchequers diminish and their trade hopes wither. They saw their political and military strength decay. They saw the shadow of the growing power of France fall over Europe.

In 1610 a lunatic killed France's able and energetic Henry IV, first of the Bourbons. Henry's successor was Louis XIII, a child nine years of age. Marie de' Medici, the clever queen mother, then became regent. She succeeded in changing abruptly the patterns of policy established by Henry IV. She turned towards Spain and stopped fighting with the Hapsburgs. She let the power of the nobles—especially her favorite Italians—steadily advance.

Meanwhile Louis increased in wisdom and stature. In 1622 he came of age. In 1624 he shrewdly chose as his first minister the noble Armand Jean du Plessis, Cardinal Richelieu (1585–1642). Richelieu was clever, dispassionate, self-disciplined, determined, Machiavellian, ruthless, and cultured—it was Richelieu who founded the famous French Academy in 1635. Always his gifts and energies were directed to increasing the power of the king and the greatness and splendor of the kingdom of France. The policies of the calculating minister were determined by cold "reasons of state" and never by emotion or prejudice or even the demands of religion.

To increase the royal power Richelieu curbed the nobility. He stopped dueling among the nobles; a few who defied him were executed. He destroyed the castles of many proud men who resented the royal demands and encroachments. He took many powers out of the hands of the nobles and gave them to more reliable *intendants,* the royal servants in the provinces—they were later to be called the "Thirty Tyrants." The support and silence of some nobles Richelieu obtained by granting them pensions. Richelieu was a realist. The nobles must be subdued, checkmated, soothed, or executed. The monarch must tower in majesty above all his subjects.

The king's first minister did not approve of the provisions of the Edict of Nantes of 1598 that gave the Huguenots the right to garrison about a hundred fortified towns, mostly in southwestern France. He wanted no partially independent units inside the state; he wanted centralization, the concentration of power in the royal hands; he wanted all roads to lead to the palace of his king. When the Huguenots rebelled, Richelieu fought and defeated them. It was not an easy task; the siege of the Huguenot port of La Rochelle lasted fourteen months. When peace was made Richelieu left religious freedom to the Huguenots by the decree of Alais of 1628. The interests of the cardinal were mainly secular. The king's minister came before the cardinal, the state before the Church.

Meanwhile Richelieu kept a watchful eye upon French resources. He encouraged trade and industry and followed the practice of Henry IV and Sully of trying to make France as self-sufficient as possible in an age of mounting mercantilism. He built up the royal navy. For the lower classes he had little concern: "All politicians agree that when the people are too comfortable it is impossible to keep them within the bounds of their duty."

All around France stood Hapsburg lands: Spain, the Spanish Netherlands, Alsace, and Franche-Comté. Beyond was the power of Austria and the Holy Roman Empire and the allied Italian states. Cardinal Richelieu, like Henry IV before him, did not like that threatening fact. He dared not move alone against the Hapsburgs. He would wait until France could get allies; then France would strike, and hard. When France finally moved into the Thirty Years' War it was as an ally not of the Roman Catholic states but of the Protestants. Cardinal Richelieu was prepared to march with any power, Roman Catholic or Protestant, that fought the Hapsburgs. His king agreed. The safety and glory of France mattered more than the religion of her allies.

The resourceful and iron-willed Richelieu died in 1642, Louis XIII in 1643. Richelieu's successor was his apt and well-trained Italian student, that man of skill and stamina called Cardinal Mazarin. The heir of Louis XIII was Louis XIV, a child of five. Mazarin, faithful to Richelieu's plans and policies, became regent and survived the rebellious challenge of mischievous French nobles, judges, and others who disliked foreigners in general and the Italian Mazarin in particular. This strange, complicated, and discreditable rebellion of the divided and jealous men of the Fronde lasted for five years (1648–1653) and then Mazarin won. The fantastic and disgraceful turmoil profited nobody in France.

Mazarin also saw Hapsburg power diminished during the last phases of the Thirty Years' War. Later in this chapter it will be seen how France drew much profit from the long years of the central European conflict between 1618 and 1648. At this point it is enough to remark that if Richelieu had lived he would have been pleased at the sharp evidences of weakening Hapsburg power contained in the Peace of Westphalia of 1648 and the Treaty of the Pyrenees in 1659. The Hapsburgs stood humbled amidst the death and rubble of war. France was now the most formidable state in western Europe.

In 1661 Mazarin died and Louis XIV began his famous period of personal rule.

Now and then in the human drama there appears a man who seems to crystallize in himself the spirit of his times and to represent it to future generations. Louis XIV of France was such a man. The "Grand Monarch" represented well the age he helped to shape and build. His dazzling and Byzantine court at Versailles symbolized for his contemporaries and for many men who came afterwards the values, ideas, and ends of the civilized classes of the seventeenth century. It is fitting that we should often call a large part of that century "The Age of Louis XIV."

Louis XIV was indeed a monarch of unique prestige. He was the absolute ruler of France and France was the leading power in Europe. In the tides of chance and time the belief in the "divine right of kings" has now been almost entirely dissolved. In the seventeenth century, on the other hand, the idea was clear and strong. "The person of the king is sacred," said Bishop Bossuet, "and to attack him in any way is a sacrilege. . . . As all perfection is united in God, so all the power of individuals is united in the person of the prince. . . . The king is the image of God, who, seated on his high throne in the heavens, makes all nature move." Not everyone, of course, accepted the doctrine that kings were divinely appointed by God and responsible only to Him. Nevertheless, thousands did believe it. Some of them fought and were killed for the cause they thought right.

Leo Gershoy has described the autocratic Louis XIV as "a handsome and dignified man of good sense who was guided in his actions towards his subjects by a sense of justice and towards God by a sense of duty." This sentence is certainly true of Louis in his younger days. And yet it did become hard, sometimes, for Louis to keep full control of his concepts of justice and duty. Surrounded by flatterers and sycophants, Louis could hardly be blamed for slipping and losing his balance. In his later days he was frequently a prig, a bigot, and a selfish snob. A smile was rarely seen to play upon the pockmarked face. Saint-Simon, whose words were often flecked with venom, wrote of "the heart which never loved anyone and which no one loved."

Louis XIV was a professional king. He worked hard at "the grand, noble, and delightful trade" of being a monarch. To him it was a serious business. He always kept his strong and self-sufficient hands upon the reins of the state. The proud and august Louis XIV believed, and firmly believed, that he had been appointed by God. To God alone he was responsible. His duty was to reign and rule. He resolutely raised the throne of France to a level of power and freedom that Europe had never seen before. The glory of his vast court at Versailles fired the imagination of men everywhere. The efficiency of his complicated government was widely honored.

Louis selected the sun as his royal symbol because the sun ruled the heavens with its power and radiance. At Versailles the orderly and elegant rituals of the formal court went on week after week, year after year. The king liked pomp and ceremony. Almost everything he did seemed an affair of state, even the selection of his numerous mistresses. Flattery and greed were his constant companions. With fortitude and sober mien Louis moved through it all. The hand that held the scepter must not waver. Was he not the absolute "Sun King," the dominant ruler of Europe, the "Grand Monarch"?

Many able men served Louis. There was Le Tellier and his son Louvois, experts in war and statesmen extraordinary. Under Louvois the French army became strong and efficient. There were Turenne and Condé, the leading generals of the century. There was the dour and indefatigable Vauban, the world's leading authority on siege warfare. There was Jean Baptiste Colbert, long-time rival of Louvois and one of the greatest financiers of Europe.

"No one had before Colbert so clear an idea of the importance of the navy, commerce, the colonies, or sound finance, or the improvement of communication by roads, rivers, and canals." The stern and chilly Colbert hated waste; to him wealth meant work. He liked efficiency and honesty and a sound tax system. His greatest weakness was his mania for regulation. Nevertheless, if the king had listened to Colbert and if the people had ranged themselves behind Colbert's courageous leadership the destiny of France would have been brighter and her power would have been prolonged and extended. The longheaded Colbert wanted to lay the foundations of a world economic and colonial empire. Louis XIV, on the other hand, burned to win military glory in Europe. Louvois, the soldier, vehemently encouraged his king. The result of the momentous decision of Louis XIV was forty years of exhausting wars. It was not given to Louis XIV to tread the paths of military glory. "The king goes as far as he can and not so far as he would."

Nor was Louis XIV able to end by royal decrees the disorderly religious divisions in his kingdom. Because he thought that all his subjects should profess the religion of the king he tried to suppress the unorthodox and enthusiastic Jansenists. Despite his persecutions he did not succeed. He also failed when he turned against the French Protestant Huguenots. At first he tried to convert them. In 1685 he revoked the Edict of Nantes of 1598 and thus ended the Huguenot right to worship freely. The result was the flight of about 200,000 solid French citizens. They took their courage and their skills to Holland, England, Prussia, and America. Those who did not flee fought on against the king. Such migration and bloodletting steadily weakened the state. Bigotry, then as always, reaped its reward.

To Louis XIV it seemed obvious that France had certain "natural frontiers" to which the boundaries of France must be extended: the Rhine, the Alps, and the Pyrenees. The theory of the "natural frontiers" fitted the dynastic and military plans of Louis very neatly. For instance, the Hapsburgs, those long-time rivals of the Bourbons, held the Spanish Netherlands. Advancing a specious and twisted legal argument—the "right of devolution"—Louis claimed for his wife the Spanish Netherlands, fought with Spain, overran Franche-Comté in 1668, and soon struck at the Spanish Netherlands and the Dutch Republic. England and Holland stopped a commercial war and joined in a Triple Alliance with Sweden to stop Louis. Louis then decided to make peace.

The peace ending the War of Devolution turned out to be a breathing spell, and in 1672 Louis struck again. The Dutch opened their dikes and fought hard under their strong leader, William of Orange. Soon they found themselves supported by other alarmed enemies of Louis and France: the Emperor Leopold, the Elector of Brandenburg, Denmark, Spain, and finally England. Again Louis was forced to make peace. By the terms of the Treaty of Nijmegen (1678) he did get Franche-Comté (the County of Burgundy) and some towns in the Spanish Netherlands. These were indeed gains; but they were not the big ones Louis craved.

Nothing ventured, nothing gained. In the next phase of French aggression Louis tried to advance legal claims to some of the lands he wanted. He set up a series of special courts called "chambers of reunion," to establish titles to disputed territory. Then he sent in his armies to enforce the decision of his courts. In that unscrupulous way he got the cities of Metz, Strasbourg, Toul, and Verdun in 1680 and 1681 and Luxemburg in 1683.

In 1686 the League of Augsburg was forged to stop the alarming advance of Louis. This League united Spain, the Holy Roman Empire, Saxony, Savoy, the Palatinate, Holland, Sweden, Bavaria, and the pope; its forces marched against Louis in 1689 after he tried to grab the Rhenish Palatinate. Meanwhile England had joined the League after the English revolution of 1688 had driven James II from the throne and had placed Holland's William of Orange upon it. The English and the Dutch joined to smash the French navy. The French army crumbled. Louis XIV signed the Treaty of Ryswick in 1697. By its terms he surrendered all the lands—except the city of Strasbourg—given him by the "chambers of reunion." He had to give up his claim to the Palatinate and get out of Lorraine. He was compelled to give the Dutch a favorable commercial treaty, to let them garrison some barrier fortresses of the Spanish Netherlands, and to recognize William III as king of England. All colonial conquests were to be restored to their original holders.

For Louis XIV the wheel of fate was to spin once more. Before the childless cretin Charles II of Spain died at last in 1700 he had named Philip of Anjou, grandson of Louis XIV, as his heir. Louis supported his grandson's claim to the throne at Madrid, seized some border forts of the Spanish Netherlands, recognized the exiled Stuart Pretender as king of England—this last step was a repudiation of his pledge at Ryswick; but the Bourbons were never ones to keep their word when it seemed to them more profitable to do the opposite.

The drums of Europe's armies were soon to roll again, the trumpets soon to sound. Was France to control Spain and the Spanish Empire through Philip of Anjou? "There are no longer any Pyrenees," Louis XIV is supposed to have told his court.

Faced by the challenge of Louis, his enemies formed the "Grand Alliance" against him. The coalition included Austria, England, Prussia, Holland and, later, Savoy. Thus began the war of the Spanish Succession, a conflict that was to last more than eleven years. In that war by land and sea Louis and his allies

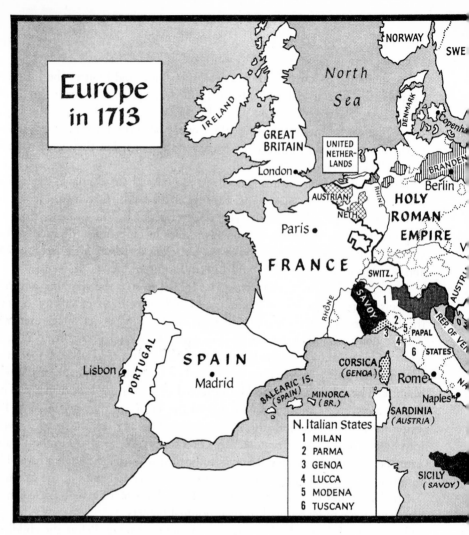

Europe
in 1713

North
Sea

NORWAY
SWE
IRELAND
GREAT
BRITAIN
London
UNITED
NETHER-
LANDS
DENMARK
Copenha
BRANDEN
Berlin
AUSTRIAN
NETH
RHINE
HOLY
ROMAN
EMPIRE
Paris
FRANCE
SWITZ.
SAVOY
AUST
RHÔNE
REP. OF VEN
PAPAL
STATES
PORTUGAL
SPAIN
Madrid
Lisbon
CORSICA
(GENOA)
Rome
BALEARIC IS.
(SPAIN)
MINORCA
(BR.)
NA
Naples
SARDINIA
(AUSTRIA)

N. Italian States	
1	MILAN
2	PARMA
3	GENOA
4	LUCCA
5	MODENA
6	TUSCANY

SICILY
(SAVOY)

—Spain, Bavaria, Portugal—were defeated. To the land war the English sent the brilliant John Churchill, Duke of Marlborough. Marlborough was a superb military strategist and tactician. He never fought a battle that he did not win or besiege a place that he did not take. At Blenheim (1704), Ramillies (1706), Oudenarde (1708), Malplaquet (1709) he rightly won a lasting fame. The collective demands of the victorious allies compelled Louis to fight on. As Louis fought, he lost still more. Not until 1713 did the general Peace of Utrecht end the War of the Spanish Succession.

The various treaties that are collectively called the Peace of Utrecht form a milestone in the history of Western Europe. The Utrecht settlement established an uneasy balance of power and a reasonable equilibrium in Europe for about forty years. By the terms of peace Philip V was recognized as king of Spain and the Spanish Empire in America on condition that the thrones of Spain and France should never be united. Austria was to have the Spanish dependencies in Europe: Milan, Naples, Sardinia, and the Spanish Nether-lands. Sicily went to the Duke of Savoy. The Dutch secured control of the

barrier fortresses. Great Britain obtained Nova Scotia, Gibraltar, Minorca, and St. Kitts. Louis XIV abandoned claims to the Hudson Bay region and Newfoundland. He recognized the Protestant succession to the English throne as established by Parliament.

The menace of Louis XIV had been met and shattered. France was nearly bankrupt. The decline of Spain had been accelerated. Britain emerged from the war the foremost of European nations. The ascendancy of France in Europe was at an end in 1713. In 1715 the dying Louis XIV said to his great-grandson: "My child, you are going to be a great king. Do not imitate me in my taste for building, or in my love of war. Strive, on the contrary, to live in peace with your neighbors."

During the years when France expanded in power and prestige the politically segmented areas of central Europe continued to bicker and battle. Much of the energy of the Germans and Slavs was drained away in conflict. For the people who lived then it was a pity that the patterns of history unrolled in such a way because the central European belt has always possessed several advantages in geographical location and natural resources. The land of the Germans, for instance, is a network of rivers. The Rhine River valley has served for centuries as a great trade artery joining other rivers that reach into Italy, Switzerland, and southern France. On its way to the Black Sea the Danube flows through the stretches of Austria and several Balkan regions. The Oder thrusts into Poland, the Elbe into the area now called Czechoslovakia. The resources of coal and iron—the twin foundations of modern heavy industry—are tremendous. Taken all together, these advantages might have promised a future of sunlit progress for many generations of men. Unfortunately, successive wars and prolonged disunity made the full use of the gifts of nature quite impossible. The hopes and wishes of thousands of people remained unrealized.

Through several centuries the main problem of the peoples of the north European plain area was essentially political. Before the alliances and arrangements of Napoleon Bonaparte in the years that bridged the eighteenth and nineteenth centuries there were more than 300 jostling German states in the strange mosaic of the Holy Roman Empire. Even Napoleon's skilled surgery only succeeded in reducing the number of states to thirty-eight. Many of those states were the tools of larger powers, the frequent victims of aggression, blackmail, bribery, fraud. The clouds and fogs of rivalry and mistrust hung heavily over the fields of battle and the palaces where the peacemakers so often prepared their treaties and their seals. The German lands were indeed lands of political discord and frequent armed clashes.

There were also religious problems. The Treaty of Augsburg of 1555 did not settle the claims and issues in dispute between the Roman Catholics and the Lutherans. Under the terms of the treaty each German ruler decided what the religion of the people in his state would be—*cujus regio ejus religio*. The result was continued tension, plots, frustration, competition, and fighting. Augsburg was not a peace; it was a brittle truce. Beneath the surface heaved the forces of disunity.

Mingled with the political and religious difficulties were the economic. The Roman Catholic bishops who had become Protestants held on to their lands. Lay rulers who had left the fold of Rome often seized Roman Catholic property. "Need," Seneca once said, "teaches things unlawful." The Roman Catholic Church, quite naturally, wanted to get back all the acres and goods that had been filched or wrested from its hands.

Meanwhile jealous and semi-independent kings, dukes, and electors watched for appropriate chances to increase their powers at the expense of the weakening Holy Roman Emperor. The new Protestant rulers, so often both ambitious and fearful, were especially anxious to see the power of the Roman Catholic emperor diminished. Across the Rhine, the leaders of France grasped every opportunity they found to foment and support disunion. They encouraged and applauded all the disruptive forces in the German states. This kind of activity remained a fairly constant factor of French foreign policy for a long time. In the judgment of the French, a divided Germany meant a stronger France in the battles and councils of Europe.

About the middle of the sixteenth century the German areas moved into an economic decline that was accelerated by the economic particularism of the separate German states in a weakening Holy Roman Empire. There were networks of tariffs inside the German regions. Each state had differing laws about weights and measures. There were several kinds of coinage and a variety of minting rights. There were more than forty toll stations on the Elbe. Under such conditions trade cannot thrive.

When Portugal, Spain, Holland, France, and England were moving to trade and colonize over the seas, the German states, having no navy and little access to the sea, moved hardly at all. Nor did they have the strength which only political and economic unity can give. States like Portugal, Spain, France, and England were unified nation-states. They could adventure and battle on a grand scale. Before the Germans could move in any semblance of unity there had to be the cooperation of all the ruling princes. Their full co-operation, if it had ever happened in the seventeenth century, would have been one of the wonders of Europe. Even the limited economic union of the Zollverein did not appear until the early nineteenth century.

As the trade centers shifted from the Mediterranean to the Atlantic the traffic on the north-south trade routes through central Europe steadily diminished. This progressive shrinking had a heavily adverse affect upon the cities of the southern German areas. The great merchant houses of such cities as Augsburg, Nuremberg, and Ulm were sometimes faced with bankruptcy. Meanwhile, the Dutch, Swedes, Danes, and English moved to hasten the demise of the once powerful Hanseatic League described in Chapter 17. The League ended as a corporate body in 1628. Several German markets were overrun by foreign merchants.

Meanwhile, too, German intellectual and artistic activities—especially in the latter part of the sixteenth century—markedly declined. After the death of Dürer (1528), Riemenschneider (1531), and Hans Holbein the Younger (1543) there was no achievement of value for a long time in German painting or sculpture. For the German lands, so filled by passion and rivalry, the latter part of the sixteenth century—and the early seventeenth—was a time of political, economic, and intellectual blight.

In 1618 there began in Bohemia, the land northwest of Vienna that was the home of the Czechs, the series of conflicts usually called the Thirty Years' War. Among the numerous causes of the war was the continued dispute about the territories of the Roman Catholic Church taken over by Protestant princes and the clerics who had abandoned allegiance to Rome. There were also bitter arguments about the fact that the Peace of Augsburg had recognized only the Roman Catholic and Lutheran religions and had failed to recognize Calvinism.

Religious differences among the numerous petty German rulers were mingled with political ambitions and jealousies. The difficulties and rivalries between many German princes—so anxious to keep their "German liberties" —and the Holy Roman Emperor darkened the scene and muddied the waters. Usually these princes wanted the emperor to be weak; he wanted to be strong. It was to be expected that many Roman Catholic princes and electors would follow the emperor. He was, after the pope, the outstanding Roman Catholic leader in Europe. Sometimes Protestant princes, for political reasons, also supported him.

Upon a wider scene, many Europeans felt that the rivalry between the Hapsburg and Bourbon dynasties could only be ended by war and that a real balance of power could only be achieved if the Hapsburgs were finally overthrown. The Bourbons of France, as we have seen, always supported that view. Against the Hapsburgs, those champions of centralism, the kingdom of France was the leader. Her allies, ready to join in an onslaught upon the emperor and his dynasty, were quite numerous. Most of them were eaten with envy. For instance, Protestant Sweden was ready to expand in the Baltic area. The king of Denmark also coveted the German lands along the Baltic. He hoped that they might soon be his and he was disposed to fight to make his hope come true.

A very large number of motives and factors—religious, personal, constitutional, political, economic—played their parts in the emerging struggle. At different times and places each took a decisive part. Perhaps the religious aspects of the war have sometimes been stressed too strongly. The relentless tide of secularism was already rolling heavily. The long age of the "reasons of state" had arrived.

In 1608 a Protestant Union of princes was formed. A year later, the Catholic League appeared. The alliances, it seemed, were being cemented and the lines of conflict drawn. The powerful Maximilian I, Elector of Bavaria, led the Catholic League—to get his help the emperor had to promise to agree to an increase in the size of Bavaria. By the side of Maximilian stood Johann Tilly, one of Europe's greatest soldiers. The Protestant Union, for its part, was supported by the mercenary troops of another famous warrior, Ernst von Mansfeld. The players were ready; the stage was set.

In 1618 the nationalist and Calvinist Protestants of Bohemia refused to put the unpopular and intolerant Roman Catholic Ferdinand of Hapsburg upon the vacant Bohemian throne. Bohemian nobles threw some imperial envoys out of the windows of the imperial palace of Prague—this was the famous event usually called the "defenestration of Prague."

The Bohemians now asked the Calvinist Frederick V, the Protestant Elector of the Palatine, son-in-law of England's James I and leader of the Protestant Union, to be their king. Frederick accepted the offer. War, so long delayed, now began. At first the conflict was a small dispute, a tiny fragment of European history. Soon it surged over most of Europe. A rock loosened upon the side of a mountain can start an avalanche. The Thirty Years' War, with its drawn-out casualty lists and drenched throughout with ugliness, brought giddy changes in the map of Europe. It also altered the personal stories of thousands of men and women who probably wanted to be left alone to live out the humble and quiet chapters of their lives, to search for food and faith, to beget children, to watch sometimes the cross and the steeple of their village church white in the moonlight, merging into the soft-starred sky. These are the people, linking their hands through the generations, who have often paid a calamitous price in tears and blood as wars and floods and famine swept all their dreams away.

Within a year Frederick was beaten. He was beaten partly because of all the Protestant rulers only the prince of Transylvania fought by his side. John George, Elector of Saxony, for instance, did not want Frederick to increase his power and territory. Frederick already held the Palatine and what did he want with Bohemia? Thus reasoned the Elector of Saxony, and this was the reason he stayed neutral. Several others had similar causes for standing aside. Frederick found himself an isolated rebel against his emperor, and despite some clever diplomatic footwork he was crushed. About 20,000 Spaniards came over from the Low Countries to help the emperor and Maximilian finish the job. The armies plundered and burned. When the soldiers did not get their pay they became more predatory still.

Frederick, soon to be called the "Winter King" because his reign was so short, lost Bohemia. He also lost the Palatinate—that fair territory along the Rhine was given to Roman Catholic Bavaria. Frederick's plight was sad.

Many German princes, both Roman Catholic and Protestant, objected to the new arrangement about the Palatine lands. They did not want to have a strong Bavaria any more than they wanted a strong Holy Roman Emperor. If they objected strongly enough, of course, they could go to war to make another settlement. There was no other way to extricate themselves from the awkward spot into which they had marched. They had been so occupied with their success in stopping Frederick that they had not considered the designs of the emperor and of Maximilian.

To our timetable and airport world the pace of the Thirty Years' War seems sometimes to be dragging and slow. Many of the facts about the

Bohemian explosion of 1618 and the following phases of the conflict are bald and uninspiring. We are sundered from them by the centuries. Dedicated students of the history of these troubled years have carefully examined the numerous spider-web strands of European diplomacy and have traced, step by step, the complicated military campaigns. They have explained, quite clearly, how it was that by 1640 the French were fighting four wars in Belgium, Italy, Germany, and Spain. They have shown, with admirable skill, the exact interests of James I and Charles I of England, of Louis XIII and Louis XIV of France, of Christian IV of Denmark and Gustavus II Adolphus of Sweden. In these pages the results of the deep and wide research of many scholars must be pressed into small spaces, sometimes capsuled into a sentence or massaged into a phrase.

The second phase of the Thirty Years' War was started in 1625 by the warlike Christian IV of Denmark and Norway. Christian, alarmed at the dangers to Lutheranism foreshadowed by Roman Catholic triumphs and anxious to hold and extend his lands in northern Germany, decided to strike first and fast. When he invaded the German lands of the empire he soon encountered the imperial forces commanded by Count Tilly and Albrecht von Wallenstein, a brilliant and enigmatic adventurer who raised a cosmopolitan mercenary army and maintained it by plunder. Christian was defeated and the peace treaty of 1629 deprived him of much of the territory he had held in northern Germany. Because he had grasped for so much Christian IV lost a large portion of what he had.

Twice the Roman Catholics had fought and won. In 1629 the emperor ordered that all lands seized from the Roman Catholics and secularized after the Peace of Augsburg of 1555 should be handed back. This blunt and drastic Edict of Restoration persuaded the Protestants to fight again for faith and property. The third phase of the Thirty Years' War began.

This time the Protestant leader was the formidable Gustavus Adolphus, king of Sweden, an excellent statesman and a brilliant soldier, the inventor of several new armaments and military tactics. The Swedish king was sincerely interested in the fate and fortunes of Lutheranism. He was also anxious to protect and extend the economic and political power of Sweden in the Baltic regions. In earlier years he had fought and defeated Denmark, Poland, and Russia and had added Finland and Estonia to his empire. The Roman Catholic expansion into the northern German states alarmed him. If once the Catholics grabbed any Baltic ports they would have powerful naval strength athwart the lines of Swedish commerce and sea power.

In 1630 Gustavus Adolphus, the "Lion of the North," invaded Pomerania. He allied Sweden with Brandenburg and Saxony, and France gave him supplies and gold. After several lightning victories—Tilly was defeated twice and died of his battle wounds in 1631—Gustavus Adolphus met Wallenstein, that greedy and intriguing champion of the Catholic League, on the foggy battlefield of Lützen in 1632. In that great duel Wallenstein's forces were defeated and Gustavus Adolphus was killed. Wallenstein lived for two years more; then he was murdered, probably at the orders of the emperor.

In 1635 the compromise Treaty of Prague provided that all territories in dispute were to be returned to those who had held them in 1627. The emperor's Edict of Restoration was thus canceled. The Roman Catholic and imperial career of victory, so strong and sure in the first two phases of the Thirty Years' War, had been checked by the obstinacy and skill of Gustavus Adolphus.

There was not to be peace. Bourbon France, long a fearful and determined opponent of the Hapsburgs of Austria and Spain, had secretly provided supplies and subsidies to Sweden, Denmark, and the German Protestant states in their battles against the Roman Catholics. True, France was a Roman Catholic nation and her famed and shrewd Richelieu was a cardinal in the Roman Church. Nevertheless, as we have seen, dynastic interests and power politics came first. The point of view of France was this: Austria and Spain must be harassed and humbled.

In 1635 the Bourbons of France moved openly against the Hapsburgs. The French armies, then under the skilled command of Condé and Turenne, struck at Philip IV of Spain in the Spanish Netherlands, in Italy, in Burgundy, even in Spain. Meanwhile, the Protestant princes of Germany engaged the imperial armies of Ferdinand III in the German arena.

In May, 1643, the swift and resolute Duke d'Enghien, at twenty-two years of age general of the northern armies of France, won the great battle of Rocroi. Some older and more experienced French officers had earlier wished to delay. "What will become of us," asked one, "if we are beaten?" The reply of the Duke d'Enghien has echoed over the hills of history for three centuries: "That will not concern me, for I shall be dead." At Rocroi the best regiments of Spain were smashed; the cavalry was routed; more than 15,000 Spaniards were killed or captured. The defeat of the Armada in 1588 had shattered Spanish strength on the sea. The battle of Rocroi decided that Spain was no longer a first-class power on the land. Spain was now nearly isolated. Her dreams of expanding power and empire were doomed.

There were other Bourbon and Protestant victories in a grisly conflict. In 1644 Turenne and the Duke d'Enghien attacked and defeated the Bavarians at the battle of Freiburg. Again and again the Austrian Hapsburgs were beaten. In 1647 and 1648 the French and the Swedes pushed about 30,000 imperialists all the way to the Danube. In 1648 the Spaniards were crushed again at Lens.

In October, 1648, a series of long negotiations brought forth a series of detailed agreements usually called the Treaty of Westphalia. Generations of students have been required to study the numerous clauses of the Westphalia peace arrangements—sometimes to their advantage, sometimes not. Not all of the clauses will certainly be mentioned here. The really significant provisions of Westphalia were only those that marked definite mileposts in European history.

In these days—and before and after, too—the princes of secular states clawed and dismembered and carried away the property of churchmen whose predecessors had once claimed sovereignty over all the princes of the planet. The voices of Gregory VII and Innocent III had been forever stilled. The whole atmosphere of the western world had been steadily changing. In the increasingly inhuman "wars of religion" of the sixteenth and seventeenth centuries there appeared, more and more, the interests and causes of kings and states. All over the Continent were storm centers. The Church of Rome was no longer a pivot and pillar of stability. Countless men had denied and mocked her spiritual claims. These men and others hastened also to speed the decline of her temporal authority. The hard fact of the weakening temporal power and prestige of the Church and the ecclesiastical states and principalities was sharply demonstrated by what happened when the peace arrangements were made at Westphalia. For the sovereign and secular nation-states the year 1648 was a time of triumph and of prophecy.

By the terms of the Westphalia agreements Calvinists as well as Lutherans were to be included in the principle of *cujus regio ejus religio* established for the German states by the Treaty of Augsburg of 1555. Each German ruler might now decide whether the official faith of his state would be Roman Catholic, Lutheran, or Calvinist. An equal number of Roman Catholic and Protestant judges were to sit in the imperial courts. All ecclesiastical property was confirmed in the possession of the Roman Catholics or the Protestants who had held that property in 1624. Steps such as these were short paces towards toleration. They also illustrated and underlined the fact that the nation-states were attempting to dictate and control, with increasing success, the status and function of the Roman Catholic and Protestant churches within their realms. Pope Innocent X denounced the Westphalian settlements as "null, void, invalid, iniquitous, unjust, damnable, reprobate, inane, empty of meaning and effect for all time." His strong adjectives did not alter the fact that the temporal powers once held by the Church belonged to the Church no more.

Both the name and the frail structure of the Holy Roman Empire were kept until 1806 when Napoleon Bonaparte wiped them away. Long before the world had heard of Napoleon the princes of Germany had become almost entirely free of even a semblance of subordination to the decisions of the emperor and the laws and rules of the empire. Napoleon was not responsible for the death of the empire. He merely presided at a funeral service that had

Europe in 1648

Austrian Hapsburgs   Spanish Hapsburgs

Boundary of the Empire

been delayed for more than a hundred and fifty years. The defunct and deceased empire no longer served a purpose in Europe.

The adjustments of territory, resources, population, and status also pointed to the hardening tendency of the age to seek and move towards territorial consolidation and extension and the organization of nation-states. Holland, Switzerland, and Sweden were formally recognized as completely independent nations. Sweden collected from the Hapsburg holdings some pieces she had long coveted: a large western section of Pomerania and the bishopric of Bremen. France took over the bishoprics of Metz, Toul, and Verdun and the "sovereignty" of Alsace. When peace was at last made with Spain in the Treaty of the Pyrenees of 1659, France got more frontier provinces in the Netherlands and along the Pyrenees. A Spanish proverb says: "Losers are always in the wrong."

The Peace of Westphalia indeed marked the end of an age. The peace-makers drew a map of Europe that was not to be greatly changed until the Peace of Utrecht in 1713. There were to be no more "wars of religion" in Europe. Religion and politics were no longer locked in the same compartment and tangled together. Men of the new centuries preferred to fight for the causes of nation-states or about conflicting political and economic philosophies.

Many of the traditional statements about the Thirty Years' War are not true and others are debatable. Usually the tale of the war is told in terms of black disaster. Contemporary quotations have been used to describe and ex-plain the wiping out of villages, the plundering, the atrocities, the butcheries and horrors. The themes of slaughter, hunger, and destruction have been repeated and passed along confidently through the generations. The sources of our information have often been poisoned springs. Many men of the seven-teenth century were interested in private or official propaganda. They were guilty of grave errors, some of them intentional. They wanted to degrade, blacken, and discredit their enemies, to describe them for their fellows and posterity as immoral and shameless men taking a unique delight in evil. In the midst of envenomed human hatreds truth is often a casualty. Exaggerations and misrepresentations multiply.

A great many of our ideas and conclusions about the Thirty Years' War need scrupulous examination and drastic revision. The devastation wrought by the Thirty Years' War was not nearly so wide or complete as many men have said. Disease, especially dysentery and typhus, killed more people than guns and swords. Probably not more than 300,000 men were slain in the 30 years of spasmodic fighting. The total decline of population was small. The un-healthy and stunted life in the German lands preceded the war and the war should not be held responsible for it.

The claims that science, art, and literature were impoverished and paralyzed by the Thirty Years' War must be handled even more gingerly than the fantastic statistics handed down to us about the loss of livestock. Scientific advances were in fact ahead of the decades before the war. Gottfried Wilhelm Leibnitz was soon to show his great genius at Mainz. So far as literature was concerned, it seems that the quantity was larger and the quality was better in the years between 1618 and 1648 than during the preceding half century. Music started to rise again as the glorious musical history of Saxony began. The first German opera was performed at the very time that Wallenstein was battling by the Baltic. True, art remained in the doldrums; but it had been in that state long before 1618.

The novel fictions written about the Thirty Years' War in the seventeenth century by men like von Grimmelshausen were accepted and repeated by German Romanticists in the nineteenth century—they liked to recite gruesome tales of slaughter and disaster. We should beware of them. Enthusiasm is not a substitute for fact.

During these years of conflict there emerged in north central Europe a new and strong state: Prussia. This newcomer to the wars and councils of Europe soon challenged the long-dominant power of Austria. Berlin's ambitious Hohenzollerns ranged themselves against the Hapsburgs of Vienna. For about three centuries they were to be bitter and obstinate rivals.

One of the early spurts of growth in the nucleus of the later Prussian state occurred shortly after Charlemagne died when a great fortress called Brandenburg was built in the north German regions. In the twelfth century this fort gave its name to a border area, the North Mark. During the fifteenth century the Emperor Sigismund sold this Brandenburg territory, which had earlier become an electorate in the Holy Roman Empire, to the hitherto insignificant Hohenzollern family. In the sixteenth century the Hohenzollerns became Lutherans and seized valuable properties of the Roman Catholic Church. In 1614 they inherited the little states of Mark and Cleves and so reached the lower Rhine. In 1614 they inherited, subject to the overlordship of the king of Poland, the duchy of East Prussia. This territory, once ruled by the militant monks of the Teutonic Knights, lay beyond the Vistula north of Poland. By the terms of the Peace of Westphalia in 1648 the Hohenzollerns added substantial areas: the eastern half of Pomerania, three wealthy secularized bishoprics and the "right of accession" to Magdeburg—they came into formal possession of Magdeburg in 1680.

In 1640 Frederick William, usually called the Great Elector, ascended the throne of Brandenburg. His scattered dominions had suffered heavily in the savage fighting of the early part of the Thirty Years' War. The soil of many areas was poor—Brandenburg was once called the "sandbox of the Holy Roman Empire." Frederick William's revenues were small. His army was almost useless. The results of the feeble rule of his father George William were everywhere obvious.

Frederick William was a hard and resolute man. He was also shrewd, coarse, heartless, and treacherous—these are perhaps desirable qualities in a ruler who wants to build a strong state. In any event, Frederick William carefully strengthened and reorganized the government of Brandenburg-Prussia and placed the center of all administration and financial control in Berlin. Frederick William wanted efficiency and efficiency he got. He insisted upon mutual toleration by the Calvinists and Lutherans in the state. He encouraged education, trade, and commerce and stimulated agriculture. He built the Frederick William Canal that joins the Oder and the Elbe. He drained marshes. He was responsible for the coming into Brandenburg of about 20,000 Huguenot refugees from France. By such a migration France lost and Brandenburg-Prussia gained.

A master of political propaganda, Frederick William deliberately tried to persuade the German peoples that their interests were identical with those of the Hohenzollerns. He hired Samuel von Pufendorf as his court historiographer and Pufendorf earned his wages as a public-relations man. Pufendorf filled his widely distributed writings with exaggerations and special pleadings. He described Frederick William as the great "defender" of the Protestants and the German "liberties" against the "foreign aggression" of the Hapsburgs. He excused the oppression of the lower classes by the Elector and the noble Junkers on the ground that such steps were necessary.

By his success in diplomatic and military affairs the tireless Frederick William also increased the prestige of Prussia. Shortly after he came to the throne in 1640 he was able, by dint of clever maneuvers, to get a Swedish army of occupation to evacuate Brandenburg at the cost of a small indemnity. When Sweden and Poland entered the "First Northern War" (1655–1660) the cunning Frederick William helped one side and then the other. At the end he persuaded the Polish king to surrender the rights of overlordship in the duchy of East Prussia. Thus Frederick William got full sovereignty over that important section of his state. In the Dutch War of Louis XIV, Frederick William defeated the Swedes—who were allied with France—and the prestige of Prussia and the fame of the Prussian army grew apace.

Frederick William the Great Elector laid many of the foundations of the later state of Germany. When he died in 1688 the territory of Brandenburg-Prussia was second only to Austria as a power in the Holy Roman Empire. A third of Frederick William's lands—they covered about 40,000 square miles —were outside the empire. The revenue of the state had been increased sevenfold in the reign of Frederick William. Its financial and credit status was high and sound. Above all, perhaps, Brandenburg-Prussia was recognized as the head of all the German Protestant states. Its army was highly efficient, disciplined, dangerous; and the rest of Europe knew it.

The momentum of Brandenburg-Prussia's advance was temporarily slackened by the ineptitude of Frederick III, ambitious, bossy, and frivolous. During his reign the states of Bavaria, Hanover, and Saxony threatened to eclipse Prussia.

Brighter hopes soon gleamed. Frederick III died in 1701. Then there came three great masters and servants of the Prussian state: Frederick I (1701–1713), Frederick William I (1713–1740), and Frederick II (1740–1786). The last of these three is usually called "the Great." If decency and morality are not considered criteria for greatness then the title is perhaps deserved.

The tale of England in these years of European conflict was not filled with chapters of gentle peace and swelling commerce. Forces of dislocation, pervasive and powerful, were everywhere at work. Protestantism paraded its numerous sects, each believing in predestination, or mysticism, or the individual priesthood of men or something else. The religious view of life in England was now not one, but many. Naturalistic philosophy and the new science challenged the authority of the classics and the synthesis of the custodians of the great traditions of Christian humanism. There were wars with France, wars with Holland, conflicts with Ireland and Scotland. The new Stuart rulers fought with pen and sword against the Parliamentarians, the Puritans, and the courts of common law.

In 1603 Elizabeth I, last of the great Tudors, was succeeded by James I, son of Mary, Queen of Scots. This first of the Stuart kings was not a worthy successor of Elizabeth. His new subjects, long accustomed to the rule of their famous queen, saw a shambling figure, unsteady in gait and unkingly in appearance. Most of them, probably, were not pleased. James was garrulous, generous in self-praise, and dogmatic. He enjoyed learned conversation, particularly if it was largely a monologue. James was not evil, a harsh and strong enemy of mankind; he was a kindly man; and he had good intentions. Only because destiny called him to be a king were his follies more important than those of his subjects.

Among the chief interests of James was his royal prerogative. He believed in the "divine right of kings." According to his theory a king was appointed by God and was responsible only to Him. His subjects might not resist the king's commands, for resistance was a sin. Under such a theory the king, as deputy of the Lord, was above Parliament, above the laws of England, above the people.

Faced by such assertions, it was not surprising that in 1604 Parliament spoke of "the ancient rights of the subjects of this realm" and stated that "our privileges and liberties are our right and due inheritance, no less than our very lands and goods." Nor is it surprising that James continued throughout his reign to haggle and quarrel with his Parliaments about such things as elections, Parliamentary privileges, and taxation. He also battled with the courts of common law and especially with the learned and obstinate Sir Edward Coke, chief justice of the Court of Common Pleas. Coke was foremost in the ranks of those who insisted that the common law controlled and limited the province of royal prerogative power. James I steadily fought such assertions, and Coke, for his part, fought back.

James I also got into trouble over the vexed questions of religion. Elizabeth's famous Anglican compromise had endured throughout the reign despite heavy assaults upon it. The hammering vehemence of dissent was mounting when James I came to the throne. Throughout the century men were to dispute loudly about the right road to Jerusalem. The numerous elements in England who were usually called "Puritans" contained some left-wing or "Broad Church" elements in the Church of England, the various kinds of Presbyterians, the Independents who did not approve of a church "system" or of priests or presbyters but stood instead for full democracy in religion, each congregation governing itself and free from outside interference. Added to these large bodies of dissent, often mixed and mingled together, were numerous smaller sects, such as the Ranters, the Muggletonians, the Family of Love. In an age of spiritual excitement men found satisfaction in many ways. There were, of course, some lunatics—Thomas Shrecker was an Anabaptist who was divinely guided to cut off his brother's head. Smith-Pigott believed he was God and fathered upon the parlormaid two children he called Power and Glory. Nehemiah Wallington kept a notebook recording God's judgments upon drunkards and "those who are killed with horses, carts, and coaches."

The Puritans painted fantastic pictures of the pomp, gluttony, and lechery of the Anglican clergy. "From plague, pestilence, and famine, from bishops, priests, and deacons, Good Lord, deliver us!" A cheap and prolific press published a spate of polemical pamphlets, written with pens dipped in vitriol, on all sides of the urgent problems of religion and politics. Across the centuries still crackle the imagery and the insults.

In seventeenth-century England, religion was more than a set of personal beliefs. An individual's profession of religion was the outward sign of a political and social attitude. The Anglican point of view was enforced, so far as possible, by the state. Dissenters were persecuted. Religion's business was held to be with social, political, and economic affairs as well as with the condition of heaven. Most of the writings of the age were both religious and political; they could not well be otherwise. The various arguments advanced for religious toleration supplied ideas for supporting democratic political theories. Men who pleaded for religious liberty and church-government reforms often pleaded also for civil liberty and political revolution. Arguments of theology and Scripture were frequently mingled with those that were political, secular, and nationalistic.

To the Puritans who came to his Hampton Court Conference in 1604, James I made it clear that he feared that the growth of Puritanism might spread a democratic temper in the state. "If you aim at a Scottish presbytery," he exclaimed, "it agreeth as well with monarchy as God with the devil. Then Jack, Tom, Will, and Dick shall meet and at their pleasure censure me and my Council. . . . I thus apply it. . . . no bishop, no king. . . . If this be all your party hath to say I will make them conform, or else I will harry them out of the land." The only happy result of the Hampton Court Conference was the Authorized Version of the Bible, completed and published in 1611. It is a masterpiece of English prose, the last great achievement of the

perfection of Elizabethan richness. To thousands of people who had no literature but the Bible the reading of God's word was a constant comfort. The
effect of Bible study on the English character cannot be calculated; through
three centuries the many-splendored poetry of the Book has been a part of
the national life.

James I was tragically unaware of the currents of social, political, and
economic forces, the flood of which no man could stay. He could not understand the sincere zeal and the militant courage of the men who opposed him
steadily. A few years later John Milton wrote his opinion of the people, in
whatever age they live, who choose to flee rather than to fight. "I cannot
praise a fugitive and cloistered virtue, unexercised and unbreathed, that never
sallies out and seeks her adversary, but slinks out of the race, where that immortal garland is to be run for, not without dust and heat."

Charles I succeeded his father in 1625. His subjects soon discovered that
he believed in the divine right of kings as his father had taught him to do.
The Puritans found that he was strongly inclined to the High Anglican
Church. Members of Parliament learned that he was contemptuous of their
rights and privileges. The common-law lawyers and judges soon saw that their
claims were scornfully denied and rejected. Heedless of public opinion, reckless of consequences, Charles defied his opponents. Such a ruler, conscientious,
unimaginative, obstinate, fish-blooded, promised to bring revolution in his
train as surely as night follows day.

With successive Parliaments, Charles battled about taxation and revenues,
religion, foreign policy, the royal favorites, the privileges of the House of
Commons. Charles was obstinate. The Parliaments and law courts were
truculent.

In 1629, Charles decided that he "abhorred the very name of Parliament."
He would govern "by those means God put into my hands." For eleven
years after 1629 no Parliament was called. Meanwhile Charles skimped and
saved and searched for every expedient by which he might keep himself independent of parliamentary grants. He continued his arbitrary levy of taxes.
Year by year the opposition grew.

So far as the Parliament and the common-law courts were concerned, such
men as John Pym, John Hampden, John Selden, Sir Edward Coke, and
Oliver Cromwell stood in the forefront of resistance to Charles. The king, like
his father before him, was also faced by the unrelenting opposition of the
Puritans as the religious issues became more bitter. Charles was supported by
William Laud, the archbishop of Canterbury who pressed forward against
the Puritans. Laud was a High Churchman who loved ritual, fine music,
stained glass, and order. Like his fellow High Churchmen, Laud wanted no
unadorned Puritan buildings, no plain services, no stern preaching of various
sectarian revelations. Laud and his followers, supported by Charles I, sought

rigid conformity everywhere. Laud hated controversy more than he loved truth. He led the High Church clergy into paths of persecution they had never trod before. He misjudged both his allies and his enemies. Some men would also say that he forgot the teachings of his Lord about mercy and charity.

In 1637 Archbishop Laud and Charles I tried to impose an Anglican liturgy upon Scotland. This was stark insanity. The Scots raised an army and dared Charles to fight. Charles than recalled the able Thomas Wentworth from Ireland, where Wentworth's ruthless policy of "Thorough" had suppressed the Irish, for a time. The king made Wentworth the Earl of Strafford and asked his advice. Strafford thought Charles should call Parliament, arguing that the English nation, long anti-Scottish, would support the king. "Scottish treason will be overcome by English loyalty."

Parliament met on April 13, 1640. It would not vote supplies; it wanted to debate grievances. It enumerated those grievances, one by one, "swarms of projecting canker worms and caterpillars, the worst of the Egyptian plagues." On May 5, 1640, Charles dissolved Parliament. "Some few cunning and some ill-affected men," said the king, "have been the cause of this misunderstanding."

In November, 1640, Charles was compelled to call the famous Long Parliament. Under the leadership of John Pym and John Hampden, the House of Commons struck first at the king's advisers, the instruments of royal government. Strafford and Laud were arrested. Strafford was soon executed; Laud's turn came three years later.

The Long Parliament proceeded with swift reforms in a divided state. Disputes with the king increased. At Nottingham, on August 22, 1642, Charles I raised the royal standard on a summer green hill. As it swung to flutter in the breeze the Civil War began.

The Civil War was not a cleavage between geographical areas or classes. Counties and classes and families were shot through with divisions. Even Parliament was divided. On both sides many entered the war with reluctance and sadness, for they were fighting no foreign foe but Englishmen.

Slowly the king's Cavaliers moved into conflict with the Roundheads. Oliver Cromwell, famous Puritan leader, recognized the importance of obtaining a Parliamentary army of enthusiasts, a force outstanding for its efficiency, strict discipline, and morale. Conscious of their divine mission, these soldiers went forward to battle for their Lord. In early 1644, a Scottish-Roundhead army fought and defeated Prince Rupert eight miles from York at the battle of Marston Moor. "God made them as stubble to our swords," wrote Cromwell.

Parliament's New Model Army, the work of Oliver Cromwell, was created early in 1645 for "a more speedy, vigorous, and effectual prosecution of the war." That task it was to perform, fearing God and keeping its powder dry. In June, 1645, it won the battle of Naseby. "God did it," said Cromwell later, "and it is wonderful in my eyes." Late in 1645 Charles had no more armies. He fled and surrendered to the Scots.

The victors soon disputed among themselves. The Presbyterians wanted a state church. The Independents, those ancestors of the modern Congregationalists, did not. "New presbyter," wrote John Milton, "is but old priest writ large." The Independents hated presbyters as much as they did bishops. Would the Presbyterians ever be inclined to give toleration to the Independents or the thousands of Anglicans? The Parliamentary party, within and without Parliament, was bitterly split. Meanwhile, Parliament calmly went ahead with its Presbyterian projects and passed bills setting up a Presbyterian Church in England. It began a bludgeoning and merciless persecution of all who were not Presbyterians, particularly the Independents, Baptists, and Anglicans. Then, early in 1647, it ordered the New Model Army to disband. By this time the New Model Army—many of the soldiers were Independents—was already infuriated by arbitrary persecution and denial of religious liberty. They had not received their back wages. To order them to go home was a dangerous step. It is always politically wise to heed the army, especially an army supported by an Oliver Cromwell.

The New Model Army did not go home. Calculations of justice and safety said otherwise. Instead, the army kidnaped Charles I.

Within the ranks of the army there were disputes between the officers and the soldiers about such things as the new democratic ideas held by the Levelers. The officers were suspicious of the common soldiers and their draft constitution called the Agreement of the People, a document inspired by Leveler principles. The officers preferred their long and conservative Heads of Proposals and decided to submit that document to Charles as a basis for negotiation. The intractable king rejected their ideas, partly because he thought he could do better still by playing off Parliament against the army and also negotiating with the Presbyterians.

In November, 1647, Charles escaped from custody. In separate negotiations with the Scotsmen he agreed to establish Presbyterianism in England for three years. The Scots kept their bargain and marched into England to aid Charles.

The gamble Charles was taking was desperate. If the Scots lost, he was lost. By this time it was becoming clear that Charles betrayed almost all with whom he parleyed. That was his darkest sin, his duplicity. To treat with him was idle; to trust him could be suicide.

The soldiers of the New Model Army now patched up their differences and went to war again. Together they came to "a very clear and joint resolution that it was our duty, if ever the Lord brought us back again in peace, to call Charles Stuart, that man of blood, to account for the blood he has shed and the mischief he has done to his utmost against the Lord's cause and people in this poor nation."

The swords of the soldiers of the New Model Army defeated the Scotsmen and ousted the Presbyterians from the Parliament in the dramatic event called "Pride's Purge." Charles I, captured again, was brought to trial for several alleged crimes, including treason against the people of England. In this event, as usual, Oliver Cromwell saw the finger of God. The outcome of the trial, made more unseemly by the prosecuting Puritan lawyer Bradshaw, was never in doubt. The court found the king guilty. "Charles Stuart, as a tyrant, traitor, murderer, and public enemy to the good people of this nation, shall be put to death by the severing of his head from his body." On January 30, 1649, Charles I stepped out into the winter sunshine to die.

In 1649 England began a series of experiments in republican government. A military despotism, led by Oliver Cromwell, seized and held power in the name of the people. Opposed to the government were most of the active champions of democracy. The people themselves were generally hostile. "I tell you, sir," shouted Cromwell to the Speaker of one Parliament, "you have no other way to deal with these men but to break them or they will break you." It seemed that it might be so. Cromwell had to rule by the sword. "The same arts that did gain the power," wrote the poet Andrew Marvell, "must it maintain."

When the Irish rose in rebellion Cromwell struck in hard vengeance. The slaughtered Protestant saints of Piedmont, whom John Milton mourned, had their Roman Catholic counterparts in Ireland. Of the massacre at Drogheda, Cromwell reported: "I think that they put to death about two thousand men." For the Irish Roman Catholics the English Puritans had no mercy. The brutality of Cromwell's terror is still a cursed memory in Ireland. The inhuman clauses of the final Cromwellian settlement in Ireland cannot be read today without horror. Cromwell slaughtered and maimed in the conviction that the Lord was avenging Himself; to the Irish Roman Catholics that could not be.

Meanwhile the Scottish attempts to restore the Stuarts failed. Meanwhile, too, England moved into a barren war with the Dutch, her great commercial rivals. In 1653 the Commonwealth crumbled before the heavy assaults at home and abroad. Cromwell drove out the members of Parliament with his musketeers. "Not a dog barked," said Cromwell. Then an Instrument of Government made Cromwell Lord Protector. He was the dictator of England, kept in power by the army. Cromwell did try to bring peace but he had to carry a sword. The saint had to be a warrior saint. How else could order be maintained? The Protector's moral "blue laws" were harshly enforced. All England felt the grim constraints of godly zeal. Meanwhile Cromwell went into an aggressive war against Spain. The Protector was at heart an imperialist. Puritan nationalism reached its peak when Roman Catholics were the enemy.

Despite a series of successes in war the economic and political scene grew darker at home. Several changes were made in the structure of the republican government and they all failed to bring happy results. Cromwell angrily dissolved his last Parliament in 1658. "I think it high time that an end be put to your sitting, and I do dissolve this Parliament. And let God judge between you and me." The sword is not a good political primer; it is a useless weapon in a moral crusade.

Oliver Cromwell died in September, 1658. Destiny had mocked his dream. He had not pleased many men. In the wreck of faiths and institutions that had marked the reigns of the first two Stuarts probably no human being could have done what Cromwell failed to do. The next century was to answer the question of James I, Charles I, and Cromwell: "How can Parliamentary government be combined with personal rule?"

The successor of Cromwell was his eldest son, Richard. He soon retired and in 1660 Englishmen brought back Charles II to be their king. Cromwell's men laid down the sword. It had not sufficed to bring to earth the Heavenly City, clean and bleak, of the Puritans. The Puritan hopes were fallen. The Puritan cause was lost.

Charles II, so long exiled, had at last come home; he did not propose to go on his travels again. Shrewd, good-humored, witty, affable, he deceived many men who mistook the appearance for the full reality. Behind the dark king's smile and easy charm there was a cynical and calculating astuteness that never left him, even in the whirling debauchery of his court.

With the return of Charles II the Puritans went out of power in Parliament and the Anglicans and Cavaliers came in. The new rulers believed in peace and order and ranged themselves behind the church and the king. They represented the conservative interests of the landed gentry who wanted some compensation for the lean years after 1649. From them was born the great Tory party. Often opposed to them were the progressive men of business, the merchants and kings of commerce. From this second group was soon to grow the Whig party, entering into conflict with the Tories and the king. The excesses of these two groups largely account for the feverish political instability of the later seventeenth century in England.

By the so-called "Clarendon Code" the Cavalier Parliament imposed narrow Anglicanism upon the nation. It punished and persecuted those who dissented from Anglican doctrines. Meanwhile England and Holland again entered into a war caused by commercial rivalry. Charles II, a secret Roman Catholic, negotiated the Treaty of Dover with Louis XIV by which he agreed to help Louis against Protestant Holland in return for money from Louis. Charles hoped that an opportunity might come to restore Roman Catholicism in England. In 1672 he tried without success to extend toleration to Catholics.

Neither the Anglicans nor the Dissenters would agree to that. Meanwhile, too, a great plague struck England in 1665 and a great fire burned a large part of London in 1666. "We beheld that dismal spectacle," wrote John Evelyn, "the whole city in dreadful flames. . . . There was nothing heard or seen but crying out and lamentation. . . . London was, but is no more!"

When the plague, the fire, and the Dutch war had passed into history, the Whig and Tory parties began to be shaped in Parliament and throughout the country. Both parties were tainted by the depravity of the age. Nevertheless, each did have a body of principles. The Tory party was based on the old Cavalier idea of devotion to the royal prerogative and the Church of England. The Whigs, on the other hand, believed in such things as toleration for Protestant Dissenters, the old Roundhead idea of Parliamentary supremacy, in commercial development, in the liberty of the subject. Through the years of political maneuvers, the fears of "popish plots" raised in part by the colossal lies of Titus Oates and the abortive schemes of the Whig Earl of Shaftesbury, the Whigs and Tories built their programs and drew their battle lines.

In 1685 Charles II died. He was succeeded by his brother James II, a king who possessed none of the swift intelligence, political sense, or tact of Charles. Charles II never went beyond the edge of safety. James, on the other hand, never knew when to stop. Fervently Roman Catholic, James II roused against him both Anglicans and Dissenters as he recklessly went ahead in his attempts to impose Roman Catholicism upon England. Through a series of dramatic events James traveled, heedless of warnings, along the road to his own ruin.

In the midst of fierce public demonstrations James II charged the archbishop of Canterbury and six bishops with seditious libel. They were acquitted. James stood alone in his realm. Both Whigs and Tories sent a formal invitation to William of Orange and Mary—the Protestant daughter of James II—to come with an army to England to aid in the restoration of English liberties. William and Mary reached England with the aid of a "Protestant wind." James II fled to France in December, 1688. He never saw England again.

Such was the "glorious revolution" of 1688. William and Mary were soon proclaimed king and queen. Parliament soon passed the famous Bill of Rights, a Toleration Act, and the Act of Settlement of 1701 that guarded against the restoration of the old Stuart line and provided for a Protestant succession to the throne of England. By such legislation the results of the bloodless revolution of 1688 were confirmed and strengthened. An essential step had been taken towards the establishment of limited constitutional monarchy and the formation of the cabinet system of government.

The facts of the gradual and constant processes of human evolution usually do not permit the honest writer to find any sound reasons for writing highly dramatic accounts of catastrophic and revolutionary alterations in man's affairs. If we take a long view of the human past we see that most change and progress have been slowly and softly blended with what went before. "Each age is a dream that is dying or one that is coming to birth."

At the same time, it is still possible to discern certain centuries and decades when the speed of men's pace increased or slackened or when the direction of their march was changed. One such time, surely, was the tumbling years of the seventeenth century in Europe. Out of the economic, religious, and political conflicts of that age emerged the forces that shaped and strengthened the nation-states of western Europe. In such lands as France and Prussia the pattern and policy of absolute government were firmly established, for a time. In England, on the contrary, the cause of absolutism was damned and destroyed and avenues of British history were opened to the men who forged the instruments of responsible cabinet government. The main important fact was this: the nation-state system in Europe was hardened and fixed by the events of the seventeenth century.

With the slow formation of national blocs of power and sentiment came several results that were as inevitable as anything human can be. The whole political history of modern Europe has been the tale of proud and jostling states, a story of the triumphs of peace mingled with the clash of arms, the thud of guns, and the laments of the desolate.

"Time will run back," said the seventeenth-century poet, "and fetch the age of gold." But Time did not run back, then or later, to bring a golden age for mankind. Nevertheless, men have continued to hope. From the springs of hope flows the balm of many ills.

...leo Galilei turned this tele-
...e upon the heavens in 1610.

[78]

Above the arc of the quadrant sits the Danish astronomer Tycho
Brahe in his observatory at Prague.

Above: The microscope of the
...ist Robert Hooke (1605-1703)

...: The manual fire engine shown
...s print of 1662 illustrates one
... of the seventeenth century
...ce in technology.

[80]

PLATE XXV

Above: "Christ Preaching," by Rembr
van Rijn (1606-1669), the Dutch genius
was one of the greatest artists in the hi.
of the world

Left: "Soldier and Laughing Girl," by
Vermeer van Delft (1632-1675). In this
istic painting Vermeer displays his fan
skill in obtaining superb effects of de
light, and atmosphere.

[82]

PLATE XXVI

PART III

Chapter 25

THE SONS
OF THE RENAISSANCE

"Man . . . hath no root, nor to one place is tied
But ever restless and irregular
About this earth doth run and ride. . . .
He knocks at all doors, strays and roams . . .
God ordered motion, but ordained no rest."
—Henry Vaughan (1622–1695),
in his poem "Man"

OVER the long centuries successive invaders had plunged into Europe. Almost always they thrust forward from the East, from Russia, from the no man's land north of the Black Sea, from the regions beyond Constantinople. Out of the East came the Huns, the Avars, the Bulgars, the Mongols, the Ottomans. These aggressive conquerors upset Bagdad, captured Constantinople, enslaved Moscow. Towards the end of the seventeenth century (1683) the Ottoman Turks surged to the gates of Vienna. There they were stopped. Western Europe was saved.

Before the seventeenth century the lands and peoples of Russia, the Near East, and North Africa had become increasingly separated from western Europe. When Rome fell, for instance, Constantinople and the Eastern Empire preserved much of the continuity of the classical culture that the West recovered only slowly during the next thousand years. The way was also opened for the religious and cultural cleavage between Rome and Byzantium. In later centuries the chapters written in the history of western Europe—such as the struggles between Church and state—had little to do with the lands to the east. After the challenge of the Turks was finally hurled back at Vienna the separation of East and West continued. Europe went its own way, its separate road. So, too, did the peoples of the Ottoman Empire and Russia; but they did not move rapidly; sometimes they hardly moved at all. While the creative energy of Europe blazed forth to transform the whole apparatus of European civilization very little of consequence was happening in the lands that lie to the east of the Mediterranean. This fact was of capital importance in the history of the world.

In the critical years following the Renaissance the whole fabric of European thought and culture was being changed; the shuttles weaving that new fabric moved back and forth year after year, relentlessly. In all the lands of the West the overlapping generations of men wrestled and labored to find new truths. Their task was not easy. When Thomas Edison, that giant of the twentieth century, was looking for a filament for his first lamp, he tried 6,000 varieties of plants before he found the right fiber. The same kind of persistence is found in the personal histories of many of the makers of the modern world who lived 300 years ago. The tides were flowing in the direction of that which was new; that which was revolutionary became that which was important. Old moorings of the mind were often broken and swept away.

One aspect of the illumination of the human mind that has rapidly increased in scope and brightness since the Renaissance is the ascendancy of science, with all its wider consequences. Today most men and women look upon science and scientific methods as unbiased, positive, exact, and impersonal, providing knowledge that is perhaps as close to truth as man can ever come. "The subtlety of nature," said Francis Bacon, "is greater many times than the subtlety of argument." Scientists observe and experiment; they scrupulously test their hypotheses by the tools of reason, by the instruments of the laboratory, by assembling and checking all of the relevant data. Their successive discoveries have enabled modern man to control and use his environment to an ever-increasing extent. Their achievements have steadily altered the shape of man's ideas about himself and the universe.

In the eyes of many of our contemporaries the scientists have displaced, or almost so, the priests, prophets, and philosophers of earlier ages. The mystic talismans of our century are test tubes, electronic devices, the creeping powers of the antibiotics, the vast and restless forces lying behind the graphite shields of the nuclear reactors. The physicists and chemists, the mathematicians and the engineers, these are the high priests of the twentieth century.

Three hundred years ago the scientists had not reached this high estate. Nevertheless, the gates were opening. Only a few men in the preceding centuries had dared to oppose the teachings of Aristotle. During the later days of the Renaissance the scholastic ideas and their holders were smitten hip and thigh. The ranks of the schoolmen were divided and they were driven over the hills. Francis Bacon's robust appeals to induction and experiment were not by any means the only forces pressing men towards the new science; but they were of much significance—Bacon was a fine publicist and publicity often aids a cause. Lamps of aspiration were lit in innumerable laboratories. A number of men, none of them in the first rank of scientists, contributed their unspectacular mites. They helped to spread new bodies of ideas, skeptical and derisive, corroding the fetters of authority, the ancient rules written "with letters of opium on tablets of lead." Truth, it seemed, was less a daughter of authority than a secret slowly to be retrieved from the womb of time.

For most human beings it is not an easy task to revolt against the established and customary way of looking at things. Men often select data to illustrate the ideas, maxims, and emotionally held preconceptions they already have in their minds. They frequently look for what they want to find. They try to confirm what they have been told or to prove that things are indeed what they assume them to be. This is a comfortable way of life; it is not the hard and rupturing road to adventure, discovery, and invention. If all human beings had lived happily the human race would probably have moved neither far nor fast.

Fortunately for human destiny the ranks of each generation have contained restless and isolated rebels, men filled with unconquerable curiosity. To these individuals—poets, mathematicians, engineers, philosophers, and all their fellows—the world owes more than most men know.

Every age, of course, has its giants of the intellect, those lonely men who stride or stumble into the unknown. One of the giants of the seventeenth century was the Florentine Galileo Galilei, who became a professor of mathematics at the age of twenty-five. Like so many of his kind, Galileo was spurred by a divine discontent. His quick brain darted from idea to idea; his eyes were keen, his judgment sharp; his hands were busy in experiment.

About Galileo many stories have been told, some of them quite untrue. For instance, Galileo did not invent the telescope; that achievement must be credited to an obscure Dutch optician named Johannes Lippershey. It is also unlikely that Galileo ever climbed the tower of Pisa in a great age of experiment to drop light and heavy round shot in order to determine the rate of acceleration of objects of different weights. It is true, of course, that the tale of Galileo and the tower of Pisa will be repeated through the generations. Men do not easily discard such stories. Folk tales are seldom destroyed by sober-suited historians.

In 1610 Galileo slanted the new little telescope—it magnified thirty times —towards the night skies and saw the pockmarks on the moon, the rings of Saturn and its phases, and the revolving satellites of Jupiter. The sunspots visible by day showed that the sun, too, was turning upon its axis. These were facts that men could see. The sun, not the earth, was surely the center of things. Who could now doubt the neat description that Copernicus had given of the universe?

It was difficult to keep science and theology apart in the seventeenth century. The philosopher and scientist Blaise Pascal (1623–1662) thought that men should "limit the areas of science and religion according to modes of knowledge." In that idea Pascal was in advance of his time. Where were the lines between the natural and the supernatural? What was the precise nature of evidence and probability? If unorthodox points of view dared to oppose the stern creeds and authority of the Church, what was the Church to do? In all the ages of man there have been different kinds and degrees of toleration. In the seventeenth century it was widely felt that men like Copernicus and Galileo were not only attacking the concepts of Aristotelian physics but were also challenging the medieval Christian view of a universe in which the earth, the dwelling place of God's children, held the central place. In 1615 the Inquisition formally condemned the teachings of Copernicus and ordered Galileo to be silent.

Galileo could not stay quiet. In 1630 he published his disturbing *Dialogues on the Two Great World Systems*. In this polemical book three characters discussed the relative merits of the Ptolemaic and Copernican systems. They also advanced all the anti-Aristotelian arguments about astronomy and mechanics. Several of the arguments were not clinched by fact and logic; there were some fuzzy passages upon such important themes as circular motion and inertia and the problems of the skies. Nevertheless, a shrewd reader could see quite clearly that Galileo was damning and mocking the ideas of Ptolemy even though the preface denounced Copernicus. The pope was furious at what he considered the duplicity of Galileo. The Inquisition compelled Galileo —he was then seventy years old—to recant, to repeat the seven penitential psalms once a week for three years, and to promise to say nothing more about Ptolemy or Copernicus or his own ideas of an earth moving around the sun. The story has long been told—it is perhaps true, perhaps not—that after his recantation Galileo whispered, "But it does move!" (*"E pur si muove!"*)

For Galileo there were other problems and discoveries. He tried, for instance, to extend the notion of velocity to non-uniform motion and arrived at the dazzling concept of instantaneous velocity. He thought that the natural tendency of a moving body was to persist in its motion in a straight line and at a uniform speed unless disturbed by some force. He began to work with such concepts as infinite processes and infinitesimal analyses. He made countless experiments with pendulums, falling bodies, and projectiles—in that distant time it seemed that precise mathematical deductions could always be disproved or validated by experiments.

In a later day Isaac Newton remarked that he had seen farther than Descartes "by standing on the shoulders of giants." One of the giants was surely Galileo Galilei.

Several other scientists probed into the mysteries of heaven and earth. For more than twenty years Tycho Brahe (1546–1601), a Danish genius, observed the planets all through their courses. He plotted the positions of nearly a thousand stars. Johann Kepler (1571–1630), Brahe's brilliant assistant, soon outpaced his master. Kepler was a man of colossal intellectual power. He delighted in mathematical relations and patterns of numbers. Of the Copernican theory he said: "I have attested it as true in my deepest soul and I contemplate its beauty with incredible and ravishing delight." Kepler did not, of course, spend his time admiring Copernicus. He formulated mathematical laws to describe the movements of the planets: the planets do not travel in circular orbits but in ellipses; the speed of each planet is affected by its nearness to the sun—the further away, the slower the pace. Kepler also stated the law that the time required by a planet to complete its journey around the sun depended upon its average distance from the sun—"the square of a planet's periodic time is proportional to the cube of its mean distance from the sun."

Johann Kepler believed that all the planets were moved on their courses by a mysterious force or virtue that flowed out of the sun. He also held some mystical ideas about the music of the heavenly spheres. It is perhaps most important to remark that Kepler looked upon the universe as a mechanistic system, an intricate and wonderful piece of clockwork. Like many of his fellow scientists he liked to move from ideas and facts to broad conclusions. In the twentieth century Professor Alfred North Whitehead once wisely remarked: "This new tinge to modern minds is a vehement and passionate interest in the relation of general principles to irreducible and stubborn facts." In that sense, Johann Kepler belonged to one of the early generations of the "modern minds."

With unhalted steps the advance of science and the scientists continued. John Napier of Scotland discovered and used and wrote a book about logarithms in 1614. Anthony van Leeuwenhoek (1632–1723) used new improved lenses in his microscope to see protozoa and blood corpuscles. The Italian physicist Evangelista Torricelli (1608–1647), a student of Galileo, determined the weight of the atmosphere and experimented with columns of mercury to contribute to the development of the barometer. There was also the micrometer, the centigrade and Fahrenheit thermometers, Huygen's pendulum clock, von Guericke's air pump. Robert Hooke (1635–1703) was the first man to see and describe the cell structure of plants; he also invented the balance wheel for the watch. Marcello Malpighi (1628–1694) kept finding out more and more about plants and animals and human anatomy. The work of William Gilbert on magnetism still further confirmed the theory of the earth's rotation. Edmund Halley studied the orbits of comets and calculated the periodicity of the one that bears his name.

Robert Boyle (1627–1691), an Irish chemist, physicist, and philosopher, attacked the ancient theories of the four elements—earth, air, fire, and water —in his *The Sceptical Chemist* (1661). He discovered and isolated "inflammable air" or hydrogen and "nitrous air" or nitrogen. He first stated the chemical distinction between elements and compounds. With the aid of a German air pump he showed that air could be weighed. The famous "Boyle's Law" is still learned by most modern students: the volume of a gas varies inversely with the pressure. More than any other man Robert Boyle raised chemistry from alchemy to the level of a natural science.

In the next century the flood of deeds and names pressed on. The Frenchman Buffon—author of the forty-four volumes of *A Natural History*—helped to systematize the study of plants and animals. That task was eased by the work of the English John Ray and the Swedish Linnaeus—author of the famous *System of Nature*. The Unitarian preacher Joseph Priestley (1733–1804) discovered oxygen; Joseph Black (1728–1799) discovered carbon dioxide. James Hutton published his *Theory of the Earth* (1795) and founded the science of geology. Antoine Lavoisier (1743–1794), the father of quantitative chemistry, demonstrated that the products of combustion were always equal to the burned substance plus the oxygen consumed in burning—this is an early statement of the law of the conservation of matter. Lavoisier was also the man who first separated water into hydrogen and oxygen. He developed a new method of naming substances; we still use many of the names he adopted: sulfates, oxides, nitrates, and the like. His nomenclature was approved by the French Academy of Sciences in 1787. Seven years later the Frenchmen guillotined Lavoisier because they found his political opinions offensive. They would have done better to have let him live.

There were still other achievements, other ideas. For instance, the methods of induction and experiment, so widely advertised in the writings of Francis Bacon, were clearly and precisely stated by another apostle of the new science: the French mathematician and philosopher René Descartes (1596–1650). In 1628 Descartes settled in Holland, that safe haven for numerous independent thinkers of the age. Nine years later he published at Leyden his famous *Discourse on the Method of Rightly Conducting the Reason and Seeking Truth in the Sciences.*

The *Discourse* opens with this sentence: "Good sense is, of all things among men, the most equally distributed: for everyone thinks himself so abundantly provided with it that even those who are the most difficult to satisfy in everything else do not usually desire a larger measure of this quality than they already possess." Since the capacity to see reason was equally distributed to all human beings, then it seemed to Descartes to follow that everybody should agree in discarding prejudices and in doubting tradition. "I thought that it was necessary for me . . . to reject as absolutely false everything to which I could imagine the least ground of doubt in order to see if afterwards there remained anything in my belief that was absolutely certain."

What did Descartes find that was "absolutely certain?" What primary truths were there, what things men could "clearly and distinctly conceive to be true," what perceptions nobody could get behind and push over? In the first place, Descartes asserted that the fact that he thought was sufficient proof of his existence: "I think, therefore I am." Secondly, Descartes held that all men were born with certain ideas given them by God. In his own mind, for instance, Descartes found the idea of a Supreme Being who was "omniscient, all-powerful and absolutely perfect." Intuitive reason, he said, compelled us to believe in the existence of a God whose image had been implanted in our minds.

From the idea and proof of God, Descartes reasoned downwards to seek explanations. In all his deductive work there is a coherence and beauty that reminds his readers of a similar unity in the work of philosophers like Aristotle and St. Thomas Aquinas. Descartes was always interested in explanations, especially those that were mathematical and logical. He was the first man to devise coordinates for plotting curves. In his analytical geometry he showed how facts could be stated in both algebra and geometry, a useful tool for finding solutions to difficult problems. Through the past three centuries men who have admired the beauty of pure logic and mathematics have revered the name and applauded the genius of René Descartes. Said Aristotle: "No one can understand nature fully nor miss it wholly; but as each contributes his part there arises a structure that has a certain grandeur."

Above all his contemporaries stood Sir Isaac Newton. To his age it seemed that Newton had settled all the chief problems of astronomy, mathematics, optics, and physics. Son of a Lincolnshire yeoman, Newton studied theology at Cambridge. Then he turned to mathematics and physics. As a mathematician he established the binomial theorem, developed a large part of the theory of equations, invented simultaneously with the German Leibnitz the theory of differential calculus. He investigated the properties of light, showing that the prismatic colors were caused by the different refrangibilities of light rays. He prepared mathematical tables showing how the future position of the moon with reference to the stars could be determined, a calculation of tremendous importance to navigation.

In 1687 Newton published his immortal *Mathematical Principles of Natural Philosophy,* usually called the *Principia.* Here he set forth, by precise demonstration, the laws of motion and of gravitation. "Every particle of matter in the universe attracts every other particle with a force varying inversely as the square of the distance between them and directly proportional to the product of their masses." This achievement, one of the greatest in the history of pure thought, provided explanation and confirmation of the theories of Copernicus and Galileo. The genius of Newton, it seemed, had discovered a "universal law of nature." He had apparently banished mystery from the world. The universe was obviously a vast mechanism, intelligible, harmonious, uniform, and thoroughly rational. It was, in the words of Newton, "a realm of

masses, moving according to mathematical laws in space and time, under the
influence of definite and dependable forces." The "forces" were tremendous:
the centrifugal power of the earth in its orbit would break a steel cable 5,000
miles in diameter. "Newton's cosmology," Alfred North Whitehead once remarked, "is very easy to understand and very hard to believe."

The impressive epitaph on Newton's monument in Westminster Abbey
speaks of his "vigour of mind almost supernatural." Of him Alexander Pope
wrote:

> Nature and Nature's Laws lay hid in Night.
> God said 'Let Newton be!' and all was Light.

William Wordsworth thus described Newton's statue at Trinity College,
Cambridge:

> The marble index of a mind forever
> Voyaging through strange seas of thought, alone.

And Voltaire said: "It is to him who masters our minds by the force of truth,
not to those who enslave men by violence; it is to him who understands the
universe, not to those who disfigure it, that we owe our reverence."

Meanwhile the knowledge of man was expanded in the field of medicine
by experiments, study, and examination. Before the sixteenth and seventeenth
centuries the body of medical knowledge and teaching—in a phrase of Professor Herbert Butterfield—was "a complex system of errors." In an era of scientific revolution men like Vesalius, Colombo, Cesalpino, and Fabricius had
invaded the kingdoms of error and used the new weapons of science with
astonishing results. Dissection and experiment gave answers that none had
found before.

Michael Servetus (1511–1553) discovered the pulmonary circulation of the
blood. What he began was finished by William Harvey (1578–1657).
Harvey, usually called the father of modern physiology, studied at Padua,
that famous university where scientific discussions from the fifteenth century
onward prepared the way—as Professor J. H. Randall's work has so admirably
shown—for the end of the undisputed sway of Aristotle. Harvey said that he
learned "not from books but from dissection." In 1628 he published his comprehensive and famous *De motu cordis* after he had assured himself of the
truth of his conclusions "by multiple demonstrations . . . for more than
nine years."

William Harvey conclusively proved that the blood, pumped by the heart,
circulated through the arteries and veins of the human body. The discovery
was so startling, "of a character so novel and unheard of," that Harvey was
in some doubt about its reception by his contemporaries. "I not only fear
injury to myself from the envy of a few but I tremble lest I have mankind
at large for my enemies, so much doth wont and custom become a second

nature." To the modern man the idea of the circulation of the blood appears obvious and simple. Scientific discoveries often seem to be easy after they have been made.

A journey through time must omit much about the claims to fame of numerous servants of man. All over Europe there was a leaping interest in science, especially among the upper classes. Learned journals, societies, and laboratories multiplied. The Academy at Florence was founded in 1661; England's Royal Society in 1662; the Academy of Arts and Sciences at Paris in 1666; the Berlin Academy in 1700. The popular imagination seized upon the wonders of science. Here, men were sure, were to be found the answers to all mysteries. Books like Fontenelle's *Plurality of Worlds* (1686) were designed to give popular explanations of the new scientific achievements and the latest ideas about the nature of the universe. James Ferguson, for instance, probably found quite profitable the book he wrote under the title clearly calculated to interest the unlearned and the unwary: *Astronomy Explained upon Sir Isaac Newton's Principles and Made Easy to Those who have not Studied Mathematics* (1756).

Thus knowledge increased and power grew. "The end of all knowledge is power," wrote England's Thomas Hobbes in the middle of the seventeenth century. "The scope of all speculation is the performance of some action or a thing to be done." Not all men would agree, then or now, with the assertion of Hobbes—there must be some place, surely, for agreement with Abraham Flexner's opinions in his remarks about "the usefulness of useless knowledge." On the other hand, the followers of Thomas Hobbes have been numerous and vocal for several generations. They have been known by many names but their theme has been unchanged: the "utilitarian" areas of knowledge are what matter; nothing else is of consequence.

Nor did all men agree with several other beliefs and values that were springing up in the new age. The interest in the classical and religious revivals that had marked the Renaissance years and the early seventeenth century began to yield to the enthusiasm about the natural sciences and the teachings of men like Descartes. What Paul Hazard has called "the broad river of incredulity" that flooded all Europe in the eighteenth century was already beginning to run. In 1695 Pierre Bayle was to say in his *Dictionary* that "the Cartesians are suspected of irreligion, and their philosophy is thought to be very dangerous to Christianity." Bishop Bossuet complained that too many men were making "their own intelligence the measure of God's purposes." He would have been pained to hear the assertions of the later Deists who demanded a natural religion without what they called superstition and a rational morality without what they called dogma.

The thoughtful and sensitive individual who looks back upon the seventeenth century can see several forces and factors that were not sharp and clear in earlier times. He is certainly aware of the increasingly secular points of view. He sees the authority of tradition and custom challenged again and again as the way is prepared for the bitter quarrel of the "ancients and the moderns." He notes the mounting complacency of men as they compare their times favorably with the days of antiquity—the past, they insisted, could not possibly have had anything to compare with the culture of the court of Louis XIV. Would not the masters of science, the rational and enlightened men of the new era, one day bring the Heavenly City down to earth?

The seventeenth and eighteenth centuries were indeed a time when there was a rising pride in man and his abilities. "By space the Universe encompasses me as an atom," said Pascal, "by a thought I encompass it." Christian faith had been nurtured in humility. In the new age of the scientific revolution— and to an increasing extent in the Enlightenment era to follow—men grew more confident in themselves and their future, in the power of human reason to set all things right. The idea of inevitable human progress was at hand. "Whatever was the beginning of this world," wrote Joseph Priestley, "the end will be glorious and paradisiacal beyond what our imaginations can now conceive."

It was inevitable that there should be attempts to reconcile the results of the new scientific movement and the theological ideas about the nature of the universe. There was an increasing tendency to defend orthodox Christianity because it was reasonable rather than because it was divinely revealed. A large number of the books and tracts of the period did not transcend the occasion of their writing; others rose above the political and doctrinal ardors and excesses of their time to make major contributions to the intellectual history of the modern world.

The work of René Descartes, mentioned earlier in this chapter, would be outstanding in any land, in any age. Descartes asserted that the material world of physical nature is a vast mechanism and subject to mathematical and physical analysis by the tools of reason. On the other hand, said Descartes, the mind and soul of man are independent of the physical world, distinct from the material universe, gifts of God.

The new rationalism and mechanism stressed on the one side of the famous dualism of Descartes with respect to mind and matter soon became widely influential in the thinking of many men in the seventeenth century and later. Into the arenas of controversy about Cartesianism scores of men moved to do battle. There were numerous points of view; several of them are still held today. The rationalist Franciscan Pierre Gassendi (1592–1650), for instance, insisted that knowledge was obtained only through the senses and that matter was indestructible. Baruch Spinoza (1632–1677), a gentle Jewish lens grinder of Amsterdam, was of the disturbing opinion that mind and matter are only different aspects of nature. Ideas and matter, God and nature, are identical. Everything is an aspect of God. Spinoza rejected all revelation, all miracles; he denied the divine inspiration of the Bible. In his stern ethical code there were few crumbs of assurance for most men. Orthodox Jews were shocked by what they considered Spinoza's rationalistic pantheism. They expelled him from the synagogue and drove him out of the tents of his people. For many years he wandered from city to city in the Netherlands, writing and talking about the unity of nature and grinding lenses. Philosophers like Spinoza and Socrates—and many priests and prophets, too—preferred to seek and suffer rather than stay home and lean back upon the cushions of conformity. Such decisions are made by wise and courageous men. To many of us the conclusions of Spinoza were wrong, quite wrong; but what he believed he fought for. Of the uncounted thousands who have done otherwise in critical hours and betrayed themselves and their causes the world knows little or nothing. We can only assume that they have had their reward.

Gottfried Wilhelm von Leibnitz (1646–1716), famous mathematician and professional librarian, tried to do two things: reconcile the teachings of Christianity and natural science; unite the Roman Catholics and the Protestants. Leibnitz said that the universe was composed of spiritual atoms called "monads." Instead of accepting the Cartesian dualism of mind and matter, Leibnitz spiritualized matter by wiping the distinction away. Such a procedure was typical of the work of Leibnitz in philosophy; he liked to shape instruments of adjustment and compromise. In mathematics he could not follow that procedure, and his work in mathematics has not been challenged and shaken. In the field of philosophy, in contrast, the conclusions of Leibnitz have been the source of much dispute. He was not able to bring the Roman Catholics and Protestants into one Church again, and he did not succeed in convincing many men that the scientists were saying the same things as the Scriptures and the various churches of God. The road of men who seek the answers of compromise are often long and hard.

There were several other problems in the scientific age of the seventeenth century. It was inevitable, for example, that the concepts of natural law would change. The old and strong idea of a natural law, stated quite simply, was that an objective and absolute standard in the universe points out right from wrong. The natural law can be discovered by human reason; it cannot be made or altered or destroyed by any man—even a king—or by any people anywhere. In the Middle Ages this natural law was considered to be one aspect of the total law of God. It was, said St. Thomas Aquinas, "the participation of a rational creature in the eternal law." In later days it was widely believed that the law stood all by itself; it could always be apprehended as an unchangeable truth by human beings who used the instrument of "right reason." The seventeenth and eighteenth centuries formed the "classic age" of the philosophy of natural law and faith in human reason.

It seemed to some men that natural law should control the activities of the sovereign nation-states whose number was increasing so appreciably. In 1625, for instance, Hugo Grotius of Holland published his masterpiece, the *Law of War and Peace*. The humane Grotius—an exiled poet, lawyer, diplomat, theologian, and historian—was gravely concerned with the growing and terrible inhumanity of Europe's wars. He argued that the ideas of reason and justice inherent in natural law should govern the relations between states in peace and war. The rules of natural law should be those of international law. "We must ask ourselves what is the nature of man, man as he is in all ages and all countries, and what is required by the conscience of this universal man."

Arguments based upon natural law can be used for many diverse purposes. Some men, like England's Thomas Hobbes, asserted that natural law justified the existence and acts of absolute governments. Other men, like John Locke, turned to natural law to explain and defend constitutional rule, toleration, and liberalism.

The *Leviathan* of Thomas Hobbes (1588–1679) is perhaps the greatest political treatise in the English language. It is an astonishing work and some men have found it admirable. Like so many political philosophers, Hobbes began his discussion by finding his answer to this question: What is the nature and origin of civil society? If men are to live in any order with one another, there must be a state. How did this state, called by Hobbes the Leviathan or "mortal god," first come to be? Hobbes declared that the state of nature existing before civil society was created was "a war of every man against every man." The life of man was "solitary, poor, nasty, brutish, and short." To Hobbes all men are filled with "a perpetual and restless desire of power after power, that ceaseth only in death." The result in the state of nature was fear and insecurity; that is the reason why men first came together to form a civil society. "Unless there is a power to keep us in awe we are in a state of war."

According to Hobbes, civil society was created when every man made a covenant with every other man and all agreed in conferring their power upon a sovereign. By the theory of Hobbes, men obey their self-imposed sovereign because he gives them protection and security. If the sovereign fails to provide protection, then Hobbes holds that the obligation to obedience and dependency on the part of the subject is ended. Thus Hobbes rejected the theory of divine right. To him a *de facto* government was also a *de jure* one; he who succeeded in ruling was the legitimate ruler. Hobbes asserted that all men act for their own advantage; they are loyal to governments only if they find it profitable to be so. Individuals are bound together in any group by two forces: a sovereign power and their own self-interest. Governments are instruments of self-protection. Only to preserve the state do people obey the law. To Hobbes all morality rests on law; it is only the dictate of reason. "Conscience is a form of indigestion." What is justice? Justice is what the sovereign says it is; he makes it. To Hobbes the essential fact in any society is law. The essential motive for creating and maintaining a society is fear. Behind the law is power, a sovereign power. Hobbes was the first political theorist to try to found the state, not on what men ought to do, but what they wanted.

Far removed from Thomas Hobbes stood John Locke. Locke, a famous Whig defender of England's revolution of 1688, set forth his theory of a government based on popular approval.

In earlier days Locke had published his *Letters on Toleration* in which he explained his ideas on religious liberty. He had also written his *Essay Concerning Human Understanding,* a book in which Locke argued that man possesses no innate ideas and that all knowledge is a construction of ideas that come from the senses as a result of experience or reflection. To this sensationalist theory of the origin of ideas Locke attached a rationalist explanation of scientific knowledge that could not be reconciled at all with the sensationalist point of view; empiricism and rationalism were woefully intermingled.

John Locke is often considered to be the father of modern psychology. Certainly he added nothing to the rationalist theories—the French philosophers had already done the spadework there. It was the rather simple sensationalist section of Locke's work that had such great influence upon later thought. Had John Locke's mind been more profound it might have been less influential.

The main parts of the political theories of John Locke are in his *Second Treatise on Government.* This book is Locke's great contribution to political thought and practice.

John Locke differed from Thomas Hobbes in asserting that all men were born free and lived in a state of reason before the appearance of the state. Nevertheless, said Locke, men were confused about the laws of reason. There were at first no laws about property, no "known and indifferent judges," no sufficient power to back their judgments and to give them execution. Men therefore agreed to contract with one another to surrender to the sovereign community their individual natural rights of enforcing the laws of reason. By this step they created a civil authority. They did it by voluntary union and mutual agreement.

In the constitution of the state—as Locke saw it—the legislature became the superior power; but it was not a power having any resemblance to the absolute sovereign of Thomas Hobbes. The powers of the legislature were limited in the beginning and are limited now by the natural rights that men have always possessed. These human rights—such as life, liberty, and property—existed before there was any government and they cannot be surrendered by any men. The basis of a government's strength, asserted John Locke, is popular consent. A government must rule by "promulgated, established laws." Its power "is in the utmost bounds of it limited to the public good of the society. It is a power that hath no other end but preservation, and therefore can never destroy, enslave." If kings or governments violate their trust, the people have a right to resist. "He who threatens liberty, threatens all."

John Locke is often said to be the father of theoretical liberalism and god-father at least of the political system of the United States. Restive in his orthodoxy and timid in his heresies, Locke foreshadowed in his life, his work, and his attitudes the prudent intellectual morality of liberal spirits everywhere. He was the mighty prophet of the wisdom of compromise and polite modera-tion.

In the Western world of art and literature there came in the seventeenth century a quiet unfolding of talent expressed on the canvas, on the printed page, in the architects' fragile dreams come true. There were a few artists of the brush whose biographies of sunlight and sorrow we can read today, the "sacred fools" of history who have known sweat, frustration, and moments of splendid vision. There were the artists of the pen whose words took flight from the page to fly singing through the minds and memories of generations of mankind. There were also, of course, the pathetic and giftless beings with lean skills and fat hopes, the fellows who tried so hard sometimes, who con-vinced few but themselves of their genius, who never came near success.

The Dutch painters of the seventeenth century have a special place in the ranks of famous men. Their brush strokes usually painted bourgeois people—especially business folk—and simple scenes from the Scriptures, the street, the kitchen, or the tavern. In this kind of work two outstanding masters were Frans Hals (1581–1666) and Jan Vermeer (1632–1675). These men liked to paint as they pleased—the tavern sot, the hopeless beggar, the grinning boy.

Even Hals and Vermeer must yield pride of place to one of the finest artists of all time: Rembrandt van Rijn (1606–1669). Rembrandt was a subtle mas-ter of the use of bold brush strokes, thick paint, diagonal composition, space in depth, molten light, and contrasting heavy shadow. What was to be ac-centuated in a painting of Rembrandt was often bathed in incorporeal radi-ance; what was to be in the background of attention was richly darkened. These brief and simple descriptive statements cannot, of course, suggest the psychological insights of Rembrandt, the sense of drama and inner excitement that his paintings convey. The reader will recall, for instance, the power of "The Denial of St. Peter," "The Holy Family," "Jeremiah Lamenting the Destruction of Jerusalem," "The Woman Taken in Adultery," "The Syndics of the Cloth Hall," "The Night Watch," and "Bathsheba"—one of the greatest of the paintings of nudes.

The fame of Rembrandt's paintings and etchings spread all over Europe. Then both fame and fortune fell. In 1656 Rembrandt had to sell his goods and his house. These disasters did not sap his fortitude; he continued to paint. Probably every biographer of Rembrandt states that he was "a painter's painter" and that he influenced Reynolds, Gainsborough, Delacroix, Ingres, and even Picasso. This statement is certainly true. It is also true that in the twentieth century the genius of Rembrandt is becoming more deeply and widely appreciated not only among the professional painters and art critics but also among the millions who claim no skills and no techniques but whose judgment is often sound and sure.

There were other kinds of painting and painters. One was Diego Rodríguez de Silva y Velásquez (1599–1660). This baroque artist did fifty paintings of the Hapsburg Philip IV. "He commemorated the dignity and courtesy of courtiers and campaigners." Men who look today at the work of Velásquez— still bathed in silvery light—may find it of little consequence to them, quite empty of meaning and character. Again, they may not. About tastes and judgments it is sometimes not wise to dispute.

In the paintings of the Flemish Anthony Van Dyck the men were always handsome, the ladies without flaw. In Van Dyck's portraits the atmosphere was one of elegance, ostentation, and conspicuous consumption. Van Dyck delighted in painting unreal people in unreal backgrounds of softness and splendor. Such was the fashion of the hour. The greengrocer must be made to look like a marquis, the bourgeois vintner like the leader of a prominent banking family. The skill of Van Dyck's brush and his easy ability in arrangement won acclaim and provoked imitation. The acclaim was not always merited and the results of the imitation did no service to the cause of art.

Greatest of all the Flemish painters was the exuberant Peter Paul Rubens (1577–1640). He was the artist who pleased the nobles and burgesses by his lavish use of rich colors, so suggestive of wealth and vitality. Several of his themes were classical, such as those in his famous "Venus and Adonis," "The Fates Spinning," and "The Rape of the Daughters of Leucippus by Castor and Pollux."

In the England of the seventeenth century there were several portrait painters and miniaturists but no landscape artists of consequence. Waves of foreign influence gave directional thrusts to all English artistic endeavors. Apart from the miniaturist work of men like Nicholas Hilliard and Thomas Flatman, English painting lacked the fineness of touch of the Continental masters. There were few painters and paintings of the highest rank; the seventeenth century, despite the enthusiasm of vigorous amateurs, was not a flourishing period of English art.

[83] "Tea at the Home of Princesse de Conti." This painting by M. B. Ollivier shows Mozart, age 11, at the clavichord.

[84] "Spinning, Reeling, and Boiling Yarn in Northern Ireland, 1791," by William Hincks

PLATE XXVII

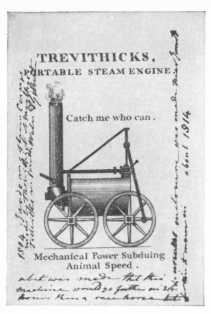

[85] Richard Trevithick of Cornwall devised the first road locomotive.

[86] Entrance to the Locomotive Engine House in Camden Town, drawing made about 1839

[87] "The Eli Whitney Gun Factory, 1826-1828." Oil painting by William G. Munson

PLATE XXVIII

The men who brought the classical style of architecture into England were Inigo Jones, the disciple of Palladio, and Sir Christopher Wren. The first fully classical building in England was the Banqueting Hall built in White-hall by Inigo Jones for James I. This magnificent structure began a new age of English architecture. After the Great Fire of London, Sir Christopher Wren, England's greatest architect, was commissioned to rebuild St. Paul's Cathedral. The result was Wren's masterpiece, a shrine of England and one of the great cathedrals of the world. He also designed fifty other London churches including St. Martin, St. Mary-le-Bow, and St. Clement Danes. The list of his prodigious achievements is long. "Architecture aims at eternity," Wren once wrote. In his hands it did.

Not until the eighteenth century and the Age of Enlightenment did the full power of the sanctions and controls of the ideals of "reason" and "nature" and "balance" and "compromise" reach their height. Nevertheless, the rules of the "classical spirit" in literature as well as art were widely observed in Europe when Louis XIV ruled in Versailles and his court declared what cultured men and women should know and do. This "classical spirit" meant a cultivated interest in the classical models of civilization, a formalized literary style and language, a deep concern with balance, poise, compromise, discipline, order, reason.

In Europe the appeal of classicism was indeed strong in the seventeenth century. There was a widespread desire for laws that would guide and protect those who were confused by successive waves of new facts sweeping over a disordered world. Men who are uncertain in the present are often comforted by the apparent certainties of the past. How fine it was to have "the constant control of reason and of a discriminating and selective taste which rejects everything in the nature of impulsive direction or adventurous fancy!"

Several men in France agreed that the classical writers had provided them with a lucid, coherent, and simple set of literary standards. Nicolas Boileau-Despréaux, critic, poet, and "legislator of Parnassus," set forth most of the rules for writing poetry. Men like Boileau approved of the idea and practice of a discreet and considered elegance in literature that would match and balance the elegant world of Versailles.

The love of reason and the rules that marked the "classical spirit" reached far beyond the boundaries of France into Germany, Italy, Spain, and, to a lesser extent, into England. It was widely said that "all culture was the culture of France." Much glory came and stayed with France because of the triumphs in poetry and drama of Jean de la Fontaine (1621–1695)—his *Fables* are still rightly famous—Pierre Corneille (1606–1684), Jean Racine (1639–1699), and Molière (1622–1673). Corneille and Racine did not depart from the rigid classical rules of tragedy. They always adhered, for instance, to the "unities" of time, place, and action. In Alexandrine rhymed couplets their tragedies moved, with insight and power, towards their dark endings. Molière—his real name was Jean Baptiste Poquelin—was the most original and able of all French writers of true comedy.

The influence of the "classical spirit" in England, as remarked above, was less considerable. It was true, nevertheless, that John Dryden, Alexander Pope, and Joseph Addison visited Boileau, and Pope declared himself to be Boileau's "disciple." And yet the fact does remain that in England there were frequent departures from the classical rules. Most English writers never abandoned the whims, disorders, and profundities that are so often the companions of inspiration and imagination. To this statement it may be replied that John Milton was an exception, that he was a classicist. Certainly the stately flow of his lofty lines and the frequent classical references lie in the classical tradition. Nevertheless, the discerning critic can see that Milton does sometimes depart from the classical rules, even in *Paradise Lost* and *Samson Agonistes*. In many respects John Milton was as much a "radical" in his poetry as he was in his prose and his life. In both his poetry and his prose he had a great deal to say to his contemporaries and to all men. Everybody who believes in toleration and democracy should read and ponder the flaming passages of the celebrated *Areopagitica*. Here is eloquence. Free men think that here is truth.

With the coming of Charles II to the English throne in 1660 there began the body of plays called Restoration drama. The Restoration years were a period of achievement in the flexible comedies of wit, repartee, intrigue, and manners. As in the plays of France's Molière, the characters were not sharply drawn. There were the easily recognizable types: the fop, the fool, the charlatan, the wild debauchee, the gallant lover, the bemused and cheated husband. The Restoration dramatists, such as the witty and eloquent William Congreve and the gross William Wycherley, often mocked at decency, morality, and virtue. They were self-consciously naughty.

In the earlier part of the century there were many prose craftsmen, among them such giants as Francis Bacon and Abraham Cowley. The plastic tongue of the Elizabethans was successfully taken in hand by the Jacobean age and the result was very important in the history of the English language. Meanwhile the printing presses were rolling forth thousands of books, sober and light. More and more writers sought to appeal to the multitude. Propaganda, pamphlets, tracts, and ballads rained over England.

Numerous poets produced lyrics, odes, epistles, satires, and epigrams, forms of poetry in which the age took considerable delight. Many readers of this book have traveled in those realms of gold. The cross-currents of English literature in the seventeenth century are many. On the one hand there is the supreme achievement of Milton's *Paradise Lost* and the stirring lines of

Dryden's *Alexander's Feast*. On the other, one may find the stumbling epigram of an amateur whose name has long since perished.

The musical world of seventeenth-century Europe had its glories and its shadows. The past merged slowly into the new age. In England, for instance, Orlando Gibbons, almost the last of the great Elizabethan makers of music, stayed on as organist in Westminster Abbey until his death in 1625. The Gentlemen of the Chapel Royal continued to be composers as well as singers —and so did the members of the Vatican Choir in Rome. Amidst such suggestions of continuity there were new threads and themes. In England the influence of the lute song swept over into the province of the madrigal. England's John Dowland, greatest of lutenist song writers, won high popularity in Denmark, the Netherlands, and Germany. The influence of the new Italian solo, particularly the examples of Monteverdi and Caccini, was felt over all western Europe. Music publishers, such as Vincenti of Venice and Phalese of Antwerp, increased their production and their wealth. Hundreds of skilled musicians traveled from country to country, especially to the royal courts. When France's Henrietta Maria came to England to be the bride of Charles I she brought eleven French musicians with her. The queens of Charles II and James II—Catherine of Braganza and Mary of Modena—brought Portuguese and Italian artists. Baltzar, the German master of the new instrument called the violin, came to live in England before the restoration of Charles II.

Italian opera excited all the musical world of Europe and strongly influenced the growth of such forms of entertainment as the English masque. Later in the seventeenth century Henry Purcell (1659–1695) gave his name to a whole musical age in England—historically Purcell's most interesting achievement was the opera *Dido and Aeneas*. Every student of music knows how his ranging genius was revealed in highly original odes, songs, sonatas, how fascinating is the complex polyphony of his fantasies for strings.

Several men were outstanding in the flourishing musical life of Europe in the early eighteenth century. One was the German genius George Frederick Handel (1685–1759). Handel was the greatest of all the numerous foreign musicians who came to cosmopolitan London. The rich gifts he gave to the world began to flow about 1710 and continued until the first performance of *Messiah* at the New Music Hall, Dublin, on April 15, 1742. In 1752 Handel's sight was ruined by the same surgeon who had blinded Bach a few years before.

Johann Sebastian Bach (1685–1750) was "the last and greatest hero of the baroque musical age." His indefatigable zeal for perfection and his superb imagination resulted in achievements as a composer, teacher, and performer that have seldom been surpassed. Students of music who read this book will know how much Bach changed the existing techniques of playing keyboard instruments, how much he was responsible for the use of the equally tempered scale, how impressive are his chorals and his masses, how just it is to say that Bach has a strong claim to be called the founder of modern organ music, of which he composed so much.

Franz Joseph Haydn (1732–1809), renowned as probably the most remarkable Austrian teacher and composer of his time, was a man whose main interest was in pure musical structure and instrumental polyphony. He stayed at the homes of his patrons Prince Paul and Prince Nicholas Esterhazy for thirty years and during that time he produced compositions in numerous musical forms: concertos, interludes, masses, operas, oratorios, overtures, quartets, sonatas, symphonies. What Haydn wrote was performed and acclaimed from London to St. Petersburg. Here was richness and color, substance and texture, beauty and freedom. The controlled formalism, so characteristic of the age, yielded to sincerity and freshness in the works of Haydn, especially in the symphonies. In his famed string quartets old Croatian folk tunes appeared and faded and appeared again, all to the astonishment and delight of those who listened and knew that what they heard was the voice of genius.

About Ludwig van Beethoven (1770–1827) learned experts like Sir George Grove and A. W. Thayer have written many volumes. Almost every biography, every article, gives a more or less graphic description of Beethoven's pathetic life as he attempted to "grapple with fate"—the phrase is his own. We read of the way in which the young Beethoven astonished Mozart at Vienna in 1787; about the grotesquely uncouth manners that alienated Haydn; about the sordid chapters—how impractical Beethoven was!—in the tale of his troubles with his dishonest brother and his dissolute nephew; about his mistakes, the painful difficulties that welled out of his own character; about the slow coming of fame; about the progress of the deafness that began about 1798 and could not be cured by skill or quackery; about his death in 1827 in the midst of a fierce thunderstorm.

Beethoven was a man of art and a man of courage. These qualities, and many more, are revealed in his music—and there alone. The depths of thought and emotional power cannot be described in the language of words. It is simple and easy to write about the varying styles or manners of Beethoven—they are usually described as three—and the result may be useful, provided that the writer and reader are both aware that the descriptive prose brings only a small measure of understanding.

Comment about the famous Seventh and Ninth Symphonies is profitable, to a point. Beethoven's music, with all its solemnity, range, and depth, provides a magnificent illustration of the fact that works of art in one medium of human communication cannot easily be explained in another. They stand alone. When we say, for instance, that Beethoven "influenced" Wagner,

Brahms, and Schumann we are quite correct. When we try to trace and analyze that "influence" we may be quite deceived and wrong. Musical criticism sometimes claims to describe and explain too much. *L'ineptie consiste à vouloir conclure.* The swallowers of formulas are always in peril.

Wolfgang Amadeus Mozart was born at Salzburg in 1756. He was a boy wonder, a prodigy—that is one word we use when we are baffled by the mysteries of genius. When Mozart was four years old he wrote his first clavier concerto; he played for the Empress Maria Theresa when he was six; he played for Louis XV and Madame Pompadour when he was seven; he composed his first opera when he was eleven. At the age of fourteen he wrote down from memory the famous Allegri *Miserere* he had heard once in the Sistine Chapel—the *Miserere* was a treasured liturgical work that nobody had been allowed to copy on pain of excommunication. The pope pardoned Mozart.

Mozart grew up to be a lively, generous, improvident young man who was often hoodwinked and swindled—he was quite incapable of striking good bargains for himself. In Marcia Davenport's *Mozart* we read of his hard struggle: "About $200 was all he ever received for *Figaro*, about $225 for *Don Giovanni* . . . and about $112 for the *Requiem*." Of his six children, two survived; both died childless. When Mozart was thirty-five, racked with typhoid and almost penniless, he struggled to finish the *Requiem*. "I have come to an end before having had the enjoyment of my talent. Life was indeed so beautiful . . . but one cannot change one's destiny." Mozart's last act, on the morning of December 5, 1791, was to puff out his cheeks in an unsuccessful effort to sound some notes in the *Requiem*. He was buried in a pauper's grave in Vienna and nobody knows where it is.

George Bernard Shaw once said that the music Mozart made for Sarastro to sing was "the only music ever written which would not seem out of place in the mouth of God." There is no question that Mozart's music came as near to perfection as human genius can hope to approach. "He contributed to every kind and shape of music," wrote Neville Cardus on the 200th anniversary of Mozart's birth, "sacred and secular, opera and symphony, all manner of chamber combinations, concerted pieces, 'occasional pieces.' . . . He remains the most enigmatic and inexplicable of all composers; we shall not know his like again. That Mozart was born, once and for all, is a happening and a consummation which beggars all understanding."

Chapter 26

THE ECONOMIC REVOLUTION:
STEAM, STEEL, AND LAND

"Gold is the child of Zeus. Neither rust nor worms can corrupt this metal, which doth astonishingly excite the minds of mortals."
—Sappho, *Fragments*

PRESENT expert estimates set the age of the planet Earth at between five and seven billion years; some authorities believe that it may be older still. *Homo pithecanthropus* first appeared here about half a million years ago, more or less. When we think of these facts it seems remarkable that only in the last five hundred years has the culture and civilization of mankind—at least a substantial part of it—changed rapidly. Not until the seventeenth century were the foundations laid for the sure and steady growth of modern science and techniques. Professor Arthur Compton once wrote that if we likened the estimated life of the universe to one year, then the last five hundred years are only two seconds. Mankind has crowded a great many experiences, with all their complex results, into those two seconds.

Throughout his history, of course, man has added to the strength of his hands new instruments of power and precision. He has tapped new sources of energy—wood, coal, water, electricity, gas, oil, uranium. He has deliberately sought to conquer the physical world. He has changed his ways of living in proportion as he has discovered new ways to master the external world of things. An increasing part of the outer world of nature has been subdued to human use. This conquest of nature forms a large part of what is usually meant by the word "progress."

From the place in the time scale at which we stand today we can observe countless men and events in the past four or five centuries that have helped to build the modern world of industry and science in Europe and America. What the future destiny of this mechanistic-scientific civilization may be no man now can say. In our present age we know that the humanistic, classical,

Renaissance arrangements are gone forever. We also know that upon what we do with our new instruments of power the fate of mankind depends.

It is usually said that the first great impetus to industrial and technological advance was given by the inventions and improvements that appeared in eighteenth-century England. There was certainly a spurt of invention and a variety of tireless achievement. Nevertheless, it should be noted that few really sudden or spectacular shifts take place in economic history. The mighty events of the eighteenth century were a long time in the making. Professors Ashton, Bining, Chapman, Gras, Heaton, Nef, and several other scholars have shown that the dramatic and sensational features of the economic alterations in the eighteenth century have often been exaggerated; that the speed of the rate of change was slower than once was believed; that there were several important inventions before the eighteenth century—such as new methods of extracting and refining metals—and a series of sharp thrusts forward, especially between 1540 and 1640; that the loved and honored words "industrial revolution" usually applied to the eighteenth century should be abandoned in the light of the enlarged mass of material discovered and explained in the last few decades.

These scholars stress the fact that the industrial and agrarian "revolutions" usually moved at a patient tortoise pace through several generations. Professor Herbert Heaton, for instance, has pointed out that only 320 Watt steam engines were used in England in 1800; that by 1830 water power was still used by a quarter of all the cotton mills in England; that only after 1850 did cheap steel, cheap electricity, cheap lubricants, and industrial chemistry come upon the stage and take command. What happened in the eighteenth century, says Professor Heaton, was "a trend rather than a tumult."

The eighteenth century certainly had this in common with other times: innumerable frustrations dogged the dreamers and the doers and countless obstacles appeared athwart their paths. On the one hand, the inquiring, persistent, and resourceful minds discovered and invented, often after many failures. On the other hand, they frequently found it difficult to spread their newly found information and to persuade people that the new devices and methods were better than the old. These men did not have the advantages of our modern tools of advertisement and communication. In all ages, of course, there are constant foes of progress and improvement and innovation: people of ignorance, apathy, blinkered conservatism, or downright obstinacy. The reader will know that these nouns describe the man around the corner or the woman in the third house down the street. We all recognize the loud gabble that reveals vacant minds uninhibited by any knowledge of the facts. Matter-of-fact knowledge, so far as we can achieve it, goes hand in hand with tolerably sound ideas. Ideas born of ignorance are usually vicious.

Despite the signals of caution contained in the previous paragraphs several valid general statements can be made about the remarkable eighteenth-century changes that were of such consequence to the world. There was a marked rise in the demands of overseas markets for industrial goods. There was a steady surge of mechanized industry and industrial production and a consequent increase of available goods and services, especially in England and, to a lesser extent, in the Netherlands, France, and southern Germany. There was a great advance in commercial activity and the exploitation of markets. There was mounting exhilaration at the manifold results of the conquests of nature and the inventions of man, especially among those whose profits increased.

Meanwhile, too, there was a continued extension of money economy institutions and a more widespread organization of economic life. One aspect of this organization, of course, was the development of capitalist arrangements with respect to finance, production, and market operations. True, there were earlier signs of such organization on capitalist lines in industry—one economic historian has pointed out that in the sixteenth century an Englishman named Henry Lee invented a small sewing machine that could make 1,500 stitches a minute; it was used at home by men and women who did piece work for their employer; thus there was an employee-employer relationship and an increase of production. The important fact, however, is that there were not many men like Henry Lee in the sixteenth century. "One swallow does not make a summer."

Whether or not the word "revolution" is used to describe what happened in eighteenth-century England, the fact still stands that Englishmen were applying mechanical power to industry on a scale never known before. Production was increased. New economic, social, and political problems were created for all Western civilization. Into every phase of English industry came new inventions, improvements, more efficient power machinery to take the place of human hands and muscles. For example, many pages could be written about the shifts and changes in the pottery industry as Josiah Wedgwood made his products an important branch of English commerce; about the linen manufacturers of Belfast; about the tin plate of South Wales.

It is always difficult, and frequently tedious, to cite a long list of the names of inventors unless their achievements are described in some detail. The meaning of the activities of some men will be swiftly illustrated here by reference to certain major inventions that transformed England's basic industries: wool, cotton, and steel.

The wool industry had been England's most important since the Middle Ages. Farmers were forbidden to export wool to feed the foreign looms of Flanders or any other country. High duties were imposed on foreign cloth so that the English clothier would be adequately protected. Englishmen were encouraged to drink port wine so that the Portuguese and Brazilian markets would remain open to English wool textiles. In rough figures the export of woolen goods probably rose from a value of £300,000 in 1720 to £5,000,000 in 1790.

Tariffs are usually defensive weapons. Inventions, on the contrary, are tools of offense—a new production device, properly used, can sometimes disturb the whole economic equilibrium of a foreign competitor; it can often shake the labor market at home; it can bring several other results, some of them happy and some of them not.

Inventions in the textile industry were both important and numerous. In 1733 John Kay of Lancashire invented the "flying shuttle," an instrument that doubled the output of the hand weaver. The growing speed and output of the weavers increased the demand for woolen yarn and cotton thread; the spinners could not meet the need. In 1764 James Hargreaves invented his multiple "spinning jenny," a machine that was in fact a large spinning wheel lying on its side and turning from eight to a hundred spindles at a time. Necessity, it seemed, had produced the invention of Hargreaves. In 1771 Richard Arkwright devised the water frame, in which a number of rollers prepared tougher threads than the "spinning jenny." In 1779 Samuel Crompton combined the merits of Arkwright's frame and Hargreaves' "jenny" in his "mule," a machine that spun a thread both fine and tough.

The production of thread and yarn was soon larger than the hand looms could handle. In 1785 the Reverend Edmund Cartwright developed a power loom. Water supplied the power needed to run the new machines. New mills sprang up by the swift streams and waterfalls on the Pennine slopes of Lancashire. But the balance between spinning and weaving was not fully restored because Cartwright's loom was not entirely successful; not until after 1820 were power looms perfected.

Meanwhile an adequate supply of cotton seemed to be assured when Eli Whitney invented his cotton gin in the United States in 1793. This machine swiftly separated the fibers from the seeds and was of high importance in the economic history of the cotton belt of the United States. In 1760 Lancashire imported nearly 8,000 tons of raw cotton; in 1800 the total had risen to about 25,000 tons; in 1861 to about 300,000 tons. The creation of new markets for American cotton in the textile factories of Great Britain helped the economy of the Southern states; it also gave an impetus to the institution of Negro slavery.

There is another reason to remember Eli Whitney. About 1798 he was making muskets at New Haven. His inventive mind led him to divide his workers into three groups and to give each group the job of making either locks, stocks, or barrels with special machines. Any three units could be fitted together to make a finished musket of a uniform pattern. Some men saw the advantages of such speed and economy. By 1815 the new method of mass production was being used in the manufacture of such things as horse pistols, iron shovels, and wooden clocks.

Slowly, very slowly, the principle of standardized interchangeable parts was adopted in the making of thousands of machine products. Men learned that the main key to mass production is accuracy in preparing standard parts. Today, for instance, more than 4,000 subcontractors manufacture the 8,854 parts that one major aircraft-engine firm fits together in making a jet engine. In the early days of the automobile there were about 800 different kinds of lock washers and 1,600 sizes of steel tubing. Today there are only 16 kinds of lock washers and 17 types of steel tubing.

It may be that the bold ideas and artful methods of Whitney and those who followed in his footsteps rank far more highly in their real importance than historians have thought and said. The ruthlessly hardheaded men of business and industry—especially in the United States—who purged away the old production systems, who admitted the urgent and dominating necessities of mass production in competition, who stamped their feet and got results, these men provide us, surely, with the raw materials from which to write more significant chapters about the history of economic enterprise. It is not enough to make gleaming phrases—such as "the challenge of events" or the "American destiny"—do duty for the precise and robust facts about what was done and who did it.

In most modern industries a satisfactory rate of production can only be achieved by making standard interchangeable parts. Our contemporary societies are increasingly dependent upon machines that do precisely that. Eli Whitney pointed the way. His statue should be placed outside the main offices of several giant industries. Too many people know nothing about him except that he invented the cotton gin.

Let us return to England and the problems of the manufacture of woolen and cotton goods in the eighteenth century. There the inventions that contributed to speed and efficiency in spinning and weaving were made more valuable by the new steam engine. In 1698 Captain Thomas Savery had invented a steam pump. In 1705 appeared Thomas Newcomen's immense fire engine. The piston of his upright machine was about five feet in diameter. The engine delivered about twenty horsepower and burned about twelve tons of coal a day. Steam was shot into the cylinder to push the piston up; then the cylinder was sprayed with cold water to condense the steam and create a vacuum inside. This enabled the atmospheric pressure on the outside of the piston head to force it down. Five-sixths of the steam energy was consumed by the alternate heating and cooling of the cylinder. This engine was used mainly to pump water out of mines.

In 1769 James Watt of Glasgow, after repairing one of Newcomen's engines, took out a patent on a horizontal steam engine in which the steam not only pushed out the piston but also pulled it in. Aided by Matthew Boulton, a hardware manufacturer near Birmingham, Watt finished a fairly efficient engine in 1775. Later improvements were made, and in 1785 the first steam engine was used to supply power for a cotton factory. The age of the steam factory began. The new source of power was now not water, but coal. England had great supplies of coal.

The first development of the iron and steel industries had been delayed in the early part of the eighteenth century because of the difficulty of obtaining an adequate fuel supply. The only known fuel for smelting purposes was wood, and England's forests were becoming exhausted. The advance of the iron industry had to wait for the discovery of new smelting methods.

Up in Shropshire three generations of Abraham Darbys used coke made from coal to make their cast-iron and copper kettles and pans. Their main difficulty was in getting a sufficient combustion of the coke to produce high-grade iron. In the end the Darbys were able to produce cast iron in large quantities with their new blast furnaces. After 1770 coke was used by other ironmasters.

In 1783 Henry Cort found a way to convert pig or cast iron into malleable or wrought-iron bars by a process known as puddling and rolling. The wrought iron had much more tensile strength than the carbon-heavy cast iron and hence could be used for a much larger number of industrial purposes. By the end of the eighteenth century England led the world in heavy industries. It was a happy accident that her coal was so close to her iron deposits in the "Black Country" of the Midlands and the north.

In the middle of the nineteenth century Sir Henry Bessemer patented a famous process for making steel in large quantities cheaply. Not until 1881, however, did the Gilchrist process enable men to use effectively the phosphorus-bearing ores of Europe.

Such were the inventions of major importance in the manufacture of textiles, iron, and steel. The patterns of inventive conquest were much the same in the other basic industries. Through years of hastening change nimble hands and quick brains made machines do things that human beings had always done before with their hands and muscles. Men drove bargains and smashed obstacles. They seized opportunities. They made things of beauty and beastliness. The wens of England's great cities sprawled ugly and dark; they enslaved the workers and the factory owners at the same time. Industrial capitalism became huge, impersonal, and efficient. Between the sweating laborer and the industrialist the gulf was fixed and wide. Was the worker worthy of his hire? Was the capitalist worthy of his profit? Around these twin questions were to turn many of the later disputes about the unsolved riddle of social justice.

The new age of the machine could not swell and prosper without a marked improvement in the British transportation system. Goods and people had to be moved more rapidly from one part of the land to another. By the end of the eighteenth century better transport increased the pace of travel. Famous road engineers, such as John Macadam and Thomas Telford, built better roads and bridges. Stage coaches were improved. A network of canals was being dug. By such transportation developments the isolation of many areas was being further broken down. Almost everywhere there was evident a broadening of horizons, a feeling of wonderful changes afoot. The old ways decayed and the new quickened and grew with remarkable speed and intensity.

Soon steamboats and railways heralded the birth of an age of speed. The steamboat came first. In 1785 a Virginia mechanic named James Rumsey drove his boat at a speed of four miles an hour on the Potomac—George Washington watched him from the shore. In 1786 John Fitch of Connecticut demonstrated his steam launch—he called it his "water beetle"—at Philadelphia and carried passengers on the Delaware. Nobody wanted to help John Fitch in his work; he was mercilessly abused for his crazy ideas; his wife was a shrew; in 1798 he walked down to the river and drowned himself.

At the end of the eighteenth century a Scotsman named William Symington invented a marine engine and in 1802 his *Charlotte Dundas* traveled twenty miles down the Clyde. In 1807 the American Robert Fulton—a shrewd and noisy salesman—made his paddle-wheel passenger steamboat *Katherine of Clermont* commercially successful on its runs along the Hudson River between New York and Albany. Regular service across the English Channel began in 1818. In 1819 the *Savannah* crossed the Atlantic, using steam power for part of the voyage. In 1827 the *Curaçao* traveled over the Atlantic using steam engines all the way. In 1838 the *Great Western* crossed from Bristol to New York in thirteen days. In 1840 Samuel Cunard founded the Cunard Line. The age of the great ocean steamships had not yet arrived; but the promise was bright.

Next came the railways. Experiments with "steam carriages" were made as early as the 1790's in both England and America. As in the case of steamship development, American and British inventors often independently came to similar conclusions. About 1800 Richard Trevithick ran a steam stagecoach over the ninety miles from London to Plymouth. In 1811 the American John Stephens saw the possibility of using steam engines running along rails by means of flanged wheels. In 1814 the Englishman George Stephenson made an engine which pulled a load of thirty tons along a road at a speed of four miles an hour. He then had the idea of an engine with cars attached traveling along rails. In 1830 Stephenson's famous *Rocket* reached a speed of thirty miles an hour.

Several conservative spirits asserted that the new railway machines were evil and unnatural. God, they said, had never intended human beings to possess and use such instruments of speed and power. He could not, surely, be pleased at what His children had done. Those who soberly condemned the new invention of the railway engine were unaware of its importance in the tale of man's conquest of distance; they had no idea that they were standing at the dawn of the railway era. Men who live in the middle of revolutions sometimes know less about them than the historians later.

There were other opponents of the new machines. The canal, stagecoach, and toll-bridge operators feared the competition of the railways, and the country gentlemen did not want their estates disfigured by "this infernal nuisance—the loco-motive Monster, carrying *eighty tons* of goods, and navigated by a tail of smoke and sulphur, coming thro' every man's grounds between Manchester and Liverpool." In 1829 one member of Parliament took a trip of five miles on the railway, once reaching a speed of twenty-three miles an hour. "It is really flying and it is impossible to divest yourself of the notion of instant death to all upon the least accident happening. It gave me a headache which has not left me yet."

The opposition to the railways was strong, but not strong enough. A number of small companies were soon formed to serve local areas. These were all later absorbed in the four great railway systems of England, which were, in turn, nationalized by the Transport Act of 1947. Huge amounts of money were invested, particularly in the "railway mania" of 1845 when more than £150,000,000 was placed for profit in railway stocks. In Europe and the United States the era of roadbeds and rails was at hand.

In 1842 England's Sydney Smith wrote words of pleasure and optimism: "Man is become a bird; he can fly longer and quicker than the solan-goose. The early Scotchman scratches himself in the morning mists of the north and has his porridge in Piccadily before the setting sun. . . . Time, distance, and delay are abolished."

Such are some of the salient facts about the multiplication of machines, the transformation of production methods, and the advance in transport and communications in the eighteenth and early nineteenth centuries.

During these years there also occurred two silent rural changes of vast significance: a revolution in the methods of English farming and the enclosure of the common fields. The old agricultural order crumbled.

Few improvements in farming methods had been made since the Middle Ages. The conservative temper of English farming past and present united with communication difficulties to prevent the spread of the few new agricultural techniques that were developed in some localities. Large areas of England were left untilled; heaths and forests blanketed wide areas of several counties.

Despite this widespread stagnation and lethargy there were a few men, not content with things as they were, who began to experiment and invent. Some were obscure individuals. Others were rich farmers whose names are now usually associated with the steps that marked the famous innovations in eighteenth-century agriculture.

One of these scientific farming pioneers was the irascible and wealthy Oxford graduate Jethro Tull. He asserted that the ground prepared for most crops should be well broken up before seed was planted and well cultivated by horse-drawn cultivators after growth had begun. Obviously those cultivators could not be used if the seed had been sown broadcast by a human sower. It was necessary to plant the seed in rows by using a drill. After the plants came up the cultivator could pass up and down between the rows. Jethro Tull showed that he could use less seed and grow bigger crops by his new methods.

A second pioneer was Lord Charles Townshend. He began experiments in crop rotation on his Norfolk estates. Townshend showed rural England that fields did not have to lie fallow one year in three. By planting root crops and clover the fertility of the soil would be restored by replacing the lost nitrogen. The roots and clover would then be fed to the livestock, ending the practice of killing off most of the cattle in the autumn. With winter food for livestock fresh meat and milk would be available throughout the year.

A third leader in agricultural experiments was Robert Bakewell of Leicestershire whose chief interest was in the improvement of sheep, cattle, and horse breeding. Formerly farmers had paid scant attention to breeding. Cattle and sheep had not been used mainly for food. Sheep had been grown for wool; cows to produce butter and milk; oxen to pull loads. In 1750, with a shrewd eye to the future meat demand, Bakewell began to experiment with longhorn cattle. In his cattle breeding Bakewell was not successful, but his imitators later developed the Durham shorthorns and the Herefords. Bakewell did succeed in developing the new breed of fat and chunky Leicestershire sheep by inbreeding large and compact animals. In these years, too, the controlled experiments with dairy cattle, hogs, and horses produced many famous breeds. The Holstein, Jersey, and Guernsey milk cows come from the eighteenth century. The Tamworth and Yorkshire hogs were developed then. After long and patient work there were bred the first of the blocky Clydesdale and Percheron horses, so useful for heavy haulage work.

Slowly the knowledge of these and other farming improvements spread over wide areas of England and beyond. The interest of the landed aristocrats steadily increased. They saw that a rising population would put a heavy pressure upon England's food supply. The mounting demand would drive food prices upwards. More and more people were moving into the cities to work in business and industry. They must be fed. Obviously men with land and enterprise could make much money in agriculture. The owners of broad acres accordingly improved their agricultural methods, confident that high profits would reward their endeavors. On the other hand, the small farmers often looked with prejudice upon the new techniques; they had a deep affection for the old ways of their fathers and were disinclined to try the new; their minds were entrapped by the past.

The great landlords wanted to put more land under cultivation; to produce as much as they could; to get high rents and high prices. By hedges and walls they enclosed more and more of the ancient common lands and open fields. Special acts of Parliament were passed to permit the enclosures—this was not difficult because the landlords controlled Parliament. In the eighteenth century nearly 3,000,000 acres of open fields and 1,000,000 acres of common waste land were enclosed. Great areas of the common and waste lands were now broken up by the plow.

Certainly the agricultural system of England was improved. The new system was obviously less wasteful than the old. With the coming of large-scale capitalistic agricultural enterprise, profits and production increased together. As more foodstuffs became available under the impetus of the new methods of scientific farming, the increasing industrial population of the cities was more adequately fed.

To the small owners and leaseholders the enclosures usually meant disaster. In the villages of England the small yeoman farmers, owning their acres by copyhold or freehold tenure, frequently found that they could not compete with the great landlords. They could not afford to buy the new livestock and machinery essential to the carrying on of successful scientific farming. They had often lost by acts of Parliament their rights in the old open fields and common lands and the compensation they received in the form, for example, of little blocks of land was not enough. To pay their debts they often had to sell what land they had, usually to large landowners. Some rented land and became tenant farmers. Some drifted to join the unsorted masses in the cities and entered industry. Others emigrated to the colonies. Still others stayed on the land as hired laborers.

The healthy and self-sufficient old village system of England slowly departed before the relentless advance of the enclosures and the demands of efficiency and modern production methods. The independent yeomanry was almost completely extinguished. Profits must be made. The cities must be fed.

The old English villages had certainly meant inefficiency and old-fashioned farming. But the lesser folk had probably been happier in the villages than they were ever to be again in a mysterious and bewildering world. The England of the yeomen and the ale house was soon gone forever. The village green might now be plowed up. The famous lines of Oliver Goldsmith's *Deserted Village* find a place in every modern anthology:

> Ill fares the land, to hast'ning ills a prey,
> Where wealth accumulates and men decay.

Into the overcast cities came thousands of men and women. Industry and commerce were hungry for workers. The smoke of William Blake's "dark, satanic mills" belched over the land. The new frontiers were in the factory.

It is perhaps difficult for the men of the twentieth century to understand and appreciate the first shocks that came to our forefathers when the new machines stepped up the rate of production with untiring efficiency and power and the vast cities began to swell and sprawl as factories marched over the green fields.

We are accustomed to a tide of technological advances, year by year. Speed and precision are our daily companions. Some men of our modern world feel lost and lonely when they are out of sight of a flashing neon sign or cannot hear the comforting roar of the city traffic. This is the world they know. This is the world they understand. This is the world into which their sons are born.

Men of the eighteenth century in England had no idea that their inventiveness and energy were opening the roads that would lead to a brave new world of nuclear energy and automation. They saw their immediate needs and the obvious advantages of swift action. As a pioneer of a mighty revolution in industrial production England opened the road to greater national wealth and power. In this she was aided by technical skills, by vast deposits of coal and iron, by the fact that she was already the first commercial and maritime power. She could produce and export more cheaply than any nation on earth. The whole world was her market and she made the most of it. The products of her indefatigable machines were exported over the seas and across the continents. From many corners of the planet she sucked up the raw materials needed by the hungry maws of her factories. The thud and beat of pistons and hammers became louder as more money made more machines and better ones. The golden streams of British capital also poured into foreign fields. London succeeded Amsterdam as the center of the international money market. Accumulated capital disposable abroad would go anywhere for profit. "There are few ways in which a man can be more innocently employed than in making money," wrote Dr. Samuel Johnson in 1775. The new world meant speed, efficiency, wealth. No man knew how big it would grow.

Nor did any man know what solutions could be found to the increasing number of insistent and nagging problems. With the increasing industrialization of many nations there came a ruthless competition among the great powers for raw materials, markets, and colonies. The life blood of empire is trade and commerce. International economic competition helped to bring diplomatic crises and war. With the rapid rise of the new industrial capitalists came also the rise of the industrial proletariat. The worker had to sell his labor in the available markets or starve. It is not surprising that the new cities were to be the seed ground of a new democracy. Soon the power of the industrial masses was to be harnessed and directed by the great labor organizations.

It was not long before the unprecedented forces released by the new ventures of Englishmen in the eighteenth century were to sweep beyond the shores of the island kingdom. Then came the churning impact of the complex industrial changes in Europe, particularly in Germany. Rapid and continuous achievements in the United States, always a land of far frontiers, helped to create an American belief in limitless progress. American zeal was incredible. Backs were strong and brains were quick; it seemed that these men were determined to change the face of the world. Here was a land of stimulating dreams, a land of becoming rather than being, filled with the incessant excitement of action.

There is an American notion, probably born of Puritan days, that he who dallies loses all. The American soul has been fed on that idea. This is the belief that has blasted time charts, turned mountains upside down, played extensive havoc with time-honored customs of commerce and trade.

The spotlight of history was soon to be focused on the new triumphs of industry and economic enterprise in the United States. The main pivots and patterns of control in the lively Western world had once been in Rome. By the mid-twentieth century they shifted to Washington and New York. The old European structure of power, once so dominant, was to crack and crumble and collapse.

Confronted with the new facts of the economic life in England it is not surprising that the finger of doubt was pointed towards several ideas and habits inherited from the past. Many old laws and customs are always at the mercy of men who make revolutions. "If the facts be so," said Oliver Cromwell, "why should we sport with them?" It seems natural enough, when we look back, that the Glasgow professor Adam Smith should have published his *Inquiry into the Nature and Causes of The Wealth of Nations* in 1776.

Adam Smith, like the French Physiocrats, opposed the controlled economy of a mercantilist system designed to increase national wealth, industry, and trade. That system had in fact been decaying long before the later years of the eighteenth century. The old laws had remained on the books; but they had not always been enforced. "The steady drift," Professor Conyers Read has written, "was towards greater freedom in economic matters. Restraints were relaxed in fact before they were relaxed in theory." By the latter part of the eighteenth century a very large number of responsible men agreed with Adam

Smith and with the natural-rights philosophers who insisted that an enlightened self-interest realizes both public and private welfare—these men were soon to be supported by the utilitarian reformers. They all said that governmental control was an obstacle to the "natural order" of society; laws of nature, discoverable by human reason, should govern all, or almost all, the political, social, and economic relations of man.

In *The Wealth of Nations* it was asserted that the natural economic laws fixed two things as the main features of a sensible economic system: private property and free competition. Any eighteenth-century English industrialist would agree with that. All through the nineteenth century the classical economists who followed Adam Smith asserted that the important task of any national economy is to produce consumable goods. The "natural economic man" assumed by the classical economists would of course produce what other men want. This "economic man," well informed, self-seeking, and intelligent, would always want to buy his goods and services in the cheapest and sell them in the dearest markets. Competition would result from the actions of a "natural economic man" living in a natural economic order. Competition and the natural economic laws, asserted the classical economists, always work together for the welfare of all. External controls interfere with the natural laws of free enterprise. Each man, pursuing his own interests, will at the same time serve best the interests of the whole community. A system of full liberty, said Adam Smith, would release tremendous economic powers. Business prospered best when left alone.

The defenders of *laissez faire* asserted that the natural laws of economics, leading capital and labor as if by an invisible hand, had decreed that certain men must grow wealthy and others must starve. In 1798 Thomas Malthus declared that population constantly tended to increase beyond the subsistence level; war, disease, and the food supply limited the increase. David Ricardo added that if wages were lifted above the subsistence level, then the workers would raise more children—or at least more would survive. Thus the labor supply would be increased and by the iron laws of economics wages would be forced down again to the subsistence level. Hence there was no advantage to anybody in raising wages. All of these theories were usually quite acceptable to the wealthy industrialists and to the governing classes because they appeared to provide a moral sanction for profits and for existing conditions generally. Inexorable laws had decreed that it was right that things should seem to be wrong in this world.

No classical economists ever held completely to the principle of noninterference in economic affairs. They did agree, for example, that the government should administer public works, education, and the like. Nevertheless, they did insist that the problems of an industrial society could best be met in the long run under a system of free exchange and association. The sagacious

Adam Smith phrased the essential principles of *laissez faire* in these words: "All sanctions either of preference or of restraint, therefore, being thus completely taken away, the obvious and simple system of natural liberty establishes itself of its own accord. Every man, as he does not violate the laws of justice, is left perfectly free to pursue his own interest his own way, and to bring both his industry and capital into competition with those of any other man, or order of men."

The Wealth of Nations, the Bible of Free Trade, had an enormously vital influence. The new capitalist industrialists liked the soothing ideas of free enterprise and the prospects of unrestricted initiative and open competition. Government interference with liberty and trade was now denounced by a respectable and sober Glasgow professor. The successful businessmen of the Western world welcomed his words and hammered and refined them to suit their own ideas and their vested interests. For many years the economic doctrines of *laissez faire* were unchallenged by any important voices. The prophet of Free Trade had triumphed. His followers were to guard and sustain a cause that they found good. Their morale, at least, was high.

Despite the arguments of all these men, nobody could fail to see the wretched consequences resulting for some men from the combination of *laissez faire* and the economic revolution. Thomas Carlyle declared that to say "button your pocket and stand still" was a policy which he would "by no manner or means believe in, but pronounce at all times to be false, heretical, and damnable if ever aught was!" Some men believed that the time had come for a massive attack on poverty, disease, and hopelessness among the ill-starred men who had not fought and scrambled into the class of the well paid and well fed. A growing number of voices said that the doctrines of *laissez faire* were unsound, unjust, and unrealistic. In far-ranging attacks they asserted that Adam Smith and his disciples had embittered the struggle between the rich and the poor and had justified and sanctioned an evil jungle competition among men. Some of their challenges were logical and penetrating; some were not.

So it was that the diverse activities of Western man in the eighteenth century hastened the scientific, economic, social, political, and intellectual changes that have marked a long revolution extending into our own times. Speed, power, mass production, intricate patterns of government, business, industry, all these emerged in the sudden acceleration of man's ability to create material goods. Disputes about the proper distribution of the expanding production of wealth soon led to furious conflicts, to discordant political and economic battle cries, to frequent confusion and despair. Into the equations of human affairs, science and its machines threw new terms. In the whirlpool of changing conditions the nature, spirits, and habits of men remained but clumsily adjusted. The tensions within and between complex and unstable societies soon added point to the proverb that it is easier for a man to take a city than to govern himself.

Man has not been a peaceful creature in the universe, despite his protestations to the contrary. When we read, for instance, about the diplomacy and wars of disordered Europe in the seventeenth and eighteenth centuries we can see several patterns of thought and action that resemble those of our own age. When we study the commerce of ideas and the tides of inventions in the days of our fathers we see inquisitive men immersed in their quarrels as well as their problems. They disputed about what was true and what was not, about what to do and how to do it. They climbed mountains, voyaged dark seas, invented machines, painted pictures, spun and knitted their philosophies, killed their fellows on the fields of battle and in the shadowed alleys. What they did, we do. Perhaps the chief difference between them and us is that we do many things upon a greater stage and grander scale. That daredevil Francis Drake sailed around the world in three years about four centuries ago (1577); our airmen fly around the world in a few hours. Probably about 300,000 men were killed in the Thirty Years' War. On August 6, 1945, one atom bomb caused the deaths of 78,150 people and destroyed three-fifths of the Japanese city of Hiroshima.

The preceding paragraphs suggest several inescapable facts that stand forth in the infinitely complicated processes that we call human history. One, surely, is this: the world owes little to caution, doubt, or faint hearts. The urgent jobs that have faced human beings in the rapid and restless days of the past were not done by men who were slowed down by cynicism, despair, or apathy. What vital and dynamic forces, what torrents of creative energy, have been released by the generations who dared to wander from the customary ways! Long ago Francis Bacon saw the dangers of fear and despair: "By far the greatest obstacle to the progress of science and to the undertaking of new tasks and provinces therein is found in this—that men despair and think things impossible." The fate of man has always depended upon courage as well as brains.

Chapter 27

COLONIES, COMMERCE, AND WAR

"Home-keeping youth have ever homely wits. . . .
I rather would entreat thy company
To see the wonders of the world abroad
Than, living dully sluggardized at home,
Wear out thy youth with shapeless idleness."

William Shakespeare, *Two Gentlemen of Verona*, I, i

THE mind of the historian travels backwards and forwards through time—and sideways and crosswise, too—discerning and tracing the courses of the thoughts and deeds of human beings. He sees impressive feats of achievement as men make new windows into reality. He sees the fates sometimes trampling on the hopes of men, killing dreams. He senses, even though he sometimes can neither describe nor explain, the deep enigmas of the subtle world where the springs of human action lie. He notes the frequently shifting balance of forces, proportions, and values. He is always aware—or should be —that surrounding all human passions and turmoils the indifferent world continues. Babies are born and graves are dug and the wind blows a little dust about the floor.

For most men of later times the unfolding drama of the seventeenth and eighteenth centuries has a particular interest. So far as the Western world is concerned, these years were a time filled with high excitement, young feelings, passions of discovery. Side by side with the wars in Europe were the bright achievements of the scientists, the philosophers, the poets and musicians swiftly described in earlier pages. Economic revolutions moved Western man towards the stage of coal and water power, increased his storehouse of technical knowledge, and looked to the coming victories of steel and steam.

There were the further triumphs of exploration, the founding of still more colonies, the expansion of commercial enterprise far over the seas of the world, the coming of more wars and revolutions as men fought in three continents for land and freedom, gold and glory. "Fame is the spur that the clear spirit doth raise."

It is often remarked, and rightly, that geography is the handmaiden of history. The words of Captain John Smith—they are quoted from his *Generall Historie of the Bermudas* (1624)—are one strong theme of the age: "For as Geography without History seemeth a carkasse without motion so History without Geography wandereth as a Vagrant without a certaine habitation."

Over the Atlantic men came from Europe to make colonies in North America. At first they settled by the seacoast or along the riverbanks. Beyond them were the trackless spaces of a vast wilderness. Slowly that wilderness was to be conquered, mile by mile, all the way to California. Hard tales of courage and survival and death are among our folk-held memories. Place names on the land are the stuff of poetry. The frontier facts and the frontier spirit are a vital part of America's heritage. The reader may now wish to look again at the tumbling lines of Walt Whitman's "Starting From Paumanok," "Song of the Redwood Tree," and "I Hear America Singing." Whitman did far more than sound his "barbaric yawp over the roofs of the world." His voice was the authentic voice of a people slowly spreading from sea to shining sea and dedicated to principles that they have never abandoned. From the woods and the prairies, as well as from the pages of John Locke and Thomas Jefferson, came the laws, the hopes, and the sure facts of liberty.

Some men said that the founding of colonies in America might drain off surplus population. Others declared that such colonies would put "a bit in the mouth of Spain." Those who claimed that they wished to be unfettered in their religion added to the flow of emigrants seeking to "find refuge in another land for God's oppressed people, where a bulwark might be raised against the kingdom of Anti-Christ." For many reasons the settlers, traders, missionaries, and adventurers came across the seas to a new world.

In 1606 the Virginia (or London) Company founded a colony at Jamestown. Slowly the settlers learned that gold and trade profits would not come easily. "Nothing is to be expected there but by labour." The character of the early settlers was poor and at first the colony did not prosper. After tobacco was planted about 1612 the prospects in agriculture brightened and enthusiasm grew. "Be not deceived with the clamorous reports of bad people," wrote Governor Dale. "I have seen the best countries of Europe; I protest to you before the living God—put all of them together, this country will be equivalent unto them, if it is inhabited by good people."

Tobacco ships sailed back to London. Virginia's economic future was assured. So far as its political future was concerned, that was foreshadowed in 1622 when "a house of burgesses broke out" to herald the approaching years of controversy. The colonists frequently objected to the "petty interference and meddlesome objection" of the London authorities. The Virginia colonists of the seventeenth century found that the English governments were strong in assertion, weak in fact. Meanwhile, of course, other English colonists and traders went to other places—to Bermuda, the Barbados, Jamaica, St. Kitts, British Guiana. English buccaneers sailed the seas, then and later. Morgan was knighted and Kidd was hanged.

In 1620 ships were coasting along the rocky shores of New England. They carried Independents who had fled to Holland in 1607 and 1608 seeking freedom of worship. William Bradford tells us that in addition to about a hundred of these men who formed "a core of true believers" there were about sixty-five who were not Independents but "persons sent over by the merchant adventurers to work and not to pray." The men and the ships were on their way to found a new colony.

They never reached their destination. It is usually said that an accidental landing at Plymouth Rock resulted in the first permanent New England settlement. The fact would seem to be that because the food supplies of the Pilgrim Fathers—"especially the beer"—were "much spent," they decided to land and stay where they did, having no more time "for further search or consideration."

"In the name of God, amen; we whose names are underwritten, the loyal subjects of our dread sovereign lord King James . . . having undertaken, for the glory of God and advancement of the Christian faith, and the honour of our king and country, a voyage to plant the first colony in the northern parts of Virginia do by these presents solemnly and mutually, in the presence of God and one another, covenant and combine ourselves into a civil body politic. . . ." These are the significant sentences of the famous "Mayflower Compact."

Not all of the Indians were unfriendly. "Friday, the sixteenth [March, 1621], there presented himself a savage, which causes an alarum. . . . He had learned some broken English amongst the Englishmen that came to fish [near Cape Cod]. . . . He asked for some beer."

Harsh and hard was the first winter. When nearly half of the Mayflower pilgrims had died William Brewster wrote: "It is not with us as with other men whom small matters can discourage, or small discontentments cause to wish themselves home again." These are noble words.

Other colonies were soon planted. "Here nature opens her broad lap to receive the perpetual accession of newcomers." It is a familiar story. The strong-sinewed founders of New England grew in number and sometimes grew in grace. By the side of Massachusetts Bay and Plymouth came Maryland (1632), New Haven (1638), the Carolinas (1663), Delaware, New Hampshire, and Maine (1664), Pennsylvania (1681—a place where there was to be "inviolably and forever freedom of conscience"), Georgia (1732) and the others. In the records of the colonies there appear names famous then and famous now: Jonathan Edwards, Cotton Mather, Roger Williams, Anne Hutchinson, Thomas Hooker.

There were the rivalries with the Dutch in the Hudson River Valley, heavy problems about such places as Manhattan and Fort Orange. There was also mounting evidence of a surging spirit of independence in the New England colonies. "They would be capable, if a drunken governor were sent over, of putting him in the stocks and sending him back again." There were alliances, expulsions, and disputes among the colonists. When some men spoke of "religious freedom" they meant freedom for their own beliefs and not for the faiths of anyone else—this is not unusual in human affairs. Sometimes there were quite violent chapters written in the pages of colonial history. In the journal of Jasper Danckaerts (1680), for instance, we read of the seizure and imprisonment of Carteret, governor of New Jersey, by Andrews, governor of New York: "They entered his home, I know not how, at midnight, seized him naked, dragged him through the window, struck and kicked him terribly and even injured him internally. They threw him, all naked as he was, into a canal, without any cap or hat upon his head, and carried him in that condition to New York, where they furnished him with clothes and shoes and stockings and then conducted him to the fort and put him immediately in prison."

Through tidewater, piedmont, and frontier the settlers, soldiers, and traders traveled. The impulse of sanctuary and the impulse of commerce merged in the frontier stream of continuous movement. Restless men wanted to know what was beyond the mountains and the prairies, the far horizons, and the canyons' rims. Westward the tides of empire moved.

Beyond the northern fringes of New England were the colonies of New France. The planting of French settlements began within a hundred years after the first discoveries of Jacques Cartier in 1524. In 1608 Samuel de Champlain founded Quebec, "the closed-up place," standing by the great St. Lawrence waterway that led to the interior of the continent. Montreal was founded in 1642, Fort Frontenac in 1673.

Champlain explored the southern reaches of the Ottawa River, the Georgian Bay and Lake Huron regions, the areas around Lake Ontario, including the lands down to the lake that bears his name. Nicolet discovered Lake Michigan in 1634. Raymbault and Jogues reached Lake Superior in 1641. Chaumonot and Brébeuf discovered Lake Erie in 1640. Grosseilliers and Radisson explored the territory near Lake Superior in 1659. Other men—some of them were mentioned in Chapter 21—pressed on to the western prairies and down the Mississippi Valley. By the early eighteenth century they had established a series of forts and trading posts from Canada to Louisiana that almost encircled the English colonies on the Atlantic coast. To the south, in Florida and along the Gulf of Mexico, was Spanish territory.

The French fur trade prospered under the Company of New France, the West India Company, and the later Canada Company. Battles with the Indians—especially the Iroquois and the Mohawks—continued steadily. Treaty arrangements were made and broken and made again. Roman Catholic missionaries, particularly the Jesuits, ranged far afield to teach their faith.

"Neighboring countries," a Frenchman once said, "are naturally enemies of each other." This statement, fortunately, is not true. It was true, however, that friendly relations did not prevail between French Canada and "the English of Boston." The French gave the Indians firearms to kill the English; the English gave them firearms to shoot the French.

The French built a thinly spread trading and military empire. The English, on the other hand, made a number of strong colonial settlements in a much smaller geographical area. On a map the French empire in America still looks impressive; it looks much more formidable than it actually was. Behind the claims and boundaries on a deceptive map there must be men and power. The English had both; the French had not. English strength increased with the coming of more colonists, with the taking of New Amsterdam, now New York, in the Anglo-Dutch War of 1664–1667, with the slow and sure profits of trade, agriculture, fishing, and industry. The French strength, on the other hand, did not advance with the years. New France was increasingly vulnerable to the guns and ships and soldiers of "the English of Boston."

On the other side of the planet the main contests for trade and power in the sixteenth century had been between the Portuguese and the Dutch. They had explored, traded, and fought in Africa and the East Indies. In India the Portuguese had a virtual monopoly of trade. Their cities of Damao, Diu, and Goa, seized from the Arabs, became important centers of commerce. Portuguese missionaries were numerous and active after King John III of Portugal decided in 1521 that it was his duty to try to bring the Cross of Christ and Rome to the peoples of the East. The zealous missionaries often tried to do too much and to convert too many. The Hindus were not pleased. Nor did they like the Portuguese guns.

The Dutch East India Company, founded in 1602, soon reached into India to challenge the Portuguese. This great Dutch enterprise, supervised by a board of directors in Amsterdam and ruled by a governor-general in Batavia, was a useful instrument of an active maritime and commercial nation. During the first fifty years of the seventeenth century about half of the seaborne commerce of Europe was carried in Dutch ships. France's Colbert estimated in the 1660's that the Dutch had 15,000 merchant ships, the English 4,000, the French 600. The Dutch East Indies Company paid yearly dividends of 200 and 300 per cent. Now the Dutch were in India; soon they were to drive the Portuguese out of Malabar and several other strategic crossroads of commerce.

The English also sought to trade with India. In September, 1599, an assembly of London merchants gathered at Founder's Hall to talk and plan—they were particularly disturbed by the Dutch control of the pepper trade. On December 31, 1600, Queen Elizabeth I signed a charter establishing "one body complete and politic, in deed and in name, by the name of the Governor and Company of Merchants of London Trading into the East Indies." The purposes of this East India Company, as declared in the charter, were these: "the Honour of our Nation, the Wealth of our People, the Increase of our Navigation, and the advancement of lawful traffic to the benefit of our Commonwealth." The new company had permission to trade in all seas and countries between the Cape of Good Hope and the Strait of Magellan except where the lands were in the possession of a Christian prince living "in amity with the Queen."

Thus there was to be no English competition with the East India Company within the specified areas. The Company was to be ruled by a governor, deputy governor, and twenty-four assistants elected annually by the 218 members. To the executive officers were given considerable powers. In each of the Company's overseas centers, or "factories," the employees of the Company lived together. They were required to be in at a certain hour at night; to say their prayers daily; to be brotherly one to another—there were to be no "brabbles." They were also instructed to be respectful to their superiors and warned of the evils of drinking, gambling, and gluttony. One dispatch from the London headquarters to an Indian station contained the interesting sentence: "For the better comfort and recreation of our employees we have sent Foxe's Book of Martyrs and Mr. Hakluyt's Voyages to recreate their spirits with a variety of history."

Despite the opposition of the Portuguese the English were permitted to establish a trading post at Surat in 1612. In 1622 the English and the Persians defeated the Portuguese, and the Portuguese bothered the English and the Dutch no more. Several English trading posts were founded through the years along the coasts. The big ones were at Madras, Calcutta, and Bombay—the strategic territory of Bombay came into England's hands as a part of the dowry of Catherine of Braganza, the queen of Charles II. In the wake of England's *Peppercorn* and *Trade's Increase* came other ships to trade; the cargoes and the dividends increased.

The encroaching Englishmen continued and extended their conflicts with the Dutch. In 1623 the Dutch seized and killed ten Englishmen at the trading post at Amboina, a deed that caused much anger in England. Thousands of copies of a picture depicting the massacre were distributed by the East India Company. Within a few decades the English had their revenge, if revenge it can be called. The religious, political, and economic wars between France and the Netherlands drained away Dutch power, a process speeded by the commercial wars with England. Exhausted Dutchmen no longer presented a formidable challenge to England in the commercial conflicts that swirled in the East Indies and India. The Portuguese power had declined. The Dutch strength was diminished. The English, it seemed, were the leaders in trade and commerce.

There remained the French. In earlier years the sons of France had not been active in Eastern trade. About the middle of the seventeenth century they began to challenge the English in India as they challenged them in America. In 1664, under the influence of Colbert, Louis XIV chartered the French East India Company, granting it a monopoly of trade for fifty years in the regions between the Cape of Good Hope and Cape Horn. Louis also gave the new company the right to make arms, to build and garrison forts, to raise troops, to declare war and make peace. Five years later a French expedition reached Surat, set up a trading post, and sent out numerous agents to buy and sell. In 1674 the French East India Company bought the Pondicherry territory about a hundred miles north of England's Madras. They established their headquarters at Chandernagor, a few miles north of Calcutta.

Throughout the latter part of the seventeenth century there was a quickening rivalry between the French and English in India, frequent clashes in America. The situation in India was worsened by the fact that the Mogul Empire was approaching its last collapse, an event described at the end of Chapter 13. When the Emperor Aurungzebe died in 1707 the final disintegration of the Mogul power came swiftly. Thomas Babington Macaulay, that master of prose and historical narrative, paints an unforgettable picture of the death agonies of the Mogul age. ("Read a page of Macaulay," wrote England's historian Freeman, "scan well his minute accuracy in every name and phrase and title; contrast his English undefiled with the slipshod jargon which from our newspapers has run over into our books; dwell on the style which finds a fitting phrase in our own tongue to set forth every thought, the style which never uses a single word out of its true and honest meaning. . . .")

> A succession of nominal sovereigns, sunk in indolence and debauchery, squandered away life in secluded palaces, chewing bang, fondling concubines, and listening to buffoons. . . . The restless and shifting elements of the state formed themselves every moment into some new combinations, which the next moment dissolved. In the course of a single generation a hundred dynasties grew up, flourished, decayed, were extinguished, were forgotten. Every adventurer who could muster a group of horse might aspire to a throne. Every palace was every year a scene of conspiracies, treasons, revolutions, parricides. . . . Desolation was in their imperial cities and famine all along the banks of their broad rivers.

In the clouded years following the decay of the Mogul Empire the competition of the English and the French continued. Hostilities broke out again and again. The stakes in India were high. In America, too, the tides of dispute were rising. A keen observer might easily have concluded that only a major war would decide the stormy contest for supremacy.

Upon the European stage the War of the Spanish Succession moved towards its climax in the Peace of Utrecht, an event already described. After Utrecht there was an interlude of rather sluggish drift in Europe, then ugly and rancorous quarrels, then war.

The conspiracies, intrigues, agitations, and alarms that continued in Europe were often far less the results of popular interests and enthusiasms than the outcome of dynastic aims and policies. Occasionally in human history the fascinating chess games of diplomacy have themselves become ends to those who played. The violent results that sometimes came were not really intended by the players. It was the game that seemed to take command. It is also true, of course, that forces of combative ambition, rivalries, and what were believed to be dynastic and national interests frequently mingled. To many men it seemed that the main problems could be solved—after a fashion and for a few decades—only by war. It was idle to suppose that little quarrels and small fluctuations of fortune could settle great issues and achieve great national ends. Only victory in an armed conflict could give sure promise of national advance and security. Such widespread and often incurable convictions and sentiments were themselves a danger to the public peace of the world.

Sensitive points of danger continued to multiply in Europe, America, and India. There was not steadily evident a strong disposition to peace. The diplomatic maneuvers mentioned above were calculated to strengthen the positions of the countries that made them and also the prestige and power of the diplomats in their own lands. They were not planned and carried out to increase the chances of collective security on the international stage. It must be added, of course, that the pressures and strains in Europe and the continents beyond the ocean were often not of a nature to be easily ended by negotiation and compromise.

In 1733 two important events occurred in Europe, each of which might have started a widespread conflagration. Spain and France formed a secret Bourbon family compact, under which they agreed to act together against Austria; there was also included in the compact a reference to the possibility of united action against Great Britain so far as commercial and colonial policies were concerned. Secondly, a limited and short European war developed over the complicated question of the succession to the throne of Poland. France and Spain supported Stanislaus Lesczinski, father of the French queen. Russia and Austria backed Augustus, the Elector of Saxony. Some of this unreasonable and unpopular war was fought on the plains of Poland. Most of the significant chapters were written in Italy. It was important, for instance, that the Spaniards drove the Austrians out of Naples and set up the dynasty of the Neapolitan Bourbons whose unsavory and tyrannical activities plagued and besmirched more than a century of Italy's history.

Despite heavy pressures from England's ally Austria, from George II, and from the English public, Sir Robert Walpole, leader of the Whig government, refused to enter the war. His tenacious efforts to effect a compromise settlement contributed greatly to the arrangements that ended the conflict in 1736. France's skilled and patient Cardinal Fleury obtained the province of Lorraine. Otherwise the political map of Europe was not altered.

Sir Robert Walpole had kept England out of the conflict. He is reported to have said to Queen Caroline: "Madam, fifty thousand Europeans were slain in Europe last year, and not one Englishman."

Even Walpole could not stand against the new and strong assaults that soon pounded against his peace policy. The old enemy Spain now became a foe once more.

British ships had been exporting thousands of tons of goods into Latin America. The Spaniards had seized several of these ships, a step they certainly had a right to take. The British complained that the Spanish were grabbing ships that were not engaged in illicit trade and that English sailors were being tortured and imprisoned. Political and emotional storms in England rose to such heights that intelligence and common sense were swamped. A sea captain named Jenkins told how the cruel Spaniards had cut off one of his ears. Contemporaries are not agreed as to whether he carried his withered ear about in a tin box, a bottle, or in his pocket. In any event, he produced it frequently and told his story. "I commended my soul to my God and my cause to my country." This silly remark, probably quite unlike the one the sailor Jenkins uttered, caught the public fancy.

Walpole at last gave way before the martial clamor and reluctantly declared war against Spain in 1739. Many Englishmen thought the conflict would be a profitable and easy affair. Spain was weak; her treasure ships were numerous. "They are ringing their bells now," Walpole is said to have remarked, "they will be wringing their hands soon." This war with Spain was to lead into a war with France; the war with France was to be followed by the revolt of the American colonies; and this, in turn, was to be succeeded by the long and dangerous struggle with Napoleon. After twenty years of peace and prosperous fatness Britain was now entering upon a series of wars destined to last intermittently for nearly seventy-five years.

In the early months of conflict Britain captured Porto Bello in the West Indies and the public was jubilant. The notes of jubilation soon were stilled when the promise of Porto Bello faded. Patronage had corrupted the armed services. Everything was rusty and out of gear. British naval expeditions to the West Indies had no good results. The attack on Cartagena failed. Combined operations on the Spanish Main were ill considered, badly conducted, and uniformly unproductive. Walpole was unjustly charged with thwarting and starving the British war effort. Then, in 1740, arose the question of the Austrian succession.

In 1740 the Emperor Charles VI, that stupid and obstinate Hapsburg, died without a male heir. He had wanted his daughter, Maria Theresa, to inherit the Hapsburg lands. Under the ancient Salic law she was excluded from the succession. Charles had tried to persuade the major European powers to accept a family agreement known as the Pragmatic Sanction which evaded the legal obstacle of the Salic law and provided for the accession of his daughter. By promises and bribes and after long negotiations, filled with diplomatic finesse, the Emperor Charles persuaded England, France, Holland, Prussia, Russia, and Spain to agree. Charles had to pay high prices to the astute and sagacious negotiators of these countries. He might suspect, but he could not know, that their promises were worth far less than he had paid to get them. In any event, Charles VI died in 1740 and the inexperienced Maria Theresa, twenty-three years old, inherited the miscellaneous and scattered Hapsburg domains.

Shortly after Maria Theresa came to the Austrian throne she was told by Prussia's Frederick II that he would join her in a firm alliance if she would give him Silesia, a strip of Austrian territory lying southeast of Brandenburg, rich in linen industries, fine waterways, and undeveloped iron ores. When Maria Theresa answered that she was prepared to defend her subjects, not to sell them, Frederick seized Silesia, after advancing a plausible claim. The greedy and cynical Prussian also remarked that there would always be lawyers and professors to justify what he had done. Maria Theresa succeeded in gathering an army; it was defeated by the Prussians at Mollwitz in April, 1741.

Several other European monarchs now became hungrily interested in the unstable state of Austria. True, some of them had accepted the Pragmatic Sanction and thus had obligations. Were obligations to take precedence over opportunities? France, Spain, Bavaria, and Saxony thought not. They decided to aid in the dismembering of Maria Theresa's inheritance. France, for instance, coveted the Austrian Netherlands. Charles Albert, the Elector of Bavaria, wanted to be Holy Roman Emperor. The French army united with the forces of Bavaria and invaded Austria. Together they marched into Bohemia in 1741 and forced the Bohemians to recognize the Elector of Bavaria as their king. In 1742 Charles Albert was elected Holy Roman Emperor at Frankfurt.

Maria Theresa, "a woman with the heart of a king," was not idle. She roused her fiery Hungarian subjects against her rapacious foes. Her armies, filled with a new enthusiasm, marched into Bavaria and seized Munich. They also defeated some French forces and forced them across the Rhine. The wheel was turning. The War of the Austrian Succession had begun.

If France took over the Austrian Netherlands, then Britain's liberal trading arrangements with the Austrian provinces would be ended. France would control territory dangerously close to the shores of England. The rival French commercial power would be increased. Economic and political interests seemed to demand that Britain support Austria with men and money. Spain, anxious to recover her former possessions in Italy ceded to Austria in 1713, supported France, Prussia, and Bavaria. France promised Spain to help regain Gibraltar and Minorca from Britain.

The War of Jenkin's Ear between Spain and England thus merged into the War of the Austrian Succession in Europe and "King George's War" in the colonies. There were really two wars: a European fight for the Hapsburg possessions; a commercial and colonial struggle between Britain on the one hand and France and Spain on the other.

For several years the conflict continued in the Austrian Netherlands, in Italy, Saxony, Silesia, in the Rhine Valley, in India, in America. From all the violent fighting there came only one firm and final decision: by the Treaty of Dresden of 1745, Frederick of Prussia kept Silesia and Glotz. Meanwhile Frederick had deserted France. "Happy are they who, having secured their own advantage, can look tranquilly upon the embarrassments of others."

The complex peace treaties of Aix-la-Chapelle, signed in 1748, settled little. Their terms provided for a return to the situation existing before the war— there were a few minor exceptions: Spain, for instance, got the Italian Duchy of Parma. Great Britain handed back Louisburg to the French; it had been taken by a British and New England expedition led by Sir William Pepperell and Admiral Warren. France, for her part, returned Madras, which had been seized from the British in India. These agreements simply meant that the question of predominance or control in India and America and upon the seas had not been decided. The arrangements at Aix-la-Chapelle marked a truce of fatigue, not a peace. The rajahs of India and the colonists of Virginia and New England were soon to see and participate in a more bitter struggle.

"It is by leagues well-concerted and strictly observed," wrote England's Sir Robert Walpole, "that the weak are defended against the strong, and bounds are set to the turbulence of ambition, that the torrent of power is restrained, and empires preserved from those inundations of war that, in former times, laid the world in ruins. By alliances . . . the equipoise of power is maintained, and those alarums and apprehensions avoided which must arise from vicissitudes of empire and fluctuations of perpetual contest." The words of Sir Robert Walpole are an excellent statement of the ideas of many men who have hoped that by treaties and alliances a balance of power might be kept in Europe and the world. Unfortunately, the facts have often bruised and broken the hopes and arguments of many generations of peacemakers. Nevertheless, the hopes of men in their changing forms have proved to be

amazingly durable. The belief in the power and safety of alliance arrangements and a balance-of-power system is not easily abandoned.

A great shift in the European balance of power came shortly after the
Treaty of Aix-la-Chapelle. It was a remarkable diplomatic revolution. The
foes of one war became the allies of the next.

The reasons are clear and the facts are simple. In the first place, it was
inevitable that Maria Theresa should cast about for help in recovering Silesia
from Frederick of Prussia. Her great diplomat Count Kaunitz, working to this
end, was able to bind France into an alliance with Austria. Secondly, it was
natural that Frederick should be alarmed at this turn of events. He turned to
England for support. The English, anxious to protect George II's Hanover,
concluded an alliance with Prussia. Thus, early in 1756, Austria and France
stood ranged against Prussia and England. The stage was set and the Seven
Years' War began.

In Europe hostilities broke out when Frederick of Prussia learned that the
Elector of Saxony had made a secret alliance with Austria. Frederick suddenly
lunged into Saxony and seized Dresden. This was the signal for the explosion
of armed conflict on three continents.

For nearly two years Britain and Prussia suffered a series of reverses. In
April, 1756, the French sailed from Toulon and landed forces on the British
island of Minorca. Britain's Admiral Byng came out of Gibraltar but did not
effect a landing to aid the defenders of Port Mahon. Byng was tried by court-
martial for failing to relieve Port Mahon and shot on his own quarterdeck.
Soon the French occupied Hanover. The forces of Russia, Austria, and France
closed in upon Frederick of Prussia. In India the British lost their post at
Calcutta. Surajah Dowlah, the native ruler of Bengal, was responsible for
the tragedy of "the Black Hole of Calcutta," where several British subjects
died as a result of his wanton and callous cruelty.

The course of the conflict that blazed in America, often called the French
and Indian War, can only be understood in the light of several facts and
factors of geography. In the first place, it must be noted that the Appalachian
Mountains stretched through New England to the Gaspé Peninsula. Through
this mountain barrier between the French and English settlements there was
only one main opening: the Hudson-Richelieu route through the Lake George
and Lake Champlain regions. It was in this general area that famous forts
were built: Carillon, Crown Point, Ticonderoga, Fort Edward, Fort William
Henry. A second inland line of contact and conflict was along the Mohawk
and the stretches up to Lake Ontario, especially from Albany to Oswego
and Montreal. A third line, running through the inland waterways, was
longer: the French traveled to Lake Erie, made a short portage to the Ohio
River, and went down to the Western slopes of the Appalachians to build
forts and check the English who moved across the mountains of Pennsylvania.

Much of the land strategy, tactics, and events of the Seven Years' War in America was dictated by such geographical facts as these.

Long before the great duel began, the English had hoped to cut the Atlantic supply lines to New France by the use of English sea power. They also planned to bottle up the French in the Gulf of St. Lawrence. The French, of course, had other ideas: they wanted to keep the mouth of the Gulf unsealed. In 1713, at the end of Queen Anne's War, England got the strategically important Shebucto, later the site of Halifax—the English began to build Halifax in 1749, the year after the end of the War of the Austrian Succession. They also deported a large number of Frenchmen from Nova Scotia to reduce the danger of French revolt in the event of war with France. Hundreds of French families left the land of Evangeline to live in Louisiana, a strange land far from the green hills of Acadia.

In 1713 the English also got Newfoundland and the Hudson Bay region firmly and finally in their hands when Louis XIV abandoned his claims. To offset these gains and to reply to these dangers the French built Louisburg in 1720. This Cape Breton fortress looked across the waters of the southern entrance to the Gulf of St. Lawrence. Earlier in this chapter it was remarked that Louisburg was taken by the British in 1745 and handed back to the French in 1748.

After 1748 the French began to extend the number and strength of their inland forts in much the same fashion as the Norman and Angevin kings had built their guardian castles in the Middle Ages. From missions, forts, and trading posts floated the flag of France. The English were apparently to be held in their coastal colonies while the unexplored West was to be left to the French. In 1756 Benjamin Franklin was to say that the "English settlements, as they are at present circumscribed, are absolutely at a stand; they are settled up to the mountains."

In 1749 England's George II gave the newly chartered Ohio Company 200,000 acres of land in the Ohio Valley. As the French attempted to extend their chain of wilderness forts to the southwest they were warned to keep off British territory. All of these conflicting claims could have but one result. In 1753 France built Fort Duquesne on the Ohio; it was a good bastion. When George Washington, acting under the orders of the governor of Virginia, tried to take Fort Duquesne in 1754 he was forced to retreat. The French started to move soldiers over the Atlantic. Two of their troop transports were seized by the British; the rest escaped. In 1755 General Braddock was sent to America with two British regiments to push the French out of the Ohio Valley.

In July, 1755, Braddock's advance guard, numbering about 1,400 men, was ambushed about eight miles from Fort Duquesne by some 900 Frenchmen and Indians. Over half the British force was killed or wounded. Braddock, shot in the lungs, died four days later. Those who escaped went back to Virginia with George Washington. The traditional view that Braddock was defeated mainly because he adhered to the column formation prescribed by British army manuals has been proved incorrect. The British authorities who ordered Braddock to take Fort Duquesne left him hampered by lack of money, supplies, transportation, and labor forces. His soldiers were wearied by the task of cutting a road westward from Fort Cumberland. He had no friendly Indian allies. It is not just to hold Braddock, an excellent general, wholly responsible for the disaster that fell upon his army.

The misfortunes that descended upon General Braddock were followed by other French successes in America after the beginning of large-scale hostilities. From Quebec, General Montcalm moved swiftly to capture Oswego. Then Fort William Henry fell into his hands.

In Britain it was widely believed that military operations had been mishandled. The Duke of Newcastle, then prime minister, was blamed for blundering and failure. Natural indignation roared about the rooftops. Under the weight of public rage the detested political machine of Newcastle collapsed. After Newcastle resigned, the nominal head of the new ministry was the Duke of Devonshire. The secretary of state and real leader of the new government was William Pitt. Pitt once said: "I am sure that I can save this country and nobody else can." He now had the chance to make good his boast. With the new man came a new spirit. The years of fumbling and sagging were over. The nation needed imagination, energy, unity of direction. Now England had all three.

Many people found Pitt's arrogance and theatricality offensive. Genius often dwells with infirmity. Pitt reminded a startled House of Commons that he was not beholden to them. "It is the people who sent me here." His arguments were powerful, his invective deadly. "The corrupt and Philistine House of Commons trembled beneath his glance."

Pitt acted at once. He had excellent ideas about the coordination of land and sea forces. He knew the importance of both speed and power. A huge naval construction program began. Large additions were made to naval personnel. New regiments were raised. Young men of ability and vigor, such as James Wolfe and Robert Clive, were given commands; old men were sent home to nurse their gout and reminisce. Efficiency became the watchword. "England has been a long time in labor," Frederick of Prussia is said to have remarked later, "but she has at last brought forth a man." Pitt, with his genius, his oratory, his patriotism, was indeed a great war leader. He was supercilious, priggish, affected, passionate, egotistical, irritable; but he was the architect of victory; he was Britain's greatest war minister before the hour of Sir Winston Churchill.

Pitt's war plans were simple, logical, and daring. In the first place, England would keep France occupied in Europe by solidly supporting Frederick of

Prussia with men and with subsidies. Frederick, son of a military maniac, was battling brilliantly and desperately against France, Austria, Russia, and Sweden. His armies were being cut down; his money was slipping away; every month his position worsened in the face of the massive forces arrayed against him. Those armies of his foes won many victories; but they never clinched them. Frederick's energy and skill in those dark months have won him undying fame among those most competent to judge. Among the admirers of Frederick's military prowess was Napoleon Bonaparte. "The king of Prussia," said England's George II, "is a mischievous rascal, a bad friend, a bad ally, a bad relation and a bad neighbor, in fact, the most dangerous and ill-disposed prince in Europe." Nevertheless, Frederick must be helped because his successes and failures were bound up with the total war effort and the fate of England's cause. "We shall win Canada," said Pitt, "on the banks of the Elbe."

The second aspect of Pitt's war plan was this: by combined operations England would isolate and overwhelm the French outposts of empire. Naval squadrons were sent out to prevent French reinforcements from reaching India and America. The French coasts were raided. Cherbourg was captured and its forts destroyed. British and Hanoverian troops fighting on the Rhine stopped the French from leaving to join the Russians and Austrians in a concerted attack on Prussia. As the flames of war leaped furiously in Europe, death and sorrow entered thousands of homes.

In 1759 Britain's Admiral Hawke won a naval victory at Quiberon Bay on the coast of Brittany and nearly wiped out the French Atlantic fleet. In the same year Admiral Boscawen crushed the French Mediterranean fleet off Lagos. The war at sea gave England naval supremacy; 90 per cent of the French navy was destroyed by 1760. The French slave trade was diminished when Britain took Senegal and Gorée in West Africa. In the West Indies, Britain seized Guadeloupe. In these years of victories Horace Walpole wrote: "It is necessary to enquire every morning what victory there is, for fear of missing one."

French power was soon to be shattered in Canada. In 1758 the British planned to move up the Hudson-Richelieu line at the same time as a land and sea attack was launched on Louisburg and the St. Lawrence was blocked. This campaign was not entirely successful. Although Bradstreet took Fort Frontenac and Forbes got Fort Duquesne—renamed Fort Pitt and then Pittsburgh—the British were defeated at Ticonderoga. Against Louisburg moved an English fleet under Admiral Boscawen and landing forces under Amherst and Wolfe. The besieged and outnumbered French defenders held out as long as they could. In July, 1758, they surrendered. The gate to the St. Lawrence was open.

In 1759 Sir William Johnson captured Fort Niagara. A British land force moved up along the Lake Champlain route under the command of General Amherst, always thorough and usually slow. The army of General James Wolfe was ferried down the St. Lawrence to Quebec. The British soldiers climbed the cliffs at night and defeated Montcalm, the French governor, in a pitched battle. Both Montcalm and Wolfe were mortally wounded.

The key to French Canada was now in the hands of the British. About 60,000 people of French blood, language, and faith passed under British rule. Britannia's flag was planted firm in a domain forever lost to France. The cost of the conquest of Canada, said Pitt, was slightly more than a thousand lives.

In India the French were led by the patriotic and able Joseph Dupleix, the governor of the French East India Company who was later so shabbily treated by his government. Dupleix had long intervened in the affairs of native Indian states with a view to increasing French commerce, influence, and political power through all southern India. He had succeeded, for instance, in setting up a puppet ruler in the Carnatic, a native state in which Madras stood.

The most effective leader of the British was Robert Clive, a man who had come out from England to India as an impoverished clerk in the East India Company, stayed to be a distinguished soldier, returned home to commit suicide at the age of forty-nine. British soldiers under Clive seized Arcot in 1751, forced a French army to surrender at Trichinopoli in 1752, pulled down the nabob of the Carnatic installed by the French and in his place put a Hindu loyal to the British. After the Seven Years' War began, Clive attacked the French and their degenerate lackey Surajah Dowlah, the ruler of Bengal whose infamous orders had been responsible for the Black Hole of Calcutta.

In 1757 Clive met Surajah Dowlah north of Calcutta at Plassey. Clive's army numbered about 3,200 British and native troops and Surajah Dowlah's about 50,000. The result was a rout, not a battle. Clive won vast Bengal at a cost of twenty men. Meanwhile, French naval units had been forced to abandon French forces in India. In 1760 the soldiers under the command of De Lally were defeated by Sir Eyre Coote at Wandewash, a spot halfway between Madras and Pondicherry. The next year Pondicherry surrendered and the French empire in India was no more.

In Europe, Britain's ally Prussia was weakening fast before the onslaughts of Austria, France, and Russia. Part of her territory was occupied by each of her enemies. Pitt had promised to stand by Prussia to the end, to make no separate peace. This was not a popular policy in England.

After Pitt learned that Spain was going to come into the war in 1762 if peace had not been agreed upon by that time, he asked the cabinet to declare war against Spain. His colleagues refused. They refused because some feared it would be difficult to defeat the combined strength of France and Spain on land; some were jealous of Pitt; some simply disliked him; some had fallen under the influence of the new king George III, and he wanted Pitt out of the way.

Pitt resigned. He was succeeded by the Scotsman Lord Bute, famed for his fine legs and his solemn elocution, a former tutor and close friend of George III. He and his king soon found that Pitt had been right in foreseeing the coalition of France and Spain. In 1762 Britain declared war on Spain. British forces took Havana, seized Manila. Meanwhile the prospects of Prussia brightened. Russia's new Tsar Peter III so admired Frederick the Great that he took Russia out of the war. Frederick's iron armies defeated Austria. When France began to negotiate with Britain, Maria Theresa saw that she could not struggle on alone. So Frederick, his obstinacy at last rewarded, kept Silesia.

Peace was made by the Treaty of Paris of 1763. In America, Britain obtained from France Canada and all territory east of the Mississippi. Spain ceded Florida to Britain in exchange for Havana and Manila; as further compensation for her losses Spain received Louisiana from France. Britain kept Senegal, Minorca, and Grenada. Guadeloupe, Martinique, and several smaller islands were returned to France. France was granted fishing rights off Newfoundland and given the two islands of St. Pierre and Miquelon.

In India all conquests made since 1749 by either Britain or France were mutually restored. France agreed to refrain from any political acts in India, to maintain no fortifications or armed forces there. French possessions in India were to be used only as commercial stations. The future lay in the hands of Britain's powerful and eager East India Company.

Thus the French surrendered most of their colonial possessions, much of their overseas trade. Only the names on the land in India and America bespeak the pride and glory that once was Imperial France. The French navy had almost entirely disappeared. The nation was nearly bankrupt.

Britain stood forth as the world's first colonial power. The Peace of Paris of 1763 marked the height of British strength in the eighteenth century—to one Englishman it was "the most honourable peace this nation ever saw." Nevertheless, there were dangers. Before 1763 Britain had always been able to rely on at least one of the European powers to act as her partner in the prolonged dance of European discord. After 1763 Britain herself was so powerful that she was no longer the natural center of coalitions against the aggressive designs of overmighty states. She had become so dangerously strong that the balance of power in Europe was upset. She had no friends on the Continent and no hopes of obtaining any. France and Spain discussed with other nations the possibility of redressing the balance of power should a convenient opportunity arise. There were other problems such as the defense and administration of the empire. England was now vulnerable in every part of the globe.

The years after 1763 provided a challenge for the highest statesmanship. It happened, however, that there were no outstanding statesmen in Europe for several years—England's William Pitt the Elder was usually ill and out of power. Most of the leaders in politics and diplomacy were rather second-rate men, often petty and fumbling and without imagination or vision. Britain was singularly unfortunate. The twenty years after 1763 are chiefly remembered in the history of the Western world because it was then that Britain lost most of her colonies in North America. A great empire was weakened and a great republic was born.

Chapter 28

CONFLICT:

BRITAIN AND AMERICA

"I do not think that any officer since the creation ever had such a variety
of difficulties and perplexities to encounter as I have."
—George Washington, quoted in Douglas Southall Freeman,
George Washington, IV, 396

IN 1714 ENGLAND's Queen Anne was succeeded by George I, first of the
Hanoverian kings. George was a cold, bullying, sensual, and stingy German.
His reign was disturbed by violent political controversies between the Whig
and Tory parties and by the rebellions of the men called Jacobites who wanted
to restore the Stuarts to the throne of England. To add to the ferment there
came the speculative mania and financial disaster called the South Sea Bubble.
Promoters and salesmen raced to speculate and sell shares at substantial profits
to greater fools than themselves. Several of the companies that were founded
in the midst of the boom were based on ideas that are best described as sheer
lunacy or brazen swindling: the importation of Spanish jackasses to breed
large mules; the manufacture of a gun that fired square bullets against infidels
and round bullets against Christians. Common sense gasped and expired as
the prices and paper profits rose to dizzy heights. Then the South Sea Bubble
burst.

To salvage the wreckage left by the exploding Bubble and to reorganize
and lead his government, George I summoned the Whig Sir Robert Walpole
in 1721. Walpole remained the leading minister until 1742.

Sir Robert wanted to maintain the internal equilibrium of the nation. He
wanted peace, appeasement, and prosperity. He was anxious to let sleeping
dogs lie, to provoke no disputes, no public fuss. Holding a low view of human
nature, Walpole believed that most men had their prices. By unscrupulous
patronage, by bribery, by interest pressures of all kinds, and by hard work, he
managed and controlled his own party. In the twenty years of his power im-

portant steps were taken in the development of the cabinet system of government, by which the executive is today rendered answerable to Parliament.
Walpole believed in the solidarity of the cabinet and in the necessity of maintaining the support of a majority in the House of Commons. Cabinet government was slowly coming to mean what it does today: party government.

After the prudent and practical Walpole was gone there came a succession
of ministries. Political machines, such as the vast and powerful creation of the
Duke of Newcastle, rose and fell. William Pitt, whose tales of triumph in the
Seven Years' War have been told on earlier pages, helped to create the conditions and gather the means for history. In the midst of those victories and
before the signing of the Peace of Paris, George III succeeded to the throne.

The new king soon revealed several undesirable qualities. He was arbitrary,
petty, and obstinate, a bundle of complexes. Compromise was a word that he
uttered with reluctance. His mistakes and his tragic fate resulted from ill-
directed abilities, from perverted ideas, from obtuse stubbornness, and from
the incompetence of several futile, pompous, and unimaginative ministers.
It is true, of course, that the able pens of the Whig historians have not always
told the exact truth in their condemnations of George III. It is also true that
some modern scholars have protested against several of the adverse judgments
that have frequently been written about that unhappy monarch. Sometimes
his modern defenders have protested and claimed too much.

George III wished to rule as a king above all parties in accordance with
what he considered to be the national welfare. As a result he was fated to do
his country incalculable damage. He opposed the reform of Parliament, the
emancipation of Roman Catholics, the relaxation of the Irish commercial laws,
and concessions to the American colonies. His exciting and nasty dispute with
John Wilkes showed what he thought of freedom of the press. He supported
the slave trade. He soon had a solid body of supporters in Parliament, sub-
servient "placemen" bound to him by ties of interest in their political and
financial futures. They were called the "King's Friends." This corrupt and pli-
able group controlled the House of Commons. Slowly cabinet government
collapsed.

These years marked the rise and advance of the American War for Independence. To the English Tories there was something darkly sinister in the
American claim "which supposed dominion without authority and subjects
without subordination." Across the Atlantic, General Thomas Gage raised
another question. "Surely the people of England," he said, "can never be such
dupes as to believe the Americans have traded with them so long out of pure
love and brotherly affection."

The Seven Years' War destroyed the French power in America. The English
colonists no longer needed British ships and soldiers to shield them from
French attack. Throughout the colonies, too, there had long been growing a

[88]

View of the Year 1765," by Paul Revere, a
on expressing an American view of the Stamp
ct and the British Parliament that passed it

w: "A View of Boston, 1768," an engraving by
Revere showing British ships landing troops.
ctober, 1768, two regiments of British regulars
were brought into Boston.

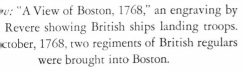

PLATE
XXIX

[89]

[90]

he Battle of Princeton," by James Peale. "On January 3, 1777, George Washington struck another
unexpected blow."

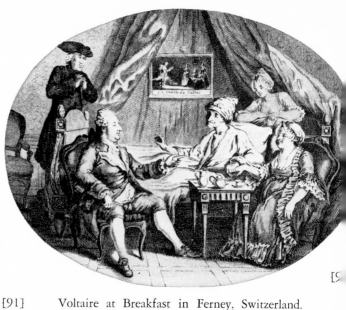

[91] Voltaire at Breakfast in Ferney, Switzerland. "We will die in the hope," said Voltaire, "that men may become more enlightened and more gentle."

"The Coffeehouse Politicians," an engraving made in 1733 by William Hogarth (1697—1764)

[93] The taking of the famous "Tennis Court" Oath of June 20, 1789, one of the first steps on the road to the French Revolution

PLATE XXX

spirit of independence. Virginia had its own Assembly in 1619. Massachusetts was an almost independent commonwealth. Note the significant words used in 1677 by the Lords of Trade and Plantations in London: "The colonists do not conform themselves to the laws, but take a liberty of trading where they see fit." Thirty years later Governor Quarry of Pennsylvania reported that "the Assembly resolved to have all the government and powers in their own hands. They insist on having the regulation of all courts and the nomination of all officers . . . so that they have banished . . . whatever is contrary to their wild notions."

In 1763 more than 2,000,000 British colonists lived in North America. There were the rough and hard frontiersmen, the toiling farmers, the small traders, the merchant aristocracy of the North and the planter aristocracy of the South. These men not only opposed and resisted many policies and laws of Britain, but they also disputed among themselves. The thirteen colonies were divided by distance, by political and social and economic differences, by mutual jealousies and provincial attitudes. In 1754 the colonial legislatures, fearful of losing their independence, refused to accept Benjamin Franklin's proposals in the "Albany Plan of Union" or to take collective responsibility in the impending war with France. During the Seven Years' War it was hard to get even a semblance of concerted action. Thousands of colonists defied, ignored, or slipped around the commercial laws and traded with their foes as well as their friends. Most provincial-minded colonists paid the local taxes imposed by their own legislatures and refused to pay anything more. Their pride and their pockets were sensitive.

As soon as the terms of the Treaty of Paris were signed in 1763 it became clear that a thorough revision of British colonial policy was imperative. There were the threatening Indian questions and the nasty difficulties about boundaries. There were also the colonial grievances springing from the chafing problems of defense, trade, and colonial administration.

The British authorities asserted that there should be permanent garrisons in America to defend the colonists against the Indian tomahawks and a possible French renewal of the war. They proposed a standing army of 10,000 men of which 2,500 would be sent to the West Indies, the remainder to the thirteen colonies. The British felt that a standing army in America would avoid the difficulty of gathering local forces. Only three colonies had provided their quota of troops in the Seven Years' War. Against such a background of fact and experience the British government felt that its proposals were sound and sane. The British were also of the opinion that the colonists should pay a part of the cost of their defense. The colonists were soon to show that they thought otherwise.

In matters of trade it had long been held that protectionist mercantilist policy must keep the colonies in a "firmer dependence" upon the mother country. By the beginning of George III's reign the whole trend of British policy was towards a greater centralization. The colonists resented the increasing interference with their trade—for more than a hundred years British commercial legislation had steadily alienated the men of the colonies, so ambitious for freedom and so hungry for profits. The old British policy rule was simple: British colonies were to import British industrial goods—they were not to manufacture even a hat or a horseshoe nail; the colonies were to export their raw materials to the mother country. It was quite natural that the British merchants and manufacturers should want to restrict the business of the colonists. After the Whig revolution of 1688 the hands and voices of men of business became more important in British affairs. On the other hand, it was also quite natural that the energetic colonists should continue to object with increasing vehemence to British control and coercion.

Many colonists did not observe the laws. It was illegal, for example, to build iron foundries in the colonies or to export iron. The colonists did both. It was illegal to import sugar from the West Indies. The colonists imported sugar. Such products as tobacco, rum, molasses, hemp, flax, and cotton moved over the seas without much heavy hindrance. So long as the British trade laws were not vigorously enforced there was not much trouble.

The age of happy illegalities was soon ended. From the British point of view the changing tides of trade made stern measures absolutely necessary. Before the Seven Years' War the main part of the British export trade slowly shifted from Portugal and the Netherlands towards the colonies. On the eve of the American revolution one-third of all Britain's exports found a market in North America.

The whole question of British trade policy and practice—and other problems, too—was complicated in the years before the War for Independence by the fact that the colonial administrative machinery in England was both corrupt and inefficient. The greatest single weakness was divided power and responsibility. The Privy Council, the Lords of the Treasury, the Customs Commissioners, the Secretaries of State, and the Boards of Trade all shared in colonial administration. Widespread indifference often prevailed about colonial affairs. Important reports from the colonies frequently remained for weeks unopened and unread.

Across the Atlantic in the colonies the representatives of the Crown suffered from this muddled and divided authority at home. In disputes with the colonists the royal agents could not be certain of constant or firm support from Westminster. Sometimes the arguments were about principle and policy. Often they were of a ridiculously personal nature. British upper-class governors and colonels did not usually mix well with democratic colonists. Class sympathies and antagonisms merged with the swirling brew of economic conflict. Benjamin Franklin had a few pertinent and unkind observations to make about some governors he had known: "their office makes them insolent; their insolence makes them odious; and being conscious that they are hated, they become malicious; their malice urges them to continued abuse of the inhabitants . . . representing them as disaffected and rebellious, and (to encourage the use of severity) as weak, divided, timid, and cowardly. . . . Their quarreling with the people is deemed a mark and consequence of their fidelity."

In the face of intermittent, blundering, and often lax control from London the colonists had in fact progressively become masters of their own internal affairs. Because the acts of trade were not steadily enforced, the colonists tended to regard themselves as possessing the substance of both economic and political independence.

It was remarked in earlier paragraphs that after the Peace of Paris in 1763 a general revision of colonial policy and a tightening up of the whole imperial organization seemed in prospect. Several unfortunate steps were taken, all of them pointing towards a new uniformity and rigidity of control. The words of a famous man of the eighteenth century contained a wisdom of which the British government was unaware: "Avoid the ancient insanity of governments —the mania of wishing to govern too much."

In 1763 George Grenville became prime minister of England. Almost immediately a royal proclamation was issued declaring that the land west of the Alleghenies was temporarily closed to settlement. One reason for establishing this frontier "proclamation line" was to conciliate the Indians by protecting them from any exploitation by greedy land-grabbers or traders. Satisfied Indians, it was argued, might help to defeat any French efforts to recover lost territory.

There were other reasons for the British decision. They were not acceptable to the colonists. Several of those colonists, especially in Pennsylvania and Virginia, had looked forward to extensive operations in the Ohio Valley. They were aggrieved and angry at what they deemed selfish and injurious restrictions. The result was a series of long and acrimonious disputes with London. If the British authorities had investigated carefully and had paid attention to these real grievances of the colonists they would have been able to avoid much trouble. Two fatal barriers to wise policy were an absence of wisdom in London and a lack of trust in the colonies. The British ministries cannot be rightly accused of deliberate evil and calculated malevolence. They can be charged, and rightly, with shambling ineptitude and a failure to grapple with the real problems, partly because they failed to understand what those problems were.

Meanwhile many frontiersmen had no patience with a policy of regulated expansion. Hardy adventurers like Daniel Boone swept beyond the Alleghenies into the Ohio Valley. Laws and proclamations were one thing; enforcement was another. The hatreds and grudges and ambitions of the truculent colonists were not to be wiped away by British denunciations and British orders. The compulsion of events that was soon to drive the British government beyond the point of no return was largely of its own making.

In 1764 Parliament passed the Sugar Act. Charles Townshend, Britain's chancellor of the exchequer, "did dazzle them by playing before their eyes the image of a revenue to be raised in America." This Sugar Act placed new customs duties on several articles, including Madeira wine, sugar, and molasses. The duty on molasses from non-English sources was reduced from the prohibitive rate of sixpence per gallon to threepence. The British authorities thought that this reduction would make smuggling less profitable; therefore more molasses from the foreign West Indies would flow through legitimate channels; and hence the total revenue would be larger than when a higher duty prevailed. Grenville hoped to obtain an annual revenue of about £45,000 from this source.

The colonial merchants of the Atlantic seaboard swiftly and loudly pointed out that this act was in fact designed to increase revenue, not to control trade. They had long been in the habit of selling their products in the West Indies and buying sugar and molasses. They had smuggled the latter into the colonies, made cheap rum, and exchanged the rum for Indian furs and slaves from Africa. When Britain reduced this trade the colonists ran short of hard money with which to purchase British goods. Few understood Britain's financial problems. Many thought that the British government, by increasing the "alarming scarcity of money" and the "stagnation of trade" and "the deluge of bankruptcies" was deliberately trying to ruin the colonial economy and limit the colonists' "rights" of self-government.

The colonists ran up large debts in London. Then they tried to issue more paper currency to make up for the hard-money shortage. The British Parliament blocked that plan by the Currency Act of 1764, an act mainly designed to check the enormous issues of legal-tender paper money earlier required to finance the Seven Years' War in America. Meanwhile, as the north coastal cities angrily denounced the tighter trade and revenue controls, the tidewater South continued to demand more liberal bankruptcy laws; the Scotch-Irish of the foothills, who had no love for England, still pressed for the removal of the galling frontier "proclamation line" of 1763.

Meanwhile Grenville went ahead with the British plans to station 10,000 British troops in North America. The home government, as remarked earlier, wanted the colonists to help defray the cost of the new military program. Surely the British taxpayer could be aided by a colonial contribution of somewhat less than one-half of the cost of the standing army! After long and fruitless negotiations with colonial representatives Grenville proceeded to carry through the Stamp Act in 1765, which required stamps purchased from the government to be placed on such articles as legal documents, calendars, advertisements, newspapers, and pamphlets.

The colonists saw many more implications in the Stamp Act than the obvious one of taxation to help maintain a standing army in America. If the British Parliament proceeded to extend its taxation system would that extension measurably decrease the "power of the purse" in the hands of the colonial assemblies? Would the proposed standing army be used to coerce the colonists as well as to defend them? If Parliament could tax the colonists for one thing could it not tax them for another? "Power to tax is power to destroy."

It is hard, in a few sentences, to seize the mood and atmosphere of those vanished years. London was astonished at the unexpected speed and violence of the colonial reaction to the Stamp Act. James Otis of Massachusetts said that this one piece of legislation did more "to stir opinion" in the colonies than all that had gone before. The Stamp Act was indeed a focal point for disaffection, especially among lawyers and men of business.

Meanwhile, in the midst of a running fire from America, the Grenville government continued to call for money to reduce outstanding colonial bills of credit. Hard money was scarce in America because it was being sent to England at a time when the colonies were in an economic depression. To many colonists it seemed that Englishmen wished to regulate commerce to their own advantage at the same time that they were taxing the colonies to get more revenue.

The stamp tax could not be collected. Westminster was far from the colonies. There was a wide gap, wider than most English statesmen knew, between their ideas about the colonies and the facts of the American situation. The colonists, rising in wealth and power, many of them living in the independent Puritan tradition of resistance, could be very formidable opponents. It was natural that they should be irritated by the swiftly changing policies of London. It was natural, too, that as British cabinets moved from one mistake and subterfuge to another, the minority of radicals in the colonies should increase in numbers and vehemence.

So far as the colonists were concerned, measures such as the Stamp Act were offensive and arbitrary. Royal officials in the colonies were attacked. British goods were boycotted. Earlier opposition to British trade regulations had been on the grounds that such controls harmed colonial trade. The challenge of the colonists to the Stamp Act rested on the basis of the new claim that it was beyond the legal right of Parliament to legislate for the colonies. The nine colonies represented in the Stamp Act Congress that met in New York in October, 1765, insisted that the Parliament at Westminster had no legal right to impose "internal" taxes. They declared that the colonial legislatures were not subordinate to Parliament but equal in status to it. Most of the legal arguments advanced by the colonists were unsound; but what mattered, in a purely practical sense, was that the conditions in the colonies made the famous "taxation without representation" issue inevitable.

In the midst of this dark march of events, the commercial and industrial interests in England complained heavily about the effects of the American boycott. On the other hand, men like Edmund Burke sympathized with the colonists. William Pitt spoke against the Stamp Act on the grounds of expediency. In 1766 the act was formally repealed because it was "attended with many inconveniences" and likely to be "productive of consequences greatly detrimental to the commercial interests in these three kingdoms."

A minority of the House of Lords objected to the total repeal of the Stamp Act because it "would make the authority of Great Britain contemptible hereafter." They were perhaps partly mollified by a Declaratory Act that was added to the repeal. It stated that Parliament "had, hath, and of right ought to have, full power and authority to make laws . . . in all cases whatsoever."

Controversies as to whether the colonies should be coerced or conciliated burst forth in successive cabinets. Grenville replaced Bute; Rockingham replaced Grenville; Pitt replaced Rockingham; then came Grafton and North. In 1767 Charles Townshend, chancellor of the exchequer, was faced with a deficit of about £500,000. To him the way to collect the needed money seemed clear. He decided to revive the policy of taxing the colonies to pay for imperial administration. He also carried out another reform of the American customs service. His Revenue Act of 1767 levied new import taxes upon such articles as tea, glass, paper, lead, and paint. British statesmen never properly understood the distinction made by the colonists between taxes imposed to raise revenue and taxes imposed to regulate commerce. Townshend's new measure set another match to the stack.

Again the colonists objected. "How is this mode," asked the Quaker lawyer John Dickinson, "more tolerable than the Stamp Act?" The nonimportation agreements in the colonies were revived. British trade slumped once more. There were riots throughout the New England colonies, especially in Boston. In October, 1768, 4,000 British troops were quartered in that restless capital of Massachusetts. Across the seas in London, William Pitt spoke against his colleagues and denounced the taxation of the colonies. "America is obstinate. America is almost in open rebellion. Sir, I rejoice that America has resisted." Edmund Burke again warned the cabinet of the dangers of its policy.

In March, 1770, the British government decided, after long debate, to repeal all of the Townshend duties except the tax on tea. Many men then hoped for a quiet return to peaceful conditions. That hope was soon blasted when a squad of British soldiers in Boston fired into a mob of young men and killed several of them. The excited youths had meant no harm. The British soldiers were guilty of a stupid and criminal mistake. Popular passions in the colonies were further inflamed by this "Boston Massacre."

Over the seas in England several voices were raised against "the impudence, the absolute madness" of the attitudes and actions of "weak, uninformed ministers and an irresponsible monarch." The British governments had certainly bungled badly. Late in the spring of 1770 the Tory Lord North became prime minister. During these dramatic months great skill and tact were needed in British administration. These qualities were not displayed. The British ministers never examined critically the bases of their decisions. The colonists could neither understand nor tolerate British policies that were alternately strong and weak, sustained and relaxed, just and unjust, astute and foolish.

At this point in an unhappy chapter of history the members of the House of Commons who had financial interests in the East India Company became concerned about the fact that their company had about 22,000,000 pounds of tea in British warehouses. A new Tea Act, passed in 1773, allowed the East India Company to send its tea directly to America and to sell it there without paying the British export duties of twelvepence per pound. Such a piece of legislation threatened to ruin many private merchants in America and to put the East India Company in a monopoly position through its selected colonial agents. The American merchants were not inclined to bow mildly before a Tea Act that threatened their interests. In Charleston they deliberately stored the tea in damp cellars. At Philadelphia and New York they compelled several ships' captains to take the tea cargoes back to England. In December, 1773, some of the followers of Sam Adams, disguised as Indians, boarded ships of the East India Company in Boston Harbor and threw overboard about 350 chests of tea valued at £15,000. The next day "tea lay strewn like seaweed along Dorchester beach." The Tea Act was a grand miscalculation.

The startled British cabinet ministers and directors of the East India Company asserted that the unexpected and violent colonial reaction to the Tea Act was an invasion of sacred property rights. The colonists must be punished. Lord North declared: "We are now to establish our authority or give it up entirely; when they are quiet and return to their duty we shall be kind." Britain must subdue "the insolent violence of those men who have so grossly violated public authority."

There was now to be no conciliation, no attempt to restore confidence. In 1774 George III and Lord North attempted to carry through a fatal and miserable policy of coercion. The charter of Massachusetts was suspended; the port of Boston was closed; the capital was moved to Salem; the right of public meeting was restricted; British officials accused of crimes were to be tried in Halifax or Great Britain; new provisions were made for quartering British troops in Boston—this was a renewal of the offensive Quartering (Billeting) Act of 1765.

The Quebec Act of 1774 gave further offense to the colonists, although it was not intended in any sense to be punitive. The act extended the boundaries of Canada to the Ohio to include the old Northwest and thus cut off the western lands coveted by Massachusetts, New York, Pennsylvania, and Connecticut. Occupation was to be discouraged and the land was to be protected for the fur trade. The French Canadians were generously allowed to retain French civil laws and to keep and practice their religion. This concession to the French Roman Catholics was especially offensive to the Puritan men of New England.

A petition from Massachusetts was dismissed by George III as "frivolous and vexatious." He wrote to Lord North; "The die is cast. The colonies must either triumph or submit. If we take the resolute part they will undoubtedly be very meek." Had not General Thomas Gage, governor of Massachusetts, assured him that the colonists would yield?

The tidal wave of punishment might have swept the colonial shores bare of resistance; but it did not; it did precisely the opposite. Hard in consequence was to be the fate of the First British Empire.

The Boston Port Act was to become effective on June 1, 1774. When the Virginia House of Burgesses declared that June 1 should be spent in prayer and fasting, the angry governor dissolved the Assembly. Several of the members then called for a Continental Congress to discuss the "united interests of America." In September, 1774, the First Continental Congress was invited to meet in Philadelphia.

To Philadelphia came representatives from all of the thirteen colonies except Georgia. After long disputes between the moderate and radical groups —the moderate Galloway Plan was defeated—the Congress issued a Declaration of Rights and Grievances which said that all of the rights of the colonists came from "the immutable laws of nature, the principles of the English Constitution, and the several charters or compacts." The British government was asked to repeal the recent "Intolerable Acts." Until grievances were redressed there was to be a constant boycott of trade with Britain. Soon British regulars and colonial militiamen began to exchange shots around Concord and Lexington.

In May, 1775, a second American Congress made a feeble gesture towards peace by sending the Olive Branch Petition to London. As this petition emphatically denied the legislative power of the British Parliament there was little hope of its success. "We are reduced to the alternative of choosing an unconditional submission to the tyranny of irritated ministers, or of resistance by force. . . . The latter is our choice. . . . We have counted the cost of this contest, and find nothing so dreadful as voluntary slavery." The Congress also appointed George Washington commander-in-chief and general of the

American Army. Washington was a conservative and aristocratic Virginia planter descended from a Norfolk county family. Able, quiet, and patient, Washington attracted to himself in an extraordinary degree the loyalty and confidence of his soldiers and the trust of most of his fellow countrymen.

The British army sent out to reconquer the angry and active colonists was commanded by Sir William Howe, the successor of General Thomas Gage. British forces totaled about 40,000 men, widely distributed over long and vague fronts. Problems of supply were tremendous. The theaters of war were widely spread. Sailing vessels had to carry much food and equipment across the Atlantic from England. The British usually had little difficulty in occupying the naked towns on the coast; but they could not seize and hold the vast spaces back from the sea.

The colonial armies were also plagued by difficulties. It was often hard to get and keep troops. The paper money issued by the Continental Congress became worthless. Some colonists preferred to sell supplies to the British, who paid in gold. Many were reluctant to go out of their own colonies to do battle with the British. Nevertheless, the colonists did achieve some early victories, and the taste of triumph was exhilarating. In May, 1775, Ethan Allen's men of Vermont took Ticonderoga and Crown Point. In November, 1775, Richard Montgomery's forces took Montreal. There were, of course, defeats; but the nimble colonial armies often melted away to fight again. More and more, their tattered banners became symbols of resolution.

Across the Atlantic the despairing voice of Edmund Burke warned of events to come. "Nobody will be argued into slavery." "The question with me is not whether you have a right to render your people miserable; but whether it is in your interest to make them happy." Many of Burke's sentences are famous still. "Magnanimity in politics is not seldom the truest wisdom." "A great Empire and little minds go ill together."

In January, 1776, Thomas Paine, that vitriolic international revolutionary, published his explosive pamphlet *Common Sense*. This was another link in a fatal chain of events. The bold and incisive Paine demanded complete separation from Britain. "Now is the time," he said, "of continental union, faith, and honor." More than 120,000 copies of his inflammatory pamphlet were sold in America within three months. Few could fail to be moved by the eloquent sentences with which Paine concluded his statement of the cause of America and, as he saw it, of mankind:

> O, ye that love mankind, ye that dare oppose not only the tyranny, but the tyrant, stand forth. Every spot of the old world is overrun with oppression. Freedom hath long been hunted round the globe. Asia and Africa have long expelled her. Europe regards her like a stranger, and England hath given her warning to depart. O, receive the fugitive, and prepare in time an asylum for mankind.

In March, 1776, Sir William Howe was compelled by George Washington to evacuate Boston, carrying off his troops by sea to Halifax. Howe's conduct on this occasion—from a military point of view—was indefensible. In the early summer he was more successful: he came south and captured New York. But the capture of New York was only a little victory in a war that was getting bigger and promised to be long.

The third American Congress now met at Philadelphia. It was there that Thomas Jefferson drafted the Declaration of Independence—the rest of the drafting committee consisted of Benjamin Franklin, John Adams, Roger Sherman, and Robert R. Livingston. By this Declaration the frayed and weakening bonds that united Britain and her colonies were cut at last.

Throughout the first part of the famous document there echoed the familiar doctrines of John Locke. "We hold these truths to be self-evident: That all men are created equal; that they are endowed by their Creator with certain inalienable rights; that among these are life, liberty, and the pursuit of happiness. That, to secure these rights, governments are instituted among men, deriving their just powers from the consent of the governed; that, whenever any government becomes destructive of these ends, it is the right of the people to alter or to abolish it. . . ." In the second part of the Declaration were listed the "injuries and usurpations" of George III, "all having in direct object the establishment of an absolute tyranny over these states." The last part of the Declaration, in magnificent and moving language, asserted "that these united colonies are, and of right ought to be, free and independent states; that they are absolved from all allegiance to the British crown, and that all political connection between them and the state of Great Britain is, and ought to be, totally dissolved."

The British soon drove Washington out of the New York area and pushed the dwindling patriot army towards Philadelphia. During the following winter Washington crossed the Delaware, captured Trenton, and won a victory at Princeton. There, in 1777, the British made a serious miscalculation. By such errors the fates of armies and the outcomes of wars have sometimes been decided. According to the British plans, Sir John Burgoyne was to move down from Canada to join Sir William Howe at Albany. A connection would thus be established between Canada and New York, and New England would be cut off. But Howe sailed away to fight the battle of Brandywine Creek and captured Philadelphia. This operation took longer than Howe had expected. Thus he was not able to put pressure upon the Americans, who were gathering and bracing themselves to oppose Burgoyne's army advancing down the Hudson. In October, 1777, Burgoyne's position had become hopeless. At Saratoga he was forced to surrender his entire army to General Horatio Gates.

Through a terrible winter of 1777–1778 at Valley Forge, George Washington's forces waited and suffered and slogged and sloshed week after week, month upon month. Stomachs were often empty, feet and bodies cold, nerves taut and raw. From the north, the Canadian raiders plunged down to kill and steal. Congress was weak. There were some self-seeking colonists who did what they could for themselves. Every war brings forth such men. They may know little of the fire and death of battle, the murderous hails of lead, the sudden knife ripping the throat. Theirs is a different world and they make the most of it. They often thrive and grow sleek. When the war is over, other men forget.

Across the seas stood France. In February, 1778, when snow and gloom lay over Valley Forge, France allied herself with America and entered the conflict on the side of the colonies. From the colonists' point of view, this was a fine event, a shining hour. For several years France had been sending munitions to aid America. Now she had moved into open war against Britain.

Let us not misunderstand the motives and reasons for the French action. France did not move into war in 1778 solely because liberty was at stake— the French Revolution was still more than ten years in the future—or to uphold and extend the ideals of the Declaration of Independence. Many Frenchmen were not unaware that here was a chance to reverse the decisions of the Seven Years' War. Others feared that France might suffer from any reconciliation between Britain and her colonies. French affection for the American colonists must not be confused with French hostility to Britain. The French were well aware of what they thought were their own interests. They were not yet the standard-bearers of liberty in Europe or anywhere else.

Early in 1778 the French attacked the West Indies and began to hamper British communications with the American mainland. American privateers, led by the famous John Paul Jones, harassed British shipping. French financial aid helped to bolster the American cause. Meanwhile George Rogers Clark used the Kentucky settlements as a base to conquer the Northwest. The small British garrisons at Kaskaskia, Cahokia, and Vincennes were overwhelmed.

In 1779 Spain came, late and eager, into the war against Britain. While Spain moved hungrily in the Mediterranean, France sent a fleet to strike at British power in India. In 1780 the Netherlands were added to the list of Britain's foes. Disputes about the rights of neutral nations to trade with all belligerents led to the formation of the League of Armed Neutrality. Russia, Prussia, Sweden, Denmark, the Holy Roman Empire, the Kingdom of the Two Sicilies, and Portugal all took measures short of war against Great Britain in "armed neutrality" arrangements. Meanwhile Britain continued to seize the ships of neutral maritime powers trading with her enemies.

The war increased in scope and violence. Britain captured St. Pierre and Miquelon and the French posts in India and defeated the French in the West Indies. When Spain tried to seize Gibraltar she failed. Meanwhile Britain's foes grabbed British territory on the west coast of Africa and in the West

Indies. Britain's foreign trade was heavily hit across the seas and in Europe. Scores of British merchant ships were captured by the enemy. Maritime insurance rates reached a height of 30 per cent. In 1781 Lord North's government floated its last war loan; the cabinet said that the British economy could stand no more. Meanwhile men were fighting in America, Africa, and Asia. They were fighting on the seas. The campaigns in North America were now only a small part of a stormy and widespread struggle.

Upon the American scene, the British obtained a limited success only in the south. In May, 1780, Sir Henry Clinton captured Charleston—Savannah had been taken in 1778. Clinton then moved by sea to New York. Through the long months the struggles in the south continued at Camden, King's Mountain, Cowpens, Guilford Courthouse, and all through the trackless swamps and mountains. In North and South Carolina, Lord Cornwallis won several battles; but he could not profit from his victories because stubborn guerrilla warfare in the interior compelled the British, again and again, to move along the coast. Up in the North the American Benedict Arnold deserted to the British and later went to fight with their forces in Virginia. His name is not in the corridors of Valhalla.

Slowly Cornwallis moved to Yorktown, that famous spot between the James and York rivers. It was at Yorktown that disaster fell upon Cornwallis in October, 1781. George Washington and Count de Rochambeau suddenly marched down from New York. At the same time, Count de Grasse, the French admiral, brought his fleet into Chesapeake Bay. Cornwallis was caught in a trap. His position was hopeless. He surrendered his entire army.

The military catastrophe at Yorktown virtually ended the war in America. Lord North declared: "It is all over!" Even George III conceded that further hostilities against the colonies would be useless. For the First British Empire this was the hour of ruin.

In 1783 peace arrangements were finally concluded at Versailles. To France, Britain returned St. Pierre and Miquelon, her West African settlements, her islands of Tobago and St. Lucia in the West Indies, her trading posts and privileges in India. To Spain was returned Florida, which she had lost in 1763, and Minorca, which she had lost in 1713. Spain, for her part, handed over the Bahamas to Britain. The British and the Dutch mutually restored all conquests, except in one minor case.

The thirteen colonies were given their independence as the United States of America. The territory of the new nation was to extend west to the Mississippi and north approximately to the Great Lakes and the St. Lawrence; the boundary west of the Great Lakes was left to be settled at a later date. To the Americans was granted the right to fish off the shores of Newfoundland. Private debts contracted before the war were to be paid. The British and the

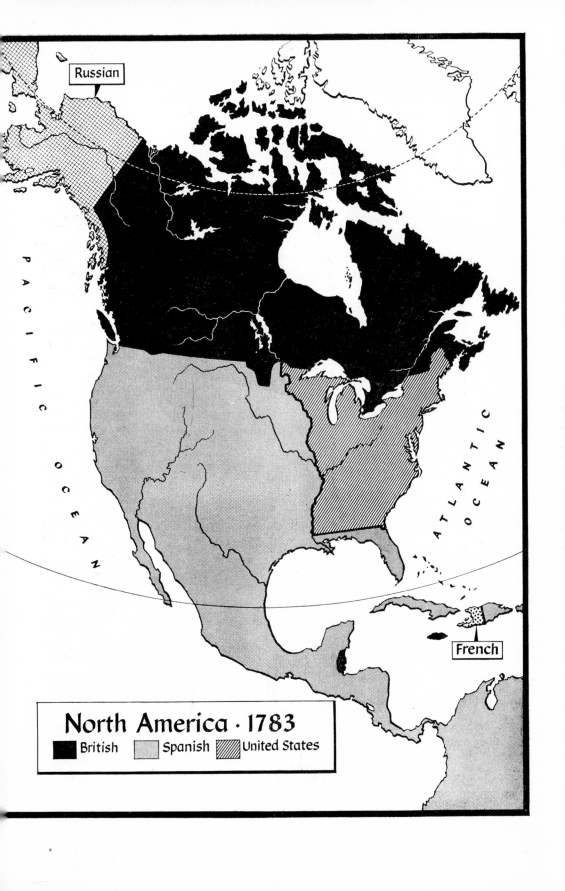

Russian

PACIFIC OCEAN

ATLANTIC OCEAN

French

North America · 1783

■ British ▨ Spanish ▨ United States

Americans were to have the right to navigate the Mississippi. Thousands of United Empire Loyalists sought safety and happiness in Canada, especially in the provinces of Ontario and New Brunswick. Across the tracts of time many descendants of the Loyalists returned to live in the United States. Harsh and bitter memories have been blurred and softened by the mists of the years.

Long before the end of the War for Independence there had been several plans for union proposed for the colonies. Now something had to be done, and soon. In 1781 the Articles of Confederation set up a "firm league of friendship and perpetual union," an ill-knit alliance of states in which the central government had no power to tax or to control commerce or the western lands. It was to be expected that there would be bitter conflict among the rival states and almost immediately the first disputes blazed forth. The main arguments were about boundaries and tariffs; there were also scores of other tangled and thorny problems. Said George Washington: "We are fast verging towards anarchy and confusion." Were the fruits of the victory over Great Britain to be lost in an internal breakdown?

At this critical hour of discontent and discord several thoughtful American leaders of will and character, including George Washington, John Jay, and James Madison, decided to try to establish a strong central government and a "more perfect union." The result, after long discussion, was the Constitutional Convention held in Independence Hall in Philadelphia between May and September, 1787, to "devise such further provisions as shall seem . . . necessary to render the constitution adequate to the exigencies of the Union." Among the fifty-five delegates were such giants as George Washington, Benjamin Franklin, James Madison, Alexander Hamilton, William Patterson, Rufus King, Robert Morris, Charles Pinckney, James Wilson, and John Dickinson.

Then, as later, there were many disputes about the projected constitution. How strong was the central government to be, how powerful the states? There were also arguments about the basic ideas and ideals that should guide and determine policy. Some of the opinions were reminiscent of the ones that had appeared in Cromwell's England a hundred and fifty years earlier. Were the propertied and well-born men to share political power with all the others, with the poor, the feckless, the loafers, the incompetent? James Madison was doubtful about the wisdom of "the unreflecting multitude." Alexander Hamilton of New York spoke, often at length, about what he called "the impudence of democracy." Hamilton saw no gains to a state in constitutional arrangements where all men met on equal terms. "All communities," he said, "divide themselves into the few and the many. The first are the rich and the well-born, the other the mass of the people . . . who seldom judge or determine right."

The voices of those who agreed with Hamilton did not entirely prevail in

1787. Nevertheless, it was true that no complete political democracy was achieved in the United States in 1787 or for several generations to come. A democratic revolution is often slow. But the road to the future was open, and the American dream beckoned and shone.

The preamble to the Constitution completed in 1787 said this: "We the people of the United States, in order to form a more perfect union, establish justice, ensure domestic tranquillity, provide for the common defense, promote the general welfare, and secure the blessings of liberty to ourselves and our posterity, do order and establish this Constitution of the United States of America." The Constitution was ratified by the required number of states when New Hampshire recorded its approval on June 21, 1788. George Washington, so often the leader of his countrymen in peace and war, was unanimously chosen President. Thomas Jefferson was Secretary of State. Alexander Hamilton was Secretary of the Treasury.

The new Constitution of the United States asserted the doctrine of popular sovereignty: all power ultimately rested with the people. It stated precisely the basic principles of federalism and the manner in which powers were divided between the state and national governments. It carefully set forth the principle and practice of the separation of powers and a system of checks and balances. It clearly stated and exactly defined the duties and responsibilities of the executive, legislative, and judicial branches of the government.

The first ten Amendments to the Constitution—the Bill of Rights—were written to protect the rights and freedoms of all individuals. In the United States no laws can be made that invade or restrict the freedom of speech, press, or religion. Every citizen is protected against arbitrary arrest or imprisonment.

The men who made the Constitution of the United States knew that they were present at a great moment in the history of the Western world. How great it was only their descendants could tell.

Thousands of books, monographs, articles, and newspaper columns have been written about the American War for Independence. Some of the writers have been men armed with knowledge and blessed with skill. They have avoided capital blunders of fact and interpretation. They have not lost sight of the shining realities by slumping over their documents and looking at little else. Distinguished modern students of American history—Samuel Eliot Morison, Douglas Southall Freeman, Henry Steele Commager, Allan Nevins, Dexter Perkins, Avery Craven, John Bartlet Brebner and their fellows—have never been unimaginative, rigid, mechanical specialists, the masters of narrow seas. They have preferred to have their business in great waters. They have also been sharply aware that a recitation of facts alone cannot convey a sense of the throbbing action and slashing ideas of a pulsing past. They have tried to catch and hold the spirit of our yesterdays as they have disputed and described in their books, in the learned journals, in the press, on radio and television programs. All this they have done with wisdom, enthusiasm, and energy. These men, and many others, have helped to continue the long and shining revolutionary tradition in the United States.

That revolutionary tradition is still strong and vigorous. Pulses are quickened today by names that leap and echo from the past: Brandywine, Saratoga, Monmouth, Valley Forge, Germantown, Cowpens, Charlestown, Long Island, Fort Washington, Trenton, Princeton, Moore's Creek Bridge. Thousands of men and women and wondering children have walked about the battlefields of Yorktown and Bunker Hill or among the restorations at Colonial Williamsburg. They have read the guidebooks and gazed upon the monuments. Others have looked at the reconstructed forts built at the spots where George Rogers Clark did his brave and desperate deeds at Vincennes and Cahokia. Still others have departed from the usual tourist and folklore roads and have become interested in such things as the strategy and tactics of the Battle of Brooklyn Heights—it is a difficult task, these days, to visualize the Battle of Brooklyn Heights or to see in the mind's eye the marching soldiers and the musket puffs when all around in Brooklyn is rolling the relentless flood of the automobiles and the sophisticated pedestrians of the twentieth century.

A few tourists and travelers may recall the words of George Washington: "My inclinations are strongly bent to arms." More, no doubt, remember that the founders of the United States of America were dedicated to certain principles that they believed were self-evident. Of such things are the fibers of patriotism and loyalty made. Despite the words of the pessimists, there are no signs that the spirit of 1776 is a weakened or dwindling thing. There is a wide understanding of the reasons that moved the colonists to fight and win the American War for Independence. There is a wide awareness, too, of the principles and the passions that have impelled generations of Americans to march, tramp, or trudge towards the present hour in the history of the world and the life of a great republic.

Thomas Jefferson once stated a significant part of the philosophy of freedom in these words: "The God who gave us life gave us liberty at the same time." He also said: "Error of opinion may be tolerated where reason is left free to combat it." In these twin statements of Jefferson stream and sing two of the national principles of the United States: liberty under God and freedom of speech. Such liberties can be defended only by those who know what they safeguard and why they fight. If they do not know, then they may find out after they have been defeated.

Chapter 29

REASON AND NATURE:
IDEAS AND IDEALS

"O Nature, sovereign of all beings! and ye, her adorable daughters, Virtue, Reason, and Truth! remain forever our revered protectors! it is to you that belong the praises of the human race; to you appertains the homage of the earth."

—Paul Henri Thiry, Baron d' Holbach,
The System of Nature

UPON this little planet Earth, whirling through the gulfs of the great night, uncounted generations of men have lifted up their eyes and wondered about the destiny of themselves and their race. Sometimes, like Pascal, they have been frightened by the silence of the infinite spaces in the vaults of immensity and the vastness of the menacing dark that hems them in. Often, too, they have knelt to worship mystery. Some have become faithful soldiers and servants of the world's religions, bearing amazing messages, spending time and tithes and energy to their soul's health, teaching men not to think of themselves more highly than they ought to think—the voice of God, says the Book of Job, asked out of the whirlwind: "Where wast thou when I laid the foundations of the earth?"

Still other men, looking at the hushed silence of the cosmos, have become convinced that in an indifferent and omnipotent universe there are no true gods to worship, no purposes, hidden or revealed. Man, they assert, is destined to perish completely in the vast death of the solar system. Man, they say, is a lonely creature in a hostile universe. Without bitterness or impotent rebellion he had best make the most of his charted destiny, which is extinction. "The slow, sure doom," wrote Bertrand Russell, "falls pitiless and dark." All men, all their "imperishable monuments," will be blotted out.

Such conflicting hopes and despairs have been present in all the rhythms of human history. Plagued by danger, disease, and doubt, harassed by relentless foes, mankind has refused to stop its advance. Man has never surrendered. He has obstinately gone on into the unexplored unknown; he has still fought onward, godlike in his persistence. His tale is a tale of grimed and gray marches and countermarches, footholds and advances won and lost. He has delighted in scoring his points against the fates. He has steadily reduced the quantum of the unknown. With all his little human frailties, he has stubbornly kept his vigils in the brooding nights.

Down a labyrinth of many roads men have pursued their individual hopes and ambitions and held their own ideas about the nature of the universe and the future of mankind. They have agreed about some things, disagreed about others. The intricate lacework of human ideas and actions can never be wholly perceived and understood. Even the facts that we can discover do not easily fit into categories or lend themselves to neat classification. The appearance of uniformity is often deceptive. The golden keys of final explanations elude our clutching fingers. Whenever a writer finds clear and certain patterns or laws in human affairs he is tiptoeing away from the difficult problems. He may have the right answers because he has asked the wrong questions.

The reader may now remark that several famous historians, philosophers, and economists have attempted to embrace all individuals and events in sophisticated systems of thought and explanation. This statement is true. It is also true that the system builders have evaded or sadly defaced the facts to suit the demands of their arbitrary arrangements. The dust of time has settled over many comprehensive philosophies of history once held by their builders to be suffused with certainty and bright with hope.

Each age sees its own enlightenments. Each generation sees how many of the final answers of yesterday were studded with errors. Albert Schweitzer once remarked: "Truth has no special time of its own. Its hour is now— always." He might have added that many of man's ideas, true and false, shift and change in ways that are unpredictable. He might have said, with Gotthold Lessing, that men have often held truth in their hands and known it not.

This chapter describes some of the beliefs and attitudes of our ancestors in the eighteenth century. We do not share all of their certainties or their optimism, but we do share some of their hope.

In the Middle Ages it was quite widely agreed that this life on earth was a pilgrimage, a preparation for the blissful hour when the faithful would be gathered together to live in felicity forever. When the Renaissance years came to Europe the pens and voices of the humanists were more concerned with man in this world and less with what happened to him in the next. The waves of secularism that surged over Europe in those hours of enthusiasm and achievement did not recede. In the eighteenth century, that era usually called the Age of Enlightenment, many men insisted that the Golden Age of man was not in the threadbare past but in the future. "The old age of the universal man must be sought in the modern world. The Greeks lived in the youth of the world." Man, said the philosophers of the eighteenth century, could build a Heavenly City here on earth. He could do it soon, given the will, knowledge, and enthusiasm. The reader of this book may recall the witty and brilliant passages of *The Heavenly City of the Eighteenth-Century Philosophers* in which Carl Becker describes the efforts of the philosophers "to finish and furnish and make resplendent the Heavenly City of their dreams."

The "climate of opinion" in the eighteenth century, the Age of Enlightenment, the Age of Reason, was one in which the magic and pervasive words "reason," "common sense," "compromise," "nature," "balance," "moderation," and "nature's laws" were accepted and respectable. God the loving and personal Heavenly Father tended to become God the Mathematician, God the Great Architect of the Universe, God the Engineer. An increasing number of men renounced or ignored the traditional revelations of the Church and the Scriptures. Once again, as so often in human history, man boldly ventured to equip the Almighty with attributes that man thought He should possess.

To the thoughtful men of the eighteenth century—especially to the educated city laity—the universe fashioned by the workmanship of the Great Architect and Engineer was an efficient and orderly machine. God had revealed His purposes in His works. The laws of God were recorded in Nature.

> All are but parts of one stupendous whole
> Whose body Nature is, and God the soul.

Upon all the cosmos the immutable laws of Nature had imposed a general harmony. Only among human beings was there dislocation, jostling rivalry, and conflict. Might there not be some principles of "moral Newtonianism" to rule the actions of men and society similar to the laws of "attraction" that Newton had discovered in the physical universe? Could these unknown principles, if they did exist, be discovered by Reason? Was Nature's universe really a system that worked together for good? In the eighteenth century, man became very much concerned about himself, about such problems as empiricism, the association of ideas, benevolence, self-love, the laws of psychology, sensationalism. Scores of treatises on moral philosophy, "natural religion," and human understanding came from the pens of reasonable men searching for new and undiscovered laws of nature and man. These years were filled with debates and explorations, with a long preoccupation with the cult of Reason, sometimes with conclusions far too simple and adulterated. "The illumination became dark with excessive light."

The Deists of the eighteenth century denied the supernatural in religion and insisted that revelation was contrary to reason. It was not proper, in this polished society, "to teach one's haggard and unreclaimed reason to stoop unto the lure of faith." Nothing, said the sagacious philosophers, was above the grasp of man's understanding. By taking thought man could lay bare the secrets of heaven and earth. God the Mathematician, God the Great Architect of the Universe, had revealed Himself in Nature. The inalienable rights of man, for instance, were to be seen in His handiwork. Said Alexander Hamilton: "The sacred rights of man are not to be rummaged for among the old parchments or musty records. They are written, as with a sunbeam, in the whole volume of human nature, by the hand of divinity itself, and can never be erased or obscured by mortal power."

Surely, said the intelligent and discontented sons of the Enlightenment, it should be possible for scrupulously reasonable men to discover and use natural laws to shape a society that would correspond to the general harmony of a rational and intelligible universe. Surely, said those who followed the physical theories of Isaac Newton and the psychological theories of John Locke, the world and society of mankind could be altered to conform with Nature's fixed and changeless logic. "The ideas, the customs, the institutions of men, if ever they are to attain perfection must obviously be in accord with those laws which Nature reveals at all times to all men."

So it was that many representative thinkers of the eighteenth century said that if restless and hopeful men used the tools of Reason they could add cubits to their stature. It was the task of creative and articulate pioneers to abandon the vague and stultifying futilities of the past and to recast all human society according to the laws of Nature and Nature's God. The Marquis de Condorcet, author of the *Outline of the Progress of the Human Mind*, asserted that there was no limit set to the perfecting of the powers of man. Honest and vigilant individuals had a moral duty to breathe a new and vigorous life into the thought, the imagination, and the social ideas of the civilized world. To defy or scorn the universal natural order was to invite disaster. Men had suffered too long from the self-inflicted wounds of ignorance. They had traveled too long upon the dreary and treacherous roads of superstition.

The busy pens of the eighteenth-century philosophers explained that the ideas of their predecessors were sweepingly wrong-headed. These invigorating philosophers, these apostles of reason and progress, were certain that with the aid of Reason they could set things right. In a regenerated society of reason, toleration, and enlightenment there would be no more evil, no more confusion and conflict. The new Kingdom of Man would be freed from the fetters of ignorance, stupidity, unreason, and superstition. The good life would be perfected on earth. The end of the long night was at hand. Said Voltaire: "Society will succeed in time in rectifying its ideas; men will learn to think." Human knowledge and human happiness went hand in hand. The political and social reformers of the Enlightenment agreed that if they rejected completely and positively all of the unreasonable heritage of the past, all the paraphernalia of dogma, then man and society would indeed be made perfect.

The Marquis de Condorcet contemplated the emerging world with enthusiasm:

> What a picture of the human race, freed from its chains, removed from the empire of chance as from the enemies of its progress, and advancing with a firm and sure step on the pathway of truth, of virtue, and of happiness, is presented to the philosopher to console him for the errors, the crimes and the injustices with which the earth is still soiled and of which he is so often the victim! It is in contemplating this vision that he . . . truly exists with his fellows in a paradise which his reason has created, and which his love for humanity enriches with the purest of joys.

Whatever is reasonable, asserted the stalwart men of the Enlightenment, should be taken as authoritative in religion as well as in science. Because God was a reasonable Being, His truth was reasonable; because man had the gift of reason, he could comprehend that truth. This conclusion is one of the main reasons that the eighteenth century was an age of skeptical toleration, an era of the skeptical idealism of Bishop George Berkeley and impregnated with the general skepticism of such men as David Hume, Edward Gibbon, and Voltaire. This is also the reason the cold Deists continued to attack revelation, miracles, and prophecy—all the Deists believed in a "natural religion" and a "reasonable morality." A concept of a mechanical universe ruled by natural laws did not harmonize with a belief in revelation or any transcendental or supernatural interference with the orderly processes established by the Great Architect. "The defect of the eighteenth century theology was not in having too much good sense, but in having nothing besides." Deism was in fact an empty word, an abstract creation of metaphysics.

It was probably inevitable that the formidable growth of rationalism should have produced a few atheists. La Mettrie and Helvétius were probably of that small group. Holbach insisted that he believed in no Supreme Being. These men were not influential. Somebody once remarked that their main "influence" was that they made men shudder. "Was there something obscene and blasphemous going on at night at Holbach's house?" Most of the important thinkers of the age stopped far short of atheism. "In the opinion that there is a God," said Voltaire, "there are difficulties; but in the contrary opinion there are absurdities."

Many streams flowed into the main flood of rationalism in the eighteenth century. The intolerance displayed by men and states in the earlier wars of religion brought its inevitable reaction. The influence of the rational thinkers of Greece and Rome had steadily broadened in the years following the Renaissance blazes of light. The critical spirit had been given still greater impetus by the march of science and the words and proofs of Locke and Newton and their fellows. Then, too, the eyes of Europeans had often been turned to far horizons. "No works were so popular during the two centuries following the discovery of America as the tales of travellers describing the marvellous new lands and strange peoples of the Far East and the Far West. Some of them told of naked savages living in piety, virtue, and happiness, without priests, Bibles, or creeds. Along with the Noble Savage the Chinese Sage became the great critic of European faith and morals." Certainly traditional religion was weakened. Secular codes of ethics were encouraged; some of them were quite independent of religious belief; this is a custom that has continued until the present day.

Thomas Paine spoke for his age when he remarked that "the insulted German and the enslaved Spaniard, the Russ and the Pole all began to think. The present age will hereafter merit to be called the Age of Reason." In 1714 Dean Jonathan Swift said that "God hath given the bulk of mankind a capacity to understand reason when it is fairly offered, and by reason they would easily be governed if it were left to their choice." The naked individual reason, it seemed, had no need to draw upon the accumulated capital of the ages. The importance of the past shriveled; what was most significant was the mind of man, moving in the Here and Now. Said Voltaire: "What light has burst over Europe during the last fifty years! . . . It is the light of common sense!"

It is difficult to stress too strongly the enthusiastic faith in reason and science and the concern for practical reforms that filled the beings of enlightened men in the eighteenth century. The following pages will show how several outstanding leaders of the Enlightenment explained and defended their belief in reason, progress, liberty, toleration, humanitarianism, service, brotherhood, equality, education and the natural rights of man. The words and actions of these men brought them into conflict with many forms of monopoly, with many traditions and crumbling dogmas, with entrenched interests, with such institutions as the Church and the monarchy, with the privileges of the proud and powerful nobles. The ideas they found and spread had deep and far-reaching consequences for all the Western world.

In the works of the philosophers of the eighteenth century we see quite clearly the cast of thought, the bias, and the doctrines characteristic of the age. These philosophers were mainly men of letters, men who popularized the heady ideas of the Enlightenment. They were often writers of impertinence and curiosity who broadcast their words of corroding doubt and satire all over Europe. They discredited old ideas. They attacked many existing institutions, often under the guise of defending them. They wrote about civil liberty and self-government. They demanded reforms.

The philosophers wrote for a reading public that was steadily widening, especially among the educated and thoughtful commercial men of the middle class. That public wanted facts and ideas set before it in stimulating, clear, and simple language. If the writers could be clever and witty, so much the better. From many of the philosophers the readers obtained what they sought. They sought books. They read pamphlets. The reforming ideas filtered and soaked and spread. The complicated censorship controls in France were evaded in scores of ways. Forbidden books and pamphlets were easily obtained. Many of them were apparently published in such places as Cologne and Amsterdam but actually printed in Paris. "The business going forward at present in the pamphlet shops of Paris," wrote Arthur Young on the eve of the French Revolution, "is incredible. . . . Every hour produces something new. Thirteen came out yesterday, sixteen today, and 92 last week. . . . Nineteen-twentieths of these productions are in favor of liberty and commonly violent against the clergy and nobility. It is easy to conceive the spirit that must thus be raised by the philosophers. The fabric they illumine and criticise may soon, I fear, be destroyed and consumed by the thunderbolt of the people."

One famous philosopher was Montesquieu, a French baron and judge who first came into the public eye when he published his brilliant *Persian Letters* in 1721. Montesquieu's book apparently contained the letters of two wealthy Persians who were describing for their friends back home what they thought about their experiences on a visit to Europe. The whole work was in fact a thinly disguised satire upon the state of things in France. "The king is a magician who persuades men to kill one another though they have no quarrel. What else but magic would make them so irrational?" In a clear reference to the expulsion of the Huguenots by Louis XIV in 1685 one of the Persians wrote of the peculiar notion that the king could "increase the number of the faithful by decreasing the number of the subjects." Here, surely, was much spice and delight for the critics of French society and government.

The work for which Montesquieu became most widely known was his *The Spirit of the Laws* published in 1748; within two years there were twenty editions. This encyclopedic volume was based upon years of research and study. Unlike many writers of his age, Montesquieu was a hard-working and serious scholar. "Study has been for me a sovereign remedy against the troubles of life, and I have never had a grief which an hour's reading will not dissipate." In *The Spirit of the Laws,* Montesquieu's great learning sometimes got in his way. The prose is often intricate and labored; there is nothing light or sprightly there.

Montesquieu carefully gathered facts about the governments and societies of the world, past and present. Then he discussed the relation of established laws to the nature of the countries in which they existed. He concluded that natural conditions determine the character of a people and that character determines what form of government will suit each country best. "Law in general," said Montesquieu, "is human reason, insofar as it governs all the nations of the earth; and the political and civil laws of each nation should be but the particular cases to which the human reason is applied." In his opinion, there is no one best form of government that will suit all nations. The nature of a people should determine whether they should have a government by aristocracy, based on moderation; by monarchy, based on honor and loyalty; by republican democracy, based on political virtue; by despotism, based on fear. He thought that the two best governments for liberty-loving peoples were monarchies and republics; monarchies should be large states, republics small. He believed that Nature intended France and England to be limited constitutional monarchies.

Montesquieu's most famous contribution to political thought was his doctrine of the separation of powers, an idea of massive consequence in the history of the United States. By dividing the system of government into three parts— judicial, legislative, and executive—and by keeping each part from encroaching upon the domain of either or both of the others Montesquieu believed that liberty could be maintained and defended. He thought that he saw this balance and division of power in the English constitutional system, a form of government he much admired. More than half a century earlier, John Locke, who was also a man of compromise and moderation, had written his opinion about the idea now put forward by Montesquieu: "It is an eternal experience that any one who possesses power tends to abuse it. In order that power should not be abused it is necessary so to arrange matters that power should be checked by power."

Most famous of all the philosophers was Voltaire, born in 1694 and christened François Marie Arouet. Throughout his long life (1694–1778) the dynamic and lynx-eyed Voltaire was a courageous and enthusiastic crusader against tyranny, stupidity, intolerance, cruelty, bigotry, and superstition. What Voltaire wrote two centuries ago has not lost its edge today. He still deserves to be read and read again. Voltaire is a great dead writer; but many of the issues he wrote about are still very much alive.

Voltaire was not a great scholar; he was no pioneer or pathfinder. He was a skeptical rationalist who had something to say and who, in saying it, excited and astounded his contemporaries. His peculiar and inimitable genius was displayed in a miraculous mastery of words, filed and polished paragraphs, a flawless felicity of style. In Voltaire's prose there are no mutinous sentences, none of the cancerous verbalisms that eat into sense. When Voltaire's piercing gaze was turned upon a man, a custom, or an institution he could describe and approve or condemn with a skill none could equal and few could imitate. His deft craftsmanship, so deceptively simple, was the envy of many of those who read his pages. His ideas flew about like sparks and threatened to ignite the dry tinder of the Old Regime in France. His wit was mordant, his anger bitter and terrible, his marching paragraphs like battalions moving through a campaign of organized demolition. The modern editions of Voltaire's work contain about ninety volumes; in those volumes are several masterpieces; they are not masterpieces because they are two centuries old, but because they were written by Voltaire.

When Voltaire was a youth he spent about a year in the Bastille because he was said to have been impertinent to the Regent; then he wrote a drama and got a pension for it; then he became royal historian to Louis XV, partly because Madame de Pompadour admired him. In 1726 he went to spend three years in England. There he found that the lower classes wore shoes and ate white bread; he also found liberty, and liberty he loved. "An Englishman," he wrote, "goes to heaven by the road he pleases." In 1734 he published his *Letters on the English Nation.* "He left France a poet; he returned to it a sage." In 1738 there appeared his *Elements of the Philosophy of Newton;* in 1751, his laudatory *Age of Louis XIV;* in 1753, his *Essay on Manners;* in 1759, *Candide;* in 1763, the *Treatise on Tolerance* ("If you would be like Jesus Christ be martyrs and not executioners.") There were, of course, scores of other works, ranging from the large *Philosophical Dictionary* (1764) to the brief paragraphs of his many pamphlets. Voltaire was a historian, critic, essayist, storyteller, dramatist, poet, and many other things besides.

The reputation of Voltaire grew rapidly as he moved brilliantly across the literary skies. It was hard—it is hard—to be neutral when confronted by his name. Some men found him subversive, combative, noisy, always making trouble and the fiery precursor of more trouble to come. They did not approve of his sharp-witted boldness, his stinging satire and irony, his flouting, bantering, and badgering—why, for instance, describe the brave and patriotic soldiers as "the regimented assassins of Europe?" Other men said that Voltaire had unique and impressive claims to be considered a sage, a tiger of rational argument, a man who epitomized the wakening, questioning, and mechanomaterialistic age in which he lived. Posterity has accepted the latter view. Men of later ages still repeat some of the epigrams and sentences that were remembered in Voltaire's day and should count for something in ours. "I do not agree with a word that you say, but I will defend to the death your right to say it." "It is forbidden to kill; therefore all murderers are punished unless they kill in large numbers and to the sound of trumpets." "Democracy seems suitable only to a very little country, which must be happily situated. Small though it be, it will make many mistakes, for it will be composed of men."

The speculative and inquisitive intelligence of Voltaire found several foes to challenge. One of his main principles, of course, was this: a man's spirit or intellect must never be compelled to yield to force. Therefore Voltaire continued, full of vitality, to attack all kinds of tyranny and unintelligent oppression, all kinds of bigotry and intolerance. He considered the feudal and ecclesiastical system of the state to be an enemy of freedom, an unlovely thing riddled with decay. His corrosive criticisms, so often quoted, were a part of a long campaign against the orthodox men and ideas of his age. Voltaire never stopped attacking the Church and the state for their defense of what he believed to be a socially pestilent system filled with intolerance and wrong. When Voltaire denounced the Church (*"Ecrasez l'infâme!"*) he was not attacking the religion of Christ. He was attacking specific evils. Many men, of course, were appalled and angered at Voltaire's belligerent and fierce mockeries, his strident and strenuous denunciations. He was execrated as a blasphemer, an enemy of the souls of men, an arch-heretic, a soul-destroying messenger of Satan, a fiend. Joseph de Maistre said that "to admire Voltaire is the sign of a corrupt soul."

It is usually easier to say what men are against than what they are for. A penetrating and considered statement about the positive beliefs of Voltaire would fill many pages. Here it is perhaps sufficient to say that Voltaire was certainly not an agnostic on the one hand or an orthodox Churchman on the other. He was tempered by Deism; but few men would venture to call him a Deist. Voltaire apparently believed, rather vaguely, in a Supreme Being, filled with "spotless purity, entire justice, inexhaustible energy." He once wrote: "If God had not existed, it would have been necessary to invent Him." A recent writer has remarked that Voltaire "missed the peculiar emotion of holiness," the feeling of awe and the impulse to worship that is at the core of all real religion. It may be so. Perhaps it is idle to speculate further. And yet, is there not something of the "emotion of holiness" in Voltaire's part in the defense of poor Jean Calas?

Voltaire has confused many men, living and dead. The makers of the French Revolution, for instance, hailed him as a prophet and put him in the Pantheon (1791). They perhaps forgot that he once had said:

> Thou hast not given us a heart for us to hate and hands for us to kill. Make us help each other to carry the burdens of a painful and passing life. Let not the small differences between the clothes that cover our feeble bodies, between all our inadequate languages, between all our imperfect laws, between all our silly opinions, let not all these nuances which distinguish the atoms called men be signals for hatred and persecution.

Far different from Voltaire was Jean Jacques Rousseau (1712–1778). Rousseau's early life was the life of an irresponsible vagabond. When he was sixteen years old he fled from the home in Geneva where he had been unhappy and neglected. All through his career Rousseau remained pathetically restless and maladjusted, cursed with deep psychological ills. He was always frustrated and bitter, always misunderstood, always running away, always filled with a sense of persecution. He fought with his mistress and he fought with his few friends. He was a morbid dreamer, a brooding anti-intellectualist, a passionate, sensual, and spontaneously bellicose being who harped on the fact that all the world was at odds with him. He trusted nobody. He was a man who never belonged, an outsider, a weak and unstable and sensitive creature who had been "turned out in the world," as David Hume phrased it, "without a skin."

It was this "self-torturing sophist, wild Rousseau," who started to set society on fire at the four corners. Madame de Staël said that Rousseau "inflamed everything." In 1750 he wrote his first *Discourse,* on the *Arts and Sciences;* and in 1753 his second, on the *Origin of Inequality Among Men.* At once he became a storm center of controversy. In these famous books Rousseau showed the "sublime creative genius"—the phrase is Mirabeau's—that has excited and disturbed several generations of men. Every page of his prose, it seemed, crackled with the ideas and eloquences of a visionary. Nothing was thin, nothing cold. Here was throbbing intensity, fierce emotion, mystic hope for men. Logic and passion were fused in the "strange and concentrated glow" that illumined Rousseau's writing. The thrusts and impulses of all of Rousseau's prose, so filled with aphorisms and epigrams, were mainly intuitive and emotional, springing from the deep wells of instinct and imagination. He often influenced the feelings of men more than their minds. In human affairs the reactions of the heart, glands, and viscera are sometimes more important than those of the brain.

The two *Discourses* of Rousseau asserted that the arts and sciences had "not tended to purify morals" and that civilization was a form of slavery, corruption, and decay, a mottled decomposition of what had once been beautiful. The modern world was a hideous and burdensome thing of misery and waste, a hideous distortion of the holy plan of Nature, a denial of the deepest cravings of man. In the vast depths of his psyche, said Rousseau, every man was essentially good; civilization had mixed and muddied ends and values and had made people evil, greedy, and immoral. These ills were the inevitable results of bad institutions and bad education. "Astronomy is born of superstition; eloquence of ambition, hatred, flattery, and lying; geometry of avarice; physics of a vain curiosity; all, and morals, too, of human pride. The arts and sciences owe their birth in our vices."

The original brotherhood of man, asserted Rousseau, was now a brotherhood no more. The emotions of fraternal sympathy and social pity had been blocked and choked by the cold-eyed scoundrels who had made the ruthless laws and conventions of civilization. Instead of a decent fraternity and companionship there was a moral spinelessness, snobbery, and corruption, swords and daggers, shot and shell, the grooved conformities of the mass mind.

> The first man who, having enclosed a piece of ground, undertook to say "this is mine," and found people simple enough to believe him, was the true founder of civil society. How many crimes, wars, murders, how much misery and horror would not he have spared the human race, who, pulling up the stakes or filling the ditch, should have cried to his fellows, "Beware of listening to that impostor. You are lost if you forget that the fruits belong to all and the land to none."

Peace, happiness, and innocence, declared Jean Jacques Rousseau, were only to be found among men living a primitive and natural life. He glorified the noble savages, the good peasants, those simple and honest people like his own Savoyard Vicar. To him the urgings of the human heart and "natural morality" were to be preferred to such things as an artificial morality declared and enforced by legislation and custom. A "natural" and simple love of the God of the heavens above and the earth below was far better than all the ritual and dogma in Europe. A "natural" education was fit and proper for a child who needed self-expression; nothing else would do. All governments, laws, customs, and institutions, asserted Rousseau, should be rebuilt and changed to conform with man's natural goodness. If anything of decent consequence was to be achieved in this world, then man must be given a free hand.

Again and again these provocative and incendiary ideas appeared in the *Discourses,* in the *New Héloïse* (1760), *Emile* (1762), and the *Social Contract* (1762). The ideal of the simple life appealed to many men who felt that the answers of Reason were not enough. The enchantment of the new gospel seized and held their hearts and minds. How could any honest individual condemn Rousseau's idea of the spontaneous virtue and the self-sufficiency of the common man, the ordinary man who toiled behind the hedges down the lane? Did not the vivid sentences of Rousseau show the passionate sincerity that must commend itself to all sensitive children of God and Nature? "Man is born free and is everywhere in chains." "It is the estate of the wealthy that steals from mine the bread of my children. . . . A bondholder whom the state pays for doing nothing is scarcely different in my eyes from a highwayman who gets a living at the expense of the passers-by." "Every idle citizen is a rogue." It is not surprising that such sentences were remembered. The leaven of Rousseau's epigrams and ideas worked among many men seeking to battle against oppression and injustice.

There were other men who did not fall under the spell of Rousseau. They were displeased and pained to see his passionate paragraphs. Voltaire, for instance, did not think well of *Emile* and Rousseau's teachings about self-expression and education. Nobody then knew how much these ideas of Rousseau were to influence Switzerland's famous Johann Heinrich Pestalozzi and, through him, America's John Dewey and thousands of his followers. "This book," wrote Voltaire, "makes me feel like going on all fours although it is more than sixty years since I lost the habit. . . . Nor can I take ship to go out and join the savages in Canada; first because the diseases that bear me down oblige me to stay near the greatest physician in Europe. . . . second because . . . the example of our nations has made the savages almost as cruel as we are."

The famous *Social Contract*, much more balanced and rationalistic than Rousseau's other works, was not read widely in his own day; its tremendous influence was in the future.

Rousseau said that the original "social contract" was an agreement unanimously accepted by all the people. Every individual surrendered his natural liberty to all his fellows, fused his will into the mystical General Will, and agreed to obey it. The General Will was sovereign, absolute, and indivisible.

Sometimes a voter could be deceived about the General Will. "If I voted the wrong way, it proves nothing more than that I was mistaken, and what I took to be the General Will was not so. If I had carried my way I should have done what I truly did not wish and then I should not have been free." Again: "No law can be unjust since no one is unjust to himself." The state could have no interest contrary to that of every citizen. True, as remarked above, the individual may not know what is right or what his real will or interest actually is; but society does know; and, if the individual does not conform, society will lock him up. "Men must be forced to be free." The individuals taken together are sovereign; taken separately they are subjects. Sometimes, indeed, even the vote of a majority did not reveal the true General Will.

When "Gracchus" Babeuf, editor of *The Tribune of the People* during the French Revolution, looked into a mirror in the morning he said that he saw "one twenty-millionth of a sovereign power and one complete slave." The mystical and ill-defined General Will was perhaps a secularized form of Oliver Cromwell's "inner light." In any event, the idea has caught and fired the imagination of millions of men during the past 200 years.

The writings of Rousseau often stimulated people to profess a disdain for the "artificial" and "unnatural" aspects of eighteenth-century civilization. Some of the denunciations of the "artificial" were themselves artificial; the hypocritical faddists are always with us. On the other hand, the teachings of Rousseau did result in a genuine and broadening interest in the human feelings of sympathy and compassion and in the common, ordinary things of life. The "cult of Rousseau" leaped over most of Europe. Rousseau became the symbol of the "man of feeling," the sensitive man, the truly natural human being uncontaminated by the stains and sins of civilization. He also became the prophet of the coming age of Romanticism, the herald of a later interest in nonrational human motivations, the harbinger of a stronger and more self-conscious nationalism.

Rousseau has often been claimed as a champion of democracy. For makers of political democracy and revolutions Rousseau certainly supplied new forms of the "popular sovereignty" theme, new surges of optimism, new slogans. On the other hand, his insistence upon the "general will" and the moral solidarity of the state persuaded some founders and followers of totalitarian theories to insist that Rousseau belonged to them. Ideas supercharged with emotion and fanaticism have often seemed to possess some thin tendrils of connection with Rousseau. In the days of the French Revolution, Robespierre defended the dictatorship of the Committee of Public Safety by saying "Our will is the general will." Karl Marx used the idea of the "general will" as a bulwark of his "class solidarity" theories. Rousseau's ethical idealism certainly stimulated the philosophical idealism of Immanuel Kant and the idealist philosophers of the nineteenth century. Wilhelm Hegel borrowed heavily from Rousseau in his exaltation of the power and glory of the state and his explanation of the mystical onmoving forces that pressed ahead inexorably to determine by the laws of the Hegelian dialectic the destinies of nations and men.

Jean Jacques Rousseau would probably have been quite surprised by certain inferences drawn from his seminal works. In Rousseau's writings, like the Book of the Revelation, the diligent searchers have usually been able to find something to support their own conclusions. They have been aided, of course, by the fact that there are several contradictory assertions and ideas in Rousseau. "Inconsistencies," Emile Boutmy once remarked, "are the characteristic quality of men who have thought much, created abundantly, and destroyed on a broad scale." It is probable, indeed, that the obvious contradictions in Rousseau have troubled the men writing about them more than they ever disturbed Rousseau.

Stanislas Girardin quoted Napoleon Bonaparte as saying: "The future will decide whether or not it would have been better for the peace of the earth if Rousseau and I had not existed."

The singular achievements of Montesquieu, Voltaire, and Rousseau shine brightly in the history of the eighteenth century. By the side of these men moved many others, each adding to human thought and knowledge and helping to shape and build the world of the Enlightenment. Denis Diderot (1713–1784), for instance, decided to "gather together the knowledge scattered over the face of the earth" and to put the vast compilation into a great encyclopedia for the edification of mankind. Perhaps, indeed, the self-consciousness of the bourgeois class might be increased and even the masses might be taught some of the truths of the new world. With the help of the scholar Jean d'Alembert, mathematician and perpetual secretary of the Academy of Sciences, Diderot began his great task of systematizing and synthesizing all the scientific and philosophical knowledge of his era. The result was the famous

Encyclopedia. The first volume appeared in 1751 and the last two—volumes 34 and 35—in 1780.

Diderot, always a man of contagious enthusiasm, was able to persuade most of the outstanding thinkers in Europe to collaborate and contribute articles: Beccaria, Buffon, Helvétius, Montesquieu, Raynal, Rousseau, Voltaire, and hundreds of others. Diderot himself wrote more than 1,100 articles; he was one of the most profound and original thinkers of his time and deserves more reading and more praise than he has had in recent years.

The *Encyclopedia* was a huge compendium of facts and ideas. There were articles on about 60,000 topics, and many of those articles were belligerent and unconventional. Several polemical pieces stressed the abuses of the government and the Church. To the whole project, in fact, the authorities of the state and the Church stood adamantly opposed. The seventh volume of the *Encyclopedia,* for example, was suppressed in 1759 because it was deemed to contain dangerous propaganda, which it did.

Again and again there was an insistence upon the great themes of human progress and perfectibility; the superiority of reason as opposed to revelation; the value of practical solutions in a materialistic world; the growth of science; naturalism in art; the evolution of government and the need for drastic reforms in the whole structure of society. Many of the articles contained constructive ideas about education, individual liberty, the decrease of upper-class privileges, the expansion of a generous humanitarianism, the reform of the laws. "It is the good legislator," said Helvétius, "that makes the good citizens." The *Encyclopedia* provides an excellent portrait of a famous age. We must not forget that it also helped to shape that age. The real makers of revolutions have often come armed with pens.

The eighteenth century was an age of practical energy as well as speculation. Scientists and mathematicians searched for more keys to unlock more doors. In the seventeenth century many answers had been found and many more mysteries revealed by such giants as Boyle, Descartes, Galileo, Harvey, Kepler, Leibnitz, and Newton. In the currents and cross-currents of the Age of Enlightenment more men appeared to write new chapters in the annals of human achievement.

There was much progress in pure and applied mathematics, especially in the development of differential and integral calculus and the practical use of it in astronomy, mechanics, artillery, and shipbuilding. Johann Bernoulli, Leonard Euler of the Berlin Academy, the geometer Joseph La Grange, the Huguenot genius Abraham de Moivre would rank highly among the mathematicians of any age. There was also much advance in astronomy. In 1781 William Herschel discovered Uranus and added about 2,500 nebulae to the

103 that had been listed earlier. Herschel also showed that the Earth was near the center of the moving solar system edged by the Milky Way. Pierre Joseph Laplace—famous for his *Système du Monde* and his five-volumed *Traité de mécanique céleste*—advanced (1796) his brilliant nebular hypothesis of the origin of the universe and supported it by mathematical calculations. Laplace put forward the idea that a great mass of whirling gas and matter had tossed off cooling pieces to form the planets. It is a far road from Herschel and Laplace to the modern concern with the problems raised by the indirect methods of measuring stellar distances, the moving clusters, the Doppler principle, the receding nebulae (if they are), finite and boundless space. Galileo and Kepler are still more remote from Baade, Minkowski, Bondi, Gold, Jeans, Jordan, Jeffreys, Hoyle, and Bethe. Such contrasts are a vivid reminder of the swift pace of man's discoveries and his adventures in ideas during the past three centuries. Event has tumbled upon event, dream upon dream.

In the field of medicine England's robust pioneer John Hunter made startling gains in his work in surgical pathology and comparative anatomy. The Swiss Albrecht von Haller studied and wrote about botany and anatomy and investigated the functions of the nerves. William Smellie, a London physician, did scientific work in obstetrics, a province hitherto belonging to midwives. Edward Jenner discovered a vaccine that gave effective protection against smallpox. Marie Bichat, a French specialist in pathological anatomy, is usually called the "father of histology." The teaching of medical science steadily improved under the stimulus provided by Leyden's Hermann Boerhave and Vienna's Gerhard van Swieten and others like them. So great were the forward strides of men of medicine in the eighteenth century that hundreds of distinguished names from that period march across the pages of the standard histories.

The scientists of the eighteenth century ranged far afield. Many of them, for instance, were interested in the newly discovered wonders of electricity. The Leyden jar was invented in 1745. Macaulay's omniscient schoolboy knows, or thinks he knows, what Benjamin Franklin did with his kite. The work of the Italians Luigi Galvani and Alessandro Volta are still recorded in the words "galvanometer" and "volt." In Chapter 25 there appeared several comments about the achievements in botany, geology, and chemistry and the names of Buffon, Linnaeus, Black, Priestley, Hutton, and Lavoisier. Enlightenment in any age can come only from dedicated and heavy thought and action. Curiosity alone is not enough.

Throughout the civilized states of Europe, especially in France and England, men and women gathered and talked in the sophisticated salons and the cultured courts. They discussed the half-certainties and the hopes of the new philosophies and the new science. The salons of France were the admiration and envy of all Europe. Wits sparkled and shone at spots like the salon of

PLATE
XXXI

[94]

An engraving of an eighteenth century London distillery and laboratory (1748)

[95]

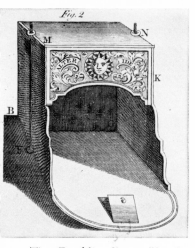

...ove: The Franklin Stove. "Serving God,"
...d Benjamin Franklin, "is doing good to men."

...ht: An eighteenth century Romage printing press,
...same model as the one used by Benjamin Franklin

[96]

Left: "Attack on the Bastille." The Bastille, frowing fortress and grim prison, was a symbol of t old régime in France. It was stormed and captur by a popular uprising on July 14, 1789.

Below: Attack on the Tuileries." On August 1792, a Paris mob, directed by a revolutionary comittee, attacked the Tuileries, then the residence Louis XVI. The king escaped. His Swiss guar were killed.

[97]

[98]

PLATE XXXII

Madame de Tencin. One met the same people or at least the same kind of people at all the salons. They all spoke the same sophisticated language. There was often a real interchange of ideas and a real circulation of results. Here assembled numerous intelligent and shrewd individuals. There were also, of course, many dilettanti, dabblers, and charlatans who moved about the orbits of the salons. Almost every age produces great little nobodies who play about the ankles of the great and are deeply concerned—in a phrase of Rudyard Kipling—"with the ego in their cosmos." They rush about vigorously and they are usually very articulate. They borrow, quote, and imitate. They flay with zeal or shoot their Lilliputian arrows at what they do not like or understand. They are often affected, weak, or vain creatures who would like to achieve greatness but who do not know quite how to do it.

The powerful forces of the Enlightenment reached far beyond the borders of France. In Germany, for instance, Gotthold Lessing (1729–1781), dramatist, writer, and philosopher, insisted upon the importance of toleration. No one religion, he insisted, possesses a monopoly of truth. The skeptical David Hume (1711–1776) extended John Locke's theory of sensationalism and claimed that only those things that can be verified by human reason can be known to be real.

In England and America there were numerous signs of the pervasive spirit of the Age of Reason. On almost every hand stood the words "reason," "balance," "moderation," "compromise," "rational progress," "Nature and Nature's laws." The world of English arts and letters flourished in a great and substantial age of materialism, so solid and secure. The work of such men as Joseph Addison, James Boswell, Daniel Defoe, Oliver Goldsmith, Dr. Samuel Johnson, Alexander Pope, Richard Steele, Jonathan Swift, and Horace Walpole will be admired as long as there are men to read the products of their consummate skill. The architects, artisans, artists, and scholars also achieved well in a vigorous age. Their names march proudly through the annals of their times: Sir John Vanbrugh, Nicholas Hawksmoor, the Adams brothers, the versatile William Kent, David Garrick, Sarah Siddons, Thomas Chippendale, Thomas Sheraton, Josiah Wedgwood, William Hogarth, Thomas Gainsborough, George Romney, J. M. W. Turner, Thomas Girtin, Sir Joshua Reynolds, Adam Smith, Edward Gibbon.

Across the seas in America lived the witty, wise, and tolerant Benjamin Franklin, a man of international fame. "Franklin," said David Hume, "is the first great man of letters for whom we are beholden to America." The cosmopolitan Benjamin Franklin was indeed a "man of letters." He was also much more: printer, orator, postmaster, shrewd wit, practical inventor, canny ambassador, statesman, maker of maxims: "Write with the learned, pronounce with the vulgar." "Eat to please thyself but dress to please others." "The most exquisite folly is made of wisdom spun too fine." "Keep your eyes wide open before marriage, half shut afterwards."

Benjamin Franklin stood before all the world of the West as a symbol of the enlightened hopes of the men of his age and land.

Not all the voices of the Age of Reason were dedicated to the principles of cold and passionless rationalism. In the German states, for instance, there rolled a strong tide of Christian evangelism. In Berlin, Leipzig, and Halle several men protested against the formal intellectual religion of later Lutheranism. Thousands of Germans heard the voices and read the pamphlets of Philip Jacob Spener, August Hermann Francke, and their fellows. The Pietists of Protestant Germany preached about the importance of an individual response of faith and self-dedication. The ardent German nobleman Count Nicholas von Zinzendorf insisted that religion should be warm, emotional, and personal. The Church of the Moravian Brethren sent its missionaries through the Western world.

In England, John and Charles Wesley began the Methodist movement early in the century. They tried to quicken the embers of emotional awareness about God and His teaching. They set out to preach the glad tidings of salvation. They visited the sick and the poor. They prayed. They talked to the masses, to the soldiers, to the colliers, to the rural workers, to "the wild, starving blasphemers" of Newcastle. They brought a religion of uplifting enthusiasm with exciting moral fervor. Great crowds up and down the land heard the messages about the brotherhood of man, the immortality of the soul, and the trumpet of faith. It was clear, surely, that men did not live by reason alone.

Meanwhile some men of letters in England and Europe began to rebel against the exact and formalized coldness of expression prescribed by the classical rules of composition. The rising middle class, for instance, was often not much interested in neatly chiseled blocks of epigrams or dramas that observed all the laws of the unities. They wanted something that would appeal to their emotions as well as challenge their wits. They wanted real human beings in their literature, people that loved and snarled and bit. Impassioned appeals to the heart now began to replace the icy darts of classical satire and the rather thinly monotonous and conventional descriptions of nature. A new cult of sentimentalism, sensibility, tenderness, and compassion slowly appeared and flourished.

In 1759 England's Laurence Sterne, that remarkable cleric, published his *Tristram Shandy*. At once he was famous. Respectable people were horrified. In 1768 he published the *Sentimental Journey*, filled with tears, love, and always laughter. The hypersensitive William Cowper decided that he would not include among his friends the man "who needlessly sets foot upon a worm." On the eve of the Romantic Age several poets, including Thomas Gray, William Collins, and Robert Burns, prepared the way for Wordsworth,

Coleridge, Keats, and Shelley and all who felt the beauty and the slow stain of the world in the blood and along the heart. In these years, too, the strange energy of William Blake burst forth. "A cistern contains," said Blake. "A fountain overflows." Blake overflowed. All but the most impudent of critics approach his engravings and his poems with an uneasy humility.

On the Continent, Johann Friedrich von Schiller (1759–1805) became a bright star in the literary firmament. Schiller, the son of an army surgeon, began to study law. Then he turned to medicine. He became the doctor of an army regiment stationed at Stuttgart. In 1783 he went to Mannheim; in 1785 he moved to Dresden; later he went to Jena. Through the years a stream of lyric poems came from Schiller's pen, poems that were exciting, terse, and beautiful. He wrote books about the history of the Netherlands and about the Thirty Years' War. He wrote volumes about philosophy and ethics. He published numerous dramas: the turbulent *The Robbers, The Maid of Orleans, William Tell, Wallenstein*. Schiller in his time was a champion of liberty and nationalism, an unrelenting opponent of tyranny in all its forms. He was also one of the greatest poets of his century.

Johann Wolfgang von Goethe (1749–1832), a friend of Schiller and Herder, was a writer of massive skill and vast imagination. Born in Frankfort, a successful law student at Leipzig and Strassburg, Goethe returned to Frankfort to begin a literary career. In 1764 he finished and published his *The Sorrows of Young Werther*, a book that brought him international fame. Uncounted readers must have been moved to tears by the trials and suicide of the lovelorn hero in that famous story. The German Romantics hailed Goethe as their master.

In 1775 Charles Augustus, Duke of Weimar, invited Goethe to come to Weimar. Goethe accepted the invitation. He became a government official and worked hard at his job. He directed the state theater. He was active in scientific studies. Meanwhile, he continued to write. He produced some of the finest songs ever to come out of Germany. Even while he was defending classical ideas and ideals he was working on his great *Faust*, a drama of tremendous power that was soon to be hailed as a triumph of Romantic art and "the national poem of the German people." All sensitive human beings share in the divine discontent of Faust. They know how much his aspirations and rebellions are symbols of universal man.

Meanwhile the enlightened despots of Berlin, St. Petersburg, and Vienna believed that by autocratic and paternal care they could improve and elevate their peoples.

The brilliant, shrewd, and cynical Frederick II (the Great) of Prussia (1740–1786), so carefully trained in the business of kingship by his father Frederick William I, steadily attempted to raise the prestige and power of the

Hohenzollerns in Europe; he also tried to be an enlightened and progressive ruler at home. He had the laws of Prussia simplified and unified and speeded up the legal machinery of the state. He constructed roads, bridges, and canals; he drained marshes; he started new villages; he encouraged immigration; he established protective tariffs and granted subsidies to stimulate domestic industries. He was an energetic and capable administrator. He worked hard. He declared that he was "the first servant of the state."

Catherine II of Russia, better known as Catherine the Great (1762–1796), succeeded her husband in 1762. Sagacious, shrewd, energetic, and quite immoral, Catherine led her vast state to a high level of prestige and power upon the European stage. She insisted that she was enlightened and benevolent in her treatment of the Russian people. She was proud of the fact that she invited artists and writers to her court. She spoke often of her plans and dreams. Not all of those dreams—the dream of establishing thousands of local schools, for instance—came true. She said that she hoped the serfs would be free some day; but she took no steps to free them. She was a realist. She knew the power of the nobles. She must not antagonize the nobles. She knew how ignorant and barbarous the people were. She must not encourage or rouse the lower classes. Catherine the Great knew that it was the gospel of folly for a despot, even an enlightened despot, to permit the reins of power to slip from the royal hands.

All of the enlightened despots—Prussia's Frederick the Great, Russia's Catherine the Great, Sweden's Gustavus III (1771–1792), Austria's Joseph II (1780–1790)—agreed that reform must come from above, not from below. Their subjects must be made happier; but there must not be too much reform and it must not come too fast. The enlightened despotism must be benevolent but not too liberal. Extreme reforms might be dangerous to monarchy.

At the same time, too, the enlightened despots advanced what they considered to be the interests of their states by such steps as the partitions of Poland in 1772, 1793, and 1795. Poland disappeared from the map of Europe. The balance of power in eastern Europe was maintained; but the balance of Europe as a whole was unsettled by the cold calculations of diplomacy and the voracious appetites of Frederick, Catherine, Maria Theresa, and Joseph. Their consciences were not tender. It is said that Maria Theresa, who had lost Silesia to the unscrupulous Frederick of Prussia, did have some qualms about the first partition of Poland. "She wept, but she kept on taking."

In the midst of all the ideas of progress there were some voices raised against the rulers of Europe. "We see on the face of the globe," wrote Holbach, "only incapable, unjust sovereigns, enervated by luxury, corrupted by flattery, depraved through unpunished license, and without talents, morals, or good qualities." Holbach overstated his charges; that was an offense of which he was often guilty. Nevertheless, a great many men agreed with him. They had quite definite ideas about the natural rights of man and the proper conduct of the affairs of states. The roads to revolution were lighted by the torches of such opinions. They appeared in 1789, in 1830, in 1848, in 1870, in many other times and places during the years of the hopes and disorders that have marked the emergence of the Western world we know.

Soon was to come the sound of the rolling tumbrils of Robespierre. To some men the French Revolution was a hard dawn showing a raw and hideous landscape. To others it marked a dream and a chance of a better world, a better life. They saw at hand a reign of virtue and the full fraternity of all men. Perhaps all the things that good men wanted were now to be achieved by legislation, by sword and gun, by the poised and relentless knife of the guillotine.

Chapter 30

REVOLUTION IN FRANCE:

HOPE AND TERROR

"We wish to fulfil the course of nature, to accomplish the destiny of mankind, to make good the promises of philosophy, to absolve Providence from the long reign of tyranny and crime. May France . . . become the model to the nations, the terror of oppressors, the consolation to the oppressed, the ornament of the universe; and in sealing our work with our blood may we ourselves see at last the dawn of universal felicity gleam before us! That is our ambition. That is our aim."

> —Maximilien Robespierre, February, 1794. P. J. B. Buchez and P. C. Roux (eds.), *Histoire parlementaire de la Revolution Francaise*, XXXI, 274

For many centuries men have gone forth to war or pushed their own governments into sudden convulsions of revolution and collapse. Filled with determination and zeal, they have done deeds of revenge, stupidity, greed, cruelty, and high courage. Men have wept and children wondered. Tombs and crosses have risen to commemorate the heroes and martyrs who died in glory. The survivors have sometimes been promised a new world of peace, perfection, and salvation here below.

Many of the men who made the French Revolution were quite certain that if they followed their formulas they could create a paradise on earth for regenerated humanity. Free men would recognize no other master but Reason. Natural men, the victors in a great crusade, would oust forever "the tyrants and the princes with their senseless and hypocritical instruments." To the National Assembly of France, Bertrand Barère said: "You are summoned to give history a fresh start."

There were many grounds for dissatisfaction in the France of the Old Regime. There were overlapping administrative units, the most important of which were the provinces, generalities, and intendancies. There were numerous other divisions corresponding to differences in customs, legal rights, and institutions. There were complicated tariff barriers and confusing networks of direct and indirect tax systems. There was a jumble of heterogeneous laws.

What was a dark crime in one part of France was but a peccadillo in another. Voltaire once remarked that men changed their laws as often as their post horses. "Must some man be right in Brittany and wrong in Languedoc?"

The cumbersome and complex territorial and legal arrangements were further complicated by the confused nature of the royal administration, an octopus of bureaucracy containing a Council of the King, a Council of State, a Council of Commerce, a Privy Council—all with interlocking directorates and functions not clearly defined. The channels of government were always sluggish, often clogged.

It is not easy to stress too strongly the confusion and maladministration that existed in the France of the Old Regime. "One cannot move a step in this vast realm without finding in it different laws, contradictory usages, privileges, exemptions from taxation, rights of every kind, overlapping, expense, and disorder."

At the center of the stage stood the king, absolute monarch and superior lord of all the feudal proprietors. Immediately below the king were two powerful and privileged classes possessing many rights and immunities: the First Estate—the clergy—and the Second Estate—the nobility. All men and women who stood outside these two groups belonged to the Third Estate.

The clergy of France, rich and strong, in fact formed "a state within a state." The regular clergy included about 60,000 monks and nuns who lived in 1,100 convents and monasteries. There were also about 6,000 Dominicans and Franciscans. The higher secular clergy numbered about 11,000 and the lower clergy—the curates and vicars—about 60,000. Most of the important work was done by the lower clergy; these men were usually sympathetic with the hopes and causes of the Third Estate.

In the secular divisions of the upper clergy there were many men and women of noble blood. There were 28 archbishops and 123 bishops in the France of the Old Regime and every one was a noble. Many of the abbots and bishops were absentees and several of the sinecures were filled with men of ignorance and immorality. "With Spanish bishops and French priests an excellent clergy could be made."

Of the total income of the Church in France it has been estimated that about 85 per cent went to the upper clergy, 15 to the lower. One of the parish priests of the eighteenth century wrote these revealing sentences: "Only rarely do the bishops pay any attention to us, their vicars. They feel that we belong to another race than themselves. They never receive us at their tables." One bishop explained why he felt so far away from the lower clergy: "The parish priests are coarse, shabby, and ignorant and one must indeed be fond of the odor of garlic in order to be happy in the society of those who ponder heaven and earth." In such circumstances it was not surprising that the humble priests did not preach resignation to their flocks but, rather, bitterness and anger.

Part of the "godlessness" of the French Revolution was caused by the Church of the Old Regime.

The nobility of the Second Estate was divided into two main groups. In the first were the nobles who were around the royal court, in the king's household, or in the army. The highest of them were often in debt; hundreds of them were bankrupt. The pensions paid to some of them cost the state 25,000,000 livres every year. The expenses of the royal household in 1787 totaled 33,000,000 livres.

The second group of nobles was composed of the impoverished men—the "sparrow hawks"—who vegetated in their modest manor houses in the country, far from the silks and fleshpots of Versailles. These men detested the higher nobility who had gobbled pensions and lucrative appointments at the court and in the Church. Because they often needed money they usually insisted upon the last jot and tittle of their manorial rights. When the waves of revolution broke into the rural areas of France the peasants disposed of a few of their problems by hanging several nobles.

Meanwhile life at the court of Versailles moved at the stately pace of the minuet, polished, polite, and pleasant. Many of the nobles had "the best of manners and the worst of morals." Only a few of the younger ones glimpsed the coming of a deluge of dark disaster for them and for their class: "And so, without regret for the past, without fear for the future, we walked gaily on a carpet of flowers that hid the abyss beneath our feet." These were the years, said Victor Hugo, of a "long-lasting feast ended by the scaffold."

Among the bourgeoisie, the untitled aristocracy of the world of business, manufacturing, and finance, profits multiplied and powers grew. The men of the bourgeois class were busy and aggressive. Most of the nobles, on the other hand, were not. For instance, they declared that trade was degrading. Even to fill their pockets, often empty and gaping, they would not condescend to enter the world of business. In this decision they followed the example of their king: "On one point the king was adamant: he would kiss no greengrocers' wives. And who shall say that it was not in part this which sealed the doom of the French monarchy?"

Meanwhile several men of the bourgeois class became giants of conspicuous consumption. It was not, perhaps, surprising that the mobs of the French Revolution often clamored for the blood of the rich bourgeoisie. On May 8, 1794, for instance, twenty-eight bankers went to the guillotine.

Louis XV (1715–1774) paid small attention to the business of government. He liked the pleasures of the court, the company of his mistresses, especially Madame de Pompadour and Madame du Barry. A wiser foreign policy in his reign might have prevented France from becoming involved in the War of the Austrian Succession and the costly Seven Years' War. But Louis XV was not deeply troubled about foreign policy. So far as the affairs of the state at home were concerned he seemed to believe that no deluge of disaster would come during his lifetime.

Louis XVI was fat, awkward, slow-witted, stolid, and weak. He usually meant to do the right thing but "he agreed with the last person who had seen him" and "changed his mind at the wrong time." His chief interests were clocks and hunting. Louis was not the kind of man or monarch that France needed at a critical hour. Nor was his queen, the "Austrian lady" Marie Antoinette, of any help. She was extravagant, silly, interfering, and very unpopular. Supported by many court nobles—including the brothers of the king —Marie Antoinette set her face against all projects of reform and persuaded Louis XVI to do likewise. Louis, slow of mind and of a gentle spirit, was easily pushed about. In the royal court there was no staunch courage or vision, few right decisions. Among the main characteristics of Versailles were apathy, obtuseness, weakness, and pride.

In 1774 Anne Robert Jacques Turgot, a physiocrat, philosopher, and practical administrator, was appointed comptroller-general. He proposed a policy of "no borrowing, no bankruptcy" and insisted that there should be no new taxes; that the tariff barriers between provinces should be swept away; that sinecures should be abolished. The nobles stood together against Turgot; every reform meant a loss of some privilege. Louis XVI once remarked: "Only Turgot and I love the people." In eighteen months Turgot saved 58,000,000 livres. Then Marie Antoinette and the court forced him to resign and his reforms were abandoned. In May, 1776, the national debt stood at 235,000,000 livres.

Turgot was followed by Cluny and Necker, the Swiss banker. They were both dismissed. After Necker came Fleury, D'Ormesson, and Charles Alexandre Calonne. Calonne was a most obliging fellow. He increased the national debt by 653,000,000 livres in three years. "The best way to borrow money," said Calonne, "is to appear to be prosperous and the best way to appear to be prosperous is to spend money." This was bad advice, bad policy. The national credit of France was collapsing.

In 1786 the Assembly of Notables was called to consider reforms in the tax structure. Calonne explained that the national deficit stood between three and four billion livres and that the budget deficit for 1786 was 120,000,000 livres. He asked if the nobles would voluntarily abandon their exemptions from taxation. Calonne, like Turgot and others before him, was faced by the unrelenting opposition of Marie Antoinette and the court. Louis XVI dismissed Calonne and called in Loménie de Brienne to devise new taxes. The Notables went home in May, 1787. The *parlements* of France refused to register the new taxes but were compelled to yield to the king's orders. There were insurrections. Louis was at last forced to call back Jacques Necker, the only man who could command any confidence.

The coming of Necker did not measurably diminish the difficulties. "France, sire," Calonne had said, "is a very imperfect kingdom, full of abuses, and in its present condition, impossible to govern."

Louis XVI now decided to summon the Estates-General, a body representing the three estates of France. The Estates-General had not met since 1614.

Nobody then could see that from the point of view of the monarchy and the upper classes Louis XVI had made a grand miscalculation in calling the Estates-General. When the members of that assembly came to Versailles a fatal chain of events began. There were released the vital impulses of anger and hope, all the intensities of exhilarated spirits that no nobles, no clergy, no absolute monarch, could ever check or stay. Men drifted and stumbled towards revolution; and then they ran. The ground rocked and trembled under the Old Regime. Proud clergy and nobles winced and wilted; some sought security in flight. Dazzled and dizzy men moved into deathgrips with events as the revolution gathered momentum. The squalid butchers who manned the guillotines worked busily to hasten the coming of the Republic of Virtue. Soldiers of France marched against Austria and Prussia and many another land. Some came home. Crosses and burdocks marked the graves of others who died. Blazing ideas shot like rockets over all of the Western world.

The Estates-General met at Versailles on May 5, 1789. There were trumpets and shouts. A great mass was celebrated. The crowds who came to watch and cheer saw an impressive procession: the Third Estate, dressed in black coats, white neckties, three-cornered hats; the nobles in their court attire, a gorgeous blaze of color; the clergy, their black robes hot and heavy.

After the members of the Estates-General gathered in a crowded hunting storage room—"the Room of the King's Minor Pleasures"—they were kept waiting for four hours. Then came three long speeches. There was no mention of reform, no remarks about the scandalous financial mismanagement, nothing but a discussion of debts and taxes. The men of the Third Estate were disappointed and suspicious. They had their own ideas. The *cahiers,* those statements of grievances and instructions prepared in their districts, had insisted upon numerous changes, including the establishment of local governments for administration, a legislative body for all France, the guarantee of certain individual liberties, the decrease of upper-class privileges, the proportionate taxation of all groups, and a series of administrative reforms. What the representatives of the Third Estate desired was in fact a limited constitutional monarchy. "Two forces must always occur—the consent of the people and the voice of the prince."

It was obvious, of course, that the court and the First and Second Estates would oppose such demands. On the other hand, the representatives of the Third Estate were well aware of the temper of the people back home, the bad harvests, the vehement complaints, the election disturbances, the pillaging, the day when the coach and horses of the Bishop of Toulon had been thrown into the sea.

Disputes arose at once. Was the Estates-General to be divided into three chambers or one? If three divisions were set up—one for each Estate—and the members voted "by order," then the First and Second Estates, the privileged orders, would always win, two to one. The Third Estate wanted to vote in one chamber and "by head." They had 621 members in the Estates-General; the clergy had 308 (200 represented the lower clergy, most of which supported the Third Estate); the nobles had 285.

The men of the Third Estate, soon at loggerheads with everybody but themselves, stubbornly refused to obey the royal commands that the Estates-General divide and vote "by order." When they found the assembly room locked on the rainy morning of June 20 they walked over to the royal indoor tennis court nearby and swore and signed the famous "Tennis Court Oath," an oath that they would not go home until they had obtained a constitution for France. They were to get that constitution; they were to get much more, too.

At the royal session of June 23 Louis XVI stated that "the King wishes that the ancient distinction of the order be preserved and observed" and ordered the Estates to sit separately. The members of the Third Estate refused. Many of the lower clergy supported them, together with a few from the upper clergy. On June 25, forty-seven nobles yielded and went over to the side of the Third Estate and twenty-seven followed the next day. Louis XVI, deafened by the racket and worried by the complaints, gave way. "They want to stay?" he asked. "Then let them stay." These were not the words of a strong king. Louis was never a leader. Once again he had failed to assert himself. Marie Antoinette and his brothers, the Counts of Artois and Provence, were telling him that the Estates-General should never have been called. Perhaps they were right; but it was too late now. The point of no return had been passed.

The Estates-General now organized itself as a single chamber. Ten days earlier the Third Estate had taken the title of the "National Assembly."

Rumors were leaping about that Louis XVI was preparing to follow the advice of the court at Versailles and dissolve the National Assembly by military force. It was true that Louis had summoned 18,000 soldiers to Versailles. What was he going to do with them? The National Assembly had declared that the deputies could not be harmed or prevented from doing their lawful business, even at the order of Louis XVI; they also said that the taxes should be paid by the people only so long as the Assembly was in session. On July 8, the famous Count Mirabeau, that champion of change, condemned the troop movements near Paris and requested the king to stop them at once. Mirabeau added that "evil counselors" were "undermining the throne."

Three days later, Jacques Necker, so widely respected, was abruptly dismissed by the king. At once there was confusion and looting in the streets and squares of Paris. Soon there were skirmishes in the provinces. The mobs were beginning to taste power, a dangerous thing.

On July 14, the Bastille, grim medieval stronghold and symbol of oppression, was attacked by mobs. Seven prisoners were released. The mayor of Paris, the governor of the Bastille, and six soldiers were murdered. Their heads were stuck on pikes and carried through the excited crowds of Paris. The usual tales about July 14 are exciting and romantic. "Bastille Day" is a symbol of many fine things, but most of the facts about that day are sordid.

Louis XVI sent away the troops. They could not be relied upon to put down the Paris mobs—they might join them. Jacques Necker was restored to his post. Louis also accepted a new city government in Paris. A "National Guard" was formed to keep order in Paris and several other cities—its commander in Paris was the Marquis de Lafayette.

When Louis went into Paris on July 17 he seemed to admit, by his words and acts, the victory of those who had opposed the court and the privileged classes.

Meanwhile, many nobles began to leave France. Most of these *émigrés* were to remain relentless foes of the Revolution. Meanwhile, too, disturbances flamed in several cities, especially in Bordeaux, Lyons, and Marseilles. Insurrection blazed in northern France. In some rural areas the curious phenomenon usually called "the Great Fear" helped speed the virtual collapse of government authority. "The men armed themselves with scythes, pitchforks, and hoes and rushed about the surrounding country in squads, hunting for the enemy which each man, fleeing from one hamlet to another, had sworn that he had seen in his own. Some of the women began boiling oil. . . ." No enemy was ever seen.

Many peasants knew exactly what they were doing and what they intended to do. They were going to wipe out the feudal and manorial arrangements by force and fire. Their excitement has been stressed too much, their calculation not enough.

It is easy to underline too heavily the dramatic and exciting themes of blood and death. In any age, such facts and fictions catch the eye and the interest. So far as these days in France were concerned, violence and murder were still the exception, not the rule. It is very misleading to suggest or to believe that the people of France had plunged into a wild world of spontaneous anarchy and murder. Then, as now, most families went to their fields and beds in peace.

A committee of the National Assembly investigated the insurrections and reported on August 3. In discussing that report the Assembly moved swiftly towards a far more complete revolution than anyone had anticipated. Faced by the challenge of events men sometimes react in ways quite unpremeditated and often unpredictable. A few liberal noblemen had agreed to surrender some of their privileges at the evening session of August 4. Nobody planned or expected the startling steps that were taken on that famous night. All was quiet and peaceful enough at the beginning of the session. Then the pace and spirit changed.

In the crowded Assembly a linen draper from Brittany spoke, tense with emotion. "You will not restore calm to a distracted France, gentlemen, until you have promised the people that you will commute all feudal payments, abolish all feudal dues." In an atmosphere increasingly charged with emotion a series of revolutionary decrees abolished numerous corporate and class privileges. The remnants of serfdom were wiped away. Tithes were abolished. All personal tax privileges were surrendered. Feudal dues were canceled and the owners were to be compensated for their losses. A summary of the long list of resolutions of this famous evening said simply: "Feudalism is abolished."

The events of the night of August 4 became an inspiration and a symbol. The men who did these things and those who saw or heard about them hoped and planned still more. An increasing number of National Assembly members "imagined that they were assembled to retrieve every fault of the past, to correct every error of the human mind, and to secure the happiness of future generations. Doubt had no place in their minds and infallibility presided perpetually over all their contradictory decrees."

In a later day Maximilien Robespierre was to remark that "man is born for liberty" and "his rights are written in his heart." This idea was to run steadily throughout the whole era of the French Revolution.

On August 26, 1789, the National Assembly, "in the presence and under the authority of the Supreme Being," issued the Declaration of the Rights of Man and the Citizen. The seventeen clauses of this interesting document were intended to be the preamble to the new constitution that would soon, it was hoped, be completed. "Men are born and remain free and equal in rights." "The aim of all political association is to preserve the natural and imprescriptible rights of man. . . . these rights are liberty, property, security, and resistance to oppression." "Social distinctions can only be based upon public utility." All men, said the Declaration, were to be equal before the law. No man was to be arbitrarily arrested or imprisoned. Taxes were to be raised by common consent. All public officials were to be held responsible for their conduct in office. There was to be freedom of thought, religion, speech, and press. "The principle of all sovereignty rests essentially in the nation" and "law is the expression of the general will." One French historian has called the Declaration of the Rights of Man and the Citizen the "death certificate of the Old Regime." The majesty of the people took the place of the majesty of the king. It should be remarked, of course, that the "people" sometimes came to be those who were in the dominant groups; the rest were traitors or individuals not worth bothering about—in the opinion of those who themselves belonged to the dominant groups.

It was one thing to publish and distribute the shining message of the Declaration of the Rights of Man and the Citizen to the people of France and the world beyond; it was quite another to translate it into action. When the makers of the new constitution worked upon their practical problems they stumbled into many controversies and thorny difficulties. They were not experienced men. There were many debates, much philosophy, frequent generalities, numerous set speeches, sharp divisions of opinion.

Should the king be given an absolute or a suspensive veto? Should there be a legislative body in one chamber or in two? One committee failed to reach any agreement. A second committee proposed to set up one chamber to be elected by all citizens of property; a new court system; several local governments to administer the laws—this step would sweep away the chaotic administrative system of the Old Regime. There was also a declaration guaranteeing the sovereignty of the people and certain rights for all individuals. The king was to be the hereditary head of the nation—"Louis by the Grace of God and the constitution of the state, King of the French"—and was to have a four-year suspensive veto. This constitution was not adopted until September, 1791.

It is immediately clear that the Constitution of 1791 was designed by the bourgeois men in the Assembly to protect their interests. It established a middle-class system of government. It strengthened privileges based on wealth. The suffrage was limited: only 3,000,000 adult males who paid a fixed level of taxes were permitted to vote. These men were called the "active" citizens because they were held to be "the real shareholders in the great social concern." All other Frenchmen were "passive" citizens, including the poor and illiterate men at the bottom who were only "machines for work." Such arrangements were somewhat different from the ideals proclaimed in the earlier Declaration of the Rights of Man and the Citizen.

There were varying opinions, then and later, about the Constitution of 1791. Alexis de Tocqueville said: "There was no reason why it should not have succeeded. . . . The weakness in the Constitution of 1791 was not so much in itself as in the condition of its birth." On the other hand, Count Mirabeau, a sturdy enemy of the courtiers and the Church, strongly opposed the new constitution—many conservatives considered Mirabeau a renegade and a dangerous demagogue. "Answer me, if you can," he said to the National Assembly, "then slander me as much as you like." So far as Mirabeau was concerned "the disorganization of the kingdom could not have been better planned" than it was in this Constitution of 1791. Gouverneur Morris was of the opinion that "the constitution is of such a nature that the Almighty himself could not make it work unless he created a new species of man."

In the months when the Constitution of 1791 was being shaped many moderate men were shocked at the rising tide of radical ideas. Was the Revolution to fall into the hands of wild doctrinaires and demagogues? Many of the "patriot" or radical leaders, on the other hand, insisted that they stood for the real and right principles of the Revolution. The "people" must come first.

Meanwhile dangerous powers grew outside the National Assembly. Newspapers multiplied in Paris to inform and agitate. Clubs were founded to move the "people" forward. The Society of the Friends of the Constitution, usually called the Jacobin Club, had a national organization—by 1793 there were about 500,000 Jacobins. These Jacobins really formed a great revolutionary body, a political party with strong ideas and programs of action. Other groups, such as the Cordelier Club and the Breton Club, mushroomed in Paris. In the membership of these associations were many men destined to play dramatic and important roles: Maximilien Robespierre, Jean Paul Marat, Camille Desmoulins, Georges Jacques Danton, and scores of others. The popular Duke of Orléans continued to foment public suspicions from the Palais Royal. The Marquis de Lafayette and the National Guard were always about, always busy. Not long after these days the Duke of Orléans was to be executed by the people whose cause he had supported and Lafayette was to be imprisoned as a revolutionary in Austria by the Austrians to whom he had fled for safety when the "red fool fury of the Seine" alarmed and frightened him.

On October 4, 1789, a riotous crowd of women walked the twelve miles from Paris to Versailles in a heavy rain. They were hungry and they wanted bread. Perhaps, they said, the king and the National Assembly could do something for them. Several of the idle and the curious went along to see what would happen.

About four o'clock the crowd reached Versailles. Some men and women went over to the National Assembly; others went to the palace. Louis XVI came back from hunting about six o'clock and received a deputation. Lafayette and a group of the National Guard arrived about midnight.

In the morning several shots were fired. The mob killed some Swiss guards at the palace. Many insisted that Louis XVI must not stay at Versailles where he was at the mercy of the unscrupulous court party. He must come back to Paris. "Jean Paul Marat sped to Versailles and returned like a streak, making as much noise as four trumpets on the Day of Judgment, crying 'Oh Dead! Awaken!' " So it was that Louis XVI, Marie Antoinette, and their son—

"the baker, the baker's wife, and the baker's little boy"—were brought back to Paris. There, surely, Louis would be safe among his beloved people; and there, in the Tuileries, he could be watched.

Soon the National Assembly followed. Outside its doors, the mobs pressed and threatened. In such circumstances, calm deliberation and wise legislation were not easily achieved.

Meanwhile the National Assembly worked at other tasks. It abolished the hereditary nobility; it destroyed the trade guilds; it declared that all citizens had equal rights to all offices, professions, and crafts. In November, 1789, it confiscated the property of the Church. By a vote of 568 to 346 the Assembly declared that "the goods of the clergy are at the disposal of the nation." Within a few months the monastic corporations were dissolved. The Assembly issued paper money, called *assignats,* with the new "national domains" as security. The *assignats* were to bear interest at 4 per cent and were to be exchanged for all interest-bearing debts of the state. The first bloc of *assignats* was issued for 400,000,000 francs. A second bloc, bearing no interest, was issued in September, 1790, for the sum of 800,000,000 francs.

The operation was not successful. Some Frenchmen, aware of the claims and the power of the Church, were reluctant to risk disaster by using the *assignats.* Inflation inevitably depreciated the value of the wildly printed currency. Within five years it was worthless. Nevertheless, the collapse of the *assignats* did not mean the end of the sale of the lands of the Church. The slow sale continued until 1793. About half of the Church lands passed into the hands of the peasants and the other half went to the rich middle class.

In July, 1790, the "Civil Constitution of the Clergy" altered the age-old relation between the Church and state. It deprived the Church of its corporate privileges. It divided France into 83 dioceses (instead of the earlier 138) to correspond with the 83 civil administrative divisions. Bishops and priests were to be elected by the citizens who had the right to vote for civil officials. All members of the clergy were to be paid by the state in the same way as other civil servants. The clergy now had the status of ordinary citizens. The Church was really a department of the government. "The service of the altar," said Count Mirabeau, "is a public function." Article 4 of the Civil Constitution stated that the pope had no jurisdiction in France except in those instances where the state approved. All public papal documents were banned.

Louis XVI was deeply troubled by the Civil Constitution of the Clergy. Was the king's conscience to be in the hands of a majority of the Assembly? The Civil Constitution of the Clergy made it impossible for the orthodox Roman Catholic to accept the Revolution. Hence the Revolution was weakened throughout France. "Refractory" parish priests who had earlier supported the cause of change and reform now became dangerous and powerful foes. About half of the clergy refused to abide by the new law. Among the "constitutional" clergy who did accept it were only seven bishops. The rest listened to the voice of Rome, and the pope was vehement in his condemnation of this part of the work of the National Assembly. The people were confused, sometimes alarmed and angry. Most of them preferred the "refractory" clergy. Some, including King Louis XVI, felt that to do otherwise would put their souls in jeopardy.

In the early autumn of 1791 "the heat was terrific and the deputies, overcome with fatigue, were anxious to be gone." The National Assembly met for the last time on September 30, 1791. Before they departed they voted that none of their members might sit in the legislature that would meet under the new constitution. This self-denying ordinance was not wise. Said one Frenchman: "They were a pack of fools."

The moderate phase of the French Revolution was ended. The violent years began.

In October, 1791, the new Legislative Assembly met in Paris. There were 745 members, ambitious, inexperienced, and "new to glory." About 265 of them were conservative or reactionary; about 135 were radical; the rest were moderates.

Early in the sessions two ill-knit factions began a bitter struggle for power. One group was the Girondins, who took their name from the fact that several of them came from the Gironde area. They stood strongly against the idea that the city of Paris should control and direct the affairs of the whole country. The second group was the Jacobins, militant men who moved in and out of their Jacobin Clubs, insisting that Paris was indeed the hub of France. They denounced the Girondins as federalists, bourgeois enemies of land reform. The Girondins, for their part, often condemned the Jacobins for being too radical; one man's idea of reform is sometimes another man's idea of anarchy. There were also several rather extraordinary clusters of men inside and outside the Girondin and Jacobin groups.

Long before the Legislative Assembly had met there had arisen a strong counterrevolutionary movement. Inside France, Queen Marie Antoinette, the reactionary nobles and clergy, and the conservative bourgeoisie made common cause. The work of the Revolution, they asserted, must be destroyed. Outside France many men feared that the ideas of the French Revolution might spread like a virulent plague. About 15,000 émigrés had fled to Prussia, Austria, and England to swell the ranks of the militant opponents of the Revolution. Many of them plotted to join in a great crusade. Scandalized reactionaries and conservatives throughout Europe believed that the time to crush the Revolution had arrived.

Within France a series of events occurred to increase divisions and fears. Louis XVI had paid Count Mirabeau to help him fight the new constitution.

After Count Mirabeau died suddenly in April, 1791, Louis decided to flee from Paris, join with loyal noblemen, and try to get help from friendly powers. At Varennes, in Lorraine, Louis and Marie Antoinette were recognized, stopped, and brought back to Paris. On June 25 the National Assembly suspended Louis from all of his functions. Anti-royalist pamphlets appeared in Paris. Many Jacobins became republicans. Most of the people in the provinces remained loyal to Louis. All over Europe his supporters made plots to free him.

Many of the Girondins felt that the Revolution should be carried further. Slowly they won control of the Legislative Assembly. For a long time, too, they had insisted that France should declare war on Austria and Prussia. "The law of equality is universal." "You embrace the cause of other peoples in embracing yours." "We must declare war against all kings and peace with all peoples." Some men also asserted that a war launched against Prussia and Austria would reveal the true position of Louis XVI: he would stand forth as a king who had no loyalty to the Revolution of his people. "From this rostrum," said Vergniaud, "we see the palace within whose walls perfidious counsels are leading the King astray. Terror and dismay have often issued from those palace doors. Let them re-enter it this day in the name of the law." It must be added, of course, that a few men were warming their private ideas and ambitions: Condorcet dreamed of a great United States of Europe; Brissot thought that he might be the leader of all France when Louis XVI was ousted.

The French reactionaries claimed that a war might restore the king's prestige; some said that if the French revolutionaries were defeated by the Prussians and the Austrians, then Louis XVI would be put back upon the throne and would be king indeed.

On April 20, 1792, the Legislative Assembly declared war on Austria "in rightful defense of a free people against the unjust aggressions of a king." There were only seven votes cast for peace. Soon France offered "fraternity and assistance" to all people who wanted "their liberty." On April 26, Prussia moved against France and was joined by Victor Amadeus of Savoy, king of Piedmont. Russia did not come in; she was busy contemplating the problems of digesting more Polish territories. Catherine of Russia and Gustavus III of Sweden did urge the allies on to crush France; but they did not aid with arms. The Revolution in France thus became a war in Europe, a power struggle and an ideological conflict in which much that was new stood against much that was old. True, the new and the old were often mingled. At what point, for example, did the new French crusade in the name of the liberties of all men meet and merge with the French national feeling and the old-new desire for territorial expansion? Only a foolish man or a knave would try to answer that question.

Disaster fell upon the French armies. Defeat followed defeat. Austro-

Prussian forces under the Duke of Brunswick pounded at French soldiers in the Austrian Netherlands and in Belgium. They threatened to invade France.

During these dark days many Parisians were asserting that Louis XVI and Marie Antoinette were supporting foreign foes. On July 27 the Duke of Brunswick issued a manifesto to the French threatening "the military execution and total annihilation" of Paris if any harm came to Louis or any other member of the royal family. This ill-judged threat probably endangered the throne of Louis still more than the previous events. On August 10 a mob demonstrated against "the treason of the Tuileries" and massacred many Swiss guards about the palace. Louis XVI, Marie Antoinette, and their son fled to the Assembly for protection. The Assembly answered by deposing them and putting them in prison. Several "patriots" in Paris and the provinces began to butcher men and women suspected of being traitors. "Blood will rain," Madame Roland had said.

Extreme measures were soon taken throughout France against those who were deemed to be counter-revolutionaries or lukewarm supporters of the new order. Terror is often a useful instrument of revolutionary policy. Moderate men usually have a hard time in revolutions. In the "September Massacres" of 1792 more than a thousand people were executed; it was a nasty episode, red and violent. "Popular justice" has sometimes been a convenient and gentle label for unbridled crime.

When Louis XVI was deposed the Constitution of 1791 obviously ceased to have any meaning. Hence a National Convention was elected to make another constitution. The 783 deputies of this National Convention met on September 20, 1792. Most of the Convention members belonged to the middle section called the Plain, a group that included the timid and vacillating, the trimmers and opportunists, the irresolute, silent, and safe men—there were about 465 of them. On the Right were the conservatives and the reactionaries, numbering about 165; more and more of them stayed away from the Convention; their absence increased their chances of safety and survival. On the Left were the Jacobins, Girondins, Cordeliers, and several other groups. Here were Robespierre, Danton, Saint-Just, Desmoulins, Marat, and the like, volatile and dangerous men.

The extremists sat far up on the left side of the Convention hall and were called "the Mountain." By this time the Girondins had split with the Jacobins more sharply than before; the Girondins said that all French citizens should pay the cost of the war; the Jacobins said that only the wealthy should pay. "Almost all our deputies," wrote Madame Roland, "go about armed to the teeth. Thousands of people warn them never to sleep anywhere except at hotels. How delightful is the liberty of Paris with its commune!"

The Convention declared that the monarchy was abolished. France became a republic "one and indivisible." Gouverneur Morris wrote in his diary:

"Nothing new today except that the Convention has met and declared that there shall be no more king."

On the same day—September 20, 1792—General Dumouriez stopped the Prussian and Austrian forces at Valmy. The Duke of Brunswick is said to have exclaimed: "We have lost more than a battle!" Rain and dysentery did more to defeat the foes of France than Dumouriez ever did; he was really a rather stupid man. Myth made Valmy a great French victory.

The "victory of humanity" was hailed as the beginning of a great French surge forward. Drunk with vainglory and made reckless by enthusiasm the Convention proclaimed a dangerous policy of aggression and international revolution in a series of decrees. "Accord fraternity and aid to all peoples who desire to recover their liberties." "Treat as enemies the peoples who, refusing liberty and equality, or renouncing them, may wish to preserve, recall, or treat with the princes and the privileged classes."

Louis XVI was condemned to death by a vote of 387 to 384. When some Girondins suggested a popular referendum on the question of the king's death Maximilien Robespierre replied that such a proposal was unsatisfactory: "Virtue has always been in a minority on earth," he said. Saint-Just remarked that Julius Caesar had been "put to death in the middle of the Senate, with no formalities beyond two and twenty dagger thrusts."

The execution of the king was carried out on January 21, 1793. A shocked Europe was even more prepared than before to suppress the explosive and dangerous forces that had been released in France. In the spring of 1793 Britain, Spain, Holland, Sardinia, and Russia joined Austria and Prussia in the war against the new republic. Before the hard blows of the allies the armies of the Convention reeled backwards. The frontier fortresses of France fell, one by one. Allied armies invaded France from Belgium, Alsace, and Spain. Inside France there were revolts against the government in Marseilles, Lyons, and Toulon. There were uprisings in Normandy. The royalist Vendée region rebelled in a violent crusade against Paris and all its works.

Two years before, England's Edmund Burke had denounced the excesses of France in his *Reflections on the Revolution in France*. Burke had declared the value of continuity in human affairs, "without which men become as flies in summer." The French Revolution was the embodiment of almost all the things Edmund Burke disliked, a revolution founded on a scorn of the past, threatening with ruin the whole social fabric that the ages had reared. For Burke the body politic of any state was a complex organism, a sublime mystery, the product of centuries of corporate life in society. The French were destroying "the old perfections of the earth," the ordered structure of classes and ranks, Church and state. In 1791 Burke had warned the world of the consequences of the ideas and deeds of the French state. In 1793 the nations of the

First Coalition set out to remedy the ills, as they saw them, of folly and delay and the failure to heed the tocsin sounded by Edmund Burke.

The Convention stood at bay, beset and beleaguered by foes within and without. The Girondins, now led by Brissot, Condorcet, and Vergniaud, quarreled furiously with the Jacobins, dominated by Robespierre, Danton, and Marat. In April, 1793, the Committee of Public Safety was appointed to direct the army, to crush the foreign foes, and to purge away all Frenchmen who were not militant supporters of the Revolution. There was no peace, surely, for the "infamous moderates in a day when virtue must be white hot." The Committee of General Security, the revolutionary tribunals, and scores of special agents brought "revolutionary justice" throughout the republic. "No one feels safe; no one is safe. If not a suspect one may be suspected of being a suspect."

Soon the Jacobins forced the Convention to decree the arrest and execution of the leading Girondins. Soon, too, the organizing genius of the Jacobin Lazare Carnot brought mass conscription and a tide of enthusiastic patriotism. The enemies of France were held back. By the end of 1793 France had recovered Belgium and had driven the Prussians out of Alsace, the English out of the harbor of Toulon. The Law of the Maximum stopped monopolies, speculation, and profiteers. All of the insurrections had been suppressed. The knives of the guillotines rose and fell.

Against the background of foreign and civil war came the Reign of Terror in France. About this period of mass emotion and tragic excesses many pages have been written, some of them so dramatic that the reader can close his eyes and see rivers of blood. Even though the descriptions of the Terror have sometimes been overwritten and inaccurate it does remain true that the purges and bloodshed formed a nasty and shocking episode in the history of Europe. Marie Antoinette, Philip of Orléans—the king's cousin—hundreds of aristocrats, and uncounted other men were the victims of swift "revolutionary justice."

Many of the makers of the Terror were zealots. Some were passionate psychotics. They were all men consumed with a flaming desire to build a Republic of Virtue. They were not prepared to accept the fact that there were then, are now, and will be tomorrow, many imperfections, injustices, fallibilities, and evils so long as human beings walk upon the earth.

The leaders of the Terror identified themselves with a mystical "general will." Under their fanatical stimulation new religious and patriotic cults arose to replace the Christian faith. The Festival of Reason was started in November, 1793, and the Festival of the Worship of the Supreme Being in May, 1794. Other national festivals, held every ten days, included celebrations in honor of such things as love, agriculture, connubial bliss, and disinterestedness. A revolutionary calendar, adopted in June, 1794, gave new names to the months. It seemed that as much as possible of the heritage of the past, so inglorious and despised by the age of Enlightenment and Virtue, was to be swept away. All was to be new and wonderful.

Maximilien Robespierre, the famous "Incorruptible," joined with Jacques Danton to march forward in the ranks of those who were determined to crush all of the foes of the Revolution. There was also Louis Antoine Saint-Just, "the exterminating angel," that handsome youth "with a mind of fire and a heart of ice" so admirably described in Geoffrey Bruun's *Saint-Just: Apostle of the Terror*. There were still others: the silver-tongued journalist Camille Desmoulins; the fiery Jean Marat; the cripple George August Couthon.

These men who sought to create a Republic of Virtue soon began to dispute among themselves. Some wanted to call a halt to mass murder. Others insisted that the Terror must continue until the head of the last suspect fell in a basket by a bloodstained guillotine. In March, 1794, a left-wing group called the "Hébertists" was executed. A little later, Desmoulins and Danton were arrested. Said Saint-Just: "If we do not guillotine them, then we shall be guillotined ourselves!" The members of the terrified Convention mouthed their agreement that Danton and several others had indeed been too "indulgent." Danton's conduct and words were confused—"Look, the Seine is running with blood!"—but he was not too confused to denounce Robespierre: "Vile Robespierre, the scaffold claims you too! You will follow me!" Later he said: "Show my head to the people! They do not see the like every day!"

Thus Danton went to the guillotine. Robespierre was master, or nearly so. And yet, with Danton gone, who in France was really "pure" and virtuous? Robespierre was probably sure that he was without fault. He would make Virtue supreme in an ideal Republic, even if he had to guillotine the whole population of France to do it. Untroubled by the mounting evidence that more and more Frenchmen were weary of bloodshed, Robespierre continued to present his proscription lists to the Convention. There must be more purges, always more purges. Meanwhile Robespierre's opponents intrigued against him.

On July 27, 1794, Saint-Just was not permitted to read a proscription list in the Convention. Robespierre's foes would not let him speak, declaring that he had it in his mind to "murder the Convention." A swift vote ousted Robespierre. He was shot and wounded at the Hôtel de Ville. Shortly afterwards he was executed. By his side in the tumbril and on the scaffold stood Saint-Just, cool and elegant and contemptuous to the end.

With the fall of Robespierre the Reign of Terror stopped.

The months following Robespierre's death are usually called the period of the Thermidorian reaction—in the new calendar of the Revolution the month of July was named Thermidor. It was an unpleasant, sterile, and colorless time. Robespierre's Goddess of Virtue went far away. The Jacobin Clubs closed.

Soon the Moderates and Royalists carried on a "White Terror" against the Jacobins, once so strong and proud. Revolutionary idealism retreated. Calculating, corrupt, and selfish men jostled for profit and power. "Government fell into an open sewer."

The Convention dissolved itself in October, 1795. A new constitution provided for a government to be headed by an executive committee, or Directory, of five men. There was to be an upper Chamber of Elders (250) and a lower Chamber of Five Hundred.

The government of the Directory was swiftly plagued by foreign wars and domestic problems. The Directors, so hard-pressed, were soon to be troubled still more. This time the source of their discomfiture was a young Corsican officer who had once expertly used a "whiff of grapeshot" to put down a royalist mob demonstrating against the Convention. His name was Napoleon Bonaparte.

Chapter 31

THE NAPOLEONIC ERA:
COHESION AND DIVERSITY

"I am no Don Quixote seeking for adventures. I am a reasonable person who does only what he believes is useful. The only difference between me and other rulers is that difficulties check their efforts, while I love to surmount them whenever I am convinced that the object is a great and noble one, worthy of myself and of the nation over which I rule."

—Napoleon Bonaparte. *Mémoires du général de Caulaincourt*, II, 217

To TAKE the place of the blood and idealism of the Terror came the corruption and incompetence of the middle-class republic called the Directory. The four-year history of this Directory (1795–1799) was at once disreputable and pathetic. It is not surprising that most Frenchmen were lukewarm in their support of the new government. Nevertheless, the majority of them were opposed to the restoration of the Bourbons. A restored Bourbon monarch might take away the advantages won by the people in the Revolution. Peasants and middle-class men might be required to hand back the lands they had obtained. Military officers who had carved careers during the Revolution might find their useful and profitable days at an end. Some politicians might face proscription. It was true that the Directory was filled with weak men and strong evils and struggles for power; but it was to be preferred to the Bourbons.

One of the many weaknesses of the Directory was this: it had no hero, no prophet, seer, messiah. The years of its rule were a time of a great vacuum. Most Frenchmen were quite ready to follow any leader who would claim to be the architect of a new France, a man chosen by destiny to guard and guide. They were willing "to accept any master who knows how to bind them by their hopes and fears." The master who was able to do this was Napoleon Bonaparte.

For fifteen years the biography of Napoleon and the tempestuous history of Europe were almost the same thing. Napoleon knit the Continent together in a vast partnership of strife and subjugation. The whole Napoleonic era possesses the cohesive unity of a great drama.

There are good reasons for saying that Napoleon Bonaparte was one of the most outstanding human beings in history. There is no doubt that he was a military man of consummate genius; those who underestimated his skill usually came to untimely ends. He was a shrewd statesman and diplomat. At the same time, Napoleon was not a man of virtue. He was ambitious, unscrupulous, hard, ruthless, cruel, double-dealing, egotistical, and greedy. In many respects his character was contemptible. To gain his ends he used and destroyed men and states. What he wanted he tried to get, whatever the cost might be. Once he remarked: "When a king is said to have been kind, the reign is a failure." This seems to have been an honest statement of his point of view.

The power that Napoleon grasped and held he obtained by force, fraud, shrewd decisions, and strength of personality. Many of his contemporaries remarked upon his confidence in himself and his destiny, his "cold gray eyes," his voice with the trenchant phrases and the sharp edge of authority. After his first meeting with Napoleon, General Augereau was confused and impressed: "This little runt of a general frightened me. It is impossible to understand how he made me feel that he was the master from the moment that he looked at me." Napoleon's generals and soldiers obeyed him; they were loyal; they were confident that under his leadership victory would be theirs; and they were usually right.

Napoleon, always a man of action, decisively shaped so many complicated events that only a series of volumes could describe and explain what he did. Under his strong hand and watchful eyes new governments, laws, and institutions were made; many of them were wisely formed; and some of them survived the collapse of Napoleon's Grand Empire. Napoleon had come, he said, to "consolidate the Revolution" and to "pacify Europe." He did both, or almost so. Because of his almost incredible series of victories on the battlefields he has taken his place beside Alexander the Great and Julius Caesar and the others who inhabit Valhalla. Nearly all of Europe bowed before his will, for a time. Some of his achievements in the arts of peace were perhaps more enduring: but it is for what he did with his swords and guns and battalions that he is most remembered. "Every man," he once said, "must fulfill his destiny."

Napoleon was born in 1769 in the little town of Ajaccio, Corsica. His shabby-genteel family sent him to school in France. Short, shy, aloof, and rather uncouth, the young Napoleon learned to take a cold and critical view of his fellow human beings in a world that he found harsh and bleak. In 1793 he received a commission as an artillery lieutenant in the French army and soon won recognition by his exploits in two events mentioned earlier: the recapture of Toulon from the English and the defense of the Convention against some persistent rebels. Early in 1796 he was appointed to the rank of general, given command of the Army of Italy, and directed to proceed to Italy.

Napoleon left his new wife Josephine de Beauharnois and led an army of 35,000 men across the Alps. There the brilliance of Napoleon's campaign dazzled his staff officers, his enemies, and later generations of war-college students.

Napoleon's foes in northern Italy were the Austrians and Sardinians. He split his enemies by marching suddenly north from Savona. "United, the two forces would have been superior to the French army. Separated, they were lost." The Sardinians were forced back upon Turin and disposed of first; the king of Piedmont-Sardinia agreed to an armistice. Then Napoleon turned against the Austrians, outflanked them, forced them into Mantua, besieged them, accepted their surrender, defeated an Austrian relief army and pursued the remnants of it almost to Vienna. With his defeated enemies Napoleon negotiated (October, 1797) the Treaty of Campo Formio—he did it himself, refusing to tolerate any interference from the Directory.

Austria now finally and formally surrendered the Austrian Netherlands that France had annexed in 1795. Austria also recognized the French frontier on the Rhine. As partial compensation for her losses Austria was given the Ionian Islands and a large slice of Venetia. Napoleon also promised the German princes on the right bank of the Rhine that he would compensate them for the lands he had seized on the left. The Italian conquests of Napoleon were organized into the dependent Cispadine Republic, Ligurian Republic, and Cisalpine Republic.

Napoleon could not let his sword rust in its scabbard. "The people of Paris," he said, "do not remember anything. Were I to remain here long, doing nothing, I should be lost. In this great Babylon everything wears out; my glory is already fading. This little Europe does not supply enough of it for me. I must seek it in the East." The Directory wanted Napoleon to attack England at once. He preferred to strike at England through Egypt and India —"I saw myself on the road to Asia, perched on an elephant, a turban in my hand." An audacious heir of Alexander the Great would march to conquer the exotic lands and fabulous wealth of the East!

In May, 1798, Napoleon transported a French army from Toulon to Alexandria, eluding in the darkness a British naval squadron under the command of Admiral Lord Nelson. Napoleon easily overran the land of the pharaohs and pyramids. Soon, however, the conqueror found himself a prisoner. On August 1, 1798, England's Admiral Nelson sank all but four ships of a French fleet in Egypt's Aboukir Bay. Napoleon's troops were completely cut off from Europe. "Had I been master of the sea," Napoleon later said, "I should have been lord also of the Orient."

Turkey now declared war. Despite his broken communication lines Napoleon invaded the Turkish province of Syria. His armies, weakened by disease and heat, slowly pushed past Gaza and Jaffa and laid siege to Acre—this was in March, 1799. Acre was a mudhole. On April 15 about 30,000 Turks were routed, an event that caused one of Napoleon's officers to exclaim: "General, how great you are!"

Even Napoleon could not stay the attacks of the weather and the diseases that cripple and slay in the Near East. In June he returned to Cairo. In July a Turkish army landed to do battle. Napoleon nearly wiped it out. The astonished Turks knew what the Austrians and Italians had learned two years before.

Meanwhile the fortunes of France had ceased to shine and glitter in Europe. Britain was sweeping French commerce from the seas; a tightening blockade throttled the ports of the French coast. Royalist revolts quickened and flamed in the French provinces as power slipped from the nerveless hands of the demoralized Directory. The Second Coalition of Britain, Austria, Russia, Naples, and Turkey was moving from victory to victory. Several French armies had been routed and the military reputation of the French Republic steadily slithered downwards. The Austrians and Russians invaded Switzerland. The Italian republics established by France were falling apart. France herself was threatened by invasion.

Many years later Napoleon wrote: "All that had been won by the Army of Italy was gone. My place was where my presence was most needed." In October, 1799, he left his marooned army in Egypt and returned to France. There are many stories of the language he used when the messengers of the Directory arrived to greet him. Some of those tales are excellent; not all of them are true.

Napoleon was hailed as a hero by enthusiastic Frenchmen who had the idea that he had conquered widely in the Near East. The popular imagination often invents; then it embroiders.

Even before the return of Napoleon there had been plots to overthrow the Directory. Napoleon swiftly allied himself with Sieyès, Talleyrand, and Fouché—master intriguers all—in a new conspiracy. Fears of Jacobin plots were deliberately built up and a political crisis was manufactured. Napoleon's troops and generals went to a special session of the legislature at St. Cloud. The plan of Napoleon and his associates to oust the government nearly miscarried when the Council of Five Hundred tried to have Napoleon outlawed. Napoleon's brother Lucien—President of the Council of Five Hundred—kept his nerve and saved the day by ordering the troops to clear the chamber and disperse the deputies. This was the famous coup d'état of November, 1799.

The Directory was swiftly overthrown. In its place was set up a new government of three consuls—the first consul was Napoleon—appointed by the Council of the Ancients. The new Constitution of the Year VIII soon established a complicated system of government containing a Legislative Body, a Tribunate, and a Senate.

The important fact was this: the Directory had been upset and driven out because France was weary of misgovernment. "The people," said a contemporary, "with the exception of a contemptible horde of anarchists, are so tired, so disgusted with revolutionary horrors and follies that all are convinced that they cannot but gain by any change." Napoleon Bonaparte had the support of nearly every class and party. He had no political past; he was a widely advertised man of talent and decision; he was popular; his military exploits had caught the public fancy. He was soon to claim that he was indeed the "son and testamentary executor of the Revolution." It was quite logical and appropriate that the Constitution of the Year VIII was ratified by a vote of 3,011,007 to 1,526. "One and all expected him to restore order and harmony, peace at home and peace abroad; they expected it from him and him alone."

Some men did not then know, of course, that when Napoleon Bonaparte became first consul he also became the virtual dictator of France. "Confidence comes from below," said Napoleon, "power from above."

Napoleon was indeed the first consul. The other two consuls were his aides, not his equals. "One will protect my right," said Napoleon, "the other my left."

The new first consul used his extraordinary skill and energy to establish a strong and efficient government upon the basis of the social and economic changes effected by the French Revolution. He was shrewd enough to see that most Frenchmen, after years of revolution and war, wanted a strong man to reduce their difficulties. They also wanted a stable and efficient government, peace, and safety.

Under the Consulate and the later Empire there were many swift reforms of administrative machinery, law, and customs. The whole administrative system of France was streamlined and tightly centralized. In each *département* Napoleon appointed new administrative officials called prefects who were directly responsible to him. The prefects, in turn, appointed the mayors in the villages and communes. The tax rolls were audited. The number of inspectors and assessors was increased. The public debt was consolidated and a sinking fund was established. A decimal monetary system was developed. Coinage was standardized. The national Bank of France was formed. Canals were dug and harbors were enlarged—vast public-works projects kept the level of employment high with consequent happy effects upon national morale. The principles of equality in taxation and equality before the law were maintained and strengthened. By such measures, sound and shrewd, Napoleon increased his prestige, his popularity, and his power.

Napoleon also settled, for a time, the disputes with the Church. Prolonged conversations between Napoleon and Pope Pius VII resulted in the famous Concordat. This agreement ended the nasty schism between Church and state in France and reconciled the refractory clergy to the Consulate. By the terms of the Concordat the Church abandoned all claims to property taken from it during the French Revolution. The French government agreed to pay the salaries of the clergy. Roman Catholicism was recognized as the religion of the majority of Frenchmen. The pope was assured that his temporal domains in Italy would remain in his hands. Members of the lower clergy in France were to be chosen by the bishops. The bishops were to be nominated by the First Consul and consecrated by the Pope.

Pius VII ratified the Concordat in December, 1801, and the French Assembly approved it in April, 1802. The reconciliation between France and the papacy was celebrated by a *Te Deum* in Notre Dame.

"Religion," Napoleon once remarked, "is a useful vaccine against social distempers." He was also aware, of course, that the faith and morals of the Church are embedded in the whole heritage of the West. Even the swift seepage of the secular ideas born of the Enlightenment could not alter that fact.

What was to be done about the maze and tangle of the laws of France? In the days of the National Convention the first steps had been taken towards a codification of the confused and often contradictory laws. Napoleon pushed that work forward, urging the legal experts to finish their tasks. The result was the famous *Code Napoléon*. Contained in it was the important Civil Code (1804) which embodied many of the fundamental changes effected by the French Revolution in the legal status of persons and property. Soon the Code of Civil Procedure (1806), the Commercial Code (1807), and the Criminal Code (1810) were completed. Throughout these codes run steadily the themes of civil equality, national unity, religious liberty. Parts of the *Code Napoléon* have been used by several countries in Latin America; by Greece, Rumania, Japan; and by some of the lands in Europe once occupied by Napoleon's armies.

For Napoleon it was not enough to be first consul. There is no doubt that he aimed at the establishment of hereditary power quite early in his dramatic career. The first step in this direction was the creation in 1802 of the Life Consulate, an act approved in a plebiscite by 3,577,259 voters and opposed by 8,374. "There will be no more factions in France," said Napoleon. "For my part, I have never seen the advantages of opposition of any kind. Whatever its nature it serves only to lessen respect for the authority in power in the minds of the people."

Many traces of the Revolution now began to disappear. "Citizen" gave way to "Monsieur." Boots were replaced by buckled shoes. The saber yielded to the sword. Meanwhile the powers of the first consul were expanded. By a series of decrees the Senate was reorganized and Napoleon controlled 80 of the 120 seats. Then he obtained the power to name his successor.

In May, 1804, the Life Consulate was transformed into the hereditary Empire. Napoleon Bonaparte became "Emperor of the French." His brothers Louis and Joseph were proclaimed Princes of France. There were also created sixteen grand dignitaries and sixteen grand marshals. To a faintly vulgar court came several people—including some of Napoleon's relatives from Corsica—who had difficulty walking on polished floors.

Another plebiscite showed that 3,572,328 Frenchmen approved the creation of the Empire and 2,569 did not. In December, 1804, the coronation of Napoleon and Josephine took place at the Cathedral of Notre Dame. Pope Pius VII, so active in the pomp and circumstance of the ceremony, did not crown Napoleon. Napoleon took the crown and placed it upon his own head. The act was symbolic.

The story has been told that when the form of the new seal of state was being discussed somebody suggested that the seal take the shape of a lion in repose. Napoleon wanted "an eagle in flight." Whether or not the tale is true it underlines the fact that Napoleon did not intend to stop at being "Emperor of the French." He would be more, and soon.

The Bourbon Louis XVIII and several of his supporters objected strongly to the new Empire and the upstart emperor. Royalist pamphlets were printed and spread about. The language of some foreign newspapers, especially the English, was strong. "Will Napoleon be able to forget the wild manners of his native land in the polish and civilization of Europe's courts? This is a little frog who is trying to be as big as a bull. He swells and swells; but the little French froggie will end by bursting." To such comments as these Napoleon had an apt and adequate reply: "Power is never ridiculous."

About the source of his personal power Napoleon had some clear ideas. This is what he said: "One must have regard for people's vanity. . . . Liberty is a pretext. Equality is a hobby. The people are pleased to have a man who has risen from the ranks for their Emperor. . . . The men who have changed the universe have never done so by capturing the leaders, but always by moving the masses. . . . Man can only be governed through the imagination. Without it he is a brute."

Napoleon Bonaparte, son and heir of the Revolution, needed success, and success he could get by military victory. If he left his arms to tarnish on the wall, then his prestige and power would decline and his fate would be sure. It was not wise, of course, for Napoleon to declare that he wanted war. It was better to assert that he wanted "the pacification of Europe" and an end to the conflict with Austria and England. The clever Talleyrand, who served so many masters and lived so many lives, phrased the whole matter well in a letter that he wrote to Napoleon on December 25, 1799. "It is always assuming a good position at the beginning of a campaign to manifest a warm desire for peace and to make every attempt towards its establishment. If the result of the campaign is favorable, one has acquired the right to show severity; if disastrous, one need not bear the reproach of having brought it on."

Late in 1799 Napoleon made a general statement to London and Vienna suggesting an end to hostilities. Austria refused. England's reply was wary and evasive: "His Majesty's Government cannot place reliance on general professions of pacific intentions. The nation of France has waged aggressive war, levied exactions and overthrown institutions in neighboring states. His Majesty's Government cannot discern as yet any abandonment of that system." Meanwhile the French still controlled the strategic area of the Low Countries, "a pistol pointed at the heart of England." Napoleon was a dangerous enemy. "England," said a contemporary, "has contracted one-half of her national debt to get the Bourbons out of France and is contracting the other half to restore them."

In June, 1800, Napoleon took the army that he had gathered at Dijon over the Alpine pass of St. Bernard and struck at the rear of the surprised Austrians. He restored the Cisalpine Republic and beat the Austrians at the battle of Marengo—a truce was signed the next day. The "freed" Cisalpine Republic was compelled to pay a monthly tax. In December, Napoleon's General Moreau defeated the Austrians at Hohenlinden—the Austrians lost 15,000 men, the French 1,500. Vienna now asked for an armistice. "Austria is done for," said Joseph Fouché, France's wily minister of police. "It rests with France alone to establish peace in Europe."

In February, 1801, the Treaty of Lunéville brought a temporary peace with Austria. Other treaties were made with lesser states: Naples, Portugal, Spain. Russia, at odds with Austria, moved out of the allied camp. The Second Coalition had crumbled. Again England stood alone. "That Bonaparte has an interest in making peace," William Pitt, the prime minister, told Parliament, "is at best a doubtful proposition, and that he has an interest in preserving it is still more uncertain." By this time Britain had taken Malta and several French, Spanish, and Dutch possessions in various parts of the world. The British fleets were victorious; the French had been stopped everywhere on the seas. On the other hand, the French had triumphed on the land. The war of "the whale and the elephant" had reached a stalemate.

Haggling negotiations for peace now began. The result was the hollow Treaty of Amiens signed in March, 1802. The treaty provided for "peace, friendship, and intelligence" between Great Britain and France. Britain kept Trinidad and Dutch Ceylon. She agreed to return the Cape of Good Hope to the Dutch and all of the French colonies to the French. The territorial integrity of Portugal and Turkey was guaranteed by both powers. No reference was made to the status of the Low Countries, one of the reasons why England had gone to war in 1793. There was no guarantee that the French-controlled European markets would be opened to British trade. England's George III said: "Do you know what I call this peace? An experimental peace—for it is nothing else." Napoleon said: "At Amiens I achieved the moral conquest of Europe." "Peace for a week," another remarked, "a truce for three weeks, and war in a month." There could be no lasting peace with Napoleon. "In the existing situation every treaty of peace means to me no more than a brief armistice; and I believe that, while I fill my present office, my destiny is to be fighting almost continuously." After one year the weary nations turned again to war.

The French stayed in Belgium. Napoleon was feverishly building naval ships; he laid robber hands on Santo Domingo in the West Indies; he sent a secret mission to India; he declared himself the President of the Cisalpine Republic, annexed the Piedmont in northern Italy, proclaimed a new constitution for Switzerland. At the same time he decided to abandon Louisiana. In April, 1803, he wrote to Talleyrand: "Irresolution and deliberation are no longer in season. I renounce Louisiana. It is not only New Orleans that I cede; it is the whole colony without reserve. . . . To attempt obstinately to retain it would be folly. I leave it to you to negotiate the affair." The government of Thomas Jefferson, anxious to control the Mississippi, paid Napoleon 60,-000,000 francs for Louisiana. In December, 1803, the flag of the United States was raised over New Orleans.

"France needs glorious deeds and hence war," Napoleon said to his Council of State in 1802. "She must be the first among states or she is lost. I shall put up with peace as long as our neighbors can maintain it, but I shall regard it as an advantage if they force me to take up my arms again before they grow rusty." He also said: "Europe cannot be at rest except under the rule of a single head who will have kings for his officers, who will distribute kingdoms to his lieutenants."

Under the terms of the Treaty of Amiens, England had agreed to give up Malta. Suspicious of Napoleon's plans, the British cabinet refused to surrender Malta, and this was the technical cause of the resumption of hostilities in May, 1803. The French historian Louis Madelin denounced the "anti-Napoleonic cutthroats" of England who were guilty of bad faith in holding on to Malta. Madelin asserted that England compelled Napoleon to go to war and to change his "wise and balanced designs." Napoleon complained that "it was England who forced us to conquer all of Europe." "I always appear to be attacking," he said, "yet what I am doing is defending myself all the time."

PLATE
XXXIII

[99]

Third of May." This painting by Spain's great artist, Francisco Goya, shows
Napoleon's soldiers executing Spanish guerrillas in 1808.

[100]

Handwriting on the Wall." This print shows an English view of the situation
Napoleon in 1803. In March, 1802, the Treaty of Amiens had been signed by
Britain and France. In May, 1803, the two nations were at war again.

[101] The Battle of Waterloo, June 18, 1815. "Napoleon's hopes had vanished with the closing cann
His last spectacular challenge had been answered."

[102]

[103]

Because the Duke of Wellington stood obstinately against reform, this contemporary cartoon shows him as being all hat, boot and spur, and very little man.

Michaelplatz, Vienna, in the early nineteenth century. This calm suggests some of the happier aspects of middle class life in the fasci capital of Austria.

PLATE XXXIV

It has already been suggested that Napoleon had been thinking for some time about the creation of a "Grand Empire" that would extend far beyond the frontiers of France. Talleyrand later said that "the extension of France to the Rhine, the Alps, and the Pyrenees was the work of the Revolution; everything else was the work of Napoleon." Napoleon may have concluded that to make his projected "Grand Empire" safe he must first subdue England. Late in 1803 he ordered the construction of flat-bottomed boats, each of which could be used to carry 100 men across the Channel. The English swiftly took countermeasures; they blockaded Brest and Toulon and protected their own coasts. "We need to be masters of the sea for only six hours," said Napoleon, "and England ceases to exist." Those hours he never got. England's Lord St. Vincent declared in the House of Lords: "I do not say, my lords, that the French cannot come. I only say, they cannot come *by sea.*"

In August, 1805, Napoleon acted upon reports that the Third Coalition of Austria, Russia, and England had been formed and that Austria was mobilizing. He suddenly shifted his Grand Army from Boulogne towards Austria. To Talleyrand he wrote: "My mind is made up. I invade Germany with 200,000 men and I do not halt until I have reached Vienna, taken Venice and everything Austria still has in Italy and driven out the Bourbons. I shall prevent the Austrians and the Russians uniting. I shall beat them before they can get together."

By forced marches Napoleon led his Grand Army down to Austria in three weeks. After a series of brilliant maneuvers he forced one Austrian army of 50,000 men to surrender at Ulm in Bavaria. Then, in December, 1805, he overwhelmed the combined Austrian and Russian armies at Austerlitz. The Austrians and Russians lost more than 25,000 men; the French lost 9,000. Austerlitz was indeed a great French triumph. Napoleon's power depended upon such victories, and he knew it. It was once remarked, for instance, that "the existence of the French in Italy depends upon a bulletin." When the Prussian ambassador congratulated Napoleon upon the outcome of Austerlitz he received the disconcerting reply: "What would the message have been had Austerlitz proved a defeat?"

Austria now signed the humiliating Peace of Pressburg by which she recognized Napoleon as King of Italy and all his changes there. Austria also lost her possessions in south Germany. Those holdings were transferred to Baden, Bavaria, and Württemberg, which, with Hesse-Darmstadt, were now allies and satellites of France. In 1806 Napoleon formed the Confederation of the Rhine. Bavaria and Württemberg were now raised to the status of kingdoms and Baden and Hesse to grand duchies. These rulers and all the other German leaders in the south accepted Napoleon as their "Protector." Napoleon compelled Francis II of Austria to surrender the title of emperor and thus the famed Holy Roman Empire, founded by Charlemagne and since the fifteenth century ruled by the Austrian Hapsburgs, was finally dissolved. The new Confederation of the Rhine agreed to accept the *Code Napoléon* and to supply 63,000 troops for the armies of the Empire. The formation of the Rhine Confederation was a step towards efficient government and the unification of the German states; but the price paid for it was independence.

The Third Coalition was apparently disintegrating. Napoleon's shattering triumphs perhaps hastened the death of England's William Pitt. "Roll up that map of Europe," he is supposed to have said. "It will not be needed these ten years."

Not all was darkness. In October, 1805, the combined French and Spanish fleets sailed out of Cadiz to meet Admiral Lord Nelson and the British navy. The result was the battle off Cape Trafalgar, the last great naval battle fought with sailing ships. Lord Nelson won the battle and lost his life. Now England's security at sea was confirmed. It was to be left unchallenged for a hundred years.

"Europe is not to be saved by any single man," said William Pitt. "England has saved herself by her exertions and will, I trust, save Europe by her example." "I cannot be everywhere," said Napoleon.

Meanwhile Napoleon continued to build his gleaming and triumphant Grand Empire in Europe. Part of his scheme for a Grand Empire by which he would "fuse all nations into one" was the creation of dependent kingdoms ruled by different members of his family. In 1805 the Cisalpine Republic became the Kingdom of Italy, ruled by Napoleon's stepson Eugène. In 1806 southern Italy became the Kingdom of Naples under Joseph Bonaparte—after Austerlitz the Grand Army had moved against Naples on the order of Napoleon: "I command you to overthrow the crippled battalions of the tyrants of the sea." The Batavian Republic became the Kingdom of Holland under Louis Bonaparte. The new nobility was expanded. To many generals and marshals Napoleon gave the titles of princes; there were 31 dukes, 308 counts, 1,090 barons, and 1,500 knights of the Empire.

The Grand Empire of Napoleon was held together by the bonds of military force. Any such arrangement is usually not a structure of unity or order at all. In his failure to understand this fact Napoleon Bonaparte was at one with other conquerors like Genghis Khan and Adolf Hitler.

Late in 1806 Prussia learned that Napoleon had secretly offered to hand Hanover back to George III of England despite the fact that he had earlier promised it to Prussia. This fact, coupled with Napoleon's alarming aggressions, drove Prussia into war, a war in which she was joined by Russia and Great Britain. The Fourth Coalition was thus formed while the graves were still fresh at Austerlitz. "It is perfectly true that Napoleon did not want to make war on Prussia in 1806 any more than on England in 1803. He only made peace impossible."

So Napoleon moved against Frederick William of Prussia. "The Prussian muskets were polished but they were the worst in Europe." On October 14, 1806, half of the Prussian army was routed by Napoleon at Jena and the rest was smashed by Davout at Auerstadt. Prussia was prostrate. Frederick William fled to East Prussia. Napoleon went to Potsdam, seized Frederick the Great's sword and sash and took them to Paris. "In politics," said Napoleon, "magnanimity is the mark of a simpleton."

In 1807 Napoleon turned against Russia. On February 18, the battle of Eylau was fought in the midst of a heavy snowstorm in the muddy stretches of the Polish marshes. For the first time Napoleon was stopped in a pitched battle. When the Russians retreated with heavy losses Napoleon claimed a victory. Soon he got about 80,000 men and boys from France—it was the third levy within a year. On June 14, 1807, he caught a Russian army at Friedland between a ravine and a river. The result was a heavy disaster for the Russians.

Napoleon now made a series of arrangements with Russia and Prussia that together constituted the Treaty of Tilsit. Alexander I and Napoleon met— it was a dramatic scene—on a raft in the Niemen River. Russia became an ally of France. The possessions of Prussia west of the Elbe, together with other German principalities, were gathered into the new Kingdom of Westphalia. The Polish possessions of Prussia became the Grand Duchy of Warsaw, nominally ruled by the King of Saxony but in fact controlled by Napoleon. The Grand Empire of Napoleon now included nearly all of Italy and Germany to the frontiers of Austria and Russia.

So it was that in an atmosphere of flattery, drama, and deception a peace was arranged between France and Russia, a large part of it at the expense of Frederick William of Prussia. Alexander I wrote to Frederick William: "It is cruel, it is painful for me to say that I shall no longer have the hope of being able to assist you in the manner my heart would wish."

Many eminent French historians—Albert Sorel, Emile Bourgeois, Frederic Masson, Edouard Driault, and others—have agreed that the Treaty of Tilsit marked a turning point in Napoleon's career, the beginning of the end. Some writers have also said that after Tilsit, Napoleon "began to attempt the impossible." Such statements are perhaps more simple than the kaleidoscopic shifting of the complex facts might seem to warrant.

A few comments may be ventured here. In the first place, it is certainly true that at the height of the Grand Empire, bulwarked by satellites and allies, Napoleon Bonaparte controlled more territory than had been under the scepter of the Emperor Charles V. Unfortunately for Napoleon, that control rested mainly upon military might. The larger the Empire grew, the longer were the military lines of communication; the longer these lines became, the less was their tensile strength.

It is also true that the Empire was not sustained by any unifying ideals and ideas acceptable to the people outside of France; it was psychologically fragmented, divided by rivalry, malice, and often by ill-veiled or open hostilities.

Of high importance and constant danger were the unpredictable forces of nationalism. The flames of nationalism only flickered at first; then they roared and leaped towards the sky. It was not then possible to rouse strong loyalties to the broad, supranational organization called the Grand Empire. Again and again, throughout Europe, Napoleon found that things kept going wrong. Some lands and peoples refused to stay beaten. Military victories brought conquests; but conquests did not bring peace.

It seemed to Napoleon that his imperial policies could never be successful unless British political and naval power was destroyed. "Lordship on land has never been able to live in peace with the lordship of the sea." Between 1803 and 1805 Napoleon's project of invading England collapsed. In a military and naval sense the islanders were unassailable. Hence Napoleon decided to begin a new and different kind of attempt to break the stalemate and end British resistance. This time he used the weapons of economic warfare.

Napoleon believed that the industry and commerce of Great Britain could be ruined if her manufactured and colonial goods could be kept out of Europe. This was the idea and purpose behind the famous "Continental System."

On November 21, 1806, Napoleon issued his drastic Berlin Decrees "with repugnance." These decrees—extended by the Milan Decrees of 1807—declared that the British Isles were in a state of blockade. They forbade all commerce between Britain and France or the states allied with France. Neutral ships that entered British ports and later came into any French-controlled ports in France, Germany, Holland, Italy, or Spain were liable to seizure.

On January 7, 1807, Great Britain replied by her Orders-in-Council declaring a blockade of all the states of Europe that submitted to Napoleon. "France by her decrees has resolved to abolish all trade with England. England now says that France then shall have no trade but with England." The Orders-in-Council stated that all ships trading between the European ports from which British ships were excluded were liable to capture and condemnation as lawful prizes. Neutral ships, however, might call at British ports for licenses to carry certain goods to French ports.

Students of the history of the United States are well aware of the repercussions in America of the French Continental System, the British countermeasures, and the terms of Jefferson's Embargo Act of 1807 and the Non-Intercourse Act of 1809. After Napoleon persuaded President James Madison that the Berlin and Milan Decrees would be withdrawn, the anger and indignation of the United States were turned against Great Britain. Despite the outcries and the opposition Britain maintained her blockade. There were searches of neutral ships and impressments, and many Americans considered these acts of the British to be crimes against persons and property. They agreed with President Madison's "crying enormity" message to Congress in June, 1812.

Napoleon's plan could not succeed without the full support of the Continent. So long as a few leaks remained in the economic dike Napoleon could not hope to triumph. On the edge of Europe he failed to obtain the cooperation he needed. British commerce flowed under neutral flags, under British licenses, under licenses issued by European authorities, even with the permission of Napoleon himself. French industry staggered beneath the burdens imposed upon it. France had to buy British goods. Many soldiers of the Empire were shod with British boots and dressed in uniforms made from British wool. In 1807 more than 50,000 of the French troops engaged in the campaign against Russia wore British overcoats. British tea, coffee, tobacco, and chocolate could not be excluded from Europe; the demand was too great, the agents of France too corruptible. British goods were smuggled through the ports of Greece, Dalmatia, Portugal, Holland, and northern Germany. As prices rose, the profits grew greater than the risks. Napoleon never got the cooperation of the people of Europe. They were most disobliging. British commerce was not effectively excluded. British warehouses were not glutted with unsold goods; her gold reserves were not exhausted; she did not founder in a sea of inflation; her credit did not collapse.

Meanwhile Napoleon tried to stop the flow of British goods through Portugal. His attempts to do so involved him in the conquest of Spain. In a drama of trickery, coercion, and fraud Napoleon shamelessly turned upon his Spanish ally in 1808 and forced the Spanish king to abdicate. Napoleon's brother Joseph was put upon the Spanish throne. "Spaniards," said a proclamation of Napoleon, "you have been ruled by traitors. I have abolished everything that was opposed to your prosperity and grandeur." The conqueror warned the Spaniards not to oppose him: "God has given me the force and will to overcome all obstacles."

Proud Spain revolted. There had never been much sympathy in Madrid or Lisbon for the liberal and irreligious doctrines of the French Revolution. Napoleon's marshals and generals were not prepared to cope with the irregular guerrilla warfare waged against them. French generalship—so well described in Sir Charles Oman's *The Peninsular War*—was mediocre, and the French artillery and equipment were inadequate. One French commander was stopped at Valencia; a second was forced to surrender near Cadiz; a third was stopped at Saragossa; a fourth was blockaded in Barcelona. Joseph was forced to get out of Madrid. A national spirit had helped France to conquer her neighbors.

The rise of new national spirits in Europe was to wreck the Grand Empire.

Events in Spain gave Great Britain an opportunity to invade the Continent. After an Anglo-Spanish alliance was signed, a British army of about 30,000 men was sent to Portugal under the command of Sir Arthur Wellesley, later the Duke of Wellington. At first the British waited and fought behind the fortified lines of Torres Vedras; their army was anchored on Lisbon; and Lisbon was supplied from the sea. By 1811 the ill-fed French had been compelled to retreat from Portugal with heavy losses; their supply and communication lines had been too long; the Spaniards had never slackened in their sniping. Steadily the Peninsular War drained French troops from other parts of Europe. London and Madrid saw to it that Napoleon did not escape from his entangling tasks in Spain.

In the fall of 1808 four kings and thirty-four "sovereign princes" assembled at the great Congress of Erfurt. Napoleon's allies were uneasy. Alexander I of Russia, for instance, had not been happy about joining the Continental System and helping Napoleon to force it upon Sweden and Denmark. Russian trade had certainly suffered. Nor had Alexander approved of Napoleon's high-handed policy in Prussia. Nevertheless, Alexander did promise at Erfurt to try to maintain peace in Eastern Europe while Napoleon was busy in Spain. The tsar also agreed that if Austria attacked France, then Russia would fight Austria.

Despite such arrangements there was no healthy confidence. Alexander I said: "It is impossible to meet Napoleon without danger, whether in negotiations or on the battlefield." Meanwhile the intriguing Talleyrand was busy betraying his master. To Alexander I he stated opinions that the tsar must have welcomed: "The French people is civilized, but its sovereign is not. The Russian sovereign is civilized but his people is not. It rests with the sovereign of Russia to ally himself with the people of France." About the same time he wrote these words to Prince von Metternich of Austria: "Napoleon's cause is no longer France's. Europe can only at last be saved by the closest alliance between Russia and Austria. . . . The interests of France itself demand that the powers which are in a position to hold Napoleon in check unite to oppose a dam to his insatiable ambition." At Erfurt, Talleyrand added to his numerous achievements in treason and treachery. His ability was great; his integrity was not. If he can be said to have loved anything it was perhaps France and certainly himself.

In February, 1809, Austria, heartened by Spanish resistance, entered the war again. "The conduct of the Austrians," wrote Napoleon later, "upset all my plans." The battle of Wagram (July, 1809) saw Austria defeated once more. Napoleon imposed what he called "a peace of violence" upon the vanquished Austrians. They were to cede territory to Bavaria and the Grand Duchy of Warsaw; to pay France an indemnity of 85,000,000 francs; to adhere to the Continental System; to reduce their army to 150,000 men. In 1810 Napoleon married the Hapsburg Archduchess Marie Louise, grandniece of Marie Antoinette. Josephine had given Napoleon no male heir and so she was put aside.

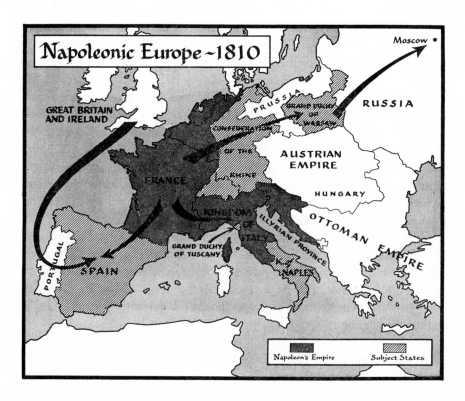

Napoleon also tried to tighten up the Continental System by annexing Holland and the north coast of Germany up to the Elbe, by establishing prohibitive duties on colonial commodities, and by setting up special courts to deal with the smugglers. It was all to no avail. The whole Continent was stirring behind its barriers.

In 1811 England was reacting to the pinch of the Continental System; but Napoleon's Europe, feeling keenly the loss of British trade, was slowly moving towards revolt. Russia, for instance, was finding that the policy of Napoleon was having increasingly unhappy results for her commerce and finance. Why should the Muscovites be deprived of necessities and comforts for the sake of Napoleon? At the same time, Alexander I was suspicious of Napoleon's intentions in Poland—he suspected, with good reason, that Napoleon intended to set up a kingdom of Poland as a military bulwark against Russia. When Napoleon made a military alliance with Austria in 1810 Alexander also feared that with the aid of Austria, Napoleon might try to incorporate the Balkans and Turkey into the Grand Empire. Alexander was further angered when Oldenburg, whose former ruler was the tsar's relative, was annexed to France.

Alexander I at last defied Napoleon by proclaiming the restoration of Poland under Russian suzerainty. Napoleon replied by attacking Russia in 1812. The Russian war ended the Continental System. It was also an important part of the end of the power of Napoleon. Meanwhile the Duke of Wellington was moving from victory to victory in Spain.

Many pages have been written about Napoleon's decision to invade Russia in 1812. Perhaps Caulaincourt's *Memoirs* came close to the heart of the matter: "Once an idea that he considered expedient lodged itself in his head, the Emperor became his own dupe. He adopted it, caressed it, impregnated himself with it. . . . When he sought to seduce you he had already seduced himself." Napoleon also said that in a crisis intuition is better than logic. Sometimes it is so, sometimes not. One can never be sure until after the event; then it is too late to change.

On June 20, 1812, a proclamation by Napoleon to his Grand Army said: "Russia's destruction shall be fulfilled. . . . Are we no more the soldiers who fought at Austerlitz?" On July 24, 1812, a proclamation of Alexander I to his people summoned them to protect Mother Russia: "You are defending your religion, your country and your liberty! I am with you and God is against the aggressor!"

About the same time that Napoleon invaded Russia the United States declared war upon Great Britain. Americans were angered at the restrictions placed upon neutral commerce and the carrying trade by the British blockade and resentful of Britain's exercise of the right of search. A few American leaders desired to conquer Florida and Canada. From a naval and military point of view the War of 1812 was not important. The American invasion of Canada failed; the British descent upon Washington was useless; the shining American victory at New Orleans in 1815 came after peace had been signed at Ghent upon the basis of the status quo.

Meanwhile Napoleon crossed into Lithuania with an army of 471,000 men. From the Prussians he had requisitioned 200,000 bushels of rye; 4,000,000 bushels of wheat; 1,200 tons of rice and dry vegetables; 35,000 tons of hay and 18,000 tons of straw; 6,000,000 pounds of gunpowder; 2,000,000 bottles of beer; 3,600 horse carts; and 15,000 horses. He hoped to defeat the Russian army and force from Russia the cession of Lithuania. But the Russians retreated. Napoleon followed them to Smolensk, to Borodino, to Moscow. He entered a deserted Moscow on September 18 and took up his residence in the

Kremlin. Two days later a great fire destroyed a large part of the city; men still argue about who started the blaze; probably the Russians did it.

Napoleon remained in Moscow for more than five weeks in the hope that Alexander I would make peace. Alexander refused: "No negotiations shall be entered into while one armed Frenchman remains in Russia." At last Napoleon retreated with the Russians fighting on his rear and flank. He reached Germany with an army of about 100,000 men. It was one of the most appalling military disasters in history. On December 3, 1812, the *Moniteur* of Paris reported that "the health of H.M. the Emperor has never been better." On December 5 Napoleon began a dash across Poland, Germany, and France upon "affairs of the highest importance."

When Napoleon reached Paris he hastened to raise new forces to maintain his control of Germany. Fortunately for Napoleon, Metternich of Austria feared Russia as much as he did France and was opposed to Prussia's schemes for extending her territories in northern Germany. When Russia and Prussia finally entered into an alliance (Treaty of Kalish, March, 1813) against Napoleon, Austria refused to join them. Meanwhile Britain promised to invade southern France from Spain—"a decision on the opposite side of Europe must be of incalculable advantage."

In May, 1813, Napoleon defeated the Russian and Prussian armies at Lützen and Bautzen. Instead of pushing his advantage, Napoleon agreed to a truce "for the sake of the hope of peace." He also tried to separate Alexander I and Frederick William III by promising to give Poland to Alexander. The suspicious tsar refused to accept the offer.

In June, Austria agreed (the Convention of Reichenbach) to join Russia and Prussia. "Men are incorrigible," said Napoleon. "Experience is lost upon them. Three times I set your Emperor upon his throne. I married his daughter . . . at the time I said I was making a blunder. . . . Fear of my soldiers alone guarantees the loyalty of princes."

The ferment in the Germanies was deep and wide. Johann Gottfried Herder (1744–1803), mentioned earlier, had long stressed the cultural unity of a Germany divided by politics and religion. He had rebuked many Germans for their uncritical aping of foreign models—"each nation is a separate species in the garden of humanity." Herder also sadly remarked: "We are working in Germany in the confusion of a Babel." The philosopher-patriot Johann Gottlieb Fichte (1762–1814) insisted that subjects must be changed into citizens. His famous *Addresses to the German Nation* declared the importance of the rising spirit of nationalism. There were other strong leaders: Baron Heinrich Friedrich Karl vom Stein (1757–1831), Prince Karl August von Hardenberg (1750–1822), Gerhard Johann David von Scharnhorst (1755–1813). Incompetence, they said, must be abolished. Apathy must be ended.

Germans must break the hold of the privileged officials and the outmoded class dictinctions. Brains must be made more important than brutality. Promotion must be by merit. The old leaders should suffer "the slow white death that waits for privilege in defeat." A new Germany must be born.

Napoleon was now fighting against thousands of roused and dedicated Germans filled with the intoxicating spirit of nationalism. For the first time, too, he was faced by the four great powers at the same time.

The allies began by moving shrewdly. They tried to avoid fighting Napoleon in person and concentrated instead upon his subordinates. They defeated Oudinot and Ney; Vandamme surrendered; Davout was shut up in Hamburg. At Dresden, Napoleon routed the Austrian and Russian armies under Count Schwarzenburg. It was his last great victory.

In the decisive four days' battle of Leipzig in October, 1813, Napoleon's army fought forces double its size. Napoleon was not well; Sokolov called him "a sick Titan." The slaughter in this "Battle of the Nations" was heavy. More than 50,000 men were killed or wounded in the bloody fighting of October 17. On October 18 the remnants of Napoleon's army were forced back into France. About 40,000 soldiers got across the Rhine; about 200,000 were left behind: the dead, the wounded, the missing, the prisoners. The immediate result of this defeat was the complete collapse of Napoleon's power in Germany.

One of Napoleon's foes concluded that "no great resistance can now be made" by the defeated emperor. He was not quite correct. The wizardry of Napoleon's defensive tactics amazed even those who understood his genius. Meanwhile the Duke of Wellington advanced northwards from Spain. When Napoleon asked on November 2 for 300,000 men to be conscripted he stated a new fact, hard and harsh: "A year ago all Europe was marching with us. Today all Europe is marching against us." The hour for which the allies—and Talleyrand—had waited so long had at last arrived. The victorious armies of the allies stood poised on the frontiers of France. Napoleon was overwhelmed. Napoleon was defeated. He would challenge Europe no more—except once, at Waterloo.

Chapter 32

VIENNA: THE GUARDS
AND THE REBELS

"My life has fallen at a hateful time. I have come into the world either
too early or too late. Now I do not feel comfortable; earlier, I should have
enjoyed the time; later I should have helped to build it up again; today I
have to give my life to prop up the moldering edifice."
— Prince Clemens von Metternich. Heinrich Ritter von Srbik,
Metternich, der Staatsmann und der Mensch, II, 298

THE Allies hesitated to invade France. Some men thought that an invasion
might rouse a strong French national resistance. Many still feared the
name and power of Napoleon. Modern men and minds may find this comment strange, perhaps ridiculous. Had Napoleon not been defeated? Was it
not true that he had been able to raise only about 120,000 men for his new
army? Did the Allies not have three armies, each containing about 125,000
soldiers, on the borders of France? An Allied leader, were one with us now,
would admit these facts. He would also remind us that there was always reason
to fear Napoleon. The terror of his name was almost unimpaired. There was
no other military leader to be compared to him. It was hard to believe in the
fall of "the man whose feet still walk the world."

There were also dissensions among the Allies. "No one can have any idea,"
wrote Alexander I, "of all the trouble to which we have been put to maintain
this coalition, to conceal the mistrust and overcome the jealousies." For four
months the march on Paris was delayed.

The Allies first offered Napoleon peace on the condition that he should
abandon Italy and confine himself to France to the Rhine. They gave him
until December 2, 1813, to accept these terms. Napoleon accepted, but his
reply did not reach the Allies by December 2. Meanwhile the Allies discovered that the French would probably not give Napoleon much support. In
Paris there was widespread apathy. The Allies also learned that a strong party
at Paris, led by Talleyrand, was in favor of a restoration of the Bourbons—

Alexander I was astonished to see that several men who had voted for the execution of Louis XVI now wanted a Bourbon monarch. Talleyrand, of course, knew that if the Allies put Louis XVIII on the throne they could not easily punish him for the crimes of Napoleon, his hated enemy. Talleyrand was soon to be president of the French provisional government. Soon, too, he was to defend France and condemn Napoleon at the Congress of Vienna. He was also to remind Louis XVIII of a remarkable fact: "There seems to be an inexplicable something in me, sire, that brings bad luck to governments that neglect me."

On December 1, 1813, the Allies issued the Declaration of Frankfort. This document carefully stated the Allied war aims and their desire for a "free, happy, and tranquil Europe." It denounced Napoleon's "thirst for conquest" and "false calculations of glory." It tried to prove to the French people that Napoleon, by refusing honorable proposals for peace, was responsible for the approaching invasion of France; that the Allies were fighting Napoleon, not the French people.

With masterly skill Napoleon resisted the Allied armies. On March 31, 1814, the Allies at last entered Paris. They had already agreed with the French leaders to a restoration of Louis XVIII, that colorless and stodgy Bourbon. Napoleon, in "the agony of Fontainebleau," would have continued the struggle. "No one ever signs his own disgrace in good faith. I will never sign the dishonor of France." The members of the provisional government declared that Napoleon was removed from the throne; they renounced their allegiance. "To a man, almost, they turned against him."

On April 5, 1814, the Allies issued a formal declaration: "Desiring to prove to the Emperor Napoleon that all animosity on their part ceases as soon as the peace of Europe is assured, and that they cannot and will not forget the place that belongs to the Emperor Napoleon in the history of his age, the Allied powers grant to him in full ownership for himself and his family the island of Elba. They assure for him an annual income of six million, three for himself and the Empress Marie Louise, three for the rest of the Bonaparte family."

Ten days later Napoleon signed a ratification of the Act of Abdication. After his abdication, Napoleon said farewell to his generals. His secretary described the scene: "Napoleon took General Petit in his arms and kissed the flag, and the silence . . . was broken only by the sobs of the soldiers."

On May 3, 1814, Louis XVIII came back to Paris. A month later Louis signed with the Allies the first Treaty of Paris, in which the boundaries of France were to be what they had been on January 1, 1792. The lands of France were thus diminished and the glory of her name was dimmed.

Napoleon sailed for Elba on the British cruiser *Undaunted*. The Empress Marie Louise had earlier fled with her son, the King of Rome. Joseph, too, had run away. To many Frenchmen the drama and the sadness of the hour were sharp and vivid. The famous French writer François René de Chateaubriand caught a part of the drama and something of the mood of France when he stressed the mutability of men's fortunes and the vanity of human affairs:

> Fifteen months ago he was in Moscow and now the Russians are in Paris. From the Pillars of Hercules to the Caucasus all Europe trembled at his word and today he is a fugitive without a home, without a place of refuge. Like the tide of the sea his might foamed over the dams and like the ebb it has receded.

Europe was at peace for the first time in more than twenty years. Soon Louis XVIII was to be placed upon the throne of France. "If they are wise, the Bourbons will change only the linen on my bed," said Napoleon. The relatives of the Corsican emperor stumbled down the steps of the thrones of Europe to make way for the legitimate rulers. "The kings crept out again to feel the sun." When the shadow of Napoleon had fallen across their courtyards they had sought security in flight or in submission. As soon as the Congress of Vienna approved, most of them would be back upon their thrones once more.

From the capitals of Europe the peacemakers gathered at Vienna.

It is not true to say that the all-embracing formula of the Congress of Vienna was simple reaction. The peacemakers of 1815 were not foolish enough to believe that they could act as if the French Revolution and the Grand Empire had never been. They did not expect to make a new Europe in the image of the old order before 1789. They were practical men. They realized that some things had happened that they could never undo. The world they had known before the Revolution had been shattered beyond repair or reconstruction.

The French Revolution and Napoleon had helped to spread liberalism and nationalism through large areas of Europe. These two forces—they were often regarded as virulent evils—brought deadly fear to many governments. Most of the rulers of Europe also agreed that the imbalance of power created by Napoleon's Grand Empire must be destroyed and a balance-of-power system revived for the good of the European body politic. A new map of Europe must be shaped. France must be weakened so that her armies could not pour over Europe again. There must be no revival of the terrors of the French Revolution and French military aggression. Steps must be taken to ensure European stability against the dangers of liberalism and destructive revolution. In the settlements at the Congress of Vienna the governing consideration was the necessity, as the Congress saw it, of maintaining order, balance, security, and peace. Finally, England, Austria, Prussia, and Russia must be compensated for the sacrifices and losses they had made to save Europe and humble Napoleon. Such were some of the challenging tasks of change and reconstruction that faced the statesmen of Europe in 1815.

Representatives of every European government except Turkey came to the deliberations at the capital of the Hapsburgs on the Danube. Among the very important persons were the emperor of Austria, the tsar of Russia, the kings of Prussia, Denmark, Bavaria, and Württemberg. There was much pomp and pageantry—the Austrian government was said to have spent about $15,000,000 in providing balls and banquets and other entertainments. Meanwhile, behind closed doors, the real and vital decisions were made by the four great powers: Austria, Prussia, Russia, England.

The hand of Prince Clemens von Metternich, Austria's foreign minister, reached everywhere. The conservative Metternich was the leader of those who were convinced that Europe needed peace and stability and that all national movements should be suppressed. Metternich's own patchwork state of Austria, so filled with different peoples, cultures, and languages, was particularly vulnerable to the explosive teachings of nationalism. Metternich and many of his associates at Vienna were also of the opinion that the liberals should be stopped from infecting others with their dissatisfactions and their ideas about changes and reforms.

Prince Metternich was an able statesman; but his ability was at least matched by his conceit and his dogmatism, always undesirable and weakening qualities. Professor Arthur J. May, one of the most highly regarded modern authorities on the Hapsburgs and their world, has said that "Metternich considered his personal judgments on international matters as infallible." Much pride went before a great fall.

In justice to Metternich it must be added that he was not so adamantly opposed to reform as many readers may believe. He did insist, however, that reform should come from above, never as the result of pressure or power from below. Of this he was never able to convince the autocratic Emperor Francis I. The very idea of reform was odious to Francis. He once said: "I won't have any innovations. Let the laws be justly applied; our laws are good and adequate. This is no time for reforms." It is also true that Metternich was less powerful in Austria than he was in the councils of Europe.

From Prussia came Prince Hardenberg, chancellor of the kingdom. From Britain came the Duke of Wellington and Viscount Castlereagh, the secretary of state for foreign affairs, hard-working, suave, and clever. From Russia came Tsar Alexander I, that dynamic and erratic Romanov who was sometimes a mystic, often a pacifist, frequently a realist and a warrior, always convinced that he had been chosen by God to undertake a series of missions for Him. Alexander was one of the most baffling characters of the nineteenth century.

As a personal representative of Louis XVIII of France came Talleyrand, slippery, subtle, and shrewd. He matched, or outmatched, the suave and calculating Metternich. Talleyrand moved with celerity and skill, a master of legerdemain with a strain of crookedness that often paid large dividends. He needed no one to hold his hand in the darkness. He was not to be trusted,

> though his tongue
> Dropped manna, and could make the worse appear
> The better reason, to perplex and dash
> Maturest counsels.

When the Allies began to dispute among themselves about the future of Saxony, Talleyrand offered to aid Austria and Britain with arms, if necessary, against Russia and Prussia. Because Austria and Britain welcomed this support, Talleyrand was able to obtain a seat for France at the councils of the victorious powers. The "Big Four" became the "Big Five."

Talleyrand insisted then, as he had insisted earlier, that the common foe had been Napoleon, not France. It was Talleyrand, too, who first presented the welcome idea of "legitimacy" to the Congress. Acting upon the principle of "legitimacy" the Congress put legitimate monarchs back upon their thrones, except where it was inconvenient to do so.

The ordered calculations of the diplomats of Vienna were sharply disturbed by an unexpected and dramatic event. Napoleon escaped from Elba—"quiet to quick bosoms is a hell"—and returned to France on March 1, 1815. "Soldiers, in my exile I listened to your voices. In defiance of all obstacles and all dangers I have hastened to you here."

Today it is difficult to imagine the excitement, and sometimes the consternation, that leaped over Europe when the news came that Napoleon was loose. Were more years of revolution, war, and aggression at hand? What deeds might Napoleon do now?

Napoleon did obtain support. Discontent had been rising and spreading in France as the vindictive and reactionary emigrés came back and led a "white terror" against the supporters of the Revolution and Napoleon. In retrospect the days of the Emperor's rule seemed more happy and glorious than in fact they had ever been. Many of the soldiers who had served under Napoleon hastened to form their ranks under his banners again.

Napoleon entered Paris and took over the government. He hastily raised an army of about 150,000 men. On June 12 he left Paris to fight and headed for Belgium. Said Fouché, once his minister of police: "This man has come back again madder than he went. . . . He can win one or two fights, crush a few Allied divisions, but he cannot gain the victory."

Against Napoleon stood England's Duke of Wellington, blocking the road to Brussels. Not far away was Prussia's Marshal Blücher, with an army of about 120,000 troops, mostly Prussians. "Blücher," Napoleon once said, "is like a bull that looks all around him with rolling eyes, and when he sees danger, charges. . . . The old rascal would always attack me with the same fury. After the most terrible beating he would be on his feet again the next moment and ready for the fray."

Wellington had an army of about 68,000 men. He himself said that it was "the worst-equipped army with the worst staff ever brought together." In it there were 29,000 British soldiers, 17,000 Belgians and Dutch, 19,000 Germans, and some others.

On June 16 the gallant old Marshal Blücher was caught by Marshal Ney at Ligny. Napoleon sent Ney a message: "The fate of France is in your hands." Ney, however, made some bad mistakes. It was Napoleon who finally split the Prussian army; the Prussians lost 12,000 men. Meanwhile Marshal Ney held Wellington back at Quatre Bras. Slowly Wellington fell back towards Brussels. The hour of the battle of Waterloo was now approaching.

On June 17, Napoleon was ill. He had trusted Marshal Ney and Marshal Grouchy with high command; each of them failed him. Their mistakes, from a military point of view, cannot easily be understood or pardoned. Commanders who show incompetence sometimes have no second chance; the soldiers who follow them also pay, often on the field of battle. On the other hand, Wellington and Blücher worked together well despite some bad staff work in Wellington's army.

On June 18, Napoleon's health was better. He hurled his infantry and cavalry—he had about 75,000 men at Waterloo—against the thin and obstinate wall of Wellington's army on the Waterloo ridge. Through the soggy cornfields the soldiers fought furiously; the cannons thundered. Shortly after four o'clock Wellington's center was torn and shaken; but he stood firmly; the line must be held. Then Marshal Blücher and General von Bülow came up and were engaged at last. As the shadows began to fall about half of the French forces started to retreat. Then the whole French army was transformed into a fleeing rabble. The French lost about 40,000 men and almost all their artillery. The British lost more than 15,000 men and the Prussians 7,000. Napoleon's hopes had vanished with the closing cannonades. His last spectacular challenge had been answered.

On July 14 Napoleon voluntarily surrendered to the captain of the British ship *Bellerophon*. The British, he said, were "the most powerful, the most unwavering, and the most generous" of his foes. Louis XVIII was entering Paris again. The last "flight of the eagle" had ended. Napoleon should never have led the French army into the gigantic task it undertook. He should also have remembered that his health was unsound. He was not the Napoleon of Marengo or Austerlitz. Time is a relentless enemy.

Elba had been close to Europe, too close. Napoleon had escaped and more than 60,000 men had died. The Allies decided that such risks should not be taken again. Hence they banished their modern Prometheus to St. Helena, a small (147 square miles), bleak, and volcanic British island in the South Atlantic. Rocky St. Helena is 700 miles away from Ascension Island—the nearest land, 1,200 miles from Mossamedes, the nearest African port, and about 4,000 miles from France. The leagued rulers of Europe had beaten Napoleon. A silent tribute to his power and their fear is the fact that they put him far away upon St. Helena.

> Then haste thee to thy sullen Isle
> And gaze upon the sea.

Napoleon was detained at St. Helena's Longwood under the sharp eyes of the watchful Sir Hudson Lowe, the British governor. There he dictated his memoirs, explained his deeds and his motives, arranged "a pose before the mirror of history." There he died in May, 1821. The house in which he had lived at Longwood was presented by Queen Victoria in 1858 to France's Napoleon III.

Soon the famous and gilded "Napoleonic legend," nourished by a literary tradition, began to grow and spread far from the remote island of St. Helena. Myths and conjurers multiplied. Facts were altered in an ever-changing epic of heroism, martyrdom, and pathos. Had not Napoleon upset thrones and slaughtered hosts of wicked enemies for the general welfare? Had this energetic "heir of the Revolution" not been overcome by the pride, the malice, and the treason of his foes? Had this dynamic "Man of Destiny" not defied many of the laws of probability for the glory of France and the people, the humble people, from the ranks of whom he had sprung? The citation of facts can never destroy legends and symbols. Many of the violent and ungracious facts about Napoleon are forgotten. The Napoleonic legend lives and grows. It is a reality. It is a fact. Even today it is difficult to write a sober and uncolored narrative about Napoleon Bonaparte. Only a heavy-livered man—or a man who has no imagination and knows no history—can stand unmoved by the tomb of Napoleon.

Talleyrand still insisted that it would be a criminal act of folly to dismember France or to punish her too heavily. The reader familiar with the documents of the Congress of Vienna will recall Talleyrand's careful treading of the razor's edge in his negotiations, the polite and deadly rapiers he used in the debates, the ways in which he asserted the importance of maintaining an equilibrium in Europe, an equilibrium that could never be achieved if France were cut or harmed. To those who seemed to be smug or complacent after the defeat of Napoleon, Talleyrand—and Metternich, too—spoke of the sad and ugly pressures and crusades of the liberals and nationalists in Europe. A strong

France, Talleyrand declared, would be an insurance against the disasters
plotted by the muttering and busy foes of conservatism, proportion, and
balance.

Those who were uncertain, hesitant, or timid were promptly reminded that
the world of Europe in 1815 was shaky; it was not wise to remove or weaken
strong props such as France; it was no time for men who should be in the same
camp to be heedless or hostile or sulky. If they wanted to stop upheavals and
ward off disaster they must be staunch supporters of balance and order. Almost
everywhere on the Continent the seeds of radicalism, resistance, nationalism,
and liberalism had been planted, especially in the years of the French Revolution and Napoleon. The harvest could be deplorable, dangerous, deadly. This
is what Talleyrand said; this is what Metternich believed.

Lord Castlereagh and the Duke of Wellington agreed to support Talleyrand. They had come to Vienna chiefly interested in two things: restoring
the balance of power and obtaining strategic colonies to protect trade routes
and the empire. To aid in achieving the former they wanted a strong France.
Castlereagh said that he wanted "to bring the world back to peaceful habits."
His chief purpose was to contribute to that end by seeing to it that no nation
became too strong among the European states. For centuries this had been a
cardinal point of British policy. It was to remain so.

The arguments of Talleyrand prevailed at Vienna. Despite the annoyance
of Prussia, who wanted revenge and more territory, the boundaries of France
were left substantially as they had been in 1789. England obtained most of the
French overseas possessions seized during the wars. After Napoleon had failed
at Waterloo the Allies restored Louis XVIII once more. They negotiated with
him a second Treaty of Paris, a settlement more severe than the first because
the French, it seemed, had shown that they were both unrepentant and incorrigible. The new treaty, signed in November, 1815, provided that France
should be occupied by Allied armies pending the payment of an indemnity
of 700,000 francs. When France had borrowed the money from England the
indemnity was paid and the occupation army withdrew (1818). There were no
other penalties placed upon France, apart from the loss of a few square miles
of land.

But France must not be too strong. Hence it was decided to create two
buffer states as guarantees against possible French aggression. Austria gave
up the Austrian Netherlands (Belgium), and they were united with Holland
to form the United Kingdom of the Netherlands. A friendly nation across
the Channel added to English security. England also restored Java and the
Dutch East Indies to the Netherlands. To create a strong state to guard the
mountain passes on the southeastern frontier of France, the states of Genoa and
Sardinia-Piedmont were joined under the house of Savoy. England and Russia

saw that this independent Italian state would also serve to check and balance Austrian power in Italy.

The Holy Roman Empire was not revived. In Germany, Napoleon had ousted about seventy princes, dukes, and counts. He had taken away the autonomy of more than forty free cities. At the same time he had strengthened states like Bavaria and Prussia. Thus Napoleon helped to stimulate German nationalism and heightened the hopes of those who dreamed of a united Germany. At Vienna such hopes were disappointed by the creation of an imperfect and impotent confederacy of thirty-nine states in which each state remained almost independent. This was done because Metternich saw that an efficient German Confederation would weaken Austria and strengthen her rival Prussia.

As compensation for her loss of the Austrian Netherlands, Austria was given Lombardy and Venetia, thus adding four million Italians to the polyglot population of the Hapsburg Empire. Otherwise no changes were made. "Austria," said Castlereagh, "is the great hinge upon which the fate of Europe must ultimately depend." The autocratic rule of the Hapsburgs must remain undisturbed.

In Italy the pope received back the states of the Church. The Bourbon Ferdinand I went to the kingdom of Naples and the Bourbon Ferdinand VII to the throne of Spain. Russia obtained the larger part of Poland. Because Denmark had supported Napoleon, Norway was taken from her and granted to Sweden in compensation for Finland, earlier conquered by Russia.

As an important part of the Vienna settlement Castlereagh claimed for England a number of small but important colonies, the strategic value of which was considerable. In the North Sea there was Heligoland; in the Mediterranean, Malta and the Ionian Islands (later given to Greece); in the Indian Ocean, Ceylon and Mauritius, strategic outposts of the eastern empire. At the foot of Africa there was Cape Colony. In the West Indies Tobago and St. Lucia were taken from France, not because they were desirable as defense posts for the empire but because they could supply sugar in abundance to the United Kingdom.

England was now the foremost power in the world. As unchallenged mistress of the seas she controlled the lanes of trade. Her colonies had steadily increased in number and importance. No foreign competitor was yet in a position to threaten her industrial and commercial supremacy. London was becoming the financial center of the world. Peace with victory had been secured. England's long years of danger were over at last.

The terms of the Vienna settlement show that the peacemakers built a nation-state structure and system out of the debris of the Grand Empire. Within that arrangement of sovereign and independent states, so familiar for many centuries, there steadily increased the power of numerous national loyalties and aspirations, part of the legacy of the French Revolution and the Napoleonic Wars.

Certainly the decisions of the Congress of Vienna were not deliberately calculated to give aid or delight to nationalists, liberals, or democrats. Many peoples were transferred from government to government and no attempts were made to find out whether they approved or not. There was no Wilsonian idea of "self-determination" or anything approaching it. The decisions at Vienna resulted in much trouble, especially as the potent forces of nationalism erupted. The hopes and achievements of many nationalists, the dreamers and the realists, form a large part of the history of Europe in the nineteenth century.

They are also of incalculable consequence in our contemporary world. In the eyes of a patriotic citizen his nation stands and shines. To him there are few earthly things more beautiful than the flag of his own land. The history and the ideals of the state are taught to the children in their impressionable years. The youths are made conscious of national principles and faiths, of great purposes shared, of a corporate life based upon values and loyalties whose demands will not be loosed until they die. No guns on the seas or land or in the air, no words spoken over the green tables of diplomacy, no teachings of international socialism, have yet measurably diminished or dimmed the power of the nation-state.

It was quite natural that Prince Metternich and his associates should have been anxious to safeguard the agreements reached at Vienna. Austria, England, Prussia, and Russia soon organized the famous Quadruple Alliance, which in fact became a Quintuple Alliance when France joined the ranks of the Big Four. Under Article 6 of the agreement it was provided that from time to time representatives of the member nations would hold "reunions devoted to the common interests and the execution of measures judged salutary for the repose and solidarity of the peoples." These diplomatic conferences were intended to facilitate cooperation in suppressing any liberal or revolutionary movements in Europe. In the triumphant age of Metternich's diplomacy the great powers were prepared to try to prevent political change, and, if necessary, to interfere and use coercion in the domestic affairs of lesser states.

Between 1818 and 1822 four international congresses were held at Aix-la-Chapelle, Troppau, Laibach, and Verona. After the conference at Laibach in 1821 an Austrian army marched into Naples to protect Ferdinand I from the liberal constitution that his subjects wanted to impose upon him. Ferdinand was soon restored to his position as an autocratic monarch. At the Congress of Verona in 1822 it was decided that Louis XVIII of France should send an army into Spain to crush some liberals who had demanded a liberal constitution.

The army of Louis marched; the revolt was crushed; hundreds of Spanish liberals were executed or imprisoned. In Spain, as in Naples, there was black reaction and uneasy peace. Until 1848 the Metternich "system" remained in a position to defend the autocratic values which Metternich called "the eternal laws of the moral world."

The Quadruple Alliance was a definite and practical agreement. Far different was the Holy Alliance, the product of the unstable and cloudy mind of Alexander I, tsar of Russia. Probably under the influence of Baroness von Krüdener, a mystic and seer, Alexander proposed that the rulers of Europe agree upon "the necessity of settling the steps to be observed by the Powers, in their reciprocal relations, upon the sublime truths which the Holy Religion of our Saviour teaches." Alexander hoped that his fellow monarchs would promise "to take for their sole guide the precepts of that Holy Religion, namely the precepts of Justice, Christian Charity, and Peace. . . ."

There had certainly been nothing like this document in European history before. Metternich said that it was a "sonorous nothing." Castlereagh said that it was "a sublime piece of mysticism and nonsense." Francis I of Austria was polite and signed the moral pledge. Prussia signed. Great Britain did not sign, saying to Alexander that His Majesty's government regretted that the British constitution forbade it. The pope refused to make an agreement with schismatics. The Sultan of Turkey was not invited to sign Alexander's Christian document.

Historians who write about the age of Robespierre and Napoleon inevitably dwell upon past politics and battles long ago. Despite the interest and importance of these dramatic events, neither writer nor reader should fail to remember that throughout these exciting years the slow currents of economic and social change were rolling upon their relentless ways. More roads and canals were built. More improvements in agriculture increased the crops. Better beef cattle were bred, better cows, sheep, hogs. Adventuring entrepreneurs built factories, railroads, steamships, banks. They traded, invested, made money, and put the profits back into more enterprises. The supplies of goods and the wealth of nations increased. The tides of migration swirled. There was work to be done, money to be made, gold to be found. Thousands of men and women, of course, continued to live simply and slowly in their native hamlets, as their fathers had done before them. In the daily rounds and common tasks they found satisfaction. Through the changeless rhythms of the seasons they lived and labored and then their tale was told.

In 1815 the long war had ended. The guns were silent and the soldiers could go home. For a time, at least, men did not need to live in fear of war and death. Now, surely, a new age of peace and a better world for the troubled children of Europe was over the near horizon. Ahead was the promise of years of progress filled with happiness and vitality, boisterous, roaring, and profitable.

These gleaming hopes soon faded. The taxes and interest rates stayed high; but many profits and prices and wages zoomed and declined, uncontrolled and shifting; the bases of prosperity were unstable when the war economy collapsed. Few men really knew what was happening or why. Some things were obvious and clear; bad weather brought bad harvests and bad harvests meant hungry people. Demobilized soldiers often found themselves without jobs or houses. Governments wrestled with currency and credit problems. Trade channels were clogged. In some parts of Europe industry was almost at a standstill. It was a bad time to try policies of economic nationalism; but several governments did. The darkness of a postwar depression spread over Europe.

To some men the shadowed scenes brought disappointment and even despair. Other men girded up their loins and were ready to fight, hard and soon. Metternich and his colleagues in the Quadruple Alliance were not only faced and threatened by the floods and forces of liberalism and nationalism. They were also challenged by the anger born of economic dislocations, the mutterings of social discontent, the unsolved riddles of social justice. It is foolish, of course, to try to separate and distinguish all the various forces of revolt and fierce dissent. Neat and defining paragraphs about nationalism and liberalism and radicalism can easily be written; but they would not be true and both writers and readers might be deceived. Unrest in any age has many causes—including sometimes the psychological and glandular conditions of leaders and men—and takes many shapes. The men who are makers of disturbances have many ends, some clear and wise, some vague and silly, and all mixed together. The scholars and others who study the anatomy of revolutions have a difficult task, especially those who do not know what they are going to find before they start to search.

The conservatives and the reactionaries naturally watched every move of the nationalists, liberals, and radicals with edgy suspicion. There were disturbances and then revolutions. Controversies, creeds, and protests poured forth with bewildering rapidity. Slogans rose and fluttered. Formulas, half-truths, and panaceas were vehemently defended and challenged. Arguments, often filled with great exaggerations, were championed by angry and articulate men. It was really absurd, said some popular leaders, to resist their claims and to deny the need for political, economic, and social reforms. A new age was struggling to be born and it would not be stopped.

From the point of view of most conservative minds the hopes and deeds of the liberals and nationalists and others of their kind were dangerous to the stability of the state and prejudicial to the interests of the upper classes. The entrenched antagonists of the reform movements of Metternich's day had one main answer: repression. They did not see that social and economic changes were creating enormous problems with which men and states had to grapple. More and more the ideals and ends of aristocracy and complete *laissez faire* were to be re-examined. Nations always march to a new order through the wreckage of the old.

The conservatives and reactionaries were almost everywhere at bay; and they defended themselves long and well. During the fifteen years before the series of revolutions that came in 1830 there were chapters of challenge and repression in most areas of Europe, all premonitory of the violent storms to come.

In 1821, the Greeks, dreaming of the hour when Greece might be free again, revolted against the Turks. A long war began. The battles were hard and the massacres and mutilations terrible. After the famous siege of Missolonghi 4,000 Greeks were slain. It was fitting that this was the town where Lord Byron died.

The fate of Greece was in the hands of her patriots and her friends. The Philhellenic enthusiasm in Europe and America rose rapidly. In October, 1827, the naval forces of Britain, France, and Russia completely destroyed the Turkish fleet at Navarino Bay. Russia sent armies to the Balkans, not for the first or last time. The French forced the Turks out of Morea. Slowly Turkey was compelled to yield, and in 1829 the sultan signed a peace treaty that acknowledged the independence of Greece. In 1833 Greece became a kingdom, and Otto, a Bavarian prince, was chosen to be "King of the Hellenes." The principle of nationalism had achieved its first triumph. The Greek war marked the first break in the Metternich system of "legitimacy."

There was also trouble in the lands west of the Rhine. German patriots were angry and disappointed when the Congress of Vienna failed to create a strong union of the German people. Liberal and progressive men asserted, often quite vehemently, their demand that constitutions should be granted to the peoples of the various German states.

At the Congress of Vienna, Prussia made it clear that she wanted the creation of a strong union in Germany in which the central government should be quite powerful. Austria, supported by almost all of the other rulers, opposed this idea. It was quite obvious that Austria, with all her various peoples, could never be a part of any real German union. She wished to be the leader of a loosely united group of nearly independent states. The constitution of the German Confederation or *Bund* shaped at Vienna came close to meeting the desires of Austria. The Confederation was simply a loose union of the "Sovereign Princes and Free Towns of Germany." The Diet that met at Frankfort contained representatives of the various German rulers who were members of the Confederation; there were no representatives of the people. The Constitution of the German Confederation could not be amended without the consent and approval of all the member states. No member could go to war against any other member. There is no need here to describe the numerous other provisions of the constitution. What mattered most was simply this: the loosely knit German Confederation did not meet the demands and aspirations of the increasing number of Germans who wanted a unified German state and more liberal governments.

Frederick William III of Prussia had promised a constitution to his subjects. But Frederick was a vacillating and fearful ruler. Again and again he was easily influenced by the warnings of Metternich and other stern and sturdy conservatives who told him why he should be afraid of the reformers and the liberals. Frederick kept hesitating; he postponed and evaded the granting of a modern constitution.

Meanwhile, throughout the Germanies, a number of restless and disillusioned university professors and students began to form college clubs and secret political societies—the *Burschenschaften*. Liberal and national ideas were easily merged. In 1817 a great youth conference was held at Wartburg. There were patriotic and rousing speeches about the future of a united Germany and the dreams of a land of liberalism. There were also a few really excited young men who burned some reactionary books. Such words and deeds of course caused wide alarm among jittery government officials. Elsewhere in Germany there were many meetings and speeches and a few skirmishes. Two years later an unstable theology student shot the dramatist August von Kotzebue, a Russian spy and a reactionary. In the state of Nassau a pharmacy student tried to shoot the head of the government; the fact that he missed his target was widely regretted.

Prince Metternich and his associates were deeply disturbed. At Carlsbad in Bohemia, Metternich gathered together the representatives of most of the larger German states and persuaded them to approve several resolutions that were later made into repressive decrees by the Diet of the *Bund*. The drastic Carlsbad Decrees of 1819 provided that professors should be watched and supervised by government agents and dismissed if their teachings could be described as dangerous and subversive. The *Burschenschaften* and the nationalistic gymnastic clubs were dissolved; strict censorship was imposed upon the contents of books, pamphlets, periodicals, and newspapers. The burning and banning of selected products of the pens and presses has always been an appalling aspect of attempts at thought control. When a professor is told by his government what he must write and teach, then he no longer lives in a free country. Truth has never yet been made by the laws of men.

In the clouds there were a few rifts. The rulers of Bavaria, Württemberg, Baden, and Hesse granted constitutions to their peoples and established parliaments. These South German rulers discovered that their popularity increased and that their effective power actually grew under the new arrangements. When Metternich tried to get them to withdraw their constitutions they refused, apparently convinced that they had little to fear from their peoples or from the harvest of constitutional reform. Besides, it was clear that they did resent the repeated interferences of Austria—and Prussia, too—in the internal affairs of their states.

In 1818 Prussia began tariff unions with several small states and slowly extended the arrangements. The result was the *Zollverein,* a customs union under Prussian leadership which by 1848 included almost all of Germany except Austria. Through the lands of the states of the *Zollverein* goods passed freely; duties did not have to be paid at every boundary line. This economic union increased the sense of German unity; it was one of the long steps towards the later political union and the creation of a German Empire. Prussia, the state that began it all, was often illiberal but seldom backward.

Meanwhile rebellion came to Russia. Against Alexander I's new reactionary policies there slowly arose an underground movement led and supported by several army officers and Russian intellectuals. When the childless Alexander died in 1825 it was not immediately clear whether he would be succeeded by his second brother, Nicholas, or his first brother, the erratic Grand Duke Constantine. Some of the men who had earlier plotted against Alexander and his policies now thought that they had a chance to obtain a more liberal government by supporting the Grand Duke Constantine. In December, 1825, a number of army officers in St. Petersburg proclaimed Constantine the new tsar in the belief that he would lead Russia along the liberal road. "Constantine and Constitution!" was their slogan.

Nicholas was the rightful heir, and Constantine had earlier surrendered any claim he might have had to the throne. An armed uprising at St. Petersburg, usually called the Decembrist Revolt, was speedily put down by some grapeshot. Five rebels were hanged; some went to Siberia. The whole rebellion was poorly organized; it was far less important at the time than it came to be in the eyes of men afterwards. Exaggerated legends and myths have been repeated for many decades about the Decembrists. Those myths certainly helped to foster the idea of a persistent Russian revolutionary tradition; and that, of course, was something of consequence.

The new Tsar Nicholas I (1825–1855) was an unsentimental ruler, quite unprepared to hear any nonsense about liberalism or reform. He believed in reaction, repression, and despotism. The student of the age knows that Nicholas was a failure as a monarch, as a statesman, as a politician, and as a man. His reign was one of the worst in Russian history; and Russia is a state in which there have been several rulers who have not added to the sum total of decency and justice in the world.

The voices and shots of the rebels against the arrangements of the world and system of Prince Metternich were heard, then, in widely separated parts of restless Europe: Spain, Italy, the German states, Russia, Greece.

In England, too, there were questions, answers, and disputes. In the spring of 1815 half a million men were demobilized. There were few jobs for them. War contracts were canceled. Steel and iron workers, gunsmiths, clothiers, and thousands of other artisans and laborers found themselves without work and wages. For many manufactured goods no markets could be found. Tons of commodities were available for export to liberated Europe; but the people of Europe had little money to pay for them. When these goods were suddenly dumped on the English market the result was a rapid glutting and stagnation; demand declined and prices fell sharply. During the next three years the paralyzing power of a great depression seized upon the United Kingdom. Two grain crops failed; factories closed; poverty, dirt, disease, ignorance, and a widespread feeling of disillusionment and frustration united to produce bitter complaints and violence.

The governing landed aristocracy of England was opposed to new ideas and the prospects of change. The members of the upper classes were angered and confused by any challenge to order, discipline, or to their monopoly of power. They had been frightened by the excesses of the French Revolution and still thought it possible that Jacobinism or some radical plague equally unpleasant would come to England. The Tory Cabinet under Lord Liverpool had no policies or plans for remedial legislation to cushion the effects of the economic maladjustments resulting from successive depressions, the pressures of the agricultural and industrial changes, the ugly dangers brought by the transition from war to peace. The ministers saw no need for major reforms or for any new approach to the domestic problems of England. They proudly insisted—how the words of their letters and diaries crackle across the years!— that they would not yield to the parading and plotting radicals. They would not be moved by the oscillations of prejudice or by arguments that appealed to feelings and distorted judgments. They might be apprehensive; they might be frightened sometimes; but they would not be compelled to swallow the shocking proposals and formulas of the radical philosophers and politicians and their kind.

Probably the fact of most importance was simply this: England's leaders, Tories and Whigs alike, did not understand what was happening to the old England they had known. So they stood together to protect themselves, their property, their power, and their way of life. The fruits of the victory over Napoleon Bonaparte and France had turned sour. There was neither peace nor prosperity, only turbulence and depression. When popular dissatisfaction brought widespread disturbances the British government sought security in repression, not relief. Eighteenth-century minds and hearts were dealing with nineteenth-century problems.

Several English workers accepted the simple explanation that the coming of the machines was responsible for their acute misery and bitterness. The answer to their troubles seemed equally simple: the machines must be destroyed. The so-called Luddite Riots took their name from Ned Ludlow, a half-witted Leicester apprentice who was said to have smashed machines to revenge himself upon his master. The Luddites damaged and destroyed probably £100,000 worth of property. It is unlikely that they would have wrecked the new labor-saving machinery or burned hayricks had they not been the victims of unemployment and low wages. In the postwar years what mattered most in England was not sedition, as the Tory government claimed, but the impact of the great depression upon the workers. Neither Tories nor Whigs —nor the Luddites—were aware of the hidden causes behind the visible and unpleasant facts. Ignorance has many faces, most of them ugly.

Meanwhile the demands for reform gradually became more insistent and the need more acute. The reformers came from many places and were of many kinds; but they did agree upon two things: their opposition to the power of aristocracy and their desire to reform Parliament. It was felt that once the reform of Parliament was accomplished many other reforms would inevitably and swiftly follow.

Many books and articles, written by such men as Jeremy Bentham and William Cobbett, were widely read, sometimes with approval and always with interest. Cobbett appealed more to the masses than the scholarly and logical Bentham. He was a violent man with a remarkable command of language. His exploding style was simple, muscular, direct, and terrific in its strength. He did not think calmly, this champion of causes. But when he wrote, his skill was magic. His *Weekly Register* had a circulation of more than 50,000 copies. In much of the writing of this "last of the great yeomen" there stands forth his prejudice against the government, unreasoned, unwearying, and fierce. To him the aristocratic system was an evil and fraudulent conspiracy against the people. He hated the whole social system. In his view the landlords and the Church made the people poor by rents and tithes; the manufacturers were ruining rural England and creating the cities, bloated and poisonous; the financiers were swindling the workers; omnipotent privilege exploited the whole state of England.

The savagery and sadness of Cobbett is perhaps best revealed in his *Rural Rides,* a description of journeys on horseback through his beloved southern England. How mighty was the flood of his prose and how strong his passion can be illustrated by passages quoted almost at random from his writings. Here is one: "Things have once been merry for the English poor and, by

God, they will be merry again despite the whole army of ministers, judges, pensioners, squires, financiers, clergy, spies, and magistrates who are the authors and maintainers of England's shame."

Such a champion as Cobbett generated heavy emotional excitement among the workers. The masses accepted his easy explanations of the reasons for the condition of England and, obeying his voice and their own inclinations, agitated for the reform of Parliament. There were, of course, several other crusaders, great and small, fighting for the cause of the depressed areas and the poorer classes. One outstanding enemy of the aristocrats and the industrialists was the famous poet Percy Bysshe Shelley.

In November, 1816, a large meeting in Spa Fields near London turned into a riot and the police broke it up. In 1817 a small army of unemployed workers, called the Blanketeers, planned to march on London; their leaders were arrested. There were other disturbances. The alarmed cabinet suspended the Habeas Corpus Act. A new Seditious Meetings Act required all public meetings to be licensed by the magistrates.

In the summer of 1819 about 60,000 people assembled to hear a speech about parliamentary reform at St. Peter's Fields near Manchester. The local magistrates, filled with prejudice and panic, sent soldiers to arrest the speaker. There was trouble. The cavalry was ordered to charge the crowd, and in the resulting stampede eleven individuals were killed; about five hundred were injured. This was the "Peterloo Massacre," a crime and a stupid blunder. The government then passed the repressive Six Acts. So far as the Tory government was concerned, the traditions of English liberty must yield to the greater cause of conservatism, safety, and the rule of the aristocracy.

The reactionary policies of the government were neither wisely conceived nor adroitly enforced. Wide gaps stood between the hopes of the people and the facts they saw all around them. Entrenched for a time upon the heights of power, the Tory cabinet punished and persecuted and stood adamantly against the reformers. Trails of bitter memories of those days remained for a long time among the workers and the lower-middle class.

If the reformers had stayed within the law for a year or two the Tories might have been forced from power. Some settlements might have been reached by evolution and compromise. Unfortunately, calm and shrewd men do not always decide what happens. The Tories had used force to defend their policies and their incompetence; some extremists among the workers replied in kind. In 1820 a gang of about twenty violent radicals plotted to murder the cabinet. The plotters in this Cato Street Conspiracy were discovered, arrested, and executed or transported to the penal colonies in Australia. For a time the cause of reform had been clouded by the desperate actions of a few foolish men.

When one looks back upon all the agitations and pressures of those decades more than a century ago it seems strange that the first steps towards effective reforms were not taken by any groups to the left of center. The men who first began to act through Parliament to bring a series of reforms were not Whigs, not radicals. They were liberal Tories. These few men, steadily opposed by the conservative and reactionary groups of their own party, continued to compel their inelastic colleagues to yield on many fronts. Several of the younger men in the Whig party cooperated with them.

One liberal Tory was the brilliant and ambitious George Canning, Secretary of State for Foreign Affairs after Castlereagh died in 1822. Canning brought a new liberalism into the field of foreign affairs, especially in relation to the revolts of the Spanish colonies in Latin America and the Greek struggle to achieve independence from Turkey. Partly as a result of Canning's policies, the Quadruple Alliance was soon torn apart through the middle. It was never to be mended again. Canning went one way, Metternich another.

Meanwhile the liberal Tory William Huskisson, president of the Board of Trade, carried on a policy of freer trade and moved away from Tory protectionism. The liberal Tory Sir Robert Peel, the Home Secretary, aided Sir James Mackintosh and others in securing the passage of five statutes abolishing the death penalty for more than a hundred offenses. The barbarous English criminal codes had long needed revision and reform and Peel and his associates began it. The result was a steady decrease in crime. Reason and humanity demanded this kind of legislation. Peel was also chiefly responsible for establishing an efficient metropolitan police force in London. For this reason London's policemen are still called "Bobbies" or "Peelers."

Step by step came a series of further reforms by Parliament. In 1825 the Combination Acts were repealed and the first chapters in the histories of the modern trade unions were soon written. In 1828 the Test and Corporation Acts were repealed. These acts, passed in the seventeenth century, had forbidden any Protestants who were not Anglicans to hold national or municipal offices. The provisions of the Test and Corporation Acts had in fact been evaded for many years by the passing of an annual Indemnity Bill. Hence the new repeal act of 1828 merely recognized a state of affairs already existing; but it was a symbol of a new spirit, slowly rising, of toleration and reform.

In 1829 the Catholic Emancipation Act was passed in a dramatic session of Parliament. The terms of the act provided, among other freedoms, that any person professing the Roman Catholic religion might sit and vote in either of the houses of Parliament upon taking an oath of allegiance to the Crown. There were many continuing currents of ill will; but nothing could alter the fact that Catholic emancipation had been granted. Another precedent, another breach with the past, had been made.

Strong demands for political reform and reconstruction continued. There were heavy attacks upon the unrepresentative character of the House of Com-

mons, the haphazard and narrow franchise requirements, the weakness of a
political structure shot through with corruption and incompetence. England
stood at the dawn of a bitter battle for parliamentary reform and the first
major political triumph of the middle class.

The new forces that were slowly shaping the face of Europe had appeared
in many lands in many guises. Later chapters will describe the revolt of the
Spanish colonies across the Atlantic and the framing of the "Monroe Doctrine"
of the United States. So far as Europe was concerned, it seemed that before the
year 1830 the alert Metternich and his cohorts had been successful in checking, on most fronts, the regiments of "revolt and crime." Apparently, too, the
bastions of the fortress of conservatism still stood, firm and strong. From the
battlements the banners of reaction snapped in the breeze.

A close scrutiny of the fortress would reveal that some portions of the walls
had been blown away; the defenders under Metternich's command were fewer
than before; the enemy had undermined several key spots; morale was often
soggy; there were no plans for new tactics and strategy. The old alliance arrangements, once so strong, were collapsing fast. Even as early as 1822 England's shrewd George Canning could see that the international scene was rapidly changing. He wrote his conclusions in a single sentence: "Things are
getting back to a wholesome state again; every nation for itself and God for
us all!"

Chapter 33

THE

TIDES OF REFORM

"History is full of the signs of this natural progress of society. We see in almost every part of the annals of mankind how the industry of individuals, struggling up against wars, taxes, famines, conflagrations, mischievous prohibitions, creates faster than governments can squander, and repairs whatever invaders can destroy. We see the wealth of nations increasing, and all the arts of life approaching nearer and nearer to perfection, in spite of the grossest corruption and the wildest profusion on the part of rulers. . . . Now and then there has been a stoppage, now and then a short retrogression; but as to the general tendency there can be no doubt. A single breaker may recede; but the tide is evidently coming in."

—Thomas Babington Macaulay, *Edinburgh Review,* January, 1830

IN THE years that followed the Congress of Vienna the Western world moved through an age of unrest to an age of revolution and reform. The swift changes, so often violent, were made by men who were excited by the tides of new ideas. Prince Metternich once said: "It is useless to close the gates against ideas; they overleap them all the same and arrive by contraband." Metternich was right. The ideas of the reformers, the revolutionaries, and the radicals flamed and roared from land to land. The makers of change saw a new glory in the sun. They would reshape and cleanse the world. They would overthrow their old masters and put up new ones. "The stairway of history is forever echoing with the wooden shoe going up, the polished boot descending."

The liberals and radicals of the early nineteenth century asserted that the Metternich system was bankrupt, a symbol of stagnation and bullying repression. They usually agreed that many governments were rickety, ill built, and incompetent; they insisted that several lands were disorderly, always unhinged and unsettled and teeming with abuses, decrepit conventions, and tyrannies. The conservatives, on the other hand, continued to denounce what they called the vague and pernicious ideas and misty calculations of the liberals and the reformers. They were unhappy and alarmed, especially when the Quadruple

Alliance withered away. They had still more cause for concern when revolutions blazed in Latin America, France, the Netherlands, Poland, Italy, the German states, and Austria. There was no violent outbreak in England; but there was a flood of reforms and a signal triumph of the middle class.

The earlier storm warnings and the rude shocks of the upheavals and revolutions of 1830 and 1848 brought all of the turbulent reactions usually produced by force and fear and hope. Meanwhile bourgeois-dominated societies multiplied. Europe moved through the first part of a period of remarkable progress. Wealth and comfort increased. Production and profits swelled. Popular education and public health improved. New class cleavages appeared, a fact swiftly noted by Karl Marx and others. The population of Europe was about 200,000,000 in 1815 and 460,000,000 in 1914. In 1815 about 20,000,000 people of European stock lived overseas; by 1914 the total had increased to more than 200,000,000. The offshoots of the mother European culture reached across many seas to many distant places. Of immense importance was the growth of an Atlantic community of people who shared the European heritage.

In the sprawling lands of Austria, Prince Clemens von Metternich was destined to serve the Hapsburgs and to "prop a falling house" for thirty years. Towards the end of those three decades he showed his awareness of how far the pendulum had swung since he had presided in dignity at the Congress of Vienna, at Aix-la-Chapelle, Troppau, Laibach, Verona. To Austria's Marshal Radetsky he wrote: "You and I are not destined to live out our days in peace."

It is not easy to convey to the reader a sense of the dynamic and inexorable thrusts and giddy confusions of the Western world from the eve of the revolutions of 1830 to the resounding disturbances of 1848, the year when all the forces of the previous decades met together in a single focus. There are many ways to describe the events that emerge with the unfolding of the great drama of political, social, and economic struggles. The theme is constant: revolution and reform. The scenes are varied: Latin America, France, the Netherlands, Poland, Italy, the German states, Austria, England.

We turn first to Latin America.

At the top of the social structure of the Spanish Empire in Latin America stood the proud and presumably competent officials sent out from Madrid. To these men were given all of the important political and military posts.

Immediately below the men from Spain were the members of the local aristocracy, the Creoles, the people of European parentage born in the colonies. There were about 3,000,000 of these men of local wealth and influence. It was natural that they should resent the coming of the streams of Spanish officials with their monopoly of political power. They did resent it; they were quite ready to hail the hour when the Spanish rulers would go back to Madrid to stay.

PLATE
XXXV

Considérant's conception of a plan envisioned by François Marie Fourier (1772-1837) for a socialist utopian community where men might live simple and harmonious lives together

[105]

irie Scene: Mirage," by Alfred J. Miller (1810-1874), who did many notable paintings of the opening of the West

European and American factories in Canton, China, around the year 1800

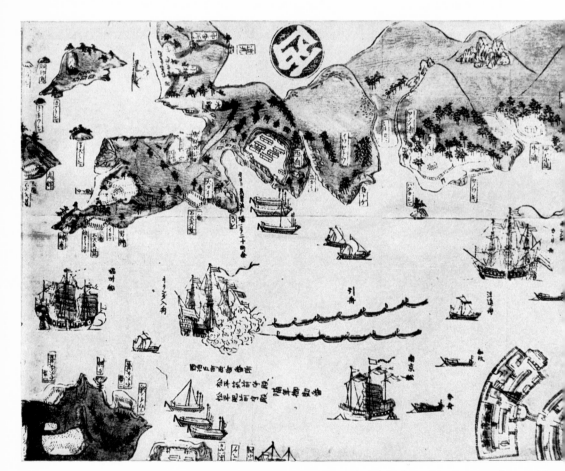

[107] Dutch ships at Nagasaki, 1802. After 1715 the Japanese allowed the Dutch to send two ships to Nagasaki.

PLATE XXXVI

Below the Spanish officials and the Creoles were the Indians, *mestizos,* and Negroes, in a social, economic, and political sense the inferior beings of the Spanish provinces.

In the early nineteenth century the population of Latin America was about 18,000,000; the population of the United States was roughly 5,500,000. About 20 per cent of the people in Latin America were white; 45 per cent were Indian; 30 per cent were of mixed blood, the *mestizos;* 5 per cent were Negro. Then, as now, the population varied considerably from region to region. For instance, in the areas now included in the states of Colombia, Chile, and Venezuela there was only a small unmixed Indian population. In Peru, Bolivia, Guatemala, and Mexico there were few Negroes; in those areas the population was approximately one-third Indian, two-thirds white. In the Caribbean regions, where there had been a steady flow of African slaves for centuries, the Negro population exceeded the total of whites and Indians. In Brazil, about half of the 3,000,000 inhabitants were Negroes, a fifth were white, and the rest were Indians or *mestizos.*

Before the early nineteenth century there had been several unsuccessful revolts against the rule of the Spaniards. The Mexicans had rebelled in 1624 and 1692. Paraguay revolted in 1721, Peru in 1780, New Granada in 1781 and 1784—this is the area that is now Colombia, Ecuador, and Venezuela. All of these revolts were crushed. There was nobody to help the Latin Americans in the eighteenth century. In that busy age most nations had other interests, other crusades and causes.

Slowly the prospects altered. In 1808 Napoleon forced Charles IV of Spain to abdicate and placed his brother Joseph Bonaparte on the Spanish throne. The Spanish Americans at once refused to accept Joseph as their sovereign. Hopeful and desperate men rose in rebellion. The ideas of the French and American Revolutions merged with private wrongs and public grievances. New nations were born.

In 1810 the Spanish viceroyalty of Rio de la Plata declared its independence. Out of this old Spanish American province came two republics: Paraguay (1813) and Argentina (1816).

A visitor to the modern city of Buenos Aires—its population is now 3,500,000—will see how the people of the capital city of Argentina still honor the memory of General José de San Martín, the leader of their first revolution. He will see the green and elegant Plaza San Martín and walk along the Avenida Libertador General San Martín. By the side of the memories of the past he will also find the attractions of the present: the high white buildings, the glass terraces, the lemon trees, the patios, parks, playgrounds, the raffia chairs in the sidewalk cafés, the tile stations and landscape murals of the subways, the round podia where the police direct the traffic, the pink stone of the Casa de Gobierno. Upon that pink stone there are bullet marks made on the

CENTRAL AMERICAN
CONFEDERATION
1823 ~ 1838

MEXICO
1821

BR.
HONDURAS

GUATEMALA

HONDURAS

SAN
SALVADOR

NICARAGUA

COSTA
RICA

PANAMA

GRAN
COLOMBIA
1822 - 1830

Bogotá

COLOMBIA
1819

Quito

ECUADOR
1822

Caracas

VENEZUELA
1829

ORINOCO

BR.

NETH.

FR.

G U I A N A

A T L A N T I C

O C E A N

AMAZON
R.

B R A Z I L

EMPIRE 1822 - 1889
REPUBLIC 1889

Bahia

PERU 1821

Lima

Cuzco

La Paz

BOLIVIA
1825

Rio de Janeiro

São Paulo

PARA-
GUAY
1813

P A C I F I C

O C E A N

CHILE 1818

ARGENTINA 1816

PARANÁ R.

URU-
GUAY
1825

Santiago

Buenos
Aires

Montevideo

Captaincy General
of Guatemala

Viceroyalty
of New Granada

(NETH.) (FR.)
GUIANA

BRAZIL
(PORTUGUESE)

Audencia
of
Lima

Viceroyalty
of PERU

Vice-
royalty
of Rio
de la
Plata

Captaincy
General
of
Chile

Patagonia

Latin
America
1789

Latin America
1825

FALKLAND IS.
(BR. 1833)

day in June, 1955, when the glory of Juan Domingo Perón was swiftly dimmed.

These facts are symbolic of the history of all of Latin America: beauty, achievements, and violence go side by side. There are still the border disputes between jealous republics. In most Latin American countries militarism and clericalism still remain the two great forces. Dictators rise and fall. Peons fight landlords and nobody really wins. Amidst all the currents and eddies of disputes there is peace, much peace, especially outside of the great cities. There is always time for the siesta. By the town squares fissured by heat there is always time to watch the green lizards slither by the blotches of little plants growing in the crevices, time to eat the yellow papaws, cut the hard mango rinds, smell the feathery mimosas.

In the early nineteenth century revolt flamed far beyond the pampas of Argentina. The dynamic Simón Bolívar, a wealthy and educated Creole, was mainly responsible for liberating five countries from Spanish control: Colombia, Bolivia, Ecuador, Peru, Venezuela. The whole continent heaved in turmoil and the great wars of liberation began. Bolívar and Francisco Miranda brought about the independence of Venezuela when a congress at Caracas decided to follow their leadership and advice. Bolívar went up the Orinoco and occupied Bogotá. He directed a revolt in Colombia. His victory at Carabobo in Venezuela in 1821 was a decisive point in the battle to free all the northern part of South America from the grasp of Spain. Bolívar was indeed the Liberator, a great soldier and a hero.

Mexico's revolt against Spain began in 1810 under the leadership of the Creole priest Miguel Hidalgo. He was caught and executed. His lieutenant, José Maria Morelos, took up the cause and won. Mexico asserted her independence in 1813. Spanish power was restored in 1815 and then overthrown again for the last time in 1821. General Augustín de Iturbide proclaimed himself emperor of Mexico in 1822. Two years later he was deposed and executed. In 1824 Mexico became a federated republic. Meanwhile, in 1823, the Central American territories broke away from Mexico and formed a loose confederation that soon failed. It was replaced by several independent republics: Guatemala, San Salvador, Nicaragua, Honduras, Costa Rica.

The short-lived restoration of Spain's authority in Mexico in 1815 marked the time when Ferdinand VII returned to the throne of Spain and decided to take the offensive in Latin America. Ferdinand sent troops and supplies across the Atlantic and proceeded to press his claims. In Mexico, Peru, and Chile, the Spaniards won, for a little while. All through the viceroyalty of Peru the power of Spain prevailed.

It was not to prevail for long. General José de San Martín, hero and patriot of Argentina, gathered 5,000 men at Mendoza, crossed over the Andes, overwhelmed the royalists at the battle of Chacabuco and helped to free Chile

(1817–1818). In this operation San Martín was aided by the famous and fascinating Bernardo O'Higgins, first director-general of Chile. His ally on the sea was England's Lord Cochrane, soon to be fighting for the freedom of Greece in the distant Mediterranean.

San Martín and his companions also moved to free Peru (1820). After a brief visit on the coast of Ecuador with Simón Bolívar, San Martín was convinced that Bolívar wanted full and complete leadership in carrying out his grand design: the building of a great confederation, powerful and united. Persuaded that Bolívar was right and that his aims were good and wise, San Martín returned to Lima, resigned as protector of Peru, and went into self-imposed exile. In the north and northwest Bolívar swept all resistance before him. Nevertheless, victory brought him no nearer to the realization of his hopes and plans and the creation of a confederation of strong republics. The peoples whom Bolívar had freed fought among themselves. In vain the Liberator tried to pacify and control and point to a larger vision beyond the local squabbles and the bickering. Bolívar failed. There was to be no strong union of republics, no union at all. The last years of Bolívar were years of bitterness and despair.

In 1819 Florida was sold to the United States. Of all the Spanish possessions in America, Puerto Rico and Cuba alone remained. The Spanish flag and the Spanish soldiers were soon to be seen no longer in Asunción, Bogotá, Buenos Aires, Caracas, Cartagena, Cuzco, Guatemala, La Paz, Lima, Montevideo, Quito, Santiago, Valparaiso.

The Portuguese rulers of Brazil were also ousted. In 1808, at an hour when the French were approaching Lisbon, the Portuguese royal family fled to Brazil. Dom Joao established his court at Rio de Janeiro. He apparently liked the bulk of the Morro do Castello, the melancholy pile of the Convent, the little tower on the top of the Church of Carmo, the thousands of church bells, the bronze spouts of the fountain from Lisbon. The people of Brazil liked Dom Joao, especially after he seized and annexed Uruguay. Most of them, particularly the Creoles, disliked the swaggering Portuguese courtiers, the officers with their tricorns and their Saragossa capes, the militiamen with their canary trousers and their white coats.

In 1816 Dom Joao became John VI of Portugal when Maria I, his insane mother, died at last. He returned to Portugal in 1821 and left his son Dom Pedro to represent him in Brazil. When a dispute arose between Portugal and Brazil, Dom Pedro was ordered home. He refused to go. In 1822 he became emperor of Brazil. In 1889 a swift rebellion sent Brazil into the ranks of the Latin American republics.

The governments of the United States and Great Britain were not displeased at these triumphs of revolutionary liberalism. They were also aware of other facts and factors of consequence. By the 1820's British and American merchants had obtained a firm foothold in Latin American markets. English and American interests would suffer a heavy blow if the new republics were broken and restored to Spain and Portugal. Then Spanish and French Bourbons would unite to keep English and American goods and ships away from South and Central America. English trade and English power would be threatened as in the eighteenth century. The balance of power in Europe had been upset. That imbalance must not be increased by the extension of French and Spanish power to the New World.

To the discomfiture of the European powers England's George Canning bluntly refused to send representatives to a Congress proposed by Spain. He would not agree to the use of European influence in the domestic affairs of the nascent states of Latin America. The British fleet, with all its massive power, stood between the allies of Metternich and Ferdinand VII and the reconquest of a lost empire. In 1822 Canning granted conditional recognition to the governments set up by the rebellious colonists.

Nor could the United States approve either the proposed extension of re-action to the New World or the possible threat to American trading and investment interests. After long negotiations with Britain—during which George Canning proposed a joint declaration of Anglo-American policy—the United States determined to make its own firm statement. On December 2, 1823, President James Monroe delivered a famous message to Congress. This "Monroe Doctrine," still a cornerstone of the foreign policy of the United States, declared that the American continents "are henceforth not to be con-sidered as subjects for future colonization by any European powers." President Monroe also said that any European intervention would be regarded as "the manifestation of an unfriendly disposition toward the United States" and "dangerous to our peace and safety."

In 1824 England formally recognized the governments of the Latin Ameri-can republics. Said Canning: "I called the New World into existence to redress the balance of the Old."

The power of Spain and Portugal in Latin America was thus gone forever as a result of the wars of liberation, the might of the British fleet, and the "Monroe Doctrine." Twenty independent states had appeared in Latin Amer-ica. In the new republics many men prospered, especially the merchants, the financiers, and the landowners. Out of the ports the ships moved with their cargoes of bauxite, copper, coffee, lead, hides, manganese, tin, wolfram, vanadium, nitrates, iron, petroleum, horns, rum, zinc. In the cities, the towns, and the country there remained the evils of poverty and disease. Through the decades since the liberation of Latin America there has been much whispering and plotting by the town squares, in the market places, and along the city streets. Revolutions start suddenly; but to prepare them takes time.

Across the Atlantic the people of Europe moved towards another prolonged battle between the forces of reaction and liberalism. Some men fought and fought hard. Some did not know what the disputes were about. Others, obviously, did not care. These comments can be made about many events in the history of our restless sphere.

In France the background of conflict was slowly shaped. There were no great and immediate troubles after Napoleon fell. France was chastened; France was meek.

Louis XVIII promised the nation peace and quiet. He kept his word. No attempt was made to change the administrative system of Napoleon or to diminish the freedoms obtained by Frenchmen during the Revolution. Louis gave the people a constitution called the "Charter," a document which said that all Frenchmen were equal before the law and equally eligible for appointment to civil or military posts. All men were to pay taxes according to their means. There was to be personal and religious liberty. France was to be ruled by the king, the House of Peers, and the Chamber of Deputies. With the aid of this Charter, Louis XVIII, a mediocre man who was often saved from heavy trouble by his common sense, kept an uneasy balance between the forces of progress and reaction.

The ultra-royalist party wanted Louis to restore the absolute monarchy and return to the nobles and the higher clergy the privileges they had once enjoyed. At first Louis XVIII opposed them. After the Duke of Berry, son of the Count of Artois, was assassinated by a lunatic liberal, Louis became gradually more amenable to the ideas and pressures of the men of the right. At the same time, the people of the middle classes wanted to hold and increase the gains that they had made during the Revolution. The city workers wanted to get better living conditions, higher wages, more human dignity. The vehement patriots spoke and dreamed of a France that would rise, phoenix-like, to triumph over all her foes. Such groups and ideas—and there were many more—were held in uneasy balance. The compromise arrangement of Louis XVIII was artificial and in many ways unpopular; but it worked; it gave France fifteen years of stability, peace, and moderation.

In 1824 Louis XVIII died and the Count of Artois came to the throne as Charles X. For years this stiff-necked and frozen-faced Bourbon had dreamed of upsetting the compromise of Louis XVIII and restoring the power of the throne and the glory of the court of Louis XIV. Now Charles X at last had his chance. He was not going to play the role of a limited constitutional monarch. He declared his belief in the divine right of kings and prepared to rule with undisguised absolutism. Heedless of the advice and warnings of friends and foes, Charles rushed ahead. He would do as he pleased, whatever the Charter might say. Poor man, there was a lot of history that he had never learned.

Charles X strengthened the power of the Church. He tried to divert public attention from the state of things at home by sending an expedition to punish rebellious tribesmen in Tunis. He proposed to raise a billion francs by reducing the interest rates on government bonds from 5 to 3 per cent. The billion francs Charles planned to hand over to the nobles to compensate them in part for the sufferings they had endured during the French Revolution. Charles was prepared for the opposition of the bankers and merchants; but he did not expect revolution. Revolution, however, was what he got.

The royalists progressively alienated more and more men by their myopic and selfish tactics. They lost their control of the Chamber of Deputies and were replaced by republicans who demanded the resignation of the unpopular Polignac ministry. Charles answered all demands and objections by defiantly dissolving the Chamber, changing the election laws so that the franchise was limited to the wealthy and the well-born landholders, ordering a new election, suspending liberty of the press. On July 26, 1830, the day after Charles X had issued these startling ordinances, several newspaper editors objected and asserted that they would not obey royal orders that destroyed the Charter of Louis XVIII and the people's freedom.

The men of Paris now moved to armed revolt. Workers from all over the city joined in the insurrection. Charles X finally promised to withdraw the ordinances; but his decision came too late. Businessmen and bankers had already decided to place upon the throne the bourgeois Louis Philippe, descendant of Henry IV through the Orléans branch of the Bourbons. Charles X abdicated and went to England, a shelter through the years for many kinds of exiles. Metternich and Mazzini and Marx all found a haven there.

Louis Philippe, the "citizen king," now ruled in France. Both the nobles and the republicans had been thwarted by the rising power of aggressive men of the middle classes, the propertied men who feared the proletariat on the one hand and a despotic king on the other. Louis Philippe, once a Jacobin, obtained the blessing and approval of the aging Lafayette, a sturdy symbol of republicanism. He also got the support of the wise and durable Talleyrand, now seventy-six years old. Talleyrand had taken no part in the revolution that had destroyed the edifice that he had toiled so hard to build in 1815. No doubt Talleyrand hated to see the Bourbon Restoration fail. He had tried to warn Charles X. It was stupid of Charles not to heed Talleyrand. It was also dangerous. Louis Philippe did not ignore him. He appointed Talleyrand French ambassador to Great Britain. Talleyrand went to London, served France well at the Court of St. James's, and became a great friend of the Duke of Wellington.

The franchise was extended to about 3 per cent of the adult males—250,-000 instead of 100,000. This was not a wide extension and meant, of course, that the vote belonged to the men who had a great deal of real estate, the big property owners, the bankers, businessmen, and industrialists. The middle class would keep a majority in the Chamber of Deputies and their interests would be protected. Freedom of the press was reaffirmed. The Chamber of Peers ceased to be hereditary. The tricolor replaced the white Bourbon banner. The European courts accepted the change of dynasty and Louis Philippe was recognized as the new "King of the French." Nicholas I of Russia, however, did not extend to Louis the usual diplomatic courtesy of calling him "my good brother." Meanwhile the new king wore a dark suit and carried an umbrella. He was very respectable, solid, safe, bourgeois.

The republicans and the socialists naturally objected to these arrangements. Most of them saw that the old class structure inherited from the Middle Ages was being replaced by new class divisions. The men of the new aristocracy, the new minority rulers, were called capitalists; they were men of wealth, investments, and influence. People who belonged to the so-called middle class were those who lived partly on property and partly on payments for services. The men of the proletariat were the wage earners, the workers, the hewers of wood and drawers of water. The opponents of the money exchange system called capitalism declared that industrial serfdom had supplanted agrarian serfdom in a new kind of feudalism. Commercial, industrial, and finance capitalism had replaced the landed wealth of the old aristocracy. All these dramatic and significant changes, said the socialists and others with similar views, did not alter the fact that the new society of the Western world resembled the old; it was still "the conspiracy of the few against the many."

When the news of the July days in France reached St. Petersburg, Nicholas I is said to have exclaimed "Gentlemen, saddle your horses! France is in revolution!" Nicholas was not the only leader who saw the imminent danger of widespread disturbance. There was almost a tradition in Europe that what happened in France had swift results in the rest of the Continent. "When France sneezes," so the proverb runs, "all Europe catches cold."

The French revolution of 1830 started a chain of explosions in western Europe. As a result of these uprisings there were a few liberal gains and victories. The Belgian revolution of 1830 brought the separation of the Belgians from the Dutch. Belgium was soon established as an independent state. Within a few years Britain, France, Austria, Prussia, and Russia recognized the independence of Belgium and guaranteed its perpetual neutrality. There were revolutions in Switzerland and in several cantons new and liberal constitutions were established. The tides of the age brought reforms in Sweden and Norway. There were violent disputes in Spain and Portugal.

In 1831 the Poles declared that Russia's Nicholas I no longer ruled in Poland. Their revolution was crushed. The Polish universities at Vilna and Warsaw were closed and thousands of Poles were exiled to Siberia. Other thousands escaped to western Europe and America, carrying their ideals and memories with them. Nicholas I, tsar and autocrat of all the Russias, was a conscientious man. He sincerely believed in the rightness of autocracy and discipline.

In Italy there were outbursts of nationalism and liberalism following the French uprisings of 1830. Revolutions came in the Papal States, in Piedmont, Parma, and Tuscany. They were all swiftly suppressed.

One of the men most deeply moved by the dreams and disaffections of his countrymen was Giuseppe Mazzini (1805–1872), a young lawyer from Genoa who organized in 1831 the secret society of "Young Italy." Said Mazzini: "Young Italy is a brotherhood of Italians who believe in a law of *progress* and *duty* and are convinced that Italy is to become a nation." In every state, declared Mazzini, the men who believed in freedom had a moral duty to rise and tear down the citadels of autocracy. "Ideas grow quickly," he said, "when watered by the blood of martyrs."

The German states were not filled with stability and calmness, the arts of peace and a cheerful silence. The heavy pressures of nationalism, liberalism, radicalism—and socialism, too—never ceased. The *Zollverein,* mentioned earlier, was slowly forging economic bonds among the states. In 1840 "The Watch on the Rhine" was written. More and more Germans hoped for free parliamentary forms of government and a unified German state. Too many of them thought that these ends could be achieved by negotiation and debate. Not for several years were they to learn that they needed swords and guns as well as words and majority resolutions.

Throughout Prince Metternich's Austria, despite the threats of much trouble ahead, the stifling controls continued. If the powers of nationalism had been allowed to range unchecked through the realms of Austria, then the fragmentation of the Hapsburg inheritance would have been fast and sure. It was highly dangerous to permit infecting nationalism to race among the Germans, Magyars, Czechs, Poles, Slovaks, Slovenes, Croats, Serbs, and all the other subject peoples of Austria.

In the Austrian court everything possible was done to maintain the old world of the years before the great French Revolution shattered the shape of the West. The rules of the court were as precise as the steps of a minuet. They remained unchanged. So, too, did the inefficiency and what Geoffrey Bruun has called the "invincible indolence." The attitude of the Emperor Francis I —he died in 1835—was clear. "Peoples? What does that mean? I know only subjects." Professor Arthur J. May once called attention to the fact that in the 1840's it was unlawful for newspapermen to print the word "constitution." It has earlier been remarked that Francis I was a much narrower and more bigoted man than Prince Metternich. The emperor did not see that reforms were ever necessary. Metternich knew that they were often needed; but he did continue to insist that they must come from above, never from below.

In England the conservative High Tories controlled the government on the eve of the key events of 1830. They did not intend to retreat very swiftly or very far or to undertake anything more than a few sedative compromises. Led by the iron Duke of Wellington, the right-wing Tories stood against remedial legislation, against a liberal foreign policy. Their own policy was one of closed-door reaction.

In 1830 the Tories were defeated and the Whigs formed a government. Lord John Russell introduced a bill to deal with "the perilous question" of Parliamentary reform. After a series of battles between the House of Commons and the House of Lords, after mobs had burned and sacked almost at will, after a raid on the Bank of England ("To stop the Duke, go for gold!"), after weeks in which England was close to civil war, the Reform Bill was passed. Not all of the details of that famous piece of legislation need be listed here. The most important facts about it were two: it made a considerable reform in the distribution of seats in Parliament; it altered the franchise provisions so that most men of the middle class were given the vote. Thomas Babington Macaulay declared: "The voice of great events is proclaiming to us, reform, that you may preserve. Renew the youth of the state. Save property divided against itself."

With the passage of the Reform Bill of 1832 the power of the aristocracy in England was broken. About one-half of the propertied middle class was enfranchised, but none of the working class. In the following decades the shift from landed aristocratic control to control by the commercial and industrial classes steadily continued. Meanwhile the laboring groups found that the middle class and the aristocracy were united, as men of property, in making common cause against the pressure of working-class movements and demands.

For several decades Adam Smith and his followers had insisted that the natural laws of economics and politics would make their own inevitable and automatic adjustments to the ultimate advantage of the state. Business, for instance, prospered best when left alone. Lord Macaulay stated the heart of the *laissez faire* theory and free-enterprise policy perhaps even more clearly than Adam Smith's *Wealth of Nations:*

> Our rulers will best promote the improvement of the nation by strictly confining themselves to their own legitimate duties, by leaving capital to find its most lucrative course, commodities their fair price, industry and intelligence their natural reward, idleness and folly their natural punishment, by maintaining peace, by defending property, by diminishing the price of law, and by observing strict economy in every department of the state. Let the Government do this. The People will assuredly do the rest.

Meanwhile English philosophers and planners like Jeremy Bentham, John Stuart Mill, and Robert Owen and popular agitators like William Cobbett were supported by many people who had no general theory about the ends and purposes of government. Voluntary associations and leagues were founded for hundreds of causes, some sane and some silly. They spread through society as arteries of public discussion and agitation in the extraordinary and dynamic world that existed in early nineteenth-century England. Confidence in the future remained secure. The Age of Progress was at hand.

In 1833 England's first Factory Act was passed. It applied to most textile mills and provided that children between the ages of nine and thirteen might not be worked more than nine hours a day; those between the ages of thirteen and eighteen might not be worked more than twelve hours in one day or more than sixty-nine hours in one week. The law also provided for medical examinations and an improvement of sanitary conditions. Similar reforms were made in the Mines Act of 1842 and the Ten Hours Act of 1847.

The year 1833 marked the end of slavery in the British Empire. In 1834 the Poor Law Amendment Act, as its title suggests, made a series of provisions for the administration of poor relief. In 1835 the Municipal Corporations Act remedied a deplorable situation in local government. In 1846, after a long and bitter controversy, the Corn Laws were repealed and the landowners no longer enjoyed the protection of a high tariff upon foreign grain. In 1849 the Navigation Acts were also repealed and England moved into a long period of a virtual free-trade policy. Meanwhile, a series of remarkable colonial reforms changed the scenes in British colonies beyond the seas, particularly in Canada and Australia. The Oxford Movement in the Anglican Church brought results of profound importance.

For eighteen years Louis Philippe ruled in France. He continued to rely upon the wealthy bourgeoisie, the only class to which the franchise had been extended. During the years of his reign the state steadily increased its industrial power behind high protective tariffs. Louis Philippe asserted that he was a liberal but became more and more suspicious of the progressive and liberal groups who had helped to put him on the throne in 1830. The French wage earners, so rapidly increasing in number, chafed under the restricted suffrage and resented their unhappy and sordid living conditions. To the discontented men of the proletariat it seemed that the bourgeoisie were multiplying their profits while the workers lived in poverty. The underprivileged commoners noted with displeasure that the bourgeois rulers of France sponsored little social legislation. In such circumstances of social and economic cleavage it was not surprising that the workers hearkened more and more to the ideas and promises of the socialists and the republicans. It was hard to believe in the sacredness of private property if you had but little of it. It was difficult to honor and obey a monarch who seemed oblivious to the needs and wishes of those among his people who had little real property, small supplies of food and clothes, and no bank accounts at all. Wrote Heinrich Heine: "In the silence one can hear a soft monotonous dripping. It is the dividends of the capitalist continuously trickling in, continuously mounting up. One can literally hear them multiply, the profits of the rich. And one can hear, too, in between, the low sobs of the destitute, and now and then a harsher sound, like a knife being sharpened."

There were many exciting and radical plans and philosophies produced in these troubled years in France. The eccentric nobleman and socialist philosopher Claude Henri de Rouvroy, Comte de Saint-Simon (1760–1825), for instance, wanted to see France governed in the interests, as he saw them, of all the people. He advocated the public ownership of industry and capital and a planned society managed by technical experts or social engineers. A second philosopher, François Marie Charles Fourier (1772–1837), wanted to create a series of small cooperative communities that he called "phalanstères." In each of these there would be 1,620 individuals, each doing the work that fitted his aptitude and inclination. All would be harmony; all would be peace. A few experimental "phalanstères" were founded in the United States, the most famous of them at Brook Farm in Massachusetts. None appeared in France.

Meanwhile, too, the lively French journalist Louis Blanc (1811–1882) asserted that the state had a duty to provide work for every healthy citizen. In his book *The Organization of Labor* (1840) and elsewhere Louis Blanc put forward the utopian idea of cooperative "social workshops" supported by the state. In these manufacturing centers the workmen would do the work and share the profits. Pierre Joseph Proudhon, a fourth social theorist, condemned private property as theft and denounced the materialism of the age and the shackles of the centralized state. No school of thinkers followed Proudhon; no cult grew up to flourish and fade; but his ideas, diffuse and imprecise as they were, did influence several radical thinkers then and later. Any rebel in any age can add to his ideas and emotions by reading the confused and fiery pages of Pierre Joseph Proudhon.

In these years there were about Paris a few German revolutionaries who had fled to France for safety. Some of them took the name of "Communists." Among them were Karl Marx and Friedrich Engels, two men who lived and wandered in Germany, France, and England and studied and wrote and taught. In their *Communist Manifesto* of 1847 and in the three volumes of *Das Kapital* (1867–1895) they provided the dogmatic explanations and answers that characterize their creed, asserting that the whole history of societies was a history of class conflicts; that the coming Communistic revolution, when the working-men of all countries would unite, would bring a final and complete triumph of the proletariat over the bourgeoisie; that then, at long last, the state would wither away; that all men would be comrades together in a Communist utopia, there in felicity to dwell forever, or at least until the end of the world.

The dominant middle classes of France wanted peace, order, and business prosperity. They insisted upon a cautious foreign policy because war would disrupt trade. When Louis Adolphe Thiers (1797–1877) tried to take strong action in the Near East he was swiftly ousted from power and replaced by François Guizot (1787–1874), a dull and stubborn conservative who was convinced that only the bourgeoisie were capable of governing France. He believed that men who had failed to make money had also demonstrated that they did not deserve the franchise; they were, surely, loafers, incompetents, or weaklings. Guizot was also of the opinion that change was usually undesirable. Among most of the conservative and reactionary spirits Guizot was popular. Among other groups he was not.

There were several opponents of the colorless and mediocre bourgeois monarchy of Louis Philippe. The Legitimists, those followers of the exiled Charles X, denied that the Orléanist title to the throne was valid. The Bonapartists dreamed of reviving the gleaming tradition of Napoleon. They reminded men of the glory that once, not so long before, had belonged to France. They polished the Napoleonic legend. In 1840 the ashes of Napoleon were brought back from St. Helena to be placed in the Invalides, that great tomb on the bank of the Seine. The power of the Bonapartists grew. Young Louis Napoleon, ambitious nephew of the Emperor, explained that he was available to serve his country if need be.

Almost all of the clergy were opposed to Louis Philippe. As they saw it, he had usurped the throne and diminished the authority and influence of the Church. For instance, he had stopped priests from teaching in the schools. Charles X would never have permitted such a triumph of secular interests. Many men of the Church regarded Louis Philippe as a godless leader. True, the bourgeoisie paid little attention to such complaints and opposition. On the other hand, thousands of peasants and humble city workers did listen to their parish priests. They believed and obeyed.

Every time Guizot and his associates refused to make reforms or grant concessions their opponents grew in numbers and strength. Numerous pamphlets and books—especially histories of the French Revolution—flowed from the presses. In 1843 the republicans and the socialists joined their forces to form one party. There were mass meetings, parades, great petitions. The mounting economic hardships increased the discontent and agitation. Political clubs, as in the days of the great Revolution, pressed the government for reforms.

A revolution against the inept and stubborn Louis Philippe started in Paris in February, 1848. The authorities had forbidden a political banquet on February 22. On the next day the people of Paris, especially the students and the angry, miserable poor, put up red flags and barricades. Fighting began. On February 24 a mob stormed the Tuileries. Guizot resigned. A British newspaper compared Guizot to Danton, "forlorn but heroic in isolation." The editor added this comment: "Guizot is a man betrayed by his uncompromising austerity into a blunder. . . . He has panted for persecution and proscription, for gags and pains and penalties, with as much intolerance and heat as if his own political theories were acts of uniformity."

Louis Philippe offered concessions. It was too late. The bourgeois king was forced to abdicate and the first phase of a swift and easy revolution was over. "Louis Philippe," said a London newspaper, "may say, 'I am a fox' but we fear that history will add for him that in the supreme event of his eventful career, he did not know how to be a lion."

Guizot and his master fled to London. In Paris a republic was proclaimed and a provisional government of socialists and republicans was set up. There were clamors for deep and wide reforms, dreams of great gains by the workers, hopes of a new justice for all the citizens of France.

The republican-socialists coalition gave no promise of stability or sense. One of the members of the provisional government was Alphonse de Lamartine, poet, historian, and inexperienced dreamer. "Can a government be consolidated with fine phrases?" Another member was Louis Blanc, the journalist, historian, and radical socialist. Blanc demanded that his national workshops be established at once. Had he not promised "the right to work" to the mobs? Louis Blanc's ideas were described by one foreign journalist as "abstractions screaming in blasphemy and dabbling in blood." The *Times* of London stated its fears of French interference with the "unalterable laws of labor" and decided that Louis Blanc's schemes and dissertations "could only obtain currency among a people with whom a fine sentence, the more unintelligible the better, is more effective than argument at any time."

Louis Blanc's less radical associates blocked his plan to create national workshops. Another program, directed by one of Blanc's political foes, was substituted. Thousands of unemployed men were hired to dig ditches and to carry dirt from one spot to another. Thus the plans of Blanc were made to appear ridiculous, expensive, and stupid.

An election in April, 1848, provided a Constituent Assembly filled with prudent and moderate individuals who reflected the mood of the country. These men were neither reactionary enough to think that all innovations were evil nor radical enough to believe that all innovations were improvements. The Paris radicals, submerged at the polls, now shouted "bread or lead" and started another uprising; this bloody affair lasted from June 23 to June 26. The terrified government ordered General Cavaignac to destroy the barricades. The rebels were stopped and crushed. Eleven thousand of them were executed or exiled over the seas. The publication of socialist newspapers was forbidden. The national workshops were closed. France became divided once more into the proscribing and the proscribed.

> On the evening of June 26, after the victory over Paris, we heard regular volleys at short intervals. . . . We all looked at one another;

our faces were green. . . . 'Those are the execution squads' we said with one voice and turned away from one another. I pressed my forehead to the window-pane and was silent. Such minutes deserve ten years of hate, a lifetime of vengeance.

The Assembly now shaped a constitution for the Second French Republic. There was to be a single legislative chamber of 750 deputies, to be elected by universal manhood suffrage; a president to be chosen by the same electorate. Some thoughtful men remembered the plebiscites that had aided the rise of the first Napoleon. "Let God and the people decide," said Lamartine.

There were three candidates for the office of President. The first was Ledru-Rollin, a socialist. The second was General Cavaignac, idol of the republicans. The third was Louis Napoleon Bonaparte, leader of the "Party of Order."

Of the 7,000,000 votes cast, about 5,500,000 supported Louis Napoleon. The memories of the imperial glories of the first Napoleon were revived. Most of the voters were voting for the first time. They had no political experience, little information. "How should I not vote for this gentleman, I whose nose was frozen at Moscow?"

Louis Blanc had warned Frenchmen against a Bonapartist restoration. "It would be the despotism without the glory, the courtiers on our necks without Europe at our feet, a great name without a great man, in a word, the Empire without the Emperor." But Louis Blanc had gone into exile after the June Days. Louis Napoleon was in Paris, the victor of the election. Soon the Empire was to be reborn.

In Vienna the power of the shrewd Prince Metternich, so often challenged and shaken, still remained unbroken. Metternich stood as a symbol of a system of control and repression that blocked the demands of the liberals and the nationalists. From the point of view of Vienna, it was clear, of course, that no concessions could be made by the Hapsburgs to the spirit of nationalism in Austria, so filled with a kaleidoscope of races, languages, and creeds. Nor could concessions be safely made elsewhere, particularly in Italy and the German states.

When news of the Paris revolution of February, 1848, came to Metternich he declared that "Europe finds herself today in the presence of a second 1793." We now know that Metternich was mistaken. At the same time, his remark conveys to us a sense of his agitation and alarm. In France, he said, "the mob is now rising against the bourgeoisie." The Emperor Ferdinand, Metternich's half-witted and harmless master, could see no immediate danger from below; but Metternich could.

Metternich did have cause to fear the running feet of the mobs. Everywhere in Europe the revolution in France encouraged the opponents of the Metternich system.

Up in the German regions the professors still lectured about liberty and the political unification of the German states. Poems and pamphlets showered over the country; many of them were seized and burned by busy and zealous policemen. Repression, it seemed, was still successful. The intellectuals and the dreamy idealists must not be permitted to harangue and to write. They must be stopped by the police and the arrogant and medieval-minded officers and men of the army.

Swiftly the patterns and prospects changed. When the Frenchmen began to shoot in Paris in February, 1848, many German liberals and nationalists thought that they, too, should join in a great revolution and crusade. Movements for rapid reform began in Baden, Württemberg, Saxony, and Bavaria. In Prussia several leaders of revolt, particularly the students and intellectuals, demanded a constitution from the timid Frederick William IV and put up barricades. Frederick William, easily intimidated, ordered the army out of Berlin, granted all the liberal demands, and then fled from the riotous city. After thinking over his "humiliation," he ordered his army to crush the rebellion; this it did, quite quickly. Nevertheless, Frederick William IV had promised his subjects a constitution and he kept his word. The constitution was not liberal; but it was better than nothing at all.

There was also strong pressure for the reorganization of the German Confederation. In May, 1848, a National Assembly, containing about 600 representatives of the German people, met at Frankfort to prepare a constitution for a German federated commonwealth. At once they began to dispute. What were to be the boundaries of this new state? Should Austria be included or not? Should the new German commonwealth be a monarchy or a republic? Should it be a loose confederation of states or a strongly centralized nation? There were other problems and difficulties. For instance, what was to be done about Prussian Poland and the duchies of Schleswig and Holstein?

When the Frankfort Assembly voted to have a constitutional monarchy about eighty sturdy republicans walked out. The results of such divisions were not happy. On the question of the inclusion of Austria in the proposed commonwealth it was agreed that the German provinces of Austria would be invited to join; the Slavs, Italians, Czechs, Poles, Magyars, and other non-German elements were to be left outside. Austria, of course, wanted to be the dominant power in the new commonwealth. It now seemed that her hopes were to be thwarted by the exclusion of the non-German areas of Austria. The Austrian delegates at the Frankfort Assembly were most unhappy.

At this point the Assembly, hopeful of building a smaller empire under Prussian leadership, offered the imperial crown to Frederick William IV of Prussia. In March, 1849, Frederick William abruptly refused the crown, partly because he did not want any trouble with Austria. To the members of the Assembly, Frederick William suggested that if the imperial title had been offered to him by his fellow sovereign princes he might have taken it; he could not accept it from an Assembly for whose existence there might be no legal justification whatever. He could not take a crown "from a gutter."

Slowly the delegates to the Frankfort Assembly went home, one by one. For many of them hope was replaced by despair and bitter disillusionment. At the same time, the sobering march of events had convinced several German leaders that there was no place in a harsh world for debates about ideals, abstractions, and involved theories. The old German liberalism was dying. Some men now said that the German states must be unified under Prussian leadership. If Austria objected, then she must be defied, perhaps defeated by arms. Twenty years later the German states did begin to move along this path. Reason and realism, it seemed, marched by the side of the Prussian armies.

In March, 1848, revolution came at last to Austria. The people of that citadel of conservatism, excited by the news from Paris, were suddenly swept into revolt. All over Austria a great flood of rebellions swirled and eddied, pushing down the walls and pillars that had been so carefully erected by the House of Hapsburg. The Magyar patriots, led by Louis Kossuth, prepared to draft a constitution that would make Hungary an almost independent state with a parliament of its own. The Czechs of Bohemia, too, demanded an elected Diet, a strong local government, freedom of the press, religious liberty, just taxation, and the like. Vienna itself was paralyzed by a rebellion, mainly led by students. The Hapsburg Empire tottered. The liberal-nationalist hopes were lightened everywhere by great blazes of triumph. Austria's minister of war was murdered. The emperor fled. Metternich followed soon.

When the news of Metternich's fall and flight reached Italy, the Milanese expelled the Austrian troops from their city. Soon almost all of Lombardy and Venetia were emptied of Austrian forces. Venetia and Milan were declared republics, freed at last from the heavy hand of Austria. The rulers of Tuscany, Piedmont, Naples, and Rome were forced—how reluctant they were!—to grant constitutions. Charles Albert, king of Sardinia, was widely hailed as the outstanding leader of Italy's battle for freedom. All seemed ready for a war with Austria, Italy's war for independence.

Then the rebels began to fight among themselves. In the seething days of revolutions, it seems, this pattern appears again and again: the radicals struggle with the moderates; the more sober moderates, often alienated by the excesses, stop to delay and consolidate; the radicals want to overthrow still more, to shoot and smash their way to the particular paradise they think they want.

There also came a sudden wave of reaction. The conservative forces began to strike back against the challenges of separation and revolution. In a divided Bohemia the Germans and Czechs were battling. The Moravians, Slovaks, and Poles were clashing in the north, the Serbs and Croats in the south. In the midst of a Pan-Slav Congress at Prague there was a local insurrection and

Austria's Prince Alfred zu Windischgrätz intervened, recaptured the city, and sent the Slavs home. Count Joseph Jellachich, a southern Slav, was shrewdly selected to lead the imperial forces against the Magyars, a people always hated by the southern Slavs. In October, 1848, the imperial troops bombarded Vienna and seized the city. Nicholas I of Russia sent soldiers to put down Kossuth's government in Hungary. Austria's veteran Field Marshal Joseph Wenzel Radetzky crushed the revolts in Italy's Lombardy and Venetia. The Italians were defeated at the battles of Custozza and Novara. Constitutions were revoked; the jails were filled; the hangmen were busy. A French military expedition restored Rome and the Papal States to the control of Pius IX.

In Vienna the Emperor Ferdinand resigned the throne to his eighteen-year-old nephew Franz Joseph. Franz Joseph began his reign by sending the members of the revolutionary assembly home. He threw out most of the constitution they had labored to shape.

It was probably inevitable that the bloody victories of the rebels in 1848 should have counted for so little in the long pull. When all of the fervor and fighting was ended, most of the revolutions of 1848 miscarried and failed. They collapsed in part because the leaders and followers of the liberal and national movements confused their hopes and dreams with the facts of their world. One of those inescapable facts was the power and prejudice of the ruling classes. A second fact was this: the conservative governments had armies, usually efficient and well trained. Against the makers of the revolutions these trained soldiers were ranged and ready. "The revolution," wrote the anarchist Pierre Joseph Proudhon, "had come before its time." It had indeed. "The German generation that came of age in 1848 rode forth on a romantic quest to rescue liberty. They turned back to marry power."

There was no revolution in Russia in 1848. There the autocratic hand of Nicholas I controlled the state; and that hand was firm and sure.

On the other side of Europe stood England. In that country there were a few episodes of bloodletting and violence and some disputes and agitation about political reform. Several forms of agitation coalesced into the strange challenge called Chartism. The main causes of the Chartist disturbances were economic and social. Some Chartists believed in moral persuasion; others advocated physical force. The voices of the demagogues supporting the "People's Charter" became louder. There were many hotly spiced Chartist articles. Several Chartist leaders delighted in garrulity and fire, noise and drama. The Chartists held mass meetings and paraded, printed pamphlets, presented petitions demanding political reforms. When the last great petition was unsuccessful in the spring of 1848, Chartism swiftly disappeared. The working class began to move towards political liberalism and to rely on existing political parties within Parliament and trade-union activity outside.

It seemed to many Englishmen that from the stage of ill-conditioned and brawling Europe came the most addled and lamentable social theories and political ideas. They saw Europe as a vast land of reactionary princes and radicals spawning revolutions. A popular British concept was that Europeans were somehow doomed to seize upon frothy and dangerous ideas fortunately unknown to Englishmen. Later in the century Benjamin Disraeli soberly noted that "an irresistible law dooms Europe to the alternate sway of disciplined armies or secret societies, the camp or the convention." So far as the English were concerned, the path of the English march towards a greater happiness for more Englishmen was not to be marked by riots and revolutions. Far away was the seventeenth century when the English had carried through two revolutions and were regarded as the most volatile people in all of Europe. We are all familiar with the British idea that constitutional freedom in their settled land must broaden down slowly, in a cautious, gradual, and evolutionary way. Neither rational progress nor ordered democracy was to be achieved, surely, by the lightning from above or the earthquake from below.

Chapter 34

NORTH AMERICA:
LANDS OF THE FREE

"It is plain enough . . . that freedom is an excellent thing. . . . There is
nothing in the world so unjust, nothing so bloody, as tyranny."
—Herodotus, *Persian Wars* (Rawlinson translation),
Book VII, Ch. 78, p. 92

IN THE early years of the rise of the United States there were many differing
judgments about the new republic, that land so filled with democratic
tumults. Some men thought that the fledgling American state would survive;
others asserted that it could not. About the newly forged Constitution there
was no unanimity. George Washington concluded that it was "a hopeful
experiment." James Madison thought that "under all the circumstances, it
was the best we could do." Probably few men then agreed with John
Marshall's judgment of 1821: "A Constitution is framed for ages to come,
and is designed to approach immortality as nearly as human institutions can
approach it."

The conflicting voices of optimistic and doubtful men were heard for several
years. France's Jacques Turgot, for instance, sent his enthusiastic words over
the seas in 1778: "This people is the hope of the human race; it may become
the model." On the other hand, Alexis de Tocqueville—he published the
four volumes of his classic *Democracy in America* between 1835 and 1839—
was quite certain that "the continuation of the American system can only be
a fortunate accident." The perspicacious Frenchman wrote many pages about
the things that he saw and thought he saw in America: the zeal and hunger
of the people for self-improvement and education, the pervasive vulgarity, the
greed, the ruthlessness and audacity of ambitious and struggling men. "America,"
he also said, "has produced very few writers of distinction; it possesses
no great historian and not a single poet." Despite such shadowed comments,
Alexis de Tocqueville did admire America. Like many a man who crossed the

Atlantic after him, de Tocqueville admitted both approval and bewilderment in the same breath.

In the works of skilled and sensitive historians the modern reader sees past generations of men and women in America pushing and plodding towards destinies they could not know. Across the years there echo the words of indignation, resentment, anger, frustration, ambition, obstinacy, happiness, hope. There are the dramas of character and men, the triumphs of vigor and freedom, the spurts of power, the simplicity and diversity of a great nation being built and consolidated in the vast stretches of the miles between two oceans, so far away from other lands and peoples.

The keen-eyed and intelligent reader also notes the constant thrusts and patterns that have made America and American nationalism, month by month, year by year: a steady sense of community duty and responsibility; opportunity; mobility; an insistence upon human dignity; an increasing awareness of the value and wisdom of moderation and compromise; a two-party political system; a diversity of regions, resources, and races; flexibility; experimentation, always experimentation; talk, always talk. There has also been that practical vision without which nations perish. Finally, of course, there has been constitutional liberty. Without liberty the price of human survival is too high. Said Thomas Jefferson: "I know no safe depository of the ultimate powers of society but the people themselves."

In April, 1789, the members of the first Congress of the United States gathered in New York. The votes of the electoral college were counted in the presence of both Houses and George Washington was notified that he had been chosen President, John Adams that he was Vice-President. Washington and Adams were competent, sagacious, and practical men. The United States was fortunate to have such leaders emerge in the critical years of her early history. There were few rosy hopes in those days, and weak and indecisive leadership might have brought disaster. States and ships need skilled and cool-headed pilots and navigators in hours of tempest and danger; if they do not have them, their chances of going under the waves are high.

The concise Constitution properly provided that there should be heads of the executive departments, men to make and use some of the tools of national policy. Congress accordingly created the offices of Attorney General, Secretary of the Treasury, Secretary of State, Secretary of War. Edmund Randolph was the first Attorney General. General Henry Knox became the first Secretary of War. Thomas Jefferson of Virginia was the Secretary of State. Alexander Hamilton, of New York, was appointed Treasurer.

The appointment of Alexander Hamilton to the first cabinet was highly important. Hamilton was patriotic and bold, a determined and hardheaded man with a finely developed economic philosophy and a passion for order and organization. Hamilton and those who supported his policy consistently proclaimed the wisdom of decreasing the powers of the states and hence increasing the strength of the central government.

Many readers of this book have studied the masterly and fascinating reports of Alexander Hamilton to Congress and his proposals regarding the payment of the national debt, the creation of a national bank and a national mint, the extension of the Federal taxing powers, the construction of a tariff system, the condition of manufacturing in the new nation. They will also recall the hard and savage battles about Hamilton's ideas and plans, especially about those that were designed to widen the powers of the Federal government. They will remember the arguments about the first Tariff Act, the problems and decisions involved in completing the first ten Amendments to the Constitution and in shaping a national court system and procedure.

Meanwhile there were political developments of considerable consequence. Several men who had once been called "Federalists" because they had championed the adoption of the Constitution joined with others of like views to form the Federalist Party. The members of the Federalist Party—their organization was completed in 1791—were men of consequence, men of property: merchants, planters, bankers, army officers. Their main strength was in New York and Philadelphia and the New England region. Led by the combative Alexander Hamilton and John Adams, these Federalists insisted that they wanted a strong central government, a national government that would obtain and use all the powers that could be claimed and held under any reasonable construction of the Constitution. They usually sympathized with the British as the islanders continued their long battle with the Jacobins. The Federalists easily became alarmed and angry about the Jacobins and their great crusade to free their fellow men.

The Federalist Party soon fell—except in Massachusetts it was dead by 1817. Its collapse and death were mainly the result of bitter quarrels between Adams and Hamilton, a multiplication of intrigues, a decline of morale, the fact that the party principles were too reactionary for a new and changing age. Many of the Federalists never really believed that the plain folk had been created equal to the people of quality. The epitaph of the Federalist Party must contain these words: "They distrusted democratic government."

Many of the ideas and members of the Federalist Party were to be taken over by the Whig Party. The Whigs, in turn, were to be absorbed by the new Republican Party that was formed in 1854.

Opposed to the Federalists stood the original Republican Party led by Thomas Jefferson—this old Republican Party was to be called the Democratic Party shortly after 1828. The Republicans wanted to limit the powers of the federal government and strongly supported what they held to be the rights of the states. Were the liberties of the people to be placed in jeopardy by a centralized federal power? Most of the Republicans also supported the makers of the French Revolution and the "rights of man." They passionately asserted that Hamilton and Adams and their Federalist fellows were aristocrats and monarchists, too pro-British, corrupt, anti-republican, un-American, led astray by their selfish ambitions and class interests. The Federalists, for their part, heatedly replied that the Republicans were dangerous advocates of revolution. It may be remarked in passing that Thomas Jefferson himself took little part in these unhappy controversies. He annoyed some of his colleagues because he was so conciliatory. In 1791 he contented himself with saying that the policy of the Federalists would leave them "all head and no body." He was right. It took a little time; but in the end he was right.

At the close of Washington's administration came the bitter election of 1796. In that contest the Federalists carried all of the seats north of the Delaware—and Delaware, too—and the Republicans captured all of the seats south of the Potomac and Pennsylvania. The new President was the Federalist John Adams; the Vice-President was the Republican Thomas Jefferson. The day after the inauguration John Adams wrote a letter to his wife: "George Washington seemed to enjoy a triumph over me. Methought I heard him say, 'Ay, I am fairly out, and you are fairly in! See which of us will be the happiest.'"

In 1793 George Washington had refused to consider still binding the treaty of alliance made with France in 1778. Despite the plans, pleas, and protests of France's Citizen Edmond Charles Genêt, who had come to America to get privateers and recruits, Washington would not change his decision. Alexander Hamilton wanted a friendly understanding with Great Britain; most of the Federalists did. Thomas Jefferson preferred one with France; most of the Republicans agreed. Washington held his course between these two points of view. He thought that the United States, at least until national development made the republic strong, should stay away from the "labyrinth of European politics." In his Farewell Address, Washington warned against "the insidious wiles of foreign influence." In his First Inaugural speech of 1801 Thomas Jefferson stated this American policy and hope: "Peace, commerce, and honest friendship with all nations, entangling alliances with none." Such themes and comments as these have frequently appeared in American history.

It was difficult to maintain American neutrality. On the lands and seas of the Western world the aims and interests of the United States clashed with those of the belligerent states. The operations of Genêt's privateers, the British seizure of American vessels and the steady interference with trade, the reprisals of Frenchmen angered by Washington's refusal to accept the agreements of 1778 as valid—all these threatened to pull the United States into the great European war. Washington was finally forced to ask France to recall

Genêt. France, in turn, asked Washington to withdraw the American minister, Gouverneur Morris, from Paris. Morris came back to America. Genêt, that busy Frenchman, was afraid to go home; he stayed in the United States and became an American citizen.

Meanwhile the malcontent farmers of western Pennsylvania launched their exciting "Whiskey Rebellion" (1794) against the new liquor tax; the Indians raided and slaughtered in the frontier regions. General Anthony Wayne—the "Mad Anthony" of the Revolution—subdued one Indian challenge at Fallen Timbers in Ohio; by the terms of the Treaty of Greenville (1795) the Indians of the Northwest surrendered eastern and southern Ohio to the American government. This treaty, the first of many such arrangements providing for the cession of Indian territory, did not end the fighting and ill will. Settlers pressed in; Indians resisted. Rival Canadian and American fur traders used the Indians to make mischief.

There were still many disputes with the British government. Britain refused to send a minister to Washington or to make any arrangements for commercial treaties or to surrender the forts in the western territory of the United States. Because the United States had no navy of consequence the British—and the French, too—were able to maul American shipping badly. In 1794 John Jay went to London to discuss a long list of grievances with what he called "good-natured wisdom." By the terms of Jay's Treaty, Britain agreed to withdraw from the western posts within two years. Britain did not agree to stop making arrangements with the Indians on the frontiers of American territory or to end her blockade and the impressment of sailors. The United States promised that it would not enter the war on the side of France. Britain still kept the lucrative British West Indian trade. The United States was to maintain the high tonnage duties on foreign ships coming into American ports. An arbitration commission was set up to decide how much damages Britain owed American merchants for the illegal seizure of their ships—the merchants later received $11,000,000. Other commissions were established to deal with boundary problems.

After much discussion, objection, and noise Jay's Treaty was ratified at Washington. Too much had been expected of Jay's mission to London. The main achievement of the new arrangements was this: peace had been kept with Britain.

Much discord now arose between the United States and France. France insisted that Jay's Treaty must be abrogated by the United States. The American "XYZ" mission to Paris was met by French threats and demands for money as a condition of peace. The Americans refused. "Millions for defense but not one cent for tribute." Even the Republican Thomas Jefferson remarked that the members of the French Directory were swindlers.

In America there were strong demands for war with France. All treaties with France were declared at an end; all trade was blocked. George Washington came out of retirement to lead a new American army. A department of the Navy was created. New ships were built. American vessels were ordered to seize any French ships that interfered with American commerce. Eighty-five French ships were captured within two years. A new song, "Hail, Columbia," reflected the popular mood and will.

The Federalists unwisely proceeded to push a series of repressive acts through Congress. A Naturalization Act raised the number of years for naturalization from five to fourteen. An Aliens Law gave the President power to deport from the United States any alien he believed to be a dangerous person. A Sedition Law provided penalties for anybody who opposed the execution of federal law or printed or published any "false, scandalous, or malicious" writings about the President, the government, or Congress. Ten Republican editors, alleged to be plotting against the government, were tried and convicted. Few Federalists, it seems, heeded the voice of Alexander Hamilton, their chief: "Let us not establish tyranny. Energy is a very different thing from violence."

Weakened and divided, the Federalists lost the disputed election of 1800. In March, 1801, the eloquent and ingenious Thomas Jefferson, leader of the Republicans, entered the White House. The Vice-President was Aaron Burr, soon to be involved in a dark conspiracy.

Many historians have rightly remarked upon Thomas Jefferson's agrarian outlook, his prejudices against cities, his dislike of manufacturers, his advocacy of diplomatic isolation, his opposition to a large navy. Despite Jefferson's errors of judgment—and not all men are agreed upon what those errors were—he was still a great national leader and President, far greater than many of his contemporaries believed him to be.

Thomas Jefferson had high ideals, courage, and determination. He had a deep faith in the honesty and common sense of the people. He believed—as every student of the University of Virginia knows—in the importance of popular education. He shared the conviction of John Locke, whose works he so much admired, that the powers of government should be where the people put them.

The exulting Republicans declared that the aims of the new administration were peace, stability, progress, prosperity. They swiftly prepared to maintain the powers of the states; to cut down the national debt and government expenditures; to repeal or allow to expire several pieces of Federalist legislation, such as the Naturalization Act, the Aliens Law, the Sedition Law. It is always dangerous for people who live in a democratic society to forget that the fountainheads of freedom may be plugged by well-meaning zealots, by ignorant men of passion and obstinacy, by the fanatics who advocate repression and coercion in the name of liberty and democracy. Every generation produces such people. Under whatever guise they come, they are enemies still.

Thomas Jefferson, the philosopher-statesman from Monticello, was now President of the United States. A new century was at hand. Douglas Southall Freeman, America's famous journalist-historian, once called that century "a muddy, bloody lake through which American life passed."

Across the green waters of the Atlantic the forces of Napoleon Bonaparte were locked in combat with successive coalitions of his foes. It will be recalled that after the collapse of the frail Treaty of Amiens of 1802 the conflict broke out again with even greater violence and then there came Trafalgar and Austerlitz, Napoleon's Continental System and the British countermeasures, the mounting British quarrels with the United States about neutral ships and trade, the British claim to the "right of search" and the impressment of merchant sailors who were supposed to be British deserters or slackers. The *Chesapeake* affair darkened the skies still more. The Embargo Act of the United States, passed in 1807, was a complete failure; it hurt the people of Britain and America alike and it helped Napoleon. The Non-Intercourse Act of 1809 had no better results.

In March, 1809, James Madison became President. The small and bald "Little Jemmy" shared the belief of his fellow Republicans that they could play Britain and France against each other and compel them both to abandon their blockades. Congress declared that the United States would trade with any nation that ended its blockade. Napoleon, always ready to promise anything, assured the United States, in a soft and saccharine statement, that the French blockade would stop at once—this was almost at the hour when he was secretly ordering the sale of confiscated American ships.

Madison and his government swallowed Napoleon's assurance. Napoleon was a skilled scoundrel, too wily for James Madison. He had no real intention of repealing his Berlin and Milan Decrees. Between 1807 and 1812 Britain seized 389 American ships. Napoleon's France seized 558.

Great Britain refused to stop either blockade or impressment. Slowly Madison's government blundered into open conflict. The seaboard states did not want war. On the other hand, several young and hotheaded men from the southern and western states did want war, and soon. These "War Hawks," led by Henry Clay and Felix Grundy, succeeded in electing the eloquent and commanding Clay himself Speaker of the House of Representatives. Fresh from their triumphs in the recent election the "War Hawks" lifted their voices.

The "War Hawks" asserted that they were anxious to end the Indian menace. Down in the Wabash Valley region Tecumseh and the Prophet, these famous Indian twins, were organizing the tribes. The tomahawks were swinging again; cabins were burned; there were shrieks and whoops in the night; scalps were drying by the tepees in the smoke and sun.

In 1811 General William H. Harrison repelled a night attack by the Indians at Tippecanoe, Indiana. The incident was a small one; but rumors grew and lies multiplied; Harrison soon became the hero of "the battle of Tippecanoe." Exciting tales of his heroism moved into the world of politics and novels and, sometimes, into history books.

The "War Hawks" said that the Indians operated from Canadian bases and were using British-made arms. The British were to blame, surely, for the power of Tecumseh. Canada must be conquered. Land-hungry settlers would have more territory if the vast stretches of Canada could be seized and annexed to the United States. The carnivorous "War Hawks" pointed out that patriotism could be profitable. Canada was near, rich, and vulnerable.

In June, 1812, Congress declared war upon Britain. The vote was 79 to 49 in the House of Representatives, 19 to 13 in the Senate. This vote gave one indication of the division that existed in the nation beyond the walls of Congress. Many men of New England denounced "Mr. Madison's War" and remarked that the real foe of the United States was Napoleon, not England or Canada.

"The conquest of Canada is in your power," Henry Clay told the men of the frontier. The militia of Kentucky, he said, could do it all alone. "It is a mere matter of marching," said Thomas Jefferson. The Canadians were of a different opinion.

The Americans mounted three offensives. General Hull thrust into Canada from Detroit, retreated, surrendered his whole army; the British took Detroit. American troops crossed the Niagara River and were pushed back. The New York militia, moving towards Montreal by the old Lake Champlain route, suddenly refused to cross the Canadian border. For the British, under the command of Sir Isaac Brock, 1812 was a satisfactory year.

In 1813 the American Lieutenant Oliver Hazard Perry built a small fleet and won the Battle of Lake Erie off Put-in Bay near Toledo, Ohio. "We have met the enemy and they are ours," he informed General Harrison. American raiders set fire to York (Toronto). The British were forced to abandon Detroit. They were pursued and overtaken by General Harrison and defeated at the Battle of the Thames in October, 1813, the same month that Napoleon was defeated at Leipzig. Tecumseh was killed in the battle. A monument stands today by a curve on the Windsor-London highway. "Here Tecumseh fought," says the brief inscription, "and here Tecumseh fell."

In 1814 about 10,000 British troops reached Canada. There were several engagements in the Niagara Peninsula—most Ontario children know about Chippewa, Lundy's Lane, and the tale of gallant Laura Secord and her cow. There was also a heavy encounter at Plattsburg in New York state. In

August, 1814, a British force captured Washington and set fire to the Capitol, the White House, and the navy yard. President Madison, who fled to the hills of Virginia, perhaps had sober second thoughts about the wisdom of the war.

The British now bombarded Baltimore—it was here that Francis Scott Key was inspired to write "The Star-Spangled Banner." Far to the south, a British expedition from Jamaica, led by General Pakenham, attacked New Orleans; the plan was to invade the United States by way of the Mississippi. General Andrew Jackson, who had just defeated the Southwest Indians at the Battle of Horseshoe Bend, left his headquarters at Baton Rouge to prepare the American defenses. Under Jackson's command was a hardy army of about 7,000 men, several of them skilled riflemen from Tennessee and Kentucky. The Americans lost about 70 men, the British about 2,000.

The Treaty of Ghent had been signed two weeks before the Battle of New Orleans. Both sides agreed to stop fighting and hand back any territory they had taken. No concessions were made by either of the belligerent powers. Neither the Americans nor the Canadians can be said to have won the War of 1812, whatever the national textbooks may say. The war was unnecessary; the campaigns were useless; the peace was a draw. At the beginning of the war the American slogan had been "On to Canada." At the end the slogan was "Not One Inch of Territory Ceded or Lost."

Except in song and story the memory of the War of 1812 soon faded on both sides of the border. The bloody episodes left in their train no long heritage of bitterness, no corrosion of hatred. This result was probably far happier, in the long pull, than the military triumph of either side.

After James Monroe succeeded James Madison as President of the United States in 1817 a series of agreements were concluded with Great Britain about Canadian boundaries and the size and number of naval forces to be maintained on the Great Lakes. In 1823 there was stated the famous Monroe Doctrine, so important in the later history of the Western world. There is no need to repeat here all of the facts that were cited and the comments that were made in earlier pages about the Message to Congress of President Monroe and the political and commercial factors involved. The important points are two. In the first place, the United States decided that it would not accept the proposal of Britain's George Canning—he had made it four times—that the United States and Great Britain should make a joint declaration opposing the subjugation of the new Latin American republics. John Quincy Adams, Secretary of State, said that it was better to act alone "rather than to come in as a cockboat in the wake of a British man-of-war." Secondly, the Monroe Doctrine, stated in the language quoted in Chapter 33, was intended to secure the Americas—South, Central, and North—from the attempts of any European power to conquer, partition, or intervene. The words were clear, the decision final. It should be added, of course, that without the British fleet the Monroe Doctrine would long have remained a paper barrier against European interference.

In 1825 John Quincy Adams, a cultivated scholar from Massachusetts, became the sixth President of the United States. Until Adams was defeated by Andrew Jackson in 1828 every President had been a man of property, good breeding, and education. Josiah Quincy once remarked that it took fifty years after the Declaration of Independence "to reach a vital belief that the people and not gentlemen are to govern this country."

Before 1828 the older states had given the franchise only to men of property. After 1828 those restrictions were gradually removed. Man's "inalienable rights" came to include the right to vote. Hence more people were enabled to have their voices heard and their votes counted. Such changes were particularly important after the power to choose the Presidential electors was taken away from the state legislatures and given to the voters.

Two main political parties fought each other in the election campaign of 1828. One was the Whig Party of John Quincy Adams, a group built out of the old Federalist Party of John Adams and Alexander Hamilton. The second was the Democratic Party of Andrew Jackson; it was really the old Republican Party of Thomas Jefferson.

A collection of several groups of voters opposed the nationalistic Adams and Clay in 1828; they supported the Democrats and elected Andrew Jackson. To men and women who remembered or had heard about George Washington, John Adams, Thomas Jefferson, James Madison, James Monroe, and John Quincy Adams it must have been a startling sight to see Andrew Jackson striding towards the White House.

For a hundred and fifty years it has been difficult to be neutral or "objective"—whatever that may be—about Andrew Jackson. Some of the reasons can easily be seen in his personality and character; others are to be found in the chapters of his varied career.

Andrew Jackson was born in 1769 in Carolina. He was taken prisoner by the British in 1781; it is said that from this event came Jackson's lifelong dislike and distrust of Britain. When the war ended the energetic Jackson studied law and became a lawyer. In 1796 he helped to frame the constitution of Tennessee. He soon became a judge in the supreme court of the state, then a senator in 1797—he was to be a senator again in 1823 and 1824. In 1813 he became a major-general in the army. Two years later he won the Battle of New Orleans and was soon a national hero. In 1818 he became military governor of Florida. In 1824 he was nearly elected President. In 1828 he was elected. Four years later he was elected again—his sad opponent was Henry Clay. In 1845 he died at the Hermitage, his home near Nashville, Tennessee.

Andrew Jackson, tribune of the people, was a skilled and swashbuckling military hero, a figure of compelling interest in his age and ours. He was energetic, brusque, uncouth, gauche, a violent and quarrelsome fellow. His disputes and duels were so numerous that they cannot be described or listed here. An adequate account of his fight against the caucus in 1824, for instance, would demand a chapter to itself.

There have been many descriptions and discussions of Jackson and his age. Familiar questions and answers appear with monotonous regularity. How far did Jackson move towards an anti-tariff position? Have the words "soft money" and "hard money" any meaning at all when applied to Jackson's ideas about such things as banks and currency? How far was the election of Jackson a delayed result of the panic of 1819 and the rising demands in the political ferment of the 1820's for a more thoroughgoing democracy?

In our own day the conflicting views about the nature and importance of what is usually called "Jacksonian democracy" are presented in scores of books and articles and on the floors of conventions, usually with vehemence and sometimes with skill. Some men have been concerned, then and now, with studying the shifting bases of a changing society and the intricate political problems posed by differing ideas about property and people. So far as "Jacksonian democracy" is concerned, some scholars have asserted that the main part of it was to be seen in the efforts of the "little man" to "restrain the power of the business community" so that political power and economic benefits could be more widely and equitably distributed. Some readers will recognize that the preceding sentences are a capsuled and incomplete statement of the coherent and logical arguments of Professor Arthur M. Schlesinger, Jr., of Harvard University. Other scholars have not agreed with Professor Schlesinger or with one another.

Despite the varying reactions to Andrew Jackson there does emerge at least one fact of consequence about which there can be no dispute: the democratic tendencies that exploded in the age of Jackson steadily moved to shape characteristic attitudes and institutions in the culture of the United States.

In 1783 the population of the United States was about 4,000,000. There were only six cities that had a population of 8,000 or more inhabitants.

By 1800 about 50,000 families had settled along the Ohio; still more thousands had moved into Kentucky and Tennessee.

Soon the tide of migration rolled into the Old Northwest territory, that land above the Ohio River and between the Appalachians and the Mississippi. The Northwest Ordinances of 1784 and 1787 provided for the survey, settlement, and government of the territory; the Land Ordinance of 1785 set the price on the land to be sold. The merchants and manufacturers of the eastern area saw new domestic markets opening up. Political parties debated the problems of cheap land that rose to take a place beside the issues of labor supply, banking, and the tariff. Into the Old Northwest came the land speculators, the traders, and the drifters, the gospel-preaching circuit riders.

Far to the south a new frontier was soon to be opened. The reader will remember that Napoleon Bonaparte's soldiers, trying to reconquer Santo Domingo, were frustrated by yellow fever and the Negro leader Toussaint L'Ouverture—he may also remember that it was about Toussaint that William Wordsworth wrote the famous words:

> Thy friends are exultations, agonies,
> And love, and man's unconquerable mind.

By 1803 Napoleon decided to withdraw from the whole region and Thomas Jefferson, Robert Livingston, and James Monroe carried through the Louisiana Purchase, earlier described; this arrangement doubled the size of the United States at a cost of $15,000,000. The Federalists objected and their leaders in New York threatened to organize a Northeastern Confederation, asserting that the United States was too big; but they did nothing and the United States grew bigger still.

Thomas Jefferson sent explorers to the West and Southwest and beyond the Rockies. The famous expedition of Meriwether Lewis and William Clark followed the Missouri north and west, pierced the Rockies and traveled along the Columbia River, earlier discovered by Captain Robert Gray, all the way to the sounds and bays of the Pacific. The journals of Lewis and Clark are exciting reading still; so are the modern pages of Bernard De Voto, a man who knew the history of the West and could convey to his readers a sense of the vastness and mystery of the deserts and the plains.

Meanwhile Zebulon Pike and others explored the upper reaches of the Mississippi and parts of the Red River valley. Pike moved into Arkansas, found the peak that was given his name, penetrated into southern Colorado, and was seized by the Spaniards. They let him go home to tell his tales.

Some boundary disputes with other nations were settled; and some were not. In 1819 Spain withdrew her claims to all of the Pacific coast lands above latitude 42°. In 1824 and 1825, by treaties with Great Britain and the United States, Russia dropped her claims to territory south of 54° 40'. The British were less obliging, insisting upon their rights and claims in the Pacific Northwest. In June, 1846, despite the slogan "Fifty-four Forty or Fight," the government of the United States agreed to accept the forty-ninth parallel as the boundary between British territory and the "Oregon country" of the United States.

The quarrels with Britain in the Pacific Northwest were thus peacefully smoothed away, or almost so. The disputes with Mexico, on the other hand, were settled by war.

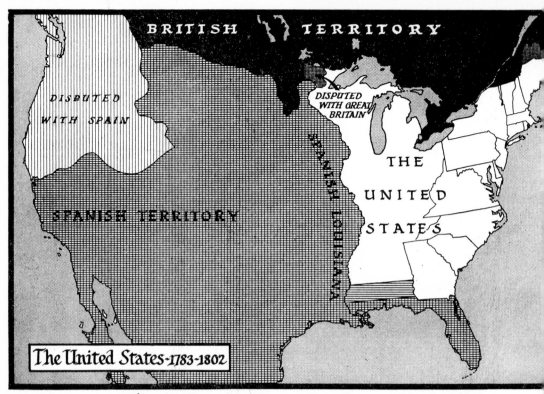

The United States·1783-1802

The Growth of the Continenta[

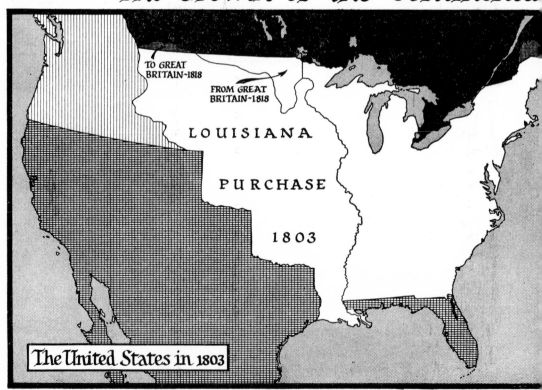

The United States in 1803

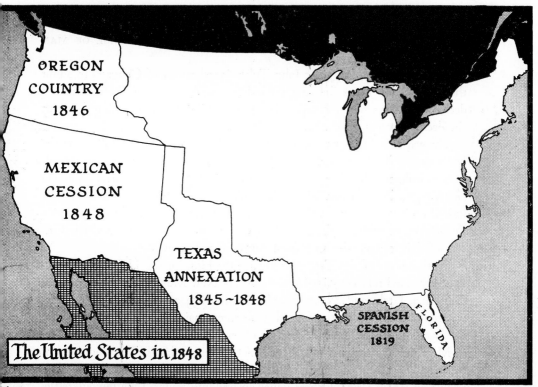

OREGON
COUNTRY
1846

MEXICAN
CESSION
1848

TEXAS
ANNEXATION
1845~1848

SPANISH
CESSION
1819

FLORIDA

The United States in 1848

United States, 1783~1853

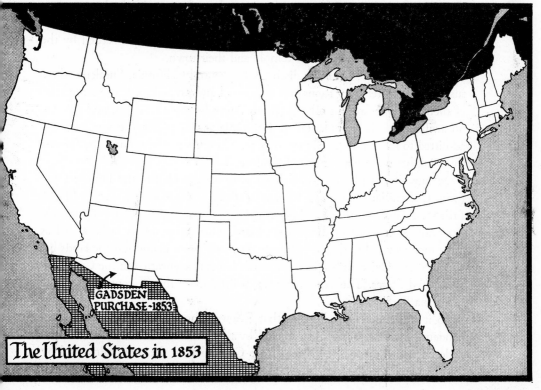

GADSDEN
PURCHASE~1853

The United States in 1853

In March, 1845, President John Tyler signed an act of Congress to admit the Republic of Texas into the United States. A year later, Mexico at last decided that she would reconquer Texas. To set about accomplishing that end, she declared war upon the United States.

The war ended after two years of fighting in the Rio Grande Valley and the lands around Veracruz and Santa Fe. Mexico was defeated, partly as a result of the brilliant soldiering of General Zachary Taylor and General Winfield Scott, especially at Buena Vista, Veracruz, and Monterrey. These days were indeed exciting. Many a youth of a later age has dreamed of the California Revolution, of riding with General Kearney, John C. Fremont, and Kit Carson, of fighting and shooting from Santa Fe to Sacramento.

By the terms of the Treaty of Guadalupe Hidalgo the United States obtained the land now contained in the states of New Mexico, Arizona, Nevada, California, Utah, and a part of Colorado. In 1853 a great block of territory was rounded out when the federal government paid Mexico $10,000,000 for the 45,000 square miles of the Gadsden Purchase.

More men, young and old, went into the western lands. The wagon trains rumbled and thumped and the dust rose. Some men went off by themselves to live on lonely farms. Others joined in building towns. One famous settlement in the conquest of the western frontier was made in Utah Valley in the year 1847. About 600 covered wagons brought into Utah the members of the Church of Latter-day Saints, followers of Joseph Smith and Brigham Young, believers in the Book of Mormon. These godly people settled by the Great Salt Lake and built their temple and their town.

In January, 1848, gold was discovered in central California. Suddenly there rushed into the territory thousands of hopeful and excited men, the same kind of men who appeared in other years in Australia, South Africa, and Alaska. So swiftly did the population of California increase that the territory was admitted to the Union as a state in 1850. Many men never found the fortune they sought; some never reached California.

Meanwhile, one by one, new states were being added to the Union: Ohio (1803), Louisiana (1812), Indiana (1816), Mississippi (1817), Illinois (1818), Alabama (1819), Maine (1820), Missouri (1821). By 1821 there were nine states west of the Appalachians. There were others to be added as more men traveled to shape their fortunes in the great plains and the lands beyond. New Mexico and Arizona were the last states admitted in the Continental United States. The year was 1912, a little more than a century after the Louisiana Purchase.

So it was that in the decades that followed the American War for Independence men exploited and explored by the banks of the Ohio, beyond the wide Missouri, along the gorges of the Columbia, in the mountains, and by the shores of the restless Pacific. The adventurers, the ambitious and land-hungry men, the aimless drifters, all these moved onwards, turning their horses towards the West. Their feet and backs were tired; but dreams and visions beckoned in their brains.

Uncounted miles of land stretched far beyond the breached barriers of the Appalachians, stretches of prairie, desert, boulders, mountains, sometimes cold, sometimes sun-scorched. Great stars burned in the western skies. In those uncharted regions a man could be lost like a mustard seed.

The overland stage coaches were not to come for several years. The Pony Express started in 1860, the transcontinental telegraph in 1861, the railroad in 1869. Before these happy achievements, the clattering wagons shook and bumped their sore and bilious passengers. Where men stopped and stayed towns sometimes grew, and cities later. Any map of the United States shows the strange new names that came to dot the land: Boise, Butte, Carson City, Dallas, Fargo, Little Rock, Los Angeles, Monterey, Oklahoma, Pueblo, Sioux City, Topeka, Tucson, Wichita, Death Valley, Grand Canyon, the Santa Fe Trail, the California Trail—how brightly shone the descriptions of Francis Parkman before our grandparents' eyes!

The Far Wanderers knew that the West was vast and wonderful; it was also sometimes merciless. Those who had an anemic inability to leave the East or were not stirred by discontent never struggled or survived—or perished—in the sprawling turbulent worlds so far from New York, Philadelphia, and Boston. "The timid never started and the weak died on the way."

Frederick Jackson Turner once wrote: "The western man believed in the manifest destiny of his country. . . . The frontiersman's dream was prophetic. . . . He had faith in man, hope for democracy, belief in America's destiny, unbounded confidence in his ability to make his dreams come true."

In 1850 there were about 3,000,000 slaves in the southern United States. True, only about 30,000 whites had slaves and only about 8,000 had more than 50 slaves. The romantic ideas about the Old South and its large plantations, great houses, happy slaves steadily singing by the magnolias and in the cotton fields is pleasant; but it is not founded in the truth.

There is a second fact: in 1790 the population of the Southern and Northern states was about equal. The two groups of states had equal representation in the Senate and had representation by population in the House of Representatives. Soon, however, the Northern states began to increase in power, progress, and population. The South stayed still, or almost so. The staple economy of the South, based upon cotton production and slaveholding, was increasingly threatened by the manufacturers and merchants of the North.

It is not surprising that the Southern states wanted to keep their representation in the Senate equal to that of the Northern states. To achieve that, the number of slave states and free states had to be even. So it was that whenever a territory in the South was admitted as a slave state, another was admitted in the North as a free state. The dividing line was the Ohio River.

In the North, the denunciations of slavery became more vehement and insistent when a controversy arose in 1820 about the admission of Missouri to the Union. Missouri was almost completely north of the Ohio River; but it had been settled mainly by Southerners; its constitution guaranteed slavery. The North refused to admit Missouri with slavery; the South refused to admit Missouri to the Union as a free state.

Henry Clay of Kentucky was widely supported when he prepared the famous "Missouri Compromise" by which Missouri was admitted as a slave state and Maine, carved from Massachusetts, as a free state. Thus the political balance between the North and South was kept. The United States stayed "half slave, half free." All the rest of the Louisiana Purchase land north of 36° 30'—the southern boundary of Missouri—was to remain forever free; slavery there was prohibited.

The decision about Missouri troubled the aging Thomas Jefferson. He always shrank from malignant and impassioned quarrels. The disputes, said Jefferson, "like a firebell in the night, awakened and filled me with terror. I considered it at once as the knell of the Union." Jefferson was not alone in his fears.

In the 1840's the disputes flamed again when the United States obtained the Oregon territory in the Northwest and Texas in the Southwest, together with all the other lands ceded by Mexico in the Treaty of Guadalupe Hidalgo. Several people in the Northern states believed the Mexican War was the result of a Southern plot to increase the slaveholding territories. This idea, the theme of James Russell Lowell's *Biglow Papers,* was a long time in dying. After 1846 arguments multiplied about what was to be done in the California, Utah, and New Mexico regions. David Wilmot, Congressman from Pennsylvania, was responsible for the "Wilmot Proviso" that was attached to an appropriation bill and said that "neither slavery nor involuntary servitude shall ever exist" in the territory taken from Mexico.

A series of compromise measures about the tightening of the fugitive-slave laws and the status of California, New Mexico, and Utah did not really settle any issues. Consider, for instance, the evasive "Compromise of 1850" and the Kansas-Nebraska Bill. The most important consequence of the Kansas-Nebraska Bill was the splitting of the Whigs; some formed the strange "Know-Nothing" Party and the rest created the new Republican Party, a group that opposed the expansion of slavery into the territories and approved such things as protective tariffs and free homesteads, thus appealing to the Eastern businessmen and the Western farmers.

In the 1850's there came the later phases of the "irrepressible conflict." The

South stood, static and agrarian; the rhythms of seedtime and harvest ruled the belt of King Cotton. The North, its economy based on free enterprise and free labor, moved forward, industrial, commercialized, expanding. It is true that the South was producing about 4,500,000 bales of cotton by 1860. Nevertheless, the power of the South, based mainly on cotton and slavery, was steadily declining. More and more, her interests were in jeopardy.

Excited voices rose in agitation and anger as men moved to the edge of violence. The Southerners were often led by strong men such as Jefferson Davis, John C. Calhoun, Edmund Ruffin, William Yancey. In 1850 Calhoun said: "The South has no compromise to offer . . . and no concessions or surrender to make." About the same time Senator Robert Toombs of Georgia had a great deal to say about the "cormorant rapacity" of the Northern shipowners. Other points of view were held by formidable men: Henry Clay, Daniel Webster, Senator Stephen A. Douglas of Illinois—Douglas was really a moderate man of compromise; he deplored sectional strife and believed that each territory should decide what it wanted to be and do on the principal of "popular sovereignty."

Meanwhile the Dred Scott decision of the Supreme Court in 1857 said that Congress had no right to exclude slavery from the territories. In 1858 there followed the famous Lincoln-Douglas debates. The South continued to fight to keep its institutions. It opposed high tariffs, often saying that such tariffs were a tax on agriculture for the benefit of the North. It stood against centralized banking, against the liberal land policy of the federal government that built up the territories, the money for internal improvements that seemed to go to the Northern states.

From the firebrand Abolitionists of the North came a stream of words and facts and arguments calculated to persuade and sway men to join a great crusade against the ills and evils of slavery. They were opposed by many moderate Northerners. The South, of course, feared and hated all the vehement Abolitionists. On both sides, moral indictments multiplied. Accusations, facts, and fantasies leaped from the printed page and the platform. The Southerners defended the "peculiar institution" of slavery and asserted that it was "highly moral" and a "positive good." The antislavery men said that slavery was a national sin and disgrace. The fanatic Abolitionist William Lloyd Garrison started his *Liberator* in 1831: "I am in earnest; I will not equivocate; I will not excuse; I will not retreat a single inch; and I will be heard." Garrison's influence has often been judged more powerful than it was in fact; it was not so great as the noise he made. More important were Theodore Dwight Weld, James G. Birney, the Quakers of Philadelphia and Indiana, Benjamin Lundy, bravely lugging his printing press about on his back, and scores of others. There was also, of course, Harriet Beecher Stowe's *Uncle Tom's Cabin* (1852), written as the fugitive slaves moved along the "underground railway" to freedom in the Northern states and Canada. In Canada's city of Chatham and the village of Lucan—once called Wilberforce—the descendants of these slaves live today with a freedom their forebears never knew this side of Africa.

There were many other dedicated and zealous men and women. After John Brown had failed in his attack on Harpers Ferry he was convicted by a Virginia court of murder and treason. Then he said (November 2, 1859): "I deny everything but what I have all along admitted—the design on my part to free the slaves. . . . I never did intend murder or treason, or the destruction of property, or to excite or incite slaves to rebellion, or to make insurrections. . . . I believe that to have interfered as I have done . . . in behalf of His despised poor, is not wrong, but right."

There were strong men and arguments on both sides. On the eve of the Civil War, John C. Calhoun said: "We cannot remain here in an endless struggle in defense of our character, our property and institutions." Some time earlier Abraham Lincoln had stated his conclusions. "A house divided against itself cannot stand. I believe this government cannot endure half slave and half free. I do not expect the house to fall, but I do expect that it will cease to be divided. It will either become all one thing, or all the other." Later in 1860 Lincoln wrote to Alexander H. Stephens of Georgia: "You think slavery is right and ought to be extended, while we think it is wrong and ought to be restricted. That, I suppose, is the rub. It is certainly the only substantial difference between us."

The difference was indeed "substantial." When men disagreed about principles, when Northern "right" met Southern "rights" head on, then trouble came, swift and violent.

In 1860 the Republicans at Chicago nominated Abraham Lincoln to be their candidate in the approaching Presidential election. The Democrats were divided. One group, led by Stephen A. Douglas, supported the idea of "popular sovereignty" by which each territory would decide for or against slavery. Opposed to them were the Southern Democrats who supported the Supreme Court's decision: slavery could go anywhere and the federal government must protect it. The Douglas wing nominated its candidates; the Southern Democrats chose theirs. Other parties and splinter groups moved into the campaign of 1860.

Lincoln and the Republicans won every free state. The two wings of the Democratic Party and the Constitutional Union Party led by Senator John Bell of Tennessee got all of the border and Southern states. In December, 1860, a convention in South Carolina of seven Southern states voted for secession when it was clear that the new President of the United States was Abraham Lincoln. They declared Jefferson Davis President of the Confederate States of America. John C. Calhoun and his supporters had always held that nullification and secession were constitutional because, in their view, the United States had never been itself a sovereign state, only the agent of the sovereign states that had ratified the contract called the Constitution. The North said that the South had no right to leave the Union; the Union was a union of peoples, not states.

The Southern states seceded because they said that Abraham Lincoln was opposed to slavery. This was not true in 1860. Lincoln was not then prepared to interfere with slavery where it was legally in existence. Many Northerners, of course, had insisted that the institution of slavery was sinful or immoral. They wanted it excluded from the territories. The principle of moral judgment runs throughout all the debates and disputes of these years.

On April 12, 1861, Southern troops shelled Fort Sumter at Charleston, South Carolina, and forced it to surrender. In the eyes of the North, this was rebellion. Three days later Abraham Lincoln called for 75,000 volunteers. The Southern states drew together: Alabama, Arkansas, North Carolina, South Carolina, Florida, Georgia, Louisiana, Mississippi, Tennessee, Texas, Virginia. General Robert E. Lee moved to command the armies of the Confederacy. Sweating soldiers in blue and gray were soon to march and kill.

In the early months of the war the Union's self-confident General George B. McClellan reorganized the Army of the Potomac and led his troops in a campaign in the mountains of West Virginia. McClellan rose rapidly to the rank of commanding general. His major weaknesses were revealed at Antietam. If he had not hesitated to commit all of his troops he probably would have smashed General Lee's forces completely. That was his great fault: delay and hesitation. In war, delay often breeds danger; hesitation may bring defeat. McClellan's bright star soon faded. In November, 1862, Lincoln dismissed him. His military career was ended. Much involved controversy arose about McClellan in his own day and later. Historians still dispute and debate about his qualities and his career. The subject is fascinating; it is hard to be neutral about McClellan.

Slowly Abraham Lincoln decided that the North was fighting not only to maintain the Union but also to free the slaves. In September, 1862, after the Union victory at Antietam, Lincoln declared that he would proclaim "forever free" all the slaves in the states still at war with the federal government. On January 1, 1863, he issued the famous Emancipation Proclamation.

Abraham Lincoln was one of those uncommon people upon whom rest so much of man's greatness. His speeches and many of the letters he wrote during these troubled years of the Civil War should be read by every civilized human being. They belong to mankind and the ages. The flashes of insight are there, the restraint and the courage, the embracing sadness.

Meanwhile the Northern states were angered by the attitude and policy of Great Britain. The British government, and still more the upper and middle classes, viewed the secession of the South with friendly eyes. The lower classes, including the textile workers who depended upon the South for their supply of cotton, were solid supporters of the North.

The premature proclamation of the extension of belligerent rights to the Southern insurgents by Great Britain was declared in itself to be a proof of animus towards the Northern states. Resentment was quickened and extended by such men as Charles Sumner and his apostles to whom England was "a soulless monster of Frankenstein." The news that England had permitted the sale of cruisers to the Confederacy was greeted with bitter anger in the Northern states. The most famous of these cruisers was of course the *Alabama*. The *Alabama* and other Confederate vessels damaged Northern shipping and attempted to break the Northern blockade of the Southern seacoast. The Northern states demanded reparations from Great Britain for letting loose the *Alabama* and her sister ships. These famous "Alabama claims" were to plague Anglo-American relations until the negotiation of the Treaty of Washington in 1871.

In February, 1862, General Ulysses S. Grant began a long, painful, and important campaign. He marched southwards through Illinois and Missouri. Then, in November, 1862, he slowly pressed in upon the strategic center of Vicksburg, Mississippi, in a series of complicated and skilled land and water operations. On July 4, 1863, the Confederate garrison at Vicksburg, 37,000 strong, finally surrendered.

The triumph at Vicksburg gave the Union forces control of the whole Mississippi River. It also separated Louisiana, Texas, and part of Arkansas from the rest of the Confederate States.

Far away in Pennsylvania, the great and grim battle of Gettysburg ended the day before Vicksburg fell.

Early in the summer of 1863 General Robert E. Lee invaded Pennsylvania; he believed that Confederate victory in the North might encourage the Northern peace party. A chance encounter between Lee's Confederate Army of Northern Virginia and General George Gordon Meade's Army of the Potomac resulted in the battle of Gettysburg, fought on the 1st, 2nd, and 3rd of July, 1863. General Lee had ordered his troops to concentrate at Gettysburg, unaware that one of Meade's cavalry divisions and two army corps had been placed in the town to screen the assembling of the Army of the Potomac a few miles to the southeast. On July 1 came the first encounters, and before the day had ended they were increasingly bitter and bloody as more and more troops came forward and were engaged.

Early on the morning of July 2 General Meade moved up to make his troop dispositions. Mainly because of faulty communication between General Lee and General James Longstreet—"General Lee's warhorse"—General Meade was given time to concentrate his forces. Longstreet has been accused of "tardiness," but the charge must not lie on Longstreet alone. If there was any blame at all, then Lee must share it.

General Meade placed his forces on a horseshoe ridge. The right flank was anchored on Culp's Hill and the left in front of an area called the Round Tops. The center was based on Cemetery Hill.

General Lee planned to attack both of the Union flanks simultaneously. General Longstreet objected, arguing that the Confederates had delayed so long and lost so much time that General Meade had established his men and position soundly. He had also been able to bring up more troops. Longstreet was right. Lee had waited too long. Richard Ewell, Lee's corps commander, also delayed and wasted time. The thrusts and waves of the Confederate attack were poorly coordinated. Federal counterattacks, supported by effective artillery fire, forced back the assaults and the few Confederates who pushed up Culp's Hill were driven off. Again and again the Confederate forces were dogged by the specter of "too little and too late."

It now seemed desirable to General Lee to strike with full force at the center of the Union line on Cemetery Ridge. He planned to do this on the morning of July 3. Once again the execution of Lee's plans was delayed. The guns that were to lay down the barrage that was to precede the infantry assault of the Confederates did not begin to fire until about one o'clock in the afternoon. Longstreet was opposed to this head-on attack. He wanted a flank assault. Lee overruled him.

The result of Lee's decision was the famous episode, so long and warmly debated, of the charge of Pickett's division in the teeth of a murderous fire from the defending Federal troops on Cemetery Hill. The Confederate attack got little artillery support. Only a few Confederate soldiers struggled and scrambled to the top of Cemetery Hill and most of them were soon cut down. The charge had no chance of success and the slaughter was terrible. Of the 4,500 men who started the attack, 3,393 officers and men fell on the field.

General Robert E. Lee had lost Gettysburg. He now began to withdraw and retreat. By the morning of July 5 Lee had turned to take the hard and heavy road that led to Appomattox. About 150,000 soldiers had fought in the famous and desperate battle of Gettysburg. There were more than 40,000 casualties. Many of the sons of the North and South gave "the last full measure of devotion."

There has been much acute analysis and sharp dispute about several phases of the battle of Gettysburg. Many professional and amateur critics and soldiers have explained what Meade, Lee, and Pickett should have done. Some men, for instance, have insisted that Meade unwisely permitted Lee to get away. Abraham Lincoln himself was of the opinion that Meade could have brought Lee to battle again and destroyed his army. Meade, for his part, thought not.

He pointed out that he did not have the means to pursue. His supplies were short and his lines were thin. To pursue and attack under such conditions was too dangerous. If Meade had tried to chase and engage Lee and Lee had turned upon him, then Meade's plans might have boomeranged. Men who look back may think that Meade was wrong. He was convinced that he was right. Those who object to Meade's decision would perhaps do well to recall that he was a distinguished professional soldier—after the Civil War he was to command successively the Military Division of the Atlantic, the Department of the East, and the Third Military District. They might also remember that Meade's adversary was no ordinary commander, but General Robert E. Lee.

Gradually the South collapsed before the pressure of the North's manpower, industrial strength, and wealth. In the campaign of 1864 General William T. Sherman, one of the ablest Northern generals, marched to Atlanta, laid waste a wide belt of land, and put his soldiers in a position to march north along the coast to meet the Union forces in Virginia. On April 3, 1865, General Grant took Richmond, capital of the Confederacy. On April 9 General Lee surrendered his army to General Grant at the Appomattox Court House. General Grant instructed his officers "to let all the men who claim to own a horse or mule take the animals home with them to work their little farms."

The victors in the Civil War never hanged Jefferson Davis "from a sour apple tree" but put him in prison for two years; he lived another twenty after they let him out. In contrast, Abraham Lincoln, President of the United States, lived less than a week after Lee's surrender. On April 14, 1865, he was shot by John Wilkes Booth. He died the next day, and his people buried him at Springfield, Illinois.

The Civil War had ended. The Union had been preserved. It is not enough to say that the North had won and the South had lost. There were other facts, other incalculable consequences. Even at the hour of military victory there was no wild exuberance in the North. In the South there was sorrow and bitterness. There was also pride. Douglas Southall Freeman once wrote a shrewd and sensitive sentence about the Southern leaders after the stillness and shadows of Appomattox: "For Lee and most of his lieutenants it was a drama of ill-fortune nobly borne and, in that way, a triumph of character over catastrophe."

To the north of the United States lies Canada. During the American Revolution 40,000 United Empire Loyalists, "abhorrers of Republicanism," had been added to Canada's population. In 1791 the Canada Act created two British provinces north of the Great Lakes and the St. Lawrence: Upper Canada, largely English, now the province of Ontario; and Lower Canada, mainly French, now the province of Quebec.

In 1837 two rebellions, led by William Lyon Mackenzie and the French-

Canadian Louis Joseph Papineau, broke out in Upper and Lower Canada. These rebellions were the Canadian challenge to a stupid and outmoded colonial policy. The Canadians demanded responsible government, by which they meant that Canadian ministers responsible to the Canadian legislature should have executive authority.

The British Government sent to Canada the brilliant and radical Lord Durham to study the Canadian situation. In his famous and long *Report on the Affairs of British North America* (1839) Durham made two important recommendations. Despairing of a federal union that would embrace the eastern colonies of Nova Scotia and New Brunswick, Durham proposed the fusion of Upper and Lower Canada. He hoped that the French-Canadians and the English in those provinces would merge into one people and would cease to be "two nations warring in the bosom of a single state." The two provinces were joined by the Union Act of July 23, 1840.

The second major recommendation of Durham's *Report* was that self-government should be granted in all matters that were the sole concern of the Canadian colonies. In 1847 Lord Elgin, Lord Durham's son-in-law, came to Canada as governor-general and in 1849 he established the principle of responsible government in domestic affairs by the simple act of signing the Rebellion Losses Bill. This was a bill to compensate those who had suffered damage in the rebellion of 1837. It was opposed by the British government and the Canadian Tories. Nevertheless, it had passed the Legislative Assembly by a large majority. Lord Elgin therefore signed it. The first step towards self-government had been taken; the precedent was established. Later in the nineteenth century the Canadians progressively obtained more control of their fiscal and foreign affairs in the gradual extension of self-government into new areas. In Canada, Australia, New Zealand, and South Africa the foundations were slowly laid for the development of the autonomous communities which today form the Commonwealth of Nations.

Meanwhile the frontiers of Canada, like those of the United States, were pushed steadily westward. English names stood side by side with French and Indian: Portage la Prairie, Poplar Point, Moosomin, Sintaluta, Broadview, Macgregor, Qu'Appelle, Red Deer, Medicine Hat, Pincer Creek, Calgary, Nanaimo, Esquimalt.

The British North America Act of 1867 created the Dominion of Canada, a federal union with the British parliamentary system of government. In this union the provinces were specifically given fifteen powers in addition to their exclusive control over purely provincial matters. All other powers, twenty-nine of which were listed, remained with the Dominion government. To the Canadian Fathers of Confederation it seemed that the American Civil War might not have happened had the residual powers in the United States been vested in the federal government rather than in the separate states. In 1867 the new Dominion consisted of four provinces: Nova Scotia, New Brunswick, Quebec, and Ontario. British Columbia and Manitoba joined in 1871; Prince Edward Island in 1873; Alberta and Saskatchewan in 1905; Newfoundland in 1949.

Swiftly the young nation grew in strength, size, self-respect, and self-reliance. By the early twentieth century the territory of Canada covered more than 3,000,000 square miles—only the Soviet Union and China are larger. Montreal is the second largest French-speaking city in the world. From the lands of the tundra to the wheat fields and the Great Lakes the years of the the twentieth century have been a period of vigor and power. Canada became the world's largest producer of newsprint, nickel, radium, platinum, asbestos; the mineral and oil resources of her vast land are beyond calculation.

Chapter 35

ASIA:

THE OPENING DOORS

"All the universe is an inn; search not specially for a retreat of peace; all the people are your relatives; expect therefore trouble from them."

—Chinese proverb

IN RECENT centuries many Europeans—traders, soldiers, travelers, and missionaries—slowly pressed and probed into the midst of the complex cultures and civilizations of the vast lands of the East. They discovered the massive importance of the forces of tradition in India, China, and Japan. They saw how the stiff and intractable laws and customs were passed from father to son as the generations folded into one another like the waves in a great sea. They learned about the wars and scars of the centuries, the decay and decline of great states, the tear-soaked years of misery, the nights of dread and the days of terror. They gazed upon the arid and savage landscapes, the fertile fields, the ancient cities, the great poverty and great wealth, the proud emperors and aristocrats, the malevolent and inefficient landlords, the priests and philosophers praying in the summer sun, the maimed and mutilated lives of many of the peasants, the faceless millions trudging towards dark horizons. All these things the Europeans weighed and measured with the eyes and values of the West. They could not easily have done otherwise.

Meanwhile the missionaries found opportunities to spread the Christian gospel. The soldiers marched to conquer and subdue. The traders bargained and bought. Europe wanted the goods of Asia. Trade meant profit.

The first heavy tides of European commerce and conquest thundered into India and the islands of the East Indian seas. Earlier pages of this book have described the busy rivalry of the intrepid Portuguese and the Dutch in the lands and waters from Bombay to the Banda Sea and beyond, the coming of the English and the French to India, the blood and shadows of the Seven

623

Years' War, the Peace of 1763, and the fall of France's star of empire in the vast subcontinent of India.

During the latter half of the eighteenth century several parts of India were filled with the fermenting excitements and tensions of challenge and change. In some areas the rich cultural inheritance was apparently forgotten as men rushed to and fro to follow leaders who promised them an end of their days of misery and a bright paradise on this earth. Several states were tormented by evil years of anarchy and violence. The law of love, *ahimsa,* was often broken. There were many wars between petty princes, volcanic eruptions of jealousy and greed. Sometimes, too, a challenge or an onslaught began a protracted struggle that extended into wide areas. There were often unpleasant years of disturbance and catastrophe, war and disease and stalking famine, strains and fears and cruel complexities, spasms of pain.

The honest historian must not stress too strongly the dramatic and exciting passages of the human story. It is true that these were troubled years in the history of India, filled with the inexorable impulses of change. It is also true that India is a large land and most of her millions of people were not in the midst of wars or languishing in complacent sterility or darkness and despair. They were grappling with their usual tasks and remembering their religions of endurance. They asked for little more than to be allowed to live from day to day and to do the unspectacular things that their fathers did before them. Calmness often survives in many corners of a tumultuous world. The rhythms of begetting and birth and death were not gravely upset. The lonely minds of priests, poets, artists, and philosophers still discovered and created, even though there were sometimes few men to hear and fewer still to comprehend. The merchants bargained by the arches; the bricks of the builders hardened in the sun.

The year 1763 was an important date in the history of India. After the Peace of Paris the powerful and eager British East India Company steadily extended its power. The directors and servants of that great enterprise obtained much profit in India; they also found much trouble.

Some of the trouble was of the Company's own making. Many of its representatives followed shameless careers of corruption and graft. Some of them were downright robbers, grabbing and gobbling without regard for morality or justice. It was not surprising that a number of angry Indian princes were soon ready to attack the British and drive them out of the country.

By 1770 a devastating famine in Bengal, increasing corruption among the British agents of the East India Company, the assaults of rebelling native princes, and the collapse of court and police administration joined to produce heavy problems. In the famine of 1770 about one-third of the population of Bengal perished. At the same time, the revenue of the East India Company in Bengal increased from £1,470,000 to £2,341,000.

Several British political leaders condemned the gathering of "unmeasured wealth" by the officers of the East India Company. Some of them insisted that Parliament should take immediate steps to control the Company and stop the accumulation of "ill-got riches" in the hands of the plunderers.

It was during this time of doubt and debate that Lord Clive, the victor of Plassey and later (1765–1767) chief representative of the East India Company in India, was accused of corruption. Lord Clive was found guilty of some of the charges made against him, although it was added that he had "at the same time rendered great and meritorious services to his country." In 1774 the man who had won India for Britain committed suicide.

In 1773 Lord North's administration passed the Regulating Act. Under this piece of legislation the presidencies of Bombay, Madras, and Calcutta were combined under the authority of a new official called the governor-general. He was to rule with the aid of a resident council of four men whose vote could limit his actions. The first governor-general was Warren Hastings.

Hastings was efficient, energetic, and hard-working. It was his misfortune that three members of his four-man council were his personal enemies, determined to oppose and thwart him. The forceful Hastings did what he could in the circumstances. He carried out a series of intelligent reforms in the administration of the East India Company. He tried to reduce corruption and moral erosion. For these policies and purposes Hastings is to be praised.

There were less pleasant aspects of the tale. The East India Company directors insisted upon their profits, and Hastings had to satisfy them. Much gold was needed to raise and maintain the military forces that were necessary if French plots were to be blocked and the borders of Bengal defended. Warren Hastings obtained the money where he could, sometimes by methods that were harsh and unfair. He did what he thought was expedient; but that which is expedient is often unjust and immoral; and it cannot stand the scrutiny of unfriendly eyes.

Hastings, shrewdly watching and reading the storm warnings in India, told his associates that there would be more trouble. When we look back from this distance in time it is hard to understand how so many of the Company officials, especially the old India hands, could have been so hidebound, unimaginative and complacent, so satisfied that what was not well would soon be better. What ideas for action and reform they did put forward were usually pale, lopsided, and bloodless. When Hastings assured the authorities at home that in his considered judgment there were several matters in India of extreme and desperate moment there was never any action, often no reply.

Then the gale struck. Hyder Ali, that "menacing meteor" who was the Moslem sovereign of Mysore, joined in an alliance with the ruler of Hyderabad, the Mahrattas, and the French to attack British territory on the Carnatic plains. "A storm of universal fire blasted every field, consumed every house, destroyed every temple. The miserable inhabitants fleeing from their villages were slaughtered. Those who escaped this tempest fled to the walled cities; but evading fire, sword, and exile, they fell into the jaws of famine." In October, 1780, the soldiers of Mysore besieged Britain's Madras. Meanwhile the British forces were being defeated far away in America. The battles in India were all part of a general war.

Warren Hastings ended the triumphant march of Hyder Ali by bribing his allies. In 1782 Hyder Ali died and his son Tipu became the ruler of Mysore and the ally of the French. Tipu signed a formal peace agreement after his defeat by the British in 1784 on the Malabar coast; but for years he plotted with the French, especially with the agents of Napoleon Bonaparte. Meanwhile the advance of the British foes in India had been stopped. This is what Hastings had planned and this is what he had done.

Many deeds of Hastings gave his opponents in India and at home excellent chances to attack him. Upon his return to England in 1785 Hastings was accused of misgoverning British India. Under the clauses of an impeachment listing twenty-two charges the weary proconsul was also accused of conquering too much territory by dubious methods. "Nations had been extirpated for a sum of money, whole tracts of land laid waste by fire and sword . . . the British government exhibited in every part of Hindustani holding a bloody scepter in one hand and picking pockets with the other." During the trial of Hastings his accusers—led by Edmund Burke, Richard Brinsley Sheridan, and Charles James Fox—raised questions that are unanswered still. The controversies about the trial of Warren Hastings continue today. There are those who insist that a man must be judged by the values of the age and place in which he lives. There are others who assert that evil is evil in all times and lands. Some men who have read all of the available documents say that the impeachment of Hastings was a crime and a tragedy. Others vehemently support a contrary point of view. Macaulay's famous and unjust essay did not close the case.

Hastings was at last acquitted. His trial lasted for seven years; it cost him more than £70,000, almost the whole of his fortune.

Several remarkably able governors-general were sent out to India between the departure of Hastings and the outbreak of the Great Mutiny in the middle of the nineteenth century. All of them, especially Lord Cornwallis and the Marquis of Wellesley, discovered that when the British wanted to keep order or prevent attacks on British territories the only effective way of doing so seemed to be by treaties of friendship or by conquest and annexation. Under successive governors-general there were many wars: wars with the Pindaris along the foothills of the Himalayas in Nepal and northern Bengal, wars with the obstinate Mahrattas, wars with the stealthy Gurkhas.

To counter menacing Muscovite plans and intrigues in Afghanistan and northern India the British captured and sacked Afghanistan's famous city of Kabul. In 1843 Sir Charles Napier invaded and annexed Sind. In 1846 Kashmir became a protected state. The part of Lower Burma that had not been annexed by the British in 1826 was taken in 1852. Most of the Punjab was annexed after the Sikh wars of 1846 and 1848–1849, and this fact ended the vile rule in the Punjab of a series of impostors, puppets, murderers, and at least two imbeciles. Lord Dalhousie, India's governor-general between 1843 and 1856, finished the conquest of the province of Oudh and ousted a moronic despot and the harpies around him.

Meanwhile more British capital moved into the Bombay and Madras regions; it also moved into other areas to stimulate cotton and jute production. The number of social and economic reforms increased. Soon there was an impressive list of public works: canals, bridges, irrigation systems, telegraph and postal services, hospitals, railways. There were also more medical aids, sanitary measures, famine relief systems. Reforms and progress in education continued. Three universities were established in 1857. In a population of about 300,000,-000 in 1900 one man in ten could read and write.

There were other reforms. The time-honored practice called *suttee,* or *sati,* was abolished—this was the custom according to which widows were expected to throw themselves upon the funeral pyres of their husbands. Officially reported in Bengal in 1818 were 839 cases of *suttee.* New regulations also forbade child marriages and decreed that no children were to be thrown to the crocodiles. Effective steps were taken to discourage the *thagi,* the secret society of stranglers who worshiped Kali, the goddess of destruction, and put into the English language the word "thug."

The natives of India often found these changes and reforms an inadequate compensation for their own customs, institutions, and religious beliefs. Some of them feared that they would be forced to abandon the ways of their fathers, to follow the road of British law and order, and to worship before strange shrines. Hindus, Moslems, Sikhs, and scores of other religious and cultural groups were bitter and unhappy. The causes of their irritation were not the same; they differed from group to group and from place to place. The peoples were united only in their discontent and their mounting objections to British policies.

By the middle of the nineteenth century discipline in the native army was very bad, especially among the troops of Bengal. Many natives were idle, restless, troubled, ready for mischief. An old Hindu prophecy had told of the end of the East India Company's rule in 1857. The Crimean War brought rumors that spread over India and damaged British prestige. Hindus feared that they would lose their caste if they served outside of India; a recent East India Company order had said that no volunteer should be accepted who would not agree to serve overseas. Tales floated and spread that Britain intended to force all India to become Christian. A new cartridge, encased in paper and greased with fat, had recently been introduced into the army. Suspicious Hindus, fearful of losing caste, became excited when rumors said that the fat was from the sacred cow. Moslems were terrified when they heard that the fat was from the unclean pig. Discontent in the breasts of thousands of soldiers and civilians prepared India for the great mutiny that crept among the Sepoys and then roared like a jungle fire through the lands of the north.

The mutiny began at Meerut and spread to Delhi. Headless and mindless mobs burned and slaughtered. At Cawnpore there was a fiendish massacre; all Europeans there were killed in the midst of primitive and savage bestialities. At Lucknow a desperate siege lasted three months. The British had been caught off guard. There were about 233,000 native troops or Sepoys in the army and about 46,000 British soldiers; but the British regiments that had been sent off to the Crimea had not returned; six regiments had been withdrawn to serve in Persia; many of the British officers who had been left behind were no credit to Britain. Had more troops been available the disasters might have been swiftly prevented. By the end of 1859 reinforcements had been sent from Britain and Persia and India was quiet again. There were no further nightmare mutinies, only the needling pertinacity and pressures of native discontent.

The dramatic nature of the famous convulsions that began in 1857 often obscures the fact that the Indian Mutiny was not an all-India uprising. It had its center in Bengal and was limited almost entirely to a belt of territory between the Himalayas and the Ganges. The native troops of Bombay and Madras, the Gurkhas of Nepal, and the Sikhs of the Punjab stood by the British. Some of them perhaps realized what chaos would come to India if the British left.

The Indian Mutiny ended the dual control of the British government and the East India Company that had been established by Pitt's India Act of 1784 and extended by subsequent legislation. All the remaining political powers of the East India Company now passed into history. By the terms of the India Act of 1858 they were transferred to the British Crown. India was henceforth to be ruled in the name of the Queen, soon to be called the Empress of India. The Viceroy of India was to be responsible to the Secretary of State for India who, as a member of the cabinet, was in turn responsible to Parliament. This chain of command remained unchanged until the creation of the two independent states of India and Pakistan in 1947.

So it was that in these dramatic years the annexations and reforms of Great Britain in India helped to bind that great land more securely to the Western world. Britain's pattern of policy increased her trade, her influence, and her wealth. It also helped India. Shrewd and thoughtful eyes watched the effects of British administration and leadership, the broadening education, the increasing Indian participation in government. Here, surely, were achievements that were laying the foundations for a future of bright promise.

With the sweeping wings of imagination we travel now to watch and weigh the forces slowly disturbing and changing the land of China a few centuries ago. Then, as now, the towers of the Forbidden City glittered in the sun, the ports were filled with the lighters and the sampans and the half-naked boatmen with their basket hats. Down the streets of the cities went the rickshas and the bullock carts. On the rivers, those great arteries of trade, glided the boats, thousands of them, large and small. Over the long caravan paths the traders moved their goods.

One of the main trade roads of the ancient world began in the Peiping and Tientsin region and twisted through the stretches of Inner Mongolia into the Tarin Basin of Sinkiang. Some caravans then followed the Himalayan passes down into the Ganges plains. Others continued westward through Afghanistan and Persia to the markets and merchants of the Near East and the ships of the West waiting in the hot harbors.

In the days of the Mongol khans, when Europe's Marco Polo was traveling through the kingdoms of Asia and the Chinese were beginning to grow the new crops of sorghum and cotton, the Christian missionaries John of Montcorvino and Friar Odoric came to the northern city of Peiping. A few centuries later more Roman Catholic missionaries, scholars, translators, and scientists, including the famous Francis Xavier and Matthew Ricci, moved through the streets of Peiping and Tokyo, teaching such things as hydraulics and mathematics and Christianity. In the early fifteenth century the Ming Emperor Yung Lo sent his admiral Cheng Ho upon seven naval expeditions to look at the world outside of China. The long, four-decked ships of Cheng Ho visited Java, Siam, Somaliland, Indochina, India—a Chinese trading station was set up at Calcutta. From Africa the Chinese brought back a giraffe, the famous "unicorn" of the misty tales told again and again through the centuries.

In 1516 the Portuguese came to China. They disgraced themselves by their lawless and silly conduct and were driven away by the Chinese. Then they improved their manners and were allowed to help the Chinese government put down the pirates on the south coast and to rent a trade base at the port of Macao, forty miles south of Canton.

Meanwhile, too, English and Dutch ships were prowling and probing along the edges of China in search of trade and profit. In 1624 the Chinese government permitted the Dutch to establish a trade center in Formosa. For thirty years the Dutch stayed; then the Chinese sent them home and no more goods flowed beween Peiping and Amsterdam. In 1637 armed English ships moved up the Pearl River to Canton.

By land and by water the goods of the Far East came into Europe: wall-paper, goldfish, lacquerware, oranges, dominoes, fans, screens, silks and spices, silkworm eggs in the sixth century, porcelain in the sixteenth century, tea in the seventeenth, plans and ideas for the tea houses, pagodas, and arches that marked the European excitements and imitations of the art and life of the East in the eighteenth century.

Not all of the chapters in the tale of the growth of trade and cultural inter-change between China and Europe were peaceful. There were too many quarrels. It is always a pity when human beings start to shout and kill and run through the corridors of history with passion-twisted faces. This is what happened in the later years of the Ming dynasty in the early seventeenth century. Sharp and strong disputes broke out among the scholars and the missionaries. The Confucians moved into quarrels with the Christians. Jesuit missionaries disagreed with those who were not Jesuits, especially about the ways in which Christianity should be taught. The Chinese who disliked the foreign "barbarians" happily joined in the noisy arguments: the more wide-spread the quarrels, the better chance there was of getting the foreigners out of China. The Chinese who wanted to encourage amicable relations with the Europeans laid their clubs about them in the name of peace. In a welter of emotions and conflicting motives the tumults increased. The European traders often became more lawless and domineering. Serenity, tolerance, tact, and good sense yielded before the pressures of the crackbrained, the nearsighted, the greedy, and the ruthless. The steady, solid, and hardheaded men were simply ignored, mocked, or thrust aside. It was all very hectic and unseemly; and it was also very dangerous.

In the midst of these floods of passion and prejudice and the tireless squab-bles of men who were not very clearheaded, the Ming dynasty collapsed. In 1644 the last Ming ruler, a flabby creature, committed suicide. The Manchus from Manchuria, those sturdy warriors of the north, seized the swords and donned the mantles of the Mings.

At first the Manchus held only four northern provinces; it was from that narrow base that they steadily expanded their power. The Manchus were re-markable rulers, efficient in war, skilled in government. They were also men who believed in conciliation as well as in force. For instance, they kept several civil servants who had been used by the Mings. They supported Buddhism, Taoism, and Confucianism. They encouraged Chinese artists and writers. They were mainly responsible for the making of *The Dictionary of K'ang Hai*, a rightly famous book that gives the pronunciation and meaning of about 45,000 Chinese characters.

Upon one point the Manchus would not bend or yield: there must be no intermarriage between the Chinese and the Manchus. The Manchus rightly feared that intermarriage would mean their absorption into the great body of

China. Then the victors would be vanquished. Such had been the fate of all of those who had conquered China in the past. Hence the Manchus insisted, with spirit and stubbornness, that Manchus and Chinese must not marry. Despite all the laws and rules the Manchus and Chinese did marry. Quietly and peacefully through the years the Manchus were absorbed. "China is a sea which salts all waters that flow into it."

In the days of the Mings and the Manchus the Chinese looked upon their ancient culture and found it superior to that of all the rest of the world. To them China was the "Central Country" surrounded by less favored lands. The foreign barbarians from Britain, Denmark, Germany, Holland, Portugal, and Sweden were permitted to enter China only under certain conditions. They must, said the Chinese, pay homage to the emperor in Peiping, the central city of all civilization. They must also bring gifts and tributes to be presented to the emperor of China according to the time-honored patterns and laws of Chinese economy.

In the early years of the Manchu dynasty many missions entered China from the lands of southeast Asia and beyond. These missions traveled a prescribed route; each mission member carried a tribute of a nature and value specified in the instructions sent from Peiping. After the various tributes were presented to the emperor he gave gifts to the members of the mission. The complicated arrangements and rituals for the exchange of tributes and gifts, so completely controlled and prescribed, resulted in an export-import flow of goods that was in fact a form of foreign trade.

The European missions to China were possible because the early Manchu emperors, especially K'ang Hsi, usually treated the foreign missionaries and traders with courtesy and kindness. During the first part of his reign K'ang Hsi was deeply interested in what the Jesuits had to say about what they believed and why. Like some of the Mings before him K'ang Hsi also welcomed the technical information the missionary-scholars brought from Europe. He was quite prepared to follow a liberal policy and to aid in the widening of the trade channels between Europe and China.

It was unfortunate that the political power of the men about the imperial court compelled K'ang Hsi to abandon his policy of friendship with the West. In 1717 a series of imperial edicts, issued under political pressure, closed China to all foreign trade except at Canton and the port of Macao, still rented by the Portuguese. There was to be no more teaching of Christianity in China. All the records of Cheng Ho's voyages were to be destroyed. The Chinese were warned to have no associations with foreigners. No Chinese was permitted to leave China. Several missionaries were deported and their property confiscated.

In the history of China there have been several periods of aloofness and isolation. The Great Wall of China was built in 216 B.C. by the First Emperor to keep out the barbarians. The wall still winds over the hills for fifteen hundred miles. It keeps out no barbarians now; but it does remain as a symbol of protection and safety. It has often been said that the people of China must guard themselves against the foes and dangers of the outside world. Long after the First Emperor had departed, several rulers of China built other kinds of walls and watched the gates. The advisers of the Emperor K'ang Hsi in the eighteenth century were convinced that it was wise to turn away from the West. In the testing and tumbling years in the middle of the twentieth century China's Mao Tze-tung used modern methods of control to limit the flow of Western ideas and trade into China.

So far as the Chinese were concerned, the blocking of the streams of intercourse with Europe meant no loss to China. To them China was the Middle Kingdom, the "Central Country," the superior state to whom all nations ought to give admiration and respect. In 1793 the Emperor Ch'ien Lung wrote these words in a letter to England's George III: "Strange and costly objects do not interest me. . . . Our dynasty's majestic virtue has penetrated into every country under Heaven, and kings of all nations have offered their costly tribute by land and sea. As your Ambassador can see for himself, we possess all things. I set no value on objects strange or ingenious, and have no use for your country's manufactures." To a Chinese gentleman of 1793 the emperor's words were right and reasonable. To a European they were irresponsible and ridiculous, clearly showing that the imperial government of China had no sense of the realities of the world, no imagination, initiative, or wisdom.

There are always pitfalls in a policy of isolation. As the world moved into the modern centuries new and improved methods of communication and transport brought Macao and Canton closer to Lisbon and London. The Chinese might deplore and denounce this sad fact; but they could not deny it. They also learned that a nation who wants to remain isolated must be strong enough to push away all comers and hold them at arm's length. By the late eighteenth century China was not strong enough to repel the foreigners clamoring at her doors.

There were urgent problems that would not go away. The population pressures upon China's food supply were tremendous. Economic difficulties multiplied. The Manchus—there were about 500,000 of them by 1800—spent much of their lives in useless indolence and drained huge sums from the state in pensions, sinecures, and interlocking corruptions. The Manchu emperors—and the mandarins, too—became weak, lax, and dishonest. A thoughtful Chinese might easily be persuaded that the Manchu emperors no longer held "the mandate of heaven" that decreed their right to rule. Unrest spread. The number of secret and subversive societies increased. Bandits on the land and pirates on the seas and rivers wounded the state.

The imperial edicts of 1717 had said that there was to be no foreign trade with China except through Macao or Canton. Foreign traders in these ports, so anxious to obtain tea, porcelain, silk, and other Chinese goods, were subject to unpleasant restrictions.

Under the "Canton system" it was provided that one official, called the "hoppo" by the foreigners, collected all the customs duties and harbor dues. Because there was no fixed system of official tariff rates, the "hoppo" often changed the level of his charges. The foreign traders found such procedures intensely irksome and provocative. They sometimes ventured to suggest that the character and ancestry of the "hoppo" were not spotless.

Only one group of thirteen Chinese merchants had been licensed by the emperor to trade with the Westerners. Protected by their monopoly powers, these Chinese merchants formed a guild or *cohong* and compelled all foreigners to trade with them. The men of the *cohong* established the commercial rules. It seemed to some indignant foreigners that these strait-jacket rules were deliberately shaped to cause trouble. For instance, if a foreigner lived down in Macao and brought a ship up the river to take on goods at Canton the Chinese authorities said that he had to have his ship tied to two small Chinese boats. He had to pay pilots' fees and interpreters' fees—the trader often spoke Chinese as fluently as the interpreter but because the law said that it was illegal for foreigners to learn Chinese the trader paid for the interpreter's services. The law also declared that a foreign merchant must not take more than 175 bales of silk on any one ship moving down the river from Canton. If a trader stayed in Canton he had to live in one of the warehouses along the river outside the city. The whole foreign community in Canton was responsible for apprehending and surrendering any foreigner accused of an offense under Chinese law.

Westerners could not understand or approve such demands and controls. Nor could they find just or intelligible the Chinese court methods. They had a steady distaste for the Chinese use of torture in judicial procedures. They objected again and again and nothing happened. They also insisted that they should have some written contracts with the Chinese merchants. They were disturbed, they said, at the fact that they had no legal protection at all. They could not ask their country's ambassadors in Peiping to help them because there were no ambassadors. Imperial China refused to enter into diplomatic relations with the Western states.

The mazes and jungles of the Chinese rules and regulations were humiliating, stupid, illogical, inconsistent, unfair, chaotic, often contradictory, almost always provocative; they caused real injury to the foreign traders. The steady complaints of the British and Americans and their fellows were well founded. They were angry men, filled with a sense of outrage. If their profits had been less, their patience would have been shorter still.

To all complaints and barbed objections the complacent Chinese replied that the foreign traders had no legal rights at all. Nobody had asked them to come to Canton. If they did come to trade, then they must accept and abide by the rigid Chinese rules. It was the foreigners who wanted to trade and to make their profits; therefore let the foreigners bow; let them petition; and let them do what the Chinese told them to do when they were within the land of China.

Behind their self-made barriers the Chinese kept trying to stand against the persistent thrusts and pressures of the West. They continued to block and blunt the numerous direct appeals and protests that flowed from Europe. In 1793, for instance, England's Lord Macartney led a large mission to Peiping to try to persuade the Chinese government to permit Western merchants to buy and sell more goods in China. The Chinese were not impressed by the English gifts of Wedgwood pottery, Sheffield knives, swords, window glass, firearms, optical instruments, and a picture of King George III. They were displeased when Lord Macartney refused to prostrate himself before the emperor. They did not want to increase their external trade. The English trade mission failed; Lord Macartney went home empty-handed. In 1816 Lord Amherst tried again; his luck was no better. Lord Napier went to Canton in 1834 to press the cause of the private British merchants. He wasted his words and time. It seemed that the gates of China were not to be opened further.

Practical men of energy and rude common sense saw that there was money in "the Chinese trade." Many of them were happy to see the charter of the East India Company lapse in 1833. They were still more pleased to see an act of Parliament end the Company's legal control of most of the commerce with China. They were delighted when the terms of the new charter of the East India Company destroyed the Company's control of the production and trade in opium. More traders, filled with hope, gravitated towards Chinese waters. More tea and silk came out of China; more opium went in.

European and Chinese smugglers busily joined in their profitable enterprises. Whatever the rules and laws of China might say, the tide of trade with the West steadily swelled. Along the coasts of China, from the Gulf of Tonghin to the Gulf of Pohai, in the bays and by the river mouths, cargoes were shifted from boat to boat by knavish men in the moonlight. Fishing sampans hung with nets in the daytime did smuggling or piracy jobs when the darkness came. Night is the mother of crime. Many a junk with patched sails seemed to be an honest vessel; but it was filled with wolves and foxes.

Meanwhile the Chinese government at Peiping was steadily growing weaker. Networks of disaffection and lawlessness continued to multiply. An abscess was created by the dope addicts in the body of the state.

In an effort to cope with the mounting drug-traffic problems the Peiping authorities jailed some British merchants and ordered them to surrender all of the opium in their possession and to sign bonds that they would import no more of the drug. The British traders handed over about 20,000 pounds of opium to the Chinese. The Peiping authorities then insisted that all vessels engaged in smuggling should be confiscated and all smugglers executed. At this point the British traders and representatives decided to leave Canton. Despite the statements of some modern writers it is not true that the British ever questioned or denied the right of the Chinese government to prohibit the importation of opium. The British did object to the Chinese treatment of British nationals. They were not unaware, of course, that British military power might spell the destruction of the Chinese rules that restricted trade.

A short war between Britain and China soon began. British gunboats moved to blockade and shell Chinese ports. In 1841 British troops moved into Canton. The conflict was ended by the Treaty of Nanking in 1842. China paid an indemnity for all British property seized or destroyed, including 1,540 opium chests. The monopoly guild of the *cohong* in Canton was ended. Peiping also agreed to accord diplomatic status to all British representatives. British merchants were granted the legal right to enter and trade in the five Chinese ports of Amoy, Canton, Foochow, Ningpo, and Shanghai. The tea, silk, pearls, brocade, and teakwood carvings could now move easily to the waiting ships and customers of Europe.

By the terms of the Treaty of Nanking, China also ceded the island and seaport of Hong Kong to Britain. To this great center and crossroads of commerce the traders and travelers came from over the seas and down through the barren red hills of China beyond the peninsula of Kowloon. Stimulated by men and gold, the city of Hong Kong steadily grew. Today, at the base of Victoria Peak, about 2,500,000 Chinese live on an island of 391 square miles, speaking the garbled dialects of the mainland. The modern visitor does not usually forget the irrigated terraces, the narrow streets and stairs, the gardens, the workshops and factories, the warehouses, the crowded docks, the roasted pigs and tin bathtubs in the congested markets, the ornate houses of the wealthy on the mountain side and the shacks and sweaty slums below, the proud bank buildings, the mysterious forces shaping human realities, the pulse beats of history as men move through time, so busy being and doing, the dimensions of meaning that are so numerous and sometimes so ill perceived.

The Treaty of Nanking of 1842 was soon followed by new demands and pressures from the West. Internal disputes in China further weakened the power of the Manchu dynasty. Some of the rebels in the T'ai P'ing (Great Peace) Rebellion (1850–1864) loudly opposed concessions to the West; but neither the insurgents nor the Peiping government, so fettered by corruption and incompetence, could defend themselves against the hammering power of Europe.

In 1856 Britain became involved in another war with China. The Chinese authorities had boarded the British schooner *Arrow* and had arrested the Chinese crew on charges of piracy. Britain demanded reparations and also insisted that the "treaty port" clauses of the Treaty of Nanking be kept by the Chinese.

France joined Britain in the war. Troops of the Western allies marched to Peiping, took reprisals for the ill treatment of British prisoners, and burned the emperor's summer palace. The Treaty of Tientsin (1858) provided that China should pay indemnities and make further trade concessions. It was also agreed that a permanent British embassy should be established at Peiping; the Chinese would set up an embassy in London. Christians in China were to be protected. The Yangtze River and five more ports were to be opened to foreign trade. Other concessions soon followed. For instance, many foreigners were permitted to learn the Chinese language. Christian missionaries were allowed to go to certain regions in China.

By the side of Britain moved France and the United States. Successful negotiations with China gave them the right to enter the "treaty ports," together with some other areas, earlier opened to Britain alone. In some cases and places extraterritorial rights were given to the foreigners. These rights soon drove deep wedges into Chinese sovereignty and prepared the way for the later "Open Door" policy.

Across the narrowing seas came more traders from the United States. Back in 1784 the *Empress of China* had sailed from New York to Canton with a cargo of American goods and had brought back some silk, tea, bamboo, and teakwood carvings. Soon several American towns and cities sent ships to China. A few individuals and companies, sensing high returns upon their investments, did the same thing. Elias Derby of Salem, Massachusetts, became a millionaire, mainly as a result of his sound judgment and good fortune in "the China trade." America's Russel and Company rose to share power and profits with England's Lent and Company and the famous Jardine, Matheson, and Company.

Chinese merchants came to the United States, and Chinese laborers crossed the seas to work in the mines and build railways. The crisscrossing destinies of men were taking Americans to Canton and Chinese to Chicago and San Francisco.

The "clipper ships," first built in Baltimore, sailed out of such busy ports as Medford, Salem, Boston, Philadelphia, Providence, New York. They were fast ships: the *Rainbow* made the trip from Canton to New York in 88 days and the *Flying Cloud,* a large vessel of 1,793 tons, usually completed its run in about 95 days. Many of the ships went round Cape Horn and up the Pacific coast to the Northwest ports, where they took on hides and furs. Then they crossed the Pacific with their full cargo of furs, glass, hides, wines, woolen goods, beeswax, cotton, clocks, and scores of other products of the Americas. Back they came with the loads from China: pepper, tea, silks, china, spices, porcelain, and numerous other things that influenced parts of American life. Professor Samuel Eliot Morison wrote these sentences in his fascinating *Maritime History of Massachusetts:* "The Northwest trade, the Hawaiian trade, and the fur-seal fisheries were only means to an end: the procuring of Chinese teas and textiles, to sell again at home and abroad. . . . Many a Boston family owes its rise to fame and fortune to the old Northwest and Chinese trade. . . . Salem became the American and for a time the world emporium for pepper. . . . Tinware that itinerant Yankees peddled throughout the Eastern states was made from Banka tin."

Some of the clipper ships were also busy in the illegal opium trade. They took Turkish opium into China. To defend themselves against the Chinese the Americans armed their clipper ships with heavy guns. There was sometimes much excitement.

These were often dramatic days in the ports and on the green seas. For good or ill, they were soon to pass away. As the Civil War ended in the United States more of the iron-clad and steam-propelled ships appeared. The realists wanted speed and dynamic efficiency and that is what they got. Slowly, one by one, the clipper ships were moored for the last time. There were some men who liked to remember how those proud ships looked when they turned seaward, their sails bellying in the wind, the gulls screaming and dipping by the masts. Nobody today can watch with envy from the dock as the nimble sailors climb the rigging of a clipper ship that is starting its three-month voyage to China, so far away, China with its redolent spices, its rivers glimmering under the stars, its fountains spurting upon the tiles. Electric lights shine harshly over the docks of New York and Canton and Shanghai in the nightime now; in the daylight the cranes swing crazily and the winches groan; the steel-studded and stimulating age of the machine is at hand and the sense of magic and wonder is dying. The last clipper ships sailed, some time ago, into the night, into the Deep of Time.

More than 500 years ago many Japanese pirates and adventurers were raiding the coasts of Korea and China to harry and steal. The Japanese who preferred the paths of peace and quiet profit set up posts to sell and trade. Some reached out to southeast Asia and started settlements and small trade centers in Indochina, Java, and Siam. Other merchants and colonists traveled past the Ryukyu Islands and Formosa to trade and live in the Philippines.

In the late sixteenth century the power of the merchants in Japan was diminished by the dominant military leaders and feudal lords; the spirit of Hideyoshi was everywhere. Nevertheless, the spirit and enterprise of those merchants was so great and they brought so much wealth to Japan that the feudal rulers rarely interfered with their activities. Osaka and Tokyo—then called Edo—became important trading cities. Trade brought profits and gold, the pillars of prosperity and hope.

When the Japanese were traveling beyond the home islands the foreigners from Europe were coming towards Japan. The Portuguese and Dutch merchants and the Roman Catholic missionaries arrived and stayed, for a time. In the early seventeenth century, however, most of the European merchants and missionaries were forced to leave—their ousting was described in Chapter 14. All ports were closed to foreign commerce. Between 1638 and 1853 only the Dutch were permitted to live and trade in Japan. They were compelled to dwell and keep their trading stations in the small Deshima district of Nagasaki.

In 1720 the Tokugawa shogunate, usually so determined to keep Japan sealed off from the outside world, did consent to the admission of Dutch books that contained no material about religion. Many Japanese, especially the young scholars, became interested in the secular Dutch learning. Books about geography, anatomy, engineering, and war were seized and studied by eager readers. No man can say what consequences came from this one little stream of learning, these few books and ideas that flowed in from the West.

Early in the nineteenth century the Russians tried to reach some profitable trading agreements with the Japanese. They jockeyed for position. They haggled. They sent diplomatic missions and naval expeditions. The Japanese were suspicious and stubborn. Every approach was fruitless. One Russian sea captain was locked up by the Japanese for more than a year.

The Russians could not ignore the black facts. It was clear that the Japanese wanted to stay in their islands untroubled by the barbarians from beyond the seas. Let the Russians go back to St. Petersburg or back to Mongolia and the felt tents and buttered tea, back to whatever regions they called home. Such was the Japanese attitude. Meanwhile the patriotic Shinto priests in Japan bowed before their shrines, the yellow-robed Buddhist monks before theirs. The followers of Confucius went upon their accustomed ways. The students of "the Dutch learning" read and debated. The barometer of their peaceful world stayed steady. Nothing was jolted or jogged. Japan was content.

In 1837 merchants from the United States and Great Britain tried in vain to open the gates that were barred and bolted. In 1846—across the seas the resistance of China was crumbling—a mission led by America's Commodore Biddle was turned away by the shogunate.

Seven years later Commodore Matthew C. Perry took a well-armed squadron of two sloops and two steam frigates into a bay near Tokyo. He brought gifts for the Japanese: guns, model railway trains, a telegraph set. He received gifts: brocades, silks, lacquerware. He said that the United States wanted to make a treaty of commerce and friendship with Japan. Then Perry wisely left Tokyo and went to China, leaving the Japanese to think about the American request and to ponder the fate of China.

In February, 1854, Commodore Perry returned to Japan with more ships and guns. The Japanese were well aware that they had to accede to his demands. On March 31, 1854, Japan signed the Treaty of Kanagawa, an agreement providing that shipwrecked sailors would be hospitalized and treated well; that any foreign vessels might stop in Japanese ports for supplies; that the two small ports of Shimoda and Hakodate should be opened to the ships of the United States; that an American consulate might be established at Shimoda.

Townshend Harris, the patient and persevering American consul at Shimoda, succeeded in 1858 in negotiating a new treaty with the evasive and sullen shogunate officials. This Harris Treaty—the final arrangements were hastened by the news of Great Britain's second defeat of China—opened five "treaty ports" in Japan. Despite the emperor's veto in 1858 the Harris Treaty became effective in 1860. Townshend Harris deserves more praise and fame than he has been given.

Soon Great Britain, France, Holland, Russia, and Prussia signed trade treaties with the shogunate. Warships, guns, diplomacy, and persistence had triumphed. For Japan the "Age of Exclusion" had ended.

Trading ships of the Western nations were soon lying anchored in the ports or moored by the docks in five of the great ports of Japan. They were also found in Canton, in Hong Kong, in Shanghai, in the waters about Bombay, and at the mouths of the Ganges. Tramp steamers from Europe and America prowled and darted along the coasts of Asia. Their business was sometimes legitimate, sometimes not. They, too, were symbols of the fact that the strange and disturbing foreigners from Europe had invaded the East. Most of them were merchants. "Trade," says the proverb, "is the mother of money."

Chapter 36

NATIONALISM:
STATES IN TURMOIL

"Mountains interpos'd
Made enemies of nations who had else,
Like kindred drops, been mingled into one."
—William Cowper, *The Task*, ii, 17

THE central decades of the nineteenth century were filled with chapters of revolution, a revolution of such complexity and depth that any brief description must use arbitrary and oversimplified language. They were a time of profoundly decisive convulsions and snappings of continuities, of force and splintering violence, of the bright hopes of the "Age of Progress." They were a time when spirits took fire and bayonets were bloody, when the drab tenements and slums and squalid corruptions sprawled over some regions like a fungus, when menacing tensions grew in the midst of protests, apologies, panegyrics, falsehoods, and agonies. They were a time of the drastic surgeries of revolutions and reforms, of progress and poverty, of spiritual restlessness, of liberalism and reaction, of imperfections and deformities, of the shifting worlds of Romanticism and Realism, of the strokes and counterstrokes of a new and violent nationalism, of gleaming triumphs and black failures.

In these years many men and women were caught up and tumbled about by new questions, new answers, and new ideas. Strange winds of doctrine overturned faiths held for centuries. Old concepts of status and contract withered and were blown away. Numerous ideas of human equality spread at a quickening pace into lands where they had never been before.

Almost every person who lived in the Western world of the nineteenth century knew and felt the turbulent power of nationalism. During these exciting years there came new ferments of national feeling. In many of the states there came, more and more, a sense of momentum, of shaping and transforming destiny. Men rose to rebel and fight, shout and shoot, destroy and build.

Sometimes their rosy hopes were mocked; and sometimes they were not. Many of those men felt that they alone knew the right road ahead. They saw themselves as the leaders and shapers of change. Those who disagreed with them must be defeated, silenced, or wiped away. Chateaubriand tells us that Danton said: "These priests and nobles are not guilty; but they must die because they are out of place; they hinder the movement of things and get in the way of the future." There are Dantons who appear, again and again, in the ranges of the past and present. They are the ones who call for the sword or the hangman's noose while timid men stand about grim-faced or nervously tittering. They are the ones who know what they want to do and what they want to get.

The core, center, and vital support of all national movements is to be found in the ideas and emotions of individuals who have been willing to speak strong words and take decisive measures. They may have been unscrupulous men; they may have been blameless men of virtue and vision; they may have been bigoted or stupid; but they were, almost always, men of passionate determination; and they did get things done. They often became national heroes and their statues stand upon the city squares.

"Nationalism" is a difficult and dangerous word. The currents and eddies of national feeling have risen from many springs. They have been moved and quickened by strong and strange forces. They have taken many forms. Their divers thrusts and intricate consequences cannot be completely calculated. The whole series of national movements was, and remains, complex and confused, erratic, unpredictable, and imperfectly understood.

From mustard seeds of truth have grown vast legends, theories, and conjectures. National heroes and conquerors—and even tyrants—have been canonized. Idiotic and extravagant partisanship, inflamed fanaticism, and narrow and exaggerated patriotism have often covered up the facts and darkened judgments. Childlike and passionate individuals have sometimes joined hands with mad and wicked men and together they have done coarse and repulsive things in the name of noble enterprise. Always, of course, there have been the honest and sober men who have done none of these things.

In the nineteenth century there were many comments and judgments about the formidable power of the new nationalism. The famous Austrian dramatist Franz Grillparzer asserted that "the path of modern culture leads from humanity through nationality to bestiality." England's Benjamin Disraeli dismissed "this modern new-fangled sentimental principle of nationality" as "dreamy and dangerous nonsense." In a later day several writers insisted that national ethics and morals were dictated by the interests of nations and classes and by military and economic power or the lack of it. For instance, Germany's Friedrich Bernhardi declared that "political morality differs from individual morality because there is no power above the state."

Statements such as these might be multiplied; they would only serve to illustrate still further the fact that nationalism and nationality and all the watchwords connected with them often meant—and mean—quite different things to different people in different times and places. Many men have placed their own contents in the word "nationalism" and have made their own definitions. Then they have added comments about such ingredients of nationalism as language, culture, traditions, myths, legends, economic interests, and the like. It is an interesting game, particularly since the rules are so few.

An accurate and full description of the floods of nationalism in the nineteenth century would contain long passages about dramatic and significant events in Belgium, Denmark, Holland, Norway, Portugal, Spain, Sweden, and Switzerland. There would also, of course, be vivid sections filled with the embittered chapters of Irish history, looking forward to the hour when "a terrible beauty was born" during an Easter Week in Dublin. The history of most of the lesser states in a world of power was marked by long and heavy struggles as their sons fought and fell for their homelands and the causes that they believed good.

In the large European states there were often restless subject peoples who chafed and fretted in what they considered to be a shameful condition. In Hapsburg Austria, for instance, the Magyars and Germans had jostled and snarled for centuries; even the formation of the Dual Monarchy in 1867 brought no sure and steady peace. Meanwhile, the heterogeneous groups within rickety and polyglot Austria plotted and rebelled, again and again. National ambitions and rivalries of minority elements were not easily pressed down or destroyed.

The Czechs, Slovaks, Slovenes, Ruthenians, Moravians, Croats, Serbs, and Italians—all these had their dreams. Fortunately for the Hapsburg dynasty and the uneasy stability of the state the numerous nationalities were seldom at peace among themselves. Nevertheless, the peril brought to Austria by the discords, hopes, fears, and ambitions of the restless nationalities was always there. It would not go away. The assassins' bullets might start a revolution; at Sarajevo they were the immediate cause of the First World War.

There were other difficulties. One of them arose from the long and steady interest of Russia in the European lands controlled by Turkey. Encouraged by the decline of the Ottoman Empire in the nineteenth century, the Russians determined to advance their frontiers in the Near East. Nicholas I, that prop and pillar of sinister despotism, was confident of the approaching demise of Turkey. He declared that he wanted an agreement with England "lest the old man should suddenly die upon our hands and his heritage fall into chaos and dissolution." Twice, in 1844 and 1853, he proposed that Turkey should be divided: England would get Egypt, Crete, and Cyprus; Russia might perhaps occupy Constantinople. With this proposal the British would have nothing to do. In the first place, it was an immoral plan of a ruler who had cruelly suppressed popular revolutions. Secondly, the dismemberment of Turkey would upset the European balance of power, threaten English interests, and further Russian designs in the Middle East and India.

In 1852 and 1853 a series of paltry disputes arose about the guardianship of the holy places in the Turkish province of Palestine and Russia's insistence that she should have a general protectorate over all Greek Orthodox Christian subjects of the sultan in European Turkey. After much truculent diplomacy, the Crimean War began. England and France, soon to be joined by Sardinia, tragically blundered into war on the side of Turkey.

After a series of chaotic and floundering campaigns Sebastopol fell to the allies. Nicholas I died and Alexander II agreed to make peace. By the terms of the Treaty of Paris of 1856 the "integrity" of the Turkish Empire was guaranteed. Turkey and Russia mutually restored to each other all conquests. Turkey declared "generous intentions" towards her Christian subjects. There were to be no warships or fortified coastal zones in the Black Sea or the Dardanelles. Moldavia, Wallachia, and Serbia were given autonomy in their domestic affairs. An international commission was to control the navigation of the Danube.

Twenty years later the Turkish provinces of Bosnia, Herzegovina, Serbia, Bulgaria, and Montenegro rebelled against Turkey. The Turkish government was mainly responsible for sickening atrocities in Bulgaria. In 1877 Russia declared war on Turkey to free the Serbs and Bulgars from Turkish control and to draw near to Constantinople. By 1878 the Russians had leaped close to Constantinople and the Turks sued for peace. Russia then imposed upon Turkey the Treaty of San Stefano. By the terms of this treaty Turkey retained only a narrow strip of land in Europe. The size of Bulgaria, now autonomous under nominal Turkish suzerainty, was greatly increased, especially by the addition of a slice of Macedonia. Montenegro, Rumania, and Serbia were to be independent. Bosnia and Herzegovina were declared to be autonomous states, also under nominal Turkish suzerainty. The heavy hand of Russia was slowly descending upon the Balkans. Turkey was almost out. Russia was moving in.

Britain's Benjamin Disraeli declared that the Treaty of San Stefano altered the terms of the Treaty of Paris of 1856—and another of 1871—and must therefore be submitted to all the powers that had signed the earlier treaties. For this purpose a European conference was necessary. Meanwhile the gray ships of a British fleet lay off Constantinople. Russia reluctantly agreed to the holding of a Congress at Berlin where the treaty of San Stefano would be revised.

Germany's Otto von Bismarck, as president of the Congress, was ostensibly the "honest broker." But Bismarck saw beyond Berlin. He saw the rivalries of Austria and Russia in the Balkans, their bitterness and overlapping national ambitions, especially in Serbia, Bosnia, and Herzegovina. He decided to support Austria, thus winning the long ill will of the Russians.

The Congress of Berlin returned Macedonia to Turkey. Bulgaria was divided into two parts. The administrative control of Bosnia and Herzegovina, still nominally Turkish, was given to Austria, ancient foe of the dismayed and angry Serbs. By a treaty with Turkey, Britain guaranteed the defense of the sultan's Asiatic territories and took control of Cyprus, the isle of Venus, and the city of Aphrodite. Meanwhile, of course, the Balkan ulcer was not healed.

Louis Napoleon Bonaparte was elected President of France in 1848. In 1852, as a result of a *coup d'état* and two tricky plebiscites, he was proclaimed Napoleon III, "Emperor of the French by the grace of God and the will of the people." The men of property, badly frightened by the excesses of the "National Workshops" and the subversive ideas of socialism spreading among the workers, were quite willing to support and anoint Louis Napoleon, "the savior of society," the bulwark against the radicalism of Paris, the strong man, the nephew of the great Napoleon who had conquered so much of the world. The workers, too, looked kindly upon Louis Napoleon, the romantic and adventurous heir of a great tradition. Would his rule not be better than a bourgeois republic? Was not the title of one of his books *The Abolition of Poverty?* Did he not favor universal manhood suffrage? Did he not declare himself to be the protector of the interests of all Frenchmen? In raising him to the highest position, France said 'I want order . . . but I want that all those who suffer may have reason to hope.' "

Napoleon III was a man who possessed a kind of chameleon character and personality. He was at once a romantic individual who delighted in sly subterranean activities, a born conspirator, cunning and crafty in some respects and very naïve in others, unscrupulous, sometimes well intentioned, vacillating, adventuresome—he had made and lost three fortunes before he had come to power in France. Some men called Napoleon III an enigma—"the Sphinx of the Tuileries." He was not really an enigma. Nor was he what Prussia's Otto von Bismarck harshly called him in a famous sentence: "a great, unrecognized incapacity." Perhaps he may be best described as a man who was usually trying to be "all things to all men."

The French emperor wanted to have real power in his own hands even while he preached and prated about the virtues and values of self-government. He insisted upon universal manhood suffrage, but few of his opponents ever got elected to office. He controlled the members of the legislature by pressures, influence, patronage, and the bribery of money and position. His bureaucracy and espionage system were efficient. Gradually the republicans were pushed out of office, often completely out of the public eye. By appropriate regulations and other devices Napoleon III slowly strangled the newspapers that opposed him, meanwhile insisting loudly that freedom of speech and freedom of thought were the pillars of a free state. He dismissed hostile university professors and ended the teachings of some courses, especially in the fields of history and philosophy. Even the mighty Victor Hugo was forced to flee from France.

All this was done quietly. There was not much fuss. Napoleon III was a despot who had no desire to describe and explain that fact to his subjects.

Meanwhile the property owners, the bourgeoisie and the peasants, were pleased to see the workers and the revolutionary socialists suppressed and peace and property protected. The French Roman Catholics were happy to note how Napoleon III supported Pope Pius IX and increased the influence of the Church in the French schools and universities. There was a rapid rise in the building of hospitals, asylums, and houses for the industrial workers. Napoleon III's government declared its interest in such things as old-age pensions, accident and sickness insurance, and other social-security measures. Public works multiplied. Large areas of Paris were completely rebuilt; broad and beautiful boulevards and squares replaced the narrow streets where mobs had once built barricades and defied the soldiers and the police. A government bank, the *Crédit Mobilier,* lent money to worthy and enterprising men of business. Many tariffs were lowered, including those on iron, steel, and wool. New railway, telegraph, and steamship lines were built. French industry, encouraged by words and aided by money, steadily expanded. France had almost everything that a great nation could desire, except liberty.

Napoleon III probably never understood why the prosperity that was mounting in France brought no increase in his personal popularity. The republicans, of course, always looked upon him with baleful eyes—was he not a renegade and a usurper? Many French Roman Catholics came to dislike the emperor's support of those Italian nationalists who wanted to strip away the pope's territories and put them into a united Italy under a king or a president. The socialists continued dissatisfied—who could ever appease the bellicose socialists? There were also some haggling and whining manufacturers who disliked the government's tariff policy.

Napoleon III now decided to permit more freedom. So began the period of "the Liberal Empire." The press laws were relaxed: political exiles were allowed to return to France; some arrogant and bumbling officials were dismissed; deportations for political reasons were stopped; the Chamber of Deputies was allowed to criticize the emperor's ministers and to determine the national budget.

It was all to little avail. The emperor's foes were not placated. The liberals still insisted that Napoleon's throne must fall. France would not long stay "the slave of one man," the emperor that Victor Hugo called "Napoleon the Little." The sinister and relentless socialists gave Louis Napoleon no quarter.

Napoleon III had said: "The Empire is peace." Meanwhile he had strengthened the army—dictators cannot starve the army.

Under the compulsion of domestic pressures Napoleon III turned his eyes abroad. He hoped to bolster his waning prestige by success in foreign wars and diplomacy. Frenchmen would surely approve and applaud the realities of military power, the sunlight glinting on the helmets of jaunty and victorious soldiers. Then the blemished records of Napoleon's government might be forgotten, or almost so. The emperor's nightmares would be ended; the gates of fear would be closed.

Napoleon III was often a bold man; he was not always a shrewd one. Vast and grand designs sometimes result in little that is vast, little that is grand.

In July, 1858, Napoleon III and Camillo Benso, Count di Cavour, prime minister of the Italian state of Sardinia, met at the French town of Plombières. There they agreed that if Austria attacked Sardinia, then France would enter at once into a war against Austria. The Sardinians and the French would unite to oust the Austrians from northern Italy. France would be rewarded by getting Savoy and Nice.

When Cavour tricked Austria into war the French army moved to support Sardinia. In the two battles of Solferino and Magenta the Austrians were defeated. Napoleon declared that he would free Italy "from the Alps to the Adriatic." For the Italian nationalists the tilt of events looked hopeful. "When France draws her sword," Napoleon III had said, "it is not to dominate but to liberate."

Suddenly Napoleon III changed his mind. The Prussians, opposed to strong French influence in Italy, mobilized along the Rhine. Napoleon III also saw that the enthusiastic revolutions breaking out in Parma, Modena, Tuscany, and a section of the Papal States might result in the creation of a united Italy, a powerful and troublesome rival of France in the Mediterranean region. The French emperor had not expected that his intervention would have such exciting results. Meanwhile the French Roman Catholics shouted their anger at Napoleon's alliance with the Italian nationalists who had declared their intention of destroying the temporal power of the pope. To the astonishment of Europe and the fury of Sardinia, Napoleon III made a sudden truce with Austria at Villafranca.

Russia had not forgotten France's part in the Crimean War, the French support of the rebellious Poles, Napoleon's share in bringing about the creation of the state of Rumania. Austria resented Napoleon's alliance with

Sardinia. Sardinia, for her part, was angered by the French emperor's abandonment of his obligations. Prussia and Britain were suspicious of Napoleon's intentions, particularly when they saw how he had added Savoy and Nice to his territories and how his active hands were moving in widely separated areas in the Near East, in Africa, and in the islands of the South Pacific.

In 1861 Napoleon III made a sensational attempt to get a foothold in Mexico. He dreamed of carving and shaping a Latin and Catholic Empire in America. His foolish and grandiose adventure began when Britain, Spain, and France decided to intervene in Mexico in an attempt to collect debts that the Mexicans owed their nationals. After the British and Spanish withdrew from Mexico, the French force stayed, overthrew the Mexican Republic, and proclaimed in 1864 a new Mexican Empire under the Austrian Archduke Maximilian.

The Mexicans objected and rebelled. As soon as the Civil War ended in the United States the Washington government demanded the immediate departure of the French. Napoleon III yielded; there was nothing else for him to do. Maximilian stayed in Mexico. In 1867 he was executed by a Mexican firing squad. His wife Carlotta died in 1927; for sixty years she lived the barren half-life of a lunatic.

The Mexican expedition was a fiasco, a reckless, useless, silly, and tragic affair. For Napoleon III and France it was a tarnished and shameful episode. Abroad and at home the star of the emperor was fading fast.

For centuries the peninsula of Italy had been a "geographical expression," a fragmented land whose peoples had heard, again and again, the hoofbeats and footfalls of invading armies. The Frenchmen, the Spaniards, and the Austrians had surged into Italy to slaughter and conquer and seize gold and jewels, thrones and lands.

Not until the nineteenth century did there appear any loud and excited demands for national unification or political freedom in the modern sense. True, the work of the secret society of the *Carbonari* had helped to keep the Italian revolutionary spirit from flickering and guttering out. Nevertheless, the *Carbonari* had never been successful in stirring large groups of people to action; webs of conspiracy spun in the darkness do not usually stimulate mass movements. Only with the coming of the *Risorgimento* were the Italians spurred to enthusiasm and action. With the *Risorgimento* came a militant desire to do something, the mingling of the memory of Rome with nationalistic and patriotic dreams and schemes for liberty and union.

The background of the *Risorgimento* is both interesting and complex. Professor Kent Roberts Greenfield and others have pointed out, and rightly, that the political aspects of the *Risorgimento* have been too heavily stressed by the historians. To understand and appreciate what ideals and ideas roused the

Italian people so strongly to fight and forge a nation-state we must look carefully at the contemporary writings, discussions, and intellectual propaganda about social and economic affairs as well as the political. In those days many men talked past the midnight hours about liberalism, nationalism, and progress; about Adam Smith's ideas on free trade; about economic reforms that seemed necessary in industry, agriculture, and commerce; about science, invention, national traditions, religion, banks, railways, the instruments of social and political action, the dreams of a united Italy, a free Italy that would rise and push aside the heels of her conquerors. Massimo d'Azelio called these years of preparation "a conspiracy in the open sun." Almost at hand was the age of new power groups, new religions and systems of ethics, new middle-class nationalists. Sardinia's Count Cavour was soon to say: "If we did for ourselves what we did for our country, what rascals we would be!"

There were several plans and ideas for the unification of Italy. One proposal, especially attractive to the more conservative groups, was advanced by Vincenzo Gioberti. In his book *On the Moral and Civil Supremacy of the Italians,* published in 1843, he said that the Italian states would be wise to unite in a confederation under the presidency of the pope. Pope Pius IX did not take kindly to the idea. The unification of Italy would probably mean war with Roman Catholic Austria and the pope did not wish for that. Nor did he wish the papal territories to be absorbed into an Italian nation-state. Pope Pius IX did not want to be the savior of Italy. "They want to make a Napoleon out of me who am only a poor country parson."

A second idea was seized and held by many Italian nationalists: all of the Italian states should be united into a liberal, unitary, secular republic with its capital at Rome. All roads should lead to republican Rome. The outstanding leader of these men was a Genoese lawyer, the great patriot Giuseppe Mazzini (1805–1872) about whom several comments were made in Chapter 33. Mazzini was a fiery crusader and mystic who came to have a tremendous moral influence upon his native land. He once said: "Character is destiny." He certainly set out to prove it. Many Italians—especially the young and eager intellectuals—joined the "Young Italy" movement started by Mazzini to advance the principles of republicanism. Soon there were about 50,000 members of the movement and many of them were writing articles and pamphlets and recruiting and addressing crowds throughout Italy. "Place the youth of the nation at the head of the insurgent masses," said Mazzini. "You do not realize the strength that is latent in these young men or what magic influence the voice of youth has on crowds."

Mazzini was a nationalist, a democratic republican, a fervent moralist, a fine writer, an eloquent speaker, often an impractical romantic. He was a man who believed, and passionately believed, that Italy could "regenerate herself through virtue and self-sacrifice."

Giuseppe Mazzini's great achievement was the rousing of the Italian people. "Each nation," he said, "has a special mission to execute." More than any other man, Mazzini was responsible for the fact that most of the land of Italy soon seethed with unrest. When pulses are speeded many things are possible.

The future did not belong to Mazzini. It did not belong to those who favored a federal union under the pope. It rested with the kingdom of Sardinia and the royal house of Savoy.

One of the most astute and able statesmen of the nineteenth century was the Piedmontese nobleman Count Camillo di Cavour (1810–1861). Cavour had served in the Sardinian army until his liberal ideas got him into trouble and into prison. The police said that he was "deeply corrupted in his political principles." In 1847 he started the nationalist newspaper *Il Risorgimento* and in its columns advocated the cause of a constitution for Sardinia. In 1848 Charles Albert, the Sardinian king, granted a constitution. In 1850 Cavour became minister of agriculture and commerce under the new king, Victor Emmanuel II, and in 1852 he became prime minister.

Cavour was a realist, a practical man who had little patience with the exuberant speeches and imaginative flights of men like Mazzini. To Cavour, Mazzini and his kind were innocent of political ability, erratic men who did not understand the realities of the world. Cavour once remarked: "I cannot make a speech, but I can make Italy."

Few men would have guessed from Cavour's physical appearance that he was one of the master statesmen of his age. Who could be favorably impressed by the sight of that short and stocky body, so carelessly dressed, the non-descript face, the unbecoming spectacles? The talented Cavour deceived many men who underestimated him, always to their sorrow.

The new prime minister of Sardinia was of the opinion that his state "must begin by raising herself, by establishing in Europe, as well as in Italy, a position of credit equal to her ambitions." The army was strengthened; it soon numbered about 50,000 well-trained and well-equipped men. More forts were built. Trade treaties were negotiated with Belgium, Holland, and Switzerland. The state financial system was reorganized. Railways were extended. A steamship line started service between Genoa and America. Many special privileges of the clergy were wiped away. The Siccardi Laws of 1850 abolished the civil jurisdiction of the ecclesiastical courts and declared that no corporation might accept any property without the consent of the state government. Marriage became a civil contract. Such reforms made a tremendous impression, exactly the impression that Cavour wanted to create. Sardinia stood before Europe and the other Italian states as a land where liberal reforms were achieved as well as talked about and where the leaders openly hoped and planned for the unification of Italy.

Cavour realized that Sardinia could never be made strong enough to oust Austria from Italy and achieve Italian unification alone and unaided. Sardinia must find and keep an ally among the great powers. To fix the eyes of Europe upon the Italian question Cavour joined Britain and France in the Crimean War. He sat in the Paris Peace Conference of 1856 and was able to speak there against the Austrian power and deeds in Italy. He was also able to prepare the way for the temporary alliance with Napoleon III described earlier in these pages.

After the war of 1859 with Austria, Cavour and King Victor Emmanuel were furious at what they considered the betrayal of Napoleon III. Nevertheless, the peace treaty with Austria gave Sardinia the rich area of Lombardy. Austria had been beaten. In a spontaneous frenzy of patriotic excitement thousands of Italians shouted and rioted against their rulers in several small Italian states. The people of Parma, Modena, Tuscany, and the papal territory of Romagna pressed for union with Sardinia. As a result of a series of plebiscites these areas were added to the lands ruled by Victor Emmanuel II. Meanwhile, of course, the prestige of Napoleon III was dimmed in Italy. It was no acci-

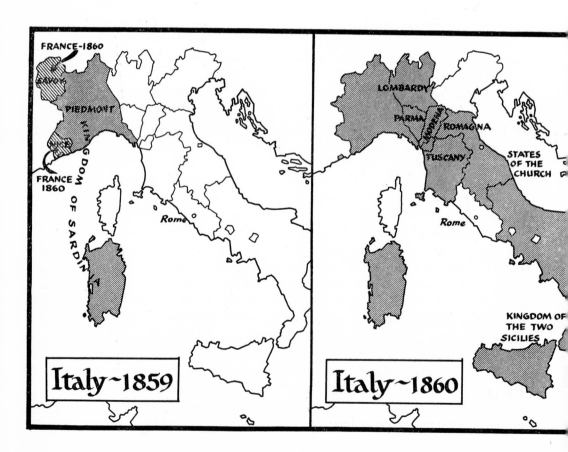

dent that not one Italian soldier came to help Napoleon in his desperate struggle with the Germans in 1870.

Upon the stage of Italian history now strode the picturesque Giuseppe
Garibaldi (1807–1882), brave, generous, patriotic, hotheaded, bold-hearted.
In earlier years he had joined the school for republican conspiracy called the
"Young Italy" movement and had marched under the banners of Mazzini.
Active in plots and rebellions, he soon attracted the attention of the police.
Condemned to death for his part in one disturbance, Garibaldi was forced to
flee from Italy in 1846. He went to South America and there he fought as a
daring guerrilla for the republican patriots. In 1848 he returned to Italy to
take his place again as a leader in the flaming revolutions. Once more he was
forced into exile. This time he went to the United States. In 1854 he came
back to Italy. His heroic exploits and his career of adventure and exile had
made his name a household word.

At last convinced that Italy could never be united in a republic, Garibaldi
decided to fight for the cause of a united Italy under Victor Emmanuel II. In
1859 he led a band of irregular fighters against the Austrians—the money

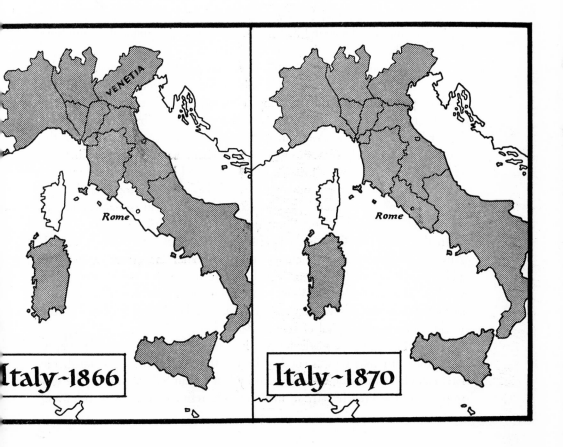

that he needed came from the money chests of Cavour. Garibaldi knew little and cared less about politics and diplomacy, but he did know how to fight. All he needed was a sword and gun.

In 1860, impatient with Cavour's peace arrangements with Austria, Garibaldi gathered about 1,100 hard, ragged, and battle-tested men, the famous Redshirts. He sailed from Genoa in two ships and invaded Sicily. After a few weeks of heavy fighting Sicily was conquered. Then Garibaldi turned towards the mainland. He landed and took Reggio from old General Gallotti —Professor G. M. Trevelyan described Gallotti as a "complete dotard." The defeated general had an interesting explanation for what had happened: "What do you expect, gentlemen; I am an old soldier, and so of course I expected Garibaldi to attack me in front, and he came from behind instead!" (*"Che volete, Signorini; io sono un vecchio soldato, a perciò m'attendeva che Garibaldi m'attaccasse di fronte, ed invece m'è capitato alle spalle!"*)

Garibaldi advanced through the wrinkled hills towards Naples. Whole armies surrendered to him without firing a shot. He entered Naples after Francis II, King of the Two Sicilies, concluded that discretion was better than valor and fled.

All southern Italy had been won by Garibaldi. That romantic daredevil nationalist and his Thousand had made their names as immortal as anything human can be.

The impetuous Garibaldi wanted to march upon Rome at once. Cavour, fearing that such an imprudent and mischievous step would alienate Roman Catholics all over the world and bring collision and conflict with the forces of Napoleon III protecting the pope, decided to stop Garibaldi. Accordingly, Victor Emmanuel led a Sardinian army down to complete the conquest of the Neapolitan regions. In November, 1860, a plebiscite decided that the Kingdom of Naples and Sicily and all the papal states around Rome should be annexed to Sardinia. King Victor Emmanuel II and Garibaldi rode together through the applauding crowds at Naples. In 1861 the first Italian parliament met at Turin and proclaimed Victor Emmanuel II "King of Italy."

In the same year Cavour died. He had lived to see Italy almost united. Austria still held Venetia. The pope still held Rome. Rome, surely, would be added to the rest of Italy soon. Shortly before his death Cavour wrote these words: "The star of Italy is Rome; that is our polar star. The Eternal City, around which twenty-five centuries have accumulated all the glories of the world, must be the capital of Italy."

Meanwhile Giuseppe Garibaldi was impatient. Twice he led volunteers to seize Rome. In 1862 he was checked by the troops of Victor Emmanuel. He later complained that he was wounded by "an Italian bullet." In 1867 he was stopped by the French garrison in Rome. He refused all offers of titles and pensions and went with his seed corn and salt cod to his farm, to hard work in the fields on the island of Caprera.

The Franco-Prussian War of 1870 was to settle the question of the future status of Rome. Napoleon III was forced to call home the French soldiers guarding the territory and interests of the pope. On September 20, 1870, Italian troops marched into the Eternal City and the citizens voted to unite with the Kingdom of Italy. The vote was 134,000 to 1,500. The pope refused to recognize the Kingdom of Italy or the annexation of papal territory. He retired before the power of the Italian state into the Vatican and remained there for the rest of his life. Meanwhile the Roman Catholic Church carried on its mission. The rise and fall of this world's kingdoms could not stay or alter that.

The Frankfort Assembly of 1848 had failed to agree upon a plan for the political union of Germany. The motley and ill-knit German Confederation still sprawled over central Europe. There was no cohesive force, no effective central power. The rival German princes still jostled one another. The liberals and nationalists still debated. "Unprofitable eloquence is like the cypress which is great and tall but bears no fruit."

After 1848 a new phase of German and European history began when Prussia moved to accomplish the unification of Germany under her leadership.

Prussian ambitions were aided by several facts. Prussia was the largest of the German states. Her political organization was strong and efficient. Her army was probably the best in Europe. The prestige of Albrecht Theodor Emil, Count von Roon, minister of war and marine, and of Helmuth Karl Bernard, Count von Moltke, famous chief of the Prussian general staff, had not been idly won. Unlike Austria, Prussia was almost entirely German in blood, language, and culture. Her industry and commerce were surging forward. Among her leading citizens were philosophers, poets, and professors who had written and were writing numerous books, articles, and pamphlets about the "historic necessity" that decreed it to be Prussia's destiny to unite Germany. The zeal and determination of many Germans to uphold and fight for the cause of German nationalism were roused and spurred through the later nineteenth century by several patriotic writers and thinkers, famous then and famous now: Johann Gustav Droysen, Heinrich von Sybel, Heinrich von Treitschke. "We have no German Fatherland," wrote Treitschke. "The Hohenzollerns alone can give us one."

It seemed to several German liberals and nationalists that the failure of the Frankfort Assembly had demonstrated the folly of relying upon exciting eloquence and metaphysical speculation to advance the cause of German unification. They concluded that national hopes would continue to be frustrated unless a common-sense attitude and realistic steps were taken in a hard and ruthless world.

King Frederick William IV of Prussia died in 1861 and his brother William I succeeded him. Most of the Hohenzollerns were soldiers, and the new king followed in their footsteps. Soon after he came to the throne he decided to increase the size of the army. The liberals feared that William I would use the enlarged and formidable army to coerce all who opposed him. In the election of 1862 the liberals triumphed and at once they refused to grant the appropriations necessary to carry William I's army plans into effect. When this happened the king was ready to abdicate.

It was at this critical hour that Otto Eduard Leopold von Bismarck (1815–1898) was appointed prime minister of Prussia. Most readers of this book have seen pictures of that extraordinary man. They will remember the tall, square frame, the great head and jowls, the shaggy eyebrows and drooping mustache, the large gray eyes. Bismarck's physical appearance suggested his keen mind, the iron will, the remarkable capacity for diplomatic intrigue. "His brain worked as if packed in ice, when feelings within were red hot."

Otto von Bismarck came from an old Brandenburg Junker family. A typical product of the reactionary landed-aristocracy class, Bismarck supported no democratic principles. He was convinced that parliamentary government was a piece of mistaken nonsense that could not fail to bring the rule of impractical and incompetent men capable only of producing chaos and weakness in the state. In Bismarck's judgment, the king must rule; the state must be supreme; Prussia under the Hohenzollerns must lead Germany.

After Bismarck finished his university career and took his law degree—he was famous then for his ability as a drinker and a duelist—he entered the Prussian civil service as a reporter in one of the Berlin courts. Bored by the weary rounds of the world of bureaucracy, he resigned and went home to manage his father's Pomeranian estates. In 1847 he became a member of the United Diet called by Frederick William IV. There Bismarck worked and talked with many liberals, and he concluded that most of them were even more irresponsible and featherbrained than he had earlier believed. During the Revolution of 1848 he planned to march with his tenants to Berlin to protect his king against the mobs. He later opposed a resolution thanking the king for granting a constitution. Bismarck had no sympathy for constitutions or democracy. He made this quite plain, for example, when he went down to Frankfort as a Prussian delegate to the Diet of the German Confederation. The liberals found him "more royalist than the king." To them he was a sneering menace, a living symbol of reaction.

Nor did Bismarck approve of the activities of several German nationalists. The well-meaning liberal nationalists who debated and planned at Frankfort were not, in Bismarck's judgment, aware of the hard truths of the world.

Throughout his life he held that view. He had no belief in the virtues of discussion and compromise. In an address to the Prussian Finance Committee in 1862 he made the famous statement so often recalled and quoted today: "Germany looks not to the liberalism of Prussia, but to its power. . . . The great questions of the time cannot be solved by speeches and parliamentary majorities—that was the mistake of 1848 and 1849—but by blood and iron!" On another occasion he remarked that "diplomacy without arms is like music without instruments."

Bismarck believed that only a war between Austria and Prussia would decide which power would control the German states and fuse them into a united whole. He spoke so vehemently upon the subject that his alarmed king sent him to be the Prussian ambassador to Russia. Bismarck was, as he said, "put on ice." In St. Petersburg he did all that he could to maintain and extend friendly relations between Prussia and Russia. He knew the importance of Russian friendship if Prussia should one day go to war with either Austria or France.

It was against the background of this extensive and varied experience that Bismarck became prime minister of Prussia in the midst of the army crisis of 1862. He immediately advised William I to tear up his abdication, to defy the legislature, to muzzle the press, and to take boldly all the money he needed for his army reforms. "The necessity for the state to exist is enough for me; necessity alone is authoritative." Against strong opposition Bismarck held his ground. He had flouted the constitution but he asserted that the end justified the action. Prussia must be strong.

For six years the parliament refused to vote the army appropriations in the budget. For six years the government collected and spent taxes without any legislative authority. Meetings of liberals were forbidden; they were often chased and beaten; their newspapers were censored or stopped. Obstinate, arbitrary, and ruthless, Bismarck had his way. Let the liberal malice boil; he would not be moved.

The policy of Bismarck now carried Prussia into three wars. The first conflict began in 1864 when Bismarck asked Austria if she would join in waging a war on Denmark to obtain the duchies of Schleswig and Holstein. These two regions had long been under Danish rule despite a series of counterclaims advanced by Prussia and Austria. The people of Holstein—a member of the German Confederation—were almost all German. Schleswig's population was partly Danish and partly German. When Denmark incorporated Schleswig in 1863 the German nationalities violently objected, denying Denmark's right to take that step. In 1864 Austria accepted Bismarck's invitation and moved with Prussia to defeat Denmark.

A series of blurred and jumbled difficulties arose about the peace arrangements and the disposition of the conquered duchies. Bismarck did not want a

peaceful settlement with Austria. He wanted war. When he annexed both
of the disputed duchies—including the fine Kiel harbor—war is what he got.

Italy was assured by Bismarck that she would get Venetia if she joined
Prussia in fighting Austria, her long-time foe. In a delightful conversation
with Napoleon III at Biarritz Bismarck gave the French emperor a vague
promise that if France stayed neutral in an Austro-Prussian war, then Napoleon
could expect to get some territory—perhaps Belgium—somewhere and sometime. Bismarck was a master of the art of committing himself to nothing.
Russia was friendly; Bismarck had strengthened that friendship three years
before when he had signed an agreement with Russia promising that Prussia
would help subdue any insurrections in Poland. The arrangements, maneuvers,
and intrigues of Bismarck had been successful. Austria was isolated.

The war that came between Austria and Prussia was finished in seven
weeks. The resistance of the German states that were allied to Austria rapidly
collapsed. The new Prussian "needle gun" fired three shots to every one of the
Austrian muzzle-loaders. At the battle of Sadowa the tactics of the efficient
Prussian army trained by von Moltke and von Roon swiftly overwhelmed the
Austrians.

Bismarck had no desire to humiliate Austria or to break up her empire. He
saw that he might need the friendship of Austria later. Despite the objections
of Prussia's William I the Treaty of Prague imposed on Austria a moderate
peace, a peace of conciliation. Austria paid a small indemnity. Italy got
Venetia. Schleswig and Holstein were to be formally united to Prussia. The
German Confederation was abolished and a North German Confederation,
dominated by Prussia, was formed. This new union contained the twenty-two
German states north of the River Main. It was a federal state in which a
lower chamber—the *Reichstag*—represented the people and an upper chamber—the *Bundesrat*—represented the princes. Of the forty-three members of
the *Bundesrat* seventeen were Prussian delegates. The president of the Confederation was the king of Prussia. The four southern states—Bavaria,
Württemberg, Baden, and Hesse-Darmstadt—stayed outside of the new association.

Napoleon III now saw that the tireless Bismarck and a tide of spectacular
events were building a powerful German state beyond the Rhine. His erratic
and ill-judged diplomacy, of which he was so foolishly proud, had failed
again. "Men shuffle cards who cannot play."

The French emperor now attempted to persuade the southern German
states that they should sign treaties of alliance with France. By hard and brilliant arguments Bismarck convinced them of the perils of negotiating with
Napoleon, and they signed secret military treaties with Prussia. They also
joined in a customs union with the North German Confederation. These were
ominous signs for France.

Many Frenchmen were alarmed. Napoleon III's regime, its earlier promise darkened by events at home and abroad, became increasingly unpopular. The emperor's personal prestige waned more and more, especially after the disastrous Mexican adventure. When he tried to get an alliance with Italy he was bluntly rebuffed. Was there not a French garrison at Rome that protected the pope and stopped Italy from seizing the papal territories? Had Napoleon III forgotten his faithlessness in 1859? Neither Austria nor Russia smiled upon Napoleon's suggestions about a possible alliance. It was clear that only an unusual threat, such as an attack upon Belgium, would bring England into a conflict in Europe. France was isolated. Napoleon III stood alone. Otto von Bismarck had seen to that. His preparations had been long, cunning, clever, unscrupulous, and successful.

In 1868 Queen Isabella II of Spain was overthrown by a revolution. Two years later the Spaniards offered the throne to a German prince: Leopold of Hohenzollern. Napoleon III told Bismarck that he could not permit a Hohenzollern to sit on the throne of Spain. When the French government formally protested the prince withdrew his candidacy.

It was then that the French leaders, all second-rate and reckless men, made a silly and dangerous mistake in their desire to hit and bite and humiliate Prussia. A chauvinistic war group, led by the Duke de Gramont and the Empress Eugénie, persuaded Napoleon III to send the French ambassador to Prussia, Count Benedetti, to the health resort of Ems where Prussia's William I was taking a holiday. Benedetti was instructed to make new demands. In a famous conversation on the promenade at Ems, Benedetti asked that no Hohenzollern should ever accept an invitation to rule Spain. His insistent and unreasonable requests were rejected by William I. A telegram was sent by the Prussian king to Bismarck informing him of the incident. This document was the famous "Ems dispatch."

Four years earlier Bismarck had wanted war with Austria. It is inaccurate to say that he now wanted war with France; he usually disliked war, partly because armed conflict was too risky and uncontrollable. Nevertheless, he had been angry and depressed when King William I had yielded to the first French demand. He knew how Napoleon had clumsily tried to block German unification. He also saw that if German patriotism could be roused against the French the unification of Germany might be hastened. The southern German states had agreed to support Prussia in the event of war. If once they joined with the north they might never go away. Who could tell what might happen when soldiers from the north and south, Germans all, marched shoulder to shoulder against a common foe?

Bismarck now proceeded to edit the "Ems dispatch," an achievement for which he has been given much fame and some honor. In his *Bismarck and the War of 1870*, Erich Eyck describes, step by step, the ways in which

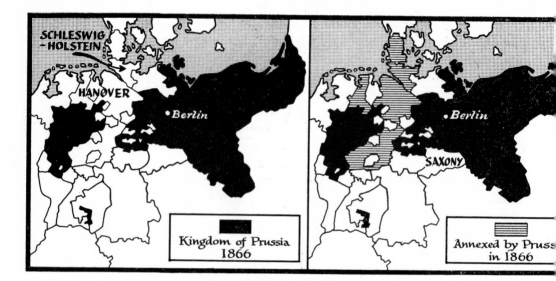

Kingdom of Prussia
1866

Annexed by Pruss
in 1866

Bismarck gave a "mature wording" to the famous telegram. Although the changes Bismarck made were not drastic, his new phrasing of the message gave the impression—quite contrary to William I's wishes—that Benedetti had intentionally been given a hard snub. To some Prussians it seemed that their elderly king—he was then seventy-three years old—had been insulted by the insolent lackey of an upstart French emperor. "Now it has a different ring," said von Moltke. "In its original form it sounded like a parley; now it is like a flourish of trumpets in answer to a challenge."

The "Ems dispatch" was published on July 14, 1870, the famous French Bastille Day. In Paris crowds pushed and paraded, demanding war at once.

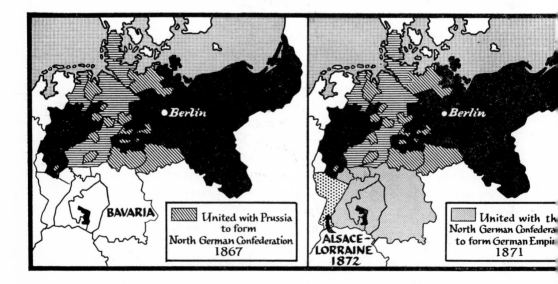

United with Prussia
to form
North German Confederation
1867

United with th
North German Confedera
to form German Empir
1871

Napoleon III was assured that all was ready, "down to the last button on the last gaiter of the last soldier." France declared war. The people shouted: "On to Berlin!"

Soldiers of the southern German states sped to join the forces of the North German Confederation. While the Germans were mobilizing a million men France nearly slipped into chaos. The bold assurances that all was ready for war were false. National morale swiftly sagged and the pulse of the state grew feeble.

The Franco-Prussian War lasted ten months. Almost everywhere the French were defeated. At the battle of Sedan a French army of 120,000 men was shattered. Some of the bravest and best Frenchmen died there. Napoleon III was captured. He sent a telegram to Empress Eugénie: "The army is defeated and captive. I myself am a prisoner." Youth, romance, power, fire, and ambition, all were gone.

Soon Paris was under siege. Meanwhile France was declared a republic, and Napoleon III fled to England. Factious and desperate men tried to form a government. They did; the republic fought bravely.

After Paris fell, a treaty of peace was arranged. This was the severe Treaty of Frankfort under the terms of which France ceded Alsace and a large part of Lorraine to Germany, paid an indemnity of five billion francs ($1,000,-000,000), and agreed to support a German army of occupation until the whole sum had been paid.

Nearly four months earlier King William I of Prussia had been proclaimed German emperor in the Hall of Mirrors in France's great palace of Versailles. The northern and southern states of Germany had joined together to form the German Empire. The unification of Germany had been achieved. The triumph of the wily and indefatigable Otto von Bismarck was complete. The end of an epoch was at hand.

PART IV

Chapter 37

THE NINETEENTH CENTURY:
THE FABRIC OF FAITH

"The beliefs which we have most warrant for have no safeguard to rest
on but a standing invitation to the whole world to prove them unfounded."
—John Stuart Mill, *On Liberty*

THE ancient Greeks and Romans saw the history of mankind as a part of
the repeated pattern of all nature, a never-ending cycle of birth, growth,
decay, and death. Individual human beings traveled through that cycle,
generation after generation. City-states, nations, and empires rose and fell.
The final destiny of men and all their social and political organizations was
fixed and sure. The "perpetual flux," the *panta rhei* of Heraclitus, was the
law of the universe. Everything changed and everything passed away. All
the ripples on the river of time had their origin and their inevitable end.

Such a view of man and his fate is one reason the twin themes of fatalism
and despair are so important in the philosophy and literature of the world of
Greece and Rome. In most of the drama, for instance, there is much terror,
very little pity, and no hope.

> Upward and back to their fountains the sacred rivers
> are stealing
> Justice is turned to injustice, the order of old to
> confusion.

The idea of progress was first brought into history by Christianity. The
Christians believed that the life of a Christian in this world was a tale of
spiritual progress, a pilgrimage to the eternity that God had prepared for the
faithful. The Christians also claimed that the acceptance of their teachings
would improve the social and political conditions in the state. Christianity, they
asserted, made good citizens. In their judgment, a good society, based upon
justice and order, was necessary to help man reach his proper spiritual and

temporal destination. St. Augustine and other Christian writers invariably insisted that proper spiritual growth of men occurs within the corporate body of the Church and state.

There was something else. According to the Christian interpretation, history was a creative process. Therefore the state and society must be steadily improved. Improvement meant progress.

In the Enlightenment of the eighteenth century the new ideas about the nature of progress and perfectibility were merely the secularized versions of the earlier Christian analysis and doctrines, especially those of St. Augustine. The philosophers relied upon Reason, Nature, and Science to bring a Heavenly City for man on this earth. To them the slowly discovered truths of science were to be preferred to the revealed truths of religion. A pervasive and rational optimism promised much. "Nature and Nature's God" would be man's help in time of trouble. Thus the faith in a secular and material theory of progress was born.

By the nineteenth century the forces of science and invention and the tools of technology were indeed bringing Nature and the material world more and more under human control. Some men came to believe that it was inevitable that the tide of progress would keep coming in and that it would never recede. The continued improvement of the lot of man, it seemed, was inevitable— or at least it was as certain as anything human can be. In some ill-defined way there was surely a law in the world that made progress and evolution necessary, an invisible force driving men onwards to new achievements and new horizons. Walter Pater simply asserted that there was "a dominant undercurrent of progress in things." Several other men wrote rather heavy treatises about human progress; they had few opponents and few readers. It appeared to be quite clear that ahead of man stretched an immense and wonderful empire. Man, it seemed, could wipe away poverty, ignorance, misery, tyranny, war. He could use the materials of the world to improve his lot; the leavens of change could increase his wealth and he would have "a good life."

Throughout all of the nineteenth century there was a wide interest in personal success, especially in Great Britain and America. Many books and articles were filled with advice and instruction about morality, perseverance, religion, punctuality, early rising, and all the techniques of right living. The titles of a few British publications suggest their contents: *Self-Help, Duty, Thrift, Character, The Way to Get On, Men Who Have Risen, Improvement of Society by the Diffusion of Knowledge.* Martin Tupper's popular *Proverbial Philosophy* was published in thirty-eight editions between 1837 and 1861. The nineteenth century remembered that a long tradition and much common sense had united to proclaim that "Satan finds work for idle hands to do" and "Take care of the pence and the pounds will take care of themselves." Mechanics' institutes, public libraries, workingmen's colleges, adult schools, and mutual-improvement societies steadily increased in number. The masses of men, of course, must not be encouraged to hope for too much from life. "It is better to be a good man than a great one." "Character matters more than wealth." "The important thing is not Success but Duty."

No accurate and just description of the nineteenth century should stress too strongly the complacent and shallow materialism, the self-indulgence, the greedy and tricky profit-seeking, the startling, ugly, and seamy realities. Nor should the century be described as an era that was priggish, prim, petulant, proud, tasteless, secular, and little more. True, all of these undesirable qualities did appear. When the tireless march of the machines and the quick brains of the aggressive men of business brought a new wealth it was inevitable that some of the more abundant money should be spent for large and un-inspiring houses, tasteless bric-a-brac and furniture, display and parade, numerous signs of vulgarity. There was frequently too much conspicuous narrowness and conscious respectability. Nevertheless, it is unwise to include only these things in a portrait of the age. There were many other exciting aspects of life in the nineteenth century, and they should not be overlooked or forgotten.

The "idea of progress" and the march of the secular spirit, so finely de-scribed by J. B. Bury and others, were indeed of high significance in the complex culture of the nineteenth century. How could it have been otherwise when new methods of communication and transportation were linking more parts of the planet together and more wealth was being made by the sleepless machinery? In such an age there could be no sense of completion or finality. Then, as now, the word "progress" contains within itself the idea of "becom-ing." It has but little place for the idea of "being." And yet, when all these things are said, it still remains true that the "idea of progress" must not be given a greater prominence than it deserves in the nineteenth century. In the midst of optimism there were sometimes raised the voices of doubt and un-certainty. Enthusiasm was frequently restrained. The confidence in the future was not unbounded. Matthew Arnold was not the only man of his age who saw and heard the ignorant armies clashing by night. Many thoughtful men remembered the long and scarring journey of mankind and looked upon the present and the future with a mingling of hope and doubt and caution.

The fact that is sometimes forgotten by scholars and students and writers is this: many different kinds of people were going about their business as the decades of the nineteenth century unrolled, all with their varying values and purposes. Along with the thrusts of secularism and materialism there were the deep currents of faith and feeling about the importance of imponderables, the moral absolutes in the life of man, the doubts and dilemmas of human beings in society, the debates about the principles and practices of man and the nature of the eternal order in the universe. It is easy, sometimes, to be overwhelmed by the magisterial utterances of the university dons or the pomp and power of politicians and newspaper editors or saddened by the silence of the thousands of conforming men in the lonely crowd. At such moments it is wise to remember that uncounted men and women, before the nineteenth century and in it, continued to ask questions and to find answers, often without trumpets or hubbub or conferences with the pressmen. They do the same thing today. The most important news about our present civilization is often not in the headlines; the most important events probably do not happen in our airplanes or on our superhighways; they happen in university laboratories, in seminars, and in churches.

When we talk and write glibly and easily about the nineteenth century as an age of secular and material progress it might be wise to pause to remark upon the fact that there were thousands of Christians, known and unknown, who once had asked the same questions that had been asked long before by the Egyptians and the Greeks, by a woman of Samarra who chanced to talk by an old stone well with a man named Jesus, by a centurion who encountered the God behind the beginning on a hill near Jerusalem. The Christian answers have always been the same, age after age. In the middle of all the materialism and progress of the nineteenth century, committed Christians, clergy and laymen alike, continued to give those answers to men clutching for assurance and safety. They continued to help the sick, the hungry, the unwanted, the unloved.

Some of the people who lived in the nineteenth century in the world of the West were individuals of note and competence, possessed of a high order of mind and spirit, creative and adventurous. Such people as these, for instance, cannot be included in any glib generalizations or embraced in a bright and brittle formula: Matthew Arnold, Jane Austen, Hector Berlioz, Henry Bessemer, Otto von Bismarck, Thomas Carlyle, Auguste Comte, William Ewart Gladstone, Oliver Wendell Holmes, Abraham Lincoln, David Livingstone, John Henry Newman, Florence Nightingale, Friedrich Nietzsche, Richard Wagner—the reader can extend the constellations of famous names, on and on. The orthodox men and women, the heretics, skeptics, and agnostics, the restless misfits, the squabbling mediocrities, the noisy individuals inflicting upon their fellows their scant and fleeting wisdom, all were there. The nineteenth century was a confused, fascinating, and complex era. Matthew Arnold called it a "multitudinous age"; and that it was.

Belief in progress was usually accompanied by a conviction that deliberate and calculated reforms of most customs and institutions could speed the steps of man towards a better and happier world. Many things that had been useful in the past were torn out and discarded. Discredited dogmas tumbled down. In almost all of Europe there was rapid social, political, economic, and intellectual change. "Better fifty years of Europe than a cycle of Cathay." There were the wounds of war and revolution. There were the tumults and turmoils of nationalism. There were the resolute and insistent challenges of liberalism and individualism demanding that the powers of government should be limited so that the individual spirit, filled with self-respect and ambition, should not wither and fade. How familiar, in those distant days, were the crusading cries about freedom of contract, freedom of speech, freedom of trade, freedom of worship, the rectification of numerous injustices, and "enlightened self-interest"!

There were many movements for political and social reform. The reader will remember the amazing flood of excitement and reform legislation described in earlier chapters of this book. Through the whole century the river of reform moved along; sometimes it slowed down, but in most lands it never stopped. When it was blocked by the dams and dikes of reaction—in Russia, for instance—it finally broke through to surge and boil over the unhappy land. In the states of Europe there were no great and prolonged disruptions in the tale of improvement and reform. In England, for instance, profound changes continued to be brought about by debate, persuasion, and voting. The reform legislation in the years of Russell, Palmerston, Derby, Gladstone, Disraeli, Rosebery, and Salisbury came to a tremendous total. These were the years of the Second Reform Bill (1867), the Third Reform Bill (1884), the growth of trade unions, reforms in the army, in education, in the courts of law, excitement and agitation in Ireland, the trumpets of imperial destiny as the hopes and glories of a great age moved towards the Victorian sunset.

The man who looks back on the nineteenth century sees numerous tensions and tragedies, the rising spirit of humanitarianism, the encouraging horizons of opportunity, the large and quickly growing bourgeois class with all its merits and defects, the unflagging toughness and realism of the self-conscious men of business and industry, the bedeviled conservatives of all lands battling hard for the old ways or brooding nervously about the sinister powers and shouting challengers outside their walls and the omens flashing warnings. The rationalists disputed with the impulsive and supple romantics and the theologians and philosophers with the erudite and professional scientists. "No age has been so rich in rival theories, so subversive of old ideas, so destructive of principles which had stood firm for many ages." If we listen carefully we can still catch the echoes of the voices and disputes. We can hear William Ewart Gladstone asserting that John Henry Newman was "the greatest figure of the century." We can also hear Thomas Henry Huxley insisting that Newman had "the brain of a moderate-sized rabbit."

Unexpected events sometimes shook the widespread faith in such things as *laissez faire* and liberal democracy. The depressions of the 1870's and 1880's were alarming to men who believed in unswerving and unhalted progress.

Why should factories be idle and the sails of so many merchant ships be furled in the harbors? The blood and iron of *Realpolitik* had its hours of triumph. Collectivist ideas increased—"the individual withers and the state is more and more." The voices of socialists and communists often became numerous and loud. The "utopian" socialists usually based their schemes on their conclusions about the essential goodness of man. Most of the "scientific" socialists had other ideas. They asserted that "the history of all hitherto existing society is the history of class struggles." They claimed that although the mortal god of the state would in time wither away, the crusaders for the cause of Communism—or "scientific" socialism—must beat down and exterminate all opponents and rivals. "Slowly comes a hungry people, as a lion, creeping nigher." The members of the capitalist bourgeois class must be elbowed out of the way or killed. In the eyes of those dedicated and violent men the revolution for which they talked and fought was inevitable. It was their task and duty, said Karl Marx, Friedrich Engels, and their fellows, to carry out the inexorable decrees of history and destiny. The proletariat was going to triumph in a great revolution and the Heavenly City of a classless society would soon be at hand.

So spoke the followers of Marx and Engels. They arrogantly usurped the prerogative of God and tried to assume His functions. Both their ideas and methods were dangerous, and remain dangerous, to democratic states. The liberal John Stuart Mill said: "If any opinion be compelled to silence, that opinion may, for aught we know, be the truth. To deny this is to assume our own infallibility." The Communist Manifesto of 1847 proclaimed: "The Communists disdain to conceal their views and aims. They openly declare that their ends can be attained only by the forcible overthrow of all existing social institutions." Between the points of view of Marx and Mill there is a wide gulf.

Many of the great expectations that glowed so warmly in the age of the nineteenth century in Europe were encouraged by the long and spectacular strides that were being taken in industry, technology, and trade. It is not difficult to describe the material achievements, the dynamic and significant technological advances, and the triumphs of the tools of precision and power in the Age of Progress. For instance, the reader may be swiftly told that iron for shipbuilding was first used in Glasgow in 1818; that the Netherlands ship *Curaçao* was the first vessel to cross the Atlantic using steam power all the way (1827); that Belgium for a time led all Europe in railway construction. The listing of such facts as these indicates that many of our great-grandfathers were scientific, clever, hardheaded, and the possessors of those qualities that are usually called practical. They were not flabby dreamers. Their world was one of quickening drama, tension, enthusiasm, adventure, and achievement.

These were the years that marked an acceleration in the industrial and commercial progress of England. That nation was becoming, more and more, the "workshop of the world." Overhead were the fair skies of prosperity. At the famous Exhibition of 1851 some of the results of an era of industrial power and inventive genius astounded and delighted an admiring public. Every year the factories turned out larger supplies of goods. More surplus capital was being invested or lent at home and abroad. In 1825, for instance, British foreign loans totaled about £100,000,000; in 1870 they were about £800,000,000. The national income rose from £515,000,000 a year in 1841 to £650,000,000 in 1852 and about £1,000,000,000 in 1872. In 1840 Britain exported £2,524,000 worth of iron and steel; in 1850 the total value was £5,350,000; in 1860 it reached £12,154,000. By the 1850's Britain was exporting nearly three billion yards of cotton cloth a year. British re-export trade steadily mounted. Almost everywhere in central England the smoke belched forth to mar the soft horizons. The railways, throbbing arteries of the body economic, spread their networks into all but the remoter shires. British ships furrowed the seas, still the highways of empire.

England had been able to use her enterprise, her strategic location, and her natural resources to become the world's greatest exporter, shipper, producer, and banker. Other nations lagged behind. Even as late as 1889 Britain's foreign trade still exceeded that of France and Germany combined and was more than double that of the United States. Then, slowly, the prospect altered. Germany and the United States surged forward. Where there had been one great industrial and commercial power, there were now three; and there were soon to be more.

In the early nineteenth century the minds and moods of many men were caught and carried off by the churning and violent currents of the Romantic Movement. These currents are far more difficult to describe and explain than the facts of industrial progress. Many scholarly scuffles and epic rows have been caused by attempts at definition and explanation. Students of the life and letters of the nineteenth century know the magnificent essays of Professor Arthur O. Lovejoy about the organic, diverse, and dynamic aspects of Romanticism. They know other works that are clean and clear and intelligent. They have also read studies that are long, bumbling, pedantic, and sterile, things written by men who forgot the words of Boileau: "The man who knows not when to stop knows not how to write."

There are several prickly and bulky problems about Romanticism that cannot be discussed here. If we are to avoid the cut and thrust and crossfire of controversy, the comments must be both few and cautious.

Romanticism stressed its opposition to the rigid literary rules of taste and writing established and held in the classical age of the eighteenth century. It

stood against complacency and smugness. It insisted upon the importance of
the emotional, the imaginative, the spontaneous, the supernatural, the irrational, the delights of misty mountains, starry nights, craggy medieval ruins,
and magic casements opening over the blue waves of fairy seas. Emile Zola
once defined art as "Nature seen through a temperament."

Many Romantic writers, some of them gifted with a miraculous mastery of
words, created literary works that have outlived detraction and neglect. These
eloquent apostles moved in a great psychological revolution against the
eighteenth century. They asserted the significance of human qualities and
creative individualism, the unweighable and unconscious swirlings deep in the
beings of men. They had no patience with anybody who tried to reduce the
world and the universe to the rules of reason or a static mechanism. They insisted upon aesthetic and emotional values and several ends denied absolutely
by the eighteenth century. They said that a personal interest and enthusiasm,
a personal feeling and faith, a personal experience of Nature and the truths
in "the deep heart of things" mattered most in the changing, imperfect, and
diverse lives of men. Those stagnant spirits who did not share such stirrings
and aspirations, those benighted rationalists who were denied the vision, were
to be kept outside the Garden.

Poetry, said the Romanticists, took "its origin from emotion recollected in
tranquillity" and was felt in the blood and the heart. Reason alone, they asserted, could never find the secret windows and the hidden fountains of truth;
it could never come near to the apprehension of total reality. Brains and logic
were not enough. "One must still have chaos in one to give birth to a dancing
star."

The tools and triumphs of science and technology enthralled and delighted
many men. The apostles of the Romantic Movement, for their part, declared
that material achievements were of little consequence to those sensitive beings
who walked in the emotional and spiritual uplands. Wrote Matthew Arnold:

> We admire with awe
> The exulting thunder of your race;
> You give the universe your law.
> You triumph over time and space!
> Your pride of life, your tireless powers
> We mark them, but they are not ours.

Every reader knows what Matthew Arnold had to say about the problems of
culture and anarchy in the nineteenth century and the problems of the ever-
present Philistines. In his "Egyptian Maid" William Wordsworth wrote of
"the degenerate grasp of modern science." In Charles Kingsley's novel *Yeast*
(1851) there is a reference to "the bottle and squirt mania mis-called
chemistry."

In the first ranks of the English Romanticists stand the names of the poets

Percy Bysshe Shelley (1792–1822), John Keats (1795–1821), the fantasy-haunted Samuel Taylor Coleridge (1772–1834), William Wordsworth (1770–1850), the tragic rebel George Gordon, Lord Byron (1788–1824). In their works are displayed the love of nature, the stormy spirit of revolt, the shifting moods and dreams of men, "the still, sad music of humanity," and the ardent search for the true and the beautiful. " 'Beauty is truth, truth beauty'—that is all Ye know on earth, and all ye need to know." The flawless grace and delicate loveliness of several of the poems of these men have never been surpassed.

In much of the prose of Sir Walter Scott (1771–1832) there is a "whispering of the last enchantment of the Middle Ages." His historical novels—and his poems and ballads, too—have delighted generations of men and youths. The pages of Scott are filled with the glamorous tales of brave knights and Crusaders and gallant Saxons and Scotsmen. The reader still can see the scimitar of Saladin, the broadsword of Richard The Lion-Hearted; the knives of the Scottish clansmen flash in the midday sun. Romantic heroes never flee or cringe. "The further those times are removed from us," wrote Chateaubriand, "the more magical they appear."

Far different from "the big bow-wow" style of Sir Walter Scott was the delicate ivorywork of Jane Austen, a lady who lived in the Romantic Age and yet was not properly of it. Jane Austen was a careful artist who gently described and satirized the middle-class people she knew in the rural world of England. Her *Sense and Sensibility* (1811) and *Pride and Prejudice* (1813) are classics. In every generation there are admirers of Jane Austen.

Two other English prose writers do belong in the Romantic tradition. The first was Thomas Carlyle (1795–1881). The second was John Ruskin (1819–1900). Both deplored the excesses, as they saw them, of democracy. Both detested the evils and ugliness of industry, the crude materialism nursed and fostered by science and invention. Both were unhappy about numerous aspects of nineteenth-century culture—and the lack of it. Both were repelled by the poverty and degradation born of industrialism. Both looked back to the Middle Ages. Both—especially John Ruskin—thought that some social reforms could be made. Man's unkindness to his fellows could be reduced, perhaps ended. The workers could be persuaded to love beauty.

In France the vigorous Romanticists were led by Victor Marie Hugo. When Hugo produced his play *Hernani* in 1830 the frenzied battle between the Romanticists and the Classicists was marked by a long and wordy warfare, riots and duels.

Victor Hugo was an officer of the Legion of Honor, a member of the French Academy, a prophet, and a rebel. Always interested in contemporary problems and democratic principles—how he hated tyrants!—Hugo was forced into exile by Napoleon III, the emperor whom Hugo called "Napoleon the Little." Napoleon III could not tolerate Hugo's eloquence and scorn.

Probably the most famous work of Victor Hugo is his *Les Misérables* (1862). His other novels are also excellent; they deserve to be more widely read. So, too, does his magnificent lyric poetry. Consider, for instance, his poem called "The Children of the Poor," a poem that inevitably suggests several of the lines of William Blake.

> Take heed of this small child of earth;
>   He is great; he hath in him God most high. . . .
> In our light bitter world of wrong
>   They come; God gives us them awhile.
> His speech is in their stammering tongue
>   And His forgiveness in their smile.

The eloquent Victor Hugo had many followers during the Romantic revolt in France: Alfred de Vigny (1797–1863); Alfred de Musset (1810–1857); Alphonse de Lamartine (1790–1869); Théophile Gautier (1811–1872); Aurore Dupin (1804–1876), famous under the pseudonym "George Sand." There was also Alexandre Dumas (1803–1870), an author still widely read today; many youths have followed their fathers and grandfathers in watching the Count of Monte Cristo as he tunnels through the rock; in spirit they ride with the Three Musketeers.

In the German states there was also vigor and excitement. Heinrich Heine (1797–1856) was a poet, essayist, critic, journalist, opponent of tyranny. "Lay on my coffin a sword," he said, "for I was a brave soldier in the Liberation War of Humanity." Witty, fluent, and shrewd, a master of pathos and irony, Heinrich Heine won many admirers and many enemies by his relentless criticism of smugness and reaction. When most of the things he said and did are forgotten he will be remembered for the strange and haunting power of his lyric poetry. Who can forget "Die Lorelei"?

In these years of tumult and dispute there was a wide interest in German history and folklore. Many of the German contemporaries of Heine were writing fairy tales based on German mythology—the most famous were the Grimm brothers. Several race-language theories were advanced about the "folk soul" of the unsophisticated tribesmen of the past. The German insistence upon the *Volksgeist* has been a frequent theme in modern history.

The most distinguished Italian writer of the Romantic Movement was Alessandro Francesco Manzoni (1785–1873), author of *The Betrothed* (*I Promessi Sposi*), published in 1827. Poland's Adam Mickiewicz wrote his rousing *Sir Thaddeus*, a trumpet call to all Polish nationalists. Denmark's Hans Christian Andersen reached into the past to find the romantic legends that have delighted children for a hundred years and more. Almost all of Europe was touched by the power of Romanticism and the moving language of the heart.

In the United States, Washington Irving (1785–1859) revived and published several old Dutch legends. James Fenimore Cooper (1789–1851) turned to the American past and the long frontier where white men and Indians stalked and skirmished. Cooper's *The Last of the Mohicans* is not forgotten yet. Meanwhile Edgar Allan Poe (1809–1849) won wide acclaim in the Western world for his bizarre and imaginative *Tales of the Grotesque and Arabesque*, "The Gold-Bug," "The Fall of the House of Usher," "The Murders in the Rue Morgue," "The Cask of Amontillado" ("I forced the last stone into its position; I plastered it up. Against the new masonry I re-erected the old rampart of bones. For the half of the century no mortal has disturbed them.") The names of America's Ralph Waldo Emerson, Henry D. Thoreau, Nathaniel Hawthorne, Herman Melville, William Cullen Bryant, Henry Wadsworth Longfellow, and Walt Whitman were soon to be known and honored in Europe. It could not now be said that the youthful United States possessed no culture and no authors of consequence.

In Russia, Alexander Sergeevich Pushkin (1799–1837) wrote excellent poetry—especially *Boris Godunov*—and one fine novel called *Eugene Onegin*. Nikolai Gogol (1809–1852) published his *Dead Souls* and the *Inspector-General*. Ivan Sergeevich Turgenev (1818–1883) wrote his graphic *The Diary of a Sportsman* and his masterpiece *Fathers and Sons*. Feodor Dostoievsky (1821–1881), that poor and sick genius, published many books, including *Crime and Punishment*, *The Brothers Karamazov*, and *The Idiot*. With understanding and sympathy Dostoevski described the harsh and tortured lives of his characters, their dark deeds and spirits, their sufferings, and the secret springs from which their emotions rose.

Count Leo Tolstoy (1828–1910) was one of the greatest writers of the modern world. His *War and Peace*, a majestic epic of the Napoleonic Wars, and his *Anna Karenina* show how the fates of the universe control the destinies of men. "Time and chance happeneth to them all." In his later days Tolstoy became an apostle of reform. He frequently asserted, especially in *The Kreutzer Sonata* and *Resurrection*, a theme that was very old in human history: "happiness consists in living for others." Modern civilization, said Tolstoy, is a failure because men believe in "the superstition of progress." Because they are not really Christians and do not believe in the Sermon on the Mount they live lives of moral disorder. All private property, Tolstoy also insisted, together with the coercive state and all its works, must be destroyed because they exist as a result of violence. Ten days before his death Leo Tolstoy left his home. He died alone, still seeking what no man can ever find.

In Romantic art there appeared the same emphasis upon emotion, imagery, and intoxicating magic that characterized Romantic literature. Nature was to be idealized, not imitated. The enthusiastic painters of the new era turned away from the sharp, restrained, firm lines and the careful and sober composition of such neoclassical artists as Jacques Louis David (1748–1825) and Jean

Auguste Ingres (1780–1867). The works of England's Joseph Mallord William Turner (1775–1851), France's Eugène Delacroix (1798–1863) and Germany's Caspar David Friedrich (1788–1857) are excellent examples of Romantic art at its best.

Other significant illustrations of the appeal and power of the Romantic artists are to be found in the works of Jean François Millet (1814–1875), famous for his landscape painting and his interest in the lives of humble men. On innumerable walls of the Western world hang copies of "The Sower," "The Gleaners," "Winter and the Crows," "The Woodcutter and Death," "Man with Hoe," "The Path Through the Wheat," and "The Angelus." The main representative of the Barbizon school, named from the Normandy village of Barbizon, was Jean Baptiste Camille Corot (1796–1875), an artist whose quiet and tender landscapes—how mysterious his lights and shadows are!—have been admired for more than a century.

Meanwhile the Pre-Raphaelite brotherhood flourished, led by Dante Gabriel Rossetti (1828–1882), William Holman Hunt (1827–1910), and John Everett Millais (1829–1896). These men tried to persuade the artists of Europe to make a more natural approach to their work and to paint with the simplicity and directness that the Pre-Raphaelites found, or thought they found, in the art of the Middle Ages and the early Renaissance. The ranks of the Pre-Raphaelites contained no really great painters. Their enthusiasm for medieval art forms and their avowed wish to find "true beauty" linked them to the Romantics of any age. On the literary side of the Pre-Raphaelite movement the writing of Algernon Charles Swinburne, William Morris, and Dante Gabriel Rossetti led them to be attacked as "the Fleshly School of Poetry."

In Romantic art the cloudy perspectives, the mists, and the shadows abound. Here and there a gleam of intense color suggests to the beholder the secret wonders, "the light that never was on sea or land." Sometimes the visionary splendor and the majestic turbulence of storms or angry waters convey a feeling of the inner mysteries of Nature and

> . . . . a sense sublime
> Of something far more deeply interfused
> Whose dwelling is the light of setting suns
> And the round ocean and the living air
> And the blue sky, and in the mind of man. . . .

Many of the sculptors of these years adhered to the classical rules. Among them were the masters Antonio Canova (1757–1822) and Albert Bertel Thorvaldsen (1770–1844). Others, including some men who helped to make the Arc de Triomphe, developed their own kinds of Romantic expression. Much of their work is interesting; most of it deserves but feeble praise. In architecture the Romantic excitement about the Middle Ages was mainly responsible for a Gothic revival. Several medieval castles, monasteries, and walls were reconstructed. New buildings in the Gothic style appeared. The most famous of these was Sir Charles Barry's Houses of Parliament, built in 1840.

In the world of music the power, passion, and poetry of Romanticism were considerable and enduring. The first quarter of the century was the age of the versatile Ludwig van Beethoven (1770–1827), whose work and genius were discussed in another context. By Beethoven's side stood Carl Maria Friedrich Weber (1786–1826), the composer of many fine and fanciful operas. There was also Franz Peter Schubert (1797–1828), famous then and now for his dreamy and delightful songs.

These three composers died at almost the same time. There followed an era dominated by the individualistic and rebellious Richard Wagner (1813–1883) —he wrote both his stirring *Tannhäuser* and his transcendent *Lohengrin* before 1850. The energetic Wagner was an extraordinary man. He never learned to play any musical instrument. If he had not been able to borrow money the world would never have had the gorgeous fabric of *Parsifal, Tristan und Isolde,* and *Die Meistersinger.*

Outstanding among Wagner's contemporaries were Felix Mendelssohn-Bartholdy (1809–1847), the resourceful Robert Alexander Schumann (1810–1856), Franz Liszt (1811–1886), Gioacchino Rossini (1792–1868), Frédéric François Chopin (1810–1849), and Giuseppe Verdi (1813–1901). Many other names shine proudly in the list of the composers of the nineteenth century: Peter Tschaikovsky, Hector Berlioz, Charles F. Gounod, Bedřich Smetana, César Franck, Antonin Dvořák, Nikolai Rimski-Korsakov, Alexander Borodin, Modeste Mussorgski, Edvard Grieg, Richard Strauss, Claude Debussy, Johannes Brahms. The nineteenth century was indeed a great age of music. What these composers did was honest and important. This statement is true of all genuine art, of any activity that has as its main purpose the discovery of some truth or the creation of something beautiful.

Slowly the power of the Romantic movement yielded to the demands and skills of Realism. The eyes of the Realists were turned away from the Middle Ages and those worlds of imagination, sentimentality, extravagance, and fantasy so beloved by the Romantics. All of the Realists asserted that they would try to write about the facts of life, hard and unpleasant though many of those facts were. In literature and art, they said, the truth must be told without evasion, fuss, or frills. The ideal was one thing; the real was another.

Many Realists also declared their interest in psychological questions, in the inner struggles of men and the frustrations they endured because they were victims of their environment and their emotional and physical weaknesses. Other writers and artists stressed the harsh realities of their world because they wanted to demonstrate the need for social or political reform.

Among the early leaders of Realism was Honoré Balzac (1799–1850). His great *Human Comedy* contains about 5,000 characters in 50 volumes, most of

Dynamos and Motors in the Palace of Electricity at the Paris Exposition, 1900

[109]

PLATE
XXXVII

King George V and Queen Mary at the Delhi Durbar in 1911

PLATE
XXXVIII

[110]

Japanese women working in a factory

[111]

Nicolai Lenin delivers a speech at the first May Day celebration. He appeals to the people with promises of land, peace, and bread and the rallying cry, "All power to the Soviets!"

them ordinary people, all of them supported by their virtues and pulled down by their vices. Some were greedy, stupid, immoral. Others were wise, honest, good. In the books of Balzac the readers could see the likenesses of people they knew. They could approve and condemn the characters in the *Human Comedy* in the same way that they applauded or denounced their neighbors.

A second master of realism was Gustave Flaubert (1821–1880). His *Madame Bovary* is a minute and vivid study of the dreary degradation of an ordinary woman in Normandy who slowly moved along the drab road of immorality, a sordid road that sloped downwards. Flaubert's masterpiece offended many people. When they objected, Flaubert replied that he was not in the book, only the human facts of life. "An artist," he said, "ought to appear in his work no more than God does in nature."

The prolific journalist and artist Emile Zola (1840–1902) was also concerned with the ordinary world of ordinary people. He is sometimes called the founder of the new school of Naturalism because his work is usually so precise and appears to be so uncolored by his own prejudices and preconceptions. The best achievements of Zola are found in his descriptions of the masses of the people of Paris and the "collective soul" of that fascinating city. Thousands of characters—the dull, the obscene, the immoral, the beastly, and the good—crowd through the pages of Zola's books. It was Emile Zola who fought so long and hard to expose the injustice and iniquity that had sent the persecuted Captain Dreyfus to Devil's Island.

Anatole France (1844–1924) was a pagan, a skeptic, a master of satire and irony. He drew back the curtains that covered the lives of apparently respectable people, and then he wrote about what he saw: intolerance, injustice, petty jealousy, wounding gossip, and much hypocrisy. In many books, especially *Penguin Island* and the *Revolt of the Angels,* the rapier thrusts of Anatole France were swift and sure and deadly.

Britain's Charles Dickens (1812–1870) made people laugh and cry. He brought pathos, humor, and irony into all his books. The poor and deluded and illiterate move through his chapters side by side with the rich and the smug. Such novels as *Nicholas Nickleby, David Copperfield, Dombey and Son, Oliver Twist,* and *Bleak House* are fine books. They are also milestones in the long efforts of Christian and sensitive men and women to try to cushion the sad results of man's inhumanity to man.

There were many other eminent realists in the England of the nineteenth century: the urbane and polished William Makepeace Thackeray (1811–1863); Anthony Trollope (1815–1882); Mary Ann Evans, known to her world and ours as George Eliot (1819–1880); George Meredith (1828–1909); and the pessimistic Thomas Hardy (1840–1928). Meanwhile the voices of such poets as Matthew Arnold, Robert Browning, and Lord Tennyson were heard throughout the lands of the West.

In the world of the drama there were such giants as Norway's Henrik

Ibsen (1826–1906), famous author of such assaults on bourgeois complacency as *The Pillars of Society, Peer Gynt, An Enemy of the People, The Wild Duck, The Doll's House.* Anton Chekhov (1860–1904) in Russia, Eugène Brieux (1858–1932) in France, and George Bernard Shaw (1856–1950) in England all aided in developing the realistic "problem play" so characteristic of the drama of the late nineteenth century.

In the United States there appeared several writers who are usually considered to be outstanding representatives of the new movements of Realism and Naturalism: Mark Twain (Samuel L. Clemens), William Dean Howells, Henry James, Stephen Crane, Frank Norris, Jack London, Theodore Dreiser. Howells, leader of the American Realists, asserted that fiction should ". . . cease to lie about life; let it portray men and women as they are, actuated by the motives and passions in the measure that we all know; let it leave off painting dolls and working them by springs and wires."

After 1860 Romanticism began to decline in art. The development of Realism began with the paintings of Gustave Courbet (1819–1877) and Honoré Daumier (1808–1879). "Show me an angel," said Courbet to his critics, "and I will paint one." Courbet and Daumier were both rebels against what they considered to be the sterility of Romanticism. They insisted upon the social importance of art. Their paintings were often damning indictments of society. They showed the poverty and misery of the lower classes and suggested the corruption and hypocrisy of the aristocrats, the fat bourgeois judges, lawyers, merchants.

About 1870 the Impressionist movement in art was begun by Edouard Manet (1832–1883). All Impressionists were in a sense Realists, for they did try to paint what they saw. Said Manet: "There is only one thing true: to paint from the first what one sees. When that is done, it is done. When it is not done, one begins all over again. Everything else is nonsense. Art is the servant of facts." It is also true, however, that the Impressionists did not study or analyze their subjects carefully, and in this they were unlike the Realists. The Impressionists tried to seize and get down upon the canvas their immediate impressions. Hence their paintings contain splotches and spots of sunlight and shadow, distorted figures, dabs of primary colors. At close range these pictures are formless masses of color; only from the other side of the room do they reveal design and structure.

The most distinguished and able of the Impressionists were Claude Monet (1840–1926) and Auguste Renoir (1841–1919). The famous landscapes of Monet, so filled with light, vaguely suggest fields, rivers, mountains, and trees. They were impressions seized in fleeting moments, nothing more. Auguste Renoir was interested in many subjects: gay boating parties on the Seine, nights at the opera, scenes at the boulevard cafés. He was particularly skilled in his use of broken colors. There is a glowing richness in the paintings of Renoir that belongs to his work alone.

In the years after 1890 Impressionism yielded before a movement usually called Post-Impressionism. The members of this school objected to the vague and formless work of their predecessors, the pure visualism and the intellectual emptiness, the lack of structure and solidity. Paul Cézanne (1839–1906), the founder of Post-Impressionism, was particularly interested in the relationship of planes and colors. He tried to paint so that the objects in his pictures would appear to have three-dimensional depth and roundness. He sought to find the geometry in nature, to "give architecture to the universe." He broke his objects into planes and used distortions and thick paint. "Everything in nature," said Cézanne, "adheres to the cone, the cylinder, and the cube."

Several revolutionary artists of the late nineteenth century cannot easily and honestly be fitted into any school, cult, or movement in the history of art. One of these men was the swashbuckling Paul Gauguin (1848–1903), the stockbroker who left his desk to become a master painter. Gauguin insisted that what mattered most in art was individual imagination and emotion. "How does that look to you? Green? All right, then use green. The greenest on your palette. And that shadow, a little bluish? Don't be afraid. Paint it as blue as you can."

In 1853 Vincent van Gogh was born. That strange and passionate genius, so suspicious and so lonely, painted pictures that have made his name immortal. From his eye, his hand, his palette, and his heart came works filled with passionate energy, violent emotional power, a remarkable understanding of space and the values of movement, a vigorous and amazing use of a wealth of pure colors. All the bright colors he loved: green, blue, violet, pink, yellow in all its shades. "How beautiful is yellow!" Yellow was the color of the sun, the source of light and warmth and life. "Oh, the beautiful sun of midsummer! It beats upon my head, and I do not doubt that it makes one a little queer"—this is what he wrote from Arles to his beloved brother Theo.

With every passing year Vincent van Gogh became more capricious and incalculable. "Dying is hard," he once said, "but living is harder still." Only in painting did he seem to find a relief from morbidity and pain and a little peace. He threatened his friend Gauguin with a razor, cut off his own ear and left it about three o'clock in the morning at a brothel. Soon he was sent to an asylum at Saint Rémy. There he painted, day after day, month upon month. Later he went to Auvers-sur-Oise. There, too, his hands and brushes were busy, busy through most of the daylight hours.

Vincent van Gogh once said to his brother: "Misery will never end." It did for him on a July day in 1890. That was the day when he went out into the sunlit fields and shot himself.

Chapter 38

THE MARCH OF SCIENCE:
NEW WORLDS FOR OLD

"On a hot summer's day, I have gone into a shop in the Strand where fragments of ice were exposed in a basin in the window; and with the shopman's permission have laid hold of the topmost piece of ice, and by means of it have lifted the whole of the pieces bodily out of the dish. Though the thermometer at the time stood at 80°, the pieces of ice had frozen together at their points of junction. Even under hot water this effect takes place; I have here a basin of water as hot as my hand can bear; I plunge into it these two pieces of ice, and hold them together for a moment: they are now frozen together, notwithstanding the presence of the heated liquid."

—John Tyndall, Lecture VI in *Heat considered as a Mode of Motion* (1863)

ALBERT EINSTEIN once remarked that the development of Western science has been based upon two great achievements: the invention of a formal system of logic by the Greeks and the Renaissance discovery that it was possible by systematic experiment to find cause-and-effect relationships. This observation is interesting and true.

Another fact is often forgotten, especially in the swirl and rush of our contemporary civilization, so dominated by machines, techniques, efficiency, speed, and the numerous slogans and watchwords that every reader knows: all civilizations have been based upon the accumulated knowledge of the past. Said Bernard of Chartres: "The generations are like dwarfs seated on the shoulders of giants and therefore able to see more things than the Ancients and things more distant."

It is also true that only a small number of individuals in any society have discovered or invented anything. The gifts of wonder and open-minded curiosity have not been given equally to all human beings. Through the centuries there has been an aristocracy of genius and high talent. "Genius does what it must and talent does what it can." Our civilization owes an incalculable debt to a few daring pioneers—the number is really very small—who breached the bounds of strange lands. When we turn the pages of history we see that it has been the spontaneous and indefeasible curiosity of these men that has lighted fires and set the world ablaze, time after time.

The way of the scientists, doers and dreamers both, has often been hard, especially when they have insisted that the truth is not always what the majority wants it to be. They have frequently suffered the censure of their fellows when they have refused to bend the knee to the smug demands of mass culture or to yield to the pressures and persuasions of the respectable individuals who have asserted that acceptance and conformity are the best assurances of safety and survival.

Men will not easily move further towards an understanding of the universe and themselves if their perspective is fogged and they try to slash and stamp down eager rebels and denounce and discredit dissent. A large part of the important chapters in the history of human thought has been written by men who have been intellectual heretics, often denounced by their more orthodox fellows as men filled with a crazy passion for change and revolution. Not by chanting in stereotypes and outmoded clichés has the character and vitality of the contemporary world been made. If the strong drugs and pressures of conformity are ever triumphant, then there can be no searching adventure, not much achievement, and few readjustments of thought.

There are always numerous individuals who are but little concerned with the words and acts of the scientists—unless those scientists discover or invent something "useful." There are also those who are quite apathetic about the pursuit of knowledge for its own sake and condemn the scientists for producing some of the new fears and terrors of the contemporary age. Still others have stood athwart the road of the advancing scientists for other reasons. In the nineteenth century, for instance, George Gissing was quite emphatic: "I hate and fear Science because of my conviction that, for a long time to come, if not forever, it will be a remorseless enemy of mankind. I see it destroying all simplicity and gentleness of life, all the beauty of the world. . . ."

The nineteenth and twentieth centuries in Western history have been nagging and turbulent times filled with great debates, vast anxieties, exciting and perilous days of triumph and pain, and an increasing lack of assurance about man's fate. They are crammed with the conquests of science. They have opened tremendous gaps between ourselves and our past.

It serves no purpose to deplore and denounce these facts. It is better to let the poets fly and sing, the barbarians of our planet trot and run around in the well-arranged frenzies of modern life, the scientists explore the vast reaches of their worlds. Meanwhile a few thoughtful and challenging individuals may perhaps continue to ponder and discuss the complexities of the universe and the validity of our assumptions about them. Men of any age reveal as much about themselves by the questions they ask as by the things they do.

"In knowledge that man is only to be condemned and despised who is not in a state of transition."

Meanwhile the anthropologists, archeologists, geologists, and historians probe backwards into time; the past of the planet and mankind is their concern. The poets and their companions use their sensitive skills and imaginations to voyage the shoreless seas of the spirit; often they come back and cannot tell the world where they have been, or what they have seen and felt in their mysterious adventures and mystical experiences. The artists, architects, sculptors, musicians, and mathematicians search for beauty of form and color, light and shadow, the pure and bleak power of equations and numbers, the fusing of sense and sound in the moving language of music. The men of science scan the space-time universe, peer into the wonders of the subatomic world, shift molecules about to please themselves and serve their fellows; they build and they destroy.

The next few pages of this book are about some men who moved in the triumphant march of nineteenth-century science. Many of them shared the conviction of Jeremy Bentham: "Experience, observation, experiment: in these three words may be seen the sources of all our knowledge."

In 1859 Charles Robert Darwin (1809–1882) published his *On the Origin of Species by Means of Natural Selection or the Preservation of Favored Races in the Struggle for Life*. In this famous volume, tremendous in its sweep and scope, Darwin set forth his conclusions about the evolution of mankind. All of his arguments were clear and logical and carefully buttressed by the evidence of long, hard, and sound scientific work. Professor J. H. Randall says that "the idea of Evolution, of change, growth, and development, has been the most revolutionary notion in man's thought about himself and his world in the last hundred years." Professor Randall is right.

In 1831 Charles Darwin had sailed on the *Beagle* on a scientific exploration trip around Patagonia and Tierra del Fuego. In 1846 he went on the *Rattlesnake* when that ship sailed to survey and chart some of the waters around Australia. On these journeys Darwin collected and sorted out masses of facts and made countless observations. During these years he also read many books and articles. One book was Sir Charles Lyell's (1797–1875) *Principles of Geology* (1830–1833), a famous and scholarly study of geological forces, the origin of fossils, and the formation of the earth's strata.

Five years after Lyell's *Principles* had been completed, Germany's Matthias Jakob Schleiden's work on cell structure presented remarkable proof of the basic unity of all organisms. The biologist Theodor Schwann reached similar conclusions. Darwin was familiar with the achievements of Schleiden and Schwann and Ernst von Baer and scores of other men that need not be mentioned here. He also knew and respected the work in paleontology of France's

Baron Georges Cuvier (1769–1832). Darwin owed much to Cuvier. So, too, do our modern paleontologists and anthropologists. True, it is a long road from Cuvier to Dubois, Koenigswald, Black, Dart, and Bloom. But Cuvier was one of the men who first began the work. We should not forget that. When we speak and write in admiration of such things as Kenneth Oakley's achievements in the fluorine-dating of fossil bones or the triumphs of Libby with carbon-14 time measurements, we should also pause to praise the men who first opened the gates and pointed the way.

In 1838 Charles Darwin read the *Essay on Population* (1798) written by Thomas Robert Malthus (1766–1834), the radical clergyman who disturbed so many people in his lifetime and later. In the *Essay on Population,* Malthus asserted that under normal conditions population increases by geometrical progression and food by arithmetical—thus the birth rate always tends to outrun the means of subsistence. What Malthus had written made a deep impression on Darwin. He concluded that "favorable variations would tend to be preserved and unfavorable ones to be destroyed. The result of this would be a formation of a new species. Here, then, I had a theory by which to work." Year after year Darwin continued to search and study.

In the year 1858 the naturalist Alfred Russel Wallace (1823–1913) was doing some research down in the Moluccas. As he was thinking about the *Essay on Population* and the conclusions of Malthus, "there suddenly flashed upon me the idea of the survival of the fittest." Darwin, as we know, had been working on the same idea for years: "There may be something left to chance, but on the whole, *the fittest will survive.*" In 1842 Darwin wrote out an abstract of his theory. Fourteen years later Wallace sent Darwin a paper he had written that stated his views; they were almost identical with those of Darwin. Two men, working independently, had reached the same conclusion, or almost so. It was an interesting coincidence.

In the *Origin of Species,* Darwin set forth the series of principles that will be connected with his name so long as there are men to read and think upon the earth. In the first place, all living vegetable and animal species, asserted Darwin, are descended from earlier and, usually, more rudimentary types. Man, for instance, "still bears in his bodily frame the indelible stamp of his lowly origin." The salt of the sea from which man came is in his blood today. In *The Descent of Man* (1871) Darwin tried to show that the human race was descended from an ancestor who was the common forebear of the anthropoid apes and men. Secondly, said Darwin, the species that are at a disadvantage in the ceaseless struggles of the world of nature—whatever those disadvantages may be—are gradually eliminated because they cannot adapt themselves to their environment. Thirdly, when certain variations or modifications of structure occur that are advantageous to the creatures possessing them —and those variations grow more marked with every generation—then those creatures have a better chance of survival. Nature decides the species that will live and the one that will perish in the dialectical process of "natural selection." Fourthly, said Darwin, a new species sometimes results from minor variations or "mutations." Finally, Charles Darwin turned his eyes from the past to a future bright with promise. "Man may be excused," he wrote, "for feeling some pride at having risen, though not through his own exertions, to the very summit of the organic scale; and the fact of his thus having risen, instead of having been aboriginally placed there, may give him hopes for a still higher destiny in the distant future."

It was later necessary to make a few modifications of Darwin's theory. For instance, Darwin had thought that sexual selection was responsible for differentiations among the various species; about that he was wrong. He had also believed that the "mutations" of which he wrote were small and that it would take a long time to produce a new species. The Dutch botanist Hugo De Vries (1848–1935) claimed, on the contrary, that evolution could proceed by sudden leaps, by abrupt and radical genetic changes that produce plants or animals quite different from anything that has appeared on earth before. In this way, said De Vries, a new species may come into existence within a few generations. This modification of Darwin's theory—De Vries put forward his ideas in 1901—was soon widely accepted. It did not, of course, alter or undermine the general validity of Darwin's conclusions.

Both Darwin and Wallace had accepted the earlier hypothesis (1802) of Jean Baptiste Lamarck (1744–1829), who said that the physical structure of organisms changed as a result of their attempts to adapt themselves to their environment and that all such changes were transmitted from generation to generation. This, too, was an error. The German zoologist August Weismann (1834–1914) flatly denied that acquired characteristics can be transmitted. His experiments showed to the satisfaction of his contemporaries—they are not entirely accepted today—that body cells and reproductive cells are completely distinct and that no changes in one kind of cell can affect the other. Thus, asserted Weismann, a parent transmits to a child those qualities that are contained in the germ plasm and nothing more.

In 1866 the Austrian monk Gregor Mendel (1822–1884) published the results of his experiments in cross-breeding tall and dwarf variations of peas. Mendel formulated his significant and complex laws of heredity, including the rules determining dominant and recessive characteristics. The theories of De Vries, mentioned above, were based on the laws of inheritance discovered by Mendel.

In later days, particularly in the twentieth century, there were long and strong discussions about some other questions. Such insistent queries as these appeared: What changes have occurred in man's dynamic vitality, his creative will, his flashing imagination, as he moved through the centuries? Why? Why has man always been able to maintain a high metabolic rate and a constant body temperature, highly important factors in his evolution? The scientists who are reading this book will have been thinking at this point of the attitudes and answers of such men as Osborn, Boule, Mayr, Simpson, McCown, Julian Huxley, and many others who ask questions and find answers.

Charles Darwin was, fundamentally, a very modest man, a quiet and retiring scholar. He cared nothing for publicity for its own sake. He did not like controversy.

By Darwin's side walked Thomas Henry Huxley (1825–1895). To the pugnacious Huxley, Darwin's friend, companion, and champion—he had been a surgeon on the *Rattlesnake*—there were few things more exhilarating than an argument, the longer and louder the better. If he were with us now, Huxley would be one of the first to agree with G. M. Young's assertion that "to a mature and civilized man no faith is possible except faith in the argument itself."

Huxley, often called "Darwin's bulldog," was an extraordinary publicist and popularizer. He was also a learned and skilled physician, zoologist, ethnologist, physiologist. "If I can convince Huxley," said Darwin, "I shall be content." He did convince Huxley; and Huxley set out to convince everybody else. In pamphlets, in books, in the press and on the platform, the tireless Huxley explained bluntly and clearly and with crushing logic the exciting and disruptive theory of natural selection and organic evolution, how it was that men and animals developed from the simple to the complex, always adapting themselves to the changing conditions of the planet. "My reflection when I first made myself master of the central order of the *Origin* was 'How extremely stupid not to have thought of that!' " Again: "The struggle for existence and 'natural selection' have become household words and everyday conceptions. . . . To anyone who studies the signs of the times, the emergence of the philosophy of Evolution . . . is the most portentous event of the nineteenth century."

The publication of the theory of evolution brought collisions and controversies. Some men looked around to salvage what they could from the wreckage of their cherished beliefs. Others felt themselves stripped bare of comfort as their old certainties dissolved; it seemed to them that their whole creed of life was crumbling into dust and nonsense. The number of pessimists and skeptics increased. Several men moved to agnosticism, to Tennyson's "sunless gulfs of doubt." Among them were a few remarkable individuals whose writings and speeches showed what Professor Basil Willey called "the poised uncertainty of the devoutly inclined agnostic mind."

Nine years after the publication of the *Origin of Species,* Thomas Huxley described the scene around him: "The consciousness of this great truth [evolution] weighs like a nightmare on many of the best minds of these days. They watch what they conceive to be the progress of materialism in such fear and powerless anger as a savage feels when, during an eclipse, the great shadow creeps over the face of the sun. The advancing tide of matter threatens to drown their souls. The tightening grasp of law impedes their freedom; they are alarmed lest man's moral nature be debased by the increase of his wisdom."

The most unrelenting opponents of the ideas of evolution and natural selection were the men who passionately believed that none of the old beliefs and traditions should be changed. They steadily refused to admit that their faiths had been jarred or blighted by the avalanche of hideous facts revealed by natural science. They girded themselves to wrestle on the side of the angels. They reviled and ridiculed Darwin and Huxley and all their works. They likened many a scientist to the "secular, faithless, heartless, ruthless" pagan that St. Paul met on the streets of Corinth and described in his letter to the Romans. They also asserted that "the spiritual cannot be judged by the unspiritual." How many concessions, they asked, must be made to rationalism?

On the other side of the battle lines moved the science-minded men who insisted that they were individuals of integrity, weary of "the stale and suffocating breath of revelation and miracle." In their judgment, the dogmas of Biblical fundamentalism were untrue and indefensible. They were content to have the laws of progress merge with the laws of evolution. Serious and sober men joined with the crackpots and cranks in the warfare between science and religion. The protracted struggle mirrored the nineteenth-century mind. In modern times, most informed and thoughtful men can look back without excitement upon the bitter disputes and storms of the days of their grandfathers. They can see that those controversies really had nothing to do with the facts and teachings about the pattern of God's way in this world. But in the nineteenth century this judgment did not prevail.

The controversies and squabbles were hard and heavy. The massed power of the truculent and defiant clergy, Roman Catholic and Protestant alike, moved into the thundering fray. Surges of prejudice rolled side by side with feelings that were genuine and powerful. Calm counsels seldom took command. Above the tumult could be heard the voice of Thomas Huxley, persuasive, vigorous, steely, and spiced with sarcasm. At a meeting of the British Association for the Advancement of Science in 1860, Samuel Wilberforce, bishop of Oxford, asked whether Huxley was "related on his grandfather's side or his grandmother's side to an ape." Huxley replied: "I would rather be descended from the humble ape than to trace my ancestry to one who used his ability and position to discredit and to crush those who sought after truth."

It was to be expected that those who accepted Genesis as a literal statement of historical fact found it impossible to agree with Darwin and his associates. Shaken out of their complacency, they resented the patient and effective way in which the scientists had produced apparently conclusive proofs, demolished myths, errors, and half-truths. Instead of moving to prayer, the opponents of Darwin's ideas started to argue, denounce, and grapple in an outburst of righteous anger. But anger was not enough. They were compelled to retreat, again and again. "Physical science goes on unconcernedly pursuing its own paths. Theology, the science whose object is the dealings of God with man as a moral being, maintains but a shivering existence, shouldered and jostled by the steady growth of modern thought, and bemoaning itself for the hostility which it encounters."

The vehement foes of the theory of evolution forgot, sometimes, that not all the truths of God had yet been revealed to them. They were blind and insensitive because they were very certain that they were right and the scientists were wrong. In their ignorance—so honest and so human—they assumed that they knew what God had meant; they thought that they knew what He had said. This is a very perilous and bigoted position for any man to take, however high and holy he may think his cause to be.

In these days of roaring tides of controversy several men declared that the theory of "evolution by natural selection" explained and justified numerous aspects of political and social history. They vehemently asserted that the idea of "the survival of the fittest" was a good reason for imperialism, wars between classes and nations, and similar conflicts and rivalries of human beings. By such struggles, they said, the "unfit" tribes, states, or classes were eliminated. It was "the way of nature" that the fit should survive and the weak perish. It was the road of progress. Many of the speculations and arguments, supported by volatile and partisan men, were muddled, haphazard, or stunted. The true scientists regarded the excited applications of Darwin's theory as invalid, often downright foolish. They might perhaps have added that the word "evolution" has a scientific meaning but the word "progress" has not.

In the animated world of nineteenth-century thought there appeared many other remarkable men. Friedrich Heinrich Alexander von Humboldt (1769–1859), for instance, was the last of the significant philosopher-scientists, an unflagging inventor, geologist, geographer, physicist, botanist, astronomer, archeologist, philologist, meteorologist, explorer—and several other things besides. This versatile and clear-sighted man—he counted stars and invented isotherms, explored the Orinoco and climbed Mt. Chimborazo—tried to put most human knowledge into one great book that he called *Cosmos* (1845–1862). He finished five volumes and then he stopped. There was too great a mass of facts, too many inescapable truths, too much specialization in Humboldt's day.

England's Herbert Spencer (1820–1903) was a madly methodical scientist and philosopher who liked to think and talk and write. Despite the fact that he was plagued by insomnia and nervous headaches, this indefatigable bachelor produced thick and heavy books in a stupendous effort to coordinate and explain all phenomena—Spencer was not a specialist in anything—in terms of the one formula of evolution. His massive and encyclopedic *Synthetic Philosophy* contains ten volumes. Spencer rejected all theology and metaphysics; he accepted matter and force, nothing else. All evolution, he asserted, is "an integration of matter and concomitant dissipation of motion, during which the matter passes from an indefinite incoherent homogeneity to a definite coherent heterogeneity and during which the retained motion undergoes a parallel transformation." Whatever we may think of this famous and clogged definition, it is true that Herbert Spencer's books, cracking under the strain of categories and facts, were not really a guide or a lamp to his age or ours. His reputation in his own day was high and formidable. Now his name is dimmed in the memories of men and his books are seldom read. William James once called him "a man unique for quaint consistency." Sober, patient, industrious, humorless—he tried to avoid reading anything opposed to his ideas—Herbert Spencer was one of the last great apostles of extreme individualism; he insisted that a policy of *laissez faire* was supported by evolution. He tried to do the impossible, and he failed. If there had been a bit of the romantic in Spencer his fate would have been less sad. He was so very sober, serious, leaden, dreary. "If Spencer ever wrote a tragedy," wrote Thomas Huxley, "it would be the slaying of a beautiful deduction by an ugly fact."

Among the restless men and minds of the nineteenth century moved Auguste Comte (1798–1857), a writer and thinker of consequence. He shaped the philosophy of positivism.

Auguste Comte was opposed to materialism on the one hand and to orthodox religion and metaphysics on the other. He thought that there should be a new moral reorganization and a new "religion of humanity." He insisted that the disquieting and neglected social problems of the world should be dealt with by the new methods of science. His first published work was *A Prospectus of the Scientific Works Required for the Reorganization of Society*. In this book Comte asserted that mankind had passed through two stages of thought, the theological and the rational, and was moving into a third stage that he called the era of positivism. Positivism, said Comte, means the use of positive knowledge to meet the challenges and problems of an industrial society.

In a complicated series of divisions—organic, inorganic, astronomical, terrestrial—Comte classified all knowledge that was positive and scientific: mathematics, astronomy, physics, chemistry, and biology. To this list he added a new science that he called sociology, the study of human beings in society. Comte insisted that a truly scientific scrutiny should be made of individuals, groups, communities, states, habits, laws, and customs. The sociologists, the new "social scientists," could do that. They could search out the laws of social order and human progress. Once those laws were discovered, then scientific reforms could be made and a new order would arise in the world of the West.

The hopes and plans of Auguste Comte attracted many men in the nineteenth century. In our contemporary world most of his lively ideas are present in various forms. A few of them have been mutilated and perverted and have become dangerous. This kind of development happens in the growth of many creeds and cults and causes. Disciples and converts sometimes have less wisdom than those who came and built first. During these tumbling years of the nineteenth century there were numerous spokesmen for ideologies and crusades. There was much wrestling with words and meanings. The legions of agnostics—Thomas Huxley and Leslie Stephen did not march alone—battled with the men who cleaved to orthodoxies, mile after mile upon a long front. New cracks and lesions continued to appear in the changing patterns of faith and action. The floods of rationality swept steadily along. Nonrational dissensions continued. Dialectical mutinies multiplied. Most philosophers of the age were more interested in the practices of men and the conduct of life than they were in speculation and theory and hence the strand of empiricism was wide and strong, especially in England. It is sometimes forgotten that German idealism, so powerful in Europe, did not appear in England among English philosophers until about 1865. The great age of the school of England's Green and Bradley, heavily dependent upon Hegel, did not begin to grow until about 1870.

Johann Gottlieb Fichte (1762–1814), the moral and political philosopher whose *Addresses to the German Nation* (1809) were described in Chapter 31, continued to assert that the spirit of the individual makes its own moral universe and to declare that the German spirit must be kept pure, uncontaminated by French culture or international influences. The followers of Immanuel Kant (1724–1804), the transcendental idealist of Königsberg, increased in number and power in Europe and America. Some awareness of Kant's complicated categories and the ideas he set forth in *The Critique of Pure Reason* (1781), *The Principles of Political Right* (1793), *Perpetual Peace* (1795), and *The Philosophy of Law* (1796) were considered to be a necessary part of the knowledge of any cultured man. The works of Georg Wilhelm Friedrich Hegel (1770–1831) were widely studied and discussed in the Western world, especially his *The Phenomenology of Spirit* (1807), *Logic* (1812–1816), and *The Philosophy of Right* (1821). Arthur Schopenhauer (1788–1860), that antirational, eccentric, pessimistic, atheistic, perverse, and lively philosopher attracted countless disciples and enemies by his *The World of Will and Idea* (1818), *On the Will in Nature* (1836), *The Two Main Pillars of Ethics* (1841).

In the writings of Fichte, Kant, Hegel, and Schopenhauer were most of the main philosophical roots of nineteenth-century idealism and pragmatism. In the pages of John Stuart Mill, Herbert Spencer, and Auguste Comte, whose works and ideas were described in earlier paragraphs, were the roots of naturalistic philosophies and positivism. In the works of Friedrich Nietzsche (1844–1900), Karl Marx (1818–1883), and Sören Kierkegaard (1813–1855)—see Chapter 33 and Chapter 37—there were the thrusts and pressures of many ideas, causes, and crusades: existentialism, communism, socialism, fascism, most of the claims of the nonrational universe as opposed to those of a reasonable universe that can be made to yield its secrets to human reason. Almost all thoughtful and sensitive men of the modern world give a large part of their philosophical allegiance to one of the original and seminal minds mentioned in the last few paragraphs.

In the nineteenth century the philosophers were not left entirely alone to inquire into such things as the theories of knowledge and truth, the validity of knowledge (realism and idealism), the sources of knowledge (rationalism, empiricism, etc.), pragmatism, vitalism, naturalism, mechanism, causality, moral and aesthetic values, formal logic, and all the concepts and values and problems that have troubled men and civilization for centuries. By taking careful thought, the radical and energetic Sigmund Freud (1856–1939) of Vienna opened the gates to modern psychiatry, a study and profession that has its own theories of knowledge and truth far different from those imbedded in the books of the philosophers. Those theories are also quite different from the ones held by several contemporary scientists who look elsewhere, especially to the chemical laboratories, for the answers to many problems of mental diseases and difficulties.

Some aspects of Sigmund Freud's intense and exciting explorations beyond the dark frontiers of the human mind are widely known. His complicated theories have had a tremendous impact upon philosophy, literature, science, art, commerce, industry, religion, morals, psychology, anthropology, and sociology. His prodigious pioneer work was *The Interpretation of Dreams* (1900), a book that shocked Europe and America. The ideas in this book and others have aided many medical men in their diagnosis and treatment of mental illness. The psychiatrists who rely today upon Freud's concepts and conclusions in their psychotherapy cannot easily be numbered. All of the outstanding psychiatrists in the modern world have borrowed from Freud as they built their own varying theories, formed their schismatic sects, and fought their bitter campaigns with wranglings and recriminations. Consider, for instance, the lives and works of Karl Abraham, Alfred Adler, Max Eitingon, Sandor Ferenczi, Erich Fromm, Karen Horney, Ernest Jones, Carl Gustav Jung, Otto Rank, Harry Stack Sullivan.

The basic Freudian theories of the psyche (divided into the conscious and unconscious, id, ego, and superego), the libido (the life energy that includes sex), the feelings of sin and guilt complexes, traumas, dreams, wish fulfillments, and numerous other aspects of the inner workings of human beings are widely studied now; they are even more extensively discussed by those who are not inhibited by any knowledge of the facts about what Freud actually said and wrote.

Some men consider the conscientious, plodding, dredging, and intolerant Sigmund Freud a genius and a major prophet and they honor him accordingly. There are also those who do not respect or admire him. Their words are words of opposition, scorn, and ridicule. It is not for amateurs and unarmed men to enter into these disputes.

In these years when Darwin, Huxley, Comte, Spencer, and Freud lived and swayed their worlds it was obvious that more and more men wished to be considered "realistic" and "scientific" about what they thought and did. In an age so filled with doubts, dilemmas, ideas, theories innumerable, and the startling facts of science it seemed sane and safe to be "realistic."

A few individuals turned with scientific interest to examine the documents behind the Bible. The "higher criticism" of the nineteenth century soon produced several interesting results. In 1835, for instance, David Friedrich Strauss published his *Life of Jesus,* a predominantly philosophical work that treated Jesus as a mythical figure. In 1863 Ernest Renan used the conclusions of the textual critics in his naturalistic *Life of Jesus,* a book that showed a Jesus quite different from orthodox views of Him.

There were many conflicts about the "higher criticism." The liberal Roman Catholics, for example, had some distinguished leaders: Acton, Newman, Dollinger, Montalembert. These men stood for a liberalization of the faith. They also believed that a scientific study of the Bible might in time lead all Christians back to the original faiths and truths that marked the beginning of their history. Many Roman Catholics, led by Pope Pius IX (1846–1878), were not prepared to compromise with liberalism. In 1864 the *Syllabus of Errors* listed eighty items of liberal belief that were held to be incompatible with the Roman Catholic faith. So far as the question of accepting new scientific discoveries was concerned, the Roman Catholic Church saw no need to state a position of hostility in the *Syllabus of Errors* or anywhere else. Unlike many Protestant groups, it had never stood for a literal interpretation of the Bible or battled against the theory of evolution.

Disputes soon arose about the nature of history and historical writing. The first of the so-called "scientific" historians was Leopold von Ranke (1795–1886), the student of Barthold Niebuhr who stressed the importance of the dispassionate study of original sources. He claimed that the historians could use the objective methods of the natural scientists. Many of his contemporaries agreed. Ranke was one of the scholars who started the seminar method of training historians, a custom that has been continued. He believed that the "facts" should be presented "as they really were." The historian should say "what actually occurred," nothing more. Modern historical writing owes a great deal to Leopold von Ranke. There was also Theodor Mommsen (1817–1903), author of the scholarly and illuminating *History of Rome,* a work rightly praised and read through many decades.

Most French, British, and American historians were prepared to use the tools of scientific methodology in their research; but few were prepared to agree completely with Ranke. Not many would assert that they could present the facts "as they really were." Such famous historians as Thomas Babington Macaulay (1800–1859), Jules Michelet (1798–1874), George Bancroft (1800–1891) were not "scientific" historians. Their works were filled with drama, imagination, bias, fire. They were artists. They were writing about human beings, and their own humanity was not lost in doing it. If they were with us now they might possibly say that the theory that history is a science is itself pseudoscientific. They might be angered at the intolerable dogmatism of those who assert that the methods and ends of the natural sciences and the "social sciences" meet in one, or that history is a "social science." They might remark that history is history and has survived and served for centuries with no other name. They might join many modern historians in asserting that it is intellectually futile to try to argue that history is a "science" unless the meaning of words and facts are massaged in a most reprehensible way.

Meanwhile the frontiers of natural science advanced. New depths were plumbed, new experiments carried out, new theories prepared, new mysteries found. Hugo von Mohl (1805–1872) gave the name "protoplasm" in 1844 to the substance inside the walls of living cells, the physical basis of life. Louis Pasteur (1822–1895) discovered the bacteria that soured wine and killed silk-worms and developed an inoculation for rabies. Ignaz Semmelweiss discovered in 1847 the values of antiseptic solutions in preventing the spread of disease. Joseph Lister (1827–1912) used phenol as an antiseptic about 1865. It was Lister who first insisted on cleanliness in surgical operations; he is considered the father of antiseptic surgery. An American surgeon, Dr. Crawford W. Long, performed the first operation with the use of ether in 1842. About 1875 Robert Koch (1843–1910) discovered the anthrax bacilli and in 1882 the rod-shaped bacilli of tuberculosis. In 1892 the diptheria antitoxin was produced by Emil von Behring (1854–1917). Slowly the victories against the deadly germs increased. Soon the scientists were to find new enemies: the viruses that belong to the borderline world between living organisms and large chemical molecules. Knowledge and tests and tools increased together. Around the necks of the physicians appeared stethoscopes. They discovered more about such things as the energy provided by food and the nature of the human nervous system. The more they found out, the more they wanted to know.

Meanwhile the geologists were pushing back the birthday of the world. The astronomers were extending their awareness of the vast immensities of the universe. More stellar distances were measured and more heavenly movements plotted. Spectrum analysis revealed the nature of the elements in some of the stars and planets. The feats of the physicists were paving the way for the greater triumphs of the future. The kinetic theory of energy was slowly developed by Bernoulli, Waterson, Joule, and Clausius. In 1847 the German Hermann von Helmholtz (1821–1894) formulated the first law of thermodynamics, the principle of the conservation of energy. ("No longer could the Germans be dismissed as a nation content with metaphysics, music, beer, and the petty politics of provincial courts.") In the 1850's Lord Kelvin (William Thomson) stated the second law of thermodynamics, the law of entropy or the dissipation of energy. The mathematicians continued to pursue their high intellectual activities. Lobachevsky invented non-Euclidean geometry; the names of Cantor, Frege, and Riemann stand proudly in the long gallery that stretches from the ancient shadows to Thales and Euclid and Pythagoras and on to Russell and Whitehead and the other mathematical giants of our modern world.

The Manchester schoolmaster John Dalton (1766–1844) discovered that when chemical compounds are built up the combining elements enter into those compounds in proportions expressible by whole numbers. Dalton therefore concluded that certain tiny particles that he called atoms were indivisible in chemical changes; that they had characteristic masses; that they must always combine in ratios of those masses or their multiples. Thus Dalton formulated a definite quantitative theory. He then proceeded to consider the numerical facts of chemical combination and to determine the atomic mass and chemical valance of certain elements. Dalton made a list of twenty atomic weights.

Several other scientists—especially Gay-Lussac and Cannizzaro—tried to discover the connection between atomic weights and physical and chemical properties. In 1869 Dmitri Mendeleev (1834–1907) drew up a periodic table in which he arranged the elements in order of ascending atomic weights. At this stage of the nineteenth century, men believed that atoms were the basic units of matter, the indestructible bedrock of reality. They could not know then that the whole structure of classical physics was soon to collapse.

A few nineteenth-century scientists began to analyze the structure of organic compounds. Then they started to break down, rearrange, and build again. The results were astounding. In 1828, for instance, Friedrich Wöhler prepared urea from cyanic acid and ammonia. Soon Unverdorben and Hoffmann separated a substance from coal tar that they called aniline. In 1856 the first aniline dye (purple) was obtained and this began Germany's great dye industry. Soon a large number of organic compounds were isolated, and many were synthesized from their elements. Several synthetic organic drugs, for instance, were produced in the late nineteenth century, including antipyrene, phenacetin, and aspirin. Then the trickle became a flood. Such achievements are often the practical results of ingenuity and widening scientific knowledge.

The history of the nineteenth century was studded with the achievements of invention, applied science, new techniques and operations: the Bessemer, Siemens-Martin, and Gilchrist-Thomas processes for making steel; the triumphs of Guglielmo Marconi, Samuel F. B. Morse, and Alexander Graham Bell in the development of the wireless, telegraph, and telephone; the streams of patents of Thomas Alva Edison. The list could be extended, on and on.

The incalculable strides of the pure scientists and mathematicians continued to speed the march of the masters of technology and manufacturing. The victories of minds and laboratories in abstract experiments and calculations brought discoveries of tremendous consequence to human societies. These remarks are an accurate comment upon several centuries of man's history; they are especially true of the recent chapters of the tale of human progress and power, the mechanization of industry, the tools of precision, the mass action and mass production, the improved agriculture, the advance in public health, the swift and effective communication and transportation, the swelling accumulations of capital for investment and production, the extension of banking and money services, the tapping of new power potentials, the enormous exchange of goods, the multiplications of man's controls over his environment. These are the pivots and pillars of the ways of living in the contemporary world.

In our modern centuries the evidences of success and failure stand forth on every hand. The startling pace of recent change can hardly be comprehended by those who remember yesterday. Men who look backwards see that the world they once knew is gone. The bridges have been blown up, the roads destroyed.

Chapter 39

THE

NEW IMPERIALISM

"Over one hundred workers signed the petition presented to the Queen in 1870 which declared that its signers had 'heard with alarm that Your Majesty has been advised to give up the Colonies.'"
—Janet Henderson Robb, *The Primrose League 1883–1906*, 178

EVERY generation of the human race has been faced by new problems. The answers to these problems, good and bad, have marked man's broadening awareness and achievement. They have changed the patterns of his life, whether he has lived in Jacques Pirenne's "maritime" civilizations or the "continental" ones, in Arnold Toynbee's linked "civilizations" or in those that have not yet been identified or named by the anthropologists, philosophers, and historians.

In modern times neither the chief problems nor the answers of men have been confined within the shifting boundaries of nation-states or even of continents. The emerging questions, plots, and patterns of reply have sometimes been hemispheric in their scope. On occasion they have embraced almost all of the habitable zones of the world.

The forms of change in the nineteenth century were particularly significant. It was then that the effects of international and interregional developments and rivalries converged to alter many aspects of the total character of the society, structure, and perspective of the Western world. Under the pressures and demands of nationalism and war the consolidation of small states into big ones continued. The desire of large states to increase their territories remained a decisive factor in almost all of the regions of the world. Expanding and restless European and American nations carried their flags, guns, techniques, and faiths in waves of expansion through continents and islands beyond the seas. Improvements in the means of transportation, the skills of men, and the numerous tools that were shaped in an age of progress, speeded the course of conquest and infiltration. No man could see or judge all of the consequences of the collective enterprises, usually called "Imperialism" or "Manifest Destiny," that leaped out of Europe and America in the nineteenth century.

The causes and explanations of the empire-building of European states are many: financial, industrial, commercial, political, humanitarian, religious, scientific, romantic. Nations with highly developed systems of commerce and industry wanted to annex territories or obtain protectorates or "spheres of influence" so that they could control and develop the natural resources of those distant areas. They needed to import raw materials for their factories, goods for their own peoples: jute, oil, tea, coffee, rubber, ivory, copper, copra—the list was long. Their quest for colonies was also determined and directed by their mounting need for export markets. They wanted to control the lands where they did business. Most European states, moving in a competitive political and economic system, wanted to be as self-sufficient as possible. They also wished to exclude from as many areas as they could the soldiers and businessmen of rival European states. In their own colonies they had no fear of foreign competition, discrimination, or tariffs.

Thus it was that expanding European states hastened to explore and exploit. England's Robert Lowe, a man always strongly opposed to imperialism, made an unkind remark that did contain some truth: "Colonies have no sentiment. They are inhabited by hard, needy, and greedy men of business who go there to make money and get away as soon as they can." Cecil Rhodes, that great British architect of empire, said this: "These islands can only support six millions out of their thirty-six millions. . . . We cannot afford to part with one inch of the world's surface which affords a free and open market to the manufactures of our countrymen." He also remarked that "Imperialism is philanthropy plus five per cent." To some other nations, especially Germany, it seemed that England wanted to bring the whole of the unclaimed world into the British Empire. "They say Christ but they mean cotton."

There were other important factors in the surge of imperialism in the latter part of the nineteenth century. Then, as always, men with capital sought fields for profitable investments. Such spots were often available in the "backward" territories of the world. In some areas the interest rates were very high, a happy situation if the investors could be assured that their money was safe. That assurance was at hand when European governments extended their political and military controls over the regions where the guns of Western man had not previously been fired and their commands had not been obeyed. The industrial revolution and the new mechanics of power made it possible for Europeans to impose their will upon wide areas of Africa and Asia. When there were Asian or African governments already in existence they were often weak and the states of Europe provided them with "resident advisers" and loans.

Thus capital went out of Europe, especially to the colonies and protectorates. The flow of money made it possible to dig mines, drill oil wells, build plantations and factories. The natives provided cheap labor. The Europeans controlled the production and distribution of goods. Meanwhile thousands of miles of railway lines were constructed in Asia and Africa. The number of steamships on the rivers and along the coast increased steadily. Cheap transportation was important.

The total export of European capital to the colonies, to the United States, Latin America, and Russia was very large. Great Britain, for instance, had more than $20,000,000,000 invested abroad in 1914. France lent Russia $2,000,000,000 in that year. After the Bolshevik Revolution in 1917 the loan was not repaid.

During this age of aggressive national rivalries the explorers adventured up strange rivers and probed into far-off lands. The eager traders made their "treaties" with native chiefs, sometimes to their own advantage. European states, steadily attempting to bring more territories into their orbits, became increasingly aware of the military importance of far-flung empires to their prestige and economic and military strength. Many Europeans asserted that colonies performed a useful function by draining away some of the surplus population; if it were not for the colonies, they said, those surplus citizens might migrate to foreign countries and be forever lost to the homeland.

The traders and adventurers were usually grasping for business, riches, gold, ivory, rubber, diamonds. The Christian missionaries were after souls. Scores of missionaries went among wild tribesmen, "half-devil and half-child," to tell them that all men were the children of God and that the Christian never dies. Medical missionaries, walking in the footsteps of the Master, helped and healed. The need was great and the medical missionaries were few. They did what they could. "And the King shall answer and say unto them, Verily I say unto you, inasmuch as ye have done it unto the least of these my brethren, ye have done it unto me."

For many Europeans these missionary activities were but one of the many tasks to be performed in the lands of "the lesser breeds without the law." It was "the white man's burden," surely, to Christianize, educate, and lift out of barbarism the primitive peoples embraced by the new empires. In some areas of Asia and Africa there was not much space left for the Christians. The Buddhists, the followers of Confucius, the men of many other faiths were there. Into several regions the Moslems had traveled long before and brought with them the teachings of Mohammed. One Moslem said to an English Christian: "God has given to you English a great many gifts. You make fine ships and sharp penknives, and good cloth and cottons; and you have rich nobles and brave soldiers; and you write and print many learned books. . . . all this is of God. But there is one thing that God has withheld from you and has revealed to us; and that is the knowledge of the true religion by which one may be saved." The Christians, on the other hand, were certain that they had "the true religion." They went into strange lands to preach and teach and heal.

The idea and practice of imperialism fired the imagination and the enthusiam of many European men. Imperialism helped to serve the ends of political ambition, economic hunger, and missionary zeal. The age of great empires was at hand.

In the latter part of the nineteenth century many men in the British Isles turned with enthusiasm to aid in the swift expansion of the British Empire. Nearly a million square miles of territory were added to Queen Victoria's possessions between 1880 and 1900. Bound to their humble tasks at home, the miner, the clerk, and the tenant farmer shared a vicarious satisfaction in the success of their fellow Britons abroad. Although personal ambitions might be frustrated, there was emotional consolation in the collective imperial adventure. Armies of journalists wrote romantic tales of the adventures of the builders of empire and the far-flung posts beyond Suez. The patriotism of the press was unrestrained. Men of letters wrote of the imperial destiny. Thousands read and quoted the works of Rudyard Kipling. From Canada to Mandalay there was the long trail of empire. The pens of the scholars and statesmen were busy. Sir Charles Dilke published his *Problems of Greater Britain* and Sir John Seeley his *Expansion of England*. The Royal Colonial Institute flourished. The Imperial Federation League was formed in 1884; its offshoots ran all over the Empire. The frontiers of far lands became more significant for thousands of Englishmen. Unowned property in Australia and Canada waited for the paupers of Lancashire; when they could emigrate they left England; with them they took their "God Save the Queen" and their memories of "the Old Country." Their sons were born far from England and the first loyalties of those sons were to the homes their fathers found. As the British Commonwealth was shaped the new worlds were again called in to redress the balance of the old.

In the beginning of the new chapter of imperialism, Britain advanced with some reluctance and hesitation down the road of empire. When strategic and economic interests were clearly challenged it seemed that steps must be taken against defiant pressure and outright blackmail. The result was a series of British political annexations of territories that otherwise would have been seized by Germany, Belgium, France, or other powers.

Early in the 1880's William Ewart Gladstone, England's Liberal prime minister, was faced with several serious external problems, especially in Egypt, the Sudan, and South Africa. The Dutch Boers of South Africa, who had founded the two republics of the Transvaal and the Orange Free State after the Great Trek earlier in the century, had refused to accept the British annexation of the Transvaal in 1877. They revolted. Britain's General Colley and a hundred British troops were killed at Majuba Hill. In 1881 Gladstone gave the Transvaal internal independence under British suzerainty. Three years later Britain abandoned her claims to suzerainty and insisted only that the external affairs of the Transvaal should be under British control.

Meanwhile the scene darkened. Many foreigners came into the Transvaal to dig for diamonds in the blue clay. Other invaders came to toil along the fifty-mile length of the great gold reef of the Rand. It is no wonder that the Boers, mindful of Majuba Hill, stubbornly clinging to the Bible, the oxcart, and the ancient ways, were ready to take up arms at the turn of the century.

There were difficulties in Egypt. The spendthrift khedive Ismail who had earlier been compelled to sell his Suez Canal shares to Britain continued to spend swiftly all the money that he could borrow abroad. The British and French took charges of Egyptian finances to pay their bondholders. In 1881 an Egyptian named Arabi headed a rebellion against the invertebrate khedive Tewfik who had replaced Ismail and against the foreigners who had assumed control of Egyptian finances. Many foreigners were killed, especially in Alexandria. France at first agreed to help Britain subdue the rebels but later changed her decision. In 1882 Britain completed the task alone. More than a thousand Egyptians were killed. There was fire and looting. Arabi was banished to Ceylon.

In 1883 the Arabs in the Egyptian province of the Sudan revolted against the tyrannical misrule of the khedive and his agents. Led by wild dervishes and a theologian who called himself the Mahdi, or prophet, they carved a bloody road through Egyptian forces. In 1884 General Charles "Chinese" Gordon was sent to Khartum, the capital of the Sudan, to speed the evacuation of the British and Egyptians. But after Gordon reached Khartum he exceeded his orders for reasons that are obscure. He delayed his return to Egypt. Khartum was cut off. The forces of the Mahdi flooded through the gates of the city. Gordon and his garrison were killed.

In 1885 British troops were withdrawn from the Sudan. Eleven years later they returned to help the Egyptian khedive to reconquer his lost provinces. An army under the command of Britain's General Kitchener accomplished this task with a victory at Omdurman in 1898. British power was now established in the Anglo-Egyptian Sudan.

In the same year there arose a conflict with France. For some time the French had been pressing eastwards from French West Africa. A small French expedition under Captain Marchand reached Fashoda, a key point standing athwart the north-south trade route. The nation that held Fashoda controlled the whole upper Nile basin.

Captain Marchand had hoisted the French flag. Kitchener, claiming Fashoda for England, told Marchand to pull the French flag down. The

French government refused to order Marchand to retreat. The British government refused to let him stay. France and Britain came close to war. After six weeks the crisis ended when France agreed to withdraw. The whole Fashoda affair was a decidedly unpleasant episode.

Meanwhile the European nations were fighting their dramatic battles for empire in almost every part of Africa. The scrambling competition was a hard and ruthless business.

For many centuries the continent of Africa had remained untroubled by foreign invaders. Africa has almost no natural harbors; there are few bays or gulfs except the Gulf of Guinea; the rivers are seldom navigable. There are no continental crossroads; the wastes of the dividing Sahara stretch wide and formidable. Upon its sandy reaches the sun beats like fire.

In the late eighteenth century the Portuguese had discovered the sources of the Blue Nile. Several men probed into the northern interior from the Red Sea, the Nile, Somaliland, and Zanzibar. In the south the Dutch had moved into the land around the Cape of Good Hope. Mungo Park discovered and explored the Niger. In 1833 Hugh Clapperton discovered Lake Chad. The Scotsman Alexander Mackay scouted through the long miles of the Uganda country. About 1856 John Speke and Richard Burton found Lake Tanganyika. David Livingstone came to Africa to bring Christianity to the people; to open good trade routes; to increase trade with the natives; to stop slavery and the slave trade. "All I can add in my loneliness," he wrote, "is may Heaven's rich blessings come down on everyone, American, English, or Turk, who will help to heal the open sore of the world." Wide interest was roused when the journalist Henry Morton Stanley searched for and found the famous missionary whom the world thought lost. But Livingstone remained at his tasks in Africa. When he died in 1873 the natives carried his body 1,500 miles to the British consul at Zanzibar; from there it was brought to lie in Westminster Abbey.

In 1876 King Leopold II of Belgium created an international company to develop the Congo Basin. Leopold II was quite unscrupulous. The native Bantus were so cruelly degraded and mistreated that the civilized world protested. In 1879 the Congo Free State was created; in 1908 it became a Belgian colony. Meanwhile the Portuguese enlarged their holdings into the protectorates of Mozambique and Angola. In 1885 the Italians occupied Eritrea, in 1892 a part of Somaliland. In 1887 and 1896 they tried to seize Ethiopia and failed.

In 1884 fourteen nations sent representatives to a conference at Berlin to establish rules for the suppression of slavery in Africa, to arrange for the free navigation of the Niger and the Congo, and to try to define what "effective occupation" of a territory should mean.

The momentum of the rush for land in Africa increased. France now entered the competition. In 1880 France took over a portion of the Congo; in 1881 Tunis was added to Algiers as a protectorate; in 1888 France occupied a section of Somaliland; in 1896 the French flag was raised in Madagascar; in 1912 Morocco became a French protectorate. The French colonial empire was now larger than all Europe.

Nor did the Germans lag. The German Colonization Society was active throughout West Africa. In 1884 German Southwest Africa, Togoland, and the Cameroons became German colonies. In the same year German agents under Karl Peters went to East Africa. When the German emperor declared German East Africa (now Tanganyika) a German protectorate, the sultan of Zanzibar protested in vain that the natives were his subjects.

Meanwhile wars and clashes between the Europeans and the African tribesmen grew more frequent and bloody. The Basuto and Zulu warriors had strong arms and many spears. So, too, did the Matabeles, Ashantis, and scores of other native fighters, sons of the jungle and the veldt.

By the side of Portugal, Belgium, France, and Germany still moved Great Britain. Chartered companies, as in the sixteenth and seventeenth centuries, were formed to build British colonies and British trade. Treaties were negotiated with the natives. The British East African Company (1888) developed what is now Kenya. Several treaties of partition and delimitation were concluded between Germany and Britain with respect to disputed areas in East Africa. A British company moved into the Guinea coast region. In 1884 Britain occupied a section of Somaliland on the Gulf of Aden and on the flank of the road to the East through Suez. In 1885 a British protectorate was established over Bechuanaland, north of Cape Colony. The Royal Niger Company (1886) extended its control of Nigeria. In 1894 Uganda became a protectorate.

In South Africa the most important of the British Empire builders was Cecil John Rhodes (1853–1902). In the Kimberley diamond mines he had made a fortune. He was a member of the international syndicate that controlled the gold mines. Rhodes had a remarkable faith in the future of the British Empire. He dreamed of a belt of British territory stretching from the Cape to Cairo and bound together by a great railway. Because he was more than a dreamer he organized the British South Africa Company for quite practical purposes in 1889. One aim was to occupy the territory north of Bechuanaland and the Transvaal. The region was soon taken; it was called Rhodesia. The Boers of the Transvaal had good cause to be angered at this political encirclement and the necessity of their finding an indirect outlet to the sea through the Portuguese harbor of Delagoa Bay.

Towards the end of the century there were several thousand European foreigners or "outlanders" in the Transvaal. Most of them had come seeking gold. Many of them could never be assimilated. The city of Johannesburg, nerve center of the region, grew into a fevered and frenzied Babel of more than 100,000 people. Some were naïve and hopeful individuals; others were tough and hard. Gamblers were busy night and day. Pickpockets stalked and slithered through the streets. Strange tales were told of gold mines that no man ever found.

Fearful and suspicious of the "outlanders" who came either as settlers or as birds of passage, the Boers refused them the franchise, taxed them heavily, subjected them to military service, made it impossible for them to become citizens until they had been residents for fourteen years. Dutch was the only official language. Harsh import duties were placed on many goods used by gold miners, and the state created a monopoly on the sale of dynamite for mining operations. The "outlanders" protested and invoked the aid of Britain.

There were plots against the Transvaal government. When Dr. Leander Starr Jameson led 660 raiders into the Transvaal in December, 1895, all of them were captured. Much has yet to be known and written about the background of this Jameson Raid and the precise parts played in the plot by Cecil Rhodes and the Boer government. A series of simple and direct answers cannot yet be found.

The Boers began to arm. The "outlanders" smuggled arms into the Transvaal. The tragic event called the Boer War was now at hand.

There were many causes of the Boer War. The reasons for the bitter disputes were complex and the usual explanations are often glibly false. Neither the Boers nor the British were solely to blame. Perhaps the greatest cause of the conflict was the fact that the desire for gold and the dancing dreams of wealth had seized upon so many men. Beyond that point, in the narrow compass of these pages, it would be unwise to go.

In the fall of 1899 the last thread of negotiation between the British and Paul Kruger, president of the Transvaal, finally snapped. An ultimatum sent to the British by President Kruger included the demand that British troops should be withdrawn from the frontiers of the Transvaal within forty-eight hours. The British government did not comply. A conflict began that was to last for nearly three years.

The Orange Free State joined the Transvaal. Together they invaded Natal and Cape Colony. From Australia, New Zealand, and Canada came contingents to swell the British forces to more than 300,000 men. The war was bloody and expensive.

On May 31, 1902, the peace treaty of Vereeniging was signed. It was a generous arrangement. The Transvaal and the Orange Free State were annexed to the British Empire. The British government gave £3,000,000— and many loans—as a gift to help the people of South Africa who had suffered in the war. The inhabitants of the Transvaal and the Orange Free State were assured that "representative institutions leading up to self-government" would soon be introduced. Full self-government was given to the Transvaal in 1906

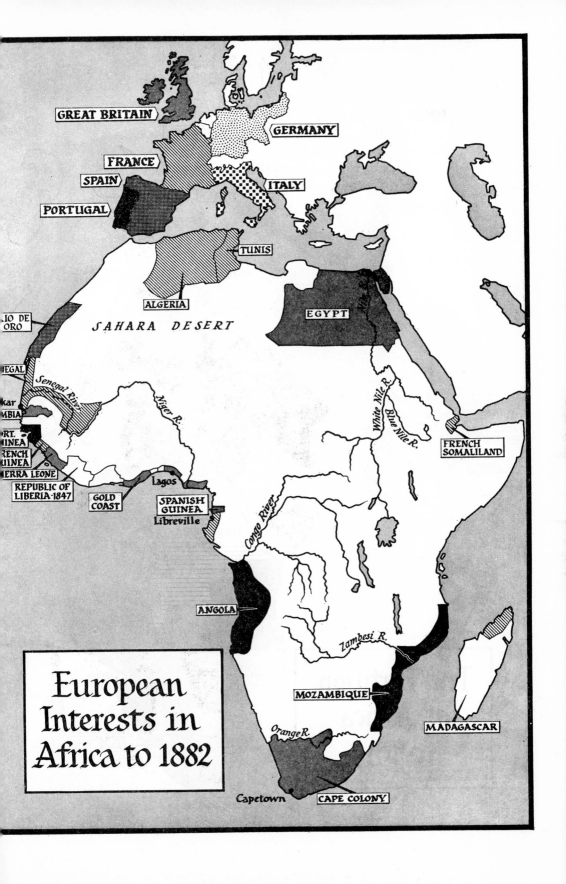

GREAT BRITAIN

GERMANY

FRANCE

SPAIN

ITALY

PORTUGAL

TUNIS

ALGERIA

EGYPT

SAHARA DESERT

RIO DE ORO

Senegal River

SENEGAL

Niger R.

White Nile R.

Blue Nile R.

Dakar

GAMBIA

PORT. GUINEA

FRENCH GUINEA

FRENCH SOMALILAND

SIERRA LEONE

REPUBLIC OF LIBERIA·1847

GOLD COAST

Lagos

SPANISH GUINEA

Libreville

Congo River

ANGOLA

Zambesi R.

MOZAMBIQUE

MADAGASCAR

Orange R.

Capetown

CAPE COLONY

European Interests in Africa to 1882

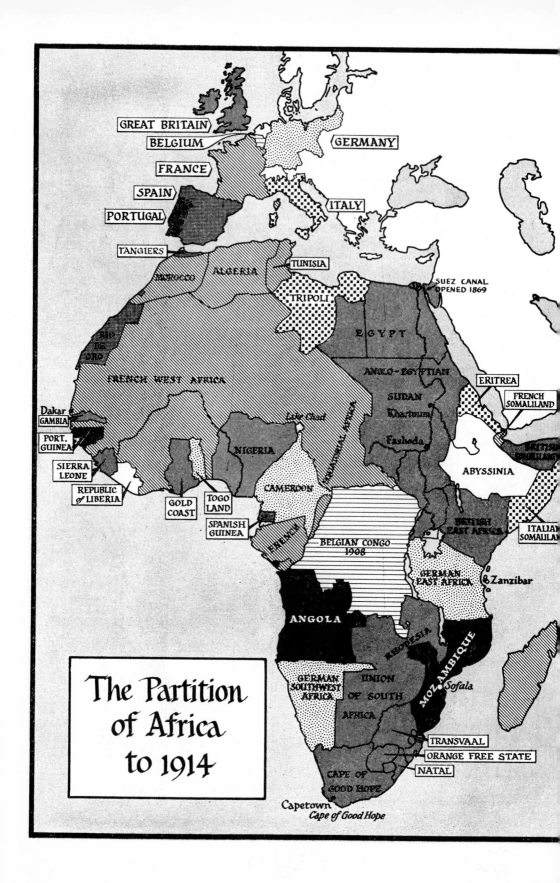

GREAT BRITAIN
BELGIUM
FRANCE
SPAIN
PORTUGAL
GERMANY
ITALY

TANGIERS
TUNISIA
SUEZ CANAL
OPENED 1869

MOROCCO   ALGERIA
TRIPOLI
EGYPT

RIO DE ORO

FRENCH WEST AFRICA

Lake Chad

ANGLO-EGYPTIAN
SUDAN
Khartoum
Fashoda

ERITREA

FRENCH
SOMALILAND

Dakar
GAMBIA

PORT.
GUINEA

SIERRA
LEONE

REPUBLIC
of LIBERIA

GOLD
COAST

TOGO
LAND

SPANISH
GUINEA

NIGERIA

CAMEROON

FRENCH

BELGIAN CONGO
1908

BRITISH
SOMALILAND

ABYSSINIA

BRITISH
EAST AFRICA

ITALIAN
SOMALILAND

GERMAN
EAST AFRICA
Zanzibar

ANGOLA

RHODESIA

MOZAMBIQUE
Sofala

GERMAN
SOUTHWEST
AFRICA

UNION
OF SOUTH
AFRICA

TRANSVAAL
ORANGE FREE STATE
NATAL

CAPE OF
GOOD HOPE

Capetown
Cape of Good Hope

The Partition
of Africa
to 1914

and to the Orange Free State in 1908. The first prime minister of the Transvaal was Louis Botha, a famous Boer general; the first prime minister of the Orange Free State was likewise a former Boer leader: General Christian De Wet. In 1910 the Orange Free State, Cape Colony, Natal, and the Transvaal united to form a great federal state called the Union of South Africa.

To the lands of southeast Asia and beyond the Europeans also came with their ships, guns, and treaties. They swept over the seas, slogged and hacked through the jungles, clambered up the hills. They fought with the natives and with one another. They prevailed over hazards and snags and reverses. The builders of empire hoisted their flags and tried to import Western ideas of order, law, and organized methods of government, to them the yardsticks of progress. They fought the treacherous tropical diseases, so numerous and deadly, that crept out of the river valleys. Some men made great profits. Several turned their eyes homeward and went back to their own lands. Others stayed and their sons stayed after them.

The Treaty of Amiens of 1802 gave the rich island of Ceylon to the British, the successors of the Dutch and the Portuguese in that fair place. After the British moved in they grew and exported much fine tea. They mined lead and dug up sapphires. Profitable cargoes of coconuts, cocoa, and rubber moved out of the port of Colombo and rice and wheat flour came in. The advancing trade and the rising curve of production in Ceylon brought pleasure and profit.

Great Britain also moved slowly into Burma. Some of the penetration was peaceful and some was not. There were two British-Burmese wars (1823–1825 and 1851–1852). In 1885 came the final British annexation of all of Burma. After Britain's conquest there was a rapid change in the patterns of Burmese living. Under the stimulation of British capital, government, law, and culture there were many improvements. British influence was particularly evident in the cities. In the delta of the Irrawaddy—the axis of Burma—the great port of Rangoon sprawled and flourished. Soon many Englishmen came there to live. In a dry lowland area far up the curving river stood Mandalay, a city with a mixed population of about 150,000 people. Mandalay was—and is—a place of many bazaars, fine roads, avenues of tall trees, a dry and healthy climate, a lot of alabaster and a few rubies, a little teak and much rice.

Southeast of Burma and south of Siam lies the peninsula of Malaya. By the late eighteenth century the British had begun to gather power and influence in that whole region, rich with rubber and tin. In 1819 Sir Stamford Raffles obtained Singapore from a Malay ruler. British power surged northwards along the peninsula, all the way to the edge of Siam. Several states became British protectorates. Thousands of Chinese entered to increase the tide of initiative and enterprise in the mines and plantations and in trade and commerce. It was not surprising that Singapore, lying on the shortest route to China from India and Europe, became one of the great ports of the world. In 1824 more than 35,000 tons of shipping cleared the harbor of Singapore. By 1850 the population reached 60,000. In 1887 Singapore, Penang, and Malacca became a crown colony.

Meanwhile the Dutch continued their advance into the East Indies; some of their giant strides were described in Chapter 35. They conquered Bali in 1849; every year they thrust further into Java—in the middle of the twentieth century Batavia became Jakarta, capital of the republic of Indonesia. About 50,000,000 people—more than half of the population of the East Indies—live in Java today. The island is about the size of New York State; it is the most densely populated area in the world.

Into all their empire in Southeast Asia, especially into Java, Sumatra, and parts of Borneo and New Guinea, the Dutch brought new standards of health and sanitation, railways, and roads. Productivity and efficiency increased. With the importation of Western commercial, agricultural, and industrial skills there also came new social and economic values among the people, new ideas and institutions, and a slowly rising restlessness. In the peasant civilizations of the fertile river deltas, in the complex tribal and family arrangements of life, in the methods of production among the metalworkers and the woodcraft men there were the beginnings of change; but the pace of alteration was very slow; the hand of the past is heavy.

France moved into Southeast Asia to extend her territory and increase her strength. The tentacles of her power first reached into the rich, rice-growing lands around Hanoi and Saigon in the peninsula that was soon to be called French Indochina. The French soon controlled, in one compact unit, all of the eastern part of Indochina: Tonkin, Annam, and Cochin-China. In the middle of the twentieth century these three regions were gathered together under the name of Vietnam. West of this area are the states of Cambodia and Laos. The French also pushed into the Chinese province of Yunnan.

Sailing ships and steamships moved in and out of the ports of the mainland and the busy islands. Their cargoes were varied and rich: coconuts, kapok, rubber, sisal, spices, sugar, tapioca, tin, tobacco. Today Southeast Asia produces two-thirds of the world's supply of tin. Before the Second World War the plantations of Southeast Asia produced more than 90 per cent of the world's rubber. From the thousands of islands in the sweep of the Pacific there still are shipped to Europe and America the cargoes of chromium, cocoa, coconuts, cotton, iron, nickel, pepper, pineapples, rice, sugar cane, yams.

Far to the south of the East Indies the British were moving forward in the development of Australia and New Zealand. In December, 1769, Captain James Cook had reached the shores of New Zealand. The natives were hostile.

Cook claimed the land for Britain, but made no landing. In March, 1770, he did land on the coast of New South Wales in Australia. In 1788 several English convicts were transported to Australia's Botany Bay. Soon several free settlers came. Slowly new colonies were planted. By 1850 six states had been established: New South Wales, Queensland, Victoria, Tasmania, South Australia, and West Australia. The discovery of gold in 1851 hastened the pace of Australia's growth. In 1850 its population was about 400,000; in 1860 it was more than 800,000; by 1914 it was about 5,000,000.

Late in the nineteenth century the six states of Australia, anxious to have a common railroad and tariff policy and nervous about the advance of German power in the lands to the north of them, especially the Bismarck Archipelago, agreed to form a federal union. The act of the Imperial Parliament creating the Commonwealth of Australia became effective in 1901.

The islands of New Zealand lie about 1,200 miles west and south of Australia. The first important settlements in New Zealand were made in 1840. More than 1,000 tough and resolute settlers were brought from Britain by the New Zealand Land Company. In the same year the British signed the Treaty of Waitangi with the Maoris, the natives of the islands. New Zealand gradually became known throughout the world for her wool, her wheat, and her remarkable achievements in democratic government, labor reforms, and social legislation.

The United States occupied the Midway Islands in 1867. After prolonged disputes with Great Britain and Germany the United States finally agreed to divide Samoa with Germany, and Britain moved out. In 1897 the United States annexed the Hawaiian Islands—these were the Sandwich Islands where Captain Cook had been killed in 1779.

At the close of the Spanish-American War the Philippine Islands—there are eleven large islands and about five thousand small ones—were ceded by Spain to the United States. Spain also surrendered Puerto Rico and Guam. For three years the Philippines continued to fight against the United States. Then they yielded and began to prepare themselves by peaceful means for the independence and self-government they later achieved.

About the annexation of the Philippines, President William McKinley of the United States wrote:

> And one night it came to me this way—I don't know how it was, but it came: (1) that we could not give them back to Spain—that would be cowardly and dishonorable; (2) that we could not turn them over to France or Germany—our commercial rivals in the Orient —that would be bad business and discreditable; (3) that we could not leave them to themselves—they were unfit for self-government—and they would soon have anarchy and misrule over there worse than Spain's was; and (4) that there was nothing left for us to do but to take

them all, and to educate the Filipinos, and uplift and civilize and Christianize them, and by God's grace do the very best we could by them, as our fellow men for whom Christ also died. And then I went to bed and went to sleep and slept soundly.

The opening phases of the race and rush of European states for concessions in China were described in Chapter 35. Once the gates of China had been opened to strangers and aliens they were not easily closed. More and more Chinese ports were entered by Western warships, troops, and traders. New areas were carved out and set aside for foreign commerce and foreign residents. In certain special sections of several Chinese port cities the European aliens obtained extraterritorial rights: Western schools and hospitals, Western judges and laws. Sometimes their own Western gunboats appeared and troops from their homelands came to visit.

It was not surprising that many Chinese leaders were angered and embittered by European pressures and the blustering and arrogant orders of some "old China hands" who knew the real weakness of China. Under the rickety and corrupt Manchu despotism many astute European businessmen shamelessly grasped and grabbed concessions wherever they could; often their methods were quite unscrupulous. These men and their manners helped to increase the obstinate and deep-rooted dislike of many Chinese for the invaders from Europe. The air was charged with hostility.

Some of the Chinese were also troubled by the mounting power of Japan. Their fears were increased when Japan defeated China on land and sea in the war of 1894–1895. The leading Chinese commanders committed suicide. By the terms of the peace treaty of Shimonoseki, China handed over to the Japanese victors the islands of Formosa (Taiwan) and the Pescadores, agreed to open four Chinese cities to trade, including the inland city of Chungking. China also declared that Korea was independent and thus open to Japanese penetration—Japan annexed Korea in 1910. Japan also got an indemnity of $150,000,000 and the Liaotung Peninsula, including Port Arthur. France, Germany, and Russia at once insisted that Japan must hand back the Liaotung Peninsula to China. Japan was forced to accede to this demand; all the rest of her rewards she kept.

The European powers did not intend that what had been denied to Japan should also be denied to them. Russia soon got a twenty-five-year lease to the strategic spots of Port Arthur and Dairen. The British obtained the harbor of Weihaiwei "for as long a period as Port Arthur shall remain in the possession of Russia." Britain also obtained the part of the Kowloon peninsula on the mainland opposite Hong Kong that had not been ceded to her in 1842. Germany used the murder of a German Catholic missionary in China as an excuse to get a lease of the Chinese port of Kiaochow (Tsingtao). France

] Ships of the German fleet built before the First World War to challenge Great Britain's command of the seas

[113]

he Invitation," by Louis Rae-
kers, a cartoon published dur-
; the First World War. The
vitation" is to an elderly Bel-
n to sign up for work in a
rman munitions factory.

PLATE XXXIX

PLATE
XL

[114]

Captured Chinese soldiers being forced to carry supplies for the Japanese in
Manchuria (March, 1932).

[115]

Anthony Eden, British Foreign Secretary, speaks before the League of Nations in July, 1936. The
power of the League is crumbling fast.

got a ninety-nine-year lease on the Bay of Kwangchow in the Kwangtung Province and several mining and railways concessions in other areas.

For several years the Russians had been pressing eastwards to Siberia and Alaska and south towards the Amur River. In 1858 China had consented to a change in the Treaty of Nerchinsk that had kept the Russians out of the Amur territory. Under the new arrangement Russia got the north bank of the Amur. Two years later Russia obtained the Primorsk region east of the Ussuri River from China and built the port and naval station of Vladivostok on the Sea of Japan. In 1896 China signed a military treaty with Russia. Russia wanted to extend her Trans-Siberian Railway (completed in 1905) through Manchuria to Vladivostok. The Chinese agreed to the building of the "Chinese Eastern Railway" to join the Trans-Siberian Railway to that Russian port.

Meanwhile a number of European nations extended their power in China by lending the Manchu government money. Russia and France advanced the Chinese the funds to pay the first installment due on the indemnity imposed on China by Japan in 1895 after the Sino-Japanese War. Britain and France made later loans. The Manchu government borrowed a total of about $160,-000,000 from Europe.

In July, 1900, John Hay, the American secretary of state, sent a circular to the major powers of the world, declaring that it was the purpose of the government of the United States "to act concurrently with the other powers" and "to seek a solution which may bring about permanent peace and safety in China, preserve Chinese territorial and administrative unity, protect all rights guaranteed to friendly powers by treaty and international law, and safeguard for the world the principle of equal and impartial trade with all parts of the Chinese Empire." This "Open Door" policy was acceptable to Great Britain, France, Germany, Italy, and Japan. Russia did not approve.

In 1900 the famous and formidable Boxer Rebellion erupted in the Chinese provinces of Manchuria, Hopei, and Shansi. The members of the secret society of the Boxers, whose proper name was "The Literary and Patriotic Order of Harmonious Fists," were determined to drive the hated aliens once and for all out of China. They used such slogans as "Protect the country, destroy the foreigner." In the disturbances that surged through China several hundred European missionaries and thousands of Chinese Christians were slaughtered. Foreign legations were besieged. Rowdy elements joined the Boxers in scenes of violence and plunder.

An international army, containing troops from six nations, was swiftly formed to answer the challenge of the defiant Chinese. This international force occupied and looted Peking and sacked the palace of the Empress Tz'u Hsi—she had fled for safety to Shensi province. The troops then marched into Hopei province, burning and killing as they went. The government of China was confronted with several demands, including one for the payment of an indemnity of $333,900,000. It may be remarked in passing that Russian troops had been moved into Manchuria to crush the Boxers there. The Russian government signed an agreement stating that these troops would be withdrawn. That promise Russia did not keep.

For more than 2,000 years China had been almost untouched by foreign influence. Now, at last, thousands of ambitious and enterprising men from outside China were sweeping into the land in steadily rising waves. The aggressive West had breached the Chinese Wall of isolationism.

To the north was Russia; the bear was prowling and hungry. Across the sea was Japan, anxious to disfigure China. Britain, France, Germany, and the United States moved in the forefront of the picture. Inside China was the weak and corrupt Manchu government, its power ebbing away. Within China, too, were the ferments and unrest among the people that no man could measure but every man could feel. The imperial Manchu government, its recent history so marred and muddled, was soon to be swept away by a republican revolution. Then there were new questions, new answers, and much new turmoil.

It is true that at the height of the years of Imperialism and Manifest Destiny there was often oppression, injustice, and the damaging exploitation of native peoples. It is also true that too much is sometimes made of these dark facts today. It must not be forgotten that there were also exciting and rewarding things done in the interests of the natives. Often the agents of Imperialism and Manifest Destiny roused in the primitive peoples a desire to rise in the scale of civilization, a wish to learn, an awareness of human dignity, an impatience to obtain political independence and to escape from the thralldom of poverty and disease. These were the first signs of the sense of urgency and enterprise that sweeps and leaps through Asia and Africa today.

In the midst of the schisms and confusions that rack our contemporary world an optimist may feel and assert that mankind is moving slowly along a road that leads to the emancipation and enlightenment of every human being and to the day when "Earth shall be fair and all her people one." This fortunate state of affairs may come to pass. On the other hand, it may not. The wise historian is not inclined to hazard his sanity and fortunes in the labyrinths of speculation about the future. The mantle of the prophet is not for him to don. Against the background of his knowledge he can point to probabilities, possibilities, and alternatives, nothing more.

Chapter 40

POWER AND POVERTY:
EAST AND WEST

"Multitudes, multitudes in the valley of decision."
—Joel, III, 14

I N SOME chapters of human history the successive generations of men did
not venture far from the paths beaten out by their ancestors. These were
years of apathy, vacillation, doldrums, peace, and sluggish quiet. At other
times men have traveled rapidly away from the familiar roads and places.
The amazing nineteenth century, for instance, was filled with the achievements of such unwearied pioneers, the enterprising pacemakers of mankind.

As the world moved towards the twentieth century the winds of change
were sweeping over Asia, Europe, and America. Those vast lands were never
the same again.

Shortly after the visit of Commodore Matthew Perry in 1854 there was a
swift and significant change in the government of the Japanese Empire. For
centuries the real ruler of Japan had been the shogun, an official whose functions and great power were described in earlier pages. The authority of the
emperor—the Mikado—had been great in theory, small in fact. In 1868 the
Tokugawa shogunate was overthrown and the young Emperor Mutsuhito
assumed again the sovereignty that had been taken away from his predecessors.

Mutsuhito was an able emperor, a realist, and a reformer. He established the
"Meiji" rule of "enlightened government" and issued a "Charter Oath" in
which he promised that the "uncivilized customs of the past" would be ended
and "learning and wisdom" would be sought "throughout the world." The
emperor and several of his advisers saw that if Japan did not put herself in a
position to compete with the West, then she would probably fall before the
assaults of European imperialism.

Soon after the fall of the shogunate there came a number of "Western" reforms in Japan. Young men were sent to Europe to study such subjects as medicine, agriculture, and engineering. Japanese leaders went abroad to look and learn. In 1872, for instance, a large Japanese mission visited Europe and the United States. "We come," said Vice-Ambassador (later Prince) Ito, "to study your strength, that by adopting wisely your better ways we may here-after be stronger ourselves." Advisers from the United States and France helped the Japanese reform their system of education. Soon the Japanese were the only literate nation in Asia. French advisers helped the Japanese build a new law code. Feudalism was abolished. Several European advisers provided technical aid in such fields as agriculture, commerce, and industry. A new civil-service system was established. The Japanese navy looked to the British navy as a model. The Japanese army looked to Germany. In 1876 a system of national conscription was adopted in imitation of the nations of Europe. "Western" banks, hotels, postal services, business methods, telegraphs, and railways appeared. In 1875 a senate was created. In 1883 a new constitution established a chancellor, a cabinet of nine ministers responsible to the emperor, a Diet composed of a House of Peers and a House of Representatives elected by limited manhood suffrage. The samurai and businessmen controlled the government. No industrial worker or peasant had a right to vote.

The new ways did not completely oust the old. The ancient ideas of loyalty, honor, endurance, patience, self-denial, obedience, and duty and the values of Shinto and Confucius were not destroyed. The old patterns of morals and ethics still prevailed. The reverence for the emperor was still unshaken. He was the focal point of the state. The constitution of 1883 stated what everybody knew to be true: "The Emperor is sacred and inviolable . . . combining in himself the rights of sovereignty. . . . He has supreme command of the Army and the Navy . . . declares war, makes peace, concludes treaties."

Meanwhile the power of Japanese industry and commerce, based upon cheap labor and astounding enterprise, advanced at a startling pace. The textile industry, for instance, challenged the mills of Lancashire in the markets of the world. As a result of the increased income brought by industry and trade, the middle-class white-collar workers, the craftsmen, and the merchants wanted the franchise and more political rights. The old samurai, for their part, disliked and feared the big cities and the resulting threat to the prestige and power of the aristocratic landlords and agriculture. A new conflict of classes was now possible in Japan. There, as in Europe and America, the whirling wheels of production had brought more unsolved problems of social justice, more steam, steel, smoke, slag, and slums. In Japan, too, were hollow stomachs and resentful hearts among the unemployed, the sick, the homeless, and the unwanted.

Meanwhile the progress of the military and naval strength of Japan was spectacular. The British and German advisers had taught the Japanese well;

Japanese skill and persistence did the rest. In 1894 Japan won a crushing victory over China in the battle of Haiyang. The Treaty of Shimonoseki, earlier described, gave Japan Formosa, a large indemnity, and extensive privileges in China. In 1902 Japan made an alliance with Great Britain. In 1904 Japan moved into war with Russia. Russia's Baltic fleet steamed around the Cape of Good Hope to be almost completely destroyed by Japan's Admiral Tojo at the battle of Tsushima. The Japanese captured Russia's "impregnable base" at Port Arthur after a siege of eight months. The Treaty of Portsmouth of 1905, also described earlier, gave Japan the southern half of the island of Sakhalin and prepared the way for Japan's annexation of Korea in 1910. It was clear that Japan was now ready to take her place in the councils and commerce and wars of the world.

Across the Sea of Japan the uncounted millions of China continued to fight for survival in the midst of contrasting scenes of incredible squalor and beauty. Most Chinese knew little and cared less about the world outside the narrow rounds of their daily lives. Their task was to get enough to eat, to have a few pleasures, and to live as long as they could in their disorderly and insecure world. The streets of the cities were filled with the old and familiar sounds: the piercing voices of the street hawkers, the sharp tones of controversy, the cries of unhappy babies. The shops and stalls still sold the tea, jade, porcelain, and silk, the lanterns and the medicines made from dried snakes and centipedes. In the country, the workers, often plagued by floods and famine, toiled in the fields as their ancestors had done before them. The patterns of habit and tradition were not easily changed. The power of the past was great. Great wealth and poverty stood side by side.

It is correct to say that the impact of the West in the nineteenth century ended the centuries of Chinese isolation. It is also true that the coming of the Europeans and Americans altered the lives of only a few of the multitudes of China. Resistance, ignorance, and apathy often went together. In later years the Chinese were to discard a lot of their culture; but those times were some distance ahead in the twentieth century.

The defeat of the Boxer uprising of 1900 meant that the Western nations drove still more wedges into the sovereignty and independence of China. Japan was able to learn from the West and at the same time to keep her independence, her emperor, her Shinto, and her army and navy. China did not try to follow the example of Japan; hard in consequence was to be her fate.

From many quarters trouble assailed the decaying Manchu government of China. Great Britain threatened China's interests in Tibet. Russia and Japan pressed in upon China's borders. After Japan defeated Russia in 1905 the Japanese seizures, pressures, and nibblings increased. The young Chinese intellectuals insisted upon the desperate need for reforms in the administration

of the state. Chinese students were studying in Japan and the United States
—the American government gave up a large part of the Boxer indemnity to
provide scholarships for Chinese students in American colleges. Many of
these students came home with keen eyes and sharp tongues. They wanted reforms and they wanted them soon. They opposed the backward-looking
Manchus, the Confucian monarchy, the old ways of doing things. They
dreamed of a new China. Secret societies began to flourish again. Vague words
were written about liberty, equality, and representative government.

There were a few reforms. Some Western administrative methods were
introduced into the central government. In 1906 an imperial decree ordered
the gradual elimination of the opium poppy; the decree also prohibited the
smoking of opium by government employees and all other men under sixty
years of age. Slavery was abolished in 1910. The first provincial assemblies
met in 1909, the first national assembly in 1910. Several patriotic Chinese
were pleased to see a boycott of trade with the United States when the Washington government placed a series of restrictions upon Chinese immigration.
Meanwhile the economic advance of China, stimulated by foreign investments,
continued swiftly. Many factories were built, especially for the manufacture of
cotton goods and matches. Iron and coal mines multiplied. Railways increased
in length and number.

In 1908 the selfish and astute Empress Tz'u Hsi died. She was succeeded
by the Emperor P'u-i, a child about three years old. The Manchu dynasty
had lasted for 264 years and now it was nearing its end. The old dragon flag
of the Manchus was soon to be pulled down and in its place was to fly the
flag of the new Republic of China, a flag of five colors—red, yellow, blue,
white, and black—representing the Chinese, Manchus, Moslems, Mongols,
and Tibetans.

For several years one of the leaders in the agitation for change had been a
Chinese Protestant patriot and philosopher named Sun Yat-sen (1867–1925).
This famous "Father of the Chinese Republic" was born on a farm near
Canton. He studied in Hawaii and Hong Kong and obtained his doctor's
degree in medicine. Later he married into the famous Soong family. Whenever
Sun Yat-sen found ideas that seemed to him to be sound and good, he made
them his own. For several years he practiced medicine in Macao. There he
helped to spread many reform ideas, so many that the authorities asked him
to leave.

Shortly after Sun Yat-sen returned to Canton the Manchus put a price upon
his head. He fled to Hong Kong. Then he went to Japan—he organized a
revolutionary society in Tokyo—and then to the United States, Great Britain,
and several European countries. In 1912 he got back to China. A few months
earlier an organized revolt had broken out against the Manchu government.
In February, 1912, the young Manchu emperor abdicated and went to live
quietly in the Forbidden City of Peking. Sun Yat-sen became the President

of the new Republic of China. The outcome of this "Chinese Revolution" was not clear in Sun Yat-sen's lifetime. The consequences were still more obscure in the years of the rule of Chiang Kai-shek and the Kuomintang. Soon the challenge of the Chinese Communists was to mark the opening phases of another revolution.

The tides of change that flowed in Japan and China were moving into most of the other lands of awakening Asia. The men from the West who carried new goods and guns to the East also brought new ideas. The stimulated leaders of Asia began to have some ideas of their own. Meanwhile the battles for land and the struggles for food went on. Famine and pestilence struck and killed. The birth and death rates stayed high. Political and religious divisions and conflicts did not diminish. True, there were improvements and reforms in many fields: law, education, medicine, agriculture, industry; but they were slow, agonizingly slow. To many intelligent and sensitive men of Asia the pace of the advance was not rapid enough. They were men in a hurry. Often their ideas and feelings about reform and progress got mixed up with the new demands of nationalism.

In India, for instance, the clamors for self-government and independence grew louder and more formidable. Such pieces of legislation as the Morley-Minto Reforms (1907, 1909) and the Indian Councils Acts (1861, 1892, 1909) did not satisfy the wishes of the Indian nationalists. There was much unrest, many demonstrations, frequent demands for sweeping changes. There were a few voices of moderation, many ones of violence.

The patriotic and religious Servants of India Society (Arya Samaj) was founded in 1875. In 1885 the first session of the India National Congress, predominantly Hindu, met at Poona and demanded Indian representatives in the government, the abolition of the salt tax, Indian officers in the army. In the latter part of the nineteenth century more members of the Congress supported direct and violent action; their radical voices often advocated the use of murder and boycott as political weapons. The extreme Hindu nationalists wanted independence from Great Britain; the moderates wanted Britain to stay with limited powers. In 1906 the All India Moslem League was formed; it demanded the creation of a separate Moslem state.

On the eve of the First World War Mahatma Gandhi returned from South Africa to his homeland. He soon proclaimed his doctrine of nonviolent opposition to the British rule in India, disobedience of all laws that he considered unjust, passive noncooperation. The saintly and subtle Gandhi was soon to show that he was one of the most remarkable human beings of the twentieth century.

The chapters of history that were written in the continent of Europe during the decades preceding the First World War were filled with disputes and frustrations and many achievements. The central themes were the same as they have been in all the long tale of mankind: continuity and change, action and reaction, growth and decay.

In Russia three tsars ruled: Alexander II (1855–1881), Alexander III (1881–1894), and Nicholas II (1894–1917).

During the early years of his reign Alexander II was a reforming liberal, to a point consistent with prudence and common sense. He emancipated the serfs in the period between 1861 and 1866, an important event in the history of Russia, even though the Emancipation Law brought less freedom than its title would suggest. Alexander also wrought changes in the law courts, local government, and imperial administration. It seemed that perhaps the grim and closed and frightened Russia of earlier centuries was slowly passing away. But hopes and dreams fade. Alexander II was disturbed by a Polish uprising (1863), the spread of revolutionary ideas, and three attempts to assassinate him. He was slowly persuaded that reaction was better than liberalism. His policy became one of heavy repression, very similar to the "Nicholas system" of his father, the ruthless tsar who had come to the throne at the hour of the famous Decembrist Revolt in 1825. In 1881 Alexander II was murdered. He was not widely mourned.

Many Russians, especially the writers and the makers of philosophies, revolted against the stifling autocracy, the society that demanded hypocrisy, conformity, and obedience. They joined in the secret societies. They supported the *narodniki* (back to the people) movement. They read and debated the writings of the anarchists Michael Bakunin (1814–1876) and Peter Kropotkin (1842–1921), especially Kropotkin's *Mutual Aid* (1902) and *The Conquest of Bread* (1888). Some of them came to believe that the coercion of the state was unnecessary and that governments were usually stupid and corrupt. Some also approved of the Nihilists with their doctrines of destruction and their weapons of terror. "Virtue marries crime in times of anarchy." The "men of the sixties"—Dobrolyubov, Pisarev (he spent twenty years in prison), and Chernyshevsky—escaped the secret police and the censors and preached the cause of violence and rebellion among the peasants. *Kolokol* (*The Bell*), the journal of Alexander Herzen (1812–1870), the father of Russian liberalism, was smuggled into Russia and was widely read, especially by the restless youth. Several of them could not resist this heady wine.

Nor could they escape the influence of many other famous and enterprising men who strode vigorously across the stage of Russian history. In Chapter 22 and Chapter 37 some of these interesting and intensely active individuals were briefly identified, defined, and described: Chekhov, Gogol, Rimski-Korsakov, Tolstoy, Tschaikovsky, Turgenev. There was also Elie Metchnikoff, who discovered that the white corpuscles in the blood can engulf and kill some of the germs that invade the body. There was Dmitri Mendeleev, the chemist who predicted the existence and properties of several unknown elements (see Chapter 38). There were others, too. Among such men as these there were many splendid gifts. Those gifts were used, with much labor and hard trials. Most creations, reforms, and discoveries are the children of struggle.

Meanwhile the vast Russian Empire expanded. The tsarist conquest of Central Turkestan (Soviet Central Asia) was finished in 1882; the colonization of Siberia grew rapidly as the Trans-Siberian Railway pushed eastward; the 6,000-mile track was completed in 1905. Thousands of Russians became excited about the bitter debates of the "Westernizers" and the Slavophiles. Should Russia turn towards Western Europe and its ways or look within to Mother Russia and the old Slav heritage?

Alexander III (1881–1894), a dull and obstinate man, insisted that "the voice of God orders us to stand firm at the helm of government" and proclaimed that an iron regime of orthodoxy, repression, reaction, and autocracy must prevail. Russia was to be "frozen." The Jews, the Poles, and the Nihilists must be crushed. Revolutionary agitation was savagely suppressed by the hands of tyranny. The secret rebels were dealt with by the secret police.

In 1894 Nicholas II (1894–1917), obstinate and weak, came to the Romanov throne at the age of twenty-six. Nicholas stood firmly against the floods of dissent. He survived the shock of defeat in the war with Japan of 1904, the strikes and violence at home, the troubles arising from the "Russification" policies, the drama of "Bloody Sunday" and the Revolution of 1905, the results of the October Manifesto, and the experiments with dumas. "Let it be understood by all," said Nicholas II, "that I shall employ all my powers in the best interest of the people but the principle of autocracy will be sustained by me as firmly and universally as it was by my never-to-be-forgotten father."

The ill-starred Nicholas II failed in the end to uphold the cause of autocracy. The reign of the last of the Romanovs came to an end in the grim days of 1917 when the Bolsheviks trained the guns of the cruiser *Aurora* on the Winter Palace, when the resourceful Gregory Rasputin died at last, when Nikolai Lenin set up his first government in the Smolny Institute, protected by artillery and machine guns. Lenin said: "The peasants want land. I will promise it to them. I will simply say—go and take it, it is yours." Soon Nicholas II, the tsar and "Little Father" of all the Russias, the Empress Alexandra, their five children, and six servants were shot to death in a cellar in central Russia. "We will now proceed to construct the Soviet order," said Lenin. And constructed it was.

The German Empire continued its rise to wealth and power. The federal government consisted of the emperor, the Bundesrat representing the states, and the Reichstag representing the people. Prussia had seventeen of the sixty-one seats in the Bundesrat. The emperor was the king of Prussia. The chancellor, who presided over the Bundesrat and guided the progress and policies of the empire, was also a Prussian: Otto von Bismarck, the man whose astute and ruthless diplomacy had forged the German Empire.

The chancellor was appointed by the emperor and was responsible to him alone. There was nothing similar to a democratic British cabinet system in Germany. The German government was enlightened, efficient, authoritarian, autocratic. In the main political party groups of the Reichstag—Conservatives, Center, National Liberals, Radicals, and Social Democrats—there appeared no outstanding leaders. The impotent Reichstag was sometimes called "the Hall of Echoes." Effective leadership in Germany was provided by one realist: Otto von Bismarck. After 1890 the Emperor William II tried to replace Bismarck; the consequences of his failure shook the world.

Bismarck sought no colonies for Germany. He wanted no naval rivalry with the British. In foreign affairs his main object was to isolate France, Germany's bitter enemy. His adroit diplomacy, described in the next chapter, shaped the Triple Alliance and the Re-insurance Treaty with Russia. When Bismarck was Germany's pilot the state was safe.

Inside Germany the imperial government steadily enlarged its functions. There was more centralization as determined attempts were made to "make the Germans sink their localisms in the common consciousness of national unity." An imperial bank was established, an imperial criminal and civil code, an imperial railway board, a new national currency. Many intolerant German nationalists denounced the Roman Catholics, the Jews, and the Socialists as "internationalists" and not loyal Germans. Many liberals felt that the *Syllabus of Errors* (*Quanta Cura*), the celebrated encyclical issued by Pope Pius IX in 1864 (see Chapter 38) and the dogma of papal infallibility in the realm of faith and morals proclaimed by the Vatican Council in 1870 were both opposed to modern ideas of liberalism and secular progress. The anti-Roman Catholic movement in Germany resulted in the bitter *Kulturkampf*. Bismarck distrusted the Roman Catholics—a third of the inhabitants of the empire—because he felt that their final allegiance was to Rome and they supported local and separatist tendencies in the state. In 1872 the Jesuits were expelled from Germany. The "May Laws" (1873–1875) passed by the Prussian Landtag against the "black international" placed the education and control of the clergy under the state. Civil marriage was made compulsory.

Pope Pius IX declared these laws invalid and asked the faithful not to obey them. Despite the heavy pressures of Bismarck and his agents the Roman Catholic Church resisted. The Catholic Center Party gained many seats in the Reichstag—and so did the Social Democrats. The National Liberals and the Radicals, the supporters of Bismarck, lost heavily. Bismarck did not want to try to govern without the Reichstag. He was also anxious about the rise of socialism, the "red international." Between 1878 and 1887 almost all of the anti-Roman Catholic legislation was revoked. Bismarck had been beaten.

Bismarck now turned against the Social Democrats, the party that wanted a socialist democratic republic. It was the "internationalist" aspect of socialism that infuriated Bismarck. Two attempts to murder William II, Bismarck blamed on the Socialists. The "Exceptional Laws" of 1878 forbade Socialist meetings, clubs, publications. Thousands of Socialists were put in prison or sought safety in flight. Nevertheless, the Social Democratic Party increased its numbers. Repression did not succeed. In 1890 the anti-Socialist legislation was repealed. Bismarck was beaten again.

Meanwhile Bismarck concluded that the industrial workers must be helped by the state "so that they will not be run over and trampled under foot on the highway of life." In the 1880's a bold and comprehensive system of social insurance was created by the Sickness Insurance Law of 1883, the Accident Insurance Law of 1884, and the Old Age and Invalidity Law of 1889. The workers, said Bismarck, must be taught to regard the state as a friend. Then they would not turn to socialism. The specters of socialism and syndicalism frightened Bismarck. The modern fear of class wars within states joined the older fear of national wars between states.

In these years there was a tremendous industrial expansion in Germany. "Tall chimneys grew like mushrooms." The progress in the coal, iron, steel, shipping, chemical, and textile industries astounded the world. Science and efficiency became and remained the watchwords of the new order. The heart-beats of several cities were the thud and thump of the industrial machines. The factories grew hungry for raw materials and markets. Competition with foreign nations increased all over the planet. In our modern world economic interdependence goes hand in hand with rivalry. From many of the battles in business and industry only a few survivors can emerge.

Beyond the Rhine stood France. The battle of Sedan of 1870 was to the French a shocking event. They were to remember that great defeat for a long time. Nor could they forget the loss of Alsace-Lorraine. *"N'en parlez jamais, y pensez toujours."*

After the fall of Napoleon III the energetic Léon Gambetta, leader of the Republicans, had tried to resist the German invaders. His difficulties were immense and he failed. The artisans and workers of Paris then formed a reckless and obstinate Commune that fought against the provisional Republican government at Versailles. Léon Gambetta and Adolphe Thiers slowly pulled down and smashed the Commune. The struggle in Paris was desperate, the destruction and brutality frightful. After the Republicans had won, thousands of their opponents were executed or exiled; more than 17,000 supporters of the Paris Commune perished in the struggle. The gulf between the working classes and the bourgeoisie was widened then; it has never been bridged or closed.

Adolphe Thiers became the "Head of the Executive Power." Thiers, a long-time bourgeois monarchist, changed his mind and championed the Republic as "that form of government which divides us least." From the beginning he was opposed by the men who marched under the banners and leaders of both the Left and the Right. In 1873 he was forced to resign.

Meanwhile Léon Gambetta, the "traveling salesman of the Republic," crusaded for the cause of the new order. Gambetta was an excellent leader. His resounding phrases stirred the hearts of those who listened, especially those who remembered his deeds. The power of his personality was tremendous; and nobody could question his love of France or his courage. The Royalists supporting the Count de Chambord almost got control of the government; but "almost" was not enough. In the end the Republicans won, and what they won they kept.

The Republican constitution, completed in 1875, provided for a Senate and a Chamber of Deputies elected by universal manhood suffrage for a term of four years. The two chambers in joint session were to elect a president for a term of seven years. The cabinet was to be responsible to the Chamber of Deputies. Because there continued to be so many small groups and parties in France the cabinets were often short-lived.

Marshal MacMahon, who succeeded Thiers, tried very hard to get the Royalists into power in 1877. "When France has spoken her sovereign voice," said Gambetta, "you will be forced to give in or give up." The Republicans won an election by a large majority and President MacMahon then "gave up." In 1879 he was succeeded by Jules Grévy. After Grévy came five presidents before the First World War: Sadi Carnot (1887–1894), Casimir Périer (1894–1895), Félix Faure (1895–1899), Emile Loubet (1899–1906), and Armand Fallières (1906–1913).

Meanwhile there were reforms in the armed services. Fortresses were built on the French frontiers. Conscription was introduced. Colonies were multiplied —by 1914 the French colonial empire was next to the British in size. Trade unions were legalized. A new system of education—free, universal, and compulsory—was established; this was the work of the anticlerical Jules Ferry. Business enterprise swiftly revived. Great advances came in several industries, especially iron and steel, silk, wine, transportation.

Not all was progress, stability, and light. The ancient quarrels between church and state often flamed. "Clericalism is the enemy!" Gambetta cried in 1877, and many Frenchmen believed him. Sometimes cracks appeared in the wall of the Third Republic. The handsome and nerveless General Boulanger, for instance, came close to seizing control of the state in 1889 and closer still to a trial for high treason. The Socialists, Syndicalists, Royalists, and scores of other groups challenged the Republican government. There were intermittent scandals—the Panama affair, for example—and feverish national disputes about the dramatic case of Captain Alfred Dreyfus, arrested in 1894 for selling military secrets to the Germans. Thousands of Frenchmen vehemently insisted that Dreyfus was guilty; thousands replied that he was not. When at last the innocence of Dreyfus was established, the ship of the Republic moved into calmer waters.

The trade unions increased in strength and number. Several factory laws and workmen's compensation acts were passed. An old-age pensions system was created. The press was free. Universal manhood suffrage was firmly fixed in the state political system. The Third Republic had survived.

As Great Britain moved towards the end of the age of imperialism the Conservative government of Lord Salisbury began to falter and fail. In 1902 Salisbury was succeeded as Conservative leader by his nephew, the brilliant and fastidious Arthur James Balfour. Balfour was confronted by heavy problems. There were difficulties about education, labor, liquor, imperial policy, and preferential tariffs. The Liberals, supported by the new and truculent Labor Party, kept up their unceasing attacks. In 1906 the Conservatives were defeated in a national election. The Liberals won 379 seats in the House of Commons; the Conservatives 132; the Irish Nationalists 83; and the new Labor Party 51.

The Liberals came into power pledged to a policy of vigorous social reform. Their cabinet was one of the ablest of modern times. The Prime Minister was Sir Henry Campbell-Bannerman, a tactful, honest, courageous, and shrewd Presbyterian. The Chancellor of the Exchequer was the erudite Henry Herbert Asquith, a Nonconformist product of Balliol and Yorkshire—he was to succeed Campbell-Bannerman as Prime Minister in 1908. The Secretary of War was Richard Burton Haldane, famous lawyer and philosopher, pugnacious Liberal imperialist. The Secretary of State for India was John Morley, celebrated author and critic. The President of the Board of Trade was David Lloyd George, filled with Celtic fervor and shrewdness. The Foreign Secretary was Sir Edward Grey, a Liberal imperialist. This cabinet has been called "the Ministry of all the Talents." It was indeed.

The years following 1906 were marked in Britain by much social legislation, many national ferments and reverberating disputes, uncounted doubts and anxieties. The titles of some significant acts of Parliament suggest their content: Workmen's Compensation Act, Trade Disputes Act, Old Age Pensions Act, House and Town Planning Act, Trade Boards Act, Labor Exchanges Act, the National Insurance Act. The Irish of southern Ireland continued to demand Home Rule; the mainsprings of Irish Nationalist policy remained the same: obstruction, sabotage, oratory, and violence. The suffragettes wanted the suffrage; the militant ones caused some trouble. The workers asked for shorter hours and higher wages and many other things besides.

The dramatic "People's Budget" of 1909—so carefully prepared by David Lloyd George—roused a storm of controversy. It included a 10 per cent death duty upon all estates valued at £200,000 or more, a tax on "undeveloped" land, a higher income tax, a tax (20%) on all increase of urban land values. The House of Lords vetoed the budget. Bitter political campaigns raged over Britain. "The landlords," said David Lloyd George, "are not in business but in blackmail." He described the House of Lords as "five hundred men, ordinary men, chosen accidentally from among the unemployed." He pleaded for the workers and "the wounded soldiers of humanity." The expanding naval program and the financial demands of the new social reforms meant a large tax increase. "Democracy," William Ewart Gladstone had said, "will prove a very costly mistress."

The British voters supported the view of the Liberals, the Irish Nationalists, and Laborites in a national election. Then the House of Lords yielded and passed the controversial budget. The veto power of the Lords was soon reduced by the Parliament Act of 1911. This act states that a money bill may not be delayed by the House of Lords for more than a month. No other bill may be delayed for more than two years. After 1911 it has not been possible for the House of Lords to thwart for long the will of the majority of the House of Commons.

Meanwhile the disputes about Irish Home Rule continued. In 1913 the Third Home Rule Bill was passed and there appeared the danger of civil war between Ulster and southern Ireland. In England there grew to ominous proportions a great social unrest, marked by a series of strikes and outbursts of violence. The problems of economic justice, of humanity and Christian kindness have troubled every generation of thoughtful and sensitive men.

Across the English Channel the clouds of war were gathering. Europe was soon to be plunged into a night darker than she had known.

Before the end of the Civil War in the United States, Abraham Lincoln had stated a hope of many of his contemporaries: "With malice toward none, with charity for all, with firmness in the right as God gives us to see the right, let us strive on to finish the work we are in, to bind up the nation's wounds. . . ."

In the South the harvest of the war was plainly visible. The economy was prostrate; the bonds were worthless; there was no gold; there was no money; there were few seed crops. Thousands of the people were homeless. About 3,000,000 slaves were free at last; but they were "turned loose, naked and hungry and destitute to the open sky."

When President Lincoln died several Northern members of Congress who wished revenge and a harsh peace raised their voices and summoned their power. President Andrew Johnson and his cabinet wanted to continue Lincoln's plans; but their opponents, led by Thaddeus Stevens and Charles Sumner, had their way. The Reconstruction Act of 1867 divided the South into five districts and placed them under military rule. By the Fourteenth Amendment the Negroes were given full citizenship. The leading Confederates were made incapable of holding federal office unless pardoned by Congress.

Many unprincipled Northern tricksters called "Carpetbaggers" grew rich with corruption, graft, and plunder. These years of darkness increased the bitterness and the political and economic disruption of the South. The United States had no cause to be proud of the "Carpetbaggers" or of the foolish programs and policies of Congress during the turmoil of the Reconstruction years before 1877 when Andrew Johnson and General Ulysses S. Grant, "the hero of Appomattox," were in the White House. Nor had it any reason to be complacent about the patterns of graft and corruption in the New York Tweed Ring, Philadelphia's Gas Ring, the deeds of "Doc" Alonzo Ames in Minneapolis, the rule in San Francisco of "Blind Boss Buckley."

When the Reconstruction ended, a new South began to emerge. The Southern whites moved into the Democratic party. There was a sudden and sound economic advance. New industries came. An agrarian revolt speeded the pace of change. The remarkable alterations in the body and face of the South have been superbly described in C. Vann Woodward's calm and judicious *Origins of the New South 1877–1913* and William B. Hesseltine's *Confederate Leaders in the New South*. Several other books—notably the numerous biographies—have been less successful; they have often helped to prolong the life of false ideas that belong in the hearts and heads of people who see through the sentimental mists the "Old South" of song and story, the land of magnolias and juleps and faithful slaves, the "Old South" that never existed at all. History must square with the facts. Sound and shrewd historians—Woodward, Hesseltine, Avery Craven, and their fellows—have helped us to see what those facts were in the lands of cotton and slavery and the belts where the Bible's fundamental truths had not been challenged by the secularism of the North.

There were six Presidents of the United States in the last quarter of the nineteenth century: Rutherford B. Hayes (1877), James A. Garfield (1881), Chester A. Arthur (1881), Grover Cleveland (1885), Benjamin Harrison (1889), Grover Cleveland (1893), and William McKinley (1897).

Many events of these years belong to the significant and interesting chapters of American history. There appeared, for instance, the long controversy about "free silver." The silver mines of Colorado, Idaho, Montana, and Wyoming produced so much silver that the money system of the United States was in jeopardy. In 1873—the year of a great depression—Congress decided to stop coining silver. The decision pushed up the price of gold and pleased the creditors and the "sound money" people who wanted to keep the gold standard. It displeased the "easy money" and debtor individuals who wanted "free silver." The disputes about currency continued almost to the end of the century when William Jennings Bryan, that famous evangelist and prophet, campaigned in 1896 for lower tariffs, an income tax, and "free silver." Said Bryan: "You shall not press down upon the brow of labor this crown of thorns, you shall not crucify mankind upon a cross of gold." Bryan always insisted that the foundation of American democracy and progress was agriculture: "Burn down your cities and leave our farms and your cities will spring up again as if by magic. But destroy our farms and the grass will grow in the streets of every city in the country."

Several new political parties rose and fell. How strong was the language of the members of the excited Populist party formed in 1892 by farmers troubled by mortgages and bad crops! "Corruption dominates the ballot box, the legislatures, the Congress. . . . The people are demoralized. . . . The fruits of the toil of millions are boldly stolen to build colossal fortunes for the few!" How sad was the fate of the Grange! How beautiful were the dreams of the men of the Greenback party—and how vehemently they demanded "easy money"! Highly exciting, too, were the numerous reform movements and the shining crusades against war, rum, and uncounted kinds of sin, the exposures of "the shame of the cities," the "evils" of giant trusts and corporations, the growth of the power of organized labor, the graft in local and national politics, the "single tax" men, the words and deeds of Carrie Nation, that Kansas suffragette who implored the farmers to "raise less corn and more hell," the crimson sins of "the Gilded Age" and the "Age of the Robber Barons."

Meanwhile General Custer and about 300 of his men were slain by the Sioux at the Little Big Horn (1876). The settlers still moved westward; the Indians retreated. In April, 1889, a land rush of 20,000 "boomers" marked the end of good free land and an unbroken frontier. The West no longer cast its spell or called in the old way to the restless spirits of the East. Out in the West the cattlemen fought with the sheep herders about the range lands and barbed wire and moved their cattle in great drives along the Chisholm Trail from the Texas grasslands towards the markets and the packers of the northlands and the east.

The United States was steadily growing in size, wealth, and population. More and more territories moved into settled statehood: Colorado (1876), Montana (1889), North Dakota (1889), South Dakota (1889), Washington (1889), Idaho (1890), Wyoming (1890). "The ever-retreating frontier of free land," wrote Frederick Jackson Turner, "is the key to American development." In 1790 the United States contained 294,000 square miles; in 1960 the total was 3,615,000 square miles. In 1790 the population of the United

States was about 4,000,000; in 1960 it was about 180,000,000. Millions of immigrants came from across the seas seeking liberty, happiness, prosperity, and power. No doubt some of them saw and remembered the words that still stand on the Statue of Liberty:

> Give me your tired, your poor
> Your huddled masses yearning to breathe free
> The wretched refuse of your teeming shore,
> Send these, the homeless, tempest-tossed, to me. . . .

The latter part of the nineteenth century in the United States was marked by much optimism, vitality, zeal, competition, ingenuity, and individualism. Several of these ideas, ideals, and practices, now so much admired, did not come into the main stream of American history until the eighteenth and nineteenth centuries. Despite the tides of tradition and legend the authoritarian New England Puritan never believed in individualism, democracy, or freedom of conscience. It was the generations that came after the seventeenth century that had new and different ideas. They changed the face of the land; and it kept on changing.

In 1869—the year that the Suez Canal was finished—the United States completed its first transcontinental railway. The steel fingers of the Great Northern reached all of the way to the Pacific coast. In 1860 there were 30,000 miles of railroads in the United States; in 1865 there were 35,000; in 1875, 75,000; in 1900, 200,000; in 1910, 240,000. In the midst of heavy immigration, court cases and rate wars, land grants and subsidies, the railway construction went on all over America. Canada finished the main line of the Canadian Pacific Railway in 1885. Upon the changing map of the United States appeared the Northern Pacific, the Southern Pacific, the Santa Fe, and many another line. There also appeared the names of many new canals and turnpikes. Not enough attention has been given by historians and others to the various revolutions in transportation that have helped to shape the history of the United States.

Great trusts and monopolies multiplied. Aggressive and efficient corporations expanded their power and profits in domestic and foreign markets. In 1901 the United States Steel Corporation was capitalized at $1,460,000,000. The massive strength of such companies as Standard Oil, American Telephone and Telegraph, International Harvester, General Electric, and the like became known to most Americans. Some men asked how it was possible to curb the power of the "aggressive" and "ruthless" giants. Was there too much control in the hands of too few men? Was it desirable to limit the activities of such financial tycoons and wizards as Carnegie, Duke, Fisk, Gould, Guggenheim, Harriman, Morgan, Rockefeller, Spreckels? Part of the answer was given by interstate commerce controls, the Sherman Act (1890) and the Clayton Anti-Trust Act (1914). There have been many attacks upon the great corporations in the United States and elsewhere. It is surprising that the strong case that can be made for most corporations has not yet been stated with coherence and skill to the world.

The stream of production steadily grew larger. By 1914 the United States was producing about 1,000,000,000 tons of coal a year; 60,000,000 tons of iron; 30,000,000 tons of steel. From over the seas of the world came raw materials to feed the factories: nickel, tin, vanadium, rubber, manganese, jute—the list was long. About twenty different metals, for example, go into the making of a modern automobile. Production, trade, and profit all increased. In 1850 the national wealth of the United States was about $7,000,000,000; by 1900 it was about $70,000,000,000.

Not all men moved in the sunshine of wealth and prosperity. There were depressions, unemployment, slums. There were riots in Pittsburgh in 1877. There were strikes: The Carnegie Steel Company Strike (1892), the Pullman Strike (1894). Eugene Debs and socialism appeared. There was the rise of labor organizations such as the Knights of Labor (1869), and the American Federation of Labor (1886) operating under a constitution written in 1881 by Samuel Gompers. The modern Committee (later Congress) for Industrial Organizations was not formed until 1935.

New machines and technological skills continued to increase the powers of man. A list of the major inventions of the age would fill many pages. Readers interested in the history of agriculture will think at once of John Deere's lightweight steel plow, Cyrus H. McCormick's reaper, the new chemical fertilizers. In other fields of man's endeavors these inventions helped to shape our contemporary world: telephone, telegraph, internal-combustion engine, Westinghouse air brake, Colt revolver, gasoline engine, electric motor, automatic coupler, electric light, rotary press, typewriter, sewing machine.

The men who stood at the edge of the twentieth century saw new devices and triumphs ahead. In 1903, for instance, an American named Wilbur Wright—it was a bleak December day at Kitty Hawk, North Carolina—flew a machine that stayed in the air for twelve seconds. It was an important event, how important nobody then could know.

In 1837 Ralph Waldo Emerson wrote: "We will walk on our own feet; we will work with our own hands; we will speak with our own minds." The words of Emerson stated a fact that is blazoned across the history of the United States. The lives of most Americans have never been sluggish or sloppy or shirking. They have believed, perhaps more than the people of any other nation, in the wisdom of risk and the sureness of change.

Chapter 41

ALLIANCES AND ARMS:
THE DARKENING SKY

"No single outstanding fact caused the war; really the grave blame rested upon the whole European system, a concatenation of alliances and treaties, a complicated network of intrigue and espionage which unerringly caught the entire family in its meshes."

—President Woodrow Wilson, October 16, 1916.
Quoted in Bernadotte Schmitt, *Triple Alliance and Triple Entente*, p. 1

BETWEEN 1871 and 1914 there were no great wars in Europe. Apart from some minor conflicts, an uneasy peace prevailed, a peace based upon the balance of power and threatened steadily by competitions for empire, struggles for trade and commerce, diplomatic crises, and staggering expenditures upon armaments.

After the empire of Napoleon III fell in 1870, Germany's Otto von Bismarck determined to keep France powerless and isolated. "As long as France has no alliances," Bismarck said, "she is not dangerous to Germany."

With his customary skill Bismarck began to organize a system of alliances designed to protect and strengthen his own state. His first step was taken in 1873 when he was the architect of the Three Emperors' League of Germany, Austria, and Russia. This League was not strong. Bismarck never trusted Russia, and Russia did not trust Bismarck. When Great Britain and Austria opposed Russian designs and pressures in the Balkans at the Congress of Berlin in 1878 Bismarck, the "honest broker," gave Russia no support. The Three Emperors' League was badly strained although its final collapse did not come until 1887.

In 1879 Bismarck turned to Austria. He negotiated with Austria's Count Andrássy the secret Dual Alliance, an important step in the building of a new system of international relations in Europe. By the terms of the agreement of 1879 Germany and Austria promised to help each other in the event of a

Russian attack. "Should, contrary to their hopes and against their loyal desire, one of the High Contracting Parties be attacked by Russia, the High Contracting Parties are bound to come to the assistance one of the other with the whole strength of their Empires and, accordingly, only to conclude peace together and upon mutual agreement."

In 1882 Italy, angered by the French acquisition of Tunis, decided to get and hold support for her colonial ambitions by joining Germany and Austria in the Triple Alliance. The agreements among the three powers were renewed and extended frequently. The members agreed to try to "fortify the monarchical principles and thereby assure the unimpaired maintenance of the social and political order in their respective states." They promised mutual assistance in case one of them was attacked by two or more great powers. If France attacked Italy, Germany and Austria promised to go to the aid of Italy. If France attacked Germany, then Italy was to join Germany. It was also agreed that if any one of the members of the Triple Alliance should move into war with a single great power, then the other two would remain neutral. Germany promised that she would help Italy if France attempted to increase her power and territory in Morocco and Tripoli. There was a special statement to the effect that the Triple Alliance was not directed against Britain.

The solid block of the Triple Alliance—Rumania joined in 1884—helped to protect Germany against a French war of revenge. It strengthened Austria against a Russian attack and supported Austrian expansion in the Balkans—after Austria had been forced out of Italy and Germany only the Balkans remained as a field for Austrian enterprise and aggrandizement. The Slav nationalists naturally resented Austria's hungry activities in the Balkan areas. Serbia, for instance, was infuriated when Austria got suzerainty over Bosnia-Herzegovina at the Congress of Berlin. The Russians, for their part, actively supported the Pan-Slav movement and encouraged Slav nationalism everywhere, even inside the borders of Austria-Hungary.

The astute Otto von Bismarck was not content to confine his diplomatic activities to the creation and maintenance of the Triple Alliance. He knew how dangerous it would be to have a powerful and hostile Russia on Germany's eastern frontier. Despite the collapse of the Three Emperors' League, Bismarck was still determined "to keep open the wires to St. Petersburg." Behind the back of his ally Austria, Bismarck negotiated a secret "Reinsurance" Treaty with Russia. The most important part of the agreement was contained in Article I:

> In case one of the High Contracting Parties should find itself at war with a third Great Power, the other would maintain a benevolent neutrality towards it, and would devote its efforts to the localization of the conflict. This provision would not apply to a war against Austria or France in case this war should result from an attack directed against one of these two latter Powers by one of the High Contracting Parties.

Germany was therefore assured of Russian neutrality if she were attacked by France. Russia was assured of German neutrality if she were attacked by either Austria or Great Britain. In this arrangement Bismarck agreed that Russian claims and interests in the eastern Balkans took precedence over those of any other state—the treaty referred to the "legitimacy" of Russia's "preponderant and decisive influence in Bulgaria and Eastern Rumelia." It also seemed clear that Germany would give "her benevolent neutrality and her moral and diplomatic support" if Russia decided to take measures to "guard the key" of the Russian Empire, i.e., Constantinople.

Of all the major powers only Britain and France remained outside of the far-reaching treaty system of Bismarck. Britain stayed in her complacent isolation, aloof and incalculable. Bismarck knew that Britain would not be roused to join in a European war unless the balance of power was threatened or a serious challenge loomed to Britain's naval and commercial power. Bismarck did not want to offend Great Britain; that is one reason he stood adamantly against the building of a big Germany navy and steadily opposed a German campaign for colonial expansion. So far as France was concerned, Bismarck supported and encouraged the French colonial enterprise in Africa because he reasoned that many Frenchmen would perhaps be more interested in colonies and commerce than in the recovery of Alsace-Lorraine. Bismarck also saw that France would get into squabbles with the British about Egypt and with the Italians about Tunis and would have little time to think about a war of revenge upon Germany. "We have tried to conciliate France," said Bismarck, "everywhere except in Alsace-Lorraine. We have no intentions and no reason to attack her."

In 1888 William I of Germany was succeeded by Frederick III, who reigned only a few months. After Frederick came William II, autocratic, volatile, headstrong, rash, and ambitious. "There is only one master in this country," asserted William II, "and I am he." He also said: "Without Germany and the German Emperor no important steps in international affairs should be taken, even beyond the seas." In 1890 he dismissed Bismarck. Then, slowly, the "nightmare of alliances" against Germany that the vigilant Bismarck had feared became a reality.

When the Reinsurance Treaty between Germany and Russia expired, Kaiser William II did not renew it, claiming that it threatened the solidarity of the Triple Alliance. Russia was now isolated. It seemed that her only possible ally was France.

For several years the relations between France and Russia had been improving. Large French loans to Russia for armaments and the building of the Trans-Siberian Railway helped to prepare the way for a practical pact. In January, 1894, such a treaty was signed. It provided that Russia should help

France if France should be attacked by Germany or by Italy and Germany; that France would aid Russia if Russia should be attacked by Germany or by Austria and Germany. Some of the terms of the treaty were quite precise. Among them, for instance, was this: "The available forces to be employed against Germany shall be, on the part of France, 1,300,000 men; on the part of Russia, 700,000 or 800,000. These forces shall engage to the full with all speed, in order that Germany may have to fight at the same time on the east and on the west." When the world learned a few of the facts about this new alliance, Otto von Bismarck, living the life of a retired gentleman, commented harshly upon the results of the emperor's policy. What Bismarck had strenuously tried to prevent had happened.

Meanwhile Great Britain's "splendid isolation" and security had been challenged by several events and circumstances in Europe and beyond the seas. The militarist spirit was rising again in Germany, spurred on by the visionary ranting of William II and the more sober tones of the professors who explained that war was a "biological necessity." Bitter disputes arose between competing British and German financial houses, especially in Turkey, Siam, Persia, and China. The relative strength of Britain's financial, industrial, and commercial power, as compared with that of Germany and the United States, was steadily declining. For example, in 1860 the total value of United Kingdom exports had been £135,000,000: of German exports £40,000,000; of United States exports £74,000,000. By 1913 the margin had narrowed. The value of exports from the United Kingdom then totaled £525,000,000; from Germany £509,000,000; from the United States £362,000,000. Colonial rivalries produced bickering and tension with Russia in the Middle and Far East; with France in Africa and the Pacific; with blustering, bumptious, and envious Germany in Africa and elsewhere. William II wanted more colonies. Germany had not been given her rightful "place in the sun." These facts—and several others—combined to disturb Great Britain.

Before the Boer War, Great Britain had gone fishing for an alliance with Germany. Some negotiations did begin, but they all failed. Berlin apparently feared that an agreement with Britain might bring Germany into war with Russia or frustrated France or both. Confident that Britain could never mend her differences with France or Russia, the German government insisted that Britain join the Triple Alliance. Britain refused and began to look elsewhere. Meanwhile more friction developed between Britain and Germany over the proposed construction of the Berlin-Bagdad railway by Germany and the increasing German influence in Turkey, by the "Kruger telegram," a congratulatory message sent by the Kaiser to Oom Paul Kruger when the Jameson raiders were captured in 1895. The British found the "Kruger telegram" very offensive.

Highly alarming to the British people and government were the streams of hostile comments coming from the neurotic German emperor, the German statesmen, and the German press. There was also the disturbing fact that German naval construction threatened to make Germany capable of challenging Britain at sea. Each German naval bill was bigger than any that had preceded it. From the British point of view the naval challenge was the most serious event of all. "Without a superior fleet," said Mr. A. J. Balfour in 1912, "Britain would no longer count as a power. Without any fleet at all Germany would still remain the greatest power in Europe. . . . If Germany had a bigger fleet she could not only defeat us at sea but she could soon be in London with her army. If our fleet is once defeated we are at the mercy of every plunderer."

The Hague Conferences of 1899 and 1907 failed to limit armaments. There were only slight gains: the establishment of a court of arbitration to which nations might submit disputes "involving neither honor nor vital interests," and one agreement about rules to be followed in laying mines, bombing unfortified towns, and the rights of neutrals.

Every British attempt to persuade Germany to reduce her naval building program—including the famous Haldane mission of 1912—failed completely. It was grimly agreed in Britain that if a war should come, then the British Navy must be ready, as of old, to defend the shores of the islands and to destroy the enemy at sea.

For a long time the British and the French had been busy with their quarrels. There had been much suspicion, dislike, and distrust. In many quarters of the planet there had been harsh and dangerous controversy. The waves of wrath that rolled during the "Fashoda Incident" of 1898 were only one dramatic illustration of the acute ill will that troubled the relations between Paris and London.

England had concluded a defensive alliance with Japan in 1902, but she needed allies in Europe. Important and dramatic steps were soon taken to reach an understanding with France. In 1903 Britain's Edward VII made a state visit to Paris. King Edward's personality, his obvious liking for the French people, for French wines and foods and opera and conversation, helped to sweep from the minds of the Parisians at least some of the darker clouds and memories of Fashoda and the Boer War. Britain's king was not warmly welcomed when he arrived in Paris, but he was cheered before he left. The royal visit was a personal and diplomatic triumph for "Edward the Peacemaker."

In a few months France's President Loubet visited London. The able Théophile Delcassé, French minister of foreign affairs, and Lord Lansdowne, the British foreign secretary, held exploratory conversations. A series of later conferences resulted in the agreement of April, 1904, known as the Entente Cordiale. The French surrendered all claims in Egypt; Britain recognized the preponderant French interests in Morocco. Other outstanding differences in

Newfoundland, Siam, Madagascar, and the New Hebrides were reconciled, or at least patched up.

France and Britain made considerable concessions to secure the understanding each desired. No formal military alliance was signed. Nevertheless, the settlement of outstanding issues marked a significant diplomatic revolution. Politics makes strange bedfellows; and so does fear.

Berlin was disagreeably surprised. Britain had reversed her policy; the years of political isolation were ended. Germany, on the other hand, complained of being "encircled" by the Franco-Russian alliance and the Entente Cordiale.

The Russo-Japanese war of 1904–1905 showed the world that Russia was less strong than many European generals and statesmen had believed. After the Russian defeat her armies were disorganized; a part of the people were in rebellion; the national debt, already tremendous, had been increased. Some men forgot that in a European conflict Russia would not be plagued by the transportation and communication problems that had multiplied her difficulties in the war with Japan. It is a long way from Moscow to the seas and battlefields of eastern Asia. Other men remembered that important fact.

The British Liberal government now felt that its earlier fears of St. Petersburg had not been fully warranted. Many shrewd and thoughtful Englishmen were afraid that Nicholas II might turn towards Germany and seek an alliance. Still others were impressed and cheered by the tsar's promises of reforms after the small-scale revolution of 1905. The British made overtures to St. Petersburg; this time they were not rebuffed.

In August, 1907, Sir Edward Grey and Alexander Isvolsky signed a treaty. Russia and Britain agreed to stay out of Tibet; the Russians promised that they would plot and incite no more in Afghanistan; Persia was divided into Russian and British spheres of influence separated by a neutral zone. There were no naval or military commitments.

The bonds uniting England, France, and Russia in the Triple Entente were slowly tightening. Confronted with this unpleasant fact, the suspicious and truculent Germans attempted to break the Entente by direct diplomatic attacks. In each case the international crisis provoked by Berlin forced the members of the Triple Entente closer together, which was exactly what Germany did not want.

The first main crisis came shortly after the formation of the Entente Cordiale between France and Britain. With the tacit consent of Britain, Spain, and Italy the French government went ahead with its plans and policies in Morocco. Baron von Holstein of Germany believed that the understanding between France and England could be weakened if Germany upset the French designs. He was certain that England would take no steps to aid her ally.

The German government pointed out that an international convention of 1880 gave Germany certain commercial rights in Morocco. William II went to Tangier, visited the sultan of Morocco, delivered a bellicose speech, and congratulated the sultan upon his independence. The German emperor insisted that the question of Morocco concerned Europe as a whole and should be discussed at an international conference of all the signatories of the convention of 1880. His was not a noble cause.

France finally agreed to the German proposal. Her ally Russia had been defeated by Japan. The Entente with England was as yet untried. Delcassé, the French foreign minister who had loudly insisted that England would fight for France, was compelled to resign. In 1906 an international conference met at Algeciras, in Spain. Germany, it seemed, had successfully promoted disorder in the ranks of the powers ranged against her.

When the game was played out the facts were otherwise. At the Algeciras Conference the British supported the French upon every issue. Spain, Russia, and Italy also stood beside France and England. France had earlier assured Italy that she would place no obstacles in the path of Italian advances in Tripoli and Cyrenaica. Let Italy turn her gaze towards those lands and France would wish her well. Italy had told France that she would not oppose French penetration in Morocco and Tunis. So it was that Germany and Austria stood alone.

The powers at Algeciras formally guaranteed the independence and integrity of Morocco. They also provided for an international police force to keep order and to protect foreigners. This police force was to be controlled by France and Spain; it was used, of course, for the extension of French and Spanish political and economic power.

Germany had won a diplomatic victory when she had compelled France to agree to an international conference. The magnitude of the German blunder was seen when the conference met. The Entente Cordiale was not shaken. Baron von Holstein was forced to resign. The secret conversations between Britain and France continued. The military experts discussed their plans in the event that Germany attacked France and Britain came into the conflict to support the French. The British government made no formal commitments of any kind. Nevertheless, some degree of moral obligation on the part of Britain was certainly incurred. Arrangements were made so that Britain could land 100,000 men in France within 12 days after the outbreak of war. The British fleet would keep the watch in the North Sea; the French fleet would move into the Mediterranean.

The next international crisis came in 1908. It arose out of the long struggle of Austria and Russia in the Balkans. There Turkey had recently fallen under German influence. Rumania's king was a Hohenzollern and hence kindly inclined towards Germany. In Serbia, however, the picture was different. Serbia's King Peter was friendly to Russia. Germany was alarmed and displeased because she feared that Serbia might block the Berlin-Bagdad railway.

Austria feared Serbia's possible part in a Pan-Slav network of plots and agitations.

Germany and Austria decided to strike at Russia and Pan-Slavism before Russia recovered from her defeat by Japan and her revolution of 1905 and before Turkey, shaken by the Young Turk revolution, could act. In 1908 Austria suddenly announced that she had annexed Bosnia-Herzegovina, the Turkish provinces placed under Austrian protection by the Congress of Berlin in 1878.

Alexander Isvolsky of Russia, a tireless intriguer, had earlier indicated to Vienna that St. Petersburg would not oppose the Austrian seizure of Bosnia-Herzegovina provided that Austria did not obstruct Russian action to open the Dardanelles. Austria, ignoring this "Buchlau bargain," went ahead with the annexation without informing Russia. Germany's menacing language and support of Austria forced Russia to yield. Russia's prestige was dimmed in the Balkans. Serbia was infuriated to see the thousands of Slavs in Bosnia-Herzegovina forced into the Hapsburg Empire.

Serbia had wanted Bosnia-Herzegovina. Now she had to bow with bitterness to the Austrian demand that she cease to agitate for an outlet to the sea and stop stirring up trouble for Vienna among the Slavs in Bosnia and Herzegovina. Serbian secret societies expanded silently across the Austrian borders. Pan-Slav movements, guided by Russia, grew stronger. "O Bosnia, orphan before the gods," ran the words of a popular song, "hast thou no patriots in thy land today?"

A third crisis came in 1911. As a result of a palace revolution in Fez the French government sent troops into Morocco on the grounds that endangered Europeans needed protection. Spain and Germany insisted that the French were violating the arrangements made at Algeciras in 1906. Germany soon sent the gunboat *Panther* to Agadir, an obscure seaport on the Moroccan Atlantic coast, claiming a strong desire to protect "German interests." Britain feared a German occupation of Agadir and the building of a German naval base on the flank of British sea lanes. Hence Britain protested vigorously. Then she warned and threatened. The German government was impressed. In the end it was agreed that the German government would accept as compensation for French advances in Morocco a portion of the French Congo which would be added to the Cameroons. This territory, about 100,000 square miles in area, was mostly desert.

Meanwhile Germany, militant, restless, and fearful of the "encircling ring of enemies," was even more bitterly opposed than before to the Anglo-French Entente. The anger and bitterness of the Germans was matched by the anger and bitterness of the French. Meanwhile, too, Germany continued to add to her military and naval strength. In 1908 William II declared that the British were "mad, mad as March hares" to suspect the German navy. He insisted that the ships were being built to protect German commerce and not to attack Britain. Nevertheless, the British were in considerable doubt about German intentions. They laid down the keels of more and more ships. The age of the superbattleship had arrived when the British launched the first *Dreadnought* in 1906. The Germans began to build their own heavily gunned and armed capital ships, and a new phase of the naval race began.

The French increased the span of military service from two to three years. Austria reorganized her army. Russia built more strategic railway lines. The diplomatic atmosphere in Europe was tense and dangerous.

In 1912 the Balkan states of Serbia, Montenegro, Greece, and Bulgaria attacked Turkey with the declared intention of liberating Macedonia from Turkish tyranny. When these allies had obtained a swift victory the great powers stepped in to arrange a peace settlement at the London Conference. Austria wanted to create a new state to be called Albania to keep Serbia from growing too large and to stop her from getting an outlet to the Adriatic. A Serbian Adriatic port might be used as a Russian naval base; it would also strengthen Serbia's economic position.

As a result of the mediation of Germany and Britain the danger of a general European war was temporarily avoided. The newly created state of Albania took possession of the disputed Adriatic ports. The Serbs were furious. Once again, as so often in Europe's history, the Slavs and Teutons waited for the battle hour.

Serbia, seeking compensation, turned to seize a large section of Macedonia. Bulgaria, Serbia's former ally, at once started a second Balkan war which involved Greece, Rumania, Serbia, and Turkey. The Turks recaptured Adrianople. Bulgaria was defeated, and the Treaty of Bucharest of August, 1913, forced her to surrender some of the territory she had taken in the first Balkan war.

The weakened Bulgarians were anxious to be revenged upon Serbia. Bulgaria had always been supported by Austria. Now both Bulgarian strength and Austrian prestige had declined together in the Balkans. The Serbs, their spirits inflamed by victory, increased their "Greater Serbia" agitation among their fellow Slavs in Bosnia and Herzegovina. Disorders in those two provinces of Austria grew in number and violence.

In June, 1914, the Archduke Francis Ferdinand, heir to the Austrian throne, traveled with his wife to Sarajevo, the capital of Bosnia. It is idle to speculate what might have happened if they had stayed at home in Vienna. Such conjectures open the doors to nowhere. The archduke and his wife did not stay home. They went down to meet their assassins in the streets of Sarajevo.

Chapter 42

WAR:

THE PLANET DIVIDED

"There is no error so monstrous that it fails to find defenders among
the ablest men. Imagine a congress of eminent celebrities such as More,
Bacon, Pascal, Cromwell, Bossuet, Montesquieu, Jefferson, Napoleon. . . .
The result would be an encyclopedia of error."

—Lord Acton, quoted by Judge Learned Hand
in *The Spirit of Liberty*, p. 261

ABOUT the causes of the First World War there have been numerous
judgments and interpretations. There are many truths, half-truths, and
fictions, all mingled together. Sometimes the facts have been selected and
weighted carefully to support arguments and conclusions reached before any
"research" began. One scholar will place a heavy blame upon the seething
nationalism of the Balkan states. A second will stress the significance of the
competition in the building of navies and armies. A third will underline the
fact that France wanted to recover Alsace-Lorraine, that Italy hoped to seize
the Austrian provinces and Trieste where numerous Italians lived—and also
to control the Adriatic. A fourth will dwell at length upon the Slav desires
and the long Russian dream of moving down to Constantinople and the Dardanelles. A fifth will describe the evils of competing alliances.

A sixth writer will be deeply concerned with the tales of the aggressive
nationalist drive for empires, the struggle between the "haves" and the "have-
nots" among the nations. A seventh will be of the opinion that the major
cause of the conflict was the commercial and economic competition. An eighth
will insist that the financiers and industrialists, plotting year by year, were
the "merchants of death" and the servants of Mars and Mammon; that they
must be charged with plunging the world into years of blood and terror. A
ninth will declare that the responsibility for the First World War must be
placed squarely upon the doorsteps of the German people. Did not General
Friedrich von Bernhardi say: "If it were not for war we should probably find

that inferior races could overcome healthy, youthful ones by their wealth and humbug"? The words of Heinrich von Treitschke will be quoted: "Man will not only sacrifice his life but the natural and justified instincts of his soul; his very self he must offer up for the sake of patriotism; here we have the sublimity of war." A tenth scholar will content himself by saying that the causes of all wars are in the human heart and that we must never underestimate the significance of the passions of men in war and peace.

No single easy and fearless theory can be made to fit all of the known and complex facts about the causes of the First World War. The most responsible authorities today agree that the responsibility for the trends and tensions and the outbreak of hostilities must be widely shared among the nations. None of the reputable authorities are willing to venture beyond this area of broad and general agreement.

On June 28, 1914, the Archduke Franz Ferdinand, heir to the throne of Austria-Hungary, and his wife were assassinated in Sarajevo, the capital of Bosnia. The murderers were Bosnians. There is no doubt that they received aid from Serbian sources and that some Serbian officials knew of the plot.

Austria asserted that Serbia was responsible for the crime; that it had been planned in Belgrade; that Serbian government men had helped in its execution. The Austrian government obtained blanket assurances from Germany in support of any steps that she might take against Serbia. Germany gave these assurances despite the fact that any strong Austrian course would clearly lead to dispute and possibly war with Russia.

On Thursday, July 23, the Vienna government presented a formidable ultimatum to Serbia. It required a satisfactory reply within forty-eight hours. The note began by asserting that Serbia had not kept her promise of March, 1909, in which she had stated that she would "live on good neighborly terms" with Austria. Instead, said the note, Serbia had supported a "subversive movement" that had ended in the murders at Sarajevo. Austria demanded that Serbia declare on July 26 that she condemned and repudiated all activity directed against Austria-Hungary and that, in addition, she accepted ten further specific Austrian demands. Among other things, Serbia was to agree to suppress all anti-Austrian propaganda; to accept "the collaboration of Austrian representatives for the suppression of the subversive movement," and to dismiss from office any individual "guilty of propaganda" against Austria. In her reply to the ultimatum (July 25) Serbia made tremendous concessions. She accepted all of the Austrian demands except those that violated her sovereignty. She offered to submit the whole question at once to the Hague Tribunal.

Austria found the Serbian reply unsatisfactory. She was determined to punish Serbia and to reduce the strength of a state that she considered dan-

gerous. Because the Serbian note did not accept the Austrian demands *in toto*
Baron von Giesl, the Austrian minister, left Belgrade at once. Francis Joseph
ordered the mobilization of eight corps, or half of the Austro-Hungarian army.
Serbia had already begun to mobilize. Austria declared war. Behind Serbia
stood Russia. "If Austria gobbles up Serbia," the Russian Sazonov had said,
"we shall make war upon her." On the evening of July 29 Tsar Nicholas II
signed the order for general mobilization. The tsar did not know, of course,
that two years earlier Nikolai Lenin had written a letter to Maxim Gorki
saying that the hope for socialism was a major war. Lenin was "afraid that
Francis Joseph and Nicholas will not give us this pleasure."

Sir Edward Grey, the British foreign secretary, had tried to get Berlin to
persuade Vienna to lengthen the time limit attached to the ultimatum to
Serbia. The German military leaders seemed reluctant to delay the steps
contemplated by Austria. They also seemed to have been persuaded that they
were ready for a war and that France and Russia were not. Great Britain also
urged Russia not to mobilize at once. Sir Edward Grey proposed mediation
between Austria and Russia by the four neutral powers of Great Britain,
France, Germany, and Italy. France stated that she could not agree, lest it
appear she was not supporting Russia; Germany could not agree because she
had promised to back Austria.

There were other proposals for mediation and discussion; all of them failed.
Germany, for instance, feared that negotiations might give Russia too much
time for mobilization. Time is a commodity of war. No nation can afford to
delay or to be outpaced by the enemy in the first hours of conflict. To be
strategically unprepared is one of the first military sins.

The huge double mobilization plan of Russia called for the movement of
troops and supplies towards the German as well as the Austrian borders.
Germany therefore prepared for mobilization and demanded that the Russians
stop their mobilization within twelve hours. On August 1, Germany declared
war on Russia and demanded of Russia's ally France an unconditional promise
of neutrality within eighteen hours. The French government replied that
France would do whatever her national interests might require. Germany declared war upon France on August 3.

Britain refused to make any commitments to Russia or to France. At the
same time, she refused to give Germany any assurance that she would remain
neutral. On July 31 Sir Edward Grey asked both Germany and France to respect the neutrality of Belgium. France agreed; Germany sent an evasive reply.
Meanwhile the Liberal government in Great Britain was divided upon the
question of possible participation in the European war. Some cabinet members
were in favor of moving at once in support of France and Russia. Others stood
against intervention. On August 2 Britain did inform France that "if the
German fleet comes into the Channel or through the North Sea to undertake

hostile operations against the French coasts or shipping, the British fleet will give all the protection in its power." Britain could do no less than this because the French fleet was in the Mediterranean as a result of arrangements reached earlier in British and French naval conversations.

The decisive event, so far as the British were concerned, was the German ultimatum to the little kingdom of Belgium, giving her twelve hours to decide whether she would allow the Germans to cross Belgium without opposition on their way to France. With dignity and firmness Belgium refused, asserting that her neutrality had been guaranteed in 1839 by the major powers of Europe, including Prussia. It was clear that the Belgians would fight if the Germans violated that pledge.

The Germans did violate it when their armies rolled into the Belgian lands. Would Great Britain go to war because Germany had torn up a treaty? When the German chancellor called that treaty "a scrap of paper" there was widespread indignation. In addition to the impulse of moral obligation there was the important fact of vital and immediate British self-interest. It had long been a pivotal point of British policy that no great power should menace or control the Belgian coast. British opinion swiftly hardened. Where there had been division there was now almost unanimity. The degree of British obligation to France and Russia, never clearly defined, was no longer a question for debate. The important thing was the indisputable treaty commitment to Belgium and the threat to British national security in the German thrust towards the coast and the narrow seas.

On August 3 the British government sent an ultimatum to Germany demanding the immediate withdrawal of her forces across the Belgian borders. Attached to the ultimatum was a time limit expiring at midnight. When Germany sent no reply Britain was at war. The British navy was ordered to "commence hostilities at once against Germany." British troops began to move across the Channel.

Within a few days after Austria's punitive attack on Serbia the sword of Damocles had fallen upon a bewildered and apprehensive world. Before the end of the year Germany, Austria-Hungary, and Turkey stood against Great Britain, France, Russia, Montenegro, Serbia, Belgium, and Japan. Italy stayed neutral, for a time.

So began the First World War. More than 10,000,000 men were to be killed in that conflict, almost a whole generation of human natural resources.

When the German forces struck westwards in a vast assault the famous plan designed by the brilliant Count Schlieffen in 1906 was put into operation. This plan provided for a hard, swift attack by five German armies across the lowlands of Belgium and northern France; two more armies were to serve as

a heavy pivotal anchor above Metz. The task of the right wing of the German forces was to tear the French flanks from their anchoring sockets and to roll them up. It was expected that France would be stunned by the swift and savage hammering in the northeast. France, surely, would be blasted out of the war before the cumbersome Russian machine could become effective. "Remember," William II had twice said to Sir Edward Grey, "we can be in Paris in a fortnight."

The Belgians were brave and obstinate. At Liége the Germans had 40,000 casualties. Then the Germans pulled out several divisions for service on the Eastern front. Their plans were disrupted. The weary German First Army reduced its arc to loop to the east and south of Paris instead of to the west and south. Into a gap that opened between von Kluck's First and von Bülow's Second Army, British and French troops poured. The Germans were stopped in the butchery of the battle of the Marne (September 5–10) and pushed back thirty miles to the Aisne River. There they dug trenches and there they stayed. Historians have usually praised France's General Joseph Joffre and General Maurice Gustave Gamelin for stopping the German drive. They do not deserve the credit. It belongs to General Gallieni and Colonel Messiny. They were the organizers of victory.

After the battle of the Marne there began the "race to the sea." The Germans took Antwerp and drove towards the seaports of Calais, Dunkirk, and Boulogne. The Allies reached these strategic places first. The Germans had lost their chance to get round the Allied flanks; the bending French, British, and Belgian lines did not break. For 600 miles, from the Belgian coast to Switzerland, the immense and dreary front became an almost rigid line, marked by twisting trenches and barbed wire, churned by shells, cursed by mud, cold, and rats. New tactics and new weapons were slowly developed as further chapters were added to the history of man's achievements in the art of organized demolition, mayhem, and homicide. Tanks and poison gas soon joined with the submarines and new artillery to add to the rising slaughter.

Germany's colonies over the seas fell, one by one, into Allied hands. New Zealand took Samoa; Australia took German New Guinea; South Africa took German Southwest Africa; France and Britain overcame Togoland and the Cameroons; Japan took Kiaochow and several Pacific islands. The British fleet bottled up the German navy at Kiel and elsewhere. The Allied nations achieved a high degree of cooperation in the economic field. Only the German merchant ships that remained moored to the docks at home were safe; the rest were captured. Economic warfare and blockade controls became the throttling process so important in the First and Second World Wars.

On the Eastern Front the Russian forces mobilized with unexpected speed. Then they lunged out of Russian Poland in a two-pronged offensive into East Prussia and eastern Galicia. A startled German High Command sent General Paul von Hindenburg to check the advance of Russia's General Rennenkampf through East Prussia. At the battle of Tannenberg (August 26–September 1) Hindenburg hurled his troops between two large Russian armies and routed each of them. He then invaded Russia, seized a large amount of supplies, and inflicted about 1,500,000 casualties on his enemy.

Meanwhile the Russians had rolled unchecked to the forts of Cracow in western Galicia. Under General von Mackensen the Germans and Austrians mounted a huge counteroffensive. The Russians were driven out of Galicia. Hindenburg captured Warsaw. Russian military power was thus being drained away. Hundreds of thousands of men were wounded or dead. Troops grew demoralized as hope fell away. The whole Russian state, it seemed, was beginning to disintegrate.

In November, 1914, Turkey entered the war on the side of the Central

Powers. This event brought a threat to the southern bastions of Russia and to the British in Egypt and the East. Because of the stalemate on the Western Front the Allies sought to find strategic and important soft spots to attack elsewhere. Now that Turkey was in the war it seemed that some Allied action might profitably be taken in the Near East. The British declared Egypt independent of Turkey and Egypt became a British protectorate. Early in 1915 the British tried to force an entrance into the Dardanelles with a view to removing the Turks from the war, opening up the Black Sea, and funneling aid to Russia. "In the East take Constantinople," said Winston Churchill. "Take it by ships if you can. Take it by soldiers if you must. But take it; take it soon; take it while time remains."

The task was hard. A strong British fleet was forced back by Turkish shore batteries. In April, 1915, British, Australian, and New Zealand troops were landed on six cruel beaches at Gallipoli; but the Turks could not be driven out of their prepared positions on the dominating slopes. At the end of the year the campaign was abandoned. From the British point of view, Gallipoli was a dark and disastrous chapter in the tale of 1915.

Soon Bulgaria joined Germany and Austria in the conquest of Serbia, Albania, and Montenegro. Greece decided to remain neutral. In May, 1915, the kingdom of Italy, anxious for territorial gains Austria was not prepared to grant, joined the Allies. Because France and Britain misjudged the value of Italian military aid they promised her parts of "unredeemed Italy," such as the Istrian Peninsula and a part of the Dalmatian coast.

Submarine warfare was Germany's answer to the British blockade. Nevertheless, the Germans were not able to sink enough Allied ships to starve England or to win the war. German submarines sent thousands of tons of Allied and neutral shipping beneath the green waves of the sea. On May 7, 1915, the *Lusitania* was torpedoed and sunk without warning. Nearly eleven hundred people were drowned, including about a hundred American citizens. The ruthless U-boat campaign was terribly effective. The inhumanity of many of the U-boat commanders also aroused the anger of several neutral powers, especially the United States. The methods used by German U-boat commanders were neither moral nor wise. Some of their deeds should not be allowed to sink into the mercy of oblivion.

On the Western Front the trench warfare continued. Great frontal attacks, such as the German thrust in the second battle of Ypres (February, 1915), failed at tremendous cost. The casualty lists grew longer and the hopes for peace were dim.

Early in the grim year of 1916 the Germans made strong and sustained efforts to break through the Allied lines on the Western Front. At Verdun

(February–June, 1916) the French and the Germans each lost about 550,000 men. The Canadian losses were also high.

In July the British and the French began a great drive along the Somme. On the first day the British under Sir Douglas Haig lost 60,000 men; it was the blackest day in British military history. In the first week they gained five miles and lost 170,000 men. They moved only slowly over the tortured earth; they fought desperately from trench to trench; then they stopped. The Germans fell back on the heavily defended Hindenburg line. Their casualties totaled 500,000; the British suffered 410,000; the French 190,000.

In May, 1916, the Italians were forced back by a relentless Austrian drive. In the same month the main sea battle of the war was fought at Jutland. For the first time out of port and on the prowl the German fleet was discovered by a squadron of British cruisers under Admiral Beatty. Behind Beatty was the main British fleet commanded by Admiral Jellicoe. The German Admiral von Hipper tried to lead Beatty towards the German High Seas Fleet under Admiral Scheer. When Jellicoe and Scheer came into the action late in the day the British vainly attempted to cut off German retreat. In the fog and the gathering darkness the German fleet escaped. The Germans had inflicted on the British heavier losses than they had suffered themselves; but the Germans knew that they had been saved from destruction only by darkness and their good fortune.

In August, 1916, Rumania joined the Allies. A short time later she was defeated and compelled to sign the humiliating Treaty of Bucharest. Her grain fields and her oil wells were now controlled by Germany.

Most of the year 1916 was a time of drag, defeat, and darkness for the Allies. Victory sat on the German standards almost everywhere. Nevertheless, the German losses had been terrible. Germany did not want the war to be prolonged. The Allies, however, had no desire to toy for long with German overtures or to accept the German terms for peace. David Lloyd George, that doughty and dogged Welshman who replaced H. H. Asquith as British prime minister in December, 1916, spoke for his country with precision and clarity: "To enter, on the invitation of Germany, proclaiming herself victorious, without any knowledge of the proposals she has to make, is to put our heads into a noose." The war continued. The skies stayed overcast.

Early in 1917 Germany announced the beginning of unrestricted submarine warfare. Any ship, Allied or neutral, was to be sunk if found in a barred zone in the waters around Great Britain, France, or Italy. The Germans thought that by this new blockade Great Britain would be brought to her knees. The British began to use convoys, "Q-boat" decoys, and depth bombs. By no great margin, but by enough, the German challenge was beaten off.

In February, 1917, the United States severed diplomatic relations with Germany. On April 2, 1917, President Woodrow Wilson declared at a special session of Congress that the United States resented the German violations of international law and Germany's irresponsible disregard for human rights. Wilson denounced Germany as a "selfish and autocratic power," an untrustworthy state, and a menace to civilization. "The world," he said, "must be made safe for democracy." On April 6 the United States declared war against Germany; later she declared war on Austria-Hungary.

It was a formidable foe that Germany's prowess in brutality had brought against her. British and American shipyards were soon producing twice as many ships as the submarines were sinking. American warships at once helped to convoy supplies to the United Kingdom. Blockade controls were tightened everywhere. The doctrine of the freedom of the seas was abandoned. American troops soon began to move over the Atlantic to France. "Life came to us in new waves," wrote a French observer, "bringing fresh strength to the almost bloodless body of France." New states joined the ranks of Germany's enemies: Brazil, China, Cuba, Greece, Liberia, Panama, Siam.

A month before the United States joined the Allies, Russia collapsed as a result of an abrupt and bloody revolution. The Romanov government, so weak, corrupt, and shot through with treason, was overthrown. Nicholas II, "The Autocrat of all the Russians," abdicated and was later murdered. (See Chapter 45.) The moderate provisional government of Prince Lvov and Alexander Kerenski was in turn destroyed by Nikolai Lenin (1870–1924), the leader of the Bolsheviks.

Nikolai Lenin (Vladimir Ulyanov) was a professional revolutionist and conspirator, clever, cold, harsh, and practical. To him the making of revolution was a science. He had no sympathy for the idealists or humanitarian dreamers. Lenin and the Bolsheviks had long claimed that no truly revolutionary party would ever gain power by using constitutional methods. That was one of the reasons the Bolsheviks had separated from the Social Democrats and cut loose from the Mensheviks (1912). The strength of the capitalist bourgeoisie, said Lenin, controls the press, the schools, the courts, the governments, the parliaments. Only by using revolutionary tactics, he insisted, can the socialists hope to seize control of the state. They should have careful plans and policies, work in small groups, infiltrate the trade unions, bore into political parties, await the chance for organized and decisive action. Then the capitalist state can be overthrown. The classless society and the dictatorship of the proletariat will be established.

When the First World War exploded in Europe, Lenin was an exile from Russia living in Germany. He refused to support the "capitalist" war. "The proletariat has no fatherland." He was in Switzerland when the Russian revolt of March, 1917, upset the state and Nicholas II. The Germans arranged to send Lenin through Germany in a sealed train to his homeland; the Germans hoped that Lenin's arrival in Russia would still further disorganize the country. So Lenin left Switzerland on April 8, 1917; then he went to Stockholm, then to Finland, and then to Petrograd. His welcome to Russia, so finely described in Edmund Wilson's *To the Finland Station,* did not delay Lenin long. After the dramatic journey, the crowds, roses, teas, and tactics, there was work to do.

The Bolshevik government that now ruled in the new Soviet Russia at once abolished private property in land and capital. Its leaders declared that the war was an "imperialist struggle for trade and territory" and opened negotiations for peace with the Central Powers. In March, 1918, the Russians signed the severe treaty of Brest-Litovsk. They agreed to "evacuate" all of the Ukraine and Finland and to surrender Poland, Lithuania, Livonia, and several regions in the Caucasus—all of these areas were now free to establish their own governments. Not every term of Brest-Litovsk was strictly observed by the Russians. Soviet governments have sometimes been less than precise in promise-keeping.

On the Western Front of 1917 the battle lines continued to sway back and forth. The tremendous losses continued. Against the defenses of the Hindenburg line the waves of Allied attacks broke in vain. The French were badly mauled at the center of the front. At the northern end the Canadians captured Vimy Ridge (April, 1917). The British renewed their attacks in Flanders' fields. The battle of Passchendaele (July–November, 1917) was fought in a horrible sea of mud; it cost the British 300,000 casualties. There followed the battle of Cambrai where tanks were used on a large scale for the first time. On the southern front a part of the Italian line fell in at Caporetto; the routed Italian Second Army was forced back all the way to the Piave River. Russia, Italy, Serbia, and Rumania were now no longer of any military significance in the war.

Only in the Near East did the Allies find some comfort in 1917. There the British seized Bagdad and chased the enemy northwards. General Allenby and T. E. Lawrence brought defeat nearer to the Turks in Palestine. Beersheba and Gaza fell. In December, 1917, General Allenby took Jerusalem.

The Eastern Front was no more. The collapse of Russia meant that more than half a million German troops were released for service in the west. The Germans now decided to strike a series of hard and heavy blows before the United States was able to bring any effective strength into the fields of battle. Through a thick fog on March 21, 1918, Germany's General Ludendorff launched a massive attack on the British near the old Somme battlefield. The numerical superiority of the Germans was nearly two to one. Ludendorff was supported by 6,000 cannon on a 43-mile front. He laid down an intense creeping barrage and then sent forward his flame throwers, machine gunners, and the gray waves of infantry. A break through the British lines would have meant the fall of the great railway center of Amiens. The French and British armies would have been separated and the British hurled back to the Channel. In two black weeks the Germans drove a salient bulging forty miles deep to within ten miles of Amiens. General Sir Douglas Haig ordered his forces to retreat no more. "There is no course open to us but to fight it out. Every position must be held to the last man; there must be no retirement." The bending British lines did not break. Meanwhile the grave dangers and the evils of divided command resulted in the selection of General Ferdinand Foch (March 28, 1919) as supreme commander of all the Allied forces on the Western Front.

On April 9 General Ludendorff struck again, this time against the British on the northern front immediately south of Ypres. The Germans intended to break through to the vital ports of Calais, Ostend, Dunkirk, and Boulogne. The British were forced back about ten miles and then they stood firmly with their "backs to the wall." Twice the Germans had been halted.

They tried once more in May. The third hammering German attack was against the French forces between Reims and Soissons. The French were defeated and the Germans advanced thirty miles to Château-Thierry on the Marne—they were within fifty miles of Paris. But again they were stopped. Two fresh and brave American divisions had arrived to bolster the French. Soon American troops were crossing the Atlantic at the rate of 250,000 a month.

On July 15, 1918, General Ludendorff made a last effort. When this German thrust was blunted General Foch struck suddenly on the German flank near Soissons. The Allied commander decided to give the Germans no rest. His great counteroffensive—the second battle of the Marne—marked the beginning of the end. The German Chancellor, Dr. Theobald von Bethmann-Hollweg, later said: "We attacked on the 15th. By the 18th even the most optimistic among us understood that all was lost. The history of the world was played out in those three days." On August 8, the British, Canadians, and Australians wiped out the German bulge in the Amiens area. "This," said General Ludendorff, "was the black day of the German army."

In September and October, 1918, the Americans, Belgians, British, and French continued to advance against stubborn German resistance. Germany's allies crumpled, one by one. Bulgaria fell. The Turks followed suit. The British and Italians struck at Austria and on November 3 Austria signed an armistice. Revolution shook Vienna. A mutiny in the German navy flared into a general German revolt. William II abdicated and sought security in flight. The German Empire of Bismarck and William I had ended.

On November 11, 1918, Germany signed an armistice in a railway dining car in a French forest. In the cities of the Allied nations people sang and danced in the streets. Some did not share the joy; they remembered their sons who would come home no more.

On November 18, England's Lord Curzon addressed the House of Lords: "The Armistice is not only the precursor, but it is the sure guarantee, of peace. Though some months may elapse before the stage is cleared of the debris that encumbers it yet peace is in no danger whatsoever. The armies have already made peace; it will remain for the statesmen to see that it is honorable and lasting."

The hungry, defeated, and embittered people of Germany now awaited the decisions of the victors.

In January, 1918, President Woodrow Wilson of the United States had stated the war aims of his country in the famous Fourteen Points. Those aims included the abolition of secret diplomacy, the freedom of the seas, equality of trade conditions, reduction of armaments, the right of self-determination of the peoples in Turkey and Austria-Hungary, the adjustment of colonial claims, the restoration of Poland, the alteration of several boundaries and the transfer of certain territories, and the establishment of the League of Nations. The desires of President Wilson and the idea of a peace without vengeance were widely praised.

In the midst of national passions inflamed by propaganda and suffering, the representatives of twenty-seven nations met at Versailles in January, 1919, to make a victor's peace. Germany, all her allies, and the powers that had stayed neutral were excluded from the conference of the peacemakers. The humiliation of the conquered enemy was complete.

After the Adriatic ambitions of Italy were thwarted and her representatives withdrew from the deliberations at Versailles the terms of peace were largely determined by the leading spokesmen of the United States, Great Britain, and France: Wilson, Lloyd George, and Clemenceau, the "Big Three." These men, aided by their staffs of experts, labored in secret councils to produce arrangements that would establish some kind of reasonable settlement. The final peace treaties were filled with self-deception. In recent years they have been widely condemned. The advantages of hindsight are great. Perhaps the verdict of Colonel E. M. House is still the best: "Looking at the Conference in retrospect there is much to approve and much to regret. It is easy to say what should have been done but more difficult to have found a way of doing it."

Clemenceau fiercely insisted that Germany must be punished and kept too weak to be dangerous; that was his chief concern. President Wilson feared that the kind of peace terms for which Clemenceau clamored would provoke another war. He placed his trust in general principles of justice bulwarked by the League of Nations. "President Wilson," wrote Carl Becker, "had no humor, no objectivity, no abiding sense of a contact with reality." The cynical Clemenceau, on the other hand, saw a great gulf fixed between the ideal and the actual. He represented the mood of an embittered France; and he wanted international guarantees, backed by political and economic sanctions and, if need be, by the sword. Of President Wilson, Clemenceau said: "He acted to the very best of his abilities in circumstances the origin of which had escaped him and whose ulterior developments lay beyond his ken." Lloyd George took a strong line only when the interests of Great Britain seemed to be concerned. In all else he urged moderation; he did not want Germany to be completely crushed. The result was an unsatisfactory compromise.

When the treaty was placed before the Germans for signature on May 6, 1919, they denounced the harshness of its terms, declaring it to be a revengeful document, a millstone handicapping not only Germany but the whole world's hope of peace. They also insisted that they would not accept the "war guilt" charges implicit in the reparations section. Their protests were futile. On June 28, 1919, the German representatives signed the Treaty of Versailles.

A new map of Europe had been drawn. Under the provisions of the peace treaty Germany returned Alsace-Lorraine to France. For fifteen years the Saar Basin, with its great coal mines, was to be controlled by a new international body, the League of Nations. Both banks of the Rhine were demilitarized. An Allied army was to occupy the left bank of the Rhine for at least fifteen years. A new Poland appeared for the first time since 1795. Germany lost West Prussia, a section of Silesia, and a part of Posen. Danzig, at the end of the "Polish corridor to the sea," was made a free port under the control of the League of Nations. As a result of a plebiscite Germany also yielded the northern half of Schleswig to Denmark.

All German colonies were surrendered to the Allies. These colonies were to be held by various states as mandates from the League of Nations. The mandates were to expire when the occupied colonies were considered fit for independence. Japan took over the German concessions in the Shantung peninsula of China and the German Pacific islands north of the equator. Australia and New Zealand administered all but one of the German islands south of the equator. The Union of South Africa virtually absorbed German Southwest Africa. Great Britain obtained as mandated territory German East Africa (Tanganyika) and divided Togoland and the Cameroons with France.

The Germans were required to surrender all shipping over 1,500 tons as well as half their ships between 500 and 1,500 tons and a fourth of their fishing trawlers. New shipping to a total of 1,000,000 tons was to be built by Germany and handed over to the Allies. The Germans were also asked to surrender 30,000 freight cars, 5,000 locomotives, thousands of trucks, agricultural implements, horses, hogs, and cattle. They gave up all their ocean cables. They promised to deliver annually thousands of tons of coal to the Allies. Germany had surrendered her fleet before her crews scuttled it at Scapa Flow. She was also required to reduce her army to a maximum strength of 100,000 men, as a prelude to a general disarmament.

The Austro-Hungarian Empire was broken up by the treaties of St. Germain and Trianon. Rumania got Transylvania from Hungary, on the famous principle of nationality or "self-determination." Serbia took the southern Slav provinces of Austria and became the kingdom of Yugoslavia. Czechoslovakia was carved out of Bohemia, Moravia, and the Slovak part of Hungary. Poland took Galicia. Italy took Trent and Istria. Bulgaria surrendered her Aegean coastline to Greece.

Out of the Russian provinces surrendered to Germany by the Treaty of Brest-Litovsk were created independent republics: Finland, Estonia, Latvia, and Lithuania. By the Treaty of Sèvres with Turkey (1920) the non-Turkish provinces of Syria and Lebanon were given as mandates to France; Iraq, Transjordan, and Palestine became mandates of Britain. Smyrna and a section of the Anatolian coast went to Greece. Constantinople and the Dardanelles were placed under international control. The Turks under Mustapha Kemal later forced a revision of this arrangement. By the Treaty of Lausanne (1923) they kept Constantinople and the whole of Asia Minor.

There remained the question of the reparations to be paid by Germany. A Reparations Commission was established to decide the total sum that might be expected from Germany. In April, 1921, the Reparations Commission recommended the collection of $33,000,000,000. There were later to be twelve international conferences about reparations. Thirty-nine cabinets in central and western Europe fell as a result of reparations controversies. All of these discussions accelerated the economic collapse of Germany that came with despair, inflation, bankruptcy, and the ruin of the middle class. A prolonged insistence upon excessive reparations brought heavy confusion and mischief to the whole world. The old disorder in Europe was not ended by the peacemakers of 1919.

At Versailles was created the League of Nations. The Covenant of the League was an integral part of the peace treaty. Hence the defeated nations did not look upon the League as a foundation stone of a new order but rather as an instrument of ruthless victors determined to maintain the peace settlements. Neither the defeated Central Powers nor Communist Russia were at first permitted to become members. The structure of the League was further deranged by the withdrawal of the United States.

In the Covenant of the League of Nations the members pledged themselves to "promote international cooperation and to achieve international peace and security." The League undertook "to respect and preserve as against external aggression the territorial integrity and existing political independence of all members." It was the duty of the League to punish aggression on the part of any of its members by "financial and economic measures" and by "armed forces." The League also undertook to labor for the limitation of armaments "to the lowest point consistent with national safety." All future international treaties were to be published; all earlier treaties incompatible with the Covenant were to be abrogated.

The Assembly of the League, in which each member had one vote, was to meet annually at Geneva to "confer, advise, and deliberate." The Council, or executive of the League, contained five permanent members representing the leading powers and four (later nine) nonpermanent members chosen by the smaller powers. All international disputes likely to cause war were to be submitted by League members to arbitration or judicial investigation. The Permanent Court of International Justice was to meet in the Palace of Peace at the Hague. The administrative Secretariat formed an international civil service.

In the beginning the League was a reasonable, earnest, and intelligent attempt to achieve collective security. The essential principle of the League was that the members composing it, while surrendering none of their sovereign independence, should recognize that they were partners in the greater unity of the human whole.

The world soon retreated from this high hope. Within a few years the Germans were to challenge the whole settlement of 1919. They removed the shackles hammered out at Versailles. Dark shadows rolled over Europe.

Chapter 43

THE AMERICAS:
NEW HORIZONS

"For our New World I consider far less important for what it has done,
or what it is, than for results to come."
——Walt Whitman, *Democratic Vistas*

WHEN the United States moved into the early years of the twentieth
century the President was the exciting Theodore Roosevelt (1901–
1909), colonel of the "Rough Riders," rancher and big-game hunter extraordinary, ex-governor of New York. Here was a leader indeed, a man famed
throughout the world for his flaring nostrils, his unflagging vitality, the ferocious gusto of his attacks upon the great trusts, the indignant blasts of his
voice as he pursued the men he considered scoundrels down the years. Some
of his contemporaries praised his tireless hostilities, his crusades for conservation and reclamation projects, his tumultuous enthusiasms, his zeal expressed
in tones healthy and loud. Others opposed him. Passions and tensions often
ran high when his name was mentioned. It was not easy to prevail against
Theodore Roosevelt. The first impulse of his opponents was usually to get out
of his way.

The conservatives of Roosevelt's day often thought him too radical; the
progressives and radicals sometimes considered him too conservative. Any
careful study of his administration reveals that Roosevelt tried to hold an even
balance between the contending elements of society. Of such stuff are statesmen made.

The tranquil and conservative William Howard Taft of Ohio inherited the
mantle of leadership of the Republican party when Roosevelt decided to depart
from the White House. In the election campaign of 1908 William Jennings
Bryan led the Democrats in his third attempt to get the Presidency. The Republican Taft was not a sturdy fighter (Said Roosevelt: "Hit them hard, old
man!"), but he won the election, obtaining 321 electoral votes to Bryan's 162;
the Republicans also controlled both the House and the Senate.

There were soon prolonged disputes about tariff revisions—the protectionist Payne-Aldrich Act was passed in August, 1909. Then there came a series of controversies about the conservation of coal areas and water-power centers— the whole Ballinger-Pinchot affair led many men to the conclusion that Taft was abandoning the Roosevelt policies. A revolt against President Taft grew swiftly despite his active part in several constructive reforms—the Sixteenth and Seventeenth Amendments, the extension of the Interstate Commerce Commission's powers by the passage of the Hepburn Act and the Mann-Elkins Act, the creation of a Department of Labor. The Congressional elections of 1910 went against the Republicans.

Soon Theodore Roosevelt came back to the battlefields of politics to oppose Taft and to seek the Republican nomination for the next Presidential election. Taft's supporters, in complete control of the Republican party machine, carried the day for their candidate on the first ballot at the Chicago Convention of June, 1911. Roosevelt's followers then left the Republican ranks to form the Progressive party. The regular Republican leaders, they said, no longer represented the people.

After forty-six ballots the Democrats chose Woodrow Wilson, reforming governor of New Jersey, as their Presidential candidate. Theodore Roosevelt and his followers—the "Bull Moosers"—were defeated. Wilson got 435 electoral votes, Roosevelt 88, Taft 8. Wilson got 41.8 per cent of the popular vote, Roosevelt 27.4 per cent, Taft 23.2.

President Woodrow Wilson (1913–1921) was a scholar, a philosopher, and a man of courage and vision. Under his leadership the Democratic party moved swiftly along the path of reform. The tariff was revised downward (the Underwood Act of October, 1913); the banking and currency system was revised (the Owen-Glass Federal Reserve Act of December, 1913); trusts were regulated more effectively (the creation of the Federal Trade Commission in September, 1914, and the passage of the Clayton Anti-trust Act in October, 1914). In the elections of 1914 the Democrats kept control of Congress.

Ahead were uncharted waters. In the summer of 1914 the First World War began. President Wilson later remarked that "Americans did not at first see the full meaning of the War. . . . We, at the distance of America, looked on at first without a full comprehension of what the plot was getting into." The election of 1916 returned Woodrow Wilson to the White House. It may be that many votes were cast for him because he had kept the United States out of war. But the conflict was not to be held back from American shores for long. In April, 1917, the United States joined the Allies as an active partner in a widening conflict. Soon American men and resources began to move across the Atlantic. We have already considered their part in the gigantic struggle.

From New York to San Francisco, from the Columbia to the Rio Grande, the triumphs of technology continued to alter the face of the nation. Complicated and tireless machines and uncounted new techniques and gadgets created more wealth, increased man's control over his environment, reshaped his society. The demands for goods and services grew steadily stronger. The networks of world investment and trade were extended. Agriculture and industry advanced together. The population increased. Between 1830 and 1930, 28,000,000 Europeans came to live and labor in the United States. The birth rate went up and the death rate went down.

In the first half of the twentieth century the productive labor per hour tripled in the United States. In 1850 more than 60 per cent of the total useful work-energy came from the muscle power of men and animals; a century later about 99 per cent came from machines. In 1935 the domestic airlines carried 679,000 passengers; in 1950 they carried nearly 30,000,000. In 1950 nearly 800,000 Americans traveled overseas. More than half of the households in the United States had at least one automobile. The automobiles and the expressways, the speed and smoke of the great cities, these were the indisputable signs of a giant's power.

With power went wealth. A famous economist wrote this sentence in 1958: "The aggregate real income of 170 million Americans probably exceeds the combined income of the 600 millions living in Europe and the Soviet Union."

In the twentieth century the "masters of capital" and the "captains of industry" gained in strength and stature. The businessmen and bankers became twin symbols of American enterprise. There was an enormous rate of capital formation. Savings and investment speeded the growth of "big business" and production. Meanwhile, too, in a great managerial revolution, management slowly began to replace ownership in the effective control of business.

With relentless steps, government reached into the world of business. There were many new ways in which the authorities of Washington and the state capitals guarded and directed and interfered. Social security, workmen's compensation, and numerous relief measures were designed to change the shape of the state. The earlier age of "free enterprise" was slowly passing away. The octopus of administrative bureaucracy extended its tentacles far and wide.

Professor Thomas C. Cochran of the University of Pennsylvania has concluded that "the evolution of the business system has led to a lessening of class distinctions and has increased economic and social democracy." In his judgment there has been "the slow ending of the idea of a self-regulating capitalist economy based on natural economic laws." Professor Cochran is undoubtedly correct. Whether or not these changes will contribute to the total national welfare in the long pull is a matter for debate and conjecture.

At the end of the First World War the United States was the most wealthy and powerful nation in the world. In 1914 the United States owed Europe about $3,000,000,000. In 1919 the foreign nations owed the United States more than $11,000,000,000. At long last the United States was a creditor nation. Nevertheless, there were shadows and difficulties. Late in 1919 it was clear that too much money was chasing goods and services, a fact that always indicates the presence of the poison of inflation in the body economic. In 1920, after speculators began selling their holdings, there was a sharp depression, filled with premonitory warnings of a greater earthquake to come. Overexpansion, high tariffs, speculation, the decline of real capital formation, these and several other sins and evils and weaknesses were to take their inevitable toll.

In January, 1919, the Eighteenth Amendment was ratified; this law, filled with difficulties for the future, prohibited the sale of intoxicating liquor. The Nineteenth Amendment, ratified in the summer of 1920, gave women the right to vote. The railways, rented by the federal government during the war, were handed back to their owners by the Transportation Act of 1920. At the same time, the control of the government over the railways was increased, particularly with respect to railway rates and wage disputes.

In 1920, against the background of depression, a national election sent the Republican Senator Warren G. Harding of Ohio to the White House. The Republican victory was decisive: Harding obtained a plurality of 7,000,000; the vote in the electoral college was 404 to 127. Calvin Coolidge, governor of Massachusetts, was elected Vice-President. The people had voted to support Harding's ambiguous platform of a "return to normalcy." They had also set their faces against joining the League of Nations. "We seek no part in directing the destinies of the world," said Harding.

Thus began a long Republican reign of twelve years, a period marked by conservatism, isolationism, reparations and war debt disputes, high tariffs, new and restrictive immigration laws, bitter domestic quarrels about such things as power problems, agriculture, the Soldiers' Bonus Bill, and scandals in government.

In 1923 President Harding died. Meanwhile Congressional investigations were uncovering the depth and extent of the graft and corruption of Harding's government. Harding himself was probably innocent of any wrongdoing; his political associates and friends were not—it was alleged that the Secretary of the Interior got about $400,000 from the oil companies for his activities in the Teapot Dome Scandal. Many other men in the upper echelons of government also deceived their leader and fleeced the people who had trusted them.

President Harding's successor was Calvin Coolidge, safe, sound, conservative, and tight-lipped. He was a strong supporter of the "business philosophy" of the era. He favored government aid to industry, high tariffs, and national isolation—"The business of the United States is business!"

The Johnson Immigration Act of 1924 heavily restricted and regulated the tide of immigration. By the 2 per cent quota system, finally adopted in 1929, immigration was limited to about 150,000 persons a year. "Our hope is a homogeneous nation. At one time we welcomed all, and all helped to build the nation. But now asylum ends. The melting pot has to have a rest. Self-preservation demands it."

The Presidential election of 1924 was fought in a time and atmosphere of peace, contentment, and prosperity—apart from a continuing depression in agriculture. At the same time, there was too much drifting and too much complacency. John J. Raskob, chairman of the Democratic National Committee, declared: "I am firm in my belief that anyone not only can be rich, but ought to be rich." Such opinions, widely held and stated, were dangerous. Complacency and pride often precede disaster.

The Democratic candidate in the election was John W. Davis. He carried only one state—Oklahoma—outside the South. Robert La Follette, leader of the Progressive Party, won in his home state of Wisconsin, nowhere else. The Republicans said "Keep cool with Coolidge" and "Coolidge or Chaos." Calvin Coolidge captured 54 per cent of the popular vote and 382 electoral votes.

President Coolidge did not choose to be the Republican candidate in the Presidential campaign of 1928. The Republicans gave the nomination to the formidable Herbert Hoover, Secretary of Commerce since 1921, head of Belgian relief after the First World War, world-famous mining engineer. The Democrats chose "Al" Smith, four times governor of New York, a colorful, competent, and liberal Irish Roman Catholic. The campaign was exciting, full of oratory, plots, and prejudice. When it was finished Herbert Hoover entered the White House. He had obtained 58 per cent of the popular vote and 444 electoral votes. Alfred E. Smith got 40.8 of the popular vote and 87 electoral votes.

President Hoover now declared: "We in America are nearer to the final triumph over poverty than ever before in the history of any land. . . ." He looked forward to the day when "poverty will be banished from this nation." In those bright hours of 1928 it was difficult to watch the clouds heaping up on the horizon or to heed the warning rumbles from behind the sun-bathed hills.

In October, 1929, the stock markets wavered and crashed downwards. Within a few days the value of stocks listed on the New York Stock Exchange fell from $87,000,000,000 to $55,000,000,000. Thousands of individuals lost all their money, all their worldly goods. The first phases of the Great Depression were at hand. Here were the early results of excessive speculation, inflated hopes, wasteful and reckless expenditures, a worship of paper profits, a reluctance to look soberly at the possible consequences of high tariffs, over-expansion, the accumulating debts and the downward slope of real capital formation. Factories and mines closed by the hundreds. The value of foreign trade soon fell from $9,000,000,000 to $5,000,000,000. Nearly 30,000 banks and businesses failed. Between 12,000,000 and 15,000,000 men and women were soon unemployed. Thousands of mortgages were foreclosed. Many men simply could not believe what was happening.

President Hoover, astounded at the sudden storm, refused to believe that it would last for long. But it did last. The skies grew darker. The flood waters rose and swirled about the weakened economic foundations of the state.

In December, 1929, controversies multiplied in Congress. A few measures were taken to bolster the sagging economy, such as the creation of the Reconstruction Finance Corporation, the Grain Stabilization Corporation and the Cotton Stabilization Corporation under the Federal Farm Board. What was done was too little. Soon the depression spread over most of the Western world.

On June 27, 1932, Franklin Delano Roosevelt, governor of New York, was selected by the Democratic party to be its candidate in the approaching Presidential elections. John Nance Garner of Texas, Speaker of the House, was Roosevelt's running mate. Roosevelt flew to Chicago to accept the nomination. "I pledge you, I pledge myself," he told the Democratic convention, "to a new deal for the American people." Throughout his aggressive campaign Roosevelt spoke of the importance of the little fellow in America, the "forgotten man" he claimed had been neglected by the Republicans and "big business." Many of the Democrats blamed the Republicans for the depression and denounced what they considered the wailing, hand-wringing incompetence of the Republican government. In vain President Herbert Hoover warned that if the Democrats came into power and put their projected tariff policy into effect then "grass will grow in the streets of a hundred cities, a thousand towns." While Hoover warned, Roosevelt promised.

In the election of 1932 Franklin Roosevelt obtained 22,821,000 popular votes and Herbert Hoover 15,761,000. Roosevelt won every state in the Union but six. The Democrats also had landslide victories in both houses of Congress.

Such was the political victory of the Democrats. A political victory, however, was not enough. "Only a foolish optimist," declared Roosevelt, "can deny the dark realities of the moment."

In his inaugural address the new President asserted: "The only thing we have to fear is fear itself." He ordered an immediate bank holiday and summoned Congress at once to Washington. In a session that lasted a hundred days Congress passed a series of laws to deal with the national emergency. These laws, together with later legislation, formed what came to be called the New Deal, a program designed to achieve recovery, reform, and relief.

The "Roosevelt Revolution" extended and strengthened the executive branch of the government. More power was centralized in the hands of the men in Washington. Millions of dollars were spent to relieve the unemployed, to construct public works, and to stimulate recovery. New agencies, armed with money and power, began their heavy tasks: the Federal Emergency Relief Administration, the Civil Works Administration, the Works Progress Administration, the Civilian Conservation Corps, the Federal Housing Administration, the National Youth Administration, the Tennessee Valley Authority, the Home Owners' Loan Corporation, the Public Works Administration, the Agricultural Adjustment Administration, the National Recovery Administration.

The authority and funds of such bodies as the Reconstruction Finance Corporation, the Interstate Commerce Commission, and the Securities and Exchange Commission were greatly increased. Federal insurance was established for all bank deposits. The farmers were aided by such pieces of legislation as the Agricultural Adjustment Acts, the Soil Conservation and Domestic Allotment Act, the Bankhead Cotton Control Act, and the creation of the Federal Surplus Commodities Corporation. Workers were aided by the establishment of a National Labor Board and a series of laws dealing with wages and hours of labor, especially the Fair Labor Standards Act (June, 1938). Thousands of Americans were given a new protection and a new hope by the Social Security Act, passed in 1935.

Despite attacks from the left and right (Senator Huey P. Long, Dr. Francis E. Townsend, Father Charles E. Coughlin, the American City League) and a series of Supreme Court decisions striking down several New Deal measures, President Roosevelt easily won the Presidential election of 1936. His opponent, Governor Alfred M. Landon of Kansas, won only two states: Maine and Vermont. Roosevelt obtained 523 electoral votes and 60.7 of the popular vote.

Meanwhile the trade unions increased in size and power. In 1935 the Committee for Industrial Organization (later the Congress of Industrial Organizations) was formed as the result of a revolt within the American Federation of Labor; two years later the CIO claimed a membership of 3,700,000 and the AFL 3,600,000. The reciprocal trade policies of President Roosevelt and Cordell Hull, the Democratic Secretary of State, resulted in trade agreements with twenty-one countries and a marked expansion of American commerce. Problems of social and race relations grew more challenging and serious. The power and influence of the press, magazines, radio, moving pictures, and the stage helped to sway and shape public opinion. The spirit of disillusion that came in the wake of the First World War and the jolting economic realities of the Great Depression were reflected in the work of several American writers: Sherwood Anderson, John Dos Passos, Theodore Dreiser, James T. Farrell, William Faulkner, Ernest Hemingway, Sinclair Lewis, Carl Sandburg, John Steinbeck, Thomas Wolfe. There were many other fine writers in these years —Robert Frost, Christopher Morley, Eugene O'Neill, Edgar Lee Masters— and the place of the United States in the international world of letters was firmly established. Meanwhile new forms of art and music appeared to challenge the public interest. There was much action and creation and invention, much debate and talk, much advertisement, much confusion.

The people and Congress of the United States were anxious to avoid any entangling commitments abroad. There was a widespread popular belief that the munitions makers and financiers and all the "merchants of death" had been mainly responsible for the entry of the United States into the First World War. The failure of most European nations to make payments upon their war debts to the United States also increased popular American suspicions and doubts about the moralities and stabilities of other nations across the seas. Isolationism was triumphant. It was wise, surely, for Americans to mind their own business behind their own stockades.

In 1935 the United States refused to join the World Court. The neutrality legislation of 1935–1937, designed to prevent the involvement of the United States in any conflict abroad, provided that no nation engaged in any war could obtain arms or ammunition from the United States. Certain goods and raw materials might be purchased on a "cash and carry" basis. American citizens were forbidden to travel on the ships of belligerents or to make any loans to the governments of states at war. President Roosevelt was opposed to this neutrality legislation; he was convinced that the isolationist Congress was making a wrong decision.

When the Second World War exploded in 1939 the policy position of the United States was slowly altered. Preparations for American defense were speeded and extended. In May, 1940, a National Defense Advisory Board was formed; in August, 1940, a permanent joint committee was created to coordinate the defense of the United States and Canada; in September, 1940, about 16,000,000 men were required to register for military service. In the same month, fifty-one overage destroyers were sent to Great Britain from the United States in return for the right granted by Britain to the United States to construct U.S. military bases under long-term leases in British Guiana, the British West Indies, and Newfoundland.

In the Presidential campaign of 1940 both President Roosevelt and Wendell L. Willkie, his Republican opponent, agreed to support Britain and France, so heavily pressed in their battle against totalitarian aggression, by "all measures short of war." In March, 1941, the Lend-Lease Act was passed by decisive majorities in both houses of Congress. The law authorized the President— Roosevelt was returned to the White House for the third time in 1940—to "sell, transfer title, exchange, lease, lend or otherwise dispose of" materials to "any country whose defense the President deems vital to the defense of the United States." Congress made an initial appropriation of $7,000,000,000 to pay for the early streams of aid to the beleaguered Allies, the "immediate, all-out aid" that Roosevelt had promised. The isolationists objected, and objected loudly; but they did not have their way.

In May, 1941, President Roosevelt said: "When your enemy comes at you in a tank or a bombing plane, if you hold your fire until you see the whites of his eyes, you will never know what hit you. Our Bunker Hill of tomorrow may be several thousand miles away from Boston." The isolationists continued to be violently opposed to the policies of the President and those who stood with him—and the supporters of Roosevelt included a large number of Republicans, led by Wendell L. Willkie. Before the Japanese attack upon Pearl Harbor the people of the United States were badly and bitterly divided. After December 7, 1941, the facts were otherwise.

South of the United States lies Latin America, a vast land with many problems and promises.

In the 7,000,000 square miles of territory between the Rio Grande and Cape Horn there dwell more human beings than are contained within the boundaries of the United States and Canada. The population level steadily rises; the annual increase is now about 3,000,000. If the present pace of population growth is maintained, about 350,000,000 people will live in Latin America in the year 2000.

It is not wise to make many broad and general statements about the twenty republics of South and Central America, so varied in their peoples and their size—Brazil is larger than the United States and Haiti is smaller than Belgium. There are great and obvious contrasts and cross-currents in Latin America, numerous ethnic, political, economic, and cultural diversities, varying ideas about government, national ideologies, society, startling differences between urban and rural populations. There are also, of course, great variations in geography and climate. Consider, for instance, the "green hell" of the humid equatorial heat of Brazil's Amazon region where the traders are kings of a river that has uncounted tributaries and flows for nearly 4,000 miles. Far to the northwest are the oil-well regions on the eastern side of Venezuela's Lake Maracaibo. To the north and northwest are the Caribbean islands and Mexico —Mexico is 2,000 miles away. About 3,000 miles to the south stretch the pampas of Argentina, so green and vast and level. To the west, beyond the Andes, Chile and Peru lie like narrow ribbons along the Pacific coast.

In every Latin American republic there are thousands of illiterate, landless, and poverty-stricken people, many of them living on poor soil and close to the subsistence level. The first Spanish and Portuguese settlers built up great landed estates and most of the fertile regions and grazing areas are still in the hands of a small part of the population. In Argentina, for instance, almost all of the land is held by about 300 families made more wealthy still by the

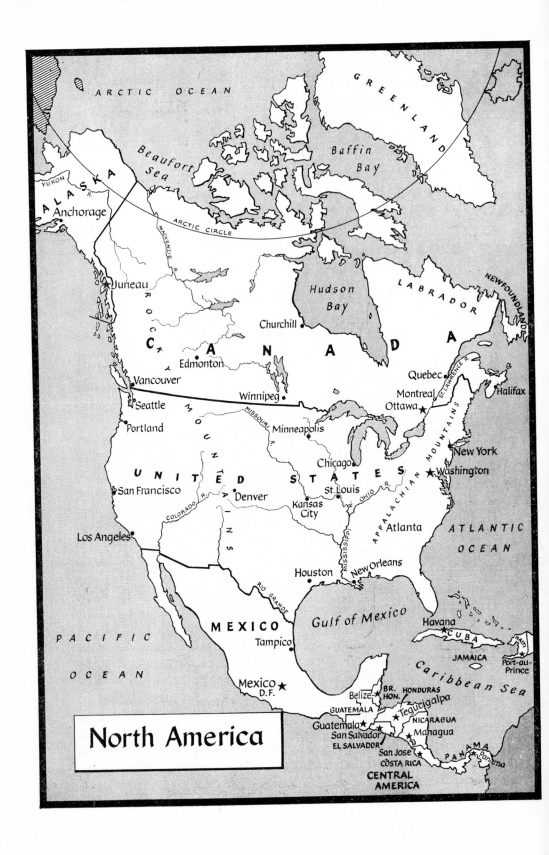

North America

South America

income from the low-cost production of meat and wheat. Almost all of the farmers are peons, tenants of the great landlords. Such conditions as these are often the mainsprings of revolution.

Only in a few areas have the evils of peonage been purged away by eager and exuberant rebels. In Mexico, for instance, a sudden uprising in 1911 overturned the regime of the dictator General Don Porfirio Díaz. The leader of the revolution, Don Francisco Madero, was assassinated in 1913. Mexico dissolved into civil war and chaos. Fanatics shouted and primed their guns; murderers crept and prowled about; soldiers and bandits wiped their reeking swords; politicians grabbed their spoils and prizes. Mexico had ten presidents in seven years. Each one hugged his power; his foes sharpened their knives and cut him down; successive governments fell to pieces. Nothing was settled except for those who died. Enterprise was strangled. Life was uncomfortable and unsafe.

Only slowly was a democratic federal government established in Mexico. The wealthy landowners were ousted and thousands of their acres of land were distributed to the peons. Similar experiments and shifts of ownership were later undertaken in Bolivia and Guatemala. In Chile, too, several large estates were broken up and sold. The urban industrial and business worlds have provided many jobs for the families that have come in from the rural areas.

The cleavage between the rich and the poor, the powerful and the weak, is still very wide in Latin America. It is easy to persuade men of many things by pointing to the high government officials in Lima and then to the Indians in the highlands of Peru, to the army officers in Buenos Aires and then to the suffering poor in the alleys of that great city. In the republic of Brazil about 5 per cent of the population—the plantation owners and the businessmen— hold about 90 per cent of the nation's wealth.

There are other difficulties. Any industrial nation depends for its driving power upon such natural resources as iron and coal. Latin America has little of either. In many areas there is an acute shortage of electricity. Only Mexico and Chile have sufficient natural resources to sustain much heavy industry. The basis of each republic's economy is still agriculture. True, there have been some industrial advances that will be mentioned later; but they are not yet of high consequence. Their chief significance is that they give promise of what may yet be done.

It is also true that the economy of each of the republics of Latin America is speculative because it is tightly tied to the production of a few commodities. It is obvious that any nation with too much speculation is in steady peril. For a long time now Brazil and Costa Rica have been too dependent upon coffee production, Chile upon such raw materials as nitrates and copper, Uruguay and Argentina upon meat and grain, Cuba upon sugar, Mexico upon oil and silver, the "banana republics" of Central America upon their export trade in fruit and a few other commodities.

When the Great Depression of 1929 struck Latin America the results were always serious, sometimes tragic. There were revolutions in seven republics within two years. Excited and tameless partisans exhorted and bludgeoned and killed. The rebel leaders sometimes became dictators and then proceeded to slaughter those whom they could not convince. They often won the acclaim and support of the poor men and women, the "shirtless ones." Some dictators and dictatorships, especially the one established in Argentina in 1946 by Juan Domingo Perón, were fairly stable. Perón's regime, supported by the Roman Catholic Church, the army, and the trade unions, rode out the storms and survived for ten years. Others were less fortunate; they rose and then they toppled. Even at the moment of their highest power the Latin American dictators could hear the sinister voices of ambition and rancor, could see in the eyes of their associates the dreaded flashes of deceit and treachery. No dictator could ever be sure that he would die in bed. The Latin American people were volatile and easily angered; the loyalty of the army officers and men was not always sure and constant.

For many years the states of Latin America have suffered from a lack of capital. Their governments have borrowed heavily abroad. Billions of British and American pounds and dollars have been invested in the lands south of the Rio Grande. Still the total of what was borrowed and invested was not enough. The governments of several of the Latin American republics were—and are— so rickety that only high interest rates would attract the wary investor. Some of the loans to Latin American countries were wisely used to build railways and refineries and the like. On the other hand, large sums were lost when some men embraced the chances to help themselves at the expense of their governments and peoples.

As the national debts mounted and the interest rates increased, many Latin Americans claimed that they were too dependent upon foreign money magnates and were losing control of their own national resources by making too many concessions. Sometimes they supported their arguments and helped their emotions by riots. Sometimes they repudiated their debts. Since the First World War, for instance, Mexico has defaulted upon more than $200,000,000 of her foreign debts and recovered all her refineries and oil wells from British and American hands. The problems of external debts and foreign ownerships and concessions will plague the relations between the governments and peoples of Latin America and the outside world for many years to come.

Sometimes the United States has found it necessary to send troops into Latin America to protect American citizens and interests. In the twentieth century, troops were sent into Cuba, Haiti, the Dominican Republic, Honduras, Mexico, Costa Rica, and Nicaragua. The Dominican Republic was occupied by United States forces from 1914 to 1922, Nicaragua from 1912 to 1925, Haiti from 1915 to 1934. Several Latin American nations felt and expressed their strong resentment at these activities of "the Colossus of the North." Tensions and doubts and suspicions were particularly strong after Cuba and Puerto Rico were freed from Spain in 1898 and then guided and guarded by the United States. The public opinion of Latin America was also inflamed after the Panama Canal was completed and after the United States swiftly recognized the Republic of Panama when Panama seceded from Colombia. Why, said many Latin Americans, did the United States move so rapidly to recognize the results of a rebellion that wounded Colombia, a friendly power?

The policies of President Herbert Hoover and Secretary of State Henry Stimson began to bring an unfamiliar spirit of good will and solidarity in the relations between the United States and the twenty republics south of the Rio Grande. President Hoover started to withdraw the marines from Haiti, and he pulled all of them out of Nicaragua. In 1930 the State Department repudiated the Roosevelt Corollary, the earlier assertion of President Theodore Roosevelt that the United States would interfere, as an "international police power," in Latin American countries to help collect debts owed to foreign countries. By 1930 it was clear that the United States was trying to change its outlook and its course. The charge and stigma of aggression, "interventionism," and imperialism could no longer rest upon Washington. The era of Dollar Diplomacy and the Big Stick of President Theodore Roosevelt was apparently about to end. In his inaugural address of March, 1933, President Franklin D. Roosevelt declared: "In the field of world policy I would dedicate this nation to the policy of the good neighbor—the neighbor who resolutely respects himself and because he does so respects the rights of others—the neighbor who respects his obligations and respects the sanctity of his agreements in and with a world of neighbors." In 1933 Cordell Hull signed an agreement at Montevideo stating that "no state has the right to interfere in the internal or external affairs of another." The Good Neighbor policy of President Roosevelt and Secretary of State Cordell Hull won a series of signal successes in Latin America. It marked a revolution in the relations between the United States and the other republics in America.

By 1934 all the marines were out of Haiti, the Platt Amendment was canceled by an agreement with Cuba, a reciprocal trade agreement was signed with Cuba and soon with six other Latin American states, and an Export-Import Bank was set up at Washington to aid in the financing and increasing of foreign trade, particularly between the United States and the Latin American republics. In 1936 the United States relinquished her earlier treaty right of intervening in Panama. It was decided that the Philippines were to be given almost full self-government for a ten-year period and then complete independence. A peaceful adjustment of the American oil claims against Mexico was reached in 1941.

Between 1933 and 1958 a series of treaties was signed by all of the republics in North and South America. These treaties were designed to strengthen and extend inter-American collaboration. In 1942 a Pan-American Conference at Rio de Janeiro was attended by representatives of all the twenty-one republics in North and South America. The extent of the almost solid front was shown by the fact that every state except Argentina and Chile either broke off relations with or went to war against the Axis powers in the Second World War.

Meanwhile there slowly appeared more heartening signs in the economic life of Latin America. A growing industrial enterprise, especially in the production of consumer goods, became evident in several Latin American states, particularly Argentina, Brazil, Chile, and Mexico. Such activities promised greater national incomes. During recent years there have also been many determined and encouraging attempts at land reform, sanitation, and education. In some countries there has appeared a middle class. The future of Latin America will probably be fairer than its past.

The first prime minister of Canada was Sir John A. Macdonald, one of the "Fathers of Confederation" and famous and able leader of the Conservative Party. For twenty-two years Macdonald stayed in office, pushing forward the railway building, carrying on his courageous and obstinate battles with the United Kingdom and the United States as Canada grew in stature and strength, maintaining the high tariffs behind which Canadian industry and agriculture were fostered and encouraged.

In 1896—the year that Republican Presidential candidate William McKinley defeated William Jennings Bryan in the United States—Sir John A. Macdonald and the Conservatives fell from power in Canada. The Liberals, led by the French-Canadian Sir Wilfrid Laurier, won the national elections of 1896, 1900, 1904, and 1908 and thus stayed in power until 1911. In Laurier's cabinets there were several Liberal giants whose names are written in the pages of Canadian history: Sir Richard Cartwright, Sir Clifford Sifton, Sir Oliver Mowat, W. S. Fielding.

The fifteen years of Sir Wilfrid Laurier's governments were marked by much railway construction, heavy immigration, settlement and exploitation, the pressing back of the wilderness, the steady advance of economic enterprise, the growth of new cities, sharp controversies about Canada's participation in the Boer War, and disputes about Roman Catholic schools in Manitoba.

Through all the years that followed the abrogation of the Canadian-American Reciprocity Treaty of 1854 the Republicans in the United States had stood opposed to all Canadian attempts to renew the reciprocity arrangements.

In 1911 Sir Wilfrid Laurier and W. S. Fielding succeeded in obtaining an agreement with the United States. The hour was too late. Canadian railway and industrial leaders objected. The Conservatives asserted that the British connection might be endangered by any close association with the United States. Several Liberals revolted against their leaders. Disputes also arose about Laurier's construction of a new Canadian navy (the Naval Act, 1910). After a violent and bitter campaign in the summer of 1911 the Liberals were defeated in a national election. There was to be no reciprocity with the United States, no free trade.

The new Conservative prime minister, Sir Robert Borden, was an honest and able man. There were more debates about naval construction on the eve of the First World War (Borden Naval Bill, 1912). These years were also marked by bad harvests and bad times. The building of the National Transcontinental Railway was finished. Then peace gave way to war.

In 1914 Canada joined the United Kingdom and her sister dominions in the long battle against Germany and her allies in the Triple Alliance. Under such leaders as Sir Arthur Currie and "Billy" Bishop thousands of Canadians went over the Atlantic to fly in the skies and fight in the mud and blood and mire of Europe. More than 60,000 Canadians lie in the graves of Flanders' fields.

In 1920 Sir Robert Borden retired and was succeeded by the Conservative Arthur Meighen. Meighen was defeated in the election of 1925. The new Liberal prime minister was William Lyon Mackenzie King. The Liberal majority was small. In 1926, believing that an election would return more Liberal members to Parliament, Mackenzie King asked Lord Byng, the governor-general, for a dissolution of Parliament. When Byng refused, King resigned. The result of these events was a famous controversy in Canadian history. Arthur Meighen tried to carry on a Conservative government, was defeated on a want-of-confidence motion, and resigned. An election returned the Liberals and Mackenzie King to power.

In the election of 1930, held in the middle of the Great Depression, the Liberals were not successful. Richard B. Bennett and the Conservatives tried to protect Canadian economic interests by a high tariff. Meanwhile new political parties, much to the left of center, appeared upon the Canadian political scene. The Cooperative Commonwealth Federation, drawing much support from the Canadian West, proclaimed platforms and doctrines of a "planned society" in some respects similar to those held and advanced by the British socialist Labor Party. In the province of Alberta, Major Douglas and William Aberhart started the Social Credit Party, a group whose startling economic theories attracted many followers.

In the election of 1935 Mackenzie King and the Liberals won a landslide victory over the Conservatives. The long reign of the Liberals began. The skillful, amazing, and enigmatic Mackenzie King, a master of political maneuver and compromise, apostle of a new Canadian nationalism, remained prime minister until his retirement after the Second World War. He was succeeded by Louis St. Laurent, who was prime minister until he retired in 1957. The successor of St. Laurent as leader of the Liberals was the brilliant and able Lester B. Pearson, Secretary of State for External Affairs and one of Canada's ace diplomats. Even the skill and brilliance of Lester Pearson and Paul Martin, the Minister of Health and Welfare, could not stem the Conservative tide. The Liberals were defeated in the election of 1958, and John Diefenbaker and the Conservatives formed a government.

During the years when these chapters in the history of mankind were being written in the United States, Latin America, and Canada the clouds of war had gathered over Europe. The might of the totalitarian states had been arrayed against Great Britain and France and free men everywhere. The challenge and curse of the crooked cross of the Nazis could not be ignored or evaded. Men left the green tables of diplomacy and moved to do battle on the fields of Mars.

Chapter 44

BETWEEN TWO WARS:

ASIA

"We may approve the feelings of the peoples for self-determination or we may condemn them, but we cannot ignore them; and they will pay little heed either to our abstract approval or condemnation."
—Alfred Cobban, *National Self-Determination*, p. 3

MANY fierce passions were unleashed in Asia during the twenty troubled years between the two World Wars. There were revolts and clashes and subversive blasts, sinister plots and sniping, much spite and malice, intricate and stubborn problems, and a great deal of hope. There also appeared a new vitality and explosive power, an enlarged perspective, a seething nationalism, a persistent and formidable desire for progress, a resentment and suspicion of anything that suggested colonialism or exploitation.

The impact of these facts upon the history of the world has been profound and irreversible. The nationalistic aspirations and intense enthusiasms of the roused peoples of Asia have produced some of the most significant transitions and revolutions in the history of mankind. From the eastern rim of the Mediterranean to the islands of Japan millions of people are marching and running. The strength of tradition dwindles. Before eager eyes there gleams and beckons the promise of the new world of tomorrow.

Not long ago the statesmen, soldiers, and traders of the West built colonies and power blocks in the Near and Far East. It is sometimes hard to believe that only yesterday these political and economic empires seemed solid, safe, and sure. In the swiftly changing decades of the twentieth century fierce and furious forces are making these empires shake and fall. Tremendous dislocations and upheavals, momentous shifts and trends and tendencies, continue to alter the face of Asia. As the events and years of the twentieth century thunder and tumble past there is a gigantic struggle for the command of the souls and bodies of millions of men.

From the point of view of the West several of the startling and convulsive changes in Asia are not entirely desirable. It is not a pleasant thing to see European and American empires and interests engulfed in disaster or menaced with destruction. It is hard to watch the work of your hands tottering and falling to pieces.

The thoughtful and sensible man knows that it is unwise to waste time weeping, shouting about catastrophes, or bewailing the loss of the sweets and spoils of trade and empire. It is a useless and dangerous idea to think that Europe and America can block or override the fierce and persistent zeal of the new Asia. Millions of men in Asia feel that they can make a new heaven and a new earth. They may not succeed. They may not be able to make anything but a lawless and bloody anarchy, filled with desperate perils. But they are determined to try to build new and better societies and civilizations. It is not wise for the nations of the West to stand in the way of Asia's advancing hopes. It is better to try to guide and direct men and ideas that cannot be stopped or fully controlled. At this stage in the journey of mankind all men need courage, wisdom, and much caution.

In the lands of the Near East there were tensions and troubles throughout the years that followed the collapse of the Central Powers in Europe and the end of the First World War. There were several attempts to overthrow existing governments; some succeeded and some did not. Malignant and unscrupulous troublemakers carried on their plots and prepared their propaganda and pressures side by side with the nationalists whose hopes and aspirations were honest and sincere. Some men sought the prizes and spoils they hoped to grab in the midst of disruption and terror. Others delighted in conspiracies and secret societies; their liking for such activities was in itself a partial explanation for what they did. They glided and padded furtively about the alleys and the market places. They met in ill-lit rooms. They threw knives and bombs. Old grievances were exhumed, old wounds remembered, old plans made again.

When Turkey had entered the First World War on the side of Germany, Great Britain had declared that Egypt, nominally a province of Turkey, was a British protectorate. During the war the Egyptian nationalism of Zaghlul Pasha and his Wafdist party spread swiftly. When peace came, the Egyptians demanded full independence. They supported their demands by oratory, riots, and murder; there was a steady blaze of trouble. The British consented to abolish the protectorate but insisted that they could not reconcile imperial necessity with Egyptian independence. Britain alone could protect the Suez Canal and foreign interests in Egypt. In 1922 the Egyptians agreed that British forces might remain.

Soon the Egyptians changed their position. In 1923 the Egyptian Parliament demanded the complete withdrawal of Britain from Egypt. In 1924 the governor-general of the Sudan was murdered in Cairo. In 1928 a treaty creating an Anglo-Egyptian alliance was rejected by the Egyptian nationalists. Not until 1936 was an agreement signed. By the terms of the treaty of 1936 Great Britain withdrew troops from Cairo and Alexandria, and kept them in the Suez Canal defense zone. A twenty-year alliance provided that Britain and Egypt would support each other in the event of war. Egypt was not required to enter any conflict by Britain's side unless she wished to do so; she did promise to place her ports and transportation facilities at Britain's disposal and to allow British forces and supplies free passage through her territory. The Egyptians were also to share in the government of the Sudan. Such treaty arrangements as these helped to reduce friction; but they did not end it. The pervasive spirit of nationalism increased.

There were also difficulties in Palestine, a British mandate after the First World War. With British aid, Palestine prospered. Behind the economic advance, however, the bitter Arab-Jewish hostility spread its malignant strength. In 1917 Britain had said that she viewed with favor "the establishment in Palestine of a National Home for the Jewish people." The Arabs objected. They regarded Palestine as their own. They clashed frequently with the Jews. No Jewish home, they declared, would ever be made on the land that the Moslem Arabs had helped to seize from the Turks. The restraining hand of Britain prevented heavy violence. British authorities continued to balance and mediate. In the end, they pleased neither Jew nor Arab.

During the First World War, Great Britain and France encouraged the restless subject peoples of Asia Minor to revolt against their Turkish rulers. To the insurgent Arabs were supplied money, arms, and technical assistance. The Near Eastern parts of the Ottoman Empire slipped away from the clutching hands of Turkey. Egypt, Mesopotamia, Syria, Palestine, and the Hejaz all escaped.

Turkey also suffered heavy losses in Europe. The earlier Balkan wars (1912–1913) had left her only Constantinople and eastern Thrace. In 1919 the Allies demanded that Turkey hand over eastern Thrace and the seaport of Smyrna to the Greeks. They imposed the Treaty of Sèvres on the sultan.

To all of these arrangements the Turkish nationalists vehemently objected. The Turkish army of Mustapha Kemal defied the Allies and expelled about a million Greeks from Asia Minor. Finally the Allies were compelled to yield to the Turkish demands. The Treaty of Lausanne (July, 1923) recognized Turkey's possession of Smyrna, eastern Thrace, and Istanbul (Constantinople). A month later the Turks deposed the sultan.

In October, 1923, a Turkish republic was established. Its new capital was at Ankara and its first president was Mustapha Kemal. Kemal was a virtual dictator, an enlightened despot. His critics were usually locked up. There was no freedom of speech or of the press. Under the leadership and iron control of the indefatigable Kemal an amazing effort was made to change Turkey, so inefficient, so ill organized and backward, into a modern, efficient, and progressive state. Almost everywhere the level of the people was raised by Kemal's constructive work.

The shrewd Kemal began at once to cope with the problem of widespread illiteracy. It was clear to him that no modern state can hope to be strong without a reasonably efficient system of education. Attendance at school was made compulsory for all children under the age of sixteen. Special schools were set up for adults who wanted to learn to read and write. The Roman alphabet was substituted for the difficult Arab characters. The Western Gregorian calendar and Arabic numerals were introduced. The ecclesiastical courts were abolished. Women were permitted to appear in public without their veils; they obtained the right to vote in 1934. Men began to discard the turban and the fez. Industrial and commercial expansion was encouraged and aided. Western law codes were introduced. Many aspects of the national life were changed. President Mustapha Kemal was elected to his high office every four years until his death in 1938.

In several other restless states of Asia Minor there were reforms in society and government. For instance, in Persia—since 1935 the official name is Iran —the shah is a constitutional monarch and the Parliament is elected. The large royalties paid by the Anglo-Iranian Oil Company helped to pay the cost of many buildings and some reforms. Riza Pahlevi, who became shah in 1925, liked to see secular progress and material achievements. The foreign engineers who built a railroad from the Caspian Sea to the Persian Gulf did a good job. The foreign experts summoned to modernize the public administration gave fine advice. Not all of it was heeded. It has not yet been possible to eradicate all of the long-standing evils of inefficiency and corruption in Iran. The extent and significance of changes and reforms in several lands must not be inflated or stressed too strongly. To put something upon paper is one thing; to make it work is quite another.

At the end of the First World War, France took Turkey's Syria and Lebanon as mandates under the League of Nations. In addition to Palestine, Great Britain obtained Iraq. In all the Arab world only Saudi Arabia remained almost completely independent under the rule of Ibn Saud (1890–1953). Throughout these Arab lands—including the state of Transjordan carved out of eastern Palestine—there raced and flashed the power of nationalism. The peoples and their leaders often envied the men and the world of the West— some Arabs had been educated there. Often they wished to imitate some of the achievements of Europe and America, especially in technology. They welcomed the money that they were paid for the oil that came out of their sands and flowed to the Western ships lying in the hot harbors. On the other hand, they feared and resented any attempts, real or fancied, at foreign control or exploitation.

The years between 1919 and 1939 were also marked by strong movements for unity in the Arab lands. During the Second World War the Arab League came into formal existence. The League embraced the seven states of Egypt, Iraq, Lebanon, Saudi Arabia, Syria, Transjordan, and Yemen. These states covered 1,000,000 square miles and contained a population of about 27,000,-000. If they had developed their resources and combined their strength they might have built a massive block of Arab power in the Near East. Instead, they remembered their rivalries, their ancient grudges, the deep suspicions that lurked beneath the smiles of courtesy.

In the vast land of India the nationalist agitation grew more formidable with every passing year. The Moslem League and the Congress Party insisted upon the justice and wisdom of their plans for self-government.

During the First World War, India helped the Allied cause and Great Britain promised major concessions as soon as the war ended. In 1918 Edwin S. Montagu, Secretary of State for India, and Lord Chelmsford, Viceroy of India, submitted their Report on Indian Constitutional Reforms. Upon this report and subsequent discussion was based the Government of India Act of 1918. This act set up a national government for India consisting of a legislative assembly and a council of state. A majority of representatives in both central bodies was to be elected and the franchise was extended to about 5,000,000 voters.

But there was no responsible government. The Indian nationalists, bitterly disappointed, turned again to violence. Meanwhile the cost of living rose and thousands died as waves of disease swept through India. Great Britain's Rowlatt Acts gave the authorities extraordinary powers to deal with plotters and agitators. But violence did not end. Obstruction did not stop.

More and more people in India insisted that they were not satisfied with small installments of political liberty. Some demanded responsible government and dominion status; others wanted full and final independence. New patterns of nationalism appeared in the midst of the baffling problems of race and religion, caste and culture, education, language, and economic advance.

Mahatma Gandhi (1869–1948), later leader of the Congress Party, had returned from South Africa to his native India in 1914. Angered by the British attempt to suppress nationalist agitation, Gandhi began a strange and vigorous campaign. In 1920, after a series of bloody riots had leaped from city to city and raced through countless villages, Gandhi headed the "Swaraj" or home-rule group and formulated the policy of peaceful noncooperation with the British, a policy soon adopted by the National Congress. The followers of

On September 1, 1939, Adolf Hitler hurled his armed Nazi might against Poland. Here a German motorized detachment rides through a shattered Polish town.

PLATE XLI

[117] After June, 1940, two thirds of France was held by the Germans. In November, 1942, they ⟨took?⟩ the whole country. This picture, taken in February, 1941, shows the expressions on some French face⟨s⟩ ⟨as the⟩ flags of France's historic regiments go into exile.

PLATE XLII

Gandhi agreed never to resist the British by violent means. Their resistance would be passive. They would silently boycott British schools and law courts; they would not take any part in the political life of India; they would not buy British goods. The saintly and stubborn Gandhi persuaded thousands to take up hand spinning and weaving as a protest against Western industrialism.

Passive resistance was not enough for some of Gandhi's followers. There were riots; bolts of British cloth were seized and burned. British troops were guilty on several occasions of errors of judgment and common humanity, especially at Amritsar. Indian nationalists continued to snipe and beat un-guarded Englishmen to death. Gandhi was sentenced in 1922 to six years in prison. He was released in 1924.

In 1924 the Indian Assembly threw out the budget when the British would not agree to grant India immediate self-government. The Viceroy thereupon put the budget into effect without legislative support. In 1927 the British government appointed the Simon Commission to report upon the problem of stabilizing the rupee, the working of the governmental system, the growth of education, and the affairs of India generally. The National Congress and most of the members of the Moslem League boycotted the Commission. In 1929 Gandhi began his famous "march to the sea" to defy the British govern-ment by making salt out of sea water. By law the making of salt was a govern-ment monopoly. At the end of his long journey Gandhi broke that law. The result was another outburst of violence.

In 1930 the Simon Report was issued. It advocated the creation of a great federation of all Indian states except Burma and the Northwest Frontier Province. Two Round Table Conferences, held in London in 1930 and 1931, agreed on the federation of the Indian native states and British India. Gandhi himself attended the Conference of 1931. There were many difficulties in all the proposals regarding representation, law, finance, and the protection of minority groups. Soon disaffection rose to new heights in India; economic distress increased; taxes were left unpaid; tongues of flaming terror licked through the Deccan and Bengal.

After a third Round Table Conference the British undertook the tremen-dous task of forming a new governmental system for India. The Government of India Act of 1935 set up an Indian federation with limited responsible government in both the bicameral federal government and in the provinces. The British government retained control of finance, foreign affairs, and the military services. The door was left open for the entrance of the native states under their princes into the federation. Negotiations to that end were proceed-ing when the Second World War began in 1939.

In India the new act was unpopular. It did not grant dominion status; it did not grant independence. Amidst ignorance and poverty, cultural and religious divisions, new leaders rose beside the old. Jawaharlal Nehru of the predominantly Hindu All-India National Congress Party demanded independence, socialism, and a strong central government for India. On the other hand, Mohammed Ali Jinnah of the Moslem League insisted that the Moslems should have an independent state, separate from the Hindus. This famous doctrine of Pakistan always took first place among the Moslem demands. Could the gulf between Hindu and Moslem elements ever be bridged? Would the British be able and willing to devise a concrete plan to satisfy India's aspirations? The answer was to come after the Second World War.

There were other disputes and difficulties in the troubled lands of southeastern Asia. The twenty million people who lived in the rich lands of French Indochina were no longer content to see the life of their land move in the ancient grooves. In Siam—soon to be modern Thailand—and in the British territories of the Malay peninsula the demands for change increased. In the Netherlands East Indies more than 70,000,000 people lived upon about 3,000 islands. Here, too, there was a mounting desire for self-government. In Burma, the long age of isolation had ended. The barges of the British Flotilla Company, carrying oil from Chauk, teak from Tenessarim, lead and silver and zinc from Mantu, chugged hundreds of miles along the Irrawaddy. Traders went far inland beyond Pegu, Kalewa, Youngoo, and Prome. Out of Burma came tons of rice—about half of the world's population lives upon a diet that is mainly rice. For uncounted centuries the rice shoots have been taken out of the nursery plots in June and transplanted to the muddy paddies by the barelegged natives. By the end of September the rice is ripe; the fields are drained in early October; the rice is cut with a scythe, threshed, hulled, polished, and sold.

In all of the undeveloped lands of Asia—and throughout the distant islands of the Pacific—millions of restless men were beginning to glimpse new worlds and to grasp for new treasures. Their old worlds had been deranged; sometimes they had been reduced to a shambles. Strangers had come to trade, to teach, and to harness human energies. The natives of the Southeast Asia regions were often men of intelligence and aptitude. They could observe; they could learn; they could alter their goals and tasks; they could aspire. The shrewd men among them could see that their countries had an acute shortage of trained labor and that steps must be taken to obtain skilled technicians and develop managerial abilities. In the twentieth century many of the people of these lands are trying to acquire, as rapidly as possible, the knowledge and skills of Western industrial countries. Sometimes the pace is too forced, the rush too wasteful and headlong. There is too much inflated and flamboyant optimism and enthusiasm, too many misconceptions, too little awareness of the complexities of the problems and the difficulties to be overcome. Meanwhile the speed and the pressures do not diminish. Burma's Prime Minister U Nu was speaking for many men beyond the borders of his own state when he said: "We should all try to do things with a strong sense of urgency, with a genuine fear of time being wasted as we fear the loss of our own lives."

For many centuries dynasty after dynasty had ruled in China. Strong men had given way to weak and empires had fallen, one by one. Such had been the experience and tradition of China. Then the intruders had come from Europe and America to defeat the Chinese in several wars, to obtain leases in important ports and provinces, to engage in economic rivalry and warfare. They also brought to China new ideas, ideas about constitutional monarchy, republicanism, socialism, and the red doctrines and dogmas of Communism. The success of the Russian revolution of 1917 had a great effect in Asia.

In 1912 China began the new and hazardous experiment earlier mentioned in Chapter 40. The old Manchu Empire fell and was replaced by a republic. General Yuan Shih-k'ai was the first president. Yuan was a man not to be trusted. He began to spin plots. He wanted to set up a new empire with himself as the first emperor.

The provisional constitution of 1912 stated that the president was to be under the control of the National Assembly. Yuan did not like that. The first National Assembly was dominated by the radical Kuomintang or Nationalist Party. Yuan did not approve of that.

A series of disputes soon arose between Yuan and the Kuomintang. For instance, the Kuomintang wanted the capital of the new republic to be in the south at Nanking. Yuan wanted it at Peking, that ancient and splendid city with nine gates at the northern end of the Yellow River plain. Yuan had his way. Then Yuan arranged a large loan through various banks in Great Britain, France, Germany, and Russia. To this loan Sun Yat-sen was opposed. He insisted that it would increase foreign influence and power in China. But Yuan completed the arrangements for the loan. He was not wise.

The revolt that had been smoldering against Yuan suddenly blazed forth when the ambitious president placed several of his personal friends and followers in key posts in the army. Yuan had made his plans carefully, and the rebellion was crushed. Sun Yat-sen, who had been one of the rebel chiefs, was forced to flee to Japan.

Yuan thought that he was now secure. He forced the Kuomintang members out of the National Assembly. A few months later he dismissed the whole National Assembly, dissolved all the provincial assemblies, selected seventy men to govern China under his direction. Early in 1915 he attempted to establish a new empire with himself as the first emperor. Rebellion flared and flamed again. This time Yuan could not beat down his foes. His gamble failed. His dream of a throne crumbled. A year later he died, disillusioned and impotent.

After the death of Yuan there came ten years of political confusion. War

lords marched and fought and tumbled about. In China's long history there
have been many such times as these.

During the years of China's weakness her predatory neighbors were not
idle. Russia attempted, not for the first time, to extend her power in Outer
Mongolia. Japan seized Kiaochow and Germany's railways in the Shantung
area. To the anger of the Chinese the peacemakers at Versailles in 1919 were
to hand these territories over to Japan.

In January, 1915, Japan made twenty-one demands upon China. If China
had yielded then she would have been a puppet of Japan. Probably Japan
would not have been allowed to bring such heavy pressures upon China if
the world had been at peace. But the world was not at peace. Most nations
were staggering under the heavy blows of war. The only world power that
was not fighting in 1915 was the United States. Washington protested to
Tokyo and the Japanese consented to withdraw some of the most objectionable
and extreme of the twenty-one demands. To the others China was compelled
to consent.

To the Chinese nationalists this capitulation before the might of Japan was
a humiliating event. There were many demonstrations and riots. Nevertheless,
there were no practical ways of stopping the Japanese encroachments. Nothing could be done against a foreign aggressor when China was so badly and
sadly divided within. There were cliques and factions almost everywhere, the
claims and counterclaims of rival war lords, the financial problems resulting
from excessive borrowings abroad, especially from Japan.

There were two governments in China, one at Peking and one at Canton.
Each claimed to be the legitimate center of authority. The Canton government elected Sun Yat-sen president in 1921. Sun Yat-sen, seeking to overthrow the Peking government, obtained money, military support, and advice
from Soviet Russia. Great Britain and the United States would give him none
—in this decision they made a major policy error. Chiang Kai-shek went to
Moscow to study military organization and some problems of strategy and
tactics. The shrewd and brilliant Michael Borodin came down to advise the
Chinese in Canton. He persuaded the Kuomintang to adopt several principles
and policies that were based upon the teachings of Marx and Lenin. In these
months there was a marked revival of the Kuomintang throughout southern
China, especially after the first National Congress of January, 1924.

In March, 1925, Sun Yat-sen died. He was a national hero. Stories about
him multiplied; not all of them were true. Sun Yat-sen became, more and
more, a symbol of Chinese republicanism and nationalism. His books were
widely read and praised. One of them, *Three People's Principles* (*San Min
Chu I*), became a handbook for many men within and without the Kuomintang. The famous three principles of Sun Yat-sen were these: nationalism,
democracy, and the economic safety of every man, woman, and child in China.

Meanwhile Chinese nationalism gained a new vitality and a greater strength. Chinese students were particularly active. Some of them had studied in Russia and had returned quite hostile to the "capitalist-imperialist" nations. Others had studied in the United States and held a different point of view. The young Chinese who had studied in the West were usually enthusiastic, informed, and obstinate nationalists. They were the leaders in the boycotts of foreign merchants. They were the leaders in the demonstrations against Japan. If they had possessed the arms they would have been the leaders in a war against the foreigners of many lands.

Several writers and teachers in the "Chinese Renaissance" used *pai hua*— the most common form of the vernacular. These men helped to stimulate interest, stir imaginations, and increase knowledge. The remarkable work of Hu Shih, for instance, helped to extend the "national speech" and to overcome the evils of the numerous and cumbersome dialects.

In 1926 the armies of the Kuomintang, led by Chiang Kai-shek, began a great drive northwards towards Peking. In this campaign the Kuomintang was supported by the Chinese Communist Party, an increasingly powerful group. Early in 1927 the Kuomintang armies swept into the Yangtze valley and seized Shanghai. In June, 1928, they captured Peking. Perhaps now, at last, all China could be united.

The alliance between the Kuomintang and the Communists soon collapsed. Nobody could have hoped that it would endure very long. The Communists were opposed to all religion and sneered at Confucian morality. Wherever Communist organizers and plotters appeared there followed strikes and violence. It was not surprising that Chiang Kai-shek and his conservative associates in the Kuomintang began to suppress the Communists. A diplomatic break with Moscow soon followed; it was not mended until 1932. The Communist advisers were sent packing home to Moscow.

A new Chinese Nationalist government was established at Nanking. The future seemed bright with promise. China was protected by the Nine-Power Treaty of 1922—the nine signatories of that treaty agreed to respect the integrity and territorial independence of China; they also agreed "to refrain from taking advantage of conditions in China in order to seek rights or privileges which would abridge the rights of subjects or citizens of friendly states. . . ." China was also a member of the League of Nations. Great Britain had allowed her treaty of alliance with Japan to lapse in 1921. The Nationalist government was in the hands of well-trained men who seemed determined to use all of their power and skills in the cause of national unity. Chiang Kai-shek strengthened his place in the state and the Kuomintang by marrying Mei-ling Soong, a sister of Madame Sun Yat-sen. With an increasingly stable government China could hope for more help from foreign bankers.

There were shadows on the sun. China was still plagued by bandits, still scourged and hurt by famines. Despite the fact that European powers and the United States handed back several of the concessions and extraterritorial rights which they had earlier obtained from China, the Chinese people, especially in the cities, did not seem to be satisfied. In 1928 and 1929 most of the Western powers agreed to the resumption of tariff authority by China. Nevertheless, there were still numerous and strong objections to the foreign intruders, especially the British. British goods were boycotted and violent hands were sometimes laid on British nationals. The prestige and trade of Britain in China steadily declined. In 1931 the British government returned Weihaiwei to China and this step perhaps helped to mollify the Chinese and reduce their resentment. There was no doubt, however, of powerful and persistent anti-foreign feeling in China. Memories of the past and fears about the future were not easily wiped away.

The Nanking government was also compelled to meet new challenges by the Chinese Communists. Some of these Communists were committed follow-ers of the teachings of Marx and Lenin; many of them had attended the uni-versity started in Moscow in 1925 to meet the needs of Chinese students. Other so-called Communists were not in fact Communists at all. They were bandits, the soldiers of local warlords, or landless peasants. To the latter, so hungry and so jealous, the message of Communism had a strong appeal.

Chiang Kai-shek tried hard to put down and keep down the menace of the Chinese Communists. He was not successful. Every month, it seemed, more Communists rose to challenge the Nanking government. In 1934 the Com-munist forces decided to evacuate southern China. They marched about 1,500 miles from Kiangsi to Yenan on the Yellow River. This was a remarkable feat. It was also a warning. The days of the "Red Star over China" might not be far distant.

A more immediate threat to China came from Japan, a state whose power had increased at a startling pace. The military and naval history of Japan was impressive—witness the Treaty of Shimonoseki, Japan's part in suppressing the Boxer Rebellion, the alliance of 1902 with Great Britain, the Russo-Japanese War and the Treaty of Portsmouth, the results of the Twenty-one demands upon China, the recognition by the Washington Conference of 1921 that the Japanese navy was the third most powerful in the world. Japan's economic and financial strength also increased the alarm of several of the Western powers. In 1931, for instance, Great Britain had $1,189,200,000 in-vested in China; Japan had $1,136,900,000; Russia had $273,200,000; the United States had $196,800,000. Japan was capturing many international textile markets. In Meiji days the business monopolies and trusts (*zaibatsu*) came to hold in their hands most of the nation's wealth. Great financial and merchant firms such as the houses of Mitsui, Yasada, Sumitomo, and Mitsubishi controlled banks, railroads, factories, power companies, and scores of other pivots of economic strength.

The population of Japan was swiftly increasing. In 1930 nearly 70,000,000 people lived in an area that is smaller than California—Japan has 142,312 square miles of land, California 158,297. In 1960 about 85,000,000 human beings lived in the same territory. Crowded Japan's birth rate in 1960 stood at 28.2 per thousand; it was 39 in 1885; the death rate was 10.9 in 1960; it was 32 in 1885.

In her islands Japan had no supplies of several important raw materials (oil, rubber, many fertilizers, scores of metals). About 20 per cent of Japan's food was imported. To pay for all her imports Japan had to export goods. Foreign trade meant survival. A lack of it meant decay and death.

In 1930—a year when Japan was hurt by the great depression—the Japanese army took over the political direction of the state. Behind the army stood the secret nationalist societies. The military men (*gumbatsu*) were supported by the business monopolies and trusts (*zaibatsu*) and the whole bureaucratic system (*kambatsu*) of the state.

In September, 1931, the Japanese army attacked China's Manchuria. The Japanese leaders expected that the foreign war resulting from "the Mukden Incident" would reduce unrest at home, increase the army's prestige, delay the unification of China, and open up new markets for Japan. China appealed to the League of Nations for help against the invader. The League appointed the Lytton Commission to investigate. The Chinese began a vast boycott of Japanese goods and fought on against the invader. In February, 1932, Shanghai fell before the Japanese power. In the same month Japan proclaimed the creation of the puppet state of Manchukuo; on the throne of the new state they put the last Manchu emperor of the Ch'ing dynasty. The Japanese also took the territory of Jehol and a section of Inner Mongolia. They continued to push southwards into China beyond the sweep of the Great Wall.

Meanwhile the Lytton Report had been submitted to the League of Nations. The Report condemned the Japanese aggression. The League refused to recognize Manchukuo, and asked Japan to stop her activities in China. The United States declared that it would not recognize any conquests made in defiance of existing treaty obligations. In March, 1933, Japan withdrew from the League of Nations.

The dream of the Japanese leaders was not of peace; it was of aggression and war and the hour when Japan would rule all of China. "China needed time," Professor Kenneth Scott Latourette has written, "and time is what the Japanese would not give her."

Japan intended to thrust and wound in a series of relentless attacks. Then, surely, the Chinese dragon would crumple. Then Japan's "new order" would be established. Soon a great "co-prosperity" sphere, controlled by Japan, would extend far into Southeast Asia.

The Japanese soon found that their aggression in Manchuria did not produce the dividends that they had expected. The factories that they built there competed with their own industries back home in Japan. Only a few Japanese could be persuaded to settle in Manchukuo. Chinese nationalists—the Japanese called them "bandits"—caused much trouble; the Japanese could seldom track them down. The Opium Advisory Committee of the League of Nations found that the Japanese tried to undermine the resistance of the Chinese by encouraging the use of narcotics. But the underground power of the Chinese did not crumble. The Japanese were blocked and baffled.

In Japan the army leaders were preparing for the next attack upon China. This time they hoped to reach and seize the rich areas of the south. The domestic situation in Japan was unpleasant. Prices, rents, and production costs were high and going higher. Foreign trade was slipping downwards—the adverse balance was a billion yen in 1936. Unrest and agitation were spreading fast. Against this tense background the radical army chiefs extended their political and economic control of the state. In 1932 they assassinated the Japanese premier and created a virtual reign of terror by murdering their opponents.

In China the Kuomintang of Chiang Kai-shek and the Chinese Communist Party agreed to stand together against the Japanese. Thus the stage was set again for war.

On July 7, 1937, an unfortunate "incident" happened when Japanese and Chinese soldiers exchanged shots at the Marco Polo Bridge near Peking. The military "incident" blazed into an undeclared war. The Japanese pushed further into Inner Mongolia and Shensi province. In August, 1937, they launched a heavy attack upon Shanghai. After a stubborn resistance the city surrendered. The Japanese then headed towards Nanking, the new Chinese capital. Nanking fell to the invading armies on December 15, 1937. The events and the atrocities in "the rape of Nanking" horrified the world. The Japanese established a provisional government at Peking. Chiang Kai-shek set his new capital at Hangkow, later at Chungking on the upper Yangtze. In 1938 the Japanese took Hangkow and Canton. Soon they drew near to Chungking. They set up a government in Nanking and put a puppet Chinese ruler —his name was Wong Ching-Wei—on a new throne. Wong Ching-Wei signed a peace agreement with Japan. China, said Wong Ching-Wei, would "cooperate" with Japan.

In November, 1937, the Far Eastern Advisory Committee of the League of Nations declared that Japan had violated the Kellogg-Briand Pact of Paris of 1928 and the Washington Treaty of 1922. The League Assembly approved the report of its committee.

Upon the European stage the aggressive tendencies of Nazi Germany and

Fascist Italy were already apparent. Early in 1936 the Japanese signed a Japanese-German Anti-Comintern Pact, an agreement ostensibly designed to strengthen the anti-Communist front in East and West. Italy's Mussolini signed the agreement in 1937. Despite the form of the treaty it was clearly calculated to show the world that Germany, Italy, and Japan were united. The Rome-Berlin-Tokyo alignment was a fact.

Japan moved ahead. Heavy pressure was brought to bear upon Western foreigners in China. British ships were fired upon and British subjects manhandled. The American gunboat *Panay* was bombed in the Yangtze. The United States began to enlarge her air, navy, and submarine bases in the Pacific and to extend financial credits to the Chinese Nationalist government. Great Britain soon began to ship goods to China along the Burma Road.

In November, 1938, Japan proclaimed the coming of a "New Order" in eastern Asia. The Nationalist government of Chiang Kai-shek was to be destroyed. The Western powers were to be driven out of China. A unified and self-sufficient economy was to be established in Japan, Manchukuo, and China.

When the Second World War began in September, 1939, the Japanese prepared to extend still further their "New Order." In September, 1940, Japan signed a military alliance with Italy and Germany, a pact directed against the United States. The Axis powers agreed "to assist one another with all political, economic, and military means when one of the three is attacked by a power at present now involved in the European war or in the Chinese-Japanese conflict." At the same time, the United States, Great Britain, China, and the Dutch East Indies began to consult about ways in which further Japanese aggression might be stopped. After the fall of France, the Vichy government allowed the Japanese to send troops into French Indochina—some "observers" had come earlier. Here they established a base that might one day be used in an attack upon Burma or Malaya or Thailand or Borneo. In 1940 the United States forbade the sale to Japan of certain commodities, including petroleum and iron products. In July, 1941, all Japanese and Chinese assets in the United States were "frozen." Great Britain and the United States warned Japan against extending her power and influence in Thailand.

In October, 1941, General Hideki Tojo became premier of Japan. In November, Saburo Kurusu came as a special envoy from Tokyo to negotiate in Washington. The negotiations were never completed. On December 7, 1941, Japanese planes attacked the naval base of the United States at Pearl Harbor.

Chapter 45

BETWEEN TWO WARS:
EUROPE

"No man is an *Iland*, intire of it selfe; every man is a peece of the *Continent*, a part of the *maine;* if a *Clod* bee washed away by the *Sea, Europe* is the lesse, as well as if a *Promontorie* were, as well as if a *Mannor* of thy *friends* or of *thine owne* were: any mans *death* diminishes *me*, because I am involved in *Mankinde;* And therefore never send to know for whom the *bell* tolls; It tolls for *thee*."

—John Donne's *Seventeenth Devotion*

THE FIRST WORLD WAR brought death and devastation and terror in the fields and streets of Europe. The treaties that closed the long conflict promised, for a brief hour, the hope of peace. This chapter is about the slow collapse of that hope, the desperate search for security, the darkening skies of Europe, and the rising challenge of the new totalitarian states.

Tyranny always means the slavery of the body, the smothering of the spirit, the dread knock on the door at night, pain, poverty, disease, death. More than a century ago Stendhal said this: "What counts is not the personality of the tyrant but the essence of tyranny. A tyrant may be intelligent or stupid, good or evil—but whatever the case, he is both all-powerful and powerless, he is frightened by conspiracies, he is flattered, he is deceived. The prisons fill, the cowardly hypocrites whisper, and the silence becomes so complete that the heart almost stops."

The words of Stendhal describe what is happening and has happened to thousands of human beings. A tree may serve today to make a house and another may be used tomorrow to erect a gallows or to shape a cross.

It is sometimes easy for free men to think that all human beings must believe in freedom. They have not in the past. They do not now. For them the dictator, the tyrant, the master of the masses, always lie in wait.

"He sitteth lurking in the thievish corners of the streets and privily in his lurking dens doth he murder the innocent; his eyes are set against the poor. . . ."

After the guns had stopped firing and the travail and convulsions of the First World War had ended at last, the hearts of some men were quickened with hope. They believed that a great moment had come in the history of the world. Others were pessimistic. Filled with fatigue and sometimes with cynicism, they gloomily insisted that men and nations had not really changed. The old and constant laws of human nature, they said, still swayed and shaped the world. They saw rising in the future the familiar conflicts of national interests, the menace of massive armaments, the short-range views, the rip tides of international hostilities, the measureless cleavages between the great intentions and the small performances of statesmen groping in confusion and uncertainty. The pessimists—they were often called realists—declared that it was nonsense to try to soothe and satisfy men by enthusiastically proclaiming the coming triumphs of peace and prosperity and progress at a time when discords were multiplying, dreams were being thwarted, plans and experiments frustrated, economies mutilated. It did nobody any good, they asserted, to pretend that all was well in the world and getting better. The blunt and practical fact was that things were bad and getting worse.

Not long after the peacemakers had left Versailles the increasingly pervasive moods of doubt and confusion began to be reflected in much of the art and literature of the Western world. Scores of outstanding writers and artists—Shaw, Joyce, Wells, D. H. Lawrence, Picasso, Chagall, Despiau, Kolbe, and their fellows—continued to rebel against several traditions and honored gods basking placidly in the sun. They were interested in the importance of widening their horizons of experience, in the urgent and anxious study of the problems of man and society, in the creation of new forms of art, in new concepts of color and design. Throughout the new realism of these painters, sculptors, and writers there was sharply evident their concern with the irrational forces and thrusts in the hearts and glands of men, with the mysterious things that went on in the private universes of the human personality. These were the years, too, of the appearance of the "social" and "psychological" novels about human beings battered by the blind fates and picked up and put down by the winds of chance and change. Here, in these pages, were descriptions of disintegrating societies where men did not seem to care very much about their fellows. There was not much kindness any more. The themes of artists and writers often reflected and described the sobering facts of the world they saw around them in the two decades of a troubled peace: the vast and impersonal state, the ruthless jungle competition of modern societies, the demands of mass culture and mass conformity, the decline of moralities.

Before the First World War the national debt of Great Britain had been about $3,500,000,000; in 1919 it was about $40,000,000,000. In 1914 the national debt of the United States stood at about $1,000,000,000; by 1924 it had reached $24,000,000,000; by 1960 it was creeping towards $300,000,-000,000. In 1919 Germany and France were almost bankrupt. The war had cost Italy about $15,000,000,000. In several European countries there were weak governments, unemployment, inflation, strikes and riots; the appeal of socialism grew stronger. The industrial machines were digesting fewer raw materials and consequently there were fewer manufactured articles to sell. Foreign and domestic trade declined; the pulse of the economies weakened. The burden of debts, trade depression, tariffs, depreciated currencies, and taxation increased.

There were also mounting problems of reparations, war debts, and disarmament. Upon the shadowed European scene there arose boundary disputes between Sweden and Finland, Poland and Lithuania, Poland and Germany in Upper Silesia, and the threat of war between Greece and Bulgaria, Greece and Italy. New alliances began to be formed in the patterns of the old. "The nations have bled at every vein," said Great Britain's David Lloyd George, "and the restlessness you get everywhere today is the fever of anaemia." Discontent seethed as capital and labor renewed their conflicts. Added to these woes were the difficulties brought by frequent political ineptitude. Less easily described were the creeping advances of crime and social degeneracy, inevitable companions of anger, doubt, and despair.

The domestic history of several European countries illustrates the perils and strains of the postwar period. Many forces were coming into conjunction as Europe moved towards another age. The voices of the dedicated exponents of radical political and economic theories were widely heard, more and more. A few men were soon preparing to ride to glory on the wings of Fascism and Nazism.

In Great Britain the postwar boom glided into a prolonged depression. The world's economic dislocation hurt Britain's foreign trade. Coal exports declined. Merchant ships reddened from rust as they lay idle in the ports. The great iron and steel industries were shaken. Cheap labor enabled the Japanese to undersell England in the Eastern cotton markets. Strikes increased in number and violence. The demoralizing tide of unemployment rose. The coalition government of Liberals and Conservatives remained in power after the election of 1918, still led by David Lloyd George, that dynamic and resilient Welsh Liberal who had been Britain's outstanding architect of victory during the war. It was unfortunate that this government could shape no coherent program to end the stagnation or ease the distress. Thousands of workers marched into the socialist Labor Party. The hopes of prosperity faded fast.

The prestige and power of the Lloyd George coalition government were also heavily bludgeoned by its difficulties and failures in foreign affairs. What should the British policy be towards Moscow and all the lands of Russia where Lenin had at last prevailed? Would the new Poland be stable and safe behind the "Curzon line" and provide an effective buffer against the red plague, a dike against the molten lava of Communism? There were recurring quarrels with Egypt and India. Southern Ireland was still disturbed by the bitter, secret, and militant Sinn Fein movement seeking not Home Rule but complete independence from Britain and the absorption, by force if necessary, of the counties of Ulster in the north. Faced by civil war, looting, and murder in Ireland, the British government tried coercion. Coercion failed, as it often does. Eamon de Valera, that frosty and selfless Sinn Fein leader, kept his 2,000 secret assassins busy. The nasty competition in crime was finally stopped, for a few years, by the creation in 1922 of the Irish Free State, a British Dominion in southern Ireland. The six counties of Ulster remained determinedly aloof. The moderates had achieved a temporary victory. For eight years no bombs exploded in Ireland and the guns were silent.

In 1922 the Conservatives under Andrew Bonar Law withdrew from the coalition government and Lloyd George at once resigned. The Canadian-born Bonar Law and the Conservatives won a national election on the slogan of "tranquillity." In the United States the slogan of President Harding was "normalcy." In Britain, too, it seemed that a disillusioned public was demanding "not surgery but serenity."

In 1923 Bonar Law retired; the cancer in his throat raced on with long and malignant strides. His successor as prime minister and Conservative leader was Stanley Baldwin, a shrewd and able industrialist and politician who delighted in being considered "the supremely ordinary man."

Meanwhile the economic situation had improved in Britain. The cost of living and the general taxation level were lower. Stanley Baldwin was of the opinion that tariff preferences and agreements within the British Empire would reduce unemployment within the United Kingdom still further. He hazarded his safe majority in a general election. Stanley Baldwin underestimated the opposition to his ideas and the staying power of his political foes. All of his enemies drew together and made common cause against him on the bitterly fought question of the tariffs. When the election was over the Liberals and the Laborites voted Baldwin out of office.

Ramsay MacDonald, an honest, humorless, and aloof Scotsman, now formed Britain's first Labor government. Upon the domestic scene, MacDonald had but slight success. In foreign affairs there was more action and achievement. MacDonald was active in supporting the League of Nations, in putting into effect the Dawes Plan for the payment of German reparations, and in championing the cause of the reduction of armaments. The Labor ministry also gave diplomatic recognition to Russia and entered into negotiations about a government loan to Moscow. The attitude of MacDonald and the Laborites towards Moscow aroused wide opposition in the United Kingdom. Meanwhile England's trade was going down and the unemployment levels were going up. Trouble stirred in the streets. Votes fell away from the Laborites.

The Conservatives won a national election held late in 1924. Stanley Baldwin was prime minister again. The wise and famous Real Property Act was passed. Several laws changed the rules governing old-age pensions and workmen's compensation. Britain returned to the gold standard.

All was not peaceful in these changing years. In 1926 a great general strike, led by a fighting alliance of trade unions, shook the whole United Kingdom. The government succeeded in maintaining vital services and the strike was throttled. In 1927 Parliament passed the Trade Disputes and Trade Unions Act which declared that all general strikes and lockouts were illegal. In 1928 the Equal Franchise Act gave women the vote on equal terms with men. The present fused into the past. The rhythms of the seasons went on.

After the election of 1929 Ramsay MacDonald was able to form the second Labor government. The new ministry was at once confronted with the rapidly darkening problems of the war debts owed to the United States; with the Young Plan, a new and serious attempt to settle the reparations controversies; and with the Washington Naval Conference of 1930. The controversies were many; the solutions were few and unfortunate.

In December, 1931, the Statute of Westminster recognized the sovereign right of each dominion in the British Commonwealth of Nations to control its own domestic and foreign affairs. The remarkable British experiment in developing political organisms abroad resulted in this unique Commonwealth of "autonomous communities in no way subordinate one to another."

In 1931, too, Britain moved into a serious financial crisis; the solidarity of the whole British financial system was soon in danger. The effects of the economic collapse in the United States had already shaken Europe. Would the British pound ride out the storm? When MacDonald proposed drastic economies, including a reduction in the expenditures for the British social services, the Labor Party divided. MacDonald and fourteen other men were thrown out of the ranks of the Laborites. Late in August, 1931, MacDonald resigned. He was then asked by King George V to form a "National Government," containing members of the three major parties, "to deal with the national emergency." The new National Government at once took swift measures to stop the gold withdrawals. In October, 1931, the country supported MacDonald in a general election and gave the National Government a "doctor's mandate" to effect national recovery. Taxes were increased and government costs reduced. Slowly the financial and economic crisis passed and the peril, for the time, was ended. Under various leaders and in various forms the National Government was to carry on through fifteen troubled years to the end of the Second World War.

Across the English Channel stood France, a land of devastation and hope.

On the one hand, there was ruin and horror, "a dreary waste with mile after mile of gaunt trees, shell holes, barbed wire entanglements, deserted fields, demolished towns, with no cattle, no houses, with no living things anywhere except in an occasional oasis where a town had in some miraculous way escaped destruction." On the other hand, France had won back the iron of Alsace, the potash of Lorraine, and the coal of the Saar. She had become the most powerful state on the Continent.

Premier Georges Clemenceau, dynamic and resolute, had helped France to win the war and triumph in the peace arrangements. The man who admires outstanding courage, resilience, and obstinacy must bow before Clemenceau. Geoffrey Bruun's magnificent little biography of Clemenceau—how sharp is Bruun's insight and how precise is his pen!—shows why the French Chamber of Deputies formally declared that Clemenceau had "deserved well of the country" when he retired early in 1920.

After Georges Clemenceau departed from politics, all of the groups that supported the Treaty of Versailles found it expedient to form the National Bloc. The Socialists, for their part, loudly trumpeted their demands for a complete revision of the conclusions of the peacemakers at Versailles. With much enthusiasm, energy, and rhetoric the members of the National Bloc attempted to draw and hold together all of the patriots who had stood together to defend France in the war. For instance, the status of the Roman Catholic Church was swiftly changed. Diplomatic relations were restored with the Vatican. The anticlerical republicans restrained their hands and muffled their voices. Several laws directed against the clergy in other days were relaxed or wiped away. Several old maxims and recipes were discarded.

The most immediate and heavy problem confronting France arose from the country's enormous war debts, especially the huge sums owed to the United States and Britain. Meanwhile the expenses of government soared. It cost much money to administer a broad empire, maintain a large army, restore the shattered regions of the homeland. There was no hope of getting back the millions lent to the Russians in other days; the Bolsheviks had refused to pay. Germany insisted that she could send no gold across the Rhine because she had none. Meanwhile France increased her taxes and floated more loans, always hoping that the payment of reparations by Germany would come to bolster and bulwark the French credit and ensure financial and economic survival.

In 1922 the militant Raymond Poincaré replaced Aristide Briand as premier and leader of the National Bloc. Poincaré was a Lorrainer; he hated Germany; he obstinately refused to consider the scaling down of the German debts. Despite British objections the inflexible Poincaré sent French armies into the Ruhr in the hope of seizing German coal and other products. The passive German resistance frustrated French aims and accelerated the German domestic collapse. The franc began to slither downwards like its neighbor the mark.

In 1924 the National Bloc was defeated by the Radical Socialists and the Socialists. Edouard Herriot became premier. He prepared to pull French soldiers out of the Ruhr and to accept the Dawes Plan for the payment of German reparations. His domestic policies were in startling contrast to his moderation in his German operations. He recognized Russia, allowed civil servants to form unions, put the remains of Jean Jaurès, the Socialist leader, in the Panthéon. But Herriot could not solve the problems of finance. After he resigned there were several tottering and stumbling governments. From 1926 to 1929 Raymond Poincaré ruled again and his drastic economies and stabilization of the franc (at 3.93 cents) helped the state grow stronger. The pace of industrialization was accelerated. Export trade increased.

In the years that followed there were many French governments. The multiplication and fragmentation of the political parties on both the Right and Left has been an outstanding and unfortunate characteristic of modern French history. To support new ideas many Frenchmen continued to propose and espouse new political groups in the state. Individuals who ceased to believe in the absolutes of the Church often came to believe in the creeds of their political parties. Here they found a new faith to fill, after a fashion, a void and vacuum in their beings, a substitute for the religion from which they had wandered and strayed, a meaning and a source of excitement in their otherwise humdrum lives.

There were numerous and bitter battles in France upon issues of small national consequence. There appeared too frequently the political rancors that are always dangerous to real democracy. There was much false rhetoric. Politicians in office, aware that forthright action might spell political defeat, often took refuge in evasion and compromise. Many observers became convinced that only a new constitution, the consolidation of political parties, much radical surgery, and the recovery of some lost moral standards could stop the progressive deterioration of the French political system and set in order the affairs of the great state of France.

When the German Empire collapsed in 1918, the Social Democratic Party, led by Friedrich Ebert and Philipp Scheidemann, established a socialist and republican government in Germany. The violent challenges and rebellions of the radical Spartacists, who proclaimed a dictatorship of the proletariat, were met and defeated. The rebel leaders Karl Liebknecht and Rosa Luxemburg were killed. Kurt Eisner, who assumed power in Bavaria, was murdered. In a national election the German voters gave strong support to all of the republican parties and a new National Assembly began its work at the town of Weimar, made famous in earlier days by Goethe and Schiller. The Assembly at once declared that Germany was a republic, chose Friedrich Ebert as the first president, made a rather complicated constitution, and prepared to sign a formal treaty of peace with the Allies.

The mines and factories and fields of Germany had not been damaged by the war. France, the victor, had suffered far more heavily. German industrial recovery was swift and sure. Her goods appeared in the markets of the world. Her new merchant marine grew rapidly. The policies of the government, controlled by the Social Democrats, stayed cautious and moderate.

General Paul von Hindenburg, famous victor of Tannenberg, became president of Germany in 1925. He defended the republic against the monarchists on the right and the Communists on the left.

The payments demanded from Germany by the Reparations Commission in 1921 totaled about $33,000,000,000. Germany at once protested that she could not pay such an exorbitant sum. France insisted that Germany must pay in full, and France's Raymond Poincaré sent French armies into the Ruhr in 1923, an event already described. It will be remembered that the passive resistance of the Germans wrecked Poincaré's hopes of getting reparations with the gun and the bayonet. In 1924, the Dawes Plan, which was finally accepted by Great Britain, France, and Germany, provided that with assistance from the United States and Great Britain, Germany should create a national bank, return to a stabilized currency, based on gold, and balance her budgets. The Allies subscribed to a German loan of $200,000,000. The Dawes Plan also provided that Germany would pay enough—the payments were to begin at $250,000,000 annually and rise to $625,000,000 in 1929—to balance the budgets of France and help France to pay Britain and the United States. The Young Plan of 1929 stated that Germany was to make annual reparations payments from 1929 until 1988.

By 1932 it was clear that Germany could not keep up these annual payments, and at the Lausanne Conference the creditor powers arranged to accept $750,000,000 in settlement of the outstanding claims. This arrangement collapsed when the Weimar Republic foundered in the Nazi storm of 1933. Germany paid no more reparations.

Meanwhile the economic situation in Germany grew threatening and dangerous. The pressure of inflation increased and the mark skidded downwards. Taxes rose sharply. The German nationalists continued to insist upon a revision of "the dictate of Versailles." The "war guilt" clauses, they asserted, should be expunged and the German colonies returned.

In the general election of 1930 the groups of the extreme Right and the extreme Left made astounding gains. The Communists, for instance, held 76 seats in the Reichstag, a gain of 22. The new National Socialist German Workers' Party, under Adolf Hitler, had suddenly become the second party in the Reichstag—the Social Democrats had 143 seats and Hitler's Nazis held

107. The enthusiastic followers of Hitler demanded that the Treaty of Versailles be changed to suit the German wishes and that reparations payments be stopped. They also proclaimed their support of conscription, more labor legislation, the ousting of the Jews, Socialists, and international bankers from places of power in the German state. The swelling tide of bitter German nationalism threatened to billow over Europe. Vast subterranean conspiracies were born. Hugenberg and Hitler snarled and plotted.

Nor was there order and calm in Italy. The Italians had been disappointed and angered at the arrangements agreed upon by the peacemakers at Versailles. Italy's gains in territory had not been large. She had obtained no mandates. It seemed to many Italians that their legitimate aspirations had been rudely thrust aside by the Allies.

In these postwar years Italy was plagued by numerous economic and political ills. The flames of discontent leaped upwards. Peasants revolted against their landlords. Strikes multiplied. Inflation shook the state. The propertied classes were alarmed at the terror in the streets.

Upon this troubled stage appeared the Fascists, a militant group founded in 1919 by Benito Mussolini, a blacksmith's son and sometime editor of a Socialist newspaper. The Fascists proclaimed the importance of patriotism; they denounced and ridiculed the internationalism of the Socialists; they insisted always upon the greatness of Italy, the noble fulfillment of a man's destiny in fighting and dying for his native land. "War," said Mussolini, "is to man what maternity is to woman." The Fascist bands of Blackshirts paraded in the streets, beat and killed Socialists, persuaded the men of property and other conservative elements that the Fascists alone promised safety and survival.

On October 20, 1922, Mussolini went to Rome with an army of Blackshirts. King Victor Emmanuel III appointed him premier. At once the new leader of Italy denounced the earlier democratic government and declared that he would give the state discipline, economy, efficiency, and honest government. Mussolini promised that he would guide the Italians to a new unity and power at home and a great empire abroad. He was their leader. He was "Il Duce." A series of laws established a corporate state under the Fascist Grand Council.

The totalitarian regime of the Fascists was worse than the evils it set out to remedy. The censorship of the press was complete. Mussolini used murder, prison, and torture as political weapons. No dictator who wants to stay in power can afford to shrink from violence. Edward Vermeil once said that Fascism was "the newest and most cruel of all the forms of exploitation of man by man."

Meanwhile Spain was filled with strikes, violence, separatist movements, government corruption, plotting, and general lawlessness. In 1923 Primo de

Rivera seized control of the government and suspended the constitution. In 1930 he resigned. A year later Alfonso XIII and the Spanish royal family were forced to flee. "Spain," said the first sentence of a new constitution, "is a democratic republic of workers of all classes which is organized as a regime of liberty and justice. The powers of all its organs emanate from the people."

In Austria the Hapsburgs had been swept away. A frail and bankrupt republican government carried on its faltering operations in Vienna. For the Austrians the postwar years were a time of poverty and near-starvation. Slowly, with the aid of foreign loans and gifts, the tangled and tottering economy was straightened out and strengthened. In Hungary a republic was formed under the presidency of the liberal Count Michael Károlyi. Early in 1919 Károlyi was compelled to resign when Hungary was dismembered by the Versailles peacemakers. Then the government was taken over by Béla Kun and the Communists. These were tortured and frightening days. Rumania attacked Hungary and seized and plundered Budapest. Hungary's Admiral Horthy, backed by the anti-Communist peasants, finally won the support of a national assembly in 1920. Hungary was proclaimed a monarchy with Horthy as "Regent"—but there was no king. Throughout the next two decades the people of Hungary continued to be disturbed and bitter and plagued by sectional, racial, and economic problems. This statement is also true of Yugoslavia, Czechoslovakia, Bulgaria, Greece, Rumania, Poland, and the Baltic states of Finland, Latvia, Estonia, and Lithuania. Spurts of violence rose and fell. In many areas of Europe there was almost always a lurking crisis.

In Russia the scene was different. There was more peace there, more quiet; sometimes the quiet was that of despair and the peace was that of death. The self-confident and ruthless Nikolai Lenin and Leon Trotsky, the men who had overthrown Alexander Kerenski and made the Bolshevik revolution, were the successors of the Tsars of all the Russias. In earlier days Lenin had written: "Democracy from below! Democracy without an officialdom, without police, without a standing army! . . . The state itself will wither away. . . ." But the state did not wither away. After Lenin came Stalin, Malenkov, Molotov, Beria, Khrushchev, and all the rest. They were dynamic men, tough and able conspirators, absolutely ruthless. Lenin had once declared: "Sentimentality is no less a crime than cowardice in war." They worked upon their theories and blueprints for the establishment of Communism in all the lands of the planet. Lenin had also said: "There can be no revolutionary action without a revolutionary theory."

The revolutionary theories of "pure" Communism soon brought trouble in Russia. Industrial production fell to about 20 per cent of its prewar level. The peasants stubbornly resisted when the crops they had grown were seized by government troops. There was famine in the Volga region.

Lenin decided that concessions must be made to the demands of the people and some wedges driven into the practice of "pure" Communism. In 1921 he started the New Economic Policy, a scheme that made great concessions to private enterprise. The peasants became almost full owners of their land. In retail trade and in some areas of manufacturing operations private ownership was permitted.

Slowly conditions in Russia began to improve. Successive planning arrangements devised by the experts of the State Planning Commission (Gosplan) were quite successful. In several areas, especially in the production of capital goods, the Russian progress was excellent. The production of consumer goods lagged. For many years there continued to be too many clogging and hampering bureaucratic controls.

Leon Trotsky was not pleased. He claimed that the Russian Communists should make plans for a world revolution at once. He asserted that the concessions made by Lenin had resulted in the growth of a bourgeois class in Russia led by men whom Trotsky regarded as pampered peasants and by the numerous public officials. Trotsky insisted, for instance, that many men in the upper echelons of the New Economic Policy administration were incompetent and unnecessary. On the other hand, Trotsky's opponents asserted that Russia must be built up as a model Communist state for all the world to see and imitate. They asserted that Trotsky's plans would throw Russia back into chaos. Leon Trotsky and Joseph Stalin became locked in a long struggle. In 1928 Trotsky fled for his life from Russia. Years later, an assassin sought Trotsky out in Mexico and drove an alpenstock into his brain. The arm of Stalin was long.

Stalin's rule in Russia was marked by the progressive and brutal wiping out of the wealthier peasants, the kulaks. About 4,000,000 of them died. There was also an increased collectivization of land, more consolidated farms, and other features of a "planned economy." In the days of Stalin's leadership there were more tractors and technicians, much emphasis upon education, much censorship, many attacks upon religion, many purges and strange public trials, the spread of Communist propaganda and agents throughout the world, the appearance of more nationalism, the establishment of a new constitution in 1936.

> How sweet it is to hate one's native land
> And eagerly await its utter ruin.
> And in its ruin to discern
> The dawn of a new life for the world.

So wrote the Russian poet Pecherin in the nineteenth century. There was another Russian named Chaadaev who said that Russia formed "a blank in the moral world order."

Si vis pacem para bellum. Weakness in a state invites aggression and conflict and tempts mighty robbers. The words of the Covenant of the League of Nations set forth a noble ideal; but those words were not in accord with the facts of a real and ruthless world. They provided no effective guarantees of the peace of the planet.

Between 1920 and 1921, fearful of a Germany that might rise again, France sought more security by allying herself with Belgium, Czechoslovakia, and Poland. About the same time, Rumania, Yugoslavia, and Czechoslovakia, apprehensive about a possible attempt by Austria-Hungary to recover her lost territories, formed the "Little Entente." Poland, suspicious of the intentions of both Austria and Russia, allied herself with France, Czechoslovakia, Rumania, Latvia, and Estonia. Rumania, anxious to protect herself against Russian designs, also joined in an alliance with France and Italy (1926). Italy later signed treaties guaranteeing the frontiers of Yugoslavia, Czechoslovakia, and Rumania. In 1926 Italy extended her control in Albania and thus dominated the entrance to the Adriatic, a matter of grave concern to Yugoslavia. Yugoslavia thereupon became an ally of France, always a rival of Italy in the Mediterranean. Meanwhile Italy signed (1927) a treaty of "peace and perpetual friendship" with Hungary. In 1925 Russia made a treaty with Turkey in which each promised to remain neutral if the other were attacked. In 1926 she made a similar arrangement with Germany. Thus a network of alliances stretched over Europe again.

Meanwhile the power of Japan grew rapidly in the Pacific. Japan was athwart the sea lanes to the Philippines. Her aggressive intentions with respect to China were quite clear. She was a serious commercial rival of the United States and Great Britain. She was building a powerful fleet. It was not surprising that suspicions and tensions rose.

In 1921 the United States called a naval conference at Washington to consider the limitation of naval construction. At this conference it was agreed to stabilize the battleship strength of Great Britain, the United States, Japan, France, and Italy in the respective proportions of 5; 5; 3; 1.67; 1.67. No agreement was reached about cruisers and smaller ships or submarines. A four-power pact to preserve the status quo in the Pacific was signed by the United States, Great Britain, France, and Japan. The London Naval Conference of 1930 could not reach agreement regarding the building of naval craft below the capital-ship level, partly because of the mounting rivalry of France and Italy in the Mediterranean. At the London Naval Conference of 1935 the Japanese insisted upon naval equality with Great Britain and the United States. When their demand was refused they withdrew from the conference.

How could safety be secured? Not by disarmament, surely, for who would disarm unless the security of each had been guaranteed by all? How could any nation, in these cold years of apprehension, confusion, cynicism, duplicity, and secret armaments, be assured that guarantees and treaties were really effective? Each state was concerned with its own interests as well as with the fair dream of the peace of the world. For instance, the Draft Treaty of Mutual Assistance of 1923 was designed to turn the League of Nations into a great defensive alliance. But the British dominions were not prepared to enter into a blanket commitment that might entangle them in conflicts far from their home shores. The United States still held aloof from the League of Nations. Again, in September, 1924, at the Fifth Assembly of the League, the Geneva Protocol was prepared, a document that carefully set up machinery for arbitration, abolished the right of nations to go to war except when ordered to do so by the League, made compulsory the submission to the World Court of cases that might lead to war. Partly because the Geneva Protocol threatened to make the League a superstate it was rejected in March, 1925, and sent to lie on the shelf by the Draft Treaty of Mutual Assistance. International bickering and tension shadowed the eyes of disillusioned men who saw the contrast between shining hopes and the travail of sordid experience.

Aristide Briand of France, Sir Austen Chamberlain of Great Britain, and the conciliatory Gustav Stresemann of Germany now began the long negotiations that culminated in the signing of eight security pacts in the Swiss town of Locarno in October, 1925. To Locarno came the representatives of seven powers: Great Britain, Belgium, Czechoslovakia, France, Germany, Italy, and Poland. Of the eight treaties the most important was the Treaty of Mutual Guarantee signed by Great Britain, Belgium, France, Germany, and Italy. The five powers agreed to settle all of their disputes without resorting to war. They all guaranteed the frontiers set up at Versailles between Germany, France, Belgium, and the Netherlands. They guaranteed the demilitarized zone established on the left bank of the Rhine in 1919. The seven subsidiary treaties guaranteed the territorial integrity of Czechoslovakia and Poland.

The Locarno pacts were widely applauded as a landmark in European history, a "splendid act of reconciliation," a vindication of man's will for general peace. Had international security at last been achieved with the new safety curtains between Germany and her neighbors? The answers were unpleasant. The "spirit of Locarno" was soon to become dead and brittle, swept away by the rising wind.

On August 27, 1928, the representatives of fifteen nations signed the agreement called the Pact of Paris; a total of sixty-two nations signed within a few months. This document, the result of a long correspondence between Aristide Briand, the French Foreign Minister, and Frank B. Kellogg, the American Secretary of State, provided that the signatory nations "condemn recourse to war for the solution of international controversies and renounce it as an instrument of national policy in their relations with one another." The reinforcement of this and other clauses of the Pact of Paris was left to the good faith and "the public opinion of mankind." But justice and morality need swords.

Heavy clouds continued to roll over the international scene. Public opinion grew weary and skeptical of the meetings of diplomats and statesmen. Slowly the world came within practical distance of almost measureless calamity. In 1932 Winston Churchill said: "We have steadily marched backwards since Locarno. Fears are greater, rivalries are sharper, military plans are more closely concerted, military organizations are more carefully and efficiently developed. Britain is weaker and Britain's hour of weakness is Europe's hour of danger."

Successive events marked the rising peril. Late in 1932 Japan left the League of Nations. Early in 1933 Germany passed under the iron control of the National Socialist German Workers' Party led by Adolf Hitler (1889–1945). "National Socialism," declared Hitler, "must, in principle, claim the right to force its principles on the whole German nation and to educate it to its ideas." The state, in other words, must be omnipotent. The secret police of Hitler moved with skill and cruelty. Some of their brutal deeds we know; the record is black. The words of Adolf Hitler, bellicose and passionate and filled with "apocalyptic anguish," rolled through Germany and echoed around the planet. His moustache and his forelock, his scowl and his open mouth became familiar sights on the platforms of Germany and in the press of the world.

The power of the leadership of Adolf Hitler in the totalitarian state of Germany was indeed great. His "Third Reich," he said, would last for a thousand years. He asserted that the enemies of Germany, within and without the state, must be destroyed. Inside the frontiers of Germany uncounted thousands of Jews were shot, starved, tortured, and gassed by the men who were said to belong to a master race. Their moral and mental debauchery has been too soon forgotten.

More than a thousand years ago the Abbot Martin of Dumes wrote a sentence that is an answer to Adolf Hitler and all of his kind who appear in any land, in any age: "An old man said, 'See that thou despise not the brother that stands by thee: for thou knowest not whether the spirit of God be in thee or in him.' "

In October, 1933, Germany withdrew from the League of Nations and secretly began to rearm. "Far away are the days of Locarno," warned Winston Churchill. "The hope is gone and we must act." With hesitation and reluctance the British increased their expenditures for the army and the navy. The grim tide of events swept on. On June 30, 1934, more than sixty of Hitler's suspected opponents were shot without trial. On July 25, the anti-Nazi Austrian Chancellor Dr. Engelbert Dollfuss was assassinated by National Socialists in Vienna. Hitler, who wanted an *Anschluss* with Austria, was preparing the way by dividing the Austrian people and slaying those who rejected his friendship. On August 3, 1934, Germany's Paul von Hindenburg died; Hitler then became president of the Reich as well as chancellor. On October 9, 1934, King Alexander of Yugoslavia and Jean Louis Barthou of France were murdered.

In January, 1935, the Saar basin was returned to Germany as a result of a plebiscite. In March, Hitler suddenly denounced the Treaty of Versailles and revealed the growing military strength of Germany. Germany was shedding the encumbrances, physical and moral, that had hitherto manacled her dangerous will to fight. The road to war was broadening. The opiate of Locarno was clearly gone. Weakness, ineptitude, and a strong desire for peace had made their invitation to aggression and tyranny.

In October, 1935, Benito Mussolini's armies marched against Ethiopia. Haile Selassie, the courageous emperor of that land, sought the protection of the League of Nations. The League had not protected Manchuria against Japan. Would Geneva act against Italy? Fearing Germany, France wanted Italian support. Britain's Anthony Eden tried in vain to persuade Mussolini

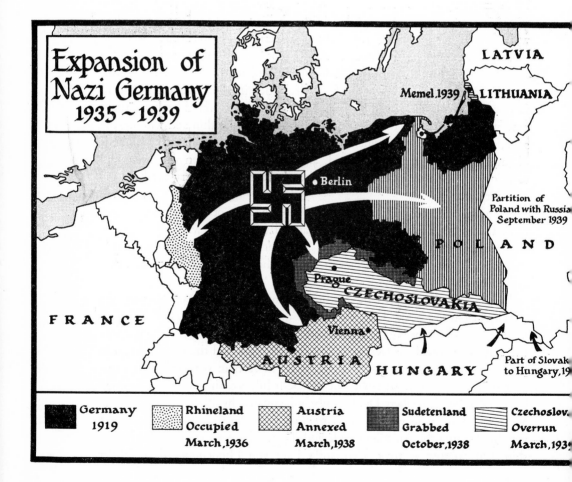

to stop his aggression. Mussolini wanted Ethiopia. The European powers did not wish for a general war. No biting sanctions, no crippling measures to halt Italy were ever applied. Mussolini got Ethiopia.

In March, 1936, Hitler occupied the demilitarized Rhineland, thus tearing up another clause of the Treaty of Versailles and a large section of the Locarno pacts. In the summer of 1936 a hard and bloody civil war began in Spain. Germany and Italy actively supported the rebel and reactionary General Francisco Franco. Russia supported Franco's foes, loyal to the Spanish government. Franco won the long war. Thousands of his opponents were swiftly shot, tortured, or jailed. Once again the foes of democracy had triumphed. Meanwhile Germany and Italy had entered into an alliance, forming the so-called Rome-Berlin Axis in November, 1936. A year later, the Japanese joined the Fascists and the Nazis.

Hitler now moved towards Austria. In March, 1938, German pressure forced the resignation of Chancellor Kurt von Schuschnigg. A German army occupied Vienna; Hitler annexed Austria. Italy, now an ally of Germany, approved. France, caught by a cabinet crisis, did nothing. Britain denounced the gangster methods of Berlin, but Hitler was not distressed by words alone. The policy of appeasement thus prevailed; its ultimate bankruptcy was almost at hand.

Czechoslovakia was the next victim of Nazi aggression. Hitler felt grave concern about some 3,000,000 Sudeten Germans who were within the Czechoslovakian frontiers. Berlin insisted that the borders of Czechoslovakia must be altered.

The crisis came in September, 1938. Neville Chamberlain of Britain and Edouard Daladier of France conferred at Munich with Adolf Hitler and Benito Mussolini. Heavy pressure was put upon the Czechs by France and Britain to accept the German demands. The final "Munich Award" gave one-fifth of Czechoslovakia to Germany. Hitler declared before the world that the revision of the Czechoslovakian borders marked his final territorial demands in Europe. (No one then quoted the words of the psalmist: "The words of his mouth were smoother than butter but war was in his heart.")

When Neville Chamberlain returned to England he dramatically declared that he had obtained "peace for our time." Peace had indeed been kept, but not for long. Many Englishmen were shocked at the terms of Munich and angered at the pilgrimage of shame that Chamberlain had made. They were certain that Hitler could not be stopped by any measures short of war. The judgments they uttered rang with urgent conviction and warning. The world balance of terror increased. The British government and people sharpened their vigilance. Anxiety whispered in their ears and the voice of hope was stilled. Above the armament factories the smoke was black and heavy.

Chapter 46

THE SECOND WORLD CONFLICT

FEODOR DOSTOIEVSKY's Grand Inquisitor said to Christ: "We have corrected Thy deed." The leaders of the totalitarian states of the twentieth century tried to do precisely that. They denied the value to mankind of the qualities of mercy, love, and justice. They exiled, imprisoned, and killed in the name of the interest of the infallible state. They tried to tear away the dignity of human beings. They treated men as living tools of dictators, nothing more. They created a joyless world of nightmare where the use of reason and the pursuit of truth were forbidden. "Whom the gods would destroy they first make mad."

Through the centuries of history there have risen conflicting voices proclaiming truths and falsehoods. Sometimes, too, there have been monstrous and malignant words and deeds that have revealed the hellish and horrible depths to which some human beings can fall. We can read, for instance, the language of the pitiless and detestable Heinrich Himmler, that cold-blooded creature of Hitler's court who tortured and exterminated thousands of helpless human beings: "What happens to a Russian or a Czech does not interest me in the slightest. . . . Whether 10,000 Russian females fall down dead from exhaustion while digging an anti-tank ditch interests me only so far as the anti-tank ditch for Germany is finished." It is fortunate that we can also turn to the contrasting words and spirit of Ugo Boccarossa, an Italian immigrant boy who survived the sinking of the *Andrea Doria* in 1956: "When I got up on deck they were taking the women and children off. They had to be first, because that is the rule, and it is right."

At the time of the Munich crisis in September, 1938, Adolf Hitler had assured the world that the revisions of the Czechoslovakian borders were his final territorial demands in Europe. He did not keep his word. In March, 1939, he seized the remainder of Czechoslovakia. "An intelligent victor," he had written, "will, wherever possible, present his demands to the vanquished in installments. He can then be sure that a nation which has become characterless —and such is every one that voluntarily submits—will no longer find any sufficient reason in any of these detailed oppressions to take to arms once more."

Great Britain and France at once declared that Germany would proceed further at her peril. Soon Hitler demanded the return of Danzig to Germany and a German road across the Polish corridor to the province of East Prussia. He accused the Poles of persecuting and killing people belonging to the German-speaking minority in Poland. Britain and France promised the Poles "all support in their power" in the event of "any action that threatened Polish independence." When Italy, on April 7, 1939, moved across the Adriatic to seize Albania, Britain and France also gave a promise of aid to Greece and Rumania in the event of Axis aggression. At the same time they sought an agreement with Russia.

On August 23 Russia suddenly made a nonaggression pact with Germany. Of the great powers, Britain and France now stood alone. Hitler sent an ultimatum to Warsaw; he did not intend that the Poles should have any time to consider it. On September 1, three highly mechanized German armies hurtled across the Polish borders. The German air force bombed the cities and towns and strafed the fleeing inhabitants. Russia struck at Poland from the east.

Britain had made a pledge to Poland. Neville Chamberlain warned Berlin that only Nazi retreat would save the peace of the world. On September 3 the British government informed Hitler that "unless not later than 11 A.M., British Summer Time, today, September 3, satisfactory assurances have been given by the German Government and have reached His Majesty's Government in London, a state of war will exist between the two countries as from that hour." Berlin did not reply. The French government declared war. Australia, Canada, New Zealand, South Africa, and all the British Empire moved into the conflict. The other nations of the world stayed neutral, for a time.

Poland fell before the end of September. Germany and Russia at once divided the unhappy land. In September, too, the Russians demanded and got mutual assistance pacts from the Baltic states of Estonia, Latvia, and Lithuania. The Russians were also permitted to occupy certain strategic areas in these three republics.

Estonia, Latvia, and Lithuania had yielded to the Russian demands. Finland refused to make any concessions. Russia attacked Finland on November 30,

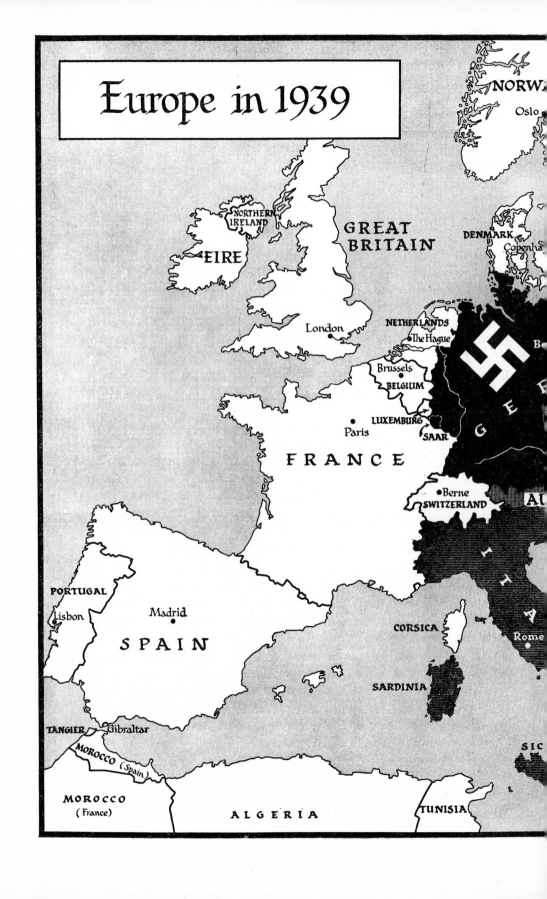

1939. The heroic and obstinate Finnish resistance, especially in the strategically important Karelian Isthmus area, astounded a watching world. Finally, of course, the heavy Russian military machine broke through the Mannerheim Line and the 4,000,000 Finns were forced to surrender (March 12, 1940). They handed over to Russia about 16,000 square miles of territory with a population of approximately 500,000 people. The annexed area included the city of Viborg and the naval base at Hangö. Finland also agreed to make no military alliances deemed by the Russians to be prejudicial to their interests and allowed the Russians the use of a railroad across Finland to Norway and Sweden.

Meanwhile the Germans swiftly undertook a savage extermination of the Jews. Later generations may perhaps not know or refuse to believe what the Nazis did in their concentration camps and their gas chambers. The facts are clear, indisputable, horrible. Men who saw the corpses stacked like firewood at Belsen and Dachau and heard the long cries of agony in the prison huts cannot forget the Nazi crimes.

The Poles, an inferior people by Nazi standards, saw many of their political and intellectual leaders taken to concentration camps. Few came back. It was not long, however, before the Germans were plagued in Poland, as they were to be elsewhere later, by a secret underground movement of stubborn and silent resistance and sabotage. Guided by patriots through the darkness, many Poles escaped to Britain to find a chance to renew the war against Hitler. Later, all over Europe, the vast underground system grew stronger, more efficient, an invisible secret state with which the Nazis could not successfully contend. Resistance at least meant hope.

The winter of 1939–1940 was a period of little activity. The British navy scoured German shipping from the seas. The *Graf Spee,* a German pocket battleship, was sunk. The naval blockade, supported by all the Allied weapons of economic warfare, continued its formidable pressures. Meanwhile Nazi submarine commanders sank thousands of tons of Allied and neutral shipping. Meanwhile, too, Hitler's clever and intellectual Dr. Joseph Goebbels relentlessly carried on his effective campaign of propaganda. By the side of Hitler moved his other aides: the persistent and power-mad Martin Bormann, the crack-brained Rudolf Hess, the devilish Heinrich Himmler, the coldly efficient Albert Speer, the Reich Marshal Hermann Goering, a contented Nero, so happy with his toga, his baton, his perfumes, and his jewels.

In the spring of 1940 the brown Nazi current rolled with terrible speed and without warning into Denmark and Norway. The Danes and Norwegians had to yield; but their spirit was not broken. In the terror of the mounting conflict streams of new weapons appeared. Speedy fighter planes streaked through the skies; mighty bombers dropped bomb loads totaled in tons;

gliders and transport planes decanted paratroopers. The intensive "flack" of anti-aircraft guns curtained about important targets; heavily armed tanks pushed about like giant beetles; huge searchlights probed through the night skies, their beams blunted against the clouds in phosphorescent discs. Soon radar, rockets, magnetic mines, new types of land mines, and "booby traps" combined to make the Second World War unlike any previous chapter of the long world disorder.

On May 10, 1940, Hitler struck at Luxemburg, the Netherlands, Belgium, and France. Those states could not hold back the Nazi flood. In the "miracle of Dunkirk" 337,130 British and French soldiers were rescued (May 26–June 3, 1940). Guns and tanks were left behind. All but 30,000 of the British troops came home. Neville Chamberlain had fallen from power in Britain (May 10, 1940). Faced by Allied disasters, Britain turned to Winston Churchill. A new National Government was formed and Churchill told the British people that he had "nothing to offer but blood, toil, tears, and sweat." The defiant words of the new leader reminded all that the cause of freedom was not yet lost. "You ask, what is our aim? I can answer in one word: victory —victory at all costs, victory in spite of all terror, victory however hard and long the road may be; for without victory there is no survival."

Under the assaults of massed tanks and infantry the French now staggered backwards. Shattered French armies fled southwards, their retreat checked by desperate civilians who clogged the highways. All roads were regularly sprayed by the bullets of low-flying German aircraft.

Early in June, as France writhed before the lashing German armies, Italy declared war on France and Britain. Benito Mussolini, always handy with a stiletto, thought that "the hour marked out by destiny" had arrived at last. The jackal joined the pack and leaped to the kill. The Germans entered Paris. France's Marshal Pétain made peace with Hitler. After the cruel and clever armistice terms had been signed Henri Philippe Pétain and Pierre Laval set up a government for unoccupied France in the southern resort town of Vichy. This government, its path stained with dishonor, cooperated with Berlin. Britain recognized the new "Free French" forces headed by the patriot General Charles de Gaulle, a cold, ambitious, and difficult man, but a brave one. De Gaulle, who had escaped the Germans, declared that France had lost a battle but not the war. Under the Cross of Lorraine he rallied Frenchmen who had neither been stunned by disaster nor lost the will to resist.

Britain stood alone against the Nazi might. The situation was desperate. The nine divisions of soldiers were too few. No weapons had been saved at Dunkirk and the supply of arms was meager. In all of Britain there were fewer than a hundred tanks. Twenty-two miles from the fortress shores of England stood Hitler's army, the mightiest in history, supported by the great German air force, the submarine wolf packs, the surface navy, the industrial power of all Europe, the Italian army, the fawning men of Vichy. Hitler could be confident.

In August and September, 1940, came the battle of Britain. There is no doubt that the Germans underestimated the ability of the Royal Air Force to keep its fighters in the air. They also miscalculated the time British airfields could be kept unserviceable by German attacks. Marshal Goering used his aircraft extravagantly and the wastage was too high. On September 7, about 400 German aircraft attacked London. About 100 were destroyed. On September 15 the Luftwaffe lost about 200 planes as a result of the deadly attacks of the British Spitfires and Hurricanes. On September 27 the Germans sent over approximately 800 aircraft. It was their last appearance in major force. Heavy German night raids continued for several months; but the battle of Britain was virtually ended by October, 1940.

It was clear that the embattled British would not yield. The indomitable Churchill had made that fact clear, again and again. After London had been bombed almost every night for nearly three months a motion to consider a German peace proposal was defeated in the House of Commons by a vote of 341 to 4. The Royal Air Force Bomber Command continued its attacks on enemy railways, docks, air fields, factories, oil refineries, and tanks in occupied Europe, in Germany, and in Italy. In British skies newly developed techniques of night fighting discouraged the Germans. The silent wastelands made by Nazi bombs in the midst of Coventry, Birmingham, Bristol, Glasgow, Hull, Manchester, Plymouth, London, and other cities made the British more dogged in their defiance. Secret preparations were made for the first Commando raids on Europe. The machines of the factories roared through the nights. Farm production was doubled in the United Kingdom. The deadly and undramatic economic warfare against Germany went on.

Meanwhile the Nazi aircraft leaped from Continental bases to wound and destroy Allied shipping; submarines prowled from their lairs along the European coast; a few German surface raiders still roamed the seas—one of them, the mighty *Bismarck,* did much damage before its tale was told.

In March, 1941, the United States Congress, convinced that the first defense line of American democracy was in Britain, passed the famous Lend-Lease Act when Britain had spent all of her dollar resources. By the late summer of 1941 the United States was giving Britain "all aid short of war."

The Italians had long been hacking at Britain's lifeline in the Mediterranean. Although Mussolini's navy was new and large it did not long remain a threat of consequence. In a battle with British forces off Cape Matapan in March, 1941, one Italian battleship was badly damaged; three 10,000-ton Italian cruisers and two 1,500-ton destroyers were sunk. Italian gunnery was inadequate; not one British ship was hit. Nor did the Italians have any more

[118] Winston Churchill inspects the ruins of Coventry Cathedral October 11, 1941.

PLATE XLIII

[119] Lord Louis Mountbatten, the last Viceroy of India, announces Indian independence at the Constituent Assembly in New Delhi on August 15, 1947.

PLATE XLIV

success on land. In December, 1940, Britain's small Army of the Nile—it contained 30,000 men under the command of General Wavell—attacked 260,000 Italians and drove them out of Egypt and Cyrenaica. The British captured 133,295 Italian soldiers; Wavell lost 600 men. In December, 1941, the Italians suffered 289,000 casualties. British Somaliland and Ethiopia were freed. Italian Somaliland and Eritrea were conquered.

The Nazis slashed into Bulgaria, Hungary, Rumania, and Slovakia. In April, 1941, they invaded Yugoslavia and Greece. The British at once drained about 75,000 men out of Africa to help the Greeks. Soon the British had lost about 30,000 of these soldiers; the rest were forced to withdraw under heavy air bombardment. The sinister shadow of the Nazi swastika fell over all of Greece. The Germans now invaded Crete, and again the British were compelled to withdraw. Crack Nazis troops poured into Libya to help the Italians. The famous Afrika Corps drove the British out of Libya, except for the port of Tobruk, held firmly for eight months by the Australians. The way seemed almost open for a final German drive on Suez, Syria, and the Near Eastern oil fields. There was an Axis-inspired revolt in Iraq. Free French forces joined with the British to squash the Vichy-controlled government in Syria, briskly spinning Nazi plots.

On June 22, 1941, Adolf Hitler suddenly attacked Russia. His left flank must be protected in his drive to the East. The "world island" of the Nazi geopoliticians must be seized. Russia, as well as the Middle East, possessed oil. The grain fields of the Ukraine awaited German reapers. Of the Russian defenses Hitler said: "You have only to kick the front door and the whole house will fall down." He also remarked that he would "cut up the giant cake" of Russia. Hitler was mistaken. The results of megalomania are usually the same. No man can escape the corruptions and stupidities of absolute power.

Britain had an ally at last. Winston Churchill declared: "Any man or state who fights on against Nazism will have our aid. Any man or state who marches with Hitler is our foe." Supplies began to move from Britain and America to Russia through southern routes and over the frozen hell of the arctic seas to Archangel and Murmansk.

The carefully planned Nazi timetable was soon upset. Successive disasters that fell upon the Germans were very annoying to Hitler—was he not the greatest strategic genius of all time? Unfortunately for Hitler, the British and the Russians were not prepared to accept his conclusions that they were defeated. When Marshal Stalin's armies were not annihilated, the Germans had to grapple with two foes of constant vigor: cold and distance. Late in 1941 the German forces were still held back from Leningrad and Moscow. In the next three years, as Churchill later declared, the Russian armies were to do "the main work of tearing the guts out of the German Army."

On December 7, 1941, the airplanes from a Japanese carrier fleet bombed the United States' naval base at Pearl Harbor in Hawaii. For the United States it was a day of disaster. For Japan, as President Franklin D. Roosevelt said, it was "a day of infamy."

Great Britain leaped at once to add Japan to its list of enemies. In a truly global war the United States and Britain became formal allies. Germany and Italy declared war on the United States.

With startling swiftness the forces of Japan surged forward. Off Malaya the British battleship *Prince of Wales* and the cruiser *Renown* were sunk. Wrote Winston Churchill later: "There were now no British or American capital ships in the Indian Ocean or the Pacific except the American survivors of Pearl Harbor who were hastening back to California. Over all this vast expanse of waters Japan was supreme, and we everywhere weak and naked." The Japanese seized Hong Kong, Malaya, Burma, the Philippines, Guam, Wake Island, the Dutch East Indies, and hundreds of other Pacific islands. They swarmed into New Guinea and threatened to attack Australia. By grasping the Burma Road they blocked the sending of supplies to China; they threatened India; they grabbed a huge supply of rubber, oil, and all the vast resources of Borneo, Java, Malaya, and Sumatra.

In 1942 the advance of the Japanese was delayed as a result of several sea battles. On May 7, 1942, the Japanese tried to penetrate the Coral Sea on the northeast coast of Australia. Their ships suffered hard damage in an encounter with American and British forces. Because the Japanese had been stopped in their attempt to cut the sea lanes between the United States and Australia, the battle of the Coral Sea was in fact a major strategic victory for the Allies. In June, 1942, the American sea and air power altered the intentions of a Japanese fleet that was steaming to conquer Midway Island. The Japanese lost four aircraft carriers, two cruisers, and three destroyers. The amphibious operations of soldiers and sailors from the United States, Australia, and New Zealand stopped the Japanese in August, 1942, at Guadalcanal, Tanambogo, Gavutu, and Tulagi in the Solomon Islands and in New Guinea. Here the Americans and their allies fought one of the most difficult campaigns in military history. The British sent reinforcements to India and seized the French island of Madagascar to protect the route to the East around the Cape of Good Hope. Slowly the Allies began a relentless drive northwards.

In Europe the Germans failed to defeat Russia in the summer of 1942 despite the power of their heavy drive beyond the Black Sea towards the rich oil regions of southeastern European Russia. True, the Russians were pushed back a thousand miles, all the way to Stalingrad on the Volga. The Germans almost reached the oil fields of Grozny and Baku; but "almost" was not enough. The Wehrmacht was stalled, blocked by the defenders of Stalingrad. The German communication lines were dangerously extended and their strength was overtaxed. Then winter came.

The logic of war is relentless. Some strategic blunders can be remedied; others never. It was one thing for the Germans to make territorial gains; it was quite another to exploit properly the implacable laws and logic of geography, strategy, production, transportation, and communication. In a global war one cogent rule remains: "The excessive expenditure of effort in one direction influences adversely the potential maximum that can be exploited in another." This military commandment the Germans did not obey. Wars are not won by the seizure of territory alone. There are also the rigid laws that govern the tensile strength of communication lines, the immutable factors that limit land transport facilities, the fixed and changeless equations of economic endurance. The danger of deep penetration into Russia had been grasped by von Falkenhayn, von Leeb, von Schlieffen, and von Seeckt. Hitler ignored the warning.

In Africa, Hitler's General Erwin Rommel, the "Desert Fox," pushed the British back almost to the Nile in the summer of 1942. In October, 1942, the British counterattacked; they leaped upon the Germans from behind the sixty-mile defense line stretching from El Alamein on the Mediterranean coast to the Qattara Depression. This mighty attack, brilliantly and carefully planned by Britain's General Sir Bernard Montgomery, was preceded by a heavy artillery barrage. On the northern end of the front there was one gun every twenty-three yards for six miles. When the battle of El Alamein was over, the Afrika Korps began its long 1,750-mile retreat, chased relentlessly by the triumphant Montgomery's British Eighth Army. The coastal road was crammed by fleeing German vehicles and men and blasted by the Royal Air Force. Montgomery captured 75,000 prisoners, 500 tanks, 1,000 guns, and the ports along the Mediterranean up to Tunisia.

On November 7, 1942, large Anglo-American forces were landed at Algiers, Oran, and Casablanca. The French, after a brief resistance, gave up Morocco and Algeria. Hitler, furious at this yielding of the French in Africa, at once (November 11) seized the southern part of France that he had earlier left in the hands of the Vichy regime. The Nazis hurried to grab the part of the French navy still stationed at Toulon. They reached Toulon too late: the angry and defiant French sailors scuttled their sixty-one ships. Hitler was foiled and frustrated; and he was not pleased.

General Rommel's men were now caught between the Anglo-American troops that had been landed in northwest Africa and the forces of General Montgomery that were pursuing the Germans along their road of retreat from Egypt. Meanwhile Allied ships and planes kept pounding and blasting at the Italian and Nazi supply lanes across the Mediterranean. The Allied vise was finally closed. Then the last Axis strongholds at Bizerte and Tunis fell. In May, 1943, the Italians and Germans in North Africa surrendered. More than 250,000 Nazi and Fascist soldiers were made prisoners, including seventeen

Axis generals. From the battle of El Alamein to the final defeat at Cape Bon the Axis had lost 427,000 men in Africa. They also lost 1,000 tanks, 3,729 airplanes, and 70,000 trucks. The "soft underbelly" of Europe was now exposed to Allied attack. The Allies were no longer on the defensive. "It may almost be said, 'Before Alamein we never had a victory. After Alamein we never had a defeat.'"

In July, 1943, 2,500 Allied ships carried 140,000 men to Sicily. That Italian island fell in thirty-eight days. Benito Mussolini was overthrown and his Fascist regime was ended. Not many years before, in the brightness of his pride, Mussolini had said: "I consider peace devitalizing and a negation of the fundamental virtues of man, which only through bloody struggles are revealed in the full light of the sun." Soon his body was to lie riddled with bullets by an Italian wall.

In early September the Italian mainland was invaded and the Italian government surrendered. The Germans, who had effectively occupied the Italian peninsula, fought on. Their resistance was long and desperate. The Allied advance was contested, month after month, past Naples, past Rome and the Anzio beachhead, all the way to the Apennines; not until the spring of 1945 were the Allied forces able to push into the Po valley.

Meanwhile a series of disasters plagued the German armies on the Russian front. Hitler refused to permit his forces to retreat before the attacks of the obstinate defenders of Stalingrad who had stalled the German onslaught. He ordered his soldiers to push on; but this they could not do. Hitler had asserted: "The occupation of Stalingrad will become a gigantic success. . . . No human being will push us away from that spot." The leader of all the Nazis was this time mistaken.

Twenty-two German divisions were destroyed at Stalingrad in January, 1943. Soon the siege of Leningrad was lifted. When the spring thaws had come and gone the Russians moved into a gigantic and continuous offensive along the whole vast front from the Crimea to the arctic wastelands. By October, 1943, they had smashed all the way to the Dnieper. Never again was Hitler able to seize the initiative.

By this time the British Commonwealth and the United States had developed careful long-range plans to coordinate their war efforts. Winston Churchill and President Franklin D. Roosevelt had met in a harbor on the coast of Newfoundland in August, 1941, in Washington soon after Pearl Harbor, and again in June, 1942. They were to hold further conferences at Casablanca in French Morocco in January, 1943, and at Quebec in August of the same year. With Russia and China, Great Britain and the United States formed the spearhead of the Allies, large and small. The armed forces of these nations were soon to carry out the massive undertakings agreed upon by Roosevelt, Churchill, Chiang Kai-shek, and Stalin in consultation with their chiefs of staff and other experts. In each major theater of war one man was placed in command of the land, sea, and air forces of all nations. For instance, the Southwest Pacific Area was commanded by General Douglas MacArthur; the Pacific Ocean Areas by Admiral Nimitz; the Southeast Asia Area by Admiral Lord Louis Mountbatten; the Middle Eastern Area by General Sir Harold Alexander; the later European Theater of Operations by General Dwight D. Eisenhower.

For many months the Russians had been pressing the British and Americans to open a second front in Europe. In August, 1942, Winston Churchill flew to Moscow to explain to Marshal Stalin that he and President Roosevelt believed that it was necessary to seize and hold control of the Mediterranean area before attempting to land forces at any place on the Continent. The decision of the United States and Great Britain to postpone the opening of a second front was never satisfactory to Stalin. The Russian leader did not understand the Anglo-American assertions that huge amphibious operations demanded more ships—tankers, troop transports, cargo vessels, landing craft—than the Allies could muster. It takes a lot of ships to move and supply a million men. Stalin continued to insist that he wanted a British-American offensive launched in Europe; he wanted Hitler's armies divided.

At last, in December, 1943, Churchill, Roosevelt, and Stalin met at a conference in Teheran, capital city of Iran. There Stalin was promised that an Anglo-American invasion of France would be mounted at the end of May or the beginning of June, 1944.

During these months of hard and heavy battles in Africa, Italy, and Russia the tide of conflict rose and fell throughout the lands and seas of the East. In northern Burma the British fought grimly and doggedly to hold back a Japanese assault. Then, suddenly, the Japanese were routed. More than 50,000 perished in the retreat. Meanwhile the Japanese fortified many of the islands they had conquered in the Pacific. They had won an empire and they were determined to hold it.

The Chinese Nationalist government under Chiang Kai-shek continued to fight the Japanese in China. In July, 1942, the Chinese defeated the invading Japanese in Kiangsi province—this event occurred a month before the landing of Allied forces, especially the American marines, in Tulagi and Guadalcanal and the other parts of the Solomon Islands mentioned earlier. In the southeastern theater of war the British and American sea and air forces continued and extended their pounding of the Japanese bases. One by one the strategic Pacific islands were torn out of Japanese hands. Other islands held by the Japanese were bypassed and the Japanese soldiers on them were left to starve or surrender—this was the famous "island-hopping" procedure that proved to be so effective in the war against Japan.

Early in 1943 the Americans and Australians advanced upon New Guinea.

Americans and Canadians recaptured the Aleutian islands of Kiska and Attu. At the beginning of 1944 the Americans moved up from the Marshall Islands to Guam, Saipan, Rota, and Tinian in the Marianas. Then came the turn of the western Carolinas. In the fall of 1944 General Douglas MacArthur launched an assault upon the central Philippines, striking first at Leyte and Luzon. By December, American bombers were flying from air fields on the Marianas to bomb the cities of Japan.

Soon the Americans turned towards the Ryukyus. In March, 1945, came the capture of the island of Iwo Jima. This event was what the Operational Narratives of the United States Marine Corps rightly call an "amphibious epic." After Iwo Jima was wrested from the hands of the Japanese, the Americans had a base 770 miles from Japan. In May, American forces attacked and seized Okinawa—that island was only about 325 miles from Japan.

The American Pacific Fleet was mauling the Japanese badly. The blockade was tightening. A steady process of attrition was wasting the Japanese air and shipping strength. A Japanese admiral later said: "Japan was beaten in the first part of 1945. That was when your submarines and naval aircraft cut off our supplies from the south." An island nation must wither and die when its sea communications are cut.

While these bloody and decisive events were happening in the East other dramatic chapters of the war were being written in Europe. The furious British and American bombing of Germany continued with unabated and devastating power. In ten days during the summer of 1943 more than 10,000 tons of bombs fell on Hamburg; three-quarters of the city was destroyed. From November, 1943, to March, 1944, the Royal Air Force dropped 33,000 tons of bombs on Berlin.

The balance of the submarine battle in the Atlantic slowly shifted to the Allied side. Late in 1941 the Germans had been sinking ships at the rate of 485,000 tons a month. By the summer of 1943 German submarines were being killed at the rate of one a day. In the first six months of 1943 new ships completed by the Allies exceeded all sinkings by more than 3,000,000 tons. Late in 1943 the *Scharnhorst* was sunk; British bombs sent the *Tirpitz* to the bottom of a Norwegian fiord.

Detailed, precise, and gigantic preparations were being made for an avalanche attack on Hitler's European fortress. Two million troops were massed in the United Kingdom. Britain was a mighty arsenal. Across the English Channel, Hitler and his henchmen prepared to defend themselves and their conquests. Their strength was still massive; they had more than 300 German divisions, excluding those of the satellite states. Hitler claimed that the Atlantic coast of Europe was an impregnable wall.

On D-Day, June 6, 1944, more than 2,000 tons of shells hurtled from Allied battleships and cruisers towards German installations on the Normandy coast.

A thousand tactical air force bombers opened their bomb bays and dropped their loads. A mighty armada of 800 warships and 4,000 landing craft carried American and British troops over the English Channel. Protecting the invaders were 11,000 Allied aircraft. Airborne troops parachuted down behind the German lines. Men and supplies poured ashore. European resistance groups and saboteurs plagued the Germans. Beachheads were won and held at five points along a sixty-mile stretch of the French coast. Within twenty days a million troops had landed. Great blockship breakwaters were built. Artificial ports, fabricated long before in England, were swiftly set up; the success of the pontoon piers probably astounded even the men who designed and made them.

In the savage battle of Normandy the Germans stubbornly held back the British and Canadians around Caen, the coastal hinge of the gateway to Paris. After capturing the ancient port of Cherbourg the Americans swept down the west side of the peninsula. The British Second Army and the Canadians finally took Caen on July 18 and the armored divisions of the American Third Army broke through the German left flank at Avranches, ripped into Brittany, swung northeast on the Seine, and outflanked Paris from the south. Paris fell on August 25. Most of western France was liberated. The Franco-American Seventh Army landed on the Riviera on August 15. It moved up towards the Rhine against the weakened German Nineteenth Army. On all the other fronts the Allies advanced with lightning speed. By the end of August the Germans had lost 400,000 men, of whom half were prisoners.

Then came the battle of Germany. The fighting was prolonged and bloody. Allied progress on all fronts slowed down. An unexpected German assault in the Ardennes sector launched by Field Marshal von Rundstedt resulted in the "Battle of the Bulge." For a time the Germans threatened to break through to Liége and Antwerp. Allied forces were rushed to stem the armored Nazi tide. At last, with tremendous effort, American and British pressure leveled out the bulge. It was the last major assault of the defiant Nazis.

In February, 1945, the British and Canadians were clearing the west bank of the Rhine. In early March a part of the American First Army reached Cologne. Other units of the First Army crossed the Ludendorff railway bridge at Remagen before the Germans were able to blow it up. The Americans rolled over the Rhine. Later in March, British and American troops crossed the Rhine at Rees and Wesel. The Canadians cleared the Germans out of the remainder of Holland. By early April, American and British forces were moving swiftly through the rich industrial areas of the Ruhr. The Russians were swirling into Germany from the east. On April 25, near Torgau, patrols of the Ukrainian First and American First Armies met. Germany was split in two.

Adolf Hitler stayed in Berlin as the Russians smashed into the city. There he died by his own hand on April 30. The Nazi "Third Reich" that Hitler had declared would endure for "a thousand years" was no more. Two days before Hitler died, Benito Mussolini and his mistress had been shot by Italian partisans and hanged by the heels in Milan. Berlin surrendered to the Russians on May 2. The Germans in Italy gave up the struggle on May 1. On the British and Canadian fronts a million German soldiers surrendered unconditionally to Britain's Field Marshal Montgomery. On May 8 the Germans made a complete and unconditional surrender at Reims. The war in Europe had ended.

In February, 1945, the Fourteenth British Army captured Mandalay, encircled large Japanese forces, swept down towards Rangoon and the many mouths of the Irrawaddy. Before the monsoon came in May, Rangoon fell and the Japanese fled. Burma was free again.

During the months of May, June, and July, the coasts of the Japanese islands were shelled by American and British naval forces. American flying fortresses bombed Japanese cities, day after day. Russia gathered her forces to lunge into Manchuria.

Then, suddenly, on August 6, 1945, the industrial city of Hiroshima was struck by a new and fearful atomic bomb. The atom had been split. Mighty power, for good or ill, had been released to mankind. The bomb dropped on Hiroshima left 78,150 human beings killed, 37,425 injured, and 13,983 missing.

On August 8, Russia declared war upon Japan and attacked Manchuria. On August 9, a second atomic bomb was dropped by the Americans on the port city of Nagasaki. Japan needed no more evidence that the prolongation of the war meant her utter destruction. The wages of Pearl Harbor had been paid. The Japanese cabinet sued for peace. On board the U.S.S. *Missouri* in Tokyo Bay the Japanese leaders surrendered in a formal ceremony. The date was September 2, 1945.

The Second World War had ended. In the holocaust of death and destruction, grief and glory, the governments of the fighting nations spent $1,117,000,000,000 for military purposes. The value of the widespread damage and destruction of property was nearly $2,250,000,000,000. More than 10,000,000 soldiers, sailors, and airmen died. About 12,000,000 civilians also perished. There were other losses of an entirely different kind. No statistics can ever measure them.

A meeting of the United Nations Security Council in New York on July 16, 1958. At this session the Council was considering the crisis in the Middle East.

PLATE XLV

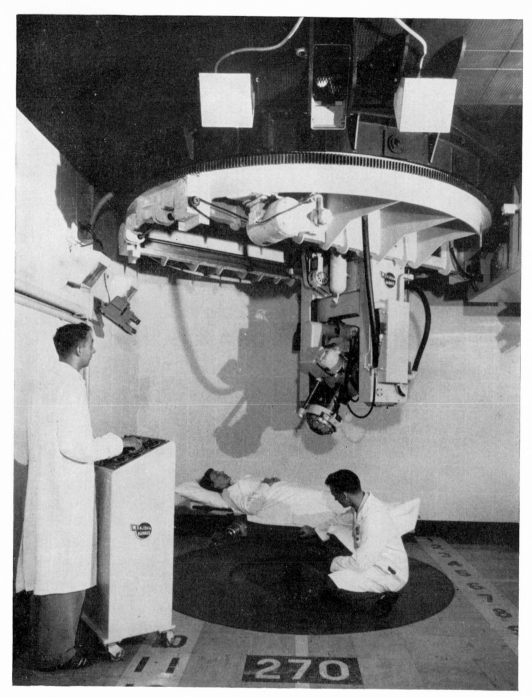

[121] Technicians work with the hectocurie Cobalt-60 teletherapy machine at the Medical Division Hospital of the Oak Ridge Institute of Nuclear Studies.

PLATE XLVI

Chapter 47

THE UNEASY

PEACE

"It would not be Christmas in our times if some unhappy dispossessed
people were not going into exile with scanty belongings and a hopeless
dread of the future. The same familiar pictures . . . of forlorn refugees
coming down the gangway with bundles and the inevitable cradle. 'Arise,
and take the child and his mother and flee.'"

—Mr. George Schwartz in *The Times* (London),
December 22, 1957

THE decades that followed the Second World War were filled with dramatic
chapters in the domestic and foreign affairs of the nation-states. A series
of complex forces fused to bring massive transformations in the modern world.
Of vital importance to all mankind were the struggles of principle and power,
the intricate networks of national rivalries and irritations, the headstrong and
dynamic nationalism of Asia, the Near East, and Africa, the fears of nuclear
warfare, the bitter and ominous disputes between the democratic and Communist nations of the world. Meanwhile population pressures increased. Economic
and financial problems multiplied. Men disputed, as always, about the distribution of wealth in the world. Uncounted troubles and tensions sprang from
man's inhumanity to man. There were many unhealthy moods and deeds.
All over the planet the faces of thousands of human beings were distorted by
hate and fear.

Through the gray years the statesmen and diplomats plodded forward with
an appearance of hope that few could feel and none could afford to discard.
The beleaguered bulk of mankind watched as the world stumbled from crisis
to crisis.

To describe contemporary events is usually not a difficult task; to judge
their long-range importance in human affairs is impossible. Even the best
of the modern minor prophets can find himself confounded in the morning
light.

When President Franklin D. Roosevelt died in 1945 the leadership of the United States passed into the hands of Harry S. Truman, a shrewd and able man who faced his tasks with courage. In the years ahead, when the passions and prejudices of political controversy have subsided, the name of Harry Truman may be included among the great Presidents of the Republic.

It is always difficult for a nation to move from war to peace. In the transition years that followed 1945 the Democratic administration was swiftly confronted with scores of problems: demobilization, inflation, labor disputes, arguments about civil rights, the mounting belligerence of Russia, the struggles between President Truman and the Eightieth Congress, and all the complaints of people who had nursed and kept too many hopes about what pleasures and profits the end of the war would bring to them.

Within the Democratic Party there appeared several divisions, especially about the liberal and pacifist ideas of Henry A. Wallace, Vice-President under Franklin D. Roosevelt and Secretary of Commerce during the first Truman administration. When Wallace broke away from the Democrats to form a Progressive party the prospects of a Democratic victory at the polls in the Presidential election seemed dim indeed.

The harassed and weakened Democrats chose Harry Truman as their Presidential candidate. His Republican opponent was Thomas E. Dewey, Governor of New York. After an amazing campaign Truman won the election. He obtained 24,105,000 popular votes and 303 electoral votes; Dewey got 21,969,000 popular votes and 189 electoral votes.

After the Democratic victory of 1948 there came several pieces of social legislation: a new Social Security Act, an amendment to the Fair Labor Standards Act, and a National Housing Act. Meanwhile prices rose. Political scandals were uncovered among the Democrats, some big, some small. The public became deeply concerned about questions of disloyalty, Communism, and subversion. Several acts of Congress were designed to bolster the internal security of the state. Unfounded and reckless charges often stimulated suspicions and roused distrust among the citizens. It sometimes seemed that too many irresponsible men were trying to seize and hold the headlines. Some individuals, of course, were really trying to watch the ramparts of the republic. But if they had had their way they might have destroyed the freedom they were ostensibly attempting to defend. Fortunately, the voices of most of the extremists were gradually muffled. In a great democracy the forces of common sense and moderation may take some time to prevail.

President Harry S. Truman was not a candidate in the Presidential election of 1952. The Democrats selected Adlai E. Stevenson, Governor of Illinois, as their leader. The Republicans chose General Dwight D. Eisenhower. Eisenhower obtained 33,824,000 popular votes and 442 votes in the Electoral College. Stevenson got 27,314,000 popular votes, 89 in the Electoral College. In

1956 Eisenhower was to win again by a decisive margin. The control of both houses of Congress remained in the hands of the Democrats. They increased their majorities in the Congressional elections of 1958.

Across the Atlantic in Great Britain the British people went to the polls in July, 1945, and defeated Winston Churchill and the Conservative party. In the storm of war Winston Churchill had been a mighty leader. Nevertheless, the British voters were unwilling to entrust Churchill and the Conservatives with the tasks of reconstruction and the winning of the peace. They turned instead to the Labor Party, the advocates of a planned and socialized economy.

Led by Clement Attlee, the Laborites embarked upon an experiment to change the battle-scarred British Isles into a stable "Socialist Commonwealth." A steady stream of remarkable legislation began to transform the face of Britain. There were new housing programs, town and country planning projects, novel and comprehensive policies and patterns in the British system of public education, radical changes in the existing programs of social insurance and allied services, new government schemes to provide full employment. The Bank of England passed under public control. Soon the coal mines were nationalized, then the railways, civil aviation, all telecommunications, the electricity industry, the gas companies.

Meanwhile the Labor government was confronted by the dark facts of British wartime losses, the accumulation of debt, defense, and European relief charges, the results of a crippled and unbalanced foreign trade. The world was short of dollars. Britain's expenses soared as she paid the high world-commodity prices. Despite loans from the United States and a drastic reduction of Britain's dollar purchases the adverse and menacing gap in Britain's export-import outlay and income widened. The stability of sterling was endangered. With every resource it could summon the Labor government battled to ride out the storm. The details of successive budgets showed how difficult was the passage to economic and financial survival.

In the virile Parliament of 1945–1950 the over-all majority of the Laborites was 140. A national election in February, 1950, reduced that majority to 7. There had been a steady erosion of Labor popularity. Many citizens felt that the unrelenting rhythm of nationalization, hailed by Labor as a sovereign specific for most ills, had shaken the state too much. The drastic economic measures of the government were widely unpopular. Nevertheless, the Labor Party, so shaken and shrunken, clung to power. But it could not hold on for long. In October, 1951, a general election turned the Laborites out of office. The Conservatives and their allies won 321 seats in the House of Commons; the Laborites, 294; the Liberals, 6; the others, 3.

In April, 1955, Sir Winston Churchill, eighty years old, resigned as Great Britain's forty-second prime minister and leader of the Conservative Party.

Europe
at mid-twentieth century

NORWAY

Oslo

GREAT

NORTHERN
IRELAND

DENMARK

EIRE

BRITAIN

Copen

NETHERLANDS

GERM

London

The Hague

Bremen

Berl

GERMAN

DEMOCR

Brussels

REPUBL

BELGIUM

FEDERAL

LUXEMBURG

SAAR

P

Paris

FRANCE

REPUBLIC

Berne

AUST

SWITZERLAND

Free Territory
(United Nations)

ITALY

PORTUGAL

Madrid

Lisbon

Rome

SPAIN

■ Communist Bloc Countries

FINLAND
Helsinki

Leningrad

Stockholm

ESTONIA

Absorbed as
Soviet
Republics

Moscow

LATVIA

LITHUANIA

S O V I E T

U N I O N

POLAND

Warsaw

Kiev

CHOSLOVAKIA

Budapest

HUNGARY

RUMANIA

Bucharest

GOSLAVIA

Belgrade

BULGARIA

Sofia

ALBANIA

Tirane

Ankara

GREECE

T U R K E Y

Athens

Dodecanese Is.
(Greece)

Churchill had lived and served under five sovereigns. His retirement marked the end of an epic span of history. The free world perhaps owed its life to this tough and dauntless Titan. From all that free world, tributes volleyed and thundered to Westminster when the incomparable Churchill departed in glory.

Sir Anthony Eden, Churchill's successor, led a strong and cohesive Conservative government into a dull and demure national election in May, 1955. The Conservatives won 344 seats, the Laborites 277. The Labor Party was badly and sadly disarrayed and divided. In 1956 Mr. Clement Attlee resigned as Labor leader and became Earl Attlee. His successor was Mr. Hugh Gaitskell.

Late in 1956 Sir Anthony Eden resigned as prime minister and leader of the Conservatives. He was followed by Mr. Harold Macmillan, a skilled and wary man. In the election of October, 1959, he led the Conservatives to another victory. His tasks were dangerous, his burdens heavy.

In 1945 Adolf Hitler's Germany had collapsed in ruin and blood. Out of the shambles in East Germany the Russians created the German Democratic Republic under Communist control. Great Britain, France, and the United States merged the zones they governed in western Germany and aided the growth of a virtually independent state. The economic recovery of West Germany was remarkable; by 1960 the value of her gross national product stood at about $50,000,000,000.

The republic of France was steadily troubled by strikes, weak coalition governments, and Communists—the underworld of Communist activity stretched thousands of miles from Moscow. Nevertheless, the industrial output of France increased about 200 per cent between 1950 and 1960. New factories, new petrochemical plants, new production of such varied items as cement and airplanes, pushed the curve of industrial achievement upwards. To supply her factory demands France sucked in great volumes of raw materials. Unfortunately, her exports failed to keep pace with her imports, partly because her domestic market sopped up so many goods. The financial ill health of France—she was sometimes at the rim of international bankruptcy—continued for several years. Again and again France kept running out of foreign exchange and seeking transfusions from abroad.

Meanwhile the French political difficulties increased. In September, 1958, the people of France and all the French Empire—except Guinea—overwhelmingly approved a constitution proposed by General Charles de Gaulle to establish the Fifth French Republic, a republic in which the executive powers of the president were to be large and strong. The voters preferred the possible dangers of dictatorship to the near-anarchy that had so often plagued the political life of France.

Italy became a republic when King Victor Emmanuel III abdicated in 1946. The moderate Alcide de Gasperi, leader of the Christian Democrats, succeeded in stopping and hurling back the challenge of the Italian Communists. Italy soon joined the North Atlantic Treaty Organization, described below, and moved towards cooperation with Great Britain, France, and the United States. After Premier de Gasperi was forced to resign in 1953 the moderate center groups still kept control in the Senate and the Chamber of Deputies. What happened in Italy was characteristic of the postwar political events in several states. In Belgium, Denmark, the Netherlands, Luxemburg, Norway, and Sweden moderate and liberal governments remained in power. In Spain and Portugal, however, the dictatorships of General Francisco Franco and Antonio Salazar stood unshaken.

Across the broad seas in all the colonial empires of the world events were soon proclaiming that the old imperial order was ended. The rising floods and storms of a new nationalism rose and surged in the colonies and they could not be stilled by decrees from the European capitals or quelled by sending gunboats and soldiers. There were sudden outbursts of violence, complicated webs of conspiracy, stubborn resistance, sometimes skillfully planned rebellions.

It is easy—especially if one looks out from the windows of London, Washington, and Paris—to forget what a tremendous gulf separates the men and cultures of Africa, Asia, and the islands of the southern seas from the Western world, how frail and modern are the links that bind the peoples of the East and West. The missionaries, the traders, and the soldiers of Europe and America did not destroy all of the ways and values of the peoples whose lands they conquered. In many parts of the colonial world, several shadowy and remote traditions, half-forgotten customs, myths, and heroic legends were remembered and in them there was no place for the ideas and teachings of Europe and America. Many tribesmen were still faithful to their old gods, and those gods were older than Woden and Thor.

As the colonial worlds moved into revolt, stirred by vital and dynamic powers that nobody can really describe or name, a few shrewd statesmen attempted to guide and direct the forces they could no longer control. Their decisions helped to change the face of the world. As they made those decisions, the pace of events grew faster.

The withdrawal of Britain from India in 1947 was a significant fact and an important symbol. When Lord Mountbatten, last of the British viceroys, departed from New Delhi he left behind him two independent states, India and Pakistan, new members of the Commonwealth of Nations brought into being by the Statute of Westminster of 1931. The world watched the successes and failures of Moslem Pakistan and Hindu India; the persecutions and massacres of Hindus and Moslems and the flights of the refugees; the looting and burning and starvation; the disputes about the status of Hyderabad and Kashmir; the rivalries and suspicions that darkened the great subcontinent; the attempts to end some of the evils of poverty, illiteracy, and disease; the tremendous tasks that faced the peoples and their governments; the plans and the promises and the hopes of a fair tomorrow.

In 1948, after a long period of British rule, Burma was given absolute independence; Ceylon became a sovereign part of the Commonwealth. In the same year Britain officially terminated her thirty-one-year rule of Palestine and the Jews proclaimed at Tel Aviv the independence of the new state of Israel. This independence was soon challenged by the Arab states of the Near East. The contending peoples of those turbulent lands began to move and march again. Decades of violence were at hand. Throughout the Near and Middle East the refugees, the uprooted and the homeless, begged for peace and asylum. Thousands of other human beings were doing the same thing in South Korea, Hong Kong, India, Pakistan, and West Berlin. Many of them are there still, always hoping to survive and to start the beautiful new life at last.

The sands of change run fast and they run at an accelerated pace. The British policies, framed to cope with numerous problems of nationalism, race, economics, and politics, were creative and dynamic. Swift thrusts of change in the Commonwealth and Empire after 1950 made nonsense out of old dogmas and habits of thought. Every year Commonwealth prime ministers and ministers of finance met in places as far apart as London, Sydney, Ottawa, and Colombo to pool their ideas, discuss their problems, and concert their policies. Changes were made in scores of governmental structures. The ministerial system was introduced in Sierra Leone. In Uganda the Legislative Council was reorganized. Nigeria was given a great degree of autonomy. In 1956 the Sudan became an independent state. A Central African Federation was formed by Northern and Southern Rhodesia and Nyasaland. In 1957 the Gold Coast became the independent state of Ghana within the Commonwealth. In 1958 the Caribbean Federation of Jamaica, Trinidad, the Barbados, and the Leeward and Windward Islands began to function. Meanwhile there were difficulties, death, and destruction as some Greeks in Cyprus demanded the cession of Cyprus to Greece and the Communists in Malaya raided and killed. Meanwhile, too, the Mau Mau organization, a secret underground of terror and dark magic, tried to oust the Europeans from Kenya. The explosive racial policy of the government of the Union of South Africa was fraught with heavy danger. Throughout South Africa were knots of passive resistance, ignorant and embittered masses, coils of tension.

Meanwhile the vast lands of the Dutch and French empires continued to be disturbed by the seething unrest described in earlier pages. New and explosive forces shivered and broke old instruments of power. At almost breakneck speed the roused masses east of Suez and in North Africa stumbled and raced towards a new world. In Algeria and Tunis and Morocco the French faced tremendous tasks and problems. The Dutch in the East Indies were plagued by questions for which no solutions could be found, by demands to which they could not accede. Many of the newly independent nations had yet to realize that with freedom came responsibility.

At the end of the Second World War the United States armed forces occupied Japan. The American authorities soon established in Japan a democratic constitution and a system of free elections. Despite American efforts, there was little alteration in Japanese habits of thought or in the social structure of the country. Meanwhile the spirit of nationalism began to rise again; it was less militant than it had been when Hideki Tojo ruled and flourished.

General Douglas MacArthur and the American occupation authorities in Japan tried to break up the great Japanese centralized trusts and holding companies. Their decrees and controls did not bring a collapse of the traditional forms of business monopolies. Many aspects of the old order, including the *zaibatsu* power, could not easily be destroyed.

In the meantime, the life of the Japanese people in the country and the great cities was not greatly changed. Almost always, it seemed, the old ways crossed and blended with the new. The cherry blossoms, the kimonos, and the Shinto shrines remained. There were also modern buses, taxis, neon lights, television networks, the chain stores and the great shopping district of the Ginza in Tokyo, the vehement voices of the trade-union leaders, the tall, earthquake-proof buildings of concrete and steel, baseball teams, suburban and underground railways—more than 500,000 passengers move through Tokyo Central Railway Station every day.

The Japanese people have long been admired for their skill and energy. After peace came in 1945 the Japanese leaders, determined to regain their lost economic strength, stimulated an intense activity in industry and commerce. Industrial production steadily increased. On the other hand, the slow expansion of trade following the postwar slump was discouraging to the Japanese. Many of the Oriental markets had been lost—only about 2 per cent of Japan's foreign trade, for instance, was with Communist China. Meanwhile the population continued to increase; by 1960 about 85,000,000 people lived in the islands of Japan, about 8,000,000 of them in Tokyo. The shrinking of trade posed a hard problem for the Japanese.

In the unfolding tale of China there were more dramatic chapters. By the terms of the Yalta agreement of February, 1945, Prime Minister Winston Churchill and President Franklin D. Roosevelt had virtually agreed to hand over to Soviet Russia Outer Mongolia, the Kurile islands, Port Arthur, and the southern part of Sakhalin, to internationalize Dairen, to allow Russia joint control with China of the Chinese Eastern Railroad. It will be recalled that President Roosevelt was very anxious to persuade Russia to depart from neu-

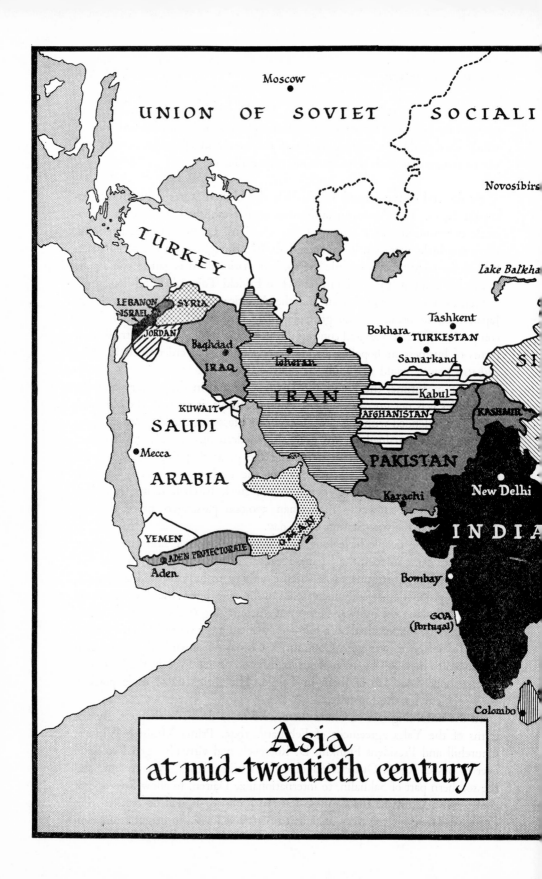

Asia
at mid-twentieth century

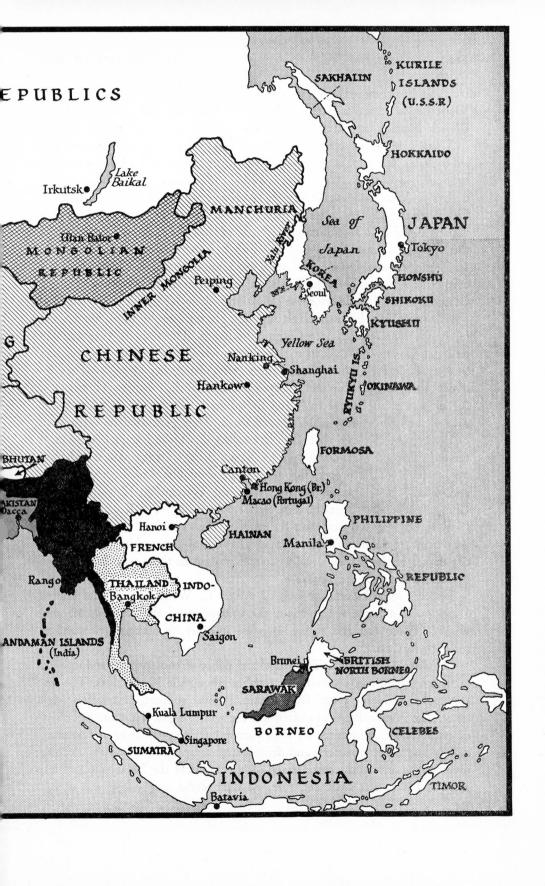

REPUBLICS

SAKHALIN

KURILE
ISLANDS
(U.S.S.R.)

HOKKAIDO

*Lake
Baikal*

Irkutsk●

MANCHURIA

*Sea of
Japan*

JAPAN

Ulan Bator ●

MONGOLIAN

REPUBLIC

INNER MONGOLIA

Peiping ●

KOREA

Seoul ●

HONSHU

Tokyo ●

SHIKOKU

KYUSHU

G

CHINESE

Yellow Sea

Nanking ●

Shanghai ●

KYUKYU IS.

OKINAWA

BHUTAN

REPUBLIC

Hankow ●

FORMOSA

PAKISTAN
Dacca

Canton ●

Hong Kong (Br.)
Macao (Portugal)

PHILIPPINE

Hanoi ●

FRENCH

HAINAN

Manila ●

Rango

THAILAND
Bangkok ●

INDO-

REPUBLIC

ANDAMAN ISLANDS
(India)

CHINA

Saigon ●

Brunei

BRITISH
NORTH BORNEO

SARAWAK

Kuala Lumpur ●

BORNEO

CELEBES

Singapore ●

SUMATRA

INDONESIA

TIMOR

Batavia ●

trality and to come actively into the war against Japan. In August, 1945, the Soviet Union signed a thirty-year treaty of friendship and alliance with the Chinese Nationalists, attacked Japan, and poured troops into Manchuria.

There were other facts of consequence. By 1945 the Chinese Communists, led by such able men as Mao Tze-tung, Chou En-lai, and Li Shao-ch'i, had succeeded in obtaining control of about one-third of China. The earlier attempts of Vice-President Henry A. Wallace and Major General Patrick J. Hurley of the United States to devise practical plans for settlement between Chiang Kai-shek's Kuomintang government and the Central Committee of the Chinese Communist Party had failed. General George C. Marshall's mediating mission at the end of 1945 was also unsuccessful. Chiang Kai-shek even ignored General Marshall's warning not to undertake overambitious military campaigns. He did try those campaigns—how foolish he was!—and lost them, one by one. Each time vast supplies, given earlier by the United States to the Nationalists, fell into Communist hands. The military disasters that fell upon Chiang Kai-shek in 1948 and 1949 were largely of his own making.

Meanwhile the Chinese Communists consolidated their strength. They increased their membership and enlarged and trained their armies. They sought the support of the intellectuals and the students. They tried to educate and discipline all the youths who followed them. They permitted no corruption. Mao Tze-tung declared that the Nationalists should be left in possession of the big cities and worn down by guerrilla attacks against their trade and communication lines. He ordered that all prisoners should be treated with kindness, and thousands of soldiers deserted from the Nationalists. Meanwhile the Chinese Nationalist forces became increasingly flabby. The Kuomintang still continued to rely too much on the landlord classes and still remained timid about trusting the masses. The ideas of Chiang Kai-shek and his cohorts about the nature of democracy usually seemed strange to those who lived in the democratic states of the West.

In July, 1947, Lieutenant General Albert C. Wedemeyer of the United States made a blunt report about the corruption of the Kuomintang and warned Chiang Kai-shek to set his house in order, to make reforms and to make them soon.

No reforms were made. The gospel and policy of conservatism and reaction prevailed. There was no worthy leadership among the Nationalists. The discredited Kuomintang rotted from within. Popular support, never strong, fell away. The Nationalist troops often lost the will to fight. Thousands of them deserted. The Communists, for their part, presented themselves as liberators, zealous and eager crusaders, and defenders of the people. When the decisive moment had arrived the collapse and disintegration of the Nationalist government of China was swift and sure. As their world and society was dying,

Chiang Kai-shek and his government fled to Formosa. All of the Chinese mainland was engulfed in a great revolution.

In October, 1949, the Communists proclaimed the People's Republic of China. In 1950 Communist China and Soviet Russia signed a treaty of mutual aid. Russia promised to get out of Dairen and Port Arthur, to hand over the Chungchun railway and to give China credits for $60,000,000 for a period of five years.

There was furious violence and much brutality at this turning point in the history of China. A ruthless reign of terror was unleashed. The Communists moved at once against the "exploiting" landlords and began a program of "land reform." The landlords, together with several other "counter-revolutionaries," were denounced as criminals, conspirators, capitalist agents, and bandits. "Public security stations" and spies helped to detect and round up for grim and spectacular mass "trials" the men and women who were to be executed; it was a degrading and indecent business. Probably about 20,000,000 were slaughtered. Thousands of acres of land were distributed among the peasants, and some of these poor people of China thought that their long tale of misery was ended at last. About 5,000,000 collective farms were created, instruments of state enterprise. Revolutions and war and world-shaking ideas have often released great energy, and this is what happened in China. They have frequently brought a message of hope; and to human beings hope is very important.

Restrictions on "bourgeois" private business were increased. Flood, famine, and health-control measures multiplied. New organs of government were set up. Inflation controls were imposed. "Labor" and "re-education" centers appeared throughout China. Much of the old culture of China seemed about to pass away. Many industrial plants were built, often equipped with Russian machinery. Thousands of Russian technicians came to aid and advise the Chinese. There were many difficulties. One of them, of course, was the problem of obtaining savings for national investment in industrial plants from a vast population that was so very poor. For many centuries, only the upper classes had known wealth and comfort. The life of all the rest of China's millions had been harsh and comfortless. Nevertheless, the Chinese determination remained: first to equal, then to excel, the West.

In four words China's Mao Tze-tung summed up a new event in the unfolding history of the world. "China," he said, "has stood up." What Mao Tze-tung said was true. Soviet Russia, for instance, knows that it is true and fears the advance of the millions of China to the day when their broad land is a powerful and industrialized state—and a hungry state. By the side of China, Russia will then be small.

Facts are stubborn things and must be in the manual of all realists. Above all, perhaps, it should be remembered that history cannot be written and life cannot be lived in a vacuum of generalities, abstractions, and good will.

When the Charter of the United Nations was adopted at San Francisco in June, 1945, it was hoped that the world, scarred and armed by experience, would end a long age of predatory exploitations and nationalistic ambitions.

The United Nations Charter contained 111 articles defining the aims of the United Nations and establishing a constitution. In the General Assembly of the United Nations each nation was given one representative and one vote. The Assembly was to meet once a year. Special sessions might be called at any time. Members of the Assembly were to discuss any problems not under consideration by the Security Council. They were to make recommendations to the Council. They were to elect the six nonpermanent members of the Security Council, the members of the Economic and Social Council, and the fifteen members of the International Court of Justice. They were to admit or expel members. In all important decisions of the Assembly, a two-thirds majority was necessary.

The Security Council contained eleven members. The United States, the USSR, Great Britain, France, and China held permanent seats; six others were elected for a two-year term by the Assembly. Each of the permanent members possessed the power of vetoing almost any proposed action by the Council, except on procedural questions. The major task of the Security Council was to investigate and discuss international disputes, to seek to prevent war, and to punish aggressive states by economic sanctions and military force.

An Economic and Social Council, consisting of eighteen members selected by the Assembly, was empowered to study and make recommendations about world social and economic conditions, particularly those that might be basic causes of international hostility and conflict. Other important bodies within the organization of the United Nations included the Secretariat, the international civil service of the United Nations, responsible for administration and research; the International Court of Justice; the International Monetary Fund; the Educational, Scientific and Cultural Organization, designed to promote understanding and cooperation among the world's peoples; the World Bank; the Food and Agriculture Organization; and the Atomic Energy Commission, which contained the eleven members of the Security Council.

The new peace of 1945 was soon placed in jeopardy by the divergent ideas and interests of the wartime allies, so edgy and suspicious. Conferences at Potsdam, London, and Moscow brought several diplomatic clashes and some deadlocks. Again and again the representatives of the Soviet Union opposed the views of the United States, Great Britain, and France. In the Security Council of the United Nations the Russian delegates repeatedly thwarted and vetoed proposals and policies they considered inimical to their interests.

The perils and pressures born of international controversies increased. There were disputes about the Soviet claim to dominance in the Dardanelles region; the peace treaties with Italy and the disposal of the Italian colonies; the control of the Ruhr Valley; the war crimes trials; the reconstruction of eastern European states; the problems of reparations and rehabilitation loans; the control of atom bomb secrets and nuclear tests; the division of Germany into four administrative zones.

Several conferences of foreign ministers resulted in more disappointments and tensions. Differences between national ideologies and interests became clearer. There were new developments of strategic doctrines, new calculations of power, new estimates of risk. National ideas and policies must always be adjusted to changing conditions. Those conditions include, of course, the shifting equations of military power. A new or improved weapon is not forgotten at a conference table. A strong nation speaks with authority because it has airplanes and ships, missiles and men. It is not enough, in our day, to be armed with honor and justice and a good cause.

The Soviet Union proceeded to extend the network of her political and economic power. Russian pressure and plotting extended from Iran to Greece and the Mediterranean shores, and the vast webs of conspiracy reached around the globe. In March, 1948, free Czechoslovakia fell as a result of Communist subversion and internal aggression. In the satellite states of Rumania, Poland, and Hungary the Russians were the masters; they could not be dislodged. When Hungary tried to break free in 1956 the Communist punishment was quick and cruel, empty of justice and mercy, revolting and inhuman and vile.

Within Russia the brutal mass murders and spectacular purges of Joseph Stalin continued. On one day a man might smile in the sunshine of the Kremlin's favor; on the next he might meet his death in silence and his comrades would see him no more. A premier, a foreign minister, a general of the army might find himself ousted from office and stripped of power. The leaders who walked by Stalin's side came and went; not many stayed for long. The tides of terror rose and fell. Stalin's dictatorship was ruthless; his career was a tale of crime and duplicity and consummate skill.

Nor were Joseph Stalin's ideas about the value of diplomacy and international agreements at all in accord with the usual views of most leaders and peoples of other nations. Stalin once wrote: "A diplomat's words must have no relation to his actions—otherwise what kind of diplomacy is it? Words are one thing, actions another. . . . Sincere diplomacy is no more possible than dry water or iron wood." The successors of Stalin have not forgotten his precepts; they, too, have broken their signed agreements and tossed aside their pledges.

From the point of view of those who believe in the teachings and doctrines of Marx, Engels, Lenin, Stalin, and their fellows, all causes and claims must yield before the demands of the Communist Party. All considerations of "bourgeois morality" must be disregarded. The actions of the state, say the Communists, must not be judged by the usual standards of right and wrong. The state has a morality all its own.

The idea is also firmly established among the Communists that the struggle for power between the capitalist and Communist states must continue. There must be no decline of determination or relaxing of effort. In 1951 Joseph Stalin said this about Russia's new Five-Year Plan: "It is sometimes asked whether it is not possible to slow down the tempo a bit, to put a check on the movement. No, comrades, it is not possible! The tempo must not be reduced! . . . We are fifty or a hundred years behind the advanced countries. We must make good this distance in ten years. Either we do it, or they crush us!"

After Stalin died in March, 1953, the Soviet government proclaimed the dawn of a new "epoch of trust and truth." Stalin's successors tried to blacken his name and wrangled and wrestled over his mantle. But they did not in fact abandon many of Stalin's principles. It would have been difficult to do so because most of the rules had been handed down by Nikolai Lenin. Changes in the strategy and tactics of the leaders in the Kremlin never meant that the long-range plans and principles of the Soviet Union had been laid aside. The fixed purpose of Communism remained the same: the bourgeois-capitalist-imperialist world must be crushed and the triumph of the "classless" society achieved.

There appeared in Russia some facts and tendencies that were not in accord with the earlier Communist creed and liturgy: the practices of state capitalism; the aristocracy of the ruling cliques, the party leaders, the bureaucrats, the managerial and professional groups, especially the engineers and scientists; the old Russian tsarist expansionist hungers. In 1849 Feodor Tyutchev wrote some sentences that the modern rulers of Russia would not find entirely offensive: "The Occident is dying, everything crumbles in the general conflagration, the Europe of Charlemagne as well as the Europe of the treaties of 1815, the Roman papacy, and all the thrones of the Occident, Catholicism and Protestantism, faith long since lost and reason reduced to absurdity. Above this vast shipwreck appears, like an Ark of the Covenant, the Russian Empire, more vast than ever."

Meanwhile the fate of the Poznan rioters in Poland and the smashing of Hungary's bid for freedom showed that the Soviet government was prepared to use any means to keep her iron grip upon her satellites. Threats and tanks and treachery, these can be deadly weapons in the hands of men to whom justice and honor and mercy are words without meaning. And meanwhile, too, the plots and purges continued in the Soviet Union. Vyacheslav Molotov, Georgi Malenkov, Lavrenti Beria, Nikolai Bulganin—such men as these rose

PLATE
XLVII

[122]

ove: The interior of the Tiros
ather satellite, one of the most
mplex electronic systems yet sent
o space by the United States

ght: "Madonna and Child," by Eng-
d's Henry Moore, one of the great-
and most versatile sculptors of the
ntieth century

[123]

[124] View of the presidential palace of President Kubitschek at Brasilia, the modern capital of Brazil. It was designed by Oscar Niemeyer, Brazil's foremost architect.

[125]

Communist Chinese Premier Chou En-lai meets in New Delhi with Indian Premier Jawaharlal Nehru (April 19, 1960).

PLATE XLVIII

and fell. Sergei Eisenstein, famous Soviet motion-picture producer, was attacked because he did not subordinate his art sufficiently to the demands of politics and the "ideological convictions" of the Communist Party. Dmitri Shostakovich was reprimanded because his Ninth Symphony was less successful as "ideological art" than his music celebrating the October Revolution and the defense of Leningrad. The peasants were harassed; there was forced labor on a great scale; there were smiles and there was murder.

The physical power of the Soviet Union steadily increased. Great iron and steel industries grew in the vast spaces of Siberia, Kazankean, and the Far East. New industrial empires appeared in the Urals. Power stations and metallurgical centers were built in the far reaches of Russia: in Bratsk, Kamensk, Novosibirsk, Krasnoyarsk, colossal enterprises on the Angara, Yenesi, and Ob river systems. In 1957 and 1958 the Soviet Union was able to place several earth satellites in orbit, an achievement that showed the world something of the level of the skills and knowledge of the Russian scientists and technicians.

The carping and jibing and barren war of nerves between the East and West continued through the years, a state of affairs that was neither stability nor strife. Heads of state, foreign ministers, and deputy foreign ministers met in frequent, prolonged, and sometimes futile discussions in Paris, London, Washington, and Geneva. Threats and insults leaped across the mountains and the seas.

Russia and China, holding the "inner line" of Asia and Europe in a military sense, were able to shift their pressure to the weakest points on the periphery or "outer line." The diverse character and interests of the "outer line" states increased their weakness and made them more vulnerable to attack, one by one, than if they had been united by a common policy and program. This was one of the problems considered by the prime ministers of Burma, Ceylon, India, Indonesia, and Pakistan at the Colombo Conference of May, 1954.

There were several nasty disputes and crises. In 1948, for instance, the Russians tried to force the Western powers out of Berlin. Despite the menacing risk of war with Russia, airplanes of the American and British "airlift" supplied fuel and food to the sectors of Berlin legally under the control of the Western powers but surrounded by the Soviet zone. In 1948 the plans of the Russians failed. Nevertheless, the Soviet government did not change its aims or ends. In 1959, for instance, a highly explosive situation arose when the Russians again demanded that the Western nations abandon West Berlin.

The Communists were seldom idle. China extended its sprawling empire by restoring its authority over Tibet in 1950, a step that gravely disturbed the Himalayan states of Nepal, Bhutan, and Afghanistan, all buffer states on the approaches to India and Pakistan. In 1959 Tibet's Dalai Lama was forced to flee to India. Early in 1954 the Communist Vietminh rebels of northern Indochina, powerful and disciplined, defeated the Vietnam and French forces in the south. Eight years of conflict were ended when an armistice was signed at Geneva by the terms of which the Indochinese state of Vietnam was partitioned near the seventeenth parallel. North of that line the Vietminh Communists remained in control. South Vietnam went to a French-supported government. Laos and Cambodia stayed as they were, nominally independent and sovereign states. Still unanswered was the problem of finding effective safeguards against acts of aggression along the southern rim of Asia.

In March, 1947, President Harry S. Truman of the United States put forward the "Truman Doctrine" and asked the Congress of his country for $400,-000,000 to assist Greece and Turkey and to protect the Middle East from Communism. "I believe that it must be the policy of the United States," said the President, "to support free people who are resisting attempted subjugation by armed minorities or by outside pressure." In September, 1948, the Committee of European Economic Cooperation estimated that the Western European nations would need aid amounting to $19,330,000,000 from the United States during the following four years. On December 19, 1948, President Truman asked Congress to appropriate $17,000,000,000 to cover the period 1948–1951. The Congress approved the bold and imaginative European Recovery Plan. The Economic Co-operation Administration was established to handle the flow of goods necessary to bring economic recovery to Europe. Aid began to move across the Atlantic on a gigantic scale. A tide of money and goods flowed to strengthen the nerves and sinews of the states and peoples who ranged themselves among the allies of the West.

Meanwhile Great Britain and the Commonwealth nations were trying to do something that might meet a part of the needs of the East. In 1950 the United Kingdom, Canada, Australia, New Zealand, South Africa, Pakistan, India, and Ceylon began the Colombo Plan, a series of seven programs costing about £2,000,000,000 and designed to help the free lands of Asia. The Commonwealth was joined in 1954 in the Colombo Plan by Thailand, the Philippines, and Japan.

Among many plans for European union proposed in the twentieth century by such leaders as President Woodrow Wilson, Aristide Briand, and Winston Churchill, none had given promise of even limited success. In March, 1948, the prospect altered. Britain, France, Belgium, the Netherlands, and Luxemburg concluded a fifty-year military, economic, and political alliance in Brussels. This "Benelux" agreement was unprecedented in the history of Europe. It provided for automatic joint defense and mutual aid against attack in Europe; for consultation in case of attack in colonial areas; for the harmonization of production, standards of living, legal systems, trade practices, and the like. The way was left open for other European nations to join. Russia claimed that the pact was "a plot against the peace of Europe." Others hoped that this regional alliance might be the forerunner of an eventual Continental federation.

Hopes are always at the mercy of facts. It is hard to drive wedges into the sovereignty of nation-states, especially when their national interests may seem to be threatened. Jeremy Bentham once remarked that "interest paves the road to faith." In the area of economic affairs the road to cooperation was long and rocky. To some nations the idea of a Free Trade Area and a Common Market in Europe was attractive. To others it was not. Several talks about trade and the proposed European Economic Community broke down. In the spring of 1959 six nations—France, the German Federal Republic, the Netherlands, Belgium, Luxemburg, and Italy—agreed to wipe away all tariff barriers between their countries and to form a Common Market. Ten nations of Europe, including Great Britain, stayed outside of this new arrangement. Some leaders in Europe stated their hope that a new era for a great European Economic Community was at hand. Others were doubtful. It was clear that the nations of western Europe were prepared to cooperate for the purpose of defense; but when they were confronted by problems of economic cooperation or integration into economic blocs they did not always move forward with celerity and enthusiasm.

In April, 1949, the final draft of the regional security pact called the North Atlantic Treaty Organization was signed by representatives of the United States, Great Britain, Canada, France, the Netherlands, Belgium, and Luxemburg. The original signatory nations were soon joined by Portugal, Norway, Denmark, Iceland. Later Turkey, Italy, Greece, and West Germany entered. Sweden, Switzerland, Ireland, and Spain remained outside. The members of the North Atlantic Treaty Organization (NATO) agreed that "an armed attack against one or more of them in Europe or North America shall be considered an attack against them all." Behind a defensive screen of men and weapons were reserves and behind the reserves were mounds of atom bombs. The Soviet Union, for its part, forged with its satellites the links of the Warsaw Pact. The Soviet world possessed great power. So, too, did the world of the West. Year by year the danger of armed conflict continued. "Let us not chop logic," said Britain's Anthony Eden in 1954. "Let us face realities."

There were scores of other treaty arrangements, born of fear and diplomacy in a complicated and dangerous world. Great Britain, for instance, made commitments for the defense of Jordan, Libya, and several other states. Turkey and Pakistan concluded a treaty of friendship. In 1954 Britain, Australia, France, New Zealand, Pakistan, the Philippines, Thailand, and the United States signed the Manila Treaty which brought into being the Southeast Asia Treaty Organization (SEATO) as a protective shield against aggression. True, the undertakings and commitments of the member states were limited. Several Asian nations—Burma, India, Ceylon, Indonesia—refused to join. Some of them felt that an alliance with the West was undesirable; several

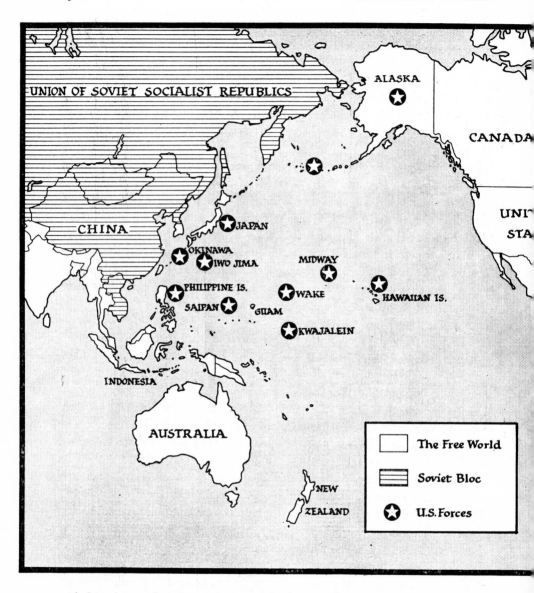

said that the results of truculence might be as unhappy as those of appeasement.

The arts of diplomacy were sometimes replaced by the skills of war. In 1950 the Republic of Korea was violently attacked by the Communist puppet government of North Korea. Within twenty-four hours, mainly as a result of the swift action of President Harry Truman of the United States, the Security Council of the United Nations branded the attack as a breach of the peace and ordered North Korea to withdraw to the boundary line of the thirty-eighth parallel. It called upon the member states of the United Nations to furnish

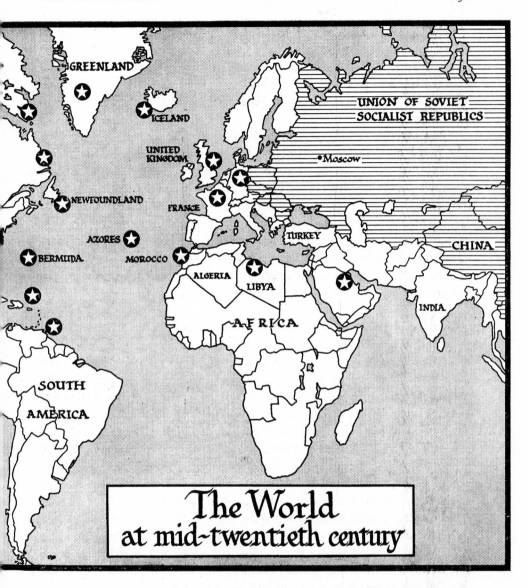

The World
at mid-twentieth century

assistance to the Republic of Korea. Fifty-two nations supported the decision of the Security Council.

Thus began a long and costly "police action" in Korea, that unhappy land where 30,000,000 people once lived in peace. The government of Communist China intervened by sending equipment and "volunteers" to aid North Korea. Tired soldiers slogged through the rice paddies. The battle lines swayed back and forth. After long delays and controversies, an armistice was signed in July, 1953. A bloodless stalemate replaced a bloody one. Korea was ruined and divided. Nevertheless, aggression had been stopped.

Soon Communist China tried to oust Chiang Kai-shek and the Nationalists from Formosa and a few islands off the Chinese mainland. The United States recognized the Nationalist government and protected Formosa, asserting that Formosa was on a perimeter line essential to the defense of the United States. In 1955 and 1958 ugly and dangerous crises arose. The balance of peace was precarious.

There were several inflamed and sensitive areas in various parts of the planet. The Suez crisis of 1956 brought the world close to war. So, too, did the bloody disputes that disturbed the lands of Iraq, Lebanon, and Jordan in 1958. Emergency sessions of the United Nations Assembly and the caution and good fortune of the world's statesman succeeded in keeping the peace of the planet. Sometimes the prospects for order and quiet seemed to gleam brightly. On one of those occasions England's Sir Winston Churchill remarked that mankind might soon be "moving along a broad, smooth causeway of peace and plenty, instead of roaming and peering around the rim of hell." But the dreams that shone at one hour were often dimmed the next.

By the middle of the twentieth century modern science had given mankind the obliterating weapons of the nuclear age. Against the thermonuclear instruments and weapons systems there was, and could be, no absolute defense. All the nations lived under the fear of bombs and rockets and guided intercontinental ballistic missiles, of blast and heat and the fall-out of radioactive particles bringing recessive genetic mutations and malignant genes and death. Twin rulers of survival were the mathematics of explosive power and aircraft ranges. The United States, Great Britain, and Russia tested their discoveries and inventions before a fascinated and shuddering world. It was clear that a global war probably meant mutual destruction. To avoid catastrophe men needed all the faith and sanity that they could summon to their aid. Of one fact only could they be certain: ahead stretched the night of the unknown.

More than 2,000 years ago a wise man of Greece said that the design and endeavor of mankind should be "to tame the savageness of man and make gentle the life of the world." Many centuries later Baruch Spinoza sadly noted that "all things excellent are as difficult as they are rare."

Chapter 48

THE CONDITION

OF MAN

"Albert Schweitzer closed his Bible and took off his glasses and looked out over the little company as he began to tell about the life of the departed friend. He was born in Hungary thirty-one years ago. He was trained as an architect and worked at it until he was exiled from his country by the new regime there. He had gone from Europe to South America but there he was stricken with such a homesickness for his native land and people that he felt he must be near some of his kin . . . and he had crossed to Africa and had been here in the hospital for over two years serving faithfully at any task that needed doing. He was on the point of going to America. His papers were in order, his passage was engaged, his bags packed, and all plans made when he had been called to make a journey which he had not expected.

Albert Schweitzer moved to the side of the grave where the mound of earth lay heaped and throwing three handfuls of earth on the wooden coffin he committed the body to the earth from which it had come and to which it now must go, and he committed the soul to the mercy of God and taking a fourth handful of earth he dropped it on the others and stepped back to the head of the grave. His furrowed cheeks and brows seemed to open and with a look of great compassion he faced the company of mourners and said the Lord's Prayer. Then each of us walked past the mound and dropped three handfuls of earth on the coffin and one of the company dropped a little bunch of flowers she had gathered near the hospital. We sang a closing hymn and filed silently back to the boat. Albert Schweitzer remained, and my last look at the steep hillside cemetery saw his tall stooped figure standing directing the shovelling in of the earth."

—Douglas V. Steere, *The Saturday Review*, June 13, 1953

PAUL TILLICH has written wisely about the fact that a sense of power and a sense of insecurity lie uneasily together in the soul of modern man. Despite the achievements and the emerging promises of science and technology there has somehow been a lack of integration in most individuals and in all societies. More and more the lord of Nature, man is not yet the master of himself.

The machines men proudly make with their minds and their hands have sometimes had dehumanizing results. More power moves side by side with

833

more doubt and more fear. Power and progress, it seems, may not mean justice, security, or peace.

The titles of many modern books suggest the nature of the main currents of thought and feeling, the problems of the lonely man and the mass minds and passions in our contemporary age of anxiety and crisis. Both prose and poetry are often filled with excitement at the trials and triumphs of man; they are also heavy with foreboding. So, too, is modern art and music. All around us are the achievements of the technicians and the scientists. All about are the tensions and disputes between capitalism and Communism. Health and wealth, disease and poverty, learning and ignorance, all these have their abode together on our planet. Terror, hatred, tragedy, contempt, immorality, misery, faltering folly, all are here. So, too, are courage, honor, kindness, wisdom, hope.

The human search for safety and salvation has lasted a long time; the goal seems still far distant. Modern man may still have the will to strive to end the evils of ignorance, hunger, disease, and poverty, and the threat of death by atomic blast and radiation; but he does not yet know the way. He walks in darkness.

As we listen to the hammering and strident voices of our century and gaze upon the inescapable realities of our bewildering world we have reason to be proud because our achievements have been so great. We have reason to be troubled because our problems are so hard and heavy. Left alone, they will not depart; they will stay and grow larger and more dangerous. Few problems are solved by men who are apathetic or careless or who sit down and wail. It is the gospel of folly to forget that fact.

It is also wise to remember that the power of the human mind, more than anything else, has brought man to the place where he now stands. The disciplined curiosity of the scientist, the bright genius of the artist, the poet, the musician, the dancing ideas of the philosophers, these forces have shaped new worlds and shaken the old, century after century. Only the human mind, the human consciousness "voyaging strange seas of thought alone," has enabled us to learn some of the laws of cause and effect in the cosmos and some of the rules that control the behavior of mind and matter. "The lonely mind of one man is the only creative organ in the world, and any force that interferes with its free function is the enemy."

Most physicists and chemists of the nineteenth century believed that the basic discoveries in science had already been made. They were mistaken. Around them the rigid and mechanical universe demanded by the classical system of physics slowly began to crumble. The heralds of a new scientific order made some fateful discoveries that showed that the laws and order of the universe were far more complex than the complacent believers in classical physics had assumed them to be. Modern magicians and high priests of physics were soon to discard, alter, or question many time-honored concepts: Newton's laws of motion, the laws of the conservation of mass and energy, the forms of mass, the nature of time and space. The Morley-Michelson ether-drift experiments of 1887 helped to destroy the idea of the existence of ether. When these things were happening, where did certainty and safety lie?

In 1886 the German scientist Heinrich Rudolf Hertz (1857–1894) proved the existence of high-frequency electromagnetic waves shooting through space with the velocity of light. At this time Hertz was working upon a theory of light earlier put forward by Britain's James Clerk Maxwell (1831–1879). In 1865 Maxwell had said that the velocity of magnetism and electricity were "so nearly that of light that it seems we have strong reason to conclude that light itself . . . is an electromagnetic disturbance in the form of waves. . . ." This Maxwell theory, linking up light, magnetism, and electricity, helped to lay a foundation for an understanding in later days of X rays, ultraviolet and infrared rays, radio waves, and the like. All this, of course, Heinrich Hertz could not know in 1886. He only knew that he had added to the work of Faraday and Maxwell and found out some facts that were important.

In 1895 the German physicist and pioneer Wilhelm Konrad Röntgen (1845–1923) discovered that certain rays, soon to be called X rays, passed through some substances that light rays would not penetrate. Less than a year later, the Frenchman Antoine Henri Becquerel (1852–1908) found that the element uranium, first discovered in 1780, emitted rays similar to those Röntgen had observed. In 1898 the Polish scientist Marie Sklodowska Curie (1867–1934) and her husband the French physicist and chemist Pierre Curie (1859–1906) found and isolated the radioactive element radium from the ore called pitchblende. They also learned that the regular streams of rays sent out by the heavy uranium and radium were not composed of atoms but of parts of atoms. The steady flow of energy from the radioactive atoms meant the spontaneous and slow disintegration of those atoms; but that breaking up and decay proceeded over a period of thousands of years.

Another important phase of the complex and technical revolution in modern science began near the end of the nineteenth century when Hendrik Lorentz asserted that matter is not composed of individual atoms and that the atoms themselves are made up of smaller particles. Britain's Sir Joseph Thomson (1856–1940) went further. He found that atoms contained what were believed to be particles carrying negative electrical charges. He called these parts of the atom "electrons."

In these exciting years there was another assertion that would have startled the classical physicists of an earlier age. Max Planck (1858–1947) noted in 1901 that energy did not move out of the atom or anywhere else in steady waves but in "spurts" or packets (*quanta*). Planck's Quantum Theory overturned many principles of physics accepted earlier. It should also be said that the ideas of Planck did not win immediate acceptance. When he advanced his quantum theory at the Prussian Academy of Science in 1901 an angry professor left the assembly hall saying "Gentlemen, this is not physics!" This professor would probably not have approved the award of the Nobel Prize to Max Planck in 1918 and he would not have been alone in his opinion. It is not only in the field of science that new ideas sometimes win acceptance slowly.

In 1905 an examiner in a Swiss patent office named Albert Einstein published two revolutionary and epoch-making papers on the special theory of relativity. In 1916 he put forward, in a highly abstract scientific paper on general relativity, his famous theory that gravitation was a property of space-time, of the German geometer Riemann's "space" of four dimensions, the fourth dimension being time; in the general theory of relativity, gravitation is represented as curvature in space.

Professor Einstein's later years were devoted to an attempt to formulate—it was an appallingly difficult task—a "unified field theory," to derive a set of equations that would embrace in a coherent and harmonious law the apparently diverse phenomena of gravitation, electromagnetic radiation—including light—and matter. If this could be done in a master theory, then a state of order and control would be shown to exist throughout all nature. Einstein believed that there must be an orderly universe and hence some human being could perhaps find a unitary theory, a complete description of nature. The reader may remember Einstein's remark: "I cannot believe that God would choose to play dice with the world."

In an appendix to the 1953 edition of *The Meaning of Relativity,* Einstein said that he had brought together electromagnetic waves and gravitation by deriving nonlinear partial differential equations for the electromagnetic force and the gravitational field. There are no means yet known to test the new theory. Any acceptance means that it is necessary to abandon Max Planck's quantum theory, and this is not easy to do. On the other hand, it is perhaps premature to assert that Einstein was wrong.

Albert Einstein died in 1956. He remains a distinguished member of the commonwealth of intellect that has no regard for geography or time, a commonwealth that contains Plato, Aristotle, Archimedes, Galileo, Leonardo da Vinci, Isaac Newton, and all of the other giants of past and present. With these men Albert Einstein shared the gift of great powers of thought and insight, a burning wonder, and a deep humility. "The truth is stronger than I," he said. He also said: "I have no particular talent. I am only extremely inquisitive."

The new physics and mathematics brought revolutionary concepts of the nature of the universe. Time and space were not absolute, said Einstein. They were both relative to the observer. The mass of a body depended upon its speed. If, for instance, any mass approached the speed of light its weight would in theory approach infinity. In the new physics of the twentieth century the constant that took the place of absolute space and absolute time was the speed of light—about 186,300 miles a second.

In 1905 Albert Einstein also stated an equation that explained the relationship of matter and energy: $E = mc^2$. This equation means that the amount of energy is equal to the mass multiplied by the square of the velocity of light. One pound of coal, if converted entirely into energy, would release the same amount of energy as would be released by burning slightly more than 1,333,-333 tons of coal. In terms of electricity, one pound of matter is equivalent to the energy of 10,000,000,000 kilowatt hours.

About 1910 the English scientist Lord Ernest Rutherford and the Danish scientist Niels Bohr described the atom as a kind of tiny solar system in which the negatively charged electrons moved in their orbits around a central positively charged nucleus—later discovered to be the seat of energy—as the planets move around the sun. It was soon discovered that the nucleus of an atom—so stupendously little—is held together by tremendously strong forces. Within it are both protons, containing a heavy positive energy charge, and the neutrons, which contain no charge at all. The lightly and negatively charged electrons always move around the nucleus in exactly the number necessary to balance or neutralize the protons in that nucleus. They are also always equal to the number of chargeless neutrons. The hydrogen atom has one electron moving around the nucleus at a speed of nearly 1,500 miles a second. The complicated uranium atom has 92 electrons, sometimes more. In the subatomic universe everything is in motion; nothing is ever at rest.

The number of protons in an atom determines its "atomic number" and the protons and neutrons together make up its "atomic weight." The heaviest atoms, such as those of uranium, weigh as much in comparison with, let us say, a pumpkin as the pumpkin weighs in comparison with the earth. The hydrogen atom, lightest of them all—its nucleus is a millionth of a billionth of the size of the atom—has no neutrons in its nucleus and only one proton. Hence its atomic number is 1 and its atomic weight is 1. Helium has two neutrons and two protons in its nucleus. The atomic number is therefore 2 and its atomic weight is 4. Uranium has 92 protons and either 142, 143, or 146 neutrons and its atomic weight can therefore be 234, 235, or 238. The variety of atoms with the same atomic numbers but different atomic weights are called "isotopes."

The scientists of the twentieth century who reached into the atom soon added the mesons to the ranks of the protons and the chargeless neutrons.

These mesons may be either positive or negative and exist within the atom for about two-millionths of a second. They are present in countless numbers in the cosmic rays that bombard the earth from outer space.

The inquisitive scientists also found strange positive electrons called positrons created out of energy by cosmic rays or by gamma rays from radioactive elements. The lives of the positrons are very short. As soon as one hits an electron both positron and electron disappear and turn back into the energy from which both are made.

By using a powerful particle accelerator and shooting a beam of about six billion volts into a beryllium target, scientists working at the University of California in 1956 were able to create anti-protons out of energy; when the anti-protons hit protons both anti-protons and protons are annihilated and turned back into energy. Anti-protons and anti-neutrons are so named because of the opposite direction of their magnetic fields from ordinary protons and neutrons.

In 1927 the German physicist Werner Heisenberg advanced his famous theory of indeterminacy, sometimes called the Uncertainty Principle. This principle was based upon Heisenberg's discovery that some electrons leap from orbit to orbit in an unpredictable fashion. Heisenberg pointed out that if we try to learn the position of an electron by peering inside the atom we cannot know the speed of that electron because the quanta or photons comprising the light rays we use alter the electron's momentum. If, on the other hand, we try to determine an electron's speed we cannot find out its position. The mechanistic principles of cause and effect, Heisenberg asserted, were no longer completely valid. At the very center of things, at the heart of the subatomic universe, was probability, indeterminacy, uncertainty. There is thus a limit to what may be known about natural phenomena. Natural events are more or less probable, never certain. Werner Heisenberg's famous principle has raised a number of fascinating and significant philosophical problems.

Various methods were soon used in bombarding the atomic nucleus in attempts to "smash" the atom. In 1919 Lord Rutherford did succeed in splitting the nucleus of the atom by bombardment and changed the element nitrogen into oxygen; his projectiles were helium atoms. In 1929 Professor Ernest O. Lawrence of the University of California invented the cyclotron, an ingenious machine that bombarded the nuclei of atoms with steady streams of protons. Three years later Professor Harold C. Urey of Columbia University discovered a heavy kind of hydrogen and used its nucleus as an atom-smashing missile. In the same year the neutron was discovered by Sir James Chadwick. The neutron, as was remarked earlier, contains no electric charge and hence, unlike the positively charged protons, it is not repelled by the positive charge in the nucleus of the atom.

In 1933 Irene Curie and her husband Professor Joliot developed artificial radioactivity by using polonium rays—polonium is a radioactive element earlier discovered by Madame Curie. About the same time Professor Enrico Fermi, the Italian physicist, began to bombard atoms with neutrons because he thought, and rightly, that neutrons would not be diverted from their course and their target by the electrical fields created by the electrons revolving around the nucleus of the atom. He also slowed the neutrons—and thus increased their penetrating power—by shooting them through paraffin sheets or similar substances. Moving at a reduced speed, the neutrons exploded better when they hit the nucleus.

It was clear that such artificial bombardments would not produce enough energy to be of much help to man. It was necessary to start a kind of atomic "chain reaction" so that atoms could be split by an initial neutron bombardment; then they would give off secondary neutrons to bombard more atoms that would, in turn, be smashed to emit more bombarding neutrons. Joliot-Curie, Halban, and Kowarski in Paris and Fermi and Szilard in the United States had proved that such a release of atomic energy was theoretically possible.

In 1939 Niels Bohr, Miss Lise Meitner, a Jewish refugee from Hitler's tyranny, and Otto Hahn, using Fermi's method, discovered that the nucleus of the uranium atom (U-235 isotope) could be split by a neutron bombardment into two almost equal parts, giving two elements near the middle of the atomic scale, a few other particles, and a tremendous release of energy— about 200,000,000 electron volts from each shattered atom. It was soon discovered that neutrons were released by this fission and a chain reaction could be foreseen. The names of Enrico Fermi, Niels Bohr, Otto Hahn, Sir James Chadwick, Lord Rutherford, Ernest O. Lawrence, Madame Curie, Lise Meitner, Harold C. Urey, Sir John Cockroft, O. R. Frisch, J. Robert Oppenheimer, Hans Bethe—and some others, too—may be remembered by our descendants long after those of other men, now famous, are recalled no more.

It was against this background of discovery that the conflicting powers in the Second World War moved towards the construction of an atomic bomb. It was necessary to build factories—at Oak Ridge, Tennessee, and elsewhere —to obtain fissionable materials. The uranium atoms which can be split are those of the uranium 235 isotope. Only seven-tenths of 1 per cent of natural uranium is of this type. On the other hand, more than 99 per cent of all natural uranium is of the nonfissionable U-238 kind. True, U-235 can be separated from U-238, but the process is long and difficult. Early in 1940 two tiny pieces of U-235 were separated by Professor A. O. Nier of the University of Minnesota. Shortly afterwards physicists at the University of California discovered that when uranium 238 is bombarded by neutrons in a nuclear pile it does not split but absorbs the neutrons and changes first into neptunium (element 92 with a half-life of sixteen minutes), and then into plutonium, an element not known on earth before. Plutonium, like U-235, is fissionable; it can release atomic energy. So, too, can thorium, an element found in fairly large quantities in Brazil, Nigeria, India, North Carolina, and Idaho. Thorium does not explode in a chain reaction but can be started by uranium. These facts about thorium were not known in 1940; they were discovered later.

In addition to the factories built at Oak Ridge, Tennessee, and at Richlands on the Columbia River in Washington, a great laboratory was constructed at Los Alamos in New Mexico. There an international team of scientists determined the "critical mass" of uranium 235 or plutonium needed to create an incredibly rapid chain reaction—a microsecond function—and a great explosion.

On July 16, 1945, the first atomic bomb was exploded on the desert in New Mexico. Not long afterwards another was dropped on the Japanese city of Hiroshima and a third on Nagasaki. The result was a hot ball of fire and a mushroom cloud, a blast and a shock wave and a hammering pressure through the air that wrecked and killed. The later hydrogen bomb, with far greater destructive power, liberated energy by transforming hydrogen into helium. The so-called cobalt bomb was a hydrogen bomb surrounded by a layer of cobalt.

The controlled fission in nuclear piles is a source of neutrons. These "thermal" neutrons are used for experimental work and to produce new kinds of atomic nuclei, especially the radioactive ones that emit the fast electrons of beta rays and are useful in medical and biological research. The radioactive isotopes produced in the atomic piles are sometimes used as "tracers" to find out whether a patient's thyroid gland is functioning normally (iodine 131). Radioisotopes can often be concentrated in certain areas where surgery is precluded to destroy malignant tissues by intense beta irradiation. Certain tracers, such as carbon 14, phosphorus 32, and sulphur 35, can be used to determine where a labeled element goes and the compounds into which it is converted by biochemical processes or chemicals. Cobalt 60 can be made in an atomic pile and it emits gamma rays similar to those of radium. It is now used in certain kinds of therapy, especially in the treatment of deeply seated malignant tumors or sarcoma. Radioactive isotopes are increasingly used for numerous chemical and industrial purposes. For instance, a radioactive isotope such as calcium 45 can be used to control the level of a liquid inside a sealed tank, the thickness of a piece of sheet metal, leather, rubber, paper, the quality of oil going through a pipe line or the dissipation of undesirable static electricity in a factory or a hospital operating room.

Around the middle of the twentieth century advanced investigation and experiments in the United States and at Britain's nuclear research center at Harwell showed that it was possible to convert the heat—the kinetic energy of the fission fragments produced in nuclear reactors—into electrical power. Several stations were built in Britain to do precisely that.

Meanwhile incalculable and monstrous perils have resulted from man's discovery of nuclear power. All human beings are exposed to unknown horrors at the narrowing rim of safety and survival. Great events are thundering by; but they do not all work together for human good. Atomic bombs or nuclear missiles may swiftly slay or maim. There is something else: any thermonuclear explosion, whether it is a high-megaton blast or a small one, releases and leaves radioactive debris. This fall-out contains countless particles of radioactive dust that can, slowly and surely, do terrifying damage to human beings. Particularly dangerous are the isotopes that combine a long life and a strong radioactivity, such as strontium 89, strontium 90, iodine 131, bismuth 210, plutonium 239, phosphorus 32, iron 55, cerium 144, caesium 137. Their dust is blown around the planet by the winds, comes down in the rain, plagues and pollutes the country gardens and the harvest fields, gets into food and water.

Radioactive dust brings disease and death. When it accumulates in human bodies it affects the bone structure, especially of young children. It contaminates the vital nucleic acid. It damages the marrow tissues, so that they produce few or abnormal cells. It increases the number of serious blood and bone diseases—the leukemia and skeletal sarcoma rate is steadily mounting now. It does irreparable damage to the spleen and the liver. It carries a genetic hazard because it can produce terrifying genetic mutations that result in congenital mental and organic defects.

Nobody knows the limits of tolerance of the human body. The threshold of danger can be easily passed. We cannot tell what we may be doing to harm the generations to come. We may be jeopardizing our own interests and theirs far more than we know. Sober and responsible men are deeply troubled, as well they ought to be.

It has been easy for some sincere people to denounce the scientists who have made possible these instruments of death. Words that damn and deplore seldom give either comfort or answers. The scientists are not responsible for what society has done with their discoveries. They must not be blamed or made the scapegoats for what has happened. If science does not remain indifferent and unprejudiced it is no longer science. The ferment of original thought is, in itself, neither moral nor immoral. The main duty and responsibility of the alert and searching scientist has been, and must be, to try to increase the sum of human knowledge and to extend man's control over his environment. The real scientist must wonder and work and study the facts that he finds, regardless of where they may lead. He must press on with his questions and challenge every assumption.

What men do with the discoveries and inventions of the scientists is a social problem. A discovery or an invention is not an evil in itself. A spade can be used for its proper purpose of digging in the ground or for bashing in the head of an opponent. Human beings decide what they will do with their tools and weapons. In the problems of our world all men are involved. We must become the civilized masters of ourselves.

There are still many things we do not know and cannot do. We have much knowledge about the crystal arrangements of solids, but we have no unified molecular picture. We have only a little thermodynamic data about liquids. We have no kinetic theory to explain completely what gases do or to predict precisely how they will act under certain conditions. We use our gifts of reason and imagination to make and manipulate things, ideas, and people. But we do not understand the nature of the life that makes these things possible. We cannot tell what forces made strange creatures rise out of the ancient slime.

New experiments have shown that life on this planet may have begun when the heat reaction from a lightning bolt or a submarine volcano suddenly synthesized the sea-water proteins, nucleic acid, and enzymes that are the basis of all living matter. After the first electrochemical reaction the chemical ingredients of life may have been manufactured and combined at lower temperatures. The secret of life probably lies somewhere in the mysteries of the polymer molecules called proteins and the amino acids found in them. Many discoveries seem to indicate that we are inching towards the answers; we do not have them yet.

The creative power of the scientists and the technicians is steadily changing the patterns of civilization. Millions of automobiles move over the roads of our shrinking planet; great trucks roar through the night; the diesel engines glide over the railways; jet engines invade the kingdom of the stratosphere. Within a few generations the gates of a new world have swung open with the coming of the telephone, motion pictures, radio, television. Complex mathematical computation and manipulating operations are performed swiftly by electronic machines. The heartbeats of our modern civilization are going faster and faster. It has sometimes been difficult to maintain intellectual coherence and stability when so many laws of nature, science, and technology seem to be valid only for short time spans. Again and again the scientists and mathematicians measure and test and revise their charts and data. Then new answers replace the old.

Only yesterday men hailed the invention of the vacuum tube. Then they praised the transistors, the differential rectifiers, the solar batteries, the feedback mechanisms of automation, the new cogs, valves, and circuits, all milestones marking progress towards a goal no man can know. They applauded the appearance of the man-made satellites that streaked around the earth, the electronic microscopes, the wonders of radar, the invasion of the realm of the atom and the seizure of some of the basic power of the universe. They admired and used the refrigerators, washing machines, incinerators, and deep-freeze units. Business and industry adopted the new automatic processing, packaging, and handling devices, the executive and personnel training methods, complex product analyses, long-term market appraisals. New service industries multiplied. Social-security programs grew. The age of the intercontinental missiles dawned.

Events and inventions tumbled upon one another. Pandora's box was turned upside down in a complex age of new processes and techniques. Man produced more and more commodities for welfare and for war.

Much was done to protect man's health. In the field of modern medicine the unrelenting struggle against physical and mental disease continued through the years with remarkable results. Public-health measures increased. The triumphs of surgery multiplied. Thousands of human beings were saved from death when Canada's Sir Frederick Banting discoverd insulin. About 1930 Sir Alexander Fleming first discovered the magic of penicillin, first of the antibiotics. The first of the sulfanilamide drugs was discovered in 1935. In 1955 a vaccine developed by Jonas Salk and his associates in the United States gave promise of halting forever the scourge of poliomyelitis. Effective serums increased in number and strength. The discovery of many secrets of human glands and hormones brought health and hope to thousands of human beings whose lives had been darkened by illness and despair. The skill of uncounted specialists in the hospitals and laboratories of the world aided in man's struggle against cancer, heart and arterial diseases and weakness, arthritis, tuberculosis and many other formidable foes of man.

As the pioneers and builders labored through the years many shrewd and thoughtful individuals began to consider the mounting pressures upon mankind in an age of continuing rearrangements and contrasts. On every hand there rose the insistent voices of those who saw how dangerous and baffling were the questions that refused to get out of the way of marching man. What could be done, for instance, about the problems of booms and depressions, the organization of trade and commerce, the complex riddles of economic cooperation, competition, and conflict, the evils of soil erosion and exhaustion, the frequently conflicting interests of industry and agriculture, the tangled arguments about production and distribution among the tariff-ridden national states of the planet? There were the constant shadows and dangers of war and the sad voices of the homeless and the hungry, the challenging problems of the conservation of water, forests, wild life, and the many other natural resources of "our plundered planet"—the phrase was first used by Fairfield Osborn.

In the books, pamphlets, and newspapers of the world uncounted questions were asked and never wholly answered. Through the skies flashed the radio and television waves carrying mingled messages of warning and of hope. Voices rolled from the platforms to try to convince their hearers—the wise and the witless and unwary—that if they used the right road maps there would be no difficulty in reaching the fat lands of the future. Truth, it was said, can still be purchased at the booths in Vanity Fair.

Meanwhile the population of the world rose steadily. There are now living upon our planet more than 2,750,000,000 human beings. The world population increase is about 93,000 a day. The population has doubled in the last century. The annual increase in 1925 was about 17,000,000; in 1950 it was about 30,000,000.

Every world population map shows that about 60 per cent of the world's people live upon less than 8 per cent of the planet's surface. More than 1,750,000,000 live in Asia and Europe, ten times the population of North America.

If we accept the opinion that a human body needs a minimum daily intake of 2,250 calories to maintain health and efficiency, then more than half of the population of the world is undernourished. The low-calorie areas are found among the scraping millions of Asia, Africa, part of the Near East, all of Latin America; the high-calorie areas are America, Europe, and the broad lands of Russia.

Two out of every three people of the world live in underdeveloped areas; their incomes are low; their diet is inadequate; their health is poor; their education is limited. Often their governments are weak, their legal systems primitive, their ignorance of modern progress tremendous. Two-thirds of the people of the world have a life expectancy at birth of less than thirty-five years. Sixty-five per cent of the world's population has only 20 per cent of the world's income. The United States, possessing less than 6 per cent of the world's population, produces and consumes more than a third of all the goods and services in the world. The annual national gross income of the United States is about 40 per cent of that of the whole world. Similar startling comparisons can be made of energy consumption and production and tools and techniques.

Very few people in the underdeveloped regions of the world know these facts. More than half of the population of our planet can neither read nor write.

Several of the inhabitants and governments of Asia and Africa are at loggerheads with the countries of the West, sometimes to an acute degree. It has been so in the past and it will be so again. But these differences have not stopped the roused lands outside of Europe and America from learning and using the technical skills without which progress is difficult. Emergency funds and technical advice and assistance provided by international and national organizations of the West are opening the gates in Asia and Africa to a world the peoples of those regions never knew.

All these things are happening at a time when the demands of new national governments east of Suez and south of the Mediterranean are speeding the pace of change. The hunger of poverty has sometimes been replaced by the hunger for power. The peace and progress of all mankind may soon depend upon an increased and sympathetic understanding between the peoples of East and West. Hu Shih once said: "Above all nations is humanity."

The speed of production and change has helped to soften and postpone some conflicts and arguments about the values and ends of the actions of men. Many individuals are concerned very much with the present, very little with the past, and only now and then with the future. For them it seems to be enough to know that practical benefits result from the continued exploitation of nature by man. They find the gifts of science sufficient for their needs. They are not troubled by the problems of religion, morals, and philosophy.

There are other men who will admit that they vaguely believe that life is futile and that human history "is no more than the meaningless resolution of blind forces which struggling men—good men and bad—do not understand and cannot control, although they amuse themselves with the pleasing illusion that they do." And there are those who do not doubt that in the fullness of time all human problems will be solved. They know that they are pilgrims towards a great river and that the land on both sides of the river belongs to God.

Only a few men ask the really significant questions as atomic machines increase, the man-made satellites of the earth go into their orbits, and the radar beams sweep the skies and the waters under the earth.

Is the trampling power of the new science bringing a disintegration of the individual personality? Are there too many captive minds and too many crowd compulsions? Do the depersonalized and pitiless gods of the machine take too much tribute? Will the machine rule man tomorrow? Are the masters of science and technology in fact the agents of doom and chaos? Is the menace of moral lethargy creeping slowly towards the forts of civilization to cripple and destroy?

"Of what use is science," Britain's Prince Philip remarked in 1958, "if man does not survive?" Prince Philip was only one human being who saw the "conflict between man and the world he has made for himself." Professor Geoffrey Barraclough posed another question: "Have we the moral qualities essential for the proper use of our immense technical knowledge?" Can man be trusted with control over the powers of nature that science gives him? Is it possible that all the progress of science is a series of steps towards the suicide of the human race? A few power-mad and evil men could begin a nuclear war and end forever the idea that technology and science will bring salvation to all mankind. Science does not give man moral wisdom. There are no equations for that.

We know very little about the mysteries of the spirit, the psyche, the soul of human beings. True, we have illusions and theories too numerous to count;

but they are not the same things as facts. Deceptive words and puny pretenses are not enough to answer and explain. The veils that cover the unique cores of personality are heavy and thick. Even the most skilled psychiatrists and psychologists cannot penetrate all of the way into the inner citadels of being. There have been too many plausible oversimplifications of the nature of man in the books and speeches of the twentieth century, too many twisted and dangerous inanities that confuse and deceive. The intoxicating vocabulary of some modern writers has not helped to reduce the vast emptiness of error and ignorance. There is much to be done. It is a naïve mistake to think that we can spend effort and time in probing the secrets of the atom and outer space and leave for another time the further exploration of the nature of the human mind and spirit. It may be later than we know.

There are other questions. How far will the forces of agnosticism, mechanized illusions, and moral neutrality threaten to overwhelm and push into oblivion the religious, rational, and ethical imperatives, the funded experience that have ruled and guided men for centuries? How did men ever come to think that scientific knowledge would enable them to wipe away every personal and social evil in their world? Is modern man being prodded and lashed along in his search for power by nameless hungers and a nagging spiritual loneliness that he cannot explain or understand? What corroding and dissolving acids eat at his soul? Is his moral awareness as great as once he believed it to be? Has he tossed away so much of his cultural heritage that he fears in the secret chambers of his being that the shining promises of material and secular progress, of triumphant nationalism and an earthly paradise will turn to ashes in his hands?

Is man's pride in the achievements of science and technology too great? Is he too proud for his own good, too blind to his own frailty? Professor Herbert Butterfield of Cambridge University has no doubts about the answer: "If our Western civilization were to collapse, even more completely than it has done, and I were asked to say upon which of the sins of the world the judgment of God had come in so signal a manner, I should specify, as the most general of the existing evils and the most terrifying in its results, human presumption and particularly intellectual arrogance." Professor Butterfield has a right to his opinion. So, too, do those who deny what he says.

What is the meaning and purpose of man? Where does the road ahead twist and end? What is the destiny that lies beyond the hills and horizons? Where are the seed plots of tomorrow's history? How many of yesterday's truths and traditions have been tossed away, diluted, or destroyed? Can no man find them now? Will tribes of new barbarians, so clever and shrewd and strong, stride out to conquer and control? What must a man do? What must he believe?

> Now, who shall arbitrate?
> Ten men love what I hate,
> Shun what I follow, slight what I receive;
> Ten, who in ears and eyes
> Match me; we all surmise,
> They this thing, and I that; whom shall my soul believe?

Some men have called the twentieth century an age of challenge. Others say that modern man is trapped in the triumphs of his own contriving and that this is an age of fear. Still others would claim that it is an era of despair. Not long before his death Mr. H. G. Wells wrote his *Mind at the End of Its Tether,* a book of black pessimism. In its pages Mr. Wells, for so long a believer and crusader in the cause of secular progress, asserted that for man there was no hope. "A remarkable queerness has come over life. It is as if the law of gravitation no longer functioned in a physical world. Everything is moving in every direction with increased velocity. . . . It is the end." Mr. Wells was prepared to ring down the curtain on the great drama of mankind. Most men are not.

Man's body is composed of a few pounds of carbon, a few quarts of water, a little sulfur, iron, phosphorus, sodium, salts, lime. From these unpromising materials are formed the blood and bones and the organs that make life possible. There are also the electromechanical calculators and nerve signal devices —the speed of human nerve signals is about 24,000 feet a minute—and the millions of circuits in the mind.

Each body is linked with a unique personality, character, spirit. The tough-minded and uncompromising realist lives by the side of the tender-minded and uncritical dreamer, and the dreamer often turns out to be the realist in the end.

Man has done much and traveled far. Badgered and bludgeoned by dangers and difficulties, he has survived. Meanwhile he wonders, works, and worships. Only the cowards surrender and only the foolish despair.

Man's achievements have been many, his vision vast. Gleams of splendor have often lighted the long road of his history. His race has met and mastered many enemies, emerged from countless hard adventures, known death and disease, the despair that corroded and stultified, the vast spiritual listlessness that sometimes swept our darkened planet, the fortitude that in the end prevailed.

The tale of the past has been told. The chapters of the present are now unfolding. Nobody can look into tomorrow.

Perhaps humanity is now moving towards a golden age of prosperity on the sunlit slopes and uplands of peace. Perhaps, on the other hand, the destiny of mankind is a swift and sure extinction. Perhaps the world will be blown to bits. Then the ashes of men will swirl in the Last Wind with the dust of what were once believed to be their imperishable achievements. Their monuments will turn into smoke that blows and billows away. New universes will stop swinging into man's ken. No longer will the scientists probe into zones of wonder or work out their equations of sunlight and savagery to astound and change the world. There will be no libraries or laboratories, those fortresses of thought and discovery. There will be no music, no poetry. Christ will not be crowned and crucified again. The writer will write no more; the reader will not read.

Some men have shielded their eyes from what they fear is the shape of things to come. They have shuddered at the prospect of collapse and barbarism and the long road back to the jungle. They have stood appalled at the thought that man's achievements may be blasted away in dust and fire and in a moment of time.

All that the fearful men and the dark prophets predict may come to pass on this planet. On the other hand, it may not. For a long time now there has been much crippling disaster in the world, much folly and crime, much danger. There has also been much intelligence, will, and faith. In the year that Albert Camus received the Nobel Prize for Literature, he wrote these words: "If we fail it will be better to have taken our stand at the side of those who want to live rather than with those who destroy."

The promises are for those who take them.

Books for Further Reading

PART 1

GENERAL WORKS

BOAK, A. E. R., *History of Rome to 565 A.D.*, 3rd ed., New York, 1946.

BOTSFORD, GEORGE W., and Robinson, Charles A., *Hellenic History*, New York, 1939.

GROUSSET, RENÉ, *The Civilization of India*, trans. C. A. Philips, New York, 1939.

LATOURETTE, K. S., *The Chinese: Their History and Culture*, 3rd rev. ed., New York, 1946.

ROSTOVTZEFF, MICHAEL I., *A History of the Ancient World*, Vol. I, Oxford, 1936.

WALKER, WILLISTON, *A History of the Christian Church*, rev. ed., New York, 1959.

CHAPTER 1. THE ASCENT OF MAN

BREASTED, JAMES H., *The Dawn of Conscience*, New York, 1934.

COON, CARLETON S., *The Story of Man*, New York, 1954.

KEITH, SIR ARTHUR, *The Antiquity of Man*, New York, 1925.

PEAKE, H. J. E., *Early Steps in Human Progress*, New York, 1933.

CHAPTER 2. THE VALLEY OF THE NILE

CERAM, C. W., *Gods, Graves, and Scholars*, New York, 1951.

EDWARDS, I. E. S., *The Pyramids of Egypt*, London, 1952.

HURST, H. E., *The Nile*, New York, 1951.

WILSON, JOHN A., *The Culture of Ancient Egypt*, Chicago, 1957.

CHAPTER 3. THE LAND BETWEEN THE RIVERS

HALL, H. R., *The Ancient History of the Near East*, London, 1932.

HOOKE, S. H., *Babylonian and Assyrian Religion*, London, 1948.

OLMSTEAD, A. T. E., *History of the Persian Empire*, Chicago, 1948.

WOOLLEY, C. LEONARD, *The Sumerians*, New York, 1928.

CHAPTER 4. BY THE SHORES OF THE GREAT SEA

ALBRIGHT, W. F., *From the Stone Age to Christianity*, Baltimore, 1940.

CERAM, C. W., *The Secret of the Hittites*, New York, 1956.

DIRINGER, DAVID, *The Alphabet*, New York, 1951.

FRAZER, SIR JAMES G., *The Golden Bough* (one-volume ed.), New York, 1958.

CHAPTER 5. INDIA: WORKS AND WORDS

BASHAM, A. L., *The Wonder That Was India*, London, 1956.

BOUQUET, ALAN C., *Hinduism*, New York, 1950.

PIGGOTT, STUART, *Prehistoric India*, London, 1957.

TSUKAMOTO, Z., *The Path of the Buddha* (ed. Kenneth W. Morgan), New York, 1956.

CHAPTER 6. CHINA: THE PACE OF CHANGE

CREEL, H. G., *Confucius, the Man and the Myth*, New York, 1949.

FITZGERALD, C. P., *China: A Short Cultural History*, rev. ed., London, 1950.

GRANET, MARCEL, *Chinese Civilization*, New York, 1930.

WALEY, ARTHUR, *Three Ways of Thought in Ancient China*, London, 1939.

CHAPTER 7. GREECE: WARRIORS DEAD

ABBOTT, EVELYN, *Pericles and the Golden Age of Athens*, New York, 1925.

KITTO, H. D. F., *The Greeks*, London, 1951.

LIVINGSTON, R. W. (ed.), *The Legacy of Greece*, London, 1928.

ROBINSON, CHARLES A., *Alexander the Great*, New York, 1947.

CHAPTER 8. PROFILES OF GENIUS

CLAGETT, MARSHALL, *Greek Science in Antiquity*, New York, 1955.

GUTHRIE, W. K. C., *The Greeks and Their Gods*, London, 1950.

HAMILTON, EDITH, *The Greek Way*, New York, 1930.

MURRAY, GILBERT, *The Literature of Ancient Greece*, Chicago, 1952.

CHAPTER 9. ROME: PRIDE AND POWER

BARROW, R. H., *The Romans*, London, 1949.

CASSON, LIONEL, *The Ancient Mariners*, New York, 1959.

HAMILTON, EDITH, *The Roman Way*, New York, 1932.

STARR, CHESTER G., *Civilization and the Caesars*, Ithaca, New York, 1954.

CHAPTER 10. THE GREAT COLLAPSE

CLOUGH, SHEPARD B., *The Rise and Fall of Civilization: An Inquiry into the Relationship between Economic Development and Civilization*, New York, 1951.

GIBBON, EDWARD, *The Decline and Fall of the Roman Empire*, 2 vols., Modern Library ed., New York, 1936.

MATTINGLY, H., *Roman Imperial Civilization*, London, 1957.

WHEELER, SIR MORTIMER, *Rome Beyond the Imperial Frontiers*, London, 1954.

CHAPTER 11. THE CROSS AND THE CRESCENT

ARNOLD, T. W. and GUILLAUME, A. (eds.), *The Legacy of Islam*, Oxford, 1931.

GIBB, H. A. R., *Mohammedanism, a Historical Survey*, New York, 1949.

GRANT, R. M., *The Sword and the Cross*, New York, 1955.

MELLONE, S. H., *Leaders of Early Christian Thought*, London, 1954.

CHAPTER 12. THE HEIRS OF ROME

AUGUSTINE, ST., *The City of God*, trans. Marcus Dods, New York, 1948.

DAWSON, CHRISTOPHER, *The Making of Europe*, London, 1932.

HUSSEY, J. M., *The Byzantine World*, London, 1957.

WADDELL, HELEN, *The Desert Fathers*, New York, 1936.

PART II

GENERAL WORKS

ARTZ, F. B., *The Mind of the Middle Ages*, New York, 1953.

FAIRBANK, JOHN K. (ed.), *Chinese Thought and Institutions*, Chicago, 1957.

KNAPTON, E. J., *Europe 1450–1815*, New York, 1958.

LATOURETTE, KENNETH S., *The Development of Japan*, New York, 1938.

STEPHENSON, CARL, *Medieval History: Europe from the Second to the Sixteenth Century*, 3rd ed., New York, 1951.

TREVELYAN, G. M., *A History of England*, 2nd ed., New York, 1946.

CHAPTER 13. INDIA: THE GOLDEN AGE AND AFTER

HALL, D. G. E., *A History of Southeast Asia*, New York, 1955.

KABIR, MUMAYUN, *The Indian Heritage*, New York, 1955.

PHILIPS, C. H., *India*, London, 1949.

SPEAR, PERCIVAL, *Twilight of the Mughals*, Cambridge, 1951.

CHAPTER 14. CHINA AND JAPAN: BOOKS AND SWORDS

GOWEN, HERBERT E., *An Outline History of Japan*, New York, 1927.

PRAWDIN, MICHAEL, *The Mongol Empire: Its Rise and Legacy*, London, 1940.

SICKMAN, LAWRENCE, and SOPE, ALEXANDER, *The Art and Architecture of China*, Baltimore, 1956.

WALEY, ARTHUR, *The Poetry and Career of Li Po*, London, 1950.

CHAPTER 15. THE FEUDAL WORLD

CROMBIE, A. C., *From Augustine to Galileo*, London, 1952.

PIRENNE, H., *Mohammed and Charlemagne*, New York, 1939.

STEPHENSON, CARL, *Medieval Feudalism*, New York, 1935.

WOODRUFF, DOUGLAS, *Charlemagne*, New York, 1935.

CHAPTER 16. POPES, KINGS, AND PEOPLE

CHESTERTON, G. K., *St. Francis of Assisi*, New York, 1934.

DAWSON, CHRISTOPHER, *Religion and the Rise of Western Culture*, New York, 1958.

HASKINS, CHARLES H., *Studies in Medieval Culture*, Cambridge, Mass., 1928.

JONES, R. M., *The Flowering of Mysticism*, New York, 1939.

CHAPTER 17. PATHS OF PEACE AND WAR

KELLY, AMY, *Eleanor of Aquitaine and the Four Kings*, Cambridge, Mass., 1950.

PERROY, E., *The Hundred Years' War*, New York, 1951.

PIRENNE, HENRI, *Medieval Cities, Their Origin and the Revival of Trade*, trans. Frank Halsey, Princeton, 1925.

RUNCIMAN, STEVEN, *A History of the Crusades*, 3 vols., Cambridge, 1951–1955.

CHAPTER 18. THE MEDIEVAL SPIRIT

ADAMS, HENRY, *Mont-Saint-Michel and Chartres*, New York, 1959.

COULTON, G. G., *Medieval Panorama*, New York, 1938.

POWER, EILEEN, *Medieval People*, London, 1951.

WADDELL, HELEN, *The Wandering Scholars*, London, 1927.

CHAPTER 19. THE RENAISSANCE: MAN IS THE MEASURE

FERGUSON, WALLACE K., *The Renaissance in Historical Thought: Five Centuries of Interpretation*, Boston, 1948.

GILMORE, M. P., *The World of Humanism 1453–1517*, New York, 1952.

HAYDN, HIRAM, *The Counter-Renaissance*, New York, 1950.

SARTON, GEORGE, *Six Wings: Men of Science in the Renaissance*, Bloomington, Indiana, 1957.

CHAPTER 20. THE REFORMATION: GOD IS THE JUDGE

BAINTON, R. H., *Here I Stand: The Life of Martin Luther*, New York, 1950.

GRIMM, HAROLD J., *The Reformation Era 1500–1650*, New York, 1954.

SMITH, PRESERVED, *The Age of the Reformation*, New York, 1920.

TAWNEY, R. H., *Religion and the Rise of Capitalism*, New York, 1926.

CHAPTER 21. BEYOND THE UNKNOWN SEAS

MORISON, SAMUEL ELIOT, *Admiral of the Ocean Sea: A Life of Christopher Columbus*, 2 vols., Boston, 1942.

NOWELL, CHARLES E., *The Great Discoveries and the First Colonial Empires*, Ithaca, New York, 1955.

PARR, C. W., *So Noble a Captain: The Life and Times of Ferdinand Magellan*, New York, 1953.

WILLIAMSON, J. A., *The Age of Drake*, London, 1938.

CHAPTER 22. RUSSIA: BLOOD AND POWER

ECKHARDT, H. VON, *Ivan the Terrible*, New York, 1949.

SUMNER, B. H., *Peter the Great and the Emergence of Russia*, London, 1950.

VERNADSKY, G., *Ancient Russia*, New Haven, 1943.

WREN, MELVIN C., *The Course of Russian History*, New York, 1958.

CHAPTER 23. EUROPE: THE NATION-STATES

BRAND, KARL, *The Emperor Charles V*, trans. C. V. Wedgwood, London, 1940.

MATTINGLY, GARRETT, *Renaissance Diplomacy*, New York, 1956.

MERRIMAN, R. B., *Suleiman the Magnificent 1520–1566*, New York, 1944.

WEDGWOOD, C. V., *William the Silent*, London, 1944.

CHAPTER 24. THE YEARS OF CHALLENGE

ASHLEY, MAURICE, *Louis XIV and the Greatness of France*, London, 1948.

BAILLY, A., *The Cardinal Dictator: A Portrait of Richelieu*, London, 1936.

OGG, DAVID, *Europe in the Seventeenth Century*, 6th ed., London, 1952.

TREVELYAN, G. M., *England Under the Stuarts*, new ed., London, 1933.

PART III

GENERAL WORKS

BUTTERFIELD, HERBERT, *The Origins of Modern Science 1300–1800*, New York, 1951.

HEATON, HERBERT, *The Economic History of Europe*, rev. ed., New York, 1948.

LATOURETTE, KENNETH SCOTT, *A History of Modern China*, London, 1954.

MORISON, SAMUEL E., and COMMAGER, HENRY STEELE, *The Growth of the American Republic*, 2 vols., 4th ed., New York, 1959.

PARRINGTON, V. L., *Main Currents in American Thought*, 3 vols., New York, 1927–1930.

SMITH, GOLDWIN, *A History of England*, rev. ed., New York, 1957.

CHAPTER 25. THE SONS OF THE RENAISSANCE

FRIEDRICH, C. J., *The Age of the Baroque 1610–1660*, London, 1952.

HALL, A. R., *The Scientific Revolution 1500–1800*, Boston, 1956.

NUSSBAUM, FREDERICK L., *The Triumph of Science and Reason 1660–1685*, New York, 1953.

WILLEY, BASIL, *The Seventeenth Century Background*, London, 1934.

CHAPTER 26. THE ECONOMIC REVOLUTION: STEAM, STEEL, AND LAND

ASHTON, T. S., *Industrial Revolution, 1760–1830*, London, 1948.

COTTRELL, F., *Energy and Society: The Relation between Energy, Social Change, and Economic Development*, New York, 1955.

HAMMOND, J. L. and B., *The Rise of Modern Industry*, London, 1937.

USHER, A. P., *A History of Mechanical Inventions*, 2nd ed., Cambridge, Mass., 1954.

CHAPTER 27. COLONIES, COMMERCE, AND WAR

NOTESTEIN, WALLACE, *The English People on the Eve of Colonization, 1603–1630*, New York, 1959.

ROBERTS, P., *The Quest for Security 1715–1740*, New York, 1947.

WOLF, JOHN B., *The Emergence of the Great Powers 1685–1715*, New York, 1951.

WRIGHT, LOUIS B., *The Cultural Life of the American Colonies 1607–1763*, New York, 1957.

CHAPTER 28. CONFLICT: BRITAIN AND AMERICA

ALDEN, JOHN R., *The American Revolution 1775–1783*, New York, 1954.

FREEMAN, DOUGLAS SOUTHALL, *George Washington: A Biography*, 6 vols., New York, 1948–1954.

MORGAN, EDMUND S., *The Birth of the Republic, 1763–89*, Chicago, 1956.

ROSSITER, CLINTON, *Seedtime of the Republic*, New York, 1953.

CHAPTER 29. REASON AND NATURE: IDEAS AND IDEALS

BECKER, CARL L., *The Heavenly City of the Eighteenth-Century Philosophers*, New Haven, 1932.

BRUUN, GEOFFREY, *Enlightened Despots*, New York, 1929.

LOVEJOY, ARTHUR O., *The Great Chain of Being*, Cambridge, Mass., 1936.

WILLEY, BASIL, *The Eighteenth Century Background*, London, 1940.

CHAPTER 30. REVOLUTION IN FRANCE: HOPE AND TERROR

BELOFF, MAX, *The Age of Absolutism, 1660–1815*, New York, 1954.

GERSHOY, LEO, *The French Revolution and Napoleon*, New York, 1933.

GOTTSCHALK, LOUIS R., *The Era of the French Revolution*, New York, 1929.

PALMER, R. R., *Twelve Who Ruled: The Committee of Public Safety During the Terror*, Princeton, 1941.

CHAPTER 31. THE NAPOLEONIC ERA: COHESION AND DIVERSITY

BRUUN, GEOFFREY, *Europe and the French Imperium, 1799–1815*, New York, 1938.

KIRCHEISEN, F. M., *Napoleon*, New York, 1932.

TARLÉ, E. V., *Napoleon's Invasion of Russia*, London, 1942.

THOMPSON, J. M., *Napoleon Bonaparte, His Rise and Fall*, London, 1952.

CHAPTER 32. VIENNA: THE GUARDS AND THE REBELS

ARTZ, FREDERICK B., *Reaction and Revolution, 1814–1832*, New York, 1934.

BRINTON, CRANE, *The Lives of Talleyrand*, New York, 1936.

BRYANT, SIR ARTHUR, *The Age of Elegance, 1812–1822*, London, 1950.

MAY, ARTHUR J., *The Age of Metternich, 1814–1848*, New York, 1933.

CHAPTER 33. THE TIDES OF REFORM

ARTZ, F. B., *France under the Bourbon Restoration, 1814–1830*, New York, 1931.

PERKINS, DEXTER, *The Monroe Doctrine, 1823–1826*, New York, 1933.

THOMSON, DAVID, *England in the Nineteenth Century*, London, 1950.

TREVELYAN, G. M., *British History in the Nineteenth Century and After, 1782–1919*, New York, 1938.

CHAPTER 34. NORTH AMERICA: LANDS OF THE FREE

CLARK, THOMAS D., *Frontier America*, New York, 1959.

DE VOTO, BERNARD, *Across the Wide Missouri*, Boston, 1952.

FREEMAN, DOUGLAS SOUTHALL, *R. E. Lee, A Biography*, 4 vols., New York, 1934–1935.

TURNER, FREDERICK JACKSON, *The Frontier in American History*, New York, 1920.

CHAPTER 35. ASIA: THE OPENING DOORS

CREEL, H. G., *Chinese Thought from Confucius to Mao Tse-tung*, Chicago, 1953.

GOODRICH, L. C., *A Short History of the Chinese People*, new ed., New York, 1951.

HUGHES, E. R., *The Invasion of China by the Western World*, New York, 1938.

REISCHAUER, E. O., *Japan, Past and Present*, New York, 1946.

CHAPTER 36. NATIONALISM: STATES IN TURMOIL

BINKLEY, R. C., *Realism and Nationalism, 1852–1871*, New York, 1935.

BROGAN, D. W., *France under the Republic: The Development of Modern France, 1870–1939*, New York, 1940.

EYCK, ERICH, *Bismarck and the German Empire*, London, 1950.

KOHN, HANS, *The Idea of Nationalism: A Study of its Origins and Background*, New York, 1944.

PART IV

GENERAL WORKS

BLACK, CYRIL, and HELMREICH, E. C., *Twentieth Century Europe*, New York, 1950.

BRUUN, GEOFFREY, *The World in the Twentieth Century*, Boston, 1948.

CHURCHILL, WINSTON, *The Second World War*, 6 vols., Boston, 1948–1953.

CLYDE, PAUL H., *The Far East*, 3rd ed. New York, 1958.

COMMAGER, HENRY STEELE, *The American Mind: An Interpretation of American Thought and Character since the 1880's*, New Haven, 1950.

SONTAG, RAYMOND J., *European Diplomatic History, 1871–1932*, New York, 1933.

CHAPTER 37. THE NINETEENTH CENTURY: THE FABRIC OF FAITH

BARZUN, JACQUES, *Darwin, Marx, and Wagner: Critique of a Heritage*, New York, 1941.

CHESTERTON, GILBERT KEITH, *The Victorian Age in Literature*, London, 1913.

EINSTEIN, A., *Music in the Romantic Era*, London, 1947.

MOWAT, R. B., *The Romantic Age: Europe*

in the Early Nineteenth Century, New York, 1937.

CHAPTER 38. THE MARCH OF SCIENCE: NEW WORLDS FOR OLD

BERNAL, J. D., *Science and Industry in the Nineteenth Century*, London, 1954.

CLARK, R. E. D., *Darwin: Before and After*, New York, 1948.

IRVINE, WILLIAM, *Apes, Angels, and Victorians*, New York, 1955.

SINGER, CHARLES; Holmyard, E. J.; Hall, A. R.; and WILLIAMS, T. I., *A History of Technology*, Volume V, *The Late Nineteenth Century, 1850–1900*, New York, 1958.

CHAPTER 39. THE NEW IMPERIALISM

DE KIEWIET, C. W., *A History of South Africa, Social and Economic*, New York, 1943.

FEIS, HERBERT, *Europe, the World's Banker, 1870–1914*, New York, 1930.

MUIR, RAMSAY, *The Expansion of Europe*, London, 1939.
WILLCOX, WILLIAM B., *Star of Empire*, New York, 1950.

CHAPTER 40. POWER AND POVERTY: EAST AND WEST

COCHRAN, THOMAS C., and MILLER, WILLIAM, *The Age of Enterprise: A Social History of Industrial America*, New York, 1942.
HAYES, CARLTON J. H., *A Generation of Materialism, 1871–1900*, New York, 1941.
KENT, P. H., *The Passing of the Manchus*, London, 1912.
PARES, BERNARD, *History of Russia*, London, 1947.

CHAPTER 41. ALLIANCES AND ARMS: THE DARKENING SKY

BRANDENBURG, ERICH, *From Bismarck to the World War*, London, 1933.
FAY, S. B., *The Origins of the World War*, 2 vols., New York, 1928.
LANGER, W. L., *European Alliances and Alignments, 1871–1890*, New York, 1931.
SCHMITT, BERNADOTTE E., *Triple Alliance and Triple Entente*, New York, 1934.

CHAPTER 42. WAR: THE PLANET DIVIDED

BAILEY, THOMAS A., *Woodrow Wilson and the Lost Peace*, New York, 1944.
CHURCHILL, WINSTON S., *The World Crisis*, 5 vols., London, 1923–1928.
NICOLSON, HAROLD, *Peacemaking, 1919*, London, 1939.
WOLFE, B. D., *Three Who Made a Revolution*, London, 1948.

CHAPTER 43. THE AMERICAS: NEW HORIZONS

BREBNER, J. B., *North Atlantic Triangle: The Interplay of Canada, the United States and Great Britain*, New Haven, 1935.
CREIGHTON, DONALD, *Dominion of the North: A History of Canada*, Boston, 1958.
HOFSTADTER, RICHARD, *The Age of Reform: From Bryan to F.D.R.*, New York, 1955.
WECTER, DIXON, *The Age of the Great Depression*, New York, 1948.

CHAPTER 44. BETWEEN TWO WARS: ASIA

FAIRBANK, JOHN K., *The United States and China*, 2nd ed., Cambridge, 1958.
GRIFFITHS, PERCIVAL, *Modern India*, New York, 1957.
SANSOM, GEORGE B., *The Western World and Japan*, New York, 1950.
VINACKE, HAROLD M., *A History of the Far East in Modern Times*, 6th ed., New York, 1959.

CHAPTER 45. BETWEEN TWO WARS: EUROPE

KNAPTON, ERNEST J., *France Since Versailles*, New York, 1952.
SCHMITT, BERNADOTTE E., *From Versailles to Munich*, Chicago, 1938.
SOWARD, F. H., *Twenty-Five Troubled Years, 1918–1943*, New York, 1943.
WOLFERS, A., *Britain and France between Two Wars*, London, 1940.

CHAPTER 46. THE SECOND WORLD CONFLICT

EISENHOWER, DWIGHT D., *Crusade in Europe*, New York, 1948.
HULL, CORDELL, *Memoirs*, 2 vols., 1948.
McINNIS, EDGAR, *The War*, 5 vols., New York, 1940–1945.
MORISON, SAMUEL ELIOT, *History of United States Naval Operations in World War II*, Boston, 1947–   .

CHAPTER 47. THE UNEASY PEACE

DEUTSCHER, ISAAC, *Stalin: A Political Biography*, New York, 1949.
GOLDMAN, ERIC, *The Crucial Decade: America 1945–1955*, New York, 1956.
HOLLAND, WILLIAM L. (ed.), *Asian Nationalism and the West*, New York, 1953.
KENNAN, GEORGE F., *American Diplomacy, 1900–1950*, New York, 1951.

CHAPTER 48. THE CONDITION OF MAN

CONANT, J. B., *Modern Science and Modern Man*, New York, 1953.
CRAMMER, J. L., and PEIERLS, R. E. (eds.), *Atomic Energy*, London, 1950.
GIEDION, S., *Mechanization Takes Command: A Contribution to Anonymous History*, New York, 1948.
RUSSELL, BERTRAND, *The Impact of Science on Society*, London, 1953.

Index

Picture Sources

ALINARI AND ANDERSON
Plate IX (33); Plate X (34); Plate XVI (53); Plate XIX (60); Plate XIX (61); Plate XX (62); Plate XXIV (75); Plate XXIV (76)

AMBROSIAN LIBRARY, MILAN
Plate XX (63), (Codex Atlanticus)

AMERICAN MUSEUM OF NATURAL HISTORY, NEW YORK
Plate I (2); Plate XXI (67); Plate XXV (77)

ANDREWS, WAYNE
Plate X (36)

ARCHIVES MUSEE GUIMET, PARIS
Plate IV (17)

ARCHIVES PHOTOGRAPHIQUES, PARIS
Plate I (1); Plate III (13) (Louvre); Plate XXVII (83), (Louvre)

ATLANTIS VERLAG, ZURICH
Plate VI (23), (From *Eternal Greece;* Photo by Martin Hürlimann)

BELFAST MUSEUM AND ART GALLERY, BELFAST, NORTH IRELAND
Plate XXVII (84)

BIBLIOTHEQUE NATIONALE, PARIS
Plate XI (37)

BRITISH INFORMATION SERVICES, NEW YORK
Plate XLIII (118); Plate XLVII (123)

BRITISH MUSEUM, LONDON
Plate II (10), (Copyright British Museum); Plate III (15); Plate V (20); Plate VII (28), (Copyright British Museum); Plate XIV (50); Plate XV (52), (Copyright British Museum); Plate XVIII (58), (Copyright British Museum); Plate XXI (68); Plate XXII (70), (Copyright British Museum); Plate XXX (91)

BROWN BROTHERS, NEW YORK
Plate XXXVIII (110) & (111); Plate XXXIX (112)

COLLECTION, NORBERT SCHIMMEL
Plate III (12)

877

COLUMBIA UNIVERSITY, NEW YORK
Plate XXVIII (85); Plate XXXIV (101), (from *Martial Achievements of Great Britain and Her Allies* by J. Jenkins. London, 1815. Butler Library)

COMBINE PHOTOS, NEW YORK
Plate XXXVII (109)

DEUTSCHES ARCHAEOLOGISCHES INSTITUT, ATHENS
Plate VII (27), (Olympia Museum)

DEUTSCHES ARCHAEOLOGISCHES INSTITUT, ROME
Plate VIII (31)

DUMBARTON OAKS COLLECTION, WASHINGTON, D. C.
Plate XI (39); Plate XII (41)

EDIZIONE A. MANLIO BRONT, CIVIDALE, ITALY
Plate X (35)

ELISOFON, ELIOT
Plate IV (18), (Copyright Eliot Elisofon)

THE FRANKLIN INSTITUTE, PHILADELPHIA, PENNSYLVANIA
Plate XXXI (96)

FREER GALLERY OF ART, WASHINGTON, D. C.
Plate V (21)

FRICK COLLECTION, NEW YORK
Plate XXVI (82), (Copyright The Frick Collection, New York)

HACHETTE, PARIS
Plate XXX (93)

HIRMER VERLAG, MUNICH
Plate XI (40), (Photo: Prof. M. Hirmer)

ITALIAN STATE TOURIST OFFICE, NEW YORK
Plate XVI (54)

METROPOLITAN MUSEUM OF ART, NEW YORK
Plate II (6); Plate II (9), (Dick Fund, 1959); Plate IV (16), (Rogers Fund, 1920); Plate VI (25), (Gift of Edmund Kerper, 1952); Plate VII (29); Plate IX (32), (Rogers Fund, 1903); Plate XII (43), (Rogers Fund, 1913); Plate XIII (44), (Fletcher Fund, 1940); Plate XIII (45), (Gift of Alexander Smith Cochran); Plate XIV (49), (Kennedy Fund, 1913); Plate XVII (55), (Gift of J. Pierpont Morgan, 1917); Plate XVII (56); Plate XVIII (57), (Musée Condé, Chantilly); Plate XVIII (59); Plate XX (64), (Bibliothèque Nationale); Plate XXVI (81), (Bequest of Mrs. H. O. Havemeyer, 1929. The H. O. Havemeyer Collection)

MUSEUM OF HERAKLION, CRETE
Plate III (14)

NATIONAL ARCHAEOLOGICAL MUSEUM, MADRID
Plate I (3)

NATIONAL MUSEUM, ATHENS
Plate V (22)

NATIONAL MUSEUM, DENMARK
Plate I (4) & (5)

NEW YORK PUBLIC LIBRARY
Plate VI (26), (from *Griechische Vasenmalerei* by Furtwangler & Reichhold.
F. Bruckmann KG Verlag, Munich. Art Division); Plate XXII (69), (from
Expeditio Francisi Draki . . . Leyden, 1588. Rare Book Division); Plate XXIII (71),
(from *Adelung's Album*, St. Petersburg, 1827); Plate XXIII (72), (from *The Father
of His Country* by W. H. Dilworth. London, 1760); Plate XXIII (73), (from
Ikona of the Holy Virgin of Vladimir . . . by Y. Poselyanin. Moscow, 1912. Sla-
vonic Division); Plate XXV (78), (from *Astronomiae Instauratae Mechanica* by
Tycho Brahe. Wandsbeck, 1598. Rare Book Division); Plate XXIX (88), (from
Paul Revere's Engravings by C. S. Brigham. Worcester, Mass., 1954. Prints Division);
Plate XXIX (89), (Stokes Collection, Prints Division); Plate XXX (92), (Prints
Division); Plate XXXI (95), (from *Experiments and Observations on Electricity* . . .
by Benjamin Franklin. London, 1774. Rare Book Division); Plate XXXII (97), (from
Gravures Historiques des Principaux Evenements . . . Paris, 1789. Prints Division);
Plate XXXII (98), (from *Les Principales Journées de la Revolution*. Paris, 1838.
Spencer Collection); Plate XXXIII (100), (Prints Division); Plate XXXIV (102),
(Prints Division); Plate XXXIV (103), (from *Das Bürgerliche Wien* Vol. I by Max
Eisler. Vienna, 1929); Plate XXXVII (108), (from *Exposition de Paris, 1900* Vol. 3.
Montgradien & Co. Paris); Plate XXXIX (113), (from *War Cartoons: The Century
Edition* Vol. 2 by Louis Raemakers. New York, 1917. Prints Division)

OAK RIDGE INSTITUTE OF NUCLEAR STUDIES, INC., OAK RIDGE, TENNESSEE
Plate XLVI (121)

OXFORD UNIVERSITY
Plate XIV (48), (Bodleian Library); Plate XV (51), (Copyright Lawrence Stone,
Wadham College)

PALESTINE ARCHAEOLOGICAL MUSEUM, JERUSALEM
Plate II (11)

PEABODY MUSEUM, SALEM, MASSACHUSETTS
Plate XXXVI (106) & (107)

PRADO MUSEUM, MADRID
Plate XXXIII (99)

PRICE, DR. DEREK J. DE SOLLA
Plate VI (24), (Copyright Dr. Derek J. de Solla Price, Yale University)

PRINCETON UNIVERSITY, PRINCETON, NEW JERSEY
Plate XXIX (90)

RADIO TIMES HULTON PICTURE LIBRARY, LONDON
Plate XXXI (94)

RCA, NEW YORK
Plate XLVII (122)

REVIEW AND HERALD PUBLISHING CO., WASHINGTON, D. C.
Plate II (8), (Review and Herald Publishing Ass'n. Washington, D. C. Courtesy
S. H. Horn)

RIJKSMUSEUM, AMSTERDAM, THE NETHERLANDS
Plate XXI (66)

SCIENCE MUSEUM, LONDON
Plate XXV (79), (British Crown Copyright); Plate XXV (80), (from *Theatrum
Machinarum Novum,* by Böckler, 1662)

SCRIBNER ART FILE
Plate XXXV (104)

SIENA TOURIST OFFICE, SIENA, ITALY
Plate XX (65), (Foto Grassi)

SVED, ETIENNES, SURESNES, FRANCE
Plate II (7)

CHARLES E. TUTTLE COMPANY, RUTLAND, VERMONT & TOKYO
Plate XIII (47), (Collection Kozan-ji, Kyoto, from *The Arts of Japan* by Hugo
Munsterberg, 1957)

UNITED PRESS INTERNATIONAL PHOTOS, NEW YORK
Plate XL (114); Plate XLI (116); Plate XLIV (119); Plate XLVIII (125)

UNIVERSITY OF EDINBURGH, LIBRARY, EDINBURGH, SCOTLAND
Plate XII (42)

UNIVERSITY OF MICHIGAN, ANN ARBOR, MICHIGAN
Plate XXVIII (86), (from *Colored Views of the Liverpool and Manchester Railway,*
by Thomas Talbot Bury. London, 1832. Transportation Library)

VATICAN MUSEUM, ROME
Plate VIII (30), (Archivio Fotografico)

VICTORIA AND ALBERT MUSEUM, LONDON
Plate V (19); Plate XI (38); Plate XIII (46); Plate XXIV (74), (All photos Crown Copyright)

WALTERS ART GALLERY, BALTIMORE, MARYLAND
Plate XXXV (105), (Copyright University of Oklahoma Press. Norman, Okla Photo, Courtesy The Walters Art Gallery)

WIDE WORLD PHOTOS, NEW YORK
Plate XL (115); Plate XLII (117); Plate XLV (120); Plate XLVIII (124)

YALE UNIVERSITY ART GALLERY, NEW HAVEN, CONNECTICUT
Plate XXVIII (87), (Mabel Brady Garven Collection)